A2 LEVEL PSYCHOLOGY

To Christine with love

Science is built up of facts, as a house is built of stones. However an accumulation of facts is no more a science than a heap of stones is a house

(Henri Poincaré, French Scientist)

A2 LEVEL PSYCHOLOGY

Michael W. Eysenck

With contributions from

Philip Banyard, Evie Bentley, Clare Charles,
Diana Dwyer, Mark Griffiths,
and Craig Roberts

Psychology Press
Taylor & Francis Group

HOVE AND NEW YORK

First published 2009 by Psychology Press

An imprint of Taylor & Francis
27 Church Road, Hove, East Sussex, BN3 2FA

http://www.psypress.com
http://www.a-levelpsychology.net

Psychology Press is an imprint of the Taylor & Francis Group, an Informa business

© 2009 by Psychology Press

AQA examination questions are reproduced by permission of the Assessment and Qualifications Alliance.

British Library Cataloguing in Publication Data
A catalogue record for this book is available from the British Library

ISBN: 978-1-84872-009-1

Cover design by Gerald Myers
Cartoons by Sean Longcroft
Typeset in India by Newgen Imaging Systems (P) Ltd
Printed and bound in Italy by L.E.G.O. SpA

CONTENTS

ABOUT THE AUTHORS

Michael W. Eysenck is one of the best-known British psychologists. He is Professor of Psychology at Royal Holloway University of London, which is one of the leading departments in the United Kingdom. His academic interests lie mainly in cognitive psychology, with much of his research focusing on the role of cognitive factors in anxiety in normal and clinical populations.

He is an author of many titles, and his previous textbooks published by Psychology Press include *AS Level Psychology, Fourth Edition* (2008), *A2 Psychology: Key Topics Second Edition* (2006), *Psychology for A2 Level* (2001), *Memory* (2009, with Alan Baddeley & Michael C. Anderson), *Fundamentals of Psychology* (2009), *Fundamentals of Cognition* (2006), *Cognitive Psychology: A Student's Handbook, Fifth Edition* (2005, with Mark Keane), *Psychology: An International Perspective* (2004), *Psychology: A Student's Handbook* (2000), *Simply Psychology, Second Edition* (2002), *Perspectives on Psychology* (1994), *Individual Differences: Normal and Abnormal* (1994), and *Principles of Cognitive Psychology, Second Edition* (2001). He has also written the research monographs *Anxiety and Cognition: A Unified Theory* (1997), and *Anxiety: The Cognitive Perspective* (1992), along with the popular title *Happiness: Facts and Myths* (1990). He is also a keen supporter of Crystal Palace football club and lives in hope that one day they will return to the Premiership.

Philip Banyard is Senior Lecturer in Psychology at Nottingham Trent University.

Evie Bentley is the Advanced Skills Practitioner for Psychology for West Sussex Adult and Community Learning, and the editor for The Association for the Teaching of Psychology.

Clare Charles is Head of Social Sciences at Lutterworth College, Leicestershire.

Diana Dwyer is Head of Psychology at The West Bridgford School.

Mark Griffiths is Professor of Gambling Studies at Nottingham Trent University.

Craig Roberts is Head of Psychology at Totton College.

Preparing for the A2 exam

By Diana Dwyer

Psychology needs no introduction. If you are using this book it is probable that you have completed the first year of your A level studies and are now ready to tackle the next leg, A2 studies.

HOW A2 DIFFERS FROM AS

Unlike the AS course, in which the entire content was compulsory, A2 contains options. These options will almost certainly have been selected by your teacher; this means that you don't need to study everything in this book.

You are a year older than when you started the AS course, and therefore you should be capable of rather more mature thought. Mature thinking is, in part, the outcome of just getting older but it is also due to your education—your AS studies have enabled you to develop new ideas and new insights. In the second year of study you can use your new knowledge to acquire a deeper understanding of psychology and apply your knowledge to new situations.

The examination for A2 is quite different from the AS examination, and this will direct how you study psychology in the A2 year. You will now have to answer essay questions in the examination rather than questions split into several parts that were used at AS level. Guidance on how to write essays constitutes a large part of this introductory chapter, but first we'll take a look at the course structure and the corresponding exams.

THE A2 COURSE AND EXAMINATIONS

The A2 course comprises two units: Unit 3 and Unit 4. There is one examination paper for each of these units, as follows:

Unit 3—PSYA3: Topics in Psychology

Three questions to be answered in 1½ hours, taken from eight topics. For each topic, there is one question. The topics are:

1. biological rhythms and sleep;
2. perception;
3. relationships;
4. aggression;
5. eating behaviour;
6. gender;
7. intelligence and learning;
8. cognition and development.

This examination can be sat in January and in June.

EXAM HINT

The minimum you must study is:
• three topics from Unit 3
• one mental disorder from Section A: Psychopathology in Unit 4
• one topic from Section B: Psychology in Action in Unit 4
• Research Methods (Section C in Unit 4), which will be examined by means of a structured question.

Unit 4—PSYA4

This exam is 2 hours long and in three sections:

*   Section A: Psychopathology: one question chosen from three.
*   Section B: Psychology in Action: there are three options:
    1. media psychology;
    2. the psychology of addictive behaviour;
    3. anomalistic psychology.

For each of these options there is one question (three questions in all, one on each). As you are unlikely to have studied more than one option, you need to consider this as a compulsory question.

*   Section C: Research Methods: one compulsory structured question.

This examination can be sat in January and June.

KNOWING HOW YOU WILL BE ASSESSED

EXAM HINT

The question numbers refer to the exam papers. It is a good idea to make a mental note of these so that you can immediately turn to the questions you will be answering in the exam.

Just as at AS, there are three main assessment objectives at A2: AO1, AO2, and AO3. You are probably familiar with these by now but just to recap:

*   **AO1 Knowledge and understanding of science and how science works**
    The examiner will look for evidence that students can:
    *   recognise, recall, and show understanding of scientific knowledge;
    *   select, organise, and communicate relevant information in a variety of forms.
*   **AO2 Application of knowledge and understanding of science and how science works**
    The examiner will look for evidence that students can:
    *   analyse and evaluate scientific knowledge and processes;
    *   apply scientific knowledge and processes to unfamiliar situations including those related to issues;
    *   assess the validity, reliability, and credibility of scientific information.
*   **AO3 How science works—psychology**
    The examiner will look for evidence that students can:
    *   describe ethical, safe, and skilful practical techniques and processes, selecting appropriate qualitative and quantitative methods;
    *   demonstrate how to make, record, and communicate reliable and valid observations and measurement with appropriate precision and accuracy, through using primary and secondary sources;
    *   analyse, interpret, explain, and evaluate the methodology, results, and impact of their own and others' experimental and investigative activities in a variety of ways.

AO1 is assessment objective 1: *knowledge and understanding* of psychological principles, theories, concepts, studies, methods, perspectives, and applications.

AO2 is assessment objective 2: *analyse and evaluate* psychological theories, concepts, studies, methods, principles, perspectives, and applications.

EXAM HINT

Know the specification well, both what is required of you in terms of skills (AO1, AO2, AO3) and content. In the exam, *you need to know two theories in depth and to be able to use others as support or counter perspectives.* It is advisable to base your study and revision on this.

THE EXAMINATIONS

Unit 3

As already mentioned, you will be required to write three essays, one on each topic area selected. Each essay is marked out of 25 marks. Of these:

- 9 marks are awarded for AO1 (i.e. demonstrating knowledge and understanding of science and how science works);
- 12 marks are awarded for AO2 (i.e. applying your of knowledge and understanding of science and how science works);
- 4 marks are awarded for AO3 (i.e. psychological implications of the above).

See the mark scheme on pages 16–17.

The questions therefore require an answer (often a single essay) that covers all of the assessment objectives. Just be careful that you do not write too much for AO1 (remember, it is 9 marks out of 25); that about half the essay is evaluation (as this is 12 marks out of 25) and that a proportion is AO3 (a discussion, for example, of the ethical and or practical issues involved in the research you have described).

Some questions are split into two parts, sometimes with one much shorter part worth 9 marks (yes, you've guessed it—this is AO1) and the second part worth 16 marks, requiring AO2 and AO3. Other "split" questions might allocate only 5 marks to the first part (likely to be AO1) and 20 marks to the second part. The second part would then be 4 marks AO1, 12 marks AO2, and 4 marks AO3.

> **EXAM HINT**
>
> Evaluation is not a "shopping list" of criticisms! Writing a "shopping list" will achieve minimal marks in the exam. So make sure your AO2 content is a more sophisticated commentary. If you use points such as "lacks ecological validity", or "it is reductionistic", show that you understand *why* the comment is relevant to the study/theory, i.e. *contextualise* your material. A few points showing good understanding will earn more marks than a longer list of points that you do not elaborate on or put into context. Further aspects of commentary are interpretation, analysis, evaluation, and conclusions.

The following are examples of the type of question you might encounter in Unit 3:

1. Describe and evaluate theories relating to the functions of sleep. (25 marks)
2. Describe and evaluate Gregory's top down/indirect theory of perception. (25 marks)
3. Discuss explanations of institutional aggression. (25 marks)
4. (a) Outline factors influencing attitudes to food and eating behaviour. (5 marks)
   (b) Outline and evaluate one or more biological explanations of one eating disorder. (20 marks)
5. (a) Outline one or more explanations of gender development. (9 marks)
   (b) Evaluate one of the theories outlined in (a) above. (16 marks)
6. Describe and evaluate research into the development of a child's sense of self. (25 marks)

Be aware that although each question will cover one topic area, it might cover more than one subsection (as in the example question on eating disorders above).

Unit 4

Unlike Unit 3, in which all the questions are equivalent to one another in terms of marks and AO1, AO2, and AO3 allocation, Unit 4 has three sections that contain very different questions:

- Section A is Psychopathology and all questions carry 25 marks: 9 AO1, 12 AO2, 4 AO3. There are three questions, of which you choose one. You are expected to study only one disorder from a choice of three (schizophrenia, depression, or anxiety disorders) so you will only be able to answer one question. An example question is:

  a. Outline clinical characteristics of schizophrenia. (5 marks)

  b. Explain issues associated with the classification and diagnosis of schizophrenia. (10 marks)

  c. Outline and evaluate one biological explanation for schizophrenia. In your answer refer to research evidence. (10 marks)

On this particular question, part (a) is 5 AO1; part (b) is 10 AO2 and part (c) 4 AO1 and 6 AO2/3 combined. Notice how the AO3 component is emphasised by pointing out that you need to refer to research evidence (and include some evaluation of it).

- Section B is Psychology in Action and also 25 marks per question: 9 AO1, 12 AO2, 4 AO3. There are three questions, of which you choose one. As in Section A, you are only expected to study one application (media psychology,

---

Psychological research and scientific methods: specimen question

You should answer *all* parts of this question.

Total for this question: 35 marks

A psychologist believed that people think of more new ideas working on their own than they do working in a group, and that the belief that people are more creative in groups is false. To test this idea he arranged for 30 people to participate in a study that involved generating ideas about how to boost tourism. Participants were randomly allocated to one of two groups. Fifteen of them were asked to work individually and generate as many ideas as they could to boost tourism in their town. The other fifteen participants were divided into three groups and each group was asked to brainstorm to generate as many ideas as they could to boost tourism in their town. The group brainstorm sessions were recorded and the number of ideas generated by each participant was noted.

The psychologist used a statistical test to find out if there was a significant difference in the number of ideas generated by the participants working alone as compared with the number of ideas generated by the participants working in groups. A significant difference was found at the 5% level for a two-tailed test ($p \leq 0.05$).

Table 1: Average number of ideas generated when working alone and when working in a group

	Working alone	Working in a group
Average number of ideas generated	14	8
Standard deviation	1.89	2.98

(a) Identify the type of experimental design used in this study. *(1 mark)*

(b) Identify **one** extraneous variable that the investigator addressed in the procedure for the study and explain how it was addressed. *(4 marks)*

(c) Name an appropriate test of statistical significance for analysing this data. Explain why this would be a suitable test to use. *(4 marks)*

(d) Explain what is meant by "$p \leq 0.05$". *(2 marks)*

(e) Give **one** reason why the psychologist used a two-tailed test. *(2 marks)*

(f) With reference to the data in **Table 1** outline and discuss the findings of this investigation. *(10 marks)*

(g) The psychologist noted that younger participants seemed to generate more ideas than older participants. Design a study to investigate the **relationship** between age and ability to generate ideas. You should include sufficient details to permit replication, for example a hypothesis, variables, detail of design and procedure, sampling. *(12 marks)*

the psychology of addictive behaviour, or animalistic psychology) so you will only be able to answer one question. An example question is:

a. Some laboratory studies indicate that feelings of hostility may rise after playing violent video games. Describe one or more such studies and discuss the findings of such research. (15 marks)

b. Outline and evaluate one or more explanations for the effectiveness of television in persuasion. (10 marks)

- Section C is Psychological Research and Scientific Method and consists of one compulsory question comprising about seven parts and is out of 35 marks. As you might expect, this is heavily weighted towards AO3, being 3 AO1, 4 AO2, and 28 AO3.

UNDERSTANDING EXAM QUESTIONS

Look very closely at the wording of the examination question. There will be one or more words that give you exact instructions. These are referred to by the examiners as *skill words*. You have met these terms at AS level but let's just recap, because they are so important.

Below is a list of skill words and what is required for each:

- *Define*: explain, in precise terms, what is meant by a particular term or concept. This is often used in short-answer questions and as a starter in essay questions that are split into sections (structured essays).
- *Outline/state*: offer a summary description in brief form without including details.
- *Describe*: provide details of a theory, study, or concept without any evaluation.
- *Explain*: this requires two separate elements. First, describe the theory or concept in terms that make it clear you understand it; second, give reasons why it came about (e.g. the underlying theory on which it is based). For example, the authoritarian personality theory of prejudice is based on Freud's theory.
- *Evaluate*: consider the positive and negative points of a theory, concept, or study in reasonable detail.
- *Discuss*: describe a theory, concept, or study and then evaluate it with reference to supporting evidence and evidence that contradicts it. Therefore this is brief description together with positive and negative evaluation.
- *Analyse/critically analyse*: examine the separate elements of the topic area and evaluate each one. Critically analyse does *not* mean that you just criticise: you need to include both positive and negative elements.
- *Assess/critically assess*: make an *informed* judgement about how good or effective a theory, method, or concept is in light of the strengths and limitations of the information and arguments presented.
- *Criticise*: critically appraise the strengths *and* weaknesses of a theory, study, or concept.
- *Evaluate/critically evaluate*: make an *informed* and systematic judgement regarding the value of a topic area. This could include some of the uses to which it could be put (such as a theory of cue-dependent forgetting being used to improve eyewitness testimony).

- *Compare/compare and contrast*: if it's just "compare", look mainly at the similarities between two or more theories, concepts, or models. For "compare and contrast" include both similarities and differences.

ANSWERING ESSAY QUESTIONS

As many of the questions in the A2 exam require you to write an essay, it is essential that you are able to do so competently. Let us consider the basic requirements of an essay.

- *Accuracy*: the information given should be correct.
- *Use of appropriate language*: psychological terminology should be used.
- *Relevance*: the essay should actually answer the question.
- *Good organisation and logical expression*: there should be an introduction, main body, and conclusion. The main body should be organised logically so that one point follows on from the previous one.
- *Good knowledge of psychology*: the essay should cover the relevant theories, studies, and methods each in sufficient detail. It should therefore demonstrate both breadth and depth of coverage.
- *Linkage and comparison*: various issues, theories, and methods should be linked, compared, and contrasted.
- *Evaluation of the content*: point out the good aspects, contributions, applications, inadequacies, and limitations of the evidence and theories presented.

> **EXAM HINT**
>
> The exam questions often ask you to discuss one or two theories. If just one is asked for, you must select a theory that you can write about at length and in depth, so be selective. If two theories are asked for, then you should present one of these in some depth and the other in slightly less detail.

Have Good Knowledge of the Material

Clearly, there is no way that you can achieve a good examination mark without the necessary knowledge. Study consistently throughout your course and revise effectively; we discussed how to do this in your AS book. The A2 year is a chance to start afresh and institute a new system of study and revision throughout the year. Don't just leave it until the month before the exam.

Use Suitable Language and Structure Your Essay in the Appropriate Way

Some of the longer questions are assessed in terms of the quality of written communication (QWC). This means that you are assessed in terms of the following:

- Legibility (whether the examiner can read your writing!), spelling, punctuation, and grammar.
- Whether the style of writing is appropriate to express the complexity of the subject matter.
- Whether the material is organised so that information is expressed clearly and coherently using specialist vocabulary when appropriate.

Obtaining Marks for the Quality of Written Communication

Essays should always be written in continuous prose and in grammatically correct language comprising only full sentences, which are organised in paragraphs. An essay should *not* contain headings, subheadings, numbered lists, or underlined points.

Use an appropriate *style* by writing only in the "third person" rather than the first person. For example, you should not say "I think that animals should not

---

How do I write effective AO1?

It is a common misconception that marks are given only for the number of points presented in an answer. This kind of "shopping list" approach does not attract high marks. You must communicate understanding and interpretation. You can demonstrate that you understand the relevance of the material by adding a sentence like:

"This shows that . . ." or "One can conclude . . .".

Other useful tips

Show a clear focus on the question:

- Use link sentences.

Be selective:

- Include only the most relevant content to the question.

Plan so your answer has structure:

- An essay plan will enable you to know what is going in each paragraph and the conclusion so that your answer has structure.

Try to provide depth and breadth:

- It is better to give fewer studies/theories/explanations and so be able to go into some detail on those you do cover than include too many with too brief and superficial a description.
- The examiner knows the time constraints and that there must be a trade-off between depth and breadth, but you should aim to achieve both by writing about either one or two things in depth and then anything else more superficially.

Try to provide synopticity:

- This can be achieved by identifying methodological approaches and criticisms, and by using counterperspectives.

---

be used in experiments if the procedures could hurt them" but rather "Some psychologists argue that it is ethically wrong to use painful procedures on nonhuman animals, especially in cases where the outcome of the research is unlikely to be of help in understanding human functioning." In textbooks, the author never expresses personal opinions. Neither should you.

Use specialist language: you have spent 2 years learning lots of technical language; now is the time to show off and use it. For example, if you are writing about standing by and not helping others, refer to it as *bystander apathy*. If experiments are not true to life, discuss the issue of *ecological validity*. If you are discussing Piaget's theory of pretend play, refer to *assimilation*, and so on. Every single topic area in psychology has its own specialist language so every essay should use that language.

Answer the Question That is Asked

Examiners constantly complain about the tendency of students to write all they know about a topic rather than answering the question set. Students sometimes believe that if they know the content they will automatically be able to answer questions in the exam. However, the danger is that they simply reproduce what they have learnt with no attempt to answer the particular question asked. What you need to do is to select the relevant material and organise it into a coherent answer.

To acquire the skills necessary to write an essay, you will need plenty of practice in essay writing during your course. This helps you to select the relevant sections from the whole of the content. When you have learnt the material, go over some sample questions on the topic and see if you can select what is necessary to answer the question set without any extra, irrelevant material. If you get used to doing this during revision, you will be able to write a good answer in the exam.

Organise the Material: Make a Plan

Making a plan is an essential part of writing a good essay. Even under exam conditions, when time is of the essence, it is well worth spending some time (2 or 3 minutes) on the planning stage. Again, it is a good idea to practice this throughout the course so that you do it quickly and efficiently in an exam. When you first start writing essays, the planning might take a considerable proportion of the total time you spend on the essay writing, but the skills you acquire by practising essay planning will soon enable you to select what is relevant in future essays, even under exam conditions. Writing a plan helps you organise the material in a logical way. This approach should also prevent you writing "everything you know" about a topic in the hope that something will get credit. The ability to be selective is a higher-order skill and one that you should demonstrate to get good marks.

As you write the plan, you might think of additional points you haven't at first considered, and you can then insert them into the correct place.

Under examination conditions, planning an essay helps you to relax somewhat during the actual writing, because you no longer have to worry about what point you will make next or whether you will forget vital information.

> **EXAM HINT**
>
> If you are asked to describe and evaluate one or two theories, be very careful how you bring in any further theories. They can be used only as counter perspectives, so simply identifying the new theory as a counter perspective and then describing it is not good enough. You must compare it with the theory/theories you've selected as your main content in a sustained manner, e.g. what insights are offered by the counter perspective that are ignored by the other theory/theories? Do the theories have similarities or differences in terms of strengths and weaknesses?

> **EXAM HINT**
>
> Do not cross out your essay plan as it will be marked if your essay is incomplete—it will be looked at more favourably having been compiled from the outset rather than simply giving a list of points at the end when you are running out of time.

Essay Structure

Use the following basic structure:

- *Introduction*: in which you "set the scene" by outlining the main points, arguments, or theories very briefly. Don't waste time making statements that mean nothing. It is pointless to start by saying "There is a lot of research into aggression". It's much better to start with something like: "There is an argument as to how much aggression is due to biological factors and how much it is due to environmental influences". At least then you have set the scene for the nature–nurture debate and for an account of research into what causes aggression. The point about not wasting time applies to any length essay but is particularly important when you are writing for only 30 minutes. Make it short and to the point: in other words, credit worthy.
- *Main body*: in which each theory or concept is discussed and evaluated, perhaps compared or contrasted if required, each in a separate paragraph.
- *Conclusion*: in which you not only summarise but attempt to answer the question and draw justifiable, but probably tentative, conclusions.

> **EXAM HINT**
>
> It is very easy to contextualise the theories and research in terms of your own experience; however, this is not relevant material for an essay. Marks are gained for informed answers and so you must make relevant use of psychological research and theory, and *not* anecdotal material.

Base Your Arguments on Sound Psychological Evidence and Theory

There is a temptation, especially with particular topics in psychology, to ignore all the basic psychology you have studied in lessons, and even written in essays during the course, and express popular but unfounded opinions such as those expressed

How do I write effective AO2?

Evaluation

Evaluation can be achieved through:

The use of research studies to provide support for an argument:

- Providing commentary on research studies, which challenges the findings because of flawed methodology or assumptions.
- Presenting alternative theories as a contrasting viewpoint.
- Suggesting useful applications.
- Considering implications and/or strengths and weaknesses.

Useful phrases in essays to introduce AO2

- So we can see that . . .
- This would imply . . .
- This suggests that . . .
- One consequence would be . . .
- One advantage of this is . . .
- An alternative explanation could be . . .
- Therefore we can conclude . . .
- This evidence provides support/contradicts the theory that . . .
- Not everyone reacts the same way, for example . . .
- There might be cultural variations . . .
- This has been applied to . . .
- There are methodological weaknesses in this research as . . .
- This study lacked internal/external validity because . . .
- The strengths of this research . . .
- There are ethical issues that must be considered . . .

EXAM HINT

In order to get in the top band of marks, try to introduce themes and debates as much as possible. In the specification for Unit 3 it reads that candidates will be expected to "develop an appreciation of issues and debates as relevant to each topic studied, for example, issues of bias, including gender and culture, the role of animals in research, ethical issues, the nature-nurture debate, free will and determinism, and reductionism." So take every opportunity to mention these. For example, if writing an essay on behavioural explanations (or therapies), mention that this very much supports the nurture side of the nature-nurture debate. When writing about psychodynamic explanations, you could mention that the methodology used does not conform to what constitutes a science. When discussing a biological approach (e.g. to aggression) you could say that this is a very deterministic view and does not allow for individuals to have much free will. When revising, think about all these issues and how you can introduce them into an essay, and you will be well on your way to top band marks!

in magazines or the popular press. You need to use research evidence in which the studies are identifiable and cite the actual evidence. So, rather than, "lots of people know that eyewitness testimony is often wrong", a much more psychologically informed answer could start with "one of the reasons why eyewitness testimony is inaccurate is the use of leading questions as demonstrated by, amongst others, Loftus and Palmer (1974) and Loftus and Zanni (1975)." You can then go on to discuss this evidence. Remember, demonstrate your knowledge of psychology, not popular opinion.

In the same way that there are no right answers for students, there are no "right" or "wrong" theories. Freud, Piaget, and Broadbent, for example, did not get it wrong. Their theories continue to be highly influential even though some elements have been criticised.

STRATEGIES YOU CAN USE TO IMPROVE YOUR AO2 MARKS

One way to think about how you can improve your marks for AO2 questions is to consider how you can evaluate the research and theories you have studied. Focus on:

- *Application.* Can the research or theories be applied to everyday life? Does the research benefit humanity?
- *Methodology.* How was the research done? Can you comment on the validity, reliability, or credibility of the research or information? What sampling technique was used, and can we generalise from this sample? Did the participants simply do what they thought the researcher wanted them to do? Could the researcher have been biased?

EXAM HINT

Note the mnemonic ECR: explain, conclude, relate. Ensure you do this with a number of evaluation points per essay.

EXAM HINT

There are many sources of AO2, most of which are generalisable, i.e. can be used in different essays. So it's a good idea to create your own AO2 revision sheet of criticisms with elaboration and commentary. Also include some useful AO2 phrases as suggested in the text.

- *Culture/gender*. How universal are the findings? Do the findings have any relevance for non-Western societies and are the findings gender specific?
- *Commentary/constructing a coherent answer*. Use evidence to support your answer. Consider the strengths and weaknesses of the evidence. Explore how psychologists have challenged different theories. Discuss how effective these challenges have been.

Don't expect the examiner to read your mind. Unless it is written down, the examiner cannot know what you intended to say. Spell out the points you are making, using statements like:

- "This research on eyewitness testimony has applications to everyday life, where mistaken identity has led to the wrong person being imprisoned . . ."
- "One major problem with this research was that the sample was male, hence it is unclear whether these findings can be generalised to females . . ."
- "It is important to recognise the limitations of this definition in that what might be seen as normal in one culture (e.g. having three wives) might be seen as abnormal in other cultures."

STRATEGIES YOU CAN USE TO IMPROVE YOUR AO3 MARKS

- *Ethics*. Did the research cause physical or psychological harm? Do you consider the research treated the participants with respect? How have psychologists used the information they have gained? For example, "Although it is clear that Milgram's research caused his participants stress, there has been some debate as to whether the means justified the ends . . ."
- *Methodology*. Can you explain or evaluate in more than one way? Can you suggest appropriate qualitative and quantitative methods and explain when and why each would be good to use? For example, for a question that asks you to explain one research method used by the biological approach to abnormality, you could choose twin studies and explain how these are done, what the rationale behind such studies is, and assess the strengths and weaknesses of this method of research, i.e. what they can and cannot tell us.

AO3 marks are research methods marks, which are spread throughout the units. These marks are for demonstrating that you have a real understanding of psychological theory and practice.

REVISION

First of all, prepare a list of topics to revise. Break each major topic area (e.g. gender) into manageable chunks. The specification is very useful in this respect and you should have a copy of this (easily available from the AQA website).

Once you have decided on your list of topics, compile a revision list: a list of topics you intend to revise. Keep it at the front of your file so that it is easily accessible, you do not loose it, and you can tick off the topics once you have:

- prepared a set of organised notes from which to revise;
- revised it once;
- revised it a second time.

Make sure that you have a set of revision notes. Before you start the process of actually learning the material, make sure you have a set of notes from which to revise. Ideally, you will have compiled these as you went along but—realistically—many people won't have done this. It is essential to prepare a set of revision notes before you start learning.

Start revising early. These exams are important and not only will you spoil your chances if you leave revision until late, you will actually suffer more misery and stress than if you had stretched it over a longer period of time. One of the awful things about revising under anxiety states is that the effectiveness of the revision is minimal.

Some students believe that if they revise too early they will have forgotten everything before the exam. Some forgetting is inevitable and if you go back to a topic a month after you have first revised it, you will probably have forgotten as much as 90% of the material. However, it will take you a very short time to relearn it compared with how long it took the first time. An added advantage is that each time you learn it, your understanding increases; you see connections both within the topic area and with other areas of the syllabus that you did not appreciate before. This enables your answers to be of a much higher standard, both in terms of understanding the particular question asked (as you can now apply the material better) and in appreciating the wider implications of the topic area.

So remember, it's never too early to start revising in a systematic and thorough manner.

Learning the Material

You should now have one set of organised notes for each topic area and, by this stage, you revise from these and nothing else. You must now *learn* the material. Do not use distraction activities such as writing out your notes more neatly, which

Where possible, plan revision to fit in with your class revision.

make you feel that you are "revising" although really you are not. The aim is to commit the material to memory—nothing else.

Draw up revision timetables

You will actually need two revision timetables.

Initially, do a timetable for the first session of learning, covering *all* the topics in all of your examination subjects. Plan it so that you do not go more than 2 weeks before the beginning of the first exam.

In those final 2 weeks you will need to be doing the second learning session, and these need to be planned after this first session has finished.

If you possibly can, try to spend one whole day between these two sessions doing no revision at all. If you really feel you cannot spare a whole day, at least have the evening off. Use a little of the time to draw up the second timetable but, after that, plan some leisure activity.

In the second timetable you obviously need to take account of the timing of the actual exams. By then you should have a better idea of the time allocation needed for each topic.

Where possible, plan your own revision to fit in with class revision. If your teacher intends to spend lesson time revising a particular topic, try to revise that topic the night *before*. This might sound like a waste of time, but it will enable you to sort out what you don't understand and ensure that your own revision is on the right lines.

Start your revision timetable with a topic you already know fairly well. This will give you confidence at the start before you start tackling the more unfamiliar areas. However, *beware "comfort" revision*—do not spend too long on these familiar topics with which you already feel comfortable.

Make your revision timetables *flexible*. This especially applies to the first timetable, because it is very unlikely that you will be able to keep to it exactly. One topic might take longer to revise than you anticipated. Don't panic about this, it will just make matters worse. Revise your timetable in the light of this.

Plan your breaks

Before you start a revision session, decide when you will finish! There is plenty of evidence to show that it is more effective to revise in lots of short learning sessions than one long one. The typical pattern that suits a lot of people is about 30–35 minutes learning, then a 5-minute break (no longer). You often won't need to watch the clock, you will feel you are no longer retaining information very well after this amount of time. When you return to work, start the next session by seeing how much of the last session you can recall without notes. Write it down (it's worth the time it takes and the paper it uses) or, if you genuinely find it more effective, say it to yourself. Then go back and check how well you did.

After about four sessions you will need a longer break, probably 20 minutes.

Try to plan your time so that you have a non-intellectual treat to look forward to at the end of the session (not half way through!). For example, buy a magazine or record your favourite TV programme and watch it before you go to bed.

Revise actively

Few people, if any, can revise effectively simply by reading through their work. Write down what you've learnt, in brief summary form. Use headings and numbered points whenever you can. Cover the notes and repeat them out loud. Try to summarise major theories in one sentence or two (this is good practice for essays). When you feel you know the material quite well, plan essays *from memory* from past paper questions.

Some people feel that it is worth the time to write whole, timed essays under examination conditions. If you do this, give them to your teacher to mark or you will not benefit from useful feedback.

USEFUL ADVICE WHEN IN THE EXAM ROOM

Time allocation

One of the most important aspects of taking an exam is to make sure that you allocate your time appropriately. Other than not revising properly, nothing is more guaranteed to lead to failure than spending too much time on one question so that the others suffer. There will be a clock in the exam room—use it! Work out *exactly* when you need to start another question and stick to it. *Don't be tempted to carry on with the same question even if you haven't finished it. Trust me—your marks will suffer if you do.* You can always leave a gap and return to finish it at the end but you *must not* leave yourself short of time to answer the last question:

> **EXAM HINT**
>
> Unit 3: 30 minutes per essay = approximately 600 words, so six paragraphs of 100 words or four paragraphs of 150 words are needed.
> Unit 4: 35 minutes for section A = approximately 700 words; 35 minutes for section B = approximately 700 words; and 50 minutes for section C = approximately 1000 words needed.

- Unit 3: spend 30 minutes on each question.
- Unit 4: spend 35 minutes on section A, 35 minutes on section B, and 50 minutes on section C.

Choice of question

Most of you will have the choices in the A2 exam fixed before you start the course. In Unit 3 you have to choose three questions from eight different topic areas. You will probably have studied only three areas so, in effect, you have no real choice. In this case, just go straight to the questions you can answer and *do not waste time reading questions on topics you have not studied*. This is important because you have no time to waste. Worse still, you might be tempted to attempt one of them: *don't*. If you have not studied the topic area, you will not be able to answer the question, so do *not* attempt it. Stick to the questions on topics you have studied. Some of you might have a little choice (if, for example, you have studied four topic areas); in this case, still ignore the questions on topics you have not studied. Read the questions on all the topics you have studied, and only those, then make a choice and stick to it.

On Unit 4 there is no real choice. This is because the course is designed to cover only one option in the first two sections (Psychopathology and Psychology in Action) so that is all you will have studied and there is only one compulsory question in the Psychological Research and Design section. Again, don't waste time reading questions you cannot do. Go straight to the relevant questions and start writing.

Make the Most of Your Time

If you finish the exam early, read through what you have done. I know you're tired after all that writing but you have studied for these exams for 2 years and they are important to your future; another 5 or 10 minutes is not much extra. Therefore make the most of every minute and just double check your answers.

Good luck! Though of course, you won't need it. Your hard work will see you through.

Mark schemes for Units 3 and 4

AO1. Knowledge and understanding of psychology (as a science) and of how science works. (9 marks)

AO2. Application of knowledge and understanding of psychology and of how science works: analysis and evaluation of knowledge and processes; application of scientific knowledge and processes to unfamiliar situations, including issues; assessment of the validity, reliability, and credibility of scientific information. (12 marks)

AO3. How science works. Psychology; candidates should be able to describe ethical, safe, and skilful practical techniques and processes; know how to make, record, and communicate reliable and valid observations and measurements; analyse, interpret, explain, and evaluate methodology, results and impact of their own and others, investigative activities. (4 marks)

In Unit 3, candidates are also required to demonstrate their understanding of the major approaches in psychology through their study of individual topics; also to develop an appreciation of issues and debates as relevant to each topic: for example, gender/cultural bias, the role of animals in research, ethical issues, nature/nurture, free will and determinism, and reductionism.

The AO3 marks are likely to be accessed through methodological analysis and evaluation of studies.

UNIT 3: TOPICS IN PSYCHOLOGY

AO1 mark bands

Marks	Content	Knowledge and understanding	Range, breadth, and depth of material	Organisation and structure
9–8	Sound	Accurate and well detailed	Good range and substantial evidence of breadth/depth	Coherent
7–5	Reasonable	Generally accurate and reasonably detailed	Range of relevant material selected. Evidence of breadth/depth	Reasonably coherent
4–3	Basic	Basic/relatively superficial	Restricted range of material presented	Basic
2–1	Rudimentary	Rudimentary, may be muddled and/or inaccurate	Material presented is brief or largely irrelevant	Lacks
0	No credit-worthy material			

AO2/AO3 mark bands

Marks	Content	Commentary and evaluation	Focus and elaboration	Issues/debates/approaches	Synopticity	Structure and expression
16–13	Effective	Demonstrates sound analysis and understanding	Well focused and shows coherent elaboration and/or clear line of argument	Used effectively	Substantial evidence of	Ideas well structured and expressed clearly and fluently. Consistently effective use of psychological terminology. Appropriate use of grammar, punctuation, and spelling

AO2/AO3 mark bands

Marks	Content	Commentary and evaluation	Focus and elaboration	Issues/debates/approaches	Synopticity	Structure and expression
12–9	Reasonable	Demonstrates reasonable analysis and understanding	Generally focused and shows reasonable elaboration and/or line of argument is evident	Used in a reasonably effective manner	Evidence of	Most ideas appropriately structured and expressed clearly. Appropriate use of psychological terminology. Minor errors of grammar, punctuation, and spelling only occasionally compromise meaning
8–5	Basic	Demonstrates basic, superficial understanding	Sometimes focused and shows some evidence of elaboration	Superficial reference to	Some evidence of	Expression of ideas lacks clarity. Limited use of psychological terminology. Errors of grammar, punctuation, and spelling are intrusive
4–1	Rudimentary	Demonstrates very limited understanding	The answer is weak, muddled, and incomplete. Material is not used effectively and may be mainly irrelevant	If reference is made it is muddled or inaccurate	No evidence of	Deficiency in expression of ideas results in confusion and ambiguity. The answer lacks structure, often merely a series of unconnected assertions. Errors of grammar, punctuation, and spelling are frequent and intrusive
0	No credit-worthy material					

UNIT 4: SECTIONS A AND B

AO1

Marks	Outline
5–4	Reasonably thorough, accurate, and coherent
3–2	Limited, generally accurate, and reasonably coherent
1	Weak and muddled

AO2 (this applies if a part-question demands just AO2 with no AO3)

Marks	Content	Explanation	Focus and elaboration	Issues/debates/approaches	Synopticity	Structure and expression
10–9	Effective	Demonstrates sound analysis and understanding	Well focused and shows coherent elaboration and/or clear line of argument	Used effectively	Substantial evidence of	Ideas well structured and expressed clearly and fluently. Consistently effective use of psychological terminology. Appropriate use of grammar, punctuation, and spelling
8–6	Reasonable	Demonstrates reasonable analysis and understanding	Generally focused and shows reasonable elaboration and/or line of argument is evident	Used in a reasonably effective manner	Evidence of	Most ideas appropriately structured and expressed clearly. Appropriate use of psychological terminology. Minor errors of grammar, punctuation, and spelling only occasionally compromise meaning

AO2 (this applies if a part-question demands just AO2 with no AO3)

Marks	Content	Explanation	Focus and elaboration	Issues/debates/ approaches	Synopticity	Structure and expression
5–3	Basic	Demonstrates basic, superficial understanding	Sometimes focused and shows some evidence of elaboration	Superficial reference to	Some evidence of	Expression of ideas lacks clarity. Limited use of psychological terminology. Errors of grammar, punctuation, and spelling are intrusive
2–1	Rudimentary	Demonstrates very limited understanding	The answer is weak, muddled, and incomplete. Material is not used effectively and may be mainly irrelevant	If reference is made it is muddled or inaccurate	No evidence of	Deficiency in expression of ideas results in confusion and ambiguity. The answer lacks structure, often merely a series of unconnected assertions. Errors of grammar, punctuation, and spelling are frequent and intrusive
0	No credit-worthy material					

AO2/AO3 mark bands (this applies if a part of a question combines AO2 with AO3)

Marks	Content	Evaluation	Focus and elaboration	Issues/debates/ approaches	Synopticity	Structure and expression
16–13	Effective	Demonstrates sound analysis and understanding	Well focused and shows coherent elaboration and/or clear line of argument	Used effectively	Substantial evidence of	Ideas well structured and expressed clearly and fluently. Consistently effective use of psychological terminology. Appropriate use of grammar, punctuation, and spelling
12–9	Reasonable	Demonstrates reasonable analysis and understanding	Generally focused and shows reasonable elaboration and/or line of argument is evident	Used in a reasonably effective manner	Evidence of	Most ideas appropriately structured and expressed clearly. Appropriate use of psychological terminology. Minor errors of grammar, punctuation, and spelling only occasionally compromise meaning
8–5	Basic	Demonstrates basic, superficial understanding	Sometimes focused and shows some evidence of elaboration	Superficial reference to	Some evidence of	Expression of ideas lacks clarity. Limited use of psychological terminology. Errors of grammar, punctuation, and spelling are intrusive
4–1	Rudimentary	Demonstrates very limited understanding	The answer is weak, muddled, and incomplete. Material is not used effectively and may be mainly irrelevant	If reference is made it is muddled or inaccurate	No evidence of	Deficiency in expression of ideas results in confusion and ambiguity. The answer lacks structure, often merely a series of unconnected assertions. Errors of grammar, punctuation, and spelling are frequent and intrusive
0	No credit-worthy material					

The mark scheme for Section C (the methods question) is specific to each question, most of which carry only a few marks. However, if you have a study for 12 marks, the following mark scheme is likely to be used. All 12 marks are AO3.

Section C

Marks	Content	
12–10	Thorough and well reasoned	Design is thorough. Design decisions are appropriate and well reasoned. Sufficient detail for the study to be implemented
9–7	Reasonable	Design is reasonable. Most design decisions are appropriate and some justification is provided. Sufficient detail for most aspects of the plan to be implemented
6–4	Basic	Design is basic. Some design decisions are appropriate. Justification provided is very limited. Insufficient detail for the plan to be implemented
3–1	Rudimentary	Design is rudimentary. Design decisions are muddled and incomplete and are not justified. The plan could not be implemented
0	No credit-worthy material	

See *A2-Level Psychology Online* for advice on studying psychology at University and the opportunities for psychology graduates.

Biological rhythms p. 21
- What is the role of endogenous (internal) pacemakers and exogenous (external) zeitgebers in the sleep–wake cycle?
- What is the role of endogenous (internal) pacemakers and exogenous (external) zeitgebers in the menstrual cycle?
- What are the consequences of jet lag and shiftwork?

Sleep states p. 43
- What are the stages and cycles of sleep?
- Is sleep necessary for survival?
- Is the primary function of sleep restoration of the brain and body?
- How does sleep change across the lifespan?

Disorders of sleep p. 61
- What are the explanations of insomnia?
- What causes sleepwalking?
- What is narcolepsy?

Biological rhythms and sleep

By Evie Bentley

We live in a rhythmic world. Night follows day, the seasons on earth and the stars above follow their annual patterns, lawn daisies close at night and open in daylight, pubs open and pubs close! Behaviour also follows rhythms, whether or not we recognise them. Swallows migrate from Africa and arrive with us every June, and return to Africa in September. Easter is still associated with lambs and chicks, even though nowadays we can manipulate breeding seasons so that lambs and chicks can be produced all the year round. Nevertheless, the natural reproductive rhythms of many non-human animals remain seasonal, so that the newborn will appear when conditions are most favourable.

BIOLOGICAL RHYTHMS

The rhythms of living things are called biological rhythms or "biorhythms". These are patterns of physiological or psychological processes that are repeated over periods of time. We both have them and are affected by them. The main types of biorhythm can be grouped according to their period or duration, that is how frequently they occur or how long they last, as:

- **Circadian**: around ("circa" means "around") a day, i.e. 24 hours.
- **Ultradian**: less than a day, i.e. cycles that occur within a day, such as mealtimes.
- **Infradian**: more than a day, including circannual rhythms (around a year).

Psychological research has focused on two aspects of biorhythms: what they are and what causes or controls them. In this chapter, we look at what psychologists have found out about, and what can go wrong with, some of these rhythms.

KEY TERMS

Circadian rhythm: a regular, repeating pattern with a 24-hour cycle, for example, the 24-hour sleep–wake cycle.
Ultradian rhythm: a regular pattern with a cycle of less than 24 hours, for example, the NREM/REM sleep cycles in a night's sleep.
Infradian rhythm: a regular, repeating pattern with a cycle that is longer than 24 hours, for example, the human monthly menstrual cycle.

EXAM HINT

This specification requires you to know about biological rhythms including circadian, infradian, and ultradian rhythms. All three are specified so make sure you revise all three rhythms.

Circadian, Infradian, and Ultradian Rhythms

Circadian rhythms

These are rhythms with a cycle or period of about 24 hours. The most obvious one (and the most researched) is our own sleep–wake cycle. In any 24-hour period, we go to sleep and wake up. The time spent in sleeping and waking varies from individual to individual and culture to culture. It also varies as you get older. We know that most babies sleep more than most adults and that most elderly people sleep even less. The possible reasons behind these variations are discussed later in the different theories of sleep. According to Green (1994), mammals possess about 100 different biological circadian rhythms. For example, temperature in humans varies over the course of the 24-hour day, reaching a peak in the late afternoon and a low point in the early hours of the morning. Another example of human circadian rhythms is the release of hormones from the pituitary gland.

Research findings

Most of the evidence, such as from Meddis (1975a), shows an average of 7–8 hours' sleep per 24 hours. We also know that there are some lucky individuals who thrive on very little sleep compared with the general population, a real example of individual differences. Records suggest that nowadays, in the twenty-first century, we are sleeping less by about one-and-a-half hours a night than did our forebears 100 years ago at the turn of the twentieth century, and Coren (1996) has suggested that many of us are right now living in a state of mild sleep deprivation. We are not sleeping less because we need less sleep but because we now overrule natural daylight. We now make our environment as light as we want whatever the time of day or season, and so we keep awake longer and sleep less.

The case of Michel Siffre is a very clear demonstration of an innate, i.e. naturally occurring, circadian rhythm in a human. In other words, the sleep–wake cycle is something we are born with and which is biologically determined. It functions in the absence of any external cues such as daylight. You might have thought that light and darkness are what make you feel tired and awake, but this study demonstrates that we go to sleep without such external cues. Such external cues are called **zeitgebers**, a German word that literally means "time giver".

Evaluation

One criticism of the Siffre case study might be that it involved only one individual and perhaps we are not justified in concluding that all humans will behave in this way. However, the results have been confirmed by other cave studies (e.g. by Kleitman, 1963), as well as one that looked at a blind individual. Miles, Raynal,

Research shows that humans sleep on average between 7 to 8 hours, per night; some survive on considerably less. Prime Minister Margaret Thatcher was well known for taking only 4 hours sleep a night.

See *A2-Level Psychology Online* to download a podcast containing an interview with Evie Bentley on the material in this chapter.

KEY TERM

Zeitgeber: An environmental factor (for example, light) that can act as a time cue.

CASE STUDY: **MICHEL SIFFRE**

Michel Siffre was studied for 7 months in 1972, when he volunteered to live underground in caves out of any contact with daylight and without any other clues about what time of day it was, such as a watch, clocks, or TV. He was safe and well fed, and the caves were warm and dry. He was always monitored via computers and video cameras, he had a 24-hour phone-link to the surface, and he was well catered for in mind and body with books and exercise equipment. In this isolated environment, he quickly settled into a regular cycle of sleeping and waking. The surprise was that this cycle was of almost 25 hours, not 24! It was a very regular 24.9-hour rhythm, so that each "day" he was waking up nearly an hour later. The effect of this was that by the end of his months underground he had "lost" a considerable number of days and thought he had been underground for much less time than had actually passed.

and Wilson (1977) described the case history of a young adult male, blind from birth, who had a strong 24.9-hour circadian rhythm. Despite being able to hear a variety of possible time cues, or zeitgebers (such as clocks and radios), this young man had considerable problems resetting his personal circadian rhythm each day. In fact, his problems were so great that he had to take stimulants in the mornings and sedatives at night to get his innate rhythm in time with the rest of the world.

Evidence that it can be difficult to override endogenous circadian rhythms was found in a study of American submariners (Kelly et al., 1999). The submariners' work schedule consisted of 6 hours on duty followed by 12 hours off duty, thus producing an 18-hour day. Despite this schedule, and their ability to control their own lighting conditions, the submariners had an average circadian rhythm that lasted just over 24 hours. Why was this? The answer is probably that the submariners in question had social contacts with people living on a 24-hour schedule and, unlike Siffre, they were aware of clock time.

However, not all studies have supported the 24.9-hour human sleep–wake rhythm. Folkard (1996) reported an interesting case study of a young woman, Kate Aldcroft, who was voluntarily isolated for 25 days without any zeitgebers. She shifted to a 30-hour rhythm, and felt well and relaxed. The researchers used a novel method of marking her rhythms—they asked her to play "Amazing Grace" on her bagpipes at what she felt were the same times, twice daily. There was a difference of hours in the actual times when she in fact played the song. Folkard reported that the participant had slept for up to 16 hours at a time and suggested that although her body temperature rhythm was a 24-hour, i.e. circadian, one her sleep rhythm might be on a 30-hour cycle.

One final note about the sleep–wake cycle. One might ask—why 24.9 hours (if that is our innate rhythm)? One suggestion is that, in the very distant past, the earth might have had a longer rotation cycle so that our days were more like 25 hours. So perhaps our internal clock is set to this rhythm and is yet to adapt. However, the fact is that the earth used to spin faster and is very gradually slowing down, so that suggestion is unsupported by fact. It seems the extra 0.9 hours of the sleep–wake circadian rhythm is adaptive because it enables us to adapt to our environment and also to stay up later without negative feelings the next day, as is discussed in the next section on disrupting rhythms.

Studies of other circadian rhythms

There is also a 24-hour cycle in metabolic rate—the personal or cellular rate of energy-use. Colquhuon (1970) found that humans had a metabolic rhythm, which peaked at about 4 p.m. and dipped 12 hours later, at 4 a.m. This rhythm correlated with many cognitive functions, such as memory and attention. Interestingly there was also a small post-lunch dip, which could be explained from the action of the **autonomic nervous system** (ANS) and digestive system. The ANS is a discrete group of nerves that control many involuntary or automatic (thus "autonomic") activities, such as heartbeat and blood pressure: we don't have to think about them consciously, they occur automatically. The ANS is divided into the **sympathetic** and **parasympathetic nervous systems**. The latter has the

> ? Are you a "morning" or an "evening" person?

> ? What reason, apart from having a different circadian rhythm, can you think of to explain why this student might have slept for so long?

KEY TERMS

Autonomic nervous system: part of the peripheral nervous system (nerves) which controls much of our involuntary behaviour, such as our heart-rate, breathing-rate, and blood pressure.

Sympathetic nervous system: the division of the autonomic nervous system that stimulates the body into "fight or flight", in other words prepares it for sudden action. Among the effects are faster heart- and breathing-rates, and more glucose in the blood. (See also parasympathetic nervous system; autonomic nervous system).

Parasympathetic nervous system: the division of the autonomic nervous system which, when activated, makes us "rest and digest", in other words calm down, slow down, and relax. (See also sympathetic nervous system; autonomic nervous system).

effect of slowing us down after we have eaten so that the body's resources can concentrate on processing the food rather than being used elsewhere—the function of the parasympathetic system is sometimes called "rest and digest". So it would make sense that, after eating a meal, there would be a dip in our metabolic rate (the post-lunch dip). Unfortunately for this simple explanation, this dip in the cognitive cycle seems to happen regardless of meals, so currently there is no good rationale for its existence. Folkard (1983) suggested that the cognitive cycle is the result of a special autonomic arousal rhythm. In other words, he sees the circadian cognitive cycle as a side-effect of the ANS cycle, so that when the ANS slows us down to rest and digest, other functions, such as mental and cognitive arousal, also reduce. Perhaps we should all alter our behaviour and have lunch followed by a siesta so we are in harmony with this innate rhythm—research suggests our cognitive performance would benefit. Burdakov, Alexopoulos, Jensen, and Fugger (2008) support this concept with findings that glucose from digested food can inhibit certain neurons (nerve cells), which produce proteins called **orexins**, small proteins that affect our wakefulness. In extreme cases a severe malfunction of orexin neurons can lead to narcolepsy. According to Burdakov et al., "This may well provide an explanation for after-meal tiredness and why it is difficult to sleep when hungry."

Evaluation. Knowledge of circadian rhythms can be applied to several everyday behaviours. Alstadhaug, Salvesen, and Bekkelund (2008) studied migraine sufferers for a year, recording data of over 2000 attacks, which challenged anecdotal evidence suggesting the greatest frequency of attacks was in the morning. They showed that there was a circadian rhythm but the peak was around midday. There are also data suggesting that changing the clocks by an hour for daylight saving, as in British Summer Time, has a measurable negative effect. Using measures of morning-ness/evening-ness (which you might know as Larks and Owls), other self-measures, and sleep diaries, Alstadhaug et al. (2008) concluded that the autumn time change was more disturbing for morning types and the late spring time change more disturbing for evening types; but that overall the disturbance caused enhanced night-time restlessness and poorer quality of sleep, which in turn affected mood and behaviour. Perhaps most significantly, our main circadian rhythm influences physiological systems that break down foreign substances such as poisons and many drugs. This breakdown by the liver, intestines, and kidneys is under rhythmic control and could be used to work out the optimum time of day for taking medication—chronotherapeutics—so that the medication stays in the system longer before being broken down, and so would be more efficacious.

Core body temperature also varies on a 24-hour rhythm because heat is a by-product of metabolism, i.e. it is a by-product of any energy turnover or use. This is why, when you are using more energy (for instance, in playing sport or running for a bus), you feel hotter. So the production of body heat follows the metabolic rhythm and peaks at 4 p.m. and dips at 4 a.m. This rhythm is well known, but evidence for it

KEY TERM

Orexins: neuropeptide hormones involved in the stimulation of hunger, as well as of energy expenditure and wakefulness; also called hypocretins.

Did you know?

The fact that there are circadian rhythms for many hormones has important applications in medicine. When a doctor takes a sample of blood or urine it is important to record the time of day at which the sample was taken to properly assess it. For example, the stress hormone cortisol is at its highest level in the morning. If an early morning sample of urine was tested for cortisol but thought to have been taken later in the day, it would be easy to assume that the person was highly stressed.

Recent research has also suggested that biorhythms should be considered when prescribing medicines. It seems that the standard practice of taking a drug at regular intervals throughout the day may not only be ineffective, but can also be counterproductive or even harmful. Evidence shows that certain medical illnesses, the symptoms of which show a circadian rhythm, respond better when drugs are co-ordinated with that rhythm (Moore-Ede, Sulzman, & Fuller, 1982).

being an innate rhythm was demonstrated by Bollani, Dolci, Montaruli, Rondini, and Caran's (1997) study of babies in the first two days of life. The researchers monitored the babies' core temperature every 10 minutes for up to 2 days, by which time all six babies were showing a clear 24-hour main rhythm, with regard to temperature. This was presumed to be due to an innate mechanism because, in that time, it was unlikely that the infants would be responding to zeitgebers.

A recent study showed a rhythm that is circadian in rats but which varies from species to species according to body size. This rhythm originates in the hypothalamus and seems to regulate bone and body size, and heart and respiration rates. Bromage et al. (2008) discovered this when studying tooth enamel development, when they found this enamel growing in a rhythm, like annual rings in a tree. The rhythm is circadian in rats but in chimpanzees is a 5-day infradian one. In humans, this rhythm takes an average of 8 days, although there is considerable variation, from 5 to 10 days, depending on body size.

Core body temperature varies on a 24-hour metabolic rhythm—the process by which higher use of energy generates heat.

Ultradian rhythms

These operate in cycles of less than 24 hours, that is, they happen more than once a day. According to Carlson (1986) there are actually numerous cycles all with a periodicity of approximately 90 minutes and all linked to a controlling mechanism, a biological clock, in the medulla. This "clock" seems to control a pattern of regular changes in our alertness and associated activity during the day, as well as the non-rapid eye movement (**NREM**) and rapid eye movement (**REM**) sleep cycles at night. The ultradian clock starts to function early in life, while still in the womb. A rhythm of central nervous system (CNS) activity—eye movements—has been observed in foetuses as young as 20 weeks, and electroencephalograph (EEG) rhythms have been recorded in pre-term neonates, although all these early ultradian rhythms last for only about 30 minutes (Simunek & Sizun, 2005).

Research findings

The Bollani et al. (1997) study also showed up shallow ultradian temperature fluctuations in many of the babies studied, in other words their temperature had a rise and dip (although the changes were small) more than once a day. A study by Klein and Armitage (1979) found ultradian rhythms in cognitive vigilance, namely a 96-minute cycle in participants' performance on verbal and spatial tasks. They called this the "basic rest–activity cycles" (BRAC) and suggested that it might be related to rhythms during sleep, and very many more recent studies have confirmed a raft of approximately 90-minute ultradian cycles.

Sleep stages. The clearest example of ultradian rhythms comes from the study of sleep cycles, which is looked at more closely later in this chapter. The data are largely from the classic study by Dement and Kleitmen (1957) conducted on nine sleeping participants for up to 61 nights in a laboratory. They all showed quite

KEY TERMS

REM: rapid eye movements which occur in one type of sleep.
NREM: non-rapid eye movements where the eyes are still during one type of sleep.

? Why do you think there are different kinds of sleep?

considerable similarity in their sleep cycles, the rhythms that occurred during sleep. Dement and Kleitman found two distinct kinds of sleep: periods when the eyes moved rapidly under closed eyelids (rapid eye movement or REM sleep) and times when the eyes were motionless (NREM sleep). These sleep periods alternated during the night's sleep. There was an observed rhythm in this alternation, starting with NREM sleep and varying between individuals but reasonably constant for any one participant. The mean was a 92-minute NREM and REM rhythm. When participants were woken from REM sleep, dreams were recalled 152 times and no dreams reported 39 times, that is dreaming was reported over 79% of the time. When woken from NREM sleep, dream recall fell to under 7% (11 out of 160 times). Therefore, the ultradian rhythm is one of alternate NREM and REM sleep, with the latter being associated with dreaming, although not exclusively so.

Evaluation

These data are sound empirical data and have been tested and found to be reliable, so the evidence for these rhythms is strong.

Infradian rhythms

These have cycles of longer than 24 hours. Examples include the human menstrual cycle, which is more or less monthly, and the reproductive cycle in cats and dogs, which occurs twice a year. There have also been suggestions of various interesting lunar effects. For example, is there a real link between mental disorders and the moon, or was the idea of a "lunatic" merely superstition? Research may eventually be able to tell us. Nevertheless, there are many confirmed instances of behaviour that is related to the moon. For instance, seashore crabs move up and down their territory in time with the tides (caused by the moon's gravitational pull on the earth's waters) even if they are kept in constant laboratory conditions (Palmer, 1989). There is also the Pacific Palolo worm, as reported by Roberts (1982, p. 393), which rises to the ocean surface— turning it white—just once a year at dawn, precisely one week after the November full moon. This could well be evidence of a lunar-influenced innate neural clock. There are also human infradian cycles, some rather unexpected. Just as women have circulating testosterone, so men have circulating oestrogen. Celec, Ostatníková, Hodosy, Skokňová, Putz, and Kúdela (2006) have found a previously unknown 12-day infradian rhythm in circulating oestrogen in young, healthy men. However, this study needs to be replicated, and with a much larger sample than the five men studied, before the findings can be considered reliable.

Findings: the human menstrual cycle

Human menstruation is the best-researched infradian rhythm. This cycle is innate in females of reproductive age, regardless of culture. It is an example of a biorhythm that is controlled by hormones—biochemical messengers synthesised by glands of the endocrine system. Hormones are released into the blood and travel in the bloodstream to their target organs—their sites of action (see Silber, 1999, for a fuller account). In the case of the menstrual cycle, the hormones are oestrogen and progesterone (the ovarian hormones) and the target organs are the ovaries and womb. There are clear individual variations in the length of this rhythm or cycle, but the average seems to be about 28 days. This does not mean

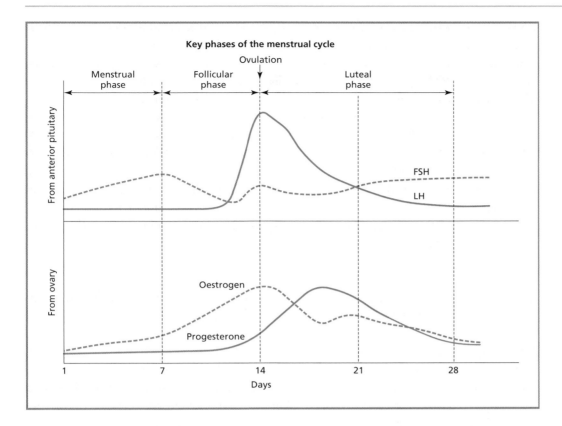

a cycle of different length is unusual or abnormal. It is not unknown to find a range of menstrual cycles from, say, 20 days to 60 days. The menstrual cycle starts with the ripening of an egg and the thickening of the lining of the womb, ready to receive a fertilised egg. Each cycle ends with menstrual bleeding, or menstruation, unless pregnancy occurs. The purpose of the cycle is to prepare the womb for the possibility of pregnancy, so a fertilised ovum can successfully grow and be nourished. The hormone oestrogen prepares the lining of the womb for this, and the hormone progesterone maintains the womb lining for a few days. Then, if there is no pregnancy, the lining is shed as menstruation. If there is a pregnancy, the womb will be freshly prepared to support the pregnancy. The lining continues to grow and, where the zygote implants, will form the placenta that will nourish the embryo.

Evaluation
It has long been observed that communities of women, such as girls in boarding schools, women's colleges, and nuns, all seem to have their menstrual cycles synchronised. It may be that the biorhythms of women who spend time together are controlled by pheromones, odourless chemicals released involuntarily by individuals and transported by the air, which carry messages within a species from one individual to another. This has been demonstrated empirically by Russell, Switz, and Thompson (1980). They collected sweat every day from one woman (the donor). This was then dissolved in alcohol to kill any bacteria and wipes of this mixture were applied under the noses of their female participants, also on a daily basis. The participants' menstrual cycles soon became synchronised with the donor's, showing a clear effect. It is thought that the natural and odourless pheromone molecules dissolve inside the nose and stimulate neurons, which in

? Can you think of any evolutionary advantages for synchronised menstrual cycles?

turn affect the hypothalamus and alter the pattern of hormone production. Why this should happen is not certain, although one suggestion might be an evolutionary one, as follows. We humans are social animals and live in social groups. We think this would also have been true of our remote hunter-gatherer ancestors. It would probably have been a real advantage for a social group to have synchronised pregnancies, which would result in several mothers breastfeeding at the same time (Bentley, 2000). This would not only mean that if a mother was ill or died another could take over feeding the baby, but that the mothers could in effect work shifts. Some could go and gather and prepare food and do other tasks, while others could feed the babies. So this synchronisation-by-proximity makes good sense in evolutionary terms. It is certainly seen in other non-human species, for instance in African lions, where lionesses in a pride operate on just such a system, and wet-nursing in humans, as well as traditional Inuit customs, show that you can continue to breastfeed even if your child was born much earlier.

Circannual Rhythms

These rhythms have a periodicity of about 1 year, that is, they are annual rhythms. They are also infradian. There is some evidence for circannual rhythms in humans. For example, Palinkas, Reed, Reedy, van Do, Case, and Finney (2001) studied men and women who spent the winter at the McMurdo Station in Antarctica. There were circannual rhythms in thryotropin-stimulating hormone and mood, with both peaking in November and July and having their lowest levels during March and April. These findings suggested that "winter-over syndrome" (involving negative moods, anxiety, and confusion) is due in part to a low level of thyroid function. Seasonal affective disorder (**SAD**; see below) can be considered to be another such rhythm—it describes people who become seriously depressed each autumn and feel better in late spring. Migrations and hibernation are other examples in non-human animals.

Seasonal affective disorder (SAD), where mood is at its lowest ebb in autumn and recovers in late spring, is an example of a circannual rhythm.

KEY TERM

SAD: seasonal affective disorder is a mood disorder, a form of clinical depression in which the sufferer develops low mood with the onset of autumn and falling light levels, only improving in mood in late spring when light levels rise again.

Research evidence: SAD and neurotransmitter systems

Some brain neurotransmitters have seasonal variations that may be circannual. The human nervous system has a large number of different neurotransmitters, some within the brain and some in the nerves. They are all chemicals that act on neurons, usually at the junctions between neurons called synapses. Neurotransmitters cross these synaptic junctions to alter the likelihood of nerve impulses occurring in the next neuron. Some facilitate or make it easier for new impulses to be generated and others inhibit or make it more difficult for the new impulses to start. Production of melatonin, a hormone and neurotransmitter produced by the pineal gland in the forebrain, varies with the quantity of natural light, that is, its concentration varies with the seasons. People who are particularly sensitive to their circulating levels of melatonin suffer in winter from the low-melatonin type of depression called seasonal affective disorder or SAD. There is more information on SAD later in this chapter.

Evaluation

Here, as before, the evidence is empirical and so can be accepted as reliable; these rhythms exist.

The Role of Endogenous Pacemakers and Exogenous Zeitgebers

It is abundantly clear that biorhythms exist, in ourselves, in non-human animals, and even in plants. This leads us to ask the main question—how are they controlled? Do we contain some sort of biological, internal clock and, if so, where is it? Or are we unconsciously sensitive to external, environmental cues (zeitgebers) which switch behaviours on and off? As we shall see, there is evidence for both internal and external clocks, and we have been able to identify the physiological mechanisms tied in with our internal clocks.

EXAM HINT

If you are asked to outline one or two biological rhythms, or to discuss research into biological rhythms, a useful way to organise your answer is to consider the evidence for the role of endogenous and exogenous factors.

Endogenous pacemakers

An internal or endogenous clock (or set of clocks) is proposed as some sort of biological mechanism that sets a periodicity or rhythm. Such biological clocks would be innate and internal, set by biological mechanisms. Their "tick" may be a 24-hour one (as for the sleep–wake cycle), an 8-hour one (as in the rhythms of sleep), or even a 12-month one (as in patterns of hibernation).

Findings

The Michel Siffre case study mentioned earlier (see page 22) is definite support for the existence of an endogenous (i.e. an innate) clock. Siffre was underground, with no natural light to tell him if it were day or night. He had videos to watch but no television, as that would have identified what time it was. He had all sorts of activities and facilities but no clock or watch and nothing that could serve as or give him any zeitgeber (time cue from outside his body). Yet he settled quickly and well into an approximately 25-hour circadian cycle (not the 24-hour cycle that might have been expected). The study by Miles et al. (1977), based on a blind man, and another by Aschoff (1965), which involved several participants living in a cave together, all confirm this approximate 25-hour rhythm when there are no external zeitgebers to indicate time of day or night. Therefore it seems that sleep–wake cycles are purely governed by internal, physiological cues.

The endogenous mechanisms involved in regulating bodily rhythms.

Non-human animal studies

Non-human animal studies also support the existence of an endogenous clock. Rae Silver and her team (cited in Blakemore, 1988) have conducted research on endogenous clocks in pigeons and in hamsters. They knew that pigeon pairs share the incubation of eggs in the nest by taking turns at sitting and they demonstrated that these turns are controlled by internal clocks, fixed in a pattern of 6-hour shifts. If one bird was delayed by, say, 2 hours in returning to take over in the nest (e.g. arriving at 3 p.m. instead of 1 p.m.) it would not leave after 4 hours, that is at 7 p.m., which would have been the "right" time for handing over if the bird was using an external cue. The bird would only leave after it had been sitting for 6 hours, that is at 9 p.m., even though the partner bird was waiting to take over. This rhythm is clearly not controlled by zeitgebers but must be determined by some internal mechanism, an extra clock perhaps, switched on by the start of the incubation shift. I say "extra" because this would be a clock that is additional to the sleep–wake cycle clock.

Evaluation

Internal clocks and the brain.   Evidence from studies of birds suggests that the sleep–wake cycle clock may be located in the pineal gland. In chickens, a pair of pineal glands lies at the upper surface of the brain, just under the thin top of the skull. Binkley (1979) showed that the glands contain light receptors. Some of the light falling on the top of the head penetrates the thin skull and stimulates the pineal gland. It is known that the pineal gland secretes the hormone melatonin in inverse proportion to the amount of light falling on the bird: as light decreases melatonin increases. This would mean that at dusk the production of melatonin is increased and that the reverse happens at dawn. Increased melatonin is associated with sleep—so we can see how changes in light can trigger an internal mechanism that governs the sleep–wake cycle. This explains why chickens become active at daybreak (also known as cock-crow!) and also would adjust the birds' activity to fit in with the seasonal variations in day length.

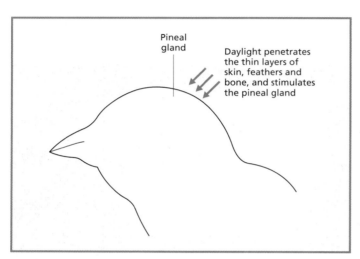

The position of the pineal gland in birds. From Bentley (2000).

Silver's experiments on hamsters have demonstrated how the internal clock may work in mammals as distinct from birds. If a tiny region of the forebrain, called the supra-chiasmatic nucleus (SCN), was removed, the hamsters' nocturnal behaviour (i.e. their circadian rhythm) disappeared. However, the behaviour was re-established if foetal SCN cells were subsequently implanted and allowed to grow. The foetal cells presumably took over the function of the lost SCN neurons. Other research involved transplanting SCN cells from mutant hamsters—animals with a different circadian rhythm giving them a diurnal rhythm—into non-mutant animals with the normal nocturnal rhythm; the recipients quickly changed their rhythm to that of the donor, mutant, SCN (Morgan, 1995). In addition, experiments with rats, which have shown a 25-hour circadian rhythm like humans, have linked damage to the SCN with complete disappearance of the circadian rhythm.

Human internal clocks.   Humans also have an SCN. It is significant that a tiny nerve branches off the optic nerve from each eye and connects with this tiny group of neurons. Whatever the amount and quality of light entering the eye, this light will generate nerve impulses that will travel out of the eye, along the optic nerve, and into the brain. Some of these impulses will go along the nerve branch to the SCN, taking along the information about the light (as shown in the figure on the next page). Thus the SCN is informed of the level of natural light. In this way, the variations and cycle of natural light can influence these special SCN neurons, which have an innate circadian rhythmic firing pattern.

The next stage of the process of biorhythm control involves the pineal gland. The SCN neurons regulate the pineal gland and its production of melatonin in the following way. If you recall, in lower animals (e.g. birds) light directly affects the pineal gland. In humans, the pineal gland is triggered into action by the SCN (which itself is triggered by light from the retina) and then produces melatonin, which builds up from dusk. A critical level of melatonin influences sleep, that is we feel the need to fall asleep when there is enough melatonin circulating in the blood.

So it seems that we have at least two endogenous mechanisms, the SCN and the pineal gland, which work together to control our circadian rhythm.

The visual pathway in the brain showing the connection to the suprachiasmatic nucleus (SCN) and onwards to the pineal gland.

More research findings: a second endogenous clock

We have behavioural and physiological evidence to support the existence of one endogenous clock— but another clock seems to exist as well. When people living in caves modify their sleep–wake rhythm to suit themselves, as opposed to relying on light and darkness, their circadian rhythms alter to fit the new sleep–wake times, with the exception of body temperature! This suggests a separate time clock for the temperature cycle (Hawkins & Armstrong-Esther, 1978). Earlier in this chapter we saw that body temperature follows a circadian rhythm with a peak at 4 p.m. and a trough 12 hours later. There is also the 90- to 96-minute cycle, found in both our REM/NREM sleep rhythms and in our cognitive vigilance during the day, which suggests another internal "clock" or pacemaker (Klein & Armitage, 1979).

The classic work in this area was carried out by Blake (1967), who asked naval ratings to perform several tasks at five different times of day (08.00 a.m., 10.30 a.m., 1.00 p.m., 3.30 p.m., and 9.00 p.m.). For most of the tasks, the best performance was obtained at 9.00 p.m., with the second-best level of performance occurring at 10.30 a.m. However, later studies found that peak performance on most tasks is reached at around midday rather than during the evening (Eysenck, 1982).

Can you think of anyone whose melatonin cycle differs from the norm?

Evaluation

Why might people perform at their best at midday rather than earlier or later in the day? Relevant evidence was obtained by Akerstedt (1977). Self-reported alertness (assessed by questionnaire) was greatest at about noon, as was the level of adrenaline. Adrenaline is a hormone associated with states of high physiological arousal in the ANS. However, it should be noted that the notion of physiological arousal is rather vague and imprecise. Furthermore, these are correlational data, and it is hard to be sure that the high level of midday performance *depends* on arousal.

After the midday peak there may be a trough. Blake (1967) found that most of his participants showed a clear reduction in performance at 1.00 p.m. compared with their performance at 10.30 a.m. This reduction in performance occurred shortly after lunch, and is commonly known as the "post-lunch dip". The explanation for this is that the physiological processes involved in digestion make us feel sluggish and reduce our ability to work efficiently. It is also noteworthy that the act of digestion is governed by the parasympathetic branch of the ANS, which leads to general relaxation, whereas physiological arousal is an effect of the antagonistic ANS branch, the sympathetic branch. The timing of this peak could depend on the morning-ness or evening-ness of the individual, being delayed in the evening-ness people, the night owls. This time-of-day effect seems to be genetic as it is directly related to the timing of a surge in cortisol in the first hour waking for the morning larks (Kudielka, Federenko, Hellhammer, and Wust, 2006).

Environmental influence, the exogenous zeitgebers

Are biological clocks all there is to control our biorhythms? Far from it. We know that various environmental cues can affect and reset our internal biological clocks. Why do we feel so ghastly when we have travelled across several time zones? Why do most of us find it difficult to work shifts, especially if these shifts change from week to week? Well, the answer to these questions seems to lie in our sensitivity to zeitgebers—environmental time cues.

Research findings

Resetting the clocks. We have to be sensitive to our environment. It is essential for survival not only in the wild but also in our "civilised" lives. For instance, if we did not alter our clothing to suit the environment we would easily succumb to hyper- or hypothermia, not to mention feeling uncomfortable and looking silly. In the wild, animals need to respond to seasonal variations by shedding hair or travelling to warmer climates. We also learn to associate points in our circadian rhythm with environmental cues such as mealtimes, coffee-breaks, and time for bed. We learn to feel hungry at certain times of day. This could explain why stomachs seem to rumble more just before mealtimes than when we are not expecting food.

There are good reasons why our biorhythms should be sensitive to *both* internal and external control. Without external control, animals would not be sensitive to seasonal variations; they would not shed hair in summer or grow extra hair in winter. Some animals sleep at night, possibly because it is safer; other animals hunt at night because they are adapted for this. In either case, the animal needs to respond to light cues. Light cues are not likely to be the only cues as far as seasonal variation is concerned. Air temperature would also be important, as it would alter the nutritional needs in order to maintain core body temperature. Thus, we can see that responsiveness to external cues enables animals to adapt to environmental conditions, which is vital for survival.

However, if animals were solely at the mercy of environmental cues we would have very irregular biological patterns and this might be life threatening.

Light as a zeitgeber. This environmental awareness extends to having an innate response to both the amount and quality of light, as described above. Psychologists believe that zeitgebers can and do reset our endogenous clocks on at least a daily basis, so that we adapt to 24-hour cycles in a 24-hour world even though we contain a 25-hour innate clock. This means that when we wake up in the morning our brain clocks are reset by morning light and our brains get ready for another day. So the morning light, which resets the chickens' pineal glands (as mentioned earlier in this chapter), is a zeitgeber for them too. In fact, light is a zeitgeber for most animals—remember those Palolo worms that respond to the November full moon. Perhaps this sensitivity to the level of light might be a factor in explaining why many of us find it so much more difficult to get up in winter, when it is darker until later in the morning—the quality of light is simply not high enough to reset our internal clock up to wakefulness! Berson, Dunn, and Takao (2002) say we have to rethink how the retina works after the finding of a new type of light-sensitive cell, different from the rods and cones and buried deeper in the retina. Like rods and cones, these cells turn light energy into nerve impulses and connect with the SCN. This research was done in rats, but mammal eyes and retinas are built on the same pattern so it is likely, although not proven, that the same system exists in humans.

Biochemicals as zeitgebers. We have seen how pheromones can reset the human menstrual cycle. This was first demonstrated by McClintock (1971), who showed a "dormitory effect" of synchronisation of menstrual cycles in the women in her university dormitory, who were thus acting as zeitgebers. A further interesting fact about how external factors may affect menstrual cycles is that women who work with men tend to have shorter menstrual cycles. This suggests that male pheromones may also be acting as zeitgebers for the female reproductive bio-clock. This could be explained in evolutionary terms: females who reproduce more often will have more offspring and therefore their genetic line is likely to become dominant. Therefore it is adaptive for females to be fertile, i.e. ovulate more often when men are about, leading to shorter menstrual cycles.

Evaluation

There is more about zeitgebers to come, but one of the most telling pieces of evidence about them is that in their complete absence (e.g. when people live underground), the normal circadian rhythm alters and becomes unsynchronised with the 24-hour rhythm of the world in which we live. This supports the view that environmental cues have a "strong" effect and, as we noted at the start of this section, it is for good reason—we need to respond to our environment to survive.

CASE STUDY: SLEEP PROBLEMS ON A SPACE STATION

In 1997, Jerry Linenger lived on the space station Mir for 5 months. He had real sleep problems because the station lights, which were meant to mimic a 24-hour light–dark cycle, were so dim. The best light cues came in through the windows, and the sun's light was very, very bright. But as Mir orbited the earth every 90 or so minutes this produced 15 day–night (i.e. light–dark) cycles every 24 hours. Jerry says he tried to cope, but couldn't, and that he'd see his Russian colleagues suddenly nod off and float around the cabin.

Monk (2001) monitored Jerry during his time in space and reported that after 90 days the astronaut's quality of sleep deteriorated very rapidly. Monk thinks the brain's endogenous pacemaker had become disrupted by the abnormal light rhythm.

Consequences of Disrupting Biological Rhythms

This section looks at what happens when bodily rhythms are disturbed. How does this affect our behaviour and what have psychologists suggested we do to cope better? The material is interesting in its own right and has important applications, e.g. considering the effects of **jet lag** on airline pilots. This chapter also provides evidence for discussing sleep states and the theories of sleep.

Humans are very adaptable. We have successfully colonised all but the most inhospitable regions of our world and are able to cope with extremes of temperature. We also can adapt to many and various day-length situations. Those who live in temperate zones cope with the changes from long days and short nights in summer to the opposite in winter, whereas those in equatorial regions have very little variation in day length. The people who inhabit the regions inside the Arctic Circle have summer weeks when the sun never sets and winter weeks of unremitting darkness. However, this latter may not be so easily adjusted to. After all, most of us cheer up and feel more positive on a sunny day and the thought of weeks of darkness is not really appealing!

Earlier, we saw that we ourselves are rhythmic, as well as being sensitive to the rhythms of the world around us, such as mealtimes and also dawn and dusk. So how do we adapt if there is no dawn and no dusk? There is a suggestion that some of us cope better than others, that there is individual difference in the extent to which we can adapt. For example, statistics in Finland, a country where the sun does not rise above the horizon for several weeks in winter, show that there is a very high suicide rate and also a large problem with abuse of alcohol. Are these signs that people are finding that the extreme rhythm of a night that lasts for weeks affects their minds and behaviour? This could be so, and there is a possible link with a recognised condition described below.

Seasonal affective disorder

This behavioural disorder, known as SAD, affects a number of people who experience serious depression as autumn approaches and shorter days set in, recovering only when spring brings more and stronger daylight. This is a serious clinical condition, far more than the slight lowering of mood many experience on

---

CASE STUDY: SEASONAL AFFECTIVE DISORDER

In a BBC documentary, Blakemore (1988) described the case of an individual with seasonal affective disorder (SAD), studied at the Maryland National Institute of Mental Health. Pat Moore had suffered from unipolar depression for many years before she became aware that her depression was seasonal, arriving with the start of winter and lifting when spring came. This was no minor mood change but a strong emotional swing so severe that her whole life was affected and her ability to function deeply impaired. In winter, she would sleep for 12 hours a day and when awake she had little energy, less enthusiasm, and felt her life held no pleasure. Blakemore suggested that humans might be sensitive to day length in the same way as some plants are, as well as many of the animals whose behaviour changes with the seasons. You have seen how the brain detects daylight and therefore, we can assume, day length also.

The idea that a factor as simple as daylight or day length could be responsible for Pat's condition was tested, with her full co-operation. As autumn arrived, she would wake early, using an alarm clock, get up and sit for a few hours listening to the radio. The key thing was that she listened to the radio sitting in front of a bank of full-spectrum lights which bathed her in bright white light as similar as possible to natural light. The result was astonishing. Pat reported feeling less down within just days of starting the treatment. After some weeks she was feeling herself again, having regained her energy and positive feelings even though it was still winter. She went from saying, "I don't seem to have a good period of time . . . and don't see a future right now" to "I feel fine now, sleeping about six hours a night . . . and then sit in front of the light box . . . I feel something has been turned on in my brain that says . . . it's time to live!" (Blakemore, 1988).

overcast or dull days. It seems the changing duration and quality of light seriously disrupts their circadian sleep–wake rhythm.

? What are the drawbacks of using case studies to collect evidence?

Evaluation

The Pat Moore case study suggests that not only is the brain very sensitive to light and day length, but it can respond to the rhythmic changes in these and sometimes this response is a negative one, producing SAD. By using extra light, the negative effect can sometimes be countered, even if this is just a temporary improvement. Therefore, it is possible that this debilitating condition can, for some sufferers, begin to be treated, at least partially successfully, with the right sort of light, and people can reclaim their lives.

A clear drawback to this research is the fact that it was a single case study and as such one should be cautious about making generalisations. It is possible that the results were due to a placebo effect—the fact that Pat expected to benefit from the light therapy might alone explain her recovery. Nevertheless, other research confirms the link between lack of daylight and SAD. For example, Booker and Hellekson (1992) found an incidence of about 9% in Alaska. Alaska lies across the Arctic Circle and so has very restricted day length and also a low quality of light during the winter months. However, Feadda, Tondo, Teicher, Baldessarini, Gelbard, and Floris (1993) found similar rates of SAD in a retrospective study of seasonal mood disorders in Italy, a Mediterranean country known for its sunshine, both in summer and most of the winter! The fact that SAD is also showing up there suggests there may be causes other than lack of daylight. It is possible that the Italian study was flawed insofar as it was retrospective and therefore memories may have been distorted. Of course, if there really is a significant occurrence of SAD in sunny countries then it may well be that this condition is far more complex than we think. For example, the key factor could be the difference between summer and winter light levels, in other words the size of the change in light quality.

It was once hoped that light therapy (**phototherapy**) would cure the SAD condition, but early experimental studies suffered from poor methodology, and what appeared to be improvements might have been unrelated to the therapy; possibly the result of experimenter expectations. Lamm (1994) reported improved methodology in the 1990s but his overview of research did not show any clear pattern, although later studies have shown a real benefit using bright light similar in wavelengths to natural light (Lam, Tam, Yatham, Shiah, & Zis 2006). Interestingly, Avery, Bolte, Cohen, and Millet (1992) and Avery et al. (1993) have shown a positive response in improving mood using dawn simulation. This involves a device that gradually increases light intensity towards the end of the time the participant is sleeping, mimicking natural dawn, and reaching a bright light level at the desired waking time. Later research has shown that using bright full-spectrum light, closely similar to natural sunlight, for a few hours following waking has very good effects on mood. The light pathway in the brain may also be linked to the neurotransmitter serotonin. Treatment with selective serotonin reuptake inhibitors (SSRIs) has also shown an improvement in mood for people with SAD.

> **KEY TERM**
>
> **Phototherapy:** therapy using bright light, usually as closely similar as possible in wavelength to sunlight, to improve mood, for example for sufferers of seasonal affective disorder.

A young seasonal affective disorder sufferer receiving phototherapy from a light box.

Air-traffic controllers have to be alert to tiny changes in flashing lights on their screens at all hours of the day or night as the lights represent aircraft. How well humans cope with disruption in sleep patterns is therefore of great concern to both industry and the general public.

Shiftwork

Many industries depend on shiftwork to keep going 24 hours a day. We obviously want our doctors, nurses, and other health professionals to be functioning at whatever hour we need them. Long-distance drivers, air-traffic controllers, and airline crew also often work through the night; many manufacturing industries also want their plant in action continuously as it makes good economic and commercial sense, and our armed forces need to have personnel alert all round the clock. But even electronic machinery requires human attention; so a human economic and psychological concern has been whether humans cope well with sleep rhythms being disrupted.

As mentioned before, our innate biological clocks are reset at least daily by environmental stimuli known as zeitgebers. The most powerful zeitgeber is light, which puts the endogenous clock mechanisms in tune with the environment, our external world. Additional zeitgebers include mealtimes and other markers of daily/nightly routines, such as clocks striking the hour and music associated with times of day. This can give rise to psychological difficulties if different zeitgebers are in conflict, for instance if twilight and sounds of evening come when someone is waking to start their "day" because they are working a night shift. We know that the innate rhythms of metabolic rate and particularly body temperature are fixed and do not vary with either zeitgebers or altered daily shifts. There could be conflict between the brain trying to work to one rhythm and the body to another. However, one cannot assume that all individuals will experience the same problems because, as Webb (1975) showed, some of us are more alert in the morning and others in the afternoon, that is there is a pattern of individual differences. In fact some of us work naturally at night (those students who stay up all night writing their essays) whereas others prefer to work in the morning.

■ Activity: The effects of shiftwork
Interview some shiftworkers using a questionnaire that comprises both fixed-response and open-ended questions. The aim is to find out what effects shift work has on your participants.

Start by establishing what their shift pattern is: is it clockwise rotating shifts (e.g. 6 a.m. to 2 p.m.; 2 p.m. to 10 p.m.; 10 p.m. to 6 a.m.); 12 hour shifts day and night; shifts that are mainly daytime, etc. Ask about sleep patterns (including how much these vary from one shift to another), mood, relationships, etc. (but be careful not to be too intrusive). Emphasise that you are mainly interested in whether the participants' mood and general sense of well-being changes according to the shift they are doing. It would also be interesting to see if they would recommend any changes in their shiftwork patterns, and compare this to Czeisler's recommendations.

Evaluation

One problem with shiftwork is often mild sleep deprivation. It can be difficult to adjust to daytime sleeping, even in a well-darkened room, when zeitgebers such as noises outside are a clear indication of the local world being awake. Akerstedt (1985) showed that people on shiftwork slept 1–4 hours less than when they could sleep normally at night. He also showed that they had a particular deficit in REM sleep. If REM sleep has a particular function then this function would also show a deficit. Burch, Yost, Johnson, and Allen (2005) found that night shiftworkers had disrupted circadian melatonin production, and that this was associated with disrupted sleep, fatigue, increased risk of accidents, and even chronic disease. The raised accident risk is discussed in the later section on performance deficits. A potential further problem is a suggestion (Furlan, Barbic, Piazza, Tinelli, Seghizzi, & Malliani, 2000) that night shiftwork is associated with an increase in heart disease.

Alleviating the effects of shiftwork

Czeisler, Moore-Ede, and Coleman (1982) have conducted a considerable amount of research related to shiftwork and found that it generally takes people 16 days to adjust to a new shift pattern. They also found that people were less tired and adjusted more easily if their shifts were rotated with the clock rather than against it, in other words a system of early shifts, then later shifts, then night shifts and then back to early shifts again. This would be working with, not against, the innate 24.9-hour clock and lengthening the day; that is, getting up later, progressively, which is less stressful than having to get up earlier. Czeisler et al.'s ideas were applied to a Utah chemical plant and workers there reported sleeping better, feeling much less tired on the job, and experiencing increased motivation and morale. Self-reporting is not empirical evidence as it is of course completely subjective, but the management also reported increased output plus fewer errors being made, so there was consensus that the new shift patterns were an improvement. Gordon (1986) reported similar improvements in a study in the Philadelphia Police Department.

Monk and Folkard (1983) also looked at the organisation of shiftwork and found that a rapidly rotating shift pattern, with workers doing only a few shifts before moving on to a different work time, could be better than the slowly rotating shift pattern where shift times changed after several days or even monthly. This is possibly because individuals might be able to maintain a fairly constant circadian rhythm in the rapid-rotation pattern, whereas the slow-rotation pattern would cause major disruptions of the circadian rhythm with each shift change.

A different approach to improving life on shiftwork was taken by Dawson and Campbell (1991), who arranged for people on their first night shift to work under a 4-hour pulse of very bright light. This seemed to help these people adjust better, as their body temperatures did not fall as much as expected during the night shifts. The hours of bright light might have partly at least reset their endogenous clocks.

> **EXAM HINT**
>
> Sleep is an ultradian rhythm and so is relevant to questions on biological rhythms. Sleep-deprivation studies can be used to illustrate the consequences of disrupting biological rhythms.

Jet lag

Anecdotal evidence has long supported sleep disturbances, headaches, and feelings of mental dullness and irritability when several time zones have been crossed. This jet lag, as the effects are known, is a feature of aircraft crews' lives and an unwelcome effect for many who travel for business and leisure. These effects do not seem to happen much if people travel from north to south or vice versa, thus staying in the same longitude and therefore the same time zone. This means that if someone flies from Manchester, Glasgow or Belfast to Accra in Ghana they should not suffer from jet lag. Even though the flight will have lasted several hours, they are staying in the same time zone and so there will be no inner "time" conflict and they will have neither gained nor lost any hours.

Jet lag can be a problem for airline staff, who frequently cross time zones in the course of their work.

Psychological knowledge about our innate clocks and zeitgebers suggests that the effects of jet lag are the result of a mismatch between our inner psychological rhythms and the outer zeitgebers, the environmental cues. For instance, if one flew from London to New York, a city 5 hours behind the UK, and arrived at 3 p.m. New York time, one's internal clock would be at 8 p.m. and when—physiologically—the body was winding down in preparation for sleep, in New York it would be late afternoon and the locals would be at their psychological circadian peak. Thus, there would be inner "time" conflict and it is this that is believed to produce the symptoms and inappropriate feelings of jet lag.

Evaluation

Jet lag is known to be more severe when flying from west to east, e.g. the shorter route from the UK to Asia, than from east to west. The suggested explanation here is linked to our 24.9-hour clock. It seems that a phase delay—delaying or putting on hold our internal clock, e.g. by staying up later—is easier to accommodate to than a phase advance—making one's internal clock skip ahead, e.g. going to bed earlier. This explanation certainly fits in well with anecdotal experience—most of us know that it is far easier to stay up late at night and feel fine at the time than it is to wake up even 1 hour earlier in the morning and feel morning-bright!

Klein, Wegman, and Hunt (1972) showed that people recover faster from jet lag after flying east–west than flying in the opposite direction. This finding suggests that it takes the endogenous mechanism and, therefore, the sleep–wake cycle about 1 day per time zone crossed to recover.

Schwartz, Recht, and Lew (1995) analysed the results of the USA baseball major league from 1991–1993 and found that teams from the west coast that had travelled east over three time zones had significantly fewer wins than teams from the east coast travelling three time zones westwards. This ties in well with the extra difficulty in adjusting when moving eastwards, a feature of jet lag, and these findings are supported by more recent research (Reilly, Waterhouse, & Edwards, 2005), although this does not explain why not everyone crossing time zones by air experiences jet lag.

Rather worryingly, Cho (2001) found a reduction on temporal lobe size and memory function in air crew who regularly flew over seven time zones, especially if only a short turn-around time was allowed. This small study challenges the view that jet lag is psychological, as it shows organic structural changes and cognitive reduction in the disorder.

The stress brought on by changing time zones and the difficulty sleeping could, in itself, be a factor in upsetting body clocks. Stewart and Amir (1998) found that rats that have been emotionally upset are not as good at resetting their innate clocks using light as the zeitgeber as rats that have not been emotionally stressed. Stewart and Amir suggested that emotional upsets could make the SCN less responsive to light. This could be a factor in humans as well, as many people find long-haul travel and its associated time changes stressful, and many people who do fly for business or pleasure are scared of being in the air. This could mean that such people take longer to accommodate to the new time zones. It could also explain why some people do not seem to experience jet lag after a long journey—such people might be those who do not experience travel and changing time zones as stressors. This hypothesis could even be applied to shiftwork, as we know that not everyone has difficulties coping with this.

? Is it easier to override endogenous cues for sleep or for waking?

See *A2-Level Psychology Online* for an interactive exercise on jet lag.

Psychologically and physiologically, the way to minimise the effects of jet lag are said to be to keep well hydrated, to avoid alcohol and caffeine (which interfere with the brain's normal functioning), and to fit in with the local zeitgebers, e.g. having meals at the "correct" time. Logically, this ought to make the adjustment to local time quicker and easier, but there are no empirical data on this.

A treatment for jet lag is available in some countries, although not the UK. This is the hormone melatonin, which is secreted by the pineal gland in the brain. Melatonin is thought to make us feel sleepy and start to wind down. Anecdotal reports suggest it can be useful in resetting the endogenous clock if small doses are taken a couple of hours before local bedtime. No real evidence is available at the moment, but research studies are in progress and so far seem to be supporting this idea.

> **?** What are the dangers with taking melatonin?

CASE STUDY: MELATONIN AND AIRCREW

Melatonin is now available in pharmacies in the US, and some claim that it can cure jet lag. Jet lag can lead to fatigue, headache, sleep disturbances, irritability, and gastrointestinal disturbances—all with a potentially negative impact on flight safety. Interestingly, reported side-effects of melatonin use include many similar symptoms. Although some researchers claim that melatonin is among the safest known substances, no large clinical evaluations have been performed on its long-term effects.

Scientists believe that melatonin is crucial for the functioning of our body clock. Studies suggest that treating jet lag with melatonin can not only resolve sleeping problems but also increase the ability of the body clock to adjust to a new time zone. However, those in the medical community advise caution. Melatonin is not a universal remedy for everyone who needs to travel over many time zones. Some physicians suggest that it should not be used unless the user intends to spend more than 3 days in the new time zone.

International aircrews will often cover several time zones, typically flying overnight west to east, spending 24 hours on the ground, then returning during the day (east to west). This cycle is likely to be repeated several times before an extended period of sleep is possible. Using melatonin to adjust the body clock in these circumstances is viewed by many scientists as inappropriate.

Timing the dose of melatonin is very important. Studies show that resynchronisation of the sleep–wake cycle occurred only if the subjects were allowed to sleep after taking the medication. In those participants unable to sleep after taking melatonin, the circadian rhythm was actually prolonged. More worryingly, the effect of melatonin on fine motor and cognitive tasks is unknown and the nature of melatonin's sedative effects are uncertain.

Unfortunately, there are no published clinical studies evaluating flying performance while taking melatonin. The US Armed Forces are actively evaluating melatonin's aeromedical usefulness. Despite ongoing research, no US military service permits the routine use of melatonin by aviators. Significantly, aircrew participating in experimental study groups are not allowed to perform flying duties within 36 hours of using melatonin.

Pre-menstrual syndrome

The monthly menstrual cycle is a normal rhythm of women between menarche and menopause. However, in all cultures some psychological fluctuations occur only in some women. The all-cultural nature of these is an indication that the fluctuations have a physiological cause and are not the product of specific cultural beliefs or behaviours. Typical changes, known collectively as **pre-menstrual syndrome** (PMS), occur a few days before the menstrual bleeding and include feelings of great energy followed by great exhaustion (Luce, 1971), plus headaches, increased irritability, depression and—for some women—also visual disturbances and mental sluggishness. Yonkers and O'Brien (2007) consider that whereas all women have some pre-menstrual symptoms, a minority is unusually sensitive to the rhythm of circulating progesterone, and that this effects a change in mood that might even lead to high levels of aggression.

Evaluation

Dalton (1964) correlated the pre-menstrual period with an increase in accidents, less achievement academically, suicide, and crime. Although a correlation cannot

> **KEY TERM**
>
> **PMS:** pre-menstrual syndrome is a condition in many women in the days preceding their monthly period when mood and emotional swings can develop.

actually infer causation, but just a possible link, in recent years PMS has been increasingly accepted by the legal world as a contributory cause of anti-social behaviour, with (in some cases) custodial sentences being reduced as a result. It is suggested that in some women the hormonal changes of the menstrual cycles adversely affect normal behaviour, but more research into PMS is needed to make clear conclusions possible and to clarify the continuum that has severe PMS as one extreme and no severe symptoms at the other.

Performance deficits

Errors or mistakes, known as performance deficits, have been linked with disturbances in our bodily rhythms, especially our sleep cycle. All of the above examples can be used as valuable comments on the psychological importance of our biorhythms.

Shiftwork, with its disruption of the daily rhythm, has the strongest links to performance deficits. Novak, Smolensky, Fairchild, and Reves (1990) studied accident rates in an industrial chemicals plant and found higher rates in shiftworkers than in day workers. Gold et al. (1992) reported sleepiness and errors in nurses on shifts, supporting Hawkins and Armstrong-Esther (1978), who monitored eleven nurses on the first seven sessions of doing a night shift. They judged the nurses' performance to have reduced significantly on the first night, although this improved as the week went on. The sample was very small indeed and there was large variation in the results, but body temperature (which had been monitored as a measure of the innate biorhythm) had not adjusted by the end of the week.

The disruption to daily rhythms and the resultant sleepiness that shiftwork imposes was reported by Gold et al. (1992) as negatively affecting the performance of the nurses in their study.

? Would you expect to find that industrial accidents are more likely to occur at certain times of the day?

Social data show that motorway accidents are particularly likely to occur when the circadian rhythms are low, at 2–4 p.m., midnight–2 a.m., and 4–6 a.m. Horne (1992) showed that a momentary falling asleep, sometimes for a few seconds only, was the probable cause, because an absence of skid or braking marks indicated that the driver had not been aware of the impending accident. This is likely to be because of a momentary lapse of consciousness, not of attention. He also found that these drivers were likely to have been awake for longer than usual, about 18 hours, and/or were sleep-deprived, as in shiftworkers.

All this has serious implications for society. As stated earlier, it is now normal for many people to work shifts—it is estimated that approximately 20% of people employed in the US work in shifts. Current psychological research suggests that many of them will therefore be under-performing at work, or before or after work. Some may be driving road vehicles or trains or planes. Some may be doctors or nurses or air-traffic controllers, yet psychological research may not always be being applied to the performance of these vital roles, despite research studies, such as that by Williamson and Feyer (2000), which show that even moderate sleep deprivation has cognitive and behavioural effects comparable to drinking alcohol, e.g. a 50% reduction in reaction speed. In the early 1970s, junior hospital doctors in the UK could be working a 100-hour week on duty. By the mid-2000s the weekly hours were down to 56 hours out of 72 hours on call in the hospital. The annual cost to the community of these changes has been in millions of pounds. But the hidden costs of not making these changes, even in terms of performance deficits, would have been vast.

EXAM HINT

You might be asked to discuss the consequences of disrupting biological rhythms. AO2 can seem daunting with this question so use the following as a guide for useful points to make:

- Draw conclusions from the research evidence about shiftwork (optimal direction and length of shift patterns) and jet lag (direction of flight, how to adjust to new time zones).
- Consider the positive applications of this research in terms of real-world usefulness and validity.
- Consider applications of the findings on light and medication times.
- Consider methodological weaknesses, such as the fact that some of the research studies are natural experiments and so we cannot confidently conclude cause and effect. Since there is a lack of control in such research other factors may influence the effects, such as individual differences (e.g. "lark" or "owl").
- Consider social factors rather than just biological ones—a shiftworker might spend little time with the family and this could lead to conflict, which might exacerbate the negative effects.

SECTION SUMMARY
Biological Rhythms

❖ Rhythms occur in the natural world. They can be categorised into:

   — Circadian rhythms, which occur once every 24 hours, e.g. the human sleep–wake and core-body-temperature cycles.

   — Ultradian rhythms, which occur more than once every 24 hours, e.g. the NREM/REM and cognitive-vigilance cycles.

   — Infradian rhythms, which occur less frequently than once every 24 hours, e.g. the human menstrual cycle; infradian rhythms lasting about 12 months are called circannual, such as SAD.

What are biological rhythms?

❖ Endogenous pacemakers are internal clocks, probably located in the brain.
❖ There are several such pacemakers.
❖ The human sleep–wake pacemaker consists of the SCN, which receives information about levels of light from branches of the optic nerves and links to the pineal gland and serotonin production.
❖ Exogenous zeitgebers are the environmental factors that can modify endogenous pacemaker activity. This enables adaptations to environmental variation. Light and pheromones are examples of exogenous zeitgebers.

The role of endogenous pacemakers and exogenous zeitgebers

❖ Biological rhythms can be disrupted in the course of everyday life.
❖ SAD is an example of unipolar depression, a psychological disorder:

   — it occurs in many countries
   — sufferers are possibly unusually sensitive to seasonal changes in light levels
   — bright full-spectrum light therapy has promising therapeutic effects, as has treatment with antidepressants, which increase serotonin activity.

Disrupting biological rhythms

Shiftwork

- ❖ People working unsocial hours might experience possible conflicts between the main zeitgeber, light, and other zeitgebers such as mealtimes, TV programmes, and clocks.
- ❖ Metabolic rate and body temperature rhythms are fixed, innate, and do not alter with shifts, so there are potential conflicts between the brain rhythm and the daily shiftwork rhythm.
- ❖ There are also individual differences such as larks and owls (Webb, 1975).
- ❖ Mild sleep deprivation, especially of REM sleep, may result (Akerstedt, 1985).
- ❖ This could contribute to an increase in accidents, and in conditions associated with physiological stress.
- ❖ Czeisler et al. (1982) found that mood, health, and performance improved if shifts changed with the clock rather than against the clock.
- ❖ Dawson and Campbell (1991) used very bright light in the first 4 hours of a night shift to help personnel adjust and found their body temperature fell less than was expected.

Jet lag

- ❖ Aircraft crews, businesspeople, and holidaymakers frequently report problems after flying east or west but not after flying north or south.
- ❖ Phase delay, i.e. staying up later, is easier for most people than phase advance, i.e. getting up earlier.
- ❖ American baseball teams flying east to west had far more wins than teams flying west to east (Schwartz et al., 1995).
- ❖ Not everyone flying across time zones experiences jet lag.
- ❖ Stress could weaken the SCN response to changes in light levels (Stewart & Amir, 1998).
- ❖ The above research was done on rats, and it is debatable how valid it is to extrapolate from such findings to humans.

Pre-menstrual syndrome

- ❖ Some women—regardless of culture—experience symptoms in the days before onset of menstruation, such as great energy followed by great exhaustion, plus headaches, increased irritability, and depression (Luce, 1971).
- ❖ Research correlates the PMS period with an increase in accidents, less achievement academically, suicides, and crime (Dalton, 1964).
- ❖ There is no empirical evidence explaining why the effects of PMS are a continuum from extreme to none, and a correlation does not infer causation.

Performance deficits

- ❖ Research supports a link between disturbing bodily rhythms and performance deficits (mistakes).
- ❖ Studies show sleepiness and errors, or higher accident rates in shiftworkers compared to day workers.
- ❖ Motorway accidents are particularly likely to occur when the circadian rhythms are low, at 2–4 p.m., midnight–2 a.m., and 4–6 a.m.
- ❖ Moderate sleep deprivation has cognitive and behavioural effects comparable to drinking alcohol, e.g. a 50% reduction in reaction speed.

SLEEP STATES

 What happens to you physiologically and psychologically when you are asleep?

The Nature of Sleep

Physiological control of biorhythms

The research described earlier in this chapter about the SCN and its links to the pineal gland is the key to the physiological control of the sleep–wake clock—both for the internal and external mechanisms. This section looks in more detail at the physiological processes.

Exogenous (external) control

It seems that morning light is received by the light-sensitive cells in the eye—the rods and cones—and stimulates nerve impulses that travel in the two optic nerves. Some impulses travel along a tiny branch off the optic nerves and reach and reset the SCN. The SCN also communicates with the pineal gland, which is located further back in the forebrain. Increased levels of light cause the pineal gland to cease producing melatonin. But from dusk the low levels of light detected in the SCN stimulate the pineal gland to produce melatonin again. As the melatonin accumulates, it influences the production of serotonin, a brain neurotransmitter involved in many pathways, including mood and sleep. Serotonin accumulates in the raphe nuclei in the hindbrain, near the pons, and stimulates the shutting down of the reticular activating system (RAS), which is closely linked with brain activity. So serotonin could be the switch to start the sleep clock. The suggested sequence could be as illustrated below.

See *A2-Level Psychology Online* for an interactive exercise on the sleep–wake cycle.

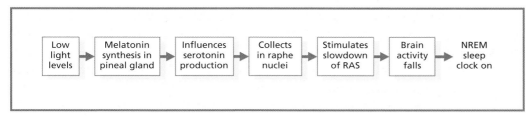

Summary of the brain mechanism involved in sleep. From Bentley (2000).

Endogenous (internal) control

Jouvet (1967) suggested that another region, the locus coeruleus in the pons, uses a different neurotransmitter, noradrenaline. In his experiments, if this area was damaged, noradrenaline levels fell and REM sleep was impaired. Jouvet proposed that each area, plus its neurotransmitter, controls one type of sleep—the raphe nuclei and its serotonin pathway control NREM sleep, and the locus coeruleus and noradrenaline pathway control REM sleep. He also hypothesised a link between the two systems so that the two types of sleep alternate. More recent research has started to understand the complicated circuitry involved (e.g. Sakai, 1985). It would appear that this circuitry involves the pons, raphe nuclei, and locus coeruleus (among others) and involves a number of different neurotransmitters, especially serotonin, noradrenaline, and acetylcholine. Supporting evidence comes from links to other brain areas. The locus coeruleus has a pathway to the cerebellum, an area known to control eye movements and muscle co-ordination—perhaps this is how the eye movements of REM are

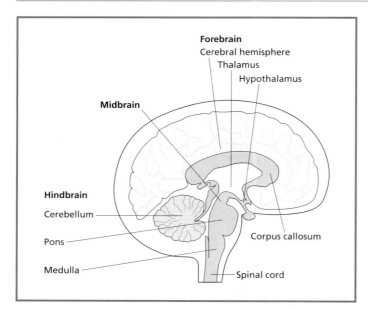

Forebrain
Cerebral hemisphere
Thalamus
Hypothalamus

Midbrain

Hindbrain
Cerebellum
Pons
Medulla

Corpus callosum

Spinal cord

The main regions of the human brain.

effected. The raphe nuclei have a pathway to the hypothalamus, which also controls body temperature and growth and repair. Electrical stimulation of a group of cells neighbouring the locus coeruleus brings about REM-style paralysis.

Unfortunately, this nice model falls down because Ramm's (1979) review of relevant research shows no ill effects on REM sleep from damage to the locus coeruleus or its pathways, although there is good evidence for the role of the raphe nuclei and their pathways on NREM sleep. Stern and Morgane (1974) suggest that REM sleep is really needed for the resynthesis of neurotransmitters, particularly noradrenaline and dopamine. This fits with the known effect of tricyclic and other antidepressants, which reduce REM sleep and increase noradrenaline levels.

Kayama and Koyama (2003) found that noradrenaline and the locus coeruleus are in fact involved with waking and with brain arousal, but that serotonin and the raphe nuclei seem to inhibit higher brain activity and so could be involved in sleep. Acetylcholine-sensitive neurons seem to have a function in inducing and maintaining REM sleep.

A further factor is a biochemical, adenosine. This builds up during wakefulness and is then broken down during sleep. It has been suggested (NINDS, 2007) that the build-up causes drowsiness and could switch the brain into preparing for sleep mode.

In conclusion

Evidence for biological clocks comes from even the simplest organisms. For instance, single-celled algae from the intertidal zone burrow up to the sand surface as the tide ebbs and go back under the sand again as the tide flows in, so that they can photosynthesise without being washed away. Evolutionary biopsychology is now suggesting that these biological clocks started as single, light-sensitive molecules in primitive bacteria and have evolved into current, complex structures (as reported by Highfield, 1996).

Our own main internal clock having a 25- not 24-hour rhythm can also be interpreted from an evolutionary perspective. Being able to adapt is critical for biological success and the human species is immensely adaptable, as our varied cultures and habitats show. By having the potential to adjust our day/night clock to suit the local conditions and being able to alter the relative timings of our own rhythms, we are successfully adapting to our environment so we fit in and live in tune with it, and work with not against it. As you will see later in this chapter, this also makes us happier.

The Nature of Sleep

The essential need for sleep in order to behave and feel "normal" is known across cultures and time. A medieval man in England who had served the years of preparation as a squire to become knighted had to spend the night before the final ceremony kneeling, awake, in vigil to prove himself able for the honour and duty of a knight. Today, when people wish to demonstrate their strong feelings in peaceful protest, an all-night vigil is often used. It is a sign of how deeply people feel that they are willing to give up their sleep. Less happily, sleep deprivation has been—and is—used as part of brainwashing techniques and even torture by authorities all over the world. On a different level, we are probably all too familiar with the mentally dull feeling after a very late night, especially if this has been followed by an early class!

A sleep deficit has well-known effects, but many people also believe we can suffer from similar mental dullness after a surfeit of sleep. However, is there any empirical evidence as to the effects of sleep disturbances? Many studies have been done on both non-human animals and our own species. Before we look at these, we will consider the extent to which sleep is both a circadian and an ultradian rhythm.

Different kinds of sleep

Sleep is an altered state of consciousness but not a state of unconsciousness—even the deepest sleeper can be woken up, although this can sometimes take quite a bit of doing! We go to sleep once a day and within this period of sleep we experience a number of different states of consciousness. Dement and Kleitman's (1957) research showed not only two types of sleep with associated brainwave (EEG) patterns, but also that the two types alternate in an ultradian rhythm and that dreaming is associated much more strongly with one of those types. The two types of sleep are rapid eye movement, or REM, sleep and non-rapid eye movement, or NREM, sleep. Dement and Kleitman found that waking participants during REM sleep was usually accompanied by reports of dreaming, whereas waking out of NREM was far less likely to produce such reports. Therefore it is a mistake to equate REM sleep with dreaming but there is a strong association.

How are sleep stages measured?

Empirical measurements are achieved using electrodes connected from an individual to a computer that receives and processes the incoming data:

- EEGs (electro-encephalograms): record brain activity from a set of electrodes temporarily attached to the skin on the head.
- EOGs (electro-oculograms): record muscle movements around the eyes.
- EMGs (electromyograms): electrodes are attached to the skin covering muscles.

The data from these gives us a picture of overall brain activity, the brainwaves, eye movements, and body muscle tone and movements.

Stages of sleep

Further research has shown that we go through four separate stages of NREM as we fall asleep. Participants who have volunteered to sleep in various sleep-research laboratories have been wired up to computers and recorders. This is usually done for several nights in succession, so that participants can get used to the artificial conditions and start sleeping more naturally. Studies have shown that after the first night, when the arrangement of sleeping is strange, participants do sleep normally (Empson, 1989). In such studies, tiny metal electrodes are taped to the skin at points on the head and wires from these discs or electrodes connect to the computer. Any tiny electrical changes from the brain are picked up by these electrodes and passed to the computers. These changes are then shown graphically as an electro-encephalogram or EEG trace and the patterns produced are called brain waves.

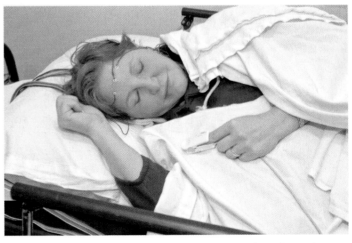

A woman undergoing a sleep research study. Tiny electrodes are attached to the head. These pick-up electrical changes in the brain to produce an EEG trace.

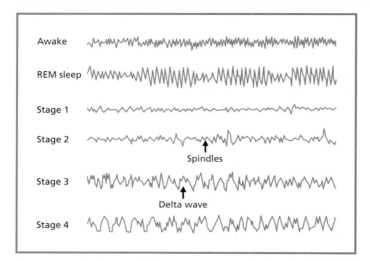

Electro-encephalogram (EEG) trace. From Bentley (2000).

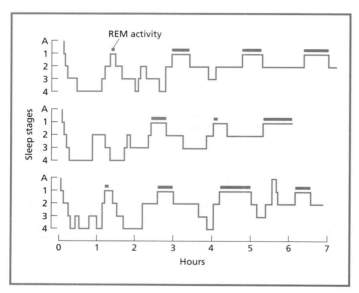

Cyclic variations in EEG during three typical nights' sleep. Note the increased REM activity as the night progresses, and reduced Stage 4 sleep.

Stages of NREM sleep

Each stage of sleep has its own corresponding EEG patterns and this is what has given us the knowledge that there are four stages in NREM sleep (which is also known as quiet sleep). When we are awake and active our brain rhythms are busy and this shows as a pattern of rapid and irregular brain waves—the EEG traces show very many, tightly packed, unsynchronised brain waves called beta waves. When we are awake and relaxed we see the presence of rhythmic waves called alpha waves in the brain EEG.

Stage 1 NREM.   Stage 1 sleep occurs when we are falling asleep and takes up to 15 minutes. Recordings show brain waves slowing down from the slow alpha waves of relaxation to even slower and more irregular theta waves (see figure above). These patterns become synchronised, that is a regular pattern emerges. The parasympathetic nervous system is active ("rest and digest") and so the heart rate slows and muscles relax. This is when we may not be aware that we are falling asleep and this state is quite similar to that of deep relaxation or meditation. It is easy to be wakened from this state and we can also jolt back into full consciousness, often thinking that something significant has happened—like the phone ringing—when in fact it hasn't. This relaxed first stage of sleep is also known as the hypnogogic state, and hallucinatory images (perceptual experiences that seem very real but which in fact are illusions) occurring here are linked to creativity.

Stage 2 NREM.   Stage 2 lasts about 20 minutes and is when the brain theta waves get slower and larger with intermittent little bursts of activity called sleep spindles; this electrical activity is also called k-complexes, and is tiny bursts of activity associated with external stimuli that do not awaken us, such as the wind whistling outside your window. Heart rate, blood pressure, and body temperature continue to fall and quiet sounds no longer waken us.

Stage 3 NREM.   Stage 3 has further falls in the heart rate and in the rate of breathing, and brain waves slow still more into delta waves with some sleep spindles. It is now quite difficult to be woken. This stage, like the previous ones, lasts for only about 15 minutes.

Stage 4 NREM.   Stage 4 is the deepest sleep. This is when growth hormone is secreted. Metabolic rate is at its lowest and it is very difficult to waken out of this state—unless there is a personally significant noise such as your own baby crying or someone shouting "Fire!" Brain waves are at their slowest too. This stage lasts typically for 30–40 minutes and is the bottom of the "sleep staircase". Although it is the deepest stage of quiet sleep, this is the stage in which sleepwalking is more likely to occur. This might seem odd, but sleepwalking is not necessarily connected with dreaming (Jacobson & Kales, 1967). Sleeptalking also occurs in deep NREM sleep, although this can also happen—less often—during REM sleep (Arkin, Toth, Baker, & Hastey, 1970).

REM sleep

After half an hour or so in Stage 4 sleep, suddenly the EEG trace speeds up the "sleep staircase" through Stages 3 and 2, showing the brain is suddenly more active. The brain waves desynchronise and become complex, as well as faster, and the brain's oxygen and glucose demands increase. The eyes start to move under closed eyelids, we go into REM (or dreaming) sleep, and are most difficult to wake.

Although we are now cerebrally very active we are physically inactive, our bodies from the neck down are almost as if paralysed. The RAS in the midbrain seems to set up a block, isolating the brain from the rest of the body. Only the

---

Sleepwalking

Dreams do not always occur in REM sleep. REM dreaming is accompanied by paralysis, probably to protect sleepers from acting out their dreams and injuring themselves. People also dream in NREM sleep, but less often, and they are not in a paralysed state. Thus, it is possible to act-out NREM dreams, which can lead to sleepwalking.

Sleepwalking is more common than one might guess; 30% of all children between the ages of 5 and 12 have walked in their sleep at least once, and persistent sleepwalking occurs in 1–6% of youngsters. Boys walk in their sleep more often than girls, and the tendency to wander during deep sleep is sometimes inherited from one of the parents.

The typical sleepwalking episode begins about 2 hours after the person goes to sleep, when they suddenly "wake" and abruptly sit up in bed. Although their eyes are wide open, they appear glassy and staring. When asked, sleepwalkers respond with mumbled and slurred single-word speech. The person may perform common acts such as dressing and undressing, opening and closing doors, or turning lights on and off. Sleepwalkers seem to see where they are going because they avoid most objects in their way, but they are unaware of their surroundings. Unfortunately, this means that they cannot tell the difference between their bedroom door and the front door, or the toilet and the wastebasket. The sleepwalker is usually impossible to awaken and does not remember the episode in the morning. The episode typically lasts 5 to 15 minutes and may occur more than once in the same night.

Although sleepwalkers avoid bumping into walls and tripping over furniture, they lack judgement. A sleepwalking child might do something like going to the garage and getting in the car, ready to go to school at 4 a.m. Sometimes, this lack of judgement can be dangerous. One sleepwalking child climbed a tree and another was found by the police walking down the street in the middle of the night. Therefore, sleepwalkers are in danger of hurting themselves and must be protected from self-injury.

Most children outgrow sleepwalking by the time they are teenagers, but for a small number of individuals the pattern continues into adulthood.

Christian Murphy escaped with cuts and bruises when he fell from his first-floor bedroom window while sleepwalking. His mother's Mercedes, which was parked below, broke his fall. Once he had landed he got up, still sleepwalking, and set off down the road.

heart and lungs seem to match the speeding-up of the brain. This REM sleep lasts for only about 10–15 minutes and completes the first sleep cycle of the night.

We then go back down through Stages 2 to 4 again, and this cycle repeats about every 90 minutes through the night, although the time spent in Stages 3 and 4 gets progressively less until only Stages 1 and 2 of NREM plus REM sleep are returned to by the end of the night.

This 90-minute cycle is the ultradian rhythm of sleep. Whether we wake up remembering what we were dreaming of may depend on whether we awaken from our last bout of REM sleep—remembering the dream—or from NREM sleep.

Other terms for REM sleep. Dement and Kleitman (1957) observed that REM sleep is associated with a highly active brain while at the same time the body's muscles are effectively paralysed so there is virtually no movement. They coined the term "paradoxical sleep" to describe this apparent contradiction. The paradox is that at a time when the brain is full of activity the body is not. Some modern researchers would prefer that REM sleep, being so different from the other stages, was called Stage 5 sleep.

Meddis (1979) used a different labelling. He called NREM sleep "quiet sleep" and REM sleep "active sleep". These terms refer to the brain activity as shown by the EEG traces. Meddis further subdivided quiet sleep into light quiet sleep (LQS) with synchronised slow patterns of EEG traces and deep quiet sleep (DQS) with larger, regular wave-like EEG traces. Stage 2 sleep would be LQS and Stage 4 would be DQS, and AS (active sleep) would include both Stage 1 and REM sleep.

Sleep-deprivation studies

One question that is asked is whether sleep is in fact necessary. Is something in the nature of sleep essential for health and healthy mental functioning? Before we look at theories of sleep we can see what research can tell us happens if sleep is restricted or completely stopped.

Non-human animals

? Is it possible to study sleep deprivation without encountering ethical difficulties?

Jouvet (1967) used cats and other animals in his experiments. He arranged flowerpots, upside down, in a large, high-sided tank of water with only a small part of the pots above the water level. When cats were put into the tank they swam quickly and got out of the water, sitting upright on the exposed pots, showing their well-known dislike of getting wet. However, they were left on the pots and eventually fell asleep. At first they were all right, seemingly dozing and presumably in NREM sleep with muscles that could still just about support the body. However, as they went into REM sleep and their muscles became slack— the effective paralysis mentioned earlier—their bodies slumped and they slid into the water. This of course woke them and they climbed out again. This cycle was repeated and quite soon the cats learned to awaken as soon as their heads began to nod.

The cats who kept themselves from going into normal REM sleep started to show abnormal behaviour, such as high levels of stress, and eventually they died. Jouvet was looking for evidence of the need for sleep, and this and similar studies were interpreted as demonstrating the essential nature of sleep, namely that REM sleep is essential for life and without it life becomes impossible.

Evaluation: Nowadays many of us would have serious ethical concerns about this sort of research, but the validity of the research has also been questioned. It has been argued that this and similar experiments had such low ecological validity that it is not possible to draw any conclusion relating to life outside the laboratory. Also, given the well-documented strong aversion cats have to getting wet, and also the fact that they were trapped in the tank, it is highly likely that they suffered from high levels of stress from the environment as well as from the lack of REM sleep. This stress alone could well have produced the abnormal behaviour and even the deaths—it certainly would have contributed. Selye's (1956) General Adaptation Syndrome (GAS) proposed that prolonged stress leads to a state of physiological and psychological collapse, which he termed the exhaustion stage.

Rats also soon die if they are deprived of sleep. They suffer physiologically, showing a breakdown of the normal control of, for example, body temperature (Hobson, 1995). Another study where rats were selectively deprived either of all sleep or of just REM sleep showed that this led to a combination of increased food intake but also weight loss, as well as the breakdown of temperature control, leading to death after 4 weeks (Rechtschaffen, Bergmann, Everson, Kushida, & Gilliland, 1989). But still it is not possible to say that all these ill effects were the results only of sleep deprivation and that other factors, such as stress, were not involved.

Human participants

An early experiment was Dement's (1960) study of eight volunteers who were monitored at night and woken every time they went into REM sleep. The first night this involved being woken an average of 12 times, but by the seventh night this went up to 26 times: more than double. This was seen as an indication of the vital nature of REM sleep, the need for REM sleep growing stronger the more the

 How do you deprive someone of NREM sleep? If the answer is that you cannot, what does this say about the validity of Dement's research?

CASE STUDY: **SLEEP DEPRIVATION: CASE STUDIES**

Two case studies of severe sleep deprivation are well known and demonstrate various effects of going without sleep for prolonged periods.

Gulevich et al. (1966) reported a 17-year-old man, Randy Gardner, who was able to stay awake for 264 hours (11 days!). For many years, this was the record for sleep deprivation. As the days went by, Gardner developed blurred speech and vision—a combination of perceptual and cognitive faults. He mistook some objects for people and showed what have been described as symptoms of mild paranoia, such as feeling people were labelling him as stupid because of his cognitive difficulties. However, he did not have a complete mental breakdown and recovered swiftly after a good sleep. He did not catch up on all the sleep he had lost, sleeping for only 15 hours the first night and in total making up just a quarter of the lost sleep. Most of this was in Stage 4 NREM and in REM sleep—two-thirds of the former and half the latter. This does indicate that these are the types of sleep that are most necessary, that have important functions, but does not, of course, tell us what those functions are; although perhaps Stages 1–3 NREM sleep are needed as the pathway into Stage 4 and REM sleep.

Peter Tripp was another case study, reported by Dement (1972). Tripp was a DJ who stayed awake for 200 hours as a publicity stunt in New York's Times Square. Dement observed

quite severe paranoid psychosis developing, with Tripp having delusions, such as of being poisoned. Tripp also tried to throw himself under traffic. His personality seemed to alter after his sleep deprivation stunt, compared with how he was before it, but some years later he resumed his positive and extravert way of life and enjoyed very successful new careers. The psychosis and personality change is very different from Gardner's experience and could, for instance, be an illustration of individual differences or of expectation, as Tripp might have expected to experience strange sensations and so on, whereas Gardner might not. Furthermore, at the time of his stunt Tripp was also involved in financial scandals associated with his DJ-ing work, and the stress from that could have been responsible for his personality change.

In these extreme cases, sleep was stopped suddenly and, as with any case study, one cannot really generalise to the normal population from isolated cases, even though there are now several reports of individuals staying awake for many days without long-term adverse effects. However, Lugaresi et al. (1986) studied a 52-year-old man who had lost the ability to sleep as the result of brain damage and who became progressively more exhausted and stressed. This condition is extremely rare, and is fatal, perhaps because of the lack of sleep, or the stress, or even the brain damage.

Peter Tripp begins his "trial by sleeplessness" in a glass-walled booth in the middle of Times Square.

participants were deprived of it. Dement reported that participants exhibited only minor and temporary behaviour changes associated with this loss of REM sleep. Although, interestingly, he initially reported some significant disturbances in behaviour, he later realised that these symptoms had been, as it were, wishful thinking—what is known as the effects of experimenter expectations—and corrected himself. He had expected that sleep deprivation would result in disturbed behaviour and these expectations apparently led him to make biased observations.

Evaluation. The final consequences of sleep deprivation in non-human animals are not necessarily seen in humans, but then human research participants are treated differently. Many studies have been done involving depriving human participants of some or all sleep and, although a temporary degree of dysfunction has sometimes resulted, this has not been life threatening or, of course, the study would have been stopped at an early stage. Researchers would not want harm to come to their participants as this would not be morally right, and also would reflect badly on them and their research. In recent years, participants have been protected from psychological or physical harm by guidelines set out by the relevant authorities. In Britain these are issued by the British Psychological Society (BPS), updated regularly (most recently, in 2007), and are binding on all psychological research in the UK from the date of publication. The BPS has also issued similar guidelines controlling the use of non-human animals.

? Many people feel that, when they are tired, they can't work at their best. What do psychiatrists suggest to be the reason for this depressed performance?

More research findings

Experimental studies have taken a less totalitarian route and have looked at a gradual deprivation of sleep—from which there seem to have been few if any major negative effects. Webb and Bonnet's (1978) studies started with participants being deprived of just 2 hours' sleep, after which they reported feeling fine, although they did fall asleep more quickly the next night and then slept for longer. Participants were also put on a 2-month programme of gradual sleep reduction, from an initial 8 hours a night sleep down to a final 4 hours. They reported no adverse effects, which does seem to indicate that we have a remarkable ability to do without sleep if we have to.

Self-reporting, however, is not a method for collecting reliable data. It is not possible to be sure of its objectivity—in fact, as Popper (1969) says, it is likely that humans cannot be truly objective. Also, there could well have been demand characteristics: the participants could have felt an expectation from the researchers for certain findings. It might also have been the case that some participants responded in a "macho" way—they could have felt that to admit to adverse effects would be seen as being wimpish.

Evaluation

Overall, the research seems to show that we do need to sleep, regularly, in order to feel and behave in our normal way. The actual amount of sleep per night

Overview of sleep-deprivation studies

Nights without sleep	Effects
1	People do not feel comfortable, but can tolerate 1 night's sleep loss
2	People feel a much greater urge to sleep, especially when the body-temperature rhythm is lowest at 3–5 a.m.
3	Cognitive tasks are much more difficult, especially giving attention to boring ones. This is worst in the very early hours
4	Micro-sleep periods start to occur, lasting about 3 seconds, during which the person stares blankly into space and temporarily loses awareness. Individuals become irritable and confused
5	As well as the effects described above, the person might start to experience delusions, although cognitive ability (e.g. problem solving) is unaffected
6	Individuals start to lose their sense of identity, to be depersonalised. This is know as sleep-deprivation psychosis

Adapted from Hüber-Wiedman (1976).

averages out at about 7–8 hours in total, but there is considerable variation between individuals. Expectation seems to be a powerful factor here, as in other of our behaviours, and if we expect to be able to cope with less sleep than usual then we are likely to find this happens. When making up lost sleep we do not show a need to catch up on all the sleep lost, but only on some of it. This is known as the REM-rebound effect as most of the caught-up sleep is REM sleep plus the Stage 4 NREM sleep leading into REM.

Hüber-Weidman (1976) produced an overview of the findings of a large number of sleep-deprivation studies, summarised in the box above. It is important to realise that the symptoms of these deprivations are more psychological than physiological for people who have been deprived of sleep for just a few days. It is also important to recognise that many, if not most, of the effects are due to REM deprivation alone rather than total sleep deprivation.

Horne (1988) proposed a model that is a bridge between a theory of sleep and sleep-deprivation studies. He suggested that most of us have more sleep than we need. It has been proposed that people sleep because their bodies need time to replenish biochemicals that have been used during the day; this "restoration theory" of sleep is described in the next section. Horne pointed out that, in fact, cell restoration takes place during the day as well as at night, so it might be that only some of our sleep is necessary, perhaps the early hours of sleep. Horne called this core sleep. He based this on an older study in which groups of participants were allowed 6 weeks on a fixed amount of sleep per night. One group slept for 4 hours nightly, a second group for 6 hours, and the third group for 7.5 hours. Participants performed a variety of cognitive tests before and after the experimental sleep period, and only the 4-hours-a-night group showed any effect at the end, a minor drop in memory. Horne concluded that we need only about 5 hours' sleep a night; the rest he termed "optional" and suggested that it could be omitted without ill effects.

Do people make up for lack of sleep during the week by sleeping longer at the weekend? Ask people to make a note of what time they go to sleep and wake up every night for at least a week. See if those who sleep comparatively little during the week make up for it at the weekends. Results can be analysed, first, by splitting the groups in two: low levels of sleep in the week and high levels of sleep in the week (you might need to discard some data if participants fall in between); then by comparing the total amount of sleep at weekends.

You need a test of difference for independent groups. It is possible that results could go either way: the idea of a sleep debt would suggest that sleep at the weekends will be greater in the "low weekday sleep" group but if sleep is determined by individual differences and/or habit, then the "low weekday sleep" group will sleep less at weekends.

If one looks back to see the pattern of sleep stages through the night, it seems that Horne is suggesting that our Stage 4 NREM sleep is vital but that only about half of our REM sleep is needed. This is a novel idea and could link in with the minor consequences of short-term sleep deprivation, but does not fit in with most other data showing the REM-rebound effect. Also, long-term loss of REM sleep is associated with psychological dysfunction such as hallucinations or waking dreams, which also does not support Horne's proposal.

A last thought

Some research has suggested an extra and different effect: that too much sleep can impair our performance and even lead to or be part of psychological disorders. Increased REM sleep is a feature of many people with unipolar depression. The tricyclic antidepressant drugs that act successfully to lift this disorder selectively block, and therefore reduce, REM sleep without interfering with NREM sleep. Pinel (1993) cites this as evidence that REM sleep deprivation is not harmful. Alternatively, it could be that the increased REM sleep before treatment was part of the problem, i.e. that it was in some way part of the depression, and that the tricyclics are beneficial by their action of reducing this extra REM sleep.

? What are the dangers with taking antidepressant drugs?

Summary

Sleep is not one phenomenon but several. It can be divided into REM sleep, when we dream the most, and NREM sleep, when the eyes are fairly still and we do not seem to dream much. NREM sleep has four stages, each with its own characteristic electroencephalogram (EEG) pattern. Stage 1 is when we start to fall asleep; Stages 2 and 3 are deeper stages of sleep, and Stage 4 is the deepest. REM sleep does not have stages. It has a fast EEG trace as the brain becomes very active, but the body is effectively paralysed and is quiet. Research has shown that deprivation is associated with detrimental effects, varying from minor, short-term perceptual problems to possible major and lasting personality changes. However, it is not clear how many of these are specifically caused by total sleep deprivation, by REM deprivation, or by other causes such as expectation. The methodology and extremely unusual conditions of many studies make it difficult to gain generalisable conclusions. Horne has suggested a different concept of core and optional sleep, which is interesting and ties in with some findings but not with others.

Functions of Sleep

The previous section explains some of what goes on when we sleep, but we also need to consider explanations of why we sleep. In addition, we should consider ideas on why it is that the amount of sleep we have varies not only with age but also individually from one person to another. According to Aristotle we sleep because, after eating, vapours from digesting food rise up and make

? Why do you think there are several stages of sleep?

the brain drowsy. However, there are two main theories of sleep now current. They are the evolutionary theory (or ecological theory) and the restoration theory.

Evolutionary explanation

The evolutionary or ecological theory, suggested by Meddis (1975a, 1975b, 1979), proposes that sleep could be a time of increased safety as animals are immobile and therefore less likely to be noticed by predators. We are all aware of how difficult it is to keep still for any length of time; movement, it is suggested, could attract unwelcome notice. So Meddis suggests that to be more or less still when it is too dark to see either food or threats could be an advantage for some animals. However, some animals do not appear, at first, to fit with this theory. What about those animals who sleep in the day and are nocturnal in habit? Some of them, such as owls, are specialised to see well in low light, and there are others, like bats, that are not dependent on light to find food or to be aware of their environment. These animals have evolved sleep patterns that fit in with

Nocturnal animals, such as bats, have evolved to sleep in the safety of a cave or burrow so that they are safe from predators during daylight hours.

their way of life, that is, they sleep during the day in places of safety such as caves or burrows. So their diurnal sleep patterns still fit in with an evolutionary theory. In addition, there are those who have no predators to fear, such as lions. Lions appear relatively happy to sleep wherever and whenever they can. Grazing animals also appear not to fit in with the theory because they sleep very little (Allison & Cicchetti, 1976). Animals such as cows and antelope spend most of their time grazing in herds. Perhaps, for these animals, remaining still in such large numbers on a wide open field or plain would present too much of a sitting target. So not remaining vigilant could be seriously maladaptive. Therefore, as they are constantly at serious risk from predators, this lack of sleep would also seem to back Meddis' theory concerning safety. However, we also know that the nutritional value of vegetation is very poor and in order to survive these grazers have to keep eating for most of each 24-hour period. If they did not—if they stopped to sleep—they would be lacking in nutrition and energy the next day.

Siegel (2005a) agrees that sleep may be adaptive because of its energy conservation, particularly in smaller mammals whose high metabolic rate is linked to high heat (energy) loss because they have a relatively high surface area to body volume ration, which could result in significant and dangerous drops in body temperature. A similar risk applies to many newborn mammals but, as they grow, they reach a body mass where greater benefit is gained from being awake, and learning.

Herbivores, such as these springbok, need to graze most of the time and be on their guard against predators, so sleep relatively little.

Evaluation

How does this relate to humans? The idea is that when we lived truly wild, when our distant ancestors were evolving, those who were able to sleep at night survived better because they were less likely to become prey for carnivores. They had conserved their energies when it was too dark to see and had been successfully hidden from predators. These survivors passed on to their descendants the ability to sleep through the night, and therefore to survive. Perhaps the adage could be rewritten as those who sleep the night away live to feed another day! So this theory suggests that sleep is an evolutionary leftover. However, if being very still and unnoticeable was the great benefit and survival tactic of sleep, then it is puzzling that so many humans sleep noisily. In fact, a whole industry has sprung up based on reducing or curing snoring! The main theory also fails to explain why after sleep deprivation we sleep for longer, perhaps even falling asleep in daylight, as it would suggest that we would not need to catch up on missed sleep if there was adequate light. Of course, evolutionary change is very, very slow and the advent of artificial light relatively recent—so perhaps our need for sleep could be an example of **genome lag**, in which case our remote descendants might not sleep much at all!

If protection was the only function of sleep, we would expect to find that animals who are likely to be attacked sleep rather little. In general, predators do sleep more than those who are preyed upon, but taken to the extreme the principle suggests that some animals wouldn't sleep at all in order to be safe.

As mentioned earlier, Horne (1988) has suggested a variation by saying that there could be two types of sleep: core, or essential, sleep and optional sleep. Each of them would have different adaptive functions. But this theory as a whole is still basically conjecture and it is difficult to see how empirical evidence could be obtained. Meddis also suggests that the much longer sleep-patterns of babies evolved to prevent exhaustion in their mothers. This certainly sounds nice, but it does not explain the survival of the non-sleepy trait in babies, nor the variation in quantities and type of sleep in people of all ages.

Empson (1989) described Meddis' theory as a "waste-of-time" theory, meaning that it suggested sleep was a waste of time (he might even have meant that the theory was a waste of time!). Empson pointed out that sleep is universal among animals, even the most successful predators, and that sleep deprivation can on occasion be fatal. This suggests that sleep has some value. However, we could ask whether it is really such an advantage, when avoiding predation, to be effectively paralysed and senseless for hours. One can see the advantage of staying still and quiet in the dark, and thus avoiding danger. But to be almost unconscious, unaware of one's surroundings, could be interpreted as being more, not less, vulnerable. Certainly, anecdotal evidence, such as the stories from India of man-eating lions preying on sleeping rather than waking victims, does not fit in with this theory. Horne also suggests that sleep might perform different functions in different species or different sizes of animal, such as in aquatic animals, grazing animals, and those with higher intellects. If this is so, then to look for a global explanation of sleep is rather pointless. However, the fact that animals such as dolphins appear to develop sleep adaptations specific to their environments suggests that there are evolutionary principles at work. Sleep must be serving a purpose and each species evolves a means of sleeping in such a way that doesn't also threaten their survival.

KEY TERM

Genome lag: the notion that some behaviour is not adaptive because genetic changes over thousands of generations have proceeded much slower than changes in our environment.

Restoration theory

Most of us would agree that after a physically or mentally strenuous day we are much more ready to go to sleep and may well sleep longer than usual. Oswald (1970, 1976, 1980) suggested that both REM and NREM sleep serve the purpose of restoring and replenishing our bodies and brains. In other words, we sleep to restore ourselves physiologically and psychologically. Oswald suggests that NREM sleep is needed more for restoring bodily processes that have deteriorated or been worn down by the day and REM sleep is the main time for renewing brain processes and replenishing neurochemicals used up in the day that need to be regenerated by protein synthesis. Horne (1988) also suggested that restoration and repair occur in relaxed wakefulness as well as in sleep.

Research findings

Restoration theory sounds both logical and sensible, and is supported by empirical evidence. Babies and foetuses sleep with both REM and NREM rhythms for a far greater proportion of their day than older children or adults, and it is in these very early stages that both bodies and neural connections are growing fastest. Not only do young babies spend on average about 18 hours a day sleeping, as opposed to about 8 hours in adults, but also they spend about half of those 18 hours in REM sleep whereas adults spend about a quarter of sleep in REM. This ties in with the larger amount of activity in the developing brain, with increased amounts of protein synthesis needed for cell and synaptic growth. Siegel (2005a) points out that if one controls for body or brain weight REM sleep is most strongly correlated with how immature the baby is at birth. Also, both physical repair and the synthesis of brain proteins are dependent on growth hormone, which is secreted after the first burst of delta activity in slow-wave sleep (Oswald, 1970, 1976, 1980). This is interesting support for the old wives' tale that we grow in our sleep! Further support of the restoration theory comes from knowledge that patients who have had physiological assaults on their brains from drug overdoses or from electroconvulsive therapy then spend an increased time in REM sleep, perhaps to synthesise the brain proteins (e.g. neurotransmitters) that have been lost or damaged, or are needed for repair. Blood flow to the brain does increase in REM sleep, the possible purpose being to bring in extra oxygen, glucose, and nutrients for the suggested protein synthesis. In addition, there is evidence from studies of learning that REM sleep is related to learning and the consolidation of memory. For example, Bloch (1976) showed that rats that were given complex maze tasks daily had increased REM sleep. Learning is related to protein synthesis.

See *A2-Level Psychology Online* for an interactive exercise on the restoration theory of sleep.

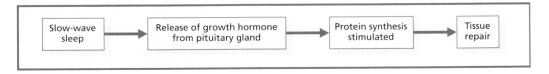

Slow-wave sleep	→	Release of growth hormone from pituitary gland	→	Protein synthesis stimulated	→	Tissue repair

Evaluation

Amino acids (the building-blocks for proteins and many neurochemicals) are not stored by the body and last for only about 4 hours in the body after a meal. This means that protein synthesis ought to halt about halfway through a night's sleep because the amino acids run out; indeed, it is definite that protein synthesis does

---

EXAM HINT

Note that the implications of sleep deprivation research can be related to the theories of sleep. The restoration theories predict negative effects of sleep deprivation and that any lost sleep will need to be regained, whereas ecological theories do not. Use this to assess their validity.

? Do you find that some worries and problems recede after a good night's sleep? Is this valid evidence for the function of sleep?

increase in the brain during slow-wave sleep. Perhaps the recent suggestion that new neurons are in fact generated, e.g. in the hippocampus, during sleep, which is facilitated by exercise, unless this neurogenesis is blocked by stress or sleep deprivation, provides a significant role for sleep in adults as well as the young.

If restoration was the only function of sleep then we would expect to find consistent effects from sleep deprivation. However, as we saw in the last section, this is not the case. People certainly don't need to make up the sleep they have lost, although they do appear to need the REM sleep or core sleep most particularly (the REM-rebound effect). It may also be that some recovery and manufacture of biochemicals takes place during the day when one is relaxed and quiet. It has been suggested that people often experience bursts of **micro-sleep** during the day. Furthermore, if restoration was the only function of sleep, we would also expect to find that the more active you were during the day the more you slept at night. Research suggests that there is no relationship. For example, Shapiro, Bortz, Mitchell, Bartel, and Jooste (1981) recorded the sleep duration of marathon runners. After a race they showed decreases in REM sleep but did show more slow-wave sleep. Horne and Minard (1985) engaged participants in numerous physical activities but found no increases in sleep, although the participants went to sleep faster. It may be that slow-wave sleep is important for recovery after vigorous activity (Carlson, 1986).

The sleep patterns of some animals raise further questions for restoration theory. If sleep serves a universal purpose, why are there so many variations in the way that animals sleep? For example, dolphins have evolved unique sleep patterns to overcome the real risk of drowning. Those in the river Indus take naps of a few seconds at a time, repeatedly, throughout the 24 hours of a day. This is probably also related to their need for vigilance at all times because so much large debris is always sweeping down the river (Pilleri, 1979) and if this hit them they could be seriously injured. A 1984 study showed that marine dolphins sleep with only one hemisphere at a time, so half the cortex is always awake, presumably to organise surfacing to breathe (Mukhametov, 1984). This is a valuable, in fact essential, adaptation in an air-breathing but aquatic animal. Empson (1993) reported similar findings for porpoises. It has been suggested (Siegel, 2005a) that the continuous motor activity of these aquatic mammals keeps the brainstem active and so they do not need REM sleep as others, like humans, do. This suggestion is based on the hypothesis that REM sleep evolved to stimulate the brainstem, whose activity reduces in slow-wave sleep, but whose activity is essential to keep us alive.

Empson's point of view is that, despite all this, the overall evidence supports sleep-as-synthesis, even though there are suggestions that the high levels of brain activity in REM sleep are likely to consume all the glucose and oxygen available, leaving no margin for growth or repair. One problem with this is that, although protein synthesis and neuron connection growth makes good sense in the immature it does not seem to apply to adults, and yet they also have REM sleep. One popular idea is that we wake more naturally from REM sleep, coming awake and alert; but when we wake from NREM sleep we and other non-human animals have a period of poor sensory–motor functioning. This would clearly not be advantageous if enemies or predators were nearby.

New ideas on the function of sleep are concerned with the brain's role in learning. Turner, Drummond, Salamat, and Brown (2007) found that sleep deprivation reduced working memory efficiency; after 4 days with only 26 minutes'

KEY TERM

Micro-sleep: Minute cat-naps or very small instants of sleep during awake periods; the instants of micro-sleep are so short-lived that the person is not aware of them.

sleep per night participants' working memory span decreased by 38% compared with the control group. Born, Rasch, and Gais (2006) found a link between late REM sleep and better procedural memory, and between early slow-wave sleep and improved declarative memory. Cirelli and Tononi (2008) hypothesised that the new synapses generated by the day's learning would be pruned during sleep, making sleep a time for reorganising memory storage, so that there would be capacity for the following day's learning. They demonstrated this in rats by measuring synaptic neuroreceptors and found a 50% reduction after sleep. Tononi calls this getting "a leaner brain . . . ready to learn anew". Of course, there are the usual reservations about assuming that what is shown in rats will also be true in humans, but this concept of sleep being needed for efficient learning is an interesting one.

Lifespan Changes in Sleep

Is there such a thing as the "correct" amount of sleep for health and happiness? There is plenty of advice around: the American Academy of Sleep Medicine guidelines are shown in the box on the right.

It must be stressed that these are only guidelines, not a definition of what is "normal". Armstrong, Quinn, and Dadds' (1994) study is referred to as the definitive work on the sleeping habits of normal children up to 38 months of age, albeit of Australian children. Over 3000 parents were surveyed over a 1-week period, with an astonishing 96.5% response rate. The findings can be summarised as follows:

Daily hours of sleep

Age	Daily hours of sleep
Infants, 3–11 months	14–15
Toddlers, 1–3 years	12–14
Pre-school, 5–6 years	11–13
School age	10–11
Adolescents	9
Adults	7–8

1. There is a wide variation of normal early childhood sleep behaviour.
2. Circadian rhythms are not well established until 4 months of age.
3. 11% of babies under 3 months of age do not have daytime sleep.
4. Daytime sleep becomes less regular as age increases, with a marked reduction at around 3 months of age.
5. Frequent night waking that disturbs parents is common from 4–12 months of age.
6. Night-time settling requires more input from parents from 18 months old.
7. Sleeping through the night varies considerably, not only from child to child but for any one child, and does not become regular until after 24 months old.

Looking at these findings one by one, it seems reasonable that childhood sleep behaviour shows variation as this mirrors human variation generally, and adult sleeping behaviour in particular as this varies from 4 to 10+ hours nightly in normal populations. Circadian rhythms are controlled by the brain and this is immature at birth, so the development of the rhythm could well be in line with early brain development and growth, especially synaptic growth. Harrison (2004) found that exposure to more light in the afternoons in 6- to 12-week-old infants promoted the development of their circadian sleep rhythm. The 11% of infants who do not sleep in the daytime might be a strain on their parents and carers but some people are more lively and energetic than others, and this is possibly a genetic feature, a behavioural trait. The frequent night wakening from 4 months could be

? How many daily hours of sleep do you need?

either a need for more food or a developing knowledge that there are more interesting things available than being asleep, especially if one can sleep in the daytime. Babies are usually hungry for experience and entertainment, brain-food as it were, and if this is provided at night then it would seem reasonable for them to demand it. Their increasing awareness of their world may also bring a need for reassurance that other people are still around, that there is comfort available, and this could be a reason for the increased demands for settling down from 18 months. Scher's (1991) study of night waking in over one hundred infants showed that at 3 months 46% were waking, at 6 months 39%, at 9 months 58%, and at 12 months 55%. So not only is night waking usual, the increase at about 9 months could relate to the socio-emotional advances being made at this time, such as the understanding and fear of strangers. Interestingly, all these data may be culture specific to Western industrialised norms and so could be examples of ethnocentrism, as studies of non-Western cultures where breast-feeding into the second year is common do not show the development of longer bouts of sleep at night time and do show shorter daily total sleep times. This could be because of the delayed weaning as breast milk is not nutritionally suitable as the sole food for older babies and/or because babies in many other cultures sleep with their mothers and not in a separate bed (Elias, Nicolson, Bora, & Johnson, 1986).

Whatever the variations in baby and child sleep patterns it is generally true that these younger people sleep more than older ones. It is also true that babies spend far more time than adults in REM sleep, up to 50% of their sleep is in REM. Young adults spend about 20% of sleep in REM and elderly adults only about 15% in REM (Zimbardo, McDermott, Jansz, & Metaal, 1993).

Van Cauter, Leproult, and Plat (2000) identified a potential issue in the decline with age of slow-wave sleep. This deterioration takes place twice, between 16 and 25 years and 35 and 50 years and, as growth hormone is secreted in slow-wave sleep these periods are also a time when growth and repair are also slowed. The sample here was 149 healthy adult males between 16 and 83 years old who were tracked over 14 years. It was not the reduction in the total amount of sleep that concerned Van Cauter et al.—a loss of 27 minutes per decade—but the implications of little growth hormone, especially as the majority of men over 45 years had very little slow-wave sleep at all, leading to loss of muscle mass and the ability to exercise plus a tendency to obesity. Of course, one study cannot ever be conclusive, but if these findings are replicated there could be investigations into stimulating slow-wave sleep and/or the production of growth hormone. The explanation for the reductions might be evolutionary, in that for our hunter-gatherer ancestors living in the wild, the lifespan would be much shorter than for ourselves today, perhaps not even half of our expectation. This means that by age 30 they would have been elderly, and few would have lived to reach their late forties, so the reduction in slow-wave sleep and growth-hormone secretion could

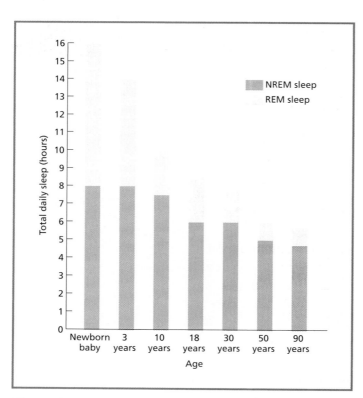

Lifespan changes in sleep. Adapted from Zimbardo et al. (1993).

be a relic of the time when the body would have been worn out and approaching death. A meta-analysis of 65 studies, representing over 3500 healthy participants, showed that it is not only slow-wave sleep that declines with age. In adults, the total time asleep and the percentage of slow-wave and REM sleep all declined significantly with age, whereas sleep latency (the time taken to fall asleep) and the percentages of Stages 1 and 2 sleep significantly increased with age. Interestingly, for school children and adolescents the total sleep time decreased with age but only on school days! However, there were very few studies on school-aged children and adolescents, and on middle-years adults, and this lack of data means that little that is useful can be concluded for these age groups.

The stereotype of elderly people often includes frequent dozing. This napping has been positively correlated with excessive daytime sleepiness and with depression, e.g. in the extensive "2003 Sleep in America" telephone poll (Foley, Vitiello, Bliwise, Ancoli-Israel, Monjan, & Walsh, 2007) but this correlation cannot show cause and effect. The daytime napping may be the result of sleepiness and/or depression, or it might be the result of these behaviours, or they might, independently, just be caused by being old. There is also the issue of a telephone poll, and the surveys and questionnaires used by other researchers. It is not possible to know how truthful respondents are, nor how influenced they might have been by social desirability or by guessing what the researchers hope to find. A contrasting study (Ancoli-Israel, 2008) surveyed over 2000 women and found that normal sleep with no perceived sleep problems was linked to healthy aging. Older women who slept well were significantly less likely to suffer from mood, attention, or memory problems and were also less likely to suffer physical problems such as cardiovascular disease and diabetes. Of course, this was a single-sex study, and might not apply to men. Furthermore, people who have difficulty sleeping might worry a lot about this and become stressed, and this could be a contributory factor in the development of cardiovascular disorders.

> **EXAM HINT**
>
> Note that the methodological limitation of much of the research on how sleep patterns change with age. First, self-reports of sleep may be biased by participant reactivity. Second, the links that are made between reduced sleep and depression are correlational and so cause and effect cannot be inferred. The lack of sleep could cause depression, depression could cause lack of sleep, or a third factor (such as worry about a relative's serious illness) could be causing them both.

Frequent napping in elderly people has been positively correlated to depression.

HOW SCIENCE WORKS: HOW MANY HOURS DO YOU SLEEP?

As you now know, there is considerable variation in the number of hours we sleep, and not just because of differences in age.

You could construct a survey of people who are parents—maybe even your own!—asking how many hours on average each of their children slept when newborn. But you need some sensitivity here; it is possible that people had a tricky time with their new babies and would rather not dwell on this, or there might have been anxiety or even tragedy because of a baby or the birth. How will you deal ethically with this? You need to minimise risk to others when carrying out experiments.

One way is to approach only people who know you, and have a prepared statement that as part of your studies you would like to ask them about their babies when newborn, and about their own sleep at that time, but also that it would not be a problem if they would rather you did not choose them for this practical work. This gives them the choice of opting out without losing face, and this is important in showing respect to participants.

Then you need to decide how you are going to label the babies and parents, because you will not want any details to identify them, such as their real names—another ethical consideration. You could use letters and/or numbers.

You also have to make your survey questions simple and clear. You could ask for the average daily time spent asleep for each baby; the amount of sleep the parent got at that time; the average number of disturbances (e.g. for feeding) during the night; how this change in sleep pattern affected how they felt and their behaviour.

When you have these data, you could ask yourself what level of data each set is, and what these data tell you. Do they support variation in hours of sleep? Do they show any effects of disturbed or reduced sleep in the adults? Can you analyse these data in any way, using descriptive statistics for instance? Can you draw any conclusions?

SECTION SUMMARY
Sleep States

The nature of sleep

❖ There are two main phases of sleep:

    — NREM sleep or slow-wave sleep has four stages of increasing slowing and synchronising of brain activity, when the eyes are motionless under the closed eyelids.

    — REM sleep is a single stage of high and random brain activity and the eyes move under the closed eyelids; the body below the neck is paralysed by a block in the RAS.

❖ The two phases alternate in a 90-minute infradian pattern through the night's sleep.

Sleep-deprivation studies

❖ Jouvet's (1967) flowerpot study found that cats deprived of REM sleep died:

    — he suggested REM sleep is necessary for life

    — similar findings came from other non-human animal studies

    — the deaths could have been die to stress, not REM sleep deprivation.

❖ Dement's (1960) study of eight volunteers deprived of REM sleep found that the participants made increasing attempts to go into REM sleep, from five times in a normal night to 12 times the first night and 26 times the seventh night:

    — this suggests REM sleep is a need

    — but does not suggest why this is so

    — these findings have been confirmed by many other studies, also sometimes showing a temporary degree of dysfunction

    — human participants must be protected from harm so these studies are not comparable for that (and other) reasons with Jouvet's work.

❖ Case studies have shown total sleep deprivation for up to 11 days with no long-term ill effects. When allowed to sleep again, more lost REM than NREM sleep has occurred, suggesting the importance of the former. Overall it seems we do need sleep to feel and function well, although the amount varies individually.

Evolutionary explanation

❖ This proposes that sleep is adaptive, i.e. increases chances of survival (Meddis, 1975a, 1975b, 1979):

    — sleeping at night when we have only poor vision not only conserves energy but also makes us less noticeable to predators and enemies

    — sleep is universal among animals and so must have some sort of function

    — this theory, as all evolutionary explanations, is conjecture because it cannot be tested empirically

    — many humans do not sleep quietly, so enemies and predators would locate them easily.

❖ Oswald (1970, 1976) suggested that NREM sleep is a time of bodily restoration, i.e. growth and repair, and REM sleep is when the brain is replenished:

    — babies who are growing and developing very fast usually sleep far more hours than older children
    — growth hormone is secreted at night, during slow-wave sleep
    — this does not explain the wide variation in the effects of sleep deprivation
    — recent research suggests sleep has a major function to do with learning.

Restoration theory

❖ There is no fixed pattern linking age and hours spent asleep.
❖ In general, babies sleep the longest, children less long, adults less still, and the elderly sleep the least and may cat-nap rather than have a single sleep period; but some suggest adolescents sleep longer than younger children perhaps because this is a time of extra learning about their world.
❖ Sleep reduction in the elderly, despite continuing needs for restoration, could be a sign that in the modern world we live artificially long; our hunter-gatherer ancestors would have been unlikely to live past their forties.

Lifespan changes in sleep

DISORDERS OF SLEEP

Explanations for Insomnia, Primary and Secondary

Insomnia is the condition where there are problems falling asleep and/or staying asleep, and the sleep that occurs tends not to be deep and is easily disturbed. Insomnia is also, unsurprisingly, linked with fatigue, poor attention, impaired judgement, decreased performance, being irritable, and with an increased risk of accidents. It is clearly an unwelcome condition, but as with many psychopathologies there are degrees of severity and insomnia can be considered a continuum rather than a single problem behaviour.

    One way of looking at insomnia is to gauge its severity as follows:

- Mild insomnia: there is little effect on work or social functioning.
- Moderate insomnia: there is a negative effect on work and social functioning.
- Severe insomnia: there is a major effect on daily functioning.
- Acute insomnia: an episode of poor sleep lasting only a few days.
- Chronic insomnia: the problem sleep lasts for months or longer; it may start in childhood and continue through adult life.

Insomnia is characterised by problems with falling and staying asleep. This can have mild or serious effects on the daily functioning of the sufferer, depending on how severe the condition.

    Another method of categorising insomnia looks at the possible causes of the sleep problem.

Clinical characteristics of primary insomnia

Category	Symptoms
Cognitive	Impaired functioning in work/social/personal life, poor concentration
Emotional	Significant stress and distress and feeling unrested, low mood (affect)
Behavioural	Difficulties in falling or staying asleep, frequent awakenings
Physiological	Significant daytime fatigue, restlessness at night

Primary insomnia is the most common form of insomnia and has no clear underlying cause. There is a sleep problem but there is no physiological or psychiatric cause, and it is likely that the sleep problem is the result of maladaptive behaviours or learning. The clinical characteristics are that for at least a month the individual would have suffered insomnia but this would not be linked with any other sleep disorder, such as parasomnia or narcolepsy, nor with another psychopathology such as clinical depression, nor with medications or substance abuse.

Unfortunately, the more the individual worries about his or her insomnia, the less likely it is that the problem will improve without some professional intervention. The condition can turn into an aggravating cycle in that the more individuals focus on their sleep problems, the less likely they may be to get good-quality sleep.

Secondary insomnia is insomnia that has a specific cause. Examples of such causes include sleep apnoea, restless legs syndrome (RLS), circadian rhythm disorders, and various medical, substance-use, and emotional problems.

Sleep apnoea is characterised by frequent interruptions of breathing when asleep followed by choking and gasping for breath, and is usually associated with loud snoring. This disorder is discussed later in the chapter. RLS is a disturbing condition in which the legs or feet twitch and jump, and there might also be feelings of burning, itching, or pulling. This is most frequent in the evenings or at night.

Circadian-rhythm disorders usually occur when an individual's innate circadian rhythm is not matched by the environmental sleep–wake schedule, e.g. in night-shiftworkers who, as described earlier, often have shorter-than-optimum hours of sleep.

Medical conditions can often be linked with insomnia because of a side-effect of drugs or because of pain. The common painkiller, codeine, has a form that interferes with sleep, e.g. in co-codramol, and its use and withdrawal can both be linked to insomnia. Other substances that cause insomnia include alcohol and other sedatives, such as benzodiazepines, and stimulants, such as caffeine.

Emotional problems produce extra worries, anxieties, and fears as well as stress so it is not surprising that these can lead to insomnia.

Factors affecting insomnia

Many of these factors are part of normal life and, as such, should not be regarded as unnatural or dangerous. A recognition that they can affect sleep and cause primary insomnia can sometimes help to control or reduce the insomnia. The basis of their interference with normal sleep patterns is often to do with preventing or interfering with the natural progression of brain activity from daytime functioning to slowing down to sleeping. This progression was described earlier in the chapter.

? Have you ever experienced insomnia? If so, what are some reasons why this could have happened?

Bedtime behaviour

In children, delaying bed-time for whatever reason—more stories, more TV, a drink—also delays settling down and calming down ready for sleep, as will night- or other fears or the need for a pacifier. Energetic or exciting activities such as rough and tumble play will also make it harder to sleep. In adults, much the same things apply, so watching exciting TV or films, allowing oneself to be physically or mentally active or restless, or just staying up later can all contribute to sleep difficulties such as insomnia. The key factor here is that if the brain is very active, if it is still alert and in daytime mode, the natural changes leading to sleep are unlikely to occur and the parasympathetic ANS, the rest-and-digest mechanism, will not switch on and calm the brain, and insomnia is the result.

? What are some ways you unwind before bedtime?

Environmental factors

Powerful stimuli, such as very bright lights, loud noises, very hot or very cold rooms, an uncomfortable bed, or a snoring companion can all contribute to insomnia because they interfere with the brain's natural calming down of neural activity, which is necessary if we are to fall to sleep. Moving to high altitudes also frequently disturbs sleep for some days, possibly because the reduction in oxygen results in more frequent breathing. This makes the blood slightly more alkaline, which in turn could interfere with normal brain activity. A change in the location where one sleeps, such as staying in unfamiliar surroundings or a hotel can also boost brain activity and lead to insomnia.

? What are some ways you can make your surrounding environment more bedtime friendly?

Stress

Acute stress, perhaps from a major life event such as an exam or a job change, can lead to insomnia, again because brain activity is heightened, the sympathetic ANS is active, and so the parasympathetic ANS cannot switch on because the two parts of the ANS are antagonistic. However, with acute stress the stressor is transitory and, when it is over, normal sleep should resume. Chronic stress is a different matter. Here the stressor persists, and so sympathetic ANS activity remains high and results in corticosteroid activity (as you know from your AS-level studies) and even to the collapse that Selye (1936) called the "exhaustion stage". This too could produce insomnia as the cortisol and then the breakdown change physiological activity. Long-term stressors can include concerns about safety or about family members or relationships, economic issues, and even worrying about not sleeping can be a powerful and unhelpful stressor. In fact, if an individual has learned an association by classical conditioning between the bed (-room) and insomnia, it might be better to relax on the sofa or anywhere else without the association with being unable to sleep.

Sleep hygiene

This term refers to habits or activities that promote the calming and slowing down of the brain in preparation for sleep. Poor sleep hygiene does not promote this progression and includes factors such as consuming caffeine or alcohol or taking in nicotine. These substances interfere with brain activity and the sleep process. Stimulating activities such as strenuous exercise or exciting mental

Stimulating activities, such as playing computer games late at night, inhibit the calming and slowing down of the neural activity of the brain in preparation for sleep.

activity will also prevent the brain from calming and slowing its neural activity. This is also likely to happen if there is no set bedtime or bedtime routine, and if the bedroom or bed is a place associated with watching TV, chatting on the phone, or doing homework then the brain is again less likely to calm down easily and quickly. Taking naps during the day is unlikely to help insomniacs as they will, obviously, feel less tired at night. These behaviours are sometimes classified as psychophysiological factors for insomnia.

Illness

Some illnesses can cause insomnia and advice from the family doctor might be needed to sort out that problem. Medications can also cause or contribute to insomnia either because of their effect as stimulants, or because of an effect when their use is discontinued, in each case because of their action on neural activity.

Sleep apnoea

It is not abnormal when asleep to have short periods without breathing. These non-breathing periods can be frightening to observers, but if the sleeping individual is breathing calmly between such periods then this is probably normal, and is known as Cheyne–Stokes breathing. It is the result of the body using so little oxygen, probably in NREM rather then REM sleep, that very little carbon dioxide is produced and so the individual does not need to breathe this out as often as when awake. Sleep apnoea is different. It is a disorder, and is not healthy. There are two types of apnoea, obstructive and central.

Obstructive sleep apnoea (OSA). The main characteristic of this disorder is fairly brief interruptions of breathing when the individual is asleep, each interruption being followed by choking and gasping as the sleeper struggles for air. The individual often snores loudly. Part of the problem may be being overweight, especially around the neck, as this weight acts as pressure on the structures inside the neck. Whatever the cause, what happens is that the upper airways collapse temporarily during sleep so that air cannot get into or out of the lungs. Typically, the chest heaves as it tries to move air in and out and obtain essential oxygen, and breathing can stop for over a minute. Blood oxygen levels may drop, and each episode ends with the person awakening to some extent and then going back to sleep. Although children and normal-weight individuals can suffer from sleep apnoea, possibly because of a smaller than usual upper airway, it is more common in overweight, middle-aged people, more often in men than in women.

As well as being worrying and straining respiratory and circulatory systems, OSA has been shown to be a threat to cognition. Macey et al.'s (2002) magnetic resonance imaging (MRI) scanning study showed small but significant reductions in brain neurons, presumably because of oxygen deprivation. Kumar et al. (2008) also used MRI scans to show that there is measurable loss of nearly 20% of the brain tissue in the mammillary bodies that lie on the underside of the brain and are part of the memory circuits. The cognitive memory deficit that results is not improved by successful treatment for OSA, which suggests that this loss is a long-lasting injury.

Children with OSA have also been studied. Many childhood sufferers of OSA have enlarged tonsils and adenoids, which press on the upper airway, resulting in the periodic collapse of the airway during sleep. The effect of this is a general reduction in health and thriving, as measured on the Children's Health Questionnaire. Surgical removal of the tonsils and adenoids produced a marked improvement in general health, as well as a major reduction in the number of interrupted breathing incidents per night, from 40 or more to only 5 or 6 (Baldassari, Mitchell, Schubert, & Rudnick, 2008). Childhood OSA is also linked to poor behaviour, growth, attention, memory and classroom performance, and lower childhood IQ scores, so this surgical treatment could transform children's lives and their future. The effects of OSA on cardiovascular health have been studied in children aged 12 to 26 months (Goldbart et al., 2007) and the disorder has been shown to start in the first year of life. As well as inflammation of the tonsils and adenoids, these children—unlike matched controls—showed high levels of ventricular heart strain. Both the inflammation and signs of heart strain reduced to normal levels following surgery removing the adenoids, but this leaves the suspicion that if untreated there could be cardiovascular problems as well as the cognitive problems mentioned earlier in childhood and adult life.

The problem with such research is always that the sample size is small, especially as the frequency of OSA in the Western world is only 5%. This means that there will always be methodological issues with interpreting the data and generalising it to the population of those with the disorder.

Central sleep apnoea. This also presents as periods of not breathing when asleep but the cause here is organic. The brain does not send the necessary normal signals to the breathing muscles, the diaphragm and the intercostals, so they do not contract frequently enough and so the individual does not take a breath often enough. It is the central control mechanism in the brainstem that is faulty, sometimes because of a stroke, but oxygen therapy can produce significant improvements in patients (White, 2005).

Personality

Why do some people and not others suffer from sleep disorders? Could personality or temperament be a causal factor? We all know that it is more difficult to get to sleep and remain asleep when we are worried and stressed. Vgontzas et al. (2001) demonstrated that there is an association between insomnia and an overall increase in stress hormones such as adrenocorticotropic hormone (ACTH) and cortisol secretion in a circadian pattern. They suggest that there is, for insomniacs, a disorder of hyperarousal in the CNS caused by chronic activation of the hypothalamic–pituitary–adrenal axis; that this leads to increased risk of chronic anxiety, depression, and physiological damage; and that therapy should be based on decreasing physiological and emotional arousal, not just sleep. This is assuming that the high stress hormone levels and CNS activity cause the insomnia, whereas it could be suggested that the equation goes the other way, and the insomnia is causing the stress and arousal. Furthermore, Bonnet and Arand (2003) used the Minnesota Multiphasic Personality Inventory (MMPI) with participants with experimentally induced insomnia and found that their levels of anxiety rose in line with their poor sleep and increasing fatigue, and this also

? What are some of the dangers of sleep disorders?

could support the concept of anxious personalities being more susceptible to insomnia—or that being a natural insomniac is anxiety-causing. However, de Sainte Hilaire, Straub, and Pelissolo (2005) hypothesised that serotonin activity could relate to both temperament as in hard-avoidance and to sleep regulation. They showed that insomniacs had more anticipatory worry than controls and greater harm avoidance, and that the latter correlated positively with sleep latency, the time taken to go from waking into deep sleep. We all know that a correlation cannot infer causation, only a relationship, but this study does suggest that the personality trait of harm avoidance might at least be a marker for primary insomnia. More data comes from the Leblanc, Beaulieu-Bonneau, Mérette, Savard, Ivers, and Morin (2007) study, which showed strong links between insomnia and high scores on depression, anxiety, neuroticism, extraversion, arousal predisposition, stress perception, and emotion-oriented coping, although such links again cannot be assumed to be causal. Similar links were found by Soehner, Kennedy, and Monk (2007) using the Eysenck Personality Inventory for extraversion and neuroticism, the Pittsburg Sleep Quality Index for quality of sleep, and the Sleep Timing Questionnaire for the duration, timing, and latency of sleep. They found links between higher neuroticism as a personality trait and the timing and poorer quality of sleep, but not with sleep duration. However, it needs to be said that the participants were not insomniacs, but normal working adults, and that the questionnaires were all self-report, mail-in ones. This could have given anonymity to encourage greater accuracy of answers, but it is not possible to know how accurate they were, nor if participants were influenced by what they supposed the researchers were looking for, nor by what they felt was socially desirable or even, perhaps, macho.

Deadly insomnia

There are, fortunately very rare, cases in which insomnia becomes not just pathological but deadly. Lugaresi et al. (1986; Montagna, Gambetti, Cortelli, & Lugaresi, 2003) followed the progression of insomnia in a man who, at the age of 52 became unable to sleep. This was a sudden onset and the sufferer became more and more exhausted, and finally developed a fatal lung infection. After death a post-mortem was done and lesions were found in two areas of the thalamus (forebrain) linked to sleep and hormonally controlled circadian rhythms. The neurons in these areas were fairly comprehensively destroyed. This case could be interpreted simplistically as death due to sleep deprivation alone. However, since the case above was first described, this genetic condition has been named as fatal familial insomnia (FFI) and it seems to have started with a mutation in an Italian known as Patient Zero who died from the disorder in 1765. Geschwind (2008) explains that the mutation affects certain proteins in the brain, particularly in the thalamus, so that they mis-fold and form prions. These prions clump together, cause neuron deaths, and the area of the brain affected develops a sponge-like structure, full of holes. Death follows, usually within a year of the first signs of the disorder developing.

Explanations for Other Sleep Disorders

Sleepwalking

Somnambulism is a relatively common sleep disorder, with estimates that it affects about 1 in 10 of us at some point in our lives. The reality of somnambulism is very different from the cartoon stereotype where the somnambulist has arms outstretched and wanders round with their eyes closed. Real-life somnambulism takes many forms, but typically the eyes are open, although often described as glazed or staring in appearance. The person moves normally, and may just wander round the bedroom, but other behaviours are known. Ebrahim and Fenwick (2008) reported treated patients who had driven cars and ridden horses while asleep, and Shakespeare's descriptions of Lady Macbeth would seem very likely.

Somnambulism is most likely to occur during NREM Stages 3 and 4, in slow-wave sleep. It can occur in REM sleep but this is much less likely, and because most NREM sleep is earlier in the sleep period episodes of somnambulism tend to be in the earlier rather than later parts of the night. Although it seems true that somnambulism is most common in childhood, peaking just before or at the time of puberty, it can continue into adulthood. An episode may last only a few seconds, or hours, and when awake the individual will have no memory of what he or she has been doing. The causes of somnambulism seem to be in part genetic, as the disorder runs in families (Horne, 1992) but triggers include fatigue, previous lack of sleep (Pilon, Zadra, Joncas, & Montplaisir, 2008), and stress or anxiety. In adults, alcohol and other drugs seem to be able to act as triggers.

> **?** Why is sleepwalking more likely to occur in NREM Stages 3 and 4?

The genetic element in somnambulism is supported by Hublin, Kaprio, Partinen, Heikkila, and Koskenvuo (1997), who used the Finnish twin cohort and found that the genetic contribution to somnambulism in childhood was 66% in men and 57% in women, and for adult somnambulism was 80% in men and 36% in women. The sex difference in childhood somnambulism does not seem significant, but it is puzzling why there is such a major difference between the sexes in adult somnambulism. Guilleminault, Palombini, Pelayo, and Chervin (2003) suggest that in child somnambulists a causal factor may be other sleep disorders, such as sleep-disordered breathing or restless legs syndrome (RLS), which fragment sleep and produce confused arousal. Certainly, RLS is known to be a genetic disorder and this could explain why somnambulism can run in families. Exactly how maladaptive genes may produce sleepwalking is not known, but Szelenberger, Niemcewicz, and Dabrowska (2005) suggest that data showing both low and declining levels of delta waves could be signs of a chronic inability to sustain slow-wave sleep. The main issue with somnambulism, apart from the

CASE STUDY: SLEEPWALKING

CK started sleepwalking as a youngster, of primary school age. His family was aware of this as he would walk from his bedroom and could be seen as he passed the living room, but his somnambulism was not at that stage any real cause for concern, and he was just doing normal behaviours such as going to the bathroom, although in his sleep. The somnambulism continued into his teens, and he recalls an occasion when he was in his mid-teens waking up in some confusion. He had been trying to get out of his bedroom and couldn't find the door handle, but woke to discover he was trying to open a solid wall. Then, in his early twenties he hurt himself quite badly. Once again, he was sleepwalking around the house at home but he must have tripped over the telephone wire and he fell and cut his face open. He still did not wake, he was not aware of the hurt and crawled into the side and curled up continuing to sleep. His sister woke because of the noise of his fall, and she and their mother failed to wake him but somehow got him back into bed. He was shocked when he did at last wake up to find himself bloodied. In adulthood, CK still on occasion has somnambulist episodes. The most serious one was when he got up at night, stood on the bed and climbed up and out of a window. This cannot have been easy as this window was very small. He managed it, however, and fell down from the first floor, waking up later, still outside on the ground—because he was cold—to find both heels, some vertebrae, and one elbow broken. There is no family history of somnambulism for CK, who is fully recovered from his fall. He is aware of the risks of still having somnambulist episodes but these are infrequent. He also knows that for him alcohol increases this risk.

anxieties it may cause, is the moderately high risk of somnambulists injuring themselves during an episode. Accounts of aggression and murder during an episode are rare whereas somnambulists bruising themselves or even breaking bones are not uncommon and further evidence that somnambulism is truly sleep-walking and not a conscious behaviour.

Narcolepsy

The frequency of narcolepsy is debated but it is rare, from about 0.02 to 0.0005% (misdiagnosis is known to be a problem) of the Western population; however, it has a profound effect. It is characterised not just by chronic sleepiness but also by muscle weakness and fatigue and abnormal rapid eye movements in REM. There may also be cataplexy, in which the muscles lose strength when the individual experiences strong emotions, sleep paralysis, and sleep hallucinations.

Narcolepsy often shows in young adulthood and the first and lifelong symptoms are of excessive sleepiness, especially when the individual is inactive or bored. Short naps of 10 to 20 minutes are common, after which the sleepy feeling is temporarily reduced, only to reappear within 2–3 hours. Cataplexy is the result of intense emotions such as anger, surprise, excitement, or laughter; or it can have no discernable cause. The body may droop or sag or even collapse as if paralysed, but there is no loss of consciousness; the individual does not faint. The episodes may be over within seconds or last some minutes. The sleep paralysis is different from cataplexy. It occurs either at the beginning of sleep or when first awakening and is a brief loss of the ability to move, apart from the breathing muscles and eye muscles. This is strange, a paradox, as breathing muscles are under involuntary control whereas eye and skeletal muscles are under voluntary control. This, although seldom lasting more than a few minutes, can be very distressing, especially as it is sometimes accompanied by a sense of fear or dread and even hallucinations. Sleep hallucinations might also occur when dropping off to sleep or when awakening. These are not the hypnogogic hallucinations that are part of normal experience, but are colours, shapes, actual figures, sounds, or may be tactile; they are frequently and unpleasantly accompanied by negative feelings such as of being under threat: attacked, fearful, and beset by dangers.

Twentieth-century research established that in non-human animals such as dogs and mice a genetic mutation can cause narcolepsy, and Lin et al. (1999) discovered that in dogs this mutation also produced a deficiently in a receptor for the neurotransmitter hypocretin. Hypocretin blocks communication between neurons, particularly messages relating to when the body should wake. Later research showed that injections of hypocretin in dogs reversed their narcolepsy, but this could not be generalised to humans as the human disorder has environmental as well as genetic causes, it is a nature and nurture phenomenon. Nishino, Okura, and Mignot's (2000) twin study showed a monozygotic (MZ) 25–31% concordance rate for human narcolepsy and 1–2% of first-degree relatives of narcoleptics suffer from the disorder compared to the very low rate in the general population. Nishino, Ripley, Overeem, Lammers, and Mignot (2000) were able to confirm that hypocretin (or orexin as it is also known) deficiency is definitely implicated in human narcolepsy and Thannickal et al. (2000) found that narcoleptics have a reduction of about 85–95% in hypocretin neurons, whereas melatonin neuron numbers are unaffected, with the hypocretin loss being degenerative and perhaps autoimmune. Longstreth, Koepsell, Ton, Hendrickson, and van Belle (2007) confirmed the selective destruction of hypocretin-producing cells in the lateral hypothalamus but only in individuals carrying one or more alleles (genes) of a type known as human leukocyte antigen (HLA). This reinforces the cause as a diathesis between genes and the environment, and one possible environmental factor has been identified. Research in South China showed that narcolepsy is more common in those born in winter, but not what it is about winter births that is the causal factor. Of course, viruses are more common in winter, so it is possible that there might be a viral interaction with the particular HLA allele(s) involved. Kim et al.'s (2008) research showed an increase in GABA levels in the medial prefrontal cortex of narcoleptics, but this could be a physiological defence mechanism activated to reduce the nocturnal sleep disturbances in narcolepsy. So although a lot more research is needed to fill in the detail, it does seem certain that narcolepsy is the product of maladaptive HLA genes, environmental factors, degenerative neurological changes, and abnormal neurotransmitter levels.

HOW SCIENCE WORKS: A SLEEP DISORDER

You might like to make a PowerPoint presentation of one of the sleep disorders, such as sleep apnoea, sleepwalking, or narcolepsy.

You could search the web, and online newspaper/magazine/radio/TV sites, for case studies as well as scientific explanations; you might find suitable graphics, perhaps even an MP3 or video clip file of a sufferer talking about the disorder. These, and explanatory text, could be integrated into a presentation for your class or a year or school meeting. The difference between what we learn from case studies and how this differs from empirical research could be explained, and the importance of a non-prejudiced or non-biased view should be clearly apparent.

SECTION SUMMARY
Disorders of Sleep

❖ Insomnia is a condition where there is difficult getting to or staying asleep, leading to fatigue, having poor attention, impaired judgement, decreased performance, being irritable, and also with an increased risk of accidents. It can be categorised as:

— mild insomnia: there is little effect on work or social functioning
— moderate insomnia: there is a negative effect on work and social functioning
— severe insomnia: there is a major effect on daily functioning
— acute insomnia: an episode of poor sleep lasting only a few days
— chronic insomnia: the problem sleep lasts for months or longer; it may start in childhood and continue through adult life.

❖ Primary insomnia is most common. The sleep problem has no physiological or psychiatric cause; it is likely that it is the result of maladaptive behaviours or learning. The clinical characteristics are that for at least a month the individual would have suffered insomnia but this would not be linked with any other sleep disorder, such as parasomnia or narcolepsy, nor with another psychopathology such as clinical depression, nor with medications or substance abuse.

❖ Secondary insomnia is insomnia that has a specific cause, such as sleep apnoea, restless legs syndrome (RLS), circadian rhythm disorders, and various medical, substance-use, and emotional problems.

Explanations for insomnia, primary and secondary

See *A2-Level Psychology Online* for some interactive quizzes to help you with your revision.

❖ Factors affecting insomnia include bedtime behaviour, environmental factors, stress, sleep hygiene, illness, sleep apnoea, and personality.

❖ Sleep apnoea may be obstructive, when the upper airways tend to collapse during sleep; or central, when there is a fault in the central control mechanism in the brainstem.

❖ Anxious personalities are more likely to develop sleep problems such as insomnia, which is also linked to a serotonin imbalance, although this may not be causal, and strong links have also been demonstrated between insomnia and high scores on depression, anxiety, neuroticism, extraversion, arousal predisposition, stress perception, and emotion-oriented coping, although such links again cannot be assumed to be causal (Leblanc et al., 2007).

Sleepwalking

❖ Somnambulism is a relatively common sleep disorder and possibly affects about 1 in 10 of us at some point in our lives.

❖ It seems to be in part genetic, as the disorder runs in families (Horne, 1992). Triggers include fatigue, previous lack of sleep (Pilon et al., 2008), and stress or anxiety. The Finnish twin cohort showed the genetic contribution to somnambulism in childhood was 66% in men and 57% in women, and for adult somnambulism was 80% in men and 36% in women (Hublin et al., 1997). The different percentages between the sexes in adulthood cannot currently be explained.

Narcolepsy

❖ This very rare condition (0.02–0.0005% of the Western population) has a profound effect. It is characterised by chronic sleepiness plus muscle weakness and fatigue and abnormal rapid eye movements in REM.

❖ There may also be cataplexy where muscles lose strength, perhaps when the individual experiences strong emotions, and that person collapses.

❖ It is partially a genetic condition, with a 25–31% MZ concordance rate (Mignot, 1998) leading to imbalances of hypocretin and GABA, but is more common in those born in winter.

FURTHER READING

Foster, R., & Kreitzman, L. (2004). *Rhythms of life.* London: Profile Books This is a very readable book that covers human rhythms including the molecular clocks we all have, our innate pacemakers, seasonal changes, sleep, SAD, rhythms, diseases, and more.

Bentley, E. (2000). *Awareness: biorhythms, sleep and dreaming.* London: Routledge. This is a useful and engaging account of redsearch into this area—the theories and the evidence.

Jarvis, M., & Russell, J. (2002). Biorhythms in *Key ideas in psychology.* Cheltenham: Nelson Thornes (pp. 24–29). This has some interesting comments on controversies and applications in this area.

REVISION QUESTIONS

In the exam, questions on this topic are out of 25 marks, and can take the form of essay questions or two-part questions. You should allow about 30 minutes for each of the questions below, which aim to test the material in this chapter. In the exam, make sure you know which topics you have covered so you can choose the correct question. Never try to answer a question unless you have been taught the topic.

See *A2-Level Psychology Online* for tips on how to answer these revision questions.

1. Discuss the role of endogenous pacemakers and exogenous zeitgebers in the sleep/wake cycle and at least one other biological rhythm (AQA, 2007).   (25 marks)

2. Discuss the nature of sleep, including two explanations or theories of the functions of sleep.   (25 marks)

3. (a) Outline with examples the different biological rhythms: circadian, ultradian, and infradian.   (9 marks)

    (b) Discuss the consequences of disrupting such biological rhythms, e.g. shiftwork, jet lag.   (16 marks)

4. Discuss explanations for insomnia, including factors influencing insomnia.   (25 marks)

Theories of perceptual organisation p. 73
- What is the top-down theory of perception?
- What is the bottom-up theory of perception?

Development of perception p. 88
- At what age to infants develop depth and distance perception?
- What do cross-cultural studies reveal about the development of perception?
- What are the influences of nature and nurture in the development of perception?

Face recognition and visual agnosias p. 101
- How do we recognise faces?
- What is prosopagnosia and what causes this?

Perception

By Michael W. Eysenck

Perceiving the world about us is of enormous importance in our everyday lives. It allows us to move around freely, to see the people with whom we are talking, to read magazines and books, to admire the wonders of nature, and to watch films and television. It is very important for our visual perception to be accurate—if we misperceive how close cars are to us as we try to cross the road, the consequences could be fatal. Thus, it comes as no surprise to discover that far more of the human brain is devoted to vision than to any other sensory modality.

Seeing our surroundings and making sense of them seems very easy. For example, we don't have to think much to know that we are on the pavement and that there are several cars moving in both directions on the road. In fact, as we will discover, making sense of (or perceiving) the environment is a major achievement.

THEORIES OF PERCEPTUAL ORGANISATION

Visual perception depends on two types of processing. First, there is **bottom-up processing**, in which processing is determined directly by external stimuli. No-one denies the importance of bottom-up processing—visual perception simply couldn't be as accurate as it is in the absence of extensive bottom-up processing. Second, there is **top-down processing**, in which processing is influenced by an individual's knowledge and expectations. The importance of top-down processing is less obvious than that of bottom-up processing. Top-down processing can distort visual perception, as can be seen if you look at the triangle shown in the figure on the right and read what is printed inside it. Unless you are familiar with the trick, you probably read it as "Paris in the spring". If so, look again, and you will see that the word "the" is repeated. Your expectation that it was the well-known phrase (i.e. top-down processing) dominated the information available from the stimulus (i.e. bottom-up processing).

PARIS
IN THE
THE SPRING

Top-down processing.

> **KEY TERMS**
>
> **Bottom-up processing:** gathering information directly from the external environment, as distinct from the effects of expectations (top-down processing).
> **Top-down processing:** processing that is affected by expectations and prior knowledge, as distinct from bottom-up processing, which is driven directly by the stimulus.

Pilots now train on computer simulators, learning how to interpret information from the optic flow about speed, height, and direction, and gaining an understanding of how the plane will react in certain situations.

An especially clear demonstration of the involvement of top-down processing comes from a study by Bruner, Postman, and Rodrigues (1951). Participants expected to see conventional playing cards presented very briefly. When black hearts were presented, some participants claimed to have seen purple or brown hearts. There was an almost literal blending of the black colour stemming from bottom-up processing and of the red colour stemming from top-down processing due to the expectation that hearts will be red.

In this section, we consider two theories of visual perception. Gibson's Direct Theory emphasises the importance of bottom-up processes. It is based on the assumption that the information provided by the visual environment permits the individual to move around and to interact directly with that environment without internal processes being involved. By contrast, Gregory's Indirect Theory of Perception focused on top-down processes. His theory is based on the assumption that perception is an active and constructive process much influenced by hypotheses and expectations.

Gibson's Bottom-up/Direct Theory

Gibson maintained that the environment provides so much rich information that there is no need for any higher or top-down processing. His Direct Theory is sometimes called the "Ecological Theory" because of the claim that perception can be explained solely in terms of the environment. Gibson's interest in perceptual phenomena developed out of being given the assignment of preparing training films for Second-World-War pilots to overcome the problems they experienced when landing. This led him to consider the sort of information available to pilots. He then spent the next 30 years studying such environmental data.

KEY TERMS

Optic array: in Gibson's theory, the pattern of light reaching the eye.
Optic flow pattern: perceptual effect in which the visual environment appears to move away from the point towards which a person is moving.

Optic array

The starting point for Gibson's theory was the notion that the pattern of light reaching the eye can be regarded as an **optic array** containing all visual information available at the retina of the eye (see the figure on the left). This optic array provides unambiguous information about the layout of objects in space. This information comes in many forms (discussed below). Perception involves "picking up" the rich information provided by the optic array in a direct way with little or no information processing involved.

Optic flow

The first kind of data that Gibson identified consisted of **optic flow patterns**—the point towards which the pilot is moving (called the "pole") seems motionless with the rest of the visual environment moving away from that point. The further any part of the landing

The optic array and how it is transformed by movement.

strip is from the pole, the greater is its apparent speed of movement. Gibson argued that the sensory information available to pilots in optic flow patterns provides them with *unambiguous* information about their direction, speed, and altitude.

Gibson was so impressed by the wealth of sensory information available to pilots in optic flow patterns that he devoted himself to an analysis of the information available in other situations.

Perception and action

Of particular importance in Gibson's theory was the assumption that there is a close relationship between perception and action. An observer can obtain valuable information about the environment by moving about. For example, optic flow patterns only exist when the individual is in motion. Previous researchers in visual perception had minimised the importance of movement. This happened in part because they carried out artificial laboratory studies in which they often prevented movement of the eyes relative to visual displays by using chin rests or other restraints.

Invariants

Gibson argued that important aspects of the optic array remain the same when observers move around their environment. These aspects are known as **invariants**. The pole (or point towards which someone is moving) is an example of an invariant. Another example is the horizon ratio relation—the ratio of an object's height to the distance between its base and the horizon is invariant regardless of its distance from the viewer. According to Gibson, this invariant helps us to estimate accurately the size of any given object whether it is close to us or far away.

Texture gradients

Another important invariant in the environment is **texture gradient**. Most objects (e.g. cobble-stoned roads, carpets) possess texture, and textured objects slanting away from us have a texture gradient—this is a gradient (rate of change) of texture density as you look from the front to the back of a slanting object. If you were unwise enough to stand between the rails of a railway track and look along it, the details would

become less clear as you looked into the distance. In addition, the distance between the connections would seem to reduce. Texture gradients provide us with information about depth and distance because they indicate which things are closer and which are further away.

Resonance

How do people detect or "pick up" the invariant information provided by the optic array? According to Gibson, there is a process of **resonance**, which he explained by analogy to the workings of a radio. In most houses throughout the Western world, there is almost non-stop electromagnetic radiation from various radio transmitters. When a radio set is switched on, there might be only a hissing sound.

Horizon ratio relation: the size of an object may get larger as you get closer, but the proportion of that object above and below the horizon remains invariant, i.e. unchanging.

Texture gradients are also perceptual invariants, and communicate distance and depth. The objects seem to become closer together as they recede into the distance.

KEY TERMS

Invariants: in Gibson's theory those aspects of the visual environment that remain the same as the observer moves.
Texture gradient: a cue to depth given by the increased rate of change in texture density as you look from the front to the back of a slanting stimulus.
Resonance: Gibson's explanation for how we detect invariant sensory information; the information is there in the environment and one simply tunes into it.

According to Gibson, the meaning that is attached to an object is directly communicated when we look at it because its potential uses are obvious. One look at a postbox and you can "see" its meaning (a place to put letters).

If tuned properly, however, speech or music will be heard clearly. In Gibson's terms, the radio is now *resonating* with the information contained in the electromagnetic radiation.

The above analogy suggests we can pick up information from the environment fairly automatically and effortlessly if we are attuned to that information. The radio operates as a single unit, in the sense that damage to any part of its circuitry would stop it working. In a similar way, Gibson argued that the nervous system works as a single unit when we are engaged in visual perception.

Affordance

A key part of visual perception involves attaching *meaning* to the visual information provided to the eyes. It is usually assumed that we perceive the meaning of things in our environment through the use of top-down processes. Relevant knowledge about objects is stored in long-term memory and we use this knowledge to decide the meaning of what we are perceiving. Gibson (1979) disagreed with this assumption. He argued that all the potential uses of an object (which he called their **affordances**) are directly perceivable. For example, a ladder "affords" ascent or descent, and a chair "affords" sitting; he even applied the notion of affordances to postboxes (Gibson, 1979, p. 139):

> The postbox … affords letter-mailing to a letter-writing human in a community with a postal system. This fact is perceived when the postbox is identified as such.

If you are somewhat sceptical about this notion of affordance, then I can assure you that you're in good company!

Most objects give rise to more than one affordance, with the particular affordance that influences behaviour being determined by the perceiver's current state. Thus, a hungry person will perceive the affordance of edibility when presented with an orange and so will eat it. Someone who is angry might look at the orange and detect the affordance of a projectile and so throw it at the person who has made them angry.

The notion of affordances is very important to Gibson's theory. It forms part of his attempt to show that all the information needed to make sense of the visual environment is *directly* present in the visual input. In addition, it conforms to the notion that there is a close relationship between perception and action.

Findings

Some of Gibson's ideas (such as those about resonance and affordance) are hard to test experimentally. However, much research has focused on his assumption that we use optic flow patterns to tell us the direction in which we are moving. To anticipate a little, the evidence generally supports the view that optic-flow information is *one* source of information that we use to work out how to move towards a target. Warren and Hannon (1988) produced films consisting of patterns of moving dots simulating the optic flow that would be produced if someone were moving in a given direction. As predicted by Gibson, observers used the optic-flow information to make accurate judgements of the direction in which they were heading.

It is probably true that we often make use of such information to make sure we are heading directly towards our goal. However, other factors *not* emphasised by

KEY TERM

Affordances: in Gibson's theory, the possible uses of objects, which are claimed to be given directly in the sensory information provided by the stimulus.

Gibson are also involved. Van den Berg and Brenner (1994) pointed out that we need only *one* eye to use optic-flow information. However, judgements about the direction in which observers were moving were more accurate when they used *two* eyes rather than only *one*. This happened because of what is known as binocular disparity—the slight difference in images on the retina of each eye allows observers to obtain additional information about the relative depths of objects.

Hahn, Andersen, and Saidpour (2003) presented observers with two photographs of a real-world scene in rapid succession. In one condition, the two photographs were presented only 50 milliseconds apart and apparent motion was perceived. In a second condition, the photographs were presented 1000 milliseconds apart and no apparent motion was perceived. When there was a fairly large change in camera position between the two photographs, judgements of heading direction were equally good in the two conditions. That is an important finding—it means that optic-flow information is *not* needed to make accurate judgements of direction of movement.

Perhaps the simplest explanation of how we move towards a particular goal is that we use information about perceived target location. In essence, we simply point ourselves at the target and try to walk directly to it—this is using the cue of visual direction. Rushton, Harris, Lloyd, and Wann. (1998) carried out an ingenious experiment in which they produced a conflict between perceived visual direction (the direction in which observers seemed to be heading) and optic-flow information. How did they do this? Observers wore prisms that provided misleading information about visual direction but accurate information about optic flow. If optic-flow information were all-important, the prisms should have had no effect on observers' direction of walking—they should have walked straight towards the target. In fact,

HOW SCIENCE WORKS: DEPTH CUES EXPERIMENT

The brain estimates depth and distance using depth cues. For this to work well in real life, the brain uses the slightly different information from each eye—the two slightly different views are the result of the eyes being a certain distance apart; this is called stereoscopic vision. You can demonstrate this for yourself by holding a pen at arm's length against a background; close first one eye and see what the pen lines up with, then close the other eye (opening the first one!) and the pen seems to have jumped against the background. This apparent—but not real—movement is called "parallax error".

An easy and amusing experiment to illustrate the importance of stereoscopic vision can be done using a ruler and three pins. Drawing pins with coloured heads are best for this, because they are easy to see. You will also need a surface into which the pins can be pushed so that they stand upright, such as a strip of wood.

Place one pin (pin A) level with zero on the ruler and a second pin (pin B) a certain distance along, e.g. 20 cm. Your participants' task is to cover one eye and then, with their open eye at the same level as the ruler and pins (this is important!) to place the third pin (pin C) at what they see is the same level as pin B. Try it yourself, it is actually quite difficult! You could record the amount of error for each participant:

- What would your hypothesis be? Would it be directional (one-tailed) or non-directional (two-tailed), and why?

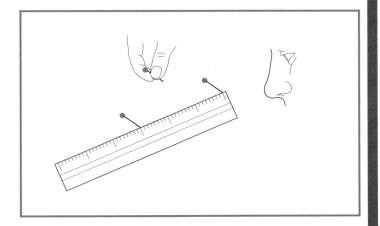

- Would you be collecting nominal, ordinal, or interval/ratio data? Can you explain this?
- What can you do with your data? You could calculate the mean error and the range, and the standard deviation.
- What would these calculations tell you about your data?
- Can you display your data in a descriptive way?
- What do your data tell you about the brain's estimation of depth/distance?

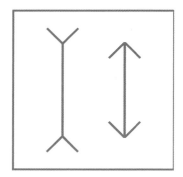

The Müller–Lyer illusion.

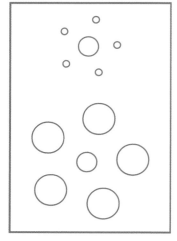

The Ebbinghaus illusion.

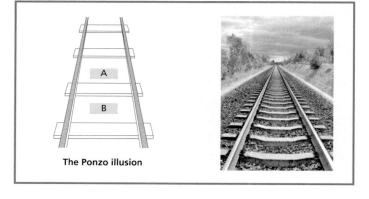

The Ponzo illusion

however, observers walked along a curved path as would be expected if they were focusing on perceived visual direction. This finding is bad news for Gibson's theory because it suggests that optic-flow information is less important than he assumed.

Gibson assumed that the visual environment provides us with so much detailed information that our perception is nearly always accurate. There is clearly some truth in this notion. Indeed, the human species would probably have become extinct a very long time ago if we often perceived the environment inaccurately (e.g. close to the edge of a precipice!). However, Gibson's approach is threatened by the existence of a large number of visual illusions in which perception is very inaccurate. In the Müller–Lyer illusion (see figure on the left), your task is to compare the lengths of the two vertical lines. Nearly everyone says that the vertical line on the left looks longer than the one on the right. In fact, however, they are the same length, as can be confirmed by using a ruler! In the Ebbinghaus illusion (see the figure on the left), the central circle surrounded by smaller circles looks larger than a central circle of the same size surrounded by larger circles. In the Ponzo illusion (see figure below), rectangle A looks larger than rectangle B although they are actually the same length.

Gibson dismissed most visual illusions as "unecological", meaning that they are irrelevant to everyday visual perception because the stimuli are two-dimensional and artificial. There is some validity in his point of view, but it isn't the whole story. According to Milner and Goodale (1995, 1998), we have *two* visual perceptual systems, although they accepted that these two systems often interact with each other and so aren't entirely separate. One system allows us to move safely around our environment without knocking into objects or falling over precipices. This vision-for-action system answers the question, "How can I interact with that object?", and is used for visually guided action. It resembles what Gibson had in mind when he argued that perception and action are very closely linked. The other system (the vision-for-perception system) is used to decide that the animal in front of us is a cat or a buffalo, or to admire a beautiful painting. This system is used to form an internal model of the world around us, and provides an answer to the question, "What is that object?"

We can apply the distinction between these two visual systems to visual illusions. The huge majority of studies on visual illusions have used measures involving the vision-for-perception system, for example, asking observers to look at visual illusions and report what they see. Such studies have obtained clear evidence of illusion effects. What would happen if we studied visual illusions using measures involving the vision-for-action system? According to Gibson's approach, we might expect there to be little or no illusion under these circumstances.

Haart, Carey, and Milne (1999) used a three-dimensional version of the Müller–Lyer illusion (see figure above). Participants were given one of two tasks to perform:

1. A matching task, in which participants indicated the length of the shaft on one figure by the size of the gap between their index finger and thumb. This task involved the vision-for-perception system.

EXAM HINT

Make sure you can explain how the vision-for-action system is consistent with Gibson's theory and how the vision-for-perception system can account for common visual illusions.

2. A grasping task, in which participants rapidly grasped the target figure lengthwise using their index finger and thumb. This task involved the vision-for-action system.

As expected, Haart et al. (1999) found a strong illusion effect with the matching task. That simply confirms the typical finding that the Müller–Lyer illusion is obtained when we consider only the vision-for-perception system. However, the findings were quite different with the grasping task involving the vision-for-action system. There was now *no* illusion effect at all! This finding has also been obtained with other visual illusions. It appears that the vision-for-action system generally operates in the accurate way assumed by Gibson.

Evaluation of Gibson's theory

What are the main strengths of Gibson's theory? First, its emphasis on the notion that the visual environment provides much more information than had previously been thought is basically correct. Second, Gibson was also right in assuming that the moment-by-moment changes in the optic array that occur when we are moving provide very useful information about the layout of the visual environment. Most previous theorists had de-emphasised the importance of movement, and had carried out studies in which the visual environment and the observer were both motionless. Third, Gibson was also right to argue that perception and action are often closely related. Some more recent theorists (e.g. Milner & Goodale, 1995, 1998) have argued convincingly that we possess an accurate perception-for-action system very similar to what Gibson had in mind when he claimed that perception is nearly always accurate. Fourth, we could use Gibson's theoretical approach to predict that there might be circumstances (i.e. focusing on the vision-for-action system) in which visual illusions are perceived accurately. The evidence supports that prediction.

What are the main limitations with Gibson's Direct Theory? First, the processes involved in identifying invariants in the environment, in discovering affordances, and in producing resonance are all much more complex than was assumed by Gibson. None of these achievements of visual perception happens as rapidly and automatically as Gibson claimed.

Second, as we have seen, Gibson exaggerated the role of optic-flow information in allowing us to move successfully around the environment. Such information is sometimes used but it is much less important than assumed by Gibson. Other factors, including visual direction (the direction we seem to be heading) and binocular disparity (slight differences in the input to the two eyes), also influence our judgements about the direction in which we are heading.

Third, Gibson's views on how we attach meaning to visual stimuli are decidedly limited. You will remember that he focused on the notion of "affordance", which relates only to the potential uses of an object. However, we can attach many other kinds of meaning to stimuli. For example, Fodor and Pylyshyn (1981) distinguished between "seeing" and "seeing as". They considered someone called Smith who is lost at sea. He sees the stars in the night sky, including the Pole Star. However, crucial to his survival is whether he sees the Pole Star as the Pole Star or as just another star. "Seeing as" involves attaching additional meaning to what is being seen. Gibson's notion of affordances was an unsuccessful attempt to explain the meaningfulness of perception. He provides a valuable account of *seeing* (especially when related to action), but he had little of interest to say about *seeing as*.

[?] Why do you think previous researchers might have minimised the importance of movement?

[?] Would you class Gibson's theory as a reductionist one?

? Is it possible that perceptual systems are different in different animals?

? Our senses can be deceived by suggestion, such as when hypnosis and relaxation techniques are used as methods of pain relief. Why do you think this is?

Fourth, a final weakness of Gibson's approach was his notion that no internal representations (e.g. memories) are needed to explain perception. Bruce, Green, and Georgeson (1996) referred to the work of Menzel (1978) to show the problems flowing from Gibson's position. Chimpanzees were carried around a field and shown the locations of 20 pieces of food. When each chimpanzee was subsequently released, it moved around the field picking up the food efficiently. As there could be no relevant information in the light reaching the chimpanzees (because they were now moving independently rather than being carried), they must have made use of stored information in long-term memory to guide their search. This is contrary to the assumptions made by Gibson.

Gregory's Top-down/Indirect Theory

Gregory's (1970, 1972) Top-down or Indirect Theory is based on the assumption that the information available to the eyes is inadequate on its own to permit detailed and accurate perception of the world around us. According to Gregory (1972), perceptions are constructions "from the fragmentary scraps of data signalled by the senses and drawn from the brain memory banks, themselves constructions from the snippets of the past." More specifically, we use the information supplied to the eyes as the basis for making inferences or forming hypotheses about the visual environment.

Gregory's theoretical approach resembles that of several previous theorists. For example, Helmholtz (1821–1894) argued that we use *unconscious inferences* to add meaning to sensory information. He assumed that these inferences were unconscious because we are usually unaware that we are making them.

Gregory's Indirect Theory makes various assumptions related to those discussed already:

1. Perception is an active and constructive process. According to Gordon (1989, p. 124), it is "something more than the direct registration of sensations . . . other events intervene between stimulation and experience." Thus, perception is more than just sensing physical data—to experience seeing something, other active processes are involved.
2. Perception is *not* directly given by the stimulus input, but also involves internal hypotheses, expectations, and knowledge, together with motivational and emotional factors. Sensory information is used as the basis for making informed guesses or inferences about the presented stimulus and its meaning.
3. The hypotheses and expectations that influence visual perception will sometimes be inaccurate, and so perception is prone to error.

Findings: expectations

Ittelson (1951) provided an illustration of how expectations can influence perception based on the Ames distorted room. It has a peculiar shape: the floor slopes and the rear wall is not at right angles to the adjoining walls. Despite this, the Ames room creates the same retinal image as a normal rectangular room when viewed through a peephole. The fact that one end of the rear wall is much further

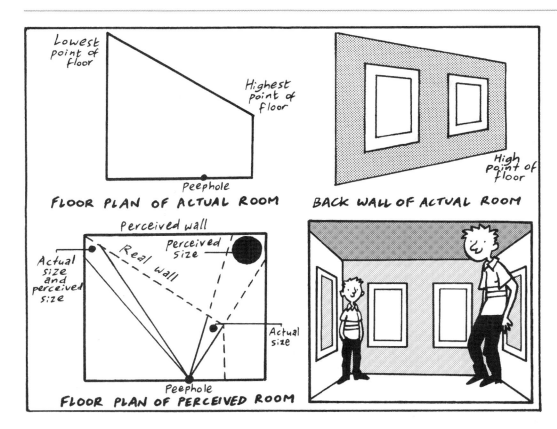

from the viewer is disguised by making it much lower. The cues suggesting that the rear wall is at right angles to the viewer are so strong that observers mistakenly assume that two adults standing in the corners by the rear wall are at the same distance from them. This leads them to estimate the size of the nearer adult as being much greater than that of the adult who is further away. If there is only one adult at the rear of the room, he or she seems to shrink or expand as he or she moves along the rear wall!

One of the most dramatic examples of expectations influencing visual perception is the "hollow face" illusion (Gregory, 1973). When a hollow face is seen from a few feet away, it is perceived as a normal face. This illusion obviously depends on our hugely greater familiarity with normal faces than with hollow ones. It is a remarkably strong illusion, and nearly everyone continues to see the hollow face as normal even when they know for certain that it is hollow.

In the real world, probably the most common way in which expectations influence visual perception is via *context*. For example, when I go to conferences, I expect to see several psychologists I know. When I see a stranger in the distance who resembles a psychologist I know, I have often initially mistaken the person for the psychologist. Palmer (1975) presented a scene (e.g. a kitchen), followed by the very brief presentation of the picture of an object. This object was either appropriate to the context (e.g. a loaf of bread) or inappropriate (e.g. a letterbox). There was also a further condition in which no contextual scene was presented. The probability of identifying the object correctly was greatest when it was appropriate to the context, intermediate when there was no context, and lowest when it was inappropriate.

Expectation probably plays a part in a phenomenon known as change blindness, in which people fail to detect changes in the visual environment. For

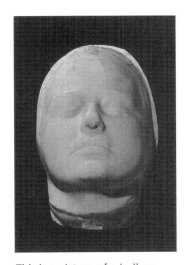

This is a picture of a hollow mask, illuminated from behind. In real life, as in this photograph, we see a normal face, with the tip of the nose nearer to us than the eyelids. Photograph by Sam Grainger.

example, in a study by Simons and Levin (1998), people walking across a college campus were asked by a stranger for directions. About 10 or 15 seconds into the discussion, two men carrying a wooden door passed between the stranger and the participant. While that was happening, the stranger was substituted with a man of different height, build, and voice wearing different clothes. Despite all these differences, half the participants failed to realise their conversational partner had changed! The reasonable expectation that they would be talking to the same stranger throughout made it harder to detect the change.

Clear-cut evidence that expectations influence our everyday perception comes from situations in which expectations produce *errors* in perception. One such situation is proofreading, in which people read through a text trying to detect spelling and other mistakes in it. Most people make numerous mistakes when proofreading. Daneman and Stainton (1993) found that errors were more common when readers were proofreading an essay handwritten by themselves rather than an essay written by someone else. Their extreme familiarity with their own writing meant that they focused less on possible errors in their own essay.

Findings: motivational factors

A central assumption of the constructivist approach is that perception isn't determined entirely by external stimuli. For example, it is assumed that current motivational and emotional states can influence individuals' perceptual hypotheses and thus their visual perception. Consider a study by Schafer and Murphy (1943). They prepared drawings consisting of an irregular line drawn vertically through a circle so that either half of the circle could be seen as the profile of a face (see figure below). During initial training, each face was presented separately. One face in each pair was associated with financial reward whereas the other one was associated with financial punishment. When the original combined drawings were then presented briefly, observers were much more likely to report perceiving the previously rewarded face than the previously punished one. In a similar study, Smith and Hochberg (1954) found that delivering a shock when one of the two profile faces was presented decreased its tendency to be perceived later.

Bruner and Goodman (1947) asked rich and poor children to estimate the size of coins. The poor children overestimated the size of every coin more than the rich children. Although this finding might reflect the greater value of money to poor children, there is a simpler explanation. The rich children would have had more familiarity with coins, and this might have made them more accurate in their size estimates. Ashley, Harper, and Runyon (1951) introduced an ingenious modification to the experimental design used by Bruner and Goodman (1947). They hypnotised adult participants into believing they were rich or poor. The size estimates of coins

The two stimulus faces and final ambiguous picture used by Schafer and Murphy to demonstrate the effects of motivation on perception.

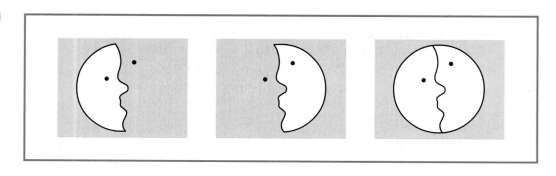

were consistently larger when the participants were in the "poor" state.

When interpreting the above findings, it is important to distinguish between effects on perception and on response. For example, it is well established from work on operant conditioning by Skinner and others that reward and punishment both influence the likelihood of making any given response. Thus, it is possible that reward and punishment in the study by Schafer and Murphy (1943) affected participants' *responses* without necessarily affecting actual visual perception. If someone offered you money for perceiving one thing and took money away from you if you perceived something else, you might be tempted to pretend to see the rewarded thing!

> **Other studies: emotional and motivational factors**
>
> Solley and Haigh (1957) examined the role of emotional factors in perception. In two sessions, one before and one after Christmas, they asked children aged between 4 and 8 to draw Santa Claus. As Christmas approached, the Santa drawings became larger and more elaborate, but after Christmas the drawings were much smaller. The emotions involved in anticipating Christmas affected how the children depicted Santa and his presents.
>
> Motivational factors were examined by Sanford (1936). Some participants were deprived of food on the day of Sanford's study and then given a word-completion task. Most hungry participants produced BREAD as the word to complete B___D, whereas non-deprived participants tended to produce the word BORED!

Visual illusions

Gregory (1970) claimed that his Indirect Theory could explain many of the visual illusions. He argued that we treat two-dimensional illusions as if they were three-dimensional, even though we know they are only two-dimensional. For example, people typically see a given object as having a constant size by taking account of its apparent distance. Size constancy means that an object is perceived as having the same size whether looked at from a short or a long distance away. This constancy contrasts with the size of the retinal image (the image on the retina inside the eye) that becomes progressively smaller as an object recedes into the distance (see figure below). According to Gregory's Misapplied Size–Constancy Theory, this kind of perceptual processing is wrongly applied to produce several illusions.

It is easiest to see what Gregory (1970) had in mind by considering the Ponzo illusion (see bottom figure on page 78). The long lines look like railways lines or the edges of a road receding into the distance. As a result, the top rectangle A can be seen as further away from us that the bottom rectangle B. If it were a three-dimensional scene, then rectangle A would be longer than rectangle B. It looks longer to us because of misapplied size constancy.

The same kind of explanation can be used with the Müller–Lyer illusion. According to Gregory (1970), the left figure looks like the inside corners of a room, whereas the right figure is like the outside corners of a building. Thus, the vertical line in the left figure is further away from us than its fins, whereas the vertical line in the right figure is closer to us than its fins. As the size of the retinal image is the same for both vertical lines, the principle of size constancy tells us that the line that is further away (i.e. the one in the left figure) must be longer. This is precisely the Müller–Lyer illusion.

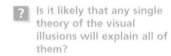

? Is it likely that any single theory of the visual illusions will explain all of them?

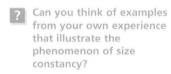

? Can you think of examples from your own experience that illustrate the phenomenon of size constancy?

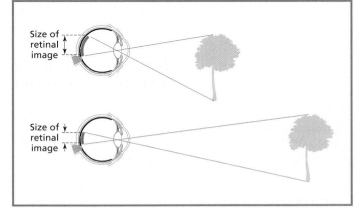

The retinal image halves in size when the distance from the eye doubles.

Findings: visual illusions

Some of the available evidence is consistent with Gregory's Misapplied Size–Constancy Theory. He argued that cues to depth are used *automatically* whether or not the figures in an illusion are seen to be lying on a flat surface. Support for this viewpoint comes from the finding that the two-dimensional Müller–Lyer figures (see page 78) do indeed appear three-dimensional when presented as luminous models in a dark room.

It might be thought that the depth cues of two-dimensional drawings would be less effective than those of photographs because fewer depth cues are present in drawings. Supporting evidence for this was reported by Leibowitz et al. (1969), who studied the Ponzo illusion and found that the extent of the illusion was greater with a photograph than with a drawing.

There are real problems with Gregory's account of the Müller–Lyer illusion. Matlin and Foley (1997) argued that our perception of visual illusions is influenced by parts of the figure not being judged. Thus, for example, the vertical lines in the Müller–Lyer illusion might seem longer or shorter than their actual length simply

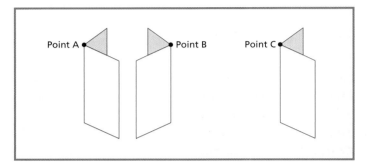

Point A   Point B   Point C

because they form part of a large or small object. Coren and Girgus (1972) reported evidence consistent with this argument—the size of the Müller–Lyer illusion was greatly reduced when the fins were in a different colour from the vertical lines. Presumably, this made it easier to ignore the fins.

DeLucia and Hochberg (1991) reported findings that are very hard (or impossible) to explain on Gregory's theory. They presented observers with three-dimensional, 2-foot-high fins placed in a line on the floor in an arrangement like that shown in the

In DeLucia and Hochberg's study, three fins that were 2 feet high were positioned on the floor and participants asked to say whether point A was closer to point B than B was C. The Müller–Lyer illusion persists even though depth is obvious in this three-dimensional situation; a fact that does not fit Gregory's Misapplied Size–Constancy Theory.

figure above. The usual illusion effect was obtained even though it was obvious that all the fins were the same distance from the observers. You can confirm DeLucia and Hochberg's findings by placing three open books in a line so that the ones on the left and the right are open to the right and the one in the middle is open to the left. The spine of the book in the middle should be the same distance from the spines of each of the other two books. Despite this, the distance between the spine of the middle book and the spine of the book on the right should look longer. I have tried this myself, and was surprised how strong the illusion was. This finding can't be explained by Gregory's Misapplied Size–Constancy Theory.

The spine of the middle book is closer to the spine of which other book? Now check your answer with a ruler.

EXAM HINT

Make sure you consider the lack of mundane realism of visual illusions as evidence for Gregory's top-down theory.

Overall evaluation of Gregory's theory

What are the strengths of Gregory's theory? First, top-down processes based on expectations, hypotheses, and so on can have a considerable influence on visual perception. Many theorists such as Gibson have emphasised the importance of bottom-up processes, and Gregory and other indirect theorists have performed the valuable service of showing that top-down processes shouldn't be ignored.

Second, Gibson's theory is wide-ranging in that it assumes that motivational and emotional factors can influence perception. As we have seen, there is supporting evidence for this assumption.

Third, according to indirect theorists, the influence of top-down processes on perception means that what we perceive is often inaccurate. That is certainly the case with the numerous visual illusions, and Gregory's Misapplied Size–Constancy Theory was specifically designed to explain the existence of these illusions. It could be argued that most visual illusions involve very artificial stimuli. However, expectations definitely play a role in everyday life, as is shown by context effects and proofreading errors.

What are the main limitations with Gregory's indirect theory? First, as we have seen, constructivist theorists predict that perception will often be in error. However, with some exceptions, such as visual illusions and proofreading errors, it seems that visual perception is generally more accurate than predicted by the theory.

Second, many of the studies carried out by constructivist theorists make use of artificial or unnatural stimuli. As Gordon (1989, p. 144) pointed out, such studies involve:

> *The perception of patterns under conditions of brief exposure, drawings which could represent the corners of buildings, glowing objects in darkened corridors ... none of these existed in the African grasslands where human perceptual systems reached their present state of evolutionary development.*

Consider, for example, studies involving the very rapid presentation of visual stimuli. Brief presentation reduces the impact of bottom-up processes, thus allowing more scope for top-down processes to operate. However, in the real world, it is rare that we have only a fraction of a second to look at an object.

Third, we have seen that Gibson was correct in arguing that the environment typically contains rich and detailed information. Gregory's view that the senses are provided only with "fragmentary scraps of data" is clearly a gross exaggeration of the true state of affairs.

Fourth, there is good evidence for the existence of two visual systems: the vision-for-perception system and the vision-for-action system. Gregory's approach is clearly of more relevance to the vision-for-perception system. It is of relatively little value in explaining the ways in which vision is associated with rapid and accurate action even with many visual illusions.

Synthesis: Neisser's Cyclic Theory

It is reasonable to conclude from our discussion so far that visual perception depends on *both* bottom-up and top-down processes, and that it is a substantial oversimplification to ignore either type of process. Accordingly, what we need is a synthesis or combination of the direct and indirect approaches to perception. Precisely this was done by Neisser (1976). In his cyclic theory, he assumed that there is a perceptual cycle involving schemas, perceptual exploration, and

What other limitations can you think of?

HOW SCIENCE WORKS: COMPARING THEORIES

It would be useful to prepare a comparison between Gibson's and Gregory's theories. You could produce a PowerPoint presentation based on constructing a flow diagram for each, then outlining the bottom-up and top-down approaches in more detail. Then you could go on to identify points they have in common, and also the differences. This is really useful in helping you understand and remember the two theories. You could even have a final section of frames with Neisser's synthesis of the two approaches. It would be useful to make the theories stand out separately, and giving the sets of frames different colour backgrounds would help with this, so long as the colours didn't interfere with the text.

The perceptual cycle as proposed by Neisser (1976)

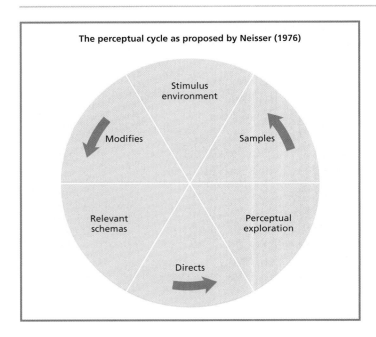

the stimulus environment (see figure on the left). Schemas contain collections of knowledge derived from past experience. These serve the function of directing perceptual exploration towards relevant environmental stimuli. Such exploration often leads the perceiver to sample the available stimulus information. If the information obtained from the environment fails to match information in the relevant schema, then the information in the schema is modified appropriately.

The perceptual cycle described by Neisser includes elements of bottom-up and top-down processing. Bottom-up processing is represented by the sampling of available environmental information that can modify the current schema. Top-down processing is represented by the notion that schemas influence the course of the information processing involved in perception.

The key notion in Neisser's theory is that of schemas or organised knowledge. According to the theory, schemas reduce the need to analyse all aspects of a visual scene. Evidence for this was reported by Biederman, Glass, and Stacy (1973). Participants could recall almost half the objects in photographs of familiar scenes (e.g. a city street) after viewing them for only one-tenth of a second, because the relevant schemas

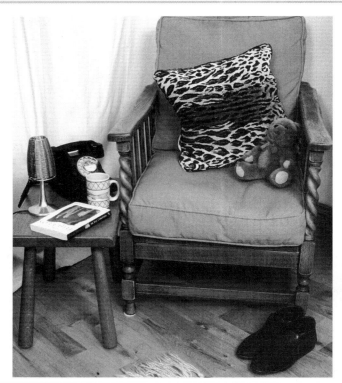

Activity: Testing Biederman et al.'s findings

Test the Biederman et al. experimental findings for yourself. Show the scene on the left to someone who has not already seen these pictures, very briefly (Biederman used one-tenth of a second), and see what objects they can recall. Try the random arrangement below on someone else, for the same time period. Again, see how many objects they can remember. Why do you have to show the two pictures to different people? How might this affect your findings?

could be used easily. In contrast, when the objects were arranged randomly in the photograph, participants found it much harder to identify and to remember them.

Evaluation

Neisser's (1976) Cyclic Theory combines some of the best features of the direct or bottom-up and indirect or top-down approaches to perception. Perception often involves top-down processes as well as bottom-up processes, and both types of processes are incorporated into Neisser's perceptual cycle. Another strength of Neisser's theory is its emphasis on schemas. Schema-relevant objects are generally perceived and remembered much better than schema-irrelevant objects.

What are the weaknesses of Neisser's Cyclic Theory? First, it is very sketchy and fails to specify in any detail the processes involved in perception. More specifically, we aren't told precisely how relevant schemas direct perceptual exploration, how perceptual exploration determines what is to be sampled in the stimulus environment, or how processing of the stimulus environment then modifies the relevant schemas. Second, it is hard to know precisely what information is contained in the various schemas.

> **EXAM HINT**
>
> Note that if the question asks you to describe and evaluate Gibson's or Gregory's theory, do use the alternative explanations as counter perspectives, but be careful—one link sentence to introduce them is not enough. You must consistently contrast the counter perspective with the explanation(s) you've covered as AO1. Do not describe the counter perspective; instead explain what insights it provides that the AO1 explanation does not. Also, consider whether the different explanations share any strengths or weaknesses, or whether the weakness of one can be used to highlight the strength of the other.

■ Activity: Comparing theories of perception

Draw up a table showing comparisons among the different theories of perception

Features of theory	Gibson	Gregory	Neisser
Major concepts			
Top-down or bottom-up?			
Generally learned or innate?			
Stored knowledge needed?			
Weaknesses			

SECTION SUMMARY
Theories of Perceptual Organisation

Gibson's Bottom-up/ Direct Theory

❖ Gibson argued that optic flow patterns provide valuable information about the direction and speed of motion.

❖ Observers "pick up" invariant information in the visual environment through a process of resonance.

❖ All of the potential uses of an object (affordances) are directly perceivable.

❖ Evaluation:

— Gibson was right that the visual environment provides very rich information.

— Visual perception is much more complex than Gibson assumed.
— Gibson tended to ignore visual illusions and the vision-for-perception system.
— Attaching meaning to objects involves complex internal processes.

Gregory's Top-down/Indirect Theory

❖ According to Gregory, observers use top-down processes to form hypotheses about the visual environment.
❖ Observers' hypotheses are sometimes inaccurate, and this makes perception prone to error.
❖ Illusions such as the Ames room and "hollow face" show how expectations can distort perception. Context can also influence visual perception.
❖ Motivational factors influence visual expectations and perception.
❖ Gregory's misapplied size-constancy theory is inconsistent with much of the evidence.

Synthesis: Neisser's Cyclic Theory

❖ According to Neisser's Cyclic Theory, visual perception depends on *both* bottom-up and top-down processes.
❖ In Neisser's theory, schemas reduce the need to analyse all aspects of a visual scene in a top-down way.
❖ Neisser's theory combines the strengths of Gibson's and Gregory's theories, but is rather vague and hard to test.

DEVELOPMENT OF PERCEPTION

? Why is it an advantage to use newborn babies in research?

Newborn infants have very limited ability to see and make sense of the world around them. However, it is obviously extremely important for their perceptual abilities to develop rapidly and effectively if they are to avoid hurting themselves by knocking into objects. Developmental psychologists have carried out numerous studies into the development of perception, and this section will consider some of their major findings. First, we consider when and how various perceptual abilities develop. Our focus will be on infants' increased ability to judge depth or distance accurately and to realise that objects remain the same size regardless of the distance from which they are observed. Second, we turn to broader issues relating to the development of perceptual abilities in infants. Most of the research has been carried out in a small number of Western countries. However, it is interesting and important to consider cross-cultural studies on perceptual development, and these studies are also discussed. Third, there has been a long-lasting controversy concerning the factors responsible for perceptual development. More specifically, there have been differing views on the importance of environmental factors versus maturational and innate factors. This is the nature–nurture debate as it relates to the issue of perceptual development.

Development of Perceptual Abilities

? Might newborn babies have had any prior perceptual experience?

Over the first few months of life, nearly all of an infant's perceptual abilities improve dramatically. One of the most important perceptual abilities is to be able to decide accurately how far away a person or object is. This is very valuable as infants move around, because they are likely to fall and hurt themselves if they don't know how far away various objects and obstacles are. Another crucially important perceptual ability is to understand that any given object remains the same size and shape regardless of how it appears on the retina. The general term "visual constancies" is used to refer to this ability. As you can imagine, the world is likely to seem very confusing to a newborn or young infant who regards the same object at different distances or orientations as two different objects!

What innate abilities are not present at birth?

Depth/distance perception

Most of us have no difficulty at all in perceiving the world around us as three-dimensional. This is more impressive than it might sound given that the retinal image used as the basis for visual perception is only *two*-dimensional and thus lacks depth. Of crucial importance to our *three*-dimensional experience is depth perception, which includes seeing some objects as closer to us than others. As a result of accurate depth perception, we can reach out and pick up objects or walk around without knocking into anything.

How does depth/distance perception develop in infants? This question was addressed in important research by Gibson and Walk (1960) using a "visual cliff" involving a glass-topped table. A check pattern was positioned close to the glass under one half of the table (the "shallow" side) and far below the glass under the other half (the "deep" side). Infants between the ages of 6½ and 12 months were placed on the shallow side of the table and encouraged to crawl over the edge of the visual cliff on to the deep side. Most failed to respond to these incentives, suggesting that they possessed some elements of depth perception. This is consistent with the evidence that binocular vision (using information from both eyes simultaneously and of proven value in depth perception) has typically developed by the age of 6 months (Teller, 1997).

Adolph (2000) argued that the development of depth perception is more complex than assumed by Gibson and Walk (1960). She argued that motor development in infancy involves a series of achievements, starting with sitting, followed by crawling, moving sideways, and then walking. Previous theorists had emphasised the notion that infants acquire *general* knowledge (e.g. an association between depth information and falling) that stops them from crossing the visual cliff. By contrast, Adolph's sway model is based on the assumption that infants' knowledge is highly *specific*. According to this model, infants learn how to avoid risky gaps when sitting, but subsequently have to learn how to avoid such gaps when they are crawling.

Adolph (2000) obtained support for her sway model by studying 9-month-old infants more familiar with sitting than with crawling. The key findings were that, "The babies avoided reaching over risky gaps in the sitting posture but fell into risky gaps while attempting to reach in the crawling posture" (Adolph, 2000, p. 290). The implication is that learning with the visual cliff is specific to a given posture (e.g. sitting) and new learning is needed when infants become more mobile. However, slightly older infants show general learning. Witherington, Campos, Anderson, Lejeune, and Seah (2005) found that newly walking infants consistently

A drawing of Gibson and Walk's "visual cliff". Babies between 6½ and 12 months of age were reluctant to crawl over the "cliff edge", even when called by their mothers, suggesting that they perceived the drop created by the check pattern.

? Would you say that depth perception was more likely to be learned or innate?

avoided the deep side of the visual cliff. These infants had learned to avoid risky gaps while crawling, and this learning simply transferred over to walking. The take-home message is that learning to avoid gaps is *specific* to a given posture in younger infants but becomes more *general* in older ones.

Arterberry, Yonas, and Bensen (1989) studied depth perception in a different way. Infants aged between 5 and 7 months were presented with two visual objects that were the same distance away from them. However, the objects were placed on a grid using linear perspective (a cue to depth based on the convergence of parallel lines to indicate increasing distance) and texture gradient (increased rate of change of texture density from front to back) to suggest that one object was closer than the other. Most 7-month-old infants showed evidence of depth perception by reaching for the "closer" objects, but 5-month-old infants did not.

Bower, Broughton, and Moore (1970) obtained evidence that infants have at least some aspects of depth or distance perception. They showed two objects to infants under 2 weeks of age. One was large and approached to within 20 centimetres of the infant, whereas the other was small and approached to 8 centimetres. The two objects had the same retinal size (i.e. size at the retina) at their closest point to the infant. Despite this, the infants were more disturbed by the object that came closer to them—they rotated their heads upwards and pulled away from it. Apparently, these infants had somehow used information about depth to identify which object posed the greater threat.

In sum, most aspects of depth perception are present by about 6 months of age. There is some evidence (e.g. Bower et al., 1970) that aspects of depth perception might be present much earlier. There is also evidence that infants' ability to use depth information effectively depends on the task and on their stage of motor development. Improvements in depth/distance perception depend at least in part on the development of binocular vision.

Visual constancies

Nearly all adults display **size constancy** and **shape constancy**. Size constancy means that a given object is perceived as having the same size regardless of its distance from us. Shape constancy means that an object is seen to have the same shape regardless of its orientation. Thus, we see things "as they really are", and are not taken in by variations in the information presented to the retina. It is of interest to discover whether infants show size and shape constancy. As we will see, there is evidence that infants have at least partial size and shape constancy.

Size constancy

Bower (1966) studied size constancy in infants between 75 and 85 days of age. The first stage of the experiment involved teaching the infants to look at a 30-centimetre cube placed about 1 metre from them. Bower then compared the length of time looking at the same cube placed 3 metres from the infant and a 90-centimetre cube placed 3 metres away. The former stimulus had the same size as the original cube, but a much smaller retinal image. In contrast, the latter stimulus had a much greater real size but the same retinal size as the original cube. Some size constancy was shown—the infants were almost three times more likely to look at the former than at the latter stimulus object. However, they failed to show complete size constancy, because they were more likely to look at the 30-centimetre cube when it was placed 1 metre away than when it was 3 metres away.

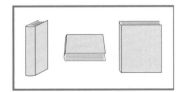

We continue to see the shape of a book as rectangular despite the fact that the retinal image is rarely rectangular—this is shape constancy.

KEY TERMS

Size constancy: objects are perceived as having a given size regardless of the size of the retinal image.

Shape constancy: objects are perceived to have a given shape regardless of the angle from which they are viewed.

Another approach to studying size constancy has involving using the **habituation method**. What happens is that a stimulus is presented until the infant no longer attends to it: this is known as habituation. When the infant shows habituation to one stimulus, he or she is shown a different stimulus. If the infant responds to the new stimulus, he or she must have discriminated between the two stimuli. Studies using the habituation method suggest that size constancy is an innate visual capacity. Slater, Mattock, and Brown (1990) familiarised newborns with a small or a large cube over a number of trials. After that, the two cubes were presented successively. The larger cube was presented at a greater distance from the newborns than the smaller cube, with the size of the retinal image being the same in both cases. All the newborns looked longer at the new cube because they had habituated to the old one. The fact that they could distinguish between the two cubes having the same-sized retinal image suggests the newborns possessed at least some of the elements of size constancy (see figure above).

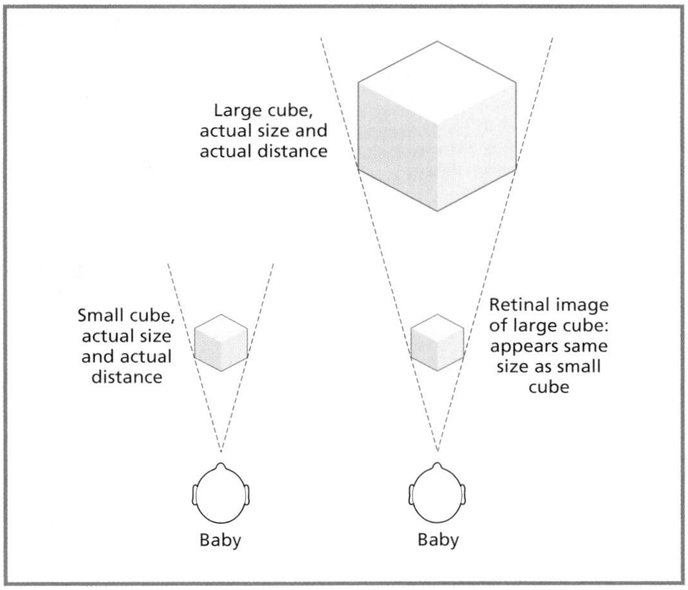

Large cube, actual size and actual distance

Small cube, actual size and actual distance

Retinal image of large cube: appears same size as small cube

Baby

Baby

Two cubes of different sizes may project retinal images of the same size, depending on their distance from the viewer.

Shape constancy

Evidence for shape constancy in 3-month-old infants was reported by Caron, Caron, and Carlson (1979) using the habituation method. Some infants were presented repeatedly with a square or a trapezoid (a four-sided shape with only two sizes parallel to each other). The square or trapezoid was presented at various angles but never face on. The experimenters arranged matters so that the trapezoid sometimes produced the retinal image of a square, and the square sometimes produced the retinal image of a trapezoid. After the infants had lost interest in looking at the shape (when they showed habituation), a square or a trapezoid was presented face on. Those infants who had previously habituated to a square that produced a trapezoidal shape on the retina immediately displayed interest in the real trapezoid. In similar fashion, those infants who had seen a trapezoid that produced a square shape on the retina were definitely interested in the real square.

What do the findings of Caron et al. (1979) mean? They indicate that the infants habituated to the *real* shape of the object rather than to the object shape projected onto the retina. This strongly suggests that these infants had developed at least partial shape constancy.

Slater and Morison (1985) also used the habituation method to study shape constancy. However, they decided to see whether there was any evidence of shape constancy in newborns (average age 1 day, 23 hours). The newborns were shown a given shape (a square or a trapezium) at various angles of slant until they had habituated to it. Then they were shown the same shape at a novel angle together with a new shape. The newborns paid much more attention to the new shape than to the same shape presented at a novel angle. Thus, there was habituation to the same shape at a novel angle, and this indicates that newborns possess at least partial shape constancy.

Do findings such as those of Slater et al. (1990) and Slater and Morison (1985) indicate that newborns possess adult levels of size and shape constancy? Not at all.

? Can you think of examples from your own experience that illustrate the phenomenon of shape constancy

KEY TERM

Habituation method: a way of assessing perception in young children based on habituation (the gradual reduction in the attention paid to a stimulus that is repeated several times).

? Which of Piaget's concepts link with shape constancy?

All that can safely be concluded is that newborns have *some* ability to discriminate between a familiar object having a given size or shape and a novel object of a different size or shape, which is a very different kettle of fish. It is probable that infants' experience and increasing mobility play some part in the development of visual constancies. However, maturational factors may well also be involved.

Infant and Cross-cultural Studies of the Development of Perceptual Abilities

We start by considering infant studies of the development of perceptual abilities. After that, we move on to consider cross-cultural studies that are relevant to the development of perceptual abilities.

Infant studies

Newborns are at a great disadvantage to adults with respect to several basic aspects of vision. According to Sireteanu (1999, p. 59), "The visual field of the newborn human infant . . . consists of a narrow tunnel around the line of vision, and the ability to resolve visual details is roughly 40 times poorer than that of adult humans." Let's consider some of the main problems with vision experienced by newborns in more detail. First, they have very poor visual acuity. We can assess visual acuity by presenting a display of alternating black and white lines, and then making the lines progressively narrower until they can no longer be separated in vision. For newborns to detect the separation of the lines, they need to be about 30 times wider than is the case for adults (Braddick & Atkinson, 1983).

Does the improvement in visual acuity over time shown by infants depend on learning or on **maturation** (changes due to genetically determined factors)? Evidence that maturation is important was reported by Maurer, Lewis, Brent, and Levin (1999), who studied human infants who had been treated for cataracts in one or both eyes. Initially, their visual acuity was at the level of newborn infants. Strikingly, however, they showed substantial improvement in visual acuity after only a 1-hour exposure to the visual world. Thus, prolonged visual experience and learning are *not* necessary for the development of visual acuity. Note, however, that infants who have had cataracts removed at an early age typically never achieve normal levels of visual acuity (Maurer, Lewis, & Mondloch, 2005).

Second, another visual limitation in newborns results from the fact that their eyes have a fixed focal length for the first 3 months. This means that they can only focus clearly on objects at a given distance from them (about 8 inches). Older children and adults show accommodation, in which the curvature of the eye's lens alters to bring objects at different distances into focus. Newborns don't show accommodation, and so only objects 8 inches in front of them can be seen clearly. As Harris and Butterworth (2002) pointed out, it is probably not a coincidence that this is approximately the distance between the infant and its mother's face when she is holding it in her arms.

Third, colour vision is either non-existent or nearly so during the first weeks of life. According to Teller (1997, p. 2197), "By two months, rudimentary colour vision has arrived. Most infants can probably discriminate red, blue, and green from each other, but not yet yellows and yellow-greens."

Fourth, newborns are deficient in binocular vision, which involves using the disparity or difference in the images projected on to the retinas of the two eyes to

? If depth perception develops around the time an infant starts crawling, does this suggest it is innately driven and due to maturation?

KEY TERM

Maturation: aspects of development in children owing little to learning or experience.

assist depth perception. Teller (1997) reviewed evidence suggesting that binocular vision is first found in infants between the ages of 3 and 6 months.

What determines the development of binocular disparity? This issue was addressed by Banks, Aslin, and Letson (1975). They studied adults who had had a problem with binocular vision because of having a squint in childhood that was subsequently corrected. Adults who had a squint at birth and received surgery by 30 months of age had good binocular disparity. Those who had a squint diagnosed between 2 and 7 years of age and surgery within 3 years of diagnosis had reasonably good binocular disparity. However, adults who had a squint at birth and surgery between the ages of 4 and 20 had little or no binocular disparity.

The above complex findings suggest that there is a critical or sensitive period for the development of binocular disparity during the early years of life. If children don't develop binocular disparity during the early years because of an uncorrected squint, then it is very difficult to develop it later. It has also proved difficult to treat **amblyopia** (impaired vision due to disuse of an eye with no obvious damage to it) in older children and adults. This finding provides more evidence of a critical period. However, visual acuity in adults with amblyopia can be improved if they receive prolonged practice on a difficult visual task (Levi, 2005), indicating that learning can be important.

Face perception

Faces (especially its mother's face) form a very important part of the newborn infant's visual environment. This has led some theorists to argue that natural selection has equipped humans with an innate bias favouring facial stimuli. For example, Morton and Johnson (1991) argued that human infants are born with a mechanism containing information about the structure of human faces. This mechanism is known as CONSPEC, because the information about faces it contains relates to conspecifics (members of the same species).

The key prediction from this theoretical approach is that newborn infants should exhibit a clear preference for facial stimuli over other stimuli. There is much supporting evidence. Johnson, Dziurawiec, Ellis, and Morton (1991) found that newborns in the first hour after birth showed more visual tracking of realistic faces than of scrambled but symmetrical faces in which facial features were moved to unusual locations within the face. This suggests that some aspects of face perception do not depend on learning.

Walton, Bower, and Bower (1992) presented infants between 1 and 4 days of age with videotapes of their mother's face and the face of a similar looking woman. Eleven out of 12 infants preferred their mother's face, indicating that infants can discriminate among faces at a very early age. Pascalis, de Schonen, Morton, Deruelle, and Fabre-Grenet (1995) replicated those findings in infants 4 days old. However, the infants could not distinguish between their mother and an unfamiliar woman when both wore scarves to hide their external facial features (e.g. hair).

The notion that there is an innate bias for faces is plausible, but there is increasing evidence it is probably wrong. An alternative view was developed by Turati and colleagues (e.g. Turati, Simion, Milani, & Umiltà, 2002). According to this view, there is nothing special about faces. Instead, newborns simply have a preference for stimuli with more *patterning* in their upper than in their lower part. This is found with faces and numerous other stimuli.

> **?** What is the role of maturation in the development of perceptual processes?

> **KEY TERM**
>
> **Amblyopia:** an eye condition in which there is impaired vision in one eye that is not due to physiological damage; commonly referred to as lazy eye.

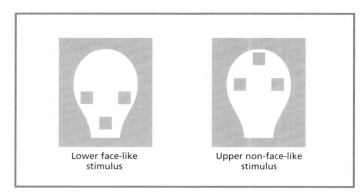

Lower face-like
stimulus

Upper non-face-like
stimulus

Newborns preferred an upper non-face-like stimulus (shown on the right) to the lower face-like stimulus (shown on the left). From Turati et al. (2002).

? Have you ever recognised someone by face, but could not remember his or her name?

Support for the above view was reported by Simion, Valenza, Macchi Cassia, Turati, and Umiltà (2002) and by Turati et al. (2002). Simion et al. found that newborns preferred visual stimuli having more elements in the top half than in the bottom half. Importantly, this was so even when the stimuli didn't look anything like faces. Turati et al. (2002) found (as predicted) that newborns aged between 1 and 3 days did *not* prefer face-like to non-face-like stimuli when the number of elements in the upper part was held constant. The key finding was that newborns preferred a stimulus consisting only of a non-face-like arrangement in the upper part to a stimulus consisting only of a face-like arrangement in the lower part (see figure on the left). These findings suggest that, "Newborns direct their gaze toward faces because they belong to a broader stimulus category that is characterised by a greater number of high-contrast areas in the upper portion of the pattern" (p. 881).

Simion, Turati, Valenza, and Leo (2006) replicated the finding that newborns prefer scrambled faces with more elements in the top area to natural faces. However, 3-month-olds preferred facial stimuli to scrambled faces. This suggests that cognitive mechanisms specialised for faces develop over the first few weeks or months of life.

Evaluation

Not surprisingly, newborns have extremely limited perceptual abilities, but these abilities develop fairly rapidly over the first weeks and months of life. For example, initially infants have very poor visual acuity, their eyes have a fixed focal length, they have practically no colour vision, and they have very deficient binocular vision. In other words, it takes several months for some of the basic mechanisms involved in vision to function effectively. Even when the basic mechanisms are fully functioning, infants still find it hard to make sense of visual information. For example, a 6-month-old infant can see the colours of traffic lights but does not understand the significance of their changing colours.

One of the few exceptions to the generally very deficient perceptual abilities shown by newborns relates to face processing. Within a few days of birth, infants show some preference for faces over other stimuli, and can discriminate to some extent between their mother's face and the faces of other people. However, there is controversy concerning whether the various findings should be interpreted as indicating that infants have an innate bias for faces.

The research on face perception in infants illustrates a problem that runs through most attempts to study visual perception in that age group. Infants can't tell us what they can see. As a result, we must rely on *indirect* evidence based on their behaviour, their gaze patterns, and so on. As a result, there is a real danger of assuming that infant visual perception is more similar to that of adults than is actually the case.

Cross-cultural studies

Much of the evidence on cross-cultural differences in perception is based on various visual illusions. For example, there is the research of Segall, Campbell, and Herskovits (1963) on the Müller–Lyer illusion (see top figure on page 78). They argued that this illusion would be perceived only by those with extensive experience of a "carpentered environment" containing numerous rectangles, straight lines, and regular corners. As was discussed earlier in the chapter, this argument ties in with Gregory's misapplied size–constancy explanation of the Müller–Lyer illusion, according to which parts of the figures are seen as corners and other rectangular features. People living in Western societies live in carpentered environments, but Zulus living in rural communities do not, and do not show the Müller–Lyer illusion. This could be because they don't live in a carpentered environment.

The above finding might simply mean that rural Zulus can't interpret two-dimensional drawings. This is unlikely in view of another of Segall et al.'s (1963) findings. They studied the horizontal–vertical illusion, which involves overestimating vertical extents relative to horizontal ones in a two-dimensional drawing. Rural Zulus showed the horizontal–vertical illusion to a greater extent than Europeans, presumably because of their greater familiarity with large open spaces. Whatever the appropriate interpretation, the fact that Zulus showed the horizontal–vertical illusion suggests that they can interpret two-dimensional drawings.

Pollnac (1977) also found that environmental factors are important in influencing the horizontal–vertical illusion by studying fishermen in the Gulf of Nicoya, Costa Rica. Those with the most experience of fishing (and who had thus spent most time at sea in large open spaces) showed the illusion most strongly.

More evidence of cross-cultural differences in visual perception was reported by Annis and Frost (1973) in a study on Canadian Cree Indians. Some of these Indians lived in tepees out in the countryside, whereas others lived in cities. Annis and Frost argued that those who lived in cities would be exposed mainly to vertical and horizontal lines in their everyday lives (the "carpentered environment"), whereas those living in tepees would come across lines in all orientations. Both groups were asked to decide whether two lines were parallel. Cree Indians living in tepees were good at this task no matter what angle the lines were presented at. By contrast, those living in cities did much better when the lines were horizontal or vertical than when they were at an angle. These findings suggest the importance of relevant experience to visual perception.

The findings of Segall et al. (1963) and of Annis and Frost (1973) suggest that relevant experience and learning play an important role in visual perception. Further support for this point of view comes from a study by Allport and Pettigrew (1957), who used an illusion based on a nearly rectangular or trapezoidal "window" fitted with horizontal and vertical bars. When this "window" revolves in a circle, it looks like a rectangular window moving backwards and forwards. People living in cultures without rectangular windows tended not to experience the rotating trapezoidal illusion. Zulus living in rural areas were less likely than Europeans or Zulus living in urban areas to see a rectangle moving backwards and forwards. This study supports the notion that what people perceive is influenced by their environmental experiences.

Some research has obtained findings that do *not* seem to fit with the research discussed above. Gregor and McPherson (1965) compared two groups of Australian Aborigines. One group lived in a carpentered environment whereas the other group lived in the open air and had very basic housing. The two groups didn't differ on either the Müller–Lyer illusion or the horizontal–vertical illusion. Cross-cultural differences in visual illusions may depend more on training and education than on whether a given group lives in a carpentered environment.

EXAM HINT

Make sure you can use infant studies to help you assess the competing influences of nature–nurture on perceptual development, and that you can use cross-cultural studies, such as Segall et al. (1963), to provide evidence for the role of learning.

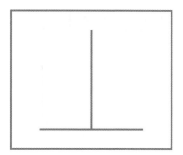

The horizontal–vertical illusion makes it look as if the vertical line is longer than the horizontal line, when in fact they are exactly the same length.

? Do cultural variations in perception support the view that we process information in a top-down or a bottom-up way?

? What is the difference between a "culture" and a "country"?

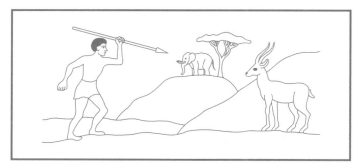

Hudson (1960) showed line drawings of three-dimensional scenes to participants from rural Africa. If they were able to use the three-dimensional depth cues in the picture, they would say that the hunter was trying to spear the antelope. However, they tended to say that the hunter was trying to spear the elephant. This lack of ability to make sense of Western drawing styles might be due to other things, such as the medium on which the drawing was presented.

? What is ethnocentrism?

? Why does ethnocentrism lead to limitations in the interpretations of cross-cultural studies?

Most of the research we have discussed so far has been concerned with visual illusions. However, there is evidence for cross-cultural differences in other aspects of visual perception. For example, most adults in Western societies can interpret two-dimensional drawings and pictures as showing three-dimensional scenes. However, black children and adults in South Africa with little previous experience of such drawings find it very hard to perceive depth in them (Hudson, 1960). There are problems with such cross-cultural research. Deregowski, Muldrow, and Muldrow (1972) found that members of the Me'en in Ethiopia did not respond to drawings of animals on paper, which was an unfamiliar material for them. This might suggest that they had poor ability to make sense of two-dimensional representations. However, when the Me'en were shown animals drawn on cloth (a material familiar to them), they were generally able to recognise them.

Evaluation

Cross-cultural research has produced many interesting and important findings. First, we have convincing evidence that there are cultural differences in perception, and this seems to be especially the case with various visual illusions. Second, some of the general factors producing cultural differences in perception have been identified. Examples include the presence or absence of a carpentered environment and degree of familiarity with open spaces. Third, specific experiences also seem to be important. Thus, for example, the rotating trapezoidal window illusion is much stronger among those living in cultures in which rectangular windows are common.

There are three major limitations with cross-cultural research on visual perception. First, it is often hard to interpret the findings. For example, cross-cultural differences in perception could be due to various factors because the experiences of people living in different cultures differ in many ways. The fact that even pigeons show the Müller–Lyer illusion (Malott, Malott, & Pokrzywinski 1967) suggests we should be careful about assuming that cultural factors are of major importance in determining how the illusion is seen! Rural Zulus might fail to show the Müller–Lyer illusion because they attend to the two lines and ignore the fins rather than because they don't live in a carpentered environment.

Second, most studies are limited because they rely on self-report measures. Some apparent cross-cultural differences in perception might occur because of cultural differences in the ability to report perceptual experiences in an accurate way. Other cross-cultural differences might depend on differences across languages rather than on actual differences in perception.

Third, much cross-cultural research has focused on two-dimensional visual illusions, and such limited research may tell us little about cultural differences in everyday perception. There are large cultural differences in the *significance* attached to various visual stimuli. For example, members of many African cultures can make much more sense of complex patterns of footprints than can members of Western societies. Similarly, Chinese texts convey much information to Chinese people but none at all to most of us.

Nature–nurture Debate in Relation to Explanations of Perceptual Development

Perceptual development is a complex matter, with different perceptual abilities developing at different ages and in different ways. Some aspects of visual perception (e.g. relating visual and auditory information, aspects of face perception, aspects of size and shape constancy, dominance of global over local features) seem to be present at birth or very shortly thereafter. Thus, these aspects reflect innate visual capacities or very rapid learning.

The eye of the beholder? Are the animals in this picture large animals against a distant background, or small animals close up?

Other aspects of visual perception (e.g. visual acuity, colour vision) develop several weeks after birth, and may well involve maturation. Maturation refers to "the emergence of instinctive behaviour patterns at a particular point in development. The genetic instructions facilitate the expression of certain behaviour patterns when a certain growth point is reached or a certain time period has elapsed" (Smith, Cowie, & Blades, 2003, p. 34). Maturation seems of importance in the development of visual acuity. As we saw earlier, infants with treated cataracts very rapidly showed reasonable visual acuity despite having had practically no visual experience (Maurer et al., 1999).

There are still other aspects of perception for which there might be a critical or sensitive period for their development (e.g. binocular disparity). Finally, there are other aspects of perception (e.g. those relating to depth perception) that develop only after several months of life, and probably require certain kinds of learning. If environmental factors are important, we might expect to find fairly large differences in visual perception across cultures, depending on important aspects of their environment. As we have seen, there are substantial cross-cultural differences in various visual illusions. Environmental factors such as whether the members of a given culture live in a carpentered environment seem to influence their susceptibility to illusions such as the Müller–Lyer. Another example is the rotating trapezoidal window illusion. Perhaps not surprisingly, cultures unfamiliar with rectangular windows don't seem to be susceptible to that illusion.

? What might be the evolutionary benefits of colour vision?

As far as the nature–nurture debate is concerned, it would be a great oversimplification to assume that all aspects of perception are totally innate or depend completely on learning. Certain basic perceptual abilities may be present at birth. However, many others are present early in infancy, whereas others take several months to develop. Most perceptual abilities depend on *both* nature and nurture, with the relative contributions of each varying from one perceptual ability to another.

Theoretical positions

One possible theoretical position is to argue that all perceptual abilities are inborn. If so, we would expect newborn infants to display these abilities. In fact, that is not at all the case. According to Teller (1997), newborn infants (sometimes called neonates) are extremely poorly equipped for visual perception because they lack many of the basic abilities that are needed:

> Their acuity and contrast sensitivity are very poor but are measurable. Their . . . eye movements reveal the capacity to analyse the direction of motion of large, high-contrast objects . . . However, they reveal no appreciation of stereo depth, no capacity to respond to low contrasts or to fine spatial details, and probably no colour vision. Their visual worlds are probably marked less by blooming and buzzing than by the haziness of low-contrast-sensitivity, the blurriness of spatial filtering, and the blandness of monochrome [black-and-white]. (Teller, 1997, p. 2196)

Why are there fairly rapid and substantial improvements in all these perceptual abilities? The most important factor is maturation, which depends on various physiological changes in the early months of life. For example, neonates' visual acuity is about one-fortieth that of adults, although it typically reaches the adult level around the age of 12 months. It is likely that the large increase in neurons in the visual cortex occurring during the first 6 months of life plays a major role.

Slater (1990, p. 262) is more upbeat in his assessment of infants' perceptual skills:

> No modality [i.e. none of the senses] operates at adult-like levels at birth, but such levels are achieved surprisingly early in infancy, leading to recent conceptualisations of the "competent infant" . . . early perceptual competence is matched by cognitive incompetence, and much of the re-organisation of perceptual representation is dependent upon the development and construction of cognitive structures that give access to a world of objects, people, language, and events.

Evidence that visual perception in newborns is influenced by cognitive incompetence was provided by Slater, Mattock, and Brown (1990), who presented newborns with a visual display in which a rod was seen moving from side to side behind a box. The newborns never saw the entire rod. Instead, they could see the top and bottom of the rod above and below the box. Adults and infants aged 3 or 4 months assume there is a *single* rod of which they can see only the ends (Kellman & Spelke, 1983). However, the newborn infants seemed to perceive the rod behind the box as a broken one.

Distortion studies

In the late nineteenth century, G.M. Stratton (1896) tested the effects of wearing a lens on one eye that turned the world upside down (he kept his other eye covered). At first everything looked unreal, but within 5 days he reported he could write and walk around with relative ease. He took the lens off after 8 days. He found that the world he saw "was immediately recognised as the old one of pre-experimental days". However, the fact that everything was now a reversal of what he had grown used to gave it a "bewildering air".

What do these findings mean in terms of an innate perceptual system? If the system is fixed, it shouldn't be possible for any adaptation to take place. Therefore, there is clearly some capacity for learning. However, it is possible that all that is being learned are new sensori-motor links. The fact that Stratton found his perception fairly intact after 8 days suggests that it hadn't really changed.

Re-adjustment studies

An important approach to the study of whether perception is innate or learned is to study individuals with cataracts preventing them seeing, who have those cataracts removed. If perception is an innate ability, we would expect such individuals to be capable of depth perception and other features of an organised perceptual system. Gregory and Wallace (1963) documented the case history of SB, described in the case study below.

The evidence from SB and other adults who have had their cataracts removed is difficult to interpret for various reasons. First, the brain areas responsible for visual processing might have degenerated or been used to facilitate the use of touch. Second, the patients have learned throughout childhood to rely on the other senses and this might interfere with their development of visual abilities. Third, as we saw in the case of SB, there can be problems of motivation when seeing seems to be difficult and frustrating.

The problems with interpreting evidence from adults who have had cataracts removed are much less when we study infants who have had cataract operations. Maurer, Lewis, and Mondloch (2005) discussed the findings from people who had cataracts removed when they were only 2 or 3 months old. When they were tested several years after the operation, some of their perceptual abilities were impaired and some were essentially normal. More complex abilities that are the slowest to mature in visually normal children were the ones most likely to be impaired. Those who had cataract operations when very young were poor at recognising faces from different viewpoints, at discriminating between faces that only differed in terms of the spacing among facial features, and at detecting small differences between shapes.

The fact that these individuals had several long-lasting deficits in visual perception suggests that early visual experience is important. The findings thus provide some support for an environmental account. Of particular importance, the lack of early visual experience led to permanent deficits for some perceptual abilities (e.g. subtle discriminations between faces) that normally develop only several months or years after the cataracts were removed. These so-called "sleeper

CASE STUDY: SB—RECOVERY FROM BLINDNESS

Some people are born blind because they have cataracts. This means that the lenses of the eye are opaque and do not let light through. In the 1950s, it became possible to replace the lens of the eye, which gave many people the chance to see for the first time. SB was a 52-year-old man who had longed to see all his life. His progress (and ultimately sad end) were recorded by Gregory and Wallace (1963). When the bandages were first removed, SB saw a confusion of colours in front of him but knew by the voice that this was his surgeon's face. Within a few days, he began to make sense of his visual sensations.

One day he looked out of his fourth-floor window and was curious about the small objects below. He tried to crawl out of the window to touch them, showing a lack of depth perception. He couldn't see depth in two-dimensional drawings, nor was he disturbed by visual illusions. He continued to touch things to help himself "see", as he had done when blind; it enabled him to match his internal concept of the object with his new perceptions. For example, when he was first shown a lathe he shut his eyes and explored it with his hands. Then he opened his eyes and said, "Now that I've felt it I can see it."

SB's story ends sadly. He never really mastered sight, preferring to use the senses he had become accustomed to and only pretending to "see". He often sat in darkness in the evenings, choosing not to turn on the light. He became very depressed and died 3 years after he gained his sight. "He found disappointment with what he took to be reality" (Gregory & Wallace, 1963, p. 114).

effects" suggest that even late-developing visual abilities depend very much on early visual experience.

Some relatively simple visual abilities were normal in individuals who had cataracts removed at an early age. These included discriminating shapes such as triangles and crosses, discriminating a face from a scrambled image, and discriminating between faces that differed in various ways from each other. These findings indicate that early visual experience is not necessary for the development of all perceptual abilities.

Evaluation

? Which do you think is more important, nature or nurture?

There is much evidence for the importance of nature or maturation *and* nurture or environment. Our current understanding of the development of the nervous system supports the view that experience is necessary for neurophysiological systems to grow. The brain requires input to mature. Thus, it is nature *and* nurture. It is also the case that each individual's particular experiences will influence his/her perceptual tendencies, as is shown by cross-cultural research. It makes evolutionary sense for an individual to adapt to the requirements of his or her own environment.

Despite what I have just said, it seems likely that the development of the basic mechanisms of visual perception (e.g. visual acuity, colour vision) depends mostly on maturational factors. In contrast, making *sense* of the visual information to which we are exposed all the time depends very much on environmental factors. A very clear example concerns the visual perception involved in reading a text. If you were to look at a Chinese text, you would perceive lines and squiggles, but you probably would have no idea what the text meant. The fact that the test would be very meaningful to Chinese speakers obviously depends on nurture or environment.

SECTION SUMMARY
Development of Perception

Development of perceptual abilities

- ❖ Research on the visual cliff indicates that infants possess some of the elements of depth perception by about 6 months of age.
- ❖ Other research suggests that a primitive ability to judge distance is present at 2 weeks.
- ❖ Infants 2 months of age have shown some size constancy but it is well short of being complete.
- ❖ The habituation method has been used to study shape constancy. It appears that 3-month-old infants have some ability to identify the real shape of objects even when they aren't viewed face on.
- ❖ The development of visual constancies probably depends on a mixture of infants' experience and maturational factors.

Infant and cross-cultural studies

- ❖ Newborns have very poor visual acuity that improves with maturation.
- ❖ Colour vision is virtually non-existent for the first few weeks of life.
- ❖ Binocular disparity and binocular vision are found only at about 3–6 months of age. Their development occurs during a critical period.
- ❖ Infants may have an innate bias for faces, but it is more likely that they have a preference for stimuli having more patterning in their upper part.

❖ There is cross-cultural evidence that people living in cultures with carpentered environments are most likely to experience the Müller–Lyer illusion.

❖ Cross-cultural studies suggest the importance of environmental factors in producing the horizontal–vertical and rotating trapezoidal window illusions.

Nature–nurture debate and perceptual development

❖ Basic visual mechanisms such as visual acuity, accommodation, and colour vision probably develop mainly as a function of maturation.

❖ Newborns have very deficient visual perception, but their visual skills develop rapidly.

❖ The finding that people can rapidly adjust to wearing an inverted lens means we have some capacity for perceptual learning.

❖ Adults who had cataracts removed when they were very young have permanent deficits on complex perceptual tasks, suggesting that early visual experience is important.

❖ Making sense of visual information (e.g. when reading) clearly depends on nurture/environment.

❖ Cross-cultural research suggests that environmental factors influence perception.

FACE RECOGNITION AND VISUAL AGNOSIAS

Recognising faces is of immense importance in our lives. We can sometimes identify people from their physique, the way they walk, or their mannerisms. Most of the time, however, we simply look at their faces. Form a visual image of someone who is important in your life. It is very likely that your image contains fairly detailed information about the person's face and its special features.

Face recognition is very important when it comes to criminal cases hinging on the memory of an eyewitness. Hundreds (perhaps thousands) of innocent people are languishing in prison because eyewitnesses mistakenly claimed to recognise them as the person who committed a crime. We know this because DNA evidence has shown conclusively, in hundreds of cases, that the person found guilty of a crime didn't actually commit it. The misery caused by mistaken face identification can be illustrated by the case of Arthur Lee Whitfield, who was sentenced to 63 years in prison for raping two women in August 1981 when he was 26 years old. However, he was released after 22 years on the basis of DNA evidence. He tried to be philosophical about his experiences: "If you're put into that position, you have to make the best of it, do things to keep your mind off what really has happened."

In this section, we consider brain-damaged individuals who have great problems with face recognition. Not surprisingly, this is a disturbing condition for those suffering from it. However, close study of such individuals has told us much about the processes involved in face recognition. After this, we focus on the most influential theory of face recognition—the one proposed by Bruce and Young (1986). As we will see, they argued convincingly that we extract several kinds of information from faces.

Patients who can't recognise faces aren't the only ones who have severe problems with visual perception. Other brain-damaged patients have much more general impairments in visual perception—they find it very hard to recognise

EXAM HINT

Note that exam questions might ask you to describe and evaluate theories of perception, or to consider the influences of nature–nurture in the development of perception, or to discuss theories and research of face recognition and prosopagnosia.

Prosopagnosics have problems recognising familiar faces. Imagine the distress it would cause to not be able to recognise your own mother.

objects, even common ones that are encountered every day. In the final part of this section of the chapter, we consider such patients.

Prosopagnosia

Imagine someone you know well has suffered from brain damage, as a result of which they can no longer recognise the faces of any of their friends and relatives. Just think how distressing that would be for them and for you. Patients with enormous problems in recognising familiar faces suffer from a condition known as "**prosopagnosia**", which comes from two Greek words meaning "face" and "without knowledge". Prosopagnosia is commonly referred to as "face blindness", and is generally (but not always) caused by brain damage. The problems it causes can be seen in the case of JK, a woman in her early thirties. She described an embarrassing incident caused by her prosopagnosia: "I went to the wrong baby at my son's daycare and only realised that he was not my son when the entire daycare staff looked at me in horrified disbelief" (Duchaine & Nakayama, 2006, p. 166).

What is really surprising is that patients with prosopagnosia can recognise most objects reasonably well despite their inability to recognise faces, and a few have excellent object recognition. However, most prosopagnosics have *some* problems with object recognition.

There are four points to bear in mind before we discuss findings from patients with prosopagnosia. First, the precise problems of face and object recognition vary from patient to patient.

Second, the origins of the condition vary. In acquired prosopagnosia, the condition is due to brain damage, and such patients had normal face recognition prior to brain damage. In contrast, developmental prosopagnosics have no obvious brain damage but never acquire the ability to recognise faces. What is true of acquired prosopagnosia might or might not also be true of developmental prosopagnosia. Most research has involved acquired prosopagnosia, and relatively little is known about developmental prosopagnosia.

Third, the fact that prosopagnosics have great problems in recognising familiar faces at the conscious levels does not necessarily mean that they fail to process such faces below the conscious level. There is a phenomenon in which a name (e.g. Stan Laurel) is recognised more rapidly when preceded by a related face (e.g. Oliver Hardy) than by an unrelated one (e.g. Robert Redford). Some prosopagnosics show this phenomenon (known as semantic priming) in spite of *not* recognising the face (Young, Hellawell, & de Haan, 1988). This shows that face processing occurred below the conscious level.

Fourth, there are various possible reasons why prosopagnosics find it much harder to recognise faces than objects. Perhaps acquired prosopagnosics have suffered damage to a part of the brain specialised for processing faces. Alternatively, it might simply be that face recognition is much harder than object recognition—face recognition involves distinguishing among members of the same category (i.e. faces), whereas object recognition generally only involves identifying the category to which an object belongs (e.g. cat, car).

KEY TERM

Prosopagnosia: a condition caused by brain damage in which the patient cannot recognise familiar faces, but can recognise familiar objects.

Findings

How could we show that face recognition involves different processes from object recognition? Suppose we found some prosopagnosics with severely impaired face recognition but intact object recognition, plus some other patients with the opposite pattern (i.e. impaired object recognition but intact face recognition). That pattern of findings is known as a **double dissociation**, and would strongly suggest that face recognition and object recognition rely on different processes.

Convincing evidence that some prosopagnosics have intact object recognition was reported by Duchaine and Nakayama (2005), who tested seven developmental prosopagnosics on various tasks involving memory for faces, cars, tools, guns, horses, houses, and natural landscapes. These prosopagnosics were required to recognise exemplars *within* each category (e.g. type of car, type of gun) to make the task of object recognition comparable to face recognition. The key finding was that some of the prosopagnosics performed in the normal range on all (or nearly all) of the non-face tasks.

Duchaine, Yovel, Butterworth, and Nakayama (2006) carried out a very thorough study on a developmental prosopagnosic called Edward, a 53-year-old married man who did very poorly on several tests of face memory. Indeed, he performed no better with upright faces than with inverted ones. However, he performed slightly *better* than healthy controls on most memory tasks involving non-face objects, even when the task involved recognising exemplars within categories.

The opposite pattern of intact object recognition but impaired face recognition has also been reported. Moscovitch, Winocur, and Behrmann (1997) studied CK, a man with impaired object recognition. He performed as well as controls on face-recognition tasks regardless of whether the face was a photograph, a caricature, or a cartoon, provided it was upright and the internal features were in the correct locations. McMullen, Shore, and Henderson (2000) tested HH, who has severe problems with object recognition as a result of a stroke. However, his face-recognition performance was good.

If there is something special about the processing of faces, we would expect to find some brain region much more involved in face recognition than in recognition of other objects. Many researchers have argued that the fusiform face area (especially the one in the right hemisphere) is specialised for processing faces. Two pieces of evidence support this conclusion. First, prosopagnosics typically have damage to this brain region (Farah, Tanaka, & Drain, 1995). Second, the fusiform face area is generally more activated when individuals are engaged in face recognition than object recognition. Downing, Chan, Peelen, Dodds, and Kanwisher (2006) presented participants with faces, scenes, and 18 object categories (e.g. tools, fruits, vegetables). The fusiform face area responded significantly more strongly to faces than to *any* of the other 19 stimulus categories. However, the differences are sometimes not that dramatic. In a study by Grill-Spector, Sayres, and Ress (2006), observers saw faces and three categories of objects (animals, cars, and abstract sculptures). More elements in the fusiform face area responded to faces than to any of the other types of objects, but the differences were not very large.

? What ethical considerations must be taken into account when studying patients with prosopagnosia?

EXAM HINT

Note that face blindness (prosopagnosia), and the deficits shown by sufferers, has greatly informed the understanding of face recognition, such as the role of the fusiform face area (especially the one in the right hemisphere) of the brain. However, some researchers do not think face recognition is very different from object recognition, and this argument can be used against the suggestion that there is a specialised area of the brain just for face recognition.

KEY TERM

Double dissociation: the finding that some brain-damaged individuals do well on task A and poorly on task B, whereas others show the opposite pattern.

Genes and face recognition

A study of between 2 and 4 generations of seven affected families (Grueter et al., 2007) found 38 cases of prosopagnosia. A sample of this group was tested for face recognition using the Warrington Recognition Memory Test for Faces, and these participants' scores were significantly below those of an age- and education-matched comparison group, suggesting a significant genetic contribution to face recognition skills. Both men and women from these families were affected, and the results could be explained by the mutation of a single gene. These findings are particularly interesting as most cases of prosopagnosia are the result of some form of brain damage. The most famous—and readable—account of this condition and others comes from Oliver Sacks in *The Man Who Mistook His Wife For a Hat* (see the case study on page 109).

In sum, while most prosopagnosics have somewhat deficient object recognition, some have essentially intact object recognition even when difficult object-recognition tasks are used. Surprisingly, a few individuals have reasonably intact face recognition in spite of severe problems with object recognition. This double dissociation is most readily explained by assuming that different processes (and brain areas) underlie face and object recognition. The great majority of prosopagnosics have damage to the fusiform face area, suggesting it is of special importance in face processing. However, as we will see, not everyone agrees that face recognition is very different from object recognition.

Are Faces Special?

According to Gauthier and Tarr (2002), many of the findings indicating that there are major differences between face and object processing should not be taken at face value (sorry!). According to them, there are two reasons why faces appear special even though they aren't. First, we typically recognise faces at the individual level (e.g. "That's my friend Nancy!"). In contrast, we often recognise objects at a more general level (e.g. "That's a pretty car", "That's a large bird"). Prosopagnosics may have special problems with face recognition because recognising *specific* examples of a category is harder than recognising the *general* category to which an object belongs.

Second, nearly all of us have considerably more experience (and thus *expertise*) in recognising faces than in recognising individual members of most other categories. According to Gauthier and Tarr (2002), the processes and brain mechanisms claimed to be specific to faces are also involved in recognising individual members of *any* object category for which we possess expertise. Thus, the fusiform face area is a brain area we use for *any* objects for which we possess expertise, not just for processing faces. We examine the evidence relevant to this expertise theory below.

According to Gauthier and Tarr (2002), prosopagnosics should have impaired ability to recognise the members of non-face categories for which they possess expertise. The reason is that their fusiform face area (or expertise area) is damaged. Some findings are inconsistent with this prediction. Sergent and Signoret (1992) studied a prosopagnosic, RM, who had expertise for cars. He had very poor face recognition but recognised considerably more makes, models, and years of cars than healthy controls. Another prosopagnosic, WJ, acquired a flock of sheep. Two years later, his ability to recognise individual sheep was as good as that of healthy controls with comparable knowledge of sheep.

The other major prediction from Gauthier and Tarr's (2002) theory is that the fusiform face area should be activated more by objects of expertise than by other objects. McKone, Kanwisher, and Duchaine (2007) reviewed eight studies, three of which reported modest support for this prediction whereas five obtained non-significant findings. Five studies addressed the issue of whether any expertise effects (i.e. more activation for objects of expertise than other objects) are greatest in the fusiform face area. Larger effects were reported *outside* the fusiform face area than inside it (McKone et al., 2007).

Evaluation

What are the strengths of Expertise Theory? First, as assumed by the theory, most people possess much more expertise about faces than almost any other object category. Second, we have more experience of identifying individual faces than individual members of most other categories. It thus seems possible that differences between face and object recognition might be attributable to differences in expertise.

What are the limitations of Expertise Theory? The greatest limitation is that none of the specific hypotheses of the theory has been supported. Of crucial importance is recognition of objects belonging to categories for which the individual possesses expertise. According to the Expertise Theory, such objects should show the same effects associated with faces (e.g. activation of the fusiform face area, impaired recognition in prosopagnosics). In fact, non-face objects of expertise typically show the same effects as non-face objects for which individuals have no expertise. The upshot is that the processes involved in face recognition differ substantially from those involved in object recognition.

Bruce and Young

The first detailed theory of face recognition (and one that has proved extremely influential) was put forward by Bruce and Young (1986). This theory was mainly intended to explain the processes involved in face recognition in healthy individuals. However, as we will see, it is also useful when it comes to understanding the problems with face recognition experienced by prosopagnosics and other brain-damaged patients.

Bruce and Young (1986) identified eight components of face recognition (see figure on the right):

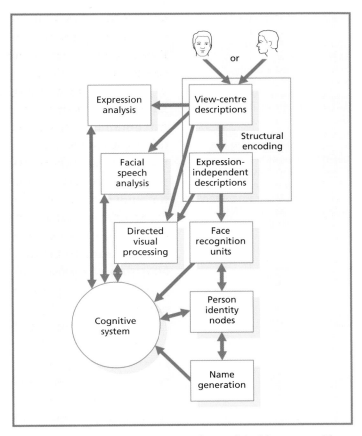

The model of face recognition put forward by Bruce and Young (1986).

1. *Structural encoding*: this produces various representations or descriptions of faces.
2. *Expression analysis*: people's emotional states are inferred from their facial features.
3. *Facial speech analysis*: speech perception is helped by observing a speaker's lip movements. This was shown clearly by McGurk and MacDonald (1976), who prepared a tape in synchronisation with lip movements indicating "ba". Participants heard "da", which is a blending of the visual and auditory information.
4. *Directed visual processing*: specific facial information is processed selectively.
5. *Face recognition nodes*: contain structural information about known faces.
6. *Person identity nodes*: they provide information about individuals (e.g. their occupation, interests).
7. *Name generation*: a person's name is stored separately.

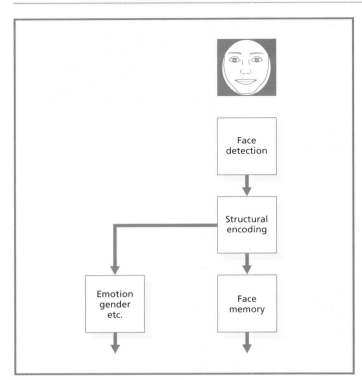

Simplified version of the Bruce and Young (1986) model of face recognition with the addition of a face detection stage. A face is first detected by a specialised module. At the next stage, a mechanism represents the structure of the face. Finally, in the last stage, this representation is matched to a memory representation. The box on the left indicates that the perceptual representation is also used for other face processing tasks, such as expression recognition and gender discrimination. From Duchaine & Nakayama, 2006.

8. *Cognitive system*: this contains additional information (e.g. most actors and actresses have attractive faces), and influences which other components receive attention.

If you are struggling with the complexities of the Bruce and Young (1986) theory, then help is at hand. Duchaine and Nakayama (2006) provided a modified version of the theory that included an additional face detection stage (see left). As its name implies, it is at this initial stage that observers decide whether the stimulus they are looking at is a face. After that, there are only three more components, about half the number proposed by Bruce and Young (1986)!

What predictions follow from the Bruce and Young theory? First, there should be major differences in the processing of familiar and unfamiliar faces. Recognising familiar faces depends mainly on structural encoding, face recognition units, person identity nodes, and name generation. In contrast, the processing of unfamiliar faces involves structural encoding, expression analysis, facial speech analysis, and directed visual processing. In terms of the simplified version of the theory put forward by Duchaine and Nakayama (2006), the face memory component (combining face recognition units, person identity nodes, and name generation) is used with familiar but not unfamiliar faces.

Evidence from prosopagnosic patients is relevant to this first prediction. Suppose that some patients have much better face recognition for familiar than for unfamiliar faces, whereas other patients have the opposite pattern (i.e. a double dissociation). Such findings would suggest that the processes involved in familiar and unfamiliar face recognition are different. Conversely, if all prosopagnosic patients showed equally poor recognition for familiar and unfamiliar faces, that wouldn't support the prediction at all.

Second, consider the processing of facial identity (who is the person?) and the processing of facial expression (e.g. what is he or she feeling?). According to the model, *separate* processing routes are involved in the two cases, with the key component for processing facial expression being the expression analysis component. If some prosopagnosic patients have very poor face recognition but relatively intact ability to process facial expressions, whereas others show the opposite pattern (a double dissociation), that would suggest the two tasks involve different processes.

Third, the processes involved in facial speech analysis (using lip movements to facilitate speech perception) differ from those used in other aspects of face processing. If some prosopagnosics are severely impaired in face recognition but have good ability to use lip movements to understand speech, that would suggest the two tasks require different processes.

Fourth, when we look at a familiar face, familiarity information from the face recognition unit should be accessed first, followed by information about that person (e.g. occupation) from the person identity node, followed by that person's name from the name generation component. Thus, familiarity decisions about a face should be made faster than decisions based on person identity nodes, and the latter decisions should be made faster than decisions concerning the individual's name.

Findings

The processing of familiar faces *must* differ from that of unfamiliar ones because we only have access to relevant stored knowledge (e.g. name, occupation) with familiar faces. If the two types of face are processed very differently, we might find a double dissociation in which some patients have good recognition for familiar faces but poor recognition for unfamiliar faces, whereas other patients show the opposite pattern. The evidence doesn't provide much support for this prediction. Young, Newcombe, de Haan, Small, and Hay (1993) studied 34 brain-damaged men. There was only weak evidence for selective impairment of either familiar or unfamiliar face recognition.

What about the second prediction? Research supports the assumption that separate routes are involved in the processing of facial identity (i.e. face recognition) and facial expression. For example, Humphreys, Avidan, and Behrmann (2007) reported very clear findings in three participants with developmental prosopagnosia (in whom there is no obvious brain damage). All three had a poor ability to recognise faces, but their ability to recognise facial expressions (even the most subtle ones) was comparable to that of healthy individuals. Young et al. (1993) found that some prosopagnosics showed good performance on identifying facial expression but poor performance on face recognition, whereas other brain-damaged patients showed the opposite pattern.

Calder, Rowland, Young, Nimmo-Smith, Keane, and Perrett (2000) obtained evidence that different processes underlie recognition of facial identity and facial expression. They presented participants with images consisting of the top and bottom halves of faces; the two halves come from the same person or from two different people. The task is to decide on the expression shown on the bottom face as rapidly as possible. If facial expression can be processed without also processing facial identity, it shouldn't matter whether the two face halves come from the same or different people. This is precisely what Calder et al. found.

What about the third prediction? It would receive support if some prosopagnosic patients with severely impaired face recognition were good at using lip movements to make sense of speech. A few such patients have been discovered. For example, Campbell, Landis, and Regard (1986) studied a woman with prosopagnosia who couldn't recognise faces and often didn't even know whether it was a male or a female face. In spite of these impairments, she could work out which phonemes were being mouthed when looking at photographs of faces.

What about the fourth prediction? According to the Bruce and Young (1986) theory, when we look at a familiar face we first access familiarity information, followed by personal information (e.g. the person's occupation), followed by the person's name. As predicted, Young, McWeeny, Hay, and Ellis (1986) found the decision as to whether a face was familiar was made faster than the decision as to whether it was a politician's face. Also as predicted, Kampf, Nachson, and Babkoff (2002) found that participants categorised familiar faces with respect to occupation faster than they could name the same faces, a finding that has also been reported by several other researchers.

The Bruce and Young theory assumes that the name generation component can be accessed *only* via the appropriate person identity node. Thus, we should never be able to put a name to a face without also having available other information about

> **EXAM HINT**
> Make sure you can explain why Bruce and Young's face recognition theory is too inflexible.

that person (e.g. his or her occupation). Young, Hay, and Ellis (1985) asked people to keep a diary record of problems they experienced in face recognition. There were 1008 incidents in total, but people *never* reported putting a name to a face while knowing nothing else about that person. If the appropriate face recognition unit is activated but the person identity node is not, there should be a feeling of familiarity but an inability to think of any relevant information about that person. In the incidents collected by Young et al. (1985), this was reported on 233 occasions.

Most published studies comparing speed of recall of personal information and names have focused exclusively on famous faces. As Brédart, Brennen, Delchambre, McNeill, and Burton (2005) pointed out, we name famous faces less often than our personal friends and acquaintances. If the *frequency* with which we use people's names influences the speed with which we can recall them, then the findings with faces with which we are personally familiar might differ from those obtained with famous faces. Brédart et al. presented members of a Cognitive Science Department with the faces of close colleagues and asked them to name the face or to indicate the highest degree the person had obtained. Naming times were faster than the times taken to provide the person information about educational level (832 ms vs. 1033 ms, respectively), which is opposite to the theory's prediction. The probable reason why these findings differed from those of previous researchers is because of the high frequency of exposure to the names of close colleagues.

Evaluation

Bruce and Young's (1986) theory has—deservedly—had a major impact on our understanding of face recognition. There are several reasons for this. First, it identifies the wide range of information that can be extracted from faces. Second, the assumption that separate processing routes are involved in the processing of facial identity and facial expression has received empirical support. Third, key differences in the processing of familiar and unfamiliar faces are identified. Fourth, the theory has contributed to our understanding of the various problems with different aspects of face recognition shown by brain-damaged patients. Fifth, as predicted by the theory, the processing of familiar faces typically leads first to accessing of familiarity information, followed by personal information, and then finally name information.

The theory possesses various limitations because it is oversimplified. First, the theory omits the initial face detection stage, at which we recognise that we are looking at a face. Some prosopagnosics with very poor face recognition can nevertheless decide whether they are looking at a face as rapidly and accurately as everyone else (Duchaine et al., 2006).

Second, the assumption that facial identity and facial expression involve totally separate processing routes is probably too extreme. The great majority of prosopagnosics have severe problems with processing facial expression as well as facial identity, suggesting that the two processing routes are only partially separate.

Third, patients with impaired processing of facial expression sometimes have much greater problems with one emotional category (e.g. fear, disgust) than others. This suggests that there might not be a single system for facial expressions, and that the processing of facial expressions involves emotional systems to a greater extent than assumed by the theory.

Fourth, the assumption that the processing of names *always* occurs after the processing of other personal information about faces is too rigid (Brédart et al., 2005). What is needed is a more flexible approach.

Which theory do you think best explains face recognition?

Visual Agnosias

There are numerous problems of visual perception associated with different areas of brain damage. So far, we have considered only prosopagnosia, but now we will consider other kinds of visual impairment. The term "**visual agnosias**" is used to refer to various conditions in which brain-damaged patients have difficulty in recognising or identifying objects.

The above definition of visual agnosias is actually too broad in two ways. First, patients who can't recognise objects because they have grossly impaired visual processes do *not* have a visual agnosia. One example is macular disease, in which a part of the retina degenerates and causes partial blindness. Second, patients who have impaired object recognition only because brain damage has partially destroyed their stored knowledge of objects also don't have visual agnosia. In their case, the problem is one of *memory* rather than *perception*. Patients with a visual agnosia generally have much stored information about objects. As a result, they can identify objects by touching them, and they can provide detailed verbal descriptions of objects when asked to do so.

Lissauer (1890) argued that there are two main types of visual agnosia:

1. *Apperceptive agnosia*: object recognition is impaired mainly because the patient has problems with complex perceptual processing.
2. *Associative agnosia*: perceptual processes are more or less intact. However, object recognition is impaired because the patients can't *access* their relevant stored information about visually presented objects. Note that relevant information is stored in long-term memory—it is simply hard to get at.

How can we distinguish between apperceptive and associative agnosia? One way is to assess patients' ability to copy objects that can't be recognised (Humphreys, 1999). Patients who can copy objects are said to have associative agnosia, and those who can't have apperceptive agnosia. The Gollin picture test has often been used to assess agnosia. In this test, patients are presented with a series of

CASE STUDY: THE MAN WHO MISTOOK HIS WIFE FOR A HAT

Mr P was "a musician of distinction, well-known for many years as a singer, and then at the local School of Music, as a teacher. It was here, in relation to his students, that certain strange problems were first observed. Sometimes a student would present himself, and Mr P would not recognise him; or specifically, would not recognise his face. The moment the student spoke, he would be recognised by his voice. Such incidents multiplied, causing embarrassment, perplexity, fear—and, sometimes, comedy."

"At first these odd mistakes were laughed off as jokes, not least by Mr P himself . . . His musical powers were as dazzling as ever; he did not feel ill . . . The notion of there being 'something the matter' did not emerge until some three years later, when diabetes developed. Well aware that diabetes could affect his eyes, Mr P consulted an ophthalmologist, who took a careful history, and examined his eyes closely. 'There's nothing the matter with your eyes,' the doctor concluded. 'But there is trouble with the visual parts of your brain. You don't need my help, you must see a neurologist.'"

And so Mr P went to see Oliver Sacks who found him quite normal except for the fact that, when they talked, Mr P faced him with his *ears* rather than his eyes. Another episode alerted Sacks to the problem. He asked Mr P to put his shoe back on.

"Ach," he said, "I had forgotten the shoe," adding *sotto voce*, "The shoe? The shoe?" He seemed baffled.

He continued to look downwards, though not at the shoe, with an intense but misplaced concentration. Finally his gaze settled on his foot: "That is my shoe, yes?"

Did he mis-hear? Did he mis-see?

"My eyes," he explained, and put his hand to his foot. "*This* is my shoe, no."

"No that is not. That is your foot. *There* is your shoe."

"Ah! I thought it was my foot."

Was he joking? Was he mad? Was he blind?

Oliver Sacks helped Mr P put on his shoe and gave him some further tests. His eyesight was fine, for example he had no difficulty seeing a pin on the floor. But when he was shown a picture of the Sahara desert and asked to describe it, he invented guesthouses, terraces, and tables with parasols. Sacks must have looked aghast but Mr P seemed to think he had done rather well and decided it was time to end the examination. He reached out for his hat, and took hold of his wife's head, and tried to lift it off. He apparently had mistaken his wife's head for his hat.

The condition Mr P suffered from is called visual agnosia and results from brain damage of some kind.

Adapted from Sacks (1985).

increasingly complete drawings of an object. Those with apperceptive agnosia have to see more drawings than healthy individuals to identify the objects.

Apperceptive agnosia

Patients with apperceptive agnosia possess some perceptual abilities despite being very poor at recognising visually presented objects. For example, they typically have normal visual acuity and can reach for moving targets. However, they have deficient visual processes that vary from patient to patient. In some cases, the problems are very great. For example, Grossman, Galetta, and D'Esposito (1997) reviewed previous research on apperceptive agnosia. One patient could only describe a circle as "lots of dots", and another couldn't discriminate between an "X" and an "O".

More evidence of reasonable visual abilities in patients with apperceptive agnosia was obtained from two patients actually studied by Grossman et al. (1997). These two patients were SZ, a 54-year-old male accountant, and AP, a 65-year-old female teacher. Both of these patients could recognise regular geometric shapes and colours despite their severely impaired ability to recognise common objects. However, both SZ and AP performed poorly when trying to recognise more complex shapes or when geometric shapes were presented upside down.

Other agnosic patients have patterns of perceptual abilities and impairments, suggesting that they are somewhere between apperceptive and associative agnosia, but perhaps closer to apperceptive agnosia. These patients have what is known as *integrative agnosia*, meaning that they have great difficulty in combining or integrating an object's features during object recognition. The integrative agnosic about whom most is known is HJA, who was studied in great detail by Humphreys and Riddoch (1987). He had a reasonable ability to produce accurate drawings of objects he couldn't recognise. However, HJA had found it extremely hard to integrate visual information: "I have come to cope with recognising many common objects, if they are standing alone. When objects are placed together, though, I have more difficulties. To recognise one sausage on its own is far from picking one out from a dish of cold foods in a salad" (Humphreys & Riddoch, 1987).

Giersch, Humphreys, Boucart, and Kovacs (2000) explored HJA's visual problems further. They tested the notion that HJA was very poor at deciding *which* features (e.g. lines) belong to *which* shapes when different shapes overlap with each other. What Giersch et al. did was to present HJA with three different kinds of stimulus array each containing three shapes. Different tasks had to be performed in different experiments. On one task, each array was followed by four shapes and the participants decided which one was the best match for the central shape in the array. On another task, the array was followed by another array that was identical to the first or in which the position of one shape had been altered.

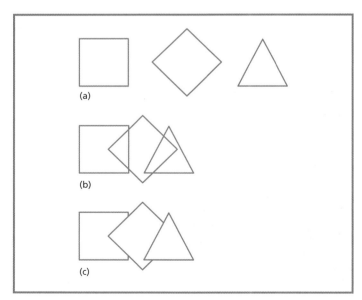

Examples of (a) separated, (b) superimposed, and (c) occluded shapes used by Giersch et al. (2000). From Riddoch and Humphreys (2001).

What did Giersch et al. (2000) find? HJA performed reasonably well on these tasks when the shapes were clearly separated from each other. However, he performed poorly with the superimposed shapes and even worse with the occluded (covered) shapes. Thus, HJA has poor ability to separate out shapes.

Associative agnosia

Patients with associative agnosia have reasonably good basic perceptual processes but are poor at *accessing* their semantic knowledge about objects even though such knowledge is stored in long-term memory. Fery and Morais (2003) discussed such a case. Their patient, DJ, was a 59-year-old man with brain damage who had previously worked as a truck driver. The finding that he could recognise only 16% of common objects when presented visually but performed at a normal level when recognising objects described verbally indicates that he was suffering from severe visual agnosia.

How do we know that DJ was suffering from associative agnosia rather than apperceptive agnosia? There were several signs that many of his perceptual abilities were reasonably intact. For example, he performed well on tasks involving shape processing, integration of object parts, and copying and matching objects. He also did very well on a complex animal decision task in which the non-animals were actual animals with one part added, deleted, or substituted (see figure on the right). DJ was correct on 93% of trials on this task.

Anaki, Kaufman, Freedman, and Moscovitch (2007) described a similar case. Their patient (DBO) was a 72-year-old man who was born in Latvia but had moved to Canada at an early age. As a result of brain damage to the left occipital lobe of the brain (at the back), he had severe visual agnosia as shown by his ability to name only 1 out of 20 common objects. However, he could identify objects when he felt them or heard their characteristic sounds, indicating that he had much stored information about common objects. DBO was also very poor at recognising famous faces.

Despite his visual agnosia, DBO performed well on various tasks involving aspects of object recognition. For example, he could match objects presented from different viewpoints and his shape discrimination was good. When presented with several faces, he was able to select the only one that was famous. The fact that he still possessed several visual perceptual skills indicates that he had associative rather than apperceptive agnosia.

In sum, patients with associative agnosia have better remaining perceptual abilities than those with apperceptive agnosia. The fact that associative agnosics generally have reasonably good perceptual abilities means that we need to look elsewhere for an explanation of their deficient object recognition. It is generally assumed that the main problem lies in accessing the stored information about objects that they possess. However, it is hard to obtain clear evidence that that is in fact the main problem.

Examples of animal stimuli with (from top to bottom) a part missing, the intact animal, with a part substituted, and a part added. From Fery and Morais (2003).

Evaluation

There is convincing evidence that the precise nature of visual agnosia varies considerably from one patient to another. The source of the problem with object recognition ranges between very early in visual processing (impaired basic perceptual processes) and much later (knowledge about visually presented objects can't be accessed from memory). The distinction between apperceptive and associative agnosia captures some of these individual differences. Identifying the precise reasons why a patient has a visual agnosia is valuable if the most appropriate form of treatment is to be used.

What are the limitations with the approach to the visual agnosias based on the distinction between apperceptive and associative agnosia? First, patients diagnosed with associative agnosia typically have better basic perceptual processes than those diagnosed with apperceptive agnosia, but their perceptual processes are also impaired. For example, consider the finding that associative agnosics often draw good copies of pictures. As Farah (1999, p. 191) pointed out, "The process by which [they] produce their good copies is invariably characterised as slow, slavish, and line-by-line".

Second, patients with visual agnosias can have problems at various stages of object processing. For example, damage to several different perceptual processes can cause impaired object recognition. Thus, it is oversimplified to categorise them all as suffering from apperceptive or associative agnosia. For example, it is not easy to categorise integrative agnosics as having either apperceptive or associative agnosia—they have better perceptual abilities than most apperceptive agnosics but inferior perceptual abilities to most associative agnosics.

Third, the distinction between apperceptive and associative agnosia is most appropriate when applied to patients having *general* deficits in object recognition. However, many patients have relatively *specific* deficits. For example, prosopagnosics are generally reasonably good at object recognition for most objects other than faces.

See *A2-Level Psychology Online* for some interactive quizzes to help you with your revision.

SECTION SUMMARY
Face Recognition and Visual Agnosias

Prosopagnosia

❖ Prosopagnosics have greatly impaired face recognition but their object recognition is generally reasonably good.

❖ Some other brain-damaged patients have poor object recognition but impaired face recognition.

❖ Prosopagnosics typically have damage to the fusiform face area, which is often assumed to be specialised for face processing.

❖ According to expertise theory, the fusiform face area is an area used to process information about any objects (including faces) for which we possess relevant expertise. The theory also claims that prosopagnosics should be poor at recognising objects for which they possess expertise. There is little support for either prediction.

❖ The available evidence strongly suggests that the processes involved in face recognition differ substantially from those involved in object recognition.

Bruce and Young

❖ According to Bruce and Young's (1986) theory, eight different components or processes are involved in face recognition.

❖ There is only weak support for the prediction that familiar faces are processed very differently from unfamiliar ones.

❖ There is good evidence that different processes are involved in the processing of facial identity and facial expression.

❖ Much of the evidence suggests that processing of a familiar face involves accessing familiarity information, then personal information, and finally the person's name.

❖ The theory has been very successful. However, it is oversimplified and processing of familiar faces doesn't always occur in the theoretically specified order.

❖ There is an important distinction between apperceptive agnosia and associative agnosia. Apperceptive agnosics have problems with object recognition mainly because of perceptual impairments. In contrast, poor object recognition in associative agnosics is due mainly to problems with accessing stored knowledge about objects.

Visual agnosias

❖ The symptoms of apperceptive agnosia vary. Some patients (those with integrative agnosia) have great difficulty in combining features during object recognition.

❖ The notion that all visual agnosics can appropriately be categorised as apperceptive or associative agnosics is oversimplified.

❖ The terms "apperceptive agnosia" and "associative agnosia" are applicable to many patients having general impairments in object recognition. However, they are much less applicable to patients (e.g. prosopagnosics) with specific problems in object recognition

FURTHER READING

Many of the topics discussed in this chapter are covered more fully in Eysenck, M.W. (2006). *Fundamentals of cognition*. Hove, UK: Psychology Press. Another useful source of information is the textbook by Sekuler, R. & Blake, R. (2006). *Perception* (5th Edn). New York: McGraw-Hill.

See *A2-Level Psychology Online* for tips on how to answer these revision questions.

REVISION QUESTIONS

In the exam, questions on this topic are out of 25 marks, and can take the form of essay questions or two-part questions. You should allow about 30 minutes for each of the questions below, which aim to test the material in this chapter. Never try to answer a question unless you have been taught the topic.

1. Describe and evaluate Gibson's bottom-up/direct theory of perception (AQA, 2007). **(25 marks)**

2. Discuss the nature–nurture debate with reference to explanations of perceptual development. **(25 marks)**

3. (a) Outline explanations of prosopagnosia. **(9 marks)**
   (b) Discuss, including case studies, Bruce and Young's theory of face recognition. **(16 marks)**

4. Compare Gregory's top down/indirect and Gibson's bottom up/direct theories of perception. **(25 marks)**

Relationships

By Evie Bentley

This chapter looks at various aspects of interpersonal relationships: how and why they begin and end, explanations of human reproductive behaviour, and the effect of parent–child relationships.

THE FORMATION, MAINTENANCE, AND BREAKDOWN OF ROMANTIC RELATIONSHIPS

Theories of Love

What is love? Is it strong liking, is it madness such as a kind of temporary insanity? Sternberg (1988, 1997) put forward a triangular theory of love, suggesting that there are three components: passion, intimacy, and commitment. Passion is the infatuation, which can be regarded as temporary insanity! It is often obsessive and overpowering but on its own is unlikely to be long lasting. Intimacy is strong liking and sharing, and commitment refers to the kind of love that does not involve passion or intimacy. Sternberg suggests various combinations of these three components, or factors, with romantic love consisting of passion and intimacy, companionate love being made up of intimacy and commitment, and fatuous love (a shallow relationship) being made up of passion and commitment. The ideal, of course, is a combination of all three factors called consummate love, passion + intimacy + commitment, but Sternberg says this is difficult to achieve.

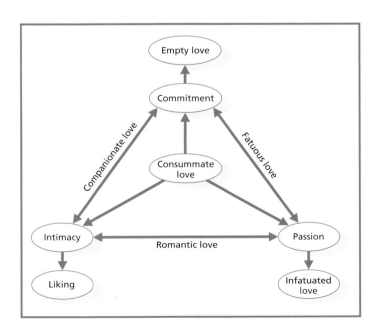

See *A2-Level Psychology Online* for an interactive exercise on Sternberg's triangular theory.

Fisher's (2004) theory is similar to Sternberg's but it is a linear stage theory, the three stages being lust, romantic love, and attachment. By lust, Fisher means desire, a powerful motivating force; romantic love means intrusive, almost obsessive, thoughts of the significant other person.

Research findings

Fisher's theory ties in with research showing that brain activity and neurochemistry is closely similar to that of obsessive-compulsive disorder (OCD); and attachment means just that, a need to be with that person in order to feel true emotional contentment. The physiological changes in the brain and hormone system caused by these stages makes the person in love the victim of a hormonal cocktail.

But is love just strong liking? Brain imaging studies suggest that the answer to that question is a definite "No". Research studies using functional magnetic resonance imaging (fMRI) scans showed different patterns of brain activity and brain chemistry for liking and for love. Aron, Fisher, Mashek, Strong, Li, and Brown (2005) found that romantic love involved dopamine activity in the motivation areas of the brain, and so suggested that this intense love is primarily a motivation system and not an emotion. Zeki (2007) and Bartels and Zeki (2004) found that romantic love activated oxytocin receptor areas associated with sex and reward systems, as well as deactivating brain areas associated with negative emotions, critical social judgement, and assessment of other people's emotions and intentions. These scans differed from those of people in non-romantic relationships.

 HOW SCIENCE WORKS: WHAT IS LOVE?
It might be interesting to see what non-psychologists think of as love. You could design and run a simple survey, perhaps with just one open question, *"How many different kinds of love do you think there are? Please list them."* You would have to decide how you would operationalise this; would you ask for a written list or would you ask people in person and record their answers yourself? It might be an idea to run a short pilot study on someone who trusts you—perhaps your mother—to see if your question is clear or whether you need to explain more. When you are satisfied that your question is clear and will not upset or stress people, you could run it for, say, 10 participants. When you have collected the responses, you could see if you can categorise them, e.g. into friendship/liking, romantic love, companionate love. Did your participants identify any other types of love? What conclusion do your findings suggest?

An alternative theory

Another way of looking at love uses similar terms but in a different way. Hendrick and Hendrick (2003) describe passionate or romantic love and companionate love. They see passionate love as intense physical attraction and strong emotional attachment, a deep relationship where one is constantly thinking of the beloved other person, and with intense sexual feelings. The other kind of love, companionate love, is psychologically more intimate as it involves sharing in-depth personal feelings and other sensitive information, plus mutual concern for the loved other person and their well-being. Interestingly, companionate love is often linked to being extremely satisfied with life, more so than passionate, romantic love.

See *A2-Level Psychology Online* for an interactive exercise on the formation of relationships.

Theories of the Formation, Maintenance, and Breakdown of Romantic Relationships

Reward/need satisfaction

The theory of reinforcement and need satisfaction is based on the notion that a key reason for forming friendships and relationships is for the rewards or reinforcements that we receive from others. These rewards often consist of approval, smiling, and so on. Foa and Foa (1975) argued that the rewards provided by other people can also include sex, status, love, help, money, and agreement with our opinions. These things are rewarding because they meet our various social needs. For example, obtaining the approval of others satisfies our need for self-esteem, being comforted satisfies our dependency needs, controlling

 List the needs that are being met in the following types of relationship: best friend, parent with child, lover.

others meets our needs for dominance, and making love satisfies our sex needs (Argyle, 1988).

Byrne (1971) argued that classical conditioning also plays an important role in determining the effects of reinforcement on interpersonal attraction. According to Classical Conditioning Theory, *any* background neutral stimuli associated with reward will come to produce positive feelings. This idea comes from Pavlov's research in which dogs that learned to associate a tone with the presentation of food salivated when the tone was presented. A study on humans was reported by Griffit and Guay (1969). They had someone give a reward or a punishment to several participants in the presence of an uninvolved bystander. The bystander was liked more by participants who were rewarded than by those who were punished.

As Skinner and others discovered many years ago, humans and animals are very responsive to rewards and punishments. Rats will press energetically on a lever if lever pressing is sometimes followed by food reward, but will stop pressing if lever pressing is followed by punishment (e.g. electric shock). In similar fashion, we typically decide to spend more time with people who provide us with rewards but as little time as possible with people who punish us.

Research support

Veitch and Griffitt (1976) tested the Reinforcement Affect Model by arranging for single participants to wait in an experimenter's office while the experimenter went on an errand. The radio was left on with music playing and, in the time alone, the participants (students) heard two news broadcasts; these contained either good or bad news. When the experimenter returned, the participants were asked to fill in a "Feelings Scale" (to assess their emotional state) and to read a questionnaire, supposedly filled in by another student, that was either in close agreement or disagreement with attitudes previously expressed by the participants in an earlier questionnaire that had been done in class. Participants also completed an "Interpersonal Judgement Scale" to rate the supposed other student. The participants exposed to the "good" news reported significantly more positive feelings than those who listened to the "bad" news. In addition, "good news" participants felt significantly more attracted to the hypothetical other student. The effect was stronger where attitudes were more similar, although it occurred where attitudes were dissimilar. This supports the idea that positive feelings increase the possibilities of interpersonal attraction, but note the artificiality of asking people to rate the attractiveness of someone they have never met!

Other research has supported this study, for example, Rabbie and Horowitz (1960) found that strangers expressed greater liking for each other when they were successful in a game-like task than when unsuccessful. However, Duck

---

Explanations of interpersonal attraction

Certain factors explain why we form relationships with one person rather than another:

Physical attractiveness: This gets generalised to other characteristics (the halo effect). The matching hypothesis suggests we are attracted to others of similar physical attractiveness to ourselves. This is supported by studies of initial attraction and established couples, but challenged by facts such as the variable individual importance of good looks.

Proximity: Can refer to physical or psychological proximity, but increased contact can foster both positive and negative relationships.

Familiarity: People generally prefer the known over the unknown, but that does not mean known equals attractive.

Attitude similarity: Similarity in leisure activities is more important in attraction than in attitudes, unless attitudes are significant for the individual.

Demographic similarity: Friendships are more likely between individuals of similar background, e.g. age, sex, social group because this could facilitate communication as well as confirm attitudes.

Similarity in personality: Having similar personalities may foster friendships; research has not supported the idea that "opposites attract"

EXAM HINT

Exam questions may ask you to consider all of the stages of relationships (formation, maintenance, and breakdown) or only one stage. Bearing this in mind, be very careful not to lose focus and give irrelevant content by linking the theory to one of the stages the question has not asked you to consider! For example, if you are asked to describe how social exchange explains the formation of a relationship just concentrate on the *formation* part of a relationship. Do not be tempted to discuss the fact that if costs outweigh rewards then the relationship may break down because factors affecting breakdown are irrelevant in answer to this question.

? What psychological harm might have been caused by this experiment?

Who do you love?

Who do we tend to love and like the most? Sternberg and Grajek (1984) found that men generally love and like their lover more than their mother, father, sibling closest in age, or their best friend. Women also loved and liked their lover and best friend more than their mother, father, or sibling closest in age. However, women differed from men in that they loved their lover and their best friend of the same sex equally, but liked their best friend more than their lover.

Sternberg and Grajek also found that the amount of love that someone has for one member of their family predicts the amount of love they will have for the other members. For example, people who love their father very much also tend to have high levels of love for their mother and sibling closest in age. However, the amount of love that someone has for their lover or best friend is not predictable from the amount of love they feel for members of their own family.

? Based on Reinforcement Theory, how would you advise someone to behave to make a good impression on, or be liked by, someone they have never met before?

KEY TERMS

Individualistic: a culture that emphasises individuality, individual needs, and independence.
Collectivistic: a type of culture where individuals share tasks, belongings, and income. The people may live in large family groups and value interdependence.

The cost–reward ratio is the means by which we weigh up the benefits versus any negative costs of a relationship. If a friend relies on us for a lot of emotional support, we would, for example, expect him or her to be there for us in our time of need.

(1992) criticises these studies because they rely on the rather artificial "bogus stranger" method; there is no actual stranger but only an imaginary one, and this might not elicit realistic responses.

Evaluation

We are more attracted to those who provide us with reinforcement than those who do not. For example, individuals who are high on rewardingness (i.e. friendly, co-operative, smiling, warm) are consistently liked more than individuals who are low on rewardingness (Argyle, 1988). However, Reinforcement Theory does not provide an adequate account of interpersonal attraction for various reasons. First, the theory is more relevant to the very earliest stages of attraction than to attraction within an ongoing friendship or relationship.

Second, as Argyle pointed out, reinforcement has not been shown to be of much importance in determining the strength of the relationship between parents and their children.

Third, Reinforcement Theory assumes that people are totally selfish and concerned only about the rewards they receive. In fact, people are often concerned about other people and about the rewards that they provide for other people.

Fourth, whether or not reinforcement increases interpersonal attraction depends to a large extent on the *context* in which the reinforcement is provided. For example, the need for sexual satisfaction can be fulfilled by a prostitute, but this does not mean that men who resort to prostitutes become attracted to them as people.

Fifth, reinforcement and need satisfaction theories are of more relevance to the **individualistic** societies of the Western world than to the **collectivistic** societies of the non-Western world (this is discussed further later). More speculatively, these theories may tend to be more applicable to men than to women. In many cultures, there is more emphasis on females than on males learning to be attentive to the needs of others (Lott, 1994).

Social Exchange Theory

Social Exchange Theory (e.g. Thibaut & Kelley, 1959) is similar to Reinforcement Theory but is more specifically relevant to interpersonal attraction and provides a more plausible account. It is assumed that everyone tries to maximise the rewards (e.g. affection, attention) they obtain from a relationship, and to minimise the costs (e.g. devoting time and effort to the other person; coping with the other person's emotional problems). Thus, we focus on the cost–reward ratio—liking is determined by what is will cost to be reinforced or rewarded by the other person. For example, if you have a friend in constant need of support and encouragement, he or she needs to provide you with plenty of rewards to make up for all the costs if the friendship is to flourish! It is also assumed that if a relationship is to continue, people expect the other person to reward them as much as they reward the other person.

Thibaut and Kelley argued that long-term friendships and relationships go through the four stages shown in the figure.

> **?** What rewards and costs are associated with the following relationships: best friend, parent with child, love?

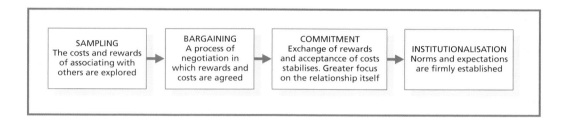

Additional assumptions are sometimes included in Social Exchange Theory. For example, how satisfied individuals are with the rewards and costs of a relationship will depend on what they have come to expect from previous relationships. In other words, they have a **comparison level** (CL; Thibaut & Kelley, 1959), representing the outcomes they believe they deserve on the basis of past experiences—so if in the past they have had very poor relationships they may expect very little from subsequent ones. In addition, their level of satisfaction will depend on the rewards (e.g. affection, sex) and costs (e.g. arguments, loss of control) that would be involved if they formed a relationship with someone else; this is known as the "comparison level for alternatives" (CLalt). All of this makes sense: if you are a very attractive and popular person, you can afford to be very choosy in your friendships and relationships.

> **EXAM HINT**
>
> Note that reward/need satisfaction theory and social exchange share some of the same criticisms because they both portray the individual as very self-centred. They both put considerable emphasis on the rewards for the individual and can be criticised on the grounds that not all relationships are based on satisfying the individual's own needs. This inter-links with cultural criticisms as such a focus on individual gain is more relevant to Western capitalist cultures than collectivist cultures.

> **KEY TERM**
>
> **Comparison level:** the outcomes that people think they deserve from a relationship on the basis of past experience.

CASE STUDY: WHAT MAKES A LONG-TERM RELATIONSHIP WORK?

Two young men travelled 12,000 miles in 72 days to ask couples, all of whom had been married for at least 40 years, how they had made their relationship work (Boggs & Miller, 2007). There was total agreement from all their interviewees—the three key factors were respect, commitment, and commitment!

- Respect was explained as showing respect and love towards each other, including making sure to listen to each other.
- Commitment meant going into the relationship with the attitude that it was going to work and never thinking that it

could always be ended if things got difficult, focusing on what was positive about their partner as well as what they had together.

- Commitment meant giving more than asking, never going to bed angry, accepting differences.

Contrast this with Peaches Geldof's (2008) statement, reported 97 days after marrying at the age of 19, "You can't ignore divorce rates. Every friend of mine has parents who are divorced. I didn't go into it with Max thinking, 'This is going to last forever'."

EXAM HINT

Reward/need satisfaction, Social Exchange Theory, and Equity Theory are each relevant to the formation, the maintenance, and the dissolution of romantic relationships, so make sure you can apply them accordingly.

Miller and Steinberg (1975) suggested that Social Exchange Theory could be regarded as a set of rules, such as for a game. These are social rules enabling each person to obtain more and increasingly accurate knowledge about the other. They suggest that initially when people meet they follow cultural rules, and therefore can assess the other's culture. If this is compatible and a relationship starts to develop then sociological rules come into play. If the relationship continues to develop, then psychological rules come into effect.

Equity theory

Some theorists (e.g. Hatfield, Utne, & Traupmann, 1979) have extended Social Exchange Theory to include more of an emphasis on fairness or equity. According to Equity Theory, people expect to receive rewards from a relationship proportional to the rewards they provide for the other person. However, imbalance can be tolerated if the two people involved in a relationship accept the situation. Walster, Walster, and Berscheid (1978) expressed the main assumptions of equity theory as follows:

- Individuals try to maximise the rewards they receive and minimise the costs.
- There is negotiation to produce fairness, e.g. one partner may do the shopping every week to compensate for going out to play sport twice a week.
- If the relationship is unfair or inequitable, it produces distress, especially in the disadvantaged person.
- The disadvantaged person will try hard to make the relationship more equitable, particularly when it is very inequitable. If this cannot be achieved, the disadvantaged person is likely to leave the relationship.

Research evidence

Hatfield et al. (1979) asked newlyweds to indicate the extent to which they felt they were receiving more or less than they should in view of their contributions to the marriage. They also indicated their level of contentment, happiness, anger, and guilt. The under-benefited (those partners who contributed more to the marriage/relationship than they received from it) had the lowest level of overall satisfaction with their marriage and tended to experience anger. The over-benefited (those partners who received more from the marriage/relationship than they contributed to it) came next (they tended to feel guilty), and those who perceived their marriage as equitable had the highest level of satisfaction. Men who were over-benefited were almost as satisfied as those in an equitable marriage, but over-benefited women were much less satisfied than women with equal benefit (Argyle, 1988).

The finding that those who perceive their marriages as equitable are happiest, and those who perceive themselves as under-benefited are least happy, was replicated by Buunk and VanYperen (1991). However, these findings applied only to those individuals high in exchange orientation (i.e. expecting rewards given by one person in a relationship to be followed immediately by rewards given by the other person). Those low in exchange orientation had fairly high marriage satisfaction regardless of whether they were over-benefited, under-benefited, or receiving equal benefit (see the box for a discussion of communal and exchange couples).

Research shows that couples who feel that they have an equitable relationship express the highest level of contentment within their marriage.

Communal and exchange relationships

Several theorists have doubted whether intimate relationships can be understood properly in terms of traditional theories. For example, Clark and Mills (1979) argued that there are two major kinds of relationships:

- Communal relationships: the main focus is on giving the other person what he or she needs; these relationships typically involve close friends or family members.
- Exchange relationships: the main focus is on the notion that what one puts into the relationship should balance what one receives; these relationships usually involve acquaintances or strangers.

According to Clark and Mills, most romantic relationships are not based on the principle of exchange. Those involved in such relationships are much more concerned about being able to meet the needs of the other person than about exchange or reciprocity.

Clark (1984) presented evidence consistent with this proposed distinction between communal and exchange relationships. Male students located sequences of numbers in a matrix with someone called Paula. Each student was told that he and Paula would receive a joint payment based on their performance, and that they must decide how much each of them received. Some participants were told that Paula was single and was taking part in the experiment to make friends. The others were told that Paula was married and that her husband was going to pick her up. Clark predicted that the former participants would tend to think in terms of a possible communal relationship with Paula, whereas the latter participants would expect an exchange relationship.

The participants found that Paula had already circled some sequences of numbers with a felt-tip pen. What was of interest was whether the participants used a pen of a different colour. It was argued that students looking for an exchange relationship would do so, because it would allow them to be paid on the basis of their contribution. By contrast, those seeking a communal relationship should use a pen of the same colour, because they were mainly concerned about their combined efforts. The findings were as predicted. About 90% of those students who thought Paula was married used a felt-tip pen of a different colour, compared with only 10% of those who thought she was single. Clark also found that pairs of friends were less likely than pairs of strangers to use different-coloured pens.

Fiske (1993) extended the line of theorising proposed by Clark and Mills. According to him, there are four types of relationship:

1. Exchange: based on reciprocity.
2. Communal: based on catering for the other person's needs.
3. Equality matching: based on ensuring that everyone receives the same; for example, giving all of the children in a family an ice cream of the same size.
4. Authority: based on the notion that one person's orders are obeyed by others.

> [?] Assessing attitudes through the use of coloured felt-tip pens is quite ingenious, but how valid do you think it is?

> [?] Does the study by Clark and Mills really show that there is a distinction between exchange and communal relationships?

Evaluation

Equity Theory seems more plausible than Social Exchange Theory. It takes more account of the rewards and costs of the other person, as well as of the individual him- or herself. The most obvious criticism of both approaches is that they assume people are very selfish and self-centred in their friendships and relationships. This assumption may possess some validity in individualist societies, e.g. the US, but is less likely to apply to collectivist societies, e.g. Europe.

Evidence of cultural differences was reported by Gergen, Morse, and Gergen (1980). European students were found to prefer equality in their relationships, with an equal distribution of rewards. By contrast, American students tended to favour equity, based on a constant ratio of rewards to inputs.

One of the more obvious predictions from equity theory is that the future quality of equitable relationships should be greater than that of inequitable ones. However, there is often no association between equity and future quality (see Buunk, 1996).

Much of the research in this area has not proved very informative. Some of the reasons for this were identified by Argyle (1988, p. 224): "[Exchange] theory has

> [?] What is the difference between equity and equality?

Cultural rules	Basic, social norms such as walking upright in the street and not crawling on all fours
Sociological rules	Sub-cultural norms, such as style of dress in school, college, or work, e.g. accountants wear suits, media people wear more edgy fashion; school pupils wear school uniform, college students wear casual clothes
Psychological rules	The interpersonal norms created between a couple in a relationship, such as using or wearing gifts given to each other as a sign of the relationship

led mainly to very artificial experiments . . . Research on real-life relationships has been hampered by the difficulty of scaling rewards."

Notions of exchange and equity are more important between casual acquaintances than they are between people who are close friends or emotionally involved with each other. Happily married couples do not focus on issues of exchange or equity. Murstein, MacDonald, and Cerreto (1977) found that marital adjustment was significantly poorer in those married couples who were concerned about exchange and equity than in those couples who were not. Furthermore, there are differences in the behaviour of communal and exchange relationships (as discussed in the box on p. 121).

Miller–Steinberg Social Exchange Rule

Miller (2005) has criticised social exchange-type theories because she feels that they are reductionist, in that they apply economic concepts to emotional relationships. She also suggests that there is a *zeitgeist* aspect to these theories because they are rooted in the freedom and openness culture of the 1970s, an approach that might not suit all relationships. Miller also points out that it should not be assumed that the aim of every romantic relationship is intimacy, nor that every relationship has a linear progression or development. She proposes that these theories, in common with many other psychological theories, show ethnocentrism and cultural bias being rooted in Western industrialised individualist culture. This means that the concepts may not be relevant to collectivist or non-Western cultures, which of course would limit their generalisation and usefulness.

As the relationship progresses these rules become increasingly personal, which means that uncertainty about each other decreases. This does not mean that intimacy is automatically the result, as increasing certainty about the other person may mean being increasingly certain that you do not actually like them much!

 HOW SCIENCE WORKS: STARTING AND ENDING RELATIONSHIPS
It would be useful, using the three theories you have read about in the textbook, to make a comparison chart as a large poster comparing the explanations each theory suggests for starting and ending a romantic relationship. You could even have a summary of each theory at the top; then underneath you could bullet point the significant factors at the beginning of the relationship; and below that you could do the same for the likely explanations for ending the relationship. Then, when you look across your chart, you have a comparison of these theories and a good plan for a "compare and contrast" type of essay.

SECTION SUMMARY
The Formation, Maintenance, and Breakdown of Romantic Relationships

❖ Sternberg's (1988, 1997) triangular theory of love suggests three components: passion, intimacy, and commitment.

❖ Fisher (2004) suggests a three-stage linear stage theory: lust, romantic love, and attachment.

❖ Hendrick and Hendrick (2003) describe passionate or romantic love and companionate love.

❖ Brain imaging studies using fMRI scans show different patterns of brain activity and brain chemistry for liking and for love: romantic love activates oxytocin receptor areas associated with sex and reward systems as well as deactivating brain areas associated with negative emotions, critical social judgement, and assessment of other people's emotions and intentions.

❖ Friendships and relationships are formed because of the reward or reinforcements we receive from others, such as smiles, help, and love, which satisfy needs such as dependency, self esteem, and sex:

Reward/need satisfaction theory

— Humans respond well to rewards and reinforcement.

— Positive feelings and experiences increase our liking of or attraction to others (Rabbie & Horowitz, 1960).

— This type of research used artificial circumstances (Duck, 1992); individuals who give more positive rewards are consistently better liked than those who give less (Argyle, 1988).

— This applies only to the early stages of a relationship, and does not affect parent–child relationships.

— This assumes people are basically selfish, which many dispute.

— This type of theory applies much more to Western individualist cultures than to collectivist cultures.

— Possibly applies more to females than to males.

❖ Relationships are focused on a cost–reward ratio, maximising rewards and minimising costs. The four stages are:

Social Exchange Theory

— sampling
— bargaining
— commitment
— institutionalisation.

❖ There is also an assessment of the rewards and costs, and expectations in order to make a comparison level:

— Very attractive and popular people can be far more choosy about their friendships and relationships than less attractive, less popular individuals.

— This explanation is economics based, and therefore reductionist, and ignores cultural and social variation; it is also a child of its times (the 1970s) (Miller, 2005).

Equity Theory

❖ This adds the following on to Social Exchange Theory (Walster, Walster, & Berscheid, 1978):

— negotiation in a relationship can bring fairness
— an unfair or inequitable relationship brings distress
— the disadvantaged person will strive for a more equitable relationship and may leave if this is not achieved.

❖ Under-benefited newlyweds were much more dissatisfied with the relationship than over-benefited partners (Argyle, 1988; Buunk & VanYperen, 1991).
❖ This is still culturally biased, as it is not supported in collectivist cultures.
❖ Happily married couples do not focus on social exchange or equity.

See *A2-Level Psychology Online* to download a podcast containing an interview with Viren Swami on his research into sexual selection and the psychology of physical attraction.

HUMAN REPRODUCTIVE BEHAVIOUR

Natural Selection and Sexual Selection

Sexual reproduction involves two parents creating a new individual by combining their genes. If an individual does not reproduce, then that is the end of his or her genes (unless an individual helps a close relative to reproduce). Therefore, any characteristic that maximises an individual's ability to reproduce successfully is highly adaptive and likely to be naturally selected. Individuals with these genes go on to form successive generations. The theory of evolution by natural selection was formulated by Charles Darwin to explain this (Darwin, 1859). At first glance, there seem to be inconsistencies with this theory. When we look at other species, some characteristics seem positively detrimental to the survival of individual animals. For example, stags have huge antlers that must be a disadvantage when trying to escape from a predator. You would think that stags with small antlers would be naturally selected and therefore we would not see any stags with larger antlers. To solve this problem, Darwin outlined the principle of **sexual selection** (Darwin, 1871). He argued that if a characteristic, such as the stag's antlers, increases the individual's chances of reproduction, then this characteristic will be adaptive because that stag will have more offspring. The antlers serve to increase the stag's reproductive fitness. The next question is, "Why would stags with larger antlers have increased chances of reproduction?" The answer is because stags fight for the right to be the dominant male and to have the right to access the harem of females.

We will start this section with a general consideration of sexual selection in non-human animals before considering the human species.

Evolutionary explanations: key summary points

According to the theory of evolution, most species are well adapted to their environment because of variation, inheritance, competition, natural selection, and adaptation.

The key to evolution by natural selection is differential reproductive success.

Evolutionary psychologists seek to apply insights from the theory of evolution to explain human behaviour.

Anisogamy and Parental Investment

Males produce sperm and females produce eggs. Sperm and eggs are both gametes, meaning reproductive cells:

KEY TERM

Sexual selection: selection for characteristics that increase mating success.

• Males produce sperm in thousands at relatively little physiological cost. Therefore, their best strategy is to mate with many females, because this should result in the maximum number of offspring to perpetuate their genetic line.

- Females produce eggs, each of which contains a store of food for the growing embryo. This incurs some cost to the female and so eggs are not generally produced in thousands.

The difference between egg and sperm is called **anisogamy**, and it results in a type of sexual reproduction in which the games or reproductive cells of the two sexes are dissimilar. It is rare to find animals in which the two gametes are the same size (isogamy), but it does occur in, for example, paramecium, a tiny freshwater organism.

Of key importance is the notion of **parental investment**, which Trivers (1972) defined as, "any investment by the parent in an individual offspring that increases the offspring's chance of surviving (and hence reproductive success) at the cost of the parent's ability to invest in other offspring". In mammals, female investment in her offspring is greater than male investment, in part because of the female's efforts during pregnancy. For example, female elephant seals are pregnant for several months before giving birth to a pup that can weigh as much as 50 kg (8 stone). After the pup is born, the mother loses up to 200 kg or 31 stone in weight during the first weeks of feeding.

It is important to note that Trivers (1972) did not argue that females in every species would have greater parental investment than males. His key notion was that the sex having more parental investment would tend to be more selective when mating than would the other sex.

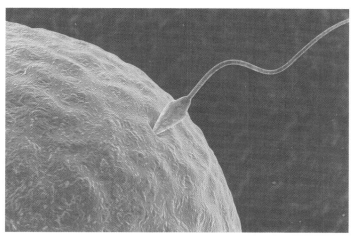

Fertilisation of a human egg by a sperm, an example of anisogamy, where the gametes of the two sexes are dissimilar.

The human species

Female parental investment is typically much greater than male parental investment in the human species. As Buss (1999, p. 102) pointed out:

A man in human evolutionary history could walk away from a casual coupling having lost only a few hours or even a few minutes. A woman in evolutionary history risked getting pregnant as a result, and therefore could have incurred the cost of that decision for years.

What are the implications of the female's greater parental investment in her offspring? According to Trivers (1972), "Where one sex invests considerably more than the other, members of the latter will compete among themselves to mate with members of the former." Thus, women will typically be more discriminating than men in their choice of sex partners, because the consequences of mating with an unsuitable partner are potentially much greater for women than for men. If males have to fight for the right to have sex with females, then natural selection would have favoured those characteristics making it easier to compete. For example, it might have led to men being larger than women, and also more aggressive physically. Similar processes based on natural selection operate in virtually all other species of mammal.

As we have seen, human males can maximise their reproductive potential by having sex with numerous females. This should lead them to seek women who are fertile. One way to do this is to seek-out younger women. By contrast, females can only bear a limited number of children, and they invest heavily in each one during the 9 months of pregnancy and for several years thereafter. It follows that they should prefer men who have good resources and who are willing to be committed to them over long periods of time.

Several studies have produced support for this view. Buss (1989) conducted a cross-cultural study to show that men and women in many different cultures follow the patterns of behaviour predicted by evolutionary theory for the factors most valued in a mate. His findings (outlined in the box below) are consistent with those of Davis (1990), who considered the content of personal advertisements in newspapers. Women advertising for a mate emphasised their physical beauty and indicated they were looking for a high-status, wealthy man. By contrast, men emphasised their wealth of other resources, and made it clear they were looking for a physically attractive younger woman. In other words, women regard men as "success objects", whereas men regard women as "sex objects". These findings fit with the much greater parental investment of women than of men. Evidence that does not fit evolutionary theory is discussed shortly.

More evidence supporting the prediction from evolutionary theory that females should be more selective than males in their choice of sexual partners was

? Why do you think that sex differences in mate preference vary between Western and non-Western cultures?

? Does this research provide strong support for the evolutionary approach?

Cross-cultural support for the evolutionary account of mate choice

One way of testing the evolutionary theory of human sexual selection is by carrying out a cross-cultural study of preferred characteristics in mates. If the theory is correct, there should be clear differences in those characteristics preferred by men and by women, and these differences should be consistent across cultures. Some support for these predictions was reported by Buss (1989), who obtained data from 37 cultures in 33 countries. He found that males in virtually every culture preferred females who were younger than them, and so likely to have good reproductive potential. By contrast, females in all cultures preferred males who were older, and thus more likely to have good resources. As predicted, females rated good financial prospects in a potential mate as more important than did males. It could be argued that males should value physical attractiveness in their mates more highly than females, because of its association with reproductive potential. Indeed, in 36 out of 37 cultures, males valued physical attractiveness in mates more than did females. Finally, males tended to value chastity in a potential mate more than did females, but the difference between the sexes was not significant in 38% of the cultures sampled.

Buss' (1989) findings are of key importance, but they are less clear-cut than they seem for three main reasons. First, they do not actually show that sex differences in mate preference are consistent across cultures. In fact, there were much smaller sex differences in more developed cultures than in less developed ones on most measures, including preferred age differences, importance of financial prospects, and the value of chastity in a mate. Second, the evolutionary approach is more concerned with behaviour than with the preferences assessed by Buss. In fact, the actual average age difference between husband and wife across cultures was 2.99 years, which is similar to the preferred age differences for males (2.66 years) and for females (3.42 years). However, it is by no means clear that there would be this level of agreement between preferences and behaviour for the other measures obtained by Buss. Third, cultural differences were about six times greater than sex differences overall. Since evolutionary psychologists largely discount cultural differences, this shows a real limitation in the evolutionary approach.

reported by Clark and Hatfield (1989). Attractive male and female students approached students of the opposite sex, and said, "Hi, I've been noticing you around town lately, and I find you very attractive. Would you have sex with me?" As you have probably guessed, this offer was received much more eagerly by male students than by female ones. None of the female students accepted the invitation, whereas 75% of the male students did. Some of the male students who declined the invitation apologised that they couldn't because they were seeing their girl-friend that night! These findings support the view that men are easily persuaded to have sex, whereas women are more choosy. However, it should be noted that we don't know whether the students' actual behaviour would have been consistent with what they said.

The Relationship Between Sexual Selection and Human Reproductive Behaviour

The two types of sexual selection are **intersexual** and **intrasexual selection**. Intersexual selection or competition concerns preferences to do with sexual partners and mate choice, and in humans generally applies more to females who choose the best mate available. Fisher (1930) proposed the **runaway process**, whereby an adaptive feature will be selected for when females choose a sexual mate resulting, after many generations, in that feature becoming increasingly exaggerated. In non-human animals, one can see that this may have been the cause of, for example, the peacock's large tail, as a bigger and more eye-catching tail could be linked to, and therefore signal, some genetic advantage such as strength and survival. In humans, this has been known as the **"Sexy Sons" Hypothesis**, suggesting that females will choose a sexual partner for successful and attractive attributes, as these then are likely to be inherited by her own sons, along with her own genes. These sons will inherit the attractiveness and be successful in mating, and so the female's own genes will also be passed on and will be perpetuated. An example of this in humans is not easy to suggest, but perhaps the preference for tallness in males would fit.

This hypothesis is challenged by Zahavi's (1977) Handicap Hypothesis, which suggests that the exaggerated feature is in fact a handicap and not an asset. The argument is that the significance of this is that any male who survives despite the handicap must be a true survivor, must have good vigour and good genes, and is therefore a preferred mate. In fact,

■ Activity: Sexist or evolutionary?

Westen (1996, p. 706) commented on the behaviour of men and women:

> Consider the Casanova who professes commitment and then turns out a few months later not to be ready for it; the man who gladly sleeps with a woman on a first date but then does not want to see her again, certainly not for a long-term relationship; or the women who only date men of high status and earning potential.

Westen suggested that all of these behaviours can be explained in evolutionary terms. Try to do this for yourself, by making a list of the different behaviours along with the evolutionary explanations for them. You also might consider why some people might find Westen's comments sexist and offensive.

EXAM HINT

A common problem when answering questions on this subject is that there is a great deal of AO1 content and you need to structure it carefully. Therefore begin with parental investment and how this determines the strategies of intra and inter-sexual behaviour. Follow this with research evidence for and against and further evaluation.

KEY TERMS

Intersexual selection: refers to the competition for a mate, mate choice, as in choosing the best mate possible.
Intrasexual selection: refers to competition between members of the same sex or sexual orientation for the best mate possible.
Runaway process: Fisher's theory that some inherited characteristics become more and more exaggerated because females actively select mates with this feature. Also called "Sexy Sons Hypothesis".
"Sexy Sons" Hypothesis: the notion that females mate with the most attractive males so that their own sons will inherit these characteristics and thus be attractive to other females. Related to the runaway process.

The size and overall impressiveness of a peacock's tail may play a part in securing a mate, as the female may see this as a sign of genetic superiority that would be passed onto male offspring.

? The terms "good taste" and "good sense" have sometimes been used to describe these theories. Considering Fisher's and Zahavi's hypotheses, which one do you think is the "good taste" hypothesis and which is the "good sense" one?

as Hamilton and Zuk (1982) suggest, a male with an exaggerated feature could only survive if he was in very good health as the feature would be a drain on energy. This could also mean that the good genes associated with that feature also confer a better protection or defence against disease.

The handicap process

According to Zahavi's (1977) hypothesis, a male adornment such as a long tail is a handicap. The argument is that a male bird that is able to survive despite having a significant handicap is likely to be genetically superior to other birds. Thus, females who prefer handicapped males may be selecting those who tend to possess good genes for survival. Thus, this theory is also called the "Good Genes" Theory, but in this case the good genes are in terms of survival and reproduction. This contrasts with Fisher's view that the good genes would be good in the sense that they would lead to attractive offspring.

The basic notion behind the handicap hypothesis can be seen if we consider a concrete example. Suppose two men are running around a track at the same speed, but one of them is carrying a heavy load. We would assume that the man handicapped by the load is stronger and fitter than the other man. Certain behaviours imply or *indicate* robust genes.

Hamilton and Zuk (1982) put forward a specific version of the handicap hypothesis. They argued that males are only likely to have a long tail or other sexual adornment if they are in good health. An individual who isn't in good health couldn't manage to survive with such an extra drain on energy. Thus, male animals with these adornments are attractive to females because they are likely to be free of diseases.

Møller (1990) tested Hamilton and Zuk's version of the Handicap Hypothesis with barn swallows in Denmark. First, Møller showed that female swallows

? Why is the research by Andersson of particular value?

Long tails in widow birds

Perhaps the most interesting form of intrasexual selection occurs when some characteristic (e.g. a long tail) evolves over the generations because it is attractive to members of the opposite sex. For example, the males of several species (e.g. peacocks, birds of paradise) are elaborately adorned, and their adornment seems to make them more attractive to females for mating purposes. This form of intrasexual selection may seem straightforward, but it is not really so. For example, the peacocks' very long and large tail reduces its chances of escaping from a predator. In addition, it has to eat more because of the weight of its tail.

It seems reasonable to assume that such adornments have developed because females find them attractive. However, it is always useful to have good evidence for any assumption. Andersson (1982) studied long-tailed widow birds in Kenya. The male of the species is fairly small (about the size of a sparrow) but its tail is about 40 centimetres (16 inches) in length. Andersson cut the tails off some males to reduce their length to about 14 centimetres or 6 inches. He lengthened the tails of other males by sticking the detached pieces of tail on to them with superglue, making their tails about 65 centimetres or 26 inches long. Andersson found that the males with the artificially lengthened tails had the greatest mating success, indicating that female widow birds are attracted to long tails in male birds.

preferred males with long tails: males with artificially lengthened tails paired up more rapidly with female swallows than did normal males. Then he found that baby swallows reared in nests containing numerous blood-sucking mites were more likely to have reduced growth or to die than were those raised in nests with relatively few mites. Finally, he found that male swallows with long tails had offspring with fewer mites on them than did males with short tails. Thus, as predicted by the handicap hypothesis, male barn swallows with longer tails are healthier than those with shorter tails, because they have greater resistance to parasites such as blood-sucking mites.

Intrasexual selection or competition refers to mate competition between members of the same sex or sexual orientation, and generally applies to males who compete with each other for sexual partners. In this section, we consider some of the key factors involved in intersexual selection (choosing a mate of the opposite sex). We start with two theories that have been applied mainly to other species but that may be relevant to the human species. After that, we focus more directly on the human species. In human sexual relations, it tends to be the female who does the choosing, and so we focus on the factors that make some men more attractive than others to women. We also consider some of the physical characteristics men find attractive in women.

Fisher's hypothesis: the runaway process

Fisher (1930) proposed that females are initially attracted to those features of males that have survival value. For example, a bird with a fairly long tail may be better at flying and so at finding food than one with a short tail. A female will prefer a male with a long tail because her offspring are likely to inherit this characteristic (assuming that the long tail was an inherited characteristic). With successive generations, males with a more exaggerated form of the long tail are the ones selected by females, so the characteristic becomes more and more exaggerated. Fisher called this the runaway process.

? According to Fisher, why will successive generations of birds have longer and longer tails?

This hypothesis has also been described as the Sexy Sons Hypothesis because females will benefit from mating with a male with desirable characteristics, as these will be passed to her sons. As a result, their reproductive chances will be enhanced because they are "sexy". Thus, the mother's genes will be perpetuated.

As long as the advantages outweigh the disadvantages, the exaggerated characteristic will be perpetuated. It is thought that one reason why the giant deer became extinct was because its antlers had simply become too large through the runaway process. Fossil records show antlers spanning as much as 3 metres. Andersson (1982) supplied experimental evidence to support this hypothesis (see the box on page 128).

Is it possible that giant deer became extinct owing to the fact that the once attractive large antlers became simply too large through the runaway process?

Does this also apply to humans? Health records and population data show that generally in a population more boys than girls are born. But males are more vulnerable than females to diseases and injuries, and so it is likely that by adulthood there will be more females than males, which does not fit the intrasexual argument. This does, however, fit basic biology as one male could, hypothetically, mate with a great number of females. A further challenge to intrasexual selection is that adult human females do not come into season but are sexually receptive at all times. However, it is accepted that human males do display and compete for female attention and, by extrapolating this behaviour, for sexual access.

Intersexual selection in humans

? Why do you think when people meet for the first time they pay particular attention to the face?

When we meet people for the first time, we generally pay a lot of attention to their face. What facial characteristics are regarded as attractive? Langlois, Roggman, and Musselman (1994) found that male and female computer-generated composites or "averaged" faces were regarded as more attractive than the individual faces from which the averaged faces were formed. One reason for this is that averaged faces are more symmetrical than individual faces, and symmetry is associated with attractiveness (Grammer & Thornhill, 1994). Of particular importance from the perspective of evolutionary psychology, individuals having average faces are thought at less risk of carrying potentially harmful genetic mutations.

Women whose faces resemble those of young children are often perceived as attractive. For example, photographs of females with relatively large and widely separated eyes, a small nose, and a small chin are regarded as more attractive. These findings are consistent with the notion in evolutionary psychology that men seek young women who are most likely to be fertile. However, wide cheekbones and narrow cheeks in women are also seen as attractive (Cunningham, 1986), and these features are not usually found in young children.

Cunningham (1986) also studied physical attractiveness in males. Men who had features such as a large, square jaw, small eyes, prominent cheekbones, and thin lips were regarded as attractive by women. These features can be regarded as indicating maturity, as they are rarely found in children. Some of these features (e.g. large jaw, prominent cheekbones) depend in part on male sex hormones (e.g. testosterone). As testosterone is thought to have adverse effects on the immune system, it could be argued that these facial features indicate men who are generally healthy and whose immune system is strong enough to cope with high levels of testosterone (Thornhill & Gangestad, 1999).

? What facial features do you find particularly attractive?

Earlier, we discussed a study by Davis (1990), who found that women advertising for a mate tended to emphasise their physical beauty, as would be predicted by evolutionary theory. However, that study begged the question of whether that kind

---

■ **Activity: Mate choice 1**

You can do a replication of Davis (1990) using "personal" ads from a local or national newspaper. Analyse 30–50 "male seeks female" ads and a similar number of "female seeks male" ones. Choose various categories that can be analysed on all the ads, such as "mentions height" (Tall man seeks . . . ; petite woman seeks . . .), other physical features (hair colour, size, etc.), and profession. You need to differentiate between what people seek and what they say about themselves. Analyse the differences by using a series of chi-squared tests (male/female × does mention characteristic/does not mention characteristic). Do not try to combine the data into one large table as it is not all independent. Your alternative hypothesis is that men and women will both seek and mention different characteristics. You need a specific hypothesis for each characteristic, such as: women will mention features associated with attractiveness more than will men, men are more likely than women to mention profession, men are more likely to seek a younger female, and so on.

There is plenty to discuss: the bias of the sample of ads, the bias of the sample of "participants" (the people writing the ads), and so on.

? Can you think of any famous people who are considered attractive, but who do not meet Cunningham's attractiveness criteria?

Natalie Portman (top left) fits Cunningham's "attractive female" characteristics—note how her features are similar to the little girl's (top right). Johnny Depp (bottom left), however, looks very different from the little boy (bottom right).

of advertisement is actually effective in attracting replies from men. Evidence that matters are more complex than might have been imagined was reported by Strassberg and Holtz (2003). Fictitious advertisements were used in which a hypothetical woman was described as "very attractive", "passionate and sensitive", or "financially successful and ambitious". Evolutionary psychologists would predict that the first advertisement would produce the most interest from men, but it was actually the last advertisement that attracted the most replies.

What physical features in women signal high fertility? Zaadstra et al. (1993) found two such features: (1) body mass index (BMI), which is based on the relationship between height and weight; and (2) waist-to-hip ratio. More specifically, they found that women with BMIs between 20 and 30 and waist-to-hip ratios under 0.70 were the most fertile on average. Of the two measures, waist-to-hip ratio was the better predictor of female fertility. According to evolutionary psychologists, features predicting fertility should be important in mate selection. Consistent with this prediction, Singh (1993) found that women with a waist-to-hip ratio of 0.70 were judged to be the most attractive. Another finding was that models and winners of pageants over a 60-year period had remarkably stable waist-to-hip ratios.

The evidence concerning BMI is less supportive of evolutionary psychology. Rubinstein and Caballero (2000) found that there had been a steady decrease in BMI for the winners of the Miss America Pageant between 1923 and 1999. Anderson, Crawford, Nadeau, and Lindberg's (1992) findings across 54 cultures are more striking. In essence, women with a slender body were preferred in cultures in which the food supply was very reliable (e.g. most Western cultures), whereas women with a heavy body were preferred in cultures in which the food supply was very unreliable. On the face of it, these large cultural differences seem inconsistent with the evolutionary approach. However, it could be argued that heavy women in cultures with very unreliable food supplies are better equipped than slender women to survive food shortages and to provide nourishment for their children.

In sum, the evidence discussed here is mostly reasonably in line with expectations from evolutionary psychology. In addition, the cross-cultural research of Buss (1989), discussed earlier, shows that women prefer older men and that men prefer younger women. However, cross-cultural studies (e.g. Anderson et al., 1992; Buss, 1989) have generally reported substantial differences across cultures, and such differences are not readily explained by evolutionary accounts. We also need to bear in mind that there may be important differences between expressed preferences when participants look at photographs and actual behaviour. Thankfully, most people whose physical features are far removed from the evolutionary ideal nevertheless manage to have sexual relationships and children.

Anderson et al. (1992): results

Preference	Food supply			
	Very unreliable	Moderately unreliable	Moderately reliable	Very reliable
Heavy body	71%	50%	39%	40%
Moderate body	29%	33%	39%	20%
Slender body	0%	17%	22%	40%

The Buss (1989) study referred to earlier was criticised by Shackelford, Schmitt, and Buss (2005), who performed a meta-analysis of Buss' data from several thousand participants in 37 cultures. They found that the original conclusion that women valued social status in men but men valued physical attractiveness in women was supported, and that these preferences seem stable across cultures. However, their criticism that preferences might not chime with actual behaviour still holds true. This was challenged by Harris (2002), whose study showed a *zeitgeist* effect. In the 1960s, research supported the Buss data but, in the twenty-first century, both heterosexual and homosexual individuals in a romantic relationship focus more on the emotional infidelity as an issue than the sexual infidelity.

Human reproductive behaviour: mate preferences

Male preferences	Female preferences
Females with youthful features suggesting fertility: big eyes, small noses, full lips	Males with resources or abilities to gain resources: material possessions
Females who look suitable for pregnancy: narrow waists but wider hips	Successful social traits, e.g. social status, dominance
Females who look successful at looking after themselves: full breasts and larger buttocks equals food reserves for pregnancy and lactation	Successful behavioural traits, e.g. intelligence, drive, ambition, strength, skills
Females who look healthy: clear skin, shiny hair, lively behaviour	Males who look healthy: clear skin, shiny hair, energetic behaviour, muscles, body size
Signs of good genes: facial and body symmetry	Signs of good genes: facial and body symmetry
Chastity and faithfulness: females with old as well as new friends	Commitment of resources, e.g. pre-mating gifts, kindness, sharing
Many sexual partners: spreading their genes widely to the next generation	Being very choosy about possible mate(s)
High-quality partners: successful children	Being attracted more by psychological factors
Exclusive sexual relationships: no sperm competition, increased paternal certainty	Exclusive emotional relationship(s): no loss of resources, more successful child-rearing

---

In response to these preferences, males exaggerate their resources and may be deceitful about commitment, and females may exaggerate their youthfulness and physical attractiveness.

> **?** Can you think of five ways each in which males and females exaggerate their attractiveness, based on the above evolutionary ideas?

■ Activity: Mate choice 2

Do all men seek the same physical characteristics in the women with whom they desire to have a sexual relationship, as implied by evolutionary theory of mate choice and supported by the research of Buss (1989)? Or are there differences based on the "fashion" of the time? One way of investigating this within one sample of men is to gather together, from magazines or the internet, a series of full-length photos of women of child-bearing age, all fairly attractive but of different shapes and possibly from different cultures and different generations (a picture of Marilyn Monroe and Greta Garbo at a fairly young age, for example). Avoid personal photos. Ask a selection of men from two different age groups to rate them on attractiveness by ranking them in order of attractiveness. If the theory is correct, you would expect no great difference in the ratings between the men, regardless of age of the men. You could analyse it by comparing men from two different generations and using a test of difference for independent groups. Use the mean score of attractiveness for each female given by each age group of men. It is the null hypothesis that you are expecting to support if evolutionary theory is correct and this has implications for the level of significance you may choose to use.

Evolutionary Explanations of Parental Investment

Parental investment differences start before birth, in fact before conception with anisogamy, followed by pregnancy and lactation and support for mother and child.

Sex differences and parent–offspring conflict

Anisogamy refers to the differences between the male sex cells (or gametes)—the sperm—and the female sex cells (gametes)—the ova or eggs. Sperm are minute and short-lived cells; really, each one is just a gamete nucleus with a cytoplasm tail, and these are produced continuously in their millions by the testes. Each ovum is very large by comparison and has both its gamete nucleus and a great deal of cytoplasm and is rich in energy and nutrients. On average, an ovum is produced every 28 days. It has been suggested that the male parental investment pre-conception is minor compared with the female parental investment because the male gametes are so small and represent a much smaller physical contribution. However, many millions of these male gametes are produced every day, whereas the single, large, nutrient-rich female ovum is produced only every few weeks. This means that it is possible to suggest that the male and female investments are not that dissimilar at this stage.

Why do you think female parental investment is so much greater than males?

However, from conception onwards the female parental investment is without doubt immensely greater than the male investment. Human gestation, or pregnancy, lasts for 40 weeks (9 months) and although during this time care from the male parent is beneficial, the female parent has considerable physical and physiological investments and costs. The foetus needs both nutrients and energy to grow and develop, and these come from the mother. If her diet is not sufficient to provide the extra then the building materials for the foetus, e.g. calcium for bones and muscles, will be taken from her body, thus weakening it. Her body also has to dispose of the foetus' waste, so her kidneys have to work harder. Furthermore, as pregnancy progresses, the woman's body will become larger and heavier and so she will need more energy to get around and might well not be able to forage and gather food so well, hence help would be needed. It is also true that for our hunter-gatherer ancestors, the early humans, and for thousands of years after them, there was no medical help during the risky procedure of human birth, which is exaggerated by the baby's large brain (and therefore head) and its immaturity at birth.

These factors are both costs and investments on the part of the mother. Lactation, the production of milk for breast-feeding, is yet another cost to the woman and investment in the baby's future. Milk is rich in fats, protein, and sugar—nutrients for energy and growth—and these come, as before, from the mother's own body. If her diet is on the sparse side, her body will give up its own nutrients for the baby, and she will be that much less strong as a result.

The male, the father, cannot contribute to birth nor to lactation and so has no costs there. However, the male does have a cost—a psychological cost—in that he has no parental certainty. The female knows the baby she gave birth to is her own flesh and blood but the male has to take this on trust. Bellis, Hughes, Hughes, and Ashton's (2005) meta-analysis of over 50 years' international data on when a father was not the biological father of his child found a variation between a 1% and 30% frequency. The general consensus was that the rate is below 10% but the estimate by Bellis' team is about 4%. This seems low but, if correct, it still means that about

Sex differences in parental investment		
	Male parent	**Female parent**
Anisogamous gametes	Millions, but minute	One at a time, but large and nutrient rich
Pregnancy/gestation	Extra care for the female	Need to provide nutrients and energy and waste disposal for the foetus
Birth	Possible support for the female	Risks of the birth process as the baby's head is large
Lactation	No contribution	Energy and nutrients such as fats needed to make milk, lactation can continue for years
Parental certainty	No certainty	Complete certainty
Commitment and resources	Possible but variable	Usually given for many years, otherwise own investment in own child would be wasted

1 in 25 families would be affected. It is likely that these paternal discrepancy figures are the result of sperm competition, where the woman has had sex with more than one man in the space of only a few days. Evolutionary theory would suggest that the reasons for the woman doing this would be either the opportunity to move to a higher-status male partner, or to gain more resources.

The effect of parental certainty or uncertainty can explain the different sexes' commitment and resources for the family. A man who is not certain that the child is biologically his is less likely to stay with the woman and child and commit resources to them, especially if there are other suitable females available, he is reasonably attractive, and the baby is healthy. It is a different story for the female, the mother, who does have parental certainty. Lactation and childcare mean her time and energies are going to be less available for gathering food and other necessities for life, and the support from a man would be crucial for her and her child to be safe and flourish. Furthermore, her already considerable investment in gestation and birth would be wasted if the child did not survive.

> **EXAM HINT**
>
> For AO2/3 consider the following:
>
> - weaknesses of the research on parental certainty
> - evidence for the sex differences
> - alternatives to evolution to explain sex differences in parental investment.
>
> Consider also:
>
> - The contradictions in the evolutionary explanation of sex differences (e.g. childless couples).
> - The contradictions in the explanations itself, e.g. on the one hand saying males should not have high investment and then, on the other, giving factors that increase male investment. Such inconsistency can be linked to the scientific criticisms.

SECTION SUMMARY
Human Reproductive Behaviour

❖ Evolutionary theory suggests that there is sexual selection in that any characteristic that increases the chance of successful mating is adaptive as more offspring will be produced.

❖ Intersexual selection or competition concerns preferences to do with sexual partners and mate choice, in humans generally applying more to females who choose the best mate available—this is the "Sexy Sons" Hypothesis:

The relationship between sexual selection and human reproductive behaviour

— females choose a sexual partner for successful, attractive attributes, e.g. tallness; these then are inherited by her own sons, plus her own genes
— the sons inherit the attractiveness and success in mating, so the female's own genes will also be passed on and perpetuated.

❖ The Handicap Hypothesis challenges that the exaggerated feature is in fact a handicap and not an asset, e.g. excessive tallness strains the heart (Zahavi, 1977).

❖ Women are more attracted by emotional fidelity and signs of resources, success and maturity signalling the ability to support a family; men are more attracted by sexual fidelity and signs of fertility such as glowing skin and an hourglass figure signalling the ability to bear children (Buss, 1989; Shackelford et al., 2005).

❖ The fidelity data were a *zeitgeist*, both males and females value emotional fidelity highest (Harris, 2002).

❖ Intrasexual selection or competition refers to mate competition between members of the same sex or sexual orientation, and generally applies to males who compete with each other for sexual partners:

— biologically speaking, one male can impregnate a large number of females
— male humans—not just non-human animals—display and compete for female attention
— although more male babies are born, they are more vulnerable to infection and stress and so by adulthood there could be more females than males.

❖ Human adult females are sexually receptive all the time, not just in a breeding season.

Evolutionary explanations of parental investment: sex differences and parent–offspring conflict

❖ Females invest more than males in parenthood before and after conception, which is why females are more choosy about sexual partners.

❖ Male gametes are minute and contain almost no nutrients whereas female gametes by comparison are very large and packed with nutrients.

❖ However, these male gametes are produced constantly, by the million, whereas a single female ovum is produced only every few weeks; so it is possible to suggest that the male and female investments at this stage are not that dissimilar.

❖ Post-conception, the female parent has considerable physical and physiological investments and costs for 40 weeks' gestation and a lengthy lactation period post-birth, plus the risks of birth, plus child-care.

❖ Females have parental certainty, males do not.

EFFECTS OF EARLY EXPERIENCE AND CULTURE ON ADULT RELATIONSHIPS

If one looks at non-human animals it can be seen that sexual mating behaviours are nature, not nurture, because these behaviours are consistent no matter where the individual species live. For example, whether one looks at American or European or Asian peacocks they always display their tails in the same upright fan, and shake the feathers to make a noise, all to attract the peahens' attention. However, it is very different in our own human species. Relationship behaviours and norms vary from group to group, from culture to culture. This means that our relationship behaviours are at least in part nurture not nature and will vary depending on the local culture and also, research suggests, on early childhood experiences.

The Influence of Childhood and Adolescent Experiences on Adult Relationships

Parent–child relationships

You will remember from AS level, in Unit 1 the study of attachment, the strong and long-lasting emotional bonding between child and a significant other person, often the mother or main carer. The most famous research on this topic was done by John Bowlby, and his theory is very relevant here. Bowlby (1969) hypothesised that early childhood experiences have a profound and life-long effect on the psyche, especially the emotional psyche. In particular, a child who has not made a secure attachment with her or his mother will be unable to make and enjoy close romantic attachments as an adult. Schwartz, Hage, Bush, and Burns (2006) suggest that one reason for this inability could be that the emotional responses of what Fisher calls lust, romantic love, and attachment are extremely similar to the emotional responses of anxiety and fear. These responses involve the activation of the sympathetic nervous system, and so heart and breathing rates increase, which could be because of excitement and anticipation to do with the beloved or could be because of anxieties, stress, and other fears. The subjective interpretation of the sympathetic symptoms could vary between those who were securely attached as children and those who were insecurely attached, and this could be a causal factor in those who were, in childhood, insecurely attached being unsuccessful in adult emotional relationships (Schwartz & Southern, 2002).

According to Bowlby (1969) a child needs a secure attachment with his or her mother in order to be able to form close romantic attachments as an adult.

A different view comes from Freud's theory of psychosexual development. In the third, or phallic, stage—approximately between ages 4 to 7—he postulated that the great challenge was to understand one's own sex-role identity through play, asking questions, and other explorations. Successful completion of this stage would bring identification with and acceptance and enjoyment of one's own sexuality and sex role. The stage begins the same for both boys and girls as they are still identifying with the mother who has provided love and security, but now psychosocial pressure to start to "be a man like Daddy" begin to affect most boys. These pressures are many and various, including the well-known saying, "boys don't cry". Western fathers traditionally would encourage rough and tumble play and other "tough" behaviours so their sons would not turn into "wimps" or "sissies". Freud suggested that these pressures, this change, could be frightening to a boy because he would feel small, weak, and powerless beside his father and would have an Oedipal complex, a strong love, and need for his mother—his warm security and provider of food—with food, of course, in Freudian terms symbolising love. If the boy is able to identify with his father, imitate male behaviour, and eventually internalise maleness, he will have successfully resolved the conflicts of the phallic stage. However, he might still have some of the Oedipal complex, so in adult life he will seek romantic relationships that include aspects of mother-love, such as from a nurturing, care-taking, and unconditionally loving woman.

? What are the stages of development according to Freud?

What about girls? Initially, Freud overlooked female psychosexual development, but when he did address it he postulated that, during the phallic stage, girls realise that they do not have a penis and so from then on suffer from penis envy. Their complex is known as the Electra complex, in which the girl desires to possess her father as her own, thus making her mother a rival. This conflict is resolved if the girl models the mother's behaviour, identifies with her, internalises female-ness, and so has female behaviours and the female sex role as an adult. How this identification and internalisation affects adult romantic relationships depends on the degree to which the sex role is accepted. Many girls remain partly identifying with their father, perhaps becoming tomboys and pursuing motor and intellectual skills, and as adults may be as comfortable around men as their sisters who have identified more completely with traditional female roles. The latter may well choose romantic partners who will cherish and care for them, the former might seek partners who will be less fatherly in their attitude.

Problems are likely to arise if the parenting has not been good and supportive and loving. Children in the phallic stage cannot distinguish between good and bad parents; parents are by definition powerful and right, and are the models for future adult behaviour. So unkind, rejecting, ignoring, or abusive parents will still provide the model for a loving relationship. The impressions from early childhood form the scripts and schemas for later life. This means that Freud was suggesting that people who have abusive, controlling, or otherwise unhappy relationships as adults behave in this way because their schemas and scripts of emotionally close relationships are based on parental behaviours in early childhood. This concept is supported by several research studies, including that by Ehrensaft et al. (2003), whose 20-year longitudinal study found that children who witness interparental violence and who also suffer from excessive punishments are likely to use violent behaviour to resolve conflicts with close emotional partners in adulthood.

What did Freud suggest for those who did not have a parental model in the phallic stage? He thought this would leave individuals with a lack of confidence in their sexual identity so that they might be uncomfortable in relationships with the opposite sex and might avoid such relationships altogether.

? What are the other stages of development according to Erikson?

Other psychodynamic views suggest that adolescence could also have important effects on adult relationships. Erikson (1968, 1980) suggested a stage theory of psychological development with adolescence as the fifth stage, during which the life crisis needing resolution is identity versus confusion. Erikson felt that in these years adolescents would work towards seeing themselves as integrated individuals with a strong personal and sexual identity.

Levinson (1978, 1986) saw adolescents as being in transition into early adulthood, exploring personal possibilities including sexuality and relationships. Earlier ideas on the person they will be are reappraised and the plan for identity and behaviour crystallises and is part of The Dream—their personal construct of where in life they are going. Gould (1978, 1981) saw adolescence as a time when false childhood assumptions should be challenged if the person was going to have a successful adult life. The main false assumption is that the emerging adult will still belong to and believe in their parents as omnipotent, and the parental world as the only correct one. Applied to relationships, this means that to have successful adult emotional relationships, the individual needs to come to an acceptance that she or he might differ from the parents or home background and that ideas and beliefs and behaviours can be different without being bad or wrong. Gould saw this challenge as a form of separation anxiety, a concept familiar to you from your study of attachments.

? Are there any similarities between Freud and Erikson's stages of development?

These psychodynamic ideas are interesting and plausible and attractive, but the main criticisms are powerful. Freud's own theory and the focus of Erikson, Levinson, and Gould, was very androcentric, with initial theorising based on males, male development, and the male world. It is also very difficult to test or measure their ideas scientifically as they are ideas, constructs, based on concepts and not on facts so they are not empirical theories. The research is based mainly on qualitative and retrospective data from questionnaires and surveys with the reservations that belong with such data. However, it needs to be said that these theories have considerable face validity.

There is, however, good scientific research on the influence of parent–child relationships. The Minnesota Longitudinal Study of Parents and Children (Collins & van Dulmen, 2005) began in 1976 with 267 mothers, and 180 of the children are still in the study. Data was collected 23 times from birth to early adulthood and included measures of parent and child characteristics, behaviours, interactions with significant others, and current environmental circumstances. These data are very informative because of the frequency and depth of information collections. The participants were monitored at every stage, including pre-school, early childhood, middle childhood, adolescence, and early adulthood. Methods used included observations, interviews, ratings from teachers and parents, written tests, school records, and public sources. Extra interviews and assessments concerned with romantic relationships were taken during adolescence and early adulthood and findings are so far consistent. Emotional expression in romantic relationships of the young adults relates to the individual's attachment experiences during their childhood social development. Securely attached infants became children with higher social competences among their peers and also closer and more secure in their friendships as adolescents, which led to being more openly expressive and emotionally attached to their romantic partners in early adulthood. This means that the quality of romantic relationships in adolescence and early adulthood is coherent with early childhood and other non-romantic relationships with significant other people (Simpson, Collins, Tran, & Haydon, 2007).

> **EXAM HINT**
>
> Remember the effects of early attachment from your studies of this at AS level. This has considerable influence on adult relationships.

Interaction with peers

In childhood, relationships tend to be involuntary: they are within the family; friends are allowed in but the main relationships are with family members. However, things change during adolescence, with powerful voluntary relationships forming and becoming of prime importance (Collins & van Dulmen, 2005). They say that romantic relationships are increasingly recognised as potentially significant in adolescent development as well as their well-being. Collins (2003) points out that such relationships can be with same-sex or opposite-sex partners.

Zani (1993) reported that about 25% of 12-year-olds have had an important romantic relationship in the past year, and for 18-year-olds this went up to over 70%. What does this mean? As with any romantic relationship, adolescents involved in such experience greater mood swings and conflict, and there may be an increase in problems relating to schooling and behaviour, but being in a relationship increases the sense of self-worth. It also raises the respect given to those in the relationship from their peers.

? What do you think are some reasons why being in a relationship increases the sense of self-worth?

? What are some positive effects of peer interaction?

? Can you think of any rules that operate in your relationships?

? Do you think peer relationships are an influential factor in romantic relationships in all cultures?

There is also the concept of adolescent relationships being a learning stage for later, adult relationships. In fact, a longitudinal study in Germany (Seiffge-Krenke, & Lang, 2002) showed a causal link between the quality of romantic relationships in middle adolescence and commitment in other relationships in adulthood. Similar research findings link positive adolescent relationships with positive later outcomes and influence development in the relationship area.

Peers are possibly the most influential factor in romantic relationships. For Western adolescents, being in a relationship is a key factor in belonging to the peer group according to Connolly, Craig, Goldberg, and Pepler (1999). Connelly, Craig, Goldberg, and Pepler (2004) suggest this may be transactional, as peer networks support early pairings and early pairings facilitate interactions with the peer group. In fact, early romantic pairings impact positively on the extensiveness of peer networks and the social and emotional development therein.

Joyner and Campa (2005) obtained teacher ratings for participants aged from kindergarten to 16, relating to how much each individual conformed to an ideal prototype for relating effectively to their peers. Not only was there coherence in measures through development but, interestingly, the research also showed that the norm of single-gender peer interaction in middle childhood is highly predictive of functioning successfully in later mixed-gender peer groups and also of having successful romantic relationships as a young adult. It is likely that the middle childhood experiences give a strong sense of gender identity and confidence, which could tie in with Freud's concept of successfully resolving the phallic stage conflicts.

Peer relations and romantic relationships

A continuing longitudinal study (Simpson et al., 2007) at the University of Minnesota has tracked 78 individuals through infancy, early childhood, adolescence, and adulthood, monitoring them at 12 months, 6–8 years, 16 years, and early adulthood. The research focus was on attachment, interaction with peers, and close friendships during childhood. The young adults' interactions with romantic partners and their expressions of emotions were also monitored. As well as supporting previous studies on attachment, e.g. that securely attached infants had higher social competence with their peers in childhood, the study has found that these positive peer relationships seem in their teens to have led to closer and more secure peer friendships. As young adults, these people were more expressive and emotionally attached to their romantic peers.

Professor Collins, leader of the research team, says that the findings highlight one developmental pathway through which significant peer-relationship experiences during the early years of life relate to the daily experiences in romantic relationships during early adulthood.

The Nature of Relationships in Different Cultures

Some aspects of romantic relationships seem constant across cultures. Buss' classic research, referred to previously, showed a great consistency across 33 countries and over 10,000 participants about what features of the opposite sex were attractive when considering a romantic relationship. This coherence is supported by Jankowiak and Fischer's (1992) cross-cultural study of 166 different societies, which found that in over 86% of them there was a belief in romantic love and relationships, showing that this is not a Western construct but more of a universal belief. This is surprising, as collectivism would seem to support arranged relationships and indeed such arranged marriages are common in some collectivist societies. Support for the perceived importance of emotional relationships comes from Endo, Heine, and Lehman's (2000) study, which found that viewing one's

See *A2-Level Psychology Online* for an interactive exercise on cultural differences in relationships.

own important relationships as more positive than those of one's peers is a feature of Japanese, Asian–Canadian, and European–Canadian participants. This belief is interesting, as it would reinforce the value of one's own relationships. However, variation or differences do exist. Japanese participants viewed their own romantic partners as more attractive than themselves, whereas the other two groups judged their partners as more like themselves.

Sprecher and Toro-Morn (2002) challenge the consistency concept in their research on approximately 700 participants in North America and a similar number in China. They found that culture differences were stronger than gender differences, although these did also exist.

Jankowiak and Fischer's (1992) study supported the idea that belief in romantic love is not a Western construct but applies across cultures.

In Western cultures, we assume that two people marry only if they are in love with each other. In the 1960s, when Kephart (1967) asked over 1000 American college students "If a boy [or girl] had all the other qualities you desired, would you marry this person if you were not in love with him [or her]?", 65% of the men but only 24% of the women answered "No". However, culture and norms are dynamic and change over time, and when later cohorts of students answered the same question, both sexes indicated that they would not marry without love, and no gender differences were found, with 80–90% of both sexes answering in the negative (Sprecher, 1994). The same question was asked in 10 other countries and the percentage of negative answers varies from 85.9% in the US and 85.7% in Brazil, to 24.0% in India.

Although China was not included in the sample, Thailand and Japan, countries similar to China in their degree of collectivism, were included. The percentages of respondents in these two countries who said they would not marry someone they did not love were 33.8% and 62.6%, respectively, which were lower than that in the US. Levine, Sato, Hashimoto, and Verma (1995) did not find any gender differences in responses, either overall or in any of the countries.

EXAM HINT

If you are asked to consider the extent to which relationships differ across cultures, try to provide evidence that argues that there are differences *and* similarities. There are more arguments for differences, so think about how you will organise this section. You could structure the material into six areas:

1. individualistic and collectivist cultures
2. voluntary and involuntary relationships
3. permanent and impermanent relationships
4. romantic relationships
5. friendships
6. family relationships.

Make sure that you provide some arguments that involve problems with the evidence, such as the fact that differences in relationships between cultures may be magnified by ethnocentric research. Consider how the weaknesses of cross-cultural research may have reduced the validity of research.

However, one limitation of Levine et al.'s study was the small sample size within each country, which ranged from 71 to 156.

Cultures affect more than the timing of romantic relationships. The selection of partners for romantic relationships, and the activities that are the norm, and therefore approved, within the relationship are culture-dependent (Murry et al., 2004). In the USA Asian-American adolescents are not as likely as other racial-ethnic groups to have had a romantic relationship in the last 18 months, compared to African-American, Hispanic, Native, and Caucasian groups (Carver, Joyner, & Udry, 2003). Reis, Collins, and Berscheid (2000) confirm previous research findings that social norms, as in community and cultural norms, regulate who is considered acceptable as a romantic "target". It is the peer group here that is so influential, as detailed above.

Giordano (2003) analysed data from the Toledo Adolescent Longitudinal Study and found that Caucasian youths experienced more awkwardness in romantic relationships than boys from other ethnic groups, although all cultures reported personal social and communicative awkwardness and becoming more emotional when interacting with relationship partners. This self-reported awkwardness was also found by Murry et al., who used several quantifiable measures, including the Dating version of the Best Friend Questionnaire, which has sections on support, positive relationship, and negative relationship. The only gender difference they found was that African–American boys were more likely to report negative aspects of romantic relationships than the same ethnic-group girls. In all the ethnic groups studied, there was a close match between the quality of the parent–adolescent relationship and adolescent romantic relationship quality. The higher levels of parental monitoring of their adolescent children correlated with the adolescents' higher self-esteem and consistently predicted higher quality romantic relationships.

Rothbaum, Rosen, Ujiie, and Uchida (2002) pursued a different line of cross-cultural study. The looked at Family Systems Theory in the US and Japan, focusing in particular on the overly close, enmeshed mother–child relationship that the theory considers unhealthy. Traditionally, Japanese culture promotes an intensely close mother–child bond, and the theory suggests this leads to maladaptive

---

Evaluation of cross-cultural research

There are several reasons for conducting cross-cultural research, i.e. research that looks at the customs and practices of different countries and makes comparisons with our own cultural norms. First, such research can tell us about what might be universal in human behaviour. If the same behaviours are observed in many different cultures, all of which have different ways of socialising children, then the behaviour might be due to innate (universal) factors rather than learning. The second reason for conducting cross-cultural research is that it offers us insights into our own behaviour: insights that we may not otherwise be aware of. Perhaps this is the appeal of watching programmes on the television that show foreign lands and different people.

There are some major weaknesses to cross-cultural research. First of all, any sample of a group of people might be biased and therefore we may be mistaken in thinking that the observations made of one group of people are representative of that culture. Second, when the observations are made by an outsider, that person's own culture will bias how they interpret the data they observe. Finally, the psychological tools that are used to measure people, such as IQ tests and questionnaires about relationships, are designed in one particular culture and based on assumptions of that culture. They may not have any meaning in another culture.

Therefore, cross-cultural research has the potential to be highly informative about human behaviour, but also has many important weaknesses.

attachments, yet evidence from Japan suggests the opposite. Research found that the very close attachment between mother and child is considered adaptive and that these children do not experience adverse effects from such relationships, and are able to go on into adult life and make healthy romantic and emotional attachments even if this would not happen in the West. This means that the Family Systems Theory is guilty of ethnocentrism, a bias in favour of Western culture and against non-Western cultures. It may hold true in its own cultural environment, but should not be applied automatically to other cultures.

SECTION SUMMARY
Effects of Early Experience and Culture on Adult Relationships

❖ Unlike most non-human species human child-rearing practices vary culturally and across time.

Parent–child relationships

❖ Early childhood experiences have a profound and life-long effect e.g. a child who has not made a secure attachment with her or his mother will be unable to make and enjoy close romantic attachments as an adult (Bowlby, 1969).

❖ Sympathetic ANS responses to lust, romantic love, and attachment are extremely similar to the emotional responses of anxiety and fear, so if not securely attached these feelings could be misinterpreted.

❖ This is challenged by Freud's view of the phallic stage of psychosexual development and the resolution of the Oedipus and Electra complexes.

❖ The Minnesota Longitudinal Study of Parents and Children has shown quality of romantic relationships in adolescence and early adulthood is coherent with early childhood and other non-romantic relationships with significant other people (Simpson et al., 2007).

Interaction with peers

❖ First relationships are involuntary, friends are allowed in but the main relationships are with family members.

❖ About 25% of 12-year-olds have had an important romantic relationship in the past year; for 18-year-olds this went up to over 70% (Zani, 1993).

❖ Research showed a causal link between the quality of romantic relationships in middle adolescence and commitment in other relationships in adulthood (Seiffge-Krenke & Lang, 2002).

❖ This may be transactional as peer networks support early pairings, and early pairings facilitate interactions with the peer group (Connelly et al., 2004).

❖ Relating effectively to peers was coherent with the quality of personal early care-giving experience (Joyner & Campa, 2005).

❖ All these data are possibly culture biased for individualist cultures.

The nature of relationships in different cultures

❖ Some aspects of romantic relationships seem constant across cultures:

— cross-cultural research data supports this (Buss, 1989; Jankowiak & Fischer, 1998)

— however, culture differences were stronger than gender differences (Sprecher & Toro-Morn, 2002).

See *A2-Level Psychology Online* for some interactive quizzes to help you with your revision.

❖ Marrying for all qualities but without love was not acceptable to 85.9% in the US and 85.7% in Brazil, 62.6% in Japan, 33.8% in Thailand, and 24.0% in India.

❖ There is a *zeitgeist* effect. In the 1960s, 65% of male US college students would marry for all qualities but without love compared to only 24% of female students.

❖ The selection of partners for romantic relationships and the activities that are the norm, and therefore approved, within the relationship are culture dependent (Murry et al., 2005):

— in the US, Asian-American adolescents are not as likely as other racial–ethnic groups to have had a romantic relationship in the last 18 months, compared with African-American, Hispanic, Native, and Caucasian groups (Carver, Joyner, & Udry, 2003)

— social norms, as in community and cultural norms, regulate who is considered acceptable as a romantic "target". It is the peer group here that is so influential (Reis et al., 2000)

— the Toledo Adolescent Longitudinal Study showed that Caucasian youths experienced more awkwardness in romantic relationships than boys from other ethnic groups (Giordano, 2003).

❖ Family systems theory would regard the traditional Japanese mother–child relationship as enmeshed and likely to lead to unsatisfactory adult relationships:

— the very close attachment between mother and child is considered adaptive and these children do not experience adverse effects from such relationships

— the children make healthy romantic and emotional attachments as adults

— family systems theory is guilty of ethnocentrism in favour of Western culture.

FURTHER READING

Bartels, A., & Zeki, S. (2004). The neural correlates of maternal and romantic love. *Neuroimage*, *21*(3), 1155–1166. This is an account of fMRI imaging showing which areas of the brain fire up and which damp down in emotional attachments.

Bernstein, D., & Nash, P. (2008). *Essentials of psychology* (pp. 556–559). Boston, MA: Houghton Mifflin. This has an interesting section on intimate relationships and love, with an excellent depiction of Sternberg's triangular theory.

Flanagan, C. (1999). *Early socialisation*. London: Routledge. This book has an interesting section on long-term effects of secure attachments in Chapter 4.

Gray, J. (1993). *Men are from Mars, women are from Venus*. London: HarperCollins. This provides a view of intersexual behaviour.

REVISION QUESTIONS

In the exam, questions on this topic are out of 25 marks, and can take the form of essay questions or two-part questions. You should allow about 30 minutes for each of the questions below, which aim to test the material in this chapter. Never try to answer a question unless you have been taught the topic.

1. Discuss **one** theory of the formation, maintenance, and breakdown of romantic relationships, e.g. reward/need satisfaction or social exchange theory. (25 marks)

2. Discuss the relationship between sexual selection and human reproductive behaviour. (25 marks)

3. (a) Outline with examples the differing parental investments of human males and females. (10 marks)

   (b) Discuss the relationship between sexual selection and human reproductive behaviour. (15 marks)

4. Discuss the influence on adult relationships of parent–child relationships and interaction with peers during childhood and adolescence. (25 marks)

5. Compare and contrast two theories of the maintenance and breakdown of romantic relationships, including research studies. (25 marks)

See *A2-Level Psychology Online* for tips on now to answer these revision questions.

Social psychological approaches to explaining aggression p. 148
- How did Bandura show that aggression might be due to observation and imitation?
- What is the role of deindividuation in aggression?
- What is institutional aggression?

Biological explanations of aggression p. 170
- Does aggression have a genetic basis?
- What is the role of hormones in aggression?
- How are brain mechanisms linked to aggression?

Aggression as an adaptive response p. 177
- Is aggression adaptive, i.e. necessary for survival?
- Are males and females jealous in different ways?
- What are the benefits of group display?

Aggression

By Evie Bentley

5

This chapter focuses on aspects of **aggression**. Why are some people aggressive? What makes them act aggressively? Why do others not act in the same way? Psychologists have psychological, biological, and **evolutionary explanations** of aggressive behaviour.

What is Aggression?

Is aggression violence against another person? Is it use of weapons? Does it have to contain the desire to harm? Well, according to Baron and Richardson (1993) it is behaviour with the intent to harm a person, or maybe even an object. After all, would you consider smashing up a bus shelter, or throwing a brick through a window to be aggressive, even if nobody was aimed at or harmed?

One way of looking at aggression is to identify different types of aggressive behaviour, for example person-oriented and **instrumental aggression. Person-oriented aggression** has causing harm to another person as the main goal, whereas instrumental aggression's main goal is obtaining some personal reward with aggression as the pathway to that reward.

On the other hand, we can also distinguish between proactive and **reactive aggression. Proactive aggression** is aggressive behaviour initiated by an individual to achieve a desired outcome; reactive aggression is a possible response to someone else's aggression.

Summary

❖ Aggression is behaviour with the intent to harm. It can be subdivided into:

  — person-oriented aggression: the aim is to cause harm to another person
  — instrumental aggression: aggression is the pathway to personal reward.

KEY TERMS

Aggression: behaviour with the intent to harm.
Evolutionary explanations (of aggressive behaviour): based on what would have been successful, or adaptive, for our remote hunter-gatherer ancestors, even if such innate behaviours are not very helpful today.
Instrumental aggression: a way of obtaining some personal reward.
Person-oriented aggression: intent to harm another person.
Reactive aggression: a possible response to someone else's aggression.
Proactive aggression: aggressive behaviour initiated by an individual to achieve a desired outcome.

? Do proactive and reactive aggression fit in with the concepts of person-oriented and instrumental aggression?

❖ or alternatively into:

— proactive aggression: aggressive behaviour initiated to achieve a desired outcome
— reactive aggression: a possible response to someone else's aggression.

The main goal of the aggression involved in mugging somebody is usually to obtain the "reward" (the bag or wallet) rather than to hurt the person. This is an example of instrumental aggression.

■ **Activity:** Examples of aggressive behaviours
Complete the table below.

Type of aggression	Example
Person-oriented	
Instrumental	
Proactive	
Reactive	

SOCIAL PSYCHOLOGICAL APPROACHES TO EXPLAINING AGGRESSION

These theories explain aggressive behaviour in terms of social influences and personal psychological factors.

Social Learning Theory

Social Learning Theory states that we learn behaviours, including aggression, by imitating successful role models. Thus, although it is possible to learn aggressive behaviour by classical or operant conditioning (Traditional Learning Theory) Social Leaning Theory suggests that observational learning can also take place, and that this is reinforced vicariously. Vicarious learning or reinforcement occurs when one sees another person—the model—rewarded for certain actions. This observation makes it more likely that one will imitate the model's action, perhaps not immediately but at an appropriate time in the future. This implicates cognitive processes, because the behaviour model has been stored for future use, a feature that is a key departure from Classical Learning Theory, which rejects any involvement of cognition in learning. Bandura (1965) promoted this explanation of aggressive behaviour, based on his experiments with nursery school children.

When aggression is imitated

Social Learning Theory states that individuals are more likely to imitate observed behaviour if:

- The model is similar to themselves, such as being the same sex or similar in age or personal style.
- The model is perceived as having desirable or aspirational characteristics, or is admired, as in the case of a media personality or celebrity, or a charismatic teacher.
- The individual has low self-esteem.

- The individual is highly dependent on others.
- Reinforcement is direct: children in particular respond most strongly to direct reward, next to seeing a model in action, and least to a recording of a model, especially a cartoon character (Bandura et al., 1963).

Punishment can also produce vicarious learning, leading to a reduced response, i.e. learning not to do an action. For example, a small child seeing another being told off for biting someone is less likely to imitate that biting behaviour. In addition, social modelling might reduce the likelihood of a response because a different response has been strengthened.

Research findings

This was demonstrated by Walters and Thomas (1963) when they recruited participants for a study on the effects of punishment on learning. The participants worked in pairs, one being the "learner" (actually a confederate of the experimenters) and one—the "true" participant—being the teacher. The teacher not only had to give the learner an electric shock following each error, but could also choose the level of shock given for the next trial. The two conditions of this experiment were the type of film seen by the "teachers" prior to the actual experiment. Participants who had watched a violent scene then went on to select higher shock levels than those who had watched a non-violent scene.

This is an example of **disinhibition**, or the weakening of inhibitions, caused in this case by what had been observed. Watching socially unacceptable behaviour in the film had weakened the normal, previously learned pro-social behaviours so the tendency to behave pro-socially was disinhibited or unlearned as a result of modelling. This is the basis of much of the criticism of aggressive and other anti-social behaviours shown in the media.

The original Bandura experiments used nursery-school children who watched an adult attacking a toy, a Bobo doll. The children were then allowed to play with the doll and Bandura found that the quality of their play tended to vary, depending on whether they had seen the adult rewarded for being aggressive, the adult being scolded (i.e. punished), or a "neutral" reaction to the aggression, i.e. no response. The children who saw the adult model rewarded were more likely to have experienced vicarious reinforcement and they were found to play more aggressively. The other two groups of children also imitated the aggression in some scenarios. Bandura (1999) pointed out that observational or social learning is the way that children learn what is, and is not, appropriate in their own social and cultural context, which explains why some cultures or sub-cultures are more aggressive than others.

More research findings
The development of aggression

The first and probably the most powerful social models for a child are her or his parents. Patterson, DeBaryshe, and Ramsey. (1989) looked at factors in a child's home environment that could relate to the

? Can you think of examples of cultures or sub-cultures in which aggression is more the social norm than in your own group? To what extent do you think that social learning explains this difference?

? Can you think of an occasion when your behaviour has been disinhibited?

> **KEY TERM**
>
> **Disinhibition:** the weakening of inhibitions caused, for example, by what has been observed.

Children watched adults behaving aggressively with a "Bobo" doll. Afterwards they were filmed imitating this behaviour.

? How else could these findings be explained?

? How important do you think observational learning is with respect to producing aggressive behaviour?

The social learning of aggression

Bandura, Ross, and Ross (1961), and Bandura (1965) carried out classic studies on observational learning, or modelling, demonstrating that aggression can be learned via social interactions (i.e. social learning). Young children watched as an adult behaved aggressively towards a Bobo doll. The children who had watched the adult model behaving aggressively were more violent (and imitated exactly some of the behaviours they had observed) than the children who had either seen no model or watched an adult model behaving in a non-aggressive manner.

Children who had seen the model rewarded, and those who had seen the model neither rewarded nor punished, behaved much more aggressively towards the Bobo doll than did those who had seen the model punished. It seems that all the children showed comparable levels of observational learning, but those who had seen the model punished were least likely to *apply* this learning to their own behaviour.

Evaluation

Bandura consistently failed to distinguish between real aggression and play-fighting, and it is likely that much of the aggressive behaviour observed by Bandura was only play-fighting (Durkin, 1995). The Bobo doll's novelty value is important in determining its effectiveness. Cumberbatch (1990) reported that children who were unfamiliar with the doll were five times more likely to imitate aggressive behaviour against it than were children who had played with it before.

Finally, there is the problem of demand characteristics. These are the cues used by participants to work out what a study is about or to guess what it is they should be doing. The demand characteristics lead participants to search for cues that might help them, and they use these cues to direct their behaviour. As Durkin (1995, p. 406) pointed out:

Where else in life does a 5-year-old find a powerful adult actually showing you how to knock hell out of a dummy and then giving you the opportunity to try it out yourself?

The Bobo doll experiment provided cues that "invited" the participants to behave in certain predictable ways.

development of aggression. They compared families with at least one highly aggressive child with other families of the same size and socio-economic status who had no problem children. The comparisons involved home observations, questionnaires, and interviews with children, parents, peers, and teachers. The key features found were termed a "coercive home environment" where little affection was shown and where family members were constantly struggling with each other and using aggressive tactics to cope. Parental behavioural control rarely involved social reinforcement or approval and instead use of physical punishment, nagging, shouting, and teasing were common. Children in such families were typically manipulative and difficult to discipline.

Patterson et al. (1989) suggested that a coercive home environment could create aggressiveness in three main ways:

1. Harsh discipline and lack of supervision disrupts bonding between parent and child and a lack of identification.
2. Parental behaviours provoked aggression in the children.
3. Children learned aggressive behaviour as a means of resolving disputes through modelling and through observational learning (Social Learning Theory).

These and similar findings have led to practical applications, such as teaching parents alternative parenting behaviours and skills, and giving children social skills training.

Video games and aggression

There have been decades of argument as to whether or not media exposure to anti-social behaviour such as aggression actually increases the chances of individuals actually behaving aggressively. According to Social Learning Theory, it would do so if the observers deemed the aggressive behaviours to be successful. This view is supported by a series of studies on American college students (Anderson & Dill, 2000), each study involving over 200 participants. In the first study, students were tested for trait aggressiveness and asked about their personal delinquent behaviours in the recent past, as well as their video-gaming habits. Those who reported playing more violent video games when school age, also admitted engaging in more aggressive real-life behaviour. The second study used independent measures, with one student group playing "Wolfenstein 3D", a violent video game, and the other group playing the non-violent "Myst". Shortly after the game playing, both groups had the opportunity to punish an opponent with a blast of noise. The Wolfenstein group used longer periods of noise blast than did the Myst group, suggesting that the video games did have an effect on their actual behaviour. Anderson and Dill (2000) suggest that the violent game primes the player's aggressive thoughts, and that there could be longer-term effects as the game playing could give practice in constructing and running aggressive scripts, which could transfer to real-life behaviour. The active nature of such game playing makes the learning effects far more powerful than passive TV or film watching.

Evidence suggests that playing violent video games can potentially lead to more aggressive behaviour in real life.

Weber, Ritterfeld, and Mathiak (2006) used functional magnetic resonance imaging (fMRI) scanning on a small sample of male participants as they were playing a latest-generation violent video game. Each participant's game playing was recorded and content analysed on a frame-by-frame basis matched to his brain-scan data. Previous studies suggested that virtual violence would suppress emotional areas of the cortex subsequent to cognitive activity whilst game playing. This study confirmed the suggestion. Further confirmation came from a repeated measures experiment comparing brain activity in participants playing games with and without virtual violence.

> **fMRI scanning**
>
> Functional magnetic resonance imaging (fMRI) is a technique that shows the level of activity in the different areas of the brain. This means that we can see where and how brain activity varies depending on what tasks the person is doing, so it gives a very valuable insight into brain functioning. The technique actually measures the rate of oxygen use in neurons, and as active neurons use more energy and therefore oxygen than inactive neurons the level of activity of different brain structures or areas is shown.

There is more about video games and aggression in Chapter 14 on media psychology.

Evaluation

Playing video games in a laboratory setting has clear low ecological validity in that the circumstances and environment are abnormal, so it is doubtful that it reflects normal behaviour. In addition, there is the issue of **demand characteristics**, as the playing of the violent/non-violent games could well have suggested the type of play behaviour that was expected. However, video games are attractive, multisensory, and exciting, and a hot topic of conversation among players, so the behaviour shown in these games could be seen as successful and therefore modelled on real life.

> **KEY TERM**
>
> **Demand characteristics:** cues from the experimental environment used by participants to work out what is expected of them and how they should behave in that situation.

There is also the problem of **self-reporting**, as there is no telling how truthful people are being or how accurate their memories are, let alone the natural desires either to impress the experimenter with how cool or edgy the individual is, or alternatively how socially desirable.

A methodological issue is that with any correlation one cannot infer causation. Perhaps the greater time spent on violent video games caused the more aggressive everyday behaviours. Or perhaps people who are naturally more aggressive in their personal behaviours choose to play more violent video games. It is a "which came first, the chicken or the egg?" puzzle. There is also the important matter of ethics. If a researcher suspects that watching violent films or playing violent games increases an individual's own level of aggression, is it ethically acceptable to do this sort of research?

However, the empirical nature of the Weber et al. (2006) research does start to establish causal associations between playing violent video games and real-life aggression. If the cognitive activity of the game playing actually damps down emotional activity and emotional responses, then this could explain both the disinhibition and the **desensitisation** effects of such games on everyday behaviour, although the sample sizes of just 13 and 11 people and the male-only sample are biases that reduce external validity.

Cross-cultural findings

Margaret Mead's classic (1935) research comparing three New Guinea tribes living fairly close to each other showed major cultural differences in behaviours. The Mundugumor were highly aggressive and had a history of killing outsiders for cannibalism. Men and women of the Arapesh were non-aggressive and co-operative in their interactions with each other and their children and would hide rather than fight. The Tchambuli had artistic, creative men and aggressive women. Could these differences be down to social learning? This is possible, but it is also possible that Mead exaggerated the extent of the differences between the sexes as even the Tchambuli males did most of the fighting in times of war. In fact, in each tribe the males were relatively more aggressive than the females, which could suggest that some aspects of aggression are biologically rather than socially determined; however, the differences in aggressive behaviour between societies do support the role of social learning in aggression. This questioning of Mead's work does not reduce the importance of her contribution to behavioural studies, as in her time it was rare for non-Western, non-industrialised societies to be studied. Even two decades later, Marshall Thomas (1958) described the !Kung culture as non-aggressive whereas later studies (Keeley, 1996) showed that the murder rate, a measure of extreme aggression, was higher in the !Kung than in most Western societies—being non-industrialised might mean few possession to fight over, but powerful conflicts over food resources, territory, mating, and status will still occur.

Empirical cross-cultural studies can also show unexpected results. Despite their stereotype of being hot-blooded Latinos, Spanish men are less likely to use physical aggression than men in the USA, and Japanese men, stereotyped as conformist and conservative, are more likely to be verbally confrontational and aggressive than men in the USA (Andreu, Fujihara, Takaya, & Ramirez, 1998). Bonta (1997) discussed 25 societies where there is virtually no violent aggression. For example, the mountain-dwelling Chewong people of the Malay Peninsula do not have any words for concepts such as fighting, aggression, or war. Bonta found beliefs and norms

---

? What do you think about this? If such research were to go ahead nowadays, what safeguards would you want to put in place?

? Does cross-cultural evidence suggest that aggression is learned, or not?

KEY TERMS

Self-reporting: the technique where participants report on themselves, such as answering questionnaires or interview questions.
Desensitisation: occurs when an individual's experiences happen repeatedly and so lose their impact on that individual.

were the key factors in 23 of the 25 peaceful societies. These believed strongly in co-operation being advantageous and competition being disadvantageous. This shows the importance of cultural expectations (known as social norms). For example, many Western social norms encourage people to be competitive and go-getting, and this could lead to the high levels of aggression in those societies.

Changes in dominant behaviour or in social status cause changes in testosterone levels. Reports of changes in testosterone of young men during athletic events, which involve face-to-face competition with a winner and a loser, reveal that testosterone rises shortly before their matches, as if in anticipation of the competition. Also, 1 to 2 hours after the competitive match, the testosterone levels of the winners are high relative to those levels of the losers (Anitei, 2006).

Evaluation

As stated above, it is possible that Mead unconsciously exaggerated cultural differences between the tribes. Further doubts on the validity of her findings come from knowing that each tribe had its own language, and Mead did not have the time to learn the different languages. Furthermore, she was with each tribe for only a few days, and might have seen a biased sample of their everyday behaviours. Finally, it is well known that when people know they are being observed they change their normal behaviours; perhaps an observer's known presence can act as a kind of demand characteristic. However, if there were real differences in aggressive behaviour between these tribes, who were quite closely related geographically, then social learning is a likely explanation of these differences in behaviour, although it would be sensible to assume that socially approved behaviours would also be reinforced by operant conditioning.

The lesser aggression shown by Spanish males compared with American males could be explained in terms of social norms, what is considered acceptable by their own cultures, or it could be that the aggressive impulses are channelled into non-contact behaviour, such as raising voices or making non-threatening gestures. This explanation could be supported by the Japanese data, as verbal confrontations and aggression could be culturally acceptable, or could express and release aggressive impulses. If the latter is true then it could even be argued that such displays are evolutionarily **adaptive**—they convey an individual's **frustration** or anger without the risk of possible damage from physical contact.

It is also debatable whether social learning on its own can explain the changes in the types of aggression. For example, comparing offences in the UK between 1998 and 2007, there were increases of 14% in murder and manslaughter, 28% in deaths from guns and weapons with blades, and 57% in deaths from punching or kicking. However, there were decreases of 24% in deaths from strangulation, 22% in deaths from poisoning, and 24% in deaths from blunt instruments, with women being far less likely to be victims than men (187 female and 547 male murder victims in 2007). This last finding could be a reflection or result of socialisation and social norms, as in our culture female aggressive behaviour has been much more disapproved of than male, or the result of the differences in testosterone, as discussed in biological explanations of aggression.

Deindividuation

Why and how do good family people change when they are in uniform, to become bullies and tyrants? Why is it that some kindly, sociable community members commit aggressive offences against powerless others? **Deindividuation** could be the answer. The term refers to the loss of personal identity and consequently personal responsibility when we are, for example, one of a crowd or wearing a mask. Diener (1980) details deindividuation as four effects of decreased self-awareness, namely:

- poor self-monitoring of behaviour
- reduced need for social approval
- reduced inhibitions against behaving impulsively
- reduced rational thinking.

So one explanation for aggressive behaviour, e.g. in a mob, is that the loss of identity when part of a crowd means that individuals feel less constrained by the norms of social behaviour, and able to behave in an anti-social way. People feel part of the crowd, not individual, and perhaps not identifiable.

Individuals in a crowd experience a sense of deindividuation and this might explain why riots may break out. However, this is not true of all "mobs", such as at a rock concert.

Some prisoners with one of the guards in Zimbardo's (1973) Stanford University Prison Experiment.

Research findings

Zimbardo (1973) explained his classic Stanford prison study findings in terms of deindividuation as a result of the social situation. The students playing the part of prison guards were in uniform. They also wore mirror sunglasses and their personal identity was partly hidden. All these young men had been pre-tested for psychological stability and were decent members of the community, but most of them acted very unpleasantly, aggressively in fact, when in the role of guard.

In a further study Zimbardo used female students to give electric shocks (which were, unknown to the participants, all fake) to other female students who were actually confederates. Some of the participants wore their own clothes and ID labels; others wore enveloping white costumes and hoods, which effectively cloaked them. The latter gave much higher levels of "shocks" than the former, which could have been because their identities were hidden by their costumes, so they were deindividuated and able to feel they could act more aggressively.

Zimbardo suggested that the aggression and brutality of the guards was because they were in uniform with mirror shades and so were deindividuated. Another factor that might also have had an effect was whether the guards were role playing, based on stereotypes of prison guards and expectations of behaviours in prisons.

Evaluation

It is possible that Zimbardo's prison guards were deindividuated, but the students acting as prisoners were also in uniform smocks and had their hair squashed down with nylon stocking caps, so they too should have been deindividuated. Furthermore, the prisoners were referred to by number not name, and yet they did not act aggressively but became obedient and apathetic, some becoming temporarily

Stanford University prison simulation experiment

In the 1960s, there were numerous reports of problems in American prisons. Many of these reports referred to brutal attacks by prison guards on the prisoners in their care. Why did this brutality occur? One possibility is that those who put themselves in a position of power by becoming prison guards have aggressive or sadistic personalities. A different possibility is that the behaviour of prison guards is due mainly to the social environment of prisons, including the rigid power structure that is found in them. These can be regarded as dispositional and situational explanations, respectively.

Philip Zimbardo (1973) studied this key issue in what is generally know as "the Stanford Prison Experiment" (SPE), because it was conducted in the basement of the psychology department at Stanford University. Emotionally stable individuals agreed to act as "guards" and "prisoners" in a mock prison. Zimbardo wanted to see whether the hostility found in many real prisons would also be found in his mock prison. If hostility were found despite not using sadistic guards, this would suggest it is the power structure that creates hostility.

What happened? The events in the prison were so unpleasant and dangerous that the entire experiment had to be stopped after 6 days instead of the intended 14 days! Violence and rebellion broke out within 2 days of the start. The prisoners ripped off their clothing and shouted and cursed at the guards. In return, the guards violently put down this rebellion by using fire extinguishers. They also played-off the prisoners against each other and harassed them almost continuously. One prisoner showed such severe symptoms of emotional disturbance (disorganised thinking, uncontrollable crying, and screaming) that he had to be released after only 1 day. On the fourth day, two more prisoners showed symptoms of severe disturbance and were released.

Changes were observed over time. The prisoners became more subdued and submissive, often slouching and keeping their eyes fixed on the ground. At the same time, the use of force, harassment, and aggression by the guards increased steadily day by day, and were clearly excessive reactions to the submissive behaviour of the prisoners. For example, the prisoners were sleep deprived, put in solitary confinement, and had to clean the toilets with their bare hands.

? Can you think of any other factors that might have encouraged these emotionally stable young men to act so aggressively?

Obedience to authority

In AS Psychology you will have learned how Milgram aimed to investigate how willing participants were to obey authority when asked to inflict pain on another person.

Forty male volunteers (a self-selected sample) took part in a controlled observational study, which they were deceived into thinking was a test of learning. The participants understood that the highest levels of shock might be fatal, especially to a man with a heart condition. The participants didn't know until the end of the experiment that no shocks were actually administered.

All participants gave shocks up to the 300-volt level, and 65% of participants continued to the highest level, 450 volts. This completely contradicted the predicted results that 3% or less would reach 450 volts. There were marked effects on the naive participants' behaviour, with most showing signs of extreme tension. For example, they trembled, sweated, stuttered, groaned, dug their fingernails into their flesh, and three had uncontrollable seizures.

The research showed that obedience to authority is due more to situational factors (the experimental setting, the status of the experimenter, and the pressure exerted on the participant to continue) than to "deviant" personality. Implications include the relevance of this research to the real-life atrocities, for example in wartime.

One can argue that the participants who took the role of the teacher acted aggressively towards the learners, but is

Photographs of Milgram's classic experiment where 65% of the participants gave a potentially lethal shock to the "learner".

this a fair comment? Ask yourself whether you think their actions were aggressive or not, and justify your judgement.

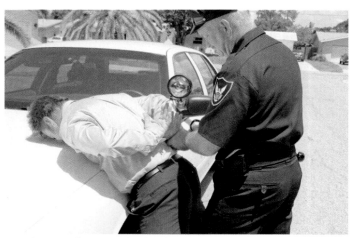

Wearing a uniform may lead individuals to conform to an expected role, as they did in Zimbardo's prison study.

It has been suggested that there is a similarity between the clothes of Zimbardo's deindividuated participants and the uniform of the Ku Klux Klan.

? There can be differences in aggressive behaviours in different sports crowds. How would you explain this?

psychologically disturbed. So the mere fact of being in uniform did not lead to aggression in all participants. It seems likely that the uniforms acted as demand characteristics, and the participants conformed to the role their uniform suggested. And it is true that some uniforms make their wearers more, not less, identifiable. Unless in a crowd of classmates, being in school uniform can help to make students more, not less, identifiable. Another relevant factor here is that in the preparation for the study Zimbardo himself, who had the role of prison supervisor, told the guards to treat the prisoners in ways to render them powerless, so the guards could well have been interpreting these instructions as directives to be aggressive.

Zimbardo's study using female students could also have a different explanation. You might have heard of the white American terrorist organisation the Ku Klux Klan (KKK). Members wear long white robes and conical hoods, and it has been suggested that the white costumes of some of the participants acted as a demand characteristic, and that the wearers (consciously or unconsciously) conformed to the role of being a member of an aggressive group. In fact, when that experiment was re-run with some girls dressed as nurses, these girls gave even lower "shocks" than those in their own clothes and ID, which supports the demand characteristic, stereotype, and role-playing explanation. This concept of conformity to a stereotypic role could also apply to the Zimbardo guards; however, it does not explain the higher levels of aggression shown in over 200 attacks in Northern Ireland where the real-life offenders were wearing disguises. These offenders had an aggressive primary purpose and so the anonymity of the disguise would be some protection from identification; this too could have led them to be more confident in not being caught, which might have increased the degree of aggression shown (Silke, 2003).

It is also very true that there are many types of crowd with different behaviours, even if the individuals in each case are much less personally identifiable. The crowds attending services led by the Pope in the USA in 2008 were not aggressive; crowds battling to get the best bargains in a sale might be aggressive; sports crowds and music concert crowds may or may not involve aggressive behaviours, depending on the actual situation.

Frustration–Aggression Hypothesis

Within any age group, from small children to older adults, aggressive behaviour can result from being in frustrating situations. In their Frustration–Aggression Hypothesis, Dollard, Doob, Miller, Mowrer, and Sears (1939) suggested that frustration links closely with aggression. According to them:

> *The occurrence of aggression presupposes frustration ... Frustration produces instigations to a number of different types of responses, one of which is an instigation to some form of aggression.*

It is worth noting that they were not suggesting that frustration always leads to aggressive behaviour, but that sometimes it might do just that.

Research findings

Doob and Sears (1939) asked participants to imagine 16 frustrating and non-frustrating scenarios. These included waiting for a bus, which then went straight past without stopping. Most participants reported feeling angry in each of the frustrating situations but this does not mean they would have acted aggressively.

Evaluation

A main criticism of this hypothesis is that it did not distinguish between frustration which is justified and that which is not. Pastore (1952) argued that it is mainly unjustified frustration that leads to anger and aggressive behaviour, and that the original experiment contained mainly examples of unjustified frustration. When he re-ran Doobs and Sears' experiment with justified frustration, such as the non-stopping bus being "out of service", the reported levels of anger were much reduced compared to the original experiment. However, there is a great difference between being asked to imagine a scenario and actually being involved in a real-life scene. We cannot be sure that people would behave in the same way in both circumstances, and so the Doob and Sears and similar studies have low mundane realism as well as low ecological or external validity.

Furthermore, in Zimbardo's prison experiment the prisoner-participants did less and less to frustrate the guard-participants, becoming increasingly more accepting and apathetic, and yet the levels of aggressive behaviour from the guards increased rapidly.

Berkowitz and LePage (1967) expanded the Frustration–Aggression Hypothesis to include the effect of aggressive cues as demand characteristics. For example, they found that if participants were giving each other electric shocks, the presence on the side of a weapon such as a gun acted to increase the average number of shocks given from 4.67 to 6.07; this increase is known as the "weapons effect". It means that the gun was acting as a demand characteristic, a cue suggesting what behaviour suited the situation. Of course, it is possible that some participants became suspicious and interpreted the weapon's presence as a suggestion that the researchers wished them to act more aggressively, but as these participants tended not to give more shocks than non-suspicious participants, it seems this effect did not happen. However, the participants who became suspicious in this way might also have had a tendency to be contrary!

Berkowitz (1989) went on to reformulate the theory as the cognitive–neoassociationist approach. He argued that the behaviour an individual displays depends on his or her interpretation of the situation. An unpleasant event causes **negative affect** or emotion (e.g. anxiety, anger) and this in turn activates tendencies towards aggression and flight. So if a person barges into you, you might feel aggrieved or angry, and want to barge them back, but if you then see that the person is blind, you are more likely to feel guilty for that negative affect and not want to be aggressive. This means that aggression is only one way of responding to frustration, which seems to fit available evidence quite well.

Social Constructionism

Most of the theories of aggression are based on the assumption that it is fairly easy to decide whether someone is behaving aggressively. However, social constructionists such as Gergen (1997) argue that we impose subjective

Berkowitz (1968) believed that the presence of guns could stimulate aggressive behaviour.

? What types of situation do you find frustrating?

? In what other ways do people respond to frustration?

KEY TERM

Negative affect: a negative mood or emotion, such as anxiety and depression.

To one team this looks like a foul; to the other, a justifiable defensive manoeuvre.

interpretations or constructions on the world around us. For example, tackles that seem like cynical fouls deserving a sending-off to the supporters of one team are regarded as perfectly fair by the supporters of the other team.

The social constructionist approach as applied to aggression is based on a number of assumptions:

- Aggressive behaviour is a form of social behaviour, and it is not simply an expression of anger.
- Our interpretation or construction of someone else's behaviour as aggressive or non-aggressive depends on our beliefs and knowledge.
- Our decision whether to behave aggressively or non-aggressively depends on how we interpret the other person's behaviour towards us.

Research evidence

The first assumption is supported by numerous cases in which an individual behaves aggressively towards someone else some time after being angered by that person. For example, in the days (thankfully past!) when teachers used to cane their students, the caning would often take place days after the student had behaved badly.

The second assumption is supported by the work of Blumenthal, Kahn, Andrews, and Head (1972), who studied the attitudes of American men towards police and student behaviour during student demonstrations. Students with negative attitudes towards the police judged the behaviour of the police to be violent, whereas the sit-ins and other actions of the students were regarded as non-violent. By contrast, men with positive attitudes to the police didn't regard their assaults on students or their use of firearms as violent. However, they condemned student sit-ins as violent acts deserving arrest. These findings suggest that our judgement that someone is behaving aggressively depends on the constructions we place on their behaviour.

How do we decide whether someone is behaving aggressively? According to the norm of reciprocity, if someone has done something to you, you are justified in behaving in the same way to that person. Evidence that the norm of reciprocity applies to aggressive behaviour was reported by Brown and Tedeschi (1976). Someone who *initiated* a hostile act against another person was seen as aggressive and unfair. By contrast, someone who attacked another person after having been provoked was regarded as behaving non-aggressively.

The third assumption of the constructionist approach was supported by Marsh, Rosser, and Harré (1978), who studied violent attacks by students in schools, and found that these attacks were neither random nor spontaneous. The attacks generally occurred in classes with less effective teachers, because the students interpreted this as a sign that the school authorities had written them off. This interpretation (although mistaken) produced anger and aggression.

Evaluation

The constructionist notion that our interpretation or construction of situations and people's behaviour determines our responses is valuable. Such interpretations

? Can you think of any recent news items that could be interpreted in different ways according to which side a person supported?

? Are there situations where the norm of reciprocity does not apply?

EXAM HINT
If you are using social constructionism as an explanation of aggression you should be able to evaluate its strengths, but also consider that it does exaggerate the differences between different individuals' constructions of what has happened.

or constructions depend on our attitudes and beliefs. Thus, we must distinguish between what *actually* happens in social situations and our interpretations.

On the negative side, social constructionists exaggerate the differences between different individuals' constructions of what has happened. There are many cases in which nearly everyone would agree that someone is behaving aggressively, for example if a defenceless old woman is suddenly attacked by a mugger and her handbag is stolen.

General Aggression Model

The research described above shows that there are several possible contributory causes for people behaving aggressively, and these have been incorporated into a General Aggression Model (Anderson, Anderson, & Deuser, 1996; Anderson & Bushman, 2002). They suggest that behaving aggressively is the outcome of a stage process.

The stages in aggression

Stage	Details
1	The individual's key factors are individual differences and situational variables, e.g. having a personality associated with several negative emotions correlated positively with aggressive/anti-social behaviour
2	What happens in Stage 2 depends on Stage 1, but could be changes in mood (e.g. hostile feelings), in brain and physiological arousal (e.g. the activation of the autonomic nervous system), and in cognition (e.g. experiencing hostile thoughts)
3	What occurred in Stage 2 then leads to appraisal processes, such as interpretation of the situation, forming possible coping strategies, and considering the possible consequences of behaving aggressively
4	As a result of Stage 3, the individual decides whether or not to behave aggressively

Evaluation

Support for this model comes from Bartholomew, Bushman, and Sestir (2006), who used weapons (hunting and assault guns) to show that these affected aggressive behaviours. The guns were clearly situational factors, which were then appraised according to individuals' personal experience. Further support is given by Anderson and Bushman's (2001) meta-analysis, which found that exposure to violent video games increased aggressive cognitions, as predicted by the model. Interestingly, the overall effect on aggressive behaviour was moderate, and of similar magnitude in males and females, children and adults.

This model has a wider scope than previous theories of aggression, making it more inclusive with greater mundane realism. There is little doubt of the influence of situational and personality factors and appraisal on determining whether or not an individual will behave aggressively, and there is some evidence supporting anti-social or aggressive personality traits, including sensation-seeking (Joireman, Anderson, & Strathman, 2003). However, negative moods and thinking, and the state of arousal, have complex and mostly unpredictable effects on behaviour. Also, the self-report nature of questionnaires used in this research does not give empirical data, so such data need to be interpreted with caution. Furthermore, these data are based on participants' conscious appraisal but it is likely that there is a lack of conscious awareness about decision-making processes. Taking this into account, it can still be said that the General Aggression Model provides a useful general framework in which to consider explanations of aggressive behaviour.

Institutional Aggression

There is no doubt that **institutionalised aggression** exists. The first question is whether this is a feature of the institution, the situation, or the environment, or whether institutions attract aggressive people. The second question is why—why might aggressive individuals be drawn to institutions or why might the institutional situation promote aggression?

The traditional view has usually been that bad things are done by bad people or, as an analogy has it, one bad apple can infect a barrel of good apples. This is known as the dispositional hypothesis, where the fault or cause lies in the person's disposition or personality. However, this view is challenged in more than one way by a wealth of psychological findings, most famously perhaps the classical research of Milgram in his obedience studies (1963, 1974), and Zimbardo in his Stanford University Prison Experiment (1973).

You will recall the Milgram study from AS, and for our purposes here we need to focus in on the fact that decent American adult males were willing to commit aggressive acts—to harm another person by giving him electric shocks of up to 450 volts. This would be lethal, and yet Milgram found that all the participants gave shocks of at least 300 volts, and that 65% gave the full 450 volts. Why did they do this? You may remember that in this experiment many of the participants turned more than once to the man they thought was the experimenter and asked if the learner, the man they thought was receiving the shocks, was "OK". Some asked if they should go and check on him, some refused to continue unless they knew he was OK. But, after protesting, the majority continued with the shocks. They had been told that the experimenter took responsibility for what they were doing, and that seemed to tip the balance to accepting the task. In Milgram's own words, "it does not take an evil man to do an evil deed" and he theorised that his participants were in the **agentic state**; a state in which they were obeying instructions and, as the responsibility was with the instructor, they were acting only as his agents. This also means that, in the agentic state, they were not responsible, or at any rate they did not see themselves as responsible. Responsibility lay with the person who issued the orders or instructions. This is psychologically interesting, as this certainly is not accepted in law, for instance those military people accused of crimes against humanity in the Vietnam conflict in the 1960s and 1970s, and in the prison atrocities committed by the American and British military in the early years of the twenty-first century.

It seems to suggest that people will do bad things, aggressive actions, if they believe (or want to believe) that these have been sanctioned or approved by those in authority above them. They are then acting in the agentic state and are not responsible for their actions. So—according to this explanation—individuals who do bad things, aggressive things, would not necessarily have an aggressive disposition but could just be in the agentic state.

> ### KEY TERMS
> **Institutionalised aggression:** occurs where aggressive behaviour has become the norm in an institution, whether a prison or in the military or elsewhere.
> **Agentic state:** the state of mind in which individuals believe they are acting for someone else, they are the other person's agent, and so they do not have personal responsibility for the actions, i.e. they are following instructions or orders.

Evaluation

Interestingly, both these views hold that individuals who are aggressive might not be bad people, and so they are rejecting the automatic application of the dispositional hypothesis.

Comments about Milgram's study are well known. He used male participants originally, which meant that his findings could not be generalised to the female half of the population, but later replications with females as participants did produce similar findings to the original experiment. The procedure was, however, well standardised and the level of obedience in making the aggressive action was clear (i.e. the maximum level of voltage given by each participant). However, the procedure lacked both mundane realism—giving a potentially lethal electric shock to another person is hardly an everyday behaviour—and ecological or external validity—the laboratory setting was an abnormal environment for the participants and so they might well not have behaved in their normal way. It is also true that culture has an important effect on behaviour, and a sample of American males may behave differently from a sample from another culture. In actual fact, when the procedure has been replicated in other cultures there has been a wide variation in levels of obedience to do the aggressive shocking both in culture and two decades later. This means that culture has a powerful effect, not just the hierarchical nature of the culture but also the social norms for blind obedience to an instruction to behave aggressively.

However, as Eysenck (2009) and others have pointed out, it is doubtful if one can assume that Milgram's participants were in fact in the agentic state. Many of them exhibited strong signs of agitation and extreme stress, such as wringing of hands, sweating, looking tense and anxious, all of which suggest they were experiencing conflict between the experimenter's instructions and their own consciences. This does not marry with being in the agentic state.

Zimbardo has a different view, a different explanation. He feels that situational factors have a great effect on what individuals do and don't do. He calls this the power of the situation. For example, he rejects the view of American military leaders that the perpetrators of the abuses in the Abu Graib prison in Iraq were "rogue soldiers" or "a few bad apples". He suggests that circumstances in the prison and cell block were such as to affect the soldiers' behaviours and affect the abusive behaviours. His classic Stanford Prison Experiment study is outlined earlier (see p. 155) and the evaluation also applies here. The aggressive guards and cloaked girls were acting in response to cues. Some of the cues might have been to do with their uniforms or hidden identities, others might have been films or other media portraying prison or KKK behaviour. These situational factors, Zimbardo suggests, are key to producing the aggressive behaviour. In support of his situational view he organised a study in which a car was abandoned in each of two neighbourhoods. One location was a university campus in the Bronx, a busy and somewhat disadvantaged area, and the other was in a campus in up-market Palo Alto, a Stanford University site. The car in the Bronx was stripped and destroyed in a matter of days by well-dressed, white adults. The car in Palo Alto was untouched even after a full week. What was the key difference between these two locations, apart from them being about 3000 miles apart? Zimbardo suggests that in the Bronx people felt anonymous, that they were not known, and that no-one would care; the Palo Alto people were a community, they looked out for each other even when a car appeared to be

> **EXAM HINT**
> Institutional aggression involves ordinary people within institutions using the situation as a reason to be aggressive. This is a very different approach from the personality theory of aggression, which explains aggression in terms of people having aggressive tendencies. It is therefore a very good evaluation point to contrast the two theories and to use one to evaluate the other.

abandoned. So this is a case of deindividuation versus identification, depending on the precise location or situation.

Despite the two different psychological explanations—agentic state or situational factors—for aggressive behaviours in groups or institutions the outcome is the same; dispositional factors are not the cause of institutional aggression. It is not that such institutions attract bad people, or that naturally aggressive people are drawn to these institutions, so there must be another cause of the aggressive behaviours seen in such environments.

Institutional factors
Socio-cognitive Theory and Social Identity Theory

Tajfel (1969) formulated a Socio-cognitive Theory of prejudice to explain the extreme intergroup prejudice and aggressive behaviour before and during the Second World War. He used Allport's (1954) ideas on stereotyping to suggest that people categorise information, e.g. about other people, into sets. Thus, according to Tajfel, we assimilate our social knowledge about each set, e.g. that group is bad or evil or a threat. The information used in such evaluations comes from the social group and is really about preferences rather than facts. Then people have a search for coherence, which is a personal explanation of the situation, and this explanation may also be shared with others. Humans like things to make sense, and this last stage is where the belief about others is justified. If this belief leads to a dispositional attribution that is unfavourable to the other group then a further belief can come into being, that one's own group need not be pro-social towards those others. It is possible that anti-social behaviour such as aggression could become an option at this stage.

Tajfel and Turner (1979) developed the original idea into **Social Identity Theory**, which states that people's membership of a group reflects on their own self-esteem. Not only do they identify with their group, they compare their own group—the **ingroup**—and consider their ingroup to be superior. This may well result in exaggerating any differences found between the groups, plus assumptions that all members of the **outgroup** are the same and less worthy than members of the ingroup; and the intergroup rivalry that usually results may become intense and violent intergroup conflict. This violence could then be regarded by the ingroup as the logical next step to punish the outgroup in some way.

Findings

Tajfel and Jahoda (1966) used games to research the attitudes of British 6- to 7-year-olds and 10-year-olds towards other countries, and found that the children agreed amongst themselves both about factual information and about their own personal preferences for the other countries. This showed that these children had assimilated information from their social groups and their families, and that even at this young age they were evaluating other social groups, other cultures. The Children's Television Workshop worked with universities in Israel and Palestine in the 1990s and found that even preschool children spoke about the other group as bad people who hurt their own group's people. This confirms that intergroup

> **KEY TERMS**
> **Social Identity Theory:** suggests that we label ourselves and others, and categorise into groups, ingroup and outgroups, as this supports personal self-esteem. We also compare these groups, assessing our ingroup as superior and this further boosts self-esteem.
> **Ingroup:** the social group to which an individual belongs, i.e. "us" as opposed to "them".
> **Outgroup:** the group(s) to which an individual does not belong, i.e. "them" as opposed to "us".

prejudice is learned at a very early age and may, in fact, be an innate tendency as it would strengthen group identity and cohesion.

Evaluation

Institutional groups are social groups, including groups such as prison officers or military people, and Social Cognitive Theory and Social Identity Theory could explain the development of aggression in such groups towards prisoners or enemies. Criminals and enemies would be likely to be stereotyped as bad people, potentially a threat, deserving punishment so their imprisonment or harsh treatment is justified as "they deserve it, they asked for it because they are criminals/enemies". This view would be reinforced by ingroup beliefs that the ingroup comprised the good people, the more righteous, who have been harmed directly or indirectly by the actions of the outgroup.

Furthermore, these institutional ingroups might well have had their views further polarised by groupthink. This is where an ingroup seeks for consensus by avoiding critical analysis of discussions, thus avoiding evaluating ideas because this could lead to internal challenges and discomfort. In this way, the group's thinking becomes increasingly more extreme, and possibly more removed from the thinking outside the group, even in those who would be regarded as "on their side". This could have happened with Zimbardo's prison guards, with real-life prison warders, and with military personnel. Interestingly, brain-scanning research (Berns, Chappelow, Zink, Pagnoni, Martin-Skurski, & Richards, 2005) shows that agreeing with your own group, even if you are doubtful, does not activate the areas of the forebrain that deal with conflict or other higher order mental activities, whereas arguing or disagreeing with your own group activates emotional areas, which Zimbardo (2007) interprets as taking on an emotional burden. This certainly suggests, surprisingly perhaps, that complying with one's own group even if one has doubts is less stressful than challenging the group.

This view is challenged by Janis (1972), who suggested eight key points for an institutional group to become extreme, for instance extremely aggressive.

These key points would, of course, lead to changes and increased polarisation of views and behaviours, but it is difficult to see how this could happen often

Janis' (1972) eight key points for a group to become extreme

Key point	Effect
Illusions of being invulnerable	Excessive optimism and risk taking
Unquestioned belief in the group's morality	Members ignore the consequences of their actions
Rationalising or ignoring warnings	Group's assumptions go unchallenged
Stereotyping	Outgroup people are weak, evil, disfigured, impotent, or stupid
Direct pressure for ingroup members to conform	Non-conformity = disloyalty
Self-censorship	Erase ideas that deviate from the apparent group consensus
Illusions of unanimity	Silence = agreement, consensus
Mind guards	Self-appointed ingroup members who block dissenting information from reaching the group

How many social identities do you have?

How many social identities can you think of that apply to yourself? Does your behaviour vary depending on which identity you are in at any one time?

without some complicity from above, i.e. from the people in charge of the group. This means that the control of the group would be involved in a causal way, which leads to the suggestion that the power system in the institution is at fault.

One problem with Social Identity Theory is that each of us has several social identities depending on what group we are with at any one time, or what we are thinking about and how we are thinking about it, in other words, on the current situation.

Dysfunctional Power Systems Theory

The hypothesis here is that there is something to do with the organisation of power in institutional situations that allows people—good people—to become aggressors in a way that is unjustified. This would be related directly to the management and its organisation.

Findings

Zimbardo (2007) describes a fast-food scam, the "strip-search scam", which has happened a number of times in the USA. Basically, a phone call is received by the assistant manager of the outlet, ostensibly from a police officer but actually from the scam perpetrator who has done his homework and so has the necessary local knowledge. The con man speaks authoritatively, accuses a new employee of theft, and insists she is isolated and searched. She is given the option of being strip-searched either there and then or after being taken to "headquarters", and she always chooses the immediate search. This develops into an intimate body search, and all the while the con man insists on being given a detailed and graphic description of exactly what is being done. This is followed by increasingly sexually degrading activities involving a male employee. The process goes on for several hours until it is obvious that the police are never going to arrive. This aggressive scam was eventually stopped when the con man was caught and convicted. The assistant managers—decent people innocently caught up in all this—were usually prosecuted and sacked.

Historical data show that in March 1942 only 20% of Holocaust victims in concentration camps had been put to death but 11 months later that figure had gone up to 80%. Who did these aggressive and murderous acts? In the main they were elderly family men, regarded in their communities as "good people".

Hersh (2004) is one of the journalists who exposed the aggression and abuses at Abu Ghraib jail, acts by American soldiers against Iraqi prisoners. The acts of aggression counted as torture and involved physical and psychological threats, humiliation, and actual harm. The soldiers did not hide their actions, they even recorded them on camera, and yet these soldiers were previously not considered bad people.

So what can psychology say to explain why and how in these and many other instances in institutions seemingly good people do aggressive and terrible acts? Factors identified in these cases are based on structural faults in how the institution is organised, with the group being insulated from the outside world and everyday life, and having a very close cohesion and agreement on their ideology. This means that everyday norms and values might not seem relevant in the particular work environment so that alternative norms and values are accepted. This would have a stronger effect if the work team was a very close one, looking inwards at itself for monitoring and with a shared focus on what they are to achieve and how they will achieve it.

German civilians viewing the dead bodies of Jewish prisoners at the newly liberated Auschwitz concentration camp. Historical data show that the executioners who murdered the prisoners like these at the concentration camps were often elderly family men who were respected in their communities.

Further factors include the situation being a very provocative one with external stressors causing high stress and huge difficulties and moral dilemmas. In such circumstances, where there is no pre-existing schema to activate and where there are emotional factors caused by the stress, people may be willing to accept and adopt behaviours that they would not normally consider appropriate, behaviours they would have said they would reject. This could explain the extraordinary behaviours in the strip-search scam.

Evaluation

It is difficult to see how a person working in a fast-food outlet could be said to be isolated from the everyday world any more than a person working in an office, nor is it easy to see how the victims in the scam were dehumanised. But the provocative situation, the stressful accusation of theft, and the threat of investigation could explain their compliance. Additionally, the sudden and unexpected responsibility for dealing with the supposed police officer and a lack of a procedure or protocol for such a situation plus being an assistant manager, not the actual outlet manager, would be likely to create major stress, difficulty, and dilemmas for that individual. This all seems to be supported by the comments later on of some of the people involved, saying that they would never have believed they would do what they had done, but that without being in that situation one could not predict how one would behave. A final point is that the culture of these fast-food outlets is to respond to what people ask for, to agree, and give them what they demand, and when shocked and stressed perhaps this automatic learned compliance of "how may I help you?" just took over.

What about the executioners of Holocaust victims? They were physically isolated from everyday life by being away from home, in fact they were taken from Germany to Poland so they were also isolated by language. They were also isolated in that they were part of the concentration camps. This could have produced an inward-looking group, and in such isolated circumstances and

---

> **CASE STUDY: WAR CRIMINALS**
>
> After the Second World War, the Allies tried many of the high-ranking Nazi officers at Nuremberg. Adolf Eichmann argued that he had only been obeying orders. He said he was not the "monster" that the newspapers described but simply an ordinary person caught up in an extraordinary situation. Eichmann was described as having no violent anti-Jewish feelings (Arendt, 1963). The argument was that he was an autonomous individual who became agentic when he joined the SS and subscribed to the military code of obedience to those in authority.

abnormal and stressful situations these men could have agreed that their orders to kill were necessary and even justified. Furthermore, dehumanising could well have been a factor in justifying their actions. For some time in their culture the Jews had been portrayed as evil beings who made life worse for others, so one could say this did dehumanise them. Also, in the Holocaust the mass killings would have gained approval as these killings were not hidden from Command but were done following orders, so this seems more an example of the agentic state. This explanation has also been put forward as a defence for soldiers and others involved in the Second World War, in Vietnam (e.g. the My Lai massacre of women and children), and in Serbia, as well as currently in Iraq, although in a court of law this does not seem to be acceptable.

Both Hersh and Zimbardo write that the chain of command in the American Army Prison System was poor, an organisational fault. The new commander of all the prisons in Iraq was female and had no experience at all of running any sort of prison. Her living conditions were so bad that she decided to move from her Abu Ghraib location and left no top-down daily supervision of what went on. She also says she was told that the prison area where the abuses took place was not her responsibility because it was "special". Being female resulted in an increase in sexist attitudes among the soldiers and a breakdown in normal discipline. The commander reports that she was visited by a team from Guantanamo who instructed her that treatment of prisoners had to toughen up as the detainees were "like dogs". This dehumanising of the prisoners would have made it easier for those dealing with them to behave more aggressively. It could also be interpreted by soldiers as justification for aggression and abuse, as this would be seen as softening up prisoners and detainees so they would reveal vital information. Another factor is that it is difficult to believe that no senior officers were aware of what was going on; in fact, some soldiers report that such officers did know, and did nothing to stop the abuses, and this would increase the belief that these actions were appropriate, allowed. Evidence obtained from interviewing lawyers who advised the American Military (Sands, 2008) supports the concept of provocative situations associated with huge stresses and dilemmas, and with the cohesion that comes from being under threat that changes even professional people's cognition of what is and what is not reasonable. So that these lawyers— good people—were able to produce arguments to bypass the Geneva convention and allow torture and extreme aggression.

However, there is evidence from a minority of highly aggressive football supporters that these people are in fact not true football supporters at all. They are those, men and a small minority of women, who have respectable,

CASE STUDY: WAR CRIMES: BUT WHO WERE THE CRIMINALS?

Spring 2004: photos of prisoners being abused in Abu Ghraib were released on a CBS news television programme; shortly afterwards General Richard B. Myers assured the American public that these abuses were not systematic and were the work of a tiny minority of "rogue soldiers".

Spring 2006: more than 400 separate investigations had to be ordered into similar allegations of mistreatment in Iraq, making the above explanation seem somewhat thin.

Summer 2006: Abu Ghraib jail was closed.

Who was responsible for the criminal abuse of prisoners? The commander, who moved to live off site because conditions were so unpleasant, was reprimanded for not doing something about the situation, but not for being aware of the abuse or the serious situation. The two generals, Miller and Sanchez, who described the prisoners as "like dogs" and gave instructions to soldiers to stop being soft on the prisoners and to use tactics to get useful intelligence from them—to get tougher—were also not held responsible for the abuses. One person who was arrested, prosecuted, and found guilty was a Staff Sergeant, Chip Frederick, who had received no training for being a guard at Abu Ghraib and who was also mocked by superiors for recommending that prisoners should be treated properly, for example being allowed to wear clothing. Despite these and many other circumstances showing lack if support for both prisoners and guards, and a strong suspicion that his superiors were aware of, encouraged, and therefore were responsible for the atrocities, Frederick was jailed for 8 years.

professional careers but who are drawn to violence, perhaps as a personality or dispositional trait. They use football events as opportunities to indulge in their acts of violence, and these occasions are meticulously planned. As Jones (2002) said about such people, "hooligans are people we all know and work with". People with such traits might be drawn to careers where the opportunities for indulging in violence and aggression are more likely, such as the armed forces. However, the evidence from sport aggression does not support this because many of those using sport as an opportunity for violence have other professional jobs, e.g. in law and finance, as you will see further on in the box about Football Firms.

Suicide bombers

Sageman (2004) considers many suicide bombers to be the "brightest and best" of their communities, but these are people who perhaps have a stronger than average need to belong to and connect with their community and also to make a special difference, to be specially effective, to reaffirm their social identity. Merari (2006) has outlined the pathway that the terrorist institutions use for such men and women:

- Identification of those who demonstrate intense patriotic/religious fervour.
- Invitations to meet with similar others to discuss their love of their community and hatred of the oppressors.
- Requests for commitment to being trained.
- Membership of a secret group (a cell) with instruction from senior people, the elders.
- Public commitment to their planned role by the making of a video for later distribution to their families.
- Assurances that they will feel no pain when they die.
- Assurances that they will have a special place in the afterlife, and that their relatives will have privileges there too, as well as financial benefits in this life.

There is an emphasis throughout on dehumanising their intended victims, taking the future bombers away from their normal environments, giving them a very tight, distinct, and different group membership.

The step-wise approach is an example of a common sales technique, the so-called foot-in-the-door. It was used in Milgram's obedience study, where each increase in shock level was only 15 volts more than the previous one, too small to seem significant. Here, each stage in the procedure is the logical next step to draw individuals in until they are in deep, too deep to think logically perhaps.

SECTION SUMMARY
Social Psychological Approaches to Explaining Aggression

❖ Social psychological approaches explain aggressive behaviour in terms of social influences and personal psychological factors.

Social Learning Theory

❖ We learn behaviours, including aggression, vicariously by imitating successful role models. This is observational learning, involves cognition, and is more likely to occur if:

— The model is similar to the observer, such as being the same sex or similar in age or personal style.
— The model is perceived as having desirable or aspirational characteristics, or is admired, as in the case of a media personality or celebrity, or a charismatic teacher.
— The observer has low self-esteem.
— The observer is highly dependent on others.
— Reinforcement is direct: children in particular respond most strongly to direct reward, next to seeing a model in action, and least to a recording of a model, especially a cartoon character (Bandura et al., 1963).

❖ Observing another being punished can also result in social learning.
❖ Parents are likely to be the first and most powerful role models.
❖ Patterson et al. (1989): aggression could be the result of a coercive home environment if:

— Harsh discipline and lack of supervision disrupts bonding between parent and child and a lack of identification.
— Parental behaviours provoked aggression in the children.
— Children learned aggressive behaviour through modelling, i.e. through observational learning (Social Learning Theory) as a means of resolving disputes.

❖ Research has focused on possible social learning of anti-social behaviour from violent video games. Disinhibition and desensitisation could contribute to learning anti-social behaviour from such sources. Weber et al. 's (2006) brain-scanning research suggests that virtual violence might suppress normal emotional responses, an observational learning effect.
❖ Mead's (1935) classic cross-cultural research suggested major differences in aggressive behaviour exist between cultures and emphasised the importance of social norms and social learning.
❖ However, the validity of her research has been questioned.
❖ Empirical research such as Bonta (1997) and Andreu et al. (1998) support the cross-cultural differences.

Deindividuation

❖ Deindividuation refers to the loss of personal identity and consequent loss of personal responsibility when an individual feels anonymous, e.g. when in uniform or when in a crowd. This results in:

— poor self-monitoring of behaviour

— reduced need for social approval

— reduced inhibitions against behaving impulsively

— reduced rational thinking.

❖ Zimbardo used the concept of deindividuation to explain his Stanford University Prison experiment.

❖ This explanation has been challenged, e.g. because of the instructions given to the guards and the apathy of the prisoners.

❖ Deindividuation does not explain the variety of crowd behaviours: some being quiet and peaceful, others joyful or full of sorrow, as well as some being aggressive.

❖ Aggression is the outcome of a build-up of frustration (Dollard et al., 1939):

Frustration–Aggression Hypothesis

— early research studies were based on imaginary situations

— later studies distinguished between justified and unjustified frustration.

❖ Berkowitz (1989) adapted the hypothesis as the cognitive–neoassociationist approach incorporating the individual's personal interpretation of the situation, such as whether it is justified or not, plus any demand characteristics.

❖ Aggression is a form of social behaviour where the individual's interpretation of that behaviour depends on his or her own knowledge, attitudes, and beliefs, and the response to that behaviour is dependent on that interpretation.

Social constructionism

❖ So describing a behaviour as aggressive is a subjective, not objective, judgement:

— this explains different interpretations of the same event

— this is an opinion, a personal judgement, and not based on empirical data.

❖ Aggressive behaviour has several possible contributory causes, which depend on the individual differences and situation variables of the person concerned.

General Aggression Model

❖ These lead to changes in mood, arousal, and cognition, followed by an individual appraisal and then action of some kind, possibly aggression:

❖ Bartholomew et al.'s (2006) study using weapons: this is generally more inclusive with good mundane realism, despite being based on non-empirical data.

❖ Such aggression could be:

Institutional aggression

— a feature of the institution, situation, or environment, or

— institutions could attract aggressive people.

❖ Research focuses on why aggressive individuals might be drawn to institutions or why institutions might promote aggression.

❖ The dispositional hypothesis suggests that aggressive people have an aggressive personality:

— Milgram's concept of the agentic state

— Zimbardo's suggestion that situational factors affect deindividuation.

❖ Social Identity Theory suggests that:

— Identification with the group one is with, the ingroup, encourages positive cognitions and emotions about the ingroup and negative, including potentially aggressive ones, for the outgroup(s).
— Stereotyping the outgroup(s) as bad people could lead to the ingroup justifying harsh, e.g. aggressive, behaviour towards that group.
— Groupthink within the ingroup could also polarise cognition and increase aggression behaviour towards the outgroup(s).

❖ Janis's (1972) model suggests eight key points for ingroup movement towards aggression:

— This seems unlikely without some consent or approval from those in charge.
— The theory as a whole does not allow for individuals belonging to more than one group, a key real-life fact, and so has low mundane realism.

Dysfunctional Power Systems Theory

❖ This addresses the problem of complicity from those in charge in the group or institution, e.g. the "strip-search" scam reported by Zimbardo, as well as many of the Holocaust atrocities and those in the Abu Ghraib jail.
❖ Structural faults in the institution's organisation include:

— The group being insulated from the outside world and everyday life.
— The group having a very close cohesion and agreement on their ideology.
— Everyday norms and values not seeming relevant in the particular work environment, so that alternative norms and values are accepted.
— The work team being a very close one, looking inwards at itself for monitoring and with a shared focus on what members are to achieve and how they will achieve it.
— The situation being a very provocative one with external stressors causing high stress and huge difficulties and moral dilemmas.
— No pre-existing schema to activate plus emotional factors caused by the stress.

❖ People may become willing to accept and adopt behaviours that normally they would not consider appropriate, behaviours they would have said they would reject.
❖ It seems to apply to aggressive organisations, such as those mentioned. Other factors, such as the fear of punishment or expectation of reward for behaving aggressively, are also relevant.

EXAM HINT

Include a discussion of the social versus the biological explanations of aggression and make a conclusion about the relative impact of nature–nurture. Draw from the physiological, genetic, and evolutionary approaches to support nature but consider how the great variety in expression of aggression across cultures suggests that social factors are also important, so an interactionist approach is necessary

BIOLOGICAL EXPLANATIONS OF AGGRESSION

These theories seek to explain aggressive behaviours in terms of biological factors. This means that faulty levels of neurochemicals such as neurotransmitters or hormones could be a cause, or maladaptive brain structures, or inherited maladaptive genes. The implications of these explanations are challenging—if the explanations are valid then do we still hold aggressive people as responsible for their actions? Do we "cure" them of their anti-social behaviours? Do we insist on suitable treatment for the illness of aggression?

Neural and Hormonal Mechanisms

Much of the basic knowledge about neural and hormonal mechanisms has been gained from non-human animal studies. These in general suggest that the basic aggressive behaviours come from the prefrontal cortex, hypothalamus, and amygdala (Gregg, 2003). The problem with this is obvious; to what extent can we extrapolate from animals such as cats to human behaviour? There is limited evidence to suggest that there are some similarities, such as the involvement of the limbic system, but it would be foolish to assume that cat brains and human brains function in exactly the same way.

> **EXAM HINT**
>
> Much of the research evidence about the biological basis of aggression is based on animal research. Make sure you assess the extrapolation issues of such research.

Haller and Kruk (2003) describe how the stress hormones—adrenaline, noradrenaline, and the glucocorticoids—are influenced by the limbic system and can result in dysfunctional behaviour such as aggression. Kruk, Halasz, Meelis, and Haller (2004) found that aggressive behaviours increased with increased levels of adrenocorticotrophic hormone (ACTH) and glucocorticoid hormones.

This suggests that intense or long-lasting stressors could lead to aggressive behaviour. Perhaps this explains the way that even generally peaceful individuals can sometime snap out of control when suddenly or long-term stressed. Haller and Kruk (2003) suggest that there is a positive correlation between noradrenaline and aggression, but, as we know, a correlation cannot infer causation, only that there is some sort of a relationship between these two variables. It is also not proven that the link between noradrenaline (and also testosterone) and aggression

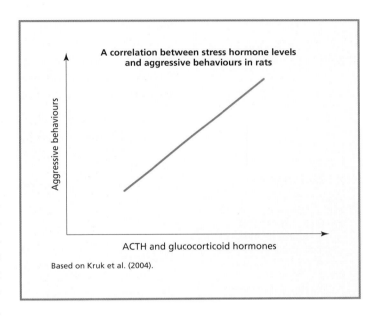

A correlation between stress hormone levels and aggressive behaviours in rats

y-axis: Aggressive behaviours
x-axis: ACTH and glucocorticoid hormones

Based on Kruk et al. (2004).

is directional as a cause of the behaviour. It is possible that the behaviour itself could cause an increase in these neurochemicals, so their raised levels could be an effect and not a cause.

Virkkunen (1985) found that habitually violent offenders show lower levels of glucocorticoids than normal people or non-violent habitual offenders. Later research has confirmed this finding in both males and females (Pajer, Gardner, Rubin, Perel, & Neal, 2001; Kariyawasam, Zaw, & Handley, 2002). Haller and Kruk (2003) suggest that the low levels of glucocorticoids lead to abnormal fears in social settings, which in turn produce an inappropriate level of aggressiveness. In rats, this is demonstrated as reduced signs of an impending aggressive response followed by attacks on the most vulnerable parts of the other animal. Normally, because contact aggression can result in life-threatening damage, there is a behavioural display of strength and/or threats, so that one or other animal can choose to retreat. The next stage is attack of non-vulnerable parts, again lessening the chances of serious injury plus the opportunity to run away.

> **?** Can you recall an instance when you or another acted aggressively and out of character due to stress?

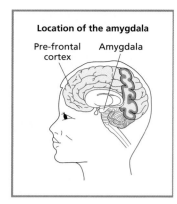

Location of the amygdala

Pre-frontal cortex   Amygdala

There is also evidence that one of the brain's neurotransmitters, serotonin, is implicated in aggressive behaviour. Virkkunen, Nuutila, Goodwin, and Linnoila (1987) showed that people with a history of criminal behaviour tend to have low levels of serotonin. Later research (Brunner et al., 1993) on a large Dutch family with a long history of violently aggressive males showed that these men have low levels of an enzyme, monoamine oxidase A (**MAOA**). This enzyme degrades serotonin and/or adrenaline and noradrenaline, so the high levels of aggressiveness could be caused by the higher levels of those neurotransmitters and hormones. This study is referred to again in the next section.

A slightly different neural aspect is brain structure and function. It has often been suggested that something basic and organic makes a person commit the ultimate aggressive act: murder. Raine, Buchsbaum, and LaCasse (1997) compared the brain structure of normal individuals and murderers and found significant differences in structure and reduced activity in both sides of the prefrontal cortex and in the amygdala of the murderers. This suggests the possibility that differences in brain structure and function could cause increases in aggression. This study is also referred to again in the next section.

It is generally accepted that men are more aggressive than women. Why is this so? It could be that aggression is at least in part the result of the hormone testosterone. This is known as a "male" hormone, despite both sexes producing it—although males do produce significantly more than females. Kalat (1998) reported that in 15- to 25-year-old men those with the highest levels of circulating testosterone also showed the highest levels of aggressive behaviour, as measured by crime statistics. It could also be significant that in non-human animals, castrated males (who therefore produce no male hormones) fight least. Some female aggression has also been linked to hormone levels; research on pre-menstrual syndrome shows that in this time of hormonal fluctuation some women can increase in irritability and hostility and are more likely to commit a crime (Floody, 1968).

Evaluation

The brain controls much of the body and a lot of behaviour, but the reductionist and determinist approaches of looking at brain structure and function alone cannot explain the wide range of aggressive behaviours we see in the everyday world. And although it seems clear that stress hormones and some neurotransmitters are implicated in aggressive behaviour, this gives no answers to the questions "how do they do this?" or "why does stress, for instance, make some people so much more aggressive than others?" Furthermore, the sheer expense of brain studies and neurochemical analyses means that sample sizes are likely to be small and therefore unrepresentative, and so findings will be biased and unlikely to be generalisable to the population at large. Thus, these studies give us useful ideas—useful pointers—but their reductionist and deterministic nature and methodological issues could be said to limit their usefulness.

Is it true that men are more aggressive than women? If it is, then is this a difference in hormonal or neural mechanisms or in socialisation? Is the

EXAM HINT
The biological explanations of aggression are both reductionist (oversimplified) and deterministic (ignore free will of the individual to control their own behaviour). Make sure that you can fully elaborate each of these criticisms.

■ **Activity: Stressors and aggression**
We all "snap" at times and say things or act aggressively and out of character. Make a list of four or five times when this has happened (naming no names!) and for each occurrence, identify some of the contributory stressors that precipitated the aggressive behaviour.

KEY TERM
MAOA: the enzyme monoamine oxidase A, which breaks down the "permissive amines" such as dopamine, serotonin, and noradrenaline (called norepinephrine in the USA). A deficiency of MAOA means that levels of these amines in the brain are abnormally high, and this could increase aggressive behaviours.

British saying "the female of the species is more deadly than the male" just a saying, or something with deeper meaning? In Sheridan and King's (1970) research, in which participants gave a real puppy painful electric shocks, few of the male participants completed the procedure and gave the strongest shocks but all the female participants gave all the shocks. This could be interpreted as the female participants giving rein to their normally hidden aggressive impulses, although it does seem more likely, given the *zeitgeist*, that they were merely obeying instructions as they were socialised to do, and were in the agentic state.

However, Archer's (1982) meta-analysis showed little difference between the sexes, with women slightly more likely than men to be physically aggressive to their partners, although the balance tipped slightly the other way for more serious aggression. These data are from Western cultures; in non-Western cultures, perhaps because the social norms there are less condemnatory of aggression and more supportive of a man's right to control his wife, male aggression is more common towards females than vice versa. This seems to challenge the general acceptance of males, testosterone-driven into being the more aggressive sex, and suggests that situational factors are the cause of any differences in levels or types of aggression.

Archer's (1982) study found that although women were slightly more likely to be physically aggressive to their partners, men were more likely to commit serious aggressive acts.

Genetic Factors

Human aggression depends in part on biological factors. Genetic influences on aggression have been clearly demonstrated in non-human animals (Cairns, Gariepy, & Hood, 1990) and twin studies on humans suggest some sort of genetic component in aggressive behaviour (Hudziak, van Beijsterveldt, Bartels, Rietveld, Rettew, & Derks, 2003). However, this is not a straightforward link, and Hennig, Reuter, Netter, and Burk's (2005) research supports a genetic link with certain dispositions or temperaments, e.g. impulsiveness, which could make actual aggression more likely. Rhee and Waldman's (2002) meta-analysis of twin and

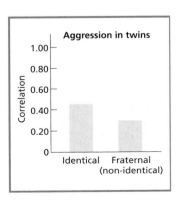

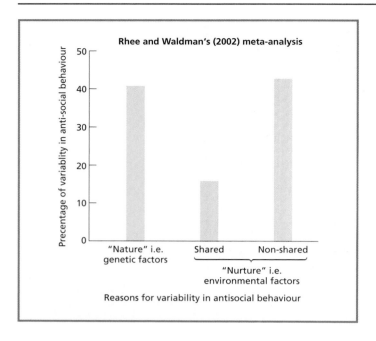

Rhee and Waldman's (2002) meta-analysis

adoption studies on anti-social behaviours, which included aggressive behaviour, found that identical twins (who share 100% of their genes) were more similar in anti-social behaviour than fraternal twins (who share 50% of their genes). This supports genetic factors as having an influence on aggressive behaviour, even allowing for the more closely similar environment of identical compared with fraternal twins. Furthermore, Rhee and Waldman (2002) found that genetic influences are the cause of 41% of the variability in anti-social behaviour.

Sex hormones (especially male sex hormones such as testosterone) influence aggressive behaviour. When transsexuals (individuals who have treatments to change sex) were studied before and after 3 months of sex hormone treatment (van Goozen, Frijda, & van de Poll, 1995), female-to-male transsexuals showed increased proneness to aggression after receiving male sex hormones, whereas male-to-female transsexuals (i.e. deprived of male sex hormones) showed decreased proneness to anger and aggression. These findings support male sex hormones as a factor in aggression.

Genes have also been linked to brain chemistry and increased aggression. MAOA is an enzyme that facilitates the breakdown of excess neurochemicals such as noradrenaline, serotonin, and other amines. Brunner et al.'s (1993) study shows that the MAOA deficiency is in fact genetic, and means that those with MAOA deficiency are likely to have raised levels of noradrenaline. This was found in four generations of males in a Dutch family. The men inherited a recessive, X-chromosome-linked gene that appears to result in aggressive, sometimes violent, behaviour including arson and attempted rape. Further support for the gene hypothesis comes from a study of 110 men who showed an association between abnormalities in the MAOA gene and aggressiveness and impulse control (Manuck, Flory, Ferrell, Mann, & Muldoon, 2000).

EXAM HINT

Make sure you can use monoamine oxidase (MAOA) deficiency to offer support for the gene hypothesis. In addition, mention the methodological weaknesses of such research, for example:

- small samples in some cases
- the fact that the environment (nurture) may explain common family behaviour rather than nature.

However, on a positive note, the identification of a specific gene obviously offers strong causal evidence for the gene hypothesis.

Evaluation

These findings are interesting because they seem to be showing a direct link between genes, brain chemistry, and aggression; but both sets of participants in the research mentioned here constitute highly biased samples. This means that we cannot assume that these findings can be generalised to the population, and so this sort of research has low ecological validity as well as low mundane realism. For example, male-only samples cannot represent females, and so ignore half the population. Furthermore, the males in question were highly unusual. Their abnormal aggressiveness does not relate to everyday aggressive behaviours and so cannot contribute a great deal to our understanding of such aggression. There is also the possibility that the unusually aggressive behaviours are now the result of

[?] Why are the samples in the above research biased? How could we overcome this?

HOW SCIENCE WORKS: EXPLANATIONS OF AGGRESSION
You will have studied biological and psychological explanations of aggression. Why not pick one set of explanations and, using your computer, produce a small series of posters to summarise each explanation, giving evidence that supports and challenges that explanation. Downloading graphics and using colour and varying your fonts, etc., would make the posters more appealing and eye-catching.

You could team up with classmates and divide-up the various explanations between you so that you produce a complete series of the explanations for display.

You could even include a separate, small scenario of aggressive behaviour, and mount this in the centre with the explanations arranged round it. Each one could then have a paragraph linking the explanation to the example of behaviour.

expectation by the extended Dutch family and community, and so aggressive acts by male children are not discouraged but accepted, which would successfully reinforce such behaviours. It also needs to be remembered that the link between raised noradrenaline levels and aggression are correlational and therefore cannot be assumed to be causal or directional, from noradrenaline to behaviour. However, the fact that the raised levels are the result of inheriting a maladaptive gene does strengthen the argument for a causal, directional link.

More research findings

Raine et al. (1997) used PET scans to examine the brains of 39 males and 2 females who were charged with the most aggressive crime, murder, and compared them with 41 controls. The participants were injected with a glucose tracer, required to work at a continuous performance task that was based around target recognition for 32 minutes, and then given a positron emission tomography (PET) scan. The scans were compared with those from the controls for the level of activity (glucose metabolism) in the right and left hemispheres of the brain in 14 selected areas. These included cortical areas such as the prefrontal, parietal, occipital, and temporal lobes (part of the cerebral cortex)] plus subcortical areas including the corpus callosum, amygdala, hippocampus, and thalamus (brain structures located beneath the cortex and constituting much of the limbic system)]. Raine et al. (1997) found significant differences in the amygdala, suggesting unusual emotional responses such as a lack of fear, which supported earlier research findings. This lack of fear could also include a lack of retribution or personal harm, or even a lack of fear of breaking social norms, all of which could increase actual aggressive behaviour.

Why do you think only two females were used in this study? Does this affect the validity of the study?

Evaluation

Differences in brain structure and/or functioning are likely to be genetic, as this study suggests. But human behaviour is very complex, as is the human brain, so it is not at all likely that a single, simple brain mechanism is the explanation for all aggressive behaviours. Also, the differences between the two groups' amygdala activity is not in doubt, although exactly what this means is not certain. It is also not clear how similar, apart from their alleged murderous acts, was that group from the control group; surely there are likely to have been powerful extraneous

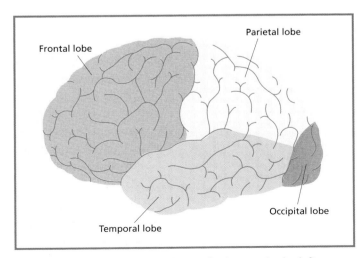

The four lobes, or divisions, of the cerebral cortex in the left hemisphere.

The limbic system. From Parkin (2001).

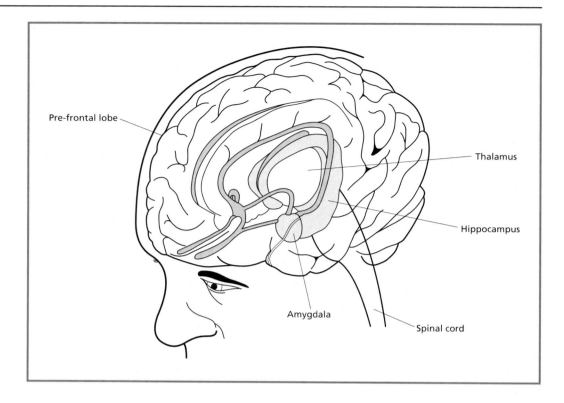

How could you explain that not all the variant MAOA males developed highly aggressive behaviours? What other factors can you suggest might be operating?

variables, perhaps confounding ones such as socio-economic background or level of education. So it cannot be concluded that aggression is caused by genetic brain differences, what McFadden (2004) calls "warrior genes" (discussed in the next section). Indeed, Caspi et al.'s (2002) study suggests a nature and nurture effect. They studied males with a variant of the abnormal MAOA gene found in the Dutch family and only those who had also suffered abuse as children were more prone to aggressive behaviour. However, not all of that group developed into aggressors, about 15% stayed within normal limits for violence and aggression.

SECTION SUMMARY
Biological Explanations of Aggression

Neural and hormonal mechanisms

❖ These mechanisms suggest that the causes of aggression are:

— faulty levels of neurochemicals, such as neurotransmitters or hormones
— maladaptive brain structures
— inherited faulty genes.

❖ Gregg (2003): basic aggressive behaviours come from the prefrontal cortex, hypothalamus, and amygdala (limbic system). However, these data come from non-human animal studies.

❖ Haller and Kruk (2003) have shown that stress hormones and glucocorticoids, which are involved in aggressive behaviour, are influenced by the limbic system.

❖ Kariyawasam et al. (2002) confirmed earlier studies that showed that habitually aggressive people have low glucocorticoid levels, and that this could give them abnormal fears, which lead to inappropriate aggressiveness.

❖ Abnormal serotonin and possibly noradrenaline levels are also linked to aggressiveness, caused by a maladaptive gene for MAOA. However, these data come from a very biased and small sample in a Dutch family.

❖ Extreme aggression, e.g. murder, has been linked to abnormal activity in the prefrontal cortex and amygdala, but again this is a small and highly biased sample, making generalisation to the population non-viable.

❖ The belief that males are innately more aggressive than females, and that this is the result of different levels of testosterone, has been largely disproved. The two sexes display aggression in different ways, rather than different amounts.

❖ Genetic components have been demonstrated clearly in non-human animals but it is not so clear for humans. Twin studies suggest some sort of genetic component in aggressiveness, and there seems to be a link with certain temperaments or dispositions (Hennig et al., 2005).

> **EXAM HINT**
>
> In the exam, you could be asked questions on the biological or social psychological explanations of aggression as an adaptive response. This means you need to consider the evolutionary basis of aggression.

AGGRESSION AS AN ADAPTIVE RESPONSE

Evolutionary Explanations of Human Aggression

Evolutionary explanations of human behaviour suggest that present-day behaviours came about because they were adaptive for our remote, human ancestors in the sense that they gave our hunter-gatherer ancestors the advantage in surviving and reproducing, and in passing on their genes. These behaviours were, and are, controlled by genes, and so the genes have been handed down from generation to generation because they conferred a benefit, and as the genes code for the behaviour, the behaviour is also handed down.

Sometimes these genes/behaviours are still advantageous but sometimes, because of the way we live nowadays, they are no longer beneficial and might even act against our best interests.

> **?** The stress response is one such behaviour. Can you think of one way it is adaptive, and one way in which it isn't? What do your classmates think?

Infidelity and jealousy

We compete in various ways, in everyday life as well as on the sports field. One way we compete is for partners—boyfriends or girlfriends: in evolutionary terms we are competing for people to mate with. Mate competition includes rivalry and can lead to feelings of jealousy and jealous behaviour. It is thought that jealousy is a genetic behaviour, that it is innate and not learned culturally. This is because jealousy is found in all human cultures; it can be regarded as a form of aggression because it often leads to outbursts of aggressive behaviour.

What is the evolutionary theory relating to infidelity, jealousy, and aggression, or sexual jealousy? It is based on biological facts and our long-ago ancestors' primitive and risky way of life. In the natural world, sex leads to babies, and thus the continuation of the family, community, or species. This would be very important for early humans, as the community or group would need a constant supply of new members if it was to continue. This is not merely a matter of sex, as pregnancy and childbirth can have complications and babies and children need all sorts of resources for successful upbringing. Even in our long-ago past, having children was expensive. However, there is a further important issue. A woman having a baby knows that the child is biologically hers. This might sound like unnecessarily stating the obvious, but the point is that for a man, until recent DNA techniques became available, this was not so; there was no way of knowing

> **EXAM HINT**
>
> Make sure you can describe evolutionary explanations for jealousy as a form of aggression. Consider the generic weaknesses of evolutionary theory, such as the lack of scientific validity, but remember to balance these against the high level of face validity and the anecdotal evidence from real-life behaviour.

if the baby was biologically his own child. For a man, parenthood had to be taken on trust because when a couple mated the woman would have parental certainty but the man would not.

How does this relate to jealousy? For the woman, the theory is that as pregnancy, childbirth, and childcare are so expensive in terms of physical resources, energy, and time, having a mate—a man—to care and provide for her and the child becomes highly significant in the struggle for survival, food, shelter, and protection. Therefore, if the man is with other women—if he is sexually unfaithful—her survival and that of her child are at risk. So she will be jealous if she suspects he is behaving in this way, and jealousy is linked to aggression. It might seem that aggression to drive off or even remove the other woman would be a successful strategy. It could well deter another woman from trying to attract that man, or even to punish the man himself. Of course, the reverse is also possible, as the other woman might feel aggressively about the existing female partner of her lover, and might translate those feelings into aggressive action to secure the man's resources for herself and any offspring. This seems still to hold true, as newspapers still report "crimes of passion" such as the murder of Jaspal Marsh by her husband's lover (BBC, 2007), and cases such as that of Lorena Bobbitt.

What about male jealousy? This is a simple matter of not wanting to devote his time and resources to another man's child. So the theory suggests that a man would be very jealous if he suspected that his female partner was being unfaithful and having sex with another man and might therefore become pregnant by this other. This could lead to actual aggression against the woman and the other man if there is any such suspicion. Furthermore, this view has been used as an explanation, although *never* a justification, of cases where a man harms his current girlfriend's child from a previous relationship (BBC, 2006). A non-tragic example of the importance of chastity and faithfulness comes from research such as Buss (1987, 1989), whose sample of 37 different cultures showed males consistently valuing female chastity highly, and also his classic lonely hearts research showing that males value faithfulness. Both of which traits would suggest the woman was less likely to have sex with a different man. Buss's research also showed that women also value faithfulness, and evolutionary theory would say that this is because faithfulness in a man means he will bring his resources home and not spend them on another woman. However, the research also showed that women are far more jealous about emotional infidelity than just sexual straying. This is because emotional infidelity is more likely to result in the man leaving, abandoning her and leaving her and her children without resources.

Is there evidence to support the evolutionary view?

The researcher Gary Brase compared sexual jealousy in different cultures and found that the most jealous men are the Brazilians and the least jealous are the Japanese (Whitehouse, 2003). What could explain this difference? Well, it seems that there is a positive correlation between the level of jealousy and the fertility rate—not that a correlation infers causation, of course. This could be seen as support for the evolutionary hypothesis, for in a country with high fertility the women are more likely to become pregnant after sexual intercourse, therefore their faithfulness to their partner is more significant. In Japan, where the fertility rate is low, sexual intercourse is far less likely to result in a woman's pregnancy, which could explain the much lower rate of sexual jealousy. These inferences do, however, depend on pregnancy being the cause of jealousy, and other data challenge this assumption, because both men and women seem to care more about emotional commitment than sexual commitment.

Evaluation

The idea that female aggressive jealousy might deter another woman from trying to attract her man could be valid, although whether and how much jealous feelings would translate into aggressive action would surely also depend on the social norms of the group and the personalities and relative strengths of those concerned. However, directing this aggression against the wandering male partner, although understandable, is possibly likely to drive him away and therefore the woman would lose her source of support for herself and any child(ren). Basically, the approach states that men don't want to invest resources in a child not possessing their genes, and so they focus on physical fidelity. By contrast, women, who are reliant on a man's resources, focus on his emotional fidelity. Buunk, Angleitner, Oubaid, and Buss (1996) obtained support for these predictions when focusing on hypothetical situations. However, Harris (2002) studied actual infidelity and found no gender differences. Men and women both focused more on emotional than on physical fidelity/infidelity. This challenges the evolutionary approach, and so its explanations need re-evaluating, perhaps as applying less to modern, industrialised societies.

Buss's research has been replicated, e.g. by Dunbar, Barrett, and Lycett (2005), and seems to apply across many cultures; thus these finding have greater validity. These and similar studies are unusual in that they investigate quite private beliefs and behaviours and yet comply with modern ethical views. This is because the research was often based on information already in the public domain: dating adverts in newspapers and, more recently, online. Of course, there is no way of knowing from these adverts how much of what people post is truthful, but that same reservation applies to interviews, questionnaires, and surveys, which have all been shown to be useful research tools.

Rape

There are two ways in which evolutionary theory can explain rape, an aggressive behaviour that is found across cultures even though it is often very severely punished. These explanations are just that, and should never be taken as in any way justifications of this violent behaviour.

The first explanation is that rape is the "last resort" of a jealous person, usually a male. This hypothesis suggests that rapists are more likely to be unmarried, resource-poor men who have been unsuccessful in attracting a mate. They are therefore jealous of their successful rivals, and the response to that emotion is directed not at those sexually successful men but at women. The victim would be a woman of good reproductive fitness, in other words young and healthy enough to be fertile, and so would possibly become pregnant as a result of the rape. In this way, the aggressive assault would be a last resort for the rapist of reproducing. This explanation has been called the Mate Deprivation Hypothesis.

The second explanation is that rape is a maladaptive version of male sexuality. Typically, males compete for females, and will use strategies to attract females and persuade them to have sex. This is based on the ease of sexual arousal in most males, plus what Clamp (2001) calls "a desire for variety in sexual partners and a readiness to engage in impersonal sex". The hypothesis suggests that these rapists would come from all socio-economic groups and would have unusually strong sex drives, and that the rape victim would, as in the Mate Deprivation Hypothesis, be at peak reproductive age. This aggression would not, then, be the result of jealousy but would stem from the desire, the drive, for infidelity, always supposing the rapist had a partner.

Research findings

Alcock (1993) analysed rape victim data from 26 American cities and found that the peak age range for rape victims was from the teens to the late 30s, which was

? Do you think a man or a woman would be more likely to express/show feelings of jealousy?

predicted by both the evolutionary approach explanations, as this matches peak female fertility. Alcock's work also found that the evidence for unusually high levels of sexual activity was supported by his data, although these findings were not sufficiently reliable to lead to a valid conclusion. Myhill and Allen (2002) found a frequency of reported rape in the UK of 1.8% in 16- to 19-year-olds, but in older cohorts up to age 59 the frequency was steady at 0.3–0.4%. These data could be interpreted as supporting evolutionary theory because peak female fertility is in the teens, although fertility declines slowly from then on rather than dropping abruptly. However, the fact that older and even postmenopausal women are also rape victims is difficult to explain using evolutionary theory, as these women have low or no fertility.

Evaluation

There is evidence that young men from lower socio-economic groups commit disproportionately more rapes than those from higher socio-economic groups, but it is also highly likely that rape by higher-ranking men might not be reported or prosecuted, making the data on socio-economic groups non-valid. People might be less keen to accuse a man of higher social standing in case the consequences of such an accusation back-fired. This means that the data on what type of person is more likely to be a rapist cannot be relied on. The case in Austria in 2008 (CNN, 2008) when an elderly man admitted raping his daughter over a period of years, can be said to support the idea that unusual behaviour by respectable people might not be reported. The anomalies of that situation—the previous conviction for sexual offences, the disappearance of the daughter, the sequential arrival of three babies on the man's doorstep, the hidden part of the house basement—which are unlikely to have gone unnoticed by neighbours and community, were never mentioned. The man's respectability and social standing seem to have protected him from investigation.

Myhill and Allen's research could also support the idea that social standing might be a factor, because they showed that women from very low-income groups, below £10,000 annual household income, were three times more likely to report suffering rape than women from households with an annual income of over £20,000. This would suggest that raping low-income women might be seen as not as reprehensible and therefore less likely to result in retribution against the rapist, as opposed to raping higher-income women. However, this does not tie in with evolutionary theory's explanation that both men and women would be looking to have the best possible circumstances for their offspring. In fact, this idea suggests the opposite: that a man would choose a higher-income woman as a potential mother for his child so that child would have a better environment in which to develop. Furthermore, as at least 25% of rape victims never told anyone about their rape, the data are significantly incomplete, and we cannot know into which socio-economic background or age group these missing victims belong.

There is also the issue of the rape of older women, as the evolutionary explanation of rape simply does not make sense for women past child-bearing. An alternative explanation is that for some male rapists their behaviour is related to great anger and hostility towards women. Psychodynamic Theory would suggest that this anger is the result of early childhood experiences, perhaps an inconsistent relationship with the mother leading to denial, displacement, and projection, but as this theory is also based on the past it is very difficult to find more than circumstantial evidence in support of it. There is certainly support for the view that the underlying cause for rape is aggression related rather than sexually related.

A different challenge to this evolutionary view is that rape was not very likely to lead to the successful production of healthy children, at least not in the world of our hunter-gatherer ancestors. This is because the rape victim would have been less likely to be successful in bearing and bringing up the child of the rape because of her own physical trauma, her reduced likelihood of attracting a good mate subsequent to the rape, and the lack of male parental care for her during the pregnancy and for the child resulting from the rape. This would really have mattered in the primitive world, and the victim's survival and that of the child would have been at risk. Unfortunately, because we cannot research the past empirically, it has to be acknowledged that evolutionary theories about any behaviour are speculative, however much they make sense. This does not mean such explanations must be rejected, but it is something to bear in mind.

Group Display in Humans

"Group display" refers here to displays of aggressive behaviour by groups, which are sometimes described as three or more people gathered together for a common purpose. Therefore, in this context psychology is looking at groups gathered together for an aggressive purpose, or groups that develop an aggressive purpose. However, it is wise to remember that crowds gather for many purposes, positive ones as well as negative ones.

If we look at animals that display aggression, it is clear that this sort of display is an adaptive response that minimises actual physical contact with its likely consequences of injury or death. When red deer stags compete for mates they have an innate procedure. First they bellow or roar loudly, as this roaring correlates with strength. Then, if they seem well matched, they pace up and down—the parallel walk—eyeing each other up. If they still judge themselves as having a chance of success they then have contact, fighting with their antlers. The stronger one usually wins and, if lucky, the loser can run off, although there is always the risk of injury, which could be life threatening. A badly damaged leg, for instance, would make foraging very difficult, as well as making the animal vulnerable to predators.

> **?** How and when do pets such as cats and dogs use aggressive display behaviours?

Findings
Warrior displays
It can be argued that the processions of martial might are an aggressive display—a chance to show off military strength and armoury. Military march-pasts are a reminder of manpower and machines, and as well as demonstrating reassurance to the nation that owns these it acts as a signal or warning to any other group considering hostile action.

Competitive sport can be said to fulfil a psychological need; a need to belong to a group and to believe that this is the best group, the ingroup. This belief then needs to be upheld in matches against other groups, other teams. Membership of one's

Military marches are a prominent display of might and prowess, and serve as a political deterrent to would-be hostiles.

Supporting a football team can be said to fulfil the psychological need to belong to a group.

ingroup is shown, for example, by the wearing of group clothing, and also by group songs and chants. But these latter behaviours can also be demonstrations of aggressive displays involving words and gestures.

Football findings

There is a clear link between aggressive crowd behaviour and college football in the USA. An empirical study of 26 of the 119 Division 1-A college football programs in 2004–2005 matched daily data on offences from the NIBRS (National Incident Based Reporting System) with the football games. Their findings suggest that the host team's community experiences a sharp increase in aggressive acts, such as assaults, vandalism, and arrests for disorderly or alcohol-related offences on game days. This increase is particularly marked if the game's result is unexpected, an upset. How does psychology explain these findings?

The traditional social learning approach suggests that the offenders are modelling the aggressive behaviours they have seen on the pitch, or on television or other recordings of games. The team players are the role models, and they have status and are perceived as being very successful, and not only in the sporting field. Their behaviour is therefore seen as successful behaviour and so on-pitch behaviour is imitated off-pitch by spectators and fans.

Further findings

The link between sport and aggression is supported by Phillips' (1986) research on 18 championship heavyweight boxing matches between 1973 and 1978. The pattern of findings was confirmed that in the 3 days following each of these prize fights there was a significant increase in American homicide rates. However, most research supports a different view, that aggression associated with sporting events is more a display than actual contact. For example, analysis of over 800 ice hockey matches (Widmeyer & McGuire, 1997) showed increased actual aggression only between teams that met more frequently.

Marsh, Rosser, and Harré (1978) and Frosdick and Marsh (2005) have alternative views. One of these, supported by participant research and much observation as well as empirical data from police records, is that, in the main,

---

Football firms

M is a respectable thirty-something lawyer, and he has counterparts all over the UK. He has spoken of his use of the internet and mobile phone to research matches, contact similar other people, plan and meet, and go to where a fight is planned. There are even football violence websites, which spring up again as soon as they are closed down.

M says: "I only go to 'hot' matches where I know there will be some violence and some opposing fans looking for the same thing as me, but that's obvious anyway" (BBC, 2005).

Groups of people like M, who associate themselves with a particular football club, are known as Firms, and belonging to one can bring unquestioning acceptance from other members, perhaps acceptance that is missing from the rest of these individuals' lives.

J is a former member of one Firm, and has spoken of the thrill and addictive nature of the violence:

If you've been involved in a situation where you have that feeling—maximum velocity—and then something happens to shut it off for a moment, it's as if your veins have been washed clean with iced water. (BBC, 2002)

actual contact aggression in football is not the norm. They quote a Strathclyde police report about a Celtic–Rangers match with a crowd of about 50,000 where the police made only five arrests, and that only 1.67% more arrests coincide with football nights compared to non-football nights. However, different research suggests that there is a separate group of fans who are fans of violence and not sport, and who use sporting events as excuses and cover for their aggression, as referred to earlier in this chapter.

Evaluation

We should always be cautious in extrapolating from non-human animals to ourselves. Although we are built to the same pattern as other vertebrates, there are major differences with our own mammal group, and even with other primates. So comparisons can be useful in generating ideas for further research, but should not be used as full explanations.

Social Learning Theory, if valid here, should apply across the board to all competitive sports, especially contact sports, but although there is good evidence of aggression in the community increasing on game days for football, boxing, and North American hockey games, there does not seem to be the same behaviour following, for example, rugby games in the UK. This lack of coherence casts doubts on the validity of Social Learning Theory as an explanation here.

The Frustration–Aggression Hypothesis could perhaps be a better explanation. If your team is not expected to win then losing, although unwanted, is not unexpected. However, if your team is expected to be victorious then losing, especially if you are the home side, is unwanted and unpleasant and quite possibly very frustrating. If this frustration is fuelled by the celebrations of the visitors because they were expected to lose but have won, then the internally pent-up emotion could explode externally as aggressive behaviour. Furthermore, such aggression could be an attempt to recoup lost self-esteem, lost because of the defeat on the field (Wann, 1993). According to Wann:

> *When individuals identify and form a strong connection with a local team, it is related to their psychological health. The more they identify with the team, the higher their self esteem, the higher their vigour or energy; the lower their fatigue, confusion, depression and alienation.*

In other words, this supporter or fan behaviour is a form of social identity and spills over into the rest of the individual's personal life; it could also explain the wearing of team shirts, etc. This identification also means the person is clearly a member of a special group, to him or her it is an ingroup, and the other team is an outgroup, and this might well be operationalised as justification for aggression. But does any of this relate to actual aggressive behaviour? There is actual violence in sports matches, but is it the norm at such events? Loud chants, abusive language, and rude gestures all count as aggressive displays designed to show the other team that one's own team is in no doubt of victory. The loudness signifies strength, comments are often designed to embarrass or humiliate the other side, but these do not involve contact aggression. Frosdick and Marsh (2005) put forward the view that the media greatly exaggerates contact aggression and ignores the aggressive displays that are both non-contact and a show and catharsis—a letting-off of emotional energy, what we call "steam". This misconception about aggression and football has led to a social construct that football aggression is rife, a common and a feared behaviour; but the facts do not support this, such as the evidence from the McElhone report in 1977 and the Strathclyde analysis of 1980. This shows that aggression then was for display, and therefore ritual, but it does not tell us what the situation is currently. For example, a Home Office report in 2004 stated that "Statistics for football-related arrests tell only part of the story and need to be placed in context". Furthermore, there is evidence for the media itself sensationalising football aggression to sell newspapers and magazines, and by doing this popularising these aggressive instances (Haley, 2001). What Marsh found 30 years ago was that ritualised aggression—aggressive display—was carefully controlled by the fans themselves. Problems tended to arise when outsiders misinterpreted the suggestions of violence as actual violence and intervened inappropriately. One example of this used to be home-team supporters pursuing the away-team supporters back to the railway station—being careful never to catch up with them, as that was not part of the display—but the accompanying shouts of murdering them, smashing their heads in, and so on would have been alarming to anyone who did not understand that this was ritual and not a call to action.

Lynch Mobs

A lynch mob is a collection of people who intend to take a person (sometimes this is someone whom they suspect of committing an offence) and to kill that person without recourse to legal action. At times, lynch-mob victims have been broken out of jail in order to execute them without trial. There are many dreadful accounts and records of such atrocities, not just in the USA but all over the world. It is not to be doubted that such events occur, the question asked here is what insights psychology can bring here.

Two different research traditions have been applied with regard to social explanations of lynching. The Sociological Power Threat Hypothesis has argued that in the southern United States lynching atrocity will increase as a function of the relative number of African–Americans in the community. So this would mean that as the minority increases in the community, they are seen as an increasing threat and blamed for bad things that happen. Alternatively, the Psychological Self-attention Theory suggests that lynching atrocity will increase as a function of the relative number of mob members. This means that the more people are gathered together when something bad happens, the more likely this gathering is to turn into a lynch mob.

A United Nations report blamed lynchings in Guatamala on previous human rights violations during the internal armed conflict and the existing levels of poverty. This view came from the facts that communities had been mistreated and were too poor to do anything to redress this abuse.

A psychodynamic perspective from Lightweis-Goff (2007) on lynching atrocities is that sublimated aggression is the cause. Aggression, according to Freud, is the natural result of the release of pent-up thanatos, an innate energy that drives a person to destruction. This energy can be released in other ways, but if held in it will eventually burst out. Thanatos could then be sublimated or rechannelled into a behaviour that allows its expression or release, and in this instance the aggression of a lynch mob could be a collective release as sublimated aggression.

Findings

Leader, Mullen, & Abrams (2007) have performed two series of analyses on American data, one using newspaper reports and the second using photographic records, applied to different and non-overlapping samples of lynching events. These produced a consistent pattern of findings that supported lynch-mob atrocities increasing as a function of the relative numbers of mob members in the mob, and not increasing as a function of the relative numbers of African–Americans in the county population. Possibly, this is a result of peer pressure, but frustrations could also be a cause leading to the aggressive act, and in a larger crowd deindividuation might well have operated. It is also possible that the fact that the accused—the victims—were black was a dehumanising factor, as many white Americans did not think of those with a dark skin as being truly human, and so didn't think that they were entitled to normal human rights, such as a fair trial.

Evaluation

In Guatamala, Mendoza's (2006) statistical analysis showed that the key factors in lynching atrocities were the size of the indigenous population and their ease of access to legal courts. The solidarity among ethnic fellows in the indigenous population correlated positively with their percentage within that population—numbers giving strength. The lower the ratio of legal courts per 1,000,000 of the population, the higher the chance of lynching atrocities. The level of poverty was not significant, and past human rights violations had only a small effect. This means that the United Nations' interpretation is challenged, because it is faulty in its findings and assumptions. Being poor did not affect the likelihood of lynching atrocities occurring, but lack of legal access and feeling part of a large enough group did. This could be because frustration at not being able to gain access to legal procedures led to aggression, the taking of the law into the mob's own hands. Alternatively, or even as well, being part of a larger group could have increased and reinforced group identity as people who have been wronged, it could have produced deindividuated cognition and led to the atrocity taking place. The impact of poverty has been challenged by Hovland and Sears (1940), who found that, in America, those years in which cotton prices were lowest tended to be the ones with the most lynchings. This was claimed as support for the Frustration–Aggression Hypothesis, and suggests that poverty is an important factor for the group's dissatisfactions, and that punishing a scapegoat could be seen as an outlet for such frustration.

Lightweis-Goff (2007) suggests that the labelling of lynching atrocities as criminal behaviours and as racist or hate crimes has ignored their collectivity. She argues that these approaches cannot explain the bloodthirsty nature of lynch mobs. Freud believed that it is possible for people to revert to being a primal horde, where the disenfranchised community can gather together in strength and attack and kill a tyrannical authority figure, taking back power to themselves. Freud also put forward the concept of contagion—not in the medical sense of infectious disease, but of thoughts or beliefs spreading through a crowd; or this sharing of similar ideas could be convergence, where people with similar thoughts gather together. However this happens, the emotion of the moment causes the ego to collapse and liberate the id, whose primitive instincts could lead to the lynching atrocity. It is possible to interpret the killing of a victim as symbolic of the destruction of a tyrant, especially in a group that has suffered wrongdoing. It is

EXAM HINT
Note that lynch mobs can be explained by evolution as a form of xenophobia. However, this can be challenged by counter perspectives such as the Psychodynamic Theory of Sublimated Aggression, the Frustration–Aggression Hypothesis, and the effects of deindividuation and dehumanisation.

? How would these different explanations of lynchings fit into the four stages of the General Aggression Model?

See *A2-Level Psychology Online* for some interactive quizzes to help you with your revision.

also possible to regard an emotional outburst as coming from basic instincts. But these suppositions, like those of thought contagion and convergence are all hypothetical constructs or ideas, and empirical evidence cannot be obtained for such because one cannot test or refute ideas. However, such constructs can produce very useful discussion, which might lead to testable hypotheses for explaining behaviours such as lynchings and eventually to a recognition of and consequent reduction in causal factors.

SECTION SUMMARY
Aggression as an Adaptive Response

❖ Evolutionary explanations of human aggression suggest that these and other behaviours came about because they:

— were adaptive for our remote, hunter-gatherer ancestors
— gave them the advantage in surviving and reproducing
— therefore, passing on the genes that controlled those behaviours from generation to generation
— what might have been adaptive then could be a problem now.

❖ The approach suggests that infidelity and jealousy are based on:

— men not wanting to invest resources in a child not possessing their genes, and so they focus on physical fidelity
— women, who are reliant on a man's resources, focus on his emotional fidelity
— doubting that fidelity brings jealousy.

❖ Much research supports the idea that the causes of jealousy vary between the sexes
❖ Recent findings challenge this as in real life males and females are both more deeply affected by emotional infidelity
❖ Evolutionary explanations of rape are based on either the rapist:

— being unsuccessful, unattractive to women, and jealous, or
— having maladaptive sexuality with regard to the drive to increase the numbers of his offspring.

❖ There is evidence both for and against these ideas, but other research suggests strongly that anger and hostility towards women drive rapists.

Group display in humans

❖ Aggressive displays by groups of humans can be a demonstration of power, as in military might or sport, or of intimidation as in warfare or sport.
❖ Links between sport and aggressive behaviour are well researched, but findings are mixed.
❖ Some sports are much more linked with aggressive behaviour than others, so Social Learning Theory and Social Identity Theory have input here, as does the Frustration–Aggression Hypothesis.
❖ Other research suggests that for a minority the sport is a cover for active aggression involving contact and a real intent to harm.

❖ Lynch mobs have a real intent to harm: to murder. Research suggests that the impetus to commit a lynching atrocity is related either to:

Lynch mobs

— an increase in the minority being targeted, or
— the size of the mob.

❖ Meta-analyses support the latter but not the former explanation. Other research supports a strong sense of injustice or non-availability of justice as a main factor.

❖ Psychodynamic Theory offers an alternative explanation, that of Thanatos. This hypothesises that a build-up of negative energy can explode as aggressive behaviour, and in a group situation individuals form a primal horde. Although lacking in empirical support, this concept seems to explain lynching behaviour by otherwise model citizens, and provides a fertile topic for discussion.

FURTHER READING

Kerr, J.H. (2005). *Rethinking aggression and violence in sport*. London: Routledge. This book has chapters on various sport and aggression-related topics, including sanctioned and unsanctioned aggression, fan violence, and sport riots.

Lorenz, K. (1966/2002). *On aggression*. London: Routledge. This reissued classic gives a wonderful broad background to the study of aggression, written by one of the greatest ethologists.

Simmons, R. (2002). *Odd girl out: The hidden culture of aggression in girls*. London: Harcourt Brace. Contains descriptions and discussions on the types and causes of girl–girl aggression, and the input of parents and teachers.

Zimbardo, P.G. (2008). *The Lucifer effect: How good people turn evil*. Roder and Co. New York: Random House. This is a fascinating account of research and theories into anti-social behaviours, especially aggression and violence, with a positive message for everyone.

See *A2-Level Psychology Online* for tips on how to answer these revision questions.

REVISION QUESTIONS

In the exam, questions on this topic are out of 25 marks, and can take the form of essay questions or two-part questions. You should allow about 30 minutes for each of the questions below, which aim to test the material in this chapter. Never try to answer a question unless you have been taught the topic.

1. (a) Outline one or more social psychological theories of aggression. (10 marks)
   (b) Discuss psychological explanations of institutional aggression. (15 marks)
2. Discuss biological explanations of aggression, such as the role of genetic, neural, and hormonal factors. (25 marks)
3. Describe and evaluate evolutionary explanations of human infidelity and jealousy. (25 marks)
4. Discuss explanations of group display, such as sports events and lynch mobs, in humans. (25 marks)

Eating Behaviour

By Evie Bentley

Eating is necessary for life! In common with most animals—and unlike green plants—humans cannot manufacture their own food, so we have to eat to obtain nutrients for growth, repair, and energy. However, we are not very limited as to what we can eat. Biologically, we are omnivores, eating both plant and animal material, even if we choose to limit our diet because of culture, mood, health concerns, or beliefs.

6

EATING BEHAVIOUR

Factors Influencing Attitudes to Food and Eating Behaviour

Culture

It is difficult to define what is meant by the term "food", except to say that it is what we eat in order to obtain nutrients. After all, there are the stories of pregnant woman craving things like coal, but one would not regard that as food! What we do know is that different cultures and different times have different views on what counts as food and this is of course based on learning. In the UK, the population generally eats meat such as lamb, fish such as pollock, shellfish such as prawns, plus vegetables and fruits. But some groups have the belief that eating certain foods is wrong. For example, to Hindus the cow is a sacred animal and so beef is not, to them, a food. And Jews have religious laws forbidding them to eat pork or shellfish, so these are not counted as food items. These examples illustrate how religious attitudes and beliefs have an effect on what we learn to regard as food.

Different sets of attitudes and beliefs apply to vegetarians. There are the ethical vegetarians who do not believe it is ethically right to kill other animals for food, so their learning is that animals are not food items. However, other vegetarians will eat fish or shellfish (i.e. they learn that these are food). What form does this learning take? It is likely that classical and **operant conditioning**, as well as social learning, are powerful in this context. Babies are weaned onto the type of food their parents eat, and so will not only associate those tastes with eating, but will be praised for eating up, so this will be reinforced operantly. As they grow older, children will be more likely to model their parents' eating habits. Social influence from peers and

> **KEY TERM**
> **Operant conditioning:** learning as a result of reinforcement, e.g. being praised for losing weight.

? There has been an increased incidence of eating disorders in recent years. Why do you think this is?

? Have you ever eaten so much of something, you now no longer like it?

advertisements and the media are also likely to add to or alter the food **schemas** that have been constructed, and this could continue throughout life.

Then there are people's likes and dislikes, which also influence their attitudes to food. Some of these likes and dislikes are impossible to explain; others can be explained using Learning Theory. For example, individuals who learn to associate a food with positive experiences, such as ice-cream with happy parties and days out, might well like that food because of its associations, learned by **classical conditioning**. However, someone who eats too much ice cream and is very, very sick, could learn, also by association (i.e. classical conditioning), a strong dislike and avoidance of that food. This type of case is called one-trial learning, because it is so powerful that to have the experience once is enough to learn the behaviour.

Garcia's classic studies in the 1950s and 1960s were based on studying the effects of radiation, including nausea. He used rats, which have a strong preference for sweet things, such as sweetened water, but who developed a strong aversion to this sweetened water if it was consumed just before they were irradiated (and suffered radiation nausea). The strength of the rats' aversion related directly to the single amount of radiation they had experienced. Given a choice of unsweetened or sweetened water, rats that received no radiation chose sweetened water 80% of the time; rats with mild radiation exposure chose it 40% of the time, and rats with strong radiation exposure chose the sweetened water only 10% of the time, even after a long time delay. This surprised the researchers, because until that time it was not known that one single trial could condition learning. The radiation-induced nausea had become associated with sweetened water, and so this water was avoided; this aversion was the result of one-trial learning.

People also construct schemas of what is food and what is not based on cultural norms. British soldiers in the Second World War were given caviar on bread, a Russian food norm, when they reached that country, but are reported to have said that "fish jam" was not what they thought of as food. It seems that they assumed that something dark, sticky, and on a slice of bread would be similar to, e.g. blackberry jam; they found the very different taste was off-putting.

In the UK, we are used to a wide range of food from various ethnic groups, but there are still some things that we might be surprised at being offered during a meal, e.g. crispy fried insects or stewed ducks' feet, both of which are considered delicacies in other cultures. Would you eat things like this? It could depend on whether your schema of foodstuffs could expand to include such items or whether your social norms about polite behaviour would allow you to refuse the food!

KEY TERMS

Schemas: mental representations of behaviours, objects, people, etc.
Classical conditioning: learning an association between two things that are not actually connected, e.g. thinness and popularity.

Not a lot of people know this!

Dandelions and nettles are really troublesome plants, unwanted in the garden, not to mention the pain of nettle stings on bare skin. Our schema of these is likely to be of weeds and not vegetables. However, they are also edible and full of useful nutrients. When the leaves are picked young, and free from chemical sprays, they can be washed, chopped, steamed, and eaten as tasty food, for example in a creamy risotto!

This area was researched by Zimbardo, Weisenberg, Firestone, and Levy (1965) using young military personnel as participants. They were asked to eat fried grasshoppers by a superior who acted either as cheerful and informal or as cool and official. The participants then had to assess this eating experience! It is interesting that nearly 60% of those given the grasshoppers by the cool and official person judged the insects to be quite tasty, whereas only about 5% of those dealt with by the cheerful superior made the same judgement. Cognitive dissonance theory would explain this by saying that people justify complying with a very odd request from someone who is not likeable by deciding that the task—such as eating fried grasshoppers—is pleasant.

Eating behaviour also varies from group to group. This can include the timing and frequency of meals, the size and type of meal, and the eating crockery and cutlery. All these things are likely to be social norms, learned as schemas from experience starting from being a child at home. So, whether you have a proper meal at lunchtime or in the evening, or eat your evening meal at 6 p.m or, as is traditional in Spain, at 11 p.m.; whether you use plates or bowls, a fork, a knife and fork, or chopsticks, these variations are the norm in some environments and not in others. Food and eating behaviours illustrate cultural diversity really well, in sub-cultures as well as in main cultures.

> **HOW SCIENCE WORKS: IS THIS FOOD?**
> You will have read in the text about the influence of culture on diet, but what does this mean in real terms? Why not do some research on the internet, looking to see what certain cultural groups do and do not regard as food? You could team up with some classmates, work separately, and then pool your findings. These could be put up as posters, with illustrations—just make sure you are all non-judgemental when you find things that are very different from your own food norms; it is unethical to show a lack of respect for other people's norms.
>
> Useful search engines are Google and Yahoo, but there are many others. Your librarian could also suggest some ideas for where to look.

Mood

Many people crave sweet or starchy foods, carbohydrates, when they are feeling low, this is the so-called comfort eating. This behaviour could be the result of various factors, which could include: (1) classical conditioning, the learned association between feeling low and compensating by eating chocolate or other sweet food; (2) operant conditioning, because of the associated feelings of happiness or pleasure even if these are only temporarily; and (3) social learning, because we see chocolate marketed as a product that brings happiness, and also because we see chocolate is given as a reward and we can reward ourselves in the same way. This latter observation would also encourage individuals to learn a schema in which chocolate brings pleasure, and in our own society giving or receiving chocolate as a reward is a social norm.

Comfort eating usually involves the consumption of starchy or high-sugar foods.

> **?** How many different cultures' food have you and your classmates tried? Have you ever refused to eat any ethnic food? Was this because of dislike or because of its strangeness as a food?

Findings

It had been widely accepted that eating carbohydrates leads to an increase in **serotonin**, one of the brain's neurotransmitters sometimes called the "happy" chemical because it is associated, among other functions, with raised mood, which would explain the comfort-eating behaviour. This belief was based on laboratory studies that showed that a high-carbohydrate diet increased the rate at which **tryptophan** enters the brain, and this then led to the increase in serotonin. Anecdotal evidence also supported the concept of eating sweet or starchy foods, like cakes, doughnuts, ice-cream, in order to cheer oneself up, although this was often reported to improve mood only very short-term.

> **KEY TERMS**
>
> **Serotonin:** a brain neurotransmitter involved in a variety of behaviours.
>
> **Tryptophan:** an amino acid present in most protein-based foods.

Evaluation. This neurochemical effect described above may not happen in everyday eating as even a small amount of protein will prevent the increased uptake of tryptophan and so would not increase serotonin levels. As little as 2–4% of the meal's calories as protein has this effect. Benton and Donohoe (1999) suggest that the food with the greatest positive effect on mood is chocolate, and that people associate chocolate with helping their mood when they feel emotionally low. If this mood improvement is not the result of the carbohydrate in chocolate, then how does this food have the reported mood-enhancing effect? Chocolate naturally contains a variety of chemicals that could affect brain function, such as anandamines, caffeine, phenylethylamine, and magnesium, but analysis shows that the actual amounts of these in chocolate are very small, too small to have any real effect on mood. In fact, there are other foods with greater quantities of these chemicals and they do not have the reputation of improving mood. So the suggestion is that eating chocolate is in itself pleasurable, because of the scent and taste and texture; and as with any pleasure, this means endorphins are released in the brain. So it is these opioid chemicals that could lift the mood and give an increased sense of well-being. An alternative explanation was suggested by Macht and Dettmer (2006) when they studied mood changes specific to eating chocolate, compared to eating apples. Their participants were all healthy and normal-weight women, and self-reported their subjective mood at intervals after eating a chocolate bar or an apple or nothing. Interestingly, both the chocolate and the apple raised the mood as well as reduced hunger, but unsurprisingly the effects of eating chocolate were more powerful. Eating chocolate also led to joyous feelings, and sometimes to guilt feelings as well. The guilt obviously reduced the pleasure from the chocolate and seemed to be related to negative cognitions about food, especially chocolate. This attitude probably linked to concerns about health, and particularly weight—even though the women were of normal, healthy weight—and might be caused by the perceived social pressures to be thin, not just normal body size. The positive mood seemed to be caused by the sensations of eating chocolate, the sensory pleasure at the time and even before that, to the anticipation of this pleasure. Perhaps "having" to eat chocolate for a worthy cause, serious research, was an extra stimulus here! Parker, Parker, and Brotchie's (2006) meta-analysis of a wide range of research into eating, behaviour, chocolate, and mood found no significant empirical evidence for the claims that chocolate is a mood-enhancing food in spite of the many claims that it is almost a drug. They distinguish between food cravings, emotional (or comfort) eating, and actual measurements of mood, and conclude that chocolate gives emotional pleasure because it satisfies certain cravings but it does not have a lasting effect on improving mood. The pleasure is transient and caused mainly by the "melt-in-the-mouth" smoothness; this silky texture comes from its cocoa butter content, as cocoa butter melts at body temperature. This means that the widespread belief that carbohydrate foods, especially chocolate, can alter and improve mood are the result of other factors as outlined at the top of this section.

Caffeine

Caffeine is another food substance that has a link to attitudes and food. In Western industrialised culture, it is very common for people to start the day with a caffeine "kick". This is usually a drink with enough caffeine in it to make the person feel energised and feel their brain is able to function more sharply. Many

? Can you think of any ethical concerns with the research discussed above?

individuals believe that they need this caffeine to be able to wake up and get going, to have a positive mood.

Findings. Smith, Brice, Nash, Rich, and Nutt (2003) looked at the effects of caffeine on mood and cognitive performance, and found that two cups of normal-strength coffee increased mood, alertness and concentration, general task performance, and memory. They also show a cause for this cognitive improvement, in that caffeine helps to maintain levels of noradrenaline centrally.

Evaluation. This prolonging of noradrenaline action would facilitate neural activity. It is one of the "permissive amines" associated with mood and low levels are implicated in mood disorders. The increased neural activity could also explain some side-effects of caffeine such as raised heart rate and blood pressure; furthermore, this effect of caffeine might also help to explain the effects of caffeine withdrawal, the well-known headaches, general fatigue, and drowsiness. However, psychological effects of caffeine use could have an additional effect on the assumption that caffeine drinks or foods improve mood and functioning (Rogers, Richardson, and Elliman 1992). Social learning could operate as children model parents' and other adults' behaviour of needing the morning cup(s) of coffee or tea. This could then be reinforced by learning, such as learning the association between the caffeine drink and the adults' improved mood. The initial bitterness of coffee or strong tea could be ameliorated using sweeteners, milk, or cream, or watering the drink down, and the younger person could then become habituated to the flavour leading to learning a liking for it because of its pleasant effects cognitively or socially, such as becoming a member of an in-group. Social aspects of caffeine use are also significant. Even if the person does not drink coffee they may use the phrases "coffee and a chat" or "relax over a cuppa" when arranging to meet a friend, signifying a pleasant association between caffeine and mood. One should also remember that not everyone enjoys caffeine drinks or the caffeine "hit". There are some who choose not to use caffeine either because they never do get to like the taste of the drinks, or because they find some of its effects, such as the raised heart rate, very unpleasant. This is an example of individual differences between humans and demonstrates the caution that is needed in generalising research findings to the population.

Overall, mood could be neurochemically linked to eating behaviour as Heath, Melichar, Nutt, and Donaldson (2006) have found that levels of serotonin (also known as 5-hydroxytryptamine; 5-HT) and noradrenaline (NA) actually alter taste perception. Their study showed that both these neurochemicals lower taste thresholds for sweetness and other tastes; in other words, raised levels of 5-HT and/or NA make food seem tastier, and lower levels of 5-HT and/or NA—as found in mood disorders such as depression—would make food less tasty. This could at least in part explain why depressives' eating behaviours change, so they may eat more than before, or less. If they eat more it is perhaps because they are searching for the tastiness that food used to have; and if they eat less it could be that food is just boring because of a lack of tastiness. This link between the permissive amines, mood, and eating behaviour could also explain why many people feel less need to eat when really happy.

Health concerns

In recent years, health issues concerned with attitudes to food and to eating have been very evident. These issues include the concept of the healthy diet, safety of

Caffeine is proven to be both a mood stimulant and concentration enhancer—perhaps this is why many crave a morning cup of coffee.

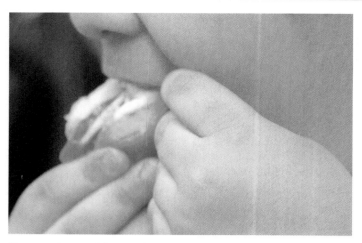

The prevalence of fatty and sugary foods combined with a lack of exercise is likely to be responsible for the fact that many UK children (27%) are overweight.

food additives such as colourings, and the inherent goodness of the food itself such as food produced without use of chemicals or hormones.

Findings

A UK government study of nearly 900 children found that although 58% of the sample aged 7–16 years did not have serious food concerns. The other 42% were concerned about food-related diseases and illness such as bird flu (in the media at the time of the survey); the fat, sugar, and salt content of their food; and the risk of food poisoning. Around 95% said that eating healthy food would make them healthy, and 82% agreed that eating healthily was personally important; 79% obtained healthy eating information from school and 31% from family or friends. The vast majority were aware that they should eat five portions of fruit and vegetables a day to stay healthy, and most were trying to cut down on sugary or fatty foods and sugary, fizzy drinks (Food Standards Agency, 2007).

Evaluation: These data from the children survey do not seem to match the data on childhood obesity; 27% of children in the UK are overweight (BBC, 2006a) and 13.7% are clinically obese (Jotangia, Moody, Stamatakis & Wardle 2005). If children know what they need to eat to be healthy then why is there an increasing number who are overweight? It seems that both poor diet—with a prevalence of fatty, sugary foods—plus lack of exercise are the probable causes. Obesity is far more common in lower socio-economic groups, which suggests that socio-economic factors might be relevant. These could include poorer access to educational resources for the parents so that norms for meals and snacks include a reliance on high-calorie, low-nutrient foods that are satisfying and cheaper. Many children outside London report having little or no choice as to what they eat, and so their knowledge may not be operationalised. Furthermore, many advertisements for sugary and fatty snacks are colourful and designed to appeal to children by associating fun things with the food in question, and the use of attractive models, fictional or real life, could encourage children's social learning that a certain food is good to eat.

Further findings

The Food Standards Agency (2008) reports that the number of UK people aware of the benefits of eating the five portions of fruit and vegetables a day rose from about 43% in 2000 to 58% in 2004, and sales of fruit and vegetables have increased this century. Furthermore, there are health concerns about the use of the 350 pesticides permitted in the UK, and the possibility of unknown long-term effects of the residues in food from the 4.5 billion litres used annually (BBC, 2008a), plus research showing that not using such chemicals and farming organically increases the nutritional value of some foods, such as potatoes, carrots, and milk. This could explain why people are buying more organic food, even though it is more expensive; organic sales grew by 22% between 2004 and 2005, and sales of boxes of organic vegetables increased by 53% over the same period.

Evaluation. Interestingly, the actual percentage of people who say they eat the five portions daily does not quite match, being 25% in 2000 and 50% in 2004. This mismatch could have a variety of reasons from the plain economic—fruit is quite expensive and many people do not enjoy eating vegetables—to a lack of belief in the information about health given out by government agencies. There is also the association between eating meat as a sign of self-worth and success, because it is more expensive than vegetables so eating meat could represent a reward for one's work and effort.

Although the increase in people buying organic food is large, and is a possible sign of health concerns, the actual amount of such food chosen is small compared with the total amount bought nationally. Wandel's (2004) survey of Norwegians showed that people's concerns about eating healthy food increased but trust in expert advice decreased. It is possible that this phenomenon is not confined to Norway. Although the study showed that people increasingly had health considerations in mind when they chose their everyday food, the uncertainty in their knowledge of nutrition because of doubts about the advice from experts possibly slowed the adoption of healthier eating. This could explain—at least in part—the difference between knowledge and actual behaviour as it could be caused by a doubtful attitude.

Final comments

It really is clear and obvious that one's social experiences will have a great influence on one's attitudes to food. We learn many attitudes at an early age, often in the home environment, by classical and operant conditioning and social learning, and, from this, we form our schema of what counts as food and our norms about food and eating. It makes sense that children would learn in this way as various substances that could be eaten might have harmful effects, so guidance from parents and others is important. The one-trial learning mentioned earlier is an adaptive or protective mechanism so that if eating a substance has real ill effects the individual concerned will know to avoid it another time; this learning is so powerful that sometimes even the thought of that substance, let alone the sight or smell, is enough to make him or her feel queasy.

> **EXAM HINT**
>
> The first area of this topic requires you to be able to discuss factors such as mood, culture, and health concerns that affect attitudes to food and eating behaviour. These factors are easy to describe but AO2/AO3 is more demanding, so think about the sources of AO2/AO3 available, for example:
>
> - Consider the methodological strengths and weaknesses of the research; the fact that the factors are not universal means individual differences apply.
> - The research evidence for the factors is correlational and so cause and effect cannot be established and other factors are likely to be involved.
> - Where there is more than one explanation for a factor, you can use the additional explanations as counter-perspectives.

Explanations for the Success or Failure of Dieting

Dieting is defined as the adoption of a particular or special diet in order to achieve a purpose. Britain has an adult obesity problem with obesity increasing nearly four-fold in the last 25 years, and it is said that about 22% of adults are considered obese and 75% overweight (Lopez-Jimenez, 2008). In everyday life, dieting usually means eating a diet that would help the individual lose weight, so it would be a lower-calorie diet than the usual one. The general overview is that dieting to lose weight may succeed in the short term but that the lost weight usually returns over the longer term. There is no doubt as to the good intentions of dieters, motivated by social norms of slimness and being attractive, as well as

Adult obesity has increased four-fold in Britain in the last 25 years.

healthier and with a likely longer lifespan, and it is psychologically interesting to look at what makes it more or less likely for dieters to succeed in their aim of long-term weight loss. Operant conditioning could reinforce dieting behaviour and weight loss if the weight loss is successful.

Findings

Mark (2006) argues that the reason dieting has low success rates for long-term weight loss is not only that environmental factors are involved, but that biological reasons make long-term weight loss difficult. He suggests that dietary initiatives are always likely to fail because they do not address the underlying biological/genetic problems such as those to do with the hormone **leptin**. This hormone has a function in regulating appetite.

Bellar and Jarosz (2008) regard obesity as a complex condition, and as such unlikely to be sorted out simply by eating fewer calories. One important factor is that people who are seriously overweight, and have been eating too many calories for a long time, have a greatly reduced ability to deal with blood sugars, because they have developed an insensitivity to the hormone **insulin**, which normally regulates blood sugar levels. This insensitivity has to be addressed if the person is to lose weight. In order to increase insulin sensitivity, this study suggests that it is important for dieters to exercise regularly, as well as to eat fewer calories. Slow weight loss is more successful in the long term than a faster weight-loss programme.

Evaluation

Havel (2000) has outlined the action of leptin on various hypothalamic areas that influence feeding behaviour and energy expenditure. Leptin seems to inhibit the release of another neurochemical, neuropeptide Y, which is the neurotransmitter stimulating hunger and eating behaviour. This means that higher leptin levels decrease hunger and eating. Humans who are eating a low-calorie diet have low levels of leptin and this is why such diets seem to produce the increased sensations of hunger, which would of course explain the weight gain so often experienced after initial weight loss, and the difficulty of maintaining that weight loss in the long term.

This is supported by Weigle et al.'s (2003) study, which shows that weight loss from a low-carbohydrate and therefore low-calorie diet results in low levels of leptin and so increases hunger and then subsequent weight gain. In addition, however, they also show that if the diet is changed to a low-fat diet, the weight loss is maintained because there is no compensatory increase in appetite. This leptin explanation of obesity seemed clear until assays showed that obese individuals usually have high levels of leptin, which should mean they would have small appetites and would not be overweight. However, further to this, Laposky, Bradley, Williams, Bass, and Turek (2007) explain that obesity seems to be linked genetically to leptin resistance. Thus, people with an abnormal leptin regulation system are insensitive to leptin and its signals to eat less, which is why they are obese in the first instance, and why dieting is not successful in long-term weight loss in the second instance. This means that there is the possibility of drug treatment or gene therapy in the future to regularise the physiological leptin system and therefore the physical obesity of such people.

There is, however, a challenge to this model, or rather to the desirability of dieting and weight reduction in the obese. A Finnish study (*The Guardian*, 2005) supported previous research showing that dieting and losing weight reduced the risk of heart disease and diabetes, but also that physiological damage can occur as a result of this dieting and can lead to long-term health risks of dying young. The sample of nearly 3000 overweight or obese people was tracked for 24 years, during which time records of health and weight and deaths were kept. Data analysis showed that those who were trying to lose weight or who gained weight had a significantly increased risk of an early death. Sørensen (2003) suggests that prevention of becoming overweight is probably the best option for a healthy population. These data are supported by recent studies such as Pischon et al. (2008).

? What are some risks of dieting?

The above biological evidence for the success or failure of dieting is very convincing, and although reductionist, is by its empirical evidence powerful, but it might not be the complete story. Truby et al.'s (2006) study for the BBC programme "*Diet Trials*" showed the importance of psychological not just biological factors. They led a 6-month randomised controlled comparison of four commercial diet programmes with a sample of overweight or obese people who were otherwise healthy. All participants had significant loss of body fat and weight over the 6 months, with an average weight loss of 5.9kg and an average loss of body fat of 4.4kg. Of course, the short duration of this study means one cannot tell if this weight and fat loss was maintained in the long term, and as—generally—50% of weight loss is regained within 1 year this missing information is important. At 1 year on, the average weight loss was 10%, which was encouraging. One diet plan was low carbohydrate and one was low fat, and yet all four plans produced significant weight loss, which does not fit in with the leptin hypothesis.

? Why do you think these programmes work so well for some, and not at all for others?

So what were the positive factors of these diet programmes? It seems that an initial and quite fast weight loss is highly motivating to continuing with the diet plan; it provides reinforcement—reward—and is an example of operant conditioning in action. However, this is typically followed by a plateau period with little or no weight loss for a while and here social support in the form of weekly meetings of dieters seems to be a critical factor. This social support gives encouragement and reassurance that the programme will continue to work and the current cessation of weight loss is a temporary stage. For those who continue with the programme, any of the four programmes, weight loss then continues. It is also likely that the knowledge of media interest, even in the majority of participants who were not going to be filmed for the television programme, also acted as encouragement to stay motivated.

Other, social, factors impact on dieting. de Castro and de Castro's (1989) participants' food diaries showed that the quantity of food eaten by an individual varies in direct proportion with the number of people present. They also demonstrated the importance of exercise, which not only burns up calories but also raises the metabolic rate even after the exercise has finished. Miller et al.'s (1997a) meta-analysis of diet, exercise, and diet + exercise weight-loss programmes found that the long-term success rate was greater for the diet plus exercise cohort. These data are supported by Ross et al. (2000), who found greater weight loss plus reduced body fat in a diet with exercise programme compared with a diet-only programme.

A further factor has been demonstrated by Lichtman et al. (1992), who demonstrated that dieters delude themselves about both their food intake and exercise levels. Obese people on a reduced-calorie diet underestimated their food intake by 47% and overestimated the amount of exercise they took by 51%. This explained their failure to lose weight!

So what is the overview of diets and their success or failure? Basically, individuals who regularly eat fewer calories than they use up each day will lose weight, particularly if this is combined with an exercise programme. Diets that produce an early noticeable weight loss will encourage dieters to persist, especially if there is good social support. Biological factors may be important, and leptin therapy may be a way forward for some dieters. But, overall, encouragement and social support for those who are truly determined to lose fat and weight probably stand the best chance of success.

EXAM HINT

Note that any explanation for the failure of diets that is based solely on biological explanations is very reductionist. Other psychological explanations can be used as alternative perspectives to illustrate the simplicity of the biological explanation. These provide valuable AO2 material.

SECTION SUMMARY
Eating Behaviour

Factors influencing attitudes to food and eating behaviour

❖ Many factors influence our eating behaviour, such as cultural influences, mood, and health concerns.

❖ Cultural influences include:

— social norms, which vary from group to group
— religious norms, which vary considerably from belief to belief
— parental and family influences
— learning—classical and operant conditioning and social learning
— schemas.

❖ Mood factors include:

— craving carbohydrates when in a low mood
— because of conditioning or social learning, or increased serotonin
— or because these foods produce an endorphin rush.

❖ Chocolate is believed to be a mood enhancer:

— it contains brain-modifying chemicals
— in too small quantities to be effective (Parker et al., 2006)
— the sensory pleasure of taste and smell and texture produce endorphin release
— learning it is a pleasure/reward by classical and operant conditioning and social learning (Macht & Dettmer, 2006).

❖ Caffeine is also believed to be a mood enhancer:

— two cups of normal strength coffee increase positive mood (Smith et al., 2003)
— caffeine supports noradrenaline activity in the brain, which would improve cognitive functioning
— noradrenaline is one of the permissive amines associated with mood.

❖ Overall, serotonin and noradrenaline could affect both mood and eating because:

— low levels of both are linked to low mood and to food being perceived as less tasty
— so people with low mood could eat more if searching for tastiness
— or eat less because food is no longer tasty, but boring.

❖ Health concerns about food include concerns about a healthy diet, food safety, and food quality.

❖ Research shows that children are informed and aware about food issues such as what constitutes a healthy diet, safe food, and quality food

— UK government survey findings
— level of overweight and obese children (Jotangia et al., 2005).

❖ Cheap food is often high in fats and sugars; availability of healthier foods is variable; advertisements for less healthy foods are often attractive to children.

❖ Fruits and organic foods are expensive and so not accessible to many.

❖ People have doubts about the veracity of government advice on diet and health.

❖ Dieting is the adoption of a particular or special diet in order to achieve a purpose.

Explanations for the success or failure of dieting

❖ In the UK 22% of adults are considered obese and 75% overweight (Lopez-Jimenez, 2008), and dieting is generally held to mean eating fewer calories in order to lose weight.

❖ Such diets can be successful short-term, but excess weight tends to return long-term, possibly because both environmental and biological factors are involved.

— overweight people are insulin-insensitive (Bellar & Jarosz 2008)
— low-calorie diets would lead to low leptin levels, which produce hunger
— obese people have high levels of leptin so should not feel hunger, although they could be leptin-insensitive; other neurochemicals might also be involved.

❖ A comparison study of four commercial diet programmes with similar, successful weight losses suggests key factors are psychological.

❖ Several studies show the importance of exercise in achieving and maintaining weight loss.

BIOLOGICAL EXPLANATIONS OF EATING BEHAVIOUR

Neural Mechanisms Involved in Controlling Eating and Satiation

Hunger, satiety, and the brain

The main centres controlling hunger have been identified in the brain (de Araujo, Gutierrez, Pereira Jr., Nicolelis, Simon, & Oliveira-Maia 2006). Hunger is the

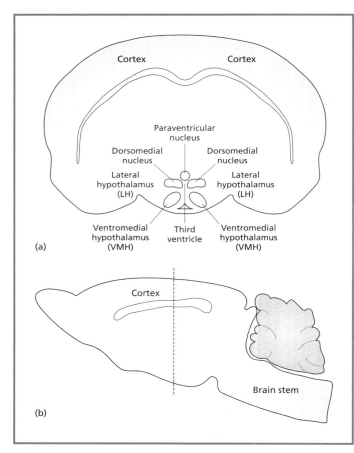

Some of the parts of the rat brain that have been found to be important in feeding behaviour. (a) Vertical cross section of the brain, (b) a side view of the brain (the front part of the brain is to the left). The vertical line shows the location of the cross-section. From Logue (2004).

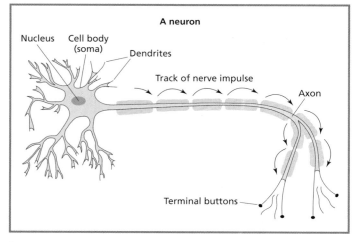

A neuron.

motivation—or drive—to start eating; satiety—the feeling of being full or replete—switches off this drive and so stops the eating behaviour. The research team implanted minute electrodes into rat brains and recorded neuronal activity through the animals' feeding cycle. They focused on the lateral hypothalamus, orbitofrontal cortex, insular cortex, and amygdala.

What they found was that they could identify individual neurons that responded to particular phases of the feeding cycle, such as a change in satiety as the rats satisfied their hunger, and in a group the bundles of these neurons reflected the hunger/satiety state of the animal. This is significant as the integration of the separate nerve impulses enables the rats to behave appropriately for their current physiological situation. Two significant eating control centres are known both to be in the hypothalamus; one is in the lateral hypothalamus (or LH), the other is in the ventro-medial hypothalamus (or VMH). Other brain areas identified as involved with feeling hunger are in the insular, parietal, and temporal cortex, and the prefrontal cortex is involved with feelings of satiety.

Research from the 1940s onwards showed that lesioning, i.e. destroying, tiny areas in the LH in rats, dogs, and other mammals led to a loss of interest in food and eating, the animals seemingly unaware that they were starving themselves. Similar lesions of the VMH led to the animals concerned eating voraciously, so they became obese. This suggested that the LH initiates eating behaviour and the VMH stops this behaviour, but as Logue (2004) and others have pointed out, destroying brain tissue, however carefully, could affect far more neurons and neural activity than that of the cell bodies in the destroyed area. For example, neurons in other areas whose dendrites or axons run through the relevant area would have their functions altered as these fibres are damaged. It is also likely that some at least of the neurons with cell bodies in the LH or VMH could be affected by sensory input relayed from other areas, and could in turn pass information on to, for example, the frontal cortex. After all, anyone with mammal pets knows that they have food preferences, as well as being aware that we do, and that in our privileged Western culture many of us can choose which foods to eat when we feel hunger so cognition also plays a part in eating and stopping eating, these behaviours are not just automatic stimulus–response drives. Then there is the evidence that starting and stopping eating also involves blood glucose levels, neurochemicals, hormones, and stretch receptor reflexes as discussed below.

So this LH and VMH control system is far from a set of simple on-off switches for hunger, eating, and satiety.

It has been known for some time that hormones such as insulin and leptin are also critically involved in eating behaviour, and animal studies showed that when blood insulin levels were low the animals ate much more than usual, whereas injections of moderate levels of insulin seemed to reduce appetite, probably by reducing hunger (Rosenzweig, Breedlove, & Leiman, 2002). It was also known that blood glucose levels affect hunger. When glucose levels—in rats or in humans—were lowered, appetite increased; when they were raised, appetite faded away (Smith & Campfield, 1993; Lavin, Wittert, Sun, Horowitz, Morley, & Read 1996). Horvath (2005) identified these brain areas and suggested that individual differences are shown in that each person has their individual set point, a balance between hunger and satiety, and this is possibly determined by a combination of genetic factors and early nutritional experience. If one imagines the line between hunger and satiety to be a continuum, with extreme hunger at one end and complete satiety at the other, then the balance point for an individual is somewhere between; but exactly where this balance point is varies. If it is nearer to hunger, then that person might have a tendency to eat more and be overweight, whereas if the balance point is nearer satiety that person will be comfortable eating less and will be unlikely to be overweight. This sounds very reasonable, and was attractive in removing the stigma of being greedy from overweight people, but it does not in any way give understanding of those annoying people who enjoy large meals and yet never put on an extra unit of fat!

Researching the details of leptin action has been difficult, but studies involving a Turkish family with a genetic deficiency that results in family members lacking leptin have been key resources. Licinio et al. (2004) used three adults from this family to demonstrate that, when they were given leptin supplements, their body weight and eating behaviour became normal. Matochik et al. (2005) showed some sustained structural changes in the cortex with the leptin supplements. London (2007) based further research on these adults to investigate the neural circuits for leptin action: these circuits allow leptin to alter human eating behaviour. The great advantage of involving this family is that, as family members produce no leptin themselves, fMRI imaging can show neural activity in the absence of leptin and then, after leptin treatment, in the presence of leptin. This brain scanning was done using visual images of food items as stimulus material, with the Turkish adults reporting their personal feelings of hunger. After the leptin treatment, there was reduced activity in the insular, parietal, and temporal cortices and increased brain activity in the prefrontal cortex. This fits in with the insular, parietal, and temporal cortex areas being concerned with hunger but the prefrontal areas being concerned with satiety.

One question has been how these chemical levels or other factors affect hunger, as the brain centres involved were known to be the LH and VMH. We have looked at the effect of leptin in the brain. Further evidence for leptin's influence on eating

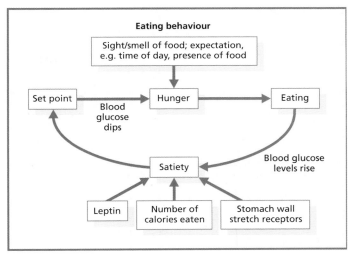

Control of eating behaviour.

The lobes of the brain and the insular cortex.

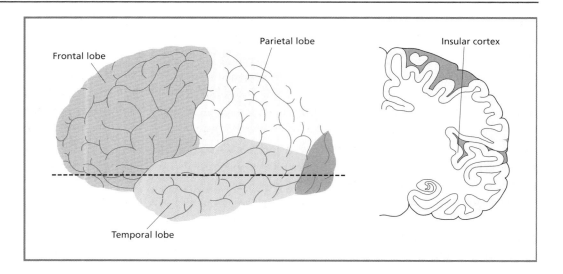

behaviour comes from studies of the Pima Indians, a population prone to obesity. Ravussin, Pratley, Maffei, Wang, Friedman, and Bennett's (1997) longitudinal study of two weight-matched groups over 3 years found that mean plasma leptin concentrations were lower in the group that gained weight than in the group that did not gain weight. This confirms leptin's influence on appetite and weight gain. This is not, however, the only mechanism. We know that the stomach sends nerve impulses to the brain when food reaches it and the stomach walls stretch to accommodate this food. Stretch receptors in the walls reflex via the vagus nerve to the hypothalamus, and these stimulate feelings of satiety. However, there is a time delay between the arrival of the food in to the stomach and these messages being sent, and this could be one reason why some individuals—especially those who eat very quickly—can continue to eat more because they still feel hungry, when in fact they have already eaten enough to be satisfied. This could be one reason why advice to eat slowly, to chew food slowly and savour it, does usually mean people eat less, because they are allowing their gut time to communicate to the brain. This challenges Johnstone et al.'s (2006) study on the drive to eat. They used rats on a strict and regular diet where food was presented for 2 hours a day. Brain activity was analysed when fasting, when anticipating feeding, and when actually feeding. The surprising results showed that appetite-stimulating neurons start firing before feeding starts; seemingly in anticipation just before the meal. The appetite-suppressing neurons started to activate as soon as food began being eaten. However, humans are not rats, and while we share many mammal features including basic brain design it cannot be assumed that what the rat brain does is the same as in the far more complex human brain.

Johnstone et al. (2006) studied brain activity in rats and found that appetite-suppressing neurons began firing as soon as food started to be eaten.

EXAM HINT
Draw a diagram of the neural mechanisms involved in eating to act as a memory aid. It doesn't have to be anatomically correct but must include: the lateral hypothalamus, ventro-medial hypothalamus, insular, parietal, temporal, prefrontal, and orbitofrontal cortex, the amygdala, and hormones leptin and insulin.

Further interesting findings come from Batterham et al.'s (2007) research using a hormone, PYY (peptide tyrosine tyrosine), which the gut releases in proportion to how many calories have been eaten. PYY is very effective in suppressing appetite. fMRI scans were done on eight participants on two occasions when they had been fasting for 14 hours. In one condition they were on a harmless saline drip, and in the other condition they were on an intravenous drip of PYY, which would mimic having recently had a good meal. Half an hour after each scan, participants were given an all-you-can-eat buffet that included their favourite foods, even high-calorie ones like spaghetti bolognese and macaroni cheese. As predicted, those participants who had been on PYY transfusion ate an average of 25% fewer calories than the individuals who had been on the saline drip. The interesting thing was that the fMRI scans showed that not only did hypothalamic centres light up for the PYY participants but so did frontal cortex areas associated with reward and pleasure. There was also a correlation between the hypothalamic activity and those on the saline drip and their calorie intake. Of course, a sample size of eight individuals is always going to be heavily biased and unrepresentative of the general population, and so one cannot justify extrapolating from Batterham's research to the community, but these finding show interesting effects of PYY, which could be taken further by later research. For example, areas for study might include PYY release after a meal for obese individuals.

> **?** What findings might you expect from PYY assays in obese people compared with similar but normal-weight people that could explain the weight gain of the obese?

It's not will power, it's my neurons, honest!

Not a lot of psychological research uses Krispy Kreme donuts! But Mohanty, Gitelman, Small, and Mesulam (2008) used them to test participants in two conditions: once when they had fasted for 8 hours and once when they had eaten as many Krispy Kreme donuts as they could, up to a maximum of eight. In each condition, fMRI scans were done as the participants looked at images of either doughnuts or toolbox screwdrivers.

It was not at all surprising that after the doughnut binge the hunger centres of the brain did not activate for the doughnut images. However, what *was* surprising was that, in the fasting individuals, it was the limbic system that became highly excited at the doughnut pictures, showing a response to what was motivationally significant. This was followed by activation of the spatial awareness networks, which, in an everyday situation, would result in the person seeking out doughnuts or similar food. Mesulam explains this process as a complex system that functions to direct our attention to what we need—if hungry, food; if not hungry, something else. Otherwise, as he says, "If we didn't have this (system) . . . every time you passed by a bakery you would have no control over your eating. If your nerve cells fired every time you smelled something edible, then you'd eat all the time, not just when you're hungry."

Mesulam also made the analogy to what we need to know, i.e. what your brain needs to be aware of. This is like being alone in an empty house or flat, when the slightest creak or other noise can seem loud and scary: it could mean danger. However, if we are there with other people, we might not even notice the noises as we are not alone and vulnerable. When we are hungry, when we need food, our brains automatically flag up any sign that food might be available.

Evolutionary Explanations of Food Preference

Evolutionary explanations focus on what factors could have been adaptive, could have helped our long-ago, hunter-gatherer ancestors survive and bear as many children as possible; food is therefore obviously one such factor. In basic survival situations it was clearly adaptive to be omnivorous, to be able to eat, digest, and use as nutrients and energy substrate both plant and animal food. In these conditions there would be a fine line between energy expenditure in hunting for and gathering food, and the energy and nutrients gained from this food. If the latter was greater than the former the individual would survive, and if the difference was great enough he or she would thrive; but if the former outweighed the latter then the result would be death. So, clearly, foods richer in energy and nutrients would be so much more beneficial to health than foods with limited energy and nutrient value. Humans all over the world have a preference for foods rich in protein, fats or oils, and sugar, and this suggests that these preferences are genetic, innate, hard-wired into us. Evolutionary theory has a very convincing explanation or why this is so.

If one looks at basic information such as the energy content of food then fats and oils contain twice as many calories as carbohydrates or proteins. This would suggest that a preference and searching for fatty foods would have been adaptive for our ancestors. Protein-rich foods would also have been necessary for health, as these are needed to repair and build body tissue, especially in pregnant or lactating (breast-feeding) women. So does this mean that humans would have a genetically controlled preference for fatty, meaty foods? This has been suggested (Eaton & Konner, 1985), and the so-called "paleolithic diet" of meat, fish, and fatty/oily foods plus fruits and vegetables has been put forward as the only healthy way for humans to eat. Starchy foods, such as cereal grains, and sugary ones, especially if processed, do not usually contain many other nutrients, whereas fatty foods have the fat-soluble vitamins such as vitamin D and so are the sources of more than just calories. Worse than this idea that carbohydrates merely give empty calories, Eaton and Konner suggested that the health problems of the industrialised world, such as hypertension, coronary heart disease, and obesity, stem from the high-carbohydrate modern diet. However, although some still hold to this view, it is now generally accepted that we humans have evolved to be flexible eaters (Leonard, 2002) and that this is a great adaptive strength as our ancestors were able to adapt to changes in climate and environment and therefore available foodstuffs. Perry et al. (2007) point out that in cultures that do eat a starch-based diet, such as the rice-eating Japanese, the genome includes extra copies of the *AMY1* gene, which codes for the enzyme amylase, which is needed to digest starch. By contrast, the Yakut of the Arctic, who eat a low-carbohydrate, fish-based diet, have fewer copies of *AMY1*. This variation shows how humans have adapted to the different foods available, and peoples with the extra *AMY1* genes would have been more successful in digesting cooked starch and so would have flourished in areas where starchy foods grew. It is, however, unlikely that this improved ability to obtain energy from starch was a driving force in the development of bigger brains, as Perry suggests, as the use of fire for cooking is relatively recent, only about 500,000 years ago, and the Yakut do not have smaller brains than other human groups.

One question that needs answering is "How do we know what these long-ago people ate?" After all, we cannot research the past by asking those people questions, and they left no written records. But many of them did leave drawings and paintings of their lives, and many of these are vivid and show people out hunting and gathering food.

Ancient cave paintings give us an idea of the kinds of hunting activities, and therefore diet, of our ancestors.

Furthermore, tooth-wear patterns from skulls can be analysed to tell us how worn down the teeth were and give an insight as to how tough was the food chewed; and there is good evidence from buried refuse heaps. These things can be dated quite accurately using radioactive isotope analysis and so we know how long ago the owners of the teeth lived, and how long ago the food refuse, such a bone and shell fragments and seed cases, was thrown away. From such data we know that our remote ancestors, the early hominids or australopithecines, ate wild plant food and occasionally scavenged animal carcasses for meat, bone marrow, etc. About 2.4 million years ago, the first of our *Homo* group emerged; these individuals were not *Homo sapiens*, like ourselves, but *Homo habilis*, who ate a wide variety of animals including deer, birds, rabbits, fish, and shellfish as well as wild plants (O'Neill, 2008). At this time, Africa's climate was changing and the environment was drying out. Forests were disappearing and grasslands were spreading so the types of food available also were changing. Searching for food would be harder and take more time, so energy needs would increase. It is estimated from modern hunter-gatherers that daily travels of up to 8 miles are needed to search successfully for food. At about the same time, the brain was starting its rapid—in evolutionary terms—increase in size. The brains of the very early hominids (the australopithecines) increased from about 400 cm^3 to 500 cm^3 over 2 million years. *Homo habilis*'s brain was abut 600 cm^3 but only 300,000 years later its descendants, *Homo erectus*, had a brain size of 900 cm^3. Our (*Homo sapiens*) brains are, on average, 1350 cm^3. These increases are extremely significant in dietary terms because the brain is a very energy-expensive structure. Not only is the modern human brain three times larger than our body size would suggest from comparisons with our primate relatives, but though it forms only 2% of our body mass it consumes 20–25% of our energy and nutrient resources.

This really shows why humans have a preference for energy-dense foods, and nutrient-dense ones too. Interestingly, the increase in brain size went hand in hand with a decrease in gut length (Aiello & Wheeler, 1995). This is known to mean that the creatures concerned—early man—were eating less tough vegetation, which requires a huge expenditure of energy to break it down to release some nutrients. This is why many herbivores seem to be eating, grazing, all the time—they are doing just that!

Studies of all primate species show that those with bigger brains eat more energy-rich diets, and humans are the extreme example of this. Modern hunter-gatherers obtain an average of 40–60% of their dietary energy from animal foods such as meat and milk. Unit for unit, meat gives more than ten times the calories of leafy vegetation and two to four times the calories of fruit. This makes the greater efforts in foraging for animal food, such as the increased distances involved, worthwhile. Modern humans living a primitive life are physically smaller then the average Westerner, 125lb compared to 160lb for males, but need more than 3000 kilocalories

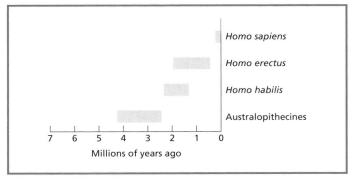

This timeline shows the rough time range in which some hominid species lived.

> **EXAM HINT**
>
> Note the two key criticisms of the research on neural mechanisms:
>
> 1. That extrapolation from animal research is an issue (in an essay elaborate on this).
> 2. In cases in which human samples have been used, the sample size is small.
>
> Both of these raise the issue of how representative the findings are for the wider human population.

[?] What are some
evolutionary changes in
human anatomy?

(kcalories) daily, rather than the 2600 kcalories the urban lifestyle requires, so for them a meat-rich diet is highly adaptive.

Evaluation

With extremely few exceptions, human evolution is accepted by the scientific community as fact. The evidence is clear and testable and supports this concept of slow change over very long periods of time. Changes in anatomy have gone together with changes in diet, particularly where brain size is concerned. In a world in which the environment has varied as humans spread out from Africa into temperate and colder zones the human ability to cope successfully with a varied diet has been a critical factor in success, it has been adaptive. This is important as the larger body size plus the moderate increase in meat consumption meant that early humans would have had to go further to forage, and spread out, moving across Africa and into the rest of the world. So the ability to vary the diet was a vital one.

The latest techniques for analysing carbon and nitrogen isotopes in hominid bones have supported the theory that these ancestral types were already obtaining almost all their dietary protein from animals (Richards, 2002). Humans have needed to seek out energy-dense and nutrient-dense foods and this, together with the ability to cook food and so make it easier and quicker to digest enabled the human gut to reduce its size and therefore its own energy demands, which would have made more dietary calories available for the bigger brains.

It is obvious that when the hunter-gatherers, who were at least partly nomadic, settled down and became farmers the efforts to forage would be reduced. The work done in caring for domesticated animals, goats, cows, and sheep for instance, and in growing, nurturing, and harvesting plants and storing food would still be considerable but not as energy-expensive as hunting and gathering. Furthermore, the majority of us in our industrial world buy our food and lead fairly sedentary lives, so our energy needs are low compared to those long-ago ancestors. But the preferences for energy-dense and nutrient-dense foods seems to be innate—genetically hard-wired into us—so we eat more than we need and we prefer crisp, fatty, creamy, or sweet foods. It is this preference that seems to have led to the current estimate that about 75% of the adult population in the UK is overweight or obese because we eat and then store the unnecessary calories as body fat.

[■] Activity:
Mechanisms involved
in eating behaviour
List the physiological
and psychological
mechanisms involved in
eating behaviour. You
might find it helpful to
present your answers in
a "mind map" format,
with "Eating" as the
central construct.

Alcohol

Alcohol has probably been known to humans for a very long time. This is because as fruits ripen, natural yeasts start to ferment the sweet juices and produce small amounts of alcohol as a by-product. Fruit seeds and stones have been found in hunter-gatherer refuse heaps, and alcohol would have given some extra calories as well as carrying the scent of the fruit further through the air making the fruit easier to find (Dudley, 2002). However, the main benefit or adaptiveness of consuming alcohol in smaller quantities seems to be associated with reducing cardiovascular disease and increased lifespan. Ridley (1999) challenges this explanation, suggesting that the adaptiveness of consuming alcohol is more to do with its disinfectant nature. He postulates that once the hunter-gatherers settled into farming communities these were likely to be fairly basic and crowded, and germs and parasites would have flourished in the dwellings and possibly also in drinking water.

In such circumstances, a moderate amount of alcohol could have acted as an adaptive factor because it might have increased the chance of an individual to survive and reproduce, and pass on the gene(s) for alcohol consumption to their offspring. Those groups which remained nomadic would not have had to deal with similar diseases as they would have moved on from place to place, from water source to water source, and so contamination of their living quarters and water sources would not have been an issue. These groups are the ancestors of modern Arabs, whose culture is historically teetotal.

Evaluation

The mere fact that many of us possess the genes that enable us to metabolise alcohol suggests that consuming this was in some way adaptive. The brain has mu opiate receptors (sensitive to alcohol) that have a circadian rhythm that peaks at about 4 p.m. (Fromme et al., 2004). When these are activated they seem to trigger a limbic-temporal lobe response to recall the steps taken in the past to have an alcoholic drink, and when the individual has that drink the biological rhythm is reset. Somewhere in our long-ago past there was a mutation that linked this opiate receptor with endorphin production, so alcohol consumption brought pleasure. If, then, the people who drank alcohol were also the people who survived better, this preference would have spread quite rapidly through populations. However, not all populations do consume alcohol, and although Arab peoples are usually abstainers, their ancestors were nomadic and so they would not have been exposed to the crowded and unhygienic conditions suggested for the settled early farmers. This makes sense, but the fact that many Orientals do not metabolise alcohol, and so are adversely affected by even small quantities, does not fit this evolutionary explanation, as historically they are a settled, agrarian culture. However, the prevalence of this condition—the lack of an enzyme that breaks down alcohol—in up to 80% of Han Chinese, Koreans, and Japanese should mean this too is in some way adaptive, despite being so unpleasant; the result of drinking alcohol for them is hot flushes and nausea. How could this lack be an advantage, adaptive? Well, the effects of drinking alcohol would make this behaviour both unattractive and unlikely, and so alcoholism is understandably less common in these ethnic groups.

> **EXAM HINT**
>
> Note that the evolutionary explanations can be criticised on the basis that they are evolutionary "stories" not facts. Even though evolution itself is a fact, we cannot be so sure about some of the assumptions that are made by evolutionary psychologists. For example, there is no fossil evidence about what food or alcohol was consumed by our ancestors, so it is difficult to have accurate knowledge of their eating behaviour. This means that the explanations lack evidence so they cannot be verified or falsified. According to Popper's definition of science, they lack scientific validity because they cannot be refuted.

SECTION SUMMARY
Biological Explanations of Eating Behaviour

❖ Hypothalamic brain centres, LH and VMH, have an important role.

❖ LH is involved with hunger leading to eating, and VMH with satiety so eating ceases:

— there are many non-human animal studies supporting these roles

— there are fewer studies on humans to support this.

Neural mechanisms involved in controlling eating and satiation

❖ Many other factors are involved, including reflexes, neurochemicals, and hormones such as leptin and insulin, blood glucose levels, stretch receptors in the stomach.

❖ Cognitive processes, e.g. food preferences also affect eating behaviour.

❖ The above factors impact on the individual set point, this latter is an example of individual differences.

❖ Studies of one family with a genetic leptin deficiency support its influence on the brain and eating behaviours (Licinio et al., 2004; London, 2007).

❖ fMRI scans show that the limbic system is activated by food images when people are hungry, but not if they are sated (Mohanty et al., 2008).

Evolutionary explanations of food preference

❖ These focus on factors that would have helped our hunter-gatherer ancestors survive and reproduce.

❖ Nutrients for energy, growth, and repair would have been in short supply, so foods that were energy-dense or rich in protein would have been extremely valuable.

❖ The preference for such foods—high in fat or sugar, and meat—would have been adaptive and could be genetic.

— humans world-wide do show preferences for high-fat and sweet foods, and high-protein foods
— some research suggests high-carbohydrate diets lead to ill health and are therefore not adaptive (Eaton & Konner, 1985)
— high-carbohydrate diet cultures have extra copies of *AMY1*, a gene coding for digesting starch, whereas low-carbohydrate cultures have fewer copies, showing that the genome evolves with the environment.

❖ The success of the high-energy, high-protein foraging could have enabled the increase in human brain size.

❖ Alcohol is another common food preference.

— its scent carries well in air thus making fermenting fruits easier to find (Dudley, 2002)
— it contains calories for energy
— it could in moderation increase survival, reducing cardiovascular problems
— it can act as a mild disinfectant
— most humans have genes which code for metabolising alcohol, supporting its adaptive usefulness
— 80% of people in the Far East do not have these genes.

EATING DISORDERS

There are several eating disorders. The most common eating disorders in the *Diagnostic and Statistical Manual of Mental Disorders* (DSM-IV) are **anorexia nervosa** and **bulimia nervosa** (discussed below). However, we could regard obesity as the most common eating disorder (S. Cave, personal communication) but—rightly or wrongly—it is *not* classified as such in DSM-IV.

Anorexia Nervosa

There are four DSM-IV criteria for anorexia nervosa:

1. The individual has a body weight less than 85% of that expected.
2. There is an intense fear of becoming fat, despite being considerably underweight.
3. The individual's thinking about his/her body weight is distorted, either by exaggerating its importance to self-evaluation or by minimising the dangers of being considerably underweight.
4. In females, the absence of three or more consecutive menstrual cycles (amenorrhoea).

Over 90% of patients with anorexia nervosa are female, and the age of onset is typically between the ages of 14 and 18 (APA, 2000). There has been an increase in the frequency of anorexia nervosa in Western societies in recent decades, with an incidence of about 0.5% in women (Cooper, 1994). Anorexia nervosa used to be very rare among African-American women in the United States, but has shown signs of a marked increase (Hsu, 1990).

Most sufferers from anorexia nervosa recover over time. However, the near-starvation that anorexics impose on themselves can produce serious and even life-threatening physiological changes. These include lowered body temperature, reduced bone mineral density, low blood pressure, and slowed heart rate.

> **?** Why do you think the majority of patients with anorexia nervosa are female?

CASE STUDY: AN EATING DISORDER

At the age of 12, JC had weighed 115 pounds and had been teased by friends and family for being "podgy". At first, JC had started to restrict her food intake by eating less at meal times, becoming selective about what she ate, and cutting out snacks between meals. Initially, JC's progressive weight loss was supported by her family and friends. However, as she began to lose pounds she would set herself new targets, ignoring feelings of hunger by focusing on each new target. In her first year of dieting, JC's weight dropped from 115 pounds to 88 pounds. Her initial goal had been to lose 10 pounds. JC's periods stopped shortly after she started her regime, her appearance changed dramatically.

In the second year of her regime, her weight loss was considered to be out of control. Her personality had also changed, and she was not the active, spontaneous, and cheerful girl she had been before dieting. Her girlfriends were less enthusiastic about coming over to her house, because JC would be stubborn and argumentative, designing strict programmes of activities for them to carry out.

JC's family asked their GP for help. He had been alarmed at JC's appearance and designed a high-calorie diet for her. However, JC believed that there was something inside her that would not let her gain weight. She would pretend to eat, often listing food she claimed to have eaten that had in fact been flushed down the toilet, or she would not swallow food she put in her mouth.

JC admitted that when she had felt down over the past 2 years she would still feel driven to lose weight and, as a result, would go on walks, run errands, or spend long periods of time keeping her room immaculate.

(Adapted from Leon, 1984)

Bulimia Nervosa

According to DSM-IV, bulimia nervosa is defined by the following five criteria:

1. Numerous episodes of binge eating, in which much more food is eaten within a 2-hour period than most people would eat, and the eater experiences a lack of control over his/her eating behaviour.
2. Frequent inappropriate compensatory behaviour to prevent weight gain (e.g. self-induced vomiting, excessive exercise, going without meals).
3. Binge eating and inappropriate compensatory behaviour occur at least twice a week over a 3-month period.

EXAM HINT

This final area of eating behaviour requires you to know the psychological and biological explanations of ONE eating disorder and so you need to choose between anorexia nervosa, bulimia nervosa and obesity. You do not need to know all three.

4. The individual's self-evaluation depends excessively on his/her shape and weight.
5. Binge eating and compensatory behaviour do not occur only during episodes of anorexia nervosa.

Binge eating is generally preceded by great tension, with the individual feeling powerless to control his/her compelling need to eat "forbidden" types of food. The binge eating itself reduces the tension, but leaves bulimics experiencing guilt, self-blame, and depression (APA, 2000).

There has been a dramatic increase in sufferers from bulimia nervosa since the late 1970s. Garner and Fairburn (1988) reported figures from an eating disorder centre in Canada. The number of patients treated for bulimia nervosa increased from 15 in 1979 to over 140 in 1986. Over 95% of sufferers from bulimia nervosa are women, and the onset is generally between 15 and 21 years of age (APA, 2000). Bulimia nervosa resembles anorexia nervosa in that both disorders are found much more in Western societies than elsewhere, and they occur more often in middle-class than working-class families.

The self-induced vomiting found in most bulimics produces various medical effects. It can damage the teeth by eroding dental enamel. It can also change the levels of sodium and potassium in bodily fluids, and these changes can be life-threatening.

Anorexia Nervosa vs. Bulimia Nervosa

There is some overlap between bulimia nervosa and anorexia nervosa, with many bulimic patients also having a history of anorexia. In addition, both disorders typically start during adolescence, and often follow a period of dieting by individuals who are very concerned about their weight, and who experience frequent feelings of anxiety and depression. Bulimics and anorexics have distorted

---

CASE STUDY: THE LIFE OF A BULIMIC

Julie's life is food. In her dingy bedsit there is scarcely space to move around among the empty drinks cans, crisp packets, piles of clothes, and ornaments. Her fridge is stuffed to overflowing with different kinds of chocolates. Eating occupies many hours of her day, but you wouldn't think it to look at her. She is a tiny thing, and when she pushes her sleeves up she reveals wrists no larger than sparrow's legs. For the best part of 20 years she has been trapped in an eating and vomiting cycle. At her lowest weight of 4 stones she found work as a dancer in a freak show. Breakfast starts her day:

> Half a box of cereal, two pints of milk, half a large sliced and buttered loaf, which I eat with a packet of bacon or ham, about three eggs and sausages. I eat the other half of the sliced loaf with butter and marmalade. I drink cooking oil with all my meals to wash the food down. After I've finished that I have a brief pause, then I need some chocolate. I eat until I can't breathe.

Then she trips out to the bathroom to collect a square plastic washing-up bowl and begins the process of bringing up all that

food. When she has finished the bowl is full. Then there is a fleeting release from the self-loathing and the yearning for food that has nothing to do with hunger.

She had a boyfriend, another bulimic, who recently died. "I need someone to love but it's too difficult with ordinary men." She loved her father until, at the age of 10, he developed schizophrenia. "From then on it was as if he hated me." It was soon after that that she started bingeing. She made herself sick and then tried to tell her mum, who could only cope by pretending it wasn't happening. Julie attempted suicide three times before the age of 19 and was then placed in a mental hospital and drip fed. She says she now wouldn't go back even to save her life, and recognises that she will probably die soon.

On Sundays, she visits her mum who lives close by but otherwise she goes out very little. When we met, she was planning a birthday treat for herself. "I get a birthday cake, little fairy cakes and biscuits and lemonade—all the things I had as a child for parties—and then I binge by myself."

(Adapted from Angela Neustatter in the *Daily Telegraph*, 7 March 1998)

views about their own appearance, and they exaggerate the importance of having an "ideal" body shape.

Despite the similarities between anorexia nervosa and bulimia nervosa, there are several important differences. First, bulimia nervosa is far more common than anorexia nervosa. Second, nearly all patients with bulimia nervosa are within about 10% of their normal weight, whereas anorexic patients (by definition) are at least 15% below their normal weight. Third, bulimics are generally more concerned than anorexics about being attractive to other people, and are more involved with others. Fourth, bulimics are more likely than anorexics to have a history of mood swings, and to have poor control of their impulses (APA, 2000).

Biological Explanations of Eating Disorders

These explanations include neural, genetic, and evolutionary approaches.

Genetic factors play a part in the development of eating disorders. Relatives of patients with eating disorders are four or five times more likely than other members of society to suffer from an eating disorder (e.g. Strober & Humphrey, 1987). Holland, Sicotte, and Treasure (1988) studied anorexia in monozygotic (identical) and dizygotic (fraternal) twins. The concordance (agreement) rate for identical twins was 56%, compared to only 7% for dizygotic twins. Kendler, Maclean, Neale, Kessler, Heath, and Eaves (1991) did a similar study on bulimia in 2163 female twins, finding a concordance rate of 23% for monozygotic twins compared with 9% for dizygotic twins.

These findings suggest that genetic factors play a part in the development of eating disorders, especially anorexia nervosa. However, the family environment experienced by identical twins is more similar than that experienced by fraternal twins (Loehlin & Nichols, 1976). Thus, environmental factors may contribute towards the higher concordance rates for identical twins.

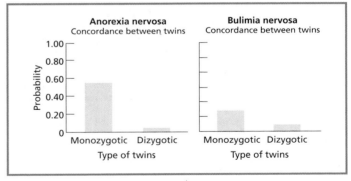

Holland et al. (1988) and Kendler et al. (1991) studied anorexia and bulimia in twins.

The recent dramatic increase in sufferers from eating disorders cannot be explained in genetic terms, because there have been no major genetic changes over the past 20–30 years. It is also very unlikely that the large differences in the incidence of eating disorders across cultures (Comer, 2001) can be accounted for by genetic factors.

The neurotransmitter serotonin may be involved in some cases of eating disorder. For example, Carrasco, Diaz-Marsa, Hollander, Cesar, and Saiz-Ruiz (2000) found that bulimics tended to have low serotonin activity. Bingeing on starchy foods containing carbohydrates can increase serotonin levels in the brain, and this may improve mood in individuals having low serotonin levels. However, patients with bulimia nervosa do not focus specifically on foods containing carbohydrates when they binge (Barlow & Durand, 1995). The finding that low serotonin levels are associated with eating disorders does not demonstrate that serotonin is important in their development. It could well be that the development of an eating disorder leads to a reduction in serotonin activity.

Bulik et al. (2008) evaluated current research and concluded that anorexia is more serious than bulimia because it has such a high mortality rate, and their view

? What are some limitations of conducting research on eating disorders?

is that it is largely a genetic disorder. The genetic influences are, however, complex. Bachner-Melman et al. (2007) have established that three genes associated with anorexia are also associated with the personality trait **perfectionism** as measured on the Child and Adolescent Perfectionism Scale (CAPS), and that these genes have neural effects on dopamine receptors and receptors for other neurochemicals such as a growth factor. However, their views are challenged by research suggesting family processes and early life experiences are also causal factors. Wade, Tiggemann, Bulik, Fairburn, Wray, and Martin's (2008) research on Australian female twins showed that—for both anorectics and bulimics—family members had made frequent comments about weight and shape while they were growing up. Interestingly, higher levels of paternal protection were uniquely associated with anorexia, whereas higher levels of parental expectation were associated with bulimia. Ringer and Crittenden's (2007) study of American females showed that all those with eating disorders were anxiously attached. They found that these participants used coercive strategies, which suggested hidden family conflicts during childhood as a cause of the maladaptive behaviours. Fairburn and Harrison's (2003) findings show a concordance rate of about 55% for monozygotic (MZ) twins and 5% for dizygotic (DZ) twins for anorexia, and 35% and 30% for MZ and DZ twins, respectively, for bulimia, which give a very clear indication of a strong genetic cause for anorexia but not for bulimia. However, these data are from clinic samples that are obviously not representative of the general population. Fairburn and Harrison's estimates for the population suggest there could be inheritance of bulimia as well as anorexia, though there is a lack of reliable data on environmental factors. Molecular genetic research is focusing on serotonin-related genes, as this neurotransmitter is known to be important in regulating eating and mood. This adds support for a genetic input into body size/weight to an earlier study from Stunkard et al. (1986) whose adoption study found that the adult body weight of adopted people correlated with that of their biological parents' and not their adoptive parents'.

Much research on eating disorders has focused on females because they are the majority of sufferers. However, research into males with these disorders also challenges purely genetic explanations for eating disorders. Chambry and Gilles (2006) suggest that anorexia could well be underdiagnosed in boys though in the main the symptoms are similar between the two sexes. The differences they found were that anorectic boys in general start off heavier than their female counterparts and indulge in more frequent excessive exercise and excessive intellectual involvement than the girls. Levels of testosterone and sexual function decline in line with the state of malnutrition and weight loss and there is a higher frequency of homosexual behaviour than in the female group. The researchers question whether a vulnerable sexual identity might predispose to male anorexia. However, the genetic causes of anorexia are supported by Wade et al.'s (2008) research into the link with temperament, which is known to be genetically controlled. They found not only that perfectionism was, as Bachner-Melman also found, co-morbid, but also a higher need for order and a sensitivity to praise and reward. Whereas such traits could be the result of family experience and culture the researchers feel these shared risk factors must be, in part at least, genetic.

Does this emphasis on neural and genetic contributory causes hold also for bulimia? Bulik and Tozzi (2004) reviewed research and put forward the claim that although sociocultural forces have an effect, neurobiological and genetic variables could represent core features of this disorder. Further research by Wonderlich et al. (2005) confirmed this idea as they investigated 179 bulimic women and found three distinct personality groups—personality being mainly genetically controlled. The three groups were a low co-morbid psychopathology cluster, an impulsive cluster with higher levels of psychopathology, and the highest psychopathology group of affective-perfectionistic types who showed type A hostile behaviour. Interestingly, these three groups did not differ in their variations of serotonin transporter genes, meaning that other genes and possibly neurotransmitters must be involved. This concept of three groups within bulimia has been supported, e.g. by Wonderlich, Crosby, Mitchell, and Engel (2007). They named the groups differently, but it is clear that their low personality pathology group is similar to the low psychopathology one; their interpersonal-emotional group to the impulsive one; and the stimulus-seeking hostile group to the affective-perfectionistic one. However, the Wonderlich team suggest that nurture might be as important as nature in the formation of these types. This view has been challenged by Nisoli et al. (2007), who established—in a group of over 100 Italian participants suffering from anorexia, bulimia, or obesity—that a gene previously associated with other psychopathologies such as alcohol and drug abuse, the *TaqA1* allele, is also a marker of a genetic psychological condition in those with a high risk of developing an eating disorder. Monteleone et al.'s (2007) study findings suggest that another gene, one involved in serotonin transmission, whilst not actually causing bulimia does seem to be involved in predisposing bulimics to a more seriously disturbed eating behaviour and higher harm avoidance (similar to behavioural inhibitions). Many of these varied studies suggest a grouping of explanations under the diathesis–stress heading. This diathesis–stress model brings together nature and nurture, suggesting that both genetic and environmental factors interact leading to either a psychopathology such as an eating disorder, or good mental health.

Evolutionary theory

Evolutionary Theory predicts that there would be some benefit for a behaviour that is passed down through the generations. This means the behaviour would be innate, that is controlled by genes. This means that the genes for anorexia nervosa, bulimia nervosa, and obesity were selected for, and that the behaviours were adaptive.

? How could these behaviours be adaptive?

Evaluation

This explanation of eating disorders is clearly problematical. Why should a disorder be adaptive? It seems a real contradiction in terms. A disorder means something is very wrong, so how can this possibly be beneficial? Behaviours that are maladaptive, or that are disordered should be selected out over time. Individuals with such behaviours would either not survive and flourish, or would not be successful in mating and producing offspring.

Bulimia could not be adaptive, bingeing and voiding could never be a healthy behaviour and so could not be called successful. However, if the gene had mutated slightly in recent centuries then it is possible to give a reasonable evolutionary explanation. Our long-ago hunter-gatherer ancestors could never have been sure of where their next meal was coming from. They had no such certainty because food would depend on what was successfully hunted or gathered at the time. Some foods would be perishable, especially things like fresh meat and ripe fruits.

Bulimia is often characterised by repeated episodes of uncontrollable binge eating followed by purging (induced vomiting). How could this be adaptive?

So, if individuals could eat very large amounts when food was plentiful and store this as body fat, then in hard times they would have energy reserves in their own bodies. This very clearly would be advantageous, would support staying alive, and so would be adaptive. This means that they could have produced more children, the women would have had better reserves to support pregnancy and lactation, and the genes for eating large amounts would have been passed on down the generations; these genes would have been an important evolutionary survival factor, so-called "thrifty genes" (Saxena et al., 2007). Then a mutation could have linked this gene for heavy eating with one that caused the stomach to empty quickly if it became very full, thus producing the voiding behaviours. Alternatively, in more recent times, perhaps because of social norms about health and a social preference for slimmer figures as shown by role models, the heavy-eating behaviour could be followed by voiding because of fears of social disapproval if bulimics became very fat.

A further idea is that the gene for eating well whenever possible could have become overexpressed or overactive in certain people, who would then binge eat, although this does not explain the voiding behaviours. A further evolutionary explanation is that the bulimia gene could lie dormant in many humans, but is only expressed—only gives rise to the behaviour—when triggered by some environmental factor. This diathesis–stress model suggests that many humans could be carriers of this gene but that if it remains dormant life-long then their own biological fitness is not compromised, and so these individuals are successful and "live long and prosper" and produce offspring who might also have the dormant gene.

Anorexia also could not be adaptive. It is not adaptive in the modern world, so in the far more challenging hunter-gatherer world it would have been a powerful disadvantage. Food was life; food was sometimes scarce; food was very, very precious. Any individual who chose to refuse food would have weakened and died early on, and indeed would have been a liability to the tribe or community as a weak person would not be able to contribute to the group and would be a drain on resources—even if they were not eating they would need time and care as they became weaker. However, it has been suggested that it could have been beneficial to the group to have an occasional person who was not interested in eating as when times became hard and food became scarce such persons would not have competed for the food resources, thus making more available for the rest of the group. This is an example of inclusive fitness, where a behaviour benefits the group and not the individual concerned. The concept is that the person's relatives would benefit, and the shared genes would still be passed on. Alternatively, in the disorder, the genes for satiety could be overactive; or they could be dormant in many humans, explanations given above for bulimia. A further evolutionary hypothesis is that anorectic behaviour would have been a sign of capitulation, of accepting defeat after some sort of conflict such as an interpersonal conflict leading to possible exclusion from the group or tribe (Gatward, 2007). This sign, refusing food and ultimately choosing not to live, would have signalled to the winner of the conflict that the anorectic individual was no longer a threat, way obviously weak, and could therefore be allowed to live and need not be killed. In this way, for the anorectic, the anorexia would have been adaptive—so long as it was not permanent and that individual could recover and thrive once more.

How likely is it that these explanations have some truth in them? It is impossible to tell. As stated at the beginning of this section we cannot research the past, especially the long-ago past. So we cannot test the evolutionary hypothesis and so it remains a hypothesis, a conjecture, a hypothetical construct, albeit a fascinating one.

Psychological Explanations of Eating Disorders

These explanations include the psychodynamic, cognitive, and cultural approaches.

There have been various psychodynamic approaches to anorexia nervosa (see Davison & Neale, 2001). The fact that the disorder is mostly found in adolescent girls suggests that anorexia might be due to fear of increasing sexual desires or to oral impregnation. Within that context, semi-starvation may reflect the desire to avoid becoming pregnant, because one of the symptoms of anorexia nervosa is the elimination of menstrual periods.

A somewhat different psychodynamic account is based on the notion that anorexia nervosa occurs in females having an unconscious desire to remain pre-pubescent. Their weight loss prevents them from developing the body shape associated with adult females, and thus allows them to preserve the illusion that they are still children.

Minuchin et al. (1978) argued that the families of anorexics are characterised by **enmeshment**, meaning that none of the members of the family has a clear identity because everything is done together. Such families prevent children from becoming independent. A child growing up in an enmeshed family may rebel against its constraints by refusing to eat. Minuchin et al. (1978) also argued that enmeshed families find it hard to resolve conflicts. Parental conflicts are reduced by the need to attend to the symptoms of their anorexic child.

It is hard to evaluate Enmeshment Theory. However, there are often high levels of parental conflict within the families of anorexics (Kalucy, Crisp, & Harding, 1977). Hsu (1990) reported that families with an anorexic child tend to deny or ignore conflicts and to blame other people for their problems. The problem is that these parental conflicts may be more a result of having an anorexic child than a cause of anorexia.

Family conflicts have also been identified in families with a child showing signs of bulimia as well as anorexia. Such families have more negative and fewer positive interactions than families with a normal adolescent (Humphrey, Apple, & Kirschenbaum, 1986). However, it is not clear whether the poor family interactions help to cause the disorder or are simply a reaction to it.

There is little support for the various psychodynamic accounts discussed, all of which seem to be based on the incorrect assumption that eating disorders only develop in adolescent females. Thus, they cannot explain eating disorders in males or in adults.

An alternative approach was taken by Bruch (1991). She argued that individuals with eating disorders generally have ineffective parents who ignore the child's needs, and make inaccurate decisions as to whether he/she is hungry or tired. This makes the children confused and helpless, and causes them to rely heavily on other people to tell them when they are hungry. Bruch (1975) found that the mothers of anorexic children said that they had always anticipated their children's needs, and so their children had never experienced hunger. Anorexics and bulimics are very worried about how they are perceived by others, and also experience a general lack of control (Vitousek & Manke, 1994). Finally, patients with bulimia nervosa sometimes mistakenly believe that they are hungry when they become anxious (Rebert, Stanton, & Schwarz, 1991).

KEY TERM

Enmeshment: a situation in which none of the members of a family has a true sense of personal identity because everything is done together.

CASE STUDY: ANOREXICS

Hilde Bruch (1971) developed a theory of anorexia based on her experience in treating such patients. The cases below are adapted from her records.

Case 1

A 12-year-old girl from a prominent upper-class family was seen when her mother consulted the psychiatrist about an older sister, who was obese. The mother felt that she wanted to punish this daughter for being overweight but spoke in glowing terms about her younger daughter, who in every way was an ideal child. Her teachers would refer to her as the "best balanced" girl in the school, and relied on her helpfulness and kindness when another child was having difficulty making friends.

Later, when the anorexia developed, it became apparent to what extent the mother's anxious and punitive behaviours had affected the way the younger daughter felt and thought about herself. She had become convinced that being fat was most shameful. As she began to put on weight in puberty, she felt horrified and that, if she was to retain respect, she would have to maintain her thinness. This led her to go on a starvation regime. At the same time, she also began to realise that she didn't have to be an ideal daughter and do what others expected of her, but she could be the master of her own fate.

Case 2

A mother sought psychoanalytic treatment because she had become depressed. Her daughter was her one great satisfaction in life. The girl (aged 14) had always been a happy child who had no problems. She had a governess, but the mother fed the daughter herself, making a special effort to provide good food and present it tastefully.

Shortly after the mother had consulted the psychiatrist, the daughter became anorexic, having started to get plump. When she visited the psychiatrist, her version of childhood was the exact opposite of her mother's account. She remembered it as a time of constant misery and that she could never have what she wanted but always had to have exactly what her mother wanted. She knew her mother had talked about what she should be eating with their doctor, and this made her feel that every bite that went into her mouth was watched. The concern about her fatness was reinforced by her father's excessive attention to appearance. Theirs was a wealthy home and there were always lavish arrays of food. Her father showed his superiority by eating very little and making snide remarks about people who ate too much.

When the girl became plump at puberty, she tried to outdo her father's haughty control. She felt she owed it to him to remain slim and aristocratic. Her life was dominated by trying to satisfy her father. She did well at school but was haunted by the fear of being found out to be stupid. She described her life as "I never deserved what they gave me" and that she was "worthless". Keeping her weight as low as possible was her only way of proving herself to be "deserving" and having "dignity".

(Adapted from Bruch, 1971)

Cognitive model

Patients with eating disorders have distorted views about themselves (e.g. their body shape and weight). Bulimics perceive their body size to be larger than do control individuals of the same size, and they also mistakenly believe that eating a small snack has a noticeable effect on their body size (McKenzie, Williamson, & Cubic, 1993). In patients with bulimia nervosa, the discrepancy between their *actual* body weight and their desired body weight is typically about the same as it is in healthy young women. However, the *perceived* discrepancy is much greater in bulimics (Cooper & Taylor, 1988): bulimics are more likely to exaggerate their body size, and their desired body size is smaller than it is for healthy women.

It is hard to interpret the above findings, because we do not know whether the cognitive distortions shown by patients with eating disorders were present *before* the onset of the disorder. The cognitive distortions may be a by-product of the eating disorder, and so play no part in its development.

Another psychological factor of relevance to eating disorders is the personality characteristic of perfectionism (a strong desire to achieve excellence). Individuals high in perfectionism may strive to achieve an unrealistically slim body shape. The mothers of girls with disordered eating often have perfectionist tendencies (Pike & Rodin, 1991). These mothers were very keen that their daughters should be thin, they were likely to be dieting themselves, and they expressed low levels of satisfaction with their family. Steinhausen (1994) found that females with eating disorders showed signs of perfectionism, as

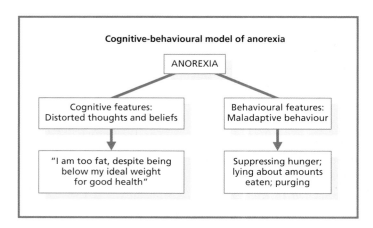

well as of compliance and dependence. Low self-esteem is also often involved (Comer, 2001).

Cultural factors

Eating disorders are considerably more common in Western than in non-Western societies (Cooper, 1994). For example, about one woman in 200 suffers from anorexia nervosa in Western Europe and the United States. In Hong Kong, by contrast, only one person out of more than 2000 Chinese people sampled had anorexia (Sing, 1994). Nasser (1986) compared Egyptian women studying in Cairo and in London. None of the women studying in Cairo developed an eating disorder, in contrast to 12% of those studying in London.

The concept of slimness as desirable is regularly reinforced in Western popular culture. Barlow and Durand's (1995) study found that Miss America contestants are on average 15% below their expected body weight.

These cultural differences are most obviously explained by the pressures on young women within Western societies to have a thin body shape, pressures that have increased greatly in recent decades. The emphasis on slimness as desirable is illustrated by the finding that a majority of Miss America contestants are 15% or more below their expected body weight (Barlow & Durand, 1995). Being underweight by that amount is one of the criteria for anorexia nervosa!

Jaeger et al. (2002) studied women in 12 Western and non-Western countries. The most extreme body dissatisfaction was found in Mediterranean countries, followed in order by northern European countries, countries in the process of westernisation, and finally non-Western countries, which demonstrated the lowest levels of body dissatisfaction. It is of interest that there was a reasonably close relationship between a country's level of body dissatisfaction and its level of eating disorders.

Cogan, Bhalla, Seta-Dedeh, and Rathblum (1996) compared the views of students in Ghana and in the United States: "Students in Ghana more often rated larger body sizes as ideal for both males and females, and also assumed that these larger sizes were held as ideal in society, than did U. S. students" (p. 98). In addition, thin females were rated by the American sample as being the happiest, whereas Ghanaians rated fat and thin males and females as equally happy.

The cultural pressures are greatest on adolescent girls for two reasons. First, they have reached the stage at which they want to appear attractive to boys. Second, most of the weight gain after puberty is in the form of fat tissue, which makes it harder for them to match the ideal shape.

Most of the distorted beliefs held by anorexic and bulimic patients (discussed above) are merely exaggerated versions of the beliefs held by society at large. Cooper (1994) argued that the self-worth of patients with eating disorders:

> . . . is seen as being evaluated largely in terms of their shape and weight: they view fatness as odious and reprehensible, they see slimness as attractive and desirable, and the maintenance of self-control is of prime importance. In addition, some attach extreme importance to weight loss . . . such beliefs are not radically different from views that are widely held.

> **CASE STUDY: MADDY**
>
> Maddy was brought up very strictly and criticised harshly as a child, especially at meal times, when she was labelled as "greedy and messy" for enjoying her food. In adult life, Maddy has had emotionally sad times and in such low moods has bought and consumed at one sitting large quantities of high-carbohydrate food such as tins of custard and packets of biscuits, and then has felt sick with disgust at herself for being messy and greedy. She says she has hated herself when she does this, and she is becoming more in control of her low-mood eating behaviour with support from her friends and from professional psychotherapists.

? How would the different explanations of eating disorders explain Maddy's behaviour?

Cultural factors cannot be the *only* reason for the occurrence of eating disorders. The great majority of young women exposed to cultural pressures towards slimness do *not* develop eating disorders. Only young women who are already vulnerable are likely to be greatly affected by such pressures.

A comparison between anorexia nervosa and bulimia nervosa

Clinical characteristics	Anorexia nervosa	Bulimia nervosa
Behavioural	Refusal to maintain body weight at least 85% of what is healthy Lying about having eaten	Recurrent bouts of binge eating and inappropriate compensating behaviours e.g. self-induced vomiting, over-use of laxatives, excessive exercising
Cognitive	Overestimation of body size Overestimation of importance of body size to self-esteem Denial of serious implications of weight loss	Self-image and self-esteem are over-influenced by body size and shape
Emotional	Intense fear of weight gain and of food	Intense fear of weight gain Fascination with food Intense guilt about bingeing
Physical/physiological	Loss of body weight Loss of secondary sexual body hair Menstruation stops for 3 consecutive months	Little if any loss of weight Acid erosion of backs of teeth Ill health due to body fluids upset by frequent vomiting

Obesity

Obesity is a physical condition in which there is too much stored body fat both under the skin and internally around the body organs. NHS Direct explains:

> *The most scientific way to measure your weight is to calculate your body mass index (BMI). This is your weight in kilograms divided by your height in metres squared . . . In the UK, people with a BMI between 25 and 30 are categorised as overweight, and those with an index above 30 are categorised as obese. People with a BMI of 40 or more are described as morbidly obese.*

Being obese puts an extra strain on the heart and is linked with cardiovascular disease, hypertension, a reduced quality of life, and an increased risk of an early death. This is why obesity is termed a disorder, and since increased body fat can only come from eating it is classed as an eating disorder. The Economic and Social Research Council (ESRC, 2007) reported that obesity has quadrupled in the UK in the last 25 years. In England in 2002, 22% of men and 23% of women were classified as clinically obese, with over half of all adults weighing more than their recommended weight. This is a world-wide, cross-cultural problem. For instance, in the USA obesity rates increased from 15% of the population in 1980 to 31% in 2000 and in Canada, almost 50% of the population is either overweight or obese; 56% of Australian adults and 27% of children are either overweight or obese. Asian immigrants to the UK also tend to have more fat around the waist, the so-called apple shape associated with increased health problems. And in the Middle East 50 to 70% of married women and 30 to 50% of married men in the Gulf States are clinically obese, with obesity rates overall much higher than in Western countries.

Possible causes of obesity include overeating or eating the wrong foods, physical inactivity, and maladaptive genes.

Psychological explanations

Psychodynamic theory

Psychodynamic explanations of behaviour are based on the teachings of Sigmund Freud, who saw behaviours as symbolic of what was going on in the mind. One Freudian idea is that food is itself a symbol, a symbol of love. This stems from the first emotional relationship or bond, which is with the mother, and the mother is also the source of food. Based on this concept, an explanation of obesity could be that people who overeat are craving love, that sufficient love is not available, and that they give themselves food as a symbol of the love they need. This means that food is

compensation for an absence of love. A problem in our society today is that being overweight is frequently disapproved of, so an overweight person might have reduced chances of finding love or affection, and so might continue to overeat; this could lead into a spiral with weight gain continuing and leading to increased obesity.

Alternatively, another Freudian or psychodynamic view is based on the concept of oral fixation. Freud believed that the first stage of psychosexual development, from birth to 1 to 2 years old, was characterised by a focus of organ-pleasure on the mouth so that not only is the child obtaining food via the mouth but is also taking in pleasure and knowledge in the same way. However, this stage can be disrupted. For example, if that child is not allowed to suckle for long enough, if she or he does not experience enough pleasure, oral fixation will result. This will demonstrate itself in various ways, but one of these is a life-long overdependence on food, meaning general overeating. This, clearly, would lead to becoming overweight or obese.

Evaluation. The foods that seem to be preferred by overweight people tend to be high in sugar and fat foods, i.e. foods that are sweet and creamy. This could be seen as support for the Freudian construct (because breast milk is fairly sweet and has a high fat content) of mother love = food.

However, even though many people find this and the oral fixation ideas attractive and convincing, these are just ideas, hypothetical constructs, and as such cannot be tested empirically. This means that we can neither prove nor disprove them, although psychodynamic therapy gives clients an understanding of what could be the underlying cause of their eating disorder, and therefore an opportunity to explore dealing with the issue.

Learning (behaviourist) theory

This theory postulates that all behaviour is learned by classical conditioning, operant conditioning, or social learning. Classical conditioning suggests that an individual can learn to associate overeating and becoming overweight or obese with something pleasant, such as one's earnings, one's ability to purchase more food than other people. This suggests a person feels a need to demonstrate their financial worth or importance.

Operant conditioning would suggest that overeating and becoming overweight or obese is learned because overeating is reinforced or rewarded, such as being praised as a child for "eating up" even if no longer hungry.

Social or observational learning would involve people having role models who overeat and become obese so that the behaviour and its consequences are seen as successful, aspirational, and are therefore imitated.

Findings. It would be completely unethical to attempt to make participants learn a behaviour that is unhealthy and possibly even life threatening, so research into overeating cannot be done this way. There is a wealth of research on the three types of learning in both non-human animals and in humans, and these types of learning are accepted. But do they account for obesity?

Evaluation. In non-industrial or less wealthy communities it is possible that, because food can at times be scarce, being overweight could be seen as associated with being successful. Indeed, it is sometimes said that having a few extra kilos of weight is just being comfortable, implying that this is not a bad thing at all and could be a sign of material comfort. The study of the people of Nauru mentioned earlier would support this explanation.

In our Western culture, we have the concept of comfort-eating, which suggests that we do have a learned association between food and comfort. However, the classically conditioned association between being obese and being successful is certainly not found throughout Western industrialised cultures and yet there are severe problems with the number of overweight or obese people in these cultures, which challenges this explanation.

It is true that often children are brought up to "eat up", in other words to finish all the food on their plates. When they comply they are frequently praised, and approval is one of the most powerful reinforcements or rewards leading to the behaviour being learned. This could lead a child to learn that eating everything is good, and perhaps this is extrapolated to a belief that eating more of everything is even better, an example of maladaptive learning.

At a traditional Hindu wedding in London, the groom's American mother was saying she wished she was more svelte, but the bride's Hindu family reassured her, saying it was good for the parental generation to be as they were, looking "comfortable and prosperous". Traditionally, Hindu culture was agrarian-based and so unlikely to be wealthy enough to eat generously or lavishly.

Many of us are brought up to finish everything on our plate before we are permitted to leave the table or to have a dessert. Could this lead us in adult life to overeat for the sake of it?

Obese role models are rare, which does not really tie in with the epidemic of obesity in our culture. Furthermore, even where there are very large role models such as the Japanese Sumo wrestlers this does not seem to affect the population as Japanese people have a low level of obesity and are generally quite slight in build, which challenges this type of learning as an explanation for obesity.

Environmental or lifestyle explanations

The huge increase in obesity rates over the last 50 years, a very short time in evolutionary terms, suggests that environmental factors are a major significant influence on obesity. The main environmental or lifestyle explanations for obesity, and in particular for the rise in obesity world-wide, focus on diet and exercise, particularly the decreasing levels of physical activity and more sedentary lifestyles, and the rise in the consumption of processed and "junk" food.

Reduced amounts of exercise (in part because most people walk less and use cars more) help to account for the steep increase in obesity. Over the past 20 years, the average daily calorie intake in several Western countries has actually *decreased* (Hill & Peters, 1998). Exercise uses up energy (and therefore calories), and anyone will put on weight if the calories he/she consumes are greater than the ones used in energy expenditure. Thus, reduced usage of calories each day could easily lead to obesity in the long run.

People gain weight when their energy intake (calories) exceeds their energy output, and lose it when the opposite is true, when their output exceeds their energy intake. For example, a loss of 0.5 kilos of body fat requires an energy output of 3500 calories. This is one reason why regular physical exercise is important.

Among the ways to lose weight outlined by the Association for the Study of Obesity (ASO) are: increasing physical activity; "energy balance", where energy intake equates with energy output; limiting portion sizes; and moderating alcohol consumption because one effect of alcohol on the brain is to stimulate the hunger centres.

Even children are becoming obese. The BBC (2006a) reports that about 27% of children are now overweight and the main problem here is a continuing reduction in the amount of exercise children take, in and out of school. Interestingly, teenage girls who diet are more likely to become obese (Stice, Cameron, Killen, Hayward, & Taylor, 1999). Nearly 700 girls were tracked in a longitudinal study over 4 years. During this time, levels of obesity rose from 16% to 21%. In fact, the girls who used the most extreme weight-loss tactics, such as laxatives and appetite suppressants, were most likely to gain weight. Why is this? It does not mean that dieting *per se* increases weight but it is suggested that a faulty perception of their own food intake is giving some girls an inaccurately low idea of their calorie intake. This is supported by Lichtman et al.'s (1992) study, which found that participants under-reported their food intake by 47% and over-reported their exercising by 51%. Alternatively, it is suggested that the girls who resorted to the more extreme dieting could be those naturally, i.e. innately, more susceptible to becoming obese. So these data could be a cognitive explanation, faulty perceptions or even not telling the truth because of a wish for social desirability; or they might be a genetic explanation.

Biological explanations
Genetics

Genetic factors help to determine who will (and will not) become obese. Grilo and Pogue-Geile (1991) reviewed evidence from thousands of twin pairs. MZ (identical) twins were much more similar to each other in weight and body mass than were DZ

Stice et al. (1999) found that teenage girls who dieted were more likely to become obese in the long term.

? What explanations can account for the differences between MZ and DZ twins?

(fraternal) twins. Similar findings were reported by Plomin, Defries, and McClearn (1997), who found that 60–70% of MZ twins were very similar in weight, compared with only 30–40% of DZ twins. The much greater genetic similarity of identical twins than fraternal twins (100% vs. 50%) probably accounts for their much greater similarity in weight.

The notion that genetic factors are of prime importance in determining body weight would receive support if family environment has little or no effect. Stunkard et al. (1986) considered the weight of adults adopted as infants. Their body weight was not correlated with that of their adoptive parents. However, it was highly correlated with the body weight of their biological parents, suggesting that genetic factors are more important than environmental ones.

One way in which heredity might influence body weight would be via metabolic rate. Individual differences in metabolic rate exist and can certainly influence body weight. Rose and Williams (1961) compared people matched for body weight, height, age, and level of activity. Despite this matching, there were pairs in which one person consumed twice as many calories as the other, and thus presumably had a much higher metabolic rate.

We should not conclude that all obese individuals simply have a low metabolic rate, although it has often been claimed that they do. Lichtman et al. (1992) studied obese individuals experiencing great difficulty in losing weight on reduced-calorie diets. Accurate measurements were made of their food intake and amount of physical activity over a 2-week period. The participants were found to have under-reported their actual food intake by 47% and over-reported their physical activity by 51%!

The ESRC (2007) also reports that children with two obese parents have approximately a 70% chance of becoming obese, while those with two lean parents have a much lower (20%) chance of obesity. This could be because of shared genes, but it could also be the result of shared dietary habits. People from certain ethnic groups may be more likely to become obese than others. Data from the USA show that people from Afro-Caribbean and Hispanic backgrounds have a much greater risk of becoming obese compared to people from Caucasian races, and there are also differences in how fat is distributed. For example, Mediterranean adult females tend to have more fat around their waists than northern European women, and Asian immigrants to the UK also tend to have more central fat. These differences may be due to cultural, genetic, or socioeconomic factors, or to a combination of all three, though there are data supporting a negative correlation between obesity and socio-economic status.

? How would you explain the causes of the negative correlation between obesity and socio-economic status? And in what ways is such a correlation useful, and not useful in understanding obesity?

Although diet cannot be ruled out as an explanation for obesity evidence is increasing for a significant genetic contribution. Mark (2006) argues that twin and adoption studies strongly support a genetic involvement in obesity, particularly as obese adoptees have been shown to share their body mass far more with their biological parents than their adopted parents. Inheriting maladaptive genes could also explain the increased levels of the hormone leptin in obese persons, and their innate leptin resistance (Block, 2005; Laposky et al., 2008). Sakkou et al. (2007) have identified a biochemical named Bsx, which is involved in spontaneous physical activity (muscle fidgeting) and food-seeking in mice. This Bsx molecule is present in humans and could fulfil a very similar function, and explain individual differences in weight gain in humans. Obesity could be the result of physical inactivity caused by having insufficient Bsx. Even though the low-Bsx mice ate less, they became fatter because of lack of exercise. Although there are many major differences between mice and humans, it is possible that Bsx works the same way in both species.

Bellar and Jarosz (2008) show that increased exercise in obese people is associated with reductions in total fat and abdominal fat and also with increased insulin sensitivity. The latter is important because insulin sensitivity is linked to hunger and satiety and therefore to amounts of food eaten. Diet is also important, especially in childhood. Spalding et al. (2008) have shown that obese young people add twice as many adipose (fat) cells a year than normal-sized others, and that this build-up starts at about 2 years of age. They were able to work this out reliably and empirically by analysing the frequency of harmless heavy carbon-14 molecules in the adipocytes. It is not possible to know whether the 2-year-olds had been given far too much food to eat or whether they had a genetic predisposition to grow extra adipocytes, and this illustrates the sometimes extreme difficulties in separating out nature and nurture influences. However, as the data from Mark (2006) suggests a genetic cause, the extra adipose cells may be the expression of the maladaptive gene(s).

Henderson (2008) describes studies that have identified a genetic variant that raises the risk of obesity. This variant seems to have a combined effect if another variant, known as FTO, is also present, when the combination leads to a weight gain of between 3.5 and 4.5kg. Particularly interesting is that the new variant is part of the 98% of the genome with no known function, the so-called "junk DNA". It is now thought that this DNA contains genetic switches that control gene activity, switching this up or down. A new variant is possible with one such switch, which lies close to another gene, *MC4R*, which is linked to a rare form of early-onset child obesity. One copy of the variant gene is possessed by 35–38% of Caucasians, and two copies by 5–6%, but one copy of this variant is significantly more common in those with Indian ancestry. This is a possible tie-in with the ESRC data on Asian immigrants referred to near the beginning of this section. However, other social or economic factors might impact on obesity. As Gibbs (1996) showed, when people on low incomes become affluent they are able to spend more on food, and on more food. For example, there was a dramatic increase in obesity in inhabitants of the island of Nauru, off the coast of Australia, within just one generation of the discovery and mining of valuable phosphate deposits.

Finally, genetics could explain the idea that obese individuals have a fault in their satiety brain centres, the set-point theory. The set-point concept is similar to the idea of a thermostat, but regulating satiety not temperature. Briefly, it suggests that there is a set point for eating which, when reached, triggers the satiety centres to stop us eating any more. Brain scans would suggest that the set point is rather a critical level, as the satiety centres are activated as soon as we eat, but a variation in the critical level/set point could well be genetically determined.

■ **Activity: Animal Studies**
Some people, including some psychologists, are not convinced that we can learn from non-human animal studies. Can you think of three ways to support generalising from mice to humans, and three ways that challenge this generalisation? How do your reasons compare with your classmates' reasons? You could pool your arguments and make a group poster—this doesn't have to be your personal beliefs, just reasonable support and challenges.

EXAM HINT

All of the explanations of eating disorder can be evaluated as:

- *Reductionist* because they are oversimplified and ignore other explanations.
- *Deterministic* because they ignore the free will of the individual to control their own behaviour.

HOW SCIENCE WORKS: PSYCHOLOGY AND EATING—THE POSTER SERIES
If you cooperate with your class, dividing up the tasks and making a display in the classroom, you could make a series of posters to illustrate what you have learned about eating behaviour. Using clear fonts for the text and colour and illustrations would make these attractive as well as informative, and help with remembering the content.

Poster 1 could be a spider diagram showing the various influences on our eating behaviour.

Poster 2 could show the neurochemical control of eating; another spider diagram perhaps with the brain at its centre and the relevant parts identified, with the factors such as hormones shown around it.

Poster 3 could show Mesulam's doughnut study—an opportunity for some luscious illustrations!

Poster 4 could show factors that explain why dieting to lose weight is unsuccessful.

Poster 5 might show the evolutionary explanation of food preferences, and the evidence and the challenges to this theory.

See *A2-Level Psychology Online* for some interactive quizzes to help you with your revision.

SECTION SUMMARY
Eating Disorders

❖ There are several eating disorders; obesity is not classified as a disorder in DSM-IV but is frequently regarded as an eating disorder.

❖ Criteria for anorexia nervosa:

— body weight is less than 85% of that expected
— an intense fear of fatness or weight gain despite being very underweight
— maladaptive thinking about one's own body weight
— amenorrhoea in females (cessation of menstrual cycles).

❖ Anorexia has increased in Western societies in recent decades, and in non-Western societies as Western influences increase.

❖ The APA (2000) estimates over 90% of patients are female with onset in the teenage years.

❖ Most sufferers recover over time but many are left with long-term physical malfunction.

❖ Criteria for bulimia nervosa:

— frequent binge eating (consuming more food with no control in 2 hours than most people would eat)
— frequent inappropriate compensatory behaviour
— binge eating and inappropriate compensatory behaviour at least twice a week over at least 3 months
— one's self-evaluation excessively dependent on own weight/shape
— binge eating and inappropriate compensatory behaviour do not occur only during periods of anorexia.

❖ Binge eating usually relieves a tension that has built up but produces guilt, self-blame, and depression.

❖ Bulimia has increased dramatically since the 1970s and over 95% of sufferers are female, with onset usually from 15 to 21 years.

❖ Self-induced vomiting tends to rot teeth but also disrupt body fluid salts balance with potentially fatal consequences.

❖ Both anorexia and bulimia are more common in middle socio-economic groups, in females, and in those preoccupied with body image.

❖ Bulimia is more common and does not disrupt weight to the same extent as anorexia.

❖ Bulimics are more likely to experience mood swings and poor self-control.

Biological explanations of eating disorders

❖ Genetic factors are involved:

— relatives of eating disorders are four or five times more likely themselves to suffer from an eating disorder
— concordance rates are 55% for MZ twins and 5% for DZ twins for anorexia, and 35% and 30% for MZ and DZ twins respectively for bulimia (Fairburn & Harrison, 2003)
— three genes associated with anorexia are also associated with the personality trait perfectionism (Bachner-Melman et al., 2007)

— early life experiences are also causal factors, especially those involving family (Wade et al., 2008)
— people with eating disorders are often anxiously attached (Ringer & Crittenden, 2007)
— adult body weight of adoptees correlates with their biological parents not their adoptive parents (Stunkard et al., 1986).

❖ Anorexia in males could be underdiagnosed; also there could be a correlation with vulnerable sexual identity.
❖ Neurochemical factors are also implicated:

— bulimics tend to have low serotonin activity (Carrasco et al., 2000)
— a serotonin transmission gene predisposes carriers to bulimia (Monteleone et al., 2007)
— But different types of bulimics share the same serotonin transporter genes (Wonderlich et al., 2005)
— The diathesis–stress model would explain these varying findings.

❖ Psychodynamic model: the causes could be:

Psychological explanations of eating disorders

— repressed fears, e.g. of increasing sexual desires or oral impregnation
— an unconscious desire to remain a child
— a lack of identity or an enmeshed family
— ineffective parents who do not listen to the child's needs.

❖ Families of sufferers often show conflicts and increased negative interactions.
❖ These explanations do not address eating disorders in males and/or in adults.
❖ Cognitive model: the causes could be maladaptive thoughts about their body shape, size etc. and about the effects of even small quantities of food:

— cognitive distortions are shown clearly by sufferers
— but these could be the effect or the cause of the disorder
— perfectionism in the mothers as well as the sufferers (daughters)
— mothers of sufferers as well as the female sufferers usually show definite signs of perfectionism and often low self-esteem
— this does not seem to apply to males with the disorder.

❖ Culture can affect eating disorders:

Cultural model

— eating disorders are far more common in Western cultures
— women in traditional non-Western cultures rarely develop the disorder
— the disorders start to become common as Western culture is introduced
— body dissatisfaction is more common in Western than non-Western cultures
— cultural pressures are greatest in adolescent girls because of natural weight gain at puberty plus becoming attracted to boys
— the majority of Western girls do not develop eating disorders
— this does not address eating disorders in males or adults.

❖ In some way eating disorders would have been adaptive for our ancestors, aiding survival and reproduction:

Evolutionary Theory

— at a time when the food supply was not reliable, bingeing when it was plentiful would have been adaptive, and a later mutation could link vomiting with feeling the stomach is very full

— genes can become overexpressed, e.g. if a double dose of a gene is inherited so hunger and eating could become much greater
— anorexia could benefit the group (inclusive fitness) as a person uninterested in food would not be a drain when food became scarce
— anorectic behaviour could have signalled acceptance of defeat after conflict and so avoided punishment
— these explanations seem weak when early humans would have prized, sought, and fought for food—food was life.

❖ Diathesis–stress suggests that the genes for eating disorders could lie dormant until activated environmentally, e.g. by personal stress.

Obesity

❖ Obesity is termed a disorder because:

— there is too much stored body fat
— it is linked to cardiovascular disease, hypertension, and a shortened life expectancy.

❖ Obesity has quadrupled in the UK in the past 25 years.
❖ It affects over 20% of men and women in the UK, and more in the USA and Middle East.
❖ Contributory factors include overeating or eating the wrong foods, physical inactivity, and maladaptive genes.

Psychological explanations of obesity: Psychodynamic model

❖ Food, as a symbol, is compensation for an absence of love
❖ The obese individual is orally fixated:

— preferred foods tend to be sweet and/or creamy like breast milk
— it is not possible to test this model empirically so it cannot be proved or refuted.

Learning Theory model (behaviourism) of obesity

❖ All behaviour even maladaptive is learned by classical or operant conditioning or social learning:

— people can learn to associate together things that are not connected, e.g. being affluent and eating too much
— in Western culture it is unlikely that people would learn to associate affluence with overeating, rather with eating more expensive food
— praise or other reward reinforces a behaviour, even overeating
— sweet/creamy/fatty foods are given as rewards, and it is polite in Western culture to finish up one's food
— people do imitate role models' behaviour, which could include overeating
— but in Western culture few role models are obese, and they seem popular despite rather than because of their weight.

Environmental or lifestyle explanations of obesity

❖ The period during which obesity has increased is too short to be genetic/evolutionary.
❖ Lifestyle changes to sedentary occupations and calorie-rich diets are the main causal factors:

— children are taking less exercise in and out of school

— research suggests that people underestimate how much they eat, and overestimate how much they exercise.

❖ Obese people are much more likely to have obese parents

Genetic factors in obesity

— but this could be due to environmental factors, such as family diet and lifestyle
— some ethnic groups are more likely to be obese
— but this too could be caused by environmental factors
— twin and adoption studies suggest a genetic contribution to obesity
— current research is focusing on genetic variants that could impact on obesity
— but some such research is done on mice so we do not know how much it can relate to humans.

FURTHER READING

http://www.bbc.co.uk/health/conditions/mental_health/disorders_eating.shtml
A good introductory site with useful information about eating disorders.

http://www.bbc.co.uk/health/conditions/obesity2.shtml
A short introduction to obesity.

http://www.nhsdirect.nhs.uk/articles/article.aspx?articleId=265
Has more information on obesity and some useful links.

Lockwood, C. (2008). *The human story: Where we come from & how we evolved.* New York: Sterling. An in-depth account of human evolution.

Mintz, S.W., & Du Bois, C.M. (2002). The anthropology of food and eating. *Annual Review of Anthropology, 31,* 99–119. An excellent and in-depth review of current thinking on this topic.

Stringer, C. (2007). *Homo britannicus: The incredible story of human life in Britain.* London: Penguin. An expert and very readable account of evolution and our early ancestors in Britain.

See *A2-Level Psychology Online* for tips on how to answer these revision questions.

REVISION QUESTIONS

In the exam, questions on this topic are out of 25 marks, and can take the form of essay questions or two-part questions. You should allow about 30 minutes for each of the questions below, which aim to test the material in this chapter. Never try to answer a question unless you have been taught the topic.

1. Discuss the factors influencing attitudes to food and eating behaviour, such as cultural influences, mood, or health concerns. (25 marks)
2. (a) Outline evolutionary explanations for food preferences. (9 marks)
   (b) Discuss the role of neural mechanisms involved in controlling eating and satiation. (16 marks)
3. Outline and evaluate **one** psychological and **one** biological explanation of a named eating disorder. (25 marks)
4. Discuss explanations for the success or failure of dieting. (25 marks)

Psychological explanations of gender development p. 230

- How does the development of our mental processes (cognition) explain gender development?
- What is androgyny and how does this develop?
- Are the causes of gender dysphoria biological or psychological?

Biological influences on gender p. 244

- Is biology destiny when it comes to gender development?
- How does Money's research support the role of biological factors even though initially he claimed the study supported the role of nurture?
- Do evolutionary roles of "man as hunter" and woman as "child bearer" explain gender differences today?
- How does the biosocial approach combine the influences of nature and nurture?

Social contexts of gender role p. 253

- How does social influence explain gender socialisation?
- How do parents and peers influence gender role development?
- How does the media affect gender development?
- What do cross-cultural studies reveal about the development of gender role?

Gender

By Diana Dwyer

When a baby is born, the key question everyone asks is, "Is it a boy or a girl?" Virtually all societies expect males and females to behave differently and to assume different roles. To meet these expectations, children must understand whether they are a boy or girl and then learn the appropriate behaviours.

Right from birth, girls and boys are treated differently and described using different language. Rubin, Provenzano, and Luria (1974) found that when parents were asked to describe their newborn infants, sons were considered strong, active, and well co-ordinated; girls as little, delicate, beautiful, and weak. Since researchers matched infants on size, weight, and muscle tone, these descriptions represent expectations rather than physical differences.

So sex-typing starts from an extremely early age and children soon start to behave differently according to their gender. By the time they are 3 or 4, children prefer same-sex friends and toys that are considered appropriate for their gender. The growing child's thoughts about itself and its place in the world are strongly influenced by whether it is male or female.

The words "**sex**" and "**gender**" are sometimes used interchangeably in everyday speech but it is important from the outset to distinguish between them.

Sex refers to the biology of being male or female. This is determined by the fact that, of a total of 23 pairs of chromosomes, males and females have one pair of chromosomes that differs between the two sexes; females have a pair described as XX, whereas males have a pair described as XY (these descriptions are based on the shape of the chromosomes).

Gender refers to the psychological characteristics associated with being male or female. Hence, we describe someone as very feminine or a behaviour as extremely masculine.

Observed Gender Differences

Maccoby and Jacklin (1974) reviewed over 1500 studies of sex differences and found only the following four main ones:

1. Girls have greater verbal ability than boys; this difference has been found at most ages during childhood.

> **KEY TERMS**
> **Sex:** the biological fact of being male or female as determined by a pair of chromosomes. Females have a pair known as XX; males have a pair known as XY.
> **Gender:** the psychological characteristics associated with being male or female, i.e. masculinity and femininity.

? Do you think nature or nurture plays a bigger role in these differences of abilities?

2. Boys have greater visual and spatial abilities than girls.
3. Boys have greater ability in abstract maths than girls, but this difference only appears from about the age of 11.
4. Boys are more aggressive than girls, both physically and verbally. In most human cultures (and most complex species) male offspring are more likely to engage in play fighting and adults more likely to fight. However, defining exactly what is meant by aggression can be a problem.

This review was very comprehensive, but no account was taken of the quality of the research and it is, of course, over 30 years old. No equivalent research, in terms of thoroughness, has been done since but a few recent, smaller-scale studies are worth consideration.

Maccoby (1990) found that girls are more compliant than boys with respect to obeying authority figures such as teachers and parents. Girls are more likely to use verbal means of getting their own way, such as by persuasion or flattery, than are boys.

Shaffer (1999) pointed out that girls show more emotional sensitivity than boys. For example, girls from the age of about 5 are more interested in and attentive towards babies than are boys.

Else-Quest, Hyde, Goldsmith, and Van Hulle (2006) carried out a meta-analysis of studies on personality differences between boys and girls. Girls scored higher than boys on effortful control and boys scored higher than girls on surgency (which is similar to extraversion).

As we shall see later, boys are far more developmentally vulnerable than are girls. They are more likely to show mental retardation, language disorders, and hyperactivity.

Gender differences in academic achievement

There have traditionally been considerable gender differences in the number of examinations passed and the subjects taken at school, but the pattern used to be that boys achieved better grades in sciences and maths whereas girls did better in English, foreign languages, and humanities. This pattern has changed considerably over the years and girls now do better than boys across the board.

With respect to GCSEs, the benchmark used is 5+ A*–C grades, and for the last 12 years approximately 10% more girls have achieved this than have boys (in 2006, 63.4% of girls and 53.8% of boys attained 5+ A*–C). The greatest gender gap is in humanities, art, and languages; the smallest is in science and maths.

Girls are more likely than boys to stay on in full-time education and are more likely to take A levels (54% of entries at A levels in 2006 were from girls). This contrasts sharply with the 1950s and 1960s when only a third of A-level entries were female.

These national assessment findings contrast sharply with the results of IQ tests and tests of reasoning in which there are small or negligible overall gender differences.

PSYCHOLOGICAL EXPLANATIONS OF GENDER DEVELOPMENT

Theories of gender development seek to explain how people develop **gender identity** (the sense of one's own gender) and how they develop **gender roles** (their ideas concerning the appropriate behaviour for males and females).

KEY TERMS

Gender identity: a child's or adult's awareness of being male or female and the implications of this. It emerges during the early years of childhood.

Gender role: a set of expectations that prescribes how males and females should think, act, and feel.

Social Learning Theory

The basic principle of **Social Learning Theory** is that children (and adults) learn by observing the behaviour of other people and imitating it. The people they imitate are known as models. This type of learning is referred to as observational learning.

Albert Bandura is the main proponent of Social Learning Theory. He argues that children learn **gender stereotypes** by observing the actions of various models of the same gender, including other children, parents, teachers, and those in the media, especially television.

Social Learning Theory acknowledges that other types of learning are also important. Children will be more likely to perform an action (such as copying someone else) if they are reinforced for it and less likely to behave in a certain way if they are punished. There are many subtle types of reinforcement and punishment apart from the obvious ones. One powerful punishment is friends mocking a child, so if a boy is seen to be behaving in what others perceive as "girlish" or "cissy" and his friends mock him, he is unlikely to repeat this behaviour. In general, boys are more strongly socialised into their gender roles than are girls. People are much more uncomfortable with boys acting like girls (e.g. a boy playing with a doll) than they are with girls acting like boys (such as a girl playing with a train set).

Evaluation

Some aspects of Social Learning Theory suggest that gender is acquired *passively* through reward and punishment. In reality, children make an active contribution to their own development and a positive aspect of this theory is that this factor is recognised in later versions of Social Learning Theory, such as Bandura's (1986) Social Cognitive Theory, in which the emphasis is on the self and the role it plays in influencing behaviour. Bandura used the term "**reciprocal determinism**", which involves the interaction of characteristics such as personality, beliefs, and cognitive abilities with the environment. For example, a girl might be encouraged in ballet dancing (direct reinforcement) and eventually chooses to go to ballet classes rather than an alternative (thus influencing her own environment), seeks out children who are also interested in ballet because they make rewarding

Some aspects of gender can be acquired passively through reward and punishment. Parents might, for example, try to discourage what they see as sex-inappropriate behaviour. This little girl is helped out of the tree, while her brother is permitted to continue climbing.

KEY TERMS

Social Learning Theory: learning by observation and imitation. In gender development, children imitate role models of the same sex.

Gender stereotypes: beliefs about the differences between males and females, based on gender roles.

Reciprocal determinism: Bandura's concept that what one learns is affected by one's characteristics (personality, beliefs, and cognitive abilities). Personality isn't simply determined by the environment, but the individual also shapes the environment.

HOW SCIENCE WORKS: WHAT DO PEOPLE THINK?

People construct all sorts of gender stereotypes; some of these might be valid and some are assumptions of questionable validity or are just plain wrong. You could test people's stereotypes using a true-or-false questionnaire in which you have a series of statements based on psychological research—perhaps illustrated with simple graphics—and tick-boxes or similar for true or false by each one.

For example: Girls are more obedient than boys ☐ True ☐ False

At the end, you could total the number of true and false judgements and compare them, perhaps using a pie chart for each statement and then an overall pie chart for the totals of all questions. It would also be useful to give a debriefing in the form of a sheet with the correct answers handed out to participants—but be prepared for some of your participants to disagree; sometimes people are very definite about their own stereotypical beliefs, even if scientific research contradicts them! You will have to remember that psychologists have to show respect to their participants even in such situations.

EXAM HINT

Social Learning Theory is not directly mentioned on the specification but it is very useful to know it in order to understand the cognitive-developmental theories which follow and some of the material later in the chapter.

companions, and so on. Thus, children are both the product and the producer of their own environment.

On the negative side, social learning theorists mistakenly assume that learning processes are very similar at any age. For example, consider young children and adolescents watching a film in which a man and a woman are eating a meal together. The observational learning of the young children might focus on the eating behaviour of the same-sexed person, whereas the adolescents might focus on his or her social behaviour. Approaches such as Kohlberg's Cognitive-Developmental Theory and Gender-Schema Theory, discussed next, are better equipped to explain developmental changes in learning and cognition.

In addition, Social Learning Theory focuses on the learning of *specific* ways of behaving. This ignores the fact that there is also a considerable amount of *general* learning. For example, children seem to acquire **gender schemas** (organised beliefs about the sexes; Martin & Halverson, 1987), and it is hard to explain how this happens in terms of social learning theory.

Maccoby and Jacklin, whose 1974 research was mentioned earlier, concluded from this extensive research that socialisation is of enormous importance. They comment:

> *We suggest that societies have the option of minimising, rather than maximising, sex differences through their socialisation practices. A society could, for example, devote its energies more toward moderating male aggression than toward preparing women to submit to male aggression, or toward encouraging rather than discouraging male nurturance activities.*

Cognitive Developmental Theories

Kohlberg

Kohlberg argues that children need to gain an understanding of gender identity *before* they begin to imitate same-sex models. Whereas Social Learning Theory states that children copy same-sex models and thereby develop a gender identity, Kohlberg argues that it is the other way round—children *first* gain a sense of gender identity and *then* copy same-sex models because their sense of gender identity makes the copying of sex-appropriate behaviour rewarding. In the words of Kohlberg (1966, p. 89), "I am a boy; therefore I want to do boy things; therefore the opportunity to do boy things . . . is rewarding."

The notion of gender identity is of great importance within Kohlberg's Cognitive-Developmental Theory. He proposed that children go through three stages in the development of gender identity:

? How do these stages compare to Piaget's stages?

1. *Basic gender identity* (age 2 to 3½ years): boys label themselves as boys and girls label themselves as girls. However, they believe it would be possible to change sex.
2. *Gender stability* (3½ to 4½ years): there is an awareness that sex is stable over time (e.g. boys will become men), but less awareness that sex remains stable across different situations, such as wearing clothes normally worn by members of the opposite sex. When a doll was dressed in transparent clothes so there was a discrepancy between its clothing and its genitals, children in this stage decided on its sex on the basis of clothing (McConaghy, 1979).
3. *Gender constancy* (4½ to 7 years upwards): children at this stage realise that sex remains the same over time and over situations.

KEY TERM

Gender schema: an organised set of beliefs about the sexes.

According to Kohlberg, children cannot be expected to show sex-typed behaviour until they have formed the necessary mental structures required to

Kohlberg's stages in the development of gender identity		
Basic gender identity 2–3½ years	Gender stability 3½–4½ years	Gender consistency 4½–7 upwards
Aware of sex, but believes it can change	Aware that sex is stable over time, but not over situations	Realises sex remains the same, regardless of time or situation

understand gender. The most important aspect of this is the understanding that gender is constant; not until children have grasped the idea that they are masculine or feminine forever will they consistently act in a sex-typed way. This means that children must acquire certain knowledge about gender before their social experiences (such as the roles that their mother and father occupy) have any influence on them.

Kohlberg based his theory on Piaget's ideas that children automatically classify the information they encounter in their environment into social categories. One of the most useful of these categories is gender, which, once it is formed, is quickly filled with all sorts of information that is relevant to gender: appearance, clothes, activities, personality characteristics. These are spontaneous—they do not require teaching by adults (this is another difference from Social Learning Theory). Once these are formed, children socialise themselves, they *actively* seeks out same-sex models and other information to learn how to act like a girl or a boy. This process of self-socialisation does not start to occur until the child reaches the gender consistency stage.

According to Kohlberg (1966), children find it rewarding to behave in line with their consistent gender identity.

Research evidence

There is evidence that children do, indeed, progress through the three stages proposed by Kohlberg. In a cross-cultural study, Munroe, Shimmin, and Munroe (1984) found that children in several cultures had the same sequences of stages on the way to full gender identity.

One of the predictions of Kohlberg's theory is that children who have reached the stage of gender consistency will pay more attention to the behaviour of same-sex models than children at earlier stages of gender development. Slaby and Frey (1975) tested this prediction. Children between the ages of 2 and 5 were assessed for gender consistency, and assigned to a high or a low gender consistency group. They were then shown a film of a male and a female performing a variety of activities. Those who were high in gender consistency showed a greater tendency to attend to the same-sexed model than did those low in gender consistency.

More evidence of the importance of gender consistency was reported by Ruble, Balaban, and Cooper (1981). Preschoolers high and low in gender consistency watched television commercials in which toys were represented as being suitable for boys or for girls. These advertisements had more effect on the attitudes and behaviour of boys and girls high in gender consistency. This offers a more complex perspective on the role of the media in gender behaviours because

 What other factors in these children's lives might have played a part?

it suggests that it is not simply a case of exposure to stereotypes in the media but what children bring with them to their media use.

Evaluation

In support of Kohlberg, gender identity does seem to develop through the three stages proposed by Kohlberg. As predicted by the theory, the achievement of full gender identity increases gender-role behaviour. In more general terms, the notion that gender development involves children actively interacting with the world around them is valuable, as is the notion that how they interact with the world depends on the extent to which they have developed a consistent gender identity.

However, there are various problems with Kohlberg's theory. First, the main one is that sex typing is well under way before a child develops a mature gender identity. Much research has demonstrated that children prefer sex-appropriate toys from at least as early as 2 years old, and that they prefer same-sex playmates from around 3 years of age, long before they begin to selectively attend to same-sex models. In other words, gender-role behaviour is shown by most boys and girls by the time of their third birthday. This is several years before they have reached gender consistency, and so it cannot be argued that *all* gender-role behaviour depends on gender consistency. It seems that only a very basic understanding of gender is necessary before children learn sex-role stereotypes and measures of gender consistency tell us little about how "sex-typed" children are (Lobel & Menashri, 1993).

Second, Kohlberg's theory tends to ignore the external factors (e.g. reward and punishment from parents) that determine much early gender-role behaviour.

Third, Kohlberg probably exaggerated the importance of cognitive factors in producing gender-role behaviour. Huston (1985) pointed out that Kohlberg's theory leads to the prediction that there should be a close relationship between beliefs about gender and gender-typed attitudes and behaviour. In fact, the relationship is not very strong, and is weaker in girls than in boys. This means that what you believe about gender roles is not necessarily reflected in your actual behaviour. As Kohlberg's theory is based on the fact that beliefs (cognitions) influence behaviour, these findings cannot be explained by his theory.

Gender-schema theory

Bem (1981) and Martin and Halverson (1987) put forward a rather different cognitive-developmental theory known as Gender-Schema Theory. This addresses the main problem of Kohlberg's theory, that sex-typed behaviour emerges long before children reach an understanding of gender consistency, and also includes elements of Social Learning Theory. They start with the same notion that children are pre-programmed to organise information in terms of schemas and that one of the most powerful schemas in nearly all societies is that of gender. These gender schemas, as they are called, consist of organised sets of beliefs about the sexes. Unlike Kohlberg, they propose that the schemas are formed as soon as children have acquired basic gender identity (i.e. from around age 2). Gender-Schema Theory uses an *information-processing approach* to explain the influence of these gender schemas. This means that once these gender schemas are formed, any information children receive about gender roles is actively used to organise and understand the larger world. The gender schemas possessed by children help to determine what they attend to, how they interpret the world, and what they remember of their experiences.

EXAM HINT

Note that a significant challenge to Kohlberg's theory is that there is not a significant relationship between children's beliefs about gender and their actual behaviour.

? Think about your own family. Are there specific domestic chores that are done by particular members of the family? Can they be categorised by gender?

The first schema that is formed is an in-group/out-group schema, consisting of organised information about which toys and activities are suitable for boys and which are suitable for girls.

Another early schema is an own-gender schema containing information about how to behave in gender-stereotyped ways (e.g. how to dress dolls for a girl).

Martin, Wood, and Little (1990) have investigated the way in which these gender schemas develop in children and suggest that they develop through three stages:

1. Children learn what type of things are associated with each sex, e.g. "boys have short hair; girls wear dresses".
2. Children begin to link gender items together and draw inferences based on the culture's view of sex-appropriate behaviour, e.g. if a person has long hair, she is also likely to wear dresses, play with dolls, enjoy helping mummy with the cooking. However, these inferences are mainly made only about their own sex. This stage is around 4–6 years.
3. From about 8 years of age, children can make these inferences about the opposite sex. So, a girl is now more likely to offer a boy a train set to play with than a doll and may assume he'd rather do things with his father than his mother.

Research evidence

According to the theory, gender schemas are used by children to organise and make sense of their experiences. If they are exposed to information that does not fit one of their schemas (e.g. a boy combing the hair of his doll), then the information should be distorted to make it fit the schema. Martin and Halverson (1983) tested this prediction. They showed 5- and 6-year-old children pictures of schema-consistent activities (e.g. a boy playing with a train) and schema-inconsistent activities (e.g. a girl sawing wood). Schema-consistent pictures were much better remembered a week later than sex-inconsistent pictures. The latter were often remembered incorrectly by changing the sex of the person and therefore making them schema consistent.

Another study that supports gender-schema theory was reported by Bradbard, Martin, Endsley, and Halverson (1986). Boys and girls between the ages of 4 and 9 were presented with gender-neutral objects such as burglar alarms and pizza cutters. They were told that some of the objects were "boy" objects, whereas others were described as "girl" objects. There were two key findings. First, children spent much more time playing with objects that they had been told were appropriate to their gender. Second, even a week later the children remembered whether any given object was a "boy" or a "girl" object.

In sum, there are two main differences between Kohlberg's theory and Gender-Schema Theory:

1. Gender-Schema Theory puts greater emphasis on the way the schemas are used to process information than does Kohlberg's theory.
2. Gender-Schema Theory holds that children do not need to have a mature understanding of gender consistency before they can show sex-typed behaviour.

Schema-consistent activities

Schema-inconsistent activities

[?] Do behaviours that are considered "boy things" and "girl things" remain constant over time? Are there illustrative examples from your childhood that are different from your parents' childhood?

Boys and girls tend to play with different toys. It's difficult to tell whether this is due to social stereotyping or to innate differences in what toys they prefer.

EXAM HINT

Make sure you can provide evidence for Gender-Schema Theory from the range of studies that show children's preferences for gender-appropriate toys and the gender bias they show in recall of gender relevant material. However, note the theory is criticised for overemphasising cognitive factors and underestimating the importance of social factors.

A study by Masters, Ford, Arend, Grotevant, and Clark (1979) also supports Gender-Schema Theory. Young children of 4 and 5 were influenced in their choice of toy more by the gender label attached to the toy (e.g. "It's a girl's toy") than by the gender of the model seen playing with the toy. As Durkin (1995) pointed out, children's behaviour seems to be influenced more by the schema, "This is a boy's toy" or "This is a girl's toy" than by a desire to imitate a same-sexed model.

Liben and Signorella (1993) demonstrated that children show gender-related bias in recall; in other words, they remember things relevant to their own sex more than those relevant to the opposite sex. Pictures and words related to "feminine" items were better remembered by girls than by boys and the converse was also true.

Evaluation

One of the main strengths of Gender-Schema Theory is that it helps to explain why children's gender-role beliefs and attitudes often change rather little after middle childhood. The gender schemas that have been established tend to be maintained because schema-consistent information is attended to and remembered. Another strength of the theory is its focus on the child as being actively involved in making sense of the world in the light of its present knowledge.

The limitations of Gender-Schema Theory resemble those of Kohlberg's theory. The theory overemphasises the role of the individual child in gender development, and de-emphasises the importance of social factors. In addition, it is likely that the importance of schemas and other cognitive factors in determining behaviour are exaggerated within the theory. Another problem is that the theory does not really explain *why* gender schemas develop and take the form they do. This is demonstrated in a study by Campbell et al. (2004), who tested children at 2 years and 3 years of age. There was no evidence that the extent of sex-typed behaviour depended on the amount of previously acquired gender-related knowledge. Thus, it is unclear whether gender knowledge *causes* subsequent sex-typed behaviour.

Finally, the theory assumes that it should be possible to change children's behaviour by changing their schemas or stereotypes but this is not necessarily true. In fact, as Durkin (1995, p.185) pointed out, "greater success has been reported in attempts to change concepts than attempts to change behaviour or behavioural intentions." In a similar way, many married couples have *schemas* relating to equality of the sexes and equal division of household chores, but this rarely has much effect on their *behaviour*!

? In what other contexts have you come across "schema"? How would you define it?

Psychological Androgyny

"**Androgyny**" is a term used to describe individuals who have both masculine and feminine qualities. Physical androgyny involves having both male and female sex organs (an extremely rare condition in humans), such individuals are also known as hermaphrodite. Psychological androgyny involves having both traits that have traditionally been associated with masculinity (such as assertive) together with traits that are traditionally viewed as feminine (such as sensitivity). Such an individual is sometimes referred to as an androgyne. In this section we will be discussing psychological androgyny.

The androgyny scale

Sandra Bem has devised a way of measuring androgyny. She compiled a list of 200 personality traits that were masculine or feminine but were neutral in terms of social desirability. Feminine items included affectionate, cheerful, childlike, and compassionate. Examples of masculine items were aggressive, analytical, dominant, and authoritative. Neutral items included adaptable, conscientious, and friendly.

Bem then asked 100 students to complete the sentence: "In American society, how desirable is it for a woman (man) to be truthful?" This was repeated with all 200 personality traits. Half the students answered the question with respect to women and half with respect to men. A Likert scale was used, rating each characteristic from 1 to 7 (1 = not at all desirable; 7 = extremely desirable). She then divided the traits into the 20 most masculine (those with the greatest gap between masculine and feminine, with it being desirable for men but not for women), the 20 most feminine (the converse), the 10 most gender neutral (no difference in their desirability for men and women) but most desirable overall, and the 10 gender neutral and most generally undesirable across the two sexes. The judgements had to be made by both men and women students in order to be selected.

Sixty traits made up the Bem Sex Role Inventory (BSRI).

Individuals completing the BSRI are asked to rate themselves on each characteristic on a scale of 1 to 7, where 1 = almost never true (of me) and 7 = always or almost always true (of me). Each person receives a masculinity score, a femininity score, and an androgyny score, which reflects the relative amounts of masculinity/femininity included in the self-description. If the scores on masculinity/femininity differs greatly, then the individual is sex-typed; if they are similar, the individual is androgynous.

In her original study (Bem 1974), Bem administered the BRSI to over 550 male students and 350 female students and found androgyny rates of 32% in the females and 39% in the males, demonstrating that, even in 1974, androgyny rates (at least amongst students) were quite high. Of course, students are by no means typical of the population as a whole. Interestingly, the correlation between androgyny score and those of desirability was virtually zero, demonstrating that this measure of androgyny is not simply measuring social desirability.

Bem believes that it is desirable to have a balance of feminine and masculine characteristics, to be, for example, ambitious, self-sufficient, nurturant, and compassionate. She maintains that this makes an individual better able to cope with life's challenges than being either extremely masculine or extremely feminine,

? What might be some of the ethical problems encountered by researchers conducting studies into the links between sexual identity and biology?

KEY TERM

Androgyny: a term used to describe individuals who have both masculine and feminine qualities. Psychological androgyny involves having both traits that have traditionally been associated with masculinity (such as assertive) together with traits that are traditionally viewed as feminine (such as sensitivity).

Characteristics used in the Bem Sex Role Inventory

1. self-reliant [M]	21. reliable [N]	41. warm [F]
2. yielding [F]	22. analytical [M]	42. solemn [N]
3. helpful [N]	23. sympathetic [F]	43. willing to take a stand [M]
4. defends own beliefs [M]	24. jealous [N]	44. tender [F]
5. cheerful [F]	25. leadership ability [M]	45. friendly [N]
6. moody [N]	26. sensitive to other's needs [F]	46. aggressive [M]
7. independent [M]	27. truthful [N]	47. gullible [F]
8. shy [F]	28. willing to take risks [M]	48. inefficient [N]
9. conscientious [N]	29. understanding [F]	49. acts as a leader [M]
10. athletic [M]	30. secretive [N]	50. childlike [F]
11. affectionate [F]	31. makes decisions easily [M]	51. adaptable [N]
12. theatrical [N]	32. compassionate [F]	52. individualistic [M]
13. assertive [M]	33. sincere [N]	53. does not use harsh language [F]
14. flatterable [F]	34. self-sufficient [M]	54. unsystematic [N]
15. happy [N]	35. eager to soothe hurt feelings [F]	55. competitive [M]
16. strong personality [M]	36. conceited [N]	56. loves children [F]
17. loyal [F]	37. dominant [M]	57. tactful [N]
18. unpredictable [N]	38. soft spoken [F]	58. ambitious [M]
19. forceful [M]	39. likable [N]	59. gentle [F]
20. feminine [F]	40. masculine [M]	60. conventional [N]

because such individuals are not constrained by the demands of rigid gender roles, whereas those who are strongly sex typed are limited in the range of behaviours available to them. Bem has commented that "In a society where rigid sex-role differentiation has already outlived its utility, perhaps the androgynous person will come to define a more human standard of psychological health".

We will now look at research into androgyny, including the evidence for and against the view that psychological androgyny does result in a more healthy psychological state than being traditionally sex typed.

Research evidence
Bem (1978) found that androgynous individuals are better able to resist social pressure and generally more flexible in their approach to situations than are sex-typed individuals. They are also better able to adjust their behaviour to the demands of the situation (Shaffer, Pegalis, & Cornell, 1992).

One of the most important indicators of psychological health is high self-esteem. Allgood-Merton and Stockland (1991) and other studies have shown that androgynous children and adolescents have higher self-esteem, are more popular with their peers, and are better adjusted than sex-typed people of the same age.

Being androgynous does not preclude appropriate masculine and feminine behaviour. Spence (1993) found that androgynous men can still feel quite masculine and that androgynous women can still be feminine even though they are capable of showing emotions and behaviour traditionally associated with the opposite sex.

Norlander, Erixon, and Archer (2000) found that students who were androgynous on the BSRI scored higher on creativity and, to a lesser extent, optimism than those who were more sex-stereotyped. Androgynous individuals have

HOW SCIENCE WORKS: GENDER ANDROGENY
Children learn their gender schema when young. The interesting thing is that whereas some individuals hold to a strict gender schema/role, others are more flexible; the latter are described as androgenous.

You could see where you come on this concept, but if you are going to ask other people to complete this task you need to remember that gender is a very socially and personally sensitive area and you will have to consider this carefully during planning for your investigation.

Look at the following list of words and phrases and decide which fit the masculine gender better, and which fit the feminine gender better. Begin by numbering them, keeping them in the same order as printed here:

independent; emotional; passive; devote self to others; rough; helpful; competitive; kind; unaware of others' feelings; give up easily; self-confident; feel inferior; don't understand others; cold towards others; can't cope with pressure.

In Bem's research the following were masculine: 1, 3, 7, 10, 11, 12, 13, 16; the others were feminine.

Do you agree? What criticisms could you make of Bem's categorisation and how would you explain this? (Clue: *zeitgeist*.)

also been found to have higher self-esteem (Lundy & Rosenberg, 1987), higher levels of identity achievement (Orlofsky, 1977) and more flexibility in dating and love behaviour (DeLucia, 1987).

However, there is research evidence that opposes the view that androgyny is a more desirable attribute than masculine identity. Orlofsky and O'Heron (1987) demonstrated that traditionally masculine traits were associated with better adjustment and higher self-esteem than androgyny. This might be because masculine traits have been more highly valued than feminine ones in most societies. Nevid and Rathus (2005) argue that the relationship between psychological androgyny and self-esteem in both men and women is not based on the combination of masculine and feminine traits, but on the presence of masculine traits such as independence and assertiveness.

Other research on androgyny demonstrates that it may change with different generations. Guastello and Guastello (2003) studied androgyny, gender-role behaviour, and emotional intelligence in 576 students and their parents. Sons were more androgynous in personality than fathers but no differences were found between mothers and daughters. Younger women were more likely than their mothers to show masculine gender-typed behaviour and less likely to show female gender-typed behaviour.

Woodhill and Samuels (2003) have suggested a reason why the data on the advantages of androgyny are ambiguous. They propose that it is useful to separate out positive and negative characteristics of androgyny. Just as there are positive traits of masculinity and femininity (such as assertiveness and nurturance, respectively), so there are negative ones (dominance, submissiveness). Androgynous people who, by definition, have a mixture of masculine and feminine traits, might not necessarily be psychologically healthy if most of these traits are negative. When Woodhill and Samuels conducted research that separated out androgynous people into

Studies show that an androgynous individual might not be psychologically healthy if most of the traits that he or she has of the opposite gender are negative; e.g. a woman having the masculine trait of aggression (negative) as opposed to assertiveness (positive).

positive and negative, they found that the positively androgynous people scored higher on indicators of mental health and well-being than negatively androgynous or negatively stereotyped people. They conclude that it is positively, not negatively, androgynous people who have the potential to live the more fulfilled and complete life that Bem (1975) originally envisaged, as negative traits may override benefits proposed for the androgynous person. It is therefore essential to differentiate between positive and negative androgyny when measuring personality rather than simply have a global score.

The clinical definition of gender dysphoria

The clinical definition of gender dysphoria is "gender identity disorder". This term is used in the two major classification systems of mental disorders, DSM-IV and ICD-10 (see Chapter 10, p. 378). DSM-IV defines gender dysphoria as "A strong and persistent cross-gender identification (not merely a desire for any perceived cultural advantages of being the other sex)".

Some people view the term "cross-gender identification" as stigmatising and therefore use only "gender dysphoria".

DSM-IV classification of gender identity disorder

1. There must be evidence of a strong and persistent cross-gender identification.
2. This cross-gender identification must not be merely a desire for any perceived cultural advantages of being the other sex.
3. There must be evidence of persistent discomfort about one's assigned sex or a sense of inappropriateness in the gender role of that sex.
4. The individual must not have a concurrent physical intersex condition (e.g. androgen insensitivity syndrome or congenital adrenal hyperphasia).
5. There must be evidence of clinically significant distress or impairment in social, occupational, to other important areas of functioning.

Gender Dysphoria

Gender dysphoria, also known as gender identity disorder, is a condition in which people are uncomfortable with the gender to which they have been assigned (dysphoria means unhappiness). In the extreme, this can lead to transsexualism, a desire to change your gender.

When a baby is born, it is identified as being a boy or girl on the basis of its genitals. These genitals indicate other biological characteristics, such as the gonads (testes in boys, ovaries in girls) and the chromosomes: XX for girls, XY for boys. As we have seen, children then develop a gender identity that provides them with expectations of gender roles, that is, the way they should behave in society. In the vast majority of cases the elements of sex, gender identity, and gender role are consistent with each other and boys are quite content to be boys and grow into men and girls are content to be girls and grow into women. However, in a few cases, individuals do not feel that they have been assigned the correct gender. Some girls feel as if they should be a boy and, conversely, some boys feel that they are a girl. This is more common in boys but occurs in both sexes.

Explanations for gender dysphoria

1. The biological explanation: the influence of prenatal hormones

One explanation of gender dysphoria is that it is caused by unusual development in parts of the brain before birth. Small areas of the brain are different in males and females and the theory is that in people experiencing gender dysphoria one of these areas has developed in a way that corresponds to the opposite sex of their other biological sex characteristics. What might cause this atypical development? Hormones are very important during foetal development and it is possible that they cause parts of the brain to develop in a way that is not consistent with the genitalia and, usually, with the chromosomes. This means that the brain has not developed in a way that corresponds to the gender assigned to the child at birth. The result is that these people are sometimes referred to as XY females (children assumed to be boys but who feel they are girls) and as XX boys (children brought up as girls who wish to be boys).

KEY TERM

Gender dysphoria (also known as gender identity disorder): a condition in which people are uncomfortable with the gender to which they have been assigned (dysphoria means unhappiness).

This mismatch between gender identity and the assigned gender is not usually recognised by the children experiencing it, never mind by other people. Younger children may feel uneasy but are unable to pin point the source of their discomfort. Only when it grows stronger during adolescence and adulthood are they are able to recognise it. Some people prefer not to acknowledge these feelings openly—they might even deny them to themselves.

Research evidence. Kruijiver, Zhou, Pool, Hofman, Gooren, and Swaab (2000) point out that males have around twice as many somatostatin neurons than do women. They found that in both male-to-female transsexuals and female-to-male transsexuals, the number of these neurons corresponded to their gender of choice, not to their biological sex. They concluded that this clearly points to a neurobiological basis of gender dysphoria.

Zhou, Hofman, Gooren, and Swaab (1995) studied one of the brain structures that is different in men and women and found that in six male-to-female transsexuals it followed a totally female pattern.

Evaluation. The research evidence cited above supports the biological explanation for gender dysphoria. However, some studies have shown no evidence of atypical biological influence on people with the condition. Rekers, Crandall, Rosen, and Bentler (1979) examined 70 "gender disturbed" boys and found no evidence for prenatal hormone treatment of the mothers nor any history of hormonal imbalance. This research is covered below as it supports the view that gender dysphoria is caused by family factors rather than biological ones, a theory that we now consider.

2. Family constellations

Stoller (1968) points out that certain family conditions are associated with gender dysphoria. For boys who want to be girls, he suggests that there is an overclose relationship with the mother and a distant father. For girls who want to be boys, he suggests that that they have a depressed mother in the first few months of their life and a father who is either not present or does not support the mother but leaves the child to try to control the mother's depression.

Rekers links gender dysphoria in boys to absence of a father figure, either physically or psychologically.

Bleiberg, Jackson, and Ross (1986) have linked the development of gender dysphoria with an inability to mourn a parent or an important attachment figure in early life.

Other suggestions are that parents have a strong desire for a child of the opposite sex and, not necessarily deliberately, reinforce gender-inappropriate behaviour (di Ceglie, 2000).

Research evidence. Di Ceglie (2000) cites the case of "James" who was looked after from 6 months to 5 years by his grandmother while his mother mainly worked

The film *Boys Don't Cry* illustrates the problem involved in gender dysphoria. It's based on the true story of a person called Brandon who has a girl's body but regards himself as a male. He lives as a boy amongst a group of teenagers and falls in love with a girl who feels the same about him. Eventually the reality of his body is revealed and, although his girlfriend accepts the new situation, others cannot. Two young men become extremely disturbed by this realisation and eventually Brandon is raped and murdered.

Hilary Swank starred in the leading role as Brandon in the film *Boys Don't Cry*.

EXAM HINT

Make sure you can cite Kruijiver et al.'s (2000) research as evidence for a biological basis to gender dysphoria. However, note the small sample size of the research and the conflicting evidence, which has found no hormonal imbalances in people with gender dysphoria. Consider the family theories as counter perspectives.

away. The grandmother involved him in many traditionally female activities such as cooking and housework. After her very sudden death, James developed gender dysphoria: he wished he were a girl, wanted to play with dolls, and fantasised about being a bride and a breast-feeding mother. He was unable ever to talk about his grandmother but, after a long period of family therapy with the aim of encouraging him to talk about her, his gender dysphoria gradually disappeared.

With respect to paternal deprivation, Biller (1974) and Hamilton (1977) have shown that gender dysphoria in boys is associated with fathers who are absent either physically or psychologically. Reker (1986) has conducted research on "gender disturbed" boys who show cross-gender identity, a history of cross-dressing, and cross-gender role-play behaviour. He found that in a group of 36 such boys, there was no father figure in the homes of 75% of the most disturbed and 21% of the least disturbed. This compared at the time with an average rate of father absence of 12% in boys of a comparable group in the USA. In those cases where the father or a father substitute was present, he was described in 60% of cases as being psychologically distant. Rekers concludes that young males with the most pronounced gender disturbances tend to be less likely to have a male role model in the home, as compared with less gender-disturbed boys.

Rekers (1986) reports that in the families of gender-dysphoria boys he has studied, 80% of the mothers had psychiatric problems and 45% of the fathers had a history of mental health problems and/or psychiatric treatment. Although he acknowledged that these percentages might be rather higher than in the total population of gender-dysphoria boys because those parents who seek help for themselves are more likely to seek help for their boys, it does still imply that the parents of such boys show unusually high levels of psychological problems.

Evaluation. The research evidence cited above does appear to link family structure with gender dysphoria, although most of the research is concerned with boys. Some of the most convincing evidence is put forward by Rekers, who associates father absence with gender disturbance in boys. Although he acknowledges that these correlational studies do not necessarily imply that the absence of a male role model in early life *causes* gender disorder, he does believe that this is not an unreasonable conclusion to draw. Nevertheless, it is very important to note the research supporting the biological explanation can be used as a criticism of this view.

In essence, we need to take account of *both* biology *and* family structure when seeking an explanation for gender dysphoria.

See *A2-Level Psychology Online* for some interactive quizzes to help you with your revision.

SECTION SUMMARY
Psychological Explanations of Gender Development

❖ The term "sex" refers to the biological fact of being male or female; "gender" refers to the psychological characteristics associated with being male or female.
❖ A "gender role" is a set of expectations that prescribe how males and females should think act and feel whereas "gender stereotypes" are beliefs about the differences between males and females based on these gender roles.
❖ Gender is a fundamental part of our self-concept.

❖ Gender identity must be established before gender roles are acquired.

❖ Children go through three stages in the development of gender identity: basic gender identity (2–3½ years), gender stability (3½–4½ years), and gender consistency (4½–7 years upwards).

❖ Achieving gender consistency leads to a predicted increase in sex-typed behaviour.

❖ However, in contradiction to the theory, children begin to acquire gender concepts before gender consistency.

❖ Other weaknesses of the theory include the tendency for it to ignore external factors (e.g. rewards and punishments from parents) and to exaggerate the role of internal, cognitive factors.

Kohlberg's Cognitive-Developmental Theory

❖ As soon as young children have acquired basic gender identity they start to form gender schemas (i.e. organised sets of beliefs about the sexes).

❖ Once these gender schemas are formed, the child actively uses information about gender roles to organise and understand the larger world. Information that is inconsistent with gender schemas tends to be misremembered.

❖ Children do not need to have a mature understanding of gender consistency before they can show sex-typed behaviour (this addresses one of the main criticisms of Kohlberg's theory).

❖ The theory also explains why children's gender-role beliefs change little after middle childhood.

❖ The limitations of the theory are otherwise similar to those of Kohlberg's, in that the theory overestimates the role of the individual child and underestimates the importance of social factors.

Gender-Schema Theory

❖ The term "androgyny" describes individuals who have both masculine and feminine qualities.

❖ Bem devised an androgyny scale to measure the extent of androgyny in individuals. She believes that it is psychologically healthy to have a balance of feminine and masculine traits.

❖ Not all the research supports Bem's view, possibly because it is necessary to differentiate between positive and characteristics of androgyny. Woodhills and Samuels argue that only people with positive androgynous traits score highly on indicators of mental health.

❖ Gender dysphoria, also known as gender identity disorder, is a condition in which people feel uncomfortable with the gender to which they have been assigned.

❖ The biological explanation for gender dysphoria is that there has been unusual development in the brain before birth such that it has not developed in a way that corresponds to the gender assigned at birth on the basis of the genitals.

❖ The neurobiological basis of gender dysphoria is supported by research evidence; however, some studies show no evidence of atypical biological influence. An alternative explanation is that family conditions contribute to the condition, e.g. an overclose relationship with the mother and a distant father.

❖ Researchers are not consistent about the specific characteristics of the family that might be linked to gender dysphoria. In support, some research found an

Psychological androgyny and gender dysphoria

unusually high incidence of mental health problems in the parents of individuals with gender dysphoria. Nevertheless, this view does possibly underestimate the role of biology as an explanation for the condition.

BIOLOGICAL INFLUENCES ON GENDER

The Role of Hormones and Genes in Gender Development

At the beginning of this chapter, we briefly mentioned the biological differences between males and females in terms of their chromosomes. This section looks at the biological differences between the sexes in more detail and considers what effect these biological factors might have on behaviour.

Prenatal sexual development

At conception, an ovum (egg) from the female is fertilised by a sperm from the male. The egg and sperm are known as gametes and each has 23 chromosomes, which code all the child's genetic material. One of the 23 is the sex chromosome, and this can be of two types, X and Y. The ova all contain an X chromosome whereas the sperm carry either an X or a Y. When a Y sperm fertilises an ovum, the embryo will have an XY pair of chromosomes and will be a boy; when an X sperm fertilises the ovum, the result is a female embryo with an XX pair of chromosomes. Hence it is always the male who determines the sex of the child.

For about the first 7 weeks of development, the external genitalia appear virtually identical in both sexes. Internally, the same two sets of ducts develop in both males and females.

After 7 weeks, the differentiation between the two sexes begins. The presence of the Y chromosome induces the developing gonads to produce hormones, including testosterone, which stimulate the development of the male internal reproductive system. If these hormones are not present, the embryo continues to develop as a female. Male hormones are essential to the development of a male whereas female hormones do not appear necessary for the development of female structures—these are capable of developing autonomously. Indeed, if a male animal embryo is castrated early enough, the animal will develop as a full biological female. In essence, normal sex differentiation depends entirely on the presence or absence of the male hormones. The period during which these hormones have their effect is known as the critical period. In humans, this is only a few days, late in the third month of pregnancy.

At about 4 months of gestation, the testosterone leads to the development of the external male sex organs, the penis and scrotum. If testosterone is not present, female external genitalia develop.

There is a rare condition, known as complete androgen insensitivity syndrome (formerly known as testicular feminising syndrome), in which genetic males (i.e. those with XY chromosomes) are insensitive to the male hormones and do not develop male genitalia. They are born looking like girls and are often brought up as girls because the condition is not usually detected until puberty when they fail to menstruate. Internally, there is a short blind-ending vagina but no uterus, fallopian tubes, or ovaries. We will look at such individuals when we consider Biosocial Theory.

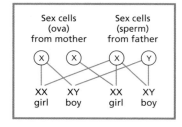

All sex cells from the mother carry X chromosomes. Half the sex cells from the male carry X and half carry Y. Therefore it is always the father who determines the sex of the child.

The influence of the sex chromosomes

The X and Y are so called because of their shape. The Y chromosome looks like an incomplete X and is one-fifth the size of the X chromosome, hence boys carry less genetic material than girls, which might be why males are more vulnerable to genetic disorders than females throughout their lives. Montagu (1968) listed 62 specific disorders that are largely or wholly due to sex-linked genes and found mostly in males, including some very serious ones such as haemophilia, as well as less important ones such as red/green colour blindness.

In most cultures, more boys than girls are conceived but more boys are miscarried, stillborn, or die soon after birth. This pattern of vulnerability continues throughout life: in communities with adequate nutrition, 54% of children who die in the first year of life are male. The life expectancy of the female at birth is almost universally higher than that of the male. Although some of this can be accounted for by lifestyle (such as men being engaged in riskier activities), this is no by means proven and females do appear to have a biological advantage over men. For example, Oakley (1985) cites a study of heavy smokers in which the females appear less at risk from coronary heart disease and lung cancer than the males.

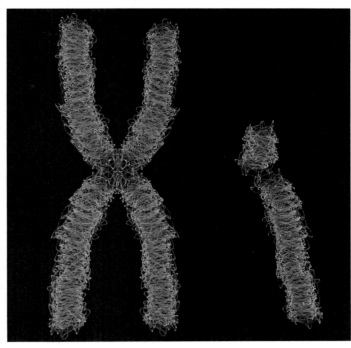

X and Y chromosomes. Human cells have 46 chromosomes, of which 22 pairs are identical in males and females. In males, the last pair is composed of an X (left) and a Y (right); females have two X chromosomes.

The role of hormones

The role of hormones in sexual development is of enormous importance so it is useful to give an overview of their effect. The number and type of hormones produced by males and females is identical—no hormones are present in one sex and not in another; the difference is in the quantity that each sex produces. Within normal biological development, females produce a preponderance of female sex hormones, oestrogen and progesterone, whereas males produce a preponderance of androgens (a collection of male hormones) of which one of the most important is testosterone.

The sex hormones are produced not only by the testes and ovaries but also by the adrenal glands. It is difficult to measure the amount of hormone produced because the male and female hormones are chemically similar and the body sometimes converts one into the other (this is why, much to their great embarrassment, rapidly developing male adolescents sometimes develop small breasts: some of the large amount of testosterone produced is converted into oestrogen which stimulates breast development).

Up to about age 8 or 10, negligible amounts of sex hormones are produced by either sex but after that both sexes produce more male *and* female hormones. From around 11 years of age, both girls and boys increase their production of female hormones but females produce far more than boys and this production eventually becomes cyclical in girls, varying on a monthly basis whereas in boys the production remains steady. With respect to male hormones, once children reach puberty both sexes increase their production rapidly but boys more so than girls.

Research evidence of the effect of biology on behaviour

It would be very surprising if the biological differences between men and women did not have some effect on behaviour but it is always difficult to separate out nature and nurture in humans. However, research—both on humans and on non-human animals—provides some clues. Testosterone appears to be linked to aggression. Male mice characteristically fight each other but females and castrated male mice will not. When the latter are injected with testosterone they will fight, as will females given a similar injection. Young, Goy, and Phoenix (1964) demonstrated that pregnant monkeys injected with androgens gave birth to females with masculinised genitalia who acted in masculine ways, such as being threatening and aggressive, engaging in rough-and-tumble play, and mounting females.

The study of the level of testosterone in foetuses can provide important clues to its function. In animals, foetal testosterone (fT) plays a central role in organising the brain and in later social behaviour. In humans it has been linked negatively with language development, eye contact, and—positively—with spatial ability. Knickmeyer, Baron-Cohen, Raggatt, and Taylor (2005) studied the fT levels in the amniotic fluid of 58 children: 35 males and 23 females. When these children were aged 4, their mothers completed a questionnaire assessing their language skills, quality of social relationships, and restricted interests. fT was negatively correlated with the quality of social relationships and positively correlated with restricted interests in the boys. This indicates that testosterone might negatively affect social relationships.

You would expect sex hormones to be related to sex drive in humans and they are, but not in the obvious way of males being affected by male hormones and females being aroused by female hormones. Instead, it is the male hormone in both sexes that appears to be linked to sex drive. Men who have had their testes removed have a much reduced sex drive but the sex drive of women is unaffected by the removal of the ovaries (which produce female sex hormones). If, however, women are injected with androgens (as they may be during courses of treatment for some medical conditions) their sex drive can increase enormously, even when they are ill.

Sex hormones are also linked to the behaviour associated with pre-menstrual syndrome, which occurs when levels of progesterone are low. Pre-menstrual syndrome/tension tends to be a catch-all phrase for a variety of symptoms. Four to five days before the onset of menses (bleeding), 60% of women experience some tangible changes, for example mild irritation, depression, headaches, decline in attentiveness. Some people experience a day or so of great energy, followed by lethargy, which disappears with the onset of bleeding. Other pre-menstrual symptoms commonly reported are weeping, insomnia, even nymphomania! Some women experience a sudden craving for sweet foods, others lose their appetite almost completely.

Dalton (1969) summarised many studies of behaviour change that could be attributed to the menstrual cycle: 63% to 84% of crimes committed by women occur in the pre-menstrual period; accident and suicide rates increase, and there is a decline in the standard of schoolwork, in scores on intelligence tests, and in speed of response.

Nevertheless, not all evidence indicates that mood changes are related to the menstrual cycle. Some researchers maintain that although a small percentage of women do suffer relatively intense periodic mood swings related to their menstrual cycle, in most women there is little relationship between the menstrual cycle and mood (McFarlane, Martin, & Williams, 1988). There may also be the influence of the **self-fulfilling prophecy**—the fact that women expect to feel moody and depressed at this time of the month may make them more likely to feel so, and be more aware of clumsiness, etc. than at other times of their menstrual cycle.

As we have seen, hormonal influences are complex and confusing. Collaer and Hines (1995) reviewed the somewhat inconsistent findings from numerous studies. They argued that there is good evidence for at least three effects. First, male sex hormones increase the likelihood that the child will enjoy rough-and-tumble play and physical activity generally. Second, exposure to high levels of male sex hormones at an early age affects sexual orientation in adolescence. Third, male sex hormones lead to an increase in aggressive behaviour.

Collaer and Hines' (1995) study showed that male sex hormones lead to an increase in aggressive behaviour.

Is biology destiny?

However important biological factors are, they can provide only a partial explanation for the development of gender roles. We have already seen how important social and cognitive factors, including the self-fulfilling prophecy, are in shaping behaviour. Biological factors cannot explain cross-cultural variations in gender roles, nor the substantial changes in gender roles that have occurred in Western societies in recent decades. Biosocial Theory, which we now consider, is an attempt to combine elements of both the biological and social approaches.

The Biosocial Approach to Gender Development

Having looked at approaches that consider the influence of upbringing (nurture) on a child's gender identity and those that consider the effect of biology, we now turn to a third approach. Rather than seeing gender differences in terms of *either* nature *or* nurture, the biosocial approach emphasises the *interaction* of these two major influences. The theory fully acknowledges the importance of biology and so involves all the biological research just covered, but it also acknowledges that social factors might interact with these biological factors to influence gender identity.

Biosocial Theory was first advanced by Money and Ehrhardt (1972), who started by proposing that there are a number of critical events that affect the early development of the child. These events begin before birth with the biological influences covered in the previous section. These biological factors obviously have a large influence on the child. However, from birth onwards, social factors also begin to play an important part. As we have already seen, once children are labelled as a boy or girl they are treated very differently and these social factors interact with the biological ones to determine the child's gender identity.

In the majority of cases, the child's biological sex matches the gender of upbringing and there are no problems. However, some individuals, known as intersex children, are born with ambiguous genitals and are not obviously one sex or the other. Money believes that, providing that a child's sex of rearing is decided

KEY TERM

Self-fulfilling prophecy: the belief that the way a person is treated, the assumptions that are made about them, and the beliefs they hold can influence their behaviour in such a way that the prophecy comes true.

before the third birthday, then social factors are so strongly influential that such children will accept their assigned gender identity. The third year is another critical period and, because a child's gender identity is established by that age, then (according to Money) it cannot thereafter be changed without causing the child serious psychological problems.

Research evidence

Early research did support the view that individuals would accept their sex of rearing and learn appropriate gender-role behaviours in association with the gender assigned at birth. Goldwyn (1979) cites the case of Mrs DW, who had androgen insensitivity syndrome and was brought up as a woman. When informed in her late teens that she was biologically male and had no internal female organs, she nevertheless felt that she was a woman and elected to stay in that role, married, and adopted two children. At no time did she ever feel masculine and was completely happy with her role as wife and mother. This, of course, is a case study of one, which makes it hard to draw firm conclusions. It also isn't entirely clear whether we can say that Mrs DW was influenced by social factors (reared as a girl) or biological ones (exposure to male hormones).

However, biological factors can have an important influence and some research contradicts Money's suggestion that sex of rearing is all important. A sad case of an identical twin boy whose penis was accidentally damaged during surgery before his first birthday demonstrates the strong influence that biology can have over upbringing. The boy was raised as a girl but always felt that he was a boy, thus contradicting Money's contention. (See the case study below.)

This poignant case study is of particular interest because it was the first one to highlight the problems of a child born developmentally normal but reassigned to another sex. Although only a single case study, it does lend strong support to the view that biology might take precedence over socialisation in cases of those born unambiguously into one sex. This, however, is not necessarily the same as cases of intersex children in which there has been atypical development with the possible influence of unusual combinations of male and female hormones.

CASE STUDY: THE BOY WHO WAS RAISED AS A GIRL; THE STORY OF DAVID REIMER

David Reimer was born a normal healthy boy, one of a pair of identical twins. At the age of 8 months he required a routine circumcision. The doctor, instead of using the usual scapel to remove his foreskin, used an electrocautery needle, which burnt off his whole penis. His devastated and confused young parents were referred to the Johns Hopkins Hospital where John Money, a leading expert in gender identity, worked. Money persuaded them that the best thing to do would be to rear the child as a girl and to have corrective surgery as necessary. David became Brenda.

Writing about the case in various published papers during the 1970s, Money reported that it had been a success. This was not, however David's experience. Despite being totally unaware of "her" sex of birth, Brenda was extremely unhappy and never felt like a girl. Even at age 2 she tore off her dress and later refused to play with dolls or to mix with girls. Often throughout her childhood she complained to her parents and teachers that she felt like a boy. By the age of 14 the psychological problems were so serious that a psychiatrist persuaded her parents to tell her the truth. This was an enormous relief. As Colapinto (2001) reports, the child said "Suddenly it all made sense why I felt the way I did. I wasn't some sort of weirdo. I wasn't crazy". David started a long and painful journey back to being a male, eventually marrying and acting as a father to three step-children. He was so incensed by the actions of Money that he courted publicity in order to highlight his plight in the hope of discouraging others from bringing up children in the "wrong" sex.

However, David could never quite get over his dreadful childhood experiences. Sadly, after experiencing marital troubles, and with history of serious clinical depression in the family, he committed suicide at the age of 38.

To read this story in detail, see Colapinto (2000).

Another study showing the influence of biology is that of Imperato-McGinley, Guerro, Gautier, and Peterson (1974), who described a family in the Dominican Republic. Four of the sons appeared—biologically—to be female when they were born, and they were reared as girls. However, at the age of about 12, they developed male genitals and started to look like ordinary adolescent males. Despite the fact that all four of them had been reared as girls, and had thought of themselves as females, they seemed to adjust well to the male role: they took on men's jobs, married, and were accepted as men. Nevertheless, it is still difficult to draw firm conclusions as the male role is more respected in this community than is the female one, so their acceptance of a changed gender identity could have been influenced by social factors as well as biological ones.

Evaluation

There is a considerable body of evidence to indicate that Biosocial Theory, with its emphasis on the interaction of biological and social factors, has a lot to recommend it. However, the more specific assertion of Money and Ehrhardt that in the first two-and-a-half to three years a child's sense of itself is flexible enough to allow its sexual label to be changed without undue disturbance is now somewhat discredited, especially in light of the only known and detailed study in which a developmentally normal child was brought up unsuccessfully as the opposite sex. Other studies in which there is a fairly direct conflict between biological and social factors, as was the case with the four children in the family from the Dominican Republic, also seem to show that biological factors cannot always be outweighed by social factors. However, cases such as that of Mrs DW demonstrate that it is quite possible to be content with the gender identity of upbringing even when it clashes with that of the chromosomal sex.

The general assertion that there is interaction between social and biological factors is of considerable value. However, it needs to be remembered that support for the biosocial approach has been obtained largely from very unusual cases, and it is difficult to know whether the findings obtained can be generalised to the ordinary population.

Evolutionary Explanations of Gender Roles

We now turn to an approach that seeks to explain differences in the behaviour of males and females in terms of evolution. **Sociobiology** applies the principles of evolution to the understanding of social behaviour. The theory argues that the behaviour of all animals has evolved so that it maximises the likelihood that individuals will pass on their genes to future generations. In human terms, this means that both women and men unconsciously behave in ways that promote conception, birth, and survival of their offspring. In pursuit of this end, the optimal mating behaviour differs dramatically between men and women (Trivers, 1972). As a man can, in theory, impregnate many women within a short time and will only waste some easily replaceable sperm if sexual intercourse does not result in pregnancy, it is in his interest to be promiscuous and seek out good child-bearers. A woman, who has to invest a great deal more in bearing each child than does a man, is likely to be far more choosy when selecting a mate. She will be coy, take her time, and choose a man who can provide for her and her infant, perhaps

> **KEY TERM**
>
> **Sociobiology:** a theory that applies the principles of evolution to the understanding of social behaviour. The theory argues that the behaviour of all animals has evolved so that it maximises the likelihood that individuals will pass on their genes to future generations.

an older man who is established in his career. In essence, she has—according to sociobiological principles—evolved strategies to differentiate between fit and unfit males so that she does not waste her costly egg and 9 months pregnancy on a child with inferior genes inherited from a sickly male.

Sociobiology also claims an evolutionary basis for other gender differences. Wright (1994) argues that women never break through the "glass ceiling" (an invisible but very real barrier to success in the workplace) because, biologically, they have less of men's innate ambition and willingness to take the risks necessary for success.

Research evidence

Buss (1989), in an extensive study of 37 cultures (in 33 countries), analysed the results of more than 10,000 questionnaires asking respondents to rate a number of factors such as age, intelligence, and sociability for their importance in a sexual partner. Consistent with sociobiological theory, men valued physical attractiveness more than did women, while women were more likely than men to value good earning potential and high occupational status. In all the cultures, both women and men preferred the man to be the older of the pair. It is worth noting, however, that gender differences in the importance of physical attraction are stronger when people estimate its importance (as in questionnaires) than when they actually interact with someone. This study is taken as offering strong support for sociobiological theory, but it is important to note the caveat in the evaluation section below.

Williams and Best (1982) explored gender stereotypes in 30 different national cultures. In each country, 100 male and female students were asked to look at a list of adjectives and state whether they were associated with men or women, or both, in their culture. Williams and Best found that there were many similarities across the various cultures. Men were seen as more dominant, aggressive, and autonomous, in a more *instrumental role*. Whereas women were more nurturant, deferent, in and interested in affiliation, being encouraged to develop an *expressive role*. This finding was also supported by earlier work by Barry, Bacon, and Child (1957).

Even some of the cross-cultural studies showing greater similarities between the two sexes than in Western culture lend some support to sociobiological theory. Within each cultural group studied by Mead (1935; reported later in the chapter), the males were generally more aggressive than the females. Even in the Tchambuli, in which gender roles showed some reversal from the usual patterns, it was the men and not the women who did most of the fighting in time of war. This supports the idea of inherited gender-role behaviours.

A study by Davis (1990) entitled "Men as success objects and women as sex objects: a study of personal advertisements" also indicates that there are consistent differences in what men and women desire in a sexual partner. Consistent with sociobiological theory, this analysis of "personal" advertisements found that men tended to emphasise their wealth or other resources while looking for women younger than themselves. By contrast, women indicated that they were looking for a high-status, wealthy man, and mentioned their own physical attractiveness. Nevertheless, physical characteristics were the most desired attributes for both men and women.

Singh (1993) found that men are attracted to women with a low waist-to-hip ratio (with the waist smaller than the hip!) and that this is related to child-bearing potential.

Singh (1993) found that men find a small waist-to-hip ratio attractive, as this is perceived as indicating optimum fertility.

Evaluation

Most cross-cultural studies have indicated that the cultural expectations and stereotypes for boys and girls are surprisingly similar in otherwise very different cultures. However, it is important to look in more detail at some of the findings. In the study by Buss (1989) there were some significant findings that have received far less attention. Both men and women placed exactly the same four attributes highest on their preference list: mutual attraction, dependable character, emotional stability and maturity, and pleasing disposition. Their rankings of qualities also placed the same four items on top: kind and understanding, intelligent, exciting, healthy (Smith & Bond, 1993). So, the support for the sociobiological view that there are large and significant differences in the attributes universally sought by males and females is not entirely convincing.

Williams and Best (1982) also do not offer unequivocal support. They found that the consensus of what women and men find desirable was true in collectivistic societies but weaker in individualistic societies where gender equality is more influential. This suggests that socialisation practices, as well as biology, can influence the characteristics men and women find desirable.

There are also important problems with the actual theory. The major limitation of sociobiological explanations in general is that they use hindsight to explain almost any behaviour in terms of why it has evolved. It is possible to argue that almost any observed gender differences are due to evolution. For example, if human females happened to be better at spatial and memory skills than males, it would be a reasonable hypothesis that they needed these skills to forage and to remember the exact location of a good food source in order to support their young. The hypotheses suggested by the sociobiologists often have no empirical evidence to support them; they are merely conjecture.

? What are the distinctive features of a collectivist society?

One important characteristic of a good theory is that it can be used to make predictions about the future, yet sociobiology has little predictive value. There are so many possibilities with regard to how behaviour may evolve that prediction becomes impossible.

Another significant problem is that it is extremely difficult to untangle the effects of culture from those of evolution. Despite Buss' work, there are significant historical and cultural differences in heterosexual mate selection. For example, men's preference for younger women was considerably greater in the past than it is now, and is greater in traditional than in modern societies (Glenn, 1989). The difficulty of separating culture from evolution will always mean that sociobiology is likely to remain controversial.

Another problem with this theory is the argument that certain patterns of behaviour are "hard wired" into us by evolution and cannot easily be influenced by other factors. Yet when we look more closely at both human and non-human animal behaviour concerning sex and infant care, we find a huge variety of behaviours within a single species and changes in environment can have a profound effect on this behaviour. Even species of birds change their mating behaviour quite drastically according to the availability of good nesting sites and food sources, so it would be very surprising if humans were less adaptable. Having plasticity of behaviour rather than rigidly determined invariant patterns can have a great survival value (Fausto-Sterling, 2000).

> **EXAM HINT**
>
> Note that evolution offers evidence of universal gender stereotypical behaviour as evidence that gender roles are the product of evolution not society. Consider this critically:
>
> * social learning can also account for universal behaviour
> * the theory is *post hoc* and is therefore based more on conjecture than empirical evidence. It is saying that behaviour has evolved because it exists, which of course is impossible to falsify. Nor can we verify that gender roles are a product of evolution because we cannot separate the influences of nature and nurture.

SECTION SUMMARY
Biological Influences on Gender

❖ There are several importance biological differences between males and females. Males have an XY chromosome composition whilst females are XX.

The role of hormones in gender development

❖ In terms of hormones, although both sexes have identical hormones, females have a preponderance of oestrogen and progesterone whereas males have a preponderance of androgens (male hormones), the most important one being testosterone.

❖ The influence of the sex hormones is complex and interacts with psychological factors, but they undoubtedly affect behaviour.

The biosocial approach

❖ This approach emphasises the interaction of biology and upbringing: of both nature and nurture.

❖ Biological factors influence whether a child is raised as a girl or a boy. In turn, this upbringing shapes the behaviour.

❖ Money argued that social factors are so strongly influential that children, regardless of biology, will accept their gender of upbringing as long as it not changed after the child's third birthday.

❖ However, the case of a child with normal genitalia at birth, who was reared as a girl even though he was biologically a boy (due to a botched operation in which his penis was destroyed) throws serious doubt on this theory as this individual was extremely unhappy with his sex of rearing.

❖ Sociobiology applies the principles of evolution to the understanding of gender-specific behaviour and argues that the two sexes have evolved different behaviour to maximise their chances of passing on their genes to the next generation.

❖ Males tend to be promiscuous and prefer attractive women (who are assumed to be healthy); conversely, it is in the female's interest to be coy and fussy so that she gets the best father for her children.

❖ However, a detailed look at the cross-cultural research evidence that supports the theory that men value physical attractiveness whereas females seek males with good earning potential, indicates more similarity than difference in what both males and females seek.

❖ There is no empirical evidence to support the general principle that evolution rather than culture is responsible for differences in male and female behaviour. Within any single species, including humans, there are vast differences in behaviour depending on the particular environment and having plasticity of behaviour rather than "hard-wired" invariant patterns can have great survival value.

Evolutionary explanations of gender roles

SOCIAL CONTEXTS OF GENDER ROLE

Social Influences on Gender Role

Throughout this chapter, we have seen that as children move through childhood and into adolescence, they are exposed to many factors that influence their attitudes and behaviour regarding gender roles. These attitudes and behaviour are generally learned first in the home and then reinforced by the child's peers, school experience, and the media, especially television. This section looks at each of these important influences, but first there is a brief overview of the processes whereby people learn gender roles.

In any learning, there are three main processes involved:

1. *Classical conditioning*: certain behaviours and roles become associated first with the mother (or main female caregiver) and eventually with other females, whereas different behaviours become associated with the father (or main male caregiver) and eventually with males in general. So, in a traditional family, mum is associated with cooking, shopping, collecting the children from school, plastering the wounds, and general nurturing behaviour whereas dad becomes associated with mending things, being out at work for most of the day, mowing the lawn, and showing an interest in sport. In other words, children learn to associate fathers and mothers with different patterns of behaviour.

2. *Operant conditioning*: certain behaviours are reinforced whereas others are punished; the types of behaviour that are reinforced or punished are likely to vary between the two sexes. Remember that reinforcers and punishments can be quite subtle, such as a small smile or a gentle pulling back, but when administered on a regular basis, they have a significant effect.

KEY TERMS

Classical conditioning: learning by association. In gender development, an example is learning to associate certain activities, such as playing football, with boys and certain activities, such as organising a tea party, with girls.

Operant conditioning: learning by consequences (by reinforcement and punishment). In gender development, both girls and boys are reinforced for gender appropriate behaviour and discouraged (punished) for gender inappropriate behaviour and in this manner learn to behave in gender-appropriate ways.

3. *Social learning*: children learn by observing the behaviour of models, the most influential models being parents (especially in the early years), same-sex peers, and media heroes and heroines. Children are also more likely to imitate those people who are reinforced for their behaviour.

The influence of parents

A child's social environment, chosen in the early years mainly by their parents, is not gender neutral but is a world full of gender stereotyping. Recall, for example, the study by Rubin et al. (1974), which demonstrated how differently parents view a newborn infant if he is a boy compared with if she is a girl. Gender stereotyping is evident in a child's physical as well as social environment. The decor of children's rooms, their clothes, and toys are chosen on gender lines, pink for girls and blue for boys (Pomerleau, Bolduc, Malcuit, & Cossette, 1990). The choice of toys also differs between the sexes: girls have more dolls and domestic items whereas boys have more tools, sports equipment, and large and small vehicles in their rooms (Pomerleau et al., 1990). Logos are also important: the appearance of an aeroplane or a flower logo clearly indicates whether the toy should be perceived as masculine or feminine (Fisher-Thompson, 1990).

Fagot and Leinbach (1989) carried out a longitudinal study on children that showed that parents encouraged gender-appropriate behaviour and discouraged gender-inappropriate behaviour in their children even before the age of 2. For example, girls were rewarded for playing with dolls and discouraged from climbing trees.

Cross-gender activity is far more discouraged in boys than in girls (people may well smile at a girl pushing a truck around the room and refer to her as a "tomboy" but they are far more uncomfortable with a boy being affectionate to a doll). Girls, therefore, have greater flexibility in cross-gender play than do boys. The responses to cross-gender activity are also different in mothers and fathers. Fagot and Hagan (1991), as well as many other subsequent studies, showed that fathers' responses to boys who engage in typical girls' play are more likely to be negative than mothers' responses. Banerjee and Lintern (2000) believe that male–female distinctions are important to younger boys most of all—they are more concerned with these distinctions than are either older boys or girls at any age.

In an interesting and somewhat surprising study, Caldera and Sciaraffa (1998) investigated the difference between mothers and fathers in the way they played with their own children with a baby doll and a clown. The average age of the children was 20 months. As expected, mothers with daughters initiated more nurturing and caretaking behaviour with the doll than mothers with sons. However, there were surprising results from the fathers. Those with sons initiated more nurturing behaviour than those with daughters, and they initiated such behaviours more with the baby dolls than with the clowns. These findings suggest that fathers can be important socialising agents for their sons, especially when it comes to feminine play. There were also differences between the way fathers and mothers played with the dolls. Typically, fathers did more tickling and engaged in more general "fun" behaviour than the mothers who were more likely to play in terms of dressing, bathing, and so on. This confirms other research (e.g. Lamb, 1997) that indicates that fathers act more as "playmates" whereas mothers are more in the caregiver role.

Moving further up the age groups, Bhanot and Jovanovic (2005) showed that when parents endorse the stereotype that maths is a male domain, their daughters underestimate their ability in this subject. These stereotypes are not deliberately imposed on the children but the parents inadvertently impose them when they give unsolicited (uncalled for) help with homework. Bhanot and Jovanovic (2005) found that girls have less self-confidence in their maths ability when their parents give intrusive support, yet this was not true for help with English homework nor if they gave maths help to their sons.

The influence of peers and school

Although parents are influential in a child's life there are, of course, other people who affect their behaviour. Perry and Bussey (1979) showed children aged 8 or 9 a film clip in which male and female adults made a choice such as selecting an apple or a pear. These choices were designed to be gender neutral yet, when given the opportunity to make their own choices, the children tended to decide in the same way as the same-sex models.

Older same-sex siblings also affect children's behaviour. Rust et al. (2000) found that young children of either sex who have older brothers become more masculine and those who have older sisters become more feminine.

Within the school setting, children inevitably become exposed to gender stereotypes and there is huge pressure on them to conform to these if they are not to become isolated and unpopular. By age 6 or 7, gender identity is established and children begin to mix in same-sex groups. This process of sex segregation is important because girls' and boys' groups socialise different behaviours and different rules (Maccoby, 1998).

Young boys in school tend to pay more attention to each other than to the teacher but that this is not true of girls. Boys are greater risk-takers than girls, more likely to break the rules, and there is support within the group for this. It is as if the boys are "showing off" to other boys by flouting rules or instructions from teachers; the rest of the group is the audience. Girls play in smaller groups than boys and this, coupled with girls' greater compliance, makes girls' groups easier for teachers to control.

Bhanot and Jovanovic (2005) found that a parent's unsolicited help with maths homework resulted in girls losing confidence in their own perceived ability.

Friendship groups also differ between the sexes. Girls appear to take greater pleasure than do boys in personal interaction. Benenson, Apostoleris, and Parnass (1997) found that at age 6, both girls and boys engage in dyadic interaction frequently (socialise in pairs), but they differ in that boys are greatly involved in co-ordinated group activity with larger groups of peers, something that is much less true of girls. Boys' friendships tend to be less intimate than those of girls, in the sense that there is less mutual self-disclosure, less physical closeness, and less eye contact. Boys' friendships appear to be based primarily on interest and participation in the same activities rather than close personal interaction. This pattern continues into adult life (as reported by Dwyer, 2000).

Benenson et al. (1997) found that 6-year-old boys socialised in larger groups of peers than girls.

Although segregation of the sexes is the rule, cross-sex interest and attraction are nevertheless there, if somewhat hidden. Such attraction often manifests itself in the form of sexualised taunting and gossip. The rule appears to be covert interest, overt avoidance.

Ruddy (2007) reported on research by Sroufe as follows:

In one study, 10-year-olds who were videotaped while at summer camp were caught co-mingling just 4 percent of the time they were observed. And those who did so were promptly taken to task by their peers. One boy made the grave mistake of loaning a radio to a girl and then, in a move that far worsened his situation, venturing into the all-girls tent to retrieve it. As he emerged from enemy territory, the boys broke into a chorus of "Oooh, you like her!" and, "Why are you with the girls?" He had to immediately hit each boy who had teased him," Sroufe says, "Kids have elaborate rituals for setting and policing gender boundaries."

Cross-sex interaction in children, especially if overt, can attract sexualised taunting and gossip among peers.

Sroufe believes that, ironically, sex segregation seems to prepare children for good cross-sex relations in later life. Those who are good at one-to-one same-sex friendships develop the communication skills necessary to eventually mix successfully with members of the opposite sex.

As children move into adolescence, the peer group in school becomes even more influential as the role of parents diminishes (although it is always important). Mac an Ghail (1994) argues that peer groups are stronger for boys than for girls when it comes to attitudes towards the value of education and whether it is worthwhile to stay on at school. He suggests that is because there is a "macho-male" culture that conveys the attitude that academic life is more suitable for girls than for boys. Similarly, Archer and Yamashita (2003) argue that that there is a male culture in some schools that is in opposition to education. Girls have rather different attitudes and their career ambition has increased considerably over the last 20 years (Francis, 2000). Gender differences also exist in the factors that influence the decision as to whether or not to stay on at school. Webber and Walton (2006) found that girls express the intention to stay on if the majority of the whole peer group (boys and girls) have those intentions but boys are influenced only by their male peers not by the whole peer group, and might even need to look for approval from other boys before they decide to continue into post-compulsory education. Moreover, this approval needs to be linked to masculinity. As Webber suggests, policies aimed at increasing students' desire to stay on at school after the age of 16 should recognise such gender specific differences if they are to have any chance of success.

The influence of media
Books
Children's books are another important influence on children's attitudes. People often imagine that "times have changed" and that modern books are less likely than those from more than 20 years ago to reflect gender stereotypes. However, this is not upheld by research. Hamilton, Anderson, Broaddus, and Young (2006) carried out extensive research into gender stereotyping in 200 top-selling and award-winning books. There were nearly twice as many male as female main

characters, with male characters appearing in illustrations more often than female ones. There were also differences in the behaviours of the two sexes conforming to traditional gender stereotypes: female main characters nurtured more than did male characters, were more often than men in no paid occupation, and were seen in more indoor than outdoor scenes. Compared with books sampled in the 1980s and 1990s, there was no reduction in sexism.

Magazines

Most magazines are aimed at one sex or the other and have a strong influence on what is seen as the "ideal" lifestyle and body. A great deal of research has looked at the influence of magazines on teenage girls. Field, Cheung, Wolf, Herzog, Gortmaker, and Colditz (1999) interviewed over 500 teenaged girls (aged 11–17) in the USA and found that pictures in magazines had a strong impact on girls' perceptions of their weight and shape: 69% reported that magazine pictures influenced their idea of the perfect body shape, and 47% reported wanting to lose weight because of magazine pictures. The majority of the pre-adolescent and adolescent girls were unhappy with their body weight and shape and this was strongly positively correlated with how often they read such magazines. The more frequently these fashion magazines were read, the more likely the girl was to have dieted and exercised to lose weight or improve body shape.

It is not only girls whose self-esteem can be damaged by media images of the "perfect" body. A study by Giles and Close (2008) indicates that men can also be made to feel physically inadequate by images of the "ideal" male form. The researchers were interested in the influence of "lad mags" (such as *Zoo* and *FHM*), which tend to make fun of men who do not have a well-toned body and place great emphasis on the importance of being successful with girls. They asked 161 young men (average age 22) how often they read such magazines and to complete a questionnaire about sociocultural attitudes towards appearance; for example, they rated their agreement with statements like "In our culture, someone with a well-built body has a better chance of obtaining success". They then completed a questionnaire about their desire and attempts to be more muscular; for example, by rating their agreement with statements like "I think that my weight-training schedule interferes with other aspects of my life". The researchers found that the more these men read lad mags, the more likely they were to accept and internalise cultural ideals regarding the male body and to strive to attain it. (The association between reading these magazines and striving to be more muscular was stronger among single men than among men who were in a relationship.) We must be cautious, however, in concluding that these magazines *cause* these attitudes. Remember that correlational studies, as this one was, do not necessarily show cause and effect; it is quite possible, as the researchers acknowledge, that men who are concerned about physical appearance tend to read these magazines more than those who are relatively unconcerned.

It is important, to note, as does Gauntlett (2008), that the mass media is widely diverse and carries very

The air-brushed body "perfection" presented in many men's and women's magazines influences the reader to desire an "ideal" body-shape that is often very difficult (if not impossible) to achieve.

many messages, often quite contradictory. He points out that, in contrast to the past, we no longer receive singular, straightforward messages about ideal types of male and female identities and that media images do indeed change over the course of 10 or 20 years.

Television

According to a report published in 2007 (Ofcom, 2007), children in Britain watch about three and half hours of television a day; in a full year this is more time than they spend at school. It would be surprising if this exposure had no impact on children's views of themselves and on gender stereotypes via observational learning. The presence or absence of role models, how women and men, girls and boys are presented and what activities they engage in have a powerful effect on how children see their role in the world. Research demonstrates that over the last few years children, girls especially, have a wider range of role models but for girls how these models look is more important than what they do.

Thompson and Zerbinos (1997) found that when young children (aged 4–9) were asked to describe cartoon characters they perceived them in very stereotypical ways: males were aggressive and active, females were domestic and concerned with appearance.

Signorielli (1997) studied the types of media most attractive to teenage girls (music magazines and videos and certain television programmes) and found that although there are positive role models of women and girls being intelligent and acting independently, the vast majority were more concerned with dating, romance, and their appearance whereas most males focus on their occupations.

Williams (1986) examined gender-role stereotypes in three towns in Canada nicknamed: "Notel" (no television channels); "Unitel" (one channel); and "Multitel" (four channels). Gender-role stereotyping was much greater in the towns with television than in the one without. During the course of the study, Notel gained access to one television channel and this led to increased gender-role stereotyping among children.

There is evidence that television can influence gender development in a non-stereotypical way (Johnston & Ettema, 1982). In the Freestyle project, there was a series of television programmes in which non-traditional opportunities and activities were modelled. These programmes produced significant attitude changes away from gender-role stereotypes, and these changes were still present 9 months later. Interestingly, the effects on actual behaviour were rather small.

Earlier, we considered the influence of magazines on body image. Television also has an impact. Tiggerman and Pickering (1996) found the amount of time an adolescent watches "soaps", films, and music videos is associated with the degree of body dissatisfaction and desire to be thin. Hargreaves (2002) found that teenage girls who watched a lot of television advertisements that featured thin-ideal women were less confident, more angry, and more

Television programmes that showed men and women taking part in non-traditional sex-typed activities have been found to produce some attitude changes among viewers, but the effects on behaviour were small.

dissatisfied with their weight and appearance than those with less exposure to such advertising. Hofschire and Greenberg (2002) showed that this does not apply only to girls. They found a positive relationship between body dissatisfaction and identification with models in girls and identification with athletes in boys.

There is little doubt that television presents largely traditional gender images, but there is mixed evidence about the impact of such images on gender attitudes and behaviour. Children are not passive recipients of television images: their existing attitudes, shaped from a host of other influences, play an important part in interpreting images of gender on television. As Durkin (2007) points out, it is too simplistic to state that because the entertainment media is full of traditional stereotypes then this media is automatically contributing to gender-role development. Durkin and Nugent (1998) have demonstrated that even by age 4 children can draw on their knowledge of how men and women are supposed to behave to comment on what they see on television.

Continuing the argument that people are not passive recipients of media messages, Durkin (2007) comments that attempts to use the media to promote gender counterstereotyped career messages have not always been successful. Adolescents tend to reject the idea that women can be plumbers or men can be secretaries. As Durkin says "The media do not shape or reshape people at will . . . the acquisition of knowledge, beliefs, values and behaviour is a complex, multifaceted and protracted affair".

The influence of gender stereotypes

Stereotypes are often portrayed as undesirable and dangerous but they are, in fact, a very necessary part of our thinking processes—we need to be able to summarise and categorise the huge amounts of information we receive and stereotypes are simply one of the schemas we use in this information processing. However, they can have a detrimental effect when they are inaccurate and pejorative and, as many gender stereotypes are exactly this, it is important to consider their influence. We might be surprised by the ways in which they can affect our behaviour and on the way we interpret behaviour.

Condry and Condry (1976) showed male and female college students a videotape of a baby reacting to different stimuli. The same tape was shown to everyone but half the observers thought the baby was a boy, while half thought it was a girl. The child was seen reacting to a jack-in-the-box, which popped out several times. The first time the child was startled, the second time it became agitated, and the third time it began to cry. Those participants who thought the baby was a girl tended to describe "her" as fearful, whereas when the infant was regarded as a boy the tears were seen as a sign of anger. Thus the simple knowledge of whether a child is a girl or boy leads to different interpretations of behaviour. (As an aside, this type of research also leads us to the important

---

■ Activity: Content analysis

A content analysis is a useful way of investigating whether sex-role stereotypes are used in children's television programmes. Choose several children's programmes from a variety of television channels. Carefully choose a coding system to use for the investigation. For example, you could look at the roles of every adult character in the programme—does it conform to a sex-role stereotype or not? Within this category, you could also look at whether the male roles are more or less likely to be sex-role stereotyped than the females. Create a table like this:

	Sex-role stereotyped	Non sex-role stereotyped	Total
Male character			
Female character			
Total			

Repeat this for your other categories.

You could also carry out the same study on children's television programmes from the past to see if there is a difference between these and the more recent programmes.

EXAM HINT

Make sure you can explain the influence of parents, peers, schools, magazines, books, and television on the development of gender. Note how pressures differ for males and females across these influences. For example, parents disapprove of cross-sex behaviour in boys more strongly than they do in girls. On the other hand, girls have more pressure from the media to conform to unrealistic standards of physical perfection.

question of whether studies of very young children showing that levels of aggression are higher in boys than in girls are more a product of the observer's interpretation than of actual aggressive behaviour.)

Gender stereotypes can also affect our memory of achievement. Chatard, Guimond, and Selimbegovic (2007) demonstrated that the gender stereotype that women are poorer at maths than men can affect students' memory of their prior maths performance. These researchers carried out a two-part study. In the first part, they found that girls who strongly believed the stereotype that boys are better at maths than girls tended to underestimate their previous performance in maths. Similarly, boys who strongly believed in the stereotype that girls are better at arts underestimated their previous scores in art exams. The researchers then put high-school students into one of two groups. The members of one group were first made aware of gender stereotypes by being asked to rate their agreement with statements like "Men are gifted in mathematics" and "Women are gifted in the arts", before rating their own abilities. Others were given what was considered a weaker reminder of gender stereotypes—they rated their own performance first, before evaluating men and women in general. The reminder of the stereotype had a strong influence on the students' memories. Both girls and boys were affected by being given the strong reminder of gender stereotypes—the girls underestimated their past performance whereas the boys overestimated theirs. No such effect was found in those who were given the stereotype after rating their past performance. With respect to the arts, all students overestimated their performance, but among those given a salient reminder of stereotypes, the girls overestimated their arts performance more and the boys far less. The researchers said these findings could have real-world implications, "It is possible that women are less likely to embrace scientific careers than men because gender stereotypes lead them to underestimate their past achievement."

Activity: Gender stereotypes
Make a list of stereotypes that are often used to describe males and females. Now categorise these in terms of gender or biology. Can any be supported by evidence, and what evidence could be considered valid?

Cross-cultural Studies of Gender Role

One of the greatest values of cross-cultural research is that it indicates whether or not patterns of behaviour are universal. If they are consistent across cultures it implies that biology is an important influence. If, on the other hand, it varies significantly, then it indicates it is culturally determined and learned. We will now take a look at research into gender roles in a variety of cultures.

In a classic study, the anthropologist Margaret Mead (1935) looked at three cultural groups in New Guinea, each of which showed very different gender roles. In the Mundugumor, both men and women were brought up to be aggressive and emotionally unresponsive, behaving in a way that is regarded as masculine in Western society. In the Arapesh, both sexes were caring, non-aggressive, and sensitive to the needs of others in a way that is associated with the feminine role. The Tchambuli showed what Western society would consider gender role reversal: males were passive, emotionally dependent, and socially sensitive whereas females were dominant, independent, and assertive. In other words, members of each of these cultures developed in accordance with the sex roles prescribed by their culture demonstrating that social forces contributed heavily to sex typing. However, there have been criticisms of Mead's work and it is not clear to what extent her observations were a true reflection of the everyday behaviour of these groups.

Many studies have demonstrated less variation between cultures with a more consistent difference in the ways males and females are socialised. Barry, Bacon, and Child (1957) studied 110 non-industrialised societies and found that in 75% of these societies there was more pressure on girls than on boys to be nurturant, with none showing the opposite pattern. Responsibility was regarded as more important in girls than in boys in 55% of the societies, with 10% showing the opposite. Obedience was stressed for girls more than for boys in 32% of societies, with 3% showing the opposite. There was more pressure on boys than on girls to achieve and to be self-reliant. Achievement was emphasised more for boys in 79% of societies (3% showed the opposite), and self-reliance was regarded as more important in boys in 77% of societies, with no societies regarding it as more important in girls.

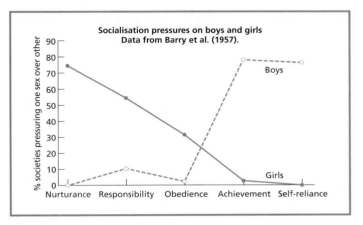

Earlier, we reported the study of Williams and Best (1982), who explored gender stereotypes in 30 different national cultures (three in Africa, ten in Europe, seven in Asia, two in North America, and six in South America). They found that in most cultures men were more dominant, aggressive, and autonomous whereas women were more nurturant, deferent, and interested in affiliation. These findings indicate that the gender-role stereotypes of females being expressive and males being instrumental (doing things) are very widespread. Related findings were obtained by Williams and Best (1990) who found that similar gender stereotypes to those found in the United States were present in 24 other countries in Asia, Europe, Oceania, Africa, and the Americas. However, the sampling process in these studies can be criticised as all the participants were University students who have much in common with each other, regardless of culture, and who are not necessarily typical of the remainder of the population. One important influence on them may be their exposure to international media images of males and females making it possible that consensus was due to this rather than other factors. It would be necessary to repeat the research on a more representative cross-section of the different cultures in order to see if this is true.

Wood and Eagly (2002) looked at cross-cultural findings relating to gender roles obtained from a large number (181) of non-industrialised cultures. Men were dominant in 67% of those cultures, especially those in which there was a lot of warfare and men's economic contribution was much greater than that of women. However, neither sex was dominant in 30% of cultures and women were dominant in 3%. There were large cultural differences in responsibility for obtaining food but this varied by gender according to other conditions. Men had the primary role in obtaining food in cultures dependent on hunting or fishing, but women had the main role when food gathering was involved. This study therefore showed important differences in the roles of men and women across these cultures and

Mbuti tribes do not distinguish sex-typed roles or responsibilities within their social structure.

EXAM HINT

Consider how you can use the many cross-cultural variations to shed some light on the nature–nurture debate in terms of gender development.

indicates that environmental conditions and practical considerations might be more influential in determining gender roles than is biology.

Societies differ considerably in the extent to which male and female roles are differentiated. We will look at an example of each extreme. The Mbuti pygmies have a social structure in which the role of biological sex has virtually no effect on social role or status. They do not even have words for "girl" or "boy", "woman" or "man"; the only language distinction between the sexes is the terms "mother" and "father". Both sexes take part in hunting and gathering; fathers are as likely as mothers to care for young children and pregnancy is no bar to hunting. Men and women share decision making equally and have the same social status.

At the other extreme are the Mundurucu Indians of central Brazil, in whom the physical and social segregation of the sexes is virtually complete. Men and boys live in men's houses separate from all females (only very young boys are part of the female homes) and the two sexes hardly interact at all. They take on different roles, have different personalities (with males being dominant), and are antagonistic towards the opposite sex.

Cultural change also applies to historical differences. There have been great changes in most Western societies in recent years. In the mid-twentieth century, many fewer women than men went to university or were in positions of power in the workforce. Nowadays, the number of female university students exceeds that of male students in several countries including Britain; there is a similar pattern in employment.

Cross-cultural research demonstrates what other research on gender indicates—that gender roles are a complex interaction between biological factors and the environment in which we are reared.

SECTION SUMMARY
Social Contexts of Gender Role

Social influences on gender role

❖ Gender roles are greatly shaped by social influences.

❖ Learning theory suggests that children learn these gender roles through classical conditioning, operant conditioning, and social learning. Important influences are parents and other role models such as teachers and peers.

❖ The media also exerts a considerable influence, especially during adolescence. Traditional gender-role stereotyping is still evident in children's books, in magazines, and on television, although there have been a few successful attempts at presenting non-stereotypical gender roles.

❖ Durkin (2007) argues that the media does not shape or reshape people at will; that other influences will always have a considerable effect. Gender stereotypes, that is, beliefs about men and women based on gender roles, also influence behaviour and can even affect our memory.

❖ Cross-cultural research into gender roles can indicate whether patterns of behaviour are universal (and therefore probably biological) or are determined by culture.

❖ Mead's classic research showed that gender roles varied enormously in three New Guinea cultural groups, indicating that culture had shaped their behaviour.

❖ Other studies have demonstrated less variation between cultures. For example, many cultures stress responsibility and obedience more for girls than for boys, whereas achievement and self-reliance are considered more important in boys than in girls.

❖ Other research indicates that in most cultures studied men were more dominant, aggressive, and autonomous whereas women were more nurturant, deferent, and affiliable.

❖ Societies differ greatly in the extent to which their social structure is influenced by biological sex with some barely distinguishing between the sexes and others having almost complete segregation between them.

Cross-cultural studies of gender role

FURTHER READING

Although now very dated, *Sex, gender & society* by Ann Oakley (1985) is still an excellent book on issues concerning gender, with a large and detailed section on cross-cultural research and fascinating case studies of individuals with problems of gender identity. This is complemented well by *Gender, nature and nurture* by Richard A. Lippa, published in 2005. This has thorough coverage of the main theories of gender identity followed by the "case for nature" and the "case for nurture", explaining the research in some detail. It concludes with an interesting "cross-examination", which looks to the future.

REVISION QUESTIONS

In the exam, questions on this topic are out of 25 marks, and can take the form of essay questions or two-part questions. You should allow about 30 minutes for each of the questions below, which aim to test the material in this chapter. Never try to answer a question unless you have been taught the topic.

1. (a) Outline and discuss cognitive development theory.   (16 marks)
    (b) In what ways does gender schema theory differ from
        cognitive development theory?   (9 marks)
2. Discuss biological explanations of gender roles, including
    the role of hormones and genes, and **either** evolutionary
    or biosocial explanations.   (25 marks)
3. Discuss the influence of social contexts on gender
    development, including social influences and culture.   (25 marks)
4. Discuss, with reference to relevant research explanations,
    psychological androgeny and gender dysphoria.   (25 marks)

See *A2-Level Psychology Online* for tips on how to answer these revision questions.

Intelligence and Learning

By Michael W. Eysenck

This chapter is concerned with intelligence, but what do we mean by "intelligence"? According to Sternberg (2004, p. 472), it involves "the capacity to learn from experience and adaptation to one's environment." The definition means we need to take account of cultural differences—what is needed to adapt successfully in one environment may be *very* different from what is required in a different environment.

Many psychologists distinguish between individualistic cultures (e.g. the United States, the United Kingdom) and collectivistic cultures (e.g. many Asian and African cultures). There is an emphasis on individuals accepting responsibility for their own behaviour in individualistic cultures but more of a focus on the group within collectivistic cultures. As we might expect, social considerations loom larger in definitions of "intelligence" in collectivistic cultures than in individualistic ones (Sternberg & Kaufman, 1998). For example, the word for intelligence in Zimbabwe is *ngware*, meaning to be careful and prudent in social relationships. In similar fashion, the Taiwanese Chinese people emphasise interpersonal intelligence (the ability to understand how to get on well with other people).

In recent years, many Western psychologists have developed the concept of intelligence to include social and interpersonal aspects. Of particular importance is the notion of **emotional intelligence**, which is "the ability to monitor one's own and others' emotions, to discriminate among them, and to use the information to guide one's thinking and actions" (Salovey & Mayer, 1990, p. 189).

THEORIES OF INTELLIGENCE

There have been many attempts to develop systematic theories of intelligence. In this section, we consider four of the main theoretical approaches. Much of the early research on intelligence was concerned with practical issues relating to the development of intelligence tests for practical purposes (e.g. personnel selection). The development of intelligence tests (and the attempt to identify the structure of human intelligence) were of central importance within the psychometric approach.

After discussing the psychometric approach, we consider the information-processing approach. It is based on the notion that many of the processes studied by cognitive psychologists (e.g. working memory) are of direct relevance to intelligence.

> **KEY TERM**
>
> **Emotional intelligence:** the ability to understand one's own emotions as well as those of others.

Next, we consider the learning approach, the central assumption of which is that intelligence is a skill. As such, it is possible to develop your intelligence as you can develop your skill at psychology or some sport.

Finally, we consider the highly influential theoretical approach of Howard Gardner. He argued that the traditional emphasis on general intelligence or IQ is oversimplified. Instead, he argued that we should identify seven intelligences, each of importance in allowing us to lead successful lives.

Psychometric Approach

The psychometric approach attaches great importance to the development of tests providing an accurate assessment of intelligence. Accordingly, we will initially focus on intelligence tests produced by this approach. The first proper intelligence test was produced in 1905 by two French psychologists, Alfred Binet and Théodore Simon. It measured comprehension, memory, and various other psychological processes. Among the well-known tests that followed are the Stanford–Binet test produced at Stanford University in the United States, the Wechsler Intelligence Scale for Children, and the British Ability Scales. These tests are designed to measure several aspects of intelligence. They often contain mathematical items, and many contain vocabulary tests in which individuals define the meanings of various words. Many tests also contain problems based on analogies (e.g. "Hat is to head as shoe is to ——"), and items relating to spatial ability (e.g. "If I start walking northwards, then turn left, and then turn left again, what direction will I be facing?").

Suppose you complete an intelligence test containing 150 items and obtain a score of 79. How well have you done? To answer that question, you must *compare* your performance against that of other people. That can only be done effectively by using a standardised test, i.e. one that has been given to a large representative sample of the population. When your score has been compared to those of others, it is possible to calculate your **intelligence quotient (IQ)**, an overall measure of intellectual ability.

How is IQ calculated? Intelligence tests are devised so that the IQs from the general population are normally distributed. The normal distribution is a bell-shaped curve in which there are as many scores above the mean as below it (see figure above). Most of the scores are close to the mean, and there are fewer and fewer scores as we move away from the mean in either direction.

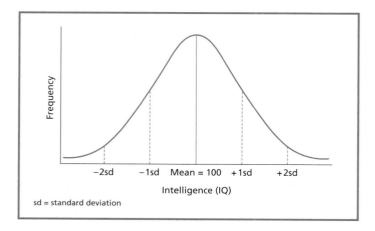

sd = standard deviation

The distribution of scores in a normal population is indicated by the **standard deviation**. In a normal distribution, 68% of the scores fall within one standard deviation of the mean, 95% fall within two standard deviations, and 99.73% are within three standard deviations. Intelligence tests are designed to produce a mean IQ of 100 and a standard deviation of about 16.

HOW SCIENCE WORKS: THE BELL CURVE
IQ scores for a population can be plotted as a bell curve, a normal distribution. This is a picture of the variation that is natural and normal in a population, whether we are talking about a type of intelligence or the length of human noses. You could see if you can collect data about a simple characteristic to see if this supports the idea of variation, and if you collaborate with others so the sample size is large, your graph might show a bell-type curve.

One issue here is time, your time. A characteristic that is really easy and quick to measure is desirable, and so a simple physical measurement of shoe size could be ideal. This means that all you need to do is ask people for their shoe size, either in traditional sizing e.g. (size 5 or 8) or in European sizing (e.g. size 38 or 41). Your finding would be put into a series of columns, one column per size, which you would total at the end.

You could even, as a practice task, work out the mean, median, and mode of your shoe size sample! Then ask yourself which of these measurements of central tendency is appropriate for your data.

When you decide you have collected enough data you need to ask yourself whether your data collection is biased—how did you choose your sample?

How could a researcher ensure that the data collection is truly representative of the target population?

Structure of intelligence: factor analysis

Psychologists using the psychometric approach (e.g. Spearman, Thurstone, Carroll) have often developed theories of intelligence by using factor analysis. This is a statistical technique used to decide on the number and nature of the factors underlying intelligence as assessed by a test. The first step in factor analysis is to give numerous items to a large number of individuals, and to obtain scores from each individual on each item. The correlations between these items are then calculated.

EXAM HINT

Make sure you can show your understanding of how science works by explaining the statistical technique factor analysis.

If two items correlate highly with each other, those who perform well on one item tend to perform well on the other one. The key assumption is that two items correlating highly with each other assess the same factor of intelligence. It is also assumed that two items correlating weakly or not at all with each other are *not* assessing the same factor of intelligence. Thus, the pattern of correlations is used to identify the main aspects of intelligence (or factors as they are known).

	Item 1	Item 2	Item 3	Item 4
Item 1	–	+.85	+.12	+.10
Item 2	+.85	–	+.08	+.11
Item 3	+.12	+.08	–	+.87
Item 4	+.10	+.11	+.87	–

We can see what happens in a simplified fashion by considering the table above. How many factors should we extract from this correlation matrix? The answer is *two*. Items 1 and 2 correlate highly with each other, and so are measures of the same factor. Items 3 and 4 correlate highly with each other (but not with items 1 or 2), and so they form a different, second factor.

Spearman vs. Thurstone

Charles Spearman was a British psychologist who put forward the first psychometric theory of intelligence. In his two-factor theory (Spearman, 1923), there is a general factor of intelligence, which he called "**g**". He argued that there

KEY TERMS

Standard deviation: a measure of the spread of scores in a bell-shaped or normal distribution. It is the square root of the variance, takes account of every score, and is a sensitive measure of dispersion or variation.
"g": the general factor of intelligence.

is a general factor because practically all the items within an intelligence test correlate positively with each other. However, most of these positive correlations are fairly low, so we can't account for all the data in terms of a general factor. Accordingly, Spearman argued there are specific factors associated with each test.

Thurstone (1938) was not convinced that it was necessary to assume that there is a general factor of intelligence. He pointed out that the general factor extracted from one intelligence-test battery might differ from that extracted from another test battery. This issue was addressed by Thorndike (1987), who assessed the correlations or loadings of tests on the general factors extracted from six different independent test batteries. The correlations between the "g" loadings in two different test batteries varied between +.52 and +.94. Thus, the general factor obtained from different intelligence-test batteries are similar but by no means identical.

Thurstone (1938) used a somewhat different approach to factor analysis from the one used by Spearman. This led him to identify seven factors of intelligence, which he termed primary mental abilities: inductive reasoning (forming generalisations from examples), verbal meaning, numerical ability, spatial ability, perceptual speed, memory, and verbal fluency. According to Thurstone, the structure of human intelligence is accurately described by these primary mental abilities, and so Spearman's general factor of intelligence wasn't required.

There was one serious problem with Thurstone's approach. All seven primary mental abilities correlate positively with each other and so can't be regarded as completely independent factors. As a result of these positive inter-correlations, factor analysis of Thurstone's seven factors produces the general factor that he claimed wasn't important (Sternberg, 1985).

Hierarchical approach

Several theorists (e.g. Carroll, 1986; Vernon, 1971) have argued that a combination of the views of Spearman and Thurstone can provide a satisfactory account of the structure of human intelligence. More specifically, they favoured a three-level hierarchical approach. At the highest level of the hierarchy is the general factor of intelligence originally identified by Spearman. At the intermediate level of the hierarchy are six or seven group factors each more specific than the general factor. Thurstone's seven primary abilities are group factors. Carroll also identified seven group factors, but disagreed somewhat with Thurstone (1938) as to their nature. According to Carroll, the seven group factors are as follows: general memory capacity; general auditory perception; general fluency; fluid ability (used to cope with novel problems); crystallised intelligence (based on acquired knowledge); general visual perception; and general speed. At the lowest level of the hierarchy, there are numerous specific factors (e.g. spelling ability) as suggested by Spearman (1923).

Carroll (1993) discussed evidence relevant to his hierarchical theory based on factor analyses of over 460 data sets obtained over a 60-year period from over 130,000 individuals. There appeared to be three levels. There was strong support for a general factor of intelligence or "g". In addition, the abilities at the intermediate level corresponded closely to those put forward by Carroll (1986).

Findings

So far, we have seen that the psychometric approach has led to the development of many intelligence tests and the identification of the structure of intelligence.

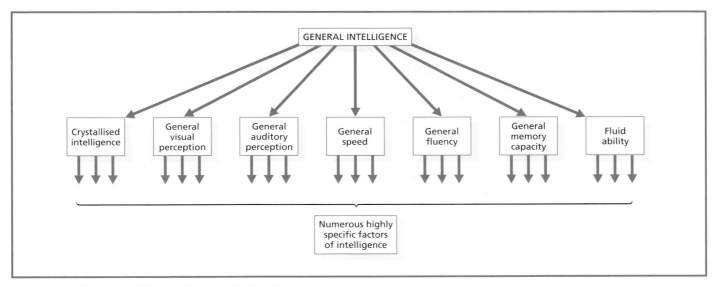

Carroll's (1986) three-level hierarchical model of intelligence.

However, what is really important is to show that the tests produced by the psychometric approach predict behaviour in the real world. The issue here is basically one of validity (the extent to which any given test measures what it is supposed to be measuring). How valid are intelligence tests? If they are valid, it is reasonable to predict that students with high IQs should have a higher level of academic performance than those with low IQs. Intelligence generally correlates about +.5 or +.6 with academic performance (Mackintosh, 1998), indicating there is a moderately strong relationship between these two variables. The correlation is reasonably impressive given that academic performance clearly depends on motivation as well as on intelligence.

Another way to assess the validity of intelligence tests is to consider the relationship between IQ and occupational performance for those working in intellectually demanding jobs. Hunter (1986) found that IQ as assessed by intelligence tests correlated +.58 with work performance among individuals with high-complexity jobs (e.g. biologist; city circulation manager). The finding that IQ predicted job performance moderately well strongly suggests that intelligence tests are at least reasonably valid.

You might think that IQ is a rather limited measure—that it doesn't take into account an individual's specific abilities. In fact, however, the evidence suggests that IQ is generally a much better predictor of job performance than are measures of specific abilities. For example, Hunter (1983) studied four very large samples of military personnel undergoing job-training programmes. In all four samples, intelligence (IQ) strongly predicted training performance and also strongly predicted specific aptitude or ability scores. Specific abilities predicted training performance to some extent. However, this only happened because measures of specific abilities correlated with IQ.

There is a final issue. Nearly all the research we have discussed has involved a very small number of cultures (predominantly the US and the UK). A section towards the end of this chapter emphasises that what it means to be intelligent varies across cultures, something that is often ignored by those working within the psychometric approach. For example, it has often been argued that most

EXAM HINT

Make sure you can assess the external validity of IQ tests positively using predictive validity and negatively using culture bias.

? Can you think of reasons why there are variances in IQ between races?

intelligence tests are biased in favour of white individuals. Williams (1972) compared white and black children who were given the Black Intelligence Test of Cultural Homogeneity (BITCH), which was designed for black Americans. White American children did no better than black American children on this test, and sometimes performed worse.

Evaluation

The psychometric approach has various successes to its credit. First, the factorial approach has produced reasonable agreement that intelligence has a hierarchical structure. Second, there is also reasonable agreement concerning the factors of intelligence at the top two levels of the hierarchy. Third, the strong evidence for a general factor of intelligence helps to justify the widespread use of IQ as a general measure of intelligence. Fourth, the intelligence tests that have emerged from the psychometric approach have been shown to have real practical value.

What are the limitations with the psychometric approach to intelligence? First, and most important, the entire approach is *descriptive* rather than *explanatory*. For example, it doesn't tell us *how* or *why* the structure of human intelligence is as it is. In addition, it sheds no light on the respective roles of genetic and environmental factors in determining individual differences in intelligence.

Second, the psychometric approach tells us very little about the cognitive processes and mechanisms underlying intelligent behaviour. This limitation has been addressed by researchers adopting the information-processing approach (see next section).

Third, factor analysis is limited in that it is like a sausage machine—what you get out of it depends on what was put into it in the first place. If, for example, no tests of creativity are included in an intelligence test, then no factor of creativity will emerge from a factor analysis of the data obtained from administering the test.

Streetwise skills such as the commercial, bargaining, and economic abilities that children such as this young street vendor possess are not measured by culturally specific psychometric tests.

Fourth, those working within the psychometric approach have often produced rather *narrow* intelligence factors. More specifically, social or emotional intelligence seems important, and yet is typically excluded from the hierarchical model—have a look back at Carroll's (1986, 1993) seven factors. Later on, we will discuss Gardner's theory of multiple intelligences, in which he identifies two intelligence factors related to social or emotional intelligence.

Fifth, the psychometric approach has almost ignored substantial cultural differences in the meaning of intelligence. There is a real danger that most intelligence tests are only directly applicable to the culture in which they were devised, and may tell us relatively little about intelligence in other cultures.

Information-processing Approach

The psychometric approach has provided a reasonable description of the structure of human intelligence. However, it has the limitation that it doesn't focus on the *processes* and mechanisms underlying intelligence. This limitation has been addressed by psychologists advocating an information-processing approach to intelligence.

How would we expect information processing in highly intelligent individuals to differ from that in less intelligent ones? The obvious prediction is that they process information faster (and more accurately) than less intelligent ones. However, there are other possibilities. For example, people have a very limited ability to retain information in short-term memory, and one reason why some people are more intelligent than others may be because their short-term memory capacity is greater. We consider these various possibilities below.

Processing speed

The assumption that individual differences in intelligence depend on the *speed* of information processing is central to most theorists who support the information-processing approach. That is a reasonable assumption. What is more controversial is the assumption favoured by many information-processing theorists that the speed of performing apparently very simple tasks can depend to a large extent on IQ. This assumption is based on the notion that performing simple processing operations faster than most other people is an important ingredient in high intelligence.

We will consider some of the findings that have been obtained by information-processing theorists. After that, we will consider possible interpretations of those findings.

Evidence

One of the easiest information-processing tasks is simple reaction time. A light or a tone is presented, after which the participant makes a simple response (e.g. pressing a button) as rapidly as possible. If individuals of high intelligence process information faster than those of less intelligence, we might expect the former to have faster reaction times than the latter. In fact, the findings from numerous early studies were disappointing (reviewed by Deary, Der, & Ford, 2001). To cut a long story short, there was typically a very small relationship between intelligence and reaction time.

There were two reasons why earlier research on intelligence and reaction time found little of interest. First, most of the participants were young, intelligent students. This is a real problem, because we can only assess the true relationship between IQ and reaction time by using a sample that covering the *full* IQ range. We can see what is happening here by considering an analogy. Suppose we want to know the relationship in men between height and basketball ability. The relationship would be much stronger if we considered men of all heights than if we limited our sample to men over 6 feet tall. In similar fashion, any relationship between IQ and reaction time will be greater if we sample across the entire IQ range than if we only use participants of above-average ability.

Second, the reaction time task was so simple that even individuals of low IQ could probably perform it fairly rapidly. If so, we must expect the association between IQ and reaction time to be weak.

Progress in the study of reaction time came when Hick (1952) studied what happens when the number of alternative stimuli increases. For example, suppose

■ Activity: Assessing reaction times
Information processing and processing speed could be related to reaction times. You could assess reaction times using a simple computer program or even the Tetris game. After deciding whether to take the best time or the mean time of three trials you could play the game—and make sure people understand it is a *game* and not yet another test—and see what variation you get.

How many factors can you think of that could affect your findings?

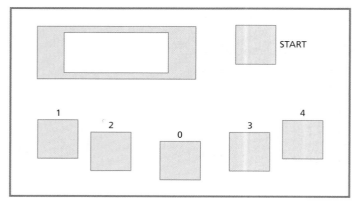

The reaction time apparatus used by Deary et al. (2001).

A commonly used inspection-time stimulus. (a) A typical inspection-time stimulus. (b) A backward mask for the inspection-time stimulus. From Deary and Stough (1996).

we have some trials on which only one light can be illuminated, others on which one out of two lights is illuminated, and still others on which one out of four (or eight) is illuminated. There is a large increase in reaction time as the number of alternatives increases reflecting the increase in stimulus uncertainty. The correlation or association between IQ and reaction time is generally greater when there are many possible stimuli than when there are few (reviewed by Deary et al., 2001).

Deary et al. (2001) reported one of the most thorough studies on IQ and reaction time. The apparatus they used is shown in the figure above. There were separate simple and four-choice reaction time tasks. On the simple task, participants rested the second finger of their preferred hand on the central "0" key and responded as rapidly as possible when a zero appeared in the display. On the four-choice task, participants rested the second and third finger of each hand on the keys labelled 1, 2, 3, and 4, and pressed the appropriate key when one of the digits 1 to 4 appeared in the display.

Deary et al. (2001) used a very large (900 people) representative sample of 56-year-olds. What did they find? First, the correlation between IQ and simple reaction time was −.31, a clear but modest relationship. Second, the correlation between IQ and four-choice reaction time was −.49, a moderately strong relationship. Third, IQ correlated −.15 with the difference between the four-choice and simple reaction times—more intelligent people showed a smaller increase in reaction time when moving from the simple to the more complex task.

How should we interpret the findings? Several explanations have been proposed (Neubauer, 1997). Perhaps the most obvious explanation is that speed of information processing within the nervous system is directly related to intelligence and to reaction time. Another possibility is that more intelligent individuals have greater powers of attention and/or motivation than those of less intelligence, and this allows them to respond faster on reaction time tasks. Both explanations are probably partially correct.

Other tasks have been used to assess speed of information processing. Of particular interest has been the **inspection-time task**, which—very briefly—presents people with two lines and they must decide which is longer. More specifically, two parallel vertical lines differing in length and joined at the top by a horizontal line are presented.

The stimulus is typically presented for less than 30 ms, and is followed by a visual mask. The inspection time has often been defined as the shortest presentation time for visual stimuli followed by at least 90% accuracy in responding. Note that speed of responding is not considered—participants are free to take as long as they want to make their decision.

The relationship between inspection time and intelligence has been assessed in many studies. Kranzler and Jensen (1989) reviewed the findings from 31 studies. The correlation between IQ and inspection time was −.50, which is moderately high. It means that more intelligent people achieve a high level of accuracy at shorter inspection times than less intelligent ones.

How can we interpret the association between IQ and inspection time? It is possible that the ability to take in information very rapidly helps to produce a high level of intelligence. Alternatively, being highly intelligent may allow individuals to take in information speedily. There is no *definitive* evidence. However, relevant findings were obtained by Deary (1995) in a 2-year study on children. There was some evidence that inspection-time differences at the start of the study causally affected differences in IQ assessed at the end of the study. There was no evidence that IQ causally affected inspection time.

Evaluation

Reaction-time studies have produced much that is of interest. The size of the correlation between IQ and reaction time (especially four-choice reaction time) is surprisingly large given that responding rapidly to a visually presented digit seems very different from the abilities (e.g. problem solving; mathematical thinking) assessed on intelligence tests. Thus, an important advantage that highly intelligent individuals have over less intelligent ones is that their basic processing speed is greater.

Inspection-time studies have also produced important findings. There is a tendency for the relationship between intelligence and inspection time to be somewhat greater than that between intelligence and reaction time. It is plausible to assume that the speed of basic visual processing is of direct relevance to individual differences in intelligence. With research on both reaction time and inspection time, there has been progress in establishing the basic mechanisms underlying intelligence.

We saw earlier in the chapter that a problem with the psychometric approach is that most intelligence tests are only directly applicable to the culture for which they were devised. In contrast, it seems likely that reaction-time and inspection-time tasks are assessing basic processes that are very similar across cultures. If so, this is a real advantage that the information-processing approach has over the psychometric approach.

What limitations with the information-processing perspective emerge from this approach? First, intelligence correlates with performance on nearly all cognitive tasks. That makes it hard to know whether findings from reaction-time and inspection-time studies are of *special* importance.

Second, there is the vexed issue of causality. Put bluntly, does high intelligence cause individuals to have fast processing speed or does fast processing speed help to cause high intelligence? At present, we simply don't know the answer, and it is possible that the causation goes both ways.

Third, the information-processing account fails to address several issues of relevance to a full understanding of intelligence. For example, the notion that processing speed is associated with individual differences in intelligence doesn't shed any light on why there are approximately seven factors of intelligence. In addition, the information-processing account doesn't reveal the role of genetic and environmental factors in the development of intelligence.

> **EXAM HINT**
> One of the assumptions of the information-processing approach is that that the speed of performing apparently very simple tasks can depend to a large extent on IQ. Make sure you can explain why this assumption is controversial. Consider both the positives (it is culture free) and the negatives (cause and effect is an issue, it doesn't explain the factors of intelligence, nor does it consider the role of genetic and environmental factors). Consider how the research on working memory capacity may be a better measure of intelligence.

Short-term memory and working memory

Humans have limited processing capacity. For example, we can hold only a few items in short-term memory. This has been shown in tests of memory span in which a series of random digits or letters is presented, after which the participant repeats back the items in the correct order. Memory span (the longest sequence of items recalled accurately at least 50% of the time) is typically about seven items (Jacobs, 1887). Perhaps more intelligent individuals have greater short-term memory capacity than other people. There is only weak support for this hypothesis. Conway, Kane, and Engel (2003) reviewed some of the evidence, and concluded there is only a very small correlation between intelligence and memory span.

All is not lost, however. In the real world, we often store information in short-term memory while at the same time processing some other information. Perhaps intelligence is related to the ability to combine these functions (i.e. processing and short-term storage). Working memory is involved when we need to store some information briefly while processing other information. Thus, we might predict that intelligence is associated with high working memory capacity.

How can we assess working memory capacity? Probably the most-used method was devised by Daneman and Carpenter (1980). People read several sentences for comprehension (processing task) and then recall the final word of each sentence (storage task). The largest number of sentences from which an individual can recall the final words more than 50% of the time is his/her **reading span**. An individual's reading span is taken as a measure of his/her working memory capacity. It was assumed that the processes used in comprehending the sentences require a smaller proportion of the available working memory capacity in individuals with a large capacity. As a result, they have more capacity available for retaining the last words of the sentences.

How strong is the relationship between working memory capacity and general intelligence ("g")? Conway et al. (2003) reviewed the relevant research. The typical correlation between working memory capacity and general intelligence was about +.6. This indicates that more intelligent individuals typically have greater working memory capacity than less intelligent ones.

Why is there such a strong association between intelligence and working memory capacity? Conway et al. (2003) argued that high intelligence and large working memory capacity both require effective attentional control, and that is why the association is so strong.

Evaluation

Most research within the information-processing approach has focused on individual differences in basic processing speed. However, the research we have discussed here suggests that individual differences in intelligence also depend on capacity differences. More specifically, working memory capacity is important but individual differences in memory span are not. The correlation between intelligence and working memory capacity is greater than that between intelligence and basic processing speed, suggesting that working memory capacity is of major importance.

There are two main limitations with research on intelligence and working memory capacity. First, the tasks used to assess working memory capacity are complex, and it is not entirely clear precisely what processes are involved in their performance. Second, there is the causality issue. We don't really know whether having high working memory capacity causes a high level of intelligence or whether a high level of intelligence produces high working memory capacity.

KEY TERM

Reading span: the maximum number of sentences that an individual can comprehend and also remember the last words of all sentences; used to assess working memory capacity or intelligence.

Learning Approach

At the start of the chapter, we saw that a very important part of intelligence is the capacity to learn from experience. Thus, we can regard individuals possessing real expertise (e.g. in chess, music, or medicine) as displaying intelligence. It is clear that learning plays a crucial role in the development of expertise—in the case of chess, it takes about 10,000 hours of practice to become a grandmaster.

The basic assumptions of the learning approach to intelligence were expressed clearly by Howe (1998, p. 3): "Learning and human abilities are closely related to each other. The abilities people gain are largely the outcome of their learning activities. Much of the learning that people do contributes to the acquisition and improvement of their abilities." Howe argued that we develop abilities as a result of two rather different kinds of learning. First, there is knowledge, which is often based on language. Second, there are skills, which take the form of actions and are typically not based on language.

Theorists who favour the learning approach argue that most people possess some fairly specific abilities, with very few people having numerous areas of expertise or ability. As a result, it doesn't make much sense to focus on general intelligence or IQ. Instead, individuals reveal their intelligence by the special abilities they have developed through learning. Ericsson, Krampe, and Tesch-Römer (1993, p. 365) (prominent advocates of the learning approach to intelligence) expressed the point as follows: "The traditional assumptions of basic abilities and capacities (talent) that may remain stable in studies of limited and short-term practice do not generalise to superior performance acquired over years and decades in a specific domain."

Everyone agrees that learning is essential for the development of outstanding abilities. However, there is less agreement in the answers to two questions following from this focus on learning. First, what kind of practice is best for the development of outstanding ability? Second, is a high level of intelligence needed as well as effective practice to develop an outstanding ability? Answers to those two questions have been provided in Ericsson et al.'s (1993) influential learning approach to intelligence to which we now turn.

Deliberate practice

Ericsson et al. (1993) and Ericsson and Lehmann (1996) addressed the issue of the most effective form of practice to promote learning and the development of abilities. They argued that numerous abilities and forms of expertise could be developed through deliberate practice. **Deliberate practice** has four aspects:

1. The task is at an appropriate level of difficulty (not too easy or hard).
2. The learner is given informative feedback about his/her performance.
3. The learner has adequate chances to repeat the task.
4. The learner has the opportunity to correct his/her errors.

According to Ericsson et al. (1993, p. 368), "The amount of time an individual is engaged in deliberate practice activities is monotonically [never decreasingly] related to that individual's acquired performance."

What exactly happens as a result of prolonged deliberate practice? According to Ericsson and Kintsch (1995), experts can get round the limited capacity of

Ericsson et al. (1993) suggested that deliberate practice was key in the development of expertise.

working memory. They proposed the notion of **long-term working memory**: experts learn how to store relevant information in long-term memory so it can be accessed readily through retrieval cues held in working memory. This does *not* mean that experts have greater working memory capacity than everyone else. Instead, they are more efficient at combining the resources of long-term memory and working memory. There are three requirements for long-term working memory to function effectively (Robertson, 2001):

1. The individual must have extensive knowledge of the relevant information.
2. The activity in which the individual is engaged must be very familiar so that he/she can predict what information will subsequently need to be retrieved.
3. The stored information must be associated with appropriate retrieval cues so that subsequent presentation of the retrieval cues leads to retrieval of the stored information.

Ericsson et al. (1993) also addressed the issue of whether the development of outstanding abilities or expertise requires high general intelligence. They claimed controversially that deliberate practice is *all* that is needed to develop expert performance. Thus, innate talent or ability has practically no influence on expert performance.

Evidence

There is evidence that experts use long-term working memory to enhance their ability to remember information. Ericsson and Chase (1982) studied a university student, SF, who was given extensive practice on the digit-span task, on which random digits are recalled immediately in the correct order. Initially, SF's digit span was about seven digits. He was then paid to practise the digit-span task for 1 hour a day for 2 years. He eventually reached a digit span of 80 digits, which is ten times the average level of performance.

How did SF do it? He reached a digit span of about 18 items by using his extensive knowledge of running times. For example, if the first few digits presented were "3594", he would note that this was Bannister's world-record time for the mile, and so these four digits would be stored as a single unit or chunk. He then increased his digit span by organising these chunks into a hierarchical retrieval structure. Thus, SF made effective use of long-term working memory by using meaningful encoding into long-term memory, developing a retrieval structure, and speed-up produced by extensive practice.

Experts in many areas seem to have excellent long-term working memory (see Ericsson & Kintsch, 1995). For example, Norman, Brooks, and Allen (1989) found that medical experts were much better than novices when unexpectedly asked to recall medical information. This is consistent with the notion that they had superior long-term working memory.

According to Ericsson and Lehmann (1996), what is important in acquiring expertise is the amount of *deliberate* practice rather than simply the time spent in practice. Charness, Tuffiash, Krampe, Reingold, and Vasyukova (2005) found among tournament-rated chess players that time spent on serious study alone, tournament play, and formal instruction all predicted chess-playing expertise. Serious study alone was the strongest predictor correlating +.50 with current playing level. Grandmasters had spent an average of about 5000 hours on serious

KEY TERMS

Working memory: a system having the functions of cognitive processing and the temporary storage of information.

Long-term working memory: used to store relevant information in long-term memory and to access it through retrieval cues in working memory.

study alone during their first 10 years of playing chess, nearly five times as much as the amount of time spent by intermediate players.

Deliberate practice is also important in the development of expertise in other contexts. Ericsson et al. (1993) reported a study on violinists in a German music academy. The key difference between 18-year-old students with varying levels of expertise on the violin was their amount of deliberate practice over the years. The most expert violinists had spent on average nearly 7500 hours engaged in deliberate practice compared to the 5300 hours clocked up by the good violinists.

The above study only showed that there is a correlation or association between amount of deliberate practice and level of performance. Perhaps those musicians with the greatest innate talent and/or musical success spend more time practising than those with less talent or previous success. However, contrary evidence was reported by Sloboda, Davidson, Howe, and Moore (1996), who compared highly successful young musicians with less successful ones. The two groups didn't differ in the amount of practice required to achieve a given level of performance. This suggests that the advantage possessed by the very successful musicians isn't due to their greater level of natural musical ability.

Tuffiash, Roring, and Ericsson (2007) obtained evidence for the importance of deliberate practice among 40 tournament-rated Scrabble players. They compared elite and average players with comparable levels of verbal ability. The elite players spent more time than the average players on deliberate practice activities (e.g. analysis of their own previous games, solving anagrams), but the two groups didn't differ with respect to other forms of practice (e.g. playing Scrabble for fun, playing in Scrabble tournaments). In addition, lifetime accumulated study of Scrabble was a reasonable predictor of Scrabble-playing expertise.

What role does innate ability or intelligence play in the development of expertise? So far as the acquisition of highly specific expertise is concerned, it seems that high intelligence is not required. For example, consider individuals who were once known by the derogatory term idiots savants (knowledgeable idiots) but are now referred to as **savants**. They have mental retardation and low IQs but possess some special expertise. Some savants can work out in a few seconds the day of the week corresponding to any specified date in the past or the future (calendar calculating). Others can perform multiplications at high speed or they know what *pi* is to thousands of places of decimals.

> Do you think musical ability is innate or a result of deliberate practice?

KEY TERM

Savants: individuals who have limited outstanding expertise despite being mentally retarded.

CASE STUDY: SAVANT

AP, an unmarried 32-year-old Hindu male, was assessed for psychiatric help because he was psychologically, socially, and physically limited. However, he demonstrated some very unusual mathematical abilities. For example, he could:

- correctly name the day of the week of given a particular date in the twentieth century, taking about 15 seconds for the correct answer
- state accurately those years in which a given date would fall on a particular day, e.g. he could name all those years in which 21 April was a Sunday.
- correctly predict future dates, e.g. that the fourth Monday in February 1993 would fall on the 22nd day of that month

- accurately recall detailed events in the field of sports, especially cricket, e.g. correctly recite all sorts of statistics, world records, batting averages, scores
- calculate correct squares, cubes, and higher powers of two-digit numbers, all answers were given almost instantaneously and often faster than the calculator
- arrange numbers in such a way that columns, rows, and diagonals added up to the same.

All this despite his difficulties in other areas of his life!

Adapted from Abhyankar, Thatte, and Doongaji (1981)

Grabner et al. (2007) found a positive correlation between intelligence and chess ranking in adult tournament chess players.

Despite the great feats of savants, their abilities are often very restricted. For example, Howe and Smith (1988) studied a 14-year-old boy who was very good at subtraction problems expressed in terms of calendar dates (e.g. "If a man was born in 1908, how old would he have been in 1934?"). However, when essentially the same subtraction problem was expressed as, "What is 34 minus 8?", he took much longer to produce an answer and the answer was often wrong!

Dramatic evidence that IQ plays little role in the development of very specific abilities was reported by Ceci and Liker (1986). They studied individuals who had spent thousands of hours acquiring knowledge of harness racing, in which horses pull a sulky (a light two-wheeled cart). These individuals could work out betting odds very accurately by taking account of up to seven variables (e.g. track size, each horse's lifetime speed). Some of these experts had IQs in the low 80s, considerably less than most people's IQs.

There is much stronger evidence for the importance of intelligence in the development of broader abilities or expertise. For example, Grabner, Stern, and Neubauer (2007) studied adult tournament chess players. They obtained a correlation of +.35 between general intelligence and ELO ranking (a measure of playing ability), indicating that intelligence was moderately predictive of chess-playing level. In addition, numerical intelligence correlated +.46 with ELO ranking. However, as predicted by the learning approach, players' chess experience (e.g. amount of practice) was an even better predictor of ELO ranking.

For most people, the broadest ability or expertise they acquire is in their career, especially those involving complex skills. As discussed earlier, Hunter (1986) found that the correlation between intelligence and work performance was +.58 for high-complexity jobs, which hardly suggests that intelligence is irrelevant. The mean IQ of those in very complex occupations (e.g. accountants; lawyers; doctors) is between 120 and 130, much higher than the population mean of 100 (Mackintosh, 1998). Note, however, that the correlation between intelligence and work performance was only +.23 with low-complexity jobs (e.g. shrimp pickers, corn-husking machine operators).

Why is job performance (especially of complex jobs) well predicted by intelligence? Hunter and Schmidt (e.g. 1996) answered this question with a theory based on four main assumptions:

1. Work performance depends to a moderate extent on job-relevant learning and knowledge.
2. Highly intelligent individuals learn more rapidly than less intelligent ones.
3. Successful job performance sometimes requires that workers respond in an innovative or adaptive fashion.
4. More intelligent workers respond more adaptively than less intelligent ones.

Hunter (1983) reported the findings from 14 studies on civilian and military groups supporting this theory. First, there was a high correlation between intelligence and job knowledge. Second, learning (i.e. job knowledge) was strongly associated with job performance. Third, there was a direct influence of intelligence on job performance not dependent on job knowledge. These findings suggest it is possible to bridge the gap between the learning approach to intelligence and the more traditional psychometric approach. Learning based on deliberate practice is crucially important for the development of high levels of

? What other types of performance may be predicted by intelligence?

ability or expertise. In addition, however, intelligence is important because more intelligent individuals learn more rapidly than less intelligent ones.

Evaluation

The learning approach to intelligence has many positive aspects. First, individuals can only behave in intelligent ways following substantial relevant learning. Second, deliberate practice is more effective than non-deliberate practice for the development of high levels of ability or expertise. Indeed, it is probably essential. Third, factors other than deliberate practice (e.g. intelligence) aren't of much importance in accounting for individual differences in narrow or low-complexity abilities. Fourth, the notion that individuals of high intelligence learn faster than those of low intelligence helps to explain why intelligence is a good predictor of performance of complex jobs.

What are the limitations with the learning approach? First, learning in the form of deliberate practice is *not* the only important factor in the development of broad, complex abilities. For example, intelligence predicts level of expertise as reflected in occupational success (Hunter, 1986) or chess-playing performance (Grabner et al., 2007).

Second, the notion that intelligence as assessed by intelligence tests is unimportant is unconvincing. As Sternberg and Ben-Zeev (2001, p. 302) argued, "Is one to believe that anyone could become a Mozart if only he or she put in the time? . . . Or that becoming an Einstein is just a matter of deliberate practice?" Why, then, does intelligence often fail to predict level of expertise? One reason may be that most experts are highly talented or intelligent, thus making it difficult for individual differences in intelligence to predict performance. For example, Bilalic, McLeod, and Gobet (2007) reported a *negative* correlation between intelligence and chess-playing expertise among elite young chess players. However, the mean IQ of this elite sample was 133, which is higher than that of 97% of the population!

Third, there are problems with most of the research showing that the amount of deliberate practice is positively correlated with ability level. What generally happened was that individuals decided how much time to devote to deliberate practice, and so the amount of deliberate practice was not under experimental control. Perhaps highly intelligent individuals or those who encounter early success in a given area (e.g. chess playing) are the ones most likely to engage in substantial amounts of deliberate practice.

Fourth, there is an important issue that has often been ignored. Why do some individuals decide to devote hundreds or thousands of hours to learning in the form of effortful deliberate practice to achieve very high levels of ability in some area? Ericsson et al.'s (1993) learning approach has identified some of the important cognitive factors involved but has been strangely silent on the crucial *motivational* factors that are also involved.

> **EXAM HINT**
>
> Can you explain why the learning theories' claim that deliberate practice alone can produce the next Mozart seems unconvincing?

Gardner's Theory of Multiple Intelligences

Howard Gardner (1983) argued strongly that most intelligence tests and most theories of intelligence are based on an excessively narrow view of intelligence. Traditionally, intelligence tests have assessed language ability, spatial ability, and mathematical ability, but haven't considered other abilities that can be of great value in coping successfully with the environment. Gardner proposed

that we possess several intelligences that are relatively separate or independent of each other.

How did Gardner decide which intelligences humans possess? In essence, Gardner (1983) argued that any proposed intelligence should satisfy general prerequisites or requirements, followed by various criteria. His starting point was that, "A prerequisite for a theory of multiple intelligences is that it captures a reasonably complete set of abilities valued by human cultures" (Gardner, 1983, p. 62). Other related prerequisites were the following: "A human intellectual competence must entail a set of skills of problem-solving . . . and must entail the potential for finding or creating problems."

Any potential intelligence fulfilling the above prerequisites then had to meet various criteria to become one of the multiple intelligences. First, it should depend on identifiable brain structures. Second, studies of brain-damaged patients should indicate that it could be impaired without disrupting other intelligences. Third, it should involve the use of distinct cognitive processes. Fourth, there should be exceptional individuals showing a remarkable ability (or deficit) with respect to the intelligence in question. Fifth, in evolutionary terms the development of the intelligence should have improved humans' adaptation to the environment. Sixth, there should be evidence for its existence from psychometric findings.

Gardner (1983) used the above prerequisites and criteria to suggest the following seven intelligences:

1. *Logical-mathematical intelligence*: of special value in handling abstract problems of a logical or mathematical nature.
2. *Spatial intelligence*: used when deciding how to go from one place to another, how to arrange suitcases in the boot of a car, and so on.
3. *Musical intelligence*: used both for active musical processes (e.g. playing an instrument, singing) and more passive processes (e.g. appreciating music).
4. *Bodily/kinaesthetic intelligence*: involved in the fine control of bodily movements in activities such as sport and dancing.
5. *Linguistic intelligence*: involved in language activities (e.g. reading, writing, speaking).
6. *Intrapersonal intelligence*: "depends on core processes that enable people to distinguish among their own feelings" (Gardner, Kornhaber, & Wake 1996, p. 211).

7. *Interpersonal intelligence*: "makes use of core capabilities to recognise and make distinctions among others' feelings, beliefs, and intentions" (Gardner et al., 1996, p. 211).

Gardner (1998) proposed adding naturalistic intelligence to the seven intelligences he had previously identified. Naturalistic intelligence is shown by individuals who can perceive patterns in nature; Charles Darwin is a famous person with outstanding naturalistic intelligence. Gardner also suggested that there might be two additional intelligences: spiritual intelligence and existential intelligence. Spiritual intelligence is based on a concern with cosmic issues, and with the achievement of the spiritual as a state of being. Existential intelligence is based on concerns about ultimate issues of existence.

 What do you think your strongest intelligence would be according to Gardner?

Evidence

In spite of its great popularity, there is surprisingly little direct evidence to support Gardner's theory of multiple intelligences. An exception is the work of Gardner (1993) in a study of creativity. He chose seven individuals who showed outstanding creativity during the early part of the twentieth century with respect to one of the intelligences. Albert Einstein was the representative of logical-mathematical intelligence; the other outstanding figures were Pablo Picasso (spatial intelligence), Igor Stravinsky (musical intelligence), Martha Graham (bodily-kinaesthetic intelligence), T. S. Eliot (linguistic intelligence), Sigmund Freud (intrapersonal intelligence), and Mahatma Gandhi (interpersonal intelligence). Nearly all of them were brought up in families that forced them to meet standards of excellence. They all had childlike qualities, showing signs of behaving like a "wonder-filled child". They were all very ambitious, which led them to sacrifice other aspects of their lives (and to cause suffering to their families).

Can you think of any other intelligences that the Gardner model does not include?

This genius-based approach to identifying intelligences is open to criticism. As Jensen (in Miele, 2002, p. 58) pointed out, sarcastically, the logic of this approach is that we could claim that, "Al Capone displayed the highest level of 'criminal intelligence', or that Casanova was 'blessed' with exceptional 'sexual intelligence'." In other words, Gardner's criteria for what constitutes an

Three of the individuals selected by Gardner (1993) to demonstrate his theory of multiple intelligence: Igor Stravinsky (for musical intelligence), Pablo Picasso (for spatial intelligence), and Mahatma Gandhi (for interpersonal intelligence).

intelligence are so lenient that almost anything goes. For example, face recognition and the ability to learn foreign languages appear to meet his criteria for an intelligence (Mackintosh, 1998).

Gardner claimed support for his theory from the study of individuals known patronisingly as idiots savants (discussed earlier). Savants generally have mental retardation and low IQs but they possess some special expertise. For example, Howe and Smith (1988) studied a 14-year-old boy who had an outstanding ability at calendar calculating. When asked to indicate the day of the week on which a past date fell or a future date would fall, he could supply the correct answer in a matter of seconds—something that the rest of us can't do! According to Gardner, savants show that intelligence can be very specific. However, it is doubtful whether the very specific abilities of savants should be regarded as intelligent— calendar calculating wouldn't be of much use when dealing with the problems of everyday life!

One of the criteria for an intelligence that Gardner (1983) suggested was the existence of psychometric support. There is certainly good support for some of his intelligences if we compare them against the seven factors identified by Thurstone. There are reasonably close matches between Gardner's spatial intelligence and Thurstone's spatial ability; between Gardner's logical-mathematical intelligence and Thurstone's numerical ability; and between Gardner's linguistic intelligence and Thurstone's verbal meaning and verbal fluency factors. However, the psychometric evidence provides less support for most of the other intelligences proposed by Gardner, especially his spiritual, existential, and naturalist intelligences.

Gardner's theory has had a considerable impact within education. An implication of the theory is that teachers should be responsive to the different patterns of abilities and personal preferences of students. Evidence for such individual differences among adults with intellectual difficulties was reported by Lisle (2007). Among these adults, 34% expressed a preference for learning through visual presentation of material, 34% through auditory presentation, 23% through kinaesthetic presentation, and 9% through multi-modal presentation. As Lisle (2007, p. 23) concluded, "This participant group requires a varied and diverse learning programme."

Evaluation

Gardner's theory of multiple intelligences possesses various strengths. First, his theoretical approach is broader in scope than that of most previous theorists. Second, there is some supporting evidence (e.g. from geniuses, from brain-damaged patients) for all seven intelligences originally proposed by Gardner. Third, Gardner's ideas have been adopted extensively within education. Educationalists are especially impressed by the notion that children can exhibit high levels of intelligence in areas other than the traditional ones such as language or mathematics. Fourth, Gardner emphasised the substantial individual differences in students' preferred ways of being taught and their patterns of abilities, and this has benefited educational programmes. Fifth, Gardner identified intrapersonal intelligence and interpersonal intelligence as two of his seven intelligences. In the years since 1983, there has been huge interest in emotional intelligence, which is basically a combination of those two intelligences (Goleman, 1995). There is evidence that high emotional intelligence is useful. For example, Rode et al. (2007) found that business students high in emotional intelligence showed greater group behaviour effectiveness and higher levels of academic performance.

Teachers often try to take Gardner's model into account. What are some ways to include various types of learning in class activities?

What are the limitations with Gardner's theory? First, the notion that intelligence consists of several relatively specific abilities is not new. As we have seen, Thurstone (1938) identified seven factors of intelligence. The philosopher Gilbert Ryle (1949, p. 48) argued that, "the boxer, the surgeon, the poet and the salesman" all have their own kinds of intelligence, which they apply "to the performance of their own special tasks."

Second, in spite of the fact that his theory was put forward well over 20 years ago, there has been no thorough experimental test of its validity. Thus, it must be regarded as somewhat speculative.

Third, Gardner used the prerequisites and criteria for selecting intelligences in a subjective and non-scientific way. In his words, "It must be admitted that the selection (or rejection) of a candidate's intelligence is reminiscent more of an artistic judgement than of a scientific assessment" (Gardner, 1983, p. 63).

Fourth, the seven intelligences correlate positively with each other, whereas Gardner (1983) assumed they were independent. This means that Gardner was wrong to disregard the general factor of intelligence. As Jensen (in Miele, 2002, p. 59) pointed out, the evidence indicates that, "A level of g [general factor beyond the 90th percentile (IQ over 120)] is probably necessary for recognised achievement in politics, the military, business, finance, or industry."

Fifth, the musical and bodily kinaesthetic intelligences are less important than the other five original intelligences in Western cultures—many very successful people are tone deaf and poorly co-ordinated.

Sixth, the theory is mostly descriptive. For example, it fails to explain *how* each intelligence works or *why* some individuals are more intelligent than others.

> **EXAM HINT**
>
> Make sure you can give a balanced evaluation of Gardner's multiple intelligences by considering:
>
> - the positive educational applications
> - the implications of emotional intelligence
> - the lack of scientific validity and explanatory power.

SECTION SUMMARY
Theories of Intelligence

❖ The psychometric approach has led to the development of intelligence tests that assess IQ with good reliability.

❖ Factor analysis suggests that the structure of intelligence is hierarchical, with general intelligence ("g") at the top.

❖ IQ correlates moderately highly with academic performance and with occupational performance, thus indicating the validity of intelligence tests.

❖ Evaluation:

— the psychometric approach is descriptive rather than explanatory
— the psychometric approach hasn't identified the cognitive processes underlying intelligent behaviour
— the psychometric approach is often rather narrow, ignoring creativity and social or emotional intelligence.

Psychometric approach

❖ According to the information-processing approach, high intelligence is associated with greater basic processing speed.

❖ The approach has been supported by research using the reaction-time task, especially in its more complex forms.

❖ The inspection-time task has provided stronger evidence that intelligence is associated with basic processing speed.

Information-processing approach

❖ Evaluation:

— the information-processing approach may be assessing basic processes that are very similar in most cultures
— it is unclear whether high intelligence causes fast processing speed or vice versa
— the approach doesn't explain why there are several intelligence factors
— high intelligence is strongly associated with high working memory capacity. Thus, good ability to combine processing with short-term storage of information is characteristic of individuals of high intelligence.

Learning approach

❖ Intelligent behaviour (e.g. expert abilities) depends crucially on a lengthy learning process.
❖ According to Ericsson et al. (1993), the learning of complex abilities depends on deliberate practice involving informative feedback and the chance to correct errors.
❖ Ericsson et al. (1993) argued that intelligence is not necessary for the development of abilities or for the development of abilities or cognitively demanding skills.
❖ Evaluation:

— deliberate practice is essential for the development of specific and broad abilities
— intelligence is more important in the development of broad abilities (especially complex ones) than specific ones
— individuals high in intelligence learn faster than those with less intelligence
— the learning approach doesn't explain why some people's motivation for learning is much greater than that of others.

Gardner's theory

❖ Gardner (1983) argued that humans possess seven separate intelligences. His theory is unusually comprehensive, including musical, intrapersonal, and interpersonal intelligences.
❖ Children with a relatively low IQ may nevertheless be gifted with respect to one or more of the seven intelligences.
❖ The study of outstandingly creative individuals provides some support for the theory.
❖ Evaluation:

— the theory has had a substantial impact in education
— Gardner anticipated subsequent developments in emotional intelligence
— Gardner's approach is rather subjective and his theory lacks strong experimental support
— the seven intelligences are *not* independent, and Gardner has not disproved the notion of general intelligence.

ANIMAL LEARNING AND INTELLIGENCE

So far, we have focused on theories designed to explain intelligence in humans. By contrast, this section is devoted to learning and intelligence in non-human species. How do other species compare to our own? According to van Schaik

(2006, p. 64), "Even though we humans write the textbooks and may justifiably be suspected of bias, few doubt that we are the smartest creatures on the planet. Many animals have special cognitive abilities that allow them to excel in their particular habitats, but they do not often solve novel problems." However, the members of other species successfully learn many things and sometimes display real intelligence.

Historically, most of the early research in non-human species focused on very simple kinds of learning, especially conditioning. Some of the most famous studies were those carried out on classical conditioning by Ivan Pavlov in Russian and on operant conditioning by the American B. F. Skinner. After we have considered the findings from conditioning research, we will move on to consider more recent research that has indicated various ways in which non-human animals may display intelligent behaviour.

Classical and Operant Conditioning

In the early years of the twentieth century, American psychologists led by John Watson established behaviourism. Their key assumptions were that it is important to study behaviour under controlled conditions and that learning can be accounted for by conditioning principles. They identified two major types of conditioning: classical conditioning and operant conditioning, both of which are discussed at length below.

Before proceeding, it is important to emphasise two points. First, the behaviourists mostly considered very *simple* forms of learning such as learning to salivate when a bell sounds or to press a lever for food reward. As a result, they discovered little of interest about what is involved in complex learning. Second, the behaviourists generally studied non-human species in their experiments. Among the various species tested, rats and pigeons were probably used more often than any others.

<aside>
EXAM HINT

Remember classical conditioning as learned associations and operant conditioning as learned consequences.
</aside>

Classical conditioning

You can see what is involved in classical conditioning by considering a visit to the dentist. As you lie down on the reclining chair, you may feel frightened. Why are you frightened *before* the dentist has caused you any pain? The sights and sounds of the dentist's surgery lead you to expect or predict that you are shortly going to be in pain. Thus, you have formed an *association* between the neutral stimuli of the surgery and the painful stimuli involved in drilling. Such associations are of central importance in classical conditioning. In essence, the fear created by the drilling is now triggered by the neutral stimuli of the surgery.

Textbook writers nearly always focus on unpleasant everyday examples of classical conditioning. Indeed, I've just been guilty of that myself! However, there are also pleasant examples. Most middle-aged people have especially positive feelings for the music that was popular when they were in their teens. Associations are formed between

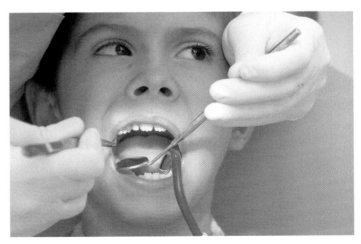

Classical conditioning helps to explain why we might feel fear in the dentist's chair before we have felt any pain.

Learned associations

Imagine something nice, something delicious, your favourite food. Is it strawberries, chocolate, a barbecue, a curry? Think about it and visualise it, and you will find your mouth is watering! There is no such food nearby, you cannot see, smell, or taste it, but you have learned that you love this food and this learned association has made you salivate. This will not happen if you are presented with a food you have never seen before, as you have not learned an association to it. If your most disliked sort of food were actually presented to you, your mouth would not water either. A different association would have been learned, and possibly a different response too.

Classical conditioning

UCS → UCR

NS + UCS paired

NS (now CS) → UCR (now CR)

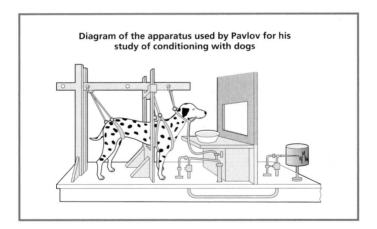

Diagram of the apparatus used by Pavlov for his study of conditioning with dogs

the music and various exciting kinds of stimuli encountered during adolescence (Marc Brysbaert, personal communication).

The best-known example of classical conditioning comes from the work of Ivan Pavlov (1849–1936). Dogs (and other animals) salivate when food is put in their mouths. What we have here is an unlearned or **unconditioned reflex** involving a connection between the **unconditioned stimulus** of the food in the mouth and the **unconditioned response** of salivation. Pavlov found he could train a dog to salivate to other stimuli. In some of his studies, he presented a tone (a neutral stimulus that becomes the **conditioned stimulus**) just before food several times, so that the tone signalled that food would arrive very soon. Finally, he presented the same tone (the test stimulus) on its own without any food following. Pavlov found that the dog salivated to the tone. The dog had learned a **conditioned reflex**, in which the conditioned stimulus (the tone) was associated with the unconditioned stimulus (sight of food), and the learned or **conditioned response** was salivation. There is a progressive increase in salivation (the conditioned response) over the course of learning.

It is essential for the food to follow very shortly after the tone for a conditioned reflex to be formed. Why is this? The conditioned stimulus produces a conditioned response because it leads the animal to *expect* the imminent arrival of the unconditioned stimulus. The conditioned stimulus couldn't make the animal expect the unconditioned stimulus if it had already been presented!

Pavlov discovered several features of classical conditioning in his research on dogs. One of these was **generalisation**. The conditioned response of salivation was greatest when the tone presented on its own was the same as the tone that had previously been presented just before food. A smaller amount of salivation was obtained when a different tone was used. Generalisation refers to the fact that the

---

KEY TERMS

Unconditioned reflex: an association between the unconditioned stimulus and the unconditioned response.

Unconditioned stimulus (UCS): a stimulus that produces an unconditioned response in the absence of learning.

Unconditioned response (UCR): an unlearned response to an unconditioned stimulus.

Conditioned stimulus (CS): a stimulus that becomes associated through learning with the unconditioned stimulus; originally it is a neutral stimulus (NS).

Conditioned reflex: the new association between a stimulus and response formed in classical conditioning.

Conditioned response (CR): a response that is produced by the conditioned stimulus after a learning process in which the conditioned stimulus has been paired several times with the unconditioned stimulus.

Generalisation: the tendency of a conditioned response to occur in a weaker form to stimuli similar to the conditioned stimulus.

strength of the conditioned response (e.g. salivation) depends on the *similarity* between the test stimulus and the previous training stimulus.

Pavlov also identified the phenomenon of **discrimination**. Suppose a given tone is paired several times with the sight of food. The dog will learn to salivate to the tone. Then another tone is presented on its own. It produces a smaller amount of salivation than the first tone through generalisation. Next the first tone is paired with food several more times, but the second tone is never paired with food. Salivation to the first tone increases, whereas that to the second tone decreases. Thus, the dog has discriminated between the two tones.

Another key feature of classical conditioning is **experimental extinction**. When Pavlov presented the tone on its own several times, there was less and less salivation. Thus, the repeated presentation of the conditioned stimulus in the absence of the unconditioned stimulus removes the conditioned response. This is experimental extinction. In approximate terms, the animal ceases to expect the conditioned stimulus to be followed by the unconditioned stimulus.

Extinction does *not* mean that the dog or other animal has lost the relevant conditioned reflex. Animals brought back into the experimental situation after extinction has occurred produce some salivation in response to the tone. This is **spontaneous recovery**. It shows that the salivary response to the tone was inhibited (rather than lost) during extinction.

What is going on in the classical conditioning situation? It might seem that two factors are of special importance. First, the conditioned and the unconditioned stimuli need to be presented very close together in time. This is sometimes known as the law of association by contiguity (contiguity means closeness in time or space). Second, there is a process of stimulus substitution: the conditioned stimulus simply acts as a substitute for the unconditioned stimulus. For example, the sight of the dentist's surgery evokes the fear originally associated with the dentist's drilling.

In fact, the above account is incorrect. It is true that conditioning is usually greatest when the conditioned stimulus is presented a short time (about ½ a second) before the unconditioned stimulus, and stays on while the unconditioned stimulus is presented. However, there is little or no conditioning if the unconditioned stimulus is presented shortly before the conditioned stimulus. This situation is known as **backward conditioning**. Thus, contiguity alone isn't enough.

Kamin (1969) showed that classical conditioning does *not* always occur when a conditioned stimulus is followed closely by an unconditioned stimulus. The animals in the experimental group received light (conditioned stimulus 1) paired with electric shock, and learned to react with fear and avoidance when

---

■ Activity: Classical conditioning

Consider the following situations and, for each, try to identify the UCS, UCR, NS, CS, CR

A puff of air is directed at your eye. Your reflex response is to blink. At the same time as the air is blown, a bell is sounded. In time, the bell produces a blink response.

As you walk into the examination room, you are filled with a sense of dread. There is a smell of roses from outside the window. A few weeks later, you smell the same perfume of roses and are filled, inexplicably, with a sense of fear.

■ Activity: The eye blink reflex

It is possible to demonstrate the classical conditioning of the eye blink reflex. Blow *carefully* (using a drinking straw or similar) a puff of air across a volunteer's eyeball. (You may have to experiment a little to get a strong, reliable blink.) Now pair the puff of air with a gentle tap on the back of the participant's hand. Record the number of pairings required to produce the eye-blink to the tap on the hand alone.

KEY TERMS

Discrimination: the strength of the conditioned response to one conditioned stimulus is strengthened at the same time as that to a second conditioned stimulus is weakened.

Experimental extinction: the elimination of a response when it is not followed by reward (operant conditioning) or by the unconditioned stimulus (classical conditioning).

Spontaneous recovery: the re-emergence of responses over time following experimental extinction.

Backward conditioning: the unconditioned stimulus is presented just before the conditioned stimulus in classical conditioning.

the light came on. The animals in the contrast group had no training. Then both groups received a series of trials with a light–tone combination followed by shock. Finally, both groups received only the tone (conditioned stimulus 2). The contrast group responded with fear to the tone on its own, but the experimental group did not.

How can we explain the above results? The control animals learned that the tone predicted shock because they hadn't previously learned something different. However, the experimental animals learned that light (conditioned stimulus 1) predicted shock, and so they formed an association between light and shock. The development of this association caused them to "block" the formation of a further association between tone and shock. The term **blocking** is used to refer to what happened with the experimental animals—a second conditioned stimulus (e.g. tone) does *not* lead to conditioned responses if another conditioned stimulus (e.g. light) already predicts the onset of the unconditioned stimulus.

What about the notion that the conditioned stimulus acts as a *substitute* for the unconditioned stimulus? Let's go back to Pavlov's research. When food is presented to a dog, it typically engages in chewing and swallowing as well as salivating (unconditioned response). However, the conditioned stimulus (e.g. tone) produces salivation but *not* chewing and swallowing. In addition, the tone often produces conditioned responses (e.g. tail wagging, looking at the place where food is usually presented) that don't occur in response to the food itself (Jenkins, Barrera, Ireland, & Woodside, 1978). Thus, the conditioned stimulus is *not* simply a substitute for the unconditioned stimulus.

Rescorla–Wagner model

We turn now to attempts to account for the classical conditioning phenomena we have been discussing. Our focus will be on the model put forward by Rescorla and Wagner (1972). Their central assumption was that associative learning between a conditioned stimulus and an unconditioned stimulus occurs when a conditioned stimulus is found to *predict* the arrival of the unconditioned stimulus. Several predictions (all strongly supported) follow from this assumption, and are discussed below.

- The theory explains why backward conditioning is so ineffective. If the conditioned stimulus is only presented after the unconditioned stimulus, then it can't predict the arrival of the unconditioned stimulus.
- The model accounts for blocking. If one conditioned stimulus already predicts the arrival of the unconditioned stimulus, then the addition of a second conditioned stimulus doesn't improve the animal's ability to predict the arrival of the unconditioned stimulus. As a result, the second conditioned stimulus is redundant and blocking occurs.
- We can make sense of the finding that dogs in the Pavlov situation respond to a tone by wagging their tails and looking at the place where food is normally presented. These are precisely the forms of behaviour that would be exhibited by a dog expecting food to be presented.

Despite the successes of the Rescorla–Wagner model, it has limitations (Miller, Barnet, & Grahame, 1995). It is assumed within the model that performance provides a *direct* measure of what has been learned. However, this assumption is incorrect. According to the model, experimental extinction occurs because there is an unlearning of the association between the conditioned and unconditioned stimuli. However, the existence of spontaneous recovery (re-emergence of conditioned responses after extinction) indicates that the association has *not* been unlearned.

Evaluation. On the positive side, the notion that associative learning occurs when a conditioned stimulus predicts the arrival of an unconditioned stimulus accounts for numerous findings in classical conditioning. In addition, the Rescorla–Wagner model led to the development of several other cognitive theories of conditioning (Gray, 2002).

On the negative side, classical conditioning is surprisingly complex, and the model fails to take account of some of these complexities (Miller et al., 1995). The key assumption that what has been learned will always reveal itself in performance has been disproved.

Role in the behaviour of non-human animals: ecological perspective

According to the standard view, there is an *arbitrary* relationship between the conditioned and unconditioned stimuli, and the optimal time gap between the two stimuli to promote good conditioning is about ½ second. Let's think about that in terms of animals living their lives in the wild. What are the chances that an animal living in the wild will encounter the same arbitrary conditioned stimulus immediately before encountering the unconditioned stimulus on numerous occasions? The answer must surely be slim or none, and Slim has just left town. Where, then, does that leave the role of classical conditioning as an explanation of animal behaviour?

According to those favouring the ecological perspective, it is much easier to produce conditioned reflexes in non-human animals with some combinations of conditioned and unconditioned stimuli than with others. According to them, animals have inherited behavioural tendencies helping them to survive in their natural environment. These behavioural tendencies are often *modified* through learning to equip animals to cope successfully with the particular environmental conditions they face. From this perspective, certain forms of learning are more useful than others, and so are acquired more easily. This approach is *very* different from the conventional one, according to which the initial relationship between conditioned and unconditioned stimulus is irrelevant.

It is vital for all animals to avoid poisonous foods, and so the ecological perspective is especially relevant to food-aversion learning. Consider, for example, the very influential research of Garcia and Koelling (1966), who studied classical conditioning using three conditioned stimuli at the same time: saccharin-flavoured water, light, and sound.

Some rats had these stimuli paired with the unconditioned stimulus of X-rays, which caused nausea. Other rats had these stimuli paired with the unconditioned stimulus of electric shock. After that, Garcia and Koelling presented each conditioned stimulus on its own. Rats that had experienced nausea showed an aversion to the flavoured water but not to the light or sound cues. By contrast, the rats exposed to electric shock avoided the light and sound stimuli but not the flavoured water. Thus, the animals learned to associate being sick with taste, and they learned to associated shock with light and sound stimuli.

What do these findings mean? There is a biological readiness to associate some stimuli but not others. For example, there is obvious survival value in learning

? Do any ethical concerns arise during conditioning experiments?

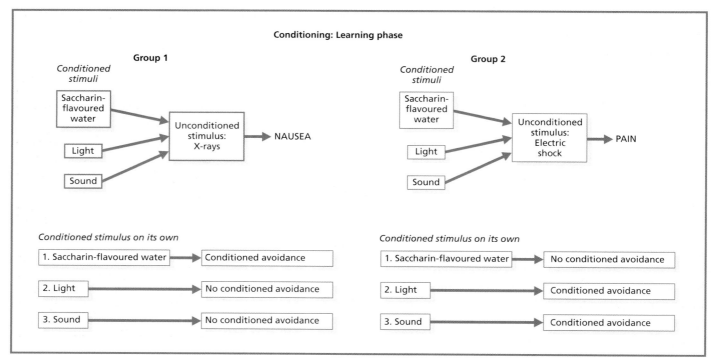

Selective conditioning of water with X-rays and nausea (food-aversion learning) and of light and sound with experience of pain. These selective forms of conditioning reflect biological readiness. Experimental design used by Garcia and Koelling (1966).

rapidly to develop a taste aversion to any food followed by illness. This is an example of the phenomenon known as **preparedness**, the notion that some forms of learning are more "natural" and easier than others.

Domjan (2005) developed the ecological perspective to explain how classical conditioning operates among animals living in their natural environment. According to him, what typically happens is that the conditioned stimulus and unconditioned stimulus are different features of the *same* object, and the conditioning produced is very strong and long-lasting. Domjan (2005) discussed findings from experiments on male Japanese quail, in which the conditioned stimulus was the stuffed head of a female quail and the unconditioned stimulus was access to a live female. Very strong conditioning was obtained in these circumstances even when the time interval between the conditioned and unconditioned stimuli increased. Indeed, conditioning was so strong that the male quail often grabbed the stuffed head and tried to copulate with it!

Evidence that classical conditioning can have substantial evolutionary value was provided by Hollis et al. (1997). Some male blue gourami fish were classically conditioned to associate a light with seeing a female gourami. Other male blue gourami fish saw the light and the female gourami, but no classical conditioning occurred because there was a gap of several hours between the two stimuli. On the test, a light was followed by an opportunity for the male gouramis to copulate with a receptive female gourami. The male fish that had been classically conditioned copulated much more than the others, and produced 10 times as many offspring. Thus, classical conditioning can enhance reproductive success.

An important function of classical conditioning is that presentation of the conditioned stimulus allows animals to interact more successfully with the unconditioned stimulus. That was certainly true of Pavlov's original research on dogs. Woods (1991) compared consuming a large meal to suffering a major physiological assault, for example, by stimulating the release of stress hormones. Classical conditioning in which the animal salivates before the arrival of food leads animals to secrete digestive hormones and enzymes before the food has reached the gut.

In sum, classical conditioning in the natural environment typically involves some pre-existing relationship between the conditioned and unconditioned stimuli. Indeed, the two stimuli are often different features of the same object. The conditioned stimulus is generally not of any special importance in its right—its importance derives from the fact that it allows the animal some time to prepare to cope effectively with the unconditioned stimulus. As a result, classical conditioning can increase reproductive success (Hollis et al., 1997).

Operant conditioning

In everyday life, people are often persuaded to behave in certain ways by the offer of reward or positive reinforcement. For example, young people deliver the morning papers because they are paid. In similar fashion, dolphins can be trained to jump through hoops to receive fish and dogs can be persuaded to beg to receive food. These are all examples of operant conditioning. Much of **operant conditioning** is based on the **law of reinforcement**: the probability of a given response occurring increases if followed by a reward or positive reinforcer such as food or praise. This is known as positive reinforcement.

According to B. F. Skinner (1904–1990), operant conditioning (especially positive reinforcement) is of enormous importance. Indeed, Skinner believed that what most species learn and how they behave are both very heavily influenced by the conditioning experiences they have had throughout their lives. The best-known example of positive reinforcement is provided by Skinner's research in which a rat in a Skinner box containing a lever received a food pellet (reward) when it pressed the lever. The rat learned that food could be obtained by lever pressing, and so pressed the lever more and more often. This is a clear example of the law or reinforcement. The effects of a reward or positive reinforcer are greater if it follows shortly after the response has been produced than if it is delayed.

The probability of a response decreases if it isn't followed by a positive reinforcer. This is experimental extinction. As with classical conditioning, there is usually some spontaneous

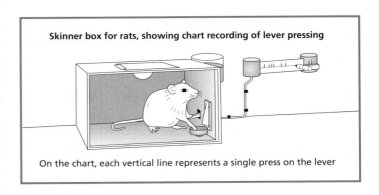

Skinner box for rats, showing chart recording of lever pressing

On the chart, each vertical line represents a single press on the lever

> **KEY TERMS**
>
> **Operant conditioning:** a form of learning in which behaviour is controlled by rewards or positive reinforcers, or by unpleasant or aversive stimuli.
> **Law of reinforcement:** the probability of a given response being produced is increased if it is followed by reward or a positive reinforcer.

Positive reinforcement: schedules of reinforcement

Humans and non-human species tend to keep doing things that are rewarded and to stop doing things that aren't rewarded. However, Skinner (1938, 1953) found some complexities in his research on operant conditioning in rats and pigeons. More specifically, he found some interesting differences in animals' response patterns depending on the precise schedule of reinforcement. The most basic schedule of reinforcement is continuous reinforcement, in which the reinforcer or reward is presented after every response. In everyday life, it is rare for members of any species to be continuously reinforced. This led Skinner to consider what happens with partial reinforcement, in which only some of the responses are rewarded. Skinner (1938) discovered four main schedules of reinforcement:

1. **Fixed ratio schedule:** every *n*th (e.g. fifth, tenth) response is rewarded. This schedule rarely occurs among animals in the wild, but human workers who receive extra money for achieving certain targets are on it.
2. **Variable ratio schedule:** every *n*th response is rewarded on average, but the gap between two rewarded responses may be very small or fairly large. Predators that dig at holes in the ground looking for prey are sometimes on this schedule, as are humans who engage in fishing or gambling.
3. **Fixed interval schedule:** the first response produced after a given interval of time (e.g. 60 seconds) is rewarded. Workers who are paid regularly every week are on this schedule—they receive reward after a given interval of time, but don't need to produce a specific response.
4. **Variable interval schedule:** on average, the first response produced after a given interval of time (e.g. 60 seconds) is rewarded. However, the actual interval is sometimes shorter than this and sometimes longer. As Gross (1996) noted, self-employed workers whose customers make payments at irregular times are rewarded at variable intervals, but they don't need to produce a specific response.

Although fruit-machine gamblers have no idea when or if they will receive a payout, they continue to play. This is an example of the most successful reinforcement—schedule—variable-ratio reinforcement.

You might imagine that continuous reinforcement (with reward available after every response) would lead to better conditioning than partial reinforcement. In fact, the opposite is the case.

recovery after extinction has occurred. There are two major types of positive reinforcers or rewards: primary reinforcers and secondary reinforcers. **Primary reinforcers** are stimuli needed for survival (e.g. food, water, sleep, air). **Secondary reinforcers** are rewarding because the person or animal has learned to associate them with primary reinforcers. Secondary reinforcers include money, praise, and attention.

[?] What are the limitations of Skinner's operant conditioning approach?

Shaping

One of the features of operant conditioning is that the required response (e.g. lever pressing) must be made *before* it can be reinforced. How can we condition

[?] Can you think of some examples of situations in everyday life involving the various schedules of reinforcement?

KEY TERMS

Fixed ratio schedule: a situation in which every *n*th response is rewarded.
Variable ratio schedule: on average every *n*th response is rewarded, but there is some variation around that figure.
Fixed interval schedule: a situation in which the first response produced after a given interval of time is rewarded or reinforced.
Variable interval schedule: on average the first response produced after a given interval of time is rewarded, but with some variation around that time interval.
Primary reinforcers: rewarding stimuli that are needed to live (e.g. food, water).
Secondary reinforcers: stimuli that are rewarding because they have been associated with primary reinforcers.

an animal to produce a complex response it wouldn't produce naturally? The answer is by means of **shaping**, in which the animal's behaviour moves slowly towards the desired response through successive approximations. Suppose we wanted to teach pigeons to play table tennis. To start with they would be rewarded for making any contact with the table-tennis ball. Over time, their actions would need to become more and more like those involved in playing table tennis to be rewarded. In this way, Skinner persuaded pigeons to play a basic form of table tennis!

Chaining

Operant conditioning can be used to produce complex sequences of behaviour. For example, suppose a rat learns that lever pressing produces food when a tone is on but not when the tone is absent. The tone becomes a **discriminative stimulus**, meaning its presence is a cue that reinforcement is available. Discriminative stimuli acquire reinforcing value, and so animals can learn to produce a given response (e.g. climbing a step) to obtain the discriminative stimulus. Thus, a rat could learn to climb a step to hear a tone that would lead to lever pressing. This learned sequence of responses is known as **chaining**. Pierrel and Sherman (1963) described an impressive case of chaining. A rat called Barnabus learned via operant conditioning to produce the following sequence of nine responses: climbing a ramp, pushing down a drawbridge, crossing a moat, climbing a staircase, crawling through a tunnel, entering an elevator, operating the elevator, raising a tiny flag, and pressing a lever for food.

Punishment: positive and negative

So far we have considered the effects of positive reinforcers or rewards on performance. However, operant conditioning can also involve unpleasant or aversive stimuli such as electric shocks or failure feedback. Humans and other species learn to behave in ways that reduce their exposure to aversive stimuli just as they learn to increase their exposure to positive reinforcers or rewards. They also learn to avoid making responses followed by the removal of positive reinforcers or reward (negative punishment).

Operant conditioning in which a response is followed by an aversive stimulus is known as positive punishment (often simply called punishment). If the aversive stimulus occurs shortly after the response, it reduces the likelihood the response will be produced in future.

Punishment can be very effective but is often applied ineffectively. For example, it is easy to punish the wrong response. Westen (1996) gives the example

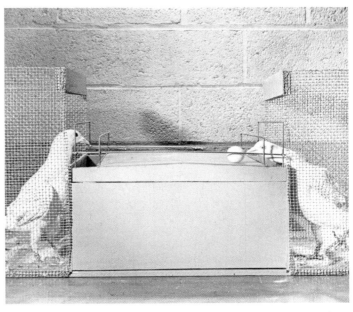

Skinner taught pigeons to play a basic form of table tennis by rewarding them every time they made contact with a table-tennis ball.

? A dog sits after being asked, you give them a treat for sitting, what type of conditioning is this?

> **KEY TERMS**
> **Shaping:** using reward or reinforcement to produce progressive changes in behaviour in a desired direction.
> **Discriminative stimulus:** a stimulus that is present when a given response will be rewarded but absent when the response will not be rewarded.
> **Chaining:** a learned sequence of responses produced by operant conditioning.

"Well, I simply trained them to give me fish by pressing this over and over again."

of someone who shouts at his dog for coming after it has been called repeatedly. The dog owner is actually punishing the desired behaviour (i.e. coming when called) rather than the undesired behaviour (i.e. refusing to come when called)! Another problem is that the animal being punished may start to fear the person delivering the punishment (due to classical conditioning) rather than fear making the undesired response.

Skinner argued that punishment can *suppress* certain responses for a while, but it doesn't produce new learning. That is sometimes the case. Estes (1944) trained two groups of rats to press a lever for food. They were then given extinction trials on which food was never available. One group only was given a strong electric shock for every lever press during the early stages of extinction. This punishment reduced the rate of responding for a while (suppression). However, in the long run the two groups produced the same number of responses, suggesting that the effects of punishment were short-lived.

Punishment often has a more lasting effect when animals can obtain positive reinforcement with some response other than the one that has been punished. For example, suppose the punished rats in the study by Estes (1944) had had access to a second lever and found that pressing that lever led to food. They would rapidly have stopped pressing the lever associated with punishment and moved to the second lever.

Avoidance learning

Nearly all drivers stop at red traffic lights because of the possibility of aversive or unpleasant stimuli in the form of an accident or trouble with the police if they do not. This is a situation in which no aversive stimulus is presented if suitable action is taken—it is an example of **avoidance learning**. Many aversive stimuli strengthen any responses that stop the aversive stimuli being presented; they are known as **negative reinforcers**.

Avoidance learning can be very effective, as was shown by Solomon and Wynne (1953). Dogs were placed in a two-compartment apparatus. A change in the lighting served as a warning that a strong electric shock was about to be presented. The dogs could avoid being shocked by jumping into the other compartment. Most dogs received a few shocks at the start of the experiment, but then generally avoided the shock for the remaining 50 or more trials.

Mowrer (1947) put forward Two-Process Learning Theory to account for avoidance learning. According to this theory, the first process involves classical conditioning. The pairing of neutral (e.g. compartment walls) and aversive stimuli (electric shock) produces conditioned fear. The second process involves operant conditioning. The avoidance

? Can you think of any situations in which avoidance learning has been incorporated into your own life?

KEY TERMS

Avoidance learning: a form of operant conditioning in which an appropriate avoidance response prevents presentation of an unpleasant or aversive stimulus.

Negative reinforcers: unpleasant or aversive stimuli that strengthen any responses that lead to the removal of those stimuli. For example, if a rat can stop electric shocks being administered by pressing a lever, the electric shocks are a negative reinforcer.

response of jumping into the other compartment is rewarded or reinforced by fear reduction.

Two-Process Learning Theory provides a plausible account of the avoidance learning. However, there are some problems with the notion that the avoidance response occurs to reduce fear. Dogs in the Solomon and Wynne (1953) study typically responded to the warning signal in about 1.5 seconds, which is probably too little time for the fear response to have developed. After the avoidance response occurred regularly, the dogs didn't behave as if they were anxious. Thus, it is hard to argue that their avoidance behaviour was motivated *only* by fear reduction.

Role in the behaviour of non-human animals: ecological perspective

You may well be thinking by now that operant conditioning is a very effective form of learning that can be used to train non-human animals to perform almost any type of behaviour. This was Skinner's view; he claimed that virtually any response could be conditioned in any stimulus situation—this is known as **equipotentiality**. In fact, the notion of equipotentiality is simply wrong. Consider the findings of Breland and Breland (1961), who trained pigs to pick up large wooden coins and insert them into a piggy bank. All went well initially, but after some time the pig "would repeatedly drop it [the coin], root it, drop it again, root it along the way, pick it up, toss it up in the air, drop it, root it some more, and so on" (Breland & Breland, 1961, p. 682). Some of the pigs began to take so long to put the coins in the piggy bank that they weren't getting enough to eat. What is going on here? Breland and Breland argued that the behaviour of the pigs can be explained by "instinctive drift":

> *Wherever an animal has strong instinctive behaviours in the area of the conditioned response, after continued running the organism will drift toward the instinctive behaviour to the detriment of the conditioned behaviour and even to the delay or preclusion of the reinforcement. (Breland & Breland, 1961, p. 683)*

Additional evidence that instinctive behaviour plays a much larger role in operant conditioning than Skinner believed was provided by Moore (1973). He took films of pigeons pecking at keys for food or water reward. Students decided what the reward was by looking at the films of the pigeons' pecking behaviour. They were correct 87% of the time. Birds pecking for food usually struck the key with an open beak, and made sharp, vigorous pecks. When pecking for water, on the other hand, the pigeons had their beak closed and there was a more sustained contact with the key. Thus, the pigeons' pecking responses were influenced by their "natural" or instinctive ways of dealing with food and water.

The above findings suggest it is useful to consider operant conditioning from the ecological perspective. This is because animals find it easier to learn forms of behaviour that enable them to cope with their natural environment. Supporting evidence was reported by Gaffan, Hansel, and Smith (1983). Rats in a T-shaped maze decided whether to turn left or right. Suppose a rat turns left and finds food at the end of that arm of the maze. According to conditioning principles, the rat has been rewarded for turning left and so should turn left on the following trial. However, in the rat's natural environment, it isn't sensible to return to a place

KEY TERM

Equipotentiality: the notion that any response can be conditioned in any stimulus situation.

HOW SCIENCE WORKS: HOW DO WE LEARN?
The traditional behaviourist theories of learning are classical and operant conditioning. You could make a PowerPoint presentation, using ICT to make the text visually interesting, e.g. with colour and movement, and with downloaded or scanned graphics. If you start with a simple explanation of each theory, you could then move on to how this could apply to a real-life example in, for instance, a child and then in an adult.

Then you could move on either by looking at alternative explanations of how we learn, or by including some in-depth variations of basic conditioning. You could even do both!

Then you might like to include factors that help us to learn—based on a small survey that you could do on family and friends by asking them what helps or hinders them when they are learning. This would suggest that learning in humans is a complex activity, and factors that affect working memory are significant.

Perhaps you could finish by asking people how they think they learn best—something we could all do with being aware of!

from which all the food has just been removed. Gaffan et al. found that rats early in training tended to avoid the arm of the maze in which they had previously found food as predicted from the ecological perspective.

Evaluation

The approach based on operant conditioning has various successes to its credit. First, operant conditioning is often very effective. The behaviour of non-human species (and humans) can be controlled by clever use of reinforcement (e.g. training of circus animals). Second, operant conditioning has been demonstrated in an amazing variety of species, including ants. Breland and Breland (1961) conditioned 38 species of animals including reindeer, whales, porpoises, and raccoons. Third, clever use of schedules of reinforcement can persuade animals to work extremely hard for food reward. For example, Kelleher (1958) used a situation in which chimpanzees had to press a key 125 times to receive a token, and had to collect 50 tokens to receive food. Thus, they produced over 6000 responses to obtain food! Fourth, techniques such as shaping and chaining have been used to produce complex behaviour the animals had never produced before in their lives.

What are the limitations of the operant conditioning approach? First, the evidence indicates strongly that Skinner's notion of equipotentiality is incorrect, as is his assumption that operant conditioning is uninfluenced by instinctive behaviour. Second, according to Skinner, the performance of a response increases when it is followed by a positive reinforcer and decreases when it is followed by a negative reinforcer. What, then, is a reinforcer? According to Skinner (1953, p. 73), "We observe the frequency of a selected response, then make an event contingent upon it and observe any change in frequency. If there is a change, we classify the event as reinforcing." That is completely circular—we only know that a stimulus is a reinforcer because it reinforces! It is not a scientific statement, because there is no way that it can be tested. Third, according to Skinner, non-

? What extraneous variables limit the operant conditioning approach?

Operant conditioning has been reported in a huge variety of animals, including reindeer, whales, and racoons!

human animals learn by performing responses that are rewarded. In fact, other forms of learning are possible. Humans often engage in observational learning—they learn simply by observing someone else being rewarded for behaving in a certain way. There is some evidence that observational learning is possible in apes. For example, Whiten (1998) found that chimpanzees learned to imitate the behaviour of a demonstrator who removed a bolt by twisting. Fourth, Skinner exaggerated the importance of *external* or environmental factors as influences on behaviour and minimised the role of *internal* factors. For example, apes have personalities and goals, and these internal factors influence their behaviour.

Evidence for Intelligence in Non-human Animals

What is the purpose of intelligence in non-human animals? As we have seen, it is important for most species to be capable of classical and operant conditioning. However, there is an additional answer to that question that applies particularly to non-human primate species, the great majority of which live in *social* groups. Among such species, what we could call "social intelligence" is really important. Individual apes or monkeys need to communicate effectively with other members of the same species to ensure they have enough food to eat and that they mate and reproduce.

"He says the downturn in world trade is adversely affecting banana supply, and warrants a reduction in interest rates".

Self-recognition

An important topic in research on human children is to assess the development of self-awareness. Much research has used a technique in which a red spot is applied to infants' noses, after which they are held up to a mirror (reviewed by Eysenck, 2004). Children between the ages of 18 and 24 months start to reach for their own nose rather than the one in the mirror, showing evidence of self-recognition or self-awareness.

A very similar technique for use with non-human animals was developed by Gallup (1970). Individually-housed chimpanzees were presented with a full-length mirror outside their cages for 10 days. For the first few days, the chimpanzees responded as if the reflection in the mirror were another chimpanzee. After that, however, the chimpanzees engaged in self-directed responses (e.g. self-grooming of parts of the body visible in the mirror). It seemed the chimpanzees had learned to recognise themselves in the mirror, which perhaps reflected their high intelligence.

Gallup (1970) followed up these intriguing observations by carrying out a systematic experiment involving the "mark test". Each chimpanzee from the previous observational study had a red mark applied to one eyebrow and the top half of the opposite ear. For some time afterwards, no mirrors were presented, and the chimpanzees rarely touched the marks. Things changed dramatically when the mirrors were re-presented. Now the chimpanzees used the reflection to guide their fingers to the marks, which they touched repeatedly. Some chimpanzees even

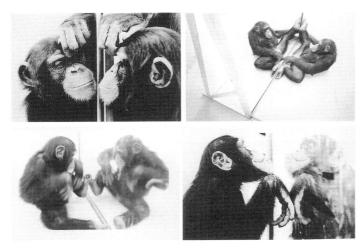

Examples of the ways in which some chimpanzees behave when they are accustomed to seeing their reflection in a mirror.

smelled their own fingers after contacting the marks. These findings with the mark test suggested strongly to Gallup that the chimpanzees had true self-recognition and probably some degree of self-awareness.

Gallup (1970) carried out the same procedures on three species of monkey, none of which showed any signs of self-recognition. Gallup, Anderson, and Shillito (2002) concluded that self-recognition on the mark test is limited to the great apes including orang-utans and bonobos as well as chimpanzees. However, not *every* ape in *every* study showed clear evidence of self-recognition, and gorillas (an ape species) show little evidence of self-recognition.

Why do monkeys fail to show self-recognition? It is not due to slow learning, because monkeys given years of almost continuous exposure to their own reflections don't show self-recognition (Gallup et al., 2002). Another possibility is that monkeys don't want to make eye-to-eye contact with their own reflection. Thus, it seems that monkeys simply lack the ability to show self-recognition.

Two species of non-human animals other than apes show self-recognition. Reiss and Marino (2001) found that two marked bottlenose dolphins used a mirror to inspect the marked parts of their body. Reiss and Marino pointed out that dolphins, great apes, and humans all have high degrees of **encephalisation** (development of cerebral cortex, especially the frontal lobes). That suggested that species have the ability for self-recognition as a consequence of a high degree of encephalisation and cognitive ability. This notion is supported by gorillas—they have a smaller frontal cortex than the other great apes, and are the only species of great ape that doesn't show self-recognition.

Plotnik, de Waal, and Reiss (2006) studied three Asian elephants called Happy, Maxine, and Patty. They all showed self-recognition, spontaneously using a mirror to touch the marks on their bodies.

It has generally been assumed that some species see their mirror image as themselves whereas other species see it as another member of the same species. De Waal, Dindo, Freeman, and Hall (2005) argued that some species occupy an intermediate position. They studied capuchin monkeys, a species that doesn't show self-recognition in the mirror test. De Waal et al. presented monkeys with their mirror image or put them in the same chamber as a same-sex stranger of the same species. The monkeys made several times more eye contact with their mirror image than with a stranger. Thus, capuchin monkeys recognise their mirror image as something of special interest and *not* simply another monkey even though they fail on the mark or mirror test.

Theoretical interpretations

How should we interpret these findings on self-recognition in apes? They suggest that apes (but not monkeys) have some level of self-awareness. This was defined by Gallup et al. (2002, p. 9) as "the ability to become the object of your own attention." Gallup et al. suggested that an important by-product of being self-aware is the ability to infer the existence of mental states in others. This ability is

KEY TERM

Encephalisation: the tendency through evolutionary development for a species to develop relatively larger brains (especially the cerebral cortex region).

often known as "Theory of Mind"—an individual's intuitive understanding of the mental states of themselves and of others, and of the differences between them (see Chapter 9).

How close is the association between passing the mark or mirror test and possessing self-awareness and even Theory of Mind? The fact that those species succeeding on the mark test typically have high levels of encephalisation suggests it is a reasonably valid measure of animal intelligence. If so, it seems likely that those species passing the mark test will possess more self-awareness (and possibly Theory of Mind) than other species.

More convincing evidence of a close link between success on the mark test and aspects of a Theory of Mind was reported by Hare, Call, and Tomasello (2001). They studied chimpanzees, a species that consistently shows self-recognition on the mark test. They carried out experiments in which a dominant and a subordinate chimpanzee competed for food. In one experiment, the subordinate chimpanzee saw the dominant chimpanzee was informed, uninformed, or misinformed about the location of food. If the subordinate monkeys understood something about the mental states of the dominant monkeys, they should have been much more likely to retrieve the food when the dominant monkeys were uninformed or misinformed rather than informed. That is precisely what Hare et al. found.

There are also various reasons why the association of success on the mark or mirror test and possessing self-awareness may *not* be very close. First, members of a given species might possess self-awareness but fail the mark or mirror test. Vervet monkeys, baboons, and macaques all fail the mirror test but possess some social awareness. Members of all three species recognise other group members as individuals, recognise dominance rank orders, and behave as if they recognise their own special place within those rank orders.

Second, members of a species might pass the mark or mirror test even with a very limited level of self-awareness. Alas, we simply don't know precisely *what* the great apes are thinking. There is a danger of attributing human characteristics or thoughts to non-human animals; this is known as **anthropomorphism**. If you were given the mark test, you would probably look into the mirror and think something like, "Goodness me, how did that mark get on my face?" We can't be sure that the great apes think something similar when given the mark test.

The success or failure of any given species on the mark test provides an approximate indication of its general intelligence or cognitive ability. In addition, those species showing self-recognition on the mark test generally show signs of some limited understanding of the mental states of others. Those species showing self-recognition on the mark test (i.e. great apes, dolphins, and elephants) are precisely those having the most empathy or sympathetic concern for the well-being of other members of the same species. Apes (but not monkeys) provide consolation to victims of aggression by putting an arm around the victim's shoulder. Elephants show empathy by trying to physically support or lift injured elephants. The evidence is least clear for dolphins. However, they are a very social species and need to make co-operative decisions about when to fish and when to sleep.

What causes this association between self-recognition and empathy? According to de Waal et al. (2005), an emotional understanding or empathy for others is much easier to achieve if the members of a species can distinguish clearly between themselves and other members of the same species. Support for this hypothesis comes from the study of human development. As de Waal et al. pointed out, the first signs of self-recognition on the mark test in young children occur at the same time as they begin to adopt the perspective of other people.

Evaluation

Research on self-recognition in non-human animals has several strengths. First, the mark test provides a valid method for assessing the presence or absence of self-recognition in any species. Second, the finding that most species showing self-recognition have a high degree of encephalisation and cognitive ability suggests that self-recognition reflects a species' level of intelligence. Third, self-recognition and self-awareness are associated with some ability to infer others' mental states. This includes knowing what others have and haven't seen and some empathy for other members of the same species. Fourth, brain-imaging research suggests that the same brain areas are involved in self-recognition and in inferring mental states in others.

What are the limitations of research in this area? First, some species failing the mark test show other evidence of possessing some social awareness. Second, we don't know precisely what animals passing the mark test are thinking when they touch the mark on their own body. Third, it has often been assumed that self-recognition is an all-or-none phenomenon. In fact, however, an intermediate state is possible (de Waal et al., 2005). Fourth, while the evidence suggests that great apes, elephants, and dolphins possess some ability to understand the mental states of other members of the same species, we must avoid exaggerating the extent of this ability. It is undoubtedly much less than that of humans.

Social learning

Members of most primate species spend much of their time in social groups. As a result, social intelligence (i.e. intelligence applied to the social world) is especially important. Much of the ability of primates to function effectively in social groups is based on social learning. **Social learning** is learning that occurs within a social context, and can involve various processes (e.g. observational learning; imitation). There are numerous forms of social learning. Two examples are learning from others about the locations of productive foraging patches or how to avoid the place in which a predator is lurking.

Whiten and van Schaik (2007) distinguished between social learning having only short-lasting effects and social learning leading on to more lasting effects in the form of traditions and culture. What is a tradition? **Tradition** is "a distinctive behaviour pattern shared by two or more individuals in a social unit, which persists over time and that new practitioners acquire in part through socially aided learning" (Fragaszy & Perry, 2003, p. xiii). A culture develops when a social group possesses numerous traditions. Whiten and van Schaik (2007) claimed that some species (especially chimpanzees and other primates) can acquire traditions and even culture, but only the human species has developed complex cultures.

Findings

Reader and Laland (2002) assessed the importance of social learning within many primate species. They assembled information from 116 primate species on frequencies of social learning, innovation, and tool use. They also considered executive brain ratio, defined as the ratio of the executive brain (neocortex + striatum) to the brainstem. There were moderately high positive correlations across the 116 species between executive brain ratio and each of social learning, innovation, and tool use, with the highest correlation being between executive brain ratio and social learning.

Observational learning is a basic form of social learning. Convincing evidence of observational learning in chimpanzees was reported by Bonnie, Horner, Whiten, and de Waal (2007). One group of chimpanzees observed another chimpanzee collect, transport, and deposit plastic tokens into a bucket to gain a food reward at a different location. In a second group, chimpanzees observed the same sequence of actions, but this time the plastic tokens were put into a pipe. After that, the chimpanzees were rewarded

Orang-utans' use of twigs as tools to extract seeds from trees shows a degree social learning.

for placing plastic tokens into the bucket or the pipe. The chimpanzees mostly placed the tokens in the same place (i.e. bucket or pipe) as the one used by the chimpanzee they had observed previously. This shows observational learning, which may be an important form of social learning in chimpanzees.

Van Schaik (2006) found evidence of social learning when studying orang-utans on the Indonesian island of Sumatra in a naturalistic observational study. These orang-utans used various tools for two main reasons. First, they used them to hunt for termites, ants, and honey. Second, they used tools to extract seeds from trees. They did this by stripping the bark off short twigs, which they then held in their mouth and inserted into cracks in the tree.

We have seen that chimpanzees and orang-utans are capable of social learning. How does their social learning compare with that of young human children? Herrmann, Melis, and Tomasello (2007) assessed the ability of chimpanzees, orang-utans, and children aged 2½ to exhibit various cognitive skills for dealing with the physical world and the social world. Using a stick to retrieve a reward that was out of reach was one task used to assess skills in the physical world. Solving a simple problem by seeing the solution demonstrated involved social learning and was a task used to assess skills in the social world.

What did Herrmann et al. (2007) find? First, young children and chimpanzees had very similar cognitive skills for dealing with the physical world, with orang-utans lagging somewhat behind. Second, the situation was very different with regard to skills for dealing with the social world, where the children performed much better than the chimpanzees and the orang-utans. This was especially true of social learning.

Herrmann et al. concluded that the findings supported the cultural intelligence hypothesis. According to this hypothesis, human adults have excellent cognitive skills, "due largely to children's early emerging, specialised skills for absorbing the accumulated skilful practices and knowledge of their social group" (Herrmann et al., 2007, p. 1360).

Evaluation

There is plentiful evidence for social learning in many non-human species from laboratory and from naturalistic studies. There is also evidence that species with a large executive brain ratio (ratio of neocortex and striatum to brainstem size) tend to exhibit the most social learning. However, there is the issue of causality here—does a large executive brain ratio promote social learning or does extensive social learning lead to an enhanced ratio?

In spite of the evidence for much social learning (especially in other primates), human social learning far exceeds that of other species. As Herrmann et al. (2007) found, social learning—even in 2½-year-old children—is substantially greater than that of other species. Humans are probably the only species in which social learning is so great that complex cultures have evolved.

Machiavellian intelligence

We have just seen that numerous species show social learning. In addition, those species that seem to be the most intelligent generally engage in more social learning than others. *What* do the members of a species need to learn to cope successfully with living in social groups? Many social skills are basically *positive* (e.g. co-operation; forming coalitions). However, other social skills are more *negative* (e.g. cheating; lying).

One of the most influential approaches focusing on negative social skills is the Machiavellian intelligence hypothesis (Byrne & Whiten, 1988, 1997). According to this hypothesis, members of species living in permanent social groups need to evolve an ability to out-wit others within the group. This can be achieved by means of **Machiavellian intelligence**—the ability to manipulate the social environment effectively by behaving in ways that deceive others. This is tactical deception and is defined as "acts from the normal repertoire of the agent, deployed such that another individual is likely to misinterpret what the acts signify, to the advantage of the agent" (Byrne & Whiten, 1997). An individual animal can gain an important advantage over others by deceiving other group members about his/her real intentions. However, it must at the same time be sensitive to deception by others. Machiavellian intelligence is fairly complex, because you can only successfully deceive others when you have a reasonable understanding of what they are thinking and/or feeling.

Findings

Non-human primates engage in several forms of behaviour that deceive others (i.e. tactical deception). Subordinate chimpanzees avoid giving food calls that might attract dominant chimpanzees to compete for the food, macaques hide themselves away from potential competitors, and chimpanzees lead approaching dominant chimpanzees away from hidden food (reviewed by Hare, Call, & Tomasello, 2006).

Is the tactical deception shown by primates intentional in that it involves a deliberate attempt to manipulate others? It may simply involve learning that positive reinforcement in the form of food is more likely to be forthcoming if they behave in certain ways. Most early research suggested that non-human primates are *not* capable of intentional deception. Woodruff and Premack (1979) trained four chimpanzees to indicate to humans where hidden food was located. After that, they introduced two experimenters. One experimenter shared any food that was found with the chimpanzees but the other one (who wore a mask) did not. Only two of the chimpanzees learned to avoid indicating the correct food location to the masked experimenter, and it took them dozens of trials. Thus, learning to deceive was a very slow process, and the chimpanzees may use the mask as a cue not to indicate the food location without really intending to deceive.

More recent research suggests that chimpanzees *can* engage in intentional deception. In research by Hare et al. (2006), chimpanzees decided which of two food items (pieces of banana) to reach for. They were in competition with a human experimenter who pulled the food out of reach if he saw them reach for it. In one experiment, the approach to one food item was visible to the experimenter whereas the approach to the other item was not. The chimpanzees preferred to be deceptive by using the route hidden from the experimenter's view.

Hare et al. (2006) reported more striking findings in a second experiment. The chimpanzees chose to move away from the food before approaching it when the experimenter could see them move away from the food but couldn't see them approach it. However, they did *not* move away from the food initially if the experimenter couldn't see them move away. The chimpanzees rapidly engaged in intentional deception when it was a good strategy.

According to the Machiavellian hypothesis, non-human primates have much larger brains than other mammals of the same size because they engage in so much complex social behaviour including deception. A reasonable prediction is that those primate species engaging in the most deception should have larger brains than those engaging in less deception. As the neocortex is the most important part of the brain for cognitive functioning, we might predict that a species' tendency to engage in deception should be positively associated with neocortex size. Byrne and Corp (2004) analysed data on brain measurements and deception from 18 non-human primate species, finding a moderately strong correlation or association between neocortex size and use of deceptive tactics.

Evaluation

The Machiavellian hypothesis has several strengths. First, it is indisputable that social intelligence is of major importance to virtually all primate species including humans. Second, tactical deception (which is sometimes intentional) is found in several species of apes. Third, as predicted by the Machiavellian hypothesis, there is a positive association between a species' tendency to engage in deception and the size of its neocortex. This suggests that the ability to deceive others of the same species *is* an important aspect of primate intelligence.

What are the limitations with the Machiavellian hypothesis? First, there is excessive emphasis on the notion that the gains obtained by those who use deception are achieved at a cost to those manipulated. This is a narrow view—members of social groups in most non-human primate species devote much time and effort to *mutual co-operation* in which the donor and the recipient both benefit. Second, there are often problems of interpretation in understanding why an animal has behaved in a misleading way. In particular, it is generally difficult to know whether it was being intentionally deceptive. Third, the correlation or association between neocortex size and use of deception is as predicted by the Machiavellian hypothesis. However, such evidence is only correlational and doesn't tell us what causes what. Primates may develop deceptive strategies because they have a relatively large neocortex, or they may through evolution develop a larger neocortex because deception is needed for survival and reproduction.

> **EXAM HINT**
> Note that the research evidence on the relationship between Machiavellian intelligence and brain size has a number of limitations:
>
> - it ignores mutual co-operation
> - the interpretation may be biased and anthropomorphic
> - it is difficult to know if the deception was intentional
> - the research provides correlational evidence so cause and effect cannot be assumed
> - it is reductionist because other factors will also influence brain size.

SECTION SUMMARY
Animal Learning and Intelligence

Classical conditioning

❖ In classical conditioning, an association is formed between the conditioned stimulus and the unconditioned stimulus.

❖ The main phenomena associated with classical conditioning include generalisation, discrimination, experimental extinction, and spontaneous recovery.

❖ According to Rescorla and Wagner's (1972) model, conditioning occurs when the conditioned stimulus predicts the imminent arrival of the unconditioned stimulus.

❖ According to the ecological approach, animals have a biological readiness to associate some stimuli (e.g. those relating to food poisoning) but not others.

❖ Advocates of the ecological approach argue that the conditioned stimulus and the unconditioned stimulus are often different features of the same object. When that happens, conditioning is typically very strong and long-lasting. The conditioned stimulus often indicates when the unconditioned stimulus will occur.

Operant conditioning

❖ The probability of a given response being produced increases when it is followed by positive reinforcement.

❖ There are four main schedules of reinforcement: fixed ratio, variable ratio, fixed interval, and variable interval.

❖ Punishment can be very effective in reducing the likelihood of a given response being produced, especially when animals can produce an alternative, rewarded response.

❖ Avoidance learning is very effective because it reduces the animal's anxiety level.

❖ Skinner mistakenly believed in equipotentiality, the notion that any response can be conditioned in any situation. It is much preferable to consider conditioning from the ecological perspective.

Self-recognition

❖ Apes, dolphins, and elephants have shown evidence of self-recognition on the mark test.

❖ Species showing self-recognition generally have high degrees of encephalisation.

❖ Species showing self-recognition often have the most empathy and concern for other members of the same species.

Social learning

❖ Social learning is generally greatest in species having a relatively large neocortex.

❖ Several species show evidence of social learning in form of observational learning.

❖ Social learning is far greater in human children than in other primate species.

Machiavellian intelligence

❖ According to the Machiavellian intelligence hypothesis, members of species living in social groups need to be able to out-wit others.

❖ Primate species engaging in the most deception tend to have larger neocortex size.

❖ It is difficult to decide whether primates' deceptive actions are intentionally so.

EVOLUTION OF INTELLIGENCE

As we have seen, intelligence is the ability to deal effectively and adaptively with the environment. During the course of human evolution, those individuals who were more intelligent were more likely to have survived and reproduced. In this section, we will focus on the evolution of human intelligence. In so doing, we will rely in part on evidence from other species to work out how human intelligence developed over millions of years. After that, we will focus on the genetic and environmental factors associated with intelligence, including the influence of culture.

Evolutionary Factors in the Development of Human Intelligence

Intelligence must have developed because it was an adaptive ability for any individual to possess. Could it be that individuals with more intelligence had greater reproductive success? Why might this be the case? Of particular importance, why has the human brain grown substantially in size in the course of evolution? There are several possible explanations. First, our ancestors must have devoted much of their time and effort to ensuring they had plentiful food supplies. According to ecological theories, brain size and the development of intelligence in any given species depended on how challenging it was for that species to have adequate access to food. Second, many primate species (including the human species) are essentially social and live in groups. According to social theories, the information-processing demands of operating effectively in social groups were important in the development of intelligence during the course of evolution.

We will shortly consider the above two theories. Before that, however, we will focus on the issue of brain size and its relation to intelligence.

Brain size

Primates have brains about *twice* as large as those of other mammals of similar size. There must presumably be some substantial adaptive advantage associated with these large brains, because large brains incur high metabolic costs. How can we explain the size of primate brains? Most primate species engage in considerably more social behaviour than non-primate mammals. Successful social interactions require a large brain able to engage in complex processing, including the ability to compete effectively against members of the group. For example, a primate who discovers a good source of food may be well advised to avoid revealing his/her discovery.

If we want to understand the evolution of human intelligence, we must consider above all else the human brain. However, we mustn't regard all its parts as being of equal relevance. MacLean (1970) argued that the human brain is a three-layered (or triune) system with each of the layers representing an important evolutionary development. The oldest of the three layers (the reptilian brain) is deep down in the brainstem. It is involved in basic functions such as breathing and eating. This layer is irrelevant to human intelligence.

Later on in evolutionary history, a second layer became wrapped around the first one. This layer is involved in preservation of the species, being concerned with functions such as pleasure seeking, emotions, feeding, fighting, and escape from pain. This layer is mostly irrelevant to human intelligence. Finally, there is

The cerebral cortex

The outer layer of the human brain is called the cerebral cortex. When you look at the brain, it is mostly cortex that you see but it is only 2mm thick. The cerebral cortex has a bumpy, folded appearance and it is these bumps that greatly increase its volume. If you flattened the cortex out it would cover a square measuring 50×50cm. It is grey in colour because it contains mostly cell bodies, rather than the axons that link one area of the brain to another.

The cortex is what distinguishes the brain of mammals from the brain of lower animals, and the human brain has a far larger frontal cortex than other mammals (darker areas in diagram below). The cortex has great importance for our ability to perceive, think, and use language, and is highly related to intelligence.

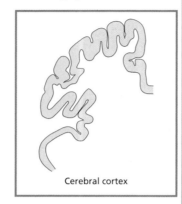

Cerebral cortex

Adapted from Fuster (1989).

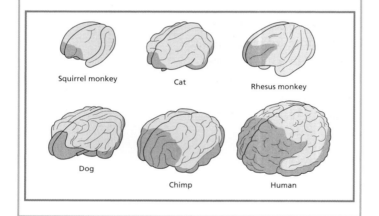

Squirrel monkey

Cat

Rhesus monkey

Dog

Chimp

Human

the third and most recent layer in evolutionary terms. This layer includes the neocortex or cerebral cortex and is overwhelmingly the most important for intelligence and thinking. We can see how crucial the neocortex is to human intelligence by considering its size relative to the more primitive parts of the brain in humans and other primates. As Dunbar (1998) pointed out, the neocortex is no larger than the medulla (part of the reptilian brain involved in breathing and swallowing) in insectivores (animals deriving nourishment from insects). However, it is 20–50 times larger than the medulla in the anthropoids (apes). In humans, the neocortex is an amazing 105 times larger than the medulla!

MacLean's (1982) notion of the triune brain provides a useful overview of the main divisions of the brain. However, his views are inevitably oversimplified given the brain's overall complexity. The brain can't really be neatly subdivided into just three parts. In addition, there are important differences within the different parts of each layer. For example, within the neocortex there are areas specialised for visual processing and other areas specialised for language processing.

The size of the human brain isn't that impressive in some ways, being only one quarter the size of the elephant brain. However, things look more promising if we consider the so-called "encephalisation quotient". This is the actual brain size of a species divided by its expected brain size on the basis of its body mass (Jerison, 1973). Humans score seven on this measure, more than any other species.

When we consider the course of evolution, we discover that the human brain has increased dramatically in size. According to Stewart (1997), seven million years ago our ancestors had a brain that was only 400 cubic centimetres (cc). Brain size didn't change much for millions of years after that. However, by the time we get to the period 2½ million years ago with *Homo habilis*, the brain size had almost doubled to about 700cc. *Homo habilis* then evolved into *Homo erectus*, who had a brain size of about 1000cc and had a socially complex life. Over the past 500,000 years, human brain size increased again and is now about 1350cc. You might imagine it is a significant advantage to have a large brain, but as mentioned earlier real metabolic costs are involved. For example, our brains consume 20% of the total energy we produce.

When psychologists first studied the links between brain size and intelligence, they found practically no relationship. However, the findings were based on inaccurate estimates of brain size (e.g. skull size). Nowadays we can obtain good measures of brain size in *living* individuals by using brain-imaging techniques such as magnetic resonance imaging (MRI). Using MRI, there is a moderate association or correlation between brain size and intelligence. McDaniel (2005) reported an average correlation between brain size and IQ of +.33 across 37 samples. Note that this is correlational evidence, and we can't use correlations to prove causes. Thus, we don't know whether possession of a large brain helps to cause high intelligence.

McDaniel's evidence is correlational. Are there any disadvantages of correlational studies?

Racial differences

Rushton and Ankney (1995) argued from MRI evidence that Mongoloid (Asian) Americans had larger brains than Caucasoid (white) Americans, who in turn had larger brains than Negroid (black) Americans. Very controversially and divisively, Rushton and Ankney claimed that these group differences corresponded to group differences in intelligence—the tested intelligence of Mongoloid Americans is higher than that of Caucasoid Americans, which in turn is higher than that of Negroid Americans.

Rushton and Ankney (1995) claimed we can explain the above differences by focusing on human evolutionary history. The ancestors of Negroid Americans lived in the warmest conditions, whereas the ancestors of Mongoloid Americans had the coldest conditions. If living in cold conditions requires more problem solving (e.g. findings shelter, gathering food), we can provide an evolutionary account of racial differences in brain size. However, this account is unsupported by any real evidence.

There are several very serious limitations with this whole approach. First, the whole concept of race is complex and controversial. Second, estimates of brain size *within* any given group often vary considerably, thus shedding doubt on the value of these estimates. Third, it is offensive and invalid to relate racial differences in brain size to differences in tested intelligence. Group differences in tested intelligence are almost entirely due to group differences in discrimination and environmental opportunities.

Ecological demands

Dunbar (1998) discussed *three* ecological hypotheses that emphasised problems primate species have to cope with when seeking food for survival. First, there is the dietary hypothesis. According to this hypothesis, primate species eating food that is distributed patchily need larger brains than primate species eating food that is more widely available. The reason they need larger brains is because of the greater demands on their memory systems when trying to locate food. In general, fruits are more patchily distributed than leaves. Thus, frugivores (fruit-eating primates and other species) should have larger brains than folivores (leaf-eating primates and other species).

Frugivorous primates tend to have larger adult brains relative to body size than is the case with folivorous primates (Clutton-Brock & Harvey, 1980). However, the dietary hypothesis received much less support from Dunbar's (1998) research. He considered the relationship between percentage of fruit in the diet and relative size of the neocortex (of key importance for intelligence) in 20 primate species. According to the dietary hypothesis, these two measures should have correlated strongly with each other. In fact, there was practically no correlation. However, Dunbar focused only on percentage of fruit in the diet. Perhaps more positive findings would have been obtained if he had considered the *importance* of fruit in each species' diet. For example, a certain fruit may provide essential nutrients for a given species even though it doesn't account for a high percentage of the diet.

Second, there is the mental maps hypothesis. According to this hypothesis, species that cover a wide area in their search for food (large range size) and/or spend a large proportion of the day foraging will have larger brains than those species that cover only a small area. The reason is that the former species need large-scale mental maps that impose additional memory loads on them. However, Dunbar (1998) found across 20 primate species that there was no correlation between range size and the size of the neocortex.

Third, there is the extractive foraging hypothesis. According to this hypothesis, primate species vary in terms of how easy or difficult it is for them to extract food. Species having difficulty in extracting food (e.g. they have to use tools to gain access to it) should have larger brains than those having immediate access to food. Dunbar (1998) divided primate species into four categories based on their use of extractive foraging: skilled; unskilled; specialised; and non-extractive foragers. Chimpanzees provide a good example of skilled extractive foragers: "Found stones are used to hammer open nuts on wood or stone anvils, sticks are used to pick up ants, stems and vines to 'fish' for termites in their mounds or ants" (Byrne, 2004, p. 34). Dunbar reported across 20 primate species that there was no relationship between complexity of extractive foraging and relative neocortex size. However, a problem with testing the extractive foraging hypothesis is that it is hard to define the difficulty of extractive foraging.

Parker and Gibson (1979) reported little relationship between complexity of extractive foraging (e.g. tool use) and intelligence across several mammal species. They argued that tool use in intelligent primate species should be thought of as a *consequence* rather than a *cause* of their high level of intelligence. However, it is hard to use correlational evidence to decide between these two possibilities.

Parker and Gibson (1979) argued that tool use in primates, such as using long sticks for extractive foraging, is a consequence rather than a cause of their high level of intelligence.

Evaluation

It seems reasonable to assume that species that have difficulty in accessing the food they need would need larger brains and more intelligence than other species. That assumption is incorporated into the dietary, mental maps, and extractive foraging hypotheses. However, as we have seen, there is very little evidence to support any of these hypotheses in studies focusing on mammals generally or on primates.

Why have these hypotheses failed? As we will see, it is likely that dealing with social problems is much more of an intellectual challenge for most primate species than the task of finding food. In other words, the hypotheses are focusing on the wrong type of challenge. However, there are other possibilities. First, neocortex size is not a direct measure of a species' intelligence, and so we may not be assessing intelligence very well. Second, it is difficult to compare the cognitive or intellectual demands of finding food across numerous species leading very different lives in very different kinds of environment.

Social complexity

We saw earlier that one aspect of social complexity (the need to use deception to out-wit other members of the species) was emphasised by the Machiavellian intelligence hypothesis. We also saw that those primate species using the most deception tend to have relatively large neocortex size (Byrne & Corp, 2004). The Machiavellian hypothesis has been broadened and extended into the social brain hypothesis (e.g. Shultz & Dunbar, 2007). According to this hypothesis, intelligence and brain size will tend to be greater in those species having complex social structures. More specifically, "The social brain hypothesis implies that constraints on group size arise from the information-processing capacity of the primate brain, and that the neocortex plays a major role in this" (Dunbar, 1998, p. 184). In other words, you need a large brain to cope with complicated social systems.

How does the social brain hypothesis differ from the Machiavellian intelligence hypothesis? The main difference is that the social brain hypothesis claims that there are several aspects to social complexity. The need for deception is one aspect, but others include the formation of coalitions, co-operative strategies, and mating strategies.

Findings

The social brain hypothesis predicts that species having complex social structures will have larger brains and be more intelligent. It is not easy to assess the complexity of social structures within a species, but Dunbar (1998) used size of social group as an approximate measure. He reported a moderately strong correlation between neocortex size and social group size across 20 primate species, thus supporting the social brain hypothesis. Dunbar carried out additional analyses to decide which processes within the neocortex are of most importance to primates in maintaining complex social structures. What really mattered was the part of the neocortex concerned with manipulating information about social relationships.

Much research has followed Dunbar (1998) in using group size as a measure of social complexity. However, it is clear that it is only an indirect measure. Recently, researchers have looked at alternative ways of looking at social complexity. Schillaci (2006) found among several primate species that those having the largest relative brain sizes had monogamous mating systems. Superficially, it looks as if this finding doesn't fit the social brain hypothesis. However, it can be argued speculatively that primate monogamy involves more complex social skills than alternative mating strategies.

Perez-Barberia, Shultz, and Dunbar (2007) carried out a very thorough test of the social brain hypothesis. They studied 206 species of mammals and found strong associations between a species' level of social activity and its relative brain size. They also found evidence that evolutionary changes in relative brain size were closely linked with changes in social activity.

What can mammals with a large neocortex do that those with a small neocortex cannot? Byrne and Bates (2007) argued that we shouldn't exaggerate their social skills. According to them, "Enlargement of mammalian neocortex confers abilities of highly discriminating perception, rapid learning in social contexts, and efficient long-term memory. The great bulk of the 'smart' social tactics of non-human primates and other species can be understood entirely in these terms" (Byrne & Bates, 2007, p. R720).

> **EXAM HINT**
>
> Make sure you can explain why social complexity may have had more impact on the evolution of human intelligence than the challenge of finding food.

Evaluation

Much evidence (including that on the more specific Machiavellian intelligence hypothesis) supports the social brain hypothesis. It makes sense to argue that the most important reason for the development of human intelligence was to cope with the intellectual challenges associated with successful and cohesive social living. When we consider numerous primate species, several aspects of social complexity (e.g. group size; deception; mating strategy) predict brain size (especially relative neocortex size). It is thus unlikely to be a coincidence that the human species has both relatively the largest neocortex of any species and is also the most intensely social species.

What are the limitations with the social brain hypothesis? First, the notion of "social complexity" is rather vague, and there are doubts as to the validity of assessing it by using measures such as group size or mating strategy. Second, we don't have any intelligence test that can be applied to all primate species, and so we have to rely on indirect measures such as relative neocortex size. Third, as Barrett and Henzi (2005, p. 1867) pointed out, the social brain hypothesis is in danger of being circular: "Primates have large brains because their social lives are cognitively demanding, and their lives are cognitively demanding because they have large brains that allow them to produce more complex forms of social behaviour." The fact that the evidence is correlational means we can't establish what causes what.

Role of Genetic and Environmental Factors

At the most general level, there are only two possible reasons why some people are more or less intelligent than others: heredity and environment. Heredity consists of each person's genetic endowment, the instructions that tell your body to produce hair of a particular colour or blood of a particular blood group or an easy or difficult temperament. Environment consists of the situations and experiences encountered by people during their lives. Individual differences in intelligence depend on both heredity (i.e. genetic factors) and environment. As we will see, many psychologists have tried to determine the relative importance of genetic factors or heredity and of environment in influencing individual differences in intelligence. However, the Canadian psychologist Donald Hebb argued that this issue is essentially meaningless. He claimed it is like asking whether a field's area is determined more by its length or by its width. Of course, its area depends equally on both length and width. In similar fashion, Hebb argued, intelligence depends equally on both heredity and environment.

Hebb's argument is less convincing than it sounds. Even though it is clear that the area of a field depends equally on its length and width, we can still reasonably ask whether the areas of different fields vary more because of differences in their lengths or in their widths. In the same way, we can ask whether individual differences in intelligence depend more on differences in genetic endowment or on environmental differences.

Those who believe in the importance of heredity draw a distinction between the genotype and the phenotype. The **genotype** is the genetic instructions that each individual is given at conception. These instructions offer a blueprint for characteristics and behaviour that are meaningless unless they can be expressed

KEY TERM

Genotype: an individual's potential in the form of genes.

Intelligence, nature, and nurture

It has been widely reported that breast-fed babies turn out as more intelligent than formula-fed infants; implying that breast milk confers some added abilities to the developing brain. There is no doubt that human breast milk is designed for optimum development of human infants, but a recent study (Caspi et al., 2007) suggests that the benefits might be nature as well as nurture. This study looked at a gene called *FADS2*, which is involved in the metabolism of fatty acids. These fatty acids are present in breast milk and other foods and are essential for the development of, among other things, healthy brain cells. It was found that 90% of the 1000 New Zealanders and 2200 British people tested had the common form of the *FADS2* gene, and of these, those who had been breast-fed scored 6.8 points higher on IQ tests than those who were formula-fed, independent of the mother's socio-economic group or IQ. The 10% who had the rarer form of this gene scored the same whether they were breast- or bottle-fed. So, whereas this supports the "breast is best" argument for infant feeding for the majority of babies, there could be a definite nature as well as nurture input here.

through the environment. The **phenotype** consists of an individual's *observable* characteristics. So far as intelligence is concerned, we can't assess the genotype. All we can do is assess the phenotype by administering an intelligence test.

There is an issue of great importance that needs to be considered at this point. It is perhaps natural to think of genetic factors or heredity and environment as having entirely separate or *independent* effects on intelligence. However, the reality is very different, because our genetic makeup influences the types of environmental experiences we have. We can see how implausible it is to assume that heredity and environment have entirely separate effects by applying that dubious assumption to basketball performance:

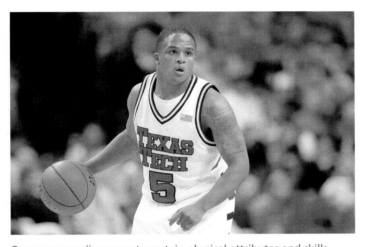

Our genes predispose us to certain physical attributes and skills, and thus influence the environments we choose to inhabit. Those predisposed to sporting prowess are more likely to indulge that predisposition by immersing themselves in the environment that supports their potential. Hence tall, well co-ordinated individuals are more likely than their shorter, less co-ordinated peers to become professional basketball players.

Good coaching, practising, preoccupation with basketball, and all other environmental factors that influence performance must be unrelated to whether genes contribute to someone being tall, slim, and well co-ordinated. For this to be true, players must be selected at random for the varsity basketball team and get the benefits of professional coaching and intense practice, without regard to build, quickness, and degree of interest (Dickens & Flynn, 2001).

In fact, of course, individuals whose genes predispose them to be outstanding at basketball are more likely to put themselves into an environment supporting excellent basketball performance than are those whose genes do not.

We can apply precisely the same logic directly to intelligence. No-one believes that the probability that a given individual chooses to read hundreds of books or go to university has nothing to do with his/her levels of genetic ability. In fact,

KEY TERM

Phenotype: an individual's observable characteristics, depending in part on his/her genotype.

individuals with the highest levels of genetic ability are much more likely to seek out intellectually demanding situations than those with less genetic ability. Thus, environmental factors are *not* independent of genetic factors but rather serve to *magnify* or exaggerate the effects of individual differences in heredity.

Plomin (1990) identified three types of interdependence between genetic factors and environment:

1. *Active covariation*: occurs when children of differing genetic ability look for situations reinforcing their genetic differences (e.g. children of high genetic ability reading numerous books).
2. *Passive covariation*: occurs when parents of high genetic ability provide a more stimulating environment than parents of lower genetic ability.
3. *Reactive environment*: occurs when an individual's genetically influenced behaviour helps to determine how he/she is treated by other people.

Evidence: twin studies

Twin studies are the most popular method of assessing the relative importance of genetic factors and environment in determining individual differences in intelligence. There are two kinds of twin: monozygotic twins and dizygotic twins. **Monozygotic (MZ) twins** derive from the same fertilised ovum (egg) and have essentially identical genotypes, and so are often called identical twins. Dizygotic (DZ) twins derive from two different fertilised ova (eggs), and so their genotypes are no more similar than those of ordinary siblings. Dizygotic twins are sometimes called fraternal twins.

What would we expect to find in a twin study? If genetic factors influence individual differences in intelligence, identical twins should be more alike in intelligence than fraternal twins. In contrast, if environmental factors are all-important, identical twins should be no more alike than fraternal twins.

The degree of similarity in intelligence shown by pairs of twins is usually reported in the form of correlations. A correlation of +1.00 would mean that both twins in a pair have essentially the same IQs, whereas a correlation of 0.00 would mean there is no relationship between the IQs of twins. Bouchard and McGue (1981; see the box on the next page) reviewed 111 studies, and reported that the mean correlation for identical twins was +.86 compared to +.60 for fraternal twins. McCartney, Harris, and Bernieri (1990) reported similar findings from a later analysis of numerous studies: the mean correlation for identical twins was +.81 compared to +.59 for fraternal twins.

On the face of it, the above findings indicate that individual differences in intelligence depend to a fair extent on genetic factors. However, there are various reasons why the interpretation of the findings is complicated. First, it is often assumed that the degree of environmental similarity experienced by identical twins is the same as that experienced by fraternal twins. However, this assumption is not correct. Identical twins are treated in a more similar fashion than fraternal twins in the following ways: parental treatment, playing together, spending time together, dressing in a similar style, and being taught by the same teachers (Loehlin & Nichols, 1976). Fraternal twins are especially likely to be treated differently if one is a boy and the other is a girl. However, most twin studies focus only on same-sex fraternal twins.

KEY TERM

Monozygotic (MZ) twins: identical twins having the same genetic make-up.

Second, there is the prenatal environment. All fraternal twins have separate placentas in the womb, whereas two-thirds of identical twins share a placenta. As a result, the prenatal environment of most identical twins is more similar than that of fraternal twins. Identical twins sharing a single placenta are more similar in intelligence than those having separate placentas (Phelps, Davis, & Schwartz, 1997). Thus, the greater similarity in IQ between identical twins than fraternal ones may depend in part on the greater similarity of prenatal environment for most identical twins.

Identical twins are relatively rare, and identical twins brought up in separate families are obviously even rarer. However, they are of particular value in assessing the roles of heredity and environment in determining individual differences in intelligence. Identical twins brought up apart should be very similar to each other in IQ if genetic factors are very important. In contrast, those favouring an environmentalist position would argue that placing twins in different environments should ensure they aren't similar in intelligence.

In their review, Bouchard and McGue (1981) found that the mean correlation coefficient for identical twins brought up apart was +.72. This seems to provide fairly convincing evidence for the importance of both genetic and environmental factors. The finding that the correlation is higher than that for fraternal twins brought up together suggests the importance of genetic factors. The finding that the correlation (+.72) is lower than that for identical twins (+.86) suggests the importance of environmental factors.

Monozygotic twins tend to experience a greater degree of environmental similarity than dizygotic twins.

Bouchard and McGue's (1981) family studies of intelligence

Relationship	Mean correlation
Identical twins reared together	+.86
Identical twins reared apart	+.72
Fraternal twins reared together	+.60
Siblings reared together	+.47
Siblings reared apart	+.24
Single parent—offspring reared together	+.42
Single parent—offspring reared apart	+.22
Half-siblings	+.31
Cousins	+.15
Adoptive parent and adopted child	+.19

In general terms, relatives who have greater genetic similarity tend to be more similar in IQ. However, relatives with greater genetic similarity tend to live in more similar environments than those with less genetic similarity, which makes it hard to interpret the findings.

However, there are problems with the evidence. Many identical twins brought up apart were brought up in separate branches of the same family, and so their environments may have been fairly similar. Other identical twins were brought up together for several years before being separated. However, Bouchard et al. (1990) found that this may not be a serious problem. They studied more than 40 adult identical twin pairs separated at a mean age of 5 months. Despite this, their IQs correlated +.75. This is still much lower than the figure for identical twins brought up together.

EXAM HINT

Consider how the interaction of nature–nurture is explained more fully by Plomin's (1990) pathways of interaction: reactive covariation, passive covariation, and reactive environment.

Heritability

What conclusions can we draw from twin studies? Psychologists trying to be as precise as possible about the contributions of genetic factors and environment to intelligence generally assess heritability. **Heritability** provides an estimate of the importance of genetic factors in determining individual differences in intelligence. The technical definition of heritability is the ratio of genetically caused variation to total variation (genetic + environmental variation), but you don't need to worry about the details. What is important is to understand that heritability is high if genetic factors are more important than environment ones in producing individual differences in intelligence, and low if environmental factors are more important. Heritability is a *population* measure (i.e. it applies to a given population). In any population, the more similar the environmental factors shared by its members, the greater will be the influence of genetic factors in determining individual differences in intelligence. Suppose that everyone in a given population were exposed to precisely the same environmental conditions. In those circumstances, all individual differences in intelligence would be due to genetic factors and so heritability would be extremely high. In contrast, in societies with enormous environmental differences between sections of the population (e.g. only some children receive schooling), the role of genetic factors in producing individual differences in intelligence would be small and so heritability would be low.

From what I have said, you won't be surprised to discover that heritability estimates vary a lot from one population to another. Mackintosh (1998) reviewed the evidence based on heritability measures. He concluded that between 30% and 75% of individual differences in intelligence in modern industrialised societies are due to genetic factors. Brace (1996) found that the heritability of intelligence was much higher among people living in affluent white American suburbs than among people living in American urban ghettoes. This occurred because the great majority of those living in affluent white suburbs enjoyed a favourable environment throughout childhood, and so individual differences in intelligence depended mainly on genetic factors.

Large differences in heritability have been found as a function of age. According to Plomin (1988, p. 420), the genetic influence on individual differences in IQ "increases from infancy (20%) to childhood (40%) to adulthood (60%)." *Why* are there these large differences? To answer that question, we need to distinguish between two types of environmental influence: shared environment and non-shared environment. Shared environment refers to all the common influences within a family that make children resemble each other; such influences include parental attitudes to education and parental income. Non-shared environment refers to all those influences unique to any given child (e.g. different experiences with peers). Twin studies indicate that shared environmental influences on intelligence are important in childhood. However, they become unimportant after adolescence (thus increasing the relative impact of genetic factors). In contrast, non-shared environmental influences have a small but fairly consistent impact on intelligence into adulthood.

A related point is that adolescents and adults *control* their own environment to a greater extent than children, and this reduces the impact of the environment on individual differences in intelligence. Thus, the increase in heritability of intelligence during the course of development may reflect what Plomin (1990) called active covariation (discussed earlier).

KEY TERM

Heritability: the proportion of the variance within a population in some characteristic (e.g. height) that is due to genetic factors.

Evidence: adoption studies

Adoption studies provide another way of assessing the relative importance of genetic factors and environment in determining individual differences in intelligence. If genetic factors are more important than environment, adopted children's IQs will be more similar to those of their biological parents than their adoptive parents. The opposite pattern will be found if environment is more important.

Horn (1983) discussed the findings from the Texas Adoption Project, which involved almost 500 adopted children. The correlation between the adopted children and their biological mothers was +.28, indicating that there was only a moderate degree of similarity in intelligence. The correlation between the adopted children and their adoptive mothers was even lower at +.15. Both of these correlations are so low that it is hard to make any definite statements about the roles played by genetic factors and environment, although the findings suggest a greater role for heredity. However, there is also evidence for the importance of environmental factors. The correlation of +.28 between adopted children and their biological mothers is much less than the correlation of +.42 between parents and children when children aren't adopted (Bouchard et al., 1981). This difference is due to environmental factors.

Loehlin, Horn, and Willerman (1989) found there were some differences in the findings when the adopted children were tested again 10 years later. Now the children showed an increased correlation with their biological mothers, but a reduced one with their adoptive mothers. Shared family environment between the adopted children and their adoptive mothers was reduced in importance. In contrast, genetic factors had a greater influence on the adopted children's intelligence than 10 years earlier.

The notion that shared family environment has less influence on intelligence as children become older received additional support in a review by Plomin (1988). The correlation between genetically unrelated children growing up together in adoptive families was about +.30 for intelligence when they were still children. However, the correlation dropped to zero in adolescence and adulthood. The major reason for this change is that environmental factors outside the home become increasingly important from adolescence onwards.

It is very hard to interpret the findings of many adoption studies because of selective placement. Adoption agencies often have a deliberate policy of placing children in homes similar to those of their biological parents in educational and social backgrounds. One of the consequences of selective placement is that some of the correlation between adopted children and their biological parents is due to selective placement rather than to genetic factors.

One of the few adoption studies involving little evidence of selective placement was by Capron and Duyme (1989). There were four groups of adopted children based on all four possible combinations of biological parents of high or low socio-economic status (SES) and adoptive parents of high or low SES. The relevance of SES is that high-SES parents tend to be more intelligent than low-SES parents and are more likely to have high IQ children. The predictions are fairly straightforward. The measured intelligence of the adopted children should be related mainly to the SES of the biological parents if genetic factors are of more importance. However, it should be related mostly to the SES of the adoptive parents if environmental factors are more important. In fact, the effects of the SES of the biological and of the adoptive parents were similar, although those of the

? What environmental factors might influence the development of IQ?

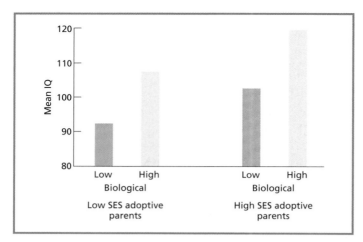

Mean IQs of adopted children as a function of socioeconomic status (SES) of their biological parents (low vs. high) and their adoptive parents (low vs. high). Data from Capron and Duyme (1989).

biological parents were slightly greater. These findings suggest genetic and environmental factors were of roughly equal importance in determining the intelligence of the adopted children.

Evidence: environmental factors

We turn our attention now to the influence of environmental factors on individual differences in intelligence. It is often assumed that the findings from twin studies indicate the importance of genetic factors. However, they also indicate that environmental factors are important! For example, Bouchard and McGue (1981) found that the correlation for identical twins brought up together was +.86 compared to +.72 for identical twins brought up apart. This difference occurs because identical twins brought up together have more similar environments than those brought up apart.

The Flynn effect

Surprising evidence that environmental factors can have a substantial effect on intelligence was reported by Flynn (1987, 1994). He discussed evidence from 20 Western countries, all showing the **Flynn effect**: a rapid rise in average IQ in many countries in recent decades. Flynn (1987) reported that there had been an increase of 2.9 points per decade on non-verbal IQ and of 3.7 points on verbal IQ. The Flynn effect is not restricted to Western countries. For example, Daley, Whaley, Sigman, Espinosa, and Neumann (2003) found significant increases in IQ among rural Kenyan children over a 14-year period.

What causes the Flynn effect? Such large and rapid increases in IQ are almost certainly due mainly to environmental factors. Embarrassingly for psychologists, we don't know precisely *why* the Flynn effect does occur. However, here are some environmental factors likely to be involved:

- Increases in the number of years of education.
- Greater access to information (e.g. internet; television).
- The provision of longer training programmes for many occupations.
- Increased cognitive complexity of the average job now compared to the past.

Other factors may be involved in the Flynn effect in non-Western countries. Daley et al. (2003) found evidence suggesting that improvements in parents' literacy, decreased family size, and improvements in children's nutrition and health all played a part in producing the Flynn effect among rural Kenyan children. As a

KEY TERM

Flynn effect: describes the rapid rise in average IQ in several Western countries in recent decades.

footnote, Sundet, Barlaug, and Torjussen (2004) found in Norway that there had been no general increase in IQ since the mid-1990s. That suggests the Flynn effect may be coming to an end.

What environmental factors are important?

Gottfried (1984) carried out a meta-analysis to assess the relative importance of several environmental factors in influencing children's intelligence. Provision of appropriate play materials, parental involvement with the child, and opportunities for variety in daily stimulation were the best predictors of children's subsequent IQs. Unfortunately, these findings were correlational in nature, and so can't show causality.

Sameroff et al. (1987, 1993) carried out a longitudinal study to investigate the factors linked to intellectual delay in young children. They assessed the children's IQs at ages 4 and 13. Sameroff, Seifer, Barocas, Zax, and Greenspan (1987) identified 10 family risk factors related to lower IQ:

1. Mother has a history of mental illness.
2. Mother didn't go to high school.
3. Mother has severe anxiety.
4. Mother has rigid attitudes and values about her child's development.
5. Few positive interactions between mother and child during infancy.
6. Head of household has a semi-skilled job.
7. Four or more children in the family.
8. Father doesn't live with the family.
9. Child belongs to a minority group.
10. Family suffered 20 or more stressful events during the child's first 4 years of life.

What did Sameroff et al. (1987, 1993) find? There was a strong negative association between the number of risk factors associated with each child and the child's IQ. At age 4, this correlation was −.58 and it was −.61 at age 13. At the age of 4, high-risk children were 24 times more likely to have IQs below 85 than low-risk children. On average, each risk factor reduced the child's IQ score by 4 points.

Sameroff et al.'s (1987) findings don't show that the environmental risk factors they identified were actually responsible for *causing* high-risk children to have low IQs. It is probable that the parents of the high-risk children were less intelligent than those of the low-risk children. This could explain, for example, why mothers might not have gone to high school or why fathers had semi-skilled jobs. In essence, there may well have been important differences in genetic potential between the low-risk

? Do you think IQs will increase as a sign of the times (e.g. technology and the internet)?

? A stimulating environment has been said to encourage a child's development. What might this environment include?

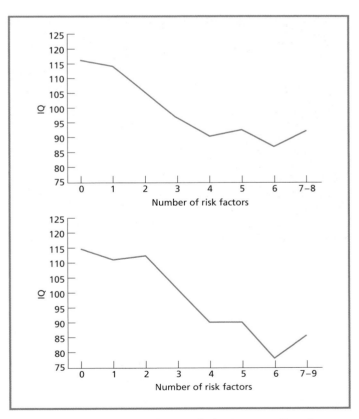

These graphs show the negative association between IQ and number of environmental risk factors. The top graph presents data for mean 4-year-old IQ scores, and the bottom graph presents data for mean 13-year-old IQ scores. Adapted from Sameroff, Seifer, Baldwin, and Baldwin (1993).

and high-risk groups of children. However, it seems likely that the adverse environmental factors identified by Sameroff et al. (1987) have *some* negative effects on children's intelligence.

Overall evaluation

The most convincing evidence we have concerning the role of genetic and environmental factors in determining individual differences in intelligence comes from twin studies. Such studies allow us to observe the effects of varying degrees of genetic similarity on intelligence. The findings from twin studies, family studies, and adoption studies consistently indicate that genetic factors and environmental factors are *both* important in influencing individual differences in intelligence.

What are the limitations of research in this area? First, genetic and environmental factors are generally positively correlated—individuals with the greatest genetic potential for intelligence tend to find themselves in environments favourable for the development of intelligence (e.g. staying at school until the age of 18, going to university). This makes it hard to disentangle the effects of genetic and environmental factors. Second, identical twins tend to have more similar environments than fraternal twins, and so the greater similarity in IQ in identical twins is not entirely due to genetic factors. Third, studies focusing on environmental factors that may influence intelligence are nearly always correlational in nature. As the environment isn't being manipulated, the available evidence doesn't clearly show that environmental factors *cause* changes in intelligence. Fourth, we have made the assumption that intelligence tests are a valid measure of intelligence. In fact, most intelligence tests are somewhat narrow in scope, failing to assess social or emotional intelligence. As a result, we should strictly say that the findings show the effects of genetic and environmental factors on individual differences in intelligence *as assessed by intelligence tests*.

Culture

In the research considered so far we have seen some of the major environmental factors that influence intelligence-test performance *within* a given culture. However, such research ignores an extremely important environmental factor—culture. What is meant by "culture"? According to Barnouw (cited in Matsumoto, 1994, p. 4), culture is "the set of attitudes, values, beliefs and behaviours shared by a group of people, communicated from one generation to the next via language or some other means of communication."

Why might we expect culture to be important? The main reason is that intelligence, "is mostly an attempt to use one's cognitive skills to achieve a state of well-being within one's cultural context" (Sternberg & Grigorenko, 2004, p. 1427). The cognitive skills that are important vary from one culture to another. Thus, for example, language skills including reading and writing are very important within most Western cultures, but more practical skills are emphasised in other cultures. There is an important consequence. As Sternberg and Grigorenko (2004, p. 1427) pointed out, "Behaviour that is considered intelligent in one culture may be considered unintelligent in another culture, and *vice versa*." Someone in a Western culture who has very good language and mathematical

? How might cultures differ in their perception of what makes someone intelligent?

skills is likely to have a high IQ. Whether that would do them much good if they were lost in the desert or the frozen wastes of Alaska is open to doubt!

What we have discussed so far matters when we consider the validity of intelligence tests. The great majority of such tests have been devised by psychologists working in the United States or in Europe. Despite this, such tests are often administered to individuals living in other parts of the world (e.g. Africa; Asia). It has sometimes been claimed that Americans and/or Europeans are more intelligent than people from most other parts of the world. This is *not* a valid conclusion to draw. As Triandis (1994, p. 58) pointed out:

> *When we measure something in another culture, we are most likely to get an answer to the question, Do they do our tricks as well as we do our tricks? rather than do they do their tricks well … Different ecologies [environments] reward different tricks.*

Findings

Conceptions of intelligence vary even within what might be regarded as a *single* culture. Okagaki and Sternberg (1993) studied ethnic groups in San Jose, California. Asian parents emphasised the importance of cognitive skills in their conception of intelligence. In contrast, Latino parents argued that social-competence skills are of particular importance in their conception of intelligence.

Most intelligence tests don't take account of the fact that cultures vary in the skills that are valued. For example, Serpell (1979) compared the performance of English and Zambian children on two tasks. The English children did better at a drawing task, whereas the Zambian children did better on a wire-shaping task. This illustrates the fact that no one culture is better than any other; there are simply variations from one culture to another.

Sternberg et al. (2001) studied Kenyan children with considerable knowledge about herbal medicines used to fight infection in that country. Such knowledge is important because more than 95% of the children living in Kenyan villages have parasitic illnesses. Sternberg et al. (2001) devised a test of practical intelligence that included an assessment of the children's ability to identify natural herbal medicines, where they come from, and what they are used for. They also administered conventional intelligence tests.

What did Sternberg et al. (2001) find? Those Kenyan children performing the best on the measure of practical intelligence performed *worse* than the other children on traditional verbal tests of intelligence. The most likely explanation is that children who devote much of their time to acquiring relevant practical knowledge tend not to engage themselves very much in school learning. Whether or not that is the correct explanation, it is clear that traditional intelligence tests were of limited value within the Kenyan context.

Cultures vary in what skills they value and deem as indicative of high intelligence. According to Sternberg et al. (2001), Kenyan children who scored highly in the practical intelligence test of rating herbal medicines and their properties did not fare so well in the conventional intelligence tests.

Grigorenko, Meier, Lipka, Mohatt, Yanez, and Sternberg (2004) studied different aspects of intelligence in Yup'ik Eskimo children living in southwest Alaska. Some of these children lived in the towns and others lived out in the country. Grigorenko et al. (2004) gave these children a test of practical intelligence (e.g. knowledge of how to travel in the virtual absence of landmarks) and traditional intelligence tests. The urban children performed better than the rural children on traditional intelligence tests. However, the rural children outperformed the urban ones on the test of practical intelligence. An important finding was that the hunting skills of the rural children were predicted better by the measure of practical intelligence than by traditional intelligence tests. Thus, the test of practical intelligence was of more relevance to the skills that the children needed in their everyday lives.

Sternberg et al. (2002) argued that children in many cultures perform poorly on conventional intelligence tests mainly because they have received very little teaching in the required skills. One way of assessing intelligence more accurately might be to use *dynamic testing*. What happens is that individuals are tested on two separate occasions with training in the skills assessed by the tests being provided between testings. Sternberg et al. (2002) used dynamic testing with children in Tanzania. There were substantial improvements in the children's performance on an intelligence test on the second testing occasion, suggesting that they had abilities and an ability to learn not revealed on the first testing occasion.

Sternberg et al. (2002) found that intelligence as assessed on the second occasion predicted the children's performance on various cognitive tasks better than intelligence assessed on the first occasion. Using dynamic testing in developing countries can provide a better assessment of intelligence than is available when there is only a single testing session.

Theory of successful intelligence

Sternberg and Grigorenko (2004) argued that their theory of successful intelligence allows us to understand how culture influences intelligence. Their starting point was that, "Intelligence, considered outside its cultural context, is in large measure a mythological construct" (Sternberg & Grigorenko, 2004, p. 1428). They pointed out that Western psychologists have emphasised the academic aspect of intelligence. In contrast, they argued that intelligence should be defined as "one's ability to achieve success in life in terms of one's personal standards, within one's socio-cultural context" (Sternberg & Grigorenko, 2004, p. 1428). There are three aspects to successful intelligence:

1. *Adaptation*: this involves modifying yourself to suit the environment.
2. *Shaping*: this involves modifying the environment to suit yourself.
3. *Selection*: this involves seeking out an environment that is better suited to your skills or values than the current one.

What is involved in successful adaptation, shaping, and selection varies considerably from one culture to another. If we want to obtain a valid

? Why do you think drawing might be less valued than a practical skill like wire-shaping in some cultures?

EXAM HINT
Make sure you can explain how the theory of successful intelligence expands on previous measures of intelligence. Consider the fact that, although this is less culturally biased, it does still have weaknesses in terms of subjectivity and researcher bias in the interpretation of what constitutes successful intelligence within one's culture. Such interpretations would be impossible to standardise so this would make any cross-cultural comparisons invalid. However, since cross-cultural research has always lacked validity, perhaps the benefit of achieving a more valid measure of intelligence within a culture outweighs this weakness.

assessment of intelligence in any given culture we must always consider the cultural context.

? Do you think IQs will increase as a sign of the times (e.g. technology and the internet)?

Evaluation

The cognitive skills needed for successful adaptation vary considerably across cultures. The reason for this is that the *demands* placed on individuals in one culture are often very different from those in another culture. Psychologists were slow to acknowledge that fact, but they have found ever increasing evidence that it is, indeed, the case. The development of intelligence tests designed to be relevant to a specific culture has been slow. However, dynamic testing is potentially a very useful way of assessing intelligence. It assesses an individual's speed of learning, which is of great importance to intelligence.

SECTION SUMMARY
Evolution of Intelligence

❖ The human species has an unusually large brain (especially neocortex) for its body size.

❖ The human brain has increased dramatically in size during evolutionary history in spite of the increased metabolic costs.

❖ There is a moderate correlation between brain size and intelligence in contemporary humans.

Brain size

❖ According to the dietary hypothesis, primate species that eat food that is patchily distributed need larger brains.

❖ According to the mental maps hypothesis, primate species that have to search for food over a wide area need larger brains.

❖ According to the extractive foraging hypothesis, primate species that have difficulty in extracting food need larger brains.

❖ There is little support for the dietary, mental maps, and extractive foraging hypotheses, perhaps because obtaining food doesn't impose great demands on cognitive or intellectual processes.

Ecological demands

❖ According to the social brain hypothesis, the brain size (or neocortex size) of a species is influenced by social complexity.

❖ There is much evidence that social complexity in the form of group size, deception, and mating strategy is associated with large brain and neocortex size.

❖ It is hard to interpret the findings because the data are correlational and so causes can't be inferred.

Social complexity

❖ We can distinguish between the genotype (genetic instructions) and phenotype (observable behaviour). With intelligence, we can only assess the phenotype.

❖ Genetic and environmental influences are *not* entirely separate or independent.

Role of genetic and environmental factors

❖ Identical twins resemble each other more in intelligence than do fraternal twins. This mostly reflects their greater genetic similarity but also their more similar environments.

Twin studies

❖ Family studies also indicate the importance of genetic factors.
❖ Heritability is a measure of the relative importance of genetic factors within a given population. It is much higher in adults than in children.

Adoption studies

❖ Adoption studies indicate that genetic and environmental factors are both important in determining intelligence.
❖ The major problem in interpreting the findings from adoption studies is selective placement.

Environmental factors

❖ Identical twins brought up apart are less similar in intelligence than those brought up together, which indicates the importance of environmental factors.
❖ The Flynn effect indicates that environmental changes have boosted intelligence. Increased number of years of education is probably the main reason for the Flynn effect.

Culture

❖ The meaning of intelligence varies considerably across cultures. As a result, it is inappropriate to use Western intelligence tests in other cultures.
❖ In many cultures, tests of practical intelligence predict successful behaviour and adaptation better than traditional intelligence tests.
❖ Dynamic testing may permit more accurate assessment of intelligence in countries in which children receive relatively little formal teaching.
❖ Successful intelligence in any culture involves adaptation, shaping, and selection.

FURTHER READING

Flynn, J. (2008). Perspectives: Still a question of black vs. white? *New Scientist*, 3 September 2008, 2672, 48–50. A discussion on environmental factors as a cause of the gap in IQ scores between black and white America.

http://www.bbc.co.uk/science/humanbody/mind/index_surveys.shtml Contains a group of interactive psychometric tests, e.g. on personality, personality traits. These are fun to take and the duration of each test is given so you can match this to what time you have available.

Taylor, A.H., Hunt, G.R., Medina, F.S., & Gray, R.D. Do New Caledonian crows solve physical problems through causal reasoning? *Proceedings of the Royal Society B: Biological Sciences*. Online. Available: http://journals.royalsociety.org/content/l7l21r228k420u59/?p=49369a8774804142b6f4ff90171a907c&pi=0 and http://journals.royalsociety.org/content/l7l21r228k420u59/?p=58f1f20978884005ad60402606b3993e&pi=0 Has a link to a short video clip showing how New Caledonian crows demonstrate evidence of causal reasoning in their learning, something it was thought only humans could do.

See *A2-Level Psychology Online* for some interactive quizzes to help you with your revision.

REVISION QUESTIONS

In the exam, questions on this topic are out of 25 marks, and can take the form of essay questions or two-part questions. You should allow about 30 minutes for each of the questions below, which aim to test the material in this chapter. Never try to answer a question unless you have been taught the topic.

1. Discuss one or more theories of intelligence. (25 marks)
2. Discuss the evidence for animal learning and intelligence. (25 marks)
3. Discuss the influence of evolutionary factors in the development of human intelligence, e.g. ecological demands, social complexity, and brain size. (25 marks)
4. (a) Discuss the role of genetic and environmental factors on intelligence test performance. (16 marks)
   (b) In what ways do cultural factors affect intelligence test performance? (9 marks)

See *A2-Level Psychology Online* for tips on how to answer these revision questions.

Development of thinking p. 325

- What are the stages of cognitive development?
- Why are young children egocentric?
- What are the similarities and differences in Piaget's, Vygotsky's, and Bruner's theories of cognitive development?
- What role should self-discovery play in education?
- How can the zone of proximal development be used to develop cognition?
- What is scaffolding and how can this be used as in peer tutoring?

Development of moral understanding p. 347

- What are the stages of moral development according to Kohlberg?
- How would you respond to the "Heinz dilemma"?
- How is Kohlberg's theory gender and culture biased?
- How does Eisenberg use role-taking skills and empathy to expand on Kohlberg's account of moral development?

Development of social cognition p. 358

- When does a child develop a theory of mind?
- How do children with autism help us to understand the development of social cognition?
- What are Selman's levels of perspective taking?
- How can we improve perspective-taking skills?
- What is the mirror neuron system and how does it influence social cognition?

Cognition and Development

By Michael W. Eysenck

Developmental psychology is concerned with fascinating issues relating to the huge changes occurring during the years of childhood. Newborn infants are almost helpless and can survive only with the almost undivided attention of their mother or other caregiver. As the years pass, however, children's progress is dramatic—for example, they rapidly become proficient at learning and at socialising with other children. At the heart of much of this progress is cognitive development, which is the central theme of this chapter.

DEVELOPMENT OF THINKING

Children change and develop in almost every way in the years between infancy and adolescence. However, some of the most dramatic changes take place in terms of cognitive development. The first systematic theory of cognitive development was proposed by a Swiss psychologist, Jean Piaget (1896–1980). There are several other major theoretical approaches to cognitive development. Later in this Section we will consider the theories of Lev Vygotsky (1896–1934) and of Jerome Bruner (born 1915).

Piaget's Theory

Piaget's central focus was on cognitive development. He was interested in how children learn and adapt to the world. For adaptation to occur, there must be constant interactions between the child and the world. According to Piaget, two processes are of key importance:

- **Accommodation:** the individual's cognitive organisation is altered by the need to deal with the environment. Thus, the individual adjusts to the outside world.
- **Assimilation:** the individual deals with new environmental situations on the basis of his or her existing cognitive organisation. Thus, the individual child's interpretation of the outside world is adjusted to fit him or her.

KEY TERMS

Accommodation: in Piaget's theory, the process of changing existing schemas or creating new schemas because new information cannot be assimilated.

Assimilation: in Piaget's theory, dealing with new environmental situations by using existing cognitive organisation.

An example of the dominance in play of assimilation over accommodation—pretending a stick is a gun.

The clearest example of the dominance of assimilation over accommodation is play. In play, reality is interpreted according to the individual's whim (e.g. a stick becomes a gun). In contrast, dominance of accommodation is seen in imitation. In imitation, the child simply copies the actions of someone else.

There are two other key Piagetian concepts: **schema** and **equilibration**. Schema refers to organised knowledge used to guide action. The first schema infants develop is the body schema, when they realise there is an important distinction between "me" and "not me". This body schema helps the infant in its attempts to explore and make sense of the world.

Equilibration is based on the notion that the individual needs to keep a stable internal state (equilibrium) in a changing environment. When a child tries unsuccessfully to understand its experiences in terms of existing schemas, there is an unpleasant state of *disequilibrium* or lack of balance. The child then uses assimilation and accommodation to restore a state of equilibrium or balance. Thus, disequilibrium motivates the child to learn new skills and knowledge to return to the desired state of equilibrium.

We can identify two extreme positions with respect to the changes occurring during cognitive development. At one extreme, the amount of knowledge available to children increases considerably, but there are no dramatic changes in *how* they think. At the other extreme, the ways of thinking found in adolescence differ profoundly from those of early childhood. Piaget identified himself with the latter position, believing there are fundamental differences in cognition among children of different ages.

Stage theory

Piaget argued that all children pass through several stages. The three main assumptions of his stage theory are as follows:

1. Large changes in the course of cognitive development permit the identification of separate processing stages.

2. All children pass through the same *sequence* of stages in the same order (although at different rates).

3. The cognitive operations and structures defining each stage form an integrated whole.

Piaget identified four major stages of cognitive development. The first is the **sensori-motor stage,**

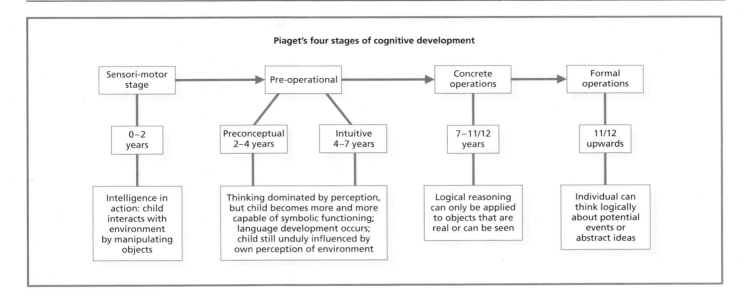

Piaget's four stages of cognitive development

Sensori-motor stage	→	Pre-operational	→	Concrete operations	→	Formal operations

0–2 years	Preconceptual 2–4 years	Intuitive 4–7 years	7–11/12 years	11/12 upwards

Intelligence in action: child interacts with environment by manipulating objects	Thinking dominated by perception, but child becomes more and more capable of symbolic functioning; language development occurs; child still unduly influenced by own perception of environment	Logical reasoning can only be applied to objects that are real or can be seen	Individual can think logically about potential events or abstract ideas

which lasts from birth to about 2 years of age. The second is the **pre-operational stage**, spanning the years between 2 and 7. The third is the **concrete operations stage**, which usually occurs between the ages of 7 and 11 or 12. The fourth stage is the **formal operations stage**, which follows on from the stage of concrete operations.

Sensori-motor stage (0–2 years)

In the first stage of cognitive development, very young children deal with the environment by manipulating objects. This means that sensori-motor development (learning to co-ordinate one's senses with one's motor responses) is basically *intelligence through action*.

The key achievement of this stage is **object permanence**. This involves being aware that objects continue to exist when no longer in view. In the early part of the sensori-motor stage, the infant has no awareness at all of object permanence: it is literally a case of "out of sight, out of mind". Object permanence develops as the child actively explores his or her environment. Towards the end of its first year, the infant starts to display **perseverative search**. This involves the infant searching for a concealed object in the place in which it was *found* some time earlier rather than in the place in which it was last *seen*. According to Piaget, this happens because the infant doesn't regard the object as existing independently of the infant's own behaviour. Perseverative search shows some features of object

Object permanence is the term used to describe the awareness that objects continue to exist even when they are no longer visible.

KEY TERMS

Pre-operational stage: the second stage in Piaget's theory of cognitive development, from 2 to 7 years. The child can cope with symbols (such as using language) but cannot cope with adult internally consistent logic (operations).

Concrete operations stage: the third stage in Piaget's theory of cognitive development, from 7 to 11 years. The child can now use adult internally consistent logic but only when the problem is presented in a concrete way.

Formal operations stage: the final stage in Piaget's theory of cognitive development, from age 11. Thinking now involves formal internally consistent adult logic and abstract thinking.

Object permanence: an awareness that objects continue to exist when they can no longer be seen.

Perseverative search: mistakenly searching for an object in the place in which it was previously found, rather than the place in which it is currently hidden.

? What reflexes are babies born with, and how might these develop into conscious activity?

? You have become very adept at sensori-motor co-ordination. Can you think of some examples?

? How could the development of a baby's first words be explained in terms of imitation?

permanence. However, full object permanence is only achieved towards the end of the sensori-motor stage.

The development of imitation is another major achievement of the sensori-motor stage. Imitation allows the infant to add considerably to its range of actions. It develops slowly and becomes more precise over time. Towards the end of the sensori-motor stage the infant shows evidence of **deferred imitation**, which is the ability to imitate behaviour that was seen before.

Pre-operational stage (2–7 years)

The child who completes the sensori-motor stage of cognitive development is still not capable of "true" thought. He or she operates largely at the level of direct action, whereas the pre-operational child becomes increasingly capable of symbolic functioning. The development of language is associated with the cognitive advances of pre-operational children. However, Piaget regarded language development as largely a consequence of more fundamental cognitive changes rather than as itself a cause of cognitive advance.

According to Piaget, pre-operational children are unduly influenced by their own perception of the environment. They tend to pay attention to only one aspect of the situation (Piaget called this **centration**). For example, they don't show **conservation**, which is the understanding that certain aspects of a visual display don't vary in spite of changes in perceptual aspects.

In addition, pre-operational children lack crucial internalised cognitive operations. One of the most important cognitive operations is **reversibility**. This involves the ability to undo or reverse mentally some operation that has been carried out. For example, reversibility allows the realisation that the effect of pouring liquid from one container into another could be negated by simply pouring the liquid back into its original container.

Piaget argued that the thinking of pre-operational children is characterised by **egocentrism**. Egocentrism is the assumption that one's way of thinking about things is the only possible way. It often involves a lack of differentiation between the self and the world, so the child can't distinguish clearly between psychological and physical events. This produces:

- *Realism*: the tendency to regard psychological events as having a physical existence.
- *Animism*: the tendency to endow physical objects and events with psychological qualities.
- *Artificialism*: the tendency to consider that physical objects and events were created by people.

Concrete operations stage (7–11 years)

Piaget argued that the shift from pre-operational to concrete operational thinking involves an increasing independence of thought from perception (the evidence of your senses). In the pre-operational stage, a child might call all red cars "Daddy's car" because Daddy has a red car. There is a certain logic. However, it is flawed and not internally consistent—it wouldn't hold up under questioning. Children at

---

KEY TERMS

Deferred imitation: in Piaget's theory, the ability to imitate behaviour that was observed at an earlier time.

Centration: attending to only one aspect of a situation.

Conservation: to understand that quantity does not change even when a display is transformed, i.e. the quantity is conserved.

Reversibility: the ability to undo, or reverse mentally, an action or operation.

Egocentrism: the sense of being the centre of everything and that one's view is the only view.

the stage of concrete operations develop various cognitive operations of a logical or mathematical nature, including the actions implied by mathematical symbols (e.g. $+$, $-$, $\times$, $>$, $<$, $=$). The term "operations" is used to describe internally consistent mental rules used in thinking. The most important cognitive operation is reversibility (described earlier), which involves the ability to cancel out the effect of a perceptual change by imagining the opposite change. During the concrete operations stage, children can use the various cognitive operations *only* with respect to specific concrete situations.

Piaget argued that cognitive operations are combined or organised into a system or structure. For example, the operation "greater than" can't really be considered independently of the operation "less than". Someone fails to grasp the full meaning of "A is greater than B" unless he or she realises that this statement means that "B is less than A". Piaget coined the term **grouping** to refer to such sets of logically related operations. For example, consider the following problem: Tom is taller than Harry; Harry is taller than Dick. Is Dick shorter than Tom? Children who understand that the question is same as "Is Tom taller than Dick?" are more likely to produce the correct answer.

The problem discussed in the previous paragraph is an example of tasks children can perform in the concrete operations stage that they couldn't perform previously. It is based on the notion of **transitivity**, which allows three elements to be placed in the correct order.

Formal operations stage (11 upwards)

In the third stage of concrete operations, the child's thinking becomes truly logical reasoning. However, this reasoning can only be applied to objects that are real or can be seen. During the final stage of formal operations, the adolescent or adult can think logically about potential events or abstract ideas. As a result, the thinking of adolescents and adults can go beyond the limitations of immediate reality. Note, however, that individuals in the formal operations stage are still able to think in the concrete way found in the previous stage of cognitive development.

Inhelder and Piaget (1958) suggested the following way to decide whether someone is using formal operations when solving a logical problem (such as the pendulum problem described below). If you ask a person to explain *how* they arrived at an answer to a logical problem, the formal operational thinker will report that they thought of a range of possibilities to account for the problem and used this range to generate hypotheses that could then be tested. By contrast, the concrete thinker will have thought of a few alternatives and tried each one out in no particular order. When one possibility doesn't work, another one is tried with no attempt to use logic to exclude certain possibilities.

Piaget's pendulum problem involves presenting participants with a set of weights and a string that can be lengthened or shortened. The goal is to work out what determines the frequency of the swings of a pendulum formed by suspending a weight on a string from a pole. The factors likely to be considered include the length of the string, the weight of the suspended object, the force of the participant's push, and the position from which the pendulum is pushed. In fact, *only* the length of the string is relevant.

KEY TERMS

Grouping: in Piaget's theory, a set of logically related operations.

Transitivity: understanding the relation between elements, for example, if x is greater than y and y is greater than z, then x is greater than z.

Children were asked to work out what would affect the frequency of the swings of the pendulum (how many times it would go back and forth in a given period). They were asked to consider changing the weights on the pendulum, the length of the string, how hard they pushed it, and which direction it was pushed in.

Concrete operational children often argue that the frequency of swinging of the pendulum is affected by the length of the string. However, they aren't able to show that the other factors are irrelevant. In contrast, many formal operational children manage to carry out the necessary tests to show that only the length of the string influences the frequency of the swings of the pendulum. According to Piaget, the ability to solve the pendulum problem requires an understanding of a complicated combinatorial system.

Testing the stage theory

How did Piaget test his stage theory? He was rather sceptical about the value of the typical experimental approach based on strict use of the experimental method. Instead, Piaget preferred a less structured and formal approach. He used the **clinical method**, in which children are questioned informally to reveal the nature of their understanding of problems.

There is one other crucial point. Piaget focused very much on describing the strengths and limitations of children's thinking at different developmental stages. However, he failed to explain precisely *why* and *how* children's thinking develops, and he attached remarkably little importance to the role of learning. Piaget's approach can be defended by arguing that we need to know *what* needs to be explained before providing an explanation.

Findings

Sensori-motor stage

According to Piaget, object permanence develops during the sensori-motor stage. As predicted, there is evidence that infants show partial object permanence towards the end of their first year. What happens is that the experimenter hides an object at location A, which the infant then finds. After that, the same object is hidden at location B, but the infant mistakenly searches at location A. This finding (perseverative search) allegedly occurs because the infant doesn't regard objects as existing independently of his or her own behaviour.

Piaget's assumption that infants show perseverative search because they don't remember where the object has been hidden is rejected by some researchers. In one study (Baillargeon & Graber, 1988), 8-month-old infants saw a toy being hidden behind one of two screens. Fifteen seconds later they saw a hand lift the toy out from the place in which it had been hidden or from behind the other screen. The infants were only surprised when the toy was lifted from behind the "wrong" screen. This indicates that they *did* remember where it had been put.

Piaget argued that imitation was a major achievement of the sensori-motor stage. Towards the end of the sensori-motor stage, the infant shows

The Swiss psychologist Jean Piaget, 1896–1980.

KEY TERM

Clinical method: a form of unstructured interview where the interviewer starts with some predetermined set of questions, but as the interview proceeds, these questions are adapted in line with the responses given. This kind of interview is used by clinicians when assessing mentally-ill patients.

evidence of deferred imitation, in which behaviour seen before is imitated. In a study by Hayne, Boniface, and Barr (2000), the experimenter demonstrated a novel action using an unfamiliar object, and infants tried to reproduce that action after an interval of time. Infants aged 6, 12, and 18 months all showed deferred imitation when the same stimulus object was used for the demonstration and the subsequent test.

Pre-operational stage

We turn now to the pre-operational stage. According to Piaget, pre-operational children pay attention to only one aspect of the total situation (centration). As a result, they don't show conservation. In his classic studies on conservation of quantity, Piaget presented children with two glasses of the same size and shape containing the same quantity of liquid. When the child agrees there is the same quantity of liquid in both glasses, the liquid from one of them is poured into a glass that is taller and thinner.

Baillargeon and Graber found that 8-month-old infants were surprised when a cup they had seen being put behind the left-hand screen was then retrieved from behind the right-hand screen.

The child is then asked if the two glasses (the original one and the new one) contain the same amount to drink, or if one contains more. Pre-operational children fail to show conservation. They argue mistakenly either that there is more liquid in the new container ("because it's higher") or that there is more liquid in the old container ("because it's wider"). In either case, the child centres or focuses on only *one* dimension (height or width).

Piaget claimed that pre-operational children fail on conservation tasks partly because of centration. However, they also fail because they lack the cognitive operation of reversibility, which involves the ability to undo (or reverse mentally) some operation. Thus, reversibility allows the realisation that the effect of pouring liquid from one container into another could be negated by simply pouring it back into its original container.

Children in the pre-operational stage often fail to show conservation. However, they possess more knowledge of conservation than seemed to be the case in Piaget's studies. Wheldall and Poborca (1980) argued that children often fail on conservation tasks because they don't understand the question. Accordingly, they devised a non-verbal version of the liquid conservation task. Only 28% of their 6- and 7-year-old children showed conservation with the standard verbal version compared to 50% with the non-verbal version.

McGarrigle and Donaldson (1974) argued that children presented with a conservation task typically assume that the experimenter deliberately *intends* to change the amount of liquid or other substance. This assumption biases them against showing conservation. It follows that children would show more evidence of conservation if the change made on a conservation task appeared to be accidental. This prediction was supported by McGarrigle and Donaldson. They presented 6-year-olds with two rows of counters with the same number of counters

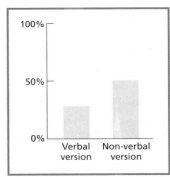

Percentages of children aged 6–7 years who showed conservation on the two versions of Piaget's conservation task (Wheldall & Poborca, 1980).

? Give a definition of operant discrimination learning and how it might be demonstrated in Wheldall and Poborca's study

McGarrigle and Donaldson found that when an experimenter rearranged one of a pair of rows of counters, relatively few 6-year-old children thought that the two rows still contained the same number of counters. However, when a teddy bear appeared to mess up the counters accidentally, most children said that the numbers in the rows were still the same.

A drawing of the model used in Piaget's three mountains task. Children were shown the model from one angle, then shown photographs of the model from other viewpoints, and asked to choose which view someone standing at one of the other labelled points would see. Pre-operational children usually selected the view from the point at which they themselves had seen the model.

? Piaget's three mountains task required children to reverse a complicated image in their heads. Do you think a failure to do this necessarily shows egocentricity, or is there another explanation?

in each row. In one condition, the experimenter deliberately messed up one of the rows. In the other condition, a "naughty teddy bear" messed up one of the rows in what looked like an accidental way. Number conservation was shown by 70% of the children in the naughty teddy condition compared to only 40% in the standard condition.

Piaget argued that the thinking of pre-operational children shows much evidence of egocentrism (thinking one's view is the only possible one). Artificialism (thinking that physical objects were created by people) is a type of egocentric thinking. An example of artificialism concerns my elder daughter Fleur, at the age of 3. We were on Wimbledon Common and I told her the sun would come out when I had counted to 10. When it did so, she was very confident that Daddy could control the sun, and often begged me to make the sun appear on overcast days!

Piaget studied egocentrism in pre-operational children by using the three mountains task (see figure on the left). Children aged between 3½ and 5 looked at a model of mountains, and decided which out of various pictures showed the view that would be seen by someone looking at the display from a different angle. Children younger than 8 nearly always selected the photograph of the scene as they themselves saw it. According to Piaget, this error occurred because young children can't escape from an egocentric perspective.

Hughes (1975) argued that children performed poorly on the three mountains task because it doesn't relate to their experience. He tested this argument by using a piece of apparatus in which two walls intersected at right angles to form what looked like a plus sign (see figure on right-hand page). A boy doll and a policeman doll were put into the apparatus, and the child was asked whether the policeman doll could see the boy doll. After that, the child was told to hide the boy so the policeman couldn't see him. Nearly all the children could do this, and any errors were corrected. Finally, a second policeman was used, and the children were told to hide the boy doll so that neither of the policemen could see him. According to Piaget, the children should have hidden the boy so they themselves couldn't see it, and so should have failed the task.

What happened in Hughes' (1975) experiment? Ninety per cent of the children performed the task successfully, a much higher figure than reported by Piaget with the three mountains task. The main reason for the difference is probably that the task used by Hughes was much more meaningful and interesting. However, it was also simpler than the one used by Piaget.

Concrete operations stage

When children move from the pre-operational to the concrete operational stage they show an increasing independence of thought from perception. Part of this change involves an understanding of conservation and of reversibility. It also involves the development of various cognitive operations of a logical or mathematical nature. We will consider two of the achievements Piaget claimed were associated with the concrete operational stage. First, there is transitivity (discussed earlier), which allows three or more elements to be placed in the correct order. For example, if Mark is taller than Peter, and Peter is taller than Robert, then it follows from the notion of transitivity that Mark must be taller than Robert. Piaget found that children in the concrete operational stage could solve such problems.

According to Piaget, children under 7 years of age shouldn't show transitivity. However, Pears and Bryant (1990) found evidence of transitivity in 4-year-olds. The children were shown several small towers, each consisting of two coloured bricks (e.g. a red brick on a yellow brick; a yellow brick on a green brick; and a green brick on a blue brick). They were told to construct a large tower in which the order of the bricks corresponded to that in the small towers. Thus, the large tower would have red at the top, followed in sequence by yellow, green, and blue. Before building the large tower, the children showed a reasonable ability to work out the correct order of the bricks, thus making transitive inferences several years earlier than assumed by Piaget.

As predicted by Piaget, children in the concrete operational stage achieve various forms of conservation. However, he de-emphasised the role of specific learning experiences and cultural factors in determining performance on conservation tasks. For example, consider conservation of volume. This can be tested by placing two identical balls of clay into two identical transparent containers filled to the same level with water. One ball of clay is then moulded into a new shape. Conservation is shown if the child realises that this won't change the amount of water it displaces. Price-Williams, Gordon, and Ramirez (1969) found that the children of Mexican potters had fast development of conservation of volume when a ball of clay was stretched into an oblong shape, because they were familiar with this substance. However, they had slow development of conservation of volume with substances with which they had less familiarity.

A drawing of the two-policemen version of Hughes' (1975) experimental set-up, in which the child is asked to hide a boy doll where neither of the policemen can see him. According to Piaget's egocentrism theory, children should hide the doll in sections A or B, where they themselves can't see him, but in fact Hughes found that 90% of children put the doll in section C—the only one the policemen cannot see.

This apparatus tests conservation of volume. Children are asked if the liquids will be at the same level again when the new shape of clay is put back into the glass. Conservation of volume is not usually attained until about the age of 11 or 12.

? What can you do now, in terms of mental activities, that you were not able to do before you were 11?

Formal operations stage

According to Piaget, children and adults in the formal operations stage have the ability to think in terms of many possible states of the world. This allows us to think in abstract terms and to escape from the world. Piaget studied formal operational thought by presenting children and adolescents with the pendulum problem (discussed earlier). Children in the concrete operations stage couldn't use abstract logical reasoning to solve this problem, whereas some adolescents and adults in the formal operations stage were able to solve the problem.

Piaget greatly overestimated the intellectual prowess of most adolescents. Bradmetz (1999) assessed formal operational thinking in 62 15-year-olds using various Piagetian tasks. Only *one* participant showed substantial evidence of formal operational thought. Bradmetz also found that overall performance on the tests of formal thought correlated +.61 with general intelligence. Thus, the cognitive abilities associated with formal thought resemble those assessed by traditional intelligence tests.

Evaluation

Piaget's theory was a very ambitious attempt to describe children's cognitive development from being irrational and illogical to being rational and logical.

The notions that children learn certain basic operations (e.g. reversibility), and that these operations then allow them to solve numerous problems, are valuable ones.

Stage theories such as Piaget's *exaggerate* the differences between stages and *minimise* the differences within stages. For example, children in the concrete operations stage show conservation of quantity for familiar materials before they show it for unfamiliar materials (Durkin, 1995). Thus, successful performance depends on *specific* learning experiences as well as on *general* cognitive operations emphasised by Piaget.

Piaget *underestimated* the cognitive abilities of young children, but *overestimated* those of adolescents and adults. However, as Lourenço and Machado (1996) pointed out, Piaget was interested in children's deep understanding of problems. Simply producing correct answers to problems at a young age doesn't necessarily require deep understanding.

Piaget provided a detailed description of the major changes in cognitive development but didn't explain adequately the processes involved. In the words of Siegler and Munakata (1993), there appears to be a "miraculous transition" from one developmental stage to the next.

Piaget de-emphasised the role of social factors in cognitive development. For example, children's cognitive development benefits from social interactions with adults and other children.

Piaget virtually ignored individual differences. He admitted, "I'm not really interested in the individual. I'm interested in what is general in the development of intelligence and knowledge" (Bringuier, 1980, p. 86).

? What problems does the clinical method pose for anyone attempting to carry out a longitudinal study of a child's development?

HOW SCIENCE WORKS: PIAGET EVALUATION

Piaget's ideas have been both hugely influential . . . and criticised.

You could produce a series of posters, using colour, different fonts, and downloaded graphics to make them eye-catching, clear, and attractive to read. Each poster would take one of Piaget's stages or concepts and present this with a short explanation. You could then give example(s) of support for the stage/concept, such as Piaget's own tasks or experiments with children, and then explain a challenge or two to it. This would not only describe and evaluate Piaget's ideas but also show how knowledge is gained and modified, and how scientific knowledge evolves.

Vygotsky's Theory

Textbook writers typically argue that Vygotsky's approach to cognitive development was radically different from that of Piaget, and there certainly are some major differences. However, we shouldn't exaggerate the scale of these differences. Smith (1996) assembled 10 quotations from Vygotsky and 10 from Piaget, and asked various experts to decide who had written each one. On average, these experts performed at little better than chance level!

In some ways, the approaches of Piaget and Vygotsky complement each other. As Shayer (2003) pointed out, Piaget was mainly concerned with determining children's thinking abilities at different stages of cognitive development. In contrast, Vygotsky was more interested in the *dynamics* of change, namely, the factors responsible for cognitive development.

One of the difficulties in discussing Vygotsky's ideas is that he kept changing his mind. However, a constant feature of his approach (and a real difference from Piaget) was his emphasis on the importance of *social* factors in influencing cognitive development. According to Vygotsky (1930/1981, p. 163), "Social relations or relations among people genetically [developmentally] underlie all higher functions and their relationships." More specifically, Vygotsky (p. 163) argued as follows: "Any function in the child's cultural development appears twice, or on two planes. First, it appears on the social plane, and then on the psychological plane." Within this approach, the child is an apprentice who learns directly from social interaction and from communication with older children having knowledge he or she lacks (Durkin, 1995).

We can contrast Vygotsky's approach with that of Piaget, who argued that children acquire knowledge through **self-discovery**. However, there are some important similarities. Vygotsky and Piaget both agreed that *activity* forms the basis for learning and for the development of thinking. In addition, they both argued that learning is most effective when the information presented to children is closely related to their current knowledge and abilities.

Vygotsky argued that there are four stages in children's formation of concepts. He identified these four stages on the basis of a study (one of the very few he carried out) in which children were presented with wood blocks having labels consisting of nonsense syllables. Each nonsense syllable consistently referred to blocks having certain characteristics (e.g. circular and thin blocks). The children had the concept-formation task of working out the meaning of each nonsense syllable. Vygotsky's four stages were as follows:

1. *Vague syncretic stage*: children fail to use systematic strategies and show little understanding of the concepts.
2. *Complex stage*: non-random strategies are used, but are not successful in finding the main features of each concept.
3. *Potential concept stage*: systematic strategies are used, but are limited to focusing on one feature at a time (e.g. shape).
4. *Mature concept stage*: systematic strategies relating to more than one feature at a time are used, and lead to successful concept formation.

Vygotsky's findings resembled those of Piaget with very different tasks. Vygotsky found that children had problems with concept formation because they focused

Lev Semeonovich Vygotsky, 1896–1934.

? What social factors do you think influence cognitive development?

? Can you relate any, or all, of these stages to some of the Piagetian concepts you read about earlier?

KEY TERM

Self-discovery: an active approach to learning in which the child is encouraged to use his or her initiative in learning.

on only one salient or obvious feature of stimuli. This is very similar to Piaget's discovery that pre-operational children fail on conservation tasks because they attend to only one aspect of the situation.

Zone of proximal development

Vygotsky emphasised the notion of the **zone of proximal development**. This was defined by Vygotsky (1978, p. 86) as "the distance between the actual developmental level as determined by independent problem solving and the level of potential development as determined through problem solving under adult guidance or in collaboration with more capable peers." In other words, the zone of proximal development involves "problem solving that is beyond one's unassisted efforts but which can be achieved with assistance" (Granott, 2005, p. 141).

Linnell and Fluck (2001, p. 215) provided a concrete example of how a mother used the zone of proximal development to assist her 32-month-old child to count out three toys and put them in a basket for Billie (a clown doll) to play with:

Mother: Right shall you give Billie some? You have to count them as you put them in.
Child: Yeah (taking one item from the basket).
Mother: Now you count them.
Child: One (takes out another toy and holds one in each hand).
Mother: That's it.
Child: Put them in there? (holding them over Billie's basket).
Mother: Yeah (child drops toy into Billie's basket). And Billie would like one more. One, two . . .
Child: Three. And this one (taking another toy out of the basket).
Mother: Go on then—give it to Billie.
Child: (Picks up another toy so he again has one in each hand).
Mother: He only wants three.
Child: (Drops both toys into Billie's basket).
Mother: That's four.

Two aspects of the zone of proximal development are of particular importance. First, children apparently lacking certain skills when tested on their own may perform more effectively in the social context provided by someone having the necessary knowledge. We have just seen an example of this with the mother helping her son to learn how to count. Second, when a given child's level of understanding is moderately challenged, he or she is most likely to acquire new knowledge rapidly and without a sense of failure. Vygotsky assumed that children differ in the size of the zone of proximal development. Those with larger zones of proximal development derive more benefit from instructions than those with smaller zones.

Language

Vygotsky argued that language develops through three stages. Language and thought are unrelated during the first stage of development. During the second stage, language and thought develop in parallel and continue to have very little impact on each other. During the third stage, children use the speech of others and talking to themselves to assist in their thinking and problem solving. By the age

[?] What other approach could the mother have taken in this scenario?

KEY TERM

Zone of proximal development: in Vygotsky's theory, capacities that are being developed but are not as yet functioning fully.

of 7, egocentric speech (i.e. speaking without heeding anyone else present) gives way to inner speech.

According to Vygotsky, language becomes increasingly central to cognitive development over the years. Berk (1994, p. 62) described some of the processes Vygotsky had in mind: "When a child discusses a challenging task with a mentor [person providing guidance], that individual offers spoken directions and strategies. The child incorporates the language of those dialogues into his or her private speech and then uses it to guide independent efforts."

Vygotsky's views on the role of language in cognitive development were very different from those of Piaget. Vygotsky argued that cognitive development depends crucially on language development and use. In contrast, Piaget argued that cognitive development typically precedes (and is little affected by) language development.

Findings

Vygotsky's notion that inner speech is of value in thinking has received support. Behrend, Harris, and Cartwright (1992) used whispering and observable lip movements as measures of inner speech. Children using the most inner speech performed difficult tasks better than children making little use of inner speech. Berk (1994) found that 6-year-olds spent 60% of the time talking to themselves while solving problems in mathematics. Those whose speech contained numerous comments about what needed to be done on the current problem did better at mathematics over the following year. This confirmed Vygotsky's view that self-guiding speech makes it easier for children to direct their actions.

Vygotsky argued that private speech becomes more internal as children's level of performance improves. Berk (1994) discussed a study in which 4- and 5-year-old children made Lego models in each of three sessions. As predicted by Vygotsky, their speech became increasingly internalised from session to session as their model-making performance improved. Thus, as Vygotsky assumed, private speech is of most value to children confronted by novel tasks they don't fully understand.

Vygotsky assumed that children don't produce egocentric or private audible speech after the age of 7. However, Girbau (2002) found evidence against that assumption. Children of 8 and 10 played in pairs with a Lego construction set. Egocentric speech was found in both age groups and was somewhat more frequent in the older group.

Evaluation

The following are the main strengths of Vygotsky's theoretical approach:

- Piaget under-estimated the importance of the social environment in cognitive development, and Vygotsky deserves credit for recognising its key role.
- Vygotsky's ideas led to the introduction of several useful teaching techniques (e.g. scaffolding; see later in chapter).
- As Vygotsky predicted, inner speech helps the problem-solving activities of young children.

Here are some of the main limitations of Vygotsky's approach:

- Many of Vygotsky's ideas were rather speculative, and he carried out very little research.

? How important do you think that private speech is in children's thinking?

? Why does private speech become less frequent when children begin to master a task?

- Vygotsky exaggerated the importance of the social environment. Children's rate of cognitive development is determined more by *internal* factors (e.g. level of motivation) than he believed.
- Vygotsky didn't specify clearly the kinds of social interaction most beneficial for learning (e.g. general encouragement vs. specific instructions).
- Social interactions aren't always beneficial to learning. As parents discover, interactions with their children can lead to confrontations and stubbornness rather than enlightenment.

Bruner's Theory

Jerome Bruner (born 1915) has made numerous contributions to our understanding of cognitive development. While his views have changed over the years, Bruner (e.g. 1986, 1990) has consistently adopted a constructivist position with respect to optimal ways for students to learn. Three of the main principles associated with his constructivist approach are the following:

1. Instruction must be concerned with experiences and contexts that make students willing and able to learn. This involves a state of readiness on the part of the student.
2. Instruction should be structured so it can be understood easily. This involves *spiral organisation*—topics are returned to at intervals at progressively more advanced levels.
3. Instruction should be designed to allow students to draw inferences and to fill in gaps in the information provided. This involves the student going beyond the information given.

Bruner was greatly influenced by Vygotsky's ideas, which were mostly consistent with his own. We will focus on the ways in which he and his colleagues have developed Vygotsky's ideas and applied them systematically in educational settings. Of key importance was an article by Wood, Bruner, and Ross (1976), in which they extended the notion of a zone of proximal development. They introduced the concept of **scaffolding**, which refers to the context provided by knowledgeable people such as adults to help children to develop their cognitive skills. Effective scaffolding means the child doesn't need to climb too far at any point. Another important aspect of scaffolding is that there is a gradual withdrawal of support as

Left to his own devices, could this boy make his sister a birthday cake? His mother uses scaffolding to create a situation in which he can begin to move to the top of a zone of proximal development.

the child's knowledge and confidence increase. Scaffolding and the zone of proximal development are closely related. However, scaffolding focuses more on the strategies used by the adult and less on changes in the child.

Granott (2005) identified four major components of efficient scaffolding:

1. It is temporary and is dismantled when the child makes sufficient cognitive progress.
2. The person providing scaffolding reduces his or her input if the child reduces its input, and increases his or her input if the child increases its input. This encourages the child to play an active role in problem solving.
3. The input of the person providing scaffolding is at a higher level than that of the child; this supports and stimulates the child.
4. Both partners should find their interactions on the task pleasant and rewarding.

? Can you think of any ways scaffolding is used in your own life?

Findings

The first systematic study of scaffolding was carried out by Wood et al. (1976). An adult female tutor taught 3-, 4-, and 5-year-old children to build a three-dimensional structure. What the tutor said and did were largely determined by the child's efforts to perform the task. Her interventions were categorised as showing (e.g. joining blocks together) or telling (e.g. asking the child whether incorrectly assembled blocks were correct). The tutor engaged in more showing than telling with the 3-year-olds, but there was much more telling than showing with the 4- and 5-year-olds. In addition, the 5-year-olds received much less help from the tutor than did the 4-year-olds, because they didn't need so much assistance or scaffolding.

Moss (1992) reviewed studies on the scaffolding provided by mothers during the preschool period. There were three main aspects to the mothers' scaffolding strategies. First, the mother instructed her child in new skills the child couldn't use on its own. Second, the mother encouraged her child to maintain useful problem-solving tactics it had shown spontaneously. Third, the mother persuaded the child to discard immature and inappropriate forms of behaviour. Scaffolding emerged as an effective technique for promoting learning in preschool children.

Conner, Knight, and Cross (1997) studied the effects of scaffolding on 2-year-olds performing various problem-solving and language tasks. Most previous studies had focused only on mothers' scaffolding, but Conner et al. also considered fathers' scaffolding. Mothers and fathers were equally good at scaffolding, and the quality of scaffolding predicted the children's performance on various tasks during the teaching sessions. The beneficial effects of good scaffolding were still evident at a follow-up session. Children who had originally received better scaffolding continued to perform better than those who had received poor scaffolding.

Evaluation

Bruner's approach to cognitive development is basically a development of Vygotsky's approach. As a result, the two approaches share the same strengths:

- Bruner's emphasis on the importance of social factors in children's cognitive development has received substantial support.
- The development of scaffolding (which made much use of Vygotsky's ideas) was probably Bruner's greatest contribution.

Bruner and his colleagues discovered the conditions under which scaffolding is generally most effective. It should be temporary, the extent of the tutor's input should be related to the child's input, the tutor's input should be at a slightly higher level than the child's current performance level, and interactions between tutor and child should be mutually rewarding.

What are the limitations in Bruner's approach?

• Bruner's focus on the importance of external social factors in promoting children's learning led him to underplay internal factors within the individual child.
• The effects of scaffolding are somewhat unpredictable. For example, the warmth or otherwise of the personal relationship between tutor and child can have a large impact on the effectiveness of scaffolding.
• Children vary in their preferred ways of learning. Many children prefer to learn with the assistance of a tutor. However, some older children prefer to acquire knowledge through reading rather than from interacting with a tutor.
• There are limitations (discussed later) with the scaffolding technique, in part because it involves complex interactions between the tutor and the child. This makes it hard to control precisely what happens in scaffolding and to identify the processes responsible for its success (or otherwise).

Comparison of the three main approaches

Vygotsky	Piaget	Bruner
Children are participating in an interactive process whereby knowledge becomes individualised through socially and culturally determined knowledge	Children's intellectual development can be seen in terms of the individual's adaptation to the environment	Social factors such as mutually rewarding adult support are vitally important in children's cognitive development

---

Applications of Piaget, Vygotsky, and Bruner to Education

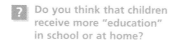 Do you think that children receive more "education" in school or at home?

The theoretical views of Piaget, Vygotsky, and Bruner have been very influential in education. We will start by considering how their influence has been felt. After that, we will discuss the cognitive acceleration through science education (CASE) programme. This programme represents an ambitious attempt to combine the insights of Piaget, Vygotsky, and Bruner to promote more effective teaching of science.

Piaget's approach

Piaget himself didn't focus very much on the usefulness of his theory for educational practice. However, many of his ideas are of clear relevance to education, and numerous educationalists have applied them to teaching. The Plowden Report, in 1967, suggested that Piaget's ideas should be used in schools (Central Advisory Council for Education (England), 1967). Years later, the Nuffield Science approach to education was based on the Piagetian notions that children should be actively involved in learning, and that concrete practical work should precede the more abstract aspects of science.

What can children learn?

According to Piaget, what children can learn is determined by their current stage of cognitive development. Thus, it is limited to what they are "ready" to learn. More specifically, children can only deal successfully with tasks making use of the various cognitive structures and operations they have already mastered. This prediction hasn't received much support. Several attempts have been made to teach concrete operations to preschool children. The ability to perform concrete operational tasks is generally learned at about the age of 7. Thus, it shouldn't be possible on Piagetian theory for much younger children to perform them successfully. However, provision of suitable training to 4-year-olds usually leads to reasonably good performance on such tasks (Brainerd, 1983). Thus, Piaget underestimated the ability of children to cope with new kinds of intellectual challenge.

How should children be taught?

According to Piaget, children learn best when engaged in a process of self-discovery involving initiative and an active approach. Children apply the processes of assimilation and accommodation to their active involvement with the world around them. Teachers can foster self-discovery in their students by creating a state of disequilibrium in which the child's existing schemas or cognitive structures are shown to be inadequate. Disequilibrium can be produced by asking children difficult questions and by encouraging them to ask questions.

Some of these ideas can be applied to playgroup practices and to children playing with toys. According to Piaget, children will obtain the most benefit from playgroups and from toys when actively involved in a process of self-discovery. In what Piaget called mastery play, the child uses new motor schemas or structures in several different situations. This helps to strengthen the child's learning.

Piaget's preferred approach can be contrasted with the traditional approach in which the teacher provides relatively passive children with knowledge. Piaget argued that this approach (**tutorial training**) is much less effective than self-discovery. In his own words, "Every time we teach a child something, we prevent him from discovering it on his own."

Brainerd (2003) reviewed the literature on self-discovery, and found it was generally less effective than tutorial training. He discussed five studies in which self-discovery of conservation concepts was compared to guided discovery, in which teachers directed students' attention to relevant features of the conservation task. Guided discovery was more effective than self-discovery in every study.

Disequilibrium

Piaget argued that disequilibrium (mismatch between new experiences and existing schemas) provides the *motivation* for children to advance in their cognitive development. The notion of disequilibrium was developed by neo-Piagetians such as Doise and Mugny (1984). They argued that cognitive development involves the resolution of socio-cognitive conflict, which is produced by exposure to the differing views of others. Thus, they emphasised social factors in learning more than Piaget did.

Evidence indicating the importance of socio-cognitive conflict was reported by Ames and Murray (1982) in a study on children aged 6 and 7 who had failed on conservation tasks. Some children were given corrective feedback. Others were exposed to children who had also failed to conserve but who had provided a

? Can you recall trying to master a skill, such as multiplication or telling the time, which seemed impossible to grasp but is now automatic?

different wrong answer from theirs. Children in the latter condition showed the greatest improvement in ability to conserve, because socio-cognitive conflict and the need to consider the task in detail were greater in this condition.

What should children be taught?

What school subjects are difficult to link with Piaget's theory? Which subjects fit well with the theory?

Piaget argued that cognitive development depends very much on children acquiring a range of schemas or cognitive structures (e.g. operations) mostly based on mathematical or logical principles. That means it should be useful for children to study mathematics and logic as well as science subjects providing illustrations of those principles at work. Of crucial importance is the notion that the learning material shouldn't be too complex or far removed from the child's existing schemas. According to Piaget, children can only learn effectively when they possess the relevant underlying schemas that can be accommodated to new experiences.

The major weakness of Piaget's position is that the cognitive structures he emphasised are of limited relevance for many kinds of learning. For example, concrete and formal operations are of little assistance in the learning of foreign languages or history. Thus, Piaget's approach applies only to some school subjects.

Evaluation

Most children in Western societies spend many years in school. What implications might this have for trying to apply Piaget's universal theory to all children?

- Piaget's ideas have influenced educational practice in several countries.
- Self-discovery and the creation of disequilibrium can both be very useful in learning, especially with intelligent students able to engage in independent thinking.
- As Piaget argued, it is often preferable for students to deal with concrete problems before proceeding to more abstract ones.
- There is evidence that more traditional approaches (e.g. tutorial training) are generally superior to Piaget's alternative approach.
- Piaget's approach can be used much more readily with subjects involving mathematical or logical principles (e.g. science; mathematics) than with subjects such as history or languages that don't involve such principles.
- It isn't easy to ascertain precisely what cognitive structures and schemas are possessed by any given child. However, this information is needed to decide the kinds of new learning for which he or she is "ready".

Vygotsky's and Bruner's approaches

Bruner's influential approach to cognitive development owed much to Vygotsky's earlier approach. We can divide up their respective influences on education as follows. Many of the general ideas from the combined approach of Vygotsky and Bruner were originally proposed by Vygotsky several decades before Bruner. However, Bruner (especially with the notion of "scaffolding") has provided innovative ways of implementing Vygotsky's ideas that have proved of benefit within education. Thus, it makes sense to discuss their approaches in the same section. As we proceed, I will do my best to make clear their respective contributions.

According to Vygotsky (1986, p. 188), "The only good kind of instruction is that which marches ahead of development and leads it; it must be aimed not so much at the ripe as the ripening functions." This can best be achieved when children's learning efforts are guided and encouraged by someone more knowledgeable. Thus, children are apprentices who are taught the necessary skills by those already possessing them. This is known as scaffolding, and we have seen it can enhance children's learning. Effective teachers reduce their control over the learning process when children are performing successfully and increase their control when children start making errors.

Peer tutoring

According to Vygotsky, those involved in teaching children should focus on the child's zone of proximal development. They should concentrate on knowledge only slightly beyond the child's current competence. The most effective tutors are often children slightly older and more advanced than those being taught. Such tutors have useful knowledge to communicate. However, they still remember the limitations in their own knowledge and understanding when they were 1 or 2 years younger. The approach described above is **peer tutoring**, and it has become increasingly popular in schools.

Peer tutoring: two brothers teach their younger sister to read.

Peer tutoring is generally effective. Barnier (1989) looked at the performance of 6- and 7-year-olds on various spatial and perspective-taking tasks. Those exposed to brief sessions of peer tutoring with 7- and 8-year-old tutors performed better than those who were not. Van Keer (2004) studied the effects of peer tutoring on the reading comprehension ability of 11-year-olds. Peer tutoring was effective when the tutor was a child older than the learner but not when the tutor was the same age. In the latter case, the knowledge of the peer tutor was insufficient to promote the learner's reading performance.

Peer tutoring has been found to work in various cultures. Ellis and Gauvain (1992) compared 7-year-old Navaho and Euro-American children performing a maze game. They were tutored by one or two 9-year-old tutors working together. The children from both cultures benefited more from the paired tutors than from the individual tutors, and the benefit was the same in both cultures.

Learning through play

Vygotsky argued that children can learn much through play. According to Vygotsky (1976, p. 552), "In play, the child functions above his average age, above his usual everyday behaviour, in play he is head high above himself." Why is this? Children at play generally make use of aspects of their own culture. For example, they may pretend to be a fire-fighter or a doctor, or they may play with toys specific to their culture. This relationship to their own culture enhances learning.

Scaffolding

Earlier in the chapter we discussed several examples of enhanced learning produced by scaffolding. Scaffolding is also involved in the successful use of peer tutoring. However, despite these successes, scaffolding has four main limitations. First, the learner may become uninvolved if the tutor has too much status. Second, scaffolding seems better suited to some kinds of tasks (e.g. construction tasks involving several steps) than to others. Howe, Tolmie, and Rodgers (1992) found that peer tutoring was of very little benefit on a task concerned with understanding

> **KEY TERM**
>
> **Peer tutoring:** teaching of one child by another, with the child doing the teaching generally being slightly older than the child being taught.

HOW SCIENCE WORKS: LEARNING TO SUBTRACT
Piaget's, Vygotsky's, and Bruner's ideas have all been applied to education. You could show how their ideas differ in practice by devising three different lessons, each one designed to teach children how to subtract, using numbers under 10. Each lesson should demonstrate how the relevant psychologist's theories would be operationalised.

• Why might it be helpful to specify the age of the children being taught?

You could present your ideas as detailed lesson plans, or clockwise spider diagrams, or even as a PowerPoint presentation.
   At the end, you could summarise the key similarities and differences of the three approaches.

motion down an incline. Third, the main focus of scaffolding is on the contribution made by the tutor to the child's understanding. In fact, however, the success (or otherwise) of scaffolding often depends crucially on the responsiveness of the tutor to the child's thoughts and actions. Fourth, scaffolding can be hard to control and to analyse because it involves complex interactions between tutor and child (Granott, 2005).

The CASE programme

It may appear that the approach to education based on Vygotsky's ideas is radically different from that of Piaget. As DeVries (2000) pointed out, Vygotsky seemed to emphasise factors *external* to the child (e.g. tutors, teachers) in promoting learning. In contrast, Piaget emphasised *internal* factors (e.g. adaptation), with the child in charge of the learning process. In fact, however, Vygotsky and Piaget were both fully aware of the importance of both external and internal factors. For example, Vygotsky's notion that tutors should teach within the zone of proximal development is a clear recognition of the importance of internal factors within the child.

Some of Piaget's and Vygotsky's ideas have been incorporated into the Cognitive Acceleration through Science Education (CASE) programme (see Shayer, 1999, for a review). This programme was originally used about 25 years ago in secondary schools in the UK and has since been developed and extended. The CASE programme has five main features, and a typical lesson involves working through them in the order listed:

1. *Concrete preparation*: involves the teacher setting the scene for what is to come. He or she ensures the students understand the scientific terms that will be used and know how to use any necessary equipment.
2. *Cognitive conflict*: is created by exposing students to unexpected ideas or findings that don't fit their preconceptions and that can't easily be understood on the basis of their current ways of thinking.
3. *Construction*: involves resolving the cognitive conflicts that have been created by discussions involving small groups or the entire class.
4. *Metacognition*: involves asking students open-ended questions requiring them to explain their thinking and focus on tricky issues. One student argued that this motivated students to have something worth saying, "Otherwise you'd feel a right prat" (Shayer, 2003, p. 482).
5. *Bridging*: involves relating students' new understanding to other aspects of science and their everyday experience. For this to work, teachers must have identified good examples to produce the required bridging.

How does the CASE approach use Piaget's and Vygotsky's ideas? First, the teacher's use of his or her greater knowledge to provide information during the concrete preparation and bridging phases is in line with Vygotsky's thinking. Second, the use of cognitive conflict resembles Piaget's emphasis on the importance of disequilibrium. Third, the phase of metacognition requires students to engage in a process resembling Piaget's self-discovery. Fourth, the construction phase resembles the peer tutoring approach based on Vygotsky's ideas.

How successful has the CASE programme been? The findings have been very impressive (Shayer, 1999). Students from numerous schools who have used the CASE programme have performed much better than other students on the nationwide General Certificate of Secondary Education (GCSE) examinations taken by 16-year-olds in the UK. This was true for students of very varying levels of ability. It was also true across science, mathematics, and English. For example, consider the 1997 GCSE results. On the basis of past performance, the percentages of CASE students predicted to obtain C grades or better were as follows: 19% in science, 18% in mathematics, and 26% in English. The actual percentages were 48% (science), 44% (mathematics), and 49% (English).

Evaluation
- The CASE programme represents an important combination of some ideas of Piaget and Vygotsky to provide an approach taking full account of external (teacher-related) and internal (child-related) factors.
- The CASE programme has proved successful across a wide range of ability and has led to substantial increases in academic performance. It has even led to increases in general intelligence (Shayer, 1999).
- Its success has led to the development of other programmes such as Cognitive Acceleration through Mathematics Education (CAME) and Cognitive Acceleration through Technology Education (CATE).
- The CASE programme incorporates five main features, and it is hard to assess the relative contributions of each feature to its overall success.
- The complexity of the CASE programme means that teachers require fairly lengthy and detailed training to use it successfully.

Summary of the different approaches to education

Piaget	Vygotsky	Bruner
Child-centred discovery ("discovery learning")	Teacher–child interaction ("social learning")	Child cognitively stretched and supported by teacher

SECTION SUMMARY
Development of Thinking

Piaget's theory

- Piaget argued that all children pass through four main stages of cognitive development.
- The sensori-motor stage: the key achievements are object permanence and imitation.
- The pre-operational stage: children focus on only one aspect of the situation (centration) and so don't show conservation. Their thinking is characterised by egocentrism.

❖ The concrete-operational stage: children show an increasing independence of thought from perception. This is associated with the development of conservation, reversibility, and an understanding of mathematical functions.

❖ The formal operations stage: adolescents can think abstractly and can envisage many possible states of the world.

❖ Evaluation:

— Piaget put forward the first comprehensive theory of cognitive development.

— Piaget exaggerated the differences between stages and minimised those within stages.

— Piaget underestimated the abilities of young children and overestimated those of adolescents.

— Piaget failed to explain how and why cognitive development occurs, and he de-emphasised the role of social factors.

Vygotsky's theory

❖ Vygotsky argued that children's cognitive development depends on social interaction and communication. Children often perform better in the presence of someone more knowledgeable than themselves.

❖ The instruction provided by others should be within the child's zone of proximal development (i.e. not too far above his or her current performance level).

❖ According to Vygotsky, language becomes increasingly central to cognitive development over the years. There is a shift from egocentric or private audible speech to inner speech.

❖ Evaluation:

— Vygotsky correctly emphasised social factors in cognitive development.

— Vygotsky's views led to the development of useful teaching techniques such as scaffolding.

— Vygotsky de-emphasised the role of internal factors.

— Social interactions aren't always beneficial to learning. They can distract attention from the task in hand or produce confrontation.

Bruner's theory

❖ According to Bruner, instruction should be easily understood and should be concerned with experiences that motivate students.

❖ Bruner emphasised the notion of scaffolding, which is the context provided by knowledgeable people to assist children's learning. Effective scaffolding involves the tutor providing input at a level slightly above the child's current performance, followed by a gradual withdrawal of support.

❖ Evaluation:

— Bruner was correct in assuming that social instruction can be very useful in promoting effective learning in children.

— Bruner identified several factors that have increased the usefulness of scaffolding.

— It is difficult to control the processes in scaffolding because it consists of complex and unpredictable interactions between tutor and child.

— The success of scaffolding depends not only on the appropriate inputs from the tutor but also on the personal relationship between the tutor and the child.

❖ According to Piaget, what children can learn is limited by their current stage of development.

❖ Piaget argued that children learn best when engaged in a process of self-discovery. Teachers can foster self-discovery by creating disequilibrium.

❖ Piaget argued that cognitive development depends very much on children acquiring schemas or cognitive structures.

❖ Evaluation:

— More traditional approaches are often more effective than self-discovery.
— Piaget's approach works better with science and mathematics than with arts subjects like history or languages.

❖ Vygotsky argued that teachers should focus on the child's zone of proximal development. One effective way in which this can be done is via peer tutoring.

❖ According to Vygotsky, children can learn much through play.

❖ Evaluation of scaffolding:

— The learner may not be involved if the tutor has too much status.
— It is less effective with some learning tasks than with others.
— Scaffolding involves complex interactions and so is hard to control.

❖ The CASE programme makes use of Piaget's and Vygotsky's ideas. It involves concrete preparation, cognitive conflict (like disequilibrium), construction, metacognition (like self-discovery), and bridging.

❖ The CASE programme is very successful. However, its complexities mean that teachers need detailed training to use it effectively.

Applications to education: Piaget

Vygotsky's and Bruner's approaches

The CASE programme

DEVELOPMENT OF MORAL UNDERSTANDING

This section considers how moral understanding develops. What is meant by the term "morality"? According to Shaffer (1993), morality implies "a set of principles or ideals that help the individual to distinguish right from wrong and to act on this distinction."

Why is morality important? Society can't function effectively unless there is some agreement on what is right and wrong. Of course, there are moral and ethical issues (e.g. animal experiments, abortion) on which individual members of a given society have very different views. However, if there were controversy on all major moral issues, society would become chaotic.

Shaffer (1993) argued that human morality has three components:

1. *Emotional component*: concerned with the feelings (e.g. guilt) associated with moral thoughts and behaviour.
2. *Cognitive component*: concerned with how we think about moral issues and make decisions about what is right and wrong.
3. *Behavioural component*: concerned with how we behave. It includes the extent to which we lie, steal, cheat, or behave honourably.

Why should we distinguish among these three components? One important reason is because there are often significant differences among them. We may

> **EXAM HINT**
>
> Questions in the exam could be on moral reasoning *and/or* pro-social reasoning, so you should make sure to cover both in your revision.

? How is moral understanding different to moral behaviour?

Shaffer's components of human morality		
Emotional	Cognitive	Behavioural
Feelings associated with moral behaviour	How we think about moral issues, and decide between right and wrong	How we behave
Theorists: Freud Eisenberg	Theorists: Piaget Kohlberg Gilligan	Theorists: Bandura Mischel
Approach: Psychodynamic/social cognition	Approach: Cognitive-developmental	Approach: Social learning

know at the cognitive level that it is wrong to cheat, but we may still cheat at the behavioural level. Some people lead blameless lives (behavioural component) but still feel guilty (emotional component). The title of this section is the "development of moral understanding": the emotional and cognitive components are part of moral understanding; the behavioural component is a means of seeing how moral understanding relates to behaviour.

The distinction between different moral components is also useful in comparing theories of moral development. We will focus mainly on the theories of moral understanding proposed by Kohlberg and by Eisenberg. Kohlberg's theory emphasises the cognitive component, whereas Eisenberg's theory focuses more on the emotional component.

Kohlberg's Theory

Lawrence Kohlberg (1927–1987) argued that we should consider children's moral development mainly from the cognitive perspective with an emphasis on understanding how children *think* about moral issues. The main experimental approach used by Kohlberg involved presenting people with various moral dilemmas. After that, they were asked a series of predetermined questions about what they would have done and why if actually faced with each dilemma. Thus, Kohlberg endeavoured to study moral reasoning—how individuals think about moral decisions—rather than moral behaviour.

Each dilemma required participants to decide whether it is preferable to uphold some law or other moral principle or to reject the moral principle in favour of some basic human need. Here is one of the moral dilemmas used by Kohlberg:

In Europe, a woman was dying from cancer. One drug might save her, a form of radium that a druggist in the same town had recently discovered. The druggist was charging 2000 dollars, ten times what the drug cost him to make. The sick woman's husband, Heinz, went to everyone he knew to borrow the money, but he could only get together about half of what the drug cost. He told the druggist that his wife was dying and asked him to sell it cheaper or let him pay later. But the druggist said "No". The husband got desperate and broke into the man's store to steal the drug for his wife.

[?] Do you think that you sometimes behave differently to your moral principles?

The moral principle in this dilemma is that stealing is wrong. However, it was the good motive of wanting to help his sick wife that led Heinz to steal the drug. It is precisely because there are powerful arguments for and against stealing the drug that there is a moral dilemma.

Kohlberg's stage theory

Kohlberg (1976) used evidence from a study using moral dilemmas like the one above to develop his stage theory of moral development. This evidence is discussed fully a little later. He assumed all children follow the same sequence of stages in their moral development. As we will see, he identified three levels, with two stages at each level.

Level 1: Pre-conventional morality

At this level, what is regarded as right and wrong is determined by the rewards or punishments likely to follow rather than by thinking about moral issues. Stage 1 of this level is based on a *punishment-and-obedience orientation*. Stealing is wrong because it involves disobeying authority and leads to punishment. Stage 2 of this level is based on the notion that the right way to behave is the one that is rewarded. There is more attention to the needs of other people than in stage 1, but mainly on the basis that if you help other people then they will help you.

Level 2: Conventional morality

The greatest difference between level 1 and level 2 is that the views and needs of other people are much more important at level 2 than at level 1. At this level,

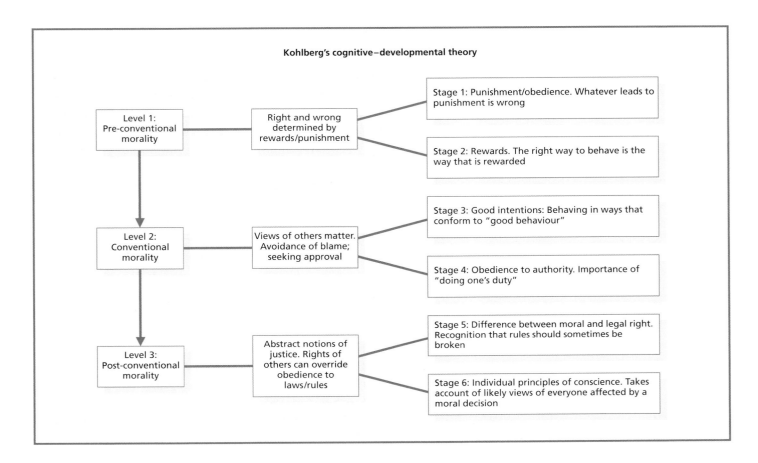

[?] In what way is moral reasoning related to moral understanding?

children really want to have the approval of others for their actions, and avoid being blamed by them for behaving wrongly. At stage 3, the emphasis is on having good intentions and on behaving in ways conforming to most people's views of good behaviour. At stage 4, children believe it is important to do one's duty, and to obey the laws or rules of those in authority.

Level 3: Post-conventional or principled morality

Those at the highest level of post-conventional or principled morality recognise that the laws or rules of authority figures should sometimes be broken. Abstract notions about justice and the need to treat other people with respect can *override* the need to obey laws and rules. At stage 5, there is a growing recognition that what is morally right may differ from what is legally right. Finally, at stage 6, the individual has developed his or her own principles of conscience. The individual takes into account the likely views of everyone who will be affected by a moral decision. Kohlberg (1981) described this as a kind of "moral musical chairs". It is very rare for anyone to operate most of the time at stage 6.

[?] Can you give examples to illustrate each of Kohlberg's six stages?

Findings

Kohlberg (1976) developed his theory of moral reasoning on the basis of a cross-sectional study. In this study, 72 boys aged between 10 and 16 were interviewed about moral dilemmas such as the "Heinz dilemma" above or the one described below:

> *In a country in Europe, a poor man named Valjean could find no work, nor could his sister and brother. Without money, he stole food and medicine that they needed. He was captured and sentenced to prison for 6 years. After a couple of years, he escaped from prison and went to live in another part of the country under a new name. He saved money and slowly built up a big factory. He gave his workers the highest wages and used most of his profits to build a hospital for people who couldn't afford good medical care. Twenty years had passed when a tailor recognised the factory owner as being Valjean, the escaped convict whom the police had been looking for back in his home town.*

The interviews consisted of a predetermined set of questions, such as "Should the tailor report Valjean to the police?", "Why or why not?", "Does a citizen have a duty or an obligation to report an escaped convict?", "Suppose Valjean were a close friend of the tailor. Should he then report Valjean?"

Each interview lasted 2 hours and allowed Kohlberg to classify each boy's level of moral reasoning. The original sample was followed for a further 20 years (Colby, Kohlberg, Gibbs, & Lieberman, 1983). The boys and men were tested six times in all at three-yearly intervals. The graph shows how moral reasoning developed. At age 10, the children displayed mainly stage 2 reasoning but there were examples of stages 1 and 3. By the age of 22,

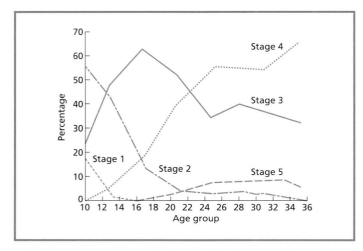

Kohlberg's moral stages studied longitudinally over a 20-year period encompassing ages 10 to 36. Adapted from Colby et al. (1983).

no-one used stage 1 reasoning and stages 3 and 4 were predominant. Most impressively for Kohlberg's theory, *all* participants progressed through the moral stages in exactly the predicted sequence. More worryingly for the theory, only about 10% of individuals in their 30s showed stage 5 moral reasoning, and there was practically no evidence of stage 6 reasoning at all.

Kohlberg's findings were confirmed by Walker, de Vries, and Trevethan (1987), who developed a modified set of nine stages to allow for the fact that reasoning often falls between two of Kohlberg's stages. They still found agreement with Kohlberg—for example, the equivalent of stage 2 reasoning dominated at age 10 and stage 3 at age 16.

To show that his moral stages were universal, Kohlberg (1969) studied the moral reasoning of children in several other countries: Britain, Mexico, Taiwan, Turkey, and USA. He found the same pattern of development, but moral development was slower in non-industrialised countries. Colby and Kohlberg (1987) reported longitudinal studies in Turkey and Israel that produced similar results.

Snarey (1985) reviewed 44 studies from 27 cultures. People in nearly all cultures went through the first four stages of moral development identified by Kohlberg in the same order and about the same time. There was little evidence of people omitting any stage of moral development or returning to an earlier stage. However, there was more evidence of stage 5 reasoning in Western cultures than in most rural or village cultures. According to Snarey, this does *not* mean that the moral reasoning of those living in Western cultures is superior to that of those living in other cultures. Instead, it reflects the individualistic emphasis of most Western cultures; for example, the greater value attached to human life.

Western cultures don't always emerge well from cross-cultural comparisons. Naito, Lin, and Gielen (2001) compared moral development in Western and East Asian cultures. East Asian adolescents reached the later stages of moral development earlier than adolescents in Western cultures. This may be due at least in part to the greater respect for authority within East Asian cultures.

Walker, Gustafson, and Hennig (2001) considered the hypothesis that *disequilibrium* or inconsistency in thinking about moral issues provides the motivation for children to advance to the next stage of moral reasoning. They carried out a longitudinal study in which children were given various moral dilemmas. The children's level of moral reasoning (based on Kohlberg's six stages) was assessed for each dilemma separately. It was assumed that children whose stage of moral reasoning differed considerably from dilemma to dilemma were in a state of disequilibrium. As predicted, children in a state of disequilibrium were most likely to show a rapid advance in moral reasoning shortly afterwards.

Kohlberg assumed that certain kinds of general cognitive development must occur before an individual can progress in his or her moral reasoning. For example, those whose moral reasoning is at stage 5 can use abstract principles (e.g. of justice), which presumably require them to be good at abstract thinking. Tomlinson-Keasey and Keasey (1974) found that girls of 11 and 12 who showed stage 5 moral reasoning were good at abstract thinking on general tests of cognitive development. However, some girls were good at abstract thinking but failed to show stage 5 moral reasoning. Thus, the ability to think abstractly is a necessary but not sufficient requirement for someone to attain stage 5 of post-conventional morality.

? Can you think of an example of how Kohlberg's levels of moral development emphasise individual rights?

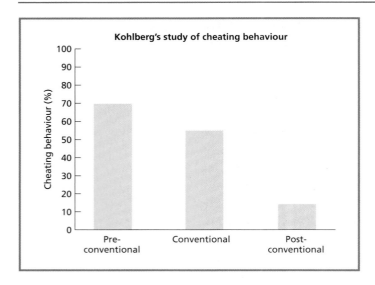

Kohlberg's study of cheating behaviour

A very important issue is whether individuals' level of moral reasoning based on what they *say* accurately reflects how they actually *behave*. The evidence is inconsistent. Santrock (1975) found that children's level of moral reasoning didn't predict whether they would cheat. However, adults' stage of moral reasoning sometimes predicts their behaviour. Kohlberg (1975) compared cheating behaviour among students at different levels of moral reasoning. About 70% of the students at the pre-conventional level were found to cheat, compared to only 15% of those at the post-conventional level. Students at the conventional level were intermediate (55% cheated). Kutnick and Brees (1982) reviewed evidence on the relationship between Kohlberg's stages of reasoning and behaviour, and concluded the relationship is generally not close.

Cross-cultural studies indicate there is more diversity in moral reasoning than suggested by Kohlberg. For example, Shweder (1990) compared Hindus in India with Americans living in Chicago. After the death of a relative, Hindus regard eating chicken or fish, or cutting one's hair, as serious transgressions. The reason is that such actions would reduce the chances of salvation. None of these acts was regarded as immoral by Americans. In contrast, many children living in Chicago regarded sexual inequality as an important moral issue, much more so than children living in India. Isawa (1992) compared the reasoning used by Japanese and American people when given the Kohlberg problem about a man stealing a drug for his wife who has cancer. The stage of moral reasoning was the same in both groups. However, the Japanese participants thought the man shouldn't steal the drug so as to make his life cleaner and purer, whereas the Americans thought the man should steal the drug to prolong his wife's life.

There is a final issue. Kohlberg claimed that any given individual's level of moral reasoning is *consistent* across different problems and different contexts. In fact, however, there is much evidence of inconsistency with moral dilemmas other than those studied by Kohlberg. Denton and Krebs (1990) gave students with an average age of 25 years Kohlberg's moral dilemmas when they were sober in an academic setting and when they had had alcohol in a social drinking setting. The level of moral reasoning was significantly lower in the social drinking than the academic setting. Thus, moral reasoning is *not* consistent but varies depending on the context. In addition, the students when sober indicated they wouldn't drive when intoxicated. However, at the end of their drinking session, all but one of the students drove home!

Gilligan's anti-Kohlberg approach

Gilligan (1977) argued that a major problem with Kohlberg's theory was its focus on male morality, an **androcentric bias**. She pointed out all the participants in Kohlberg's original study were male, and she claimed that essentially Kohlberg had produce a theory centred on how men approach moral decisions. According to Gilligan (1982), boys develop a **morality of justice** focusing on the use of laws and moral principles. In contrast, girls develop a **morality of care**, in which

KEY TERMS

Androcentric bias: a bias in favour of males. An androcentric theory is based on research data on males and then applied to all human behaviour.

Morality of justice: this is a form of morality in which the emphasis is on the importance of laws and moral principles.

Morality of care: this is a form of morality in which the emphasis is on showing compassion for others and focusing on human well-being.

their main focus is on human well-being and compassion for others. Kohlberg showed sexist bias by regarding the morality of justice as superior to the morality of care.

Gilligan and Attanucci (1988) assessed moral reasoning in the context of real-life dilemmas to make their findings more valid. Eighty men and women aged between 14 and 77 were asked various questions about moral conflict and choice. Sample questions were "Have you ever been in a situation of moral conflict where you had to make a decision but weren't sure what was the right thing to do?"; "Could you describe the situation?"; "What did you do?"; "Do you think it was the right thing to do?"; and "How do you know?". Each participant was interviewed individually for 2 hours, and their answers classified as care only, care focus (more than 75% care considerations), care justice (less than 75% of either), justice focus, or justice only.

What did Gilligan and Attanucci (1988) find? As predicted, far more men were in the justice focus or justice only categories: 65% vs. only 2%. Also as predicted, more women (35%) than men (30%) were in the care focus or care only categories. However, they used a relatively small number of women (34) and the method of interviewing was unsystematic and potentially biased.

Jaffee and Hyde (2000) carried out a meta-analysis of 113 studies focusing on possible gender differences in moral orientation. Overall, there was only a very small tendency for males to show more justice reasoning than females, and a slightly larger (but still small) tendency for females to show more care reasoning than males. According to Jaffee and Hyde (p. 719):

> *The small magnitude of these effects [the ones just described], combined with the finding that 73% of the studies that measured justice reasoning and 72% of the studies that measured care reasoning failed to find significant gender differences, leads us to conclude that, although distinct moral orientations may exist, these orientations are not strongly associated with gender.*

Evaluation

Kohlberg's theory of moral reasoning has several strengths. First, he provided a reasonably detailed and accurate account of moral development. Second, children in nearly all cultures work through the various stages of moral reasoning in the order specified by Kohlberg. Third, as Kohlberg had suggested, disequilibrium motivates children's developments in moral reasoning (Walker, Gustafson, & Hennig, 2001). Fourth, there is evidence of an association between developments in moral reasoning and general cognitive development.

The main limitations of Kohlberg's theory are as follows. First, few people seem to develop beyond stage 4 (Colby et al., 1983; Snarey, 1985), suggesting that stages 5 and 6 are much less important in real life than the preceding stages. Second, Kohlberg focused on moral judgements in response to artificial dilemmas rather than on actual moral behaviour. This is a problem because such judgements typically fail to predict behaviour accurately (Kutnick & Brees, 1982). Third, moral reasoning is less consistent across different types of moral problems than assumed by Kohlberg. Fourth, Kohlberg didn't consider the emotional component of morality in any detail. For example, the development of emotions such as shame and guilt is important within moral development (reviewed by Eisenberg,

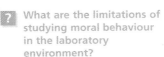

? How could you measure moral development in a way that is not gender specific?

? What are the limitations of studying moral behaviour in the laboratory environment?

? How are empathy and sympathy different?

? What do you think personal distress leads to?

2000). Fifth, Kohlberg paid insufficient attention to differences in moral reasoning across cultures.

Eisenberg's Theory

Nancy Eisenberg felt that Kohlberg's emphasis on justice and fairness overlooked a key aspect of morality—pro-social moral reasoning. We can start to gain an understanding of what that means by considering a definition of pro-social behaviour: "Any voluntary, intentional action that produces a positive or beneficial outcome for the recipient regardless of whether that action is costly to the donor, neutral in its impact, or beneficial" (Grusec, Davidov, & Lundell, 2002, p. 2). Thus, pro-social moral reasoning involves responding in a positive way emotionally and behaviourally when someone else is in need.

Eisenberg argues that **empathy** is a fundamental part of moral development and pro-social moral reasoning. Empathy is "an affective response that stems from the apprehension or comprehension of another's emotional state or condition, and is identical to or very similar to what the other person is feeling" (Eisenberg & Fabes, 1998, p. 702). In order for individuals to behave in a caring way towards others, it is very important for them to feel empathy. However, empathy is not enough on its own. There are two major possible consequences of empathy:

1. **Sympathy**, which "consists of feelings of sorrow or concern for the other" (Eisenberg, 2002, p. 33).
2. **Personal distress**, which is "a self-focused, aversive affective reaction to the apprehension of another's emotion, e.g. discomfort, anxiety" (Eisenberg, 2002, p. 33).

According to Eisenberg, sympathy generally leads to pro-social or helping behaviour whereas personal distress does not.

Eisenberg believed, like Kohlberg, that changes take place in moral reasoning in parallel with the maturation of general cognitive abilities. Eisenberg especially emphasised the growth of role-taking skills—the ability to assume the perspective and take the part of another person. These skills in turn assist in the growth of empathy and thus pro-social moral reasoning. According to Eisenberg, Lennon, and Roth (1983), there are five levels or stages in the development of pro-social reasoning:

- Level 1: the child "is concerned with self-oriented consequences rather than moral considerations" (Eisenberg et al., 1983, p. 850). The child focuses on direct gains to himself/herself and the likelihood that any assistance provided will be reciprocated in the future.
- Level 2: the child "expresses concern for the physical, material, and psychological needs of others" (Eisenberg et al., 1983, p. 850). However, this concern doesn't involve role taking or expressions of sympathy.
- Level 3: the child focuses on stereotyped views of the behaviour of good and bad people, and wants the approval of others.
- Level 4: the individual shows empathy and sympathy, role taking, and experiences positive emotion if help if given. Helping (or not helping) is justified by internalised values and norms.

Levels in the development of pro-social reasoning

- Level 5: the individual's justifications for helping or not helping are more strongly based on internalised values and beliefs. He or she focuses on living up to his or her own values.

Findings

Eisenberg's theory has been tested by asking children of different ages to decide what they would do if faced by various dilemmas. Here is one of the dilemmas:

One day a girl named Mary was going to a friend's birthday party. On her way she saw a girl who had fallen down and hurt her leg. The girl asked Mary to go to her house and get her parents so that they could come and take her to the doctor. But if Mary did . . . she would be late for the party and would miss the ice cream, cake, and all the games. What should Mary do?

Eisenberg-Berg and Hand (1979) found that young children were self-centred. Most of them decided Mary should go to the party and leave the injured girl on her own. In contrast, older children generally decided it was more important to help the injured girl than to go to the party. Of course, the opinions expressed by children when given such dilemmas may not correspond to their actual behaviour in everyday life. However, Eisenberg-Berg and Hand obtained some evidence that the level of pro-social reasoning revealed by the dilemmas *does* predict actual behaviour. Sharing behaviour was more common among children at level 2 of pro-social reasoning than among those at level 1.

If we are to obtain clear evidence about developmental changes in pro-social reasoning it is useful to carry out longitudinal studies in which the *same* children are followed up for several years. Precisely that was done by Eisenberg et al. (1983), who assessed the same group of children at average ages of 55, 73, and

? If Mary went to the party, what level of Eisenberg's theory is she on?

? If Mary thinks by helping the girl she will be told how brave and thoughtful she acted and so she decides to help, what level of Eisenberg's theory is she on?

The amount of spontaneous sharing exhibited in preschool children predicted levels of pro-social empathy all the way through childhood until adulthood.

91 months. There was a progressive decrease in self-centred pro-social reasoning with increasing age, coupled with an increase in needs-oriented pro-social reasoning. These changes were as predicted by the theory. There was only a moderate association or correlation between pro-social moral reasoning and moral reasoning as assessed by Kohlberg's moral dilemmas. Thus, the two approaches focus on somewhat different aspects of moral reasoning.

Eisenberg, Fabes, Shepard, Guthrie, Murphy, and Reiser (1999) reported findings on some of the children studied by Eisenberg et al. (1983) through to the age of 19 or 20. What did they discover? First, there were stable individual differences in pro-social reasoning and behaviour. The amount of spontaneous sharing that children showed in preschool predicted their pro-social responding and sympathy all the way through to early adulthood.

Second, as predicted by Eisenberg's theory, children showing the most pro-social behaviour also tended to have the highest levels of sympathy. Indeed, the main reason why early spontaneous sharing predicted later pro-social behaviour was that young children who shared had more sympathy than those who did not.

Third, also as predicted theoretically, personal distress was negatively associated with pro-social behaviour. However, the effects were only modest.

What types of parenting are associated with children's development of pro-social reasoning? This question was addressed by Eisenberg et al. (1983) in a study we discussed earlier. They discovered that the answer varies somewhat as a function of the child's age. Younger children's pro-social reasoning develops most rapidly when they receive supportive and empathic mothering. In contrast, pro-social reasoning in older children develops best when the mother is non-authoritarian and encourages independence in her child.

According to Eisenberg's theory, empathy only develops fully at about the age of 12. In fact, however, most of the ingredients of full empathy are present several years earlier. For example, Radke-Yarrow and Zahn-Waxler (1984) found evidence of empathy and sympathy in children as young as 18 months. Here is an example:

> *A neighbour's baby cries. Jenny [18 months old] looked startled, her body stiffened. She approached and tried to give the baby cookies. She followed him around and began to whimper herself. She then tried to stroke his hair, but he pulled away. Later, she approached her mother, led her to the baby, and tried to put her mother's hand on the baby's head. He calmed down a little, but Jenny still looked worried. She continued to bring him toys and to pat his head and shoulders. (Radke-Yarrow & Zahn-Waxler, 1984, p. 89)*

Additional evidence was reported by Zahn-Waxler, Robinson, and Emde (1992) in a study on children in three age groups: 13–15 months; 18–20 months; and 23–25 months. When a child witnessed another child's distress, the oldest children were far more likely than the youngest children to react with pro-social behaviour (49% vs. 9% of the time). Empathy or sympathy in response to another child's distress also increased from 9% of occasions in the youngest group to 25% in the oldest group, whereas personal distress decreased from 15% to 7%. These findings show the theoretically predicted changes in pro-social development but at much younger ages than those assumed by Eisenberg.

Which is of greater usefulness: a theory of moral reasoning or moral behaviour?

Evaluation

Eisenberg's theory of pro-social reasoning has several successes to its credit. First, it provides a different perspective on the development of moral understanding from Kohlberg. It emphasises the *positive* aspects of morality, whereas Kohlberg focused on issues to do with laws, rules, punishment, and obligations. Second, despite the differences, Eisenberg's approach can be regarded as a broadening of Kohlberg's original approach with an increased emphasis on emotional factors. Third, the evidence broadly supports Eisenberg's stage-based approach to the development of pro-social reasoning. Fourth, Eisenberg's approach is of value to parents in that it shows how to raise helpful and altruistic children. For example, emphasising that the consequences of an action matter, and acting as pro-social models for children's behaviour, are both useful approaches for parents to adopt.

What are the limitations of Eisenberg's approach? First, it is difficult to distinguish among internal emotional states such as "empathy", "sympathy", and "personal distress", all of which involve the child experiencing negative emotional states. Second, the prediction that personal distress should be negatively related to pro-social behaviour has received only modest support. Third, Eisenberg failed to produce a comprehensive theory of moral reasoning because she ignored those important aspects of moral judgement when laws and rules are involved. Fourth, there is evidence of sympathy and empathy in children several years earlier than predicted by Eisenberg et al. (1983). Fifth, Eisenberg assessed children's stage or level of pro-social reasoning by using hypothetical dilemmas. The stage of pro-social reasoning only predicts behaviour to some extent, because behaviour is also influenced by other factors (e.g. desire to impress other people).

> **EXAM HINT**
>
> You may be asked to cover either moral understanding or pro-social reasoning. Make sure you know both Kohlberg's and Eisenberg's theories in equal depth so that you are prepared to answer a question on either or both.

SECTION SUMMARY
Development of Moral Understanding

❖ Kohlberg assessed moral development from the cognitive perspective using hypothetical moral dilemmas.

Kohlberg's theory

❖ Kohlberg argued that all children proceed through the same sequence of three moral levels (two stages at each level): pre-conventional morality; conventional morality; and post-conventional morality. He found in a study that all his participants progressed through the moral stages in the predicted sequence.

❖ Evaluation:

— There is reasonable cross-cultural support for the theory.
— Moral judgements often fail to predict moral behaviour.
— Individuals' levels of moral reasoning across different problem types are less consistent than predicted.
— Kohlberg de-emphasised the role of emotional factors in moral behaviour.

Eisenberg's theory

❖ Eisenberg argued that empathy is a fundamental part of moral development. Empathy can produce sympathy or personal distress, with only the former leading to pro-social behaviour.

❖ There are five levels or stages in the development of pro-social reasoning. According to the theory, children show an increased concern and empathy for other people rather than focusing exclusively on themselves.

❖ As predicted, children show a steady decrease in self-centred pro-social reasoning and an increase in needs-oriented pro-social reasoning.

❖ Mothers who are non-authoritarian and who encourage independence promote pro-social reasoning in their older children.

❖ Evaluation:

— Eisenberg focused on the positive aspects of morality.
— Pro-social reasoning can develop earlier than predicted by Eisenberg.
— There is little evidence that personal distress is negatively related to pro-social behaviour.

DEVELOPMENT OF SOCIAL COGNITION

As children grow up, they have a rapidly developing sense of who they are. They also have a large increase in their social involvement with other people, and a clearer sense of their place in society. What underlies these developments? In part, they occur as children develop emotionally. However, they also depend very much on children's cognitive development, and this will be our main focus in this section. More specifically, children gradually acquire an increasing ability to understand the thoughts, feelings, and intentions of other people. Many theorists have argued that this ability is of crucial importance in explaining children's social development. The argument is that you will find it much easier to interact successfully with someone else if you can see how things look from their point of view.

The three approaches discussed in this section are all based on the assumption that an ability to "read the minds" of other people is of enormous value in social interaction. According to the first approach we will consider (Baron-Cohen's **Theory of Mind**), young children assume that other people's beliefs are the same as their own. It is only when they start to realise that other people often have *different* beliefs that they show real progress in social development.

Selman's perspective-taking theory is the second approach we will consider. The basic assumptions resemble those of Theory of Mind. It is assumed that children gradually acquire the ability to adopt other people's perspective, and that this greatly increases the likelihood of children interacting successfully with other children.

Finally, we will consider the biological approach. What is exciting about this approach is that parts of the brain involved in understanding others' intentions have apparently been identified. As we will see, there are reasons for arguing that a system in the brain known as the **mirror neuron system** plays a key role in allowing us to make sense of other people's behaviour.

KEY TERMS

Theory of Mind: having an understanding that others' thoughts and emotions are different from one's own.

Mirror neuron system: it consists of numerous neurons in the brain that respond in a very similar way whether an individual performs a given action or observes someone else perform the same action; this system is allegedly important in imitation behaviour and developing an understanding of others' actions.

Development of Child's Sense of Self

It is hard to exaggerate the significance of the development of a sense of self within social development. According to Schaffer (1996, pp. 154–155), "Of all social concepts that of the self is the most basic . . . It has a key role because it determines how each of us construes reality and what experiences we seek out in order to fit in with the self-image." Many factors are involved in the child's developing sense of self. One of the most important is the child's gradual realisation that other children and adults have beliefs, thoughts, and emotions differing from his or her own. An extremely influential theoretical approach here is Simon Baron-Cohen's Theory of Mind, which will be the central focus in this section. By the way, Simon Baron-Cohen *is* related to Sacha Baron Cohen (they are first cousins). Sacha Baron Cohen is most famous for two of the characters he has played—Ali G and Borat.

Theory of Mind

One crucial difference between most 5-year-olds and most 2- or 3-year-olds is that the former understand that other people's beliefs about the world may differ from their own. This is really important, because social communication is extremely limited if a child assumes everyone else has the same beliefs. Research in this area revolves around the notion of Theory of Mind, which "conveys the idea of understanding social interaction by attributing beliefs, desires, intentions, and emotions to people" (Astington & Jenkins, 1999, p. 1311). In other words, children and adults possessing Theory of Mind are "mind readers" who are reasonably good at understanding what other people are thinking and feeling.

Theory of Mind has been assessed using various false-belief tasks. For example, Wimmer and Perner (1983) used models to present children with the following story. A boy called Maxi puts some chocolates in a blue cupboard. While he is out of the room, his mother moves the chocolate to a green cupboard. The children indicated where Maxi would look for the chocolate when he returned to the room. Most 4-year-olds argued mistakenly that Maxi would look in the green cupboard. This indicates an absence of theory of mind, because these children simply assumed that Maxi's beliefs were the same as their own. In contrast, most 5-year-olds produced the right answer.

Wellman, Cross, and Watson (2001) reported a meta-analysis based on 178 false-belief studies. Most 3-year-olds performed poorly on false-belief tasks whereas a substantial majority of 5-year-olds were correct. The findings were similar in seven different countries (United States, United Kingdom, Korea, Australia, Canada, Austria, and Japan), except that a Theory of Mind developed slowest in Austria and Japan. Thus, a Theory of Mind develops at about the age of 4.

? How might these similarities and differences be explained?

Flynn (2006) studied the development of Theory of Mind over several months. Young children, most of whom were 3 years old at the start of the experiment, showed a gradual development in the understanding of false beliefs on theory-of-mind tests. For some time before the children could explain other people's behaviour with reference to their false beliefs, they were in a state of confusion and failed to provide any explanation.

How can we explain children's development of Theory of Mind? We will focus on two explanations. First, Baron-Cohen (1995) emphasised the importance of a "shared attention mechanism", which involves combining information about your

The shared attention mechanism allows a child to determine whether they and another person are attending to the same object.

direction of gaze with that of someone else. Children using this mechanism can think along the following lines: "I see that X sees the object; X sees that I see the object." The shared attention mechanism allows children to decide whether they and another person are actually attending to the same object. It also allows them some insight into the mental state of another person (e.g. "Mummy sees the toy").

Second, Astington and Jenkins (1999) argued that language development is central to children's development of theory of mind. Findings supporting that viewpoint are discussed below.

Findings

While it is generally assumed that Theory of Mind typically develops around the age of 4, some aspects of Theory of Mind may develop earlier. O'Neill (1996) carried out a study in which 2-year-old children watched an attractive toy being placed on a high shelf in the presence or absence of their parent. The children subsequently asked their parent to let them have the toy. Those children whose parent had been absent previously were much more likely to name the toy and to gesture towards it than were those whose parent had been present. Thus, even 2-year-olds may have some awareness of the knowledge possessed by others.

Some research has focused on Baron-Cohen's (1995) notion that Theory of Mind in children is facilitated by the earlier development of a shared attention mechanism. This hypothesis was tested by Charman, Baron-Cohen, Swettenham, Baird, Cox, and Drew (2000) in a longitudinal study. Children's ability to show shared or joint attention with an adult was assessed when they were 20 months, and their performance on Theory-of-Mind tasks was assessed at 44 months. As predicted by Baron-Cohen's hypothesis, shared or joint attention at 20 months predicted Theory of Mind performance 2 years later. This finding suggests that shared attention is one of the abilities needed for Theory of Mind to develop.

The role of language ability in Theory of Mind was examined by Lohmann, Carpenter, and Call (2005) on two false-belief tasks with 3- and 4-year-old children. Performance on both tasks was better among children with higher vocabulary and grammar scores. Astington and Jenkins (1999) carried out a longitudinal study on 3-year-olds to test the assumption that language development underlies improvement on false-belief tasks with age. The children were given various Theory-of-Mind tasks (e.g. false-belief tasks) and measures of language competence over a 7-month period. Language development at one time predicted later Theory-of-Mind performance. Thus, language ability may play a causal role in the development of Theory of Mind.

Autism

Autism is a serious condition characterised by very poor social interaction (e.g. a failure to develop peer relationships, not actively participating in play, preference for solitary activities), impaired communication (e.g. delay in the development of

EXAM HINT

Make sure you can explain how the shared attention mechanism and language are causally linked to Theory of Mind.

KEY TERM

Autism: a severe disorder involving very poor communication skills, deficient social and language development, and repetitive behaviour.

language; reluctance to maintain a conversation), and repetitive patterns of behaviour. About 70% of autistic children also have mental retardation, and 40% have IQs below 50 (lower than over 99% of the healthy population).

According to Baron-Cohen (e.g. Baron-Cohen, Leslie, & Frith, 1985), the central problem of autistic children is that they lack a Theory of Mind. More specifically, they don't understand that other people have different ideas and knowledge from their own, and they don't appreciate that behaviour is influenced by beliefs and thoughts. As a result, autistic children can't make sense of the social world, which prevents them from communicating effectively with other people. Baron-Cohen (1995, p. 5) argued that autistic children suffer from "mindblindness", in that "they fail to develop the capacity to mindread in the normal way."

Suppose that Baron-Cohen is correct in assuming the central problem in autistic children is that they lack a Theory of Mind. The implication is that typical social development including the development of friendships and effective communication with other people depends very heavily on the possession of Theory of Mind. That seems reasonable—how can you interact successfully with other people if you can't understand what they are thinking or feeling?

According to Baron-Cohen (1995), an important reason why autistic children fail to develop Theory of Mind in the same way as other children is because they lack a shared attention mechanism. As discussed earlier, Baron-Cohen assumed it is important for children to develop a shared attention mechanism as a first step towards Theory of Mind. The shared attention mechanism allows children to gain insight into the mental state of other people by working out what they are attended to. If autistic children lack a shared attention mechanism, this would greatly reduce their chances of developing Theory of Mind.

CASE STUDY: AUTISTIC TALENTS

Not all aspects of autism are as negative as might be imagined. Some autistic children have startling artistic abilities and can produce drawings in full detail and perspective much earlier than other children.

An autistic girl named Nadia was studied by Selfe (1983). When she was only 5 years old, Nadia could draw realistic pictures of horses, cockerels, and cavalrymen from memory, although she did not speak and had various severe motor problems.

Other talents shown by autistic children and adults include feats of mental arithmetic, for example being able to calculate the day of the week for any given date in the previous 500 years. There have also been gifted autistic musicians who learn to play musical instruments by ear, with no formal training.

These talents may all be linked in some way to the autistic child's narrow focus on the world, through which they can become preoccupied with certain objects or processes in great detail.

Kanner (1943) called gifts like these "islets of ability", which suggests that other aspects of autistic children's intelligence are hidden beneath the surface of a sea of difficulties.

Drawings by 5-year old Nadia, who is autistic (left), and an average 6½-year-old child (right).

Findings

Baron-Cohen, Campbell, Karmiloff-Smith, Grant, and Walker (1995) studied typically developing 4-year-old children as well as older autistic and Down's syndrome children with a mental age of at least 4. All these children were given the following false-belief task designed to assess Theory of Mind:

Sally puts her marble in the basket. Then she goes out. Anne takes Sally's marble, and puts it into her box. Then Sally comes back from her walk and wants to play with her marble. Where will she look for her marble?

More than 80% of the typically developing and Down's syndrome children correctly pointed to the basket, but only 20% of the autistic children did. Thus, most of the autistic children didn't understand that other children may have a different perspective from their own—they seemed to lack Theory of Mind.

The fact that 20% of the autistic children in the study by Baron-Cohen et al. (1995) appeared to show Theory of Mind seems inconsistent with the theory that a lack of Theory of Mind is *always* central to the problems of autistic children. However, autistic children don't solve Theory-of-Mind problems in the same way as healthy children. When they succeed on such problems, they seem to use deliberate strategies to work out the correct answers in a laborious way, whereas typically developing children produce correct answers rapidly and without deliberation (Happé, 1995).

More evidence that nearly all autistic children have major problems with Theory of Mind was reported by Baron-Cohen (1989) using a more complex Theory-of-Mind task. He found that 90% of typically developing children (mean age = 7½ years) solved this problem correctly. In contrast, 0% of the autistic children produced the right answer even though they were several years older than the typically developing children.

The Sally–Anne test. C denotes the child observer, and E is the experimenter.

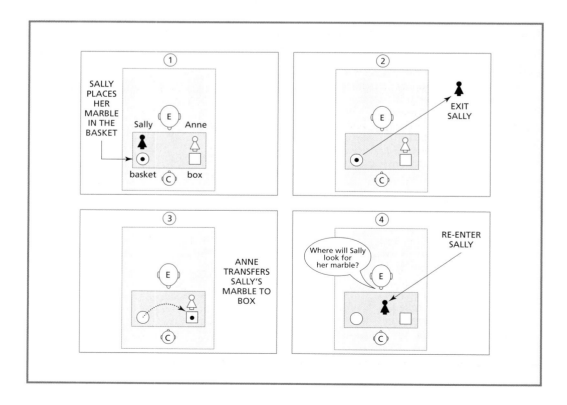

Baron-Cohen's (1995) theoretical ideas about autism and the shared attention mechanism have been tested in several studies. For example, Baron-Cohen et al. (1995) found that most young children know that if someone looks at one out of four blocks of chocolate, that is the one that person wants. As predicted theoretically, autistic children didn't realise that that was the case.

Baron-Cohen et al. (1996) administered five tests (including a test of shared attention) to 16,000 18-month-old infants. Nearly all the 12 infants who failed every test were diagnosed with autism by the age of 42 months. These findings are consistent with the notion that autistic children fail to develop Theory of Mind at least in part because they lack the shared attention mechanism.

Dawson et al. (2004) studied autistic children, developmentally delayed, and typically developing children. Three different aspects of attention were assessed in these three groups: (1) joint or shared attention; (2) social orienting (greater attention to social than to mechanical stimuli); and (3) attention to another's distress. The autistic children performed at a lower level than the other two groups on all tests. However, the group differences were greatest on the joint or shared attention task. This suggests that autistic children have a special difficulty with shared attention rather than simply with attention itself.

Baron-Cohen assumed that autistic children's poor performance on false-belief tasks is due to a fairly *specific* cognitive deficit, namely, mindblindness. However, the problems autistic children have with false-belief and other tasks may also reflect fairly *general* cognitive deficits. Performance on false-belief tasks depends on executive functions such as planning and inhibition of dominant responses (e.g. Müller, Zelazo, & Imrisek, 2005), and autistic children are impaired with respect to these executive functions (see Hill & Frith, 2003, for a review). Hughes and Russell (1993) used a task in which participants had to turn a knob or flick a switch to obtain a marble in a box, but couldn't obtain it by reaching into the box. Autistic children found it much harder than children with learning difficulties to inhibit the response of reaching immediately for the marble. Planning in autistic children has been studied by observing their performance on the Tower of Hanoi, in which discs have to be moved according to various rules to attain a specified goal state. Autistic children show very poor planning on this task (Hill & Frith, 2003).

Another *general* cognitive deficit that may help to explain the problems of autistic children relates to **central coherence**. Central coherence refers to the tendency to use *all* the available information when interpreting a situation. For example, someone may say something unkind, but the smile on their face indicates they don't mean it seriously. Frith and Happé (1994) argued that autistic children lack central coherence. Instead, they attend to only parts of the

> **KEY TERM**
>
> **Central coherence:**
> using all of the available information to make sense of a social situation; autistic children lack this ability.

> ■ Activity: Autism
>
> H is a 20-year-old man with autism and mild learning disability. He would like to have friends but has an idealistic concept of friendship, as he thinks a friend is a person "you'll do anything for", with no exceptions. He has been recruited as a lookout by a local gang while they break into cars and he has been very efficient at this, giving appropriate warnings so his friends get away. However, he himself was caught because he had no concept of the need to look inconspicuous, and also failed to flee when the others did. H is likely to co-operate with any demands his friends make because he values their friendship so strongly.
>
> How does your knowledge of autism explain H's attitude and behaviour in this example?

information. The devastating effect that can have is shown in this quotation from Donna Williams, who is an autistic adult:

> *It is hard to care or be interested in what a person feels when you perceive a body and then a hand and an eye and a nose and other bits all moving but not perceiving in any connected way, with no perception of the context. (Williams, 1994, p. 49)*

Overall evaluation

The theoretical approach of Baron-Cohen and others on Theory of Mind possesses several advantages: First, the development of a Theory of Mind is of real importance in allowing children to communicate well with other people. Second, there is considerable support for the major assumptions of the theory. As Rajendran and Mitchell (2007, p. 231) pointed out, "The essential clinical picture that individuals with autism have difficulties understanding their own and others' mind seems unquestionable." Third, some aspects of cognitive development associated with the development of a theory of mind have been identified. Language development seems to be of particular importance. Fourth, autistic children's difficulties with false-belief tasks reflect at least in part problems with general executive functions and are thus of wide significance. These include the shared attention mechanism, planning, and inhibition of dominant responses.

The Theory-of-Mind approach also possesses some limitations: First, false-belief tasks are complex. There is no agreement concerning the balance of general and specific processes underlying performance on such tasks when performed by healthy individuals (Apperly, Samson, & Humphreys, 2005). Baron-Cohen may have exaggerated the importance of Theory of Mind in explaining performance on false-belief tasks.

Second, Baron-Cohen has emphasised the importance of specific cognitive deficits in explaining autistic children's Theory of Mind. However, motivational factors are probably also involved. Autistic children may not achieve Theory of Mind in part because they are less motivated than typically developing children to understand others' thoughts and feelings.

Third, Baron-Cohen argues that autistic children have a specific cognitive deficit relating to Theory of Mind. However, there is good evidence that autistic children also have general cognitive deficits in executive functioning and in central coherence.

Fourth, the Theory-of-Mind approach doesn't account for *all* the problems faced by autistic children. As Smith, Cowie, and Blades (2003, p. 481) pointed out, "It is not obvious how specific language problems . . . , obsessive behaviours, or 'islets of ability' [in autistic children] could be linked to a lack of understanding minds."

Development of Children's Understanding of Others: Selman's Perspective-taking Theory

If children are going to understand other children, to communicate effectively with them, and to make friends, they need to have some ability to take other people's perspective. That was the central assumption that Robert Selman (1976,

1980) incorporated into his perspective-taking theory. This assumption is similar to Baron-Cohen's emphasis on the importance of developing a Theory of Mind that permits children to read the minds of others. Selman also argued that developing good perspective-taking abilities enables children and adolescents to negotiate more effectively with other people and to resolve interpersonal conflicts.

The other major assumption was that children generally proceed through a series of levels or stages in which they become progressively better able to adopt the perspective of other children and of adults. Selman identified five levels that children go through. When they are very young, they have little or no idea what someone else might be thinking or feeling. They gradually come to understand that other people can interpret a given situation or event very differently from them. This allows them to realise that other people's *emotional* reactions to that situation or event may also differ from their own. As noted already, there are clear similarities here with the Theory of Mind approach discussed in the previous section. Finally, most older children and adolescents can compare two people's perspectives on a situation at the same time. The details of these five levels (together with the approximate ages at which they occur in brackets) are shown in the box below.

Selman's (1976) levels of perspective taking

Level 0: Egocentric viewpoint (ages 3–6)

Children at this level have some recognition they can have different thoughts and feelings from others. However, they don't distinguish between their social perspective (thoughts and feelings) and that of the other person.

Level 1: Social-informational role taking (ages 6–8)

Children at this level or stage understand that other people can have access to different information, and that this difference can produce different perspectives. However, they generally focus on just one perspective rather than co-ordinating perspectives.

Level 2: Self-reflective role taking (ages 8–10)

Children at this level can "step into another person's shoes" and see their own thoughts, feelings, and behaviour from that person's perspective. They realise that mentally putting oneself in someone else's place is an effective way of working out their intentions and likely actions.

Level 3: Mutual role taking (ages 10–12)

Children at this level realise that they and the other person can mutually and simultaneously adopt each other's roles. They can move outside the two-person interaction and view it mentally from the perspective of a third person.

Level 4: Social and conventional system role-taking (ages 12–15+)

Older children and adolescents at this level or stage realise that mutual perspective-taking is not guaranteed to lead to full understanding. They regard social conventions as important, because these conventions are understood by everyone and help to increase mutual understanding.

How did Selman (1976) identify these levels or stages in the development of social role-taking? One approach was to present children with various social dilemmas involving conflicting feelings. One dilemma concerned a child, Holly. She had to decide rapidly whether to climb a tree to rescue a friend's distressed kitten or to honour her promise to her father that she would never engage in

Selman's (1976) "kitten stuck in the tree" study posed a dilemma to test a child's response to interpersonal conflict.

reckless tree climbing. Children were asked questions such as the following: Does Holly realise how her friend feels about his kitten? How will Holly's father feel if he discovers that she climbed the tree? What would you do in that situation?

More recent research has used the Interpersonal Negotiation Strategies Interview (Schultz, Yeates, & Selman, 1988), which involves a series of hypothetical dilemmas involving interpersonal conflicts. This measure shows good reliability over time. When two raters assess children's responses on this Interview, they generally show a high level of agreement (Yeates, Schultz, & Selman, 1991).

We might imagine that children with superior perspective-taking ability would generally display better social negotiating skills and be more popular than those with less ability. However, Selman, Lavin, and Brion-Meisels (1982) argued that how children use their perspective-taking ability in everyday life is also important. Successful social interaction requires knowing *what* behaviour is appropriate in a given situation as well as having good perspective-taking ability. Thus, perspective-taking ability is necessary but not sufficient for harmonious social relations with other people.

Findings

According to Selman's theoretical approach, children should advance through the various levels as they grow older. Gurucharri and Selman (1982) reported the findings from a longitudinal study in which interpersonal understanding was assessed at the start of the study, 2 years later, and then 3 years after the second assessment. Between the first and second assessments, 40 out of 48 children showed some advance in interpersonal understanding, and none showed a reduction in understanding. Data were available for 41 children and adolescents for the second and third assessments. Altogether, 38 showed an advance in interpersonal understanding, 2 showed no change, and only 1 had a decline. Finally, every child who took part in the whole study showed some advance in interpersonal understanding over the 5-year period.

As discussed earlier, Selman and his colleagues have typically assessed children's perspective-taking ability by analysing their reactions to various hypothetical social dilemmas. It is important to show that perspective-taking ability as revealed by such artificial dilemmas predicts actual *behaviour* in the real world. This issue was addressed by Selman, Schorin, Stone, and Phelps (1983). In their study, girls in small groups performed activities such as making puppets and putting on puppet shows. Girls who showed superior perspective-taking skills when given an artificial dilemma tended to communicate more competently than the other girls in group discussion.

More evidence that perspective-taking ability predicts social behaviour was reported by Yeates et al. (1991) using the Interpersonal Negotiation Strategies Interview discussed earlier. Scores on this Interview correlated highly with measures of social competence (+.66 for boys and +.58 for girls). Interview scores also correlated with behaviour problems (−.33 for boys and −.17 for girls). Such findings suggest perspective-taking ability can be assessed with good validity.

What circumstances might prevent children and adolescents from developing good perspective-taking skills? Maltreated children are less interpersonally sensitive and empathic than non-maltreated ones (Bolger, Patterson, & Kupersmidt, 1998), which could be due in part to their deficient social perspective-taking abilities. Burack, Flanagan, Peled, Sutton, Zygmuntowicz, and Manly (2006) studied children (average age = 10 years) and adolescents (average age = 15 years) whose families were chronically dysfunctional. Both groups showed substantially worse perspective-taking abilities than controls. Indeed, the average level of perspective-taking ability in the maltreated adolescent group was similar to that of non-maltreated children 5 years younger.

Why did the maltreated children and adolescents show such limited perspective-taking abilities? The low level of verbal interactions between children and parents and the stressfulness of the family environment both probably played a part. Another likely factor was that the maltreated participants observed very socially inadequate behaviour by their parents.

Burack et al. (1996) found that children from chronically dysfunctional families showed less empathic ability than their non-maltreated peers. One possible reason being that they had observed socially inadequate behaviour in their parents.

Selman's theory emphasises the important role played by cognitive processes in social interaction. As a result, we would expect cognitive development and intelligence to play a part in the development of perspective taking. Some research has focused on the relationship between perspective taking and the stages of cognitive development identified by Piaget (e.g. Keating & Clark, 1980; see start of this chapter). Children who haven't reached the concrete operational level are generally at stage 0 of perspective taking. Children exhibiting concrete operational thought but not formal operational thought are mostly at Selman's stages 1 and 2. Finally, older children showing evidence of formal operational thought tend to be at Selman's stages 3 and 4. Walker (1980) found that any given stage of Piagetian cognitive development was achieved *before* the related stage of perspective taking. This suggests that advances in perspective taking may depend on prior cognitive development. However, there is only an association or correlation between stages of cognitive development and of perspective taking, and so we don't know that one causes the other.

Evidence relating perspective-taking ability to intelligence was reviewed by Yeates, Schultz, and Selman (1990). The typical correlation between IQ and perspective tasking is about +.45, indicating the existence of a moderately strong association between the two variables.

Evaluation

Selman's perspective-taking theory has various successes to its credit. First, children's increasing ability to take the perspective of other people is important in their social development. Second, the development of perspective taking proceeds approximately through the successive stages identified by Selman. Third, perspective-taking ability is associated moderately strongly with various aspects of social behaviour. This is important, because a measure of perspective-taking ability that didn't predict children's behaviour in social situations would be of little value. Fourth, the very poor perspective-taking abilities of maltreated children and adolescents may help to explain why they lack social skills and interpersonal sensitivity. Fifth, as predicted, the rate of development of perspective-taking ability is predicted by children's cognitive development and by their IQ.

What are the limitations of Selman's approach? First, it is very cognitive, focusing on children's increasing ability to understand other people's thoughts and beliefs. While perspective-taking abilities are important in social interactions, they are *not* the whole story. An individual's cognitive processes don't *always* predict his or her behaviour very well. For example, some children having good perspective taking abilities aren't very successful in social interactions because they lack the motivation to use those abilities.

Second, there is the issue of how children proceed through the various stages of perspective taking. What factors cause children to develop their perspective-taking abilities? We don't really know, and the factors involved probably vary from one child to another.

Third, many of the findings are correlational, so causal interpretations aren't warranted. For example, maltreated children are less interpersonally sensitive and empathic than healthy controls, and they also have deficient perspective-taking skills. It is tempting to conclude that their inadequate perspective-taking skills are partly responsible for their low level of interpersonal sensitivity. However, it isn't valid to draw such a conclusion on the basis of an association or correlation between interpersonal sensitivity and perspective-taking skills.

Fourth, Selman's approach de-emphasises the role played by individual differences in personality in accounting for the competence of children's social behaviour. Consider the two dimensions of emotionality (tendency to experience intense emotional states, especially negative ones) and emotion regulation (ability to control and manage emotional reactions). Children having low emotionality and high emotion regulation at one point in time were more socially competent than other children at a later point in time (Eisenberg et al., 1997). Such factors aren't considered by Selman.

> **EXAM HINT**
> Consider how individual differences in emotionality and emotion regulation can be used to evaluate Selman's perspective-taking theory.

Biological Explanations of Social Cognition Including Role of the Mirror Neuron System

So far we have considered the development of social cognition mainly in terms of the psychological processes involved. Recently, however, there has been a rapid increase in research on biological explanations of social cognition. There is no real conflict between these biological explanations and previous psychological ones. Indeed, there are encouraging signs that the biological approach can enrich and enhance our understanding of social cognition based on more psychological approaches. The role of the mirror neuron system has played a central role in recent biological explanations, and so we will focus our attention on that biological system.

Mirror neuron system

Understanding the actions of others is of great importance to humans (and also other primates). We couldn't succeed socially if we lacked the ability to make sense of other people's behaviour. Indeed, as we have seen, humans lacking that ability (e.g. individuals with autism) find social life extremely difficult.

There is another reason why it is important for us to pay close attention to the actions of other people. Much of our learning occurs through imitation, which requires careful observation of what other people are doing. Bandura (1965) emphasised the importance of what he called observational learning. He discovered that children were much more likely to imitate the actions of an adult model when those actions were rewarded than when they were punished.

There was a breakthrough in our understanding of the above issues by Gallese, Fadiga, Fogassi, and Rizzolatti (1996). They assessed monkeys' brain activity in two situations:

1. The monkeys performed a particular action (e.g. grasping).
2. The monkeys observed another monkey performing a similar action. Gallese et al. discovered that 17% of the neurons in area F5 of the premotor cortex were activated in *both* situations. They labelled these neurons "mirror neurons".

Findings such as those of Gallese et al. (1996) led theorists to propose the notion of a mirror neuron system. This mirror neuron system is formed of neurons activated when animals perform an action *and* when they observe another animal perform the same action. According to Gallese et al., this system facilitates imitation and understanding the actions of others. Subsequent research confirmed the importance of area F5 and also indicated that the superior temporal sulcus forms part of the mirror neuron system in monkeys.

Gallese et al.'s (1996) study of brain activity in monkeys led to the proposal of the mirror neuron system, whereby neurons are activated during both performance and observation of an action.

So far as understanding social cognition in humans is concerned, there are two crucial issues. First, it is important to show that humans possess a mirror neuron system resembling the one found in monkeys. As we will see, there is much controversy on this issue, and the findings are not clear-cut.

Second, if there is a human mirror neuron system, we need to discover its functions. It has been argued that the activation of mirror neurons when observing someone else's movement allows you to simulate yourself performing that movement using your own motor system. This then allows you to access the intentions, goals, and emotions you would have if you performed that movement, all of which are then assigned to the individual you are observing. This suggests that the mirror neuron system may be centrally involved in understanding the behaviour and emotional states of others and may even underlie Theory of Mind. Gallese, Keysers, and Rizzolatti (2004, p. 396) argued as follows: "The fundamental mechanism that allows us a direct experiential grasp of the mind of others is . . . direct simulation of observed events through the mirror mechanism [mirror neuron system]".

However, the human mirror neuron system (assuming it exists) may fulfil much more modest functions. It may be a fairly primitive system that only permits mindless imitation of the actions performed by others. For example, parrots can imitate what a human has just said, but they don't understand what they are saying.

Findings

As so much of the research on the mirror neuron system has been done on monkeys, we briefly consider that research before moving on to human research.

? What are the limitations of this research?

Given that our brains are much more complex than those of monkeys, we are likely to match (or surpass) most of the mental abilities possessed by monkeys.

How can we show that mirror neurons are involved in actual *understanding* rather than merely allowing us to recognise others' actions without understanding? In other words, is the mirror neuron system involved in working out *why* someone else is performing certain actions as well as deciding *what* those actions are? Umiltà et al. (2001) found that mirror neurons discharged when the participant couldn't see the action but could infer or work out what it was likely to have been. They used two main conditions. In one condition, the experimenter's action directed towards an object was fully visible to the monkey participants. In the other condition, the monkeys saw the same action but the same (and most important) part of the action was hidden from them behind a screen. Before each trial, the monkeys saw the experimenter place food behind the screen so they knew what the experimenter was reaching for.

What did Umiltà et al. (2001) find? First, over half of the mirror neurons tested discharged in the hidden condition. Second, about half of the mirror neurons that did discharge in the hidden condition did so as strongly in that condition as in the fully visible condition. Thus, many mirror neurons responded to the monkeys' *understanding* of the experimenter's actions rather than merely to what could be seen. Third, Umiltà et al. used a third condition that was the same as the hidden condition except the monkeys knew that no food had been placed behind the screen. In terms of what the monkeys could see of the experimenter's actions, this condition was identical to the hidden condition. However, mirror neurons that discharged in the hidden condition did *not* discharge in this third condition. Thus, the *meaning* of the observed actions determined activity within the mirror neuron system.

? Do you think the results of Umiltà et al.'s research are applicable to humans?

Is there a mirror neuron system in humans? Much research is supportive, but definitive evidence is lacking. Consider a study by Dinstein, Hasson, Rubin, and Heeger (2007). Activation in many brain areas was assessed while human participants observed the same movement being made repeatedly or performed that movement repeatedly. Five brain areas (including ventral premotor cortex, anterior intraparietal cortex, and superior intraparietal cortex) were affected in similar fashion by the observation and motor tasks. These brain areas may form the human mirror neuron system. However, all that Dinstein et al. found was that neurons within the same brain *areas* responded on both tasks. Convincing evidence for a mirror neuron system requires that the same *neurons* are activated whether observing a movement or performing it. However, this hasn't been demonstrated in studies on humans.

Iacoboni, Molnar-Szakacs, Gallese, Buccino, Mazziota, and Rizzolatti (2005) argued that our understanding of the intentions behind someone else's actions is often helped by taking account of the *context*. For example, someone may shout loudly at another person because they are angry or because they are acting in a play. Iacoboni et al. wanted to see whether the mirror neuron system in humans was sensitive to context as well as the actions being observed. Iacoboni et al. used three conditions:

1. Intention condition: There were films clips of two scenes involving a teapot, mug, biscuits, a jar, and so on—one scene showed the objects before being used (drinking context) and the other showed the object after being used

(cleaning context). A hand was shown grasping a cup in a different way in each scene.

2. Action condition: The same grasping actions were shown as in the Intention condition. However, the context wasn't shown, so it wasn't possible to understand the intention of the person grasping the cup.
3. Context condition: The same two contexts were shown as in the Intention condition, but no grasping was shown.

There was more activity in areas forming part of the mirror neuron system in the Intention condition than in the Action condition. This suggests that the mirror neuron system is involved in understanding the intentions behind observed actions, because it was only in the Intention condition that the participants could work out *why* the person was grasping the cup.

Emotional states

Is the mirror neuron system (or a similar system) involved in our ability to experience and understand the emotional states of other people? Relevant research has looked at disgust. The anterior insula cortex (part of the limbic system close to the brainstem) is activated strongly when someone is exposed to disgusting stimuli. What is of interest is whether the anterior insula cortex is also activated when someone looks at the disgusted facial expressions of others. That is indeed the case. Phillips et al. (1997) found the amplitude of the response of the anterior insula increased progressively the more disgusted the observed facial expression was. This finding suggests the human mirror neuron system is responsive to emotional states. However, since Phillips et al. didn't demonstrate that the *same* neurons were activated when participants were exposed to disgusting stimuli or observed others' disgusted facial expression the evidence is inconclusive.

Autism

As we saw earlier, children with autism have severe deficits with abilities such as imitation and Theory of Mind. If the mirror neuron system plays a major role in Theory of Mind and imitation, we might expect autistic children to have impaired functioning of that system. Dapretto et al. (2006) showed autistic children and typically developing children faces expressing five different emotions: anger, fear, happiness, neutrality, or sadness. There were two conditions: (1) simply observe the face; or (2) imitate the expression on the face. There was much less activity in the mirror neuron system in autistic children than in typically developing ones on both the observation and imitation tasks. In addition, those autistic children having the greatest number of symptoms of social deficits had the least activity in the mirror neuron system. Thus, it seems that the mirror neuron system in autistic children is impaired.

What conclusions can we draw from the above findings? According to Dapretto et al. (2006, p. 28), "A dysfunctional 'mirror neuron system' may underlie the social deficits observed in autism." However, there is an issue about causality here. It is possible that an impaired mirror neuron system plays a role in the development of autism, but it may be that the development of autism prevents the mirror neuron system from functioning effectively.

Additional evidence supporting the hypothesis that the mirror neuron system is impaired in autistic children was reported by Hadjikhani, Joseph, Snyder, and Tager-Flusberg (2006). They focused on brain areas (e.g. the inferior frontal cortex; inferior parietal lobe; and superior temporal sulcus) believed to form part of the human mirror neuron system. Autistic children (compared to healthy children) showed evidence of cortical thinning in those brain areas.

There are two reasons why we should be cautious in accepting the hypothesis that impaired functioning of the mirror neuron system is of central importance in autism. First, autistic children have several problems including social and communication deficits, repetitive behaviour, and a restricted range of interests. It isn't clear that an impaired mirror neuron system could account for most of these problems. Rogers, Hepburn, Stackhouse, and Wehner (2003) found that autistic children's ability to imitate (regarded as an important part of the function of the mirror neuron system) wasn't correlated with their language development or their adaptive behaviour. Thus, an inability to imitate may *not* be central to autistic children's difficulties.

Second, several studies have compared brain activation in autistic and healthy children while performing observation and imitation tasks (reviewed by Dinstein et al., 2008). In about half of these studies, autistic children had similar activation to healthy children in brain areas associated with the mirror neuron system.

Evaluation

Research on the mirror neuron system (especially in monkeys) suggests strongly it is part of the mechanism involved in allowing us to imitate the actions of others. More importantly, it has provided exciting evidence suggesting the mirror neuron system probably plays an important role in social cognition (especially our understanding of other people's intentions and actions). It also seems that the mirror neuron system takes account of information about the context in which the actions of others are performed. More speculatively, impairments in the mirror neuron system may help to explain the deficits in social cognition and understanding shown by autistic individuals.

What are the limitations of research on the mirror neuron system? First, most research has involved functional magnetic resonance imaging (fMRI). This isn't precise enough to identify what is happening at the level of individual neurons. According to Agnew, Bhakoo, and Puri (2007, p. 288), "There is no direct evidence of human neurons that respond to action."

Second, the mirror neuron system may well be used in processing information about the changing intentions and emotional states of other people. However, when we try to understand someone else's intentions, we often take account of their stable characteristics (e.g. personality). For example, if Will walks rapidly towards us, we expect he will be warm and friendly because he has an agreeable personality. However, if Dave walks rapidly towards us, we expect him to be distant and businesslike because he has a rather cold personality. The mirror neuron system doesn't take account of these stable characteristics.

Third, most evidence on the detailed functioning of the mirror neuron system has come from studies on monkeys. What is true of the monkey brain is not necessarily true of the human brain. In addition, even

---

EXAM HINT

Make sure you can explain how the mirror neuron system may underpin Theory of Mind and evaluate this claim using research evidence from animal and human research.

EXAM HINT

Note that in an exam question that asks you to describe and evaluate research into the development of children's perspective taking you can potentially write about the development of Theory of Mind, Selman's perspective-taking theory and/or the mirror neuron system. However, you could not write about all three equally and achieve depth, so you would have to plan which one you would cover in depth and which to cover in less depth.

though monkeys have a mirror neuron system, they are much less skilful than we are at inferring other people's intentions. That suggests one of two things: (1) the human mirror neuron system is more complex than that of the monkey; or (2) some of our ability to infer others' intentions doesn't involve the mirror neuron system.

Fourth, it isn't clear whether autistic children have an impaired mirror neuron system. Even if we accept the functioning of the mirror neuron system is impaired in autistic children, this doesn't provide *direct* evidence of causality. As mentioned earlier, that finding could occur because a deficient mirror neuron system helps to cause autism, or because the presence of autism causes deficiencies in the mirror neuron system.

Mirror neurons and understanding emotions

Enticott, Johnston, Herring, Hoy, and Fitzgerald (2008) compared brain activity when viewing videos of non-facial clips, such as thumb movement, with those of pairs of human faces. The face task was recognition of either same faces or same emotions. Increased mirror neuron activity was associated with the emotion recognition task but not the face recognition task, meaning that people who are good at recognising facial expressions have mirror neurons that are more active, and therefore these people would be better able to work out others' intentions and emotions—and this would bring increased empathy. So mirror neuron activity boosts understanding other people's actions and intentions and is also involved in understanding emotions.

SECTION SUMMARY
Development of Social Cognition

Theory of Mind

❖ According to Baron-Cohen, achieving Theory of Mind is of central importance in social development. Those with Theory of Mind are "mind readers".
❖ Theory of Mind is often assessed by false-belief tasks, and emerges at about the age of 4.
❖ Children's acquisition of Theory of Mind depends on the development of a shared attention mechanism and on language skills.
❖ According to Baron-Cohen, autistic children are severely delayed in the acquisition of Theory of Mind. Their "mindblindness" helps to explain their lack of social skills.
❖ Evaluation:

— As predicted, autistic children have a deficient shared attention system and Theory of Mind.
— Autistic children have general cognitive deficits (e.g. in executive functioning and central coherence) in addition to specific problems with Theory of Mind.
— Theory of Mind deficits don't explain all the symptoms of autism.

Perspective-taking theory

❖ According to Selman, successful social development requires that children have the ability to take other people's perspective.
❖ Selman identified five levels or stages through which children proceed. Children start with an egocentric stage but then become more skilled at mutual role-taking.

❖ Maltreated children and adolescents have very deficient perspective-taking abilities, which may help to explain their poor social skills.

❖ Evaluation:

— The level of perspective taking predicts actual social behaviour.
— Perspective taking develops approximately as suggested by Selman.
— Selman emphasised cognitive factors and de-emphasised motivational ones.
— Little is known of the factors causing children to develop their perspective-taking abilities.

Mirror neuron system

❖ The mirror neuron system consists of neurons that fire when animals or humans perform an action or when they observe another animal/human perform the same action. This system may be involved in imitation and in understanding others' intentions.

❖ The evidence for a mirror neuron system is stronger in monkeys than in humans. In monkeys, it seems to be involved in understanding others' actions, and the same is probably true in humans.

❖ There is some evidence that the mirror neuron is impaired in autistic children.

❖ Evaluation:

— The mirror neuron system probably plays an important role in social cognition.
— The mirror neuron system is more likely to be used to interpret changing intentions of others rather than their intentions based on relatively unchanging characteristics (e.g. personality).
— Even if the mirror neuron system is impaired in autistic children, this doesn't prove that autism is caused in part by that impaired system.

FURTHER READING

McNair, T. (2007). Autism and Asperger syndrome. http://www.bbc.co.uk/health/conditions/autism1.shtml Has a factual and easy to understand account of the autism spectrum.

New Scientist (2004). http://www.newscientist.com/article/dn6323-chaotic-homes-hamper-child-development.html Chaotic homes hamper child development reports a study comparing MZ and DZ twins which suggests that chaos has more effect than poverty on cognitive development.

Szalavitz, M. (2008). Do supercharged brains give rise to autism? *New Scientist*, *2674*, September 19. Gives an overview of a novel theory suggesting a hyperactive brain that makes every sensory input overwhelming can explain all the characteristics of autism.

See *A2-Level Psychology Online* for some interactive quizzes to help you with your revision.

REVISION QUESTIONS

In the exam, questions on this topic are out of 25 marks, and can take the form of essay questions or two-part questions. You should allow about 30 minutes for each of the questions below, which aim to test the material in this chapter. Never try to answer a question unless you have been taught the topic.

1. Discuss one or more theories of cognitive development.   (25 marks)
2. Discuss applications of theories of cognitive development
    to education.   (25 marks)
3. Discuss one or more theories of moral understanding.   (25 marks)
4. (a) What is meant by "Theory of mind"?   (10 marks)
    (b) Discuss aspects of the development of social cognition,
         including perspective-taking and mirror neurons.   (15 marks)

See *A2-Level Psychology Online* for tips on how to answer these revision questions.

Psychopathology: Schizophrenia

By Michael W. Eysenck

10

The term "schizophrenia" comes from two Greek words: *schizo* meaning "split" and *phren* meaning "mind". Schizophrenia is a very serious condition and it is only fairly recently that effective forms of treatment have been developed. It is a form of **psychosis**, a term that refers to disorders in which there is some loss of contact with reality. About 1% of the population of the United Kingdom suffer from schizophrenia during their lives; the figure is similar elsewhere. Schizophrenia is slightly more common in men than in women, but the difference is minimal.

Here is an account by a 23-year-old man with schizophrenia:

> . . . In my flat I began to get delusions. I was a storekeeper at the time . . . I kept thinking the Mafia were out to get me, and the FBI were protecting me, ready to send me away to be trained. I kept thinking my parents were Jews. I would ask my landlady, in my loneliness, if I could watch her television and I would cry all the way through the programmes . . . The police picked me up and I made a false confession of murder so that they would incarcerate me and protect me from the Mafia . . . my doctor said I needed a rest. (Birchwood & Jackson, 2001, pp. 2–3)

It used to be assumed that it was almost impossible to treat schizophrenia successfully. However, as we will see later in the chapter, that assumption has thankfully been proved wrong. Encouraging evidence emerged from the International Study of Schizophrenia (Harrison et al., 2001) in which patients with schizophrenia were followed up over 15 and 25 years. Patients were classified as recovered if they were employed and had resumed their former role function, were not seen as mentally ill by their family, and had no obvious psychotic symptoms. On these relatively stringent criteria, 48% of the patients were deemed to have recovered—a much higher figure than many people would have guessed.

KEY TERM

Psychosis: a broad category of mental disorder covering those with a partial or total loss of contact with reality.

EXAM HINT
You need to know the clinical characteristics of schizophrenia but you should only use this material in the exam if it has been asked for in a sub-part (a) AO1 question. Do not include them if the question asks you to consider the explanations because just describing the clinical characteristics is not part of the explanations.

CLINICAL CHARACTERISTICS OF SCHIZOPHRENIA

The onset of schizophrenia is typically between the late teens and the mid-30s. The symptoms vary somewhat but typically include problems with attention, thinking, social relationships, motivation, and emotion. One of the most important classificatory systems for mental disorders, including schizophrenia, is the *Diagnostic and Statistical Manual, 4th edition* (DSM-IV), which was published in 1994 and revised in 2000 (DSM-IV-TR). DSM-IV contains about 400 mental disorders, each defined by descriptive and observable symptoms.

According to DSM-IV-TR, the criteria for schizophrenia include:

1. Two or more of the following symptoms, each of which must have been present for a significant period of time over a 1-month period: delusions; hallucinations; disorganised speech; grossly disorganised or catatonic (rigid) behaviour; and negative symptoms (lack of emotion, lack of motivation, speaking very little or uninformatively). Only one symptom is needed if the delusions are bizarre or if the hallucinations consist of a voice commenting on the individual's behaviour.
2. Continuous signs of disturbance over a period of at least 6 months.
3. Social and/or occupational dysfunction or poor functioning.

Another very important classificatory system is the International Classification of Diseases (ICD), the tenth edition of which (ICD-10) was published by the World Health Organization in 1992. The criteria used in ICD-10 to diagnose schizophrenia are similar to those used in DSM-IV. The main difference so far as schizophrenia is concerned is that DSM-IV requires evidence of continuous disturbance for at least 6 months, whereas ICD-10 requires that symptoms must be present for most of the time over a 1-month period.

People with schizophrenia generally have confused thinking and often suffer from delusions. Many of their delusions involve "ideas of reference", which means that they attach great significance to external objects or events. Thus, for example, when an individual with schizophrenia sees his neighbours talking, he can be convinced that they are plotting to kill him. People with schizophrenia often also suffer from delusions of grandeur, for example, thinking they are Napoleon even though they can't speak French.

Individuals with schizophrenia often suffer from hallucinations. Whereas delusions arise from mistaken interpretations of actual objects and events, hallucinations arise in the absence of any external stimulus. Most schizophrenic hallucinations consist of voices, which are usually saying something of personal relevance to the patient.

Language impairments characterise schizophrenia. Patients might repeat sounds (echolalia) or use invented words (neologisms). Their speech can seem illogical and involves abrupt shifts from one theme to another. In some cases, the patient's speech can be so jumbled that it is described as a "word salad".

People with schizophrenia often suffer from delusions and misinterpret ordinary events, such as conversations between other people, as being about themselves.

CASE STUDY: *A BEAUTIFUL MIND*

Too many people think schizophrenia means having a split mind, whatever that is, or being seriously deviant, dangerous, and unable to live any form of normal life. This is not true, especially for those who benefit from medical therapies and social support. The film *A Beautiful Mind* is based on the true story of the mathematician John Nash, a Princeton professor and Nobel Prize winner, whose early to middle years were blighted by the disorder but who survived to flourish later on. Nash isn't typical of schizophrenics any more than he is of the normal population—how many of us are Nobel Prize winners? But his experiences and symptoms as shown in the film illustrate problems such as the failure of many medications to give much relief and the cognitive stress and social withdrawal of many sufferers.

Watch the film if you can, and then see what you can find out about how understanding and treatments of schizophrenia today differ from Nash's time.

Russell Crowe portrayed John Nash in the 2001 film *A Beautiful Mind.*

Finally, some patients with schizophrenia have even more bizarre behaviour. One of the most common behavioural abnormalities is to remain almost motionless for hours at a time. Some patients make strange grimaces or repeat an odd gesture over and over again.

The symptoms of schizophrenia are said to be "positive" and "negative". Positive symptoms ("pathological excesses") include delusions, hallucinations, and bizarre forms of behaviour. Negative symptoms ("pathological deficits") include an absence of emotion and motivation, language deficits, general apathy, and an avoidance of social activity. The positive symptoms are more important than the negative ones when diagnosing a patient with schizophrenia—of the five categories of symptom identified within DSM-IV, four are positive and only one is negative. However, patients with several negative symptoms often respond poorly to drugs and are generally hard to treat.

From what has been said so far, you might have the impression that everyone who is categorised as "schizophrenic" is basically similar; this is *not* the case. About one-third of patients have a single episode or a few brief episodes of schizophrenia and then recover fully. Another one-third have occasional episodes of the disorder throughout their lives and function reasonably effectively between episodes. The remaining third deteriorate over a series of increasingly incapacitating episodes. Those patients for whom schizophrenia comes on suddenly tend to have a better prognosis (outlook); the same is true for patients in whom the positive symptoms predominate.

A distinction is sometimes drawn between type I and type II schizophrenia. Type I schizophrenia is dominated by positive symptoms, whereas type II schizophrenia mainly involves negative symptoms. Type I schizophrenia has a later onset than type II, and there is a greater chance of recovery. There is some evidence to suggest that type I schizophrenia tends to involve biochemical abnormalities, whereas type II schizophrenia involves structural abnormalities in the brain (Birchwood & Jackson, 2001).

According to DSM-IV-TR, there are five main types of schizophrenia:

1. *Disorganised schizophrenia*: involves great disorganisation, including delusions, hallucinations, incoherent speech, and large mood swings.
2. *Catatonic schizophrenia*: the main feature is almost total immobility for hours at a time, with the patient simply staring blankly.
3. *Paranoid schizophrenia*: involves delusions of various kinds.
4. *Undifferentiated schizophrenia*: a broad category that includes patients who don't belong clearly to any other category.
5. *Residual schizophrenia*: consists of patients who don't have any prominent positive symptoms (e.g. hallucinations, delusions) but who have various negative symptoms (e.g. lack of emotion). Patients diagnosed with other types of schizophrenia whose symptoms have reduced in number and in strength often have their diagnosis changed to residual schizophrenia.

? What clinical characteristics of schizophrenia can be seen in this Case Study of WG (below)?

CASE STUDY: A PATIENT WITH SCHIZOPHRENIA

A young man of 19 (WG) was admitted to the psychiatric services on the grounds of a dramatic change in character. His parents described him as always being extremely shy and with no close friends, but in the last few months he had gone from being an average-performing student to failing his studies and leaving college. Having excelled in non-team sports such as swimming and athletics, he was now taking no exercise at all. WG had seldom mentioned health matters but now complained of problems with his head and chest. After being admitted to hospital, WG spent most of his time staring out of the window and—uncharacteristically—not taking care over his appearance. Staff found it difficult to converse with him and he offered no information about himself, making an ordinary diagnostic interview impossible. WG would usually answer direct questions, but in a flat, emotionless tone. Sometimes his answers were not even connected to the question, and staff would find themselves wondering what the conversation had been about. There were also occasions when there was a complete mismatch between WG's emotional expression and the words he spoke. For example, he giggled continuously when speaking about a serious illness that had left his mother bedridden. On one occasion, WG became very agitated and spoke of "electrical sensations" in his brain. At other times, he spoke of being influenced by a force outside himself, which took the form of a voice urging him to commit acts of violence against his parents. He claimed that the voice repeated the command "You'll have to do it".

Adapted from Hofling (1974).

SECTION SUMMARY
Clinical Characteristics of Schizophrenia

Symptoms

❖ Two major diagnostic systems are DSM-IV and ICD-10. There are positive symptoms (e.g. delusions, bizarre behaviour) and negative symptoms (e.g. lack of motivation, lack of emotion).

❖ Schizophrenics often have hallucinations and various language impairments.

❖ According to DSM-IV-TR, there are five types of schizophrenia: disorganised, catatonic, paranoid, undifferentiated, and residual.

ISSUES SURROUNDING THE CLASSIFICATION AND DIAGNOSIS OF SCHIZOPHRENIA

KEY TERM

Reliability: the extent to which a method of measurement or a research study produces consistent findings across situations or over time.

For any diagnostic system to work effectively, it must possess reliability and validity. **Reliability** means that there is good *consistency* over time and between the individuals (the raters) who are using the system to rate patients. If two therapists often disagree in their diagnosis of patients based on one of the main diagnostic systems, this would suggest a low reliability for that system.

Validity means that a diagnostic system assesses what it claims to be assessing. In the case of schizophrenia, it means that patients who are diagnosed as suffering from schizophrenia actually have that mental disorder. If a diagnostic system is to be valid, it must also have high reliability.

The great majority of diagnostic systems (including DSM-IV and ICD-10) are based on categories. Such systems assume that all mental disorders are distinct from each other. Patients who fulfil the relevant criteria for any given disorder are categorised as having that disorder. It is an all-or-none approach—either you have the disorder or you don't. If the assumptions underlying the categorical approach are sound, it should be fairly easy to diagnose any mental disorder (including schizophrenia). However, two kinds of evidence discussed below suggest that reality is not as neat and tidy as assumed within the categorical approach.

First, there is **comorbidity**—this term describes a patient who suffers from two or more mental disorders at the same time. Patients with schizophrenia often show comorbidity, having other disorders such as major depressive disorder or bipolar disorder (see Chapter 11) or an anxiety disorder (see Chapter 12). Sim et al. (2006) studied 142 hospitalised schizophrenic patients, 32% of whom had an additional mental disorder. Those with comorbidity had less awareness of their condition and poorer outcomes than those without.

Comorbidity occurs in part because the symptoms of different mental disorders often overlap with each other. For example, major depressive disorder and schizophrenia both involve very low levels of motivation. This creates problems of reliability—does the low motivation reflect the existence of depression, or schizophrenia, or both?

Second, there is accumulating evidence to suggest that the categorical approach should be replaced by the continuity approach, according to which there is no sharp dividing line between individuals with schizophrenia and those not suffering from the condition. If this were the case, it would make it difficult to diagnose schizophrenia with high reliability.

The continuity approach has been tested by using questionnaires that include items that refer to some of the positive and negative symptoms of schizophrenia. Such questionnaires assess **schizotypy**, which is a proneness to develop psychosis (especially schizophrenia). Chapman, Chapman, Kwapil, Eckblad, and Zinser (1994) found that apparently normal individuals who had high scores on schizotypy were more likely than other people to develop a psychosis (typically schizophrenia) over the following 10 years.

The findings of Chapman et al. (1994) support the continuity hypothesis. Further supporting evidence comes from a consideration of a mental disorder known as **schizotypal personality disorder**. Individuals with schizotypal personality disorder (which is classified as a mental disorder) have a mild form of several symptoms of schizophrenia. It is sometimes hard to decide whether an individual's symptoms are severe enough to justify a diagnosis of schizophrenia or sufficiently mild that schizotypal personality disorder is the appropriate diagnosis. The blurred boundary between the two diagnoses reduces the reliability with which schizophrenia is diagnosed.

? What is the difference between validity and reliability?

? What are some problems with diagnosing strictly on the basis of the DSM-IV criteria?

? What concerns may arise when treating a patient with psychiatric comorbidity?

KEY TERMS

Validity: the extent to which something is true. This may be applied to a measurement tool, such as a psychological test, or to the "trueness" of an experimental procedure both in terms of what goes on within the experiment (internal validity) and its relevance to other situations (external validity).
Comorbidity: the presence of two or more disorders in a given individual at the same time.
Schizotypy: a dimension of personality that relates to a proneness to develop **psychosis** (especially schizophrenia).
Schizotypal personality disorder: a mental disorder in which many of the symptoms are milder versions of those characteristic of schizophrenia.

The assumption that there are five types of schizophrenia raises various issues; most of these relate to reliability, but some also relate to validity. First, the diversity of symptoms associated with each type of schizophrenia poses problems for the notion of "schizophrenia". For example, patients with catatonic schizophrenia and paranoid schizophrenia often have no symptoms in common—why should they both be regarded as different forms of the same disorder?

Second, there are problems concerning undifferentiated schizophrenia. This is basically a "rag bag" category for all those patients with schizophrenia who are hard to classify. As a result, patients diagnosed with undifferentiated schizophrenia can have a wide range of different symptoms, and two patients with undifferentiated schizophrenia might have no common symptoms.

Third, there are questions concerning the diagnosis of residual schizophrenia. It is a matter of fine judgement to decide whether the symptoms of a person who was originally diagnosed with another type of schizophrenia have reduced sufficiently in strength and number to warrant changing the diagnosis to undifferentiated schizophrenia. When the symptoms reduce further, it can be difficult to decide whether the patient should retain the diagnosis of undifferentiated schizophrenia or should be regarded as recovered.

Rosenhan (1973) challenged the notion that schizophrenia can be diagnosed with high validity and reliability. Eight healthy individuals (five men and three women) tried to gain admission to twelve different psychiatric hospitals. They all complained of hearing indistinct voices saying "empty", "hollow", and "thud". Even though this was the only symptom they reported, seven of them were diagnosed as suffering from schizophrenia. After these healthy individuals were admitted to psychiatric wards, they all said they felt fine and no longer had any symptoms. However, it took an average of 19 days before they were discharged, nearly all of them being classified as having "schizophrenia in remission".

Rosenhan (1973) next decided to see whether abnormal individuals could be classified as normal. He told the staff at a psychiatric hospital that pseudo-patients (normal individuals pretending to have schizophrenic symptoms) would try to gain admittance. No pseudo-patients actually appeared, but 41 genuine patients were judged with confidence to be pseudo-patients by at least one member of staff! Nineteen of these genuine patients were suspected of being frauds by one psychiatrist plus another member of staff. Rosenhan concluded, "It is clear that we cannot distinguish the sane from the insane in psychiatric hospitals."

Rosenhan's findings seem to show that psychiatrists cannot diagnose schizophrenia with any validity. However, there are various reasons for disagreeing with this conclusion. First, Kety (1974) made the following excellent point:

If I were to drink a quart of blood and, concealing what I had done, come to the emergency room of any hospital vomiting blood, the behaviour of the staff would be quite predictable. If they labelled and treated me as having a bleeding peptic ulcer, I doubt that I could argue convincingly that medical science does not know how to diagnose that condition.

 Can you think of any problems with the validity of the Rosenhan study?

HOW SCIENCE WORKS: DIAGNOSING SCHIZOPHRENIA

An issue with diagnosis, for example with schizophrenia, is that it involves making judgements about an individual's behaviours. You will know of Rosenhan's (1973) famous research, and in fact can read his research paper *On Being Sane in Insane Places* on the web; you can also illustrate this issue yourself. Make a table with the positive and the negative symptoms of schizophrenia in one column, and have two more columns, one for "normal" and the other for "pathological" behaviours, you can then survey your classmates for examples of what they would consider a normal behaviour and what they would consider pathological for each symptom—such as for bizarre behaviour. It might be interesting then to see what a different group, such as a different age group, would give as examples, to see if social norms about what is normal or acceptable could affect judgement.

Second, psychiatrists do not expect totally healthy people to try to gain admittance to a psychiatric hospital. Although errors of diagnosis were made under the very unusual conditions of Rosenhan's study, this does not mean that psychiatrists cannot distinguish between the normal and the abnormal under more typical circumstances.

Third, Rosenhan's (1973) findings are less dramatic than they seem. The diagnosis "schizophrenia in remission" is used very rarely, and suggests that the psychiatrists were unconvinced that the patients had really suffered from schizophrenia. This is confirmed by the fact that these normal patients were released within a few days of admission.

We turn now to validity. Davison, Neale, and Kring (2004) argued that we should consider three types of validity when evaluating diagnostic or classification systems. First, there is *content validity*, which refers to the extent to which an assessment measure covers the range of symptoms of schizophrenia. An interview, checklist, or other form of assessment possesses content validity if it obtains detailed information from individual patients regarding all of the symptoms of schizophrenia.

Second, there is *criterion validity*. Any form of assessment for schizophrenia possesses good criterion validity if those diagnosed as having schizophrenia differ in predictable ways from those not diagnosed as schizophrenic. For example, as individuals with schizophrenia typically have low motivation, low emotion, and bizarre behaviour, we might reasonably predict that they would be less likely than other people to be happily married or to have a full-time job.

Third, there is *construct validity*. This type of validity involves testing hypotheses based on the diagnosis of schizophrenia. For example, as we will see shortly, some researchers have argued that individuals with schizophrenia have high levels of dopamine. If those receiving a diagnosis of schizophrenia based on a given form of assessment were found to have higher dopamine levels than those not receiving a diagnosis of schizophrenia, this would provide some evidence for construct validity. A problem arises when the hypothesis is *not* supported, in which case it would be hard to know whether this failure occurred because the diagnosis was wrong or because the dopamine hypothesis is wrong.

A fourth type of validity, known as *predictive validity*, is also important. Predictive validity concerns our ability to predict the eventual outcome for patients who receive a diagnosis of schizophrenia. Schizophrenia is generally regarded as a very severe mental disorder. Accordingly, there would be evidence for predictive validity if the great majority of those diagnosed with schizophrenia took several years to recover or failed to recover.

Assessment: Evidence

So far, we have identified various issues that might cause problems for the reliable and valid diagnosis of schizophrenia. In fact, the main approaches to diagnosing schizophrenia have proved themselves to be reasonably reliable. For example, Jakobsen et al. (2005) used the Operational Criteria Checklist (OPCRIT), a symptom checklist with a glossary providing clear and explicit descriptions of the symptoms, to study patients with a history of psychosis. There was good agreement on the diagnosis of schizophrenia when the diagnoses of OPCRIT were compared against those of ICD-10, indicating a high level of reliability. There was

Activity: Diagnosis
Imagine that you are in a situation where you have been wrongly diagnosed as suffering from a mental disorder such as schizophrenia. How would you react to such a situation? Would you be incredulous? Furious? Tearful? Shocked and withdrawn? How might these emotions be interpreted by those people whose job it is to assess your mental condition?
In Rosenhan's classic study, what normal behaviour was labelled by the staff as pathological?

? What is the difference between criterion validity and construct validity?

? Can you think of any problems with the reliability of the Rosenhan study?

? What are some benefits of using an Operational Criteria Checklist (OPCRIT)?

also good agreement (and thus high reliability) when ICD-10 and DSM-IV diagnoses were compared.

Vares, Ekholm, Sedvall, Hall, and Jonsson (2006) considered various methods used to diagnose schizophrenia, including structured interviews, OPCRIT, and medical records. They reported that OPCRIT was a very reliable way to assess schizophrenia. They also found that patients diagnosed with schizophrenia on the basis of an interview typically received the same diagnosis based on medical records, which provides more evidence of good reliability.

What about validity? First, we consider content validity (i.e. the extent to which an assessment measure covers the range of symptoms of schizophrenia). Measures such as standard semi-structured interviews or the Operational Criteria Checklist possess good content validity because they involve working through all of the symptoms associated with schizophrenia and with other related mental disorders.

Most forms of assessment for the diagnosis of schizophrenia possess reasonable criterion validity, meaning that those diagnosed as schizophrenic differ in predictable ways form those not diagnosed as schizophrenic. Keith, Regier, and Rae (1991) found that nearly 3% of those who are divorced or separated have been diagnosed as schizophrenic at some point, compared with 1% of married individuals. People with schizophrenia are much less likely than non-schizophrenics to be in full-time employment and to have a strong social network (Comer, 2001). These kinds of evidence are not especially convincing—individuals suffering from almost *any* mental disorder are more likely than healthy individuals to experience social, relationship, and job problems.

There is another issue relating to evidence for criterion validity. Pilgrim (2000, p. 302) argued that diagnosis is unhelpful in answering the central question, "How do we account for this person's actions and experience in this particular context?" Thus, individuals with schizophrenia might have marital and social problems because they are living in poverty and have few opportunities in life, and not because they are suffering from schizophrenia. At the very least, it is hard to decide whether schizophrenia causes the problems or the problems help to cause the schizophrenia.

Construct validity involves testing predictions about schizophrenia based on some hypothesis or theory. We will be discussing theoretical explanations of schizophrenia shortly. For present purposes, we will focus on the hypothesis that genetic factors are important in schizophrenia. There is evidence for reasonable construct validity in the consistent support for the genetic hypothesis in twin and family studies. Indeed, genetic factors are probably more important in the development of schizophrenia than almost any other mental disorder.

Predictive validity refers to the ability to predict patients' eventual outcomes on the basis of the diagnosis they receive. The predictive validity of a diagnosis of schizophrenia is reasonable, but there are some concerns about it. At one extreme, up to 20% of those diagnosed with schizophrenia never have a recurrence of the disorder after the first episode (Birchwood & Jackson, 2001). At the other extreme, about 10% of schizophrenics commit suicide (Birchwood & Jackson, 2001).

What is lowering predictive validity? One reason is that the eventual outcome depends in part on the precise symptoms that the patient has in the first place. As mentioned earlier, the outcome tends to be better if a patient has mostly positive symptoms, rather than if he or she has predominantly negative symptoms.

Another reason concerns the length of time for which there must be continuous disturbance, which is 6 months in the DSM system but only 1 month in the ICD system. Mason, Harrison, Croudace, Glazebrook, and Medley (1997) wanted to see what would happen if they changed the duration criterion to 1 month for the DSM system and to 6 months for the ICD system. Overall, predictive validity was reasonably high, but it was higher for both systems when the 6-month period was used than when the 1-month period was used. The problem with the 1-month criterion is that many individuals with a brief, never-to-be-repeated disturbance are categorised as having schizophrenia.

Finally, we will briefly consider two possible biases that could reduce reliability and validity. First, there is a danger of social class bias. Keith et al. (1991) reported that 1.9% of lower-class people, 0.9% of middle-class people, and only 0.4% of upper-class people were diagnosed with schizophrenia. Some experts argue that these differences reflect social class bias. For example, Johnstone (1989) claimed that lower-class individuals tend to be diagnosed with more severe mental disorders (such as schizophrenia) than middle-class people with essentially the same symptoms. However, the supporting evidence is rather weak. The alternative hypothesis—that there are genuine differences in the incidence of schizophrenia across the social classes—remains plausible.

Second, there is ethnic bias. Keith et al. (1991) also found that 2.1% of African–Americans are diagnosed with schizophrenia, compared with 1.4% of white Americans. McGovern and Cope (1987) carried out a study in Birmingham in the United Kingdom. Two-thirds of psychotic patients held in hospitals were African–Caribbean, compared with only one-third who were white and Asian. Such findings suggest ethnic bias, but it is hard to interpret the evidence. Let's go back to the Keith et al. findings: African–Americans on average are more likely than white Americans to live in poverty and to suffer marital separation. When these factors were controlled for, it turned out that there was no difference in the incidence of schizophrenia in the two groups.

> The symptoms listed in the clinical characteristics of schizophrenia include delusions, hallucinations, disorganised speech, grossly distorted or catatonic behaviour, lack of emotion, lack of motivation, and speaking very little or uninformatively. This at first seems clear, but to what extent do these behaviours have to be shown for the individual to have schizophrenia?
>
> - Joss didn't speak so much as grunt replies, and seemed often morose, lost in personal thoughts.
> - Maz prays many times a day and expects an eternity spent in paradise after this life is over.
> - Sam slurs speech, gets words muddled together, and has real difficulty expressing ideas and feelings.
> - Dai just isn't bothered, isn't sick, but doesn't make any efforts with work or even social life.
>
> Are these four people schizophrenic? Or is Joss a typical teenager, or someone who has had a shock or loss? Is Maz delusional or deeply religious? Is Sam drunk or suffering from a different disorder such as dyspraxia (inability to perform deliberate motor actions)? And is Dai unhappy or even depressed? What other explanations are there for these behaviours?
>
> How would you separate out true schizophrenics from the rest of the community so they could obtain appropriate treatment and support?

SECTION SUMMARY
Issues Surrounding the Classification and Diagnosis of Schizophrenia

❖ Good diagnostic systems need to be reliable (consistent) and valid (assess what they claim to assess).

❖ DSM-IV and ICD-10 are categorical systems. However, comorbidity and psychosis-prone healthy individuals go against the notion of neat-and-tidy categories.

Classification and diagnosis

❖ There are five subtypes of schizophrenia, and it can be hard to distinguish among them.

❖ Rosenhan apparently found that psychiatrists can't distinguish between schizophrenics and normals, but his study was flawed.

Assessment: evidence

❖ Structured interviews and symptom checklists based on DSM-IV and ICD-10 have shown good reliability.

❖ Most standard forms of assessment have good content validity.

❖ There is evidence for criterion validity, but many of the social and other problems of schizophrenics are found in patients with other mental disorders.

❖ The diagnosis of schizophrenia has construct validity, as is shown by the consistent support for the genetic hypothesis.

❖ Predictive validity is fairly high, but up to 20% of those diagnosed with schizophrenia differ from the majority of schizophrenics in having no recurrence of the disorder.

❖ It has been claimed that biases (e.g. social-class bias, ethnic bias) reduce reliability and validity. However, the evidence remains unconvincing.

BIOLOGICAL EXPLANATIONS OF SCHIZOPHRENIA

Biological explanations have been offered of many mental disorders. However, such explanations have proved more successful in accounting for the development of schizophrenia than most other disorders. In this section, we consider four kinds of biological explanation. First, we focus on the genetic factors that might be involved in producing schizophrenia. Second, we consider possible biochemical factors that could play a role in the development of schizophrenia. Third, the possibility that brain structure and early development are involved is discussed. Fourth, we analyse evolutionary explanations, which are much more general and speculative than the other three explanations.

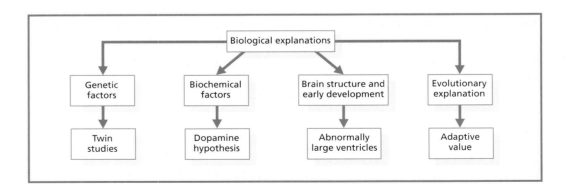

There is one point I would like to make at this juncture. Although these four types of explanation are discussed separately, this does not mean that they are unrelated. For example, if there are biochemical differences between those with schizophrenia and those without, it might very well be that these differences have been produced as a result of genetic factors. In addition, evolutionary pressures

? To what extent do you think that it is important to relate the different types of schizophrenia to the different explanations?

The four major models of abnormality

Your AS level studies covered four major models of abnormality. Each of these provides explanations of the origins of mental disorders, and each is associated with certain forms of treatment.

The *biological model* proposes that the causes of mental disorders resemble those of physical illnesses. Clusters of symptoms can be identified and a diagnosis made, followed by suitable treatment. There is some evidence that infection, genetics, biochemistry, and/or neuroanatomy can account for mental disorders. If the causes are physical then the treatments should be physical as well, and the biological model recommends direct manipulation of the body processes, such as using drugs or electroconvulsive therapy. This model is less appropriate for disorders with psychological symptoms, such as phobias.

The *behavioural model* suggests that mental disorders are caused by learning maladaptive behaviour via conditioning or observational learning. Logically, anything that is learned can be unlearned using the same techniques. The approach is best for explaining (and treating) those disorders that emphasise external behaviours, such as phobias. The behavioural model is oversimplified and more appropriate to non-human animal behaviour. Ethically, there are advantages, such as the lack of blame attached to a person with a mental disorder, but the treatments can be psychologically painful and manipulative.

According to the *psychodynamic model*, the roots of mental disorder are to be found in unresolved conflicts and traumas from childhood. This model might focus too much on the past at the cost of understanding current problems, and too much on sexual problems rather than on interpersonal and social issues. Ethical concerns include the problem of false memory syndrome and the sexist nature of the theory. The approach is best for conditions in which patients have insight, such as some anxiety disorders, although it has not proved very effective with phobias.

The *cognitive model* takes the view that distorted and irrational beliefs are crucially involved in most mental disorders. Limitations of the cognitive model include the problem of whether distorted thinking is a cause or an effect, and the circularity of the explanations. The model suggests that individuals are in part to blame for their problems. The cognitive-behavioural model is a recent and popular development, combining both cognitive and behavioural approaches.

have undoubtedly had a major impact on the genes that we have inherited and on our biochemical systems.

Genetic Factors

There are various ways of trying to decide whether genetic factors are important in schizophrenia. Below, we consider three approaches: twin studies, family studies, and adoption studies. After that, we evaluate the evidence to see what conclusions it is reasonable to draw.

Assumptions of biological explanations

- All mental disorders have a physical cause (micro-organisms, genetics, biochemistry, or neuroanatomy).
- Mental illnesses can be described in terms of clusters of symptoms.
- Symptoms can be identified, leading to the diagnosis of an illness.
- Diagnosis leads to appropriate physical treatments.

Twin studies

Striking support for genetic factors was reported by Rosenthal (1963), who studied quadruplets—the four girls were identical to each other. Amazingly, all four developed schizophrenia, although they did differ somewhat in age of onset and the precise symptoms. They were known as the Genain (dreadful gene) quadruplets. However, they had a dreadful childhood (including neglect and abuse) so it is *not* clear that only genetic factors were involved.

The most convincing evidence for the involvement of genetic factors in schizophrenia comes from the study of twins, one of whom is known to be schizophrenic. Researchers want to establish the probability that the other twin is also schizophrenic—a state of affairs known as **concordance**. Gottesman (1991)

KEY TERM

Concordance: when a disorder or condition is found in both twins.

> **Expressing inheritance**
>
> Psychologists use a variety of measures to explore the extent to which a characteristic is inherited.
>
> The **concordance rate** expresses the extent to which two measures are in agreement. For example, if 20 twin pairs are studied and in 18 of them both had developed schizophrenia, this would produce a concordance rate of 18/20 or 90%, which is very high concordance. Alternatively, one can correlate the IQ scores of two individuals, and the degree of correlation shows us how concordant they are.
>
> Monozygotic (identical) twins have the same genes (100% concordance) whereas dizygotic (non-identical) twins and siblings are genetically 50% similar.
>
> **Heritability** is a measure of the relationship between: (1) the variance of a trait in the whole population; and (2) the extent to which that variance is due to genetic factors. It is expressed as a heritability ratio and calculated by dividing the genetic variance of a characteristic by the total variance (genetic variance/total variance). The genetic variance is calculated using, for example, concordance rates. This percentage is then divided by the amount of variance within the population.
>
> A heritability of 1.0 means that all the variance in a population can be accounted for in terms of genetic factors. However, such a figure has never been achieved in practice. So far as schizophrenia is concerned, heritability estimates make considerable use of information from twin studies. However, it is difficult to disentangle genetic and environmental effects because individuals with a genetic vulnerability for schizophrenia tend to live in poor and deprived conditions. It has been estimated that the heritability of schizophrenia is about +0.8 (O'Donovan, Williams, & Owen, 2003), which indicates that the development of schizophrenia depends strongly on genetic factors. Note that any assessment of heritability is specific to a given population—it is not a universal figure that applies to all cultures at all times.

? Can you think of any reasons for the sharp difference in concordance rates between twin studies, other than genetic factors?

summarised about 40 studies that included considerable differences in severity of the symptoms of schizophrenia. The **concordance rate** was 48% when a monozygotic (MZ) or identical twin had schizophrenia, but only 17% when a dizygotic (DZ) or fraternal twin had schizophrenia. These findings strongly suggest that genetic factors are important—the reason why identical twins have a much higher concordance than fraternal twins is because they are much more similar genetically (100% similarity vs. 50% similarity, respectively). Gottesman also reported that the concordance rate for identical twins brought up apart was very similar to that for identical twins brought up together. This suggests that the high concordance rate for identical twins is *not* due to them being treated in a very similar way within the family.

Torrey (1992) argued that many twin studies were inadequate. He reviewed eight studies in which representative samples were used and allocation of twin pairs to identical or fraternal was done with reasonable certainty. Overall, the concordance rate for identical or MZ twins was 28%, compared with only 6% for fraternal or DZ twins. These figures are much lower than those reported by Gottesman (1991) but in line with figures reported by Joseph (2003). Joseph considered the nine most recent twin studies on schizophrenia, finding that the concordance rate was 22.4% for identical twins and 4.6% for fraternal twins. These figures are much lower than the concordance rates found by Gottesman (1991). However, we need to take into account the fact that the lifetime risk of schizophrenia in the general population is only 1%. Even on the figures of Torrey and of Joseph, you have a substantially increased chance of schizophrenia if you have a twin (especially identical) with the condition.

Family studies

Gottesman (1991) reviewed concordance rates from family studies of schizophrenia. If both your parents have schizophrenia, then you have a 46% chance of developing schizophrenia as well. The concordance rate is 16% if

KEY TERMS

Concordance rate: if one twin has a disorder or condition, the likelihood that the other twin also has it.

Heritability: the proportion of the variance within a population in some characteristic (e.g. height) that is due to genetic factors.

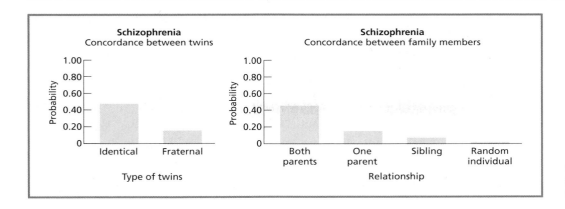

Research by Gottesman (1991) indicates that schizophrenia tends to run in families.

only one of your parents has schizophrenia; it is 8% if a sibling has schizophrenia. These concordance rates are all considerably higher than the 1% probability of someone selected at random suffering from schizophrenia at some point in their life.

Zimbardo, McDermott, Jansz, and Metaal (1995) gathered together data from numerous studies. The concordance rate among first-degree relatives (close relatives

---

What environmental factors might be of importance in triggering schizophrenia?

The fact that there is only a concordance rate of around 50% in identical twins reared together has raised interesting questions for psychologists. What environmental factors could possibly be so different that an identical genetic vulnerability could trigger this debilitating disease in one twin and not the other?

In a fascinating article, Ingram (2004) uses the case study of one pair of identical male twins, Corven and Michael, to speculate on the nature of these risk factors. He likens the genetic vulnerability to a speeding car and the risk factors to speed cameras: activating a single speed camera causes a little upset in terms of points on the licence, but not a great deal; it can be thought of as the equivalent of developing mildly eccentric behaviour, whereas triggering several cameras can lead to loss of a driving licence, the equivalent of full-blown schizophrenia.

So what might these risk factors be? Ingram emphasises that the suggestions he makes are tentative but nevertheless gives a picture of "how the genetic car drives through the speed cameras of life".

The fertilised egg that developed into Michael (the non-schizophrenic twin) arrived in the womb 2 hours ahead of Corven. The two zygotes developed separate placentas: Michael's placenta was larger and more effective than Corven's, which meant that he received more nutrients. The twins had identical genes but their prenatal environments were quite different.

Both twins have a gene that breaks down an essential component of nerve cells. The nutrients that counteract this effect are mainly found in fish and meat, neither of which their mother ate because she is a vegetarian. Normally, this would not be a problem because these nutrients are available in small amounts in vegetables and nuts. However, competing as the twins were for these nutrients, Michael, with the larger placenta, took the lion's share and Corven did not get an adequate amount; thus, Michael's nerve cells grew satisfactorily while Corven's did not. For Corven, the first speed camera had been triggered.

The twins also have a gene that slows down the growth of glia cells, cells that maintain connections between nerve cells in the brain. Five weeks into her pregnancy their mother developed influenza and the virus from this, together with antibodies used to fight it, entered the twins' bloodstream via the placenta. Again, for a single healthy developing embryo, this is not usually a problem. However, the virus further weakened the action of the glia cells—an effect that was more severe in Corven than in Michael because of Corven's existing deficiency in nutrients. This virus was the second speed camera.

Later speed cameras are even more speculative and might never be known, but pressures of work, stress of personal relationships, even cannabis, can all be risk factors.

The parents of individuals with schizophrenia often agonise over why this has happened and whose fault it is. But it might be no-one's fault—just too many speed cameras on the route to adulthood. But remember—risk factors can be biological and prenatal—they are not necessarily life-event or family-induced stressors.

What are the limitations of twin and family studies of schizophrenia?

having many genes in common) was higher than that among second-degree relatives (who have fewer genes in common). Among first-degree relatives, the concordance rate was 9% for siblings, 6% for parents, and 13% for children. Among second-degree relatives, it was 2% for uncles and aunts, 4% for nephews and nieces, and 5% for grandchildren.

Gottesman and Bertelsen (1989) found that their participants had a 17% chance of being schizophrenic if they had a parent who was an identical twin with schizophrenia. This could be due either to heredity or to environment (e.g. both twins brought up in the same very deprived conditions). However, they also studied participants with a parent who didn't have schizophrenia but had an identical twin with schizophrenia. These participants also had a 17% chance of having schizophrenia. Thus, what is of most importance is the genes handed on by your parents rather than the environment in which you grow up.

Adoption studies

The notion that genetic factors are important in producing schizophrenia is supported by adoption studies. One approach is to look at adopted children, one of whose biological parents has schizophrenia. Tienari (1991) did this in Finland. He managed to find 155 schizophrenic mothers who had given up their children for adoption. These children were compared with 155 adopted children who did not have a schizophrenic parent. There was a large difference in the incidence of schizophrenia in these two groups when they were adults. In all, 10.3% of those children with schizophrenic mothers developed schizophrenia, compared with only 1.1% of children without schizophrenic mothers.

Wahlberg et al. (1997) reported additional findings from the study started by Tienari, this time showing that environmental factors are important. They studied the environment provided by the adopted families in terms of whether it was low or high in communication deviance (a tendency to communicate in unclear and confusing ways). Children at genetic risk because their mothers had schizophrenia had very good psychological health if raised by adopted families low in communication deviance. Indeed, they were even healthier than children with no genetic risk! By contrast, children who were at genetic risk and were raised by adopted families that were high in communication deviance showed high levels of thought disorder. Thus, the chances of developing schizophrenia depended on an *interaction* or combination of genetic factors and environmental ones.

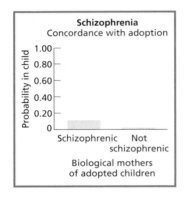

Schizophrenia
Concordance with adoption

Probability in child: 1.00, 0.80, 0.60, 0.40, 0.20, 0

Schizophrenic — Not schizophrenic

Biological mothers of adopted children

Evaluation

We will start by evaluating the evidence from twin studies. Despite large differences in the concordance rates reported across studies, two findings have been obtained repeatedly:

1. Identical and fraternal twins who have a co-twin with schizophrenia are much more likely than random members of the population to suffer from schizophrenia.
2. Among twins having a co-twin with schizophrenia, identical twins are at significantly greater risk than fraternal twins.

These two findings strongly suggest that genetic factors play a role in the development of schizophrenia. However, recent findings suggest that the role might be less than was assumed on the basis of the early twin studies.

Twin studies also provide much ammunition for those arguing that environmental factors are important. If genetic factors were all important, the concordance rate for identical twins would be 100% if diagnosis were perfect. In fact, the concordance rate for identical twins is somewhere between 22 and 48%, figures that are substantially lower than 100%.

As Joseph (2003) pointed out, use of the twin-study method is based on the equal environment assumption—identical twins are treated no more alike than fraternal ones. This assumption is hard to test. However, Joseph discussed six studies in which concordance rates of fraternal twins were compared with those of non-twin siblings. As the genetic similarity is the same in both cases, we might predict that the concordance rates would be the same. In fact, the concordance rates were consistently higher for fraternal twins than for non-twin siblings. This suggests that there might be something special about twins, making it dangerous to draw general conclusions from them.

Identical (monozygotic) twins are not only genetically identical; they are also more likely to be treated identically by their family.

The evidence reported by Gottesman clearly indicates that schizophrenia runs in families. Furthermore, as predicted by the genetic hypothesis, the concordance rate is much higher between relatives who have high genetic similarity. However, family members who are more similar genetically tend to spend more time together and are more likely to live together. As a result, environmental factors are also involved.

The evidence from adoption studies indicates that genetic factors are important in the development of schizophrenia. However, an important qualification to this was reported by Wahlberg et al. (1997). Children at high genetic risk did very well if their adopted families provided a supportive environment. Thus, we must consider genetic *and* environmental factors together to predict accurately how likely any given person is to develop schizophrenia.

In sum, the evidence from twin, family, and adoption studies indicates that genetic factors are of real importance in the development of schizophrenia. The consistency of the evidence is impressive. However, there are two other major conclusions. First, environmental factors are clearly important; indeed, they might well be more important than genetic ones. Second, if we are to understand fully what determines schizophrenia, it is essential to study genetic and environmental factors at the same time.

> **EXAM HINT**
>
> All three major approaches to investigating the role of genetic factors in schizophrenia (twin, family, and adoption studies) have their own strengths and limitations. The limitations can make it hard to interpret the findings. Family studies are often the most difficult to interpret, because genetic and environmental similarity tend to go together. In adoption studies, children are sometimes adopted by members of their extended family or live in the same area and have contact with their biological family. This makes it hard to disentangle nature and nurture. However, the good news is that the findings are broadly similar across all three approaches.

Biochemistry

Genetic factors can lead to differences in brain chemistry; this would make the brain chemistry the immediate causal factor of schizophrenia. Biochemical abnormalities might be important in the development and maintenance of schizophrenia. For example, schizophrenia might result in part from abnormally high levels of the neurotransmitter dopamine (Seidman, 1983). A slightly different view is that neurons in the brains of patients with schizophrenia are oversensitive to dopamine.

Dopamine hypothesis

According to the original version of the dopamine hypothesis, patients with schizophrenia have excessive levels of dopamine. Dopamine is a neurotransmitter (chemical substance), and there are various reasons for arguing it that it might play a role in schizophrenia. First, there is strong evidence that the main antipsychotic drugs (discussed later) share the ability to block dopamine receptors. This is entirely consistent with the dopamine hypothesis. However, the fact that schizophrenia can be treated successfully by drugs that block dopamine receptors does not prove that excessive dopamine levels are the main cause of schizophrenia.

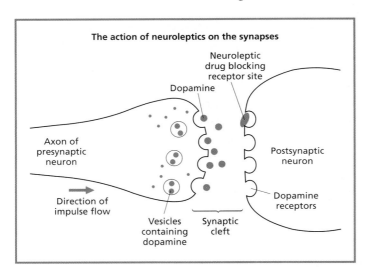

The action of neuroleptics on the synapses

Second, the drug L-dopa, which increases dopamine levels, can produce many of the symptoms of schizophrenia. L-dopa has been given to patients suffering from Parkinson's disease, which is caused by low levels of dopamine in parts of the brain. It is effective in treating some of the symptoms but an unwanted side effect is the presence of various schizophrenic symptoms.

Third, there is evidence on the effects of amphetamine. This drug produces a functional excess of dopamine; the brain responds as if there were too much dopamine. High doses of amphetamine can produce some of the symptoms of schizophrenia (e.g. paranoia, auditory hallucinations). In similar fashion, the symptoms of patients with schizophrenia often become worse when they are given amphetamine, which activates dopamine (van Kammen, Docherty, & Bunney, 1982). Stronger evidence was reported by Laruelle, Abi-Dargham, Gil, Kegeles, and Innis (1999), who administered amphetamine to individuals with schizophrenia and those without. The patients with schizophrenia showed a greater increase in dopamine transmission in response to the amphetamine than the individuals who did not have schizophrenia.

Fourth, there is more direct evidence based on studying the brains of patients with schizophrenia. Post-mortem (after death) examination showed that such patients had a greater density of dopamine receptors in certain parts of the brain (the caudate nucleus putamen) than individuals not suffering from schizophrenia (Owen, Crow, Poulter, Cross, Longden, & Riley, 1978). More recent research has suggested that what is happening is rather complex. Winterer and Weinberger (2004) discussed research focusing on dopamine receptor types D1 and D2, both of which assist in producing stable representations of external and internal stimuli. Schizophrenics often have an abnormal dopamine D1 : D2 ratio, which causes disruption and leads to some of the symptoms of schizophrenia.

Problems with the dopamine hypothesis

It is hard to assess brain levels of dopamine in patients with schizophrenia. Indeed, this can only be done in a *direct* way by post-mortem assessment. Such assessment has generally indicated that individuals with schizophrenia have more dopamine receptors than healthy individuals (Seidman, 1990).

It is also possible to assess dopamine levels in an *indirect* way. However, this involves inserting a needle into the spine, which can be dangerous. The findings have generally been negative—patients with schizophrenia do not seem to produce more dopamine than other people.

Some supporters of the dopamine hypothesis have argued that the dopamine receptors of patients with schizophrenia are more *sensitive* than those of healthy controls. That could explain why individuals with schizophrenia seem to behave as if they had high levels of dopamine. Brain-imaging studies have produced rather variable results. One study, by Gjedde and Wong (1987), found that individuals with schizophrenia have more than twice as many dopamine receptors of a given type than controls; however, no difference between schizophrenics and controls was found in another study (Farde et al., 1990).

In sum, dopamine is probably of importance in understanding schizophrenia. However, the notion that schizophrenics typically have much higher dopamine levels than healthy individuals is clearly too simple-minded. It looks increasingly as if there are various complex differences in dopamine functioning (e.g. D1 : D2 activation ratio) between those with schizophrenia and healthy individuals. There is also the causality issue. If we find an association between having schizophrenia and having high levels of dopamine, the excessive dopamine levels might have played a part in causing the schizophrenia. However, it is also possible that elevated dopamine levels are in part a consequence of having schizophrenia.

Brain Structure and Early Development

Several researchers have argued that brain abnormalities might be involved in schizophrenia. There are several sophisticated techniques for studying the brain, some of which have been used to study brain structure in schizophrenics. Pahl, Swayze, and Andreasen (1990) reviewed almost 50 studies, the great majority of which found abnormally large lateral ventricles (liquid-filled cavities) in the brains of patients with schizophrenia. Further evidence of the involvement of the ventricles was reported by Suddath, Christison, Torrey, Casanova, and Weinberger (1990), who used magnetic resonance imaging (MRI) to obtain pictures of brain structure from identical twin pairs in which only one twin had schizophrenia. The twin with schizophrenia generally had more enlarged ventricles and reduced anterior hypothalamus. Indeed, the differences were so large that the twin with schizophrenia could be identified readily from the brain images in 12 out of 15 twin pairs.

Enlarged ventricles can occur because the brain areas surrounding them have decreased in volume. There is much evidence that the brain volume of people with schizophrenia is generally less than that of healthy individuals, and also that there are progressive decreases in brain volume over time. For example, Mathalon et al. (2001) found that adult patients with schizophrenia had more rapid reductions in total brain volume than did healthy controls.

There is one large problem so far as interpreting the above findings is concerned: the data are essentially correlational. We know that there is an *association* between being schizophrenic and having various brain abnormalities. However, we don't know whether the brain abnormalities preceded and helped to cause the schizophrenia or whether these brain abnormalities are merely a consequence of

> **?** Does the evidence indicate whether schizophrenics might have excess dopamine (or serotonin), or are just more sensitive to it?

> **?** Could you use this knowledge to diagnose schizophrenia? How reliable would the diagnosis be?

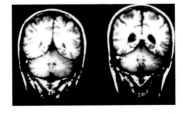

Magnetic resonance imaging of monozygotic twins shows marked enlargement of the lateral ventricles in the schizophrenic twin (right). Images courtesy of Drs. E. Fuller Torrey, M.D., and Daniel Weinberger, The Treatment Advocacy Center.

having schizophrenia. Some progress in addressing the causality issue has been made by researchers examining the neurodevelopmental hypothesis (see below).

Neurodevelopmental hypothesis

According to the neurodevelopmental hypothesis, brain lesions occurring very early in development (possibly before birth) can make the individuals affected vulnerable to schizophrenia. This hypothesis found support in a study by Wright, Takei, Rifkin, Murray, and Shaw (1999), who reported data from several countries on the incidence of schizophrenia in children born to mothers who had flu during pregnancy. There was an elevated risk of schizophrenia in these children. This was especially the case when the mother had flu between the fourth and seventh months of the pregnancy.

Similar findings were reported by Sham, O'Callaghan, Takei, Murray, Hare, and Murray (1992), who focused on patients with schizophrenia admitted to hospital in England and Wales between 1970 and 1979. There was a tendency for these patients to have been exposed to a flu epidemic between the third and the seventh months after conception.

Susser et al. (1996) considered the effects of a severe famine lasting several months in parts of Holland during the Second World War. Children conceived during the famine had twice the normal risk of developing schizophrenia subsequently. Presumably, nutritional deficiency was responsible.

Patients with schizophrenia are disproportionately likely to have been born in late winter and less likely than those without schizophrenia to have been born in the summer or autumn (Birchwood & Jackson, 2001). It is not clear how to interpret this finding. However, seasonal viruses that affect newborn babies and can increase the chances of adult schizophrenia are most prevalent in the winter.

O'Callaghan et al. (1992) reported that several perinatal (shortly before or after birth) and birth complications are associated with schizophrenia. These complications include premature birth, low birth weight, prolonged labour, and foetal distress.

Walker, Savoie, and Davis (1994) studied family home movies taken during the early childhoods of children who did or did not develop schizophrenia subsequently. At a very early age (sometimes as young as 2), those children who would develop schizophrenia had more motor abnormalities, more negative emotional expressions, and more odd hand movements. This is intriguing evidence that there might be early signs that someone will develop schizophrenia many years later.

Evaluation

Various factors occurring prior to birth, shortly after birth, or in the early years of childhood can significantly increase the risk of developing schizophrenia in late adolescence or early adulthood. According to the neurodevelopmental hypothesis, many of these factors can cause brain lesions, and these brain lesions in turn play a role in the development of schizophrenia. At present, we don't have a detailed account of how these factors cause brain lesions. Indeed, we don't even have clear evidence that they actually do cause brain lesions. However, the findings that patients with schizophrenia have larger ventricles and smaller brain volume than healthy controls suggest that it is fruitful to consider brain abnormalities when trying to explain schizophrenia.

? If one of your relatives has suffered from a mental disorder, what reasons are there for you not to worry that you may also develop the same disorder?

Evolution

Group-splitting hypothesis

Several experts have put forward evolutionary explanations of schizophrenia. For example, Stevens and Price (1996, 2000) developed the group-splitting hypothesis. According to this hypothesis, our distant ancestors formed groups that tended to increase in size. As group size increased, however, so did risks from predation, difficulties in finding enough food, and rivalries within the group. Dunbar (1996) estimated that between 100 and 150 was the optimal group size. It is possible that individuals with schizophrenia—with their bizarre beliefs, mood changes, hallucinations, delusions, and strange speech—could have acted as leaders and enabled subgroups to split off from the main group.

How plausible is the group-splitting hypothesis? In its favour, some people with schizophrenia have delusions of grandeur, hallucinations, and bizarre beliefs that might have been appealing to members of a group that had become too large. Equally, however, people with schizophrenia often have incoherent speech and a relative absence of emotion and motivation—not the most obvious characteristics of a charismatic leader!

Shamanism

An alternative to the group-splitting hypothesis is the notion that schizophrenia is associated with shamanism (Polimeni & Reiss, 2002). A shaman is a medicine man or key religious figure, such people are often believed to be able to communicate with spirits. Some of the characteristics of schizophrenia (e.g. auditory hallucinations; delusions of grandeur) might have been useful qualities for shamans to have. As with the group-splitting hypothesis, this is a speculative viewpoint and lacks convincing evidence to support it. It would appear that most people with schizophrenia do not have the personal qualities needed in a charismatic shaman.

Could this have made schizophrenia adaptive?

Many genes exist in two forms, or alleles. One such is the *COMT* gene, which has a val and a met form. This means an individual could be homozygous for either or heterozygous, i.e. val-val, met-met, or val-met. Both allelles are common in the population, meaning they have been conserved as we evolved, so they must confer some advantages as well as disadvantages. For example, met-met people have more dopamine activity in the prefrontal cortex, making them both more likely to be highly anxious as well as having really good working memory and attention functions. Val-val individuals have abnormally low prefrontal activity, and so poorer working memory, but they are less easily startled or put off balance by emotionally challenging stimuli. This val-val pattern slightly biases those people to schizophrenic-type brain activity as people with the val-val variant show reduced prefrontal dopamine activity and less efficient prefrontal information processing typical of the disorder. Of course, this does not mean that val-val causes schizophrenia, but that this genetic combination might predispose an individual to be vulnerable to developing the disorder.

Language Hypothesis

Crow (2000) argued that the central paradox with schizophrenia is that, despite the fact that the disorder should reduce reproductive success, this apparently genetic condition persists. Crowe addressed this paradox in his language hypothesis. His starting point was that language has clear adaptive advantages in terms of enabling the users to engage in precise communication. Crow's central

? The ability to use language is usally adaptive. When might this not be true?

claim was that there are close links between schizophrenia and language—schizophrenia involves a breakdown in the brain's internal linguistic controls, leading sufferers to use unusual language or to believe they are hearing voices. Putting these ideas together led Crow to conclude that schizophrenia is the price that humans pay for having language.

According to Crow (2000), a genetic mutation more than 150,000 years ago led to the development of both language and schizophrenia. In some individuals, language is not lateralised (i.e. located only in the left hemisphere, which is the usual state of affairs). This disrupts certain mechanisms of language, such as people's ability to distinguish their thoughts from the speech output that they generate and the speech input that they receive and decode from others. According to Mitchell and Crow (2005, p. 971), "The language deficits of patients with schizophrenia can best be understood as abnormalities of lateralisation."

Crow's language hypothesis is interesting. The proposed linkage between schizophrenia and language is strengthened by the finding that there is reduced lateralisation of language to the left hemisphere in schizophrenics (Mitchell & Crow, 2005). It is also true that several symptoms of schizophrenia involve language abnormalities, and it is likely that language skills contribute to reproductive success.

There are several limitations with Crow's hypothesis. First, it is not very clear how the deficient language skills of individuals with schizophrenia are associated with evolutionary success. Second, most of the symptoms of schizophrenia have very little to do with language; for example, lack of emotion and motivation, disorganised movements, and social impairments. Third, most genetic changes occur over very long periods, lasting hundreds of thousands of years. This makes it unlikely that genetic changes leading to language and to schizophrenia occurred rapidly.

SECTION SUMMARY
Biological Explanations of Schizophrenia

Genetic factors

❖ The much higher concordance rate for identical than for fraternal twins provides some of the strongest evidence that genetic factors are important. However, some recent studies have produced less impressive findings than earlier studies.

❖ The genetic hypothesis is also supported by family and adoption studies.
❖ Many family studies are open to an environmental interpretation. The fact that the concordance rate for identical twins is substantially below 100% means that environmental factors are very important.

Biochemistry

❖ It has been claimed that individuals with schizophrenia have excessive levels of dopamine or that their receptors are oversensitive to dopamine.
❖ The evidence indicates that dopamine is important for an understanding of schizophrenia. There seem to be various differences between those with schizophrenia and healthy individuals in dopamine functioning, but the complexities involved remain unclear.

Brain structure and early development

❖ Individuals with schizophrenia tend to have abnormally large lateral ventricles in their brains. This might help to cause schizophrenia or it could be that having schizophrenia affects the brain.
❖ The risk of someone developing schizophrenia is increased by various perinatal and birth complications. Much research is needed to work out what viral or other factors are responsible.

Evolution

❖ Evolutionary accounts claim that schizophrenia had some adaptive value in our ancestral past.
❖ According to the group-splitting hypothesis, individuals with schizophrenia in the past acted as leaders to prevent groups from becoming too large.
❖ It is not clear that the lack of motivation and incoherent language of individuals with schizophrenia equip them to become leaders.
❖ According to Crow's language hypothesis, schizophrenia is the cost humans pay for having language. More specifically, a genetic mutation led to development of language and of schizophrenia.
❖ The association between schizophrenia and language is supported by the language impairments of those with schizophrenia. However, major symptoms of schizophrenia such as lack of motivation and emotion can't easily be explained on the language hypothesis.

PSYCHOLOGICAL EXPLANATIONS OF SCHIZOPHRENIA

Many different psychological explanations of schizophrenia have been put forward. Here we will only discuss some of the most important ones. We will start by considering psychodynamic explanations initially proposed about 100 years ago. After that, we will discuss cognitive explanations. Finally, we will focus on various socio-cultural explanations including those emphasising life events, interpersonal communication within families, and possible effects of lower social class.

> **EXAM HINT**
>
> The question will usually stipulate whether biological or psychological explanations are to be considered. You can use the alternative explanations to evaluate the one you are writing about but be careful—one link sentence to introduce them is not enough. You must consistently contrast the alternative explanation with the explanation(s) you've covered as AO1. Do not simply describe the alternative explanation; instead explain what insights it provides that the AO1 explanations do not. Also consider whether the different explanations share any strengths or weaknesses, or whether the weakness of one can be used to highlight the strength of the other.

Psychodynamic Explanation

Here we consider Sigmund Freud's explanation of the factors involved in the development of schizophrenia. This explanation depends on his theory of

Sigmund Freud, 1856–1939.

Useful mnemonic

To help you remember Freud's stages of psychosexual development, the following mnemonic is made from the initial letter of each stage:

- **O**ld **A**ge **P**ensioners **L**ove **G**reens!

---

psychosexual development, so I will discuss that briefly to provide context for Freud's views on schizophrenia.

Freud argued that all children go through a series of stages of psychosexual development. First is the oral phase, which lasts from birth up to about 18 months of age, during which the infant obtains satisfaction from eating and sucking. Second is the anal stage (approximately 18–36 months), during which the child derives satisfaction from the anal region (e.g. withholding faeces). Third is the phallic stage (3–6 years), during which the genitals become a source of satisfaction. Fourth is the latency stage (6–puberty), during which boys and girls spend little time together. Fifth is the genital stage (onset of puberty onwards), in which the genitals are the main source of sexual pleasure.

If a child experiences severe problems or excessive pleasure at any stage of development, this leads to **fixation**, in which basic energy or libido becomes attached to that stage for many years. Later in life, adults who experience very stressful conditions show **regression**, in which their behaviour becomes less mature and like that displayed during a psychosexual stage at which they fixated as children.

We need to consider one other aspect of Freud's general theory before turning to his explanation of schizophrenia. One of the key parts of the mind is the **ego**, which is associated with conscious, rational processes. The ego develops during the first 2 years of life. It works on the reality principle, meaning that it strives to accommodate environmental demands in a realistic way.

We are now ready to discuss Freud's explanation of schizophrenia. This consists of three major assumptions. First, most adults with schizophrenia experienced very harsh childhood environments, often because their parents were very cold and unsupportive. This means that they often fixated at the early stages of psychosexual development.

Second, schizophrenia develops when the adult regresses to the earliest stage of development before his or her ego had developed. That means that the person ceases to operate on the basis of the reality principle, and so loses touch with reality. The regression to very early childhood leads to symptoms such as delusions of grandeur and the creation of neologisms (new words).

Third, when individuals with schizophrenia find themselves reduced to an infantile state, they try hard to regain contact with reality and a degree of ego control. For example, auditory hallucinations might be one way of substituting for a lost sense of reality.

KEY TERMS

Fixation: in Freud's theory, spending a long time at a given stage of development because of problems or excessive gratification.

Regression: returning to earlier stages of development when severely stressed.

Ego: the conscious, rational mind; one of the three main parts of the mind in Freud's theory.

Evaluation

On the positive side, Freud's theoretical account of schizophrenia was one of the first systematic attempts to explain its origins. A key feature of schizophrenia is that it involves a loss of contact with reality. This is addressed by Freud's assumption that people with schizophrenia regress to a period of early childhood in which infants have no proper notion of reality. Finally, Freud was able to account for some of the symptoms of schizophrenia (e.g. delusions of grandeur, neologisms) within his theory.

We turn now to the limitations of Freud's approach. There has been little research on Freud's explanation of the development of schizophrenia. However, it is clear that his explanation isn't very satisfactory for various reasons. First, to put it mildly, it doesn't make any sense to argue that schizophrenics resemble very young children. For example, most infants have enormous curiosity and interest in the world around them—this is a world away from the rigid or catatonic behaviour, lack of emotion, and lack of motivation often found in schizophrenics.

Second, most mothers of schizophrenics are not harsh and withholding as Freud assumed. Waring and Ricks (1965) found that mothers of schizophrenics tended to be anxious, shy, withdrawn, and incoherent. Thus, the mothers of schizophrenics tend to be inadequate in various ways but not those assumed by Freud.

Third, Freud's theory of schizophrenia is very complex. It involves assumptions about fixation, regression, stages of psychosexual development, and so on. There is very little support for any of these assumptions, and it would be exceptionally difficult to prove that experiences in the first 2 years of life contribute to the development of schizophrenia 20 years later.

Fourth, the psychodynamic approach de-emphasises the importance of biological factors in the development of schizophrenia. For example, it doesn't explain why schizophrenia often has a sudden onset in late adolescence or early adulthood. As a result, it provides a very limited understanding of the disorder. This helps to explain why psychodynamic therapy for schizophrenia has generally proved to be unsuccessful (Comer, 2001). As a result, psychodynamic therapy will not be discussed when we turn our attention to major forms of therapy for schizophrenia.

> **Assumptions of the psychodynamic explanation**
>
> - Much of our behaviour is driven by unconscious motives.
> - Childhood is a critical period in development.
> - Mental disorders arise from unresolved, unconscious conflicts originating in childhood.
> - Resolution occurs through accessing and coming to terms with repressed ideas and conflicts.

Cognitive Explanations

Many different cognitive explanations for the development of schizophrenia have been put forward. However, they all assume that the various cognitive impairments shown by people with schizophrenia (e.g. poor attentional control; language deficits; disorganised thinking) play an important role in the development and maintenance of schizophrenia. For example, McKenna (1996) argued that many of the symptoms of schizophrenia occur as a result of a defect in selective attention. Symptoms such as disorganised speech, speaking uninformatively, delusions, and hallucinations might all depend at least in part on the poor ability of a person with schizophrenia to concentrate.

Frith (1992) argued that important cognitive factors are associated with the development of schizophrenia. He claimed that positive symptoms of schizophrenia (e.g. delusions of control, auditory hallucinations) might occur because individuals with schizophrenia have problems with self-monitoring, and so fail to keep track of their own intentions. As a result, they mistakenly regard their own thoughts as alien and as having come from someone else. This provides an explanation of the auditory hallucinations experienced by people with schizophrenia. According to Frith, similar failures of self-monitoring can lead

? What are the limitations of the cognitive approach?

them to attribute agency for some of their motor movements to other people. Frith speculated that these problems might occur as a consequence of an irregularity in the neuronal pathways running between the septo-hippocampal system and the prefrontal cortex.

Frith (1992, p. 121) argued that individuals with schizophrenia have another important cognitive deficit: "The schizophrenic knows well that other people have minds, but has lost the ability to infer the contents of these minds: their beliefs and intentions." The ability to understand other people's mental states is often called Theory of Mind (see Chapter 9). If individuals with schizophrenia lack a Theory of Mind, this could help to explain some of their delusions and also why paranoid schizophrenics are suspicious of others' intentions.

Hemsley (1993, 2005) put forward a cognitive theory of schizophrenia. His starting point was that perception and memory combine effectively in healthy individuals but fail to do so in individuals with schizophrenia. In our everyday lives, we use stored knowledge (much of it in the form of schemas or packages of information) to allow us to predict what is going to happen next. Memory tells us that when we are in a restaurant a waiter or waitress will give us a menu, take our order, bring the food, and so on. More generally, memory helps to ensure that we attend to and perceive the most important stimuli in the environment. It also helps us to keep track of our current goals.

By contrast, there is a substantial breakdown in the relationship between memory and perception in schizophrenics. In the words of Hemsley (2005, p. 43), "A range of genetic and environmental influences contributing to the disorder [schizophrenia] may operate through a . . . failure to integrate contextually appropriate stored material with current sensory input and ongoing motor programmes." As a result, people with schizophrenia are often unable to predict what will happen next, their concentration is poor, and they attend to unimportant or irrelevant aspects of the environment. More generally, their poor integration of memory and perception leads to disorganised thinking and behaviour.

Findings

Several of the main symptoms of schizophrenia (e.g. disorganised speech, delusions, hallucinations) can be explained in terms of deficient self-monitoring or a breakdown between perception and memory. In addition, however, Frith's theory in particular has been investigated in several studies, and we will briefly consider the relevant evidence.

McGuigan (1966) found that the larynx of patients with schizophrenia was often active during the time they claimed to be experiencing auditory hallucinations. This suggests that they mistook their own inner speech for that of someone else. McGuire, Silbersweig, Wright, Murray, Frackowiak, and Frith (1996) also studied patients with schizophrenia who suffered from hallucinations. They were found to have reduced activity in those parts of the brain involved in monitoring inner speech.

Johns et al. (2001) carried out a more thorough test of self-monitoring theory using three groups: (1) individuals with schizophrenia with verbal hallucinations and delusions; (2) individuals with schizophrenia with delusions but no hallucinations; and (3) healthy controls. All participants read words aloud under four conditions: (1) reading aloud; (2) reading aloud with acoustic distortion of their own voice; (3) reading aloud while hearing someone else's voice (alien feedback); and (4) distorted alien feedback. After participants had said each word, they indicated the source of the word they heard. Both groups of individuals with schizophrenia were more likely than controls to misattribute the source of their own distorted voice, but there were no group differences in attributing the source with alien feedback. The misattribution of the source of their own distorted voice was more common among individuals with schizophrenia with hallucinations than in those with delusions, especially when the words were insulting.

Johns et al.'s (2001) findings confirm that individuals with schizophrenia who experience hallucinations have impaired verbal self-monitoring. They also indicate that individuals with schizophrenia who have delusions but no hallucinations also show some tendency towards impaired verbal self-monitoring.

The notion that individuals with schizophrenia have a deficient Theory of Mind (discussed fully in Chapter 9) was tested by Drury, Robinson, and Birchwood (1998). As predicted, patients tested during a schizophrenic episode performed very poorly on measures designed to assess Theory of Mind. These findings suggest that individuals with schizophrenia have deficits in Theory of Mind. However, another possibility is that their performance occurred simply because they experience information-processing overload when faced with complex tasks.

Evaluation

The cognitive approach provides a reasonable account of many of the positive symptoms of schizophrenia. For example, the existence of verbal hallucinations is one of the most puzzling symptoms of schizophrenia, and the cognitive approach has shed considerable light on why schizophrenics have such hallucinations. The notion that schizophrenics have impaired awareness of their own internally generated thoughts also helps to explain why they often have disorganised speech and delusions. The finding that schizophrenics seem to have deficits in Theory of Mind is also of potential significance.

> **Assumptions of cognitive explanations**
>
> - Maladaptive behaviour is caused by faulty and irrational cognitions.
> - It is the way you think about a problem, rather than the problem itself, that causes mental disorder.
> - Individuals can overcome mental disorders by learning to use more appropriate cognitions.
> - Aim to be positive and rational.

What are the limitations with the cognitive approach? First, it doesn't explain the negative symptoms of schizophrenia (e.g. showing little motivation, being very unemotional). Second, the direction of causality is not very clear. Attentional and other cognitive problems might play a role in triggering schizophrenia but it is also possible that having schizophrenia produces cognitive deficits. Third, many brain-damaged patients have problems with attention or with the relationship between memory and perception. Despite having these cognitive deficits, however, they fail to develop the symptoms of schizophrenia. Fourth, several factors having little relevance to cognitive deficits influence the development of schizophrenia. Examples include genetic factors, stressful life events, and various social factors.

Socio-cultural Explanations

Various socio-cultural explanations of the origins of schizophrenia have been proposed. These explanations cover many social and cultural factors that might play a role in the development of schizophrenia. It seems reasonable to assume that individuals who have to deal with major life events (e.g. the death of a loved one, serious illness, divorce) would be more vulnerable to developing schizophrenia and other mental disorders. Another socio-cultural explanation focuses on interpersonal communication (especially within the family). For example, if family members are very expressive emotionally, this may trigger schizophrenia or increase the chances of relapse. Finally, another possible explanation is based on the assumption that poor, working-class individuals lead more stressful lives than other people. If so, the stressfulness of their living conditions might make them vulnerable to being schizophrenic.

Life events

One of the first studies to consider the possible impact of life events on schizophrenia was carried out by Brown and Birley (1968). They studied patients with schizophrenia who had recently had a schizophrenic episode. Their key finding was that 50% of these patients had experienced at least one major life event in the 3 weeks beforehand. By contrast, only 12% had experienced a life event in the preceding 9 weeks. Very few healthy controls reported any life events over the same 12-week period. These dramatic findings suggested that life events can rapidly trigger a schizophrenic episode.

There were several limitations with this study and other early research on life events and schizophrenia. First, the patients' reports of the nature and timing of the life events they had experienced were obtained *retrospectively*, i.e. some time after they had happened. It is thus possible that some of the patients might have distorted the timing of life events to "explain" their schizophrenic episode.

Second, what matters is the significance a major life event has for the individual rather than simply the event itself. For example, the impact of marital separation differs depending on whether the individual concerned already has a new partner whom they love. Thus, we need to relate life events to the individual's personal *context*.

Third, we must distinguish between life events that are *independent* of schizophrenia and those occurring as a consequence of the disorder. For example, marital separation might occur because the spouse of a person with schizophrenia cannot put up with his or her bizarre behaviour and lack of emotion. Only life events that are *independent* of the disorder can play a role in the development of schizophrenia, but Brown and Birley (1968) didn't distinguish clearly between independent and non-independent events.

Hirsch et al. (1996) carried out a study dealing with all the limitations of the Brown and Birley (1968) study. Theirs was a prospective study in which they obtained regular information on life events throughout the course of 1 year. They took account of the context in which life events occurred by using the Life Events and Difficulties Scale, which uses independent raters to assess how severe a life event is taking account of the individual's personal circumstances. Finally, they decided the extent to which each life event was independent of the patient's illness.

Marital separation might arise from an individual's inability to cope with his or her partner's erratic behaviour. In this sense the life event is not causal (and therefore independent of the disorder) but consequential.

What did Hirsch et al. (1996) find? First, 23% of the risk of patients having a relapse during the 1-year period was due to life events. Second, the risk was 41%

for patients who had twice the average number of life events. Third, in contrast to the findings of Brown and Birley (1968), there was no evidence that life events were especially likely immediately before a schizophrenic episode. Instead, the risk of having a schizophrenic episode increased cumulatively as the number of life events increased over time.

How do life events increase the probability of patients with schizophrenia having a relapse? This issue was addressed by Myin-Germeys et al. (2003), who focused on the ways in which patients in remission responded to the hassles of everyday life. Patients with schizophrenia who had experienced recent major life events didn't differ from those who hadn't in the perceived stressfulness of daily events and hassles. However, those with recent major life events showed more intense negative emotional reactions to daily hassles. These emotional reactions presumably make patients with recent major life events more vulnerable to relapse.

? Why do you think life events increase the risk of a relapse of schizophrenia?

Evaluation

The early studies were relatively unsophisticated and failed to provide convincing evidence that life events play a role in producing relapse in schizophrenic patients. However, later studies (e.g. Hirsch et al., 1996) established that the occurrence of major life events does increase patients' vulnerability to relapse. In addition, part of the reason why major life events increase the probability of relapse is because they lead patients to respond more negatively to the numerous hassles of everyday life.

There are various limitations with research in this area. First, the onset of a schizophrenic episode does not depend *only* on life events. If that were the case then every patient who experiences severe life events would have a schizophrenic episode. Thus, the onset of a schizophrenic episode depends on a combination of major life events *and* some specific vulnerability within the individual patient. Second, there are many types of life event, and some types are probably more likely than others to trigger a schizophrenic episode. However, this issue has not been examined in detail. Third, it is likely that genetic and other biological factors help to determine the impact of life events on patients with schizophrenia, but the life-event approach does not consider such factors.

Interpersonal communication within families

Some theorists have argued that there are abnormal and inadequate patterns of communication within the families of patients with schizophrenia. Bateson, Jackson, Haley, and Weakland (1956) put forward a double-bind theory, according to which the members of families of individuals with schizophrenia communicate in a destructively ambiguous way. For example, the mother will tell her child that she loves him but in a tone of voice that doesn't indicate love. The double-bind theory accounts in part for the confused thinking of patients with schizophrenia. However, it suffers from the serious problem that little evidence supports it. For example, Ringuette and Kennedy (1966) asked clinicians to analyse letters written by parents to their hospitalised children. The extent to which these letters contained double-bind communication was the same regardless of whether the children suffered from schizophrenia or from some other disorder.

Despite the failure of double-bind theory, the families of individuals with schizophrenia do tend to have inadequate interpersonal communication. Mischler and Waxler (1968) found that mothers talking to their schizophrenic daughters were rather aloof and unresponsive. However, the same mothers behaved more normally and responsively when talking to their healthy daughters. Thus, the presence of a patient with schizophrenia in the family might result in poor communication patterns, rather than the other way around.

Expressed emotion

Despite the lack of support for double-bind theory, the interactions within families might still play a key role in maintaining the symptoms of patients already suffering from schizophrenia. What is important is the extent to which a family engages in expressed emotion—this involves criticism, hostility, and emotional over-involvement. In one study (Kavanagh, 1992), schizophrenics living in families with high **expressed emotion** were nearly four times as likely to relapse as those living in families with low expressed emotion. Butzlaff and Hooley (1998) carried out a meta-analysis of several studies. Expressed emotion within families was a good predictor of schizophrenic relapse, especially for those with more chronic or long-lasting schizophrenic symptoms. However, the impact of expressed emotion on relapse was greater for depression and for eating disorders than for schizophrenia, so expressed emotion has negative effects on several mental disorders.

The notion of expressed emotion might help to explain a fascinating cross-cultural difference, namely, that individuals with schizophrenia in developing countries are much less likely than those in developed countries to suffer relapse. This is counterintuitive, given that patients generally have better access to treatment and medication in developed countries. A plausible explanation is that levels of expressed emotion within the families of individuals with schizophrenia are significantly lower in developing countries than in developed ones. Supporting evidence was reported by Leff et al. (1990), who found high levels of expressed emotion in only 23% of families of individuals with schizophrenia in Chandigarh, India, compared with 47% of families in London.

It is sometimes claimed that studies on expressed emotion indicate that the family causes the patient to relapse. This is a gross oversimplification. In fact, expressed emotion results from *interactions* between family members and the patient that develop over a considerable period of time. According to Patterson, Birchwood, and Cochrane (2000), the development of expressed emotion typically goes through three stages. At the first stage, the family members experience a sense of "loss" of the person they once knew. At the second stage, the family members engage in emotional over-involvement in an attempt to resolve the emotional issues caused by adjusting to the patient's serious condition. At the third stage, if emotional over-involvement has failed to resolve important issues, family members often become angry and critical.

Evaluation

There is strong evidence that expressed emotion is associated with relapse for patients with schizophrenia. However, most studies in this area have not successfully identified the direction of causality. One possibility is that expressed emotion within the family causes relapse. Another possibility is that individuals in poor psychological shape are more likely to provoke expressed emotion from members of their family. What is most likely is that expressed emotion emerges as a result of family interactions over time as the family members struggle to adjust to the situation. Thus, processes involving the entire family cause expressed emotion rather than the specific activities of any individual family member.

Expressed emotion is of importance in understanding why patients with schizophrenia relapse. However, many other factors including genetic influences,

KEY TERM

Expressed emotion: a way of describing the behaviour of certain families. These behaviours include too much criticism, hostility, and emotional overprotectiveness.

cognitive deficits, and life events are also involved but are not considered by this approach.

? What are the practical applications of theories of schizophrenia?

Social causation hypothesis

Individuals belonging to the lower social classes, and African–Caribbean people, are much more likely than whites belonging to the middle class to be diagnosed with schizophrenia. This suggests that social class and deprivation might be important factors in causing schizophrenia. In fact, however, there are three plausible ways to explain the association between schizophrenia on the one hand and social class and ethnic status on the other.

First, there might be bias, with clinicians being more willing to diagnose schizophrenia when considering the symptoms of patients from the lower social classes or from African–Caribbean countries. As discussed earlier, Johnstone (1989) claimed that lower-class patients are more likely than middle-class ones to receive a diagnosis of schizophrenia or some other serious condition even when there were few (if any) differences in symptoms. However, there is no strong evidence to support this position, or the notion that ethnic bias leads to an over diagnosis of schizophrenia among people of African–Caribbean descent.

Second, there is the social causation hypothesis. According to this hypothesis, members of the lower classes in a society experience more stressful lives than other people because of poverty, poorer physical health, and so on. Stress is also more likely to arise through discrimination, because ethnic and racial minorities in many cultures often belong to the lower social classes. The high level of stress makes people more vulnerable than members of the middle class to schizophrenia.

Third, there is the social drift hypothesis, according to which individuals who develop schizophrenia are likely to lose their jobs, and so their social status is reduced. Thus, schizophrenia *causes* reduced social status rather than low social status causing schizophrenia. If so, then schizophrenics should belong to a lower social class than their parents. Turner and Wagonfeld (1967) found this when comparing schizophrenics and their fathers. However, the fathers also tended to belong to the lower social classes themselves, as predicted by the social causation hypothesis.

Dohrenwend et al. (1992) tested the social causation and social drift hypotheses. They compared two immigrant groups in Israel: (1) European Jews who had been settled in Israel for some time; and (2) more recent immigrants from North Africa and the Middle East. The latter group experienced much prejudice and discrimination, and so should have had higher rates of schizophrenia according to the social causation hypothesis. In fact, the advantaged (former) group had a higher rate of schizophrenia, especially among those in the lower social class. This fits the social drift hypothesis if we assume that members of an advantaged group are likely to find themselves in the lowest social class because they have developed schizophrenia.

In recent years, stronger evidence supporting the social causation hypothesis has been obtained in the United Kingdom. Four of the main findings (reviewed by Cooper, 2005) are as follows. First, schizophrenia is found much more often in decaying inner-city areas than in poor rural areas, suggesting that being born or brought up in a poor inner-city area is a risk factor. Second, schizophrenia and other psychoses are almost seven times more common in African–Caribbean people than in white people. Third, the incidence of schizophrenia in Caribbean countries is similar to that of white people in this country. Fourth, the incidence of schizophrenia in second-generation African–Caribbean people in the UK is higher than that of first-generation African–Caribbean people.

Why is the rate of schizophrenia among African–Caribbean people in the UK so high? Many live in conditions that are more stressful and deprived than in the countries from which they came. The risks increase as a function of the amount of time spent in such conditions, which is why the incidence of schizophrenia is higher in second-generation than first-generation African–Caribbean people.

Evaluation

It is improbable that there is any *single* explanation of the fact that schizophrenia is more prevalent among lower-class people and those from African–Caribbean countries. There is evidence to support the social causation hypothesis, but the social drift hypothesis has also received some support. The strongest evidence in favour of the social causation hypothesis is found in African–Caribbean people, whose high incidence of schizophrenia is due mainly to social deprivation.

What are the limitations of the social causation hypothesis? First, much of the evidence is hard to interpret and is consistent with the social causation and social drift hypotheses. Second, several factors (e.g. discrimination, poverty, decaying inner-city environment) increase the probability of developing schizophrenia, but the relative importance of these factors remains somewhat unclear. Third, we must not exaggerate the importance of social deprivation in causing schizophrenia. The overwhelming majority of those living in poor and severely deprived conditions *do not* develop schizophrenia. Fourth, the social causation hypothesis focuses on one important factor in causing schizophrenia but ignores the role played by genetic factors, life events, and cognitive deficits.

Conclusions

You might have become bewildered because the development of schizophrenia is influenced by so many very different factors. Hopefully, I can eliminate some of this bewilderment by fitting most of the findings into what is known as the **diathesis–stress model**. According to this model, the occurrence of psychological disorders depends on two factors:

1. *Diathesis*: a genetic vulnerability or predisposition to disease or disorder.
2. *Stress*: some severe or disturbing environmental event. The term "stress" is used here in a very broad sense. It might include, for example, drug taking or any event placing an extra burden on the individual psychologically and/or physically.

The key notion in the diathesis–stress model is that both diathesis or genetic vulnerability *and* stress are necessary for any psychological disorder (including schizophrenia) to develop.

The diathesis–stress model can readily be applied to the development of schizophrenia. There is clear evidence of a diathesis or genetic vulnerability for

---

EXAM HINT

A useful way to conclude an essay on schizophrenia is to say that because some researchers argue that schizophrenia is not a single illness, one single explanation is not sufficient; instead multiple perspectives are needed.

A Danish study has found a link between being born with minor physical irregularities and developing schizophrenia as young adults. A total of 265 babies was examined for physical problems (such as a high palate, curved fifth finger, low-set ears, or wide-set eyes) at birth. Many of these babies had one parent who had schizophrenia. Those with several minor physical deviations were more likely to suffer from schizophrenia by the time they were 19 years old than those with no mental disorder or those with other mental problems. It is hypothesised that these minor physical irregularities might in some way interact with the genetic predisposition to schizophrenia to increase the likelihood of developing the disorder later in life. If this is so, it is a classic example of the diathesis–stress model.

KEY TERM

Diathesis–stress model: the notion that psychological disorders occur when there is a genetically determined vulnerability (diathesis) and relevant stressful conditions.

schizophrenia. However, not everyone who inherits the genetic component (e.g. a non-schizophrenic whose identical twin has schizophrenia) becomes schizophrenic. We can explain this in terms of the psychological factors that trigger the disorder such as troubled families or stressful life events. There are also biological factors to take into account, such as the possible role of dopamine. In addition, as is emphasised in the neurodevelopmental hypothesis, brain lesions at an early age might make individuals more vulnerable to developing schizophrenia many years later. What is indisputable is that several factors play a part in causing schizophrenia, and so a multi-dimensional approach is essential.

> **EXAM HINT**
>
> Do some research on epigenetics (the study of gene–environment interactions) to help understand the variations in types of schizophrenia and within the families of schizophrenics. This explanation can better account for such variations because it offers a more in-depth understanding of the diathesis–stress model. It suggests that although there is a diathesis/genetic predisposition, the genes might or might not be switched on, depending on the individual's life experiences. The whole life course needs to be considered: prenatal, early and later childhood, and adulthood, as there are risk factors across the life stages.

Another way of considering the factors associated with schizophrenia is whether they occur a long time before its onset (as with a diathesis) or occur only shortly beforehand (as with stress). Genetic factors and early brain lesions are examples of factors occurring a very long time prior to schizophrenia. By contrast, factors such as stressful life events or disrupted communications patterns may exert their influence immediately prior to the onset of schizophrenia.

An important reason why it is important to understand the causes of schizophrenia is that such understanding influences decisions concerning the appropriate form of treatment. Biological explanations tend to lead to biological methods of treatment whereas behavioural explanations lead to behavioural methods of treatment.

SECTION SUMMARY
Psychological Explanations of Schizophrenia

❖ According to Freud's psychodynamic approach, most individuals with schizophrenia had harsh childhoods. They regress to the earliest stage of development.

Psychodynamic explanations

❖ Evaluation:

— Individuals with schizophrenia do not resemble very young children.

— Most mothers of schizophrenics are anxious rather than harsh.

— The psychodynamic approach de-emphasises genetic and social factors.

❖ According to Frith, individuals with schizophrenia have problems with self-monitoring and don't keep track of their own intentions.

Cognitive explanations

❖ According to Hemsley, there is a breakdown in the relationship between memory and perception in schizophrenia. This causes attentional problems and disorganised thinking and behaviour.

❖ Frith's theory is supported by evidence showing that individuals with schizophrenia often mistake their own inner speech for that of someone else. There is also evidence that they have a deficient Theory of Mind.

❖ Evaluation:

— Cognitive explanations don't account for the negative symptoms of schizophrenia.

— It isn't clear that cognitive deficits help to trigger schizophrenia rather than the opposite.
— The cognitive approach de-emphasises genetic factors and life events.

Life events

❖ There is much evidence that major life events increase the probability of a schizophrenic episode.

❖ Some early research was limited because it relied on retrospective reports of events, didn't assess the personal significance of events, and didn't focus on events that occurred independently of the disorder.

❖ Life events may increase the probability of a schizophrenic episode by increasing individuals' emotional sensitivity to daily hassles.

❖ More needs to be discovered about the genetic and other factors making some individuals more vulnerable than others to life events.

Interpersonal communication in families

❖ According to double-bind theory, families of individuals with schizophrenia communicate in a destructively ambiguous way. There is little evidence for this.

❖ Expressed emotion (e.g. hostility, emotional over-involvement) is associated with relapse in schizophrenia.

❖ Expressed emotion results from complex interactions between family members and the patient over a long period of time.

❖ Evaluation:

— The higher incidence of relapse in developed than in developing countries might depend on cultural differences in expressed emotion.
— It is hard to establish causality in studies on expressed emotion.
— Genetic factors, life events, and cognitive deficits are de-emphasised as factors contributing to relapse in schizophrenia.

Social causation hypothesis

❖ According to the social causation hypothesis, schizophrenia is more prevalent among the lower classes and ethnic groups because their lives are stressful.

❖ An alternative interpretation is that schizophrenia causes individuals to lose their jobs and so reduces their social status.

❖ Findings on African–Caribbean people in the UK strongly support the social causation hypothesis.

❖ Evaluation:

— Much of the evidence is hard to interpret.
— We don't know which aspects of social deprivation are most important in increasing the chances of developing schizophrenia.
— The fact that the overwhelming majority of individuals living in deprived social conditions don't develop schizophrenia means that other factors are also important.

Conclusions

❖ The evidence strongly indicates that we need a multi-dimensional approach to explain the development of schizophrenia.

❖ According to the diathesis–stress model, schizophrenia depends on diathesis (predisposition) and on stress. More generally, some factors occur a long time before the disorder (diathesis) whereas others occur only shortly beforehand (stress).

BIOLOGICAL THERAPIES FOR SCHIZOPHRENIA

The main form of biological therapy for schizophrenia is drug therapy. Overall, drug therapy is probably more effective than any other form of therapy in the treatment of schizophrenia. Another form of biological therapy is electroconvulsive therapy (ECT), which involves passing electric currents through the brain to cause convulsions. We will consider both forms of biological therapy here.

Drug Therapy

When discussing drug effects on schizophrenia, we need to distinguish between the positive and negative symptoms of schizophrenia; the positive symptoms include delusions and hallucinations, whereas the negative symptoms include lack of motivation, lack of emotion, and social withdrawal. Some drugs are more effective at reducing the positive symptoms than the negative ones. There are two main categories of drug: (1) conventional or neuroleptic drugs; and (2) the newer atypical drugs.

Neuroleptic drugs

Neuroleptic drugs (drugs that reduce psychotic symptoms but produce some of the symptoms of neurological diseases) are conventional drugs often used in the treatment of schizophrenia. Common neuroleptic drugs include Thorazine, Prolixin, and Haldol. These drugs block the activity of the neurotransmitter dopamine within 48 hours, and their effects on dopamine are believed to be important in therapy. However, it takes several weeks of drug therapy before schizophrenic symptoms show substantial reduction. The major neuroleptic drugs are of real value in treating schizophrenia. However, their effectiveness is greater in reducing positive symptoms than negative ones. Indeed, Birchwood and Jackson (2001) concluded that there is no good evidence that neuroleptic drugs are effective in treating the negative symptoms of schizophrenia. Overall, however, these drugs "reduce schizophrenic symptoms in the majority of patients . . . the drugs appear to be a more effective treatment for schizophrenia than any of the other approaches used alone" (Comer, 2001, p. 457).

Neuroleptic drugs generally have their strongest beneficial effects within the first 6 months. However, there can be serious problems if patients with schizophrenia stop taking the drugs, even after several years. For example, Sampath, Shah, Krska, and Soni (1992) studied patients with schizophrenia who had been taking neuroleptic drugs for 5 years. One group then switched to a **placebo** (an inactive substance), whereas the other group continued to take the drug. In the placebo group, 75% of the patients relapsed within 1 year, compared with 33% of patients who continued to receive the drug.

Neuroleptic drugs produce side effects. Windgassen (1992) found that 50% of patients with schizophrenia taking neuroleptics reported grogginess or sedation, 18% reported problems with concentration, and 16% had blurred vision. In addition, many patients with schizophrenia on neuroleptic drugs develop symptoms closely resembling those of Parkinson's disease (e.g. muscle rigidity, tremors, foot shuffling). Approximately 2% of patients with schizophrenia (especially elderly ones) taking neuroleptic or conventional drugs develop neuroleptic malignant syndrome. This involves muscle rigidity, altered

What are some risks associated with the use of neuroleptic drugs?

KEY TERMS

Neuroleptic drugs: drugs that reduce psychotic symptoms but can produce some of the symptoms of neurological diseases.

Placebo: an inactive substance (e.g. salt tablet) given to patients to see whether the mere fact of apparently receiving drug treatment improves their symptoms.

Informed consent

There is a proven link between the use of neuroleptic drugs and the onset of Parkinson's disease, in which the midbrain fails to produce enough dopamine (a chemical that helps to control movement). What ethical issues with regard to informed consent are raised by this fact?

consciousness, and fever, and can be fatal. Drug treatment is halted as soon as there is a suspicion that the patient might be developing this syndrome.

Most of the above side effects occur within a few weeks of the start of drug therapy. However, more than 20% of patients who take neuroleptic drugs for over a year develop the symptoms of **tardive dyskinesia**. These symptoms include involuntary sucking and chewing, jerky movements of the limbs, and writhing movements of the mouth or face. These effects can be permanent.

What can be done to reduce unwanted side effects of neuroleptic drugs? One obvious answer is to use low doses of the drugs, and there are generally fewer side effects with low doses than with higher ones (Barondes, 1993). However, the problem is that neuroleptic drugs tend to produce greater patient improvement at higher doses (Barondes, 1993). Thus, it is a difficult juggling act to try to maximise the beneficial effects of the drugs while avoiding as many side effects as possible.

Atypical antipsychotic drugs

Schizophrenia is increasingly treated with atypical antipsychotic drugs (e.g. Clozaril, Risperdal, Zyprexa). These drugs resemble the neuroleptic or conventional drugs in that they block activity of the neurotransmitter dopamine. However, they also affect serotonin activity. Atypical antipsychotic drugs are generally of comparable overall effectiveness to the conventional neuroleptic drugs. However, they have various advantages over the conventional drugs. First, they have fewer side effects than the neuroleptic drugs. Second, they benefit 85% of patients with schizophrenia, compared with 65% given neuroleptic drugs (Awad & Voruganti, 1999). Meltzer (1999) found that about one-third of patients who had shown no improvement with neuroleptic drugs responded well to the atypical drug clozapine. Third, the atypical drugs are of much more use in helping schizophrenic patients suffering mainly from negative symptoms (Remington & Kapur, 2000). Fourth, many side effects of the conventional drugs (especially tardive dyskinesia) are absent with the atypical drugs.

However, the atypical drugs can produce serious side effects. For example, schizophrenic patients who take clozapine have a 1–2% risk of developing agranulocytosis. This involves a substantial reduction in white blood cells, and the condition can be life threatening. However, olanzapine (which is another atypical drug) does not seem to cause agranulocytosis.

Effectiveness

Drug therapy for schizophrenia is effective in various ways. First, it has proved itself to be probably more effective than any other form of therapy in the treatment of this serious mental disorder. Second, drug therapy often reduces the symptoms of schizophrenia more rapidly than psychological therapies. Third, drug therapy allows patients with schizophrenia to live relatively normal lives; in the old days, many were restrained in straitjackets.

However, there are three problems relating to the effectiveness of drug therapy. First, drug therapy is not effective in every respect. Curative treatments are effective at reducing the symptoms of a disorder because they reduce or eliminate the underlying processes responsible for the disorder. By contrast, palliative treatments are effective because they suppress the symptoms of a disorder *without* addressing the underlying processes. Drug therapy for schizophrenia is basically a

KEY TERMS

Tardive dyskinesia: some of the long-term effects of taking neuroleptic drugs, including involuntary sucking and chewing, jerky movements, and writhing movements of the mouth or face.

DRUG THERAPY FOR SCHIZOPHRENIA

Drug/group of drugs	How they work	Drawbacks
Neuroleptic drugs (e.g. Thorazine, Prolixin, Haldol)	Block the activity of dopamine. This reduces delusions, hallucinations	Little effect on lack of motivation and emotional and/or social withdrawal. Some patients report grogginess, sedation, difficulty concentrating, dry mouth, blurred vision. Many also experience symptoms similar to Parkinson's disease
Atypical antipsychotic drugs (e.g. clozapine)	As neuroleptics, but also affect serotonin activity. Fewer side effects than neuroleptic drugs	Expensive. Produce fatal blood disease in 1–2% of patients

---

palliative treatment. As the underlying processes are not eliminated, patients often have to take drugs for many years. Second, some patients are resistant to drugs, and so the drugs are not effective with everyone. However, as we have seen, patients who do not respond to neuroleptic drugs sometimes respond to atypical drugs. Third, the neuroleptic drugs are not effective in treating the negative symptoms of schizophrenia.

Appropriateness

Drug therapy is appropriate in that schizophrenia has more of a genetic and biological basis than almost any other mental disorder. This is a good reason for assuming that drug therapy might be especially appropriate in the treatment of schizophrenia. There is another important reason why drug therapy is appropriate. As we saw earlier, patients with schizophrenia exhibit abnormalities in dopamine functioning, although many of the details remain unclear. The main drugs used to treat schizophrenia (neuroleptic and atypical antipsychotic drugs) both block dopamine receptors. It is appropriate to use drugs that target parts of the physiological system (i.e. dopamine receptors) that function abnormally in schizophrenics.

In what ways is drug therapy for schizophrenia inappropriate? First, there are problems with side effects, some of which (e.g. tardive dyskinesia, agranulocytosis) are potentially very serious. Unfortunately, the most obvious way of reducing side effects is by resorting to low doses of drugs, but low dosages are less effective in treatment. Second, there are problems with compliance. The existence of side effects means that patients with schizophrenia are sometimes reluctant to take drugs when they should. There have been tragic results in some cases when patients with schizophrenia stopped taking their medication. Third, the drugs used to treat schizophrenia basically treat the symptoms rather than the underlying reasons. As the drugs don't *cure* the patient, he or she might need to continue taking drugs intermittently for life. That seems somewhat inappropriate given the increased likelihood of disabling side effects when the drugs are taken over prolonged periods of time. Fourth, there are considerable individual differences in responses to drugs. Even the newer atypical antipsychotic drugs aren't effective with 15% of patients.

> **Compulsory medication**
>
> The reduction of the more severe symptoms of schizophrenia has obvious advantages for the carers and families of schizophrenics. Does this mean that patients could or should be given medication without their consent? Are there any differences between the human rights of a schizophrenic person and those of any other patient visiting his or her doctor? Should the human rights of one person take precedence over those of another person?

Electroconvulsive Therapy (ECT)

Many of the positive symptoms of schizophrenia such as hallucinations, delusions, and disorganised speech seem to involve deficient functioning of the cognitive system. In addition, negative symptoms such as lack of motivation and emotion presumably involve deficient functioning of the brain as a whole. As a result, it can be argued that it is worth considering forms of therapy having direct effects on brain functioning. This line of thinking has led to the use of electroconvulsive therapy (discussed below) in the treatment of schizophrenia.

Electroconvulsive therapy (ECT) involves passing an electric current through the head to produce brain seizures. It used to result in broken bones, patient terror, and memory loss. However, several improvements have been made over the years (see Chapter 11), one of which is the use of strong muscle relaxants to minimise the magnitude of convulsions. In addition, there has been a move away from administering ECT to both brain hemispheres to applying it only to the non-dominant hemisphere to reduce any memory loss. Finally, patients sometimes used to become extremely anxious before and during ECT. Increasingly, this problem is addressed by using anaesthetics so that patients are asleep while receiving ECT.

This 1956 photo shows a patient receiving electroconvulsive therapy. The treatment has undergone several improvements over the years, which have served to reduce the unpleasant side effects.

Findings

ECT is used in the treatment of schizophrenia, but much less frequently than in the treatment of depression (see Chapter 11). Tharyan and Adams (2005) carried out a meta-analysis on the effects of ECT in treating schizophrenia. It had beneficial effects in the short-term, but smaller than those obtained with drugs. It wasn't clear that ECT produces long-term benefits to patients with schizophrenia. Tharyan (2005, p. 1) summarised the evidence as follows: "ECT, combined with treatment with antipsychotic drugs, may be considered an option for people with schizophrenia, particularly when rapid global improvement and reduction of symptoms is desired. This is also the case for those with schizophrenia who show limited response to medication alone."

Braga and Petrides (2005) reviewed 42 articles in which ECT had been used in combination with antipsychotic drugs (mostly neuroleptic drugs) to treat schizophrenia. The general findings were encouraging: "The combination [of antipsychotics and ECT] is a safe and efficacious treatment strategy for patients with schizophrenia, especially those refractory [resistant] to conventional treatments" (Braga & Petrides, 2005, p. 75).

More encouraging evidence for the value of ECT was reported by Chanpattana (2007). Patients with schizophrenia who had previously proved resistant to treatment received ECT on its own or in combination with neuroleptic drugs. ECT produced a marked reduction in positive symptoms, especially when used in combination with drug therapy. ECT plus drug therapy also led to significant improvements in quality of life and social functioning. In general, the beneficial effects of ECT were greater when used three times a week than when used only twice. However, ECT had no effect or led to a worsening of *negative* symptoms.

Effectiveness

ECT has proved itself to be a moderately effective form of treatment for schizophrenia. It is typically effective in producing a rapid improvement in the symptoms of schizophrenia. Patients with schizophrenia who have shown very little response to antipsychotic drugs often derive benefit from ECT. There is reasonable evidence that the combination of ECT and drug therapy is more effective than either form of treatment on its own. Recent evidence suggests that ECT is more effective in treating the positive symptoms of schizophrenia than the negative ones. This makes sense, given that ECT affects the brain in a direct fashion and most of the positive symptoms involve some form of cognitive impairment.

In the previous paragraph, we focused on the ways in which ECT therapy is effective in the treatment of schizophrenia. However, there are circumstances in which ECT is less effective. First, it is less effective when used on its own rather than in combination with drug therapy. Second, ECT is relatively ineffective in treating the negative symptoms of depression, such as lack of motivation and emotion. Third, ECT therapy is less effective in the long-term than in the short-term. Fourth, although ECT reduces the symptoms of schizophrenia, it does not produce a cure. Thus, it is a palliative rather than a curative treatment.

Appropriateness

In very general terms, the use of ECT to treat schizophrenia can be regarded as appropriate. There is much evidence that biological factors are of particular importance in schizophrenia, and ECT is a biological form of treatment. As mentioned earlier, most of the symptoms of schizophrenia seem to involve deficient functioning within the brain, and so a form of treatment that alters brain functioning may well prove to be appropriate. Finally, schizophrenia was historically regarded as a mental disorder that was especially difficult to treat, and this made it appropriate to think in terms of radical forms of therapy such as ECT.

In what ways is ECT inappropriate in the treatment of schizophrenia? First, there are various side effects, including memory loss, other cognitive impairments, and possible neurological damage. The circumstances in which ECT is generally most effective (strong current to both hemispheres) are those in which the side effects tend to be the greatest. However, the good news is that most side effects are relatively short lasting.

? What are some risks associated with the use of electroconvulsive therapy?

KEY TERM

Electroconvulsive therapy (ECT): a form of therapy used to treat depressed patients, in which brain seizures are created by passing an electric current through the head.

EXAM HINT
Use the treatment aetiology fallacy to evaluate treatments. This refers to the fact that just because the treatment works this does not mean that whatever the treatment targets (such as biochemical imbalances in the case of drugs and ECT) was the cause of the disorder in the first place. A useful analogy is that an aspirin treats a headache but it is not a lack of aspirin that causes the headache.

Second, ECT seems somewhat inappropriate because we don't have a clear understanding of *why* it is effective. It is probable that it affects neurotransmission and produces structural changes in neuronal networks, but we don't know the details. This lack of knowledge makes it difficult to devise more effective ways of using ECT.

Third, the use of ECT is inappropriate in the sense that it raises ethical issues. Most patients dislike receiving ECT, and some might be put under excessive pressure to become involved in this form of therapy.

Fourth, the central goals of therapy for the patient and for the therapist are to reduce or eliminate all the major symptoms of schizophrenia and for recovery to be long lasting. ECT generally does not satisfy these two goals: it is not very effective in eliminating the negative symptoms of schizophrenia, and its beneficial effects haven't been convincingly shown to last on a long-term basis.

SECTION SUMMARY
Biological Therapies for Schizophrenia

Drug therapy

❖ Neuroleptic or conventional drugs block dopamine and are effective at reducing positive symptoms but not negative ones.
❖ Patients who stop taking neuroleptic drugs often experience relapse.
❖ Side effects with neuroleptic drugs include grogginess, muscle rigidity, impaired concentration, and tardive dyskinesia.
❖ Atypical antipsychotic drugs benefit more patients than neuroleptic drugs, they have fewer side effects, and they reduce negative as well as positive symptoms.
❖ Evaluation:

— Much of the evidence is hard to interpret.
— There are problems with compliance.
— Some patients are resistant to drugs.

Electroconvulsive therapy (ECT)

❖ ECT often produces a rapid improvement in symptoms, and is often effective in combination with drug therapy.
❖ ECT is more effective in treating the positive than the negative symptoms of schizophrenia.
❖ Evaluation:

— The benefits of ECT seem to be mostly short-term rather than long-term.
— ECT does not produce a cure for schizophrenia.
— Ethical issues are raised because patients dislike receiving ECT and it is potentially dangerous.

PSYCHOLOGICAL THERAPIES FOR SCHIZOPHRENIA

Until the 1960s, it was widely believed that schizophrenia was such a serious disorder that psychological therapies were doomed to failure. However, the picture began to change with the introduction of new techniques of behavioural therapy in the middle of the 1960s. Since then, there have been various exciting developments in psychological therapies for schizophrenia. After discussing behavioural therapy, we will consider two of those developments. First, there is cognitive-behavioural therapy, which, as the name implies, focuses on producing cognitive as well as behavioural changes. Second, there is family therapy, which is based on the assumption that family interactions play a key role in schizophrenia.

Behavioural Therapy

Behavioural therapy (often called behaviour therapy) developed during the 1950s and 1960s. It was based on the assumptions that most forms of mental illness occur through maladaptive learning, and that the best treatment consists of appropriate new learning. Behaviour therapists believe that abnormal behaviour develops through conditioning, and that it is via the use of the principles of conditioning that clients can recover (see Chapter 8). Thus, behavioural therapy is based on the assumption that classical and operant conditioning can change unwanted behaviour into a more desirable pattern. Behavioural therapy focuses on *current* problems and behaviour and on attempts to remove any symptoms the patient finds troublesome. This is a major difference from psychodynamic therapy, in which the focus is on uncovering unresolved conflicts from childhood.

There are various forms of behavioural therapy; here, we will consider token economies, but other forms of behaviour therapy have been developed. For example, Marder et al. (1996) compared the effectiveness of social skills training (a form of behaviour therapy) with group psychotherapy in the treatment of schizophrenia. Over a 2-year period, social skills training was more effective in improving social adjustment.

> **EXAM HINT**
>
> Note that you need to have covered the issues of classification and diagnosis, clinical characteristics, explanations, and treatments of schizophrenia fully as you do not know which area will be asked about in the exam. A question that is divided into parts might ask you about the issues of classification and diagnosis in one sub-part, the clinical characteristics in another, and the explanations in another.

> **What is unwanted behaviour?**
>
> The term "unwanted behaviour" leads to questions about who decides what behaviour is disliked, unwanted, or abnormal. Usually, the client himself or herself will decide that symptoms (e.g. phobic reactions) need treatment. Some behaviour is so antisocial that everyone agrees it is undesirable. However, it is possible for behaviour that those in authority decide is unacceptable to be labelled as "mental illness". Could the behaviour of rebellious young people, trade union activists, or lonely old people be construed as "ill" and in need of modification? Has this ever happened as far as you know?

Token economy

Most forms of behavioural therapy have not been used extensively in the treatment of schizophrenic patients. An exception is the **token economy**, a form of therapy based on the use of selective positive reinforcement or reward. This tends to be used with institutionalised patients, who are given tokens (e.g. coloured counters) for behaving in appropriate ways. These tokens can later be used to obtain various privileges (e.g. cigarettes, watching television). Ayllon and Azrin (1968) reported a classic study in which female patients with schizophrenia, who had been hospitalised for an average of 16 years, were rewarded with plastic tokens for actions such as making their beds or combing their hair. The tokens were exchanged for pleasant activities, such as seeing a film or an additional visit to the canteen. This token economy was very successful. The number of chores the patients performed each day increased from five to over forty when this behaviour was rewarded with tokens.

Paul and Lentz (1977) used a token economy with hospitalised patients with long-term schizophrenia. The patients developed various social and work-related skills, they became better able to look after themselves, and their symptoms were reduced. These findings are all the more impressive in that they were achieved at the same time as a substantial reduction in the number of drugs that were being

> **KEY TERM**
>
> **Token economy:** institution-based use of operant conditioning to change the behaviour of mental patients by selective positive reinforcement of rewards.

Token economies, where desirable behaviour is rewarded with a coloured token, have proven to be moderately effective in the treatment of institutionalised patients with schizophrenia.

given to the patients. After $4\frac{1}{2}$ years, 98% of the patients in the token economy had been released, compared with only 45% who received no specific treatment.

Dickerson, Tenhula, and Green-Paden (2005) reviewed 13 studies of token economies being used with patients with schizophrenia; beneficial effects were reported in 11 of these studies. Dickerson et al. concluded that token economies are especially effective when used in combination with psychosocial and/or drug therapy.

Effectiveness

Token economies are of historical importance: they were among the first forms of hospital-based treatment to show clear evidence of reducing the symptoms of schizophrenia. Token economies have proved moderately effective with institutionalised patients resistant to other forms of therapy, as shown in Dickerson et al.'s (2005) meta-analysis. More specifically, they are successful in increasing the frequency with which patients with schizophrenia produce various kinds of desired behaviour.

In what ways is the effectiveness of token economies limited? First, their beneficial effects are often greatly reduced when good behaviour is no longer followed by the rewards the patients have become used to receiving. There is no easy answer to this problem. Token economies work because the environment is carefully structured so that good behaviour is consistently rewarded and bad behaviour is not. The outside world is very different, and patients find it hard to transfer what they have learned in a token economy to the much less structured environment outside the institution.

Second, the effectiveness of token economies is limited because they focus on only a few of the symptoms of schizophrenia. Token economies increase certain kinds of behaviour but do not address cognitive symptoms of schizophrenia, such as hallucinations, delusions, or disorganised speech.

Third, there is a danger that token economies might produce only token (i.e. minimal) learning. For example, it is possible that what patients with schizophrenia learn in token economies is merely to *imitate* normal behaviour without any accompanying changes in their thoughts and beliefs.

Appropriateness

Token economies are in some ways an appropriate form of treatment for schizophrenia. The symptoms of schizophrenia include catatonic behaviour, in which the patients remain rigid, and negative symptoms such as lack of motivation and a general disengagement. Providing patients with schizophrenia with the incentive to behave in desirable ways can have direct effects on these symptoms. In other words, the patients behave as if there isn't enough positive reinforcement or reward in their lives, and token economies are specifically designed to provide adequate rewards to increase their motivation. As Dickerson et al. (2005) pointed out, token economies are probably most appropriate when used in combination with other forms of therapy designed to address other symptoms of schizophrenia.

In what ways are token economies inappropriate? First, there are ethical issues. The "desired behaviours" or goals are decided by the psychologists or by the institution, and might not be acceptable to the patient if he or she had a free choice.

Second, token economies are an inappropriate form of treatment when dealing with several of the problems experienced by patients with schizophrenia. Token economies are not likely to improve symptoms such as delusions, hallucinations, and lack of emotion. In addition, token economies do not focus on some of the factors (e.g. genetic factors, biochemistry, poor communication within the family) that play important roles in producing schizophrenia.

Third, it is most appropriate to use token economies within various institutional settings, because it is possible for therapists to exert the necessary level of environmental control in such settings. However, the great majority of patients with schizophrenia nowadays are treated in the community, and token economies are much less effective in community settings.

Fourth, one of the goals of therapy is to produce long-lasting beneficial changes. However, token economies often produce rather short-lasting and even superficial changes in behaviour that fail to generalise well to the outside world.

> **Assumptions of behavioural therapy**
>
> - All behaviour is learned, and maladaptive behaviour is no different.
> - This learning can be understood in terms of the principles of conditioning and modelling.
> - What was learned can be unlearned, using the same principles.
> - The same laws apply to human and non-human animal behaviour.

Cognitive-behavioural Therapy

We will start by discussing the key features of cognitive-behavioural therapy before moving on to consider its application to the treatment of schizophrenia. Therapists using cognitive-behavioural therapy assume that patients often have irrational thoughts and beliefs about themselves and about the world around them. These irrational thoughts (e.g. "It is essential that everyone likes me", "I must be perfectly competent and achieving to consider myself worthwhile") are typically negative and self-defeating. It is assumed that such irrational thoughts contribute to the development and maintenance of mental disorders. Accordingly, a central goal of cognitive-behavioural therapy is to eliminate these irrational thoughts and beliefs by challenging them and demonstrating they are wrong.

Changing patients' thoughts and beliefs is one of the two main goals of cognitive-behavioural therapy. The other main goal is to change behaviour in desirable ways. This can be accomplished by giving the patient "homework" to carry out. For example, a patient with social phobia (excessive fear of social situations) might be instructed to have a short conversation with everyone with whom they work every single day. The underlying assumption is that the benefits of therapy are likely to be greater when the patient's cognitive processes and behaviour are both changed than when only cognitive processes or behaviour are changed.

It used to be thought that schizophrenia was such a serious mental disorder that it would be a waste of time talking to patients and attempting to persuade them to modify their irrational thoughts. In fact, however, cognitive-behavioural therapy has made substantial progress in the past 10–15 years. We will briefly mention two important factors influencing this progress. First, the great majority of patients with schizophrenia receive long-term drug therapy, and are more responsive to cognitive-behavioural therapy than they would be in the absence of drugs.

Second, it was discovered that many patients with schizophrenia actively engage in coping strategies to control their delusions and hallucinations. For example, Tarrier (1987) found that 75% of patients experiencing delusions and/or hallucinations reported using coping strategies. The strategies used included the use of distraction, concentrating on a particular task, and positive self-talk. About

? What are some beneficial feelings a patient may have after completing their "homework"?

Tarrier (1987) found that 75% of schizophrenic patients engaged in coping strategies, such as turning up the television to drown out voices.

one-third of the patients used behavioural strategies (e.g. drowning-out voices by turning up the television set, engaging in solitary activities). Almost three-quarters of the patients using strategies (72%) reported that at least one of their strategies was fairly successful in controlling their symptoms. Those patients using a number of coping strategies were most likely to perceive coping as effective.

Cognitive-behavioural therapy for schizophrenia has focused mainly on the positive symptoms of hallucinations and delusions, and is rarely designed to reduce the negative symptoms of schizophrenia (such as lack of emotion, lack of motivation, speaking very little). One approach to reducing (or at least controlling) hallucinations and delusions is Coping Strategy Enhancement. Initially, the therapist asks detailed questions to establish the content of the patient's delusions and hallucinations, the triggers for these thoughts, and the coping strategies they use. Finally, patients rate each of their coping strategies in terms of their effectiveness.

Cognitive-behavioural therapy based on Coping Strategy Enhancement has five main features. First, the therapeutic situation is set up as one in which the therapist and the patient work together to improve the patient's coping strategies. Second, it is emphasised that having delusions and hallucinations does not mean that the patient is mad. Healthy individuals have hallucinations when very stressed, when sleep deprived, or when under hypnosis. Third, one of the patient's delusions or hallucinations is selected for treatment, often because it is one for which the patient already possesses moderately effective coping strategies. The therapist and patient might try to identify additional coping strategies. Fourth, the patient is given the "homework" of applying one or more coping strategies whenever the target delusion or hallucination is experienced. Fifth, the therapist and patient discuss ways of making the coping strategies more effective.

Other forms of cognitive-behavioural therapy incorporate aspects of Coping Strategy Enhancement, but also focus on trying to change patients' delusions and hallucinations. Initially, the therapist questions the patient's irrational beliefs, and asks the patient to think of alternative explanations for his or her beliefs. After this, there is "reality testing": therapist and patient plan an activity that is designed to test the validity of a delusional belief; this is then performed by the patient. For example, a patient called Nigel claimed he had special powers that allowed him to make things happen simply through thinking. The therapist and Nigel decided to test these special powers in the following way. Several video recorders were set to pause at different times, and Nigel predicted which one would pause next. In over 50 attempts, his guess was never right! This led him to the reasonable conclusion that he did not really possess special powers (Chadwick, Birchwood, & Trower, 1996).

Effectiveness

Tarrier, Beckett, Harwood, Baker, Yusupoff, and Ugarteburu (1993) tested the effectiveness of Coping Strategy Enhancement. Patients with schizophrenia showed significantly more reduction in positive symptoms than patients on a waiting list for treatment, and the improvement was still there 6 months after the end of treatment. The patients showed an improvement in coping skills, and this improvement was associated with decreased hallucinations and delusions. The main problem was that almost half of the patients scheduled to take part in the study refused to participate or dropped out.

There have been numerous subsequent attempts to assess the effectiveness of cognitive-behavioural therapy. The results indicate it is effective in treating some of the symptoms of schizophrenia. For example, Tarrier (2005, p. 136) came to the following conclusion after reviewing 20 studies: "There is consistent evidence that CBT [cognitive-behavioural therapy] reduces persistent positive symptoms in chronic patients and may have modest effects in speeding recovery in acutely ill patients." However, it was not clear whether cognitive-behavioural therapy was effective in reducing relapse rates.

Similar findings from a meta-analysis of several studies were reported by Pfammatter, Junghan, and Brenner (2006). Cognitive-behavioural therapy was moderately effective in reducing positive symptoms and also led to slight improvements in social functioning. However, Pfammatter et al. (2006, p. S74) pointed out that we don't know *why* cognitive-behavioural therapy is effective: "Specific therapeutic ingredients within the overall toolbox of cognitive-behaviour therapy for positive symptoms still need to be identified." In other words, there are several different aspects of treatment in cognitive-behavioural therapy, and it has not been established which are the most important ones.

There is another issue concerning the interpretation of the findings. In the great majority of studies, cognitive-behavioural therapy has been compared against some control treatment (e.g. routine therapy) and found to be superior. This difference could occur either because cognitive-behavioural therapy is especially effective or because the control treatment is inadequate. Control treatments are sometimes (but not always) given by non-experts (Turkington, Kingdon, & Chadwick, 2003). Thus, the use of inadequate control treatments might explain some of the findings.

Appropriateness

Cognitive-behavioural therapy is an appropriate form of treatment for schizophrenia in various ways. First, several symptoms of schizophrenia are mainly cognitive in nature; for example, delusions, hallucinations, and disorganised speech.

Second, as many patients with schizophrenia use coping strategies to control their hallucinations and delusions, it is reasonable to develop therapeutic techniques to improve those coping strategies. Third, patients with schizophrenia are often especially concerned about their bizarre delusions and hallucinations. Their realisation in therapy that similar delusions and hallucinations sometimes occur in healthy individuals is useful in improving their mental state.

In what ways might cognitive-behavioural therapy be inappropriate? First, it is specifically designed to reduce only certain positive symptoms of

> **EXAM HINT**
>
> Remember to assess the appropriateness of treatments by considering the following:
>
> - how effective the treatment is across different symptoms
> - the patient's level of functioning
> - the effect of the treatment on relapse rates
> - the patient's motivation to use the treatment versus drop-out rate
> - if the action of the treatment is fully understood
> - ethical issues.

schizophrenia. Thus, cognitive-behavioural therapy is not an appropriate form of therapy for reducing or eliminating negative symptoms (e.g. lack of emotion and lack of motivation). Second, at best, cognitive-behavioural therapy has only modest beneficial effects on relapse rate. This is unfortunate, given the importance to the well-being of patients with schizophrenia of avoiding relapse. Third, cognitive-behavioural therapy does not take into account the biological factors (e.g. biochemistry) associated with schizophrenia. Fourth, the appropriateness of cognitive-behavioural therapy is reduced because many patients with schizophrenia drop out of therapy. Fifth, the appropriateness (and effectiveness) of cognitive-behavioural therapy would be increased if we could find out in more detail *which* aspects of therapy are most important in producing beneficial changes.

Family Therapy

We saw earlier in the chapter that high levels of expressed emotion (e.g. hostility; excessive criticism) within the families of patients with schizophrenia are associated with relapse and negative outcomes. That suggests that therapy with a focus on social dynamics within the family might prove beneficial. Accordingly, Falloon et al. (1985) devised a form of family management to be used when the patient returned home from hospital. The emphasis was on teaching everyone in the family how to be constructive, undemanding, and empathic in their dealings with each other and with their schizophrenic relative. In addition, they were told that they should not have high expectations of the family member with schizophrenia and should avoid stressful interactions with him or her. This form of therapy was used with patients with schizophrenia who came from families rated high in expressed emotion. The findings of the study are discussed below.

Effectiveness

The patients with schizophrenia who received family therapy in the study by Falloon et al. (1985) were compared against others who were receiving individual therapy from a therapist. With these patients, the therapist rarely saw any of the other family members. Note that all the patients with schizophrenia, in both groups, were also on drug therapy, and the focus of the study was on what (if anything) family therapy contributed to reducing the relapse rate.

Falloon et al. (1985) found that the relapse rate was markedly lower among those patients with schizophrenia receiving family therapy than those receiving individual therapy. In terms of hospital re-admission rates within 1 year, 50% of those in the individual-therapy group returned to hospital compared with only 11% of those in the family-therapy group. Similar (but less dramatic) findings were reported in subsequent studies in which family therapy was used with patients with schizophrenia from families with high expressed emotion. In their review, Birchwood and Jackson (2001) found that the relapse rate over 12 months was 60% for patients with schizophrenia receiving routine treatment, but was between 25% and 33% for those receiving family therapy.

The general approach adopted by Falloon et al. (1985) can be described as **family psychoeducation**. This involves several factors, including:

- Family members are taught how to provide ongoing support and empathic engagement.
- Clinical resources are available if required in a crisis.
- Patients are given advice in enhancing their social network and developing good communication skills.

In a nutshell, family psychoeducation involves treating families as part of the solution rather than as part of the problem.

McFarlane, Dixon, Lukens, and Lucksted (2003) carried out a review of the literature on the effects of family psychoeducation on patients with schizophrenia. They concluded that it was associated with reduced relapse rates, improved recovery, and improved family well-being.

More recently, Falloon and colleagues have developed a family-centred therapy for patients with schizophrenia known as the Optimal Treatment Project. This involves providing education for caregivers and patients to allow them to cope with stressors, training in social skills for patients, effective drug therapy, and monitoring patients' condition to enhance the effectiveness of treatment. As with other forms of family therapy, patients with schizophrenia treated within the Optimal Treatment Project typically receive drug therapy at the same time. The Optimal Treatment Project has been used in over 20 different countries, and the evidence indicates that it is significantly more effective than traditional ways of managing schizophrenia (Falloon et al., 2004). However, as Hayman-White and Happell (2007) have pointed out, trials of the Optimal Treatment Project have generally taken place at specially selected sites where the therapists and administrators were highly motivated.

Family therapy has proved its worth by reducing the relapse rate of patients with schizophrenia and making it less likely that they will have to return to hospital. However, we must not exaggerate what can be achieved. Even patients who do not relapse sufficiently to be re-admitted to hospital nearly always continue to require drug therapy. In addition, their level of social adjustment is markedly lower than that of healthy individuals.

Appropriateness

Family therapy for schizophrenia is very appropriate in various ways. First, 65% of patients with schizophrenia return from hospital to live with their families. This figure is far higher than in the past, and means that establishing a secure and relatively stress-free family environment for patients with schizophrenia is more important than ever. Second, the evidence that expressed emotion within families increases the risk of relapse indicates the value of having therapists focus on family dynamics in therapy. Third, many of the symptoms of schizophrenia (e.g. disorganised speech, speaking very little, lack of emotion) help to isolate patients with schizophrenia socially, and so therapy that emphasises social functioning is appropriate.

In what ways is family therapy for schizophrenia inappropriate? First, it is limited, because it does not consider genetic or biochemical factors relevant to

 HOW SCIENCE WORKS: PSYCHOLOGICAL THERAPIES FOR SCHIZOPHRENIA
It is interesting to see that under the banner heading psychological therapies there are in fact several different approaches. You could look at two or three psychological therapies and produce a poster comparing them. You could include brief outlines of the therapies themselves, where and how they differ and are similar, and also assess the usefulness of each therapy, i.e. assess the therapeutic success of each one. It could be quite a challenge to use text, colour, and graphics to make your poster as engaging as possible, as this is quite difficult subject matter.

See *A2-Level Psychology Online* for some interactive quizzes to help you with your revision.

schizophrenia. Second, family therapy would probably not be successful on its own, but needs to be used in conjunction with drug therapy. Third, many patients with schizophrenia are unmarried and do not belong to a functioning family, and so family therapy cannot be fully implemented. Fourth, family therapy probably cannot provide a cure for schizophrenia. It generally benefits patients with schizophrenia, but is a long way from making their social functioning comparable to that of healthy controls.

SECTION SUMMARY
Psychological Therapies for Schizophrenia

Behavioural therapy

❖ Token economies involve the use of selective positive reinforcement to increase desirable behaviour in patients with schizophrenia.

❖ Token economies increase the frequency of various kinds of behaviour but do not address cognitive symptoms.

❖ The effects of token economies often fail to generalise to everyday life.

	Schizophrenia					
	Biological				Psychological	
Theories	Genetic	Biochemistry	Brain structure	Evolutionary	Social	Behaviourist
Main evidence	Twin studies	Dopamine hypothesis	Abnormally large lateral ventricles	Assumptions that there was a link with language development	(1) Inadequate patterns of communication (2) Lower social status	Early experience of punishment may lead to schizophrenia
Support	High level of concordance for monozygotic twins	Neuroleptic drugs block dopamine which seems to reduce schizophrenic symptoms	MRI scans of identical twins found schizophrenic twin had more enlarged ventricles	Sufferers have language impairments	(1) Mothers of schizophrenics less responsive (2) Lower classes have more stressful lives	Labelling theory: bizarre behaviour may be rewarded by attention
Criticism	Environmental similarity, may be the cause of similar behaviour	Relationship between dopamine and schizophrenia is only correlational (cause and effect uncertain)	Other parts of the brain may be involved	Poor language skills do not seem to be adaptive or confer leadership. Low motivation and emotion do not seem associated with language	(1) Schizophrenic children may cause poor communication (2) Developing schizophrenia may lead to reduced social status	Doesn't explain acquisition of symptoms. Rejects genetic evidence. Trivialises a serious disorder

Theories of schizophrenia: strengths and weaknesses.

❖ One approach to cognitive-behavioural therapy involves improving the patient's coping strategies when dealing with hallucinations and delusions.

❖ An alternative form of cognitive-behavioural therapy involves reality testing, in which patients with schizophrenia are made aware of the limitations in some of their beliefs.

❖ Cognitive-behavioural therapy is effective in treating the positive symptoms of schizophrenia.

❖ It is much less effective in treating negative symptoms. There are doubts as to its effectiveness in reducing the relapse rate.

Cognitive-behavioural therapy

❖ Family therapy based on everyone in the patient's family being empathic and understanding has proved effective, and has led to a substantial reduction in the relapse rate.

❖ Falloon and colleagues have developed the Optimal Treatment Project, which involves providing patients and caregivers with useful social and other skills. It has proved effective in over 20 countries.

❖ Family therapy is generally only effective when used in conjunction with drug therapy. Although it has beneficial effects, it leaves patients with schizophrenia with deficient social functioning.

Family therapy

FURTHER READING

All the main issues relating to the explanation of (and treatment for) schizophrenia are discussed in a very accessible way by Birchwood M., & Jackson C. (2001). *Schizophrenia*. Hove, UK: Psychology Press.

REVISION QUESTIONS

In the exam, questions on this topic are out of 25 marks, and can take the form of essay questions or multi-parted questions. You should spend about 35 minutes on each of the questions below, which aim to test the material in this chapter. In the exam, make certain you know if you have covered an anxiety disorder, schizophrenia, or depression as your psychopathology topic, and then choose the correct question.

1. (a) Briefly describe the clinical characteristics of schizophrenia. (5 marks)

    (b) Discuss the issues which apply to classifying and also diagnosing schizophrenia. (10 marks)

    (c) Outline and comment, using research evidence, on one or more explanations of schizophrenia. (10 marks)

2. Discuss **one** biological and **one** psychological explanation of schizophrenia. (25 marks)

3. Discuss the use of biological and psychological therapies for the treatment of schizophrenia. (25 marks)

See *A2-Level Psychology Online* for tips on how to answer these revision questions.

Psychopathology: Depression

11

By Michael W. Eysenck

Most people have experienced mild depression at one time or another. Even though mild depression is a long way from the intensity of depression found in patients, it is a miserable experience. Someone suffering from mild depression feels sad and pessimistic, has low self-esteem, and lacks motivation.

We can see what is involved in depression by considering the thoughts of Martha Manning (1994), a therapist who suffers from depression:

> *The house is deserted. I search for things to do. It is all I can do just to empty the dishwasher and sweep the floor. Then I lie on the couch and stare into space, vacant and deadened. I have a haircut appointment that I am already dreading, even though it's three hours away. How will I keep up a conversation with my effusive hairdresser? It will be a monumental effort just to move my lips into a smile. My face is simultaneously waxy and frozen. The muscles have gone on strike.*

How many people suffer from depression? It is one of the most common mental disorders, and the number of people (especially young people) suffering from depression has increased in recent years. There is a large sex difference—in most cultures and at most ages, women are twice as likely as men to suffer from depression. Around the world, over 120 million people suffer from depression serious enough to qualify as a mental disorder. As a result, there are greater financial costs and mortality associated with depression than with any other mental disorder.

It is very worrying that depression is very common among adolescents. For example, Saluja, Iachan, Schedit, Overpeck, Sun, and Gledd (2004) found among adolescents aged between 11 and 15 that 25% of the females and 10% of the males had depressive symptoms. More detailed analysis revealed that depressive symptoms were more common among the older adolescents than the younger ones. Among 11-year-olds, 13% of the females and 7% of the males had depressive symptoms; among 15-year-olds, however, 34% of the females and 14% of the males had depressive symptoms.

CLINICAL CHARACTERISTICS OF DEPRESSION

The first important point to make is that there are different kinds of depression. The key distinction is between **major depressive disorder** (sometimes called unipolar depression) and **bipolar disorder** (also known as bipolar depression).

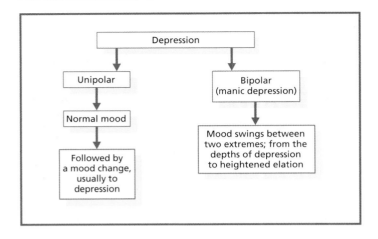

? What are some problems with diagnosing strictly on the basis of the DSM-IV criteria?

? What are the benefits of having classification systems based on categories?

KEY TERMS

Major depressive disorder: a disorder characterised by symptoms such as sad depressed mood, tiredness, and loss of interest in various activities.
Bipolar disorder: a mood disorder in which there are depressive and manic (elated) episodes.
Dysthymic disorder: a condition involving depressive symptoms that occur much of the time over a period of at least 2 years.

According to the revised fourth edition of the *Diagnostic and Statistical Manual* (DSM-IV-TR), which was published in 2000, the diagnosis of major depressive disorder requires the presence of a major depressive episode. In turn, the diagnosis of a major depressive episode requires that five symptoms (including depressed mood or loss of interest or pleasure) occur nearly every day for a minimum of 2 weeks. The symptoms are as follows:

- *Emotional symptoms*: sad, depressed mood; loss of pleasure in usual activities.
- *Motivational symptoms*: changes in activity level, passivity, loss of interest and energy.
- *Somatic symptoms*: difficulties in sleeping (insomnia) or increased sleeping (hypersomnia), weight loss or gain, tiredness.
- *Cognitive symptoms*: negative self-concept, hopelessness, pessimism, lack of self-esteem, self-blame, and self-reproach; problems with concentration or the ability to think clearly; recurring thoughts of suicide or death.

Some individuals have many of the above symptoms but at a less severe level and without having major depressive episodes. If these symptoms are not absent for more than 2 months at a time during a 2-year period, the individual may be diagnosed as suffering from **dysthymic disorder**. Finally, some patients have some symptoms of depression but do not meet the criteria for either major depressive disorder or for dysthymic disorder. They might fit one of several categories of "depression not otherwise specified". For example, a patient who has had fewer than five depressive symptoms for a period of at least 2 weeks might be diagnosed with minor depressive disorder.

Another very important classificatory system is *International Classification of Diseases*, the tenth edition of which (ICD-10) was published by the World Health Organization in 1992. The criteria used in ICD-10 to diagnose a depressive episode are similar to those used in DSM-IV. Severe depressive episodes must include the following symptoms over at least a 2-week period: depressed mood most of the day and nearly every day, loss of interest or pleasure in activities that are generally regarded as pleasurable, and increased fatigue or reduced energy. Other symptoms must also be present, but no single symptom is essential. These additional symptoms can include loss of self-esteem, sleep disturbance, change in appetite, and excessive guilt.

Patients with bipolar disorder experience both major depressive episodes and manic episodes. According to DSM-IV-TR, manic episodes involve "a period of abnormally and persistently elevated, expansive, or irritable mood, lasting at least one week." They also experience significant distress or impairment and at least three of the following symptoms: inflated self-esteem or grandiosity; more

---

CASE STUDY: MANIC BEHAVIOUR IN MANIC DEPRESSION

Robert B had been a successful dentist for 25 years, providing well for his wife and family. One morning he woke up with the idea that he was the best dental surgeon in the world, and that he should try to treat as many people as possible. As a result, he set about enlarging his practice from 2 chairs to 20, planning to treat patients simultaneously. He phoned builders and ordered the necessary equipment. After a day of feeling irritable that there had been delays, he decided to do the work himself and began to knock down the walls. When this proved difficult, he became frustrated and began to smash his X-ray equipment and washbasins. Robert B's family were unaware of his behaviour until patients began to phone his wife after being turned away from the dental surgery. When she mentioned the phone calls to him, Robert B "ranted and raved" at her for 15 minutes. She described her husband as looking "haggard, wild-eyed, and run down", and his speech was "over-excited". After several days of this behaviour, Mrs B phoned her daughters and asked them to come over with their husbands to help. On the evening of their visit, Robert B began to "brag about his sexual prowess and make aggressive advances towards his daughters". When one of his sons-in-law tried to intervene he was attacked with a chair. Robert B was admitted to hospital, and subsequently it was found that he had had a history of such behaviour.

---

talkativeness than usual; a decreased need for sleep; flight of ideas; distractibility; an increase in activity or psychomotor agitation; and an excessive involvement in pleasurable activities, which has much potential for painful consequences.

In major depressive disorder there is a distinction between reactive and endogenous depression. Reactive depression is caused by some *external* stressful event(s) such as the death of a close friend. The event triggers an episode of depression. Endogenous depression is caused by something *internal*, i.e. within the person (e.g. hormonal imbalances). This distinction is not found in the classification schemes DSM-IV-TR or ICD-10 but it is important for understanding the causes of depression. Endogenous depression is linked to biological factors. With reactive depression, by contrast, an individual might have a genetic predisposition to depression but psychological factors are a primary cause.

There are important differences between major depressive disorder and bipolar disorder other than the precise symptoms involved. First, major depressive disorder is much more common than bipolar disorder. In any given year, approximately 7–8% of those living in Western cultures suffer from major depressive disorder, compared with only 1–1.5% who suffer from bipolar disorder. Second, major depressive disorder is at least twice as common in women as in men, whereas men and women are equally susceptible to bipolar disorder. Third, bipolar disorder is a more serious disorder than major depressive disorder and is much more difficult to treat successfully.

Note that when I refer to "depression" in this chapter, I am referring to major depressive disorder (i.e. unipolar depression).

> **?** If a person is depressed because he or she is going through a divorce, is this reactive or endogenous depression?

> **?** Why do you think depressive disorder is more common in women?

Seasonal Affective Disorder

A final type of depression should be discussed briefly at this point. Many people feel more cheerful and active during the summer months than during the winter, but in some cases there are pronounced mood changes across the year. **Seasonal affective disorder** is a condition in which there are seasonal fluctuations in symptoms of clinical depression (see also Chapter 2 on biological rhythms). These symptoms typically occur during the autumn and winter and not during the spring and summer. In addition, seasonal affective disorder involves various physiological symptoms, including a lack of energy, sleeping longer than usual, increased appetite, and weight gain.

Seasonal affective disorder is much more common in women than in men. Indeed, some studies have reported that four times as many women as men suffer

> **KEY TERM**
>
> **Seasonal affective disorder:** a disorder that nearly always involves the sufferer experiencing severe depression during winter months.

EXAM HINT

Note the different types of depression: unipolar, bipolar, seasonal affective, premenstrual, post-partum. This diverse range means that the different explanations of depression must combine in various ways to explain these different types of depression.

from the condition. More specifically, seasonal affective disorder is most common among women in their childbearing years. Finally, the occurrence and severity of seasonal affective disorder tend to be greater in parts of the world further from the equator, suggesting that the disorder is caused by a reduction in the hours of daylight during the winter months. For example, Terman (1988) found that nearly 10% of those living in New Hampshire (a northern State of the USA) suffered from seasonal affective disorder, compared with only 2% in the southern State of Florida. However, the relationship between latitude and symptoms of seasonal affective disorder is much weaker in Europe than in North America. This suggests that other related factors, such as seasonal variations in temperature and weather conditions, might also be involved.

SECTION SUMMARY
Clinical Characteristics of Depression

❖ According to DSM-IV-TR, major depressive disorder requires five symptoms, including depressed mood and loss of interest or pleasure to occur nearly every day for 2 weeks.

❖ Dysthymic disorder involves less severe symptoms occurring over a 2-year period.

❖ Bipolar disorder involves manic episodes as well as major depressive episodes.

❖ Seasonal affective disorder involves seasonal fluctuations in the symptoms of clinical depression, with the symptoms being worst in the autumn and winter.

ISSUES SURROUNDING THE CLASSIFICATION AND DIAGNOSIS OF DEPRESSION

? What is the difference between validity and reliability?

Two major factors need to be considered when deciding whether the classification and diagnosis of depression are adequate. First, there is **reliability**, the extent to which the diagnosis of depression is *consistent* over time and between therapists or other raters. Second, there is **validity**, the extent to which a diagnostic system assesses what it claims to be assessing. Thus, for example, in a valid system, patients who are diagnosed as suffering from major depressive disorder actually have that disorder. For diagnoses to be valid, it is necessary but not sufficient that they are reliable. If a system isn't reliable, then it can't be valid.

Several factors can reduce the reliability and validity of diagnosis of major depressive disorder (unipolar depression). First, classification systems such as DSM-IV-TR and ICD-10 are *categorical* systems. This is an all-or-none approach in which patients are assumed to have (or not to have) a given mental disorder (e.g. major depressive disorder). This can produce real problems. For example, a patient

EXAM HINT

Remember that reliability refers to *consistency*. This means that DSM or ICD is reliable if clinicians using it give patients with similar symptoms the same diagnosis (e.g., the same type of depression). A lack of reliability inevitably reduces validity because this refers to whether they have been given the correct diagnosis.

KEY TERMS

Reliability: the extent to which a method of measurement or a research study produces consistent findings across situations or over time.
Validity: the extent to which something is true. This can be applied to a measurement tool, such as a psychological test, or to the "trueness" of an experimental procedure both in terms of what goes on within the experiment (internal validity) and its relevance to other situations (external validity).

must have five symptoms nearly every day for at least 2 weeks to be diagnosed as having major depressive disorder. Thus, a patient who has six symptoms every day for 13 days, or a patient who has four symptoms every day for 8 weeks, is not deemed to be suffering from major depressive disorder! Clearly, there is an arbitrary element to such a system.

There is also an arbitrary element when deciding whether patients have any given symptom. For example, loss of pleasure in usual activities is a symptom of major depressive disorder, but *how much* loss of pleasure is needed to qualify? Other examples include deciding whether a patient's difficulties in sleeping are sufficiently great to count as a symptom, or whether his/her weight gain or loss is sufficient.

Second, it is sometimes assumed that mildly depressed individuals who don't receive a diagnosis of major depressive disorder or minor depressive disorder are functioning well. This assumption is incorrect and dangerous. For example, Horwath, Johnson, Klerman, and Weissman (1992) found that over 50% of new cases of major depressive disorder (unipolar depression) had previously reported less severe symptoms of depression. Expressed differently, individuals with mild depressive symptoms were 4.4 times more likely than non-depressed individuals to develop major depressive disorder over the following 12 months.

Comorbidity describes the presence of two or more mental disorders at the same time; such as agoraphobia and major depressive disorder.

Third, there is the issue of comorbidity. **Comorbidity** means that a given individual has two or more mental disorders at the same time. It occurs in part because the symptoms of different mental disorders often resemble each other. For example, depression and anxiety are both unpleasant mood states and many people suffer from both at the same time. Barlow (1988) looked at comorbidity among patients suffering from various anxiety disorders: agoraphobia (fear of public places), panic disorder, and generalised anxiety disorder (persistent excessive worrying and anxiety about numerous events). He found that 39% of patients with agoraphobia also had major depressive disorder or dysthymic disorder, as did 35% of those with panic disorder and 17% of those with generalised anxiety disorder.

> **EXAM HINT**
> Note the comorbidity of depression with other forms of mental disorder. This shows us that the different mental disorders are not completely discrete conditions, and so there are likely to be both general causes, which play a part in different mental disorders, and specific causes for the particular mental disorder.

Comorbidity creates problems for classification and diagnosis. Why is this? First, it casts doubt on the notion that all the diagnostic categories in DSM-IV and ICD-10 are quite distinct and different from each other. Second, if a patient has, say, three mental disorders, it makes it difficult for the therapist to know *which* disorder to focus on early in treatment. Third, comorbidity means that we can't regard all patients suffering from major depressive disorder (unipolar depression) as having comparably severe conditions. For example, Lewinsohn, Rohde, and Seeley (1995) studied adolescents suffering from depression. Those who had one or more additional disorders had received more mental health treatment, had made more suicide attempts, and had worse academic performance.

? What concerns may arise when treating a patient with psychiatric comorbidity?

> **KEY TERM**
> **Comorbidity:** the presence of two or more disorders in a given individual at the same time.

I have focused on problems with respect to the classification and diagnosis of major depressive disorder (unipolar depression). However, these problems aren't necessarily very serious. If the diagnosis of depression were very unreliable and invalid, then many patients receiving treatment for depression would not actually have the disorder. As a result, treatment would be unlikely to be of much benefit. In fact, as we will see, various forms of therapy for depression have proved successful, which reduces concerns about the reliability and validity of diagnosis.

Diagnosis: Semi-structured Interviews

Patients are generally diagnosed on the basis of one or more interviews with a therapist. Some interviews are very unstructured and informal. This can produce good rapport between the patient and the therapist, but reliability and validity of diagnosis tend to be low (Hopko, Lejuex, Armento, & Bare, 2004). The most reliable and valid approach involves the use of semi-structured interviews in which patients are asked a largely predetermined series of questions. We now consider two of the most used semi-structured interviews for depression.

The Structured Clinical Interview for DSM-IV-Patient Version (SCID-I/P) is a semi-structured interview that takes about 60–90 minutes to complete. It starts with an open-ended interview, which is followed by systematic questions concerning symptoms and current and lifetime disorders; clinical judgement is required to interpret the patient's answers. Inter-rater reliability and diagnostic accuracy were both high with the SCID-I/P (Ventura, Liberman, Green, Shaner, & Mintz, 1998), and—surprisingly—were as good for relatively inexperienced interviewers as for experienced ones.

The Anxiety Disorder Interview Schedule for DSM-IV (ADIS-IV) is also a semi-structured interview. As its name suggests, it is mainly designed to diagnose anxiety disorders. However, given that so many anxious patients suffer from depression, it also provides an assessment of depression. Many of the symptoms assessed by the ADIS-IV are initially rated on a yes/no basis, with degree of severity being rated for those symptoms that are present.

Brown, DiNardo, Lehman, and Campbell (2001) studied the reliability of assessment of major depressive disorder in a study in which 1400 patients were given the ADIS-IV twice by two therapists close together in time. Inter-rater reliability was good (i.e. the two therapists showed good agreement) but somewhat lower than for most of the anxiety disorders. What factors caused diagnostic disagreements and so reduced reliability? The most important was a tendency for patients to report different symptoms during the two interviews. The second most important factor was a difference in the diagnosis by the two therapists. For example, sometimes one therapist would diagnose major depressive disorder whereas the other diagnosed generalised anxiety disorder (chronic worry in several domains of life). The third most important factor involved the so-called "threshold issue". One of the criteria for major depressive disorder is that the patient experiences significant distress or impairment. Therapists sometimes disagreed as to whether the symptoms exceeded this threshold.

How valid are the diagnoses produced by assessment procedures such as SCID-I/P and ADIS-IV? Davison, Neale, and Kring (2004) identified three kinds of validity. First, there is *content validity*, which refers to the extent to which an

? What is the benefit of having a structured interview?

assessment procedure obtains detailed relevant information. SCID-I/P and ADIS-IV are clearly both high in content validity.

Second, there is *criterion validity*, which refers to the extent to which there are predictable differences between those diagnosed with, say, major depressive disorder and those not receiving that diagnosis. As we might expect, patients diagnosed with major depressive disorder are less likely to be in a long-lasting relationship, to have a full-time job, or to have many friends (Hammen, 1997). This provides some evidence for criterion validity, but note that poor social and work functioning are found in those suffering from most mental disorders.

Third, there is *construct validity*, which is the extent to which hypotheses about a given disorder are supported by the evidence. For example, it is often assumed that depression is associated with a lack of involvement in pleasurable activities, and the evidence supports that assumption (Lewinsohn, Munoz, Youngren, & Zeiss, 1992). Overall, then, it seems that the main ways of diagnosing major depressive disorder possess reasonable content, criterion, and construct validity.

We have seen that the SCID-I/P and the ADIS-IV both assess depression with good reliability and validity. Hopko et al. (2004) argued that the ideal approach to classification and diagnosis is a multi-method approach involving cognitive, behavioural, and physiological assessments of the individual patient. For example, therapists can learn much from direct observation of the patient. In addition, self-report measures such as the Beck Depression Inventory (BDI) can be of value. The BDI assesses the number and intensity of depressive symptoms, and patients with major depressive disorder typically have considerably higher scores than healthy individuals (Hammen, 1997). Note that the BDI is *not* used directly in diagnosis, partly because depressive symptoms are found in many mental disorders. However, it would clearly be a cause for concern with regard to the reliability and validity of diagnosis if a patient diagnosed with major depressive disorder had a fairly low score on the BDI!

> What is the difference between criterion and construct validity?

HOW SCIENCE WORKS: DIAGNOSING DEPRESSION
A problem with psychopathologies such as depression is that they don't have physical symptoms that can be measured. Depression is a mood disorder, and diagnosis depends heavily on an individual describing their mood, their feelings, in self-report techniques.

You could produce a series of posters, one for each of the self-report diagnostic techniques, giving a summary of the technique and then an evaluation as a short list of plus and minus points such as for the methodological strengths and weaknesses. You could use ICT and word processing, colour and various other tools, and download graphics to make your posters attractive and to liven up an important area of psychopathology.

SECTION SUMMARY
Issues Surrounding the Classification and Diagnosis of Depression

❖ Diagnostic systems need to be reliable and valid.

❖ Problems of reliability stem from the use of categorical systems, deciding on the severity of any symptom, and comorbidity.

❖ Despite the problems, semi-structured interviews (e.g. SCID-I/P; ADIS-IV) have good reliability.

❖ Problems of reliability with the ADIS-IV include changes in patients' symptoms over time and overlapping symptoms between mental disorders.

❖ SCID-I/P and ADIS-IV possess reasonable content, criterion, and construct validity.

BIOLOGICAL EXPLANATIONS OF DEPRESSION

It has often been argued that major depressive disorder (unipolar depression) and bipolar disorder depend at least in part on biological factors. We will start by considering depression from the evolutionary perspective. After that, we consider the notion that genetic factors influence the development of depression. Finally, we focus on various possible biochemical explanations based on the notion that depressed individuals differ from non-depressed ones in terms of the levels of various neurotransmitters or hormones. Although these explanations are considered separately, it is *really* important to note that they are closely related in some ways. For example, genetic factors might explain individual differences at the biochemical level. In addition, our genetic and biochemical make-up depends very much on the evolutionary history of the human race.

Evolutionary Explanations

Several evolutionary theories have been put forward to explain why depression (especially major depressive disorder) evolved. We will consider two of the main ones: the rank or social competition hypothesis and the social navigation hypothesis.

According to the social competition hypothesis (e.g. Price, Sloman, Gardner, & Rohde, 1994), an individual who is the loser in a contest (i.e. loses rank) should accept the loss. This prevents further injury from re-engaging with the person who has defeated him or her, and so represents "damage limitation". According to this hypothesis, the adaptive significance of depression is that it allows the individual to adjust to the new situation. When people accept that they have lost rank or their position in the dominance hierarchy, it is natural for them to become depressed, to become lethargic or lacking in energy, and to engage in self-doubt.

The rank or social competition hypothesis accounts for many of the symptoms of depression. For example, the lack of motivation shown by depressed individuals is easily explained if depression is triggered by the need to adjust to being demoted in the social dominance hierarchy. As predicted, recovery from depression often occurs only when the individual finally abandons some unobtainable goal (Nesse, 2000).

The rank or social competition hypothesis, does not take into account the fact that a depression-related lack of motivation (to care for your child, for example) is a maladaptive behaviour.

However, the hypothesis has serious limitations. First, it isn't made clear why depression can last for several years—how long would we expect a process of adjustment to take? Second, bear in mind that depression can be caused by many factors, including genetic ones. The social competition hypothesis focuses on important environmental factors (i.e. major losses) triggering depression, but this is only part of the story. Third, lack of motivation and inability to function have generally been very maladaptive in nearly all cultures at all periods of human history. For example, there have been a few (thankfully rare) cases in which a mother was too depressed to feed or care for her child, who died as a result of her neglect. In exceptional cases, mothers suffering from extreme depression have been known to kill their newborn child (infanticide).

Social Navigation Hypothesis

According to the social navigation hypothesis (Watson & Andrews, 2002), depression is adaptive because it leads to appropriate attempts to decide what should be done after an important loss. According to Watson and Andrews, depression serves two valuable functions. First, it increases the focus on accurate analysis and solution of the individual's major problems. This is known as the social rumination function, and it involves the individual thinking at length about their problems and what to do about them. Second, the obvious distress and unhappiness displayed by depressed individuals might help to persuade other people to help them. This is known as the social motivation function.

It follows from the social navigation hypothesis that depressed individuals should recover when their social problems are resolved. As predicted, recovery from depression is faster when depressed individuals have strong social support (Brugha, Bebbington, Stretch, MacCarthy, & Wykes, 1997). There is some evidence that depressed individuals can be more realistic than non-depressed ones in their thinking (depressive realism). For example, non-depressed individuals have a self-serving bias—they attribute success to their own ability but failure to bad luck. By contrast, depressed individuals often seem more realistic, in that they are less inclined to take all the praise when things go well or to refuse to accept responsibility when things go badly (Ackermann & DeRubeis, 1991).

What are the limitations of the social navigation hypothesis? First, severe depression is associated with extremely low levels of motivation. This hardly sounds like the ideal state to be in to engage in complex social problem solving! Second, the hypothesis is far too optimistic about what happens to depressed individuals. Depressed people who make their partner's life a misery often find themselves losing their partner rather than receiving the help they seek. Third, the fact that 5% of clinically depressed individuals commit suicide (Bostwick & Pankratz, 2000) is hard to reconcile with the alleged adaptive functions of depression emphasised by the social navigation hypothesis. Fourth, other reasonable explanations are available. For example, Nesse and Williams (1995) argued that rates of depression are increasing because depression is a result of life in highly developed, competitive urban societies. People (especially young people) are presented with many images of ideal lives and material possessions by the media, which can make individuals feel dissatisfied and depressed.

> **?** If one of your relatives has suffered from a mental disorder, what reasons are there for you not to worry that you may also develop the same disorder?

Bipolar Disorder

We turn now to bipolar disorder. As we have already discussed the possible evolutionary value of depression, our focus will be on the manic phase of the disorder. It has been argued that this phase is related to creativity, lack of inhibition, and charismatic leadership, and is thus adaptive. Many species hibernate during the winter and are most active during the summer months. In that context, it is interesting that nearly all individuals with seasonal affective disorder suffer from severe depression during the winter months. It is also of interest that patients with bipolar disorder are more likely to have manic phases in the warmer months. Carroll (1991) found that the peak time for manic episodes was early spring for one group of bipolar patients and late summer for another group. Perhaps there is adaptive value in being most active during the time of the year when there are the most hours of daylight, and food is plentiful.

Creativity and bipolar disorder are believed to be genetically linked. Does this help to explain why many famous comedians, artists, and politicians such as Stephen Fry, Vincent Van Gogh, and Winston Churchill, have all been said to be sufferers from manic depression?

Winston Churchill, Abraham Lincoln, Vincent van Gogh, Graham Greene, Ludwig van Beethoven . . . the list of sufferers from manic depression or bipolar disorder is apparently endless. The argument is that creativity is linked to the same genes that underlie bipolar disorder. Without one, we might not have the other.

Evaluation

Various accounts suggest that depression and bipolar disorder are adaptive. However, we need to ask ourselves whether the severe disadvantages of such a debilitating disorder outweigh any possible adaptive value it might have. The fact that some famous people suffered from bipolar disorder doesn't prove that there is a causal connection—perhaps they would have been equally successful without bipolar disorder. However, it is possible that some tendency towards mood swings might have adaptive value. Indeed, women who experience moderate mood swings are happier than those who don't (Diener, Suh, Lucas, & Smith, 1999).

Genetic Explanations

There are three main kinds of studies that can be carried out to establish whether genetic factors are important in the development of depression: twin studies, family studies, and adoption studies. First, we will consider the relevant evidence and then evaluate it.

Twin studies

The clearest evidence for the role of genetic factors in the development of major depressive disorder and bipolar disorder comes from studies on monozygotic, or identical, twins and dizygotic, or fraternal, twins. If one twin has depression, what is the probability that the other twin has the same disorder? This is the **concordance rate**. Suppose that genetic factors are important. As identical twins share 100% of their genes whereas fraternal twins share only 50%, the concordance rate should be higher for identical twins. If identical and fraternal twin pairs have the same concordance rate, then the implication would be that environmental factors are all-important.

Allen (1976) reviewed the relevant studies. For major depressive disorder, the mean concordance rate was 40% for identical twins and only 11% for fraternal twins. For bipolar disorder, the mean concordance rate was 72% for identical

> **Genes, depression, and gender**
>
> With regard to depression, genes seem to affect women more than men. A meta-analysis of well-run twin studies, in which the twins were brought up apart, found that genes were responsible for 42% of the development of depression in women but for only 29% of depression in men (Kendler, Gatz, Gardner, & Pedersen, 2006). The reason for these findings is unclear, and although it does seem that more women than men suffer from depression, it is not known whether this is genetically controlled or is an environmental or even a social effect.
>
> What environmental factors might produce this difference between the sexes, and what social factors?

twins and 14% for fraternal twins. More recent studies have produced similar findings. McGuffin, Katz, Watkins, and Rutherford (1996) found the concordance rate for major depressive disorder to be 46% compared with 20% for fraternal twins. Craddock and Jones (1999) found that the concordance rate for bipolar disorder was 40% for identical twins and between 5% and 10% for fraternal twins, siblings, and other close relatives. In the population at large, about 7% are diagnosed with major depressive disorder and 1% with bipolar disorder, and *all* figures for identical and fraternal twins are much higher.

? What are the limitations of twin studies of depression?

These findings suggest that genetic factors are involved in both types of depression, and that their involvement is probably greater for bipolar disorder than for major depressive disorder. Berrettini (2000a) linked bipolar disorder to genes on chromosomes 4, 6, 11, 12, 13, 15, 18, and 22. Problems of interpretation with these findings are discussed in the Evaluation section below.

Family studies

Family studies also suggest the involvement of genetic factors. Gershon (1990) presented the findings from numerous family studies in which depression was assessed in the first-degree relatives of patients with depression. For both major depressive disorder and bipolar disorder, the rates of depression were about two to three times the rates in the general population. Sullivan, Neale, and Kendler (2000) reported similar findings in a review of several family studies.

Egeland et al. (1987) studied the Amish, a small religious community in Pennsylvania. The community has a relatively low incidence of major depressive disorder compared to the surrounding communities. However, one family had an extremely high level of bipolar disorder, with 11 out of 81 members being affected. On examination of their genes, two marker genes on chromosome 11 appeared to be different. Importantly, these genes were "neighbours" of the genes involved in the production of monoamines, a biochemical implicated in depression (see later). However, Hodgkinson (1987), who studied extended families in Iceland, couldn't find any evidence of the different genes in relation to bipolar disorder.

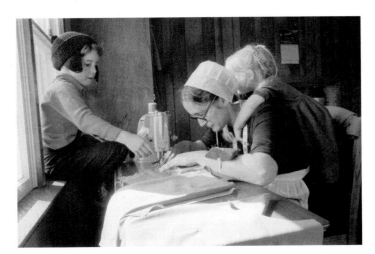

The Amish people of Pennsylvania have a relatively high incidence of bipolar disorder. One study found that this predisposition may be carried on chromosome 11, but the finding has not been replicated.

Adoption studies

Wender, Kety, Rosenthal, Schulsinger, Ortmann, and Lunde (1986) found that the biological relatives of adopted sufferers from major depression were seven times more likely than the sufferer's adoptive relatives to have had major depression. In similar fashion, it was found that the biological parents of adopted children who later developed depression were eight times more likely than the adoptive parents to have suffered from clinical depression (Wender et al., 1986).

Sullivan et al. (2000) discussed two other adoption studies on major depressive disorder, neither of which produced strong evidence for a genetic influence on major depression. However, the studies were limited—one diagnosed major depression in a very indirect way and the other had very little information about the biological parents.

Overall evaluation

Twin studies can provide the most convincing evidence concerning genetic influences on major depressive disorder (unipolar depression) and bipolar disorder. As we have seen, the concordance rates for both types of depression are much higher for identical twins than for fraternal twins, suggesting that genetic factors are important. The concordance figures are more convincing for bipolar disorder than for major depressive disorder, suggesting that genetic influences are stronger for bipolar disorder. However, it isn't known whether the identical and fraternal twin pairs experienced equally similar environments. As a result, some of the higher concordance rate for identical twins might reflect environmental rather than genetic influences—perhaps these twins tend to grow up in stressful family environments.

The data from family studies are harder to interpret. Relatives who are the most genetically similar tend to spend the most time together. Thus, it is hard (or even impossible) to disentangle genetic and environmental effects. Of particular importance, an individual in close contact with a relative suffering from clinical depression might be more vulnerable to depression because of the stressful environment rather than because of genetic factors. Thus, the findings from family studies can provide no more than weakish evidence that genetic factors are involved in producing major depressive disorder and bipolar disorder. The findings from adoption studies are somewhat inconsistent. Wender et al. (1986) reported striking findings that suggested a strong genetic influence on major depression, but other researchers have obtained less convincing findings.

Biochemical Explanations

Biochemical and genetic explanations overlap with each other because the functioning of our biochemical system depends in part on genetic factors. If someone has a genetic vulnerability to develop depression, this vulnerability might have an impact on their biochemical system, and this in turn could lead to depression.

Much emphasis has been placed on the potential role that might be played by various **neurotransmitters** ("chemical messengers") in the development of depression. Most of the interest has centred on monoamine neurotransmitters such as serotonin, noradrenaline, and dopamine. For example, Kety (1975) put forward a permissive amine theory of mood disorder, according to which the level

KEY TERM

Neurotransmitters: chemical substances that are released at the junction between neurons (a synapse) and that affect the transmission of messages in the nervous system.

Depression and diet

Explanations of depression that are based on biological factors are generally related to endogenous depression, i.e. depression that is caused by internal factors. There is some evidence that what you eat might affect your mood and could, in extreme cases, lead to depression.

Tryptophan is a substance that is found in some foods, such as maize and other starchy foods. Delgado, Charney, Price, Aghajanian, Landis, and Heninger (1990) found that acute tryptophan depletion (ATD) induces a temporary relapse in patients suffering from major depressive disorder. This is supported in a study by Smith, Clifford, Hockney, and Clark (1997), who found that women experienced depression when tryptophan was removed from their diets. In addition, it has been suggested that serotonin might be involved in some cases of eating disorder, and that the reason why bulimics often eat a lot of starchy foods is to increase their levels of tryptophan and serotonin.

---

of noradrenaline is generally controlled by the level of serotonin. When the level of serotonin is low, however, noradrenaline levels are less controlled and so might fluctuate wildly. A third neurotransmitter, dopamine, is also involved.

As already stated, noradrenaline, serotonin, and dopamine are all neurotransmitters of the monoamine group, which explains the name "permissive amine" theory. Neurotransmitters act at the synapses or junctions between neurons in the brain. They facilitate or block nervous transmission. Noradrenaline is associated with physiological arousal in general, a fact you might recall from studying stress at AS level. Serotonin is also related to arousal and sleep—increases in serotonin generally reduce arousal. Dopamine is generally inhibited by serotonin and has been linked with schizophrenia (see p. 392). Under typical conditions, all three neurotransmitters play a role in arousal and are also related to mood.

Kety's (1975) theory assumed that serotonin levels are low in depression as a result of inherited individual differences. The low levels of serotonin prevent adequate control of the other two neurotransmitters. Numerous studies have investigated the levels of these various neurotransmitters, with varying results. Teuting, Rosen, and Hirschfeld (1981) compared the substances found in the urine of depressed patients and healthy controls. Compounds produced as a by-product of the action of enzymes on noradrenaline and serotonin were present in smaller amounts in the urine of depressed patients. This finding suggests that depressed patients have lower levels of noradrenaline and serotonin.

Subsequent research, however, has produced findings that don't fit the theory. For example, Thase et al. (2002) found that depressed patients (especially those with severe depression) had increased levels of noradrenaline. This is the opposite of what was predicted theoretically.

What has been established is that we are dealing with an extremely complex system. Given that, there are unlikely to be any very simple biochemical differences between depressed and non-depressed individuals. For example, Rampello, Nicoletti, and Nicoletti (2000) found that patients with major depressive disorder had an imbalance in several neurotransmitters, including noradrenaline, serotonin, dopamine, and acetylcholine.

Hormonal factors

The **endocrine system** produces hormones, which influence a huge range of behaviours: growth, menstruation, sleep, sexual activity, and so on. Various

? What role is suggested for dopamine to play in depression?

KEY TERM

Endocrine system: a system of a number of ductless glands located throughout the body that produce the body's chemical messengers, called hormones.

? Is PPD likely to be due entirely to biological factors?

The massive hormonal changes that a woman undergoes after childbirth might go some way to explaining the prevalence of short-term depressive symptoms in 20% of new mums.

? Could you use this knowledge to diagnose depression? How reliable would the diagnosis be?

conditions that are linked to hormone changes have depression as a major symptom, for example premenstrual syndrome (PMS), postpartum depression (PPD, after a woman has had a child), and seasonal affective disorder (discussed earlier in the chapter).

The female menstrual cycle involves changes in the levels of oestrogen and progesterone. In the week or two before menstruation, some women develop symptoms such as irritability, bloating, breast tenderness, mood swings, impaired concentration, and headache. These changes are related to the hormonal fluctuations.

Abramowitz, Baker, and Fleischer (1982) studied the female admissions to a psychiatric hospital. They found that 41% entered on the day before (or the first day of) their menstrual period. Another study, this time looking at women in the healthy population, found depressive symptoms during the premenstrual period in 43%.

The link between premenstrual syndrome and depression could explain in part why more women than men suffer from depression. However, there are several other explanations. More women than men have suffered from child abuse, and such abuse predicts adult depression (Butcher, Mineka, & Hooley, 2004).

About 20% of women report moderate depression shortly after giving birth and a few of these women become chronically depressed. In extreme cases, severe depression has led mothers to commit infanticide. Symptoms of postpartum depression include sadness, anxiety, tearfulness, and trouble sleeping. These symptoms usually appear within a few days of delivery and go away by 10–12 days after the birth.

Women who have recently given birth undergo massive hormonal changes, which is one possible explanation for postpartum depression. However, women who become depressed after childbirth have often had previous emotional problems. This suggests that their depression is sometimes attributable to marital difficulties or the stresses involved in having a child (Gotlib, Whiffen, Wallace, & Mount, 1991).

Cortisol (a human stress hormone) might have an important role in depression. Levels of cortisol tend to be elevated in depressed patients. For example, elevated blood plasma levels of cortisol have been found in 30% of depressed outpatients and 70% of depressed hospitalised patients (Thase et al., 2002). This is not very surprising given that stressful life events often play a role in triggering depression.

The notion that cortisol might be relevant to depression has been examined by using the dexamethasone suppression test. Dexamethasone is synthetic cortisol and it suppresses cortisol secretion in healthy individuals. However, about 50% of depressed patients show very little suppression (Howland & Thase, 1991). Ribeiro, Tandon, Grunhaus, and Greden (1993) reviewed numerous studies on depression and the dexamethasone suppression test. Depressed patients who show little suppression, even after treatment, are more likely than other depressed patients to suffer rapid relapse.

The above findings suggest that the levels of cortisol are so high in depressed patients that they can't easily be suppressed. However, high levels of non-suppression are also found in patients suffering from other mental disorders (e.g. schizophrenia). Thus, non-suppression might reflect general mental distress rather than being specific to depression.

General evaluation

Depressed patients often have disrupted functioning of various neurotransmitters. However, no simple theory fits the facts, and findings opposite to theoretical predictions greatly weaken the permissive amine theory. Findings such as those of Rampello et al. (2000) provide some indication of the true complexity of the biochemical differences between depressed and non-depressed individuals.

Hormonal factors are probably of relevance in depression. First, studies on premenstrual syndrome and postpartum depression indicate that major hormonal changes can be associated with depression. However, women who suffer postpartum depression have often had previous episodes of clinical depression. This suggests that postpartum depression is a combination of hormonal imbalance and a pre-existing predisposition to depression. Lack of emotional support, low self-esteem, and unrealistic ideas about motherhood are also found in cases of postpartum depression, suggesting that psychological factors are important. Major life changes can be stressful even when the events themselves are basically positive, because we have to adjust to the new situation. This might be relevant so far as postpartum depression is concerned.

Second, studies on cortisol have provided interesting evidence that most severely depressed patients have elevated levels of cortisol. However, there are limitations to the cortisol research. Reduced suppression on the dexamethasone suppression test is also found in other mental disorders, and so high levels of cortisol aren't specific to depression. Second, high cortisol levels may be a result of depression rather than forming part of the cause.

As we will see later, suggestive evidence supporting the biochemical approach comes from drug therapy for depression. The monoamine oxidase inhibitors (MAOIs) increase the active levels of noradrenaline and serotonin in depressed patients and reduce the symptoms of depression. Currently, the most prescribed antidepressant drugs are selective serotonin re-uptake inhibitors (SSRIs), of which the most celebrated is Prozac. The SSRIs are chemically unrelated to the older MAOIs but also tend to increase the availability of serotonin.

Finally, lithium carbonate, which is very effective in reducing manic symptoms in bipolar disorder, is thought to decrease the availability of noradrenaline and serotonin.

Avoid the treatment aetiology fallacy. Aspirin may cure headaches but lack of aspirin is not a cause of headaches.

None of these drug effects can provide *direct* evidence of what causes depression. For example, aspirin is effective in curing a headache but it would be absurd to argue that an absence of aspirin causes the headache! MacLeod (1998) called this the **treatment aetiology fallacy**—the mistaken notion that the success of a given form of treatment reveals the cause of the disorder.

There is a final important point. There are generally problems of interpretation even when significant differences in the level of some neurotransmitter or hormone are found in depressed patients and healthy controls. The reason is that it is unclear whether the difference played a part in the development of depression or whether the difference is merely a consequence of patients having developed depression.

> **KEY TERM**
>
> **Treatment aetiology fallacy:** the mistaken belief that the effectiveness of a form of treatment indicates the cause of a disorder.

SECTION SUMMARY
Biological Explanations of Depression

Social competition hypothesis

❖ According to the social competition hypothesis, it is adaptive for someone who loses social status to accept the loss.
❖ The hypothesis explains the lack of motivation shown by depressed individuals but does not account for long-lasting depression.
❖ The hypothesis minimises the problems caused by the loss of motivation associated with depression.

Social navigation hypothesis

❖ According to the social navigation hypothesis, depression is adaptive because it fulfils social rumination and social motivation functions.
❖ As predicted, social support speeds up recovery from depression and depressed individuals often seem more realistic in their thinking.
❖ Evaluation:

— The lack of motivation shown by depressed individuals seems ill suited to social rumination and complex social problem solving.
— Depression often drives other people away rather than leading to offers of help.

Bipolar disorder

❖ The manic phase of bipolar disorder might be related to creativity and charismatic leadership; several famous people suffered from bipolar disorder.
❖ Famous people with bipolar disorder might have been just as famous without the bipolar disorder.

Genetic factors

❖ Twin studies strongly suggest that genetic factors are involved in major depressive disorder and bipolar disorder because of the higher concordance rate for identical than fraternal twin pairs. However, it is possible that identical twins experience more similar environments.
❖ The rates of depression are significantly higher among the first-degree relatives of patients with depression than in the population at large. This can be explained in both genetic and environmental terms.
❖ Adoption studies have shown that the chances of an adopted person developing depression depend more on whether the biological, as opposed to the adoptive relatives have had depression.

Neurotransmitters

❖ According to the permissive amine theory, low levels of serotonin in depressed individuals prevent adequate control of noradrenaline and dopamine levels.
❖ The evidence indicates that any biochemical differences between depressed and non-depressed individuals are very complex.

Hormonal factors

❖ Various conditions involving depression (e.g. premenstrual syndrome; postpartum depression) are linked to hormonal changes.
❖ Levels of the stress hormone cortisol are elevated in depressed patients.
❖ Elevated cortisol levels may reflect general mental distress rather than being specific to depression.
❖ The existence of an association between hormonal levels and depression could occur because depression produces elevated hormonal levels rather than the other way around.

PSYCHOLOGICAL EXPLANATIONS OF DEPRESSION

Various biological explanations of depression have made a valuable contribution to our understanding of the causes of depression. However, there are also several influential psychological accounts of depression, including psychodynamic, behavioural, cognitive, life-event, and socio-cultural explanations. It is certainly not the case that only *one* of these explanations can be correct—it is much more likely that all of the explanations have some contribution to make to our overall understanding of the causes of depression.

> **EXAM HINT**
> The question will usually stipulate whether biological or psychological explanations are to be considered. You can use the alternative explanations to evaluate the one you are writing about, but be careful—one link sentence to introduce them is not enough. You must consistently contrast the alternative explanation with the explanation(s) you've covered as AO1. Do not simply describe the alternative explanation; instead explain what insights it provides that the AO1 explanations do not. Also consider whether the different explanations share any strengths or weaknesses, or whether the weakness of one can be used to highlight the strength of the other.

> **HOW SCIENCE WORKS: EXPLAINING DEPRESSION**
> In science, it is important to test a hypothesis or explanation to see if it is right or wrong, and so to increase our knowledge scientifically. You could choose either biological or psychological explanations of depression and produce a PowerPoint presentation using a combination of text and graphics such as downloaded images to outline each explanation and then give the supporting and the challenging evidence, finishing each explanation with an overall conclusion or judgement. When you do this presentation, you could also ask your class to vote for the explanation they find more convincing.

Psychodynamic Explanation

Freud's psychoanalytic theory is an example of the psychodynamic approach to understanding depression. He argued that depression is like grief in that it often occurs as a reaction to the loss of an important relationship. However, there is an important difference, because depressed individuals regard themselves as worthless. According to Freud, what happens is that the individual identifies with the lost person, so that repressed anger towards the lost person is directed inwards towards the self. Note that **repression** involves forcing painful, threatening, or unacceptable thoughts and memories out of consciousness into the unconscious mind. This inner-directed anger reduces the individual's self-esteem, and makes him or her vulnerable to experiencing depression in the future.

Freud distinguished between actual losses (e.g. death of a loved one) and symbolic losses (e.g. loss of a job), which are equated with loss of a loved one. Both kinds of losses can produce depression by causing the individual to re-experience childhood episodes when they experienced loss of affection from some significant person (e.g. a parent).

To avoid loss turning into depression, the individual needs to engage in a period of mourning work. During this period, he or she recalls memories of the lost one. This allows the individual to separate himself or herself from the lost person, and so reduce the inner-directed anger.

Who is most susceptible to depression? According to Freud, there are two kinds of person. First, those whose parents failed to fulfil their needs during the oral stage in infancy. As a result, they develop low self-esteem and are too dependent on others in adult life. Second, those whose parents gratified their

> **KEY TERM**
> **Repression:** the process of forcing very threatening thoughts and memories out of the conscious mind in Freudian theory; motivated forgetting.

needs to excess during the oral stage. Such individuals are reluctant to move on and develop a sense of independence.

What about bipolar disorder? According to Freud, the depressive phase occurs when the individual's superego or conscience is dominant. By contrast, the manic phase occurs when the individual's ego or rational mind asserts itself and he/she feels in control.

Findings

There is reasonable evidence that depression is caused in part by loss events. Kessler (1997) found that childhood adversities and traumatic stresses were associated with depression starting before the age of 20. However, they were *not* associated with depression starting later in adulthood, which seems inconsistent with Freud's theory.

Freud's emphasis on the importance of childhood in determining an individual's susceptibility to depression was also supported by Kendler, Pedersen, Farahmand, and Persson (1996). Adult female twins who had experienced parental loss through separation in childhood had an above-average tendency to suffer from depression in adult life. In similar fashion, Bifulco, Harris, and Brown (1992) studied women who had lost mothers through separation or death before they were 17 (see the box below).

Separation and loss

You might also consider anaclitic depression, from your AS level studies, which is a state of resigned helplessness and loss of appetite in young children who have been separated from their mothers. Bowlby's (1969) theory of attachment proposed that there might be long-term emotional damage as a consequence of early loss. Bifulco et al. (1992) offered support for this in a study of about 250 women who had lost their mothers, through separation or death, before they were 17. They found that loss of their mother through separation or death doubles the risk of depressive and anxiety disorders in adult women. The rate of depression was especially high among those whose mothers had died before the child reached the age of 6.

There is a danger of exaggerating the importance of major losses as a trigger for depression. This can be seen if we simply consider the statistical evidence—fewer than 10% of individuals who experience major losses go on to develop clinical depression.

Freud would predict that the repressed anger and hostility of depressed individuals would emerge at least partly in their dreams. However, Beck and Ward (1961) found no evidence of this. Freud would also predict that depressed people should express anger and hostility mainly towards themselves. In fact, however, they express considerable anger and hostility towards those close to them (Weissman, Klerman, & Paykel, 1971).

Evaluation

Some of Freud's most general assumptions are approximately correct. First, major losses increase the probability of an individual developing major depressive disorder. Second, childhood experiences play an important role. Children who have unhappy childhoods because of parental indifference, separation, or death are at increased risk of becoming depressed as adults. Third, there are clear individual differences in vulnerability to depression after experiencing a major loss, and Freud at least addressed this issue by focusing on children's very different experiences in infancy.

What are the limitations with Freud's approach? First, the evidence relating childhood experiences and adult depression is based on finding an association or correlation between the two factors. However, this does not prove that adult depression is *caused* by adverse childhood experiences. Second, Freud argued that depressed individuals direct anger and hostility towards themselves. However, the evidence suggests that these negative emotions are directed more towards other people. Third, the details of Freud's theory are fanciful. Freud emphasised the importance of the oral stage of development, which lasts for the first 18 months of life. It stretches belief that subsequent childhood experiences are of minor significance compared to what happens during the oral stage. In addition, it doesn't seem very likely that symbolic losses are regarded by those affected as resembling the loss of a highly valued person.

Behavioural Approach

Advocates of the behavioural approach (e.g. Lewinsohn; Seligman) focus on the fact that depressed individuals lack motivation and engage in far fewer activities than non-depressed individuals. According to the behavioural approach, depressed people are unresponsive because they doubt whether being involved in activities would be rewarding. However, as we will see, Lewinsohn and Seligman differ in terms of the precise mechanisms thought to be involved.

Reinforcement

Lewinsohn (1974) put forward a behavioural theory based on the notion that depression occurs because of a reduction in the level of **reinforcement** or reward. This relates to the psychodynamic view that depression is caused by the loss of an important relationship, because important relationships are a major source of positive reinforcement. There is also a reduction in

> **KEY TERM**
>
> **Reinforcement:** a behaviour is more likely to re-occur because the response was agreeable. Both positive and negative reinforcement have agreeable consequences.

CASE STUDY: MAJOR (UNIPOLAR) DEPRESSION

Paul was a 20-year-old college senior majoring in chemistry. He first came to the student psychiatric clinic complaining of headaches and a vague assortment of somatic problems. Throughout the interview, Paul seemed severely depressed and unable to work up enough energy to talk with the therapist. Even though he had maintained a B+ average, he felt like a failure.

His parents had always had high expectations for Paul, their eldest son, and had transmitted these feelings to him from his earliest childhood. His father, a successful thoracic surgeon, had his heart set on Paul becoming a doctor. The parents saw academic success as very important, and Paul did exceptionally

well in school. Although his teachers praised him for being an outstanding student, his parents seemed to take his successes for granted. In fact, they often made statements such as "You can do better". When he failed at something, his parents would make it obvious to him that they not only were disappointed but felt disgraced as well. This pattern of punishment for failures without recognition of successes, combined with his parents' high expectations, led to the development in Paul of an extremely negative self-concept.

From: Sue, D., Sue, D., & Sue, S. (1994). *Understanding abnormal behaviour*. Boston: Houghton Mifflin.

reinforcement with other losses (e.g. being made redundant). However, Lewinsohn and other behaviourists argued that the lack of social rewards is especially important in creating depression.

There is evidence supporting this theoretical approach. For example, Lewinsohn, Youngren, and Grosscup (1979) found that depressed individuals reported fewer rewards than non-depressed ones. In addition, the mood of depressed individuals improved when they began to experience more rewards.

Lewinsohn's behavioural theory oversimplifies the causes of depression. For example, many people experience major losses without becoming depressed, and the theory fails to explain how this happens. The theory also omits any consideration of other causes of depression such as genetic factors. In addition, it focuses on *external* factors (i.e. the patterns of behaviour exhibited by depressed individuals) and doesn't consider sufficiently *internal* factors (e.g. dysfunctional thoughts and beliefs).

Most importantly, evidence that depressed individuals have fewer positive rewards or reinforcements and experience more negative events does not prove that these factors *cause* depression. Perhaps individuals who are already depressed have low activity levels and so fail to receive much positive reinforcement. It is known that non-depressed people often find it unrewarding to interact with depressed individuals. For example, Gotlib and Robinson (1982) found that people interacting with a mildly depressed individual became less verbal, supportive, and cheerful.

Evidence suggesting that a reduced level of reinforcement accompanies or results from depression rather than helps to cause depression was reported by Lewinsohn, Hoberman, and Rosenbaum (1988). They assessed over 500 non-depressed people at the start of the study for various factors associated with depression (e.g. reductions in reinforcement; negative thinking; life stress). They then re-assessed them 8 months later to see who had become depressed. The key finding was that reductions in positive reinforcement did *not* predict subsequent depression—that makes it unlikely that lack of positive reinforcement causes depression.

Learned helplessness

Seligman's (1975) theory and research on learned helplessness have been very influential and have been developed into a more cognitive approach (see next section). **Learned helplessness** refers to the passive behaviour shown when animals or humans believe punishment is unavoidable. In his original studies, Seligman exposed dogs to electric shocks they couldn't avoid, sometimes by strapping them into a hammock. After that, the dogs were put in a box with a barrier in the middle. They were given shocks after a warning signal, but could escape by jumping over the barrier into the other part of the box. However, most of the dogs passively accepted the shocks and didn't learn to escape. Seligman described this as learned helplessness, and argued that it was very similar to the behaviour shown by depressed people.

Similar findings have been reported in studies on humans. For example, Hiroto (1974) used three groups of human participants: (1) those exposed to a loud noise they couldn't stop; (2) those exposed to a loud noise they could stop by pushing a button; and (3) those who didn't hear a loud noise. All participants were then placed in front of a rectangular box with a handle on of it and exposed to loud noise. Unknown to the participants, the noise could be switched off by

? Why might Seligman's experiments be considered unethical today?

? What is wrong with applying the results of a laboratory experiment on dogs to humans in society?

KEY TERM

Learned helplessness: passive behaviour produced by the perception that punishment is unavoidable.

moving the handle from one side to the other. Only the group previously exposed to a loud noise they couldn't stop showed learned helplessness by failing to move the handle.

How might the idea of learned helplessness be applied to domestic violence?

Learned helplessness is an important phenomenon, and the passive behaviour shown by dogs and humans in the learned helplessness situation resembles that shown by depressed individuals. It seems likely that a perceived inability to control stressful situations is common to learned helplessness and depression. It has been found that humans exposed to the learned helplessness situation subsequently have elevated scores on a depressive mood survey (Miller & Seligman, 1975). However, there are some limitations with this research. First, most of it has been done with non-human species, and we can only speculate on their emotional states. Second, depression in humans revolves around a lack of social rewards rather than physical punishment. Third, uncontrollable shocks nearly always produce anxiety as well as helplessness, but depression in humans is sometimes not accompanied by anxiety.

Cognitive Explanations

Abramson, Seligman, and Teasdale (1978) developed Seligman's learned helplessness theory into a much more cognitive theory by focusing on the thoughts of people experiencing learned helplessness. Abramson et al. started by arguing that people respond to failure in various ways:

- Individuals attribute the failure to an *internal* cause (themselves) or to an *external* cause (other people; circumstances). For example, your boyfriend finishes your relationship. You are convinced it is because of your moodiness (internal cause) or the fact that you live a long way apart (external cause).
- Individuals either attribute the failure to a stable cause (e.g. "My relationships will always fall apart) or to an unstable cause (e.g. "OK, he's gone, but there will be someone for me eventually").
- Individuals either attribute the failure to a *global* cause (e.g. "Everything always goes wrong) or to a *specific* cause (e.g. "My relationship has gone wrong, but my studies are going well").

Individuals suffering from depression see themselves as failures, and often attribute this to faults within themselves that cannot be changed.

People with learned helplessness attribute failure to internal, stable, and global causes. In other words, they feel personally responsible for failure, they think the factors causing that failure will persist, and they think that those factors will influence most situations in future. In view of these negative and pessimistic thoughts, it is no wonder that sufferers from helplessness are depressed.

The above cognitive theory was modified by Abramson, Metalsky, and Alloy (1989). They attached less importance than Abramson et al. (1978) to specific attributions and more importance to the notion that depressed individuals develop a general sense of hopelessness.

Beck and Clark (1988) put forward a cognitive theory resembling that of Abramson et al. (1978, 1989). They agreed that depressed individuals have unduly negative thoughts about themselves and the world around them. They described depressive schemas (mental representations) consisting of organised negative information stored in long-term memory. According to Beck and Clark (1988, p. 26):

> *The schematic organisation of the clinically depressed individual is dominated by an overwhelming negativity. A negative cognitive trait is evident in the depressed person's view of the self, world, and future . . . As a result of these negative maladaptive schemas, the depressed person views himself [sic] as inadequate, deprived and worthless, the world as presenting insurmountable obstacles, and the future as utterly bleak and hopeless.*

The term "cognitive triad" is used to refer to the three elements: the depressed person's negative views of himself or herself, the world, and the future.

Evaluation

Depressed individuals undoubtedly have the kinds of negative thoughts described by Abramson et al. (1978) and by Beck and Clark (1988). However, the crucial issue is whether these negative thoughts help to cause depression or whether they occur as a result of being depressed. The cognitive approach is much more important if the former is the case.

Much of the evidence suggests that negative thoughts and attitudes are caused by depression rather than the opposite direction of causality. However, reasonable evidence that negative and dysfunctional attitudes are involved in the development of major depressive disorder was reported by Lewinsohn, Joiner, and Rohde (2001). They measured negative or dysfunctional attitudes (e.g. "My life is wasted unless I am a success"; "I should be happy all the time") in adolescents not having a major depressive disorder at the outset of the study. One year later, Lewinsohn et al. assessed the negative life events experienced by the participants over the 12-month period. They also assessed whether they were suffering from major depressive disorder. Those who experienced many negative life events had an increased likelihood of developing a major depressive disorder only if they were initially high in dysfunctional attitudes. As dysfunctional attitudes were assessed *before* the onset of major depressive disorder, dysfunctional attitudes seem to be a risk factor for developing that disorder when exposed to stressful life events.

Supportive findings were reported by Evans, Heron, Lewis, Araya, and Wolke (2005), who assessed negative or dysfunctional self-beliefs in women in the

The cognitive triad

"I am helpless and inadequate"

"The world is full of insuperable obstacles"

"I am worthless, so there's no chance of the future being better than the present"

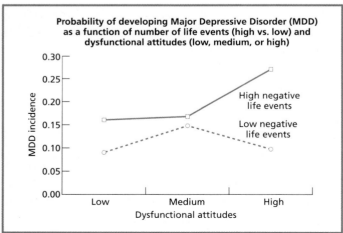

Probability of developing Major Depressive Disorder (MDD) as a function of number of life events (high vs. low) and dysfunctional attitudes (low, medium, or high)

High negative life events

Low negative life events

MDD incidence / Dysfunctional attitudes (Low, Medium, High)

Adapted from Lewinsohn, Joiner, and Rohde (2001).

eighteenth week of pregnancy. Women with the highest scores for negative self-beliefs were 60% more likely to become depressed subsequently than those with the lowest scores. They even found that negative self-beliefs predicted the onset of depression 3 years later, which is strong evidence that negative or dysfunctional beliefs can play a role in causing depression.

The cognitive approach to understanding the development of depression is limited in various ways. First, it is not clear why individuals develop negative or dysfunctional attitudes in the first place. Second, the cognitive approach ignores the role of genetic and other biological factors in the development of depression. Third, the cognitive approach tends to exaggerate the importance of cognitive factors at the expense of social factors (e.g. close personal relationships).

■ **Activity: Responding to everyday problems**

Compile a set of everyday situations or problems (e.g. not doing well in a particular subject, being late for school, not handing in homework). Ask each other about these problems and decide from the participants' answers which factors are involved. Draw up a table of responses like the examples here.

Example:

Question 1. Are there any subjects that you are not doing well in, and if so, why do you think this is?

Participant A: I'm hopeless at maths, it's my own fault. (Internal factor)

	Internal	External	Stable	Unstable	Global	Specific
Q1	✓					
Q2						

Participant B: I'm doing badly in maths, because the teacher is awful. (External factor)

	Internal	External	Stable	Unstable	Global	Specific
Q1		✓				
Q2						

Life Events

Individuals suffering from major depressive disorder often experience an above-average number of stressful life events before the onset of depression. Brown and Harris (1978) carried out an interview study on married women in London. They found that 61% of the depressed women had experienced at least one very stressful life event in the 8 months before interview, compared with 19% of non-depressed women. However, many women manage to cope with major life events without becoming clinically depressed. Of those women who experienced a serious life event, 37% of those without an intimate friend became depressed, compared with only 10% of those who had a very close friend.

The findings of Brown and Harris (1978) have been replicated several times. Brown (1989) reviewed the relevant studies. On average, about 55% of

Brown and Harris's (1978) study concluded that women who had the support of a very close friend after a serious life event were much less likely to become depressed than those who did not.

? What are the practical applications of theories of depression?

depressed patients had at least one severe life event in the months before onset compared to only about 17% of healthy controls.

The probability of life events leading to depression depends in part on each individual's cognitions or thoughts. Segal, Shaw, Vella, and Kratz (1992) studied ex-patients who had recovered from depression. The patients were assessed for the presence of dysfunctional attitudes (e.g. believing that partial failure is as bad as total failure) and then followed up for 12 months. Those patients who experienced the greatest number of life events were most likely to relapse into depression, especially when there was a *match* between the type of life event and the patient's particular concerns. More specifically, life events involving problems with achievement triggered a relapse most often in patients who were very self-critical, and life events involving interpersonal problems triggered a relapse most often in patients who were dependent.

Evaluation

There are three main limitations with most life-event studies. First, the information is obtained retrospectively several months afterwards, and so there might be problems remembering clearly what happened. Second, it is often unclear whether life events have caused depression or depression caused the life events. For example, marital separation might cause depression, but depression can play an important role in causing marital separation. Third, the meaning of a life event depends on the *context* in which it happens. For example, losing your job is very serious if you have a large family to support, but might be much less serious if you are nearing the normal retirement age and have a large pension. This third limitation doesn't apply to the research of Brown and Harris (1978), because they took full account of the context in which the life events occurred when assessing their seriousness.

Socio-cultural Factors

According to socio-cultural theorists (e.g. Nolen-Hoeksema, 1990), the incidence of major depressive disorder is influenced strongly by social and cultural factors. There is much supporting evidence. For example, we have seen that women experiencing serious life events are much less likely to develop depression if they have an intimate friend (Brown & Harris, 1978).

Another important social factor is marital status. Blazer, Kessler, McGonagle, and Swartz (1994) found that divorced individuals were more depressed than individuals who were married or who had never been married. It is hard to interpret this finding. It is possible that divorce helps to trigger depression. However, it is also possible that being depressed makes someone more difficult to live with and that this can lead to divorce.

Some cultural differences in rates of depression have been reported (Hammen, 1997). However, it is often difficult to interpret the findings. One reason is that the precise symptoms associated with depression vary across cultures. In general terms, depressed individuals in non-Western countries report mostly physical symptoms (e.g. fatigue, sleep disturbances), whereas guilt and self-blame are more common symptoms in Western countries.

One of the most striking facts about major depression is that it is twice as common in women in most countries of the world (Hammen, 1997). Why is there this gender difference? There are more explanations than you can shake a stick at, many of which assume that women's lives are more stressful than men's. There are various reasons why this might be so. First, women on average have fewer opportunities and are sometimes regarded as having lower status. Second, women are exposed to more stressors than men. Third, women are more likely than men to find themselves in situations providing limited control over their lives.

There is much support for the above assumptions. Women tend to be poorer than men, to have lower-status jobs, to have less adequate housing, and to face more discrimination, all of which are associated with depression (Brems, 1995). In addition, women typically spend more of their time than men engaged in child care and housework.

Women in many societies are more likely than men to be victims of sexual assault and child abuse. More generally, Kendler, Neale, Kessler, Heath, and Eaves (1993) found that women reported significantly more negative life events than men in the past year in several areas of life including marital problems, financial problems, interpersonal difficulties, work problems, and events happening to those in their social network. There is also evidence for gender differences in perceived control. LeUnes, Nation, and Turley (1980) found that women were more likely than men to show learned helplessness (discussed earlier) under laboratory conditions.

So far, we have focused on the societal pressures experienced by women. There is also evidence that the ways in which women cope with depression may increase its intensity. Nolen-Hoeksema (1991) found that depressed women tend to spend a lot of time thinking about their problems and to focus excessively on their emotions. By contrast, men are more likely to engage in problem solving or distraction (e.g. drinking alcohol).

Several social and cultural factors influence the development of depression. However, other factors are at least as important. For example, there are genetic factors, biochemical factors, behavioural factors, and cognitive factors.

? How might the diathesis-stress model be used to explain depression?

Conclusions

In this section and the previous one, we have seen that many factors contribute to the development of depression. Indeed, there are so many that you might be feeling somewhat bewildered. It helps to make sense of the findings if we relate them to the **diathesis–stress model**, according to which the occurrence of depression (or any other mental disorder) depends on two factors:

> **EXAM HINT**
> Use the fact that depression is not a single illness to conclude that to understand the causes a multiple perspectives are needed. The behavioural and cognitive explanations of depression can be linked, so use the fact that traditional behavioural explanations do not account for cognition as a criticism. Remember that there are different types of depression so you should link this to the need for an idiographic (individual-based) approach rather than a nomothetic (universal) approach.

1. *Diathesis*: a genetic vulnerability or predisposition to disease or disorder.
2. *Stress*: some severe or disturbing environmental event. Within this model, the term "stress" has a very broad meaning.

What is most important about this model is that diathesis or genetic vulnerability *and* stress are both necessary for major depressive disorder or bipolar disorder to develop.

The diathesis–stress model assumes that the development of depression involves a combination of *internal* factors (i.e. factors inside the individual) and

Diathesis–stress model: the notion that psychological disorders occur when there is a genetically determined vulnerability (diathesis) and relevant stressful conditions.

EXAM HINT

Do some research on epigenetics (the study of gene–environment interactions) to understand the variations in types of depression and within the families of depressives. This explanation can better account for such variations because it offers a more in-depth understanding of the Diathesis–Stress Model. It suggests that although there is a diathesis/genetic predisposition, the genes might or might not be switched on, depending on the individual's life experiences. The whole life course needs to be considered—prenatal, early and later childhood—as well as adulthood, because there are risk factors across the life stages.

external factors (i.e. environmental factors). Internal factors making an individual vulnerable to depression include genetic factors, biochemical factors, pre-existing dysfunctional beliefs, and lack of social support. External factors that can help to trigger depression include severe life events (especially major losses) and failures. This type of multi-factor approach to understanding depression is much more realistic than any single-factor approach focusing on only one determinant of depression.

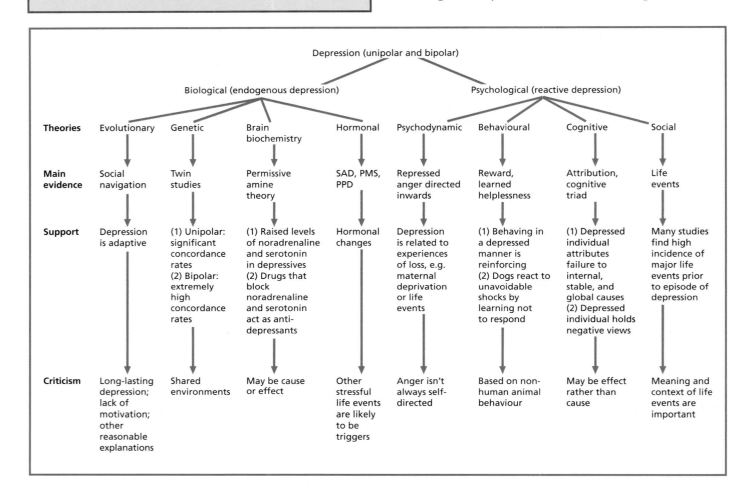

	Biological (endogenous depression)				Psychological (reactive depression)			
Theories	Evolutionary	Genetic	Brain biochemistry	Hormonal	Psychodynamic	Behavioural	Cognitive	Social
Main evidence	Social navigation	Twin studies	Permissive amine theory	SAD, PMS, PPD	Repressed anger directed inwards	Reward, learned helplessness	Attribution, cognitive triad	Life events
Support	Depression is adaptive	(1) Unipolar: significant concordance rates (2) Bipolar: extremely high concordance rates	(1) Raised levels of noradrenaline and serotonin in depressives (2) Drugs that block noradrenaline and serotonin act as anti-depressants	Hormonal changes	Depression is related to experiences of loss, e.g. maternal deprivation or life events	(1) Behaving in a depressed manner is reinforcing (2) Dogs react to unavoidable shocks by learning not to respond	(1) Depressed individual attributes failure to internal, stable, and global causes (2) Depressed individual holds negative views	Many studies find high incidence of major life events prior to episode of depression
Criticism	Long-lasting depression; lack of motivation; other reasonable explanations	Shared environments	May be cause or effect	Other stressful life events are likely to be triggers	Anger isn't always self-directed	Based on non-human animal behaviour	May be effect rather than cause	Meaning and context of life events are important

Depression (unipolar and bipolar)

SECTION SUMMARY
Psychological Explanations of Depression

Psychodynamic explanation

❖ According to Freud, depressed individuals react to the loss of an important relationship by directing repressed anger at the lost person towards themselves.

❖ Individuals whose needs weren't met or were gratified to excess during the oral stage are vulnerable to adult depression.

❖ Evaluation:

— Depression is caused in part by loss events.

— Depressed people direct anger at others rather than themselves.

— It is improbable that events during the oral stage influence the development of adult depression.

❖ Lewinsohn argued that depression results from a reduction in the level of reinforcement.   *Behavioural approach*

❖ Evaluation:

— Depression seems to cause a reduction in positive reinforcement rather than the other way around.
— There is insufficient emphasis on internal factors such as dysfunctional beliefs.

❖ Seligman argued that depression results from learned helplessness and perceived inability to control stressful situations.

❖ Evaluation:

— Learned helplessness is an important phenomenon.
— Depression in humans is typically associated with a lack of social reward rather than physical punishment.
— Seligman's approach de-emphasises cognitive factors.

❖ It has been argued that depressed individuals attribute failure to internal, stable, and global factors.   *Cognitive explanations*

❖ Beck argued that depressed people have the cognitive triad consisting of negative views about themselves, the world, and the future.

❖ Evaluation:

— As predicted, there is evidence that dysfunctional beliefs can help to trigger depression.
— It is unclear why people develop dysfunctional beliefs in the first place.
— Genetic and social factors are de-emphasised.

❖ Depressed patients often experience one or more severe life event in the months before onset of depression.   *Life events*

❖ Evaluation:

— It is often not clear whether life events have caused depression or depression has caused life events.
— The meaning of a life event depends on the context in which it occurs—this is often ignored.

❖ Social support can help to prevent depression.   *Socio-cultural factors*

❖ Women are much more likely than men to become depressed. This might be because they are exposed to more stressors and are regarded as having lower status.

❖ Other factors (e.g. genetic; cognitive) are also important

BIOLOGICAL THERAPIES FOR DEPRESSION

Biological therapies for depression mostly involve the use of drugs. As different drugs are used to treat patients with major depressive disorder (unipolar depression) and those with bipolar disorder, we will consider drug therapy for these two disorders separately. Patients with major depressive disorder are also sometimes treated with electroconvulsive therapy (ECT), and we will also consider the effectiveness of that form of treatment.

Drug Therapy: Major Depressive Disorder

Drug therapy has been used extensively in the treatment of patients suffering from major depressive disorder. The drugs used to treat major depression are also relevant to treating the depressed phase of bipolar disorder. We saw earlier that some experts have argued theoretically that depression involves a shortage of monoamines, which are a type of neurotransmitter including serotonin and noradrenaline. The evidence is inconsistent regarding the correctness of this theory, but it suggested that an effective therapy for depression might involve developing drugs that increase the supply of these neurotransmitters. Two groups of such drugs are the monoamine oxidase inhibitors (MAOIs) and the tricyclic antidepressants. The MAOIs work by inhibiting the enzyme monoamine oxidase, which results in increased levels of neurotransmitters such as noradrenaline and serotonin. Tricyclics also enhance the action of monamines in a slightly different way.

It could be argued that the tricyclics and the MAOIs are simply stimulants producing physiological activation rather than drugs that correct depressed patients' biochemical deficits. However, most of the evidence is inconsistent with that notion. Neither the tricyclics nor the MAOIs have much effect on the mood of healthy individuals who do not have chemical deficits or imbalances.

A third group of drugs for depression, the selective serotonin re-uptake inhibitors (SSRIs), is specific to serotonin. For example, fluoxetine (trade name Prozac) prevents the re-uptake of serotonin by the presynaptic neuron, so leaving the serotonin to have an enhanced effect on the postsynaptic neuron. The SSRIs were developed more recently than the MAOIs and tricyclics, but are now the most commonly used drugs to treat depression.

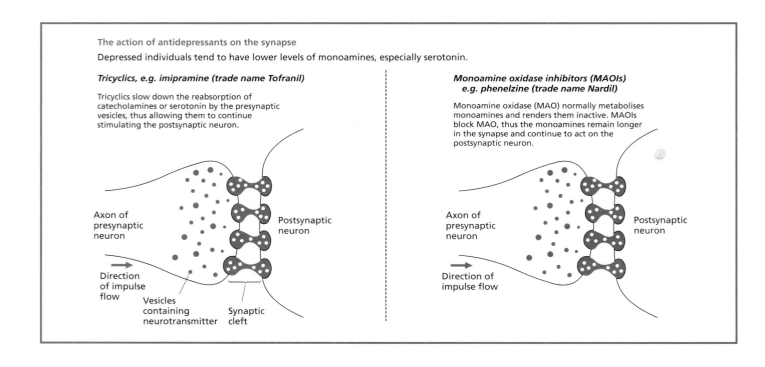

The action of antidepressants on the synapse
Depressed individuals tend to have lower levels of monoamines, especially serotonin.

Tricyclics, e.g. imipramine (trade name Tofranil)

Tricyclics slow down the reabsorption of catecholamines or serotonin by the presynaptic vesicles, thus allowing them to continue stimulating the postsynaptic neuron.

Axon of presynaptic neuron

Postsynaptic neuron

Direction of impulse flow

Vesicles containing neurotransmitter

Synaptic cleft

Monoamine oxidase inhibitors (MAOIs) e.g. phenelzine (trade name Nardil)

Monoamine oxidase (MAO) normally metabolises monoamines and renders them inactive. MAOIs block MAO, thus the monoamines remain longer in the synapse and continue to act on the postsynaptic neuron.

Axon of presynaptic neuron

Postsynaptic neuron

Direction of impulse flow

Effectiveness

The MAOIs, the tricyclics, and the SSRIs have proved consistently effective in the treatment of major depressive disorder, but the tricylics are generally more effective than the MAOIs, and produce fewer side effects. However, the tricyclics can produce dizziness, blurred vision, and dryness of the mouth, and can impair driving to a dangerous extent. It is not clear why the various drugs are ineffective with some patients. However, the tricyclics tend to be more effective with fairly severe forms of depression, perhaps because abnormalities in the levels of monoamines are most likely to be found in severely depressed patients. There can be a high relapse rate with tricyclics unless therapy is continued over a long period of time (Franchini, Gasperini, Perez, Smeraldi, & Zanardi, 1997).

The SSRIs are at least as effective as the tricyclics but possess some advantages. Depressed patients taking SSRIs are less likely to suffer from dry mouth and constipation than those taking tricyclics, and it is harder to overdose on SSRIs. The fact that there are fewer side effects with SSRIs than with the MAOIs or tricyclics means that problems of non-compliance (i.e. discontinuing medication, disregarding instructions on dosage and timing) are reduced. However, SSRIs conflict with other forms of medication and some side effects have been reported. For example, some depressed patients taking an SSRI reported reduced sex drive, nausea, insomnia, and excessive sweating (Dimidjian et al., 2006).

> **EXAM HINT**
>
> Use the treatment aetiology fallacy to evaluate treatments. This refers to the fact that just because the treatment works this does not mean that whatever the treatment targets, (such as biochemical imbalances in the case of drugs and ECT) was the cause of the disorder in the first place. A useful analogy is that an aspirin treats a headache but it is not a lack of aspirin that causes the headache.

Hollon, Stewart, and Strunk (2006) identified two types of effective treatment. First, there are treatments that work because they reduce or eliminate the processes causing the disorder (curative treatments). Second, there are treatments that work because they suppress the symptoms of a disorder without changing the underlying processes (palliative treatments). The beneficial effects achieved by curative treatments should remain after the end of treatment, whereas palliative treatments are likely to be followed by relapse. As we will see, the evidence suggests that drug therapy for major depressive disorder is palliative rather than curative.

DeRubeis et al. (2005) compared cognitive therapy with drug therapy involving mainly paroxetine (one of the SSRIs). Patients with major depressive disorder received 16 weeks of treatment with cognitive therapy or with paroxetine. Approximately 58% of the patients in each group showed considerable improvement as a result of treatment.

Hollon et al. (2005) studied those depressed patients who responded to treatment in the DeRubeis et al. (2005) study for a 12-month continuation period afterwards. There were three groups: (1) those who had received cognitive therapy but had no treatment during the continuation period; (2) those who had received drug therapy but had no treatment during the continuation period; and (3) those who had received drug therapy and continued to receive drug therapy throughout the continuation period.

Hollon et al. (2005) were most interested in how likely it was that patients in the three groups would relapse (i.e. have a recurrence of most of their symptoms). Of those withdrawn from cognitive therapy, 31% suffered a relapse, as did 47% of those who received drug therapy throughout. However, the most striking finding was that 76% of those withdrawn from drug therapy suffered a relapse.

? How would you explain
the fact that drugs
typically don't have the
same effect on all people?
What other factors might
be involved?

These findings strongly suggest that drug therapy is mainly a palliative treatment whereas cognitive therapy is a curative treatment. Thus, drug therapy is effective only for as long as depressed patients continue to take medication.

How effective is drug therapy in the treatment of patients with major depressive disorder who have previously received drug treatment? Typically, there is a poorer response to drug therapy among such patients. Leykin, Amsterdam, DeRubeis, Gallop, Shelton, and Hollon (2007) considered the effectiveness of drug therapy using the selective serotonin reuptake inhibitor paroxetine in patients with major depression. The recovery rate was nearly 60% among those who had never received drug therapy before but was under 20% among those who had received drug therapy for depression twice or more in the past.

Why was drug therapy for depression so ineffective with patients who had been given it in the past? The simplest possibility is that these patients are especially difficult to treat, which is why they had to return for more therapy. However, that explanation is wrong. Leykin et al. (2007) administered cognitive therapy to patients with major depressive disorder who had never received drug therapy in the past or had received it at least twice. Approximately 40% of patients in both groups recovered, indicating that those who have received much drug therapy previously are not very hard to treat. It is more likely that drug therapy affects biochemical functioning so that subsequent drug therapy has less impact on those patients who have received it previously.

Appropriateness

Drug therapy using any of the drugs we have discussed has repeatedly proved to be effective in the treatment of major depressive disorder. However, there are issues concerning the appropriateness of drug therapy. First, no antidepressant drug is effective with *all* depressed patients. Typically, about 30% of patients fail to respond to any given drug or show only very modest beneficial effects. However, patients who do not respond to one drug often respond to a different one, and drug therapists generally change a patient's drug if their first choice doesn't reduce his or her symptoms.

Second, it is not altogether clear *why* the various antidepressants reduce the symptoms of major depressive disorder. The MAOIs and tricyclics increase the levels of noadrenaline and serotonin, and the SSRIs increase serotonin levels. However, it would be an oversimplification to argue that low levels of these neurotransmitters are of central importance to the development or maintenance of depression.

Third, most drug therapy for depression is palliative rather than curative. That raises serious questions about the appropriateness of drug therapy given that patients want to be cured rather than having to continue taking drugs over long periods of time. However, it is likely that drug therapy is curative for some patients, even though it seems to be only palliative for most.

Fourth, and related to the third point, depressed patients treated by drug therapy often relapse because the therapy inappropriately fails to identify and treat the underlying factors responsible for depression. For example, depressed patients are typically concerned about past losses and their personal relationships, but these are not the focus of drug therapy.

Fifth, drug therapy is less effective in treating depression among those patients who have previously received drug therapy than among those who have not. The

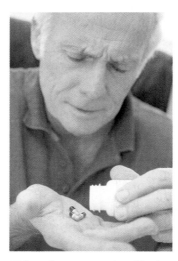

Although proven to be effective at reducing symptoms, the fact that most drug therapy for depression is palliative rather than curative raises questions about its appropriateness as a treatment.

finding that patients given drug therapy in the past are much more likely to recover if given cognitive therapy rather than more drug therapy suggests it is inappropriate to give drug therapy to such patients.

Electroconvulsive Therapy: Major Depressive Disorder

Electroconvulsive therapy (ECT) has been used extensively in the treatment of major depressive disorder. In ECT, an electric current is passed through the head to produce a convulsion. ECT used to produce broken bones, patient terror, and memory loss. However, various changes in treatment have almost eliminated these problems. First, the patient is given strong muscle relaxants to prevent or minimise convulsions. Second, the current is generally only passed through the non-dominant brain hemisphere rather than through both hemispheres. This reduces the danger of memory loss, although it also reduces the effectiveness of treatment. Third, anaesthetics are used to put patients to sleep during ECT, thus reducing substantially the chances of experiencing terror.

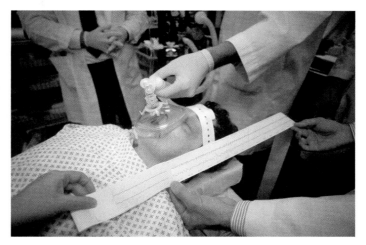

Electroconvulsive therapy (ECT) has been found to be quite effective in cases of severe depression, although the reasons why it might be effective are uncertain.

Many studies designed to assess the effectiveness of ECT have compared it against simulated ECT, in which patients are exposed to the equipment and believe falsely that they have received ECT. This is done to ensure that the beneficial effects of ECT are genuine and not simply a **placebo effect**—seeing the equipment and believing that you are receiving shocks might be enough to reduce symptoms in the absence of any actual shocks.

When is ECT used rather than antidepressant drugs in the treatment of major depressive disorder? The great majority of patients are treated initially with antidepressant drugs rather than by ECT. However, some patients have poor tolerance of antidepressants, or don't respond when given them; these patients are sometimes given ECT. Janicak, Davis, Gibbons, Ericksen, Chang, and Gallagher (1985) found that 80% of all severely depressed patients responded well to ECT, compared with 64% given drug therapy.

ECT is also often the treatment of choice in the case of patients with very severe depression when rapid reduction in symptoms is especially important. This can be essential in cases of severe depression in which suicide attempts are possible.

Effectiveness

How effective is ECT in the treatment of depression? The findings are encouraging. For example, Petrides et al. (2001) reported that between 65% and 85% of depressed patients had a favourable response to ECT. Pagnin, de Queiroz, Pini, and Cassano (2004) carried out a **meta-analysis** in which the effectiveness of ECT was compared with various types of antidepressant drugs and simulated ECT. ECT was more effective in

> **KEY TERMS**
> **Electroconvulsive therapy (ECT):** a form of therapy used to treat depressed patients, in which brain seizures are created by passing an electric current through the head.
> **Placebo effect:** positive responses to a drug or form of therapy based on the patient's beliefs that the drug or therapy will be effective, rather than on the actual make-up of the drug or therapy.
> **Meta-analysis:** an analysis in which all of the findings from many studies relating to a given hypothesis are combined for statistical testing.

the treatment of depression than antidepressants or simulated ECT. The findings led Pagnin et al. (2004, p. 13) to conclude that, "ECT is a valid therapeutic tool for treatment of depression, including severe and resistant forms." ECT is used mostly with patients suffering from major depressive disorder, but patients with bipolar disorder are sometimes exposed to it. Grunhaus, Schreiber, Dolberg, Hirshman, and Dannon (2002) compared the effectiveness of ECT with both groups. They found that 57% of the patients responded positively to ECT and there was no difference between the patients with major depressive disorder and those with bipolar disorder in responsiveness to the treatment.

> [?] What clinical characteristics of depression can be seen in Lucy Case Study?

CASE STUDY: ECT WAS MY MAGIC WAND

Lucy (a pseudonym) had her first bout of serious depression at university when she was only 20. Now 30 years old and a successful PA, she describes her twenties as a time of black despair. "It was actively horrific, all the time, every minute of every day. My depression always took the same form. It started with anxiety and morphed into black despair. I would wake up early and feel sick. Then I would feel a physical change coming over my body—my chest felt heavy and my limbs rinsed through with a mixture of worry and inertia", she says. Within a couple of days she would stop functioning properly, unable to wash her hair, prepare food, or think rationally. Even music became unbearable because it seemed so trite and unimportant. Through these years, she had had various therapies including about half a dozen different antidepressant drugs, cognitive-behavioural therapy, counselling, group therapy, art and drama therapy, and in-patient treatment.

Last year the depression got even worse. After 5 months, Lucy wasn't getting any better and her doctor recommended the last resort—ECT—and warned about side effects. Lucy agreed, and was too numb to feel much anxiety or apprehension. However, as soon as she awoke from the first ECT session she felt her old self, her old personality had returned, although she did feel a bit confused. She had more sessions, and although she did have memory problems and felt her brain was working more slowly, her doctor assured her that these were normal side effects and would pass, and they did. Brain imaging has shown that following ECT treatment brain-wave patterns are abnormal for about 3 months.

Lucy's experience is very encouraging but ECT isn't so good for every patient. However, Lucy says, "I'd urge anyone with serious depression to try it. If you truly are at absolute rock bottom, you shouldn't be put off by fear, because it isn't possible for you to feel any worse. They press a switch, and it makes you better."

What kinds of patient benefits most from ECT? This issue was addressed by de Vreede, Burger, and van Vliet (2005) in a study on patients with major depression. They identified four patient factors predicting good response to ECT: age above 65 years, the absence of a psychotic depression (involving more severe symptoms), the absence of a personality disorder, and responding well to antidepressants.

Appropriateness

ECT is often an effective form of treatment for major depressive disorder. However, there are concerns about its appropriateness. First, there is still no detailed understanding of precisely *why* ECT is effective. It has numerous effects on the brain, including affecting neurotransmission and probably producing structural changes in neuronal networks. However, it is hard to establish *which* effects are important in reducing depression. It seems reasonable to assume that a better understanding of how ECT has its beneficial effects would allow therapists to improve its effectiveness.

> [?] Given that the full implications of ECT are poorly understood, do you think it is ever right to administer such treatments to vulnerable patients?

Second, ECT is associated with various side effects, including memory loss and other cognitive impairments, which raise issues about its appropriateness. However, most of these problems are short-term rather than long-term.

Third, ECT is generally most effective at reducing symptoms when given to both hemispheres at a high dose. However, these are the conditions in which side effects are most common. Thus, therapists selecting the optimal dose have to strike a delicate balance between effectiveness on the one hand and unwanted side effects on the other.

Fourth, ECT seems to be less effective in the treatment of depression in patients who are below 65 years of age, who respond poorly to antidepressants, and who have psychotic depression and a personality disorder (de Vreede et al., 2005). Thus, the appropriateness of ECT depends on various personal characteristics of the patient.

Drug Therapy: Bipolar Disorder

It has proved considerably more difficult to find effective treatments for bipolar disorder than for major depressive disorder. Probably the most effective form of treatment for bipolar disorder is drug therapy based on lithium carbonate (sometimes referred to simply as lithium). Lithium stabilises levels of the neurotransmitter glutamate in the brain, and has beneficial effects on both manic and depressive episodes. Various suggestions have been made as to the mechanism by which it exerts its effects. One notion is that lithium alters potassium and sodium ion activity in neurons and hence transmission of nerve impulses.

> **? It has sometimes been suggested that manic depression is higher among very creative people, and that the manic phase of the disorder can particularly heighten creativity. How might this affect some sufferers' decisions about whether or not to take drug treatment such as lithium carbonate?**

CASE STUDY: STEPHEN FRY

The actor, presenter, and comedian Stephen Fry suffers from bipolar disorder. He was first referred to a psychiatrist when still at school. His condition was not diagnosed until he was 37, and he experienced despair, a suicide attempt, and self-abuse with alcohol and cocaine. "I always heard voices in my head saying what a useless bastard I am, but the voice is my own," he says. "It is my own voice, telling me what a worthless lump of shit I am."

Bipolar disorder, also known as manic depression, affects at least 1 in 100 people, so there are hundreds of thousands of sufferers in the UK, and about two thousand a year successfully commit suicide. Most bipolar people do not have therapeutic care; about 5% have psychological therapy and only a third have their mental state assessed annually.

Fry himself has rejected treatment as, although the depressions are dark and threatening, the manic episodes are valuable to him. He says, "I love my condition too. It's infuriating I know, but I do get a huge buzz out of the manic side. I rely on it to give my life a sense of adventure, and I think most of the good about me has developed as a result of my mood swings. It's tormented me all my life with the deepest of depressions while giving me the energy and creativity that perhaps has made my career."

Effectiveness

Lithium carbonate produces rapid improvement in most manic patients, and can delay the onset of depressive episodes in patients suffering from bipolar disorder. It reduces the occurrence of manic and depressed episodes in 80% of patients with bipolar disorder (Gerbino, Oleshansky, & Gershon, 1978). Lithium carbonate is also effective in preventing relapse. For example, Suppes, Baldessarini, Faedda, and Tohen (1991) found that the relapse rate for successfully treated bipolar disorder patients was 28 times greater among those who stopped taking lithium compared to those who continued to take it! In similar fashion, bipolar patients treated successfully with lithium were 24 times more likely to commit suicide if they stopped taking lithium than if they did not (Baldessarini, Tondo, & Hennen, 1999).

Geddes, Burgess, Hawton, Jamison, and Goodwin (2004) carried out a meta-analysis of studies on lithium therapy for bipolar disorder. Lithium was effective in preventing relapses after most of the symptoms had been eliminated, but its effectiveness was greater in preventing relapses of manic symptoms than of depressive symptoms.

Lithium also has the advantage of producing rapid results—it often produces significant improvements in patients' moods within 5–14 days. Before lithium was introduced, the suicide rate for bipolar disorder patients was about 15%, whereas it is now much lower.

Unfortunately, lithium can have serious side effects on the central nervous system, the cardiovascular system, and the digestive system. In addition, an overdose can be fatal. Discontinuation of lithium carbonate increases the chances that the symptoms of bipolar disorder will recur, so it tends to be used continously. However, the chances of relapse are much less if lithium is taken after the elimination of manic symptoms (Viguera, Nonacs, Cohen, Tondo, Murray, & Baldessarini, 2000).

Appropriateness

Lithium carbonate is an appropriate form of therapy for bipolar disorder in various ways. First, the symptoms of bipolar disorder are serious, and lithium typically reduces these symptoms rapidly. Second, the rapid action and overall effectiveness of lithium mean that there is a substantial reduction in the number of bipolar disorder patients committing suicide. Third, there is generally a long-term reduction in both manic and depressed episodes in patients who continue taking lithium.

In what ways is drug therapy based on lithium inappropriate? First, therapy is very limited, in that the dysfunctional beliefs and personal concerns of bipolar patients are not considered during the course of treatment. Second, lithium-based

? What are the risks associated with taking lithium?

Disorder	Drug/group of drugs	How they work	Drawbacks
Major depressive disorder (unipolar depression)	Monoamine oxidase inhibitors (MAOIs)	Inhibit oxidation of monoamines (neurotransmitters, including dopamine, serotonin, and noradrenaline), so that levels increase	A range of side effects
	Tricyclic antidepressants	As MAOIs	Dizziness, blurred vision, dry mouth
	SSRIs (e.g. Prozac)	As MAOIs, but mainly affect levels of serotonin	Preoccupation with suicide and violence
Depression (bipolar)	Lithium carbonate	Anti-mania, but mechanism is imperfectly understood	Side effects on central nervous system, cardiovascular, and digestive systems. Overdose can be fatal

therapy produces unwanted side effects involving the central nervous system, the cardiovascular system, and the digestive system. Third, there is a substantial risk of relapse if bipolar disorder patients stop taking lithium, which means that many patients take it over long periods of time. However, prolonged medication with lithium increases the chances of severe side effects.

SECTION SUMMARY
Biological Therapies for Depression

❖ Drugs used to treat depression include the MAOIs, the tricyclics, and the SSRIs.

❖ The SSRIs are at least as effective during treatment as the tricyclics and MAOIs, but have fewer side effects.

❖ The relapse rate following successful treatment is much higher following drug therapy than following cognitive or cognitive-behavioural therapy.

❖ Evaluation:

— Drug therapy is limited because it doesn't consider the psychological problems suffered by depressed patients.

— Drug therapy tends to be palliative rather than curative, and so often fails to produce long-term recovery.

— Drug therapy tends to be less effective when patients undergo a second or third course of treatment, perhaps because drug therapy alters biochemical functioning.

Drug therapy: major depressive disorder

❖ ECT involves passing an electric current through the patient's head to produce convulsions.

❖ It is used mainly with patients who do not respond well to drug therapy.

❖ ECT is generally effective in treating depression, especially in older patients without psychotic depression or personality disorder.

❖ Evaluation

— It remains unclear *why* ECT is effective.

— ECT can produce memory loss and is often regarded as a frightening procedure.

— ECT is typically not very effective with patients who respond poorly to antidepressants or who have personality disorder or psychotic depression.

Electroconvulsive therapy: major depressive disorder

PSYCHOLOGICAL THERAPIES FOR DEPRESSION

Psychodynamic Therapy

As we saw earlier, Freud argued that depression is caused by major actual or symbolic losses. Actual losses often involve the death of someone who was very important in the patient's life or the end of an intimate relationship. Individuals who are excessively dependent on other people are especially likely to develop depression after such a loss.

The original form of psychodynamic therapy was psychoanalysis, which was developed by Sigmund Freud 100 years ago. Freud argued that individuals whose needs weren't met during the oral stage of psychosexual development are vulnerable to developing depression in adulthood. The reason is that the failure to have their needs met causes low self-esteem and excessive dependence. Individuals whose needs were met to excess during the oral stage are also vulnerable to depression because they might become too dependent on others. In addition, depressed individuals have often lost someone who was very important in their lives. The repressed anger they feel towards the lost person is redirected to themselves.

Freud argued that it is crucial in therapy to uncover depressed patients' repressed memories and allow them to gain insight into the factors causing their depression. How can this be done? One of Freud's main methods was **free association**, which involves the client saying whatever comes into his or her mind. This method often doesn't work very well because the client might be reluctant to say what he or she is really thinking. However, long pauses in what the client says indicate that he or she is moving close to an important repressed idea. Skilled therapists regard the presence of long pauses as an indication that additional questioning and discussion are required.

Freud also made much use of dream analysis. According to him, we are much more likely to gain access to repressed material while dreaming than when we are awake. The reason for this is the existence of a censor in our minds that is more vigilant when we are awake—perhaps it nods off when we are asleep? Repressed material is included in our dreams, although generally in disguised form because of its unacceptable nature. Freud drew a distinction between the manifest content of dreams (the content as reported by clients) and the latent content of dreams (their true or underlying meaning). Part of psychodynamic therapy involves questioning clients about the manifest content of dreams to work out their latent content.

Freud's concepts were quite revolutionary for his time.

Psychodynamic theory and dream analysis

Freud hypothesised that in our dreams we realise those ideas, wishes, and needs that we have buried or repressed from our conscious mind because they are in some way unacceptable to us: perhaps they are socially unacceptable, or would for some other reason fill us with guilt or anxiety. Examples of this could be the inner conflicts between our id (primitive self), ego (socialised self), and super-ego (idealised self), or those between our libido (biological desires) and thanatos (turning away from pleasure), or others such as penis envy in females or Oedipal sexual desires for the opposite-sex parent. Dreams represent these thoughts and desires and their fulfilment in a form that does not threaten us or cause us pain (Freud, 1933).

Jung, a follower of Freud who later diverged to form his own psychodynamic theories, suggested that in our dreams we are able to access the stored memories of all humanity, dating back to our primeval ancestry, He called this the "collective unconscious". This could perhaps explain the dreams of inescapable pursuit or of falling as memories of highly emotionally charged events from other people in other times. He also believed that a main motivator or driving force was not sex but the search for the spiritual and mystic. Perhaps this combination of thoughts from the collective unconscious with desires for the awesome and wondrous could explain the apparently illogical narratives of dreams.

From Bentley, E. (2000). *Awareness: Biorhythms, sleep and dreaming*. Routledge, London.

KEY TERM

Free association: a technique used in psychoanalysis, in which the patient says the first thing that comes into his/her mind.

In the years since Freud developed psychoanalysis, numerous forms of psychodynamic therapy have emerged. There are two major differences between these newer forms of psychodynamic therapy and Freud's original approach. First, Freud focused on the patient as an individual and de-emphasised the importance of the patient's social relationships. By contrast, psychodynamic therapists nowadays accept that many of the problems experienced by depressed individuals revolve around their social relationships. Second, Freud was especially interested in exploring patients' childhood experiences in order to understand the origins of their depression. Contemporary psychodynamic therapists argue that the emphasis should be on patients' current problems because those problems are of central interest to patients.

Effectiveness

We will start by considering the use of psychodynamic therapy to treat major depressive disorder and then move on to bipolar disorder. In general, psychodynamic therapy (in line with most other forms of therapy) is more effective in treating major depressive disorder than bipolar disorder.

Many of the early studies on psychodynamic therapy in treating major depressive disorder suggested that it was of very limited effectiveness. However, the findings have been more encouraging with more modern forms of psychotherapy. Elkin et al. (1989) compared psychodynamic therapy focusing on the patient's current social interactions with cognitive-behavioural therapy. Both were of some effectiveness in reducing depressive symptoms and promoting recovery.

Psychodynamic therapy provides patients with insight into themselves and focuses on cognitive and emotional problems. It has been proven effective in the treatment of major depressive disorder.

Stronger evidence for the effectiveness of psychodynamic therapy in the treatment of major depressive disorder was discussed by Leichsenring (2001), who used the findings from a meta-analysis based on several studies to compare the effectiveness of psychodynamic therapy and cognitive-behavioural therapy. Leichsenring (2001, p. 401) concluded as follows: "In 58 of the 60 comparisons (97%) . . . no significant differences could be detected between STPP [short-term psychodynamic psychotherapy] and CBT/BT [cognitive-behavioural therapy/behaviour therapy] concerning the effects in depressive symptoms, general psychiatric symptomatology, and social functioning." Both forms of therapy were moderately effective in reducing the symptoms of depression.

What about the effectiveness of psychodynamic therapy in treating bipolar disorder? Much of the evidence is negative. For example, Colom, Vieta, Martinez, Jorquera, and Gasto (1998) considered studies in which psychodynamic therapy and cognitive-behavioural therapy had been used. There was no clear evidence that either form of therapy was effective across various measures such as hospitalisation, recurrence of the disorder, and suicidal behaviour.

The great majority of patients with bipolar disorder receive drug therapy. Typically, the drugs used can have serious side effects, leading many patients to discontinue treatment or to take their drugs on an irregular basis. Sajatovic, Valenstein, Blow, Ganoczy, and Ignacio (2007) argued that patients receiving only drug therapy often feel poorly informed about their condition and have little opportunity to use their self-management skills. Combining psychodynamic therapy with drug therapy not only makes patients better informed but also increases the chances they will take a more active role in managing their disorder. Sajatovic et al. discuss research indicating that psychodynamic therapy is of some value in treating bipolar disorder when used in combination with drug therapy.

Appropriateness

There are various ways in which psychodynamic therapy for depression seems appropriate. First, many of the problems experienced by depressed patients are cognitive in nature. Psychodynamic therapy focuses on providing patients with insight into themselves and their problems that will change their cognitive beliefs about themselves. Second, patients are most concerned about their current difficulties with personal and social relationships, and psychodynamic therapy increasingly focuses directly on such difficulties. Third, the fact that psychodynamic therapy is often effective in treating major depressive disorder provides support for its appropriateness.

In what ways is psychodynamic therapy inappropriate in the treatment of depression? First, many of the problems faced by depressed patients revolve around their loss of motivation and disengagement from the world. However, psychodynamic therapy doesn't address the motivational issue in a direct fashion.

Second, psychodynamic therapy focuses on cognitive and emotional problems experienced by depressed patients. As a result, it doesn't emphasise sufficiently patients' behavioural problems, such as their very low involvement in pleasurable activities.

Third, successful psychodynamic therapy requires the patient to participate fully in complex discussions with the therapist. However, depressed patients are often too passive and lacking in motivation to do this.

Fourth, psychodynamic therapy is designed to produce changes in the ways in which depressed patients regard themselves and the world, and such changes typically take a fairly long time to produce. As a result, depressed patients (whose outlook on life is generally pessimistic) often become discouraged when they don't experience any rapid improvement in their condition.

Fifth, psychodynamic therapy is less appropriate in the treatment of bipolar disorder than of major depressive disorder. As we have seen, bipolar disorder differs in many ways from major depressive disorder. It is a more serious condition and has proved much harder to treat. The "talking cure" that psychodynamic therapists provide is of limited usefulness when applied to the complexities of bipolar disorder.

Behaviour Therapy

Various forms of behaviour therapy have been used in the treatment of depression. For example, Lewinsohn et al. (1992) argued that a central problem for depressed individuals is the relative lack of positive reinforcement or reward in their lives. Accordingly, therapy needs to focus on persuading clients to become more involved in pleasurable events and activities. In addition, it is important to

> **EXAM HINT**
> Remember to assess the appropriateness of treatments by considering the following:
> - how effective the treatment is across different symptoms
> - the patient's level of functioning
> - the effect of the treatment on relapse rates
> - the patient's motivation to use the treatment versus drop-out rate
> - if the action of the treatment is fully understood
> - ethical issues.

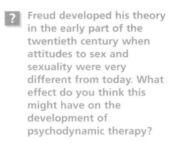 Freud developed his theory in the early part of the twentieth century when attitudes to sex and sexuality were very different from today. What effect do you think this might have on the development of psychodynamic therapy?

reward their non-depressive behaviours and not to reward their depressive ones. The therapist does this by praising the depressed client's constructive ideas and behaviour and ignoring his or her depressive ideas and behaviour. Finally, it is often useful to improve depressed patients' social skills.

Therapists use the client's responses on a Pleasant Events Schedule and an Activity Schedule to select activities that the client regards as pleasurable. The client is then encouraged to set up a weekly schedule for engaging in those pleasurable activities. The mood of depressed individuals often improves when they engage in additional pleasurable activities (Leenstra, Ormel, & Giel, 1995). However, the beneficial effects of Lewinsohn et al.'s (1992) version of behaviour therapy are generally greater when all the various techniques are used rather than just one (Jacobson et al., 1996).

A somewhat similar approach is based on behavioural interventions recommended by Beck, Rush, Shaw, and Emery (1979) and is sometimes known as behavioural activation. The central notion is that depressed individuals often remain depressed because they exhibit withdrawal and avoidance of interpersonal situations, distressing thoughts, distressing feelings, and so on. Behavioural activation involves becoming engaged in activities and situations that provide reinforcement or reward and that fit in with the individual's long-term goals. The client schedules daily activities, rates how much pleasure and sense of achievement are associated with each activity, and explores different forms of behaviour designed to achieve his or her goals.

Effectiveness

Behaviour therapy of the kinds we have discussed is of moderate effectiveness in treating major depressive disorder. However, two qualifications need to be made. First, depressed patients receiving behaviour therapy often exhibit less improvement than those receiving cognitive or drug therapy (Comer, 2001). Second, it has generally been argued that behaviour therapy is mainly effective with patients who have relatively mild depression. For example, the treatment guidelines of the American Psychiatric Association state that drug therapy should be used with moderately and severely depressed patients.

Evidence suggesting that behaviour therapy may be of more value than generally assumed was reported by Dimidjian et al. (2006) in a major study on patients with major depressive disorder. They compared the effectiveness of behavioural activation based on Beck et al.'s (1979) recommendations with that of cognitive therapy and of drug therapy using the SSRI paroxetine. There were no differences in improvement between the various treatments for patients who were less severely depressed at the outset. However, there were clear group differences for the more severely depressed patients. Full recovery among these patients was achieved by 56% of the patients receiving behaviour therapy compared to only 36% of those receiving cognitive therapy and 23% of those receiving drug therapy.

Behaviour therapy is of very little effectiveness in treating bipolar disorder. This is not altogether surprising if we consider the manic episodes experienced by patients with bipolar disorder. When patients are in a manic episode, they typically show increased activity and substantial involvement in pleasurable activities. Thus, they are not in need of behaviour therapy designed to increase the number of pleasurable activities in which they engage!

In any therapy, how does one know if effectiveness is due to the personal characteristics of the therapist rather than the therapy itself?

Appropriateness

Behaviour therapy for the treatment of major depressive disorder is generally appropriate. Some of the main symptoms of depression relate directly to motivation—depressed individuals are rather passive, and exhibit low levels of interest and of energy. It thus seems entirely appropriate for therapy to focus on persuading depressed patients to engage in activities they personally find reinforcing or rewarding. Most patients can see the value of increasing their involvement in such activities and this encourages them to continue with treatment.

In what ways is behaviour therapy inappropriate for the treatment of major depressive disorder? First, behaviour therapy doesn't directly address the various *cognitive* symptoms of depression, including feelings of hopelessness and helplessness, a negative self-concept, and recurring thoughts of suicide or death.

Second, it would seem appropriate in treatment to start by identifying *why* a patient has a very low level of motivation and numerous negative thoughts about themselves and the world. By contrast, the emphasis in behaviour therapy is on changing the patient's behaviour rather than focusing on the reasons for his/her depressed state.

Third, there is a danger with behaviour therapy that the underlying problems (e.g. loss of an important relationship) are not addressed. As a result, patients may show recurrence of their depressive symptoms.

Cognitive and Cognitive-behavioural Therapy

The person who has probably contributed most towards the development of cognitive therapy for depression is Aaron Beck. In 1976, Beck argued that therapy for depression should involve uncovering and challenging the negative and unrealistic beliefs of depressed clients. Earlier, we discussed Beck's notion of the "cognitive triad", which consists of negative thoughts that depressed individuals have about themselves, about the world, and about the future. Depressed clients typically regard *themselves* as helpless, worthless, and inadequate. They interpret events in the *world* in an unrealistically negative and defeatist way, and they see the world as posing obstacles that cannot be handled. The final part of the cognitive triad involves depressed individuals seeing the *future* as totally hopeless, because their worthlessness will prevent any improvements occurring.

According to Beck et al. (1979), the first stage of cognitive therapy involves the therapist and the client agreeing on the nature of the problem and the goals for therapy. This stage is called collaborative empiricism. The client's negative thoughts are then tested out by the therapist challenging them or by the client engaging in certain forms of behaviour between therapy sessions. It is hoped that the client will come to accept that many of his or her negative thoughts are irrational and unrealistic. For example, a depressed client who argues that people are always avoiding him or her can be asked to keep a diary of specific occasions on which this happens. It is very likely that it happens much less often than the patient imagines.

Cognitive therapists differ among themselves in their approach towards their clients. However, the main common features were identified by Beck and Weishaar (1989, p. 308):

Cognitive therapy consists of highly specific learning experiences designed to teach patients: (1) to monitor their negative, automatic thoughts (cognitions); (2) to recognise the connections between cognition, affect,

See *A2-Level Psychology Online* to download a podcast containing an interview with Dr Mark Williams on Mindfulness-based Cognitive Therapy (MBCT)—a new framework for treating depression.

? In what ways might a person's thoughts about themselves influence the way they react in a particular situation?

Think of an occasion when you felt helpless or worthless. Could you try to reinterpret the situation in a more positive way?

Common irrational beliefs

- I must be loved or liked by every significant person I meet
- I must be perfect if I am to be worthwhile
- The world will end if things are not as I want them to be
- My unhappiness is not under my own control and I am powerless to change things
- I should worry about bad things happening
- It is better to put off dealing with anything unpleasant than to face it
- I need a stronger person to depend on
- My problems are the result of my past

and behaviour; (3) to examine the evidence for and against distorted automatic thoughts; (4) to substitute more reality-oriented interpretations for these biased cognitions; and (5) to learn to identify and alter the beliefs that predispose them to distort their experiences.

Increasingly over the years, cognitive therapists have realised that it is important to focus on changing depressed individuals' behaviour as well as their ways of thinking about themselves and the world around them. As a result, cognitive therapy nowadays generally has sufficient emphasis on behavioural change to make it better described as "cognitive-behavioural therapy". Thus, cognitive-behavioural therapy builds on cognitive therapy. Kendall and Hammen (1998) identified the four basic assumptions underlying cognitive-behavioural therapy:

1. Patients typically respond on the basis of their *interpretations* of themselves and the world around them rather than on the basis of what is *actually* the case.
2. Thoughts, behaviour, and feelings are all interrelated and all influence each other. Thus, it would be wrong to identify one of these factors (e.g. behaviour) as being more important than the others.
3. For therapeutic interventions to be successful, they need to clarify and to change the ways people think about themselves and the world around them.
4. It is very desirable to change both the client's cognitive processes and his or her behaviour, because the benefits of therapy are likely to be greater than when only cognitive processes or behaviour are changed.

■ **Activity: How do you feel?**
It's your birthday and friends have arranged a get-together, but just before you go out to meet you get an e-mail from your closest friend saying he or she won't be there. No "sorry", no explanation, just a full stop.

	Irrational/negative	Rational/positive
Thoughts	S/he has sent a very offhand e-mail, why is s/he being so unpleasant?	Maybe s/he has had a bad day at work, or broken up with a friend, or had a row at home
Emotions	Hurt, upset, feeling not respected or liked, feeling rejected as a friend	Disappointed, don't understand, but hope to meet up very soon to sort this and be friends again and have fun
Behaviour	Be too cool to notice her/him next time you meet, act like you are just an acquaintance	Call her/his mobile and be nice, arrange to meet for a chat and a laugh

Effectiveness

There is convincing evidence that cognitive and cognitive-behavioural therapy are both effective in treating major depressive disorder. One of the largest studies was reported by Elkin (1994). Depressed patients were assigned to various groups, including Beck's cognitive therapy, treatment with the tricyclic antidepressant drug imipramine, and a placebo group that received no specific treatment. Cognitive and drug therapy both led to almost total elimination of depressive symptoms in about 55% of patients who completed treatment. This was a much higher recovery rate than achieved by the placebo group. The main difference between the cognitive and drug therapy groups was that there was a reduction in depressive symptoms more rapidly in the drug group.

Cognitive therapy and drug therapy were compared in more recent research by deRubeis et al. (2005) and Hollon et al. (2005). As these studies were discussed in the section on drug therapy, I will mention the key findings only briefly. Consistent with the findings of Elkin (1994), deRubeis et al. found that cognitive therapy and drug therapy were comparably effective by the end of treatment, with 58% of patients showing considerable improvement. However, the findings were very different when those patients who had responded well to treatment were followed up by Hollon et al. (2005) over the following 12 months. The relapse rate was 31% among patients who had received cognitive therapy, but it was far higher (76%) among those who had received drug therapy. Even those who continued to receive drug treatment during the 12-month period were more likely to relapse (47%) than patients who had previously received cognitive therapy.

The above findings suggest that cognitive therapy is a curative treatment that focuses on the mechanisms underlying depression. By contrast, drug therapy is mostly a palliative treatment that suppresses depressive symptoms only as long as drugs continue to be administered. Supporting evidence was reported by Segal, Kennedy, Gemar, Hood, Pedersen, and Buis (2006). Drug therapy and cognitive-behavioural therapy were equally effective by the end of treatment, and there was a comparable reduction in dysfunctional or negative attitudes in patients receiving each type of therapy. After the end of treatment, patients who had recovered from depression were made to feel sad. This led to an increase in dysfunctional or negative attitudes in patients who had received drug therapy but not in those who had received cognitive-behavioural therapy. These findings suggest that the cognitive changes were much more superficial and easily disrupted among patients given drug therapy than those given cognitive-behavioural therapy.

Segal et al. (2006) related the changes in dysfunctional attitudes produced by an induced sad mood to relapse into depression over the following 18 months. Regardless of the form of treatment, those individuals who showed the greatest increase in dysfunctional attitudes were most likely to relapse. If we put all these findings together, we can see why cognitive and cognitive-behavioural therapy are so effective. They produce long-lasting beneficial changes in patients' dysfunctional attitudes so they are relatively unlikely to relapse back into depression.

How effective are cognitive and cognitive-behavioural therapy in treating bipolar disorder? These forms of therapy have been used much less often in treating bipolar disorder than major

EXAM HINT

Compare the effectiveness of different treatments to better assess their effectiveness. Note how Segal et al. (2006) made a direct comparison with cognitive-behavioural therapy versus drug treatments. Prepare a revision aid of the effectiveness and appropriateness of each form of treatment so that you can draw comparisons about which treatments are most effective.

depressive disorder, and have typically been used in combination with drug therapy. The limited evidence suggests that both forms of therapy are moderately effective. Lam, Tam, Shiah, Yatham, and Zis (2000) compared patients with bipolar disorder receiving only drug therapy with patients receiving cognitive therapy as well as drug therapy over a 30-month period. There were two main findings. First, the cognitive therapy patients spent 12% less time than the drug-only patients in bipolar episodes. Second, the patients receiving cognitive therapy reported better mood states and social functioning, and fewer dysfunctional attitudes about goal attainment.

Jones (2004) reported similar findings from studies in which cognitive-behavioural therapy was or was not combined with drug therapy in the treatment of bipolar disorder. Patients who received cognitive-behavioural therapy had fewer depressive symptoms, better social functioning, and a lower risk of relapse.

Innovations in CBT for depression

Researchers at Oxford University are addressing one of the criticisms of cognitive-behavioural therapy (CBT): that it neglects the cognitive symptoms of depression, such as maladaptive thinking. Two maladaptive cognitive processes involved in depression are negative interpretation bias, where a sufferer interprets an ambiguous event (such as a friend walking past him or her without a look or greeting) as hurtful, and negative intrusive mental imagery, which involves involuntary and very distressing mental images about the past or future, such as being rejected or humiliated. These negative cognitions lead to increased depth of depression and challenging them by asking for alternative explanations of behaviours, or learning to pair a different cognitive task with the upsetting image so as to interfere with and overcome that image, are promising strategies being explored. The focus is on developing access to positive information and positive mental image development.

Appropriateness

Most of the symptoms of patients with major depressive disorder are basically cognitive. They have dysfunctional attitudes and beliefs about themselves, the world, and the future, and these attitudes create a sense of hopelessness and helplessness. Thus, it is entirely appropriate for cognitive therapy to have as a central goal the changing of such negative and irrational attitudes into ones that are more positive and realistic. Cognitive-behavioural therapy is even more appropriate in that it also focuses on increasing depressed patients' involvement in pleasurable and rewarding activities.

In what ways are cognitive and cognitive-behavioural therapy inappropriate? First, it is important to consider precisely *why* depressed patients have negative beliefs about themselves, the world, and the future. If (as is often the case) those beliefs are based on realistic concerns, then it seems inappropriate for therapy not to emphasise those concerns. Second, the central problems experienced by depressed patients often revolve around personal relationships, especially close ones. Cognitive and cognitive-behavioural therapists sometimes don't consider these relationships sufficiently. Third, many depressed patients successfully treated by cognitive or cognitive-behavioural therapy subsequently show relapse and a re-occurrence of their symptoms. This suggests that therapy might sometimes simply suppress patients' negative and dysfunctional beliefs

EXAM HINT

Note that you need to have covered the issues of classification and diagnosis, clinical characteristics, explanations, and treatments of depression fully because you do not know which area will be asked about in the exam. A question divided into parts could ask you about the issues of classification and diagnosis in one sub-part, the clinical characteristics in another, and the explanations in another.

rather than eliminating them. However, recent findings indicating that the relapse rate is much less following cognitive or cognitive-behavioural therapy than following drug therapy suggests this is not a major problem.

SECTION SUMMARY
Psychological Therapies for Depression

Psychodynamic therapy

❖ Psychodynamic therapy has moved from a focus on the individual and childhood experiences to one on social relations and current experiences.
❖ Psychodynamic therapy has become increasingly effective in treating major depressive disorder.
❖ Evaluation:
  — Psychodynamic therapy doesn't focus directly on patients' loss of motivation and non-involvement in pleasurable activities.
  — Patients receiving psychodynamic therapy sometimes become discouraged at the slow rate of improvement in their condition.

Behaviour therapy

❖ Behaviour therapy is based on the assumption that depressed patients have insufficient positive reinforcement in their lives and so need to become more engaged in pleasurable activities.
❖ Behaviour therapy has generally been found to be more effective with mildly depressed patients than with severely depressed ones.
❖ Evaluation:
  — Behaviour therapy doesn't directly address the cognitive symptoms of depression.
  — Since behaviour therapy doesn't focus on patients' underlying problems, there is a danger that the symptoms of depression will recur.

Cognitive and cognitive-behavioural therapy

❖ Cognitive therapists assume that depressed patients have unrealistically negative beliefs about themselves, the world, and the future.
❖ Cognitive-behavioural therapy involves changing patients' behaviour as well as their cognitive beliefs.
❖ Cognitive and cognitive-behaviour therapy are often as effective as drug therapy, but with the advantage that the relapse rate is much lower.
❖ Evaluation:
  — These forms of therapy don't pay sufficient attention to the reasons why depressed patients have dysfunctional beliefs in the first place.
  — Cognitive therapy sometimes suppresses rather than eliminates dysfunctional beliefs.

FURTHER READING

There is very thorough but easy-to-read coverage of all aspects of depression in Hammen, C. (1997). *Depression*. Hove, UK: Psychology Press.

See *A2-Level Psychology Online* for some interactive quizzes to help you with your revision.

REVISION QUESTIONS

In the exam, questions on this topic are out of 25 marks, and can take the form of essay questions or multi-parted questions. You should spend about 35 minutes on each of the questions below, which aim to test the material in this chapter. In the exam, make certain you know if you have covered an anxiety disorder, schizophrenia, or depression as your psychopathology topic, and then choose the correct question.

1. (a) Discuss the issues which apply to diagnosing
       depression.   (5 marks)
   (b) Outline psychological explanations for depression.   (10 marks)
   (c) Comment, referring to research studies, on one
       explanation of depression.   (10 marks)
2. Describe and evaluate, referring to research studies,
   biological explanations of depression.   (25 marks)
3. Discuss the use of biological and psychological therapies
   in the treatment of depression.   (25 marks)

See *A2-Level Psychology Online* for tips on how to answer these revision questions.

Psychopathology: Anxiety Disorders—Phobias

By Michael W. Eysenck

A number of disorders are classified as "anxiety disorders" because they share one clinical characteristic: anxiety. Anxiety is an adaptive response that is important to ensure survival. It is sometimes very valuable for an animal (or human) to experience anxiety because anxiety places it in a state of heightened arousal ready to respond to an immediate danger. However, anxiety can become a chronic (long-lasting) and disabling response. An individual with an anxiety disorder experiences an intensity of anxiety very disproportionate to any threat that is posed. Anxiety disorders are worryingly common. For example, more than 20 million Americans and about 5 million British people are affected by an anxiety disorder every year, with women being more likely to be affected than men.

DSM-IV-TR [the *Diagnostic and Statistical Manual*, 4th edition, revised; American Psychiatric Association (APA), 2000] and ICD-10 [*International Classification of Diseases* (WHO), 1992] are the main systems for diagnosing and classifying mental disorders. According to these publications, the anxiety disorders include:

- phobias: phobic anxiety disorders
- obsessive compulsive disorder
- generalised anxiety disorder
- panic disorder
- reaction to severe stress and adjustment disorder (e.g. post-traumatic stress disorder).

We will be considering the various phobic disorders in this chapter; obsessive compulsive disorder is discussed in Chapter 13.

Phobias involve a high level of fear of some object or situation, with the level of fear being so strong that the object or situation is avoided whenever possible. Indeed, the main characteristic the phobias have in common is avoidance of the feared stimuli or situations. There are various different categories of phobia: specific phobia, **social phobia**, and **agoraphobia**. There are some important

> **KEY TERMS**
> **Social phobia:** a disorder in which the individual has excessive fear of most situations, and will often avoid them.
> **Agoraphobia:** an anxiety disorder in which there is fear of public and other situations from which it might be hard to escape in the event of a panic attack.

? What are some problems with diagnosing strictly on the basis of the DSM-IV criteria?

similarities between them, but also some important differences. For example, social phobia and agoraphobia are both serious disorders because they involve avoiding social situations and public places, respectively. By contrast, specific phobias often involve avoidance of certain creatures (e.g. spiders), which typically has a much less disruptive effect on the patient's everyday life. Accordingly, when discussing any given issue, I will sometimes deal with each type of phobia in turn before providing an overall summary.

CLINICAL CHARACTERISTICS OF PHOBIC DISORDERS

We will consider the clinical characteristics of the three types of phobia in turn, starting with specific phobia, which involves strong and irrational fear of some specific object or situation. Specific phobias include fear of spiders and of snakes, but there are hundreds of different specific phobias. The following is an account of what specific phobia is like from a patient with spider phobia (Melville, 1978, p. 44):

Unusual phobias include triskaidekaphobia, the fear of the number 13; batophobia, fear of being close to high buildings; and nephophobia, a fear of clouds.

Seeing a spider makes me rigid with fear, hot, trembling, and dizzy. I have occasionally vomited and once fainted in order to escape from the situation. These symptoms last 3 or 4 days after seeing a spider. Realistic pictures can cause the same effect, especially if I inadvertently place my hand on one.

DSM-IV-TR identifies four major subtypes of specific phobia:

1. Animal type.
2. Natural environment type: this includes fear of heights, fear of water, and fear of storms.
3. Blood-injection-injury type.
4. Situational type: this includes fears about being in various situations such as in a plane, a lift, or an enclosed place.

More unusual phobias: dextrophobia, fear of objects at the right side of the body; xanthophobia, fear of the colour yellow; and genuphobia, fear of knees.

In addition, a fifth category, labelled "other type", covers all specific phobias that don't fit any of the four major subtypes. According to DSM-IV-TR (APA, 2000), the following are the major diagnostic criteria for specific phobia:

? What are the benefits of having classification systems based on categories?

- Marked and persistent fear of a specific object or situation.
- Exposure to the phobic stimulus nearly always produces a rapid anxiety response.
- The individual recognises that his or her fear of the phobic object or situation is excessive.
- The phobic stimulus is either avoided or responded to with great anxiety.
- The phobic reactions interfere significantly with the individual's working or social life, or he or she is very distressed about the phobia.
- In individuals under the age of 18, the phobia has lasted for at least 6 months.

EXAM HINT

You need to know the clinical characteristics of phobias but you should only use this material in the exam if it has been asked for in a sub-part (a) AO1 question. Do not include them if the question asks you to consider the explanations because simply describing the clinical characteristics is not part of the explanations.

There are fewer criteria for specific phobia in ICD-10, but they overlap with those in DSM-IV-TR. First, anxiety must be restricted to the presence of the phobic object or situation. Second, the phobic object or situation is avoided whenever possible. Third, the symptoms produced must be directly caused by anxiety.

CASE STUDY: A PHOBIA

A young student in his first year at university was referred to a therapist after seeking help at the student health centre. During initial interviews he spoke of feeling frightened and often panicking when heading for his classes. He claimed he felt comfortable in his room but was unable to concentrate on his work or to face other people. He admitted to fears of catching syphilis and of going bald. These fears were so intense that at times he would compulsively scrub his hands, head, and genitals so hard that they would bleed. He was reluctant to touch door handles and would never use public toilets. The student admitted that he knew his fears were irrational, but felt that he would be in even more "mental anguish" if he did not take these precautions.

In later sessions with the therapist, the student's history revealed previous concerns about his sexual identity. As a child he harboured feelings of inferiority because he had not been as fast or as strong as his peers. These feelings were reinforced by his mother, who had not encouraged him to play rough games in case he got hurt. At puberty, the student had also worried that he might be sexually deficient. At a summer camp he had discovered that he was underdeveloped sexually compared with the other boys. He had even wondered if he was developing into a girl. Although he did in fact mature into a young man, he worried constantly about his masculine identity, even fantasising that he was a girl. The student admitted that at times his anxiety was so great that he considered suicide.

Adapted from Kleinmuntz (1974).

Approximately 11% of Americans develop a specific phobia at some point in their lives (Comer, 2001). In Europe, the United States, and Canada at least twice as many females as males develop specific phobia (Comer, 2001). Specific phobia is generally not a very serious condition, which explains why almost 90% of people with a specific phobia don't seek treatment for it. Specific phobias generally start during childhood.

Social phobia

Social phobia involves extreme concern about one's own behaviour in social situations and about the reactions of others. Halgin and Whitbourne (1997, p. 215) provided a concrete example of someone suffering from social phobia:

> *Ted is a 19-year-old college student who reports that he is terrified at the prospect of speaking in class. His anxiety about this matter is so intense that he has enrolled in very large lecture classes, where he sits at the back of the room . . . Sometimes he rushes from the classroom and frantically runs back to the dormitory.*

The DSM-IV-TR (APA, 2000) diagnostic criteria for social phobia are as follows:

- Marked and persistent fear of social or performance situations involving exposure to unfamiliar people or possible scrutiny by others lasting at least 6 months. There is concern about humiliating or embarrassing oneself.
- Anxiety is usually produced by exposure to the social situation.
- There is a recognition that the fear is excessive and/or unreasonable.
- There is significant distress or impairment.

The diagnostic criteria for social phobia in ICD-10 resemble those in DSM-IV-TR. One criterion is

Stage-fright: an example of fear when facing the scrutiny of others.

Yet more unusual phobias: captoptrophobia, fear of mirrors; lachanophobia, fear of vegetables; pogonophobia, fear of beards.

that anxiety is restricted to particular social situations, and another is that there is frequent avoidance of those social situations.

Social phobia is a serious condition because the phobic reactions of social phobics interfere significantly with their working and/or social life. Social phobia is more common in females than in males with about 70% of sufferers being female. In any given year, approximately 8% of people experience social phobia. Patients with social phobia tend to be relatively young (late teens to late twenties), unmarried, and of lower socio-economic class.

Agoraphobia

Agoraphobia is an anxiety disorder in which there is great fear of open or public places. This fear can be so great that agoraphobics are often reluctant to leave the safety of their own homes. Agoraphobia on its own is rather rare. In most cases, patients who develop agoraphobia already suffer from panic disorder, and so the disorder becomes panic disorder with agoraphobia. The fact that agoraphobics typically also suffer from panic disorder is important in understanding agoraphobia—agoraphobics try to avoid open or public places from which escape would be difficult if they were to experience a panic attack. Thus, they are frightened of what might happen to them in public places rather than the public places themselves.

Before discussing the criteria for panic disorder with agoraphobia, we will consider the definition of a panic attack. According to DSM-IV-TR (APA, 2000), a panic attack involves intense fear or discomfort, with four or more bodily symptoms suddenly appearing. These symptoms include palpitations, shortness of breath, accelerated heart rate, a feeling of choking, nausea, sweating, chest pain, feeling dizzy, and fear of dying. Panic attacks can be distinguished from other types of anxiety by the fact that they are typically short in duration and of great intensity.

The DSM-IV-TR criteria for panic disorder with agoraphobia are as follows (APA, 2000):

- Recurrent unexpected panic attacks.
- At least one panic attack has been followed by at least 1 month of worry about the attack, concern about having more panic attacks, or changes in behaviour resulting from the attack.
- Agoraphobia, in which there is anxiety about being in situations from which escape might be hard or embarrassing in the event of a panic attack.
- The situations are either avoided, endured with marked distress, or manageable only with the presence of a companion.

According to ICD-10, one of the main criteria for agoraphobia is that anxiety is largely restricted to: crowds, public places, travelling away from home, and travelling alone. Another criterion is that there is frequent avoidance of the situations causing anxiety.

Approximately 3–4% of people develop panic disorder with or without agoraphobia during the course of their lives. Similar percentages have been found in many countries and ethnic groups. About 75% of those suffering from agoraphobia or panic disorder with agoraphobia are female. One likely reason why men show less agoraphobic avoidance than women is because they are more likely to drink heavily so that they can go out in public.

Panic disorder
↓
Produces anxiety that an attack might occur
↓
Embarrassment about having an attack out in public
↓
Agoraphobia + panic attack

? Can you suggest reasons why more women are agoraphobic than men?

CASE STUDY: LYNN, AN AGORAPHOBIC FOR 8 YEARS

Friday 19th December
Today has been the biggest challenge. I woke up and immediately felt anxious. Too much time in bed and too much time to think have caused this. From 7 a.m. all I could think about was "I need to go out, I haven't been out in 2 days, what if I can't do it again". I sat and thought about it, and thought about it and thought about it. In the end I was so worked up that I could feel the panic attack getting closer. I ran to my bedroom and got dressed and went out. I knew if I just faced the problem instead of sitting thinking about it, I would feel much better. It worked. I went out and walked my usual route and felt fine. I enjoyed it actually even though it was freezing and pouring with rain. I ended up back in bed after this. Still not well at all and while suffering from the cold it is probably not a great idea to walk in the rain. But mentally I feel far better.

Saturday 20th December
Arrrghhh maybe that walk was a bad idea. I. AM. SO. ILL!!! There is no hope of me leaving my bed today. But I can rest easy and not obsess about not getting out again. I also have the added joy of looking after my three nephews tonight. I can barely look after myself right now.

Sunday 21st December
I feel sooo much better! Got up and took two of the boys out for a walk. We were out for quite a while. On returning home I learned my dad was heading out to do some Christmas shopping. I quickly jumped in the car with him and asked him to take me for a spin. I haven't been in the car since Tuesday so I wanted to prove to myself that I can still do it. We went around the usual route and then for some reason my dad took a wrong turn. Well of course the panic hit me immediately. I shouted that he would need to find somewhere to turn. The panic really does come over me in waves. One minute I felt it rise from my tummy to my head and then it would go down again. I think if I can mentally talk myself through this I will be ok but when taking the wrong turn my head just went "NO NO NO".

How does Lynn's account tie in with what you know about agoraphobia?
http://www.livingwithagoraphobia.blogspot.com/

SECTION SUMMARY
Clinical Characteristics of Phobic Disorders

❖ Specific phobia involves strong and irrational fear of some specific object. It is generally not a very serious condition.

❖ Social phobia involves extreme concern about one's own behaviour in social situations and about the reactions of others. It interferes significantly with working and social life.

❖ Agoraphobia involves great fear of open or public places. The fact that it is nearly always accompanied by panic disorder suggests that agoraphobics are frightened of having a panic attack in public.

ISSUES SURROUNDING THE CLASSIFICATION AND DIAGNOSIS OF PHOBIC DISORDERS

Two important issues relating to classification and diagnosis are reliability and validity. **Reliability** is the extent to which a measure (e.g. diagnostic system) produces *consistent* or accurate findings. For example, a diagnostic system would be highly reliable if patients are assigned to the same diagnoses on different occasions or with different clinical psychologists or psychiatrists making the diagnoses.

Validity is the extent to which a measure is actually measuring what it is intended to measure. For example, do patients receiving a diagnosis of social phobia actually have that mental disorder rather than a different one? Any diagnostic system designed to assess the various phobias needs to have good reliability and validity. Note that it isn't possible to have high validity in the

KEY TERMS

Reliability: the extent to which a method of measurement or a research study produces consistent findings across situations or over time.
Validity: the soundness of the measurement tool; the extent to which it is measuring something that is real or valid.

? What is the difference between validity and reliability?

absence of reliability—if a diagnostic system produces very inconsistent diagnoses over time, then it can't be valid. However, a diagnostic system can be reliable but not valid—it can produce consistent results but fail to be assessing what it claims to be assessing.

We now move to a more detailed analysis of validity with regard to evaluating diagnostic or classification systems. Four types of validity will be considered, the first three of which were emphasised by Davison, Neale, and Kring (2004):

- *Content validity*: high content validity means that the given form of assessment, such as interview or checklist, succeeds in eliciting adequate information from patients concerning all of the symptoms of the phobia in question.
- *Criterion validity*: involves considering various aspects of the behaviour of those diagnosed with a given phobia. High criterion validity means that those with a diagnosis of, say, social phobia, differ in predictable ways from those not receiving that diagnosis.

? What is the difference between criterion and construct validity?

- *Construct validity*: this type of validity is more theoretical in nature than the others. It involves testing hypotheses based on our understanding of the particular phobia. For example, we might predict that patients diagnosed with social phobia would underestimate their own social skills. It is sometimes hard to know what to do if a hypothesis isn't supported. In the example, it might mean that the diagnostic assessment was inaccurate or that the hypothesis itself was at fault.
- *Predictive validity*: this is concerned with the extent to which we can use the diagnosis of, say, social phobia, to predict the eventual outcomes for patients. Suppose, for example, that most social phobics respond well to a given form of treatment but that nevertheless it generally took a long time for recovery to occur. Since we would be able to predict the eventual outcome (in this case recovery) reasonably well from the diagnosis, this would indicate high predictive validity.

EXAM HINT

Remember reliability refers to *consistency*. This means that DSM or ICD is reliable as a means of diagnosing phobias if clinicians using it give patients with similar symptoms the same diagnosis, both in terms of actually diagnosing phobic disorder and the subtype. A lack of reliability inevitably reduces validity because this refers to whether they have been given the correct diagnosis.

Validity?

Sam gets really embarrassed by little mistakes, such as stumbling on an uneven bit of pavement. She feels people are looking at her and thinking she is stupid or clumsy. When she did stumble, she didn't go out into town again for days. She also finds it really daunting to speak out in front of others, such as at work, and even avoids going out for a coffee or a drink to relax after work because it's not relaxing for her, but fills her with anxiety about her own behaviour and the response from others.

Do you think Sam has a disorder?

How could you explain her behaviour if she was 15 years old?

Would your view be different if Sam was in fact 30 years old? Why?

This shows that other factors can affect diagnosis—such as being an adolescent!

We will now consider some general problems with reliability and validity of diagnosis. After that, in the "Assessment" section, we will move on to more specific issues relating to the four types of validity we have just discussed. As indicated earlier, DSM-IV and ICD-10 are the two major systems for the classification and diagnosis of mental disorders. They are both categorical systems, with diagnosis leading patients to be assigned to a given category or mental disorder. Categorical systems are limited because they assume that having a given disorder (e.g. agoraphobia) is all-or-none—you have or have not got the disorder. In fact, reality is not that neat and tidy, as is indicated by two kinds of findings discussed below.

First, many individuals who aren't diagnosed with a phobia because they don't meet all the relevant criteria nevertheless have many of the symptoms. For example, according to DSM-IV, one criterion for social phobia is that the patient has had marked and persistent fear of various social situations for at least 6 months. This means that someone who has marked and persistent fear of such situations for 5 months hasn't got social phobia! More generally, there are millions of shy and socially anxious individuals who lead normal lives despite having most of the symptoms of social phobia. In similar fashion, there are also millions of people who are very frightened of snakes and/or spiders, but the fear isn't quite strong enough to qualify as a specific phobia. The validity of DSM-IV and ICD-10 is reduced by the strict and arbitrary criteria used in diagnosis. Why are these strict criteria used, then? The answer is reliability is increased by using very explicit and detailed criteria.

Second, there is considerable evidence for **comorbidity**, in which a patient has two or more mental disorders at the same time. For example, about 50% of social phobics have one or more related disorders such as depression, substance abuse, agoraphobia, or generalised anxiety disorder (Rachman, 2004). Many individuals with social phobia also have avoidant personality disorder, in which there is persistent anxiety in social situations and great sensitivity to being evaluated negatively by others. One of the few differences between social phobia and avoidant personality disorder is that those with social phobia accept that they have a problem and would like to overcome it (Rachman, 2004). Comorbidity is also found with other phobias. For example, patients with agoraphobia often suffer from panic disorder or depression.

> ? What concerns may arise when treating a patient with psychiatric comorbidity?

Many social phobics also suffer from avoidant personality disorder. Comorbidity complicates the process of making an accurate diagnosis, owing to the overlap in symptoms.

Why does comorbidity cause problems for reliability and validity of diagnosis? It suggests there is overlap between the symptoms of any given phobia and those of various other disorders, which makes it hard to discriminate between disorders. As a result of comorbidity, we can't assume that all patients with a given phobia have equally severe symptoms. Those with a given phobia and other mental disorders are generally more difficult to treat than those who only have the given phobia.

Assessment

There are various ways in which patients can be assessed to decide on the appropriate diagnosis. The methods used include interviews, checklists, and medical records. However, patients are generally diagnosed mainly on the basis of one or more interviews with a therapist or other expert. Some interviews are unstructured and informal. This can help to establish good rapport between patient and therapist. However, it is difficult to assess the information obtained from unstructured interviews, and so reliability and validity of diagnosis are generally both low (Hopko, Lejuex, Armento, & Bare, 2004).

Semi-structured interviews are probably the best form of assessment, and we will discuss two examples of such interviews. First, there is the Structured Clinical Interview for DSM-IV-Patient Version (SCID-I/P). This is a semi-structured interview that typically lasts just over 60 minutes. An open-ended interview is

> **KEY TERM**
>
> **Comorbidity:** the presence of two or more disorders in a given individual at the same time.

? What are the benefits of using an interview schedule?

followed by systematic questions concerning symptoms and current and lifetime disorders. It is a reasonably reliable and valid assessment procedure (Comer, 2001).

Second, there is the Anxiety Disorder Interview Schedule for DSM-IV (ADIS-IV). Many of the symptoms assessed by the ADIS-IV via semi-structured interview are initially rated on a yes/no basis, with degree of severity being rated for those symptoms that are present. Brown, DiNardo, Lehman, and Campbell (2001) carried out a thorough investigation of the reliability of DSM-IV as a way of diagnosing the anxiety disorders and depression. What happened was that 1400 patients were interviewed twice with the second interview occurring within 2 weeks of the first one. The interviews were based on the criteria for the various disorders contained in DSM-IV.

Brown et al.'s (2001) found that reliability in the form of inter-rater agreement was excellent for specific phobia, social phobia, and panic disorder with agoraphobia. Inter-rater agreement was higher for the various phobias than for other mental disorders such as generalised anxiety disorder and major depressive disorder. Why was that? All the phobias are associated with a clear behavioural symptom (avoidance of the feared stimulus or situation) that makes it relatively easy for therapists to diagnose them.

Brown et al. (2001) examined the factors associated with diagnostic disagreements between the two interviewers. Three factors were of particular importance. First, the main reason for unreliability of diagnosis with specific phobia and social phobia related to the "threshold" issue—did the patient's symptoms cause sufficient distress or interference with his or her life to warrant a phobia diagnosis? Sometimes one interviewer would decide that the threshold level of distress or interference had been exceeded whereas the other did not.

Second, patients' reports of their symptoms sometimes changed between interviews, even though they occurred close together in time. Most of these changes probably reflected genuine changes in patients' symptoms over time.

Third, the interviewers sometimes made errors. For example, patients would describe their symptoms in the same way on both interviews, but the interviewers would categorise them in different ways. Alternatively, the interviewers would simply miss important information being communicated by the patient.

We turn now to issues relating to validity. What about content validity, which refers to the extent to which a diagnostic system addresses all of the relevant symptoms of any given disorder? Major semi-structured interviews such as ADIS-IV and SCID-I/P have high content validity because they have been carefully constructed to cover all symptoms of phobias contained in DSM-IV.

Criterion validity refers to the extent to which those receiving a given diagnosis (e.g. agoraphobia) differ from those not given the diagnosis in predictable ways. There is evidence for criterion validity. For example, agoraphobia and social phobia are both serious conditions because they greatly limit patients' ability to function properly in their social and working lives. As expected, most of those diagnosed with agoraphobia or social phobia report significant problems of work and social adjustment (Mataix-Cols et al., 2005). There was less evidence of impaired adjustment in specific phobics, because it is generally a much less serious condition. Schneider et al. (1994) found that over 50% of people with social phobia reported impairment in areas of life including education, employment, family relationships, marriage/romantic relationships, and friendships. The fact that patients with a wide range of other mental disorders also have impairments in several areas of life means these findings provide only weak evidence for criterion validity.

Construct validity is concerned with the extent to which theoretical predictions concerning a given disorder are supported by the evidence. The diagnosis of the phobias has reasonable construct validity. For example, as is discussed more fully later, cognitive theorists argue that a central problem in social phobia is that patients have the mistaken belief that their social behaviour is less adequate than is actually the case. Rapee and Lim (1992) obtained support for this prediction. Social phobics rated their own social performance as being significantly worse than the ratings given by independent judges.

Finally, we consider predictive validity, which is the ability to predict eventual outcomes (e.g. recovery). Agoraphobia and social phobia are much more serious conditions than specific phobia. As a result, we would expect that successful treatment for agoraphobia and social phobia would generally be harder to achieve and would take much longer than for specific phobia. As predicted, social phobia and agoraphobia typically require several months' treatment, and some patients don't respond well to treatment. By contrast, Ost (1989) used one-session exposure to their feared stimuli with specific phobics. He reported that, "90% of the patients obtained a clinically significant improvement . . . which was maintained after an average of 4 years."

HOW SCIENCE WORKS: RESEARCHING DISORDERS
A psychological disorder can make life personally and socially difficult for both the sufferer and for his or her family and friends. This means that researching the disorder has special ethical concerns as this general area of psychopathology is what is known as socially sensitive. You could produce a pamphlet as an advice tool, aimed at researchers into this sort of area. You would need to identify the social sensitivity of such research, and give advice, including the British Psychological Society (BPS) guidelines, on how to deal with the sufferers, their families, and other involved people—what to do, how to do it, what to avoid. Obviously this needs to be very clear, whilst not interfering with research ideas. You might also want to include other advice such as the importance of having your ideas evaluated by others before they are operationalised.

SECTION SUMMARY
Issues Surrounding the Classification and Diagnosis of Phobic Disorders

❖ A good diagnostic system should be reliable. It should also possess good content, criterion, construct, and predictive validity.

❖ Comorbidity makes it hard to discriminate among mental disorders and causes problems for reliability and validity.

❖ Semi-structured interviews such as the SCID-I/P and ADIS-IV have very high reliability. This is so in spite of difficulties concerning whether a patient's symptoms are sufficiently serious to justify diagnosing phobia.

❖ Major semi-structured interviews have good content validity. They also have reasonable criterion validity in terms of predicting how impairing a given phobia will be.

❖ Construct validity is good, because theoretical predictions have been supported. Finally, predictive validity is good, with recovery generally being achieved much faster for specific phobia than for social phobia or agoraphobia.

BIOLOGICAL EXPLANATIONS OF PHOBIC DISORDERS

Many explanations of the development of phobias have been offered. They can be divided broadly into biological explanations and psychological explanations, although some explanations combine biological and psychological factors. I will consider biological explanations in this section of the chapter, and will then move on to psychological explanations in the next section.

Genetic Factors

Much research on biological factors associated with phobias has focused on possible genetic factors. Most evidence has come from twin studies, although some family studies have also been carried out. Twin studies distinguish between monozygotic or identical twins and dizygotic or fraternal twins. Identical twins share 100% of their genes, whereas fraternal twins share only 50% of their genes. The crucial measure in twin studies is the **concordance rate**—the chance that one twin has a given condition given that the other twin does. If genetic factors are important, then the concordance rate will be higher for identical than for fraternal twins.

Specific phobia

Specific phobias probably depend in part on genetic factors. Fyer et al. (1990) found that 31% of close relatives of individuals with specific phobias also had a phobia. More striking findings were reported by Ost (1989) in a study on people with blood phobia. In 64% of the cases, these blood phobics had at least one close relative who also suffered from blood phobia. The findings from these studies are consistent with the notion that genetic factors are involved. However, if you observe a relative with a specific phobia, it may increase your chances of developing a specific phobia. If this is the case, it would provide evidence for the importance of observational learning (discussed later).

? If one of your relatives has suffered from a mental disorder, what reasons are there for you not to worry that you may also develop the same disorder?

The four major models of abnormality

There are four major models of abnormality, which were covered in your AS level studies. Each of these models provides explanations of the origins of mental disorders, and each is associated with certain forms of treatment.

The *biological model* proposes that the causes of mental disorders resemble those of physical illnesses. Clusters of symptoms can be identified and a diagnosis made, followed by suitable treatment. There is some evidence that infection, genetics, biochemistry, and/or neuroanatomy may account for mental disorders. If the causes are physical then the treatments should be physical as well, and the biological model recommends direct manipulation of the body processes, such as using drugs or electroconvulsive therapy (ECT). This model is less appropriate for disorders with psychological symptoms, such as phobias.

The *behavioural model* suggests that mental disorders are caused by learning maladaptive behaviour via conditioning or observational learning. Logically, anything that is learned can be unlearned using the same techniques. The approach is best for explaining (and treating) those disorders that emphasise external behaviours, such as phobias. The behavioural model is oversimplified and more appropriate to non-human animal behaviour. Ethically, there are advantages such as the lack of blame attached to a person with a mental disorder, but the treatments can be psychologically painful and manipulative.

According to the *psychodynamic model*, the roots of mental disorder are to be found in unresolved conflicts and traumas from childhood. This model may focus too much on the past at the cost of understanding current problems, and too much on sexual problems rather than interpersonal and social issues. Ethical concerns include the problem of false memory syndrome ("remembering" non-existent childhood traumas) and the sexist nature of the theory. The approach is best for conditions where patients have insight, such as some anxiety disorders, though it has not proved very effective with phobias.

The *cognitive model* takes the view that distorted and irrational beliefs are crucially involved in most mental disorders. Limitations of the cognitive model include the problem of whether distorted thinking is a cause or an effect, and the circularity of the explanations. The model suggests that individuals are in part to blame for their problems. The cognitive-behavioural model is a recent and popular development, combining both cognitive and behavioural approaches.

KEY TERM

Concordance rate: if one twin has a disorder or condition, the likelihood that the other twin also has it.

Expressing inheritance

When psychologists explore the extent to which a characteristic is inherited they use a variety of measures.

The concordance rate expresses the extent to which two measures are in agreement. For example, if 20 twin pairs are studied and in 18 of them both had developed schizophrenia, this would produce a concordance rate of 18/20 or 90%, which is very high concordance. Alternatively one can correlate the IQ scores of two individuals, and the degree of correlation shows us how concordant they are.

Monozygotic (identical) twins have the same genes (100% concordance) whereas dizygotic (non-identical) twins and siblings are genetically 50% similar.

Heritability is a measure of the relationship between: (1) the variance of a trait in the whole population; and (2) the extent to which that variance is due to genetic factors.

This is expressed as a heritability ratio and calculated by dividing the genetic variance of a characteristic by the total variance (genetic variance/total variance). The genetic variance is calculated using, for example, concordance rates. This percentage is then divided by the amount of variance within the population. A heritability ratio of 1.0 means that all the variance in a population can be accounted for in terms of genetic factors.

So far as the phobias are concerned, heritability estimates make considerable use of information from twin studies. However, it is difficult to disentangle genetic and environmental effects because identical twins generally experience more similar environmental conditions than fraternal twins as well as being more similar genetically. Distel, Vick, Willemsen, Middeldorp, Merckelback, and Boomsma (2008) studied the heritability of blood-injury, agoraphobic, and social phobic fears, and came up with heritability estimates of between +0.36 and +0.51. These estimates suggest that genetic factors are of moderate importance in producing phobias. Note that any assessment of heritability is specific to a given population—it is not a universal figure that applies to all cultures at all times.

Stronger evidence based on twin studies involving 1708 female twins was reported by Kendler, Karkowski, and Prescott (1999). They obtained estimates of heritability (a measure of the involvement of genetic factors in which the higher the figure the greater the role of genetic factors). Heritability was moderately high for blood-injury phobia, animal phobia, and situational phobia.

Social phobia

As far as social phobia is concerned, Fyer, Mannuzza, Chapman, Liebowitz, and Klein (1993) discovered that 16% of the close relatives of social phobics developed the same disorder against only 5% of the relatives of individuals without social phobia. However, Skre, Onstad, Torgersen, Lygren, and Kringlen (1993) found that the concordance rate for social phobia was similar in identical and fraternal twin pairs, leading them to conclude that social phobia is caused mainly by environmental influences. Kendler et al. (1999) argued that the involvement of genetic factors in various phobias had been *underestimated* because unreliability of diagnosis of phobias reduces the concordance rate. They took account of this when analysing the data from numerous female identical and fraternal twins. They concluded that genetic factors are moderately important in the development of social phobia.

? What type of environmental influences may be associated with the development of a phobia?

Agoraphobia

As far as panic disorder with agoraphobia is concerned, Torgersen (1983) considered pairs of identical and fraternal twins at least one of whom had the disorder. The concordance rate was 31% for identical twins against 0% for fraternal twins, but the

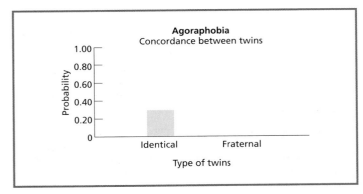

Torgersen (1983) studied twins suffering from agoraphobia.

sample size was small. Harris, Noyes, Crowe, and Chaudhry (1983) found that the close relatives of agoraphobic patients were more likely to be suffering from agoraphobia than were the close relatives of non-anxious individuals. Noyes, Crowe, Harris, Hamra, McChesney, and Chandry (1986) found that 12% of the relatives of agoraphobics also had agoraphobia, and 17% suffered from panic disorder. Both of these percentages figures are significantly higher than for healthy controls, thus supporting the genetic argument.

Phobias compared

From the evidence discussed so far, it seems that genetic factors play some role in the development of most phobias. Are there any important differences in the genetic factors influencing different phobias? Bienvenu, Hettema, Neale, Prescott, and Kendler (2007) recently provided a positive answer in a study on 7800 twins. They found close links between the genetic factors influencing social phobia and those influencing individual differences in extraversion and neuroticism (susceptibility to negative mood states). More specifically, individuals genetically liable to be introverted and high in neuroticism are most likely to develop social phobia. Precisely the same pattern was true of agoraphobia. However, there were much weaker links between the genetic factors influencing personality and those influencing the development of specific phobia. Thus, the genetic factors underlying specific phobia differ from those underlying agoraphobia and social phobia.

Evaluation

What are the limitations of twin and family studies of phobic disorders?

The evidence from twin and family studies suggests that genetic factors are of moderate importance in determining panic disorder with agoraphobia, specific phobia, and social phobia. In their twin study, Kendler et al. (1999) found very little difference in the importance of genetic factors in determining social phobia and various specific phobias. However, genetic factors were somewhat more important in agoraphobia.

There are various limitations with the evidence. First, as Kendler et al. pointed out, we can have confidence in concordance rates if the reliability of diagnosis is high. However, this is often not the case. Second, it may be misleading to assume that genetic factors are specific to a *single* form of phobia. There is evidence that genetic vulnerability is more general than that; for example, if you have a twin suffering from social phobia you might be at risk of developing panic disorder with agoraphobia as well as social phobia (Kendler, 1995). However, there is also some specificity. As we have seen, genetic liability to low extraversion and high neuroticism is associated much more with agoraphobia and social phobia than with specific phobia (Bienvenu et al., 2007).

Third, environmental factors may explain at least some of the reported effects. For example, a close relative of someone suffering from a phobia may develop the same phobia because he or she imitates the behaviour displayed by the patient or because they are both exposed to the same environment (observational learning). With twins, the higher concordance rates for identical than for fraternal

Assumptions of biological explanations

All mental disorders have a physical cause (micro-organisms, genetics, biochemistry, or neuroanatomy)

- Mental illnesses can be described in terms of clusters of symptoms.
- Symptoms can be identified, leading to the diagnosis of an illness.

Diagnosis leads to appropriate physical treatments.

twins may occur in part because identical twins are exposed to more similar environments. The fact that twins have a sibling of exactly the same age as themselves may in and of itself affect their thoughts and behaviour. If that is the case, it is dangerous to *generalise* from what is true of twins to everyone else.

Evolutionary Explanation

One of the most intriguing facts about specific phobias is that people rarely develop phobias for potentially dangerous objects invented only fairly recently. For example, few people have car phobia, even though around the world tens of thousands of people a year are killed by cars. However, millions of people in Western cultures have spider or snake phobias, even though they have very rarely seen spiders or snakes, and most of the ones they have seen are harmless.

Seligman (e.g. 1970) used the term **preparedness** to describe the tendency for members of a species to be more likely to develop phobias to some objects than to others. According to Seligman and Hager (1972, p. 450), "The great majority of phobias are about objects of natural importance to the survival of the species . . . The theory does not deny that other phobias are possible, it only claims that they should be less frequent, since they are less prepared." We are most likely to develop phobias to objects that have "threatened survival, potential predators, unfamiliar places, and the dark" (Seligman & Hager, 1972, p. 465).

The notion that we are biologically predisposed to acquire certain conditioned responses more easily than others can be applied to the main phobias of humans. For example, objects that were probably associated with danger to primitive humans include insects, heights, and small animals. Consider poisonous snakes, for example—you may only have one chance to escape and so there should be survival value in having an innate predisposition to avoid them. This line of thinking helps to explain many specific phobias.

The concept of preparedness is useful in explaining agoraphobia, which involves a fear of public places. It may have been advantageous for our remote ancestors to spend most of their time in their own territory thus avoiding the dangers of straying too far from it. In similar fashion, our remote ancestors may have had much to fear from other people, and this could help to explain the origins of social phobia.

> **■ Activity: Are you ready?**
> You can test the suggestion that we are born biologically prepared to fear certain animals.
> You will need to draw up a list of 20 animals, ones that you feel people think are truly harmful, e.g. a tiger, and ones that you think are harmless, e.g. a worm. Then you can ask your sample to rate each animal on a kind of Likert scale: 1 = not really frightening, 2 = quite frightening, 3 = extremely frightening.
> Collate your findings and ask yourself, "Do the findings support the idea that humans are born with a readiness to fear animals that are genuinely a threat to us?"

Findings

Tomarken, Mineka, and Cook (1989) presented participants with a situation in which various stimuli were sometimes followed by electric shock. The stimuli used included snakes, spiders, and a damaged electrical outlet. Participants exaggerated how often snakes and spiders had been followed by electric shock but didn't do so with the damaged electrical outlet. Thus, we are more likely to associate the fear of an electric shock with objects dangerous in our evolutionary past (e.g. snakes, spiders) than with potentially dangerous objects that have only recently come into existence (e.g. damaged electrical outlets).

EXAM HINT

Note that the evidence for genetic factors comes mainly from twin and family studies. However you should also consider the evolutionary explanations of learned preparedness as evidence for a genetic basis.

KEY TERM

Preparedness: the notion that each species finds some forms of learning more "natural" and easier than others.

Monkeys are prepared to fear dangerous objects, but not neutral objects

Cook and Mineka (1989) reported good evidence for preparedness in a study on laboratory-bred monkeys who had never previously encountered a snake. The monkeys watched a monkey reared in the wild reacting with strong fear to a snake. After that, they very rapidly acquired a fear of snakes when shown a toy snake. However, no fear developed in these monkeys when they saw a wild-reared monkey apparently reacting with strong fear to a rabbit. Presumably the monkeys responded so fearfully to the toy snake because of biological preparedness.

The notion of preparedness has not fared so well when used in clinical contexts. In the first place, we have no way of being certain about the extent to which various fear stimuli were actually dangerous in our ancestral past. This issue is often addressed by asking experts in Darwinian theory to produce ratings of such stimuli. We would expect that most of the specific phobias treated by therapists would be prepared ones rather than non-prepared ones. The evidence is mixed, but much of it fails to support that prediction (Davey, 1995).

Another reasonable prediction is that specific phobias which we are biologically prepared to develop would be more serious and resistant to treatment. This is *not* what has been found. Davey (1995, p. 290) concluded his review of the evidence as follows: "Degree of preparedness was found to be unrelated to outcome of therapy, duration of phobia, suddenness of onset . . . and severity of impairment."

Evaluation

The notion of biological preparedness seems to provide a plausible account of many findings, such as our greater susceptibility to snake and spider phobia than to car phobia. In addition, there is reasonable laboratory evidence indicating that we develop fear responses more readily to snakes and spiders than to other stimuli.

What are the limitations with the evolutionary approach based on the notion of preparedness? First, there is much stronger evidence for a fear of spiders in cultures such as those in Europe than in other cultures (e.g. those in Africa). This doesn't fit the theory because we would expect on the preparedness view that fear of spiders would be universal.

Second, several relatively rare phobias can't easily be explained in evolutionary terms. For example, consider arithmophobia (fear of numbers), triskaidekaphobia (fear of the number 13), and cherophobia (fear of gaiety). However, note that Seligman didn't suggest that biological preparedness explains *all* phobias.

Third, we must often speculate when applying the notion of preparedness. For example, consider carnophobia (fear of meat) and myrmecophobia (fear of ants). Do these phobias exist because our remote ancestors had to deal with meat that could poison them and with dangerous ants? The only honest answer is that we don't know.

Fourth, biological preparedness hasn't proved of much value when we try to understand patients' specific phobias. Contrary to prediction, many of their phobias are non-prepared rather than prepared. In addition, there is very little evidence to suggest that prepared phobias are more serious than non-prepared ones, or that they are more difficult to treat.

SECTION SUMMARY
Biological Explanations of Phobic Disorders

❖ Twin studies have suggested that genetic factors are important in blood-injury phobia, social phobia, and situational phobia. Twin and family studies also suggest that genetic factors are important in social phobia and agoraphobia.

Genetic factors

❖ According to Seligman, we are most likely to develop phobias to objects that were very threatening in our evolutionary past. This is known as preparedness or biological preparedness.

Evolutionary explanation

❖ Laboratory evidence in humans and other species provides support for the notion of preparedness.

❖ Evaluation:

— The prediction that most specific phobias should be prepared rather than non-prepared hasn't received much support.

— The predictions that prepared phobias should be more serious and harder to treat than non-prepared phobias haven't been supported.

— It is often a matter of speculation as to whether any given object was or wasn't very threatening in evolutionary history.

PSYCHOLOGICAL EXPLANATIONS OF PHOBIC DISORDERS

Several psychological explanations for phobias have been put forward. We will be considering four types of psychological explanation. We start with behavioural explanations based on conditioning theory. After that, we discuss the historically important psychodynamic explanation originating in the work of Sigmund Freud. Next, we turn our attention to the cognitive explanation of phobias. Finally, we consider social factors involved in the development of phobias.

Behavioural Explanations

According to most of those favouring behavioural explanations, phobic fears are acquired by classical conditioning. **Classical conditioning** is a form of learning first shown by Ivan Pavlov (discussed at length in Chapter 8). In essence, a neutral or conditioned stimulus (e.g. a tone) is paired repeatedly with a second or unconditioned stimulus (e.g. presentation of food). After a while, the natural or unconditioned response to the second or unconditioned stimulus (e.g. salivation) comes to be made to the neutral stimulus when presented on its own. This learned response is known as the conditioned response. According to the behavioural account, what happens in the development of a phobia is that the conditioned or phobic stimulus (e.g. spider) is associated with a painful or aversive stimulus creating fear.

In a classic study, Watson and Rayner (1920) showed that emotions could be classically conditioned like any other response. Their participant was an

> **KEY TERM**
>
> **Classical conditioning:** basic form of learning in which simple responses are associated with new stimuli.

Types of conditioning

Classical conditioning

- Unconditioned stimulus (UCS), e.g. food → reflex response, e.g. salivation
- Neutral stimulus (NS), e.g. bell → no response
- NS and UCS are paired in time (they occur at the same time)
- NS (e.g. bell) is now a conditioned stimulus (CS) → a conditioned response (CR) (a new stimulus–response link is learned, the bell causes salivation)

Operant conditioning

- A behaviour that has a positive effect is more likely to be repeated
- Positive and negative reinforcement (escape from aversive stimulus) are agreeable
- Punishment is disagreeable

Watson and Rayner taught a boy ("Little Albert") to fear white fluffy objects by striking a metal bar (unconditioned stimulus) every time he touched the previously unfeared object (neutral stimulus), demonstrating that fear could be learned through classical conditioning.

? Can a conditioning account explain the relative frequency of different phobias?

11-month-old boy called "Little Albert", who was reared almost from birth in a hospital. Watson and Rayner found out initially that items such as a white rat, a rabbit, and white cotton wool didn't trigger any fear response. In other words, they could all be regarded as neutral stimuli. Watson and Rayner then induced a fear response (unconditioned response) by striking a steel bar with a hammer (unconditioned stimulus). This startled Albert and made him cry. After that, they gave him a white rat to play with. As he reached to touch it, they struck the bar to make him frightened. They repeated this three times, and did the same 1 week later. After that, when they showed the rat to Albert he began to cry, rolled over, and started to crawl away quickly. Classical conditioning had occurred, because the previously neutral or conditioned stimulus (i.e. the rat) produced a conditioned fear response. The suggestion is that Albert had developed a phobia for the rat.

Watson and Rayner found that now the sight of any white and furry object (e.g. a white fur coat; a Father Christmas beard) provoked a fear response. This is called **generalisation**—Albert had learned to generalise his fear of the white rat to other similar objects. Although they intended to "re-condition" Albert to eliminate these fearful reactions, he was taken away from the hospital before this could happen.

Mowrer (1947) developed a two-process theory to explain the origins of phobias. The first stage involves classical conditioning (e.g. linking the white rat and the loud noise). The second stage involves operant conditioning. What happens here is that avoidance of the phobic stimulus reduces fear and fear reduction is reinforcing or rewarding. As a result, patients generally avoid phobic stimuli.

A key prediction of the behavioural account is that patients with phobic disorders should be much more likely than other people to have had a frightening experience with the phobic object. There is some support for this prediction. Barlow and Durand (1995) reported that about 50% of individuals with specific phobia for driving remember a traumatic experience while driving (e.g. a car accident) as having caused the onset of the phobia. Hackmann, Clark, and McManus (2000) found that 96% of social phobics remembered some socially traumatic experience that had happened to them (often in adolescence). For example, they were harshly criticised in public or couldn't stop blushing on an important social occasion.

KEY TERM

Generalisation: in classical conditioning, the tendency to transfer a response from one stimulus to another that is quite similar.

Thorpe and Burns (1983) carried out a study on agoraphobics, 70% of whom reported an anxiety-provoking event that seemed to trigger the disorder. However, in only 55% of these patients was the event described in a way consistent with an explanation of agoraphobia based on conditioning.

Other evidence is less supportive of the conditioning account. Keuthen (1980) reported that half of all phobics couldn't remember any highly unpleasant experience relating to the phobic object. Those favouring a conditioning account have argued that phobics often forget conditioning experiences that happened many years previously. To reduce this problem, Menzies and Clarke (1993) carried out a study on children suffering from water phobia. Only 2% of them reported a direct conditioning experience involving water. In defence of the behaviourist view, it could be argued that children often have very poor recall of the events of early childhood. Alternatively, they may not have realised that the event involved water (e.g. the traumatic event may have taken place beside a stream and thus the sound of water created a phobia).

There is a final problem. In many studies, there was no control group of non-phobics, and so we don't know whether the phobic patients had experienced more unpleasant events involving the phobic object than other people. For example, DiNardo et al. (1988) found that 50% of dog phobics had become very anxious during an encounter with a dog, which apparently supports conditioning theory. However, 50% of healthy controls without dog phobia had also had an anxious encounter with a dog! Thus, dog phobia doesn't seem to depend on having had a frightening encounter with a dog.

Menzies and Clarke (1993) found that phobias do not necessarily develop as a result of a frightening encounter directly with the phobic object. Many people are phobic of snakes, despite never having encountered a real one.

? How might one explain why only some individuals go on to develop a phobia after a fearful experience?

Modelling and information transmission

Bandura (1986) developed conditioning theory by showing the importance of modelling or observational learning. Individuals learn to imitate the behaviour of others, especially those whose behaviour is rewarded or reinforced. Mineka, Davidson, Cook, and Kuir (1984) found that monkeys could develop snake phobia simply by watching another monkey experience fear in the presence of a snake.

Another possible way in which phobias could be acquired is through information transmission. What happens is that fear-producing information about the phobic object leads to the development of a phobia. Ost (1985) described the case of a woman who was a severe snake phobic. She had been told repeatedly about the dangers of snakes, and had been strongly encouraged to wear rubber boots to protect herself against them. She finally reached the point at which she wore rubber boots even when going to the local shops.

Some phobias can be acquired through modelling or information transmission. However, modelling or observational learning seems to be less important in producing specific phobias in humans than in other species, and there are only a few well-documented cases in which information transmission has led to phobias. However, Merckelbach, de Jong, Muris, and van den Hout (1996) reported evidence that modelling and negative information transmission are important in producing small-animal phobias and blood-injection-injury phobia.

Assumptions of the behavioural model

- All behaviour is learned, and maladaptive behaviour is no different.
- This learning can be understood in terms of the principles of conditioning and modelling.
- What was learned can be unlearned, using the same principles.
- The same laws apply to human and non-human animal behaviour.

Overall evaluation

There is reasonable evidence that phobias can (and sometimes do) develop as suggested by advocates of the behavioural approach. More specifically, classical conditioning of the fear response has been demonstrated as has development of a phobia via observational learning. In addition, many phobics when questioned can remember a traumatic experience that could have triggered the phobia. Finally, the hypothesis that avoidance behaviour in phobic individuals is reinforced or rewarded provides a fairly convincing explanation.

What are the limitations with behavioural explanations of the development of phobias? First, it has proved hard to obtain strong support for the conditioning approach in the laboratory. As Rachman (2004, p. 82) concluded, "It is possible to produce conditioned fear responses in humans under laboratory conditions, but the responses tend to be weak, transient, and incomplete." For example, attempts to replicate the findings of Watson and Rayner (1920) have generally failed (e.g. Valentine, 1946).

Second, many phobic patients can't remember any traumatic event that could have caused their phobia via classical conditioning. The linkage between traumatic events and phobias is further weakened by the fact that the great majority of civilians exposed to air raids in time of war fail to develop any phobic reactions (Rachman, 2004).

Third, behavioural explanations of phobias leave much that is important out of account. For example, genetic factors, social factors, and cognitive factors all seem to play significant roles in the development of phobias but aren't considered directly in behavioural explanations.

> ■ Activity: The behavioural model and phobias
> Which of the following phobias are most likely to be the consequence of classical conditioning?
>
> - Claustrophobia (fear of enclosed spaces).
> - Agoraphobia (fear of open spaces).
> - Arachnophobia (fear of spiders).
>
> Are there any problems with this approach? What are the weaknesses of the behavioural model as an explanation for mental disorders?

Psychodynamic Explanation

> ? Freud developed his theory in the early part of the twentieth century when attitudes to sex and sexuality were very different from today. What effect do you think this might have on the development of psychodynamic therapy?

Freud originated the psychodynamic approach within psychology. According to him, phobias are a defence against the anxiety produced when the impulses of the id or sexual instinct are repressed or forced into the unconscious. These repressed impulses and ideas subsequently turn into symbolic representations. According to Freud (1950, p. 120), "The main point in the problem of phobias seems to me that phobias do not occur at all when the *vita sexualis* [sexual life] is normal."

Various psychodynamic explanations have been offered of the existence of specific phobias. For example, the psychodynamic theorist Abraham (1927), who worked closely with Freud, argued that spider phobia occurs because of an unconscious fear of the sex organs: "the penis embedded in the female genitals."

The most famous psychodynamic case study on phobia is that of Little Hans (discussed in detail on the next page). Little Hans suffered from horse phobia (a specific phobia), and Sigmund Freud argued that this phobia could be explained in terms of his theory of childhood sexuality. Even though Freud discussed the case of Little Hans in detail, he actually had surprisingly little to do with assembling the relevant evidence. This was done by the father of Little Hans, a supporter of Freud's called Max Graf.

Freud argued that the evidence of the case study indicated that Little Hans was sexually attracted to his mother. However, Hans was very frightened that his father would punish him for being sexually attracted to his mother. Horses resembled his father in that their black muzzles and blinkers looked like his moustache and glasses. As a result, Little Hans transferred or displaced his fear of his father on to horses. In other words, Hans' unacceptable sexual desires for his mother and his fear of retribution from his father were turned into the much more acceptable fear of horses.

Little Hans showed his fear of horses only when he saw them pulling a cart at speed—he was not frightened of horses without carts, or of horses pulling carts at a walking pace.

Freud's account of Hans' fear of horses is interesting but very fanciful. In fact, Hans himself suggested a very simple explanation for his horse phobia. He said that it started when he observed a serious accident involving a horse and cart moving at high speed. As Hans' fear of horses started immediately after seeing the horse collapse, this seems like a very plausible explanation. Note that Hans *only* showed his phobia when he saw a horse pulling a cart at high speed. This is exactly what we would expect on Hans' own explanation of his horse phobia. If his fear of his father had been transferred to horses, Hans should have shown a phobic reaction every time he saw a horse.

CASE STUDY: LITTLE HANS

The case study of Little Hans (the 5-year-old phobic boy) is unusual for several reasons. It is Freud's only analysis of a child rather than an adult. This enabled Freud to test his hypotheses about child sexuality. The case study was also unusual in that Freud's analysis was indirect as almost all of the interviews and observations were made by the boy's father and passed on to Freud. Hans' father was Max Graf, a music critic and early supporter of Freud and member of the Psychoanalytic Society. Hans' father wrote to Freud when the boy was 5 years old, describing the main problem: "He is afraid a horse will bite him in the street, and this fear seems somehow connected with his having been frightened by a large penis." Freud met Hans on only two occasions. The recording of information and direct interviews were undertaken by Hans' father who then corresponded and discussed the case at length with Freud. The chief features of the case history (chronologically) are outlined below:

- Hans was fascinated by his "widdler" (his penis). He observed that animals had big ones and it was likely that his parents had big ones too because they were grown up.
- Hans spent a lot of time alone with his mother over the summer holiday and realised he liked having her to himself. He wished his father would stay away. He also felt hostile towards his new baby sister, who further separated Hans from his mother. He expressed this indirectly in his fear of baths because he thought his mother would drop him (in fact, he *wished* his mother would drop his little sister, a desire that was projected elsewhere because of the anxiety it aroused).
- There were two strands to his anxiety about horses. First, Hans once heard a man saying to a child "Don't put your finger to the white horse or it'll bite you." Second, Hans asked his mother if she would like to put her finger on his widdler. His mother told him this would not be proper. Therefore, it is suggested that Hans learned that touching a white horse or a widdler was undesirable. Hans' desire (libido) for his mother created a sense of anxiety and fear that she might leave him if

he persisted. Unconsciously, this anxiety was projected elsewhere: he became afraid of being bitten by a white horse.
- More anxiety was created by the fact that Hans' mother told Hans that if he played with his widdler it would be cut off. Hans' father told Hans that women have no widdler. Hans reasoned that his mother's must have been cut off—and she might do the same to him.
- There were two pieces of symbolism. First, Hans had a dream about two giraffes, he took away the crumpled one and this made the big one cry out. This might represent Hans' wish to take away his mother (crumpled one) causing his father to cry out (big giraffe—possible symbol of penis). Hans sat on the crumpled one (trying to claim his mother for himself). Second, Freud suggested to Hans that the black around the horses' mouths and the blinkers in front of their eyes were symbols for his father's moustache and glasses. Hans might envy these symbols of adulthood because they could give him the right to have a woman's love.
- Hans developed further anxieties about horses. Hans told his father that he was afraid of horses falling down, and if they were laden (e.g. with furniture) this might lead them to fall down. Hans also remembered seeing a horse fall down and thinking it was dead; as he secretly wished his father would fall down dead this made Hans feel more anxious.
- Hans now became preoccupied with bowel movements ("lumf"). His sister was lumf-like, as was a laden cart. So laden vehicles represented pregnancy and when they overturned it symbolised giving birth. Thus the falling horse was both his dying father and his mother giving birth.
- In the end, Hans became less afraid of horses. He developed two final fantasies that showed that his feelings about his father were resolved: (1) "The plumber came and first he took away my behind with a pair of pincers, and then he gave me another, and then the same with my widdler"; (2) Hans told his father that he was now the daddy and not the mummy of his imaginary children, thus showing that he had moved from wishing his father dead to identifying with him.

? How would you suggest that a behaviourist might explain Hans' fear of horses (you might consider the accident that Hans witnessed)?

Evaluation

Individuals with phobia often have little conscious awareness of the processes involved in the development of their phobia. This suggests that Freud was right to argue that unconscious processes are sometimes involved in the development of fears. He was also probably right that phobics' fears can have symbolic elements associated with them. Finally, the account of Little Hans is of historical importance because it was the first systematic description of specific phobia.

It is generally accepted nowadays that the psychodynamic approach to explaining phobias is severely limited in several ways. First, many individuals with phobias have perfectly satisfactory sexual lives, and so shouldn't suffer from phobias at all according to Freud. Second, the 5-year-old Hans' account of the origins of his horse phobia is much more plausible than Freud's because it is much simpler and more consistent with the evidence. Third, as Freud (1910, p. 246) admitted, "It is true that during the analysis Hans had to be told many things which he could not say himself, [and] that he had to be presented with the thoughts that he had so far showed no signs of possessing." Such an approach casts considerable doubt on the value of this case study as evidence for Freud's theory. Fourth, the psychodynamic approach ignores the genetic and social factors associated with the development of phobias. Fifth, many of the claims made by advocates of the psychodynamic approach lack any real evidence to support them. For example, Abraham's notion that spider phobia occurs because of an unconscious fear of sexual organs seems to say more about Abraham than about spider phobia.

Assumptions of the psychodynamic model

- Much of our behaviour is driven by unconscious motives.
- Childhood is a critical period in development.
- Mental disorders arise from unresolved, unconscious conflicts originating in childhood.
- Resolution occurs through accessing and coming to terms with repressed ideas and conflicts.

Assumptions of the cognitive model

- Maladaptive behaviour is caused by faulty and irrational cognitions.
- It is the way you think about a problem, rather than the problem itself, that causes mental disorder.
- Individuals can overcome mental disorders by learning to use more appropriate cognitions.
- The model aims to be positive and rational.

Cognitive Explanation

According to cognitive explanations, what is of central importance is that phobics have irrational and dysfunctional beliefs causing them to experience intense fear when exposed to phobic stimuli and/or situations. More specifically, phobics have **interpretive biases**, meaning they interpret ambiguous stimuli and situations in much more threatening ways than other people. We will consider this hypothesis with each of the phobias in turn. Before we do so, note that phobics have some awareness that their reactions to phobic stimuli are excessive. Thus, they are *not* totally convinced that their phobic stimuli are genuinely very threatening.

Specific phobia

Several studies have considered interpretive biases in specific phobias. For example, Thorpe and Salkovskis (1995) asked spider phobics, non-spider phobics, and controls to rate statements on the Phobic Beliefs Questionnaire while imagining that their phobic object was in the room with them. Large numbers of the spider phobics (percentages are in brackets) believed they would experience the following thoughts if confronted by a spider: I would make a fool of myself (62%); I would go mad (56%); I would be hysterical (68%). In contrast, very few

---

KEY TERM

Interpretive biases: the tendency shown by most anxious and depressed patients to interpret ambiguous stimuli and situations in a negative or threatening way.

of the non-spider phobics indicated that they would have any of these irrational thoughts.

Why do individuals with specific phobias have interpretive biases for their phobic stimuli? It is assumed that these biases arise because of negative experiences involving the phobic stimuli. That assumption shares with the behavioural explanation the emphasis on previous negative experiences. However, there is an important difference. According to the behavioural account based on classical conditioning, the conditioned stimulus is the phobic object and the unconditioned stimulus is some aversive event. The unconditioned stimulus has to follow very shortly after the conditioned stimulus for conditioning to occur. In contrast, the cognitive account argues that a much wider range of negative experiences could play a role in producing specific phobia.

Agoraphobia

We saw earlier that nearly all patients with agoraphobia also suffer from panic disorder, and the fear of having a panic attack in public plays an important role in producing the agoraphobia. Kamieniecki, Wade, and Tsourtos (1997) presented participants with ambiguous scenarios relating to bodily sensations. Patients who had panic disorder with agoraphobia produced more anxiety-related interpretations of these scenarios than did controls, indicating the existence of interpretive biases. This is entirely consistent with the typical clinical finding that patients mistakenly believe that a panic attack means they may well have a heart attack and die.

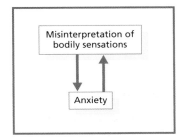

Why do these patients have interpretive biases for bodily sensations? Verburg, Griez, Meijer, and Pols (1995) came up with a plausible answer. They argued that a history of respiratory disease would cause many normal individuals to become very concerned about their own bodily sensations and thus to develop interpretive biases for those sensations. They found that 43% of patients with panic disorder with or without agoraphobia had suffered from at least one respiratory disease in their lives. This was much higher than the figure of 16% found among patients with other anxiety disorders. However, the fact that over half the patients who had panic disorder with or without agoraphobia had never suffered a respiratory disease means that other factors are generally involved.

Why don't patients who have panic disorder with agoraphobia realise that their bodily symptoms are harmless? Instead, they engage in various **safety-seeking behaviours**, such as sitting down or breathing slowly and deliberately to prevent the onset of a heart attack or other serious physical symptoms (Eysenck, 1997). They mistakenly believe that these safety-seeking behaviours "save" them from disaster.

Social phobia

We turn now to social phobia. One of the most influential cognitive accounts of social phobia was a model put forward by Clark and Wells (1995). They argued that there are several reasons why social phobics have greatly exaggerated fears about social situations. First, most of their attention is self-focused rather than directed at other people. As a result, they don't have accurate feedback concerning the impact of their social behaviour on others.

Second, they make excessively negative interpretations about the adequacy of their social behaviour (a form of interpretive bias). For example, social phobics often regard what they say as being wrong and/or incoherent when that is not the case.

Third, the cognitive model answers the following puzzling question: "Why do social phobics maintain interpretive biases and the feeling that they could easily experience social catastrophes year after year in the face of considerable contrary evidence?" According to the model, social phobics believe mistakenly that they manage to avoid social catastrophes because they use various safety-seeking behaviours designed to minimise anxiety. The most obvious safety-seeking behaviour is simply avoiding stressful social situations. However, there are also several more subtle safety-seeking behaviours within social situations; for example, avoiding eye contact and saying very little.

Findings

Much evidence supports this cognitive model. Stopa and Clark (1993) asked social phobics, patients with other anxiety disorders, and healthy individuals to speak out loud the thoughts they had had during a previous social interaction. The social phobics reported several times more thoughts concerning negative evaluations of themselves and their own behaviour than were found in the other groups. Rapee and Lim (1992) asked social phobics to give a public talk and then asked observers and the participants themselves to rate their public-speaking performance. Social phobics rated their performance as much worse than did the observers, which is clear evidence of an interpretive bias.

Clark and Wells (1995) didn't directly address the issue of precisely *why* social

Introverted individuals are less socially skilled and have fewer friends than extraverted individuals.

phobics developed interpretive biases in the first place. However, two kinds of findings suggest what may be involved. First, in a study discussed earlier, Hackmann et al. (2000) found that 96% of social phobics recalled a socially traumatic event that may have helped to trigger the social phobia. It is likely that such events could lead to interpretive biases regarding the social adequacy of one's behaviour. Second, individuals who are introverted are less socially skilled and have fewer friends than those who are extraverted, and this might lead them to develop interpretive biases. As predicted, Bienvenu et al. (2001) found that social phobics were more introverted than patients with other anxiety disorders. Note that the direction of causality is unclear—having social phobia may make people introverted *or* being introverted may help to trigger social phobia.

Evaluation

The cognitive approach has various strengths. First, phobic patients do have irrational thoughts about their phobic stimuli. More specifically, they typically have strong interpretive biases. Second, experiences that might plausibly lead to the development of phobias (e.g. respiratory disease; negative experiences involving phobia stimuli; inadequate social skills) have been identified. Third, there is reasonable evidence that phobic individuals maintain their interpretive biases over long periods of time because they use safety-seeking behaviours that prevent them from discovering how mistaken their biases are.

The cognitive approach has various limitations. First, there is the causality issue: do interpretive biases help to trigger phobias or is it simply that having a phobia leads to relevant interpretive biases? If the latter is correct, then interpretive biases may play little role in the development of phobias. Second, the cognitive approach doesn't focus sufficiently on phobics' behaviour. The central symptom of phobia is avoidance behaviour, and yet the cognitive approach fails to provide a detailed explanation of such behaviour. Third, and more generally, the cognitive approach doesn't consider various factors (e.g. genetic, social) that have been shown to influence the development of phobias.

? What are the limitations of the cognitive approach?

Social Explanations

Several social factors might be involved in the development of phobia. However, we will focus on two main ones: (1) parenting styles; and (2) life events and experiences.

Parental styles

There is evidence suggesting that parental practices play a role in the development of social phobia. Arrindell, Kwee, Methorst, van der Ende, Pol, and Moritz (1989) found that social phobics reported that their parents were rejecting, lacking in emotional warmth, or overprotective. This may mean that children find it hard to show healthy social development if they feel unloved (rejecting parents) or have little control over their social lives (overprotective parents). Note, however, that Arrindell et al.'s evidence is only correlational and so we can't be confident about causality—perhaps children born with an anxious temperament cause their parents to be overprotective.

Another limitation with Arrindell et al.'s (1989) findings is that they were based on *retrospective* reports by adult social phobics of how they had been treated by their parents as children. Such reports could be deliberately distorted (e.g. the phobics might want to blame their parents for their disorder) or they might be distorted because of the fallibility of memory. These problems were largely overcome by Lieb, Wittchen, Hofler, Fuetsch, Stein, and Merikangas (2000), who interviewed parents to assess their parenting styles. Their key findings largely replicated those of Arrindell et al. (1989): "Higher parental overprotection and higher parental rejection were significantly associated with increased rates of social phobia in offspring" (Lieb et al., 2000, p. 862).

There are other ways in which parents may influence the development of social phobia. Adult social phobics report that their parents overemphasised the opinions of others, failed to stress the importance of family sociability, and tended to isolate their family from others (Bruch & Heimberg, 1994).

Overbeek, ten Have, Vollebergh, and de Graaf (2007) considered parenting styles with respect to several mental disorders including some of the phobias. Parental lack of care and overprotection were both associated with an increased risk of phobia. The risk was similar regardless of whether it was the mother or the father that showed a lack of care or was overprotective.

? Why might some therapists prefer to use the term "client" instead of "patient"?

Life events and experiences

Phobic patients tend to experience more serious life events than healthy controls in the year or so before the onset of the phobia. Kleiner and Marshall (1987) found that 84% of agoraphobics reported having experienced family problems in the months before their first panic attack. Andrews (1988) considered four studies that indicated that agoraphobia and panic often follow a period of severe stress.

Marteinsdottir, Svensson, Svedberg, Anderberg, and Von Knorring (2007) studied the relationship between life events and social phobia. Patients with social phobia reported more negative life events than healthy controls during the year preceding the onset of social phobia. In addition, female social phobics (but not male ones) were more likely than healthy controls to have experienced the death of a relative or close friend during the same time period.

There is also evidence that patients with phobias have experienced more negative life events and experiences than healthy controls in the course of their lives. Magee (1999) discovered that unpredictable and uncontrollable events causing physical harm (e.g. life-threatening accidents; a natural disaster) had been experienced by more agoraphobics than healthy controls. Social phobics were more likely than healthy controls to have experienced sexual assault by a relative or verbal aggression between parents. Finally, more specific phobics than healthy controls had experienced somewhat predictable but hard-to-control childhood experiences (e.g. chronic parental violence).

Overall evaluation

Several studies have found that phobic patients are more likely than non-phobics to have had parents who were rejecting or overprotective. There is also some evidence that the risk of developing a phobia is comparable whether it is the father or the mother who is rejecting or overprotective. There is also evidence that phobics tend to experience more life events in the months preceding the onset of the phobia than do non-phobics. All these findings are consistent with the notion that social factors in childhood and in adulthood play a role in the development of phobia.

There are various limitations with much of the research. First, information about the phobic's experience is typically obtained some time after the events or experiences in question. That is especially the case when adult phobics are asked about the parenting styles they were exposed to as children. As a result, some information about the parenting styles they experienced or about life events may be forgotten or remembered in a distorted form.

Second, we basically have an *association* between parental styles experienced in childhood or life events preceding the onset of phobia on the one hand and various phobias on the other hand. This doesn't provide a solid basis for establishing causality. For example, genetic factors may help to explain the association—rejecting or overprotective parents may tend to be anxious, and so are likely to have children who are also anxious and thus liable to develop phobia.

Third, there is often a possibility that high levels of anxiety played a part in causing the life events or experiences. For example, someone in the early stages of developing social phobia might avoid social occasions and be so unapproachable that his or her behaviour triggers the severe life event of marital separation.

? What are the practical applications of theories of phobic disorders?

Conclusions

Many biological and psychological factors play a role in the development of a phobia. Indeed, there are so many factors that you could be excused for feeling unsure about what conclusions should be drawn. Hopefully, such feelings can be reduced by relating the various factors to the **diathesis–stress model**. According to this model, the occurrence of phobia or any other mental disorder depends on two factors:

? *How might the diathesis–stress model be used to explain phobias?*

1. *Diathesis*: a genetic vulnerability or predisposition to disease or disorder.
2. *Stress*: some severe or disturbing environmental event. Within this model, the term "stress" has a very broad meaning.

The most important assumption of the diathesis–stress model is that diathesis or genetic vulnerability *and* stress are both necessary for a phobia to develop.

At the most general level, the diathesis–stress model assumes that the development of a phobia involves a combination of *internal* factors (i.e. factors inside the individual) and *external* factors (i.e. environmental factors). Internal factors that might make an individual vulnerable to developing a phobia include genetic factors, factors based on our evolutionary history, and pre-existing dysfunctional beliefs. External factors that might be involved in triggering a phobia include conditioning experiences, serious life events, or deficient parenting. This multi-factor approach to understanding the development of phobia is more realistic than any single-factor approach focusing on only one determinant of phobia.

> **EXAM HINT**
>
> Do think about the fact that there are several subclasses of phobias in your conclusion. This means that you probably need more than one explanation to cover all phobias.

> **EXAM HINT**
>
> Do some research on epigenetics (the study of gene–environment interactions) to help understand the variations in types of phobias and within the families of phobics. This explanation can better account for such variations because it offers a more in-depth understanding of the diathesis–stress model. It suggests that whilst there is a diathesis/genetic predisposition, the genes may or may not be switched on depending on the individual's life experiences. The whole life course needs to be considered, prenatal, early and later childhood, as well as adulthood as there are risk factors across the life stages. Consider the influences of nature–nurture as part of this conclusion.

SECTION SUMMARY
Psychological Explanations of Phobic Disorders

❖ According to the behavioural account, phobias develop when a conditioned or phobic stimulus is associated with an aversive stimulus creating fear.

❖ Phobic stimuli are avoided because avoidance reduces fear and thus is rewarding.

❖ It is predicted that phobic patients should have had conditioning experiences involving phobic stimuli.

❖ Phobias can also develop through modelling or observational learning.

❖ Evaluation:

— The avoidance of phobic stimuli is typically motivated by fear reduction.

— The role of modelling in the development of phobias seems to be greater in other species than in humans.

— Behavioural explanations de-emphasise genetic, social, and cognitive factors.

Behavioural explanations

> **KEY TERM**
>
> **Diathesis–stress model:** the notion that psychological disorders occur when there is a genetically determined vulnerability (diathesis) and relevant stressful conditions.

Psychodynamic explanation	❖ According to the psychodynamic account, phobias are a defence against the anxiety produced when the impulses of the id are repressed. ❖ Evaluation: — Unconscious processes are sometimes involved in the development of phobias. — Against the psychodynamic explanation, many phobics have satisfactory sexual lives. — The psychodynamic explanation is not very detailed, and is rather far-fetched and implausible. — Genetic and social factors are de-emphasised.
Cognitive explanation	❖ According to the cognitive account, phobics have irrational beliefs in the form of interpretive biases. ❖ These interpretive biases are often triggered by specific experiences. For example, some social phobics have experienced traumatic social events. ❖ Phobic patients often maintain their interpretive biases for several years because they engage in safety-seeking behaviours. ❖ Evaluation: — There is convincing evidence that phobics have interpretive biases for their phobic stimuli. — Many phobics have had experiences that could plausibly have produced interpretive biases. — It is not clear interpretive biases help to produce phobias—it may well be that interpretive biases are a consequence of having a phobia. — The cognitive explanation pays insufficient attention to genetic and social factors.
Social explanations	❖ According to one social explanation, the parents of phobic patients showed lack of care or were overprotective. ❖ There are associations between parenting style and phobia, and this is the case for fathers as well as mothers. However, the data are typically retrospective and causality can't be established. ❖ Phobic patients tend to experience more serious life events than healthy controls in the year before the onset of phobia. ❖ In addition, phobic patients on average have experienced more serious events in the course of their lives than most other people. ❖ It is difficult to explain the association between life events and phobia. It is possible that high anxiety increases the probability of experiencing life events and developing a phobia.
Conclusions	❖ The factors involved in the development of phobias can be considered within the framework of the diathesis–stress model. According to this model, diathesis (predisposition) and stress (some external event) are *both* needed for a phobia to develop. ❖ More generally, the diathesis–stress model assumes that external *and* internal factors combine to produce any mental disorder including phobia.

THERAPIES FOR PHOBIC DISORDERS

So far, we have considered the various factors associated with the development of phobias. We now move to a discussion of the main forms of therapy devised to treat phobias. At a very general level, it is possible to identify two major categories of therapy. First, there are biological therapies (e.g. those involving the use of drugs to treat phobias). Second, there are psychological therapies designed to change patients' ways of thinking and/or their behaviour. They include psychodynamic, behavioural, and cognitive therapies.

Biological Therapies for Phobic Disorders

Drug therapy is overwhelmingly the most common form of biological therapy used in the treatment of phobic disorders. Accordingly, that will be the focus of our discussion. When we discuss the effectiveness of drug therapy for phobic disorders, bear in mind that treatments can be effective in two ways. A treatment can be effective because it reduces or eliminates the symptoms of a disorder and also eliminates the underlying processes. Patients receiving such treatments, which Hollon, Stewart, and Strunk (2006) described as "curative", remain recovered even a long time after treatment. Alternatively, a treatment can be effective because it suppresses the symptoms of a disorder while it is applied. However, as it doesn't focus on the underlying processes responsible for the disorder, recovery often doesn't continue after treatment has finished. Hollon et al. described such treatments as "palliative".

Various drugs have been used in the treatment of social phobia. For example, there are the benzodiazepines such as Valium and Librium. These are anti-anxiety drugs that are effective at reducing anxious symptoms. Monoamine oxidase inhibitors (MAOIs) are another class of drug used with social phobics. These drugs are also used in the treatment of depression. They inhibit the oxidation of monoamines (neurotransmitters including dopamine, serotonin, and noradrenaline) so that the levels increase. In recent years, drug therapy for social phobia has increasingly made use of selective serotonin reuptake inhibitors (SSRIs). The SSRIs include fluvoxamine, fluoxetine (Prozac), sertraline, and paroxetine, and are also used in the treatment of depression. Antidepressant drugs are often used in drug therapy for social phobia because social phobics often have high levels of depression (Rachman, 2004).

Various drugs have also been used in the treatment of panic disorder with agoraphobia. As with social phobia, benzodiazepines and SSRIs are often used. Tricyclic antidepressants, which increase the activity of noradrenaline and serotonin, are also used to treat panic disorder with agoraphobia. As with social phobia, an important reason for using antidepressant drugs with patients suffering from panic disorder with agoraphobia is that they frequently have many depressive symptoms.

Drug therapy has seldom been used in the treatment of specific phobia. There are various reasons for this. First, many individuals with specific phobias aren't generally anxious but merely experience great fear to certain specific stimuli. Thus, they don't really need drugs that will reduce their anxiety in all situations. Second, most patients and therapists don't regard specific phobia as a serious

> **EXAM HINT**
> Use the treatment aetiology fallacy to evaluate treatments. This refers to the fact that just because the treatment works this does not mean that whatever the treatment targets, (such as biochemical imbalances in the case of drugs) was the cause of the disorder in the first place. A useful analogy is that an aspirin treats a headache but it is not a lack of aspirin that causes the headache.

condition, because it typically has much less impact on the patient's life than social phobia or agoraphobia. As a result, it is generally felt that the condition doesn't warrant the use of drugs. Third, as we will see, behavioural therapy for specific phobia is very effective and so is the therapy of choice.

Effectiveness

Most drugs that have been used in the treatment of social phobia are at least moderately effective. For example, Heimberg et al. (1998) compared the effects of phenelzine (a monoamine oxidase inhibitor) and cognitive-behavioural therapy. Phenelzine started to produce beneficial effects faster than cognitive-behavioural therapy. However, the two forms of therapy reduced the symptoms of social phobia to a comparable extent by the end of treatment. Blomhoff et al. (2001) compared drug therapy using sertraline (an SSRI) with behaviour therapy in the form of exposure (discussed below). Drug therapy was superior to **exposure therapy** at the end of treatment. Bandelow, Seidler-Brandler, Becker, Wedekind, and Ruther (2007) reviewed six studies in which drug therapy was compared with psychological forms of therapy in the treatment of social phobia. Drug and psychological therapy both led to similar substantial improvements.

So far, I have only discussed the effectiveness of drug therapy at the end of treatment for social phobia. What patients want, of course, is for the gains derived from therapy to be maintained long after the therapy itself has ended. However, there are indications that drug therapy is less effective than other forms of therapy in the period after the end of treatment. Liebowitz et al. (1999) carried out a follow-up of the patients studied by Heimberg et al. (1998) in a study discussed above. Patients who had responded positively to drug therapy or cognitive-behavioural therapy were followed up for 6 months after treatment had terminated. None of those receiving cognitive-behavioural therapy suffered a relapse during that period compared to 33% of the patients who had received drug therapy. Thus, drug therapy was a palliative rather than an entirely curative treatment in the terms used by Hollon et al. (2006).

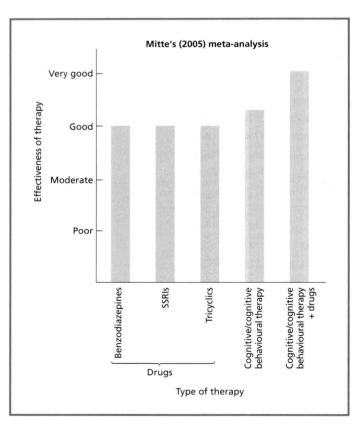

The effectiveness of different types of therapy in treating agoraphobia with panic disorder. Based on data in Mitte (2005).

We turn now to the effectiveness of drug therapy in the treatment of panic disorder with agoraphobia. Mitte (2005) reported a meta-analysis focusing on the effectiveness of benzodiazepines, SSRIs, and tricyclics. She obtained four main findings. First, all types of drugs were equally effective in treating panic disorder with agoraphobia. Second, cognitive or cognitive-behavioural therapy was at least as effective as (or slightly more effective than) drug therapy. Third, the drop-out rate was significantly higher for drug therapy than for cognitive or cognitive-behavioural therapy (20% vs. 15%). Fourth, adding drug therapy to cognitive or cognitive-behavioural therapy increased the effectiveness of treatment.

The gains produced by drug therapy in treating panic disorder with agoraphobia may not be maintained following the end of treatment. Marks et al.

KEY TERM

Exposure therapy: a form of therapy in which patients are exposed to the object or situation they fear for lengthy periods of time until their anxiety level is substantially reduced.

Drug therapy for anxiety disorders		
Drug/group of drugs	How they work	Drawbacks
Barbiturates	Treat symptoms of anxiety: palpitations, shortness of breath, accelerated heart rate, feeling of choking, nausea, dizziness, etc.	Problems of concentration, lack of co-ordination, slurred speech Addictive: withdrawal symptoms include delirium, irritability
Benzodiazepines (e.g. Valium, Librium)	Have a sedative effect on the CNS	Drowsiness, lethargy, impairments of long-term memory Withdrawal symptoms and possible addiction
Antidepressants (e.g. MAOIs, SSRIs, tricyclics)	Increase action of serotonin and similar amines	Expensive, some side effects Shorter-term benefits than cognitive therapy, focus on symptoms not causes

? In what instances might a GP feel justified in prescribing drugs such as Valium or Librium? What does "tolerance" to drugs mean and what are the problems associated with this and the treatment of anxiety disorders?

(1993) compared drug therapy using alprazolam (a benzodiazepine) and behavioural therapy (exposure) on their own or in combination. Exposure was somewhat more effective than drug therapy at the end of treatment, and the combination of drug plus exposure therapy was slightly more effective than exposure on its own. However, the story was different over a 6-month period following the end of treatment. Most of the gains achieved by drug therapy were lost during follow-up, whereas those achieved by exposure therapy were maintained. While exposure therapy was slightly more effective during treatment when combined with alprazolam, the opposite was the case during follow-up. Thus, the benefits of drug therapy were short-term, strengthening the argument that drug therapy tends to be mainly palliative.

We saw earlier that there are various reasons for not using drug therapy to treat specific phobia; however, it has occasionally been used. For example, Benjamin, Ben-Zion, Karbofsky, and Dannon (2000) assessed the effect of using paroxetine (a selective serotonin reuptake inhibitor) over a 4-week period as a treatment for specific phobia. There were significant reductions in anxiety, but no attempt was made to see whether these reductions were maintained after treatment.

Appropriateness

There are some ways in which drug therapy for phobias is appropriate. Most patients with phobias are very concerned or distressed at the extreme levels of anxiety they experience when confronted by the phobic object or situation, and drugs successfully reduce that anxiety. As a result, social phobics and patients with agoraphobia find that their lives are much less restricted and constrained than before treatment. Another point is that phobic patients seeking treatment typically hope that the therapist will be able to deal rapidly with their symptoms. Many patients find that drug therapy is appropriate for their needs because the drugs act quickly and effectively.

Despite the above considerations, there are various ways in which drug therapy for the phobias is not appropriate. First, while drug therapy is effective during treatment, the gains obtained are often lost very quickly afterwards. The

Specific phobias (such as arachnophobia), even though they can cause extreme distress to the individual when confronted with the phobic object, are considered to have little serious impact on daily life, and tend not to be treated with drug therapy.

? What are some risks associated with taking anti-depressants?

main effect of drug therapy is to suppress phobic patients' symptoms, and this suppression effect stops when drug treatment comes to an end.

Second, drug therapy doesn't address the underlying mechanisms responsible for producing the phobia. Each anxiety disorder has its own specific underlying mechanisms, but the same anti-anxiety and antidepressant drugs are given to patients almost regardless of their specific anxiety disorder. Such an indiscriminate or blunderbuss approach isn't likely to cure the underlying problems. In the terms used by Hollon et al. (2006), drug therapy for phobias is palliative rather than curative.

Third, all the drugs used in the treatment of phobias possess unwanted side effects. For example, the SSRIs can cause insomnia, reduced sex drive, and nausea (Dimidjian et al., 2006); the tricyclics can cause blurred vision, dry mouth, and dizziness; and the benzodiazepines can cause drowsiness and lethargy. The MAOIs can block the production of monoamine oxidase in the liver, leading to an accumulation of tyramine and increased blood pressure.

Fourth, many patients dislike taking drugs over prolonged periods of time. As we have seen, phobic patients receiving drug therapy are more likely than those receiving cognitive or cognitive-behavioural therapy to drop out of treatment (Mitte, 2005). A common reason for dropping out of drug therapy is because of the various side effects of drugs.

Drug therapy

SECTION SUMMARY
Biological Therapies for Phobic Disorders

❖ Social phobia and panic disorder with agoraphobia are treated with anti-anxiety drugs (e.g. benzodiazepines) and/or antidepressants. Drug therapy is rarely used with specific phobia, in part because of the rapid effectiveness of exposure therapy for that condition.

❖ Drug therapy for social phobia and for panic disorder with agoraphobia has proved effective and comparably effective to other forms of therapy. However, it is less effective than other therapies with respect to long-term improvement.

❖ Evaluation:

— Drug therapy seems to suppress the symptoms of phobias rather than to produce a cure.

— Drug therapy is somewhat unfocused, with the same anti-anxiety and antidepressant drugs being given to patients with different disorders.

— Most drugs have unwanted side effects (e.g. insomnia, dizziness, drowsiness), and there are often fairly high drop-out rates.

Psychological Therapies for Phobic Disorders: Behavioural Therapy

? How might a fear response in a child be rewarded or reinforced?

According to behaviour therapists, what is key in the treatment of phobias is to eliminate patients' avoidance of their phobic stimuli and situations. This is often hard to do because patients find their avoidance behaviour is rewarded. For example, when a social phobic decides to avoid a social situation or a specific phobic decides to avoid an encounter with his or her phobic object, there is an almost immediate reduction in fear or anxiety. This reduction in fear is rewarding—it is like the relief we experience when we discover that some threatening event isn't actually going to happen.

Behaviour therapists argue that phobias are acquired by means of classical conditioning, in which the phobic stimulus is associated with a painful or aversive stimulus that creates fear. This fear can be reduced by avoiding the phobic stimulus. Joseph Wolpe (1958, 1969) was a behaviour therapist who devised a technique for treating specific phobias known as **systematic desensitisation**. It involves the attempt to replace the fear response to threatening stimuli with a new response incompatible with fear. This new response is usually muscle relaxation.

The first stage in systematic desensitisation is to provide clients with relaxation training in which they learn how to engage in deep muscle relaxation. This prepares them for the subsequent stages of treatment.

Second, clients construct a fear hierarchy with the assistance of their therapist. A fear hierarchy consists of a list of situations or objects producing fear in the client, starting with those causing only a small amount of fear and moving on to those causing increasingly great levels of fear. For example, the first item on the list of a snake phobic might be a small, harmless snake 50 feet away, with subsequent items featuring larger and more dangerous snakes closer to the client.

Third, clients learn to use their relaxation techniques while imagining the objects or situations they fear, starting with those at the bottom of the fear hierarchy. The therapist describes the object or situation, and the client then forms as clear an image as possible of it. An alternative approach is to present the actual object or situation itself (known as in vivo desensitisation). In addition, the client often places himself or herself in progressively more frightening real-life situations between sessions.

When the client can imagine the less-feared items in the fear hierarchy without experiencing fear, he or she moves on to the next items. Eventually, the client can confront the most feared object or situation in the fear hierarchy without fear, at which point he or she is regarded as cured.

Systematic desensitisation puts demands on the expertise of the therapist. For example, the success of systematic desensitisation depends on the therapist identifying the reasons for the client's anxiety. Consider someone who is very fearful of social situations. This fear may be totally irrational or it may occur because the individual concerned lacks social skills. If the latter is the case, then training in social skills is required in addition to systematic desensitisation.

How does systematic desensitisation work? Wolpe (1958) argued that individuals learn through a process of conditioning to associate certain specific stimuli (e.g. snakes) with anxiety. They need to learn to produce a response incompatible with anxiety (e.g. deep muscle relaxation) in the presence of the anxiety-evoking stimulus. Wolpe used the term **reciprocal inhibition** (also known as counterconditioning) to refer to this process of inhibiting anxiety by substituting some competing response. For relaxation to inhibit the client's anxiety, the amount

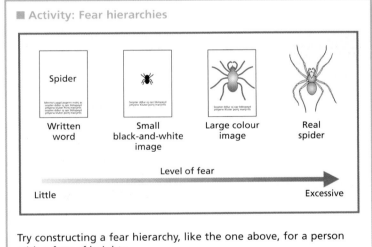

■ Activity: Fear hierarchies

Level of fear

Little — Excessive

Spider → Small black-and-white image → Large colour image → Real spider

Written word

Try constructing a fear hierarchy, like the one above, for a person with a fear of heights.

KEY TERMS

Systematic desensitisation: a form of behaviour therapy designed to treat phobias, in which relaxation training and a fear hierarchy are used.

Reciprocal inhibition: the process of inhibiting anxiety by substituting a competing response.

Fear of cats

If an individual has a fear of cats, systematic desensitisation could be used to overcome this. The client might have learned their fear in the following way

- Unpleasant scratch (unconditioned stimulus: UCS) → fear (unconditioned response: UCR)
- Cat (neutral stimulus: NS) paired with UCS, becomes conditioned stimulus: (CS) → fear (now conditioned response: CR)

This can be overcome by associating the cat with a new response—relaxation.

- Cat (CS) → fear (CR)
- Cat paired with new UCS (relaxation) → pleasant feelings (CR)

In exposure therapy, individuals are gradually exposed to the object or situation they fear.

of anxiety triggered by imagining the phobic stimulus mustn't be too great. That explains why systematic desensitisation starts with stimuli creating only a small amount of anxiety.

Wilson and Davison (1971) suggested a simpler explanation. According to them, the crucial process is one of **extinction**, which occurs when a response that is repeatedly produced in a given situation in the absence of reinforcement loses its strength. More specifically, imagining the phobic stimulus produces the anxiety response but there are no adverse consequences (e.g. being bitten by a snake). This lack of consequences eventually leads to a reduction in the strength of the anxiety response. According to this explanation, *all* that matters is repeated non-reinforced exposure to the phobic stimulus. There is a crucial difference in prediction between the reciprocal inhibition and extinction accounts—according to the former, deep muscle relaxation is essential, whereas it is almost irrelevant according to the latter.

This kind of thinking led to the development of exposure therapy. In **exposure therapy**, phobic individuals are exposed to the object or situation they fear (often gradually increasing the threateningness of the object or situation) for lengthy periods of time until their anxiety level is substantially reduced. For example, patients with a specific phobia may be given one 3-hour exposure session or five 1-hour sessions (Choy, Fyer, & Lipsitz, 2007). Presenting the feared object or situation itself in this way is known as in vivo [in living] exposure. It differs from the typical procedure with systematic desensitisation, which involves *imagining* the feared object or situation.

In recent years, in-vivo exposure therapy has been developed into virtual reality exposure therapy. What happens with virtual reality exposure is that a computer programme produces a virtual environment simulating the phobic situation. Exposure therapy provides maximal scope for extinction to occur but doesn't involve muscle relaxation. If extinction is the crucial process in curing phobias, exposure therapy should be very effective. However, if muscle relaxation is essential, then exposure therapy shouldn't be effective.

Effectiveness

Choy et al. (2007) reviewed the literature on the effectiveness of systematic desensitisation in the treatment of specific phobia. Systematic desensitisation was generally moderately effective in reducing anxiety levels. However, its effects on avoidance of the feared object or situation were less consistent. For example, Rosen, Glasgow, and Barrera (1976) found in a study on animal phobia that clients treated with systematic desensitisation were as likely as controls to continue to avoid the feared animals.

Four studies have assessed the long-term effects of systematic desensitisation. According to Choy et al. (2007), the treatment gains (decreased anxiety and avoidance) present at the end of treatment were maintained at follow-up. For example, Denholtz, Hall, and Mann (1978) found that 60% of clients who were treated for flying phobia continued to fly during the 3½-year follow-up period.

KEY TERM

Extinction: elimination of a conditioned response when the conditioned stimulus is not followed by the unconditioned stimulus or a response is not followed by a reward.

Does systematic desensitisation work because of reciprocal inhibition (with muscle relaxation inhibiting the anxiety response) or because of extinction (non-reinforced exposure to the feared stimulus)? We can answer this question by comparing systematic desensitisation with and without relaxation. Levin and Gross (1985) reviewed the relevant literature. The picture was confused. In 10 studies, systematic desensitisation without relaxation was as effective as desensitisation with relaxation. However, there were a further 15 studies in which relaxation did contribute to the success of systematic desensitisation!

In more recent years, exposure therapy has consistently been found to be effective in the treatment of specific phobia, with traditional exposure therapy and virtual reality exposure therapy producing similar success rates. Both forms of exposure therapy are often more effective than systematic desensitisation (Choy et al., 2007). However, there is one problem with exposure therapy. Prolonged exposure to feared stimuli can create intense levels of anxiety, and so the dropout rate is sometimes rather high.

Exposure therapy has also proved effective in the treatment of social phobia and panic disorder with agoraphobia (Comer, 2001). So far as social phobia is concerned, Clark et al. (2006) reviewed eight studies in which the effectiveness of exposure therapy and cognitive therapy had been compared. Both forms of therapy were consistently effective, and in six of the studies there was a non-significant difference in their effectiveness. However, as is discussed in more detailed later, Clark et al. (2006) found that an enhanced version of cognitive therapy was substantially more effective than exposure in the treatment of social phobia, and there was still a large difference between the two forms of therapy at a 1-year follow-up.

So far as panic disorder with agoraphobia is concerned, Salkovskis et al. (2007) used exposure therapy lasting for a total of just over 3 hours. Exposure in their study involved patients entering various feared situations initially accompanied and then subsequently alone. Exposure therapy was carried out under two different conditions: (1) exposure therapy on its own; (2) exposure therapy designed to produce cognitive change—instructing patients not to use safety-seeking behaviours during exposure to increase their cognitive awareness that the feared situations weren't dangerous. Patients receiving the second form of exposure therapy showed less avoidance than those receiving the first form when walking through a market and entering a crowded pedestrian precinct.

How should we interpret Salkovskis et al.'s (2007) findings? Some behaviour therapists have argued that exposure therapy is effective because it produces extinction of the fear response. The claim is that the fear response isn't rewarded because it is no longer followed by avoidance behaviour. A similar notion is that exposure therapy causes **habituation** of the fear response—habituation involves a reduced response (e.g. fear response) when a particular stimulus is presented repeatedly. Since there was ample opportunity for extinction and/or habituation to occur, we might expect that both forms of exposure would be comparably effective. The fact that they weren't suggests that cognitive processes play an important role in determining the effectiveness of exposure therapy.

Appropriateness

Systematic desensitisation and exposure therapy can both be regarded as appropriate forms of treatment for phobias for various reasons. First, they both

---

EXAM HINT

Compare the effectiveness of the different types of therapies, for example research suggests that traditional exposure therapy, and virtual reality exposure therapy are more effective than systematic desensitisation but then an enhanced form of cognitive therapy has been found to be more effective than exposure for social phobia.

KEY TERM

Habituation: the gradual reduction in the amount of attention paid to a stimulus when it is presented several times; it can also refer to reduced physiological or emotional responses to an aversive stimulus that is presented repeatedly.

have a solid theoretical foundation. Systematic desensitisation is based on the notion that through conditioning individuals could learn to replace the anxiety response to feared stimuli with a relaxation response. Exposure therapy is based on the notion that it produces extinction or habituation of the fear response.

Second, it is obviously important in treatment of phobias to reduce or eliminate their avoidance behaviour. Note that exposure therapy and systematic desensitisation focus directly on reducing avoidance behaviour.

Third, and related to the second point, much of the anxiety and distress experienced by social phobics and by agoraphobics occurs because their avoidance behaviour often restricts their social and working lives. As a consequence, dealing directly with phobics' avoidance behaviour is appropriate because it can have beneficial effects on their anxiety levels.

There are some reasons for doubting the appropriateness of systematic desensitisation and exposure therapy. First, these forms of behavioural therapy don't consider all the relevant factors. For example, individuals suffering from social phobia often have limited social skills and low self-confidence that aren't treated within behavioural therapy. The importance of considering social skills has been revealed in studies in which social phobics receiving social skills training showed more recovery than those not receiving such training (Rachman, 2004). It could also be argued that behaviour therapy doesn't focus sufficiently on changing phobics' cognitive processes and beliefs.

Second, exposure therapy deliberately creates high levels of anxiety and this can upset patients so much that they drop out of treatment. Exposure therapy raises ethical issues concerning acceptable levels of suffering by patients.

Third, the appropriateness of any form of treatment depends in part on having a good understanding of *how* it works. Behaviour therapists assume that exposure therapy works because it causes extinction or habituation of the fear response. However, cognitive processes (e.g. disconfirming patients' beliefs about the threateningness of phobic stimuli) may also be important. If so, it should be possible to develop exposure therapy into a more effective and appropriate form of treatment.

CASE STUDY: ACROPHOBIA—FEAR OF HEIGHTS

Acrophobics have an overpowering fear of heights, a phobic fear that produces intense anxiety, panic attacks, and sends heart rate and blood pressure sky high. Traditionally, therapy has been based on the usual approaches—psychodynamic, behavioural, cognitive, bio-medical, and so on. However, a novel and highly successful new technique, virtual reality (VR), has been developed in California by Lamson (2004).

Sixty participants were recruited from advertisements and were assigned randomly to either the experimental (VR) or the control (drugs) group. Each participant set themselves a target to be reached after a week's therapy, and over 90% of the VR group achieved theirs.

The VR group wore headsets that took them into a café with an open terrace. During the 50-minute therapy session the participant had to "walk" across the terrace and over a plank that led to a bridge set in a hilly scene. Lamson monitored participants' blood pressure and heart rate, and found that the fear response did subside during the 50-minute session.

This therapy is a development of exposure therapy, but avoids the extreme anxiety of confronting the phobic stimulus in reality. It also avoids the risks, such as side effects, of even successful drug therapy.

Perhaps one of the strengths of VR therapy is that it gives the clients confidence; they have been successful in the virtual world so this encourages them to be optimistic about success in the real world. As Lamson says, "within 3 months the woman who could barely start up a step ladder was on the roof cleaning the gutters."

Fourth, exposure therapy is generally more effective than systematic desensitisation in the treatment of phobias. This has led to a marked reduction in the use of systematic desensitisation in recent years. The implication is that systematic desensitisation is unnecessarily complicated, and that muscle relaxation often adds nothing to treating phobias.

Psychological Therapies for Phobic Disorders: Cognitive Therapy

We saw earlier that the cognitive explanation of phobias is based on the assumption that phobic patients have irrational beliefs or interpretive biases with respect to their phobic stimuli. Thus, for example, social phobics mistakenly interpret their own social behaviour as being far more inadequate than it is. Such interpretive biases cause phobics to experience intense fear when confronted by phobic stimuli, and this leads them to avoid situations in which they are likely to experience these stimuli. If interpretive biases are of central importance in the development and maintenance of phobias, then treatment designed to reduce or eliminate these biases should lead to recovery. That is precisely how cognitive therapy attempts to cure phobic patients.

Social phobia

Cognitive therapy has been used to treat social phobia more often than specific phobia or agoraphobia. Accordingly, we will start by considering cognitive therapy for social phobia before discussing briefly its application to other phobias. Earlier we discussed the cognitive model of social phobia proposed by Clark and Wells (1995). According to this model, social phobics have several cognitive problems:

- They focus excessively on their own social behaviour, especially on its deficiencies. Thus, they have attentional biases for negative aspects of their own behaviour.
- They misinterpret their own social behaviour as being much less adequate than is actually the case. This is an example of interpretive bias.
- They maintain their unrealistic fears about potential social catastrophes by safety-seeking behaviours. For example, social phobics often believe that they can avoid being negatively evaluated by others by saying very little and "melting into the background".

David Clark and his colleagues have devised a form of cognitive therapy that seeks to resolve the above problems. First, patients are given training in focusing their attention externally rather than on themselves in social situations. Second, patients watch video evidence of themselves in social situations to demonstrate that their social behaviour is more socially skilled than they believed. Third, patients are instructed to avoid using all their habitual safety-seeking behaviours in a social situation.

Specific phobia

Cognitive therapy as applied to specific phobia focuses on eliminating the interpretive biases that patients have for their phobic stimuli. For example, many patients suffering from a flying phobia believe that their lives are in serious danger every time they fly anywhere. This interpretive bias can be addressed by persuading them to reconsider the probability of a plane crash using actual statistics, and by comparing the dangers of travelling by plane against the dangers associated with other forms of travel. Patients with animal phobia generally believe that there is a high probability that animals belonging to a given species may harm them or even cause their death. Such interpretive biases can be confronted if the therapist provides detailed information about the true level of danger posed by the species in question.

Agoraphobia

When it comes to cognitive therapy for agoraphobia, remember that agoraphobics nearly always also suffer from panic disorder. More specifically, it is generally accepted that for most patients agoraphobia arises as a consequence of already having panic disorder. As a result, as Rachman (2004, p. 128) pointed out, "Tackling the panic disorder first and then 'mopping up' the agoraphobic avoidance has become the preferred approach to treatment." In practice, cognitive therapists typically start the treatment of patients having panic disorder with agoraphobia by reducing patients' interpretive biases relating to panic disorder. For example, patients often misinterpret a fast heart rate as indicating they are going to have a heart attack and may well die.

How does cognitive therapy proceed? First, patients are told about the actual causes of bodily sensations and their tendency to misinterpret those sensations. Second, they are taught how to interpret those bodily sensations rapidly and accurately in stressful situations. Third, cognitive therapists often instruct patients to distract themselves from potentially anxiety-provoking bodily sensations by, for example, starting a conversation. Fourth, the symptoms of agoraphobia are generally treated by means of behaviour therapy involving exposure to public places. However, this is not always necessary. Hedley, Hoffart, and Sexton (2001) studied the effects of cognitive therapy in patients having panic disorder with agoraphobia. Reductions in patients' fear

CASE STUDY: SARAH—A CASE OF AGORAPHOBIA

Sarah, a woman in her mid-30s, was shopping for bargains in a crowded department store during the January sales. Without warning and without knowing why, she suddenly felt anxious and dizzy. She worried that she was about to faint or have a heart attack. She dropped her shopping and rushed straight home. As she neared home, she noticed that her feelings of panic lessened.

A few days later she decided to go shopping again. On entering the same shop, she felt herself becoming increasingly anxious. After a few minutes, she had become so anxious that a sales assistant asked her if she was OK and took her to a first-aid room. Once there her feelings of panic became worse and she became particularly embarrassed at all the attention she was attracting.

From then on, she avoided going to this large shop again. She even started to worry when going into smaller shops because she thought she might have another panic attack, and this worry turned into intense anxiety. Eventually she stopped shopping altogether, asking her husband to do it for her.

Over the next few months, Sarah found that she had panic attacks in more and more places. The typical pattern was that she became progressively more anxious the further away from her house she got. She tried to avoid the places where she might have a panic attack but, as the months passed, she found that this restricted her activities. Some days she found it impossible to leave the house at all. She felt that her marriage was becoming strained and that her husband resented her dependence on him.

Adapted from Stirling and Hellewell (1999).

of bodily sensations and panic attacks were often followed by reductions in agoraphobic symptoms.

Effectiveness

We will first consider the use of cognitive therapy in the treatment of social phobias, after which we will move on to specific phobia and agoraphobia. In the great majority of treatment studies, cognitive therapy was very effective in the treatment of social phobia. We can see how effective it is by considering studies in which cognitive therapy has been compared against exposure therapy, which has sometimes been regarded as the "gold standard" for the treatment of social phobia. Clark et al. (2006) discussed the eight studies that predated their own study. There were no differences in effectiveness of the two therapies in six of the studies and only minor differences in the others.

Clark et al. (2006) decided to test the effectiveness of a more complete form of cognitive therapy based on the Clark and Wells (1995) model and including the avoidance of safety-seeking behaviours. They compared its effectiveness with exposure plus applied relaxation in the treatment of social phobia. There was also a wait-list control group receiving no treatment. The findings were clear-cut. Of those receiving cognitive therapy, 84% no longer met the criteria for social phobia after treatment. For those receiving exposure plus applied relaxation, the figure was 42%, and it was 0% for those in the control group. These differences were still present 1 year after the end of treatment. It is impressive that cognitive therapy was substantially more effective than exposure therapy, suggesting that the latest developments in cognitive therapy have enhanced its effectiveness.

What about cognitive therapy in the treatment of specific phobia? Choy, Fyer, and Lipsitz (2007) reviewed studies on the use of cognitive therapy for specific phobia. This form of therapy was effective in five out of six studies. For example, Ost et al. (2001) used cognitive therapy in the treatment of claustrophobia (fear of enclosed spaces). Approximately 80% of patients receiving cognitive therapy showed strong signs of recovery compared to only 18% of controls. In addition, 93% of those receiving cognitive therapy maintained their treatment gains over a follow-up period of 14 months. However, cognitive therapy is often less effective than exposure therapy in treating specific phobia (Choy et al., 2007).

Choy et al. (2007) discussed other findings suggesting that cognitive therapy is sometimes of limited value in treating specific phobia, especially when its long-term effects are considered. For example, dental phobics who had received cognitive therapy showed long-term reductions in subjective anxiety associated with dental treatment. However, many of them still avoided seeking dental treatment. Muhlberger, Wiedemann, and Pauli (2003) found that only 45% of flying phobics treated by cognitive therapy reported flying when questioned 6 months

---

HOW SCIENCE WORKS: ACROPHOBIA (PHOBIC FEAR OF HEIGHTS)

You know about various therapies for helping people with serious anxieties. One such is the phobic fear of heights, acrophobia. It would be helpful to you, both for understanding and remembering, to apply the knowledge in this textbook to this phobia as an example of an anxiety disorder. This could be done by making some large posters.

Poster 1: You could make a spider diagram with a summary of the phobia in the centre. Then on one side you could have the biological explanations and on the other the psychological explanations. You would find extra information from the internet and/or your library.

Poster 2: Here again, you could summarise the phobia in the centre but now focus on therapies—both the biological and the psychological ones.

You could make these posters more attractive and interesting by using different fonts and colours and including some suitable graphics. You would need to decide whether you were targeting people with some psychological knowledge or those without, for whom you would need to make particularly clear explanations.

after the end of treatment. This figure was only slightly (and non-significantly) higher than the 27% of patients who hadn't received any treatment.

What about cognitive therapy in the treatment of panic disorder with agoraphobia? Cognitive therapy has proved very effective in treating panic disorder. Comer (2001) referred to studies in which 85% of panic patients given cognitive therapy had no panic attacks for as long as 2 years after treatment, compared to only 13% of control patients. However, cognitive therapy on its own is often less effective in the treatment of panic disorder with agoraphobia (Rachman, 2004). As a result, exposure therapy is often added to cognitive therapy. The combination of cognitive and exposure therapy is highly effective (Rachman, 2004). However, as discussed earlier, part of the reason why exposure therapy is effective may be because of the effects it has on cognitive processes.

Support for the above point of view was reported by Salkovskis et al. (2007). They predicted that, "Situational exposure will be most beneficial when it helps the person to experience a disconfirmation of the catastrophic misinterpretations which occur within such situations" (Salkovskis et al., 2007, p. 878). Thus, they argued that exposure therapy should be most effective when it produces *cognitive* change within the patient, reducing his or her interpretive biases about threatening situations. Accordingly, Salkovskis et al. compared exposure therapy that was or wasn't designed to maximise the chances that patients' interpretive biases would be disconfirmed. As predicted, exposure therapy led to a greater reduction in agoraphobic symptoms (assessed by patients' ability to walk along streets and through crowded areas) when it was based on a belief-disconfirmation approach including avoidance of safety-seeking behaviours.

Appropriateness

There are several reasons for arguing that cognitive therapy is an appropriate form of therapy for phobia. First, there are important differences at the cognitive level between phobics and healthy controls. More specifically, phobics undoubtedly possess the various cognitive biases (especially interpretive biases) assumed to be of central importance by cognitive therapists. For example, social phobics have attentional biases leading them to focus too much on themselves in social situations, and interpretive biases leading them to exaggerate the inadequacies of their social behaviour.

Second, it is plausible to assume that these cognitive biases play an important role in maintaining phobias, because they enhance the fear experienced when phobics encounter the feared stimuli or situations. There is some support for that assumption in the fact that cognitive therapy has proved successful in the treatment of phobias, perhaps especially social phobia (Clark et al., 2006).

Third, an important reason why phobics continue to misinterpret the threateningness of phobic stimuli is because their use of safety-seeking behaviours prevents them from developing more realistic interpretations. That means that it is appropriate for cognitive therapists to persuade phobic patients to avoid using safety-seeking behaviours. The fact that therapy is more effective when patients stop using

---

EXAM HINT

Remember to assess the appropriateness of treatments by considering the following:

- how effective the treatment is across different symptoms
- the patient's level of functioning
- the effect of the treatment on relapse rates
- the patient's motivation to use the treatment versus drop-out rate
- if the action of the treatment is fully understood
- ethical issues.

safety-seeking behaviours (e.g. Clark et al., 2006; Salkovskis et al., 2007) helps to indicate the appropriateness of cognitive therapy in this respect.

In what ways may cognitive therapy for social phobia be inappropriate? First, the cognitive approach focuses too much on the patient's beliefs and not enough on reality. For example, social phobics often have genuine reasons for being concerned about their social behaviour. Some social phobics have poor social skills, and social skills training can be effective (Comer, 2001).

Second, one criterion for social phobia and for specific phobia (see discussion at start of the chapter) is that the patient recognises that his or her fear of the phobic object or situation is excessive. Thus, even before treatment has started, phobic patients "know" at some level that the objects or situations they fear are less threatening than their emotional reactions suggest. Thus, much of the information communicated by cognitive therapists may already be known by phobic patients.

Third, appropriate treatment for phobia involves producing cognitive change (e.g. removing interpretive biases) and behavioural change (e.g. stopping avoidance behaviour). Cognitive therapy isn't wholly appropriate because it doesn't directly address behavioural change. Supporting evidence comes from studies on specific phobia. Cognitive

> **EXAM HINT**
>
> Note you need to have covered the issues of classification and diagnosis, clinical characteristics, explanations, and treatments of phobias fully as you do not know which area will be asked in the exam. Sub-parted questions may ask you about the issues of classification and diagnosis in one sub-part, the clinical characteristics in another, and the explanations in another.

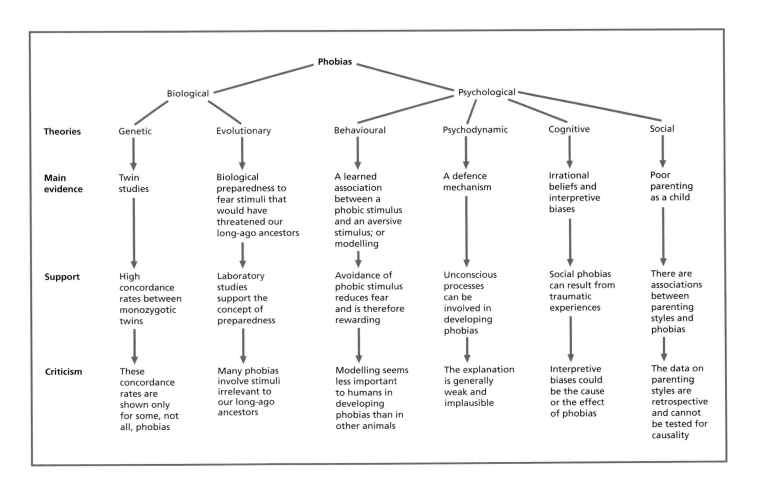

	Biological		Psychological			
Theories	Genetic	Evolutionary	Behavioural	Psychodynamic	Cognitive	Social
Main evidence	Twin studies	Biological preparedness to fear stimuli that would have threatened our long-ago ancestors	A learned association between a phobic stimulus and an aversive stimulus; or modelling	A defence mechanism	Irrational beliefs and interpretive biases	Poor parenting as a child
Support	High concordance rates between monozygotic twins	Laboratory studies support the concept of preparedness	Avoidance of phobic stimulus reduces fear and is therefore rewarding	Unconscious processes can be involved in developing phobias	Social phobias can result from traumatic experiences	There are associations between parenting styles and phobias
Criticism	These concordance rates are shown only for some, not all, phobias	Many phobias involve stimuli irrelevant to our long-ago ancestors	Modelling seems less important to humans in developing phobias than in other animals	The explanation is generally weak and implausible	Interpretive biases could be the cause or the effect of phobias	The data on parenting styles are retrospective and cannot be tested for causality

therapy for specific phobia sometimes produces long-term reductions in subjective anxiety but has much more modest long-term effects on avoidance behaviour (Choy et al., 2007).

SECTION SUMMARY
Psychological Therapies for Phobic Disorders

Behaviour therapy

- ❖ Systematic desensitisation involves the attempt to replace the fear response to phobic stimuli with a response incompatible with fear (e.g. muscle relaxation). The technique is applied to the items in the patient's fear hierarchy, which are imagined in turn.
- ❖ Exposure therapy involves exposing patients directly to their phobic stimuli or situations for long periods of time. It is claimed that it produces extinction or habituation of the fear response.
- ❖ Exposure therapy is generally more effective than systematic desensitisation in treating phobias, and is about as effective as any other form of therapy.
- ❖ Evaluation:

  — Exposure therapy can create intense levels of anxiety leading to high drop-out rates.
  — Behaviour therapy doesn't focus directly on producing cognitive change.
  — Systematic desensitisation is used much less than it used to be, partly because it is unnecessarily complicated.

Cognitive therapy

- ❖ Cognitive therapists assume that phobic patients have interpretive biases that are maintained by safety-seeking behaviours.
- ❖ Cognitive therapy involves trying to eliminate interpretive biases, in part by stopping patients from using safety-seeking behaviours.
- ❖ Cognitive therapy is very effective in treating social phobia. It is moderately effective in treating specific phobia and agoraphobia, but probably less so than exposure therapy.
- ❖ Evaluation:

  — Cognitive therapists sometimes attach too little importance to the genuine problems of patients.
  — Most phobic patients are aware before treatment that their fears are excessive.
  — Cognitive therapists don't focus directly on producing behavioural change.

See *A2-Level Psychology Online* for some interactive quizzes to help you with your revision.

FURTHER READING

Rachman, S. (2004). *Anxiety* (2nd Edn). Hove, UK: Psychology Press. Has excellent introductory coverage of all phobias.

REVISION QUESTIONS

In the exam, questions on this topic are out of 25 marks, and can take the form of essay questions or multi-parted questions. You should spend about 35 minutes on each of the questions below, which aim to test the material in this chapter. In the exam, make certain you know if you have covered an anxiety disorder, schizophrenia, or depression as your psychopathology topic, and then choose the correct question.

1. (a) Outline biological explanations for **one** anxiety
        disorder.   (10 marks)
    (b) Evaluate, using research evidence, the explanations
        you have described in part (a).   (15 marks)
2. Discuss the use of **one** biological and **one** psychological
    therapy for the treatment of an anxiety disorder.   (25 marks)
3. Describe and evaluate psychological explanations
    of an anxiety disorder.   (25 marks)

See *A2-Level Psychology Online* for tips on how to answer these revision questions.

Psychopathology: Anxiety Disorders—Obsessive Compulsive Disorder

By Michael W. Eysenck

As we saw in Chapter 12, several anxiety disorders share the clinical characteristic of "anxiety". Anxiety is useful when it makes us aroused and alert and ready to respond to immediate danger. However, with individuals suffering from anxiety disorders, anxiety becomes a long-lasting and disabling response. An individual with an anxiety disorder experiences an intensity of anxiety that is disproportionate to any threat being posed. Very large numbers of people (5 million in the UK and over 20 million in the US) suffer from an anxiety disorder in any given year.

There are several anxiety disorders including the following: phobias (phobic anxiety disorders), obsessive compulsive disorder (OCD), generalised anxiety disorder, panic disorder, and reaction to severe stress and adjustment disorder (e.g. post-traumatic stress disorder). We discussed the phobias in the last chapter and will be considering obsessive compulsive disorder in this chapter.

Individuals suffering from obsessive compulsive disorder often exhibit a range of obsessions and also compulsive behaviour in the form of rituals. However, there are substantial individual differences. Wilner, Reich, Robins, Fishman, and van Doren (1976) found that 69% of obsessive compulsive patients had both obsessions and compulsions, 25% had obsessions only, and 6% had compulsions only. Why is obsessive compulsive disorder classified as an anxiety disorder? The reason is because the great majority of patients with obsessive compulsive disorder typically experience high levels of anxiety. Patients' obsessional thoughts create anxiety, and their compulsive behaviour occurs to try to reduce anxiety.

Obsessive compulsive disorder is a very severe condition. Consider the following findings based on a large British sample (Torres et al., 2006). Obsessive compulsive disorder was associated with more serious social and occupational impairment than other anxiety disorders. Even more disturbingly, about 25% of patients with obsessive compulsive disorder had tried to commit suicide at some point in the past.

It used to be thought that obsessive compulsive disorder was a relatively rare disorder affecting less than 1% of the population. However, recent estimates are that the lifetime incidence of obsessive compulsive disorder is between 2% and 3% (Rachman, 2004). Men and women are equally likely to suffer from it, and it generally starts in late adolescence or adulthood.

Obsessive–compulsive spectrum disorders

"Obsessive compulsive disorder" is an umbrella term that includes a variety of disorders on the obsessive–compulsive spectrum. The driving force for these is a build-up of tension to a point where the obsessive compulsive behaviour takes over and the tension is released—until the next time. The spectrum includes:

- Trichotillomania: an overwhelming urge to pull out hair, resulting in noticeable hair loss
- Body dysmorphic disorder (BDD): believing one has a defect in his/her physical appearance, e.g. a badly scarred face from acne, or a feeble-looking chin. Sufferers are likely frequently to look in the mirror or try to camouflage or hide the problem
- Kleptomania: irresistible impulses to steal random objects not personally or financially needed
- Compulsive sexual behaviour: uncontrollable sexual thoughts or even behaviour, which distresses the sufferer and may cause personal, work, or criminal problems
- Compulsive shopping: excessive and unnecessary shopping leading to personal, work, or financial difficulties
- Pathological gambling: serious, problem gambling habits leading to significant financial, personal, and/or legal problems
- Intermittent explosive disorder: sudden, violent outbursts of rage that can result in serious assaults and damage and destruction of property
- Pyromania: an uncontrollable desire to start fires, associated with a release of tension

CLINICAL CHARACTERISTICS OF OBSESSIVE COMPULSIVE DISORDER

What are the main symptoms associated with obsessive compulsive disorder? First of all, we need to distinguish between obsessions and compulsions. Obsessions are persistent thoughts, impulses, or images that keep intruding into an individual's consciousness. In contrast, compulsions are rigid, repetitive actions that individuals feel compelled to perform to reduce their anxiety level. In a mild way, most people have obsessions and compulsions. Muris, Murckelbach, and Clavan (1997) found that 75% of people routinely button their shirts top to bottom, 50% always brush their teeth up and down, and 34% typically sleep on their left side. These routine behaviours are so well established that 40% of people are irritated if forced to abandon them.

You can see clearly what is involved in obsessive compulsive disorder by considering Kraines' (1948, p. 183) account of a woman with the disorder who:

> . . . complained of having "terrible thoughts". When she thought of her boyfriend she wished he were dead; when her mother went down the stairs, she "wished she'd fall and break her neck"; when her sister spoke of going to the beach with her infant daughter, the patient "hoped they would both drown". These thoughts "make me hysterical. I love them; why should I wish such terrible things to happen? It drives me wild, makes

EXAM HINT

You need to know the clinical characteristics of obsessive compulsive disorder but you should only use this material in the exam if it has been asked for in a sub-part (a) AO1 question. Do not include them if the question asks you to consider the explanations because simply describing the clinical characteristics is not part of the explanations.

me feel I'm crazy and don't belong to society; maybe it's best for me to end it all than to go on thinking such terrible things about those I love."

Diagnosing Obsessive Compulsive Disorder

One of the main systems of classifying mental disorders is DSM-IV (*Diagnostic and Statistical Manual*, fourth edition), which was first published by the American Psychiatric Association (APA) in 1994 and then in a revised edition (DMS-IV-TR) in 2000. The other main classificatory system is ICD (*International Classification of Diseases*), the tenth edition of which—ICD-10—was published by the World Health Organization (WHO) in 1992. According to DSM-IV-TR, the diagnosis of obsessive compulsive disorder requires the following symptoms to be present:

- Recurrent obsessions or compulsions.
- Past or present recognition that the obsessions or compulsions are excessive or unreasonable.
- Obsessions or compulsions cause marked distress, take up more than 1 hour a day, or interfere significantly with the individual's normal functioning.

Within DSM-IV-TR, obsessions are defined on the basis of four criteria, all of which must be present. First, there are recurrent and persistent thoughts, impulses or images that are experienced as intrusive and that cause marked anxiety. Second, there are thoughts, impulses, or images that differ from excessive worries about real-life problems. Third, the individual tries to ignore, suppress, or neutralise obsessions with some thought or action. Fourth, the individual recognises that obsessions are a product of his or her own mind.

What are some problems with diagnosing strictly on the basis of the DSM-IV criteria?

Within DSM-IV-TR, compulsions are defined on the basis of two criteria, both of which are required. First, there are repetitive behaviours (e.g. hand washing, checking) or mental acts (e.g. counting, praying) the individual feels compelled to perform in response to an obsession or according to rigid rules. Second, there are behaviours or mental acts designed to prevent or reduce distress or to prevent some dreaded event or situation.

What are the benefits of having classification systems based on categories?

ICD-10 (WHO, 1992) uses similar but less detailed criteria. Obsessions and compulsions have to share all of the following four criteria. First, they are recognised as originating in the mind of the patient. Second, they are repetitive and unpleasant, and at least one obsession or compulsion is recognised as excessive or unreasonable. Third, the patient must try to resist their obsessions and compulsions. Fourth, the patient must experience their obsessive thoughts or compulsive acts as "not pleasurable".

We will now consider the nature of obsessions and compulsions in more detail. Obsessions are thoughts or images that are intrusive and feel foreign or alien to the person experiencing them. These obsessions can involve wishes (e.g. that an enemy would die), images (e.g. of disturbing sexual activities), impulses (e.g. desire to attack one's boss), ideas (e.g. that one's illegal actions will be discovered), or doubts (e.g. that a crucial decision was wrong). Akhtar, Wig, Varma, Pershad, and Verma (1975) found that most obsessions fell into five categories. The most frequent one was concerned with dirt and contamination, followed in order by aggression, orderliness of inanimate objects, sex, and religion.

An indication that an individual is suffering from obsessive compulsive disorder is the presence of repetitive behaviours that the individual feels compelled to perform as a means of reducing or avoiding distress; such as excessive hand washing.

Common compulsions

- Cleaning: spending hours washing and scrubbing hands or cleaning household surfaces
- Checking: repeatedly checking and rechecking whether lights and appliances are switched or turned off, or unplugged
- Counting: spending hours counting meaningless strings of numbers
- Arranging: needing objects such as towels, cutlery, ornaments, or furniture placed in a certain way
- Repeating: speaking words or sentences again and again
- Completing: performing a task in a precise order repeatedly, until it is done perfectly (and if interrupted, often needing to start all over again from the beginning)
- Hoarding: collecting objects that are useless

Common obsessions

- Fears about being contaminated by dirt, germs, or chemicals
- Fears of causing the house to flood, something to catch fire, or being burgled
- Aggressive thoughts about physically harming a loved one
- Anxieties about things being exactly right or symmetrical
- Intrusive thoughts or urges about sex
- Excessive doubts about one's own religious beliefs or morals
- An unfounded need to ask, tell, or confess

Compulsions are actions that are performed repetitively because the patient believes there may be dire consequences if he or she doesn't perform them. These repetitive actions often take the form of compulsive rituals in which the same set of actions is performed in exactly the same way on every occasion. Cleaning compulsions (e.g. constant washing of the hands) and checking compulsions (e.g. endless checking that the front door is locked or the oven is turned off) are very common forms of compulsions. Indeed, Akhtar et al. (1975) found these were the two most common types of compulsions.

Most patients with obsessive compulsive disorder experience both obsessions and compulsions. One reason for this is because compulsive behaviour is often produced to reduce the anxiety associated with their obsessions. For example, someone who has obsessional thoughts about contamination may deal with them by engaging in elaborate cleaning rituals.

Obsessive compulsive disorder is included among the anxiety disorders for various reasons. Patients with this disorder find that their obsessions cause high levels of anxiety. In addition, patients' anxiety levels increase if they try to inhibit their obsessions or compulsions.

When you were reading about the apparently very diverse symptoms of obsessive compulsive disorder, you may have wondered whether there is any common thread to them. Rasmussen and Eisen (1991) argued that obsessive compulsive disorder is a "what if" disorder. Patients with the disorder spend much of their time worrying that something terrible will happen. In the words of Rasmussen and Eisen (1991, p. 37), "The very fact that it is within the realm of possibility, however unlikely, that I will stab my baby, or poison my child, is enough to terrify me so that I can think of nothing else no matter how hard I try."

There is a final issue to discuss—is obsessive compulsive disorder similar in different cultures? Fontenelle et al. (2004) obtained evidence that the answer is yes. They compared patients with obsessive compulsive disorder in Brazil, North America, Latin America, Europe, Africa, and Asia. There was generally an early onset of the disorder in nearly all cultures, and most patients in all cultures had a mixture of obsessions and compulsions. However, more patients had aggressive obsessions in Brazil than elsewhere, and there were many religious obsessions in the Middle East. Overall, Fontenelle, Mendlowicz, Marques, and Versiani (2004, p. 403) concluded that, "The core features of OCD [obsessive compulsive disorder] are probably relatively independent of cultural variations."

SECTION SUMMARY
Clinical Characteristics of Obsessive Compulsive Disorder

❖ According to DSM-IV, the symptoms of obsessive compulsive disorder include recurrent obsessions or impulses that are recognised as excessive or unreasonable.

❖ Obsessions are recurrent thoughts, impulses, or images that the individual tries to neutralise with some thought or action.

❖ The most common obsessions are concerned with dirt and contamination, followed by aggression, orderliness of inanimate objects, sex, and religion.

❖ Compulsions are repetitive behaviours that individuals feel compelled to perform.

❖ Cleaning and checking are the two most common types of compulsions. They serve to reduce patients' anxiety about their obsessions.

ISSUES SURROUNDING THE CLASSIFICATION AND DIAGNOSIS OF OBSESSIVE COMPULSIVE DISORDER

The most important issues surrounding the classification and diagnosis of obsessive compulsive disorder relate to reliability and validity. **Reliability** is concerned with the extent to which the same diagnosis is made consistently on different occasions or by different judges or by different forms of assessment (e.g. interview vs. checklist). A diagnostic system can't be of much value if it produces inconsistent diagnoses. **Validity** refers to the extent to which a diagnostic system assesses what it is claimed to assess. For example, does a patient who receives a diagnosis of obsessive compulsive disorder genuinely suffer from that mental disorder rather than a different one? For a diagnostic system to be valid, it must also be reliable—if patients' diagnoses keep changing from day to day or week to week, there is something seriously wrong with the diagnostic system.

The great majority of diagnostic systems (including DSM-IV and ICD-10) are based on categories. This is basically an all-or-none approach—either you have a given disorder, such as obsessive compulsive disorder, or you haven't. Unfortunately, reality is not as neat and tidy as suggested by these categorical approaches. For example, there is **comorbidity**, which occurs when

> **EXAM HINT**
> Remember reliability refers to *consistency*. This means that DSM or ICD is reliable as a means of diagnosing obsessive compulsive disorder if clinicians using it give patients with similar symptoms the same diagnosis, both in terms of actually diagnosing obsessive compulsive disorder and the subtype. A lack of reliability inevitably reduces validity because this refers to whether they have been given the correct diagnosis.

> **KEY TERMS**
> **Reliability:** the extent to which a method of measurement or a research study produces consistent findings across situations or over time.
> **Validity:** the soundness of the measurement tool; the extent to which it is measuring something that is real or valid.
> **Comorbidity:** the presence of two or more disorders in a given individual at the same time.

? What concerns may arise when treating a patient with psychiatric comorbidity?

someone suffers from two or more different mental disorders at the same time. Patients with obsessive compulsive disorder often show comorbidity. Steketee (1990) found that many patients having obsessive compulsive disorder also suffered from one or more personality disorders (e.g. histrionic, avoidant, schizotypal, dependent, obsessive compulsive). Obsessive compulsive disorder often occurs along with other anxiety disorders, especially social phobia, panic disorder, generalised anxiety disorder, and post-traumatic stress disorder (Kessler et al., 2005).

The fact that comorbidity is common causes problems for reliability and validity of diagnosis. It suggests that there is overlap between the symptoms of obsessive compulsive disorder and those of several other disorders, and so there are problems of *discriminating* among disorders. It means we can't regard all sufferers from obsessive compulsive disorder as having symptoms of comparable severity, given that many of them have the symptoms of one or more other disorders as well.

So far the focus has been on reliability and it is now time to consider validity. Davison, Neale, and Kring (2004) identified three types of validity that they argued are important when evaluating diagnostic or classification systems. First, there is content validity. Any form of assessment (e.g. interview, checklist, medical records) possesses content validity if it obtains detailed information from individual patients regarding all of the symptoms of obsessive compulsive disorder.

? What is the difference between criterion and construct validity?

Second, there is criterion validity. The assessment of obsessive compulsive disorder possesses good criterion validity if those diagnosed with obsessive compulsive disorder differ in predictable ways from those not receiving that diagnosis.

Third, there is construct validity. This is a type of validity that involves testing hypotheses based on the diagnosis of obsessive compulsive disorder. A problem arises when the hypothesis is *not* supported. For example, we might form the hypothesis that obsessive compulsive patients perform rituals to reduce their anxiety level. If we found that wasn't the case, it would be hard to know whether this failure occurred because the diagnosis was wrong or because our original hypothesis was wrong.

In addition to the three types of validity emphasised by Davison et al. (2004), there is a fourth type of validity known as predictive validity. Predictive validity concerns our ability to predict the eventual outcome for patients receiving a diagnosis of obsessive compulsive disorder. It is generally regarded as a severe mental disorder that is hard to treat effectively. Accordingly, there would be evidence for predictive validity if the great majority of those diagnosed with obsessive compulsive disorder took a long time to recover.

We will consider these various types of validity in more detail shortly. This will be done in relation to a discussion of some of the main forms of assessment used in diagnosis.

Assessment

Patients are generally diagnosed mainly on the basis of one or more interviews with a therapist. There are various kinds of interviews. Some are unstructured and informal, which can help to establish good rapport between patients and therapists. However, the problem is that reliability and validity of diagnosis tend to be low with such interviews (Hopko, Lejuex, Armento, & Bare, 2004).

A much more reliable and valid approach involves the use of semi-structured or structured interviews in which patients are asked a largely pre-determined series of questions. We will consider two examples here. The Structured Clinical Interview for DSM-IV-Patient Version (SCID-I/P) is a semi-structured interview that takes a little over 1 hour to administer. An open-ended interview is followed by systematic questions concerning symptoms and current and lifetime disorders. The evidence suggests that it is a reasonably reliable and valid assessment procedure (Comer, 2001).

What is the difference between validity and reliability?

The Anxiety Disorder Interview Schedule for DSM-IV (ADIS-IV) is also a semi-structured interview. Many of the symptoms assessed by the ADIS-IV are initially rated on a yes/no basis, with degree of severity being rated for those symptoms that are present. Brown, DiNardo, Lehman, and Campbell (2001) carried out two interviews on 1400 patients with a gap of under 2 weeks between interviews. These interviews were based on the criteria for various anxiety disorders and depression contained in DSM-IV. The inter-rater agreement for obsessive compulsive disorder was excellent, indicating that this disorder can be diagnosed with high reliability. Indeed, the reliability of diagnosis for obsessive compulsive disorder was as high or higher than for almost any other anxiety disorder or type of depression. The most likely explanation is that compulsions provide a clear behavioural indication of the presence of obsessive compulsive disorder, and this assists therapists in diagnosing the condition.

What were the main sources of unreliability in the diagnosis of obsessive compulsive disorder? The most important source was differences in the symptoms reported by patients on the two interviews. The second most important factor was the "threshold" issue—therapists had to decide whether a patient's symptoms exceeded the threshold of causing "marked distress" or impairment. Sometimes one therapist would decide that they did whereas the other one didn't. The third factor was interviewer error, in which the interviewer simply made a mistake in categorising the patient's responses.

> ■ **Activity: An exercise in categorisation**
> Most people can recall an occasion when they have felt compelled to return home to check that the gas has been turned off or the front door locked. Today, more people than ever before buy disinfecting products to combat germs. These are behaviours that can be taken to extremes in obsessive compulsive disorder.
>
> How might you distinguish between behaviours that apply to most people sometimes, and behaviours that are symptomatic of obsessive compulsive disorder?

Steinberger and Schuch (2002) compared DSM-IV and ICD-10 in their diagnoses of children and adolescents having symptoms of obsessive compulsive disorder. There were large differences between the two systems, suggesting there are problem with reliability of diagnosis. Using DSM-IV criteria, 95% of the patients were diagnosed as obsessive compulsive compared to only 46% using ICD-10 criteria. Why did this difference occur? According to Steinberger and Schuch, the criteria used in ICD-10 are less detailed and clear than those of DSM-IV, and so the DSM-IV system is preferable.

There is a final issue relating to reliability. It has often been argued that there are biases in diagnosis. For example, there is ethnic bias, in which members of some groups are more likely to receive a given diagnosis than members of other groups even when they have the same symptoms. There is also gender bias, in which the members of one sex are disproportionately likely to receive a given diagnosis. In fact, there are no clear signs of bias with respect to obsessive compulsive disorder. Steketee and Barlow (2002) found a similar incidence of obsessive compulsive disorder across several cultures. Men and women are about equally likely to receive a diagnosis of obsessive compulsive disorder, which doesn't suggest the existence of gender bias.

Validity

? Can something be valid but not reliable?

What about validity? We start by considering content validity, the extent to which diagnostic assessment covers the entire range of symptoms. Assessment procedures such as SCID-I/P and ADIS-IV have high content validity, because they exhaustively address all the DSM-IV symptoms for obsessive compulsive disorder.

Criterion validity is high if those diagnosed with a given disorder show predictable effects. In view of the seriousness of obsessive compulsive disorder, we would predict that those diagnosed with the condition would have major life problems. Karno, Golding, Sorenson, and Burnham (1988) found that patients with obsessive compulsive disorder were more likely than healthy controls to be divorced or separated. They were also more likely to be unemployed. Such findings are as predicted. However, they don't provide strong evidence for the validity of a diagnosis of obsessive compulsive disorder. The reason is that patients with many (or most) mental disorders experience a high level of interpersonal and occupational difficulties.

? Can something be reliable but not valid?

Construct validity is high if patients diagnosed with obsessive compulsive disorder show effects predicted by one or more hypotheses. It has been hypothesised that a major reason why patients engage in elaborate rituals is to reduce the level of anxiety caused by their obsessional thoughts. It can then be predicted that preventing patients from producing these rituals should initially lead to high anxiety. However, when patients discover that their obsessional thoughts don't actually have any dire consequences, then their level of anxiety should reduce. Both of these predicted effects have been obtained (Comer, 2001).

There is some evidence relating to predictive validity, which is the ability to predict the eventual outcome for patients diagnosed with obsessive compulsive disorder. Thus, there would be high predictive validity if most obsessive compulsive patients responded comparably to treatment. In fact, however, predictive validity is reduced by the finding that some patients with obsessive compulsive disorder are harder to treat than others. For example, Lochner and Stein (2003) found that obsessive compulsive disorder with comorbid tics (recurrent stereotyped movements) had an earlier onset than obsessive compulsive disorder on its own and it was more resistant to drug therapy.

SECTION SUMMARY
Issues Surrounding the Classification and Diagnosis of Obsessive Compulsive Disorder

❖ Patients with obsessive compulsive disorder often have other disorders, which creates problems for reliability of diagnosis.

❖ Semi-structured interviews based on DSM-IV (e.g. SCID-I/P; ADIS-IV) provide reliable and valid diagnoses of obsessive compulsive disorder. However, a source of unreliability concerns decisions as to whether the patient's symptoms cause marked distress or impairment.

❖ DSM-IV is preferable to ICD-10 in the diagnosis of obsessive compulsive disorder because it is more detailed and clearer.

❖ The diagnosis of obsessive compulsive disorder shows reasonable content and construct validity. It is hard to assess criterion validity, and there are some problems with predictive validity.

BIOLOGICAL EXPLANATIONS OF OBSESSIVE COMPULSIVE DISORDER

What are the factors causing obsessive compulsive disorder? As we will see, many answers have been offered to this question. Several of these answers involve biological explanations, and we will be considering three main types of such explanations. First, there are explanations based on the assumption that genetic factors are important in the development of obsessive compulsive disorder. Second, there are explanations based on an evolutionary perspective. These explanations argue that the origins of obsessive compulsive disorder lie in our ancestral past. Third, there are various biochemical and/or anatomical hypotheses. Note that these explanations are not necessarily incompatible with each other. For example, the genetic factors of relevance to obsessive compulsive disorder may well have been influenced by what happened during the course of evolution.

The four major models of abnormality

There are four major models of abnormality, which were covered in your AS level studies. Each of these models provides explanations of the origins of mental disorders, and each is associated with certain forms of treatment.

The **biological model** proposes that the causes of mental disorders resemble those of physical illnesses. Clusters of symptoms can be identified and a diagnosis made, followed by suitable treatment. There is some evidence that infection, genetics, biochemistry, and/or neuroanatomy may account for mental disorders. If the causes are physical then the treatments should be physical as well, and the biological model recommends direct manipulation of the body processes, such as using drugs or ECT. This model is less appropriate for disorders with psychological symptoms, such as obsessive compulsive disorder.

The **behavioural model** suggests that mental disorders are caused by learning maladaptive behaviour via conditioning or observational learning. Logically, anything that is learned can be unlearned using the same techniques. The approach is best for explaining (and treating) those disorders that emphasise external behaviours, such as phobias. The behavioural model is oversimplified and more appropriate to non-human animal behaviour. Ethically, there are advantages such as the lack of blame attached to a person with a mental disorder, but the treatments can be psychologically painful and manipulative.

According to the **psychodynamic model**, the roots of mental disorder are to be found in unresolved conflicts and traumas from childhood. This model may focus too much on the past at the cost of understanding current problems, and too much on sexual problems rather than interpersonal and social issues. Ethical concerns include the problem of false memory syndrome and the sexist nature of the theory. The approach is best for conditions where patients have insight, such as some anxiety disorders, though it has not proved very effective with obsessive compulsive disorder.

The **cognitive model** takes the view that distorted and irrational beliefs are crucially involved in most mental disorders. Limitations of the cognitive model include the problem of whether distorted thinking is a cause or an effect, and the circularity of the explanations. The model suggests that individuals are in part to blame for their problems. The cognitive-behavioural model is a recent and popular development, combining both cognitive and behavioural approaches.

Genetic Explanation

Twin studies and family studies have been carried out to decide whether genetic factors are important in the development of obsessive compulsive disorder. What happens with twin studies is that comparisons are drawn between identical and

HOW SCIENCE WORKS: TWIN STUDIES AND GENETICS

Twin studies are done to investigate how much of a behaviour is genetic as opposed to environmental; i.e. nature rather than nurture. One twin study of individuals with obsessive compulsive disorder show an 87% concordance rate for identical twins and a 47% rate for fraternal twins.

It would be a good exercise to make a poster showing how and why identical and fraternal twins differ genetically, including the difference in shared genes.

You could also incorporate the concordance rates for obsessive compulsive disorder and explain what the significance of the difference in rates tells us. This would not only make these facts clear to you, they would, if presented clearly and well, be an asset to the class.

? What other factors may contribute to this concordance rate?

fraternal twins. Identical twins share 100% of their genes whereas fraternal twins share only 50% of their genes. The most important measure is the **concordance rate**—if one twin has obsessive compulsive disorder, what is the probability that the other twin also has it? If genetic factors are important, then the concordance rate will be higher for identical twins than for fraternal twins.

Carey and Gottesman (1981) found that identical twins showed a concordance rate of 87% for obsessive symptoms and features compared to 47% in fraternal twins. This difference suggests that genetic factors are moderately important. van Grootheest et al. (2005) reviewed twin studies on obsessive compulsive disorder. All of the studies reported higher concordance rates for identical than for fraternal twins, and the overall conclusion was that there is a moderate genetic influence on the development of obsessive compulsive disorder. However, the concordance rates for identical twins were well short of 100%, indicating that environmental factors are of major importance.

Family studies typically involve interviewing the relatives (especially close ones) of patients with obsessive compulsive disorder. Most of these studies have provided additional support for the importance of genetic factors. For example Pauls, Alsobrook, Goodman, Rasmussen, and Leckman (1995) identified a sample of patients with obsessive compulsive disorder and interviewed all their available first-degree relatives (i.e. those sharing 50% of their genes with the patients). The rate of obsessive compulsive disorder was much higher among these relatives than among the relatives of healthy controls (10.3% and 1.9%, respectively). In similar

Expressing inheritance

When psychologists explore the extent to which a characteristic is inherited they use a variety of measures.

The **concordance rate** expresses the extent to which two measures are in agreement. For example, if 20 twin pairs are studied and in 18 of them both had developed schizophrenia, this would produce a concordance rate of 18/20 or 90%, which is very high concordance. Alternatively one can correlate the IQ scores of two individuals, and the degree of correlation shows us how concordant they are.

Monozygotic (identical) twins have the same genes (100% concordance) whereas dizygotic (non-identical) twins and siblings are genetically 50% similar.

Heritability is a measure of the relationship between: (1) the variance of a trait in the whole population; and (2) the extent to which that variance is due to genetic factors. This is expressed as a heritability ratio and calculated by dividing the genetic variance of a characteristic by the total variance (genetic variance/total variance). The genetic variance is calculated using, for example, concordance rates. This percentage is then divided by the amount of variance within the population. A heritability ratio of 1.0 means that all the variance in a population can be accounted for in terms of genetic factors.

So far as obsessive compulsive disorder is concerned, heritability estimates make considerable use of information from the many twin studies that have been carried out. However, it is difficult to disentangle genetic and environmental effects because identical twins generally experience more similar environmental conditions than fraternal twins as well as being more similar genetically. However, the evidence discussed by van Grootheest et al. (2005) suggests that heritability for obsessive compulsive disorder is moderately high. Note that any assessment of heritability is specific to a given population—it is not a universal figure that applies to all cultures at all times.

KEY TERM

Concordance rate: if one twin has a disorder or condition, the likelihood that the other twin also has it.

fashion, Nestadt et al. (2000) found that the lifetime incidence of obsessive compulsive disorder was higher in the relatives of patients with obsessive compulsive disorder (11.7%) than in the relatives of healthy controls (2.7%).

Evaluation

Twin and family studies have consistently found evidence that genetic factors are of importance in determining the development of obsessive compulsive disorder. However, it is totally clear for various reasons that environmental factors are very important. First, part of the reason why the concordance rate is higher for identical than for fraternal twins may be because the environments in which identical twins are brought up tends to be more similar than those in which fraternal twins are brought up. Second, environmental factors probably also play a role in explaining why the incidence of obsessive compulsive disorder is higher among the relatives of patients than among the relatives of healthy controls. Close contact with a relative suffering from obsessive compulsive disorder may be very stressful and the stress thus created may increase the chances of developing the disorder. Third, if genetic factors were all-important in the development of obsessive compulsive disorder, then the concordance rate for identical twins should theoretically be 100%. The actual figure is consistently far lower than that (generally about 50–60%), indicating that environmental factors may be important.

Evolutionary Explanations

In principle, there is an almost infinite list of obsessions and compulsions from which patients with obsessive compulsive disorder might suffer. In practice, however, most (but nothing like all) of their compulsions revolve around washing and checking. Why is this the case? Throughout most of human history, many (or even most) people died prematurely because they lived in unhygienic conditions that led to disease. Accordingly, it was totally adaptive for individuals to be very concerned with hygiene issues and to wash themselves thoroughly several times a day. Historically, too, most human beings until fairly recently lived in potentially dangerous environments with little protection from wild animals or adverse climate. As a result, it was sensible for them to check carefully that everything in their environment was in order.

Abed and de Pauw (1998) offered an evolutionary account of obsessive compulsive disorder based on some of the ideas discussed above. They argued that obsessions are uncontrollable thoughts that produce strong aversive states (e.g. disgust, fear). These obsessional thoughts are the product of a brain system that Abed and de Pauw termed the "Involuntary Risk Scenario Generating System". This system allows individuals to work out

> **Trichotillomania**
>
> Trichotillomania (compelling urge to pull one's hair out) is one of the more common serious disorders on the obsessive–compulsive spectrum. It seems to be linked to a gene known as *Hoxb8*. In mice, a litter was bred without this gene and the animals licked and nibbled at their fur until they had made themselves bald (Woods & Twohig, 2008). They carried on with these behaviours and their skins started to develop sores. Humans are very different from mice, but these findings suggest that a similar genetic lack might be implicated in obsessive compulsive disorders.

 What type of environmental factors do you think may play a role in obsessive compulsive disorders?

> **EXAM HINT**
>
> Note that the evidence for genetic factors comes mainly from twin and family studies. However, you should also consider the evolutionary explanations of obsessive compulsive disorder as evidence for a genetic basis.

 Can you think of some ways OCD may be adaptive?

> **HOW SCIENCE WORKS: EVOLUTION AND OBSESSIVE COMPULSIVE DISORDER**
>
> Evolutionary explanations for the persistence of obsessive compulsive disorder down the generations is based on the concept that the obsessions and compulsions could have been adaptive, though perhaps in a milder form.
>
> You could make this clear by constructing a PowerPoint presentation with the obsession and compulsion as the frame title and the adaptive function of this as the text box. You would need to research as many obsessions and compulsions as you can, using internet sources—online archives from newspapers such as the tabloids can also be useful here.
>
> Then you need to think of a possible adaptive value to our hunter-gatherer ancestors, and you could also discuss these possibilities with your classmates. If you do make the presentation then you have the opportunity to use colour and graphics to attract attention and enhance what you are communicating.

ways and means of avoiding harm in safety without having to confront real-life dangers. According to Abed and de Pauw, obsessive compulsive disorder involves the over-activation of warning signals related to stimuli and situations that were potentially dangerous in our evolutionary history.

A related evolutionary account of obsessive compulsive disorder was offered by Szechtman and Woody (2004), who began by arguing that most obsessional thoughts and images, and most compulsions, revolve around the idea of security or safety. We have a security motivation system designed to detect potential dangers and prevent them turning into emergencies. More specifically, this system has an "easy-to-turn-on, hard-to-turn off quality", which makes evolutionary sense, "because repeated false alarms are much less costly than even a single failure to prepare for upcoming danger". In essence, what distinguishes patients with obsessive compulsive disorder from healthy individuals is that they find it much harder to turn off their security motivation system.

It has been argued that obsessive compulsive disorder may have an adaptive function; that of ensuring safety. Repeatedly checking the gas oven is turned off is preferable to the potential danger of leaving it on once accidentally.

If, as evolutionary accounts emphasise, the obsessions and compulsions of patients with obsessive compulsive disorder fulfil an adaptive function, then we might expect this disorder to be found in nearly all cultures. This is, indeed, the case. If these obsessional thoughts and compulsions are adaptive, then we might expect many healthy individuals to report them. Rachman and de Silva (1978) found that 80% of healthy individuals reported obsessional thoughts and/or compulsions, with 54% reporting both.

Evaluation

The evolutionary accounts we have discussed have various strengths. First, they explain why patients with obsessive compulsive disorder have certain obsessions and compulsions rather than others. Second, it is likely (but not certain) that some obsessions and compulsions fulfilled an adaptive function in our ancestral past, and the evolutionary approach is the only one to emphasise this notion. Third, the notion that obsessive compulsive disorder is associated with an overactive warning system seems plausible.

What are the limitations of the evolutionary perspective? First, the obsessional thoughts and compulsions of patients with obsessive compulsive disorder are often very disturbing and severely disrupt their everyday functioning. Thus, we mustn't exaggerate any adaptive value they may have. Second, some of the thoughts and actions of patients with obsessive compulsive disorder seem to have no possible adaptive value. For example, some patients wish repeatedly that their spouse would die, and others have repeated urges to shout out obscenities at work. Third, it is very difficult to test the evolutionary approach. Abed and de Pauw (1998) and Szechtman and Woody (2004) have put forward plausible evolutionary accounts of the origins of obsessive compulsive disorder. However, it isn't clear how we might decide which account is closer to the truth. Fourth, the evolutionary approach is designed to explain why obsessive compulsive disorder exists within human cultures. It is less relevant to explaining why certain individuals develop obsessive compulsive disorder.

Biochemical and Anatomical Explanations

Those who favour biological explanations of obsessive compulsive disorder often argue that it is associated with differences in brain functioning. Several different theories have been proposed, but we will focus on two of them. First, we will consider the notion that patients with obsessive compulsive disorder suffer from biochemical abnormalities. Second, we will turn to theories that identify particular regions of the brain that are allegedly different in obsessive compulsive patients than in healthy controls.

Biochemical explanations

The most influential biochemical explanation of obsessive compulsive disorder has been the serotonin hypothesis. According to this hypothesis, individuals with obsessive disorder have reduced levels of the neurotransmitter serotonin or have deficient serotonin metabolism. What seemed like strong support for the hypothesis came from studies of drug therapy for the disorder. As is discussed later in the chapter, two classes of drug have proved effective in the treatment of obsessive compulsive disorder:

> **Assumptions of biological explanations**
>
> - All mental disorders have a physical cause (micro-organisms, genetics, biochemistry, or neuroanatomy).
> - Mental illnesses can be described in terms of clusters of symptoms.
> - Symptoms can be identified, leading to the diagnosis of an illness.
> - Diagnosis leads to appropriate physical treatments.

serotonin reuptake inhibitors (SRIs) and selective serotonin reuptake inhibitors (SSRIs). Both classes of drug increase serotonin levels, which suggests that an important part of the problem with obsessive compulsive disorder might be a low level of serotonin. Further support was provided by the finding that drugs that mainly affect neurotransmitters other than serotonin are of little or no value in treating obsessive compulsive disorder.

Despite the apparent support for the serotonin hypothesis, however, there are serious problems with it. First, discovering that drugs that increase serotonin levels reduce the symptoms of obsessive compulsive disorder doesn't prove that a low level of serotonin caused the disorder. Drugs can be effective for many different reasons. For example, aspirin cures headaches, but no-one believes that a lack of aspirin is what causes headaches in the first place!

Second, studies in which serotonin levels in obsessive disorder patients have been assessed have typically found no differences between them and healthy controls. As Rachman (2004, p. 75) concluded, "There is no evidence that patients with OCD [obsessive compulsive disorder] have more or less serotonin than non-patients, or more or less serotonin than patients with other forms of anxiety disorder." In addition, there is no evidence that patients with relatively low levels of serotonin respond better to drug therapy than patients whose serotonin levels are higher.

Third, there is much evidence indicating that SSRIs have to be taken for at least 6 weeks or more before there is any reduction in the symptoms of obsessive compulsive disorder (Dougherty et al., 2002). Indeed, there is often an *increase* in symptoms early in drug therapy. These findings seem strange if the main problem is insufficient serotonin.

Fourth, there is now reasonable support for what is almost the opposite of the serotonin hypothesis! While it is true that SSRIs initially increase serotonin levels, what happens after that is that the drugs' effects on serotonin receptors produce a functional decrease in the availability of serotonin (Dolberg, Iancu, Sasson, & Zohar, 1996). That helps to explain why the beneficial effects of SSRIs on the symptoms of obsessive compulsive disorder take a long time to occur.

Evaluation

It is clear that the neurotransmitter serotonin is of some importance to an understanding of obsessive compulsive disorder, but the details are still unknown. It is also clear that the serotonin hypothesis is wrong. There are several reasons for saying this. First, in addition to all the evidence that is inconsistent with it, the hypothesis doesn't explain why and how patients with obsessive compulsive disorder have low levels of serotonin in the first place.

Second, the symptoms of which obsessive compulsive patients complain involve obsessions and compulsions, and it is unclear how low levels of serotonin would produce these symptoms.

Third, there is plentiful evidence that psychological therapies are effective in the treatment of obsessive compulsive disorder. As there is no reason at all for supposing that these therapies produce increased serotonin levels, their effectiveness is mysterious on the serotonin hypothesis.

Fourth, even if the evidence supported the serotonin theory, that wouldn't prove that low serotonin levels help to cause obsessive compulsive disorder. Such evidence would be basically correlational. As a result, we wouldn't know whether low serotonin levels are one cause of obsessive compulsive disorder or whether having obsessive compulsive disorder leads to reduced serotonin levels.

Anatomical explanations

Another biological explanation is based on the assumption that there are differences in brain anatomy and functioning between obsessive compulsive patients and healthy controls. Much of the focus has been on the orbital region of the frontal cortex (which is close to the eyes) and on the caudate nucleus (located within the basal ganglia just below the cerebral cortex). According to Baxter et al. (1992), the orbital frontal cortex and the corpus striatum (which includes the caudate nucleus) are of central importance in obsessive compulsive disorder. Two main processes are involved:

1. Primitive urges concerning sex, aggression, danger, and hygiene—"the stuff of obsessions" according to Baxter et al. (1992)—all originate in the orbital frontal cortex. Patients with obsessive compulsive disorder have an overactive orbital frontal cortex and so suffer from many more obsessions than other people.
2. Dysfunction of neural circuits, including the corpus striatum, in patients with obsessive compulsive disorder reduces inhibitory processes and leads to inappropriate repetitive behaviour.

What evidence is there to support the above hypothesis? First, it has been found that there is increased brain activity in the brain areas identified by Baxter et al. (1992) when obsessive compulsive symptoms are produced by relevant phobic stimuli (Evans, Lewis, & Iobst, 2004).

Second, there are various anatomical differences in the brain between patients with obsessive compulsive disorder and healthy controls (reviewed by Soriano-Mas et al., 2007). More specifically, areas such as the orbital frontal cortex and the caudate nucleus are sometimes larger in obsessive compulsive patients than in controls. However, we must not exaggerate the extent of the differences. Soriano-Mas et al. (2007) tried to categorise obsessive compulsive patients and healthy controls using detailed information about brain structure. Their overall accuracy was 77%, indicating that brain anatomy alone doesn't provide a very precise way of determining whether someone has obsessive compulsive disorder.

Third, obsessive compulsive symptoms often seem to increase or decrease when the orbital region and/or the caudate nucleus are damaged through either illness or accident. Comer (2001) discussed the case of an obsessive compulsive patient who shot himself in the head in an attempt to commit suicide. Even though he survived, there was extensive damage to brain areas such as the orbital region and the caudate nucleus. After his injury, the patient reported a dramatic reduction in his symptoms.

Fourth, supporting evidence has been obtained through the use of brain imaging. Saxena and Rauch (2000) reviewed the relevant studies, most of which found that obsessive compulsive patients have elevated activity in the orbital region and the caudate nucleus compared to healthy controls. After treatment, activity in these brain areas reduces to a level comparable to that of controls.

> ? Could you use this knowledge to diagnose OCD? How reliable would the diagnosis be?

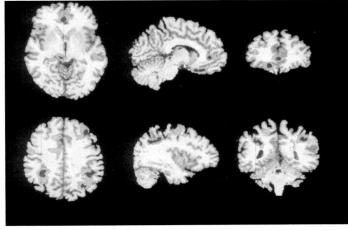

Coloured PET (positron emission tomography) scans of a human brain, showing active areas in obsessive compulsive disorder. In this patient, positive correlations (activity increases as symptoms get stronger) are in the top row, seen coloured in the left orbital region, prefrontal, left frontal gyri, and thalamus. Negative correlations (activity decreasing as symptoms strengthen) are in the bottom row in the right frontal gyrus and parietal regions.

Evaluation

There is fairly consistent evidence from brain-damaged patients and from brain imaging indicating that certain brain regions such as the orbital region and the caudate nucleus or corpus striatum are associated with obsessive compulsive disorder. The involvement of these brain areas in thinking and in action means that it is reasonable to assume that they play a role in obsessive compulsive disorder. Baxter et al. (1992) have provided a plausible explanation of the precise roles that different brain regions may play in obsessive compulsive disorder.

The anatomical hypothesis possesses a number of limitations. First, there are several studies in which no differences in brain anatomy were found between obsessive compulsive patients and controls. Even when significant differences are found between patients and controls, there are typically many obsessive compulsive patients whose brain anatomy isn't distinguishable from that of healthy controls (e.g. Soriano-Mas et al., 2007).

Second, when brain activity is assessed, what we have is an *association* between elevated activity in certain brain areas and obsessive compulsive disorder. As it is only an association, it doesn't show that those brain areas play a role in *causing* obsessive compulsive disorder. Indeed, it seems at least as likely that having obsessive compulsive symptoms leads to increased brain activity in areas concerned with thinking and action.

Third, the hypothesis doesn't provide a comprehensive account of the origins of obsessive compulsive disorder. For example, environmental factors (e.g. life events) are important in producing obsessive compulsive disorder. However, it seems improbable that environmental factors could influence brain anatomy, and it is unclear how they might influence brain activity.

BIOLOGICAL EXPLANATIONS OF OBSESSIVE COMPULSIVE DISORDER

Explanation	Evidence	Strengths	Weaknesses
Genetics: inheriting maladaptive genes	Twin studies; family studies	Empirical, testable data	Does not include environmental factors
Evolutionary: adaptive for our ancestors	Adaptive rationale, risk awareness leading to avoidance and survival	Face validity; found in most cultures; a behavioural extreme	Conjecture; does not explain why only some individuals are affected
Biochemical and anatomical: maladaptive brain functioning	Serotonin is implicated because SSRIs improve OCD symptoms	Serotonin is known to affect mood and behaviour	Serotonin levels do not seem low in sufferers; SSRIs take 6 weeks to have an effect
	Brain malfunction in the orbitofrontal cortex and caudate nuclei	Sufferers have an over-active and sometimes enlarged orbitofrontal cortex and dysfunction of inhibitory processes in the caudate nuclei	These differences are not found in all sufferers; OCD might cause the extra brain activity

---

SECTION SUMMARY
Biological Explanations of Obsessive Compulsive Disorder

Genetic explanation

❖ Twin and family studies indicate that there are genetic influences on the development of obsessive compulsive disorder.
❖ Evaluation:

— Environmental factors may account in part for the higher concordance rate for identical than for fraternal twins.
— The finding that the concordance rate for identical twins is far below 100% means that environmental factors are very important.

Evolutionary explanations

❖ According to evolutionary explanations, washing and checking compulsions had adaptive value in our ancestral past.
❖ Obsessive compulsive disorder may involve the over-stimulation of warning signals related to stimuli that were dangerous in our evolutionary history. Alternatively, we may have a security motivation system designed to detect dangers.
❖ Evaluation:

— Some of the thoughts and actions of patients with obsessive compulsive disorder don't seem to have any possible adaptive value.
— It is very hard to test evolutionary accounts.
— Evolutionary accounts don't directly explain why only certain individuals develop obsessive compulsive disorder.

❖ According to the serotonin hypothesis, obsessive compulsive patients suffer from low serotonin levels; this is why SSRIs are effective.

❖ Evaluation:

— Serotonin is relevant to an understanding of obsessive compulsive disorder.

— Obsessive compulsive patients don't have low levels of serotonin.

— Whereas SSRIs initially increase serotonin levels, they subsequently produce a functional *decrease* in the availability of serotonin.

Biochemical explanations

❖ According to Baxter et al. (1992), obsessive compulsive patients have an overactive orbital frontal cortex leading to numerous obsessions. Dysfunctional neural circuits including the corpus striatum lead to inappropriate behaviour through reduced inhibition.

❖ Evaluation:

— On average, there are only small differences in brain anatomy between obsessive compulsive patients and healthy controls.

— The existence of an association between obsessive compulsive disorder and brain abnormalities doesn't establish causality.

— The approach is limited in that it ignores important environmental factors helping to trigger obsessive compulsive disorder.

Anatomical explanations

PSYCHOLOGICAL EXPLANATIONS OF OBSESSIVE COMPULSIVE DISORDER

We saw in the last section that much can be understood about obsessive compulsive disorder by considering various biological explanations of its development. In this section, we will see that there is also much mileage in considering major psychological explanations of the disorder. We will be discussing four psychological explanations. First, there is the psychodynamic explanation originally proposed by Sigmund Freud approximately 100 years ago. Second, there is the behavioural explanation. According to this explanation, the reason why obsessive compulsive patients have compulsions and ritual behaviour is because they fulfil the function of reducing their level of anxiety. Third, there is the cognitive explanation, according to which an excessive sense of personal responsibility is at the heart of obsessive compulsive disorder. Fourth, there are social explanations of obsessive compulsive disorder. For example, it may be that individuals who experience serious life events may be more vulnerable than other people to the development of obsessive compulsive disorder.

> **EXAM HINT**
>
> The question will usually stipulate whether biological or psychological explanations are to be considered. Do use the alternative explanations as counterperspectives, but be careful—one link sentence to introduce them is not enough. You must consistently contrast the counterperspective with the explanation(s) you've covered as AO1. Do not describe the counterperspective; instead explain what insights it provides that the AO1 explanations do not. Also consider whether the different explanations share any strengths or weaknesses, or whether the weakness of one can be used to highlight the strength of the other.

Psychodynamic Explanation

Psychodynamic explanations of obsessive compulsive disorder originally go back to Freud, but have since been developed by other psychodynamic theorists. It is assumed that the ego (the conscious, rational mind) of patients with obsessive compulsive disorder is disturbed by their obsessions and compulsions. This leads to the use of various ego defence mechanisms including isolation, undoing, and reaction formation. Isolation involves patients regarding their unwanted thoughts as being alien and not belonging to them. The basic idea in undoing is that an undesirable impulse can be cancelled out by performing certain acts. For example, patients who have undesirable sexual impulses may literally cleanse themselves by washing their hands repeatedly. Finally, there is reaction formation, in which the patient adopts a lifestyle that is completely opposite from that suggested by their undesirable impulses. For example, a man with obsessive compulsive disorder may become a monk to repress his obsessive sexual desires.

Freud argued that the anal stage of development, which occurs at about 2 years of age, was of particular importance. It is during this stage that children are toilet trained. If children's parents are too harsh in their approach to toilet training, they may retaliate by becoming aggressive and deliberately soiling their clothes. This can lead to further pressure from the parents causing the child to feel dirty and ashamed. There is a danger of a major conflict within the child between wanting to soil his or her clothes and wanting to retain faeces, and this conflict can ultimately lead to obsessive compulsive disorder.

More generally, Freud (1949, p. 336) argued as follows: "It remains uncontestable that for the average human being anxiety is closely connected with sexual restriction." When an individual's sexual needs can't be satisfied, it is "discharged through being converted into dread" (Freud, 1949, p. 339).

The psychodynamic explanation doesn't have much to recommend it for various reasons. First, it is true as Freud claimed that many children experience conflicts with their parents during toilet training. However, the notion that these conflicts escalate into obsessive compulsive disorder several years later is fanciful and there is practically no evidence supporting it. Second, Freud's account seems less relevant to some obsessions and compulsions than others. For example, it is not altogether clear how an obsession with the orderliness of inanimate objects or engaging in compulsive checking are relevant to toilet training or sexual constraints.

Third, even if were the case that certain experiences during toilet training were associated with obsessive compulsive disorder, that wouldn't establish causality. For example, it could be that obsessive compulsive disorder and problems with toilet training both reflect a certain type of personality that some children inherit. Fourth, several factors (e.g. genetic ones, life events) that seem to be important in the development of obsessive compulsive disorder are ignored within the psychodynamic approach.

? Freud developed his theory in the early part of the twentieth century when attitudes to sex and sexuality were very different from today. What effect do you think this might have on the development of psychodynamic therapy?

Assumptions of the psychodynamic model

- Much of our behaviour is driven by unconscious motives.
- Childhood is a critical period in development.
- Mental disorders arise from unresolved, unconscious conflicts originating in childhood.
- Resolution occurs through accessing and coming to terms with repressed ideas and conflicts.

Behavioural Explanation

Solomon and Wynne (1953) carried out important research that paved the way to a behavioural explanation of obsessive compulsive disorder. Dogs were placed in shuttle boxes consisting of two small compartments divided by a hurdle over which the dog could jump. Ten seconds after a light was turned on, the dog received an electric shock unless it had jumped into the other compartment during

? Why might this experiment be considered unethical today?

the 10-second interval. After several trials, the dogs (very sensibly!) got in the habit of jumping into the non-electrified compartment shortly after the light was turned on.

After the conditioned response of jumping had become established, the experimenters disconnected the electricity so that the dogs couldn't receive any more shocks whether or not they jumped over the hurdle. Perhaps surprisingly, the dogs continued to jump over the hurdle for hundreds of trials. Presumably this happened because jumping the hurdle was strongly reinforced or rewarded because it reduced the dogs' anxiety or distress.

It is claimed that a very similar process is involved in the development of obsessive compulsive disorder. Fear in individuals with obsessions and compulsions is triggered by fear associated with stimuli (e.g. unwashed hands, obsessional thoughts) that are very unlikely to cause real harm. Patients with obsessive compulsive disorder manage to reduce their level of fear by compulsive rituals (e.g. hand washing), and this behaviour is reinforced or rewarded by fear reduction.

Mowrer (1947) developed a two-process theory along these lines. First, neutral stimuli become associated with threatening thoughts or experiences through classical conditioning, and this leads to the development of anxiety. For example, shaking hands may become associated with the anxiety-provoking notion of contamination for someone with obsessive compulsive disorder. Second, the individual discovers that the anxiety that is created can be reduced substantially by washing his or her hands.

Rachman and Hodgson (1980) obtained support for the above explanation. Patients with obsessive compulsive disorder were exposed to situations triggering their obsessions (e.g. shaking hands if they had an obsession about contamination). As predicted, this produced a high level of anxiety. However, more importantly, when the patients performed their compulsive rituals (e.g. hand washing) when exposed to such situations, their level of anxiety rapidly decreased.

? What is wrong with applying the results of a laboratory experiment on dogs to humans in society?

Assumptions of the behavioural model

- All behaviour is learned, and maladaptive behaviour is no different.
- This learning can be understood in terms of the principles of conditioning and modelling.
- What was learned can be unlearned, using the same principles.
- The same laws apply to human and non-human animal behaviour.

Evaluation

The notion that patients with obsessive compulsive disorder produce compulsive rituals because these rituals serve to reduce their anxiety levels makes sense, and is supported by the evidence. As is discussed later, one of the most effective forms of therapy for obsessive compulsive disorder is exposure and response prevention. This involves exposing patients to situations they fear while preventing them from engaging in their usual anxiety-reducing compulsive rituals. This technique seems to work because it allows patients to see that their fears and anxieties are groundless, and so their compulsive rituals aren't needed. For present purposes, the key point is that the success of exposure and response prevention is entirely consistent with the behavioural explanation of obsessive compulsive disorder.

Behavioural explanations of obsessive compulsive disorder are limited in several ways. First, behavioural explanations fail to take account of genetic factors known to be involved in the origins of obsessive compulsive disorder. Second, behavioural explanations don't explain why so many of the rituals of obsessive patients relate to washing and checking rather than to other possible ritualised forms of behaviour. Third, while behavioural explanations indicate why compulsive rituals are maintained, they don't really offer a clear account of how these rituals originate in the first place.

Cognitive Explanation

From a cognitive perspective, it has often been argued that an inflated sense of personal responsibility plays a major role in producing the obsessions and compulsions found in patients with obsessive compulsive disorder. For example, Salkovskis (1991, pp. 13–14) suggested that the behaviour patterns of these patients "reflect an attempt to prevent themselves from being responsible for adverse consequences that might arise from not acting on the content of the thought (prevention of harm through, for example, washing and checking)." More succinctly, Salkovskis (1996, p. 121) expressed the same idea as follows: "OCD [obsessive compulsive disorder] patients show a number of characteristic thinking errors linked to their obsessional difficulties. Probably the most typical and important is the idea that 'Any influence over outcome = responsibility for outcome'."

Where does this inflated sense of personal responsibility come from? Undoubtedly, numerous factors are involved and it is impossible to provide a general answer to that question. However, women who are pregnant or who have recently given birth find themselves in a situation in which they have enormous responsibility for the well-being of their child. According to the theoretical approach of Salkovskis, we might expect pregnant women to show an increase in obsessive compulsive symptoms. Buttolph and Holland (1990) found that 69% of female patients with obsessive compulsive disorder had the onset or worsening of symptoms during pregnancy or childbirth. Neziroglu, Anemone, and Yaryuratobias (1992) found that 39% of female patients with obsessive compulsive disorder with children reported an onset of the disorder during pregnancy.

What are the limitations of the above cognitive explanation of obsessive compulsive disorder? First, as Tallis (1995) pointed out, if an inflated sense of personal responsibility was the only factor involved in obsessive compulsive disorder, then many more people would suffer from it. Second, given the huge range of behaviour of which humans are capable, it seems very odd that an excessive sense of personal responsibility predominantly leads to washing and checking rather than other forms of behaviour. Third, patients with obsessive compulsive disorder may feel excessively responsible for negative events, but very rarely seem to feel excessive responsibility for positive events.

We have discussed some of the major irrational and dysfunctional thoughts and beliefs that cognitive theorists believe are at the heart of obsessive compulsive disorder. Other dysfunctional beliefs (most of which depend to some extent on an exaggerated sense of personal responsibility) were discussed by Abramowitz (2006):

1. Belief that thoughts can help to cause events (e.g. "If I wish someone dead, that increases the chances they will die"). The notion that having a negative thought about doing something wrong is equivalent to actually doing it is known as *thought–action fusion*.

Assumptions of the cognitive model

- Maladaptive behaviour is caused by faulty and irrational cognitions.
- It is the way you think about a problem, rather than the problem itself, that causes mental disorder.
- Individuals can overcome mental disorders by learning to use more appropriate cognitions.
- Aim to be positive and rational.

2. Belief that negative events are extremely likely and would be disastrous (e.g. "One day I will leave my door unlocked, everything I own will be stolen, and everyone will disapprove of me").

3. Belief that mistakes and imperfection are intolerable (e.g. "I must ensure that I always do the right thing").

Why do patients with obsessive compulsive disorder have persistent compulsions? According to Salkovskis (1996), there are two main reasons. First, as assumed by the behavioural approach, compulsions are rewarded or reinforced by immediate reduction of distress or anxiety. Second, patients' compulsions prevent them from discovering that their obsessions are dysfunctional and wrong. For example, they are so obsessed with checking everything so they don't make any mistakes that they never find out that they wouldn't actually be held personally responsible for any mistake they were to make. Some of the ideas put forward by Salkovskis resemble those of the behavioural explanation. However, he attaches more significance to the *cognitive* processes involved.

One of the major irrational beliefs commonly held by obsessive compulsive disorder sufferer is that imperfection is intolerable. David Beckham has spoken of his struggle with such compulsions, revealing that he has the overwhelming desire to have everything in straight lines or in pairs. In a televised interview he said that if there happened to be two cans of soda in his fridge, one would have to be removed and placed elsewhere as he prefers everything to be in pairs.

Evaluation

The cognitive approach correctly emphasises the range of dysfunctional beliefs possessed by obsessive compulsive patients. It is also reasonable to argue that obsessive compulsive patients typically have an exaggerated sense of personal responsibility for negative outcomes. Finally, the existence of compulsive rituals makes it very hard for obsessive compulsive patients to realise that their obsessions and dysfunctional thoughts about danger are incorrect.

Despite attractive features of cognitive explanations of obsessive compulsive disorder, there are several limitations with such explanations. First, what we know is that patients with obsessive compulsive disorder typically have many dysfunctional beliefs and exaggerate their personal responsibility for bad events. Such evidence is basically in the form of an association, and so doesn't tell us what causes what. It is entirely possible that having obsessive compulsive disorder leads to dysfunctional beliefs, and it may be that having dysfunctional beliefs doesn't play any role in the development of obsessive compulsive disorder.

Second, the cognitive account ignores the role of genetic factors. Twin and family studies indicate that the development of obsessive compulsive disorder depends to some extent on genetic factors, but such evidence isn't considered in the cognitive account.

Third, the cognitive account fails to explain many of the detailed facts about obsessive compulsive disorder. For example, why do patients with obsessive compulsive disorder accept excessive responsibility for negative outcomes but not for positive ones? Why do most of the compulsive rituals of these patients revolve around washing and checking?

? If one of your relatives has suffered from a mental disorder, what reasons are there for you not to worry that you may also develop the same disorder?

Social Explanation: Life Events

It has been found that individuals experiencing severe life events (e.g. divorce, job loss) are more likely than other people to develop numerous mental disorders. This is not a surprising finding—it seems commonsensical that someone who has to deal with distressing events is more vulnerable in many ways than someone who doesn't. Note, however, that it is generally assumed that life events are very rarely the *only* factor triggering a mental disorder. When life events help to trigger a mental disorder, it is more a case of the final straw that breaks the camel's back.

There is some evidence that life events play a role in the development of obsessive compulsive disorder. Khanna, Rajendra, and Channabasavanna (1988) discovered that patients with obsessive compulsive disorder had experienced significantly more negative life events than healthy controls in the 6 months prior to the onset of the disorder. Most of these events were undesirable and uncontrolled events in the areas of health and bereavement.

McKeon, Roa, and Mann (1984) found evidence that the relationship between life events and obsessive compulsive disorder is more complicated. In their study, they took account of whether the patient had had an anxious or non-anxious personality before the onset of obsessive compulsive disorder. Patients who had had a non-anxious personality experienced three times as many life events as healthy controls in the year before onset of the disorder. By contrast, those with an anxious personality hadn't experienced a surplus of life events on average. These findings suggest that life events *or* an anxious personality can contribute to the development of obsessive compulsive disorder.

There is also evidence that exposure to traumatic life events at some point in life is associated with obsessive compulsive disorder. For example, Saunders, Villeponteaux, Lipovsky, Kilpatrick, and Veronen (1992) found that those who had experienced childhood sexual abuse were about five times more likely than non-abused individuals to develop obsessive compulsive disorder. Cromer, Schmidt, and Murphy (2007) found that patients with obsessive compulsive disorder who had experienced one or more traumatic life events at some point in their lives had more severe symptoms than those who hadn't experienced any.

It is important to note that all of the above studies simply show an association between life events and obsessive compulsive disorder; and an association does not prove that there is a causal relationship. This means that it isn't necessarily the case that the life events helped to cause the disorder, and that alternative explanations are possible. For example, individuals who are very anxious and stressed a few months before developing obsessive compulsive disorder might, through their own behaviour, help to create life events such as losing their job or marital separation. In the Saunders et al. (1992) study, it may be that individuals who experienced childhood sexual abuse typically had several other serious problems to deal with in childhood. Perhaps it is those other problems rather than the sexual abuse that played a role in triggering obsessive compulsive disorder years later.

There are two other potential problems with life-event data. First, the information is generally obtained retrospectively several months or even years after the events in question. That opens up the possibility that distortions of memory may be involved. Second, most studies on life events and obsessive compulsive disorder have failed to take account of the significance of the life events for the individual. For example, the stressfulness of divorce depends in part on whether the individuals concerned have formed an intimate relationship with someone else.

SECTION SUMMARY
Psychological Explanations of Obsessive Compulsive Disorder

❖ According to the psychodynamic approach, patients with obsessive compulsive disorder react to their obsessions and compulsions with various defence mechanisms (e.g. isolation, undoing).

❖ Freud argued that the anal stage of development was especially important for the subsequent development of obsessive compulsive disorder.

❖ Evaluation:

— There is little evidence that the anal stage is important for the subsequent development of obsessive compulsive disorder.

— The existence of an association between problems with toilet training and obsessive compulsive disorder wouldn't prove that there was a causal link.

— Psychodynamic explanations ignore genetic factors and life events.

Psychodynamic explanations

❖ According to the two-process theory, obsessions develop through classical conditioning. The anxiety associated with obsessions can be reduced by compulsive rituals.

❖ Evaluation:

— The success of therapy involving exposure and response prevention is consistent with the behavioural explanation.

— It isn't clear how compulsive rituals develop in the first place.

— The behavioural explanation ignores the role of genetic factors and life events in triggering obsessive compulsive disorder.

Behavioural explanation

❖ According to the cognitive account, many of the problems of obsessive compulsives stem from an exaggerated sense of personal responsibility. This can be triggered in women by pregnancy and childbirth.

❖ It isn't clear why an excessive sense of personal responsibility leads to washing and checking rather than other forms of behaviour. The association between exaggerated personal responsibility and obsessive compulsive disorder doesn't prove there is a causal relationship.

❖ According to the cognitive account, patients' compulsive rituals prevent them from realising that their obsessions bear little resemblance to reality.

Cognitive explanation

❖ There is evidence that obsessive compulsives have a greater average number of life events than healthy controls in the months or years before onset.

Social explanation: life events

❖ There is the issue of causality—it is not clear whether the life events helped to cause the disorder or vice versa.

❖ Life events are usually assessed several months afterwards, so what is remembered may be distorted.

THERAPIES FOR OBSESSIVE COMPULSIVE DISORDER

So far we have focused on the range of factors involved in the development of obsessive compulsive disorder. It is now important to move on to a consideration of the main forms of therapy that have been devised to treat the disorder. At one time, it was thought to be a disorder that was extremely hard to treat. Thankfully, that hasn't been the case for the past 15 years or more. However, even now only a small percentage of obsessive compulsive patients recover completely as a result of treatment.

At the most general level, we can identify two major categories of therapy. First, there are biological therapies (e.g. those involving the use of drugs to treat obsessive compulsive disorder). Second, there are psychological therapies that focus on changing patients' ways of thinking and/or behaviour. As we will see, there are several different psychological therapies, including psychodynamic, behavioural, cognitive, and cognitive-behavioural.

> **EXAM HINT**
>
> Note you need to have covered the issues of classification and diagnosis, clinical characteristics, explanations, and treatments of obsessive compulsive disorder fully as you do not know which area will be asked in the exam. Sub-parted questions may ask you about the issues of classification and diagnosis in one sub-part, the clinical characteristics in another, and the explanations in another.

Biological Therapy: Drug Therapy

The great majority of forms of biological therapy used in the treatment of obsessive compulsive disorder involve the administration of drugs. For many years, most of the drugs used were serotonin reuptake inhibitors (SRIs), of which the most effective seemed to be clomipramine. This was noteworthy, because clomipramine has greater effects on the neurotransmitter serotonin than do the other SRIs. There were two main consequences of the discovery that clomipramine was especially effective. First, there was a systematic attempt to produce other drugs that would also increase serotonin levels. That led to the development of selective serotonin reuptake inhibitors (SSRIs). The SSRIs include fluvoxamine, fluoxetine (Prozac), sertraline, and paroxetine.

The second consequence was that it was assumed theoretically that patients with obsessive compulsive disorder have low levels of serotonin. That seemed to make sense given that drugs that apparently increase serotonin levels are effective in treating the disorder.

As discussed earlier in the chapter, the two key assumptions that used to be made about SRIs and SSRIs (and the reasons why they are effective) are incorrect. First, patients with obsessive compulsive disorder generally don't have low serotonin levels (Rachman, 2004). However, it is possible that various brain structures in obsessive compulsives show increased sensitivity to serotonin. Second, whereas SSRIs initially seem to increase serotonin levels, this is not the case when the drugs are taken over a relatively long period of time. Dolberg et al. (1996) found that over time the effects of SSRIs on serotonin receptors actually

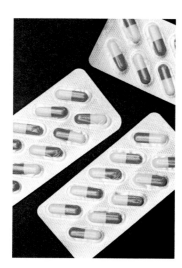

For a long time, serotonin reuptake inhibitors (SRIs) were the most commonly prescribed drugs for the treatment of obsessive compulsive disorder.

produced a functional *decrease* in the availability of serotonin. The current situation is that the SRIs and the SSRIs are both effective in treating obsessive compulsive disorder, but the precise mechanisms that are involved are unclear.

? What is the natural function of serotonin?

Effectiveness

One possible implication of what was said above is that SRIs and SSRIs are most likely to have beneficial effects when they start to produce decreases in the availability of serotonin. In other words, they shouldn't be effective early in treatment (when they increase serotonin levels), but should become effective some time later on. Precisely that pattern has been found. For example, Dougherty et al. (2002) found that SSRIs sometimes produced an increase in the symptoms of obsessive compulsive disorder early in treatment. After 6 weeks or more, however, SSRIs began to be effective at reducing symptoms.

Eddy, Dutra, Bradley, and Westen (2004) considered the effectiveness of various classes of drugs including tricyclics, anti-anxiety drugs, SSRIs, and SRIs. The findings were clear: the SSRIs and SRIs were more effective than the other drugs in terms of improvement from pre- to post-treatment. The most effective drug of all was the SRI clomipramine. However, there are three problems with clomipramine. First, patients taking it are more likely than those taking the SSRIs to drop out of the study because of its side effects. These side effects include dry mouth, drowsiness, sedation, and sweating. Second, only a minority of patients were willing to take clomipramine over a 1-year period. Third, clomipramine can pose dangers when it is taken by patients who have heart problems or who are at risk of attempting suicide.

What is the optimal form of drug therapy given the different strengths and limitations of the various drugs available? One recommended approach (Schruers, Koning, Luermans, Haack, & Griez, 2005) is to start for 10–12 weeks with an SSRI. If that drug isn't effective, then switch for the following 10–12 weeks to a different SSRI. If that also proves ineffective, then switch for the final 10–12 weeks to clomipramine.

An alternative approach has been suggested for patients who don't seem to be responding well to SRIs. This approach involves administering atypical antipsychotic drugs as well as an SRI. Preliminary evidence (reviewed by Kenneman, Pokos, Weerasundera, & Castle, 2005) suggests that this combination is often more effective than SRIs on their own. Why is this? Kenneman et al. suggest that the neurotransmitter dopamine is involved. More specifically, some patients with obsessive compulsive disorder have abnormalities in dopamine function, and atypical antipsychotic drugs act to produce dopamine blocking. There is increasing evidence that dopaminergic and serotonergic pathways are both involved in the development and maintenance of obsessive compulsive disorder, and the dopamine and serotonin systems interact with each other in complex ways.

? How would you explain the fact that drugs do not always have the same effect on all people? What other factors might be involved?

How effective is drug therapy for obsessive compulsive disorder in the long term? Hollon et al. (2006) pointed out that treatments can be effective in two different senses. Some effective treatments are palliative—they suppress the symptoms of a disorder but do not focus on the processes producing the disorder. Other effective treatments are curative—they reduce or eliminate the symptoms of a disorder *and* the underlying processes.

The limited evidence available suggests that drug therapy for obsessive compulsive disorder is palliative rather than curative. Simpson et al. (2004) compared groups of patients with obsessive compulsive disorder administered behaviour therapy (exposure and response prevention) or drug therapy (clomipramine) who responded successfully to treatment. During the 12 weeks following the end of active treatment, 45% of the patients who had received clomipramine relapsed back into the disorder compared to only 12% of those who had received exposure and response prevention. Thus, the beneficial effects of drug therapy often don't last for long after treatment has ceased.

There is a final point. While it is generally the case that drug therapy is used on its own, it is also possible to combine drug therapy with psychological forms of therapy. More specifically, as is discussed later, there have been several studies in which use of SRIs or SSRIs has been combined with exposure and response prevention. There have been mixed results when this combined treatment is compared with either form of therapy on its own. However, one of the problems with exposure and response prevention is that it can cause high levels of anxiety and so lead to drop out. Adding drug therapy to exposure and response prevention can reduce the drop-out rate, and thus add to the overall effectiveness of treatment (Hill & Beamish, 2007).

EXAM HINT

Use the treatment aetiology fallacy to evaluate treatments. This refers to the fact that just because the treatment works this does not mean that whatever the treatment targets (such as biochemical imbalances in the case of drugs) was the cause of the disorder in the first place. A useful analogy is that an aspirin treats a headache but it is not a lack of aspirin that causes the headache.

[?] What are some risks associated with taking SRIs and SSRIs?

Appropriateness

There are various reasons for arguing that drug therapy for obsessive compulsive disorder is appropriate and justifiable. First, it has shown itself to be effective by reducing anxiety levels and reducing many of the symptoms of obsessive compulsive disorder. In the eyes of patients, that is sufficient evidence of drug therapy's effectiveness. Second, drug therapy is appropriate in view of the increasing evidence that obsessive compulsive disorder is associated with complex abnormalities of serotonin and dopamine function. In other words, part of the problem in obsessive compulsive disorder is biochemical, and drug therapy is thus appropriate as a form of treatment that produces biochemical changes. Third, drug therapy seems to be appropriate when used in combination with exposure and response prevention, because it reduces anxiety levels sufficiently so that the drop-out rate is reduced.

What reasons are there for doubting the appropriateness of drug therapy in the treatment of obsessive compulsive disorder? First, it doesn't seem to have much effect on the underlying mechanisms responsible for obsessive compulsive disorder. As a result, drug therapy seems to reduce the symptoms of the disorder while patients take drugs but often fails to produce benefits that continue afterwards. This means that patients often need to take drugs for several years, which doesn't seem desirable. Second, we don't really know in detail *why* serotonin reuptake inhibitors and selective serotonin reuptake inhibitors are successful in reducing

Drug/group of drugs	How they work	Drawbacks
SRIs, e.g. clomipramine, and SSRIs, e.g. Prozac, paroxetine	Prolong the action of serotonin at nerve endings in the brain, so increasing the effect of serotonin	Side effects, especially for clomipramine, such as dry mouth, sweating Patient unwillingness to take the drug for 1 year. Possible increased risk of heart problems and suicide

obsessional and compulsive symptoms. Third, the appropriateness of drug therapy for obsessive compulsive disorder is reduced by the fact that many patients drop out of treatment because of drug side effects such as dry mouth and drowsiness. Fourth, there are some types of patients (e.g. those with heart problems or in danger of committing suicide) for whom drug therapy is totally inappropriate.

SECTION SUMMARY
Biological Therapies for Obsessive Compulsive Disorder

Drug therapy

- ❖ SRIs and SSRIs are used to treat obsessive compulsive disorder. It used to be assumed that patients had low levels of serotonin and that the drugs increased serotonin levels.
- ❖ In fact, patients with obsessive compulsive disorder don't have low levels of serotonin, and SSRIs over time produce a functional decrease in the availability of serotonin.
- ❖ SRIs and SSRIs are effective in the treatment of obsessive compulsive disorder, but the beneficial effects often start only after a few weeks of treatment.
- ❖ Evaluation:

  — Drug therapy seems to suppress the symptoms of obsessive compulsive disorder rather than curing the disorder.
  — SRIs and SSRIs often produce a range of unwanted side effects.
  — We only have a limited understanding of how the SRIs and SSRIs produce their beneficial effects.

Psychological Therapy: Psychodynamic Therapy

As we saw earlier in the chapter, Freud in his psychodynamic theory of obsessive compulsive disorder focused on the anal stage of psychosexual development. According to him, young children at that stage often find themselves in a conflict situation between wanting to retain faeces and wanting to soil their own clothes. This conflict can form the basis for the later development of some of the symptoms of obsessive compulsive disorder (e.g. cleaning rituals, anger). The conflicts and negative experiences of childhood are repressed (forced into the unconscious). Of central importance to psychodynamic therapy is the attempt to recover these repressed memories and provide the patient with insight into his or her disorder.

How can we uncover repressed memories and allow the client to gain insight? One method used by Freud was **free association**, in which the client said the first thing coming into his or her mind. Free association is ineffective if the client shows resistance and is reluctant to say what he or she is thinking. Nevertheless, the presence of resistance (revealed by long pauses) suggests that the client is getting close to an important repressed idea, and that further probing by the therapist is needed.

Another method is the analysis of dreams, which Freud described as "the *via regia* [royal road] to the unconscious". Freud argued that the mind has a censor that keeps repressed material out of conscious awareness. This censor is less vigilant (it nods off?) during sleep, and so repressed ideas from the unconscious

? Why might some therapists prefer to use the term "client" instead of "patient"?

KEY TERM

Free association: a technique used in psychoanalysis in which the client says whatever comes immediately to mind.

are more likely to appear in dreams than in waking thought. However, these repressed ideas usually emerge in disguised form because of their unacceptable nature. As a result, the therapist has to work with the client to decide on the true meaning of each dream.

The psychodynamic approach to therapy is more difficult to use with patients suffering from obsessive compulsive disorder than from some other disorders. Obsessive compulsive patients often tend to be suspicious of therapists, whom they suspect of invading their private thoughts and threatening their security by questioning them.

Effectiveness

There is general agreement that Freud's original psychoanalytic treatment (and subsequent developments in psychodynamic therapy) are no more than very modestly effective in the treatment of obsessive compulsive disorder. That was the conclusion that Salzman (1980) came to in his review of the evidence. There isn't much evidence that things have changed in the years since then. According to Esman (2001, p. 145), since 1969, "Virtually nothing has appeared in the psychoanalytic literature that has added to our understanding of the disorder or enhanced the very limited therapeutic influence on such cases."

Why has psychodynamic therapy been ineffective in the treatment of obsessive compulsive disorder? We will discuss three answers to that question. First, psychodynamic therapy is generally not very effective in the treatment of mental disorders. Fonagy et al. (2005) carried out a thorough review of the evidence, and concluded that there have been remarkably few studies in which psychodynamic therapy was shown to be significantly more effective than alternative forms of therapy.

Second, there is no convincing evidence that the psychodynamic approach, with its emphasis on the anal stage of development, provides a valid basis for therapy. Most of the beneficial effects of therapy with the more severe mental disorders (of which obsessive compulsive disorder is one) are due to specific factors—these are aspects of therapy specific or unique to that form of therapy. If the unique features of psychodynamic therapy are misconceived, then treatment won't be effective. Why is psychodynamic therapy moderately effective with less severe disorders? Some of the effectiveness of therapy with such disorders depends on factors (e.g. therapist warmth, therapeutic alliance between therapist and client) common to most forms of therapy. In other words, a psychodynamic or other therapist *only* needs to be friendly and sympathetic to assist patients with minor disorders. However, this is not enough to help patients with severe problems such as obsessive compulsive disorder.

Third, obsessive compulsive patients often have a tendency to "think too much" because of their tendency to focus on details and on accuracy. The lengthy discussions between therapist and patient that characterise psychodynamic therapy may actually be counterproductive by encouraging

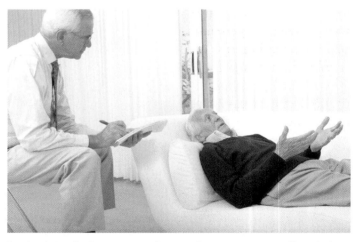

Psychodynamic therapy, as a therapy that encourages self-analysis, might be counterproductive in the treatment of the obsessive compulsive sufferer, who already has a tendency to excessively focus on detail and accuracy by nature.

patients to think excessively about the details of their problems. As Salzman (1985, p. 156) expressed it, "It often appears as though the patient were deliberately confusing the situation by introducing new issues when there is a real danger of clarifying his or her experience."

? In any therapy, how does one know if effectiveness is due to the personal characteristics of the therapist rather than the therapy itself?

Appropriateness

The success of other psychological therapies for obsessive compulsive disorder indicates that it is appropriate to treat the disorder by psychological means. This means that psychodynamic therapy is appropriate in a very general sense. There is plenty of evidence indicating that an important reason why patients engage in compulsive rituals is to reduce the anxiety produced by their obsessions. About 100 years ago, Sigmund Freud put forward a similar idea. He argued that one reason why patients perform compulsive behaviours is in order to undo or cancel out their urges. It is appropriate for psychodynamic therapy to focus on patients' strategy of undoing.

It is perhaps not altogether surprising that a form of therapy originally devised about 100 years ago has turned out in many ways not to be appropriate. There are several reasons why psychodynamic therapy is inappropriate for the treatment of obsessive compulsive disorder. First, it seems inappropriate for therapy to focus on patients' early childhoods, given that there is practically no evidence that early childhood is of any real relevance in producing the disorder. Second, most patients with obsessive compulsive disorder are distressed by their own behaviour (e.g. compulsive rituals). However, psychodynamic therapy does not directly focus on changing behaviour. Third, the obsessions of obsessive compulsive patients are based on wildly exaggerated beliefs. It would be more appropriate to challenge these dysfunctional beliefs head on rather than only indirectly through an emphasis on repressed childhood memories.

Psychological Therapy: Behavioural Therapy

The most important form of behavioural therapy for obsessive compulsive disorder is exposure and response prevention. This involves exposing patients to situations evoking obsessional distress until their anxiety levels decrease. At the same time, patients are instructed to resist performing the rituals they would typically use to reduce anxiety (i.e. response prevention). The combination of exposure to anxiety-evoking situations and response prevention eventually leads to extinction of the fear response.

Therapists using exposure and response prevention usually start by assessing the patient's obsessional thoughts and impulses, the stimuli or situations that trigger the obsessions, and his or her compulsions. They also ask the patient to indicate the anticipated negative consequences if feared stimuli are confronted without him or her performing his or her compulsive actions. Then the therapist explains why exposure and response prevention is a useful form of therapy, emphasising the reduction of distress that should follow prolonged exposure. After that, the therapist and patient discuss the specific types of exposure that will be used.

> **EXAM HINT**
>
> Why is the behavioural treatment exposure and response prevention so successful? But why does it not work for some patients? Prepare a revision aid of the effectiveness and appropriateness of each form of treatment so that you can draw comparisons about which treatments are most effective.

? What sort of ethical problems does behavioural therapy present?

Exposure usually starts with only moderately distressing stimuli and situations so that it is relatively easy for the patient to manage his or her distress. After the patient seems to be coping successfully with such situations, he or she is exposed to the most distressing situations. At all stages, patients are strongly encouraged to resist the temptation to perform their rituals. At the end of each treatment session, the therapist tells the patient to practise exposure for several hours alone before the next treatment session.

Exposure therapy with prevention is anxiety-provoking and can be distressing for patients. As a result, this form of therapy isn't suitable for all patients with obsessive compulsive disorder. For example, it can be dangerous if used with patients suffering from substance abuse, active psychosis, or who have thoughts of committing suicide.

Behavioural therapy: steps in exposure and response prevention

- Therapist assesses client's obsessional thoughts and compulsive impulses.
- Client discusses their worst-case scenario(s).
- Therapist outlines the therapy, emphasising the ultimate reduction in distress.
- Therapist takes the client through a hierarchy of distressing stimuli from less → moderately → greatest with support each time to manage and cope with the anxiety and distress without performing their ritual compulsion.
- This takes many sessions, and the client has homework, i.e. practising the technique on their own.
- Outcome: this is very successful and is based on extinction of learned fear responses.

? What are some reasons for assigning clients homework?

As we will see shortly, exposure and response prevention has proved to be very successful in treating obsessive compulsive disorder. *Why* is it successful? According to most behaviour therapists, it is successful because it provides an opportunity for conditioned fear responses to extinguish. More specifically, exposure to distressing situations creates fear, and the failure of negative consequences to happen in those situations leads to a gradual reduction in the amount of fear that is experienced. However, cognitive therapists have pointed out that there is an alternative explanation. Perhaps exposure and response prevention is effective because it helps to change their dysfunctional beliefs about the threats posed by situations they find distressing.

Effectiveness

There is strong evidence that therapy based on exposure and response prevention is effective. Eddy et al. (2004) carried out meta-analyses in which they compared the effectiveness of behaviour therapy (exposure + response prevention), cognitive therapy, and cognitive behavioural therapy. All three forms of therapy were moderately effective, but exposure and response prevention was slightly more effective than cognitive or cognitive behavioural therapy. For example, consider mean scores on the Yale–Brown Obsessive-Compulsive Scale. Untreated controls had a mean score of 22.00, whereas post-treatment means were 14.15 for patients treated with cognitive behavioural therapy, 13.10 for those receiving cognitive therapy, and 12.48 for those given exposure plus response prevention.

Despite these encouraging findings, exposure and response prevention therapy doesn't benefit all patients with obsessive compulsive disorder. About 25–30% of patients who start exposure and response prevention therapy drop out, mostly because of the high levels of anxiety that are created in the therapeutic situation. Among those patients who remain in treatment, 20% or more fail to derive much benefit from it. These figures mean that about 50% of patients aren't significantly improved by exposure with response prevention.

What can be done to reduce the drop-out rate? As mentioned earlier, there are promising indications that adding drug therapy to exposure and response prevention can persuade more patients to persevere with behavioural therapy (Hill & Beamish, 2007). That seems very reasonable given that drugs reduce patients' anxiety levels and so make it easier for them to tolerate exposure and response prevention.

Abramowitz (1998) identified three factors influencing the effectiveness of exposure and response prevention. First, the beneficial effects were greater when the therapist rather than the patient controlled the exposure situations. Second, the effects are greater when response prevention is total rather than partial. That is reasonable because total response prevention maximises the likelihood of the fear response extinguishing. Third, exposure and response prevention therapy is especially effective with patients suffering mostly from compulsions, presumably because the emphasis is on changing behaviour. Those who suffer mainly from obsessions sometimes benefit from having drug therapy in addition to exposure and response prevention.

Most of the studies we have considered so far have been somewhat artificial. They have typically involved patients suffering only from obsessive compulsive disorder who were all treated in the same way and often received the same number of therapy sessions. Seligman (1995) used the term **efficacy studies** to describe this scientific and well-controlled approach. He contrasted such studies with **effectiveness studies**, which involve the messy state of affairs found in actual clinical practice. For example, many patients with obsessive compulsive disorder also suffer from one or more other mental disorders (the presence of two or more disorders is known as comorbidity). Comorbidity is common in effectiveness studies but typically missing from efficacy studies. In addition, the therapy received by patients in effectiveness studies often varies somewhat and there is no standardisation of the number of therapy sessions.

Should researchers carry out efficacy studies or effectiveness studies? Both kinds of studies are worthwhile. Efficacy studies allow us to identify factors responsible for benefit to patients and thus to interpret the findings with confidence. However, it is difficult to *generalise* the findings from such controlled studies to typical clinical practice. The strengths and weaknesses of effectiveness studies are exactly the opposite. They are informative about the typical outcomes in clinical practice. However, the uncontrolled nature of such studies makes it hard to be sure about the interpretations of the findings. Our confidence in any given form of therapy would clearly be greatest if it produced good outcomes in efficacy and effectiveness studies.

Franklin, Abramowitz, Kozak, Levitt, and Foa (2000) carried out a large-scale effectiveness study on exposure and response prevention on obsessive compulsive patients, 50% of whom had comorbid conditions. Therapy produced a substantial improvement in the patients: on average, there was a 60% reduction

KEY TERMS

Efficacy studies: assessments of therapeutic effectiveness based on well-controlled investigations of well-defined clinical problems.

Effectiveness studies: assessments of therapeutic effectiveness based on typical clinical practice; see **efficacy studies**.

in symptoms. Thus, exposure and response prevention has proved to be a very useful form of therapy in both efficacy and effectiveness studies.

Appropriateness

In general, exposure and response prevention therapy is an appropriate form of therapy for obsessive compulsive disorder. Most patients are very concerned about the numerous compulsive rituals they perform almost every day, and this therapy focuses directly on these rituals. More specifically, response prevention shows patients that no dire consequences follow if they fail to perform their usual rituals. In addition exposure and response prevention therapy demonstrates to patients that it is possible to control and to reduce the anxiety they experience when confronting distressing situations.

There are some ways in which behaviour therapy for obsessive compulsive disorder can be regarded as inappropriate. First, prolonged exposure combined with response prevention is deliberately designed to create high levels of anxiety in patients. This often leads to fairly high drop-out rates, with such patients not deriving much benefit from the therapy. However, this problem can be partially resolved by adding drug therapy to treatment.

Second, it can be argued that it is unethical for therapists to set out to create high levels of anxiety in the vulnerable individuals they are treating. Patients do give informed consent to therapy, but sometimes they underestimate how unpleasant the situation is going to be.

Third, behaviour therapists claim that exposure and response prevention therapy is effective because it leads to extinction of the fear response. However, it is probably not appropriate to ignore the contribution of cognitive factors to its effectiveness. As mentioned earlier, cognitive therapists argue reasonably enough that exposure and response prevention therapy works in part because it produces cognitive changes (e.g. in dysfunctional beliefs involving exaggerated fears).

Fourth, exposure and response prevention therapy focuses more on compulsions than on obsessions, suggesting that this form of therapy may be less appropriate for patients whose symptoms consist mainly of obsessions. There is some evidence that patients who mostly have obsessions are often not treated successfully by exposure and response prevention (Rachman, 2004).

> **EXAM HINT**
> Remember to assess the appropriateness of treatments by considering the following:
>
> - how effective the treatment is across different symptoms
> - the patient's level of functioning
> - the effect of the treatment on relapse rates
> - the patient's motivation to use the treatment versus drop-out rate
> - if the action of the treatment is fully understood
> - ethical issues

Psychological Therapy: Cognitive Therapy

It should be pointed out at the outset that there are various forms of cognitive therapy. Some of them have been combined with exposure and response prevention to produce cognitive behavioural therapy. I won't be discussing that form of cognitive therapy, mainly because it hasn't so far proved to be of much value. As Hill and Beamish (2007, p. 507) concluded in their review, "Integrating cognitive components with behavioural approaches does not result in additional therapeutic gains." However, as is mentioned later, cognitive therapy can help to reduce the drop-out rate from behavioural therapy.

Most forms of cognitive therapy focus on changing patients' dysfunctional and irrational beliefs. Early in cognitive therapy, patients are told that it is important for them to recognise that many of their beliefs are dysfunctional. When they have done that, it is important for them to take steps to make these beliefs more realistic. One approach within cognitive therapy is the **pie technique**. With this technique, the patient indicates the degree of responsibility that various people would have if a threatening outcome happened. After that, the patient's degree of responsibility is given by the amount of "pie" not accounted for by others' responsibility. This is typically much less than the patient's perception of the extent of his or her responsibility. For example, a patient believed that he would be 100% responsible if there were a bad car crash after his bicycle fell down in the street. After detailed questioning, he admitted that the car driver would be 45% responsible, the weather 25%, the approaching car 20%, and the car mechanic 5%. This left the patient with only a 5% responsibility for the car crash, which should be compared against the patient's original perception of 100% responsibility.

Various other approaches are also used by cognitive therapists. One is the "double standard" technique discussed by van Oppen and Arntz (1994). The therapist focuses on some threatening outcome or event (e.g. the car crash following the patient's bicycle falling down in the street). Typically, the patient believes that he or she would be totally responsible and guilty if that happened to them. The patient is then asked whether he or she would find someone else responsible and guilty if the same threatening event happened to the other person. Typically, the patient wouldn't hold the other person responsible for the event. The major discrepancy between that view and the very high level of responsibility that the patient feels for his or her thoughts and behaviour is pointed out to the patient. This often causes the patient to feel less responsible than before for unfortunate outcomes.

Freeston, Rheaume, and Ladouceur (1996) developed several ways of challenging the dysfunctional beliefs of obsessive compulsive patients. Patients often overestimate the importance of their obsessional thoughts, based on the illogical belief: "It must be important because I think about it, and I think about it because it is important" (Freeston et al., 1996, p. 437). This belief can be challenged by asking patients to record their thoughts to show that many unimportant thoughts occur every day. Another method is to ask patients to attend closely to something obviously unimportant (e.g. the tip of their nose). This shows that it is entirely possible to spend much time thinking about matters that have very little importance.

Freeston et al. (1996) also developed ways of challenging patients' belief that thoughts can increase the probability of an event. This can be done by asking the patient to buy a lottery ticket and to spend 30 minutes a day thinking repetitively about winning the jackpot. Another method is to for the patient to identify a household appliance that is known to be in good working order. The patient is told to think 100 times a day that the appliance will break down within the next week. Of course, if patients did win the lottery or their household appliances did break down, their belief that thoughts can influence events would be greatly strengthened!

Freeston et al. (1996) also developed ways of changing the excessive sense of personal responsibility that is often experienced by obsessive compulsive patients. Situations are identified in which excessive responsibility is perceived. Patients are

? In what ways might a person's thoughts about themselves influence the way they react in a particular situation?

KEY TERM

Pie technique: a form of treatment in which obsessive compulsives use an imaginary pie to indicate how responsible various people or factors would be if a threatening event were to occur.

asked to predict their reactions if responsibility were transferred to someone else who was paid a large amount of money to take care of the situation. Patients usually indicate that they would be much less anxious and concerned in those circumstances.

Effectiveness

As we saw earlier, Eddy et al. (2004) found in a meta-analysis that cognitive therapy was nearly as effective as exposure and response prevention in the treatment of obsessive compulsive disorder. However, the effectiveness of cognitive therapy depends somewhat on the symptoms that need to be treated. Generally speaking, cognitive therapy tends to be more effective in treating obsessions than in treating compulsions.

Cottraux et al. (2001) found that the findings varied depending on whether effectiveness was assessed at the end of treatment or at a 1-year follow-up. Cognitive therapy and exposure and response prevention produced comparable levels of improvement at the end of treatment. One year later, however, only those patients treated with exposure and response prevention showed further improvement.

One of the advantages of cognitive therapy over exposure and response prevention is that the drop-out rate is typically lower. The reason for this is that cognitive therapy typically creates significantly less anxiety than does exposure and response prevention. Adding some elements of cognitive therapy to exposure and response prevention can help to reduce drop-out rates and benefit treatment (Abramowitz, 2006). For example, patients are often unconvinced that exposure to situations that will make them anxious will actually benefit them. Cognitive therapy (e.g. focusing on patients' tendency to overestimate danger) has proved useful in making patients more accepting of exposure therapy.

Appropriateness

Nearly all obsessive compulsive patients have dysfunctional beliefs and obsessions. As a result, it is entirely appropriate that cognitive therapists challenge these beliefs and obsessions in order to make them more accurate. More generally, cognitive

---

CASE STUDY: OCD

Mike was a "normal" teenager who went to school and college, although he says he always felt shy and rather anxious. What was he anxious about? He worried that he'd forgotten to shut the front door firmly so it locked when he left the house, and that he would lose his door key. He was anxious about how others perceived him, what they thought of him, anxious about being laughed at or mocked in other ways. This doesn't sound abnormal—most adolescents, and many adults—have anxieties like these. But Mike then found he could control his anxiety for a while by performing repetitive behaviours. When he entered a room Mike would have to touch each wall, tapping it seven times, and he would need to do this discreetly so it was not noticed. He also had to wash his hands frequently, even if they seemed not dirty; and he'd need to soap and then rinse them vigorously seven times. He had to tap the light switches in any room he was in, and there were numerous other little behaviours that he would need to do to feel calmer and safe. However, this feeling of calmness, the lessening of his anxieties, would only last

for a finite time and then he would feel the anxiety start to increase in him again.

When Mike got to 19 years old he started to think more positively about himself and decided he needed to be back in charge of his behaviour, not ruled by anxieties and fears. He had some CBT (cognitive-behavioural therapy) sessions, which supported him in questioning the logic of his obsessions and the usefulness of his compulsions. Mike did realise his behaviour was personally unhelpful as well as unrealistic, and was able, gradually, to stop the compulsive actions without being overcome by his fears.

He describes his freeing himself from OCD as a long and difficult struggle, but in his twenties he is a quiet person, working successfully in IT and enjoying life, although he says he is still a worrier!

Mike could have a personality that predisposes him to being anxious, but what might have triggered everyday anxiety into becoming a disorder?

factors are very important in obsessive compulsive disorder—individuals with obsessive compulsive disorder spend excessive amounts of time thinking about issues in great detail. This justifies a therapeutic approach focusing mainly on changing cognitive processes and beliefs. Much cognitive therapy is based on the assumption that individuals with obsessive compulsive disorder have a grossly exaggerated sense of personal responsibility for negative outcomes. That is appropriate given the extensive evidence that this assumption is basically correct. Finally, cognitive therapy is acceptable to the great majority of obsessive compulsive patients, as is shown by the relatively low drop-out rates usually found with it.

In what ways is cognitive therapy for obsessive compulsive disorder not appropriate? First, the great majority of those with obsessive compulsive disorder have a mixture of cognitive (i.e. obsessions) and behavioural (i.e. compulsive rituals) problems. It can reasonably be argued that cognitive therapists often focus on the cognitive problems rather than the behavioural ones.

Second, cognitive therapists focus on changing dysfunctional beliefs without considering in detail *why* patients developed these beliefs. There is a case for arguing that it would be more appropriate (and probably more effective) to base therapy on a clearer understanding of the origins of these dysfunctional beliefs.

Third, the emphasis on reducing exaggerated concerns about personal responsibility is only partially appropriate given that patients' concerns about personal responsibility don't extend to situations producing positive outcomes. Perhaps obsessive compulsive patients have low self-esteem, and so blame themselves for negative outcomes but accept no credit for positive ones. If that is

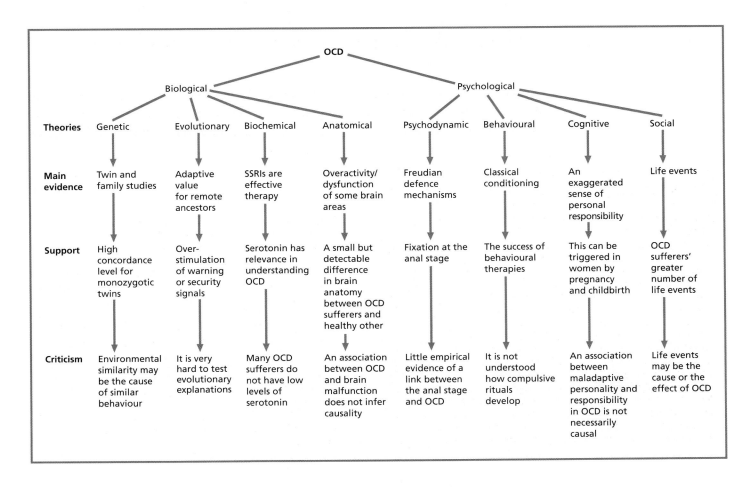

Which type of therapy do you think is most effective for treating obsessive compulsive disorders?

the case, it would be appropriate for cognitive therapists to focus more on enhancing patients' self-esteem.

SECTION SUMMARY
Psychological Therapies for Obsessive Compulsive Disorder

Psychodynamic therapy

❖ Psychodynamic therapy involves the use of free association and other techniques to uncover repressed memories and allow patients to gain insight.
❖ Psychodynamic therapy traditionally focused on patients' experiences during the anal stage of development, which are probably of little or no relevance to adult obsessive compulsive disorder.
❖ Psychodynamic therapy is significantly less effective than other forms of treatment for obsessive disorder. Reasons include patients' suspiciousness of their therapist and the lack of focus on the patients' patterns of behaviour.

Behavioural therapy

❖ The main form of behavioural therapy involves exposing patients to stressful situations and persuading them to avoid producing compulsive rituals in those situations.
❖ Exposure and response prevention is very effective because it allows patients' conditioned fear responses to extinguish. It is especially effective when patients control the exposure situations and when response prevention is total.
❖ There is a fairly high drop-out rate because of the high levels of anxiety created. However, this can be reduced by adding drug or cognitive therapy.
❖ Exposure and response prevention raises ethical issues, and it doesn't focus sufficiently on obsessions.

Cognitive therapy

❖ Cognitive therapy focuses on changing patients' dysfunctional and irrational beliefs, of which the most important one is an exaggerated sense of personal responsibility.
❖ Methods used by cognitive therapists include the pie technique, the "double standard" technique, and real-world testing of irrational beliefs.
❖ Cognitive therapy is almost as effective as behavioural therapy, and has the advantage of a lower drop-out rate.
❖ Evaluation:

— Cognitive therapy is less effective in dealing with behavioural symptoms (compulsions) than cognitive ones (obsessions).
— There is little attention to the reasons why patients developed irrational beliefs in the first place.

See *A2-Level Psychology Online* for some interactive quizzes to help you with your revision.

FURTHER READING

Rachman, S. (2004). *Anxiety* (2nd Edn) Psychology Press: Hove, UK. An excellent introductory coverage of all the anxiety disorders.

REVISION QUESTIONS

In the exam, questions on this topic are out of 25 marks, and can take the form of essay questions or multi-parted questions. You should spend about 35 minutes on each of the questions below, which aim to test the material in this chapter. In the exam, make certain you know if you have covered an anxiety disorder, schizophrenia, or depression as your psychopathology topic, and then choose the correct question.

See *A2-Level Psychology Online* for tips on how to answer these revision questions.

1. (a) Outline biological explanations for **one** anxiety
       disorder.   (10 marks)
   (b) Evaluate, using research evidence, the explanations
       you have described in part (a).   (15 marks)
2. Discuss the use of one biological and one psychological
   therapy for the treatment of an anxiety disorder.   (25 marks)
3. Describe and evaluate psychological explanations of
   an anxiety disorder.   (25 marks)

Psychology in Action: Media Psychology

14

By Michael W. Eysenck

When we use the term "media", we are referring to any medium of communication: books, newspapers, magazines, music (pop songs), the internet, CDs, DVDs or videotapes, films, and television. Most research in this area has focused on the last two kinds of media, but we must remember that *all* media have strong influences. There was a fear in Victorian times that very cheap short novels ("penny dreadfuls") would damage vulnerable minds. The medium has changed but the fear hasn't.

Many experts have increasing concerns about the impact the media have on our lives. This is partly because of the enormous increase in the media to which we are exposed on a daily basis. For example, until the early 1950s, only one television channel was available in the UK! Nowadays, the number of television channels is so great that it would be very difficult to work out a precise number. In addition, of course, there has been an explosion in the availability of video games, DVDs, and the internet. More than ever, we live in a 24/7 society.

MEDIA INFLUENCES ON SOCIAL BEHAVIOUR

This section is concerned with media influences on social behaviour. Unsurprisingly, these influences can be beneficial or harmful. That is, the media can promote either pro-social or anti-social behaviour. How can we explain the media's impact? We will first consider some possible explanations, and then see how well these explanations account for the findings from studies on pro- and anti-social behaviour.

Explanations of Media Influences on Pro- and Anti-social Behaviour

Some of the main explanations of media influences on social behaviour are based on the following notions: social learning, disinhibition, **desensitisation**, **cognitive priming**, **stereotypes**, **counter-stereotypes**, and stimulation. We will consider each

> **KEY TERMS**
> **Desensitisation:** the process of becoming less sensitive to stimuli the more they are encountered.
> **Cognitive priming:** the idea that cues, e.g. violent TV programmes, lead to thoughts and feelings that produce aggression.
> **Stereotypes:** social perception of an individual in terms of readily available features, such as skin colour or gender, rather than his or her actual personal attributes.
> **Counter-stereotypes:** positive stereotypes, such as a lawyer in a wheelchair, used to counter the negative effects of stereotyping.

EXAM HINT

Note that the topic area Psychology in Action requires you to know about:

* pro- and anti-social behaviour
* persuasion and attitude change
* the psychology of "celebrity".

The exam questions might be on just one of any of these areas or a question might be sub-divided so that, for example, one part is on media influences on anti-social behaviour and the other part might ask you to consider research into intense fandom.

of these explanations in turn. Note that there are similarities and overlaps between these explanations. In addition, most studies have not been designed in such a way that we can be confident that only one of the possible explanations provides the most appropriate interpretation of the findings.

Social Learning Theory

According to Bandura (1977), one of the factors in media influence is observational learning or modelling. We learn ways of behaving aggressively or altruistically from observing people on television and imitating their behaviour subsequently. This is especially likely if the behaviours are reinforced and/or the observer identifies with the characters on television, either because they are similar in terms of gender or age, or because they are admired. This might lead us to question the extent to which we would imitate cartoon characters, as we are unlikely to identify with them.

Two main predictions stem from Social Learning Theory. First, the behaviour produced by viewers of television or other media will resemble the behaviour they have observed. For example, if a character in a television programme stares angrily when frustrated, we would expect viewers to copy this angry stare rather than exhibit other kinds of aggressive behaviour. Second, we would expect observers to show a greater tendency to imitate a given character's behaviour if it is rewarded rather than punished. As we will see, there is much support for both of these predictions.

Disinhibition

The effects of cartoons can be explained in terms of disinhibition. Much of the time, we exert conscious control over our behaviour, and feel we should inhibit

Bandura's Bobo doll study emphasised the importance of observation and imitation as part of the learning process.

Observational learning

Of the hundreds of studies for which Bandura was responsible, one group stands out above the others—the Bobo doll studies. Bandura made a film of one of his students, a young woman, essentially beating up a Bobo doll. In case you don't know, a Bobo doll is an inflatable, egg-shaped balloon creature with a weight in the bottom that makes it bob back up when you knock it down. Nowadays, it might have Darth Vader painted on it, but back then it was simply "Bobo" the clown.

The woman punched the clown, shouting "sockeroo!" She kicked it, sat on it, hit it with a little hammer, and so on, shouting various aggressive phrases. Bandura showed his film to groups of kindergartners who, as you might predict, liked it a lot. They then were let out to play. In the playroom, of course, were several observers with pens and clipboards in hand, a brand new Bobo doll, and a few little hammers.

As you might predict, what the observers recorded was a lot of little kids beating the daylights out of the Bobo doll. They punched it and shouted "sockeroo!" kicked it, sat on it, hit it with the little hammers, and so on. In other words, they imitated the young woman in the film, and quite precisely at that.

This might seem like a real nothing of an experiment at first, but consider: these children changed their behaviour without first being rewarded for approximations to that behaviour! And while that might not seem extraordinary to the average parent, teacher, or casual observer of children, it didn't fit so well with standard behaviouristic learning theory. Bandura called the phenomenon observational learning, or modelling, and his theory is usually called Social Learning Theory.

From http://www.ship.edu/~cgboeree/bandura.html

anti-social behaviours. High levels of violence in the media promote the view that such behaviour is common and acceptable, and this reduces our normal inhibitions about behaving in this way. For example, you watch a scene showing a son hitting his father when the father says the son must stay at home. This then decreases your normal inhibitions about behaving in such a way.

This applies generally to anti-social rather than to pro-social behaviour. However, we might imagine that where people normally feel inhibited about helping in an emergency situation, portrayal of such behaviour in a television programme might disinhibit it in future. For example, normally we would feel inhibited about stepping in between two lovers having a quarrel. However, a programme on television that showed how this might be helpful might reduce our normal inhibitions, i.e. it would disinhibit us.

> **?** Can you think of an occasion when your own behaviour has been disinhibited?

Desensitisation

Desensitisation differs from disinhibition. Here, it is suggested that violent acts reduce our responsiveness. As Franzoi (1996) pointed out, we gradually become less responsive to, and emotionally concerned by, acts of violence because we have seen so many on television. In a study by Thomas, Horton, Lippincott, and Drabman (1977), two groups of children watched a videotape of young children behaving aggressively. Their physiological reactions to this videotape were recorded. Those children who had seen a television programme containing a lot of violence just before watching the videotape became less aroused physiologically than did those who had just watched a programme containing no violence. Such reduced responsiveness may be associated with an increased acceptance of violent behaviour.

> **?** How might you use the concept of desensitisation to explain an increase or decrease in pro-social behaviour?

On the basis of this approach (as with the disinhibition effect), we would expect that increased viewing of violent programmes should increase viewers' tendency to behave aggressively. However, what causes this to happen is different. It is assumed here that the viewers become less sensitive to (and so less concerned about) violence when they watch it repeatedly.

Cognitive priming

One reason why media violence might play a part in producing aggressive behaviour is because of cognitive priming. The basic notion is that the aggressive cues presented in violent television programmes lead to aggressive thoughts and feelings. When college students were asked to write down their thoughts while watching violent films (e.g. *The French Connection*), they reported numerous aggressive thoughts, increased anger, and a high level of physiological arousal (Bushman & Geen, 1990).

Convincing evidence for the importance of cognitive priming was reported by Josephson (1987). Some Canadian boys watched a television programme involving violence in the form of a gun battle in which the snipers communicated with each other using walkie-talkies; other boys watched a non-violent programme about a motocross team. After they had watched the television programme, all the boys played floor hockey. Before

In Bushman and Geen's (1990) study, students reported an increase in aggressive thoughts, anger, and physiological arousal whilst watching violent films, such as *The French Connection*.

? What ethical concerns arise from this study?

the game started, the referee gave the boys instructions by walkie-talkie or in a tape recording. The boys who watched the violent programme and received instructions by walkie-talkie were more aggressive during the hockey game than those who watched the same programme but received instructions by tape recording. Thus, the walkie-talkie acted as a cognitive prime or cue to aggression.

The same principle could be applied to pro-social behaviour. However, relatively little research on the effects of television on either pro-social or anti-social behaviour has focused specifically on cognitive priming.

Stereotypes

Another way the media influences our behaviour is through the use of stereotypes. All communications media need to put across a great deal of information in a relatively short time, so they use standard cultural and sub-cultural stereotypes, such as foreigners being given roles of the "enemy" (using foreign-sounding names and/or accents) and portraying men as criminals or aggressors more often than women. There are positive stereotypes as well, such as overweight people being depicted as "jolly" and women portrayed as caring.

? What are some other common stereotypes?

Mulac, Bradac, and Mann (1985) analysed the content of several children's programmes. They found strong gender stereotyping: males were more dynamic and female characters had greater socio-intellectual status and aesthetic quality. These stereotypes can be anti-social insofar as they maintain prejudices. They may also be pro-social if they try to break down existing stereotypes.

Counter-stereotypes

One way to deal with the problem of stereotypes is to replace them with counter-stereotypes. For example, many years ago, there was a television series called *Ironside*, in which the central character was a successful lawyer in a wheelchair. Other examples of counter-stereotypes are women judges and single fathers. Greenfield (1984) found that *Sesame Street*'s use of ethnic and disabled minorities helped children from minority groups to have greater cultural pride.

Stimulation hypothesis

There has been much controversy about the dangerous effects that the media can have on people, especially young children. However, the media has enormous potential for education, which can be in terms of providing suitable models for children to imitate. However, it can be most effective when individuals find

---

Television and the reduction of prejudice

The Children's Television Workshop (CTW) does more than make the *Sesame Street* series. In a research project with Israel Educational Television and Al-Quds University's Institute for Modern Media in east Jerusalem, the Workshop made a similar set of television programmes for preschoolers aimed at Israeli and Palestinian children (Rechov Sumsum/Shara'a Simsim Research Symposium, 1999). Prejudiced attitudes towards the other culture had been found in children as young as 4 years old. The agenda of the programmes was to emphasise similarities between children in the two cultures and to break down negative cultural stereotypes; it was supported by outreach materials for schools. The series Rechov Sumsum/Shara'a Simsim (the Hebrew and Arabic translation, respectively) was broadcast to viewers in Israel and the West Bank in 1998. A follow-up study (Cole et al., 2001) showed a small but real reduction in the prejudiced attitudes of child viewers. A further assessment of Jewish children some years later showed a clearly more positive, even optimistic, interpretation as a result of the programmes (Warshel, 2007).

themselves in commonplace situations and ways of resolving those situations are provided. Thus, for example, an individual is shown behaving anti-socially and the television character deals with the situation in a pro-social way. A programme on American television, *Freestyle*, aimed to reduce sex-role stereotypes in children by presenting characters who engage in non-stereotypical behaviours even though they find this hard to do. Eventually, the difficulties are overcome and the character is rewarded (Johnston & Ettema, 1986).

The danger with this type of approach is that children imitate the anti-social behaviour and disregard the resolution! Lovelace and Huston (1982) claimed that the most effective way of communicating a pro-social message might be to present the pro-social behaviour without any contrasting conflict or anti-social behaviour. However, the conflict-resolution strategy can be effective at conveying pro-social behaviour: if various models show pro-social actions, if the pro-social resolution is given sufficient time and attention, and if viewing conditions are adequate.

A somewhat different technique, the presentation of unresolved conflict, can be useful in classroom or therapeutic situations where an adult can guide post-viewing discussion and activity. However, this technique has unknown effects in unsupervised conditions.

> ? Which past or present television programmes do you consider to be pro-social?

General Aggression Model

The General Aggression Model put forward by Anderson and Dill (2000) is discussed in detail in the section on the effects of video games and computers on young people. However, although the model has often been applied to explain the effects of violent video games on aggressive behaviour, it is also of direct relevance to understanding the effects of the media on anti-social behaviour. This model is fairly comprehensive—it focuses on situational and personality characteristics; cognitive, physiological, and emotional factors; and on the central role played by an individual's cognitive appraisal or interpretation of the situation. It is definitely worthwhile looking at the General Aggression Model when considering explanations for media influences on pro- and anti-social behaviour.

> ? Identify the three different ways that aggression can be learned.

Pro-social behaviour: findings

Increased pro-social or helping behaviour as a result of media influence has been found in children of various ages. Friedrich and Stein (1973) studied American preschool children who watched episodes of a pro-social television programme called *Mister Rogers' Neighborhood*. These children remembered much of the pro-social information contained in the programmes. They behaved in a more helpful and co-operative way than children who watched television programmes with neutral or aggressive content.

Sprafkin, Liebert, and Poulos (1975) studied 6-year-old children, some of whom watched an episode of *Lassie* in which a boy risks his life to rescue a puppy from a mine-shaft. Other groups of children saw a different episode of *Lassie* in which no help was involved, or an episode of a situation comedy called *The Brady Bunch*. After watching the programme, all the children had the chance to help some distressed puppies. However, to do so they had to stop playing a game in which they might have won a big prize. Children who had watched the rescue from the mine-shaft spent an average of over 90 seconds helping the puppies, compared with under 50 seconds by the children who had watched the other

> **EXAM HINT**
>
> The debate about anti-social behaviour is often misperceived as more important than the one on pro-social behaviour, but make sure you are equally ready for a pro-social or an anti-social question, as you could be asked to consider either.

The study by Sprafkin, Liebert, and Poulos (1975) monitored the effects of an episode of *Lassie* in terms of its potential to influence pro-social behaviour in 6-year-olds.

programmes. These findings suggest that the first group of children imitated specific acts they had seen as predicted by Social Learning Theory with its emphasis on observational learning.

Baran, Chase, and Courtright (1979) studied older children between the ages of 8 and 10. These children watched an episode of *The Waltons*, in which there was much emphasis on helping behaviour. They were then found to behave in a more helpful or pro-social way than other children who had not seen the programme.

Rosenkoetter (1999) argued that pro-social television will influence children's pro-social behaviour only if they understand the moral message being communicated. Children who watched the most pro-social television programmes exhibited the most pro-social behaviour, especially if they had a good understanding of the programmes' moral lessons.

Rauterberg (2004) reviewed numerous studies on the effects of television on pro-social behaviour, and came to the following conclusions. First, children exposed to pro-social television programmes have more positive social interactions, have more self-control, and show more altruistic behaviour (voluntary helping behaviour that is costly to the individual). Second, the beneficial effects of pro-social programmes were greater on altruistic behaviour than on social interactions or self-control. Third, the effects of pro-social television content on behaviour are stronger when viewing is combined with discussion. Fourth, the effects of pro-social television programmes are stronger on kindergarten and primary-school-aged children than on adolescents.

How long lasting are the effects of pro-social television programmes on children's behaviour? Hearold (1986) reviewed over 100 studies on the effects of pro-social television programmes on children's behaviour, and concluded that such programmes generally make children more helpful. Indeed, the beneficial effects of pro-social programmes on pro-social behaviour were almost twice as great as the adverse effects of television violence on aggressive behaviour. This may be because pro-social programmes are more likely to be designed specifically to produce certain effects on viewers. However, helping behaviour was usually assessed shortly after watching a pro-social television programme, and only a few studies focused on possible long-term effects.

It is not clear whether pro-social television programmes have long-term effects on children's pro-social behaviour. In a study by Sagotsky, Wood-Schneider, and Konop (1981), children of 6 and 8 saw co-operative behaviour being modelled. Children of both ages showed an immediate increase in co-operative behaviour. However, only the 8-year-olds continued to show increased co-operative behaviour 7 weeks later. Wiegman, Kuttschreuter, and Baarda (1992) carried out a longitudinal study in Holland. The viewing of pro-social behaviour on television didn't have any effect on subsequent pro-social behaviour.

Evidence that observational learning from a film can produce beneficial longer-term changes in behaviour was reported by O'Connor (1980). Children who avoided playing with other children were shown a film of children playing happily together. Every child who saw the film played more with other children afterwards, and this effect was lasting. Perhaps the effects were long lasting because the children's initial experiences of playing with other children were so positive.

Evaluation

Research concerned with media influences on pro-social behaviour has produced several consistent findings. There are general beneficial short-term effects on

? What characters in television programmes do children imitate today?

altruistic behaviour and positive social interactions. However, any long-term effects are smaller or non-existent. There are greater effects on pro-social behaviour when children have a good understanding of the relevant moral or other issues. Finally, media influences on pro-social behaviour are generally greater when the recipients are younger children than when they are adolescents. Most of the findings are consistent with Social Learning Theory, according to which individuals imitate positive behaviour they have observed.

What are the limitations with media research on pro-social behaviour? First, different studies have focused on very different kinds of pro-social television (e.g. rescuing a puppy from a mine-shaft; children playing happily). Little is known about the extent to which the beneficial effects of pro-social television depend on the type of pro-social behaviour displayed or its intensity. Second, most research focuses on short-term effects of watching pro-social television, but what matters most in real life is whether the beneficial effects are long lasting. Third, there is much support for Social Learning Theory, according to which we imitate others' behaviour (especially if it is rewarded). However, we are most likely to imitate someone else's behaviour if we understand *why* they are behaving in a given way (Rosenkoetter, 1999), and Social Learning Theory doesn't really explain this.

> **■ Activity: Media influences on pro-social or anti-social behaviour**
>
> One way of looking at media influences on the young is to do a content analysis of the amount of pro-social behaviour and the amount of anti-social behaviour on children's TV. You could do these separately and make a comparison between the two.
>
> You must decide exactly what constitutes anti-social behaviour and then break these behaviours into categories (e.g. one person hitting another, one cartoon character being hit by another, etc.). Do the same for pro-social behaviour.
>
> You can then use the data in a variety of ways, for example, a comparison of the content of different programmes, of groups of programmes aimed at different age groups, of the types of anti-social behaviour shown, of the types of pro-social behaviour, and of the amount of time spent in pro-social as compared to anti-social behaviour.

Anti-social behaviour

The violence shown on television differs in two main ways from violence in real life. First, violent crime is far more prevalent on television than in the real world. For example, the average 16-year-old in Western society has seen 13,000 violent murders on television. As Gerbner (1994) pointed out, "We are awash in a tide of violent representations the world has never seen . . . drenching every home with graphic scenes of expertly choreographed brutality." If real people were murdered at the same rate as characters shown on television, the entire population would be wiped out in about 50 days!

Second, television typically minimises the effects of violence on the victim, as was shown by the National Television Violence Study (1997) in its analysis of thousands of violent programmes shown on American television. During fist-fights, people who were knocked down typically recovered almost immediately and came back stronger. In 58% of violent scenes, the victim wasn't shown experiencing any pain. In children's programmes, two-thirds showed violence as amusing, and only 5% indicated that violence can have long-term consequences.

Not surprisingly, there is a positive association or correlation between the amount of television children have seen and their aggressiveness. However, it is very hard to interpret this correlational evidence. It may be that watching violent programmes causes aggressive behaviour. On the other hand, it may be that naturally aggressive children choose to watch more violent programmes than non-aggressive children. In what follows, I focus on studies that have had some success in addressing the causality issue.

The issue of whether there is a correlation between violence on television and aggressive behaviour is frequently debated in the media.

[?] Can you see any ethical issues in the Leyens et al. study?

[?] Do you think watching television violence can make people more violent in real life?

Findings

One of the most thorough studies of the effects of media violence on physical and verbal aggression was reported by Leyens, Camino, Parke, and Berkowitz (1975). The participants were juvenile delinquents at a school in Belgium. They lived in four dormitories, two of which had high levels of aggressive behaviour and two of which had low levels. During a special movie week, boys in two of the dormitories (one high in aggression and the other low) watched only violent films, whereas boys in the other two dormitories watched only non-violent films.

There was an increased level of physical aggression among the boys who saw the violent films, but not among those who saw the non-violent films. The findings were more complex for verbal aggression. This increased among boys in the aggressive dormitory who saw violent films, but it actually *decreased* among boys from the non-aggressive dormitory who saw violent films. In addition, the effects of the violent films on aggression were much stronger shortly after watching them than later on. However, a limitation of this study is that the experimenters didn't distinguish clearly between real and pretend aggression.

Coyne, Archer, and Eslea (2004) argued that there is an important distinction between direct aggression (i.e. violent behaviour) and indirect aggression (e.g. spreading rumours). Indirect aggression is present in more programmes on British television than is direct aggression, but there has been remarkably little research on the effects of indirect aggression. Coyne et al. presented children aged between 11 and 14 with videos showing direct or indirect aggression, both of which triggered aggressive behaviour in the children. However, viewing direct aggression led to more directly aggressive responses whereas viewing indirect aggression produced more indirectly aggressive responses. These associations between the type of aggression viewed and children's subsequent aggressive behaviour is as expected on Social Learning Theory.

Eron (1982) and Huesmann, Lagerspetz, and Eron (1984) reported on a major longitudinal study. First, the amount of television watched and levels of aggressiveness were assessed in some young children. Then aggressiveness and the amount of television watched were re-assessed in the same children several years later. The amount of television watched at a young age predicted the level of aggressiveness (measured by the number of criminal convictions by the age of 30). This suggests that watching television violence can cause aggressive behaviour, which is consistent with expectations from the desensitisation and disinhibition hypotheses discussed earlier. In addition, children who were aggressive when young watched more violent television programmes several years later. This suggests that more aggressive individuals choose to watch more violent television programmes.

Johnson and Young (2002) carried out an important study on more than 700 young Americans followed up over a 17-year period. They related the amount of television watched at the age of 14 with aggressive acts (e.g. assault; robbery) between the ages of 16 and 22. Those who watched more than 3 hours of television daily at age 14 were five times more likely to commit aggressive acts between 16 and 22 (29% vs. 6%, respectively), which is consistent with the disinhibition and desensitisation hypotheses. This finding does not prove a causal relationship. However, the finding remained intact when Johnson and Young controlled for other factors (e.g. childhood neglect, neighbourhood violence, previous aggressive behaviour, parental income) that might have played a part in producing the association between television watching and aggression.

We will now discuss two meta-analyses combining findings from many research studies before turning to other research approaches. Wood, Wong, and Chachere (1991) reviewed 28 laboratory and field studies concerned with the effects of media violence on aggression in children and adolescents. In both field and laboratory studies, exposure to media violence led to more aggressive behaviour towards strangers, classmates, and friends, but the effects were stronger under laboratory conditions.

Comstock and Paik (1991) reviewed more than 1000 findings on the effects of media violence. There were generally strong short-term effects, especially with respect to minor acts of aggression. In addition, there were rather weaker long-term effects. Five factors increased the effects of media violence on aggression:

1. Violent behaviour is presented as being an efficient way to get what one wants. This emphasis on rewarded violence is predicted by the social learning approach with its emphasis on observational learning.
2. The person behaving violently is portrayed as similar to the viewer.
3. Violent behaviour is portrayed realistically rather than, for example, in cartoon form.
4. The suffering of the victims of violence isn't shown.
5. The viewer is emotionally excited while watching the violent behaviour.

> **?** Bearing in mind Comstock and Paik's five factors, what advice would you give filmmakers who do not wish to provoke aggression in their audiences?

CASE STUDY: MOVIE VIOLENCE

Since its release in 1994, the film *Natural Born Killers* has been surrounded by controversy and has sparked a long-standing debate about the effect of viewing intense violence on the human mind. The film follows the story of Mickey and Mallory Knox, a young couple who go on a killing spree across America, claiming 52 lives at random. Their flippant attitude towards the crimes they commit is portrayed as exciting and thrilling by the media and, as a result, their murderous behaviour catches the imagination of a generation of young impressionable people who idolise them.

The notion of admiring cold-blooded killers may seem to be far-fetched, but alarming similarities have emerged between the reaction to the fictional Mickey and Mallory and other real-life killers. *Natural Born Killers* has been linked to at least a dozen murders, including two cases in France where the defence has blamed the film as providing inspiration for the crime.

In October 1998, the French courts sentenced Florence Rey to 20 years in prison for her part in a shoot-out that left five people dead. She had committed the crime with her boyfriend, Audry Maupin, who was killed in the shoot-out. Publicity material from the film was found in the flat that Rey shared with her boyfriend at the time of the shootings. The press latched on to this and called the pair "France's Natural Born Killers" and, as in the film, the vulgarity of the multiple murder was lost and replaced by a glamorous image of rebellion that was both enticing and thrilling. Before long, young Parisians were wearing a picture of the convicted woman on their T-shirts. This was the first time a real-life murderer had been idolised in public.

Stronger links between the film and a murder were discovered in the case of Véronique Herbert and her boyfriend Sébastian Paindavoine, who lured their victim into a trap and then stabbed him to death. There was no motive for the attack and Herbert placed the blame on *Natural Born Killers*. She said, "The film coincided with my state of mind. Maybe I muddled up dream and reality. I wanted to eliminate someone, as if by magic . . . The idea of killing invaded me." In the light of such a testimony, can anyone deny the link between the sort of violence depicted in *Natural Born Killers* and Herbert and Paindavoine's gruesome act?

The pro-censorship lobby says that the film and the subsequent murders provide conclusive evidence that screen violence is translated rapidly into street violence. The image of killing, especially in a fictional world where the characters do not have to live with the consequences of their actions, can become a reality. Such allegations against a film cannot be dismissed and the controversy surrounding the subject matter has been fuelled by the similarities between Mickey and Mallory and the real-life murderers. However, the argument against censorship states that *Natural Born Killers* was intended as a satire on the bloodlust of the media and American society and that it is society that should be held responsible for any acts of violence rather than the film itself.

A different way of trying to establish the effects of violent television is to compare levels of anti-social behaviour *before* and *after* the arrival of television. For example, television arrived in some parts of the United States several years before others. According to FBI crime statistics, the level of violent crime was no greater in those areas that had television than in those that did not, which seems inconsistent with the desensitisation and disinhibition hypotheses. Furthermore, the introduction of television into an area did not lead to an increase in violent crime. However, the introduction of television was followed by an increase in the number of thefts (Hennigan, Del Rosario, Cook, & Calder, 1982). This may have occurred because television advertisements made many people more determined to acquire material possessions.

A similar study was carried out on St Helena, in the south Atlantic (the island is best known for the fact that Napoleon spent the last few years of his life there). The inhabitants of St Helena received television for the first time in 1995, but there were no adverse effects on the children. Some of the evidence consisted of secret videotaping of the children playing at school. Charlton reported that, "Bad behaviour is virtually unheard of in the playground, and our footage shows that what is viewed is not repeated." The main factors thought to prevent television violence from influencing the children of St Helena were: stable home, school, and community situations.

Most research on the effects of media violence has been carried out in the US or the UK. Thus, we don't really know whether the findings would be the same in other cultures. Huesmann and Eron (1986) carried out one of the few cross-cultural studies. They tested children and parents over a period of 3 years in Finland, Israel, Poland, and Australia. In the first three countries (but not in Australia), the amount of television violence seen by young children predicted their subsequent level of aggression even when their initial level of aggression was controlled for statistically. These findings suggest that media violence increases aggressive behaviour in most countries.

I will make two final points. First, there are individual differences in the effects that media violence has on people's behaviour. For example, children are probably especially vulnerable to media violence because they have unformed personalities and are very susceptible to the effects of disinhibition, desensitisation, and social

? Do you think that children from St Helena would identify with characters in American television programmes? How does this affect the impact of the findings?

CASE STUDY: ST HELENA

A study was carried out on the island of St Helena in the south Atlantic. Its inhabitants received television for the first time in 1995, but there is no evidence of any adverse effects on the children. According to Charlton (1998):

> The argument that watching violent television turns youngsters to violence is not borne out, and this study on St. Helena is the clearest proof yet. The children have watched the same amounts of violence, and in many cases the same programmes as British children. But they have not gone out and copied what they have seen on TV.

What are the factors preventing television violence from influencing the children of St Helena? According to Charlton (1998):

> The main ones are that children are in stable home, school and community situations. This is why the children on St Helena appear to be immune to what they are watching.

HOW SCIENCE WORKS: DOES WATCHING VIOLENT TV MAKE YOU AGGRESSIVE?
Good ethical practice and decent morals make it impossible to encourage people to watch violent television programmes and then to wait and see if they become more violent in real life! However, you could do a correlation that, although not entirely real-life (like much of the research), would give interesting findings.

If you were to draw up a list of violent films and television programmes from the present and recent past, and ask participants to tick any they have watched in the last year, you could then count the ticks for each individual. These scores would give you one co-variable. Then you might construct a written scenario—or even illustrate this with downloaded graphics—such as someone trying to snatch your briefcase, bag, or wallet, with a choice of how you would choose to respond. One choice would be to let go, do nothing, let the thief get away; this is the non-violent choice. You could give three more choices with increasing violence, and one very violent choice, such as punching and kicking the assailant. If you scored each response with the non-violent one scoring 1 and the very violent one scoring 5, you would then have values for your second co-variable. You could then construct a table of results and a scattergraph, and even put in the line of best fit to give you an idea of the value of the correlation.

- It is quite easy to calculate the correlation coefficient so you would know the precise size of your correlation.
- What are the drawbacks to asking people to give personal information, such as their viewing habits?
- What are the possible sources of error in asking people to say how they might behave in a hypothetical situation?

models. Individual differences in personality are also important. Zillmann and Weaver (1997) showed films containing scenes of violence to male participants. Only those high in psychoticism (a personality dimension involving coldness and hostility) showed greater acceptance of violence as an acceptable way to resolve conflicts after watching the films.

Second, violence and aggression are not the only anti-social behaviours associated with the media. Prejudice can be inflamed by newspaper and other media reports. Televised role portrayals and inter-racial interactions contribute to the development and maintenance of stereotypes, prejudice, and discrimination among children. Limited portrayals of ethnic groups and of inter-ethnic interaction mean that children develop stereotypical views of our society.

Can you think of any concerns that may arise when conducting a study of this nature?

Evaluation

Most of the evidence consistently shows that media violence increases anti-social behaviour. These effects are generally stronger in the short-term than in the long-term, but studies carried out over a period of years suggest there are genuine long-term effects. Real progress has been made in identifying the factors determining the strength of the effects of media violence on anti-social behaviour. For example, anti-social behaviour is most common when a violent person is rewarded for behaving violently, when the depiction of violence is realistic, and when the victim's suffering isn't shown.

What are the limitations of research in this area? First, there is often a failure to distinguish among different types of violence. For example, there is a huge difference between the fictional violence shown in cartoons such as *Tom and Jerry* and the factual violence shown in news coverage of a war zone. Second, many studies report an association or correlation between exposure to media violence

? What are some examples of direct violence? Indirect violence?

and anti-social behaviour; such findings can't show there is a causal link. Third, many studies involve exposing participants to a single violent programme—such an approach tells us little about the long-term effects of exposure to violent programmes. However, longitudinal studies go some way to dealing with this criticism. Fourth, there has been a great emphasis in research on the viewing of *direct* violence. However, we also need to consider what happens when people view *indirect* aggression. Fifth, most research focuses on how individuals react to media violence they have watched on their own. In the real world, however, our responses to media violence are often influenced by peer-group pressure or our family environment. Sixth, the effects of media violence undoubtedly depend on factors such as age, sex, ethnicity, and culture, but these factors are rarely studied. It is also very likely that delinquents are particularly susceptible to the effects of media violence. Seventh, there are important ethical issues in exposing individuals to media violence given that the effects of such exposure may be negative and damaging.

Effects of Video Games and Computers on Young People

As everyone knows, there has been a marked increase in the last few years in the amount of time that young people spend playing video games and using computers. Most research in this area has focused on video games, and our discussion will reflect that. However, there has been some research on computer-based gaming. For example, Griffiths, Davies, and Chappell (2003) studied the characteristics of those playing games on the internet. They found that 85% of the players were male and that more than 60% of them were over 19 years of age. Thus, those playing games on the internet are somewhat older than those playing video games.

The *Grand Theft Auto series* has sparked controversy over its violent content amid concerns that this 18+ rated video game glorifies criminal violence and might fall into the hands of younger children. The NPD Group, which monitors sales of US video games, named *Grand Theft Auto* the best-selling video game since the firm began tracking sales in 1993.

In recent years, there has been a substantial increase in the violent content of video games. In addition, video-game graphics have improved dramatically, making players' experience of violence much more realistic. Millions of parents are concerned that excessive playing of video games might damage their children. One possibility is that young people might become more aggressive after prolonged playing of video games. Another possibility is that they may become addicted to playing video games and so neglect their studies and their friends.

We focus mainly on the effects of playing violent video games, although many non-violent games are available. There are three main reasons. First, the great majority of research in this area has been on video games involving violence. Second, when 10-year-olds were asked to report their favourite video game, 73% of boys and 59% of girls chose violent ones. Third, there is much concern about the negative effects that playing violent video games can have on young people, and important ethical issues are raised.

Note that there are *positive* aspects to playing video games—they can encourage learning and education. As Gentile and Anderson (2003) pointed out, "Health video games can successfully teach health behaviours, and flight simulation video games can teach people how to fly." In addition, video games can assist in children's socialisation process. According to Durkin (1995), adolescents who don't play video games may become socially isolated as a result.

Anderson and Dill (2000) put forward a four-stage general aggression model to explain the effects of video violence:

Stage 1: At this stage, the key variables are situational cues (e.g. guns present) and individual differences (e.g. aggressive personality).

Stage 2: What happens at Stage 1 produces various effects at Stage 2, including affect (e.g. hostile feelings), arousal (e.g. activity in the autonomic nervous system, and cognition (e.g. hostile thoughts).

Stage 3: What happens at Stage 2 leads to appraisal processes (e.g. interpretation of the situation; consequences of behaving aggressively).

Stage 4: Depending on what happens at Stage 3, the individual decides whether to behave aggressively or non-aggressively.

Most research on the effects of video games on young people has focused on aggression. However, video games may have various other effects on social behaviour. For example, most early video games had white men in the leading parts, which may well have served to reinforce unfortunate stereotypes (oversimplified generalisations) about gender and race. Of course, there are some exceptions. Lara Croft in *Tomb Raider* is an example. She gave name to the **Lara phenomenon**, in which powerful female characters play central roles in video games. Jansz and Martis (2007) studied the Lara phenomenon by analysing the introductory films to 12 recent video games. Female characters appeared in leading parts as frequently as male characters, which represents real progress. However, there was a tendency to emphasise female bodily characteristics (e.g. breasts) and all the heroes in these video games were white.

Findings

Anderson and Bushman (2001) carried out a meta-analysis of studies on violent video games. They tested predictions from their general aggression model, and concluded that the findings strongly supported it. First, the situational cues provided by violent video games were associated with aggressive behaviour. The magnitude of the effect was similar in males and females, and in children and adults. Second, according to the general aggression model, aggressive cognitions or thoughts play a central role in the development of the aggressive personality. As predicted, exposure to violent

HOW SCIENCE WORKS: A CONTENT ANALYSIS OF VIDEO OR COMPUTER GAMES

Researchers have reported considerable bias in video and computer games; you could do a small investigation to see if this is true for a game with which you are familiar or one that you know is popular. One way of doing this is to make a series of categories as columns headed, for example:

- violence by male
- violence by female
- violence towards male
- violence towards female
- number of white characters
- number of non-white characters.

When you have made your choice of columns, watch/play the game and tick the columns for each relevant instance.

At the end, after totalling the columns, look at your data to see what it tells you.

- Do your data agree with the published research?
- Is anything different?
- Why might this be so?

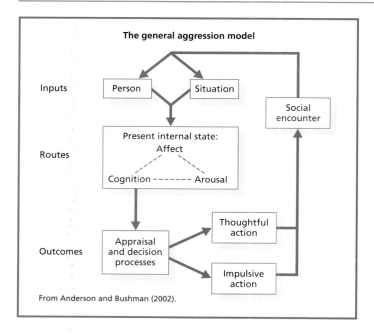

The general aggression model

Inputs

Routes

Outcomes

From Anderson and Bushman (2002).

video games reliably increased aggressive cognitions. Third, exposure to violent video games produced aggressive affect or emotion and increased physiological arousal, both predicted by the model.

In their General Aggression Model, Anderson and Dill (2000) argued that characteristics of the person (e.g. his or her personality) influence the effects of exposure to violence. Unsworth, Devilly, and Ward (2007) carried out a relevant study. Adolescents played a violent video game called *Quake II*. Some participants had increased anger ratings after the video game and others had decreased anger ratings, but the majority showed no change. Participants with personalities prone to aggression were most likely to have increased anger ratings.

Cognitions or thoughts are of central importance in the general aggression model. For example, it is assumed that repeated exposure to violence can create a **hostile expectation bias,** in which individuals come to expect others to behave aggressively. Bushman and Anderson (2002) exposed participants to violent video games (e.g. *Mortal Kombat*) or non-violent ones (e.g. *3D Pinball*), after which they read ambiguous stories in which it was unclear what the main character would do next. For example, in one study the main character has a minor traffic accident after he brakes at traffic lights. He then walks towards the other driver. Participants who had played violent video games expected the main character to feel angrier and to behave more aggressively than those who had played the non-violent games.

According to Social Learning Theory (discussed earlier), individuals imitate the behaviour of other people when it is rewarded but won't imitate punished behaviour. Carnagey and Anderson (2005) tested whether these predictions apply to the playing of violent video games. Young people played one of three versions of the same video game involving racing cars. In one version, violence was always rewarded, in another version violence was always punished, and the third version was non-violent. Measures were taken of the participants' hostile emotion, aggressive thoughts, and aggressive behaviour.

What did Carnagey and Anderson (2005) find? As expected, the video game in which violence was rewarded led to increased hostile emotion, aggressive thinking, and aggressive behaviour. By contrast, punishing violent behaviour led to increased hostile emotion, but did *not* increase aggressive thinking or aggressive behaviour. These findings show that video violence doesn't necessarily have similar effects on emotions, thoughts, and behaviour. In addition, violent video games must increase aggressive thinking if they are to increase aggressive behaviour, as predicted by the General Aggression Model.

Have changes in video games in recent years (e.g. more violent content, more realistic graphics) increased the negative effects of these games on young people? This question was addressed by Ferguson (2007), who carried out a meta-analysis taking account of the year in which each study was carried out. He found that violent video games increased aggressive behaviour, aggressive thoughts, aggressive emotions, and physiological responses. However, the magnitude of these effects had *not* increased in recent years. Perhaps surprisingly, the effects of violent video games on aggression were smaller on younger people than on older ones.

According to Ferguson (2007), although violent video games did increase aggressive behaviour and cognitions, these effects were lesser in younger people than older ones.

? Have you ever felt more aggressive after playing a violent video game or after watching a violent programme?

Despite Ferguson's (2007) findings, the effects of violent video games on aggression sometimes depend on how realistic the games are. Persky and Blascovich (2007) compared the effects of violent video games played in an immersive virtual environment (highly realistic) and on a desktop computer (much less realistic). Aggressive feelings and physiological reactions were both significantly higher among participants playing in the immersive virtual environment. Ivory and Kalyanaraman (2007) compared the effects of older and newer video games. The newer ones were experienced as more real and more involving. They produced more physiological and self-reported arousal and slightly more hostility.

What happens when individuals play violent video games repeatedly? Barlett, Harris, and Baldassaro (2007) studied the changes occurring when people engaged in increased play of such video games. There were progressive increases in aggression and hostility.

To what extent do young people who play video or computer games become addicted? Grusser, Thalemann, and Griffiths (2007) found in a large sample of adolescents that 12% of them appeared to have computer/video game addiction. Perhaps surprisingly, addicted individuals didn't display more aggressive behaviour than non-addicts.

Evaluation

Research into the effects of computer and video games has produced several interesting and important findings, most of which can be understood within the General Aggression Model. First, the effects of violent games depend on both the situation and the characteristics of the person playing them. Second, playing violent video games has several effects: increasing arousal, hostile emotions, and aggressive behaviour. Third, exposure to violence influences an individual's subsequent appraisals or interpretations (the hostile expectation bias). Fourth, the effects of violent videos on aggressive thoughts and behaviour are sometimes greater when the graphics and situation are more realistic. Fifth, although there is evidence of addiction to video games, it isn't clear that such addiction leads to more aggressive behaviour.

What are the limitations with the research into violent video games and aggression? First, many of the studies have only looked at short-term effects rather than possible long-term effects. Second, many researchers have only observed children's free play activity after playing video games, so we don't know much about the effects of these games in other situations. Third, many studies have reported a positive association or correlation between the amount of playing of video games and aggression. We can't be sure about causality with such findings. It is possible the video games caused the aggression, but it is also possible that naturally aggressive children choose to spend far more of their time playing violent video games. Fourth, there are obvious ethical reasons why researchers shouldn't expose children to violent video games. Indeed, in a press release issued in 2005, the American Psychological Association called for a significant reduction in the levels of aggression in video games (http://www.apa.org/releases/videoviolence05.html).

SECTION SUMMARY
Media Influences on Social Behaviour

What is the media?

- ❖ The "media" is any means of communication: books, magazines, films, television, and video games. The media can have effects on pro-social and anti-social behaviour.

Explanations of media influence

- ❖ *Social Learning Theory*: our behaviour is based on observational learning or modelling. Individuals copy behaviour they see or read about in the media, especially when it is reinforced or rewarded.
- ❖ *The disinhibition effect*: exposure to certain behaviours in the media reduces our normal inhibitions. This is likely to result in anti-social behaviour but could lead to pro-social behaviour as in reducing our reluctance to intervene in a lovers' quarrel.
- ❖ Desensitisation occurs when our normal sensitivities are dulled by overexposure.

Pro-social behaviour

- ❖ Pro-social television often increases children's pro-social behaviour (especially altruistic behaviour).
- ❖ There is support for the Social Learning Theory prediction that observational learning causes individuals to imitate behaviour they have seen.
- ❖ Pro-social television produces more pro-social behaviour when the issues are discussed so as to increase children's understanding.
- ❖ Evaluation:

  — There is relatively little evidence concerning the long-term effects of pro-social television.
  — Social Learning Theory provides a plausible account of many findings. However, it does not explain the importance of children understanding why someone else has shown pro-social behaviour.

— The relative effectiveness of different kinds of pro-social television in enhancing viewers' pro-social behaviour is unknown.

Anti-social behaviour

❖ Violent media coverage minimises the victim's suffering and often increases anti-social behaviour.
❖ As predicted by Social Learning Theory, watching direct aggression leads viewers to display direct aggression whereas watching indirect aggression leads to indirect aggression.
❖ There are stronger effects on anti-social behaviour when violent behaviour is seen to be rewarded, the victim's suffering isn't seen, and the violent behaviour is realistic.
❖ Evaluation:

— Less is known about long-term effects than short-term ones.
— Social factors (e.g. peer group pressure) often influence behaviour in response to violent television in the real world, but haven't been studied in the laboratory.
— We know rather little about the extent to which the effects of violent television depend on age, sex, and culture.

Effects of video games and computers

❖ Despite the Lara phenomenon, video games often promote unfortunate stereotypes.
❖ Violent video games often produce aggressive cognitions, aggressive emotion, and increased physiological arousal, especially when violence is rewarded.
❖ Repeated exposure to violent video games can lead to hostile expectation bias, in which ambiguous situations trigger hostile reactions.
❖ Evaluation:

— Most research on video games has focused only on short-term effects.
— There is evidence that adverse effects of playing violent video games increase with increased time devoted to playing.
— There are ethical issues associated with violent video games, especially when they are played repeatedly or addictively.

PERSUASION, ATTITUDE, AND CHANGE

There has been a considerable amount of research within social psychology on **persuasion, attitude,** and change. Before proceeding, we need to define "persuasion" and "attitude". According to the *Oxford Dictionary of Psychology*, persuasion is "the process by which attitude change is brought about." The same dictionary defines attitude as "an enduring pattern of evaluative responses towards a person, object, or issue." Evaluative responses involve deciding whether our feelings about someone or something are generally positive (e.g. "I really like him") or negative (e.g. "He gives me the creeps!").

The area of persuasion and attitude change is important because we spend so much of our lives exposed to persuasive messages from television, radio, movies,

> **KEY TERMS**
>
> **Persuasion:** the range of processes involved in producing changed attitudes.
> **Attitude:** beliefs about some person, group, or object, with these beliefs having an evaluative component (good vs. bad).

? What are some things you have been persuaded to do?

the internet, and so on. It is also important because of its relevance to applied psychology; for example, advertisers are very keen to understand how to devise advertisements that will persuade us to buy their products.

The main focus in this section is on various major theories. Some of these theories were put forward to understand the factors producing attitude change when persuasive messages are presented. Other theories are concerned more with the influence of attitudes on decision making. Finally, as television has a major impact on most people because of the hundreds of hours a year they spend watching it, we consider ways of explaining why television is effective in producing attitude change.

Hovland–Yale Model

The power of persuasive communications to change people's attitudes was shown in a frightening way by the success of Nazi propaganda during the 1930s. This played a part in the United States War Department decision to fund Carl Hovland to study factors influencing the effectiveness of persuasive communications. After the end of the Second World War, Hovland moved to Yale University and continued this line of research. This research led in 1953 to an important book by Hovland, Janis, and Kelley entitled *Communication and Persuasion*, in which the Hovland–Yale Model of persuasion and attitude change was discussed.

The central thrust of the Hovland–Yale Model is that several factors jointly determine the extent to which a persuasive communication changes people's attitudes. First, there are characteristics associated with the communicator or source. For example, they predicted that the effectiveness of a communicator would depend on his or her expertise, trustworthiness, likeability, status, and race.

Second, there are features of the communication or message. The impact of a message depends on whether its appeal is emotional, on the order in which the arguments are presented, whether the arguments are one-sided or two-sided, and whether the communication contains an explicit conclusion.

Third, there are characteristics associated with the audience or recipients of the communication. The extent to which a persuasive communication produces attitude change depends on the initial position of the recipients, their intelligence, their personality, their self-esteem, and their persuasibility.

Hovland et al. (1953) argued that recipients of a communication go through four successive processing stages. First, there is the amount of attention paid to the communication. Second, there is the extent to which the communication is comprehended. Third, there is the amount of acceptance of the message being communicated. Fourth, there is the amount of retention or memory for the communication.

Finally, Hovland et al. (1953) pointed out that persuasive communications produce various changes within the recipients. These include opinion change, behaviour change, knowledge change, perception change, and emotion change. Persuasive messages may produce changes in some or all of these measures.

Findings

There is a considerable amount of support for most assumptions of the Hovland–Yale Model. For example, the importance of the communication source was shown by Hovland and Weiss (1951). Participants were given information about drug taking and were led to believe the source was a prestigious medical journal or a newspaper. The amount of attitude change produced by the communication was more than twice as great when the source was thought to be the medical journal.

Even a casual study of the advertisements we see on television shows that advertisers attach great importance to their choice of individuals to present products. Attractive, well-liked celebrities are used in television commercials to persuade members of the public of the desirability of owning whatever products they are endorsing. Such communication sources are effective in boosting demand for consumer products (Chaiken & Eagly, 1983).

Another important characteristic of the communication source is his or her trustworthiness. Priester and Petty (1995) manipulated trustworthiness by having the source of a persuasive message argue in favour of a self-serving position (untrustworthy condition) or a position that opposed the source's self-interests (trustworthy condition). Individuals low in need for cognition (i.e. not enjoying effortful thinking) accepted the source's arguments without scrutiny when the source was trustworthy. However, they engaged in more thorough processing of the message when the source was untrustworthy.

When trying to persuade other people of a given point of view, we might decide to present only one side of the argument. Alternatively, we could present both sides of the argument, but try to identify weaknesses in the opposing side. Which approach is more effective? Hovland, Lumsdaine, and Sheffield (1949) studied American soldiers who listened to a radio broadcast claiming that the war against Japan would last for more than 2 years. The broadcast presenting both sides of the argument produced more attitude change than the one-sided broadcast among soldiers who initially believed the war would last less than 2 years. They were already familiar with arguments in favour of a rapid end to the war, and so found the one-sided broadcast biased. By contrast, those soldiers who initially believed the war would last for a long time were more influenced by the one-sided message. Thus, attitude change depends on the nature of the communication and on characteristics of the recipients (their initial position).

Are emotional messages more persuasive than non-emotional ones? In general, a threatening message can be very effective if recipients believe they can avoid the negative consequences contained in it. Sturges and Rogers (1996) had young adults listen to persuasive messages arguing that the dangers of tobacco were modest or great, and that it was easy or hard to keep away from tobacco. The greatest change in attitude towards cigarette smoking occurred among participants exposed to the high-threat message (i.e. dangers of tobacco are great) arguing that avoiding tobacco was easy.

Much research has focused on various characteristics of recipients that make them more or less likely to be influenced by persuasive messages. Cacioppo, Petty, and Morris (1983) considered individual differences in need for cognition. Those high in need for cognition enjoy engaging in effortful thinking and so would be

? What are some currently running advertisements featuring celebrities?

Sturges and Rogers' (1996) study found that the greatest change in attitude towards cigarette smoking occurred among those exposed to high-threat messages and who believed they could easily avoid the negative consequences.

EXAM HINT

Make sure you can fully explain the factors identified by the Hovland–Yale model as affecting the extent to which the communication is persuasive, such as the characteristics of the communicator, the impact of the message, and the characteristics of the audience.

? Why do you think individuals with high self-esteem are more easily persuaded than those with low self-esteem?

expected to process persuasive messages more thoroughly than those low in need for cognition. Participants read an editorial that was worded either strongly or weakly. As predicted, individuals with a high need for cognition were influenced more than those with a low need for cognition by strong arguments but were less influenced by weak arguments.

Are women more easily persuaded by messages than men? Eagly and Carli (1981) found that what matters is the relative familiarity of the subject of the message. Women are influenced more than men by messages on topics with which men are familiar. However, the opposite is the case with messages on topics with which women are more familiar. Thus, familiarity and knowledge make us less susceptible to attitude change.

According to the Hovland–Yale model, individuals high in self-esteem should be more resistant to attempts at persuasion than those low in self-esteem. However, most research has failed to support this prediction. For example, Baumeister and Covington (1985) found that those high in self-esteem were as easy to persuade as those low in self-esteem. However, individuals high in self-esteem were less willing to admit to having been persuaded.

Kinder, Pape, and Walfish (1980) discussed evidence that persuasive messages can produce changes in only some of the major outcomes (e.g. knowledge, attitudes, behaviour). They considered the effects of mass-media programmes designed to reduce the social problems caused by drugs. These programmes significantly increased people's comprehension and knowledge about drugs but had very modest effects on their attitudes and behaviour.

In general, the relationship between attitudes and behaviour is rather weak. For example, you probably know people who have been persuaded by media coverage that exercise is good for them, but who nevertheless take no exercise! Wicker (1969) summarised the findings from 32 studies, finding that the average correlation between attitude and behaviour was only +.15. As Wicker (1969, p. 65) concluded, "Taken as a whole, these studies suggest that it is considerably more likely that attitudes will be unrelated or only slightly related to overt behaviour than that attitudes will be strongly related to actions." However, attitudes might be more related to behaviour if we considered behaviour associated with deep-seated, important attitudes.

Evaluation

The Hovland–Yale Model represented the first systematic approach to understanding the factors responsible for attitude change. The emphasis within the model on characteristics of the source, features of the message, characteristics of the message recipients, and different kinds of potential change provides a useful framework. Many specific predictions of the model have been supported. For example, attitude change depends on the expertise, trustworthiness, and likeability of the source; on whether the message arguments are emotional and are one- or two-sided; and on the intelligence and personality of the recipients. Finally, as the model indicates, attitude change depends on the processes (e.g. attention, comprehension) that recipients use when presented with a message.

What are the limitations of the Hovland–Yale Model? First, it is difficult to assess the overall model. It identifies numerous factors influencing attitude change but doesn't indicate clearly how all these factors *influence* each other. Second, the prediction that individuals high in self-esteem are less susceptible to attitude change has been disproved. Third, the notion that message recipients respond to persuasive messages by proceeding through successive stages of attention, comprehension, acceptance, and retention is too neat and tidy. For example, our understanding of the message during the comprehension process may cause us to re-direct our attentional processes to different aspects of the message. Fourth, researchers testing the Hovland–Yale Model mostly focused on the *external* factors (e.g. source attractiveness; message emotionality) claimed to influence attitude change rather than on the underlying *internal* processes (e.g. attention; comprehension). As we will see, more recent theoretical approaches such as the Elaboration Likelihood Model have focused much more on these crucial internal processes.

Elaboration Likelihood Model

We turn now to the Elaboration Likelihood Model (e.g. Petty & Cacioppo, 1986). According to this model, people are generally motivated to hold correct attitudes. However, they might be unable or unwilling to process persuasive messages thoroughly for various reasons (e.g. lack of relevant knowledge, low personal relevance of the message). According to the model, recipients of messages can be persuaded in two different ways involving two distinct processing routes:

1. *Central route*: this involves detailed consideration and elaboration of the persuasive message.
2. *Peripheral route*: this involves being influenced more by non-content aspects of the message (e.g. the number of arguments produced) and by the context (e.g. the attractiveness of the communicator) than by the message content. Individuals using this route pay relatively little attention to the persuasive message.

What determines which processing route will be used? People often use the peripheral route because they have limited time to devote to most messages. However, they use the central route if their motivation and ability are high. Thus, individuals interested in the topic discussed in the message who possess relevant background knowledge are especially likely to engage in central processing.

According to the Elaboration Likelihood Model, most factors influencing attitude change can produce effects in various ways. Let us consider reasons why there is generally more attitude change when the communicator is attractive. Bohner (2001) used the example of an attractive model advertising the

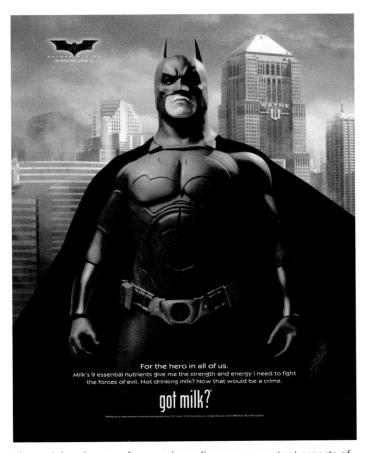

> **EXAM HINT**
>
> Remember that the Elaboration Likelihood Model consists of two forms of processing: the central route and the peripheral route. Make sure you can explain differences in which form of processing is preferred based on need for cognition.

For the hero in all of us.
Milk's 9 essential nutrients give me the strength and energy I need to fight the forces of evil. Not drinking milk? Now that would be a crime.

got milk?

The peripheral route of persuasion relies on non-content aspects of the message to sway the recipient. This striking image of Batman was used in the *Got Milk* campaign and is designed to encourage the audience to buy milk without having to think carefully about its benefits.

advantages of a particular brand of shampoo. She might influence attitude change via the peripheral route because her attractiveness creates a positive association with the shampoo. Alternatively, she might influence attitude change by encouraging recipients of the message to pay close attention so that their hair will look as nice as hers. Finally, the use of an attractive model might increase recipients' motivation to attend to her message.

A final assumption of the Elaboration Likelihood Model is that there are consistent individual differences in the need for cognition. Individuals high in need for cognition are motivated to engage in effortful thinking on many topics. Such individuals should be more likely than those low in need for cognition to engage in central-route processing.

According to the Elaboration Likelihood Model, central processing typically produces stronger and longer-lasting attitudes than peripheral processing. Why is this? According to Petty (1995, p. 230):

> When we do a lot of thinking before changing our attitudes, we are likely to be accessing the attitude and the corresponding knowledge structure quite frequently. This cognitive activity should tend to increase the number of linkages and strengthen the associations among the cognitive elements in the underlying attitude structure. This would tend to make the attitude structure more internally consistent, accessible, and enduring.

Findings

Petty, Cacioppo, and Goldman (1981) tested the Elaboration Likelihood Model. Students read a message that strongly supported the notion that a new large-scale examination should be introduced. All students would need to pass this examination to graduate. Some participants were told this examination might be introduced the following year to provide them with strong motivation to use the central route. The other participants were told there would be no change for 10 years, and thus any changes wouldn't affect them personally. This was designed to produce low motivation to process the message thoroughly so they would use the peripheral route.

Petty et al. (1981) prepared several versions of the message. It was either attributed to a source high in expertise (the Carnegie Commission on Higher Education) or low in expertise (a local high-school class). The quality of the arguments in the message was also varied. There were either strong arguments based on statistics and other data or weak arguments based on personal opinion and anecdotes.

What did Petty et al. (1981) find? For students expected to use the central route, the quality of the arguments was the main factor determining how persuaded they were. By contrast, for those students expected to use the peripheral route, the source of the message was the main factor influencing its persuasiveness. Thus, there are two separate routes to persuasion.

We might expect distraction to reduce the impact of a persuasive communication on attitude change—if the recipient is distracted, he or she will take in less of the message. However, distraction sometimes *increases* attitude change. Petty, Wells, and Brock (1976) studied distraction effects in the context of the Elaboration Likelihood Model. Their main manipulation was the quality of the arguments put forward in two different communications, both advocating an

? Do persuasive messages influence you via the central or the peripheral route?

increase in tuition fees at the university attended by the student participants. The message with high argument quality (strong message) claimed there had been a 2-year investigation into the issue and that increasing tuition fees would greatly increase graduates' starting salaries. The message with low argument quality (weak message) claimed there had been a 2-month investigation and increased tuition fees would lead to better lighting in classrooms.

Petty et al. (1976) predicted that distraction would *reduce* persuasion when the message was strong. The reason for this prediction was that the strong message produced favourable responses through central-route processing, and distraction reduced the amount of such processing. Petty et al. predicted that distraction would *increase* persuasion when the message was weak. The weak message would mainly elicit counterarguments, and distraction would reduce the counterarguments considered by participants. Both predictions were supported by the data.

The notion that any given factor can influence attitude changes in different ways in different situations has received support in other research (Petty, Brinol, & Tormala, 2002). For example, attractive and expert sources produce *more* attitude change in recipients of persuasive messages when the arguments are strong. However, they produce *less* attitude changes when the arguments are weak.

According to the Elaboration Likelihood Model, individuals high in need for cognition are motivated to understand communications thoroughly and so are more likely than those low in need for cognition to use central-route processing. The evidence indicates that those high in need for cognition engage in more central-route processing (reviewed by Cacioppo, Petty, Feinstein, Jarvis, & Blaire, 1996). In addition, and also as predicted by the model, individuals high in need for cognition are less affected than those low in need for cognition by peripheral cues (e.g. communicator attractiveness).

The Elaboration Likelihood Model assumes that people using the peripheral route are mainly influenced by non-content aspects of a persuasive message. For example, they may use various simple heuristics or rules of thumb when presented with a persuasive message. Axsom, Yates, and Chaiken (1987) compared the persuasiveness of a message apparently supported by many other people or by relatively few. There was more attitude change when many other people agreed with the message because the participants used the heuristic or rule of thumb, "If so many people agree, it must be true."

? What kinds of motivational factors might lead someone to pay close attention to a persuasive message?

Evaluation

The Elaboration Likelihood Model possesses various strengths. First, it represents clear progress when compared with the Hovland–Yale Model. In particular, there is much more focus on the internal processes underlying attitude change. Second, the notion that two routes are involved in producing attitude change is more realistic than the previous view that only one process is involved. Third, it is important to know that attitude change often depends on contextual information (e.g. likeability of the communicator). Fourth, the model takes account of individual differences (e.g. need for cognition) that influence how people process persuasive communications. Fifth, the notion that the impact of any given factor (e.g. distraction, communicator expertise, and attractiveness) varies from situation to situation has received much support and is a definite advance on the Hovland–Yale Model.

What are the weaknesses of the Elaboration Likelihood Model? First, the notion that there are two forms of processing of persuasive messages is oversimplified. As Petty (1995, pp. 208–209) admitted, "It is best to view the central and the peripheral routes as falling along a continuum [continuous line] of attitude change strategies that differ in the amount of effortful message evaluation they require."

Second, it is assumed that central and peripheral processes can occur at the same time. However, it isn't made clear how these processes interact and combine with each other.

Third, the model is complex, and it is assumed that several factors can influence either the central or peripheral route. As a result, it is often difficult to predict beforehand which processing route will be used by most people.

Fourth, the model focuses on factors determining the type of processing in which message recipients are most likely to engage. However, there has been a partial failure to consider, "those processes that determine when message processing will cease . . . or there will be a shift from one [processing] mode to another" (Petty et al., 2002).

Cognitive Consistency/Dissonance

One of the most influential approaches to an understanding of attitudes (and the relationship between attitudes and behaviour) is Festinger's (1957) **Cognitive Dissonance** Theory. According to this theory, someone holding two cognitions or thoughts that are psychologically discrepant experiences cognitive dissonance (an uncomfortable or negative emotional state produced by a discrepancy between two cognitions or thoughts). This state motivates the person to reduce the dissonance. People generally feel a need for cognitive consistency, and are willing to take steps to achieve it. Dissonance can be reduced by changing one or both of the cognitions, or by introducing a new cognition.

A commonplace example of cognitive dissonance is found in smokers. They have the cognition or thought that smoking can cause several diseases and they also have the cognition that they frequently engage in smoking behaviour. How can they reduce cognitive dissonance? One way is to stop smoking, but most smokers find it extremely difficult to do that. An alternative approach is for smokers to persuade themselves that smoking is less dangerous than is usually assumed. Gibbons, Eggleston, and Benthin (1997) found that smokers about to quit smoking regarded it as very dangerous, and this was a factor in them deciding to quit. However, when the same individuals started to smoke again, they perceived smoking to be much less dangerous than before! This change of attitude helped them to justify their decision to start smoking again. This study shows clearly the importance individuals attach to having consistency between their decisions and their attitudes.

Faller, Schilling, and Lang (1995) focused on smokers with lung cancer. More than 80% of these patients justified their decision to smoke by doubting the relevance of smoking as a cause of their illness. For example, they would point to the possibility that "toxins in the workplace" might be responsible, or they would emphasise that some non-smokers get lung cancer. Faller et al. summarised the patients' attitude as follows: "Obviously smoking is usually the cause, but it is not really so in my particular case!"

One way a smoker who does not wish to quit may try to reduce the cognitive dissonance they experience from habitually doing something that they understand can cause many diseases, would be to claim that smoking is less dangerous than usually assumed.

KEY TERM

Cognitive dissonance: an unpleasant psychological state occurring when someone has two discrepant cognitions or thoughts.

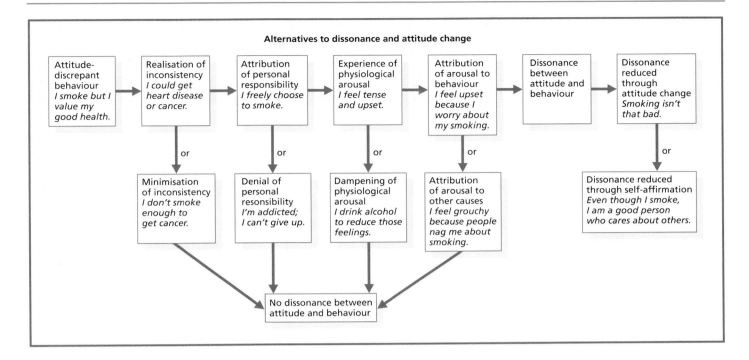

Festinger (1957) argued that people will often resolve a discrepancy between their attitudes and behaviour by altering their attitudes. Thus, rather than attitudes determining behaviour, behaviour sometimes determines attitudes. How can we create a discrepancy between someone's attitudes and their behaviour? One approach is **induced compliance**, in which people are persuaded to behave in ways inconsistent with their attitudes. Another approach is **effort justification**. What happens here is that people exert much effort to achieve some fairly trivial goal, and then have to justify having put in all that effort.

? What are some examples of induced compliance?

Findings

One of the most influential studies on induced compliance is that of Festinger and Carlsmith (1959). Participants spent 1 hour performing very boring tasks (e.g. emptying and refilling a tray with spools). After that, the experimenter asked each participant to tell the next participant that the experiment had been very enjoyable. The participants were offered $1 or $20 to lie in this way. Finally, all the participants were asked by the experimenter how much they liked the tasks they had performed.

Which group do you think expressed more positive views about the experiment? Advocates of operant conditioning (see Chapter 8) might well argue that the experiment was more rewarding for participants receiving $20 (a lot of money in the 1950s), and so they should have viewed the experiment more positively. In fact, those receiving only $1 had much more favourable opinions about the study than those receiving $20 or other control participants not asked to lie at all (see figure overleaf).

What is the reason for Festinger and Carlsmith's (1959) findings? Those participants who received $20 could argue that the money was sufficient justification for lying, and so there was little cognitive dissonance. By contrast, those receiving $1 had considerable cognitive dissonance. They said the experiment was very enjoyable when they knew it wasn't, and the small amount of money couldn't really justify lying. They couldn't change the lie, so the only way to reduce dissonance was by

KEY TERMS

Induced compliance: creating a conflict between an individual's attitudes and behaviour by persuading him or her to behave in ways that aren't consistent with his or her attitudes.

Effort justification: creating a conflict between attitudes and behaviour when people make great efforts to achieve a modest goal.

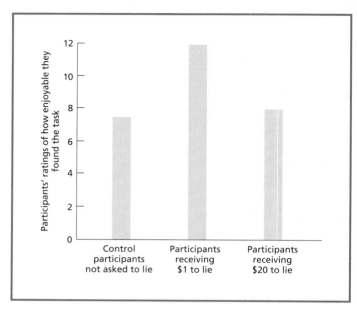

Data from Festinger and Carlsmith (1959).

changing their attitude towards the experiment, deciding that it was actually fairly enjoyable.

Aronson and Mills (1959) carried out a study on effort justification. Female college students had to undergo an initiation to join a group discussing the psychology of sex. One group read aloud non-obscene words related to sex whereas the other group read aloud obscene words followed by vivid descriptions of sexual activity. After that, both groups listened to an extremely boring discussion of mild sex behaviour in animals involving the group to which they wanted to belong. Which group do you think evaluated the boring discussion more highly? According to cognitive dissonance theory, the female students who had read out the obscene words should have rated it more highly. They were in a state of dissonance: they had agreed to join a group but had been very embarrassed for the sake of joining it. They could only justify the effort they had put in by deciding that the very boring group discussion was actually pretty interesting—which is what happened.

Festinger (1957) claimed that people will change their attitudes when they experience cognitive dissonance and when this unpleasant internal state is attributed to the discrepancy between their attitudes and their behaviour. Support for these assumptions was reported by Zanna and Cooper (1974). Participants were given a placebo (inactive) pill, which they were mistakenly told would cause them to feel aroused. When these participants were put into an unpleasant state of cognitive dissonance, they attributed this state to the pill rather than to cognitive dissonance. As a result, they failed to show the typical attitude change produced by cognitive dissonance.

Other research has focused more directly on the notion that dissonance effects produced by discrepant attitudes occur because individuals strive to reduce the negative affect or emotion caused by the discrepancy. There is much evidence that individuals given freedom of choice about behaving contrary to an important attitude report high levels of negative affect. However, this high level of negative affect is sometimes not followed by changed attitudes (Devine, Tauer, Barron, Elliot, & Vance, 1999). Burris, Harmon-Jones, and Tarpley (1997) carried out a study in which individuals' religious beliefs were disconfirmed. After this, they could reduce cognitive dissonance by means of additional information that accounted for the disconfirmation. Those participants who reported the greatest reduction in dissonance also tended to report the lowest levels of negative affect, which is as predicted by Festinger's theory.

Evaluation

Cognitive dissonance has several strengths. First, it is a very general theory that has been applied successfully to numerous situations involving discrepancies between an individual's attitudes and his/her behaviour. Second, there is much evidence in favour of the apparently paradoxical prediction from Cognitive Dissonance Theory that the weaker the reasons for behaving inconsistently with one's attitudes, the stronger the pressure to change those attitudes (e.g. Festinger & Carlsmith, 1959).

Third, previous theorists had typically assumed that attitudes cause behaviour. Festinger accepted that that is often the case. However, he showed convincingly that the direction of causality is sometimes the other way around—behaviour can cause changes in attitudes.

What are the limitations of Festinger's theory of dissonance? First, there are many situations in which cognitive dissonance and dissonance reduction simply don't occur when they should according to the theory. For example, people are often unconcerned about having inconsistencies between their attitudes and behaviour. Several specific examples of circumstances in which little or no attempt is made to reduce cognitive inconsistency are discussed below.

Second, the induced-compliance effect found by Festinger and Carlsmith (1959) wasn't replicated by Hiniker (1969) with Chinese participants or by Choi, Choi, and Cha (1992) with Koreans. These failures to replicate might have occurred because the need for cognitive consistency is less strong in collectivistic cultures (which emphasise group solidarity) than in individualistic ones (which emphasise personal responsibility). Kashima, Siegal, Tanaka, and Kashima (1992) found that Australians believed that consistency between attitudes and behaviour is more important than did the Japanese. People in collectivistic cultures focus on behaving in a socially acceptable way even when it conflicts with their beliefs.

Third, Festinger's approach ignores important individual differences. Nail, Correll, Drake, Glenn, Scott, and Stuckey (2001) presented participants with a scenario in which a friend failed to turn up at a restaurant and subsequently offered either a good or a poor reason for standing them up. As predicted by Festinger's theory, the participants indicated that they would regard the other person as less of a friend when he or she offered a poor reason. However, this effect was stronger among participants who on a questionnaire expressed a high preference for consistency.

Fourth, people can often live much more comfortably with cognitive inconsistency than Festinger assumed. If we don't accept personal responsibility for the inconsistency, then we aren't likely to experience dissonance and change our views (Cooper & Fazio, 1984). In addition, if after making a decision we feel we can reverse it at any time, then we aren't likely to experience any dissonance.

Fifth, as we will see shortly, many findings supporting Cognitive Dissonance Theory also support Bem's (1972) Self-perception Theory. Dissonance Theory is sometimes less successful than Self-perception Theory at explaining findings when individuals argue for a position fairly close to their initial attitudes.

Self-perception Theory

Bem (1967, 1972) argued that there was a different way to explain how people resolve differences between their attitudes and behaviour. According to his Self-perception Theory, we often use our own behaviour to *infer* our attitudes: "Individuals come to 'know' their own attitudes, emotions, and other internal states partially by inferring them from observations of their own overt behaviour and/or the circumstances in which this behaviour occurs" (Bem, 1972, p. 5). For example, if you realise you have eaten a lot of yoghurt recently, you might conclude that you have positive views about yoghurt as a food. If we use own behaviour to infer our attitudes, there will typically be consistency between them.

Bem (1967, 1972) accepted that we don't *always* infer our attitudes from our own behaviour. Suppose that you have a very strong positive attitude towards a

? Why might the need for cognitive consistency be less strong in collectivist cultures?

In Nail et al.'s (2001) study, participants considered the other person as less of a friend if he or she offered a poor reason for standing them up. However, some felt more let down than others, depending on how highly they rated consistency.

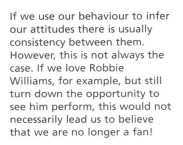

If we use our behaviour to infer our attitudes there is usually consistency between them. However, this is not always the case. If we love Robbie Williams, for example, but still turn down the opportunity to see him perform, this would not necessarily lead us to believe that we are no longer a fan!

well-known singer, but you turn down the chance to see her or him perform. It is rather unlikely that such a strong attitude would be changed by drawing inferences from your apparently unenthusiastic behaviour. Thus, we mainly infer our attitudes from our own behaviour when our attitudes were initially rather weak or ambiguous.

The assumption that an individual's attitudes are influenced by his or her behaviour (and by the context in which that behaviour occurs) is common to Self-perception Theory and to Cognitive Dissonance Theory. What, then, are the key differences? First, Festinger focused on the importance of *motivation* in producing attitude change, arguing that people strive for cognitive consistency to reduce the negative arousal associated with dissonance. By contrast, Bem argued that it wasn't necessary to assume the existence of such a negative state to account for cognitive consistency. Second, Festinger assumed that we generally know our own attitudes, whereas Bem argued that we often only know what our attitudes are by inferring them from our own behaviour. The easiest way of seeing how the two theories differ is to consider the relevant evidence, to which we now turn.

Findings

Bem (1967) reported an experiment that was a modified version of the one carried out by Festinger and Carlsmith (1959). He gave participants a written description of one of the conditions in that experiment and asked them to guess the attitude of someone in that condition. These guessed attitudes corresponded closely to those reported by participants in the original experiment. Bem explained these findings as follows—participants in the original experiment and the simulated one used information about the behaviour of the original participants and the context in which it occurred to infer attitudes. Crucially, the participants in the simulated experiment made their inferences *without* experiencing any unpleasant dissonance. That led Bem to conclude that consistency between attitudes and behaviour does *not* require dissonance. However, it is entirely possible that the original participants did experience dissonance.

Salancik and Conway (1975) carried out a more direct test of Bem's Self-perception Theory using two groups of students who were asked questions about their frequency of religious observance. In one group, the questions made participants focus on all the occasions when their behaviour indicated religious observance. In the other group, the questions made participants focus on their numerous failures to show religious observance. As predicted by Self-perception Theory, those participants who focused on their religious behaviours reported more favourable attitudes towards religion than those who focused on their failures to display religious behaviours. This is a clear example of attitudes being inferred from behaviour.

Self-perception Theory can explain the success of the **foot-in-the-door technique.** The essence of this technique is that it is easier to persuade someone to comply with a large request if you have previously persuaded them to comply with a smaller one. We will first consider a study involving this technique and then relate it to Self-Perception Theory. Sherman (1980) asked individuals living in Bloomington, Indiana, if they would hypothetically be willing to volunteer to spend 3 hours collecting money for the American Cancer Society. Three days later, a different experimenter called the same individuals and asked them to provide actual help. Over 30% of these individuals agreed to help, compared with only 4% of a control group of individuals who were approached directly. Thus, the foot-in-the-door technique produced a seven-fold increase in actual volunteering. According to Self-Perception Theory, the behaviour of hypothetically agreeing to volunteer led participants in the foot-in-the-door condition to infer that they had positive attitudes to charitable work. This made them more willing to engage in actual charitable work.

It seems plausible to explain the success of the foot-in-the-door technique with reference to changes in self-perception resulting from complying with a small request. However, changes in self-perception have rarely been measured, and so there is relatively little *direct* evidence to support this explanation of the foot-in-the-door effect. Some of the best evidence was reported by Burger and Caldwell (2003). Initially, they increased some participants' self-perception that they were altruistic by telling them they were helpful individuals. These individuals were more likely than control participants to volunteer to deliver canned food to the homeless. Burger and Caldwell decreased other participants' self-perception that they were altruistic by paying them $1 to sign a homelessness petition. These individuals were less likely than participants not paid to sign the petition to volunteer to deliver food to the homeless. Thus, changes in self-perception influence the extent to which the foot-in-the-door effect is obtained.

It is assumed within Self-perception Theory that individuals use information about their own behaviour to infer their attitudes. Suppose, however, that someone's *actual* behaviour is not helpful, even though their *intended* behaviour was helpful. Would they regard themselves as helpful because of their positive intention or non-helpful because of their behaviour? In a study by Dolinski (2001), participants were asked to give directions to a non-existent street. After that, someone else asked them to look after a heavy bag for a few minutes. Most of the participants responded positively to this second request, despite their previously unhelpful behaviour. Thus, participants seemed to draw inferences based on their *intentions* rather than on their *behaviour* itself.

Not everyone is susceptible to the foot-in-the-door technique. Guadagno, Asher, Demaine, and Cialdini (2001) used a questionnaire to identify individuals varying in their preference for consistency. When the attention of individuals low in preference for consistency was drawn to their compliance with a small request, it actually *reduced* their willingness to comply with a larger request. Guadagno et al. called this the reverse foot-in-the-door effect, and it is clearly inconsistent with Self-perception Theory.

> [?] Can you give some examples of the foot-in-door-technique in action?

KEY TERM

Foot-in-the-door technique: an approach to persuasion in which someone who has previously complied with a small request is more likely afterwards to comply with a larger request.

Does behaviour always influence our attitudes? The answer is, "No!" As Bem (1967, 1972) argued, it is mainly when our pre-existing attitudes are weak or non-existent and the situation is fairly trivial that we infer our attitudes from our behaviour. Consider, for example, a study by Taylor (1975). Female participants viewed pictures of men while receiving fake feedback on their physiological reactions (heart rate) to each one. Women who did not expect to meet any of the men based their liking of them on the fake heart-rate information. However, the findings differed for women who did expect to meet the man they liked the most. These women, for whom the consequences of their attitudes were more important, did *not* infer their attitudes from their own alleged physiological reactions.

Is Self-perception Theory more or less adequate than Dissonance Theory? It is hard to say, given that both theories have attracted a considerable amount of support. Another point is that there are many situations in which both theories make the same predictions. A useful contribution to this issue was provided by Fazio, Zanna, and Cooper (1977), who argued—with supporting evidence—that Dissonance Theory provides a better account than Self-perception Theory of attitude change when individuals behave in ways that differ considerably from their attitudes. It is in such circumstances that dissonance is most likely to be created. By contrast, however, Self-perception Theory was superior to Dissonance Theory in predicting attitude change accurately when people's behaviour differed only slightly from their attitudes.

Self-perception

Self-perception has an interesting link to the reported incidence of illness or morbidity. Kerala is one of the wealthiest provinces of India, with high levels of education and life expectancy, but also a high morbidity rate (Kumar, 1993). However, in Bihar, a poorer region of India with very little and poor-quality education, and a low life expectancy, the morbidity rate is also low. This suggests that having good education and general health enables people to become more self-aware, to use this information to infer attitudes and beliefs about their own daily health (Bajpai, 2003). It is not that poor people have less illness but simply that they report less illness. They are just in a poor position, with regard to knowledge and resources, to perceive their personal condition on a daily basis, if at all. This could explain the dissonance between their life expectancy (poor) and their reported morbidity (low) (Sen, 1998). However, it could be that these people are fully occupied in every way in the daily struggle for survival, and that self-perception of their personal health is an unaffordable luxury.

EXAM HINT

Note the foot-in-the-door effect supports the Self-perception Theory because it shows how our attitudes can be influenced by our perception of our own behaviour. But remember that this influence is fairly limited as behaviour influences attitudes only when the pre-existing attitude is weak or non-existent.

Evaluation

There is much support for the main assumptions of than Self-perception Theory. First, discrepancies between attitudes and behaviour can be resolved in the absence of any dissonance or negative affect. Second, attitudes are sometimes inferred from behaviour. Third, as predicted by Bem, we are more likely to use our behaviour to infer our attitudes when our attitudes are weak. Fourth, it can explain the success of the foot-in-the-door technique. However, there is relatively little direct evidence that this technique is effective because complying with a small request produces changes in self-perception.

What are the limitations with than Self-perception Theory? First, we often don't use our behaviour to infer our attitudes. Examples include situations in which our pre-existing attitudes are strong and unambiguous and those in which there is a relatively large discrepancy between our attitudes and behaviour.

Second, there are situations in which Dissonance Theory works better than Self-perception Theory (e.g. when there is a large discrepancy between attitudes and behaviour; Fazio et al., 1977). Third, Self-perception Theory doesn't take sufficient account of individual differences. The theory predicts the foot-in-the-door effect but individuals low in preference for consistency show the reverse foot-in-the-door effect (Guadagno et al., 2001). Fourth, it is hard to predict what inferences people will draw from their own behaviour when that behaviour is somewhat ambiguous. For example, what inferences will be drawn when someone intends to be helpful but their behaviour is not helpful (e.g. Dolinski, 2001)?

Explanations for the Effectiveness of Television in Persuasion

We might expect television to be especially effective in persuasion and producing attitude change. Television combines moving visual displays with an auditory input (words and sounds), whereas other media—such as print or radio—involve only a single sense modality. It seems likely that the effectiveness of a means of communication in persuasion would be greater when individuals receive information through two sense modalities rather than one. Dijkstra, Buijtels, and van Raaij (2005) presented advertisements for a book and a brand of wine on television, in print, and on the internet. Participants exposed to the advertisements on television had better memory for them than did those exposed to the advertisements in print or on the internet.

? How effective is television in changing people's attitudes?

Worchel, Andreoli, and Eason (1975) compared the effectiveness of television, radio (audiotape), and written material in producing attitude change. Some participants received a message disagreeing with their initial position communicated by a relatively trustworthy person (a newscaster) or an untrustworthy person (a candidate for political office). The trustworthy communicator changed attitudes *more* in the television condition than the other two conditions, but the untrustworthy communicator changed attitudes *least* in the television condition. Thus, the trustworthiness of the communicator mattered most when television was used because their personal characteristics are most obvious in that condition. Worchel et al. (1975, p. 157) concluded that, "Television may be the most involving medium."

Other research has suggested that what is going on may be more complex. Chaiken and Eagly (1983) considered whether the effectiveness of television or videotape compared with audiotape and written material depends on message complexity. When the message was easy to understand, the television style of presentation (i.e. videotape) produced the greatest amount of attitude change. However, when the message was hard to understand, the written material produced significantly more attitude change than did videotape. This happened because readers could go back over written information if they didn't understand it fully, which was impossible with television and videotape.

The power of television to change Americans' views on issues on which most people have strong opinions was investigated by Slater, Rouner, and Long (2006). Participants watched two television dramas, one advocating the death penalty and the other advocating gay marriage. The former drama was effective in increasing support for the death penalty, with those having a liberal ideology being most likely to change their opinion. By contrast, the latter drama did *not* change opinions about gay marriage, perhaps because initial opinions were held so strongly.

Why was the drama on the death penalty so effective? It focused on the importance of a crime-free society and the beneficial effects of having the death penalty. Watching the drama caused participants with a liberal ideology to attach more importance to a crime-free society, and this led them to become more positive about the death penalty. This framing effect demonstrates that changing the framework within which individuals consider an issue can make them change their opinions. In this study, liberals focused on the frame of a crime-free society (in which they strongly believed), and this made them more accepting of the death penalty (to which they were opposed in the absence of that frame).

We will shortly consider theories explaining the effectiveness of television in persuasion. However, some of the theories we have already discussed are relevant. For example, the Elaboration Likelihood Model (Petty & Cacioppo, 1986; discussed earlier) works when messages are presented on television. Kirby, Ureda, Rose, and Hussey (1998) considered the effectiveness of a message encouraging women to have regular mammograms that was embedded within the *Oprah Winfrey Show*. The arguments presented were strong or weak, and the peripheral cues were either favourable (shown in colour, much liked background music) or unfavourable (shown in black and white, disliked background music). According to the model, individuals not highly motivated to attend to the message should focus on peripheral cues to a greater extent than those who are highly motivated. As predicted, women with fewer concerns about breast cancer were more influenced by the peripheral cues than those with greater concerns.

Long running TV dramas and soap operas such as *EastEnders* are considered to be incredibly powerful in influencing social norms. However, such dramas offer a distorted version of reality that, over time, is assimilated by the audience, resulting in the cultivation effect, where our attitudes to the real world become similarly distorted.

Cultivation theory

One of the most influential theories on the effects of television on persuasion is Cultivation Theory (Gerbner, Gross, Morgan, & Signorielli, 1986). Its first assumption is that television provides a systematically distorted view of reality. The second assumption is that long-term viewing of these distortions causes viewers' attitudes to become similarly distorted (the cultivation effect). Thus, the effectiveness of television in persuasion is very *general* and biases our attitudes about the world around us.

What causes the cultivation effect? Shrum (2001) argued that two factors are involved. We can see how his explanation works by considering the concrete example that heavy television watchers exaggerate the incidence of violent crime. First, heavy television watchers find it easy to think of examples of violent crime because they have seen so many on television. Second, when people are asked how much violent crime there is, they often answer quickly and so don't focus on the *source* of their information. Perhaps if they focused on the fact that most examples of violent crime that come to mind are from television programmes they have watched, they would be less inclined to exaggerate the amount of violent crime.

Findings

Television often portrays a systematically distorted view of the world. For example, women on television are typically younger and more attractive than men (Signorielli, 1989) and overt acts of crime or violence occur about five times an hour on American television. This rate of portrayal of crime and violence on television is 10 times greater than its incidence in the real world (Gerbner et al., 1986).

Those who watch the most television tend to have the most distorted attitudes and perceptions about the world (reviewed by Shrum, 1999). For example, heavy television watchers are more likely than light television watchers to exaggerate the incidence of violent crime, their personal crime risk, and the prevalence of divorce, prostitution, alcoholism, and drug abuse. Sotirovic (2001) studied attitudes towards Americans receiving welfare. Participants who often watched television cable news and entertainment shows had biased views, believing that welfare recipients are mostly young, non-white, and female.

? What are the limitations of this study?

There is a serious limitation with the evidence discussed in the previous paragraph: it is correlational and so cannot establish causality. People who watch the most television might live in areas where there is a considerable amount of crime. If so, it might be their direct experience of crime rather than their watching of television that leads them to perceive the overall crime level as higher than is actually the case.

How can we decide how best to interpret the evidence? One approach is to select participants carefully so that heavy and light watchers of television are equated for possibly relevant factors such as direct experience, age, education, and income. When this is done, those watching the most television still have more distorted attitudes than those who watch less television, but the association between television watching and attitude distortion is reduced (Shrum, 1999). Overall, the findings provide support for cultivation theory, but indicate the need to control for various factors.

As discussed earlier, Shrum (2001) argued that heavy watchers of television might show less of a cultivation effect if they focused on the fact that much of their information about social issues comes from television. Shrum, Wyer, and O'Guinn (1998) tested this notion by telling participants that the topics they were going to be asked about often form a part of television programmes and this might influence their answers. The usual cultivation effect (i.e. heavy watchers having more distorted views) disappeared in this condition.

Evaluation

Cultivation Theory suggests that television can substantially distort our knowledge about (and our attitudes to) the world. Much of the evidence supports this theory. Heavy television watchers perceive the world to be more dangerous than is actually the case, and often have distorted stereotypical views about various minority groups. Most previous theories of persuasion had focused on specific effects of individual messages or other communications, but Cultivation Theory has directed our attention to much broader and more general forms of persuasion. Another strength of Cultivation Theory is that it has emphasised that many effects of television on persuasion are cumulative ones developing over long periods of time. That is a welcome change from most laboratory research, which focuses on very short-term effects.

What are the limitations with Cultivation Theory? First, most of the evidence is inconclusive because it is only correlational. Second, Cultivation Theory is basically descriptive and doesn't have much to say about *why* and *how* television distorts watchers' views and attitudes. Third, Shrum (2001) argued with supporting evidence that heavy television watchers have distorted attitudes only when they don't think about the source of their information about the world. This suggests that these distorted attitudes are less deep-rooted than assumed by Gerbner et al. (1986). Indeed, Shrum (2001) found that the attitudes of heavy television watchers were no more distorted than those of light watchers when they were all instructed to be as accurate as possible in their attitudes and were told they would have to justify their answers.

Agenda setting and priming

Several theorists have argued that television systematically influences people's attitudes in ways additional to those emphasised by cultivation theory. For example, Iyengar and Kinder (1987, p. 117) argued that the power of television (and the media generally) lies in "commanding the public's attention (agenda setting) and defining criteria underlying the public's judgements (priming)." According to Iyengar and Kinder (1987, p. 63), research on priming indicates that, "By calling attention to some matters while ignoring others, television news influences the standards by which governments, presidents, policies, and candidates for public office are judged."

In sum, television influences *what* we think about (i.e. agenda settings), and also helps to determine the factors influencing *why* we arrive at certain attitudes and judgements.

McCombs and Shaw's (1972) study of news coverage revealed a level of agenda setting by the media.

Findings

McCombs and Shaw (1972) obtained support for the notion that television and the media produce agenda setting in a study of news coverage of the 1968 US presidential election campaign. There was a close correspondence between the amount of attention that specific issues received on television and the importance the public attached to those issues.

The study by McCombs and Shaw (1972) was limited because it didn't establish causality. More specifically, it wasn't clear whether the media influenced the public's views or whether the public's views influenced media coverage. This issue was addressed by Iyengar and Kinder (1987). Participants watched newscasts (some of which had been altered) over a period of 1 week. They ranked several issues in order of importance at the start and end of the week. Media coverage influenced the participants—issues emphasised in the newscasts were perceived as being more important at the end of the week than the beginning.

Television also influences people's judgements via priming (focusing attention on certain issues). Krosnick and Kinder (1990) considered assessments of American President Ronald Reagan's performance at different points in time. During his presidency, there was the Iran–Contra affair, in which officials high up in the American administration illegally diverted funds from the secret sale of arms to Iran to the Nicaraguan Contras. As a result of extensive television coverage of this affair, people's assessments of Reagan's job performance were more influenced by his foreign policy than before.

Evaluation

Television probably has a major impact in determining people's views about the world. Part of what is involved is agenda setting—because people obtain so much of their knowledge of the world from television, the issues emphasised by television tend to be the issues they perceive as important. Another part of what is involved is priming, with the judgements that we make (e.g. about politicians) being strongly influenced by the (often biased) information we obtain from watching television.

What are the limitations with theories emphasising agenda setting and priming? First, the terms "agenda setting" and "priming" are imprecise. The notion of agenda setting has been applied to numerous issues, ranging from those of short duration (e.g. a major burglary) to those of very long duration (e.g. global warming). Second, the *processes* by which agenda setting and priming lead to persuasion and attitude change have not been explored in detail. For example, are the processes conscious or non-conscious? How different are the processes underlying agenda setting and priming? Third, the reasons why agenda setting and priming have more effect on some kinds of attitude change than on others are unclear. For example, Krosnick and Kinder's (1990) finding that the Iran–Contra scandal reduced people's assessments of President Reagan's job performance indicates the power of priming. However, the scandal had less effect on assessments of Reagan's character, although we don't know why.

SECTION SUMMARY
Persuasion, Attitude, and Change

❖ According to the Hovland–Yale Model, communicator effectiveness depends on his/her expertise, trustworthiness, likeability, and status.

Hovland–Yale Model

❖ Communication effectiveness depends on its emotional appeal and whether arguments are one- or two-sided.

❖ The impact of a communication depends on the initial position of the recipients and their intelligence and personality.

❖ According to the Hovland–Yale Model, recipients of a communication go through stages of attention, comprehension, acceptance, and memory.

❖ Evaluation:

— The model provides a useful framework, and most of the factors predicted to produce attitude change have been shown to do so.

— The various factors interact with each other in complex ways not made explicit in the model.

— The processing of persuasive messages doesn't proceed neatly and tidily through successive stages of attention, comprehension, acceptance, and retention.

— Research on the Hovland–Yale Model didn't focus enough on internal processes such as attention and comprehension.

❖ According to the Elaboration Likelihood Model, persuasive messages are processed through a central route and/or a peripheral route.

Elaboration likelihood model

❖ The central route involves message elaboration and is used if recipients' motivation and ability are high.

❖ The peripheral route involves superficial processing of non-content aspects of the message (e.g. attractiveness of the communicator).

❖ Evaluation:

— There is much evidence for different kinds of message processing.
— The model is oversimplified.
— It is often hard to predict which route will be used in any given situation.

Cognitive dissonance

❖ According to Festinger, discrepant cognitions or thoughts produce cognitive dissonance, which motivates the individual to reduce the dissonance.

❖ Evaluation:

— There is much evidence that people often resolve a discrepancy between their attitudes and behaviour by altering their attitudes.
— Dissonance Theory works less well in collectivistic cultures, which attach less importance to consistency.
— If individuals feel no personal responsibility for a cognitive discrepancy, they often experience little or no dissonance.

Self-perception Theory

❖ According to Bem's Self-perception Theory, we often only know what our attitudes are by inferring them from our own behaviour.

❖ Evaluation:

— As predicted by the theory, discrepancies between attitudes can be resolved in the absence of dissonance or negative affect.
— There is evidence that attitudes are sometimes inferred from behaviour.
— The success of the foot-in-the-door technique can often be explained by Self-perception Theory.
— The predictions of the theory are unclear when there is a discrepancy between intended and actual behaviour.
— Individuals low in preference for consistency sometimes fail to conform to theoretical predictions.
— Dissonance theory works better than Self-perception Theory when there is a large discrepancy between attitudes and behaviour.

Effectiveness of television

❖ Television is often more effective in persuasion than other media because it combines visual and auditory input and is involving.

Cultivation Theory

❖ According to Cultivation Theory, television provides a distorted view of reality, and heavy television watchers are strongly influenced by this distorted view.

❖ Evaluation:

— Television can distort watchers' attitudes about reality.
— Much of the evidence is correlational and doesn't establish causality.
— Cultivation Theory doesn't have much to say about the processes leading television to produce distorted views.

Agenda setting and priming

❖ Television can also change people's attitudes by agenda setting and priming due to its emphasis on certain issues and de-emphasis on other issues.

❖ Evaluation:

— The terms "agenda setting" and "priming" are vague.

— The processes causing agenda setting and priming to influence television viewers' behaviour are unclear.

THE PSYCHOLOGY OF "CELEBRITY"

What is a "celebrity"? According to *Chambers Dictionary*, a celebrity is "a person of distinction or fame." Celebrity and the worship of celebrity have existed for a very long time. As Giles and Maltby (2006, p. 82) pointed out, "This bizarre state of affairs—a small group of human beings idolised by a much larger number—has existed in most societies to some extent through history." Royalty and military leaders were often celebrities several centuries ago. However, there have been two dramatic changes in the area of celebrity in recent decades. First, there has been a huge increase in the number of celebrities, especially in the West. This is due in part to an explosion in the information that is readily available about thousands of people through the media.

In recent years, the definition of celebrity has shifted to incorporate the "ordinary" celebrities produced by reality TV shows such as *Big Brother*.

Second, there has been a definite shift in the characteristics of celebrities. The growth of reality television and do-it-yourself celebrity websites has led to a marked increase in the percentage of "ordinary" celebrities who are mostly famous because they are well-known. Turner (2006) used the term "the demotic [popular or vulgar] turn" to refer to this substantial reduction of any important differences between the famous and everyone else.

Individuals differ enormously in terms of how attracted they are to celebrities. This raises the question: how many types of celebrity worship are there? Maltby, Day, McCutcheon, Houran, and Ashe (2006) addressed this issue by using the Celebrity Attitude Scale, a modified version of the Celebrity Worship Scale produced by McCutcheon, Lange, and Houran (2002). They identified *three* dimensions of celebrity worship:

1. *Entertainment–social*: this aspect involves individuals regarding their favourite celebrity as a source of entertainment and of social interaction. Sample item: "Keeping up with news about my favourite celebrity is an entertaining pastime."
2. *Intense–personal*: this aspect involves individuals having intense and compulsive feelings about (and devotion to) their favourite celebrity. Sample item: "I consider my favourite celebrity to be my soul mate."
3. *Borderline–pathological*: this aspect involves uncontrollable fantasies and forms of behaviour relating to their favourite celebrity. Sample item: "I would gladly die to save the life of my favourite celebrity."

In this section, I start by considering various explanations of celebrity. As we will see, there are various reasons why people are attracted to celebrities. Some are basically social psychological, whereas others have more of an evolutionary basis. After that, I turn to the more worrying phenomena (e.g. pathological celebrity worship, stalking) associated with very intense attachments to celebrities or other people.

The Attraction of "Celebrity"

In some ways, it seems strange that tens of millions of people are attracted to celebrities. After all, the great majority of fans of celebrities never meet the object of their intense interest. Even if they do meet the celebrity of their choice, it is likely to be very briefly (e.g. while the celebrity signs his or her name). What, then, is the intense appeal that celebrities have for so many people? We will consider two possible answers. First, fans may derive pleasure from having a "pretend" relationship with their favourite celebrity. Such a relationship has various advantages over real relationships. For example, your favourite celebrity is not going to evaluate or criticise you in the way that often happens with real relationships!

Second, we can account for the attraction of celebrity using evolutionary explanations. The favourite celebrity for many millions of individuals is someone of the opposite sex who appears to possess precisely the qualities that have proved of value in our evolutionary history. Thus, the attraction of celebrity may reflect ancient evolutionary pressures. Of course, there could be some mileage in both explanations.

Social psychological explanations

The great majority of close relationships involve two people, both of whom are intensely emotionally involved with each other. However, there is another type of relationship, known as a **parasocial relationship**. The essence of a parasocial relationship is that it is one-sided—one person has an emotional investment in someone else, but the other person is often unaware even of the existence of the first person. The overwhelming majority of relationships between fans and celebrities are parasocial ones. The fan possesses considerable knowledge about a celebrity and has some degree of emotional commitment to that celebrity, but the celebrity lives in blissful ignorance of the fan's existence.

When any close relationship is threatened or comes to an end, those involved typically experience various negative emotional states (e.g. distress, depression). The same should be true of parasocial relationships if they resemble "real" relationships. This hypothesis was tested by Eyal and Cohen (2006), who assessed viewers' reactions after the showing of the last-ever episode of the comedy series, *Friends*. The amount of break-up distress reported by viewers was best predicted by the intensity of their parasocial relationship with their favourite character in the series.

Convincing evidence that parasocial relationships can resemble "real" ones was obtained by Thomson (2006). With real relationships, the strongest attachments are those in which each person's needs for autonomy (independence), relatedness (a sense of closeness), and competence (a sense of mastery and achievement) are

KEY TERM

Parasocial relationship: an entirely one-sided relationship between two people in which one person feels strongly attached emotionally to the other person, who is typically completely unaware of the existence of the first person.

Eyal and Cohen (2006) found that the break-up distress reported by viewers of the last ever episode of *Friends* reflected the extent of their parasocial relationship with the show's characters. There were reports of emotional scenes when the series' finale was broadcast live in Times Square, New York (above).

met (LaGuardia, Ryan, Couchman, & Deci, 2000). Thomson focused on these three factors in predicting individuals' attachment strength to a celebrity. All three factors were strongly predictive, thus revealing impressive similarities between real and parasocial relationships. More specifically, it seems that parasocial relationships fulfil some of the main needs fulfilled by real relationships.

I have already identified one advantage that parasocial relationships have over real ones. Another advantage was identified by Gaffney (2001), who argued that with celebrities we should distinguish between the person (what someone is really like) and the persona (how they appear when in public). The persona typically consists of the most attractive characteristics of the celebrity, with the less attractive ones hidden from view, and it is the persona that celebrity worshippers see. In real relationships, by contrast, we typically experience the other person "warts and all".

Evidence: personal factors

What kinds of people are most likely to seek strong parasocial relationships with celebrities? It is often argued that those most attracted to celebrities tend to be lonely and shy individuals. Loneliness and shyness are deterrents to establishing real relationships but not to establishing pretend relationships with celebrities. There is modest support for this position. Ashe and McCutcheon (2001) found that shyness and loneliness in young adults were both weakly associated with the strength of participants' parasocial relationships with celebrities. In a study already discussed, Eyal and Cohen (2006) found that lonely participants experienced more distress than non-lonely ones after the last episode of *Friends*.

An important factor influencing attraction towards celebrities is age. Adolescents and young adults are much more likely than older adults to engage in celebrity worship (Giles, 2000). One likely reason is that younger people are less likely to have an established social network. As a result, they feel a greater need to extend their social relationships by fantasising about establishing a close relationship with a celebrity. Supporting evidence was reported by Giles and Maltby (2004) in a study of British adolescents aged between 11 and 16. Those adolescents who had an intense–personal interest in a celebrity reported low levels of security and closeness to others and low attachment to parents. These findings suggest that intense interest in a celebrity was motivated by a desire to reduce some of the deficiencies in their everyday lives. In the words of Giles and Maltby (2004, p. 813), "Celebrities provide adolescents with a secondary group of pseudo-friends during a time of increasing autonomy [independence] from parents."

The notion that celebrity worship may generally have greater effects during the years of adolescence rather than later was supported by Maltby et al. (2006). Adolescents, undergraduate students, and adults selected a same-sexed celebrity whose body and figure they admired. They then completed a revised version of the Celebrity Attitude Scale and questionnaires relating to body shape. The female adolescents were the only group for whom intense–personal celebrity worship was associated with a negative body image. The most likely explanation is that only female adolescents were so strongly influenced by their perceptions of their favourite celebrity that it had a negative impact on their own body image.

Another important factor in determining the intensity of an individual's parasocial relationship with a celebrity is his or her attachment style. The best-known way of categorising attachment styles was introduced by Ainsworth (e.g.

? Why do you think people form parasocial relationships?

Ainsworth, Blehar, Waters, & Wall, 1978) on the basis of her research on infant attachments using the Strange Situation. Ainsworth identified three major types: (1) secure attachment (strong and positive); (2) avoidant attachment (insecure: fearful and withdrawing); and (3) resistant or ambivalent (insecure: seeking contact + resistance to contact). Cole and Leets (1999) found that students having ambivalent attachment were most likely to form a parasocial relationship with a celebrity, and those having avoidant attachment were least likely to do so. Securely attached students were in the middle.

How can we explain the above findings? Individuals with a resistant or ambivalent attachment style are often very emotional but have negative views about themselves. Intense attraction to a celebrity allows them to express their emotions without the fear of rejection. By contrast, individuals with an avoidant attachment style are generally less inclined to invest emotionally in relationships because of their past experiences. Securely attached individuals often have satisfactory real-life relationships and so do not seek an additional relationship with a celebrity.

Evidence that individuals with ambivalent or resistant attachment invest more heavily than other people in parasocial relationships was reported by Cohen (2004). Israeli participants completed questionnaires indicating how they would react if their favourite television characters were taken off the air. Their negative reactions resembled those that people experience after the end of "real" social relationships. Of greatest relevance, the most negative emotional responses were obtained from participants having ambivalent or resistant attachment.

Evaluation

The notion that individuals who worship a celebrity often have a parasocial relationship with that celebrity has received considerable support. Such parasocial relationships are surprisingly similar to "real" relationships in which both people are very actively involved in the relationship. Some of the characteristics associated with someone engaging in celebrity worship have been discovered, including being adolescent, being shy and/or lonely, and having ambivalent attachment.

What are the limitations with the social psychological approach? First, there is a real danger of oversimplifying matters. There is no *single* answer to the question, "What kinds of people engage in parasocial relationships?" any more than there is to the question, "What kinds of people engage in close personal relationships?" Many different motivational and other factors determine any given individual's level of attraction to a celebrity.

Second, it is easy within the social psychological approach to assume that individuals have a *consistent* attachment style across their major relationships based on their personality and early experiences. This is a substantial oversimplification. Ross and Spinner (2001) obtained questionnaire measures concerning adults' attachment styles (secure, fearful, preoccupied, and dismissing) in four relationships. For most of the participants, there were significant differences in attachment styles across their different attachment relationships.

Evolutionary explanations

Many millions of individuals are intensely attracted to glamorous celebrities of the opposite sex. This suggests that a major reason why people worship celebrities

EXAM HINT

Note that celebrity attraction can be explained by an interaction of nature (evolutionary theories) and nurture (social psychological theories), which means both biological and learning factors can be accounted for. Remember that a key criticism of evolutionary theories is that they are speculative and lacking evidence. Bear this in mind as you read about these theories.

is because they are perceived as especially desirable as sexual and/or romantic partners. What characteristics make someone especially attractive to members of the opposite sex?

Reasonably clear answers to this question have been proposed by evolutionary psychologists (e.g. Buss, 1999). One of their main assumptions is that there are excellent evolutionary reasons why men and women value different characteristics in potential mates. As Buss (1999, p. 102) pointed out:

> *A man in human evolutionary history could walk away from a casual coupling having lost only a few hours or even a few minutes. A woman in evolutionary history risked getting pregnant as a result and therefore could have incurred the cost of that decision for years.*

The ability to wrestle with a mammoth went down well with the ladies.

In more technical terms, men and women differ in **parental investment**, which is the time and effort a parent devotes to rearing his/her offspring. In humans, the parental investment of women is much greater than that of men. What are the implications of sex differences in parental investment? Females can only bear a limited number of children, and they invest heavily in each one during the 9 months of pregnancy and for several years thereafter. Women should prefer men having good resources, and who are willing to be committed to them over long periods of time. By contrast, human males can maximise their reproductive potential by having sex with numerous females. This should lead them to seek fertile women. One way of doing this is to seek younger women. Both male and female mating strategies are designed to maximise the probability that the individual's genes will survive.

What are the implications of the evolutionary approach for understanding celebrity worship? Females should be most attracted to male celebrities who command high levels of resources (e.g. money). More generally, "Culturally successful men are preferred as mating and marriage partners. These men wield social influence and have control over resources that women can use for themselves and their children" (Geary, Vigil, & Byrd-Cranen, 2004). There is evidence that the children of culturally successful men have lower mortality rates in childhood than the children of less successful men. They also have better psychological and physical health and live longer (Geary et al., 2004).

The evolutionary approach would dictate that females should be most attracted to male celebrities who are culturally and financially successful.

Males should be most attracted to female celebrities who are fertile. One of the main signs of fertility is age, with women in their late teens and early twenties being more fertile than younger or older women. Zaadstra et al. (1993) found that body mass index (BMI) and waist-to-hip ratio were associated with fertility in women. Women with a BMI between 20 and 30 and a waist-to-hip ratio under 0.70 were the most fertile on average.

There might be stronger support for the evolutionary approach with the pretend relationships between fans and celebrities than with the real ones of everyday life. Male fans are free to select female celebrities who are very young

KEY TERM

Parental investment: the time and effort devoted by a parent to rearing his/her offspring.

and outstandingly beautiful, and female fans are free to select male celebrities who are incredibly successful and wealthy. In the real world, however, compromise is generally the order of the day. Although a physically unattractive woman might *prefer* to have a wealthy mate, or a man lacking resources might *prefer* a very attractive young mate, their own lack of sexual attractiveness means that their *actual* choices often deviate substantially from their *preferred* choices. By contrast, fans' actual celebrity choices can coincide exactly with their preferences.

There are other possible evolutionary explanations for the attraction of celebrity. Mark Schaller (2006) argued that in our evolutionary past it was very important to distinguish between friends and enemies. Familiarity was a very useful cue, because friends are more likely than enemies to be familiar. Schaller went further and pointed out that our ancestors used familiarity and similarity to determine kinship. Of course, celebrities are very familiar to us. According to Schaller, "I've seen Bruce Willis . . . in his underwear, in bed with his wife . . . I've seen him in my own house dozens of times." He knows rationally that Bruce Willis isn't a member of his family. However, he reacts to him as if he were family, describing the neural processes involved as, "the highly automatised, non-conscious residue of our ancient evolutionary past."

> ■ **Activity: Westen (1996, p.706) commented on the behaviour of men and women:**
>
> *Consider the Casanova who professes commitment and then turns out a few months later not to be ready for it; the man who gladly sleeps with a woman on a first date but then does not want to see her again, certainly not for a long-term relationship; or the women who only date men of high status and earning potential.*
>
> Westen suggested that all of these behaviours can be explained in evolutionary terms. Try to identify such behaviour for yourself by making a list of the different behaviours along with the evolutionary explanations for them. You also might consider why some people might find Westen's comments sexist and offensive.

Evidence

One of the main predictions from the evolutionary approach is that females are attracted to male celebrities because they are culturally successful and have access to considerable resources. The fact that most celebrities fulfil these criteria is consistent with this approach, although many other factors could be at work. It follows from the evolutionary approach that male celebrities should generally enjoy much more success with women *after* becoming celebrities than they beforehand. There is massive anecdotal evidence supporting that prediction. Townsend, Kline, and Wasserman (1995) found that both sexes agreed that males' sexual attractiveness depended more than females' sexual attractiveness on their status. More importantly, males who achieved high status (e.g. via athletic stardom) became much more sexually attractive to females and had a greatly increased number of sex partners.

According to evolutionary theory, men focus mostly on *external* physical attributes when assessing the sexual attractiveness of women, whereas women focus more on *internal* factors (e.g. social status; access to resources). As external attributes are easier to judge than internal ones, it follows that men's ratings of the sexual attractiveness of female celebrities should be more similar than women's ratings of male celebrities. As predicted, Townsend and Wasserman (1997) found that women showed more variability than men when rating the sexual attractiveness of celebrities of the opposite sex.

We can obtain some idea of what men are seeking in women and women are seeking in men by considering "lonely hearts" advertisements. The differences predicted by evolutionary theory are typically found. Waynforth and Dunbar (1995) found that women offering physical attractiveness in their advertisements made higher demands on the type of man they wanted than women not offering

All the above celebrities featured in the 2006 *New Woman* "World's sexiest male" poll. Women show more variability than men when rating the sexual attractiveness of celebrities, as this is not purely based on external factors, but also on internal factors, such as sense of humour, intelligence, and financial prowess.

physical attractiveness. However, there was no difference in the demands made by men offering or not offering physical attractiveness. Men offering good resources made higher demands on the type of woman they wanted than men not offering good resources. However, level of resources did not influence women's demands on the type of man they wanted. The implication is that we might expect to find that male celebrities are very wealthy and female celebrities are young and very physically attractive. That is approximately the case, although there are some obvious exceptions.

The evolutionary approach is approximately correct, but doesn't take sufficient account of variations across cultures. Consider the prediction that men should prefer slender women. Anderson, Crawford, Nadeau, and Lindberg (1992) reviewed findings from 52 cultures. Whereas women with a slender body were preferred in cultures in which the food supply was very reliable (e.g. most Western cultures), women with a heavy body were preferred in cultures in which the food supply was very unreliable. It could be argued from the evolutionary perspective that heavy women in cultures with very unreliable food supplies are better equipped than slender women to survive food shortages and to provide nourishment for their children.

On the evolutionary hypothesis, we might expect that celebrity worship would generally involve fans selecting a very sexually attractive celebrity of the opposite sex. McCutcheon (2002) carried out a study on young adults with an average age of about 20. Of the female participants, only 61% selected someone of the opposite sex in a glamorous profession as their favourite celebrity. Among male participants, only 24% chose an opposite-sexed celebrity in a glamorous profession. Presumably, people's favourite celebrities are often selected because of specific skills they possess (e.g. singing, guitar playing) rather than because of their sexual attractiveness.

The notion that there are similarities between friendship and kinship was investigated by Ackerman, Kenrick, and Schaller (2007), who found that close friendship can activate emotional processes resembling those generally associated with kinship, especially with women. They asked men and women to imagine sexual contact with kin, friends, and strangers. The women responded to the friends more like kin than like strangers, whereas the men responded to the friends more like strangers. It is generally accepted that celebrities are treated in many ways like friends, and these findings suggest that celebrities might also be treated like kin, especially by female fans.

Evaluation

The evolutionary approach offers interesting insights into the reasons why people are attracted to celebrities. The fact that fans are entirely free to choose their favourite fantasy sexual partner from literally hundreds or thousands of celebrities means we can see their genuine preferences freed of the constraints of everyday reality. By and large, the evidence is consistent with the notion that male celebrities are attractive to women because they have high social status and resources, whereas female celebrities are attractive to men because they are young and very attractive physically. More generally, female fans focus on internal features of male celebrities, whereas male fans focus on external features of female celebrities. In addition, part of the attraction of celebrities may be that our great familiarity with them and with their lives means that we accept them not only as if they were friends but almost like members of our own family.

What are the limitations with the evolutionary approach? First, it is most applicable when fans are intensely interested in a celebrity because he or she is sexually attractive. However, that is often *not* the case, as we saw in the study by McCutcheon (2002). Nevertheless, sexual attraction probably plays a larger role when fans are intensely involved with their favourite celebrity.

Second, there are various ways of interpreting the findings, some owing little to the evolutionary approach. Women's preference for men who are culturally successful and wealthy can be explained by their desire to have a mate who will provide for their children. However, it is not hard to think of other explanations. Women might find successful and wealthy men attractive because they would be able to buy whatever they wanted for themselves or because of the envy they would attract from other women.

Third, the assumption that our mate preferences fundamentally reflect our strong motivation to ensure the survival of our genes is dubious. The birth rate in several European countries has been going *down* steadily for many years. Indeed, in some countries (e.g. Spain; Italy), it is now so low that their populations are starting to decrease. Such changes are difficult to explain in evolutionary terms.

Fourth, the evolutionary approach is a general one offering some explanations of why individuals might be strongly attracted to a celebrity. However, it doesn't indicate why a given person is strongly attracted to one celebrity but not to numerous others who are equally attractive sexually. In addition, it doesn't provide a clear explanation of why many millions of people have no strong attraction to any celebrity.

? What other factors can you think of that might make a celebrity attractive?

Research into Intense Fandom

So far, we have focused mainly on the largely innocuous or even healthy interest that millions of people have in celebrities. However, there is a dark side to celebrity attraction, which can come to the fore when individuals become obsessed by their favourite celebrity. At its most extreme, such obsessions can lead to stalking and even attempts to kill the celebrity in question. We will first discuss the nature of celebrity worship and then turn to the issue of stalking.

Celebrity worship

We are bombarded with very detailed information about thousands of celebrities. This was shown strikingly in a study by Aron, Aron, Tudor, and Nelson (1991) in which the participants generated visual images of various individuals. The image they formed of the singer and actress Cher was more vivid than that of their own mother!

Common sense would suggest there are various kinds of celebrity worship, and some are more dangerous than others. For example, it seems perfectly healthy for an adolescent to become very interested in a particular musical celebrity and to buy his or her CDs, to go to his or her concerts, and to become very knowledgeable about his or her life and interests. However, it is much less healthy when individuals devote most of their waking hours to obsessional thoughts about a given celebrity. When their favourite celebrity dies, such individuals often experience bereavement hallucinations as part of their sense of grief and loss closely resembling those found in individuals when a close family member dies (Rosenblatt, Walsh, & Jackson, 1976).

A reality television show in the United States reveals just how far some celebrity worshippers are willing to go. The show is called, *I Want a Famous Face*, and the participants have all undergone plastic surgery to look as similar as possible to their favourite celebrity. For example, Mike and Matt both wanted to look like Brad Pitt, and young women wanted to look like Pamela Anderson, Britney Spears, or Victoria Beckham.

Some individuals who are obsessed with a particular celebrity develop a mental disorder known as **erotomania**. This is a mental disorder in which the individual has delusions that someone of higher social status (often a celebrity) has fallen in love with him or her and has made romantic advances. Most patients suffering from erotomania are isolated and don't have a partner or a full-time job (Kennedy, McDonough, Kelly, & Berrios, 2002), and 75% of sufferers are female; they often have other mental disorders. The fact that other family members often have mental disorders suggests a genetic basis to erotomania (Kennedy et al., 2002). In some cases, erotomania can lead to stalking (discussed later).

The potential dangers associated with celebrity worship were shown by Cheng et al. (2007). M.J. Nee, a famous male television actor in Taiwan, committed suicide by hanging himself from a tree in April 2005. During the 3-week period of extensive media reporting after this suicide, there was a 55% increase in the number of suicide attempts. The impact of Mr Nee's suicide was especially great on individuals who had made a previous suicide attempt in the year preceding the media reports of his death. Many attempting suicide following Nee's suicide referred directly to it as a factor in their decision. One said, "Life is like on the stage, a big star has gone, why not me?", and another said, "Suicide can be a glorious act like his became" (Cheng et al. 2007, p. 864).

Findings

Who is most prone to celebrity worship? According to Maltby, Houran, and McCutcheon (2003), the answer depends on which aspect or dimension of

It is quite natural for adolescents to express devotion to a pop group, with a bedroom wall plastered in posters, for example. However, some individuals become obsessional and delusional about the celebrity and their relationship with them; a condition known as erotomania.

KEY TERM

Erotomania: this is a mental disorder in which the individual concerned deludes himself or herself into believing that someone of much higher status has made romantic advances to him or her.

? Are certain personality types more prone to celebrity worship?

celebrity worship we consider. They related scores on the three celebrity worship dimensions described earlier (entertainment–social, intense–personal, borderline–pathological) to the three personality dimensions identified by H.J. Eysenck (e.g. 1967). These three dimensions are as follows: extraversion (mainly concerned with sociability); neuroticism (tendency to experience negative emotional states); and psychoticism (tendency to be cold and hostile).

What did Maltby et al. (2003) find? First, entertainment–social celebrity worship was positively associated with extraversion. This makes sense given that extraverts are more interested in social interactions and gossip than introverts. Second, intense–personal celebrity worship was positively associated with neuroticism. This also makes sense given that individuals high in neuroticism have more intense emotional states (especially negative ones) than those low in neuroticism. Third, borderline–pathological celebrity worship was positively associated with psychoticism. However, the association was weak.

Individual differences in cognitive functioning are important in explaining who does or doesn't worship celebrities. Levy (1979) found that those scoring high on a measure of celebrity adulation tended to have had several years' less education than those who scored low. Fujii, Ahmed, and Takeshita (1999) discussed findings from several cases of erotomania (a pathological romantic obsession with a celebrity). Most of these patients showed various cognitive deficits and a lack of flexibility in thinking. McCutcheon, Ashe, Houran, and Maltby (2003) focused on the relationship between scores on the Celebrity Attitude Scale and various measures of cognitive ability (e.g. verbal creativity, spatial ability, crystallised [knowledge-based] intelligence). High scorers on all three dimensions of celebrity worship (entertainment–social, intense–personal, and borderline–pathological) had lower cognitive ability than low scorers. Thus, celebrity worshippers are less intelligent on average than those who don't worship celebrities.

Absorption-Addiction Model

How can we explain the existence of celebrity worship? One answer was provided by McCutcheon et al. (2002), who put forward the Absorption–Addiction Model. The first stage on the road to celebrity worship is absorption, which can be defined as "a total attention, involving a full commitment of available perceptual, motoric, imaginative and ideational resources to a unified representation of the attentional object" (Tellegen & Atkinson, 1974, p. 274). Individuals with a weak sense of identity are more likely to show absorption with a celebrity, with this absorption leading them to discover as much as possible about the celebrity and to develop closeness with him or her.

The second stage involves addiction. The motivational forces leading to absorption can produce a state of addiction in which the individual craves greater and greater closeness to his or her favourite celebrity, and indulges in increasingly extreme delusional forms of thinking and behaviour. Part of the impetus behind this addiction is the desire to achieve a full sense of identity and a social role.

Evidence supporting this model was reported by Houran, Navik, and Zerrusen (2005), who argued that the absorption and addiction shown by celebrity worshippers involve an excessive identification with their favourite celebrity. This implies that they don't perceive clear boundaries between themselves and other people, and might also indicate a failure to distinguish clearly between emotions and thoughts. Houran et al. (2005) predicted that celebrity worshippers have unclear or thin boundaries in these (and other) respects. As predicted, there were significant positive correlations between unclear or thin boundaries and each of the three dimensions of celebrity worship. Individuals high in borderline–pathological celebrity worship had especially weak boundaries at the interpersonal level.

Overall evaluation

Research on celebrity worship has several successes to its credit. First, it has established that there are three different kinds of celebrity worship: entertainment–social, intense–personal, and borderline–pathological. Second, each type of celebrity worship is associated with a different major personality dimension. Third, the Absorption–Addiction Model provides an account of celebrity worship based on absorption with a celebrity leading to an addictive compulsion to achieve greater closeness to him or her.

What are the limitations of research on celebrity worship? First, nearly all the evidence is correlational in nature and so we can't infer causality. For example, intense celebrity might alter someone's personality rather than personality helping to determine whether someone engages in celebrity worship.

Second, it is assumed that the same processes are involved regardless of the characteristics of the celebrity being worshipped. As Giles and Maltby (2006) pointed out, celebrity worshippers might simply be attracted by celebrity status. However, people are attracted to some celebrities (e.g. the late Pavarotti, Stephen Hawking) because of their outstanding abilities rather than because they are famous and attractive.

Third, the Absorption–Addiction Model describes rather than explains celebrity worship. Almost by definition, individuals exhibiting borderline–pathological celebrity worship are very absorbed with the celebrity of their choice and have an obsessional and addictive focus on that celebrity.

People can be attracted to celebrities because of their abilities, for example musical skills, rather than because they are famous and attractive.

Stalking

According to *Chambers Dictionary*, a stalker is "someone who obsessively follows another person, often with a sinister purpose." This definition captures part of what is involved, but for a more complete picture we need to consider legal definitions. According to Spitzberg and Cupach (2007, p. 66), such definitions "typically identify stalking as an (a) intention pattern of repeated behaviours towards a person or persons (b) that are unwanted, and (c) result in fear, or that a reasonable person (or jury) would view as fearful or threatening." According to this definition, the relationship the victim has (or has had) with the pursuer is irrelevant. Thus, repeated unwanted behaviour that frightens the victim is stalking even if the pursuer and victim used to have a romantic relationship.

Stalking can involve many different kinds of behaviour. Cupach and Spitzberg (2004) identified eight different categories of stalking behaviour: hyper-intimacy, interactional contacts, surveillance, harassment, intimidation, coercion and threat, aggression, and mediated contacts. Most (but not all) of those categories are self-explanatory. Hyper-intimacy behaviours often involve excessive courtship activities (e.g. giving numerous lavish presents). Mediated contacts are attempts at communication with the victim via technologies such as e-mail and the internet; it is sometimes known as cyber-stalking. Threats are involved in 54% of cases of stalking, physical violence in 32% of cases, and sexual violence in 10% of cases (Spitzberg & Cupach, 2007).

How common is stalking? Spitzberg and Cupach (2007) reviewed findings from 175 samples. Approximately 25% of individuals have experienced stalking, with females more likely than males to be the victims of stalking (28.5% vs. 11%, respectively). On average, stalking lasts for 22 months. In about 80% of cases, the pursuer and the victim knew each other beforehand. Indeed, in 50% of cases, the pursuer and victim had had a romantic involvement. Thus, the media's notion that stalkers are all totally insane or psychopathic is well wide of the mark.

Celebrity stalking

There have been a few well-publicised cases in which celebrities have been stalked. For example, John Hinckley was a lonely young man who became infatuated with the film actress Jodie Foster, who starred in several films including *Taxi Driver* and *The Silence of the Lambs*. He stalked her while she was studying at Yale University, including sending her love letters and talking to her on the phone.

A famous case of dangerous celebrity infatuation is that of John Hinckley who developed an obsession with and began stalking Jodie Foster after repeatedly watching *Taxi Driver*. Hinckley went on to attempt to assassinate President Ronald Reagan in a desperate bid to grab Foster's attention, but was found not guilty by reason of insanity in his 1982 trial.

Only a few days before he tried to assassinate President Ronald Reagan, Hinckley wrote a letter to Foster asking, "Don't you maybe like me just a little bit?" then on 30 March 1981, he stood outside the Washington hotel where President Reagan had just given a speech. As Reagan emerged from the hotel, Hinckley stepped forward, pulled out a gun, and fired six times. One of the bullets damaged Reagan's left lung but he was able to leave hospital 2 weeks later. After the assassination attempt, Hinckley asked Secret Service agents, "Is it on TV? Am I somebody?" At his trial, he was found not guilty because of insanity, and was sent to a psychiatric hospital in Washington, DC.

As we will see, stalkers vary in terms of the main motives for their stalking behaviour. In the case of Hinckley, one of his motives was to become famous. Ironically, he became famous for all the wrong reasons.

Arthur Jackson was another celebrity stalker. He was born in Scotland and spent most of his life there. He became obsessed by the American actress Theresa Saldana (who starred in the film *Raging Bull*) when he saw her in a film. He travelled to the United States to track her down. He managed to obtain Theresa Saldana's address by phoning her mother and pretending that he needed to contact her in connection with a film role. On 15 March 1982, Jackson stabbed Theresa Saldana viciously ten times, and would have killed her but for the intervention of Jeff Fenn, a bottled water deliveryman. Jackson was sentenced to 14 years in prison for the assault. He once described himself as "the benevolent angel of death", and was found to be mentally ill. His mental illness obviously helps to explain his behaviour.

Despite the extensive media coverage of celebrity stalking, the overwhelming majority of cases do *not* involve celebrities. As a result, most research has focused on individuals stalking non-celebrities, and we now focus on the main findings emerging from this research. It is probable that similar psychological factors motivate most stalkers regardless of whether their victim is or isn't a celebrity.

Findings: motives

The first issue I will consider is that of motive: *why* do stalkers pursue innocent victims? Spitzberg and Cupach (2007) reviewed 175 studies of stalking. They identified four very general motive categories: intimacy motives, aggression motives, disability-based motives (e.g. drugs, mental illness), and issue-based motives (e.g. dispute over money). Intimacy motives were most important in 32% of cases, aggressive motives in 22% of cases, disability-based motives in 12% of cases, and issued-based motives in 13% of cases (these percentages don't add up to 100 because the motives of some stalkers didn't fall into any of the above categories).

CASE STUDY: ANNA KOURNIKOVA

In January 2005, a stalker named William Lepeska swam naked across Biscayne Bay to the home of the tennis player Anna Kournikova, his celebrity obsession. Fortunately for her, he ended up on the wrong pool deck at the wrong house, shouting for her to come and rescue him. Like John Hinckley, who stalked the actor Jodie Foster, Lepeska was judged unfit to plead and sent to a treatment facility for 6 months.

At a more specific level, most stalkers have several motives. This explains why summing the various percentages gives a figure much higher than 100. The most common specific motives within each of the general categories are as shown on the right.

Three things are striking about these figures. First, they indicate that most stalkers are not mentally ill. Second, stalkers vary enormously in the motives that caused them to engage in stalking, and so we mustn't think of all stalkers as being alike. Third, the behaviour of most stalkers is influenced by various motives, and the precise pattern of motives varies from stalker to stalker. This contrasts with the common belief that stalkers are motivated only by revenge or love. In sum, it is important to avoid thinking of all stalkers as being basically similar in their underlying motives.

Intimacy motives	Aggression motives
Obsession (55%)	Anger/revenge (32%)
Dependency (42%)	Control/possession (23%)
Reconciliation (35%)	Attack (18%)
Disability-based motives	**Issue-based motives**
Drugs (16.5%)	Share information (39%)
Mental illness (8%)	Personal dispute (25%)
	Gain access to children (23%)

Findings: who becomes a stalker?

Who is most likely to become a stalker? One approach is to focus on individual differences in personality. There are five major personality factors (openness, conscientiousness, extraversion, agreeableness, and neuroticism), and we can compare stalkers with non-stalkers on all of them. Kamphuis, Emmelkamp, and de Vries (2004) found that stalkers were extremely low on agreeableness, moderately low on conscientiousness, and moderately high on neuroticism (i.e. low emotional stability). They didn't differ from non-stalkers on extraversion or openness (a personality dimension involving openness to experience). These findings suggest that personality is of real relevance in determining who becomes a stalker. However, it is possible (but not very likely) that engaging in stalking behaviour produces changes in a stalker's personality.

Another approach to identifying those most likely to become stalkers is to regard stalking as involving serious problems of attachment. After all, stalkers greatly desire a relationship with someone else who doesn't want to have a relationship with them. There is much indirect evidence supporting the notion that stalkers have particular problems with attachment. In a small sample of imprisoned stalkers, Kienlen, Birmingham, Solberg, O'Regan, and Meloy (1997) found that most had lost a parent in childhood. They also reported that many of the stalkers had suffered the loss of an important personal relationship in the few months before they started stalking. Lewis, Fremouw, Del Ben, and Farr (2001) compared a group of stalkers with a healthy control group. Stalkers were significantly more likely than controls to be insecurely attached.

An influential approach is based on Bartholomew and Horowitz's (1991) research on attachment styles in adulthood. They argued that any individual's attachment style depends on two factors: (1) his or her self-image (positive or negative); and (2) his or her image of others (positive or negative). The combination of these two factors produces four main attachment styles. One of these styles involves a negative self-image and a positive other-image, and is known as **preoccupied attachment**. Preoccupied attachment is characterised by "an over-involvement in close relationships, a dependence on other people's acceptance for a sense of personal well-being, a tendency to idealise other people, and incoherence and exaggerated emotionality in discussing relationships" (Bartholomew & Horowitz, 1991, p. 228).

There is much support for the assumption that stalkers tend to have preoccupied attachment (reviewed by Spitzberg & Cupach, 2007). Langhinrichsen-Rohling, Palarea, Cohen, and Rohling (2000) studied people's behaviour after the end of a romantic relationship. Stalkers were more likely than non-stalkers to have preoccupied attachment. Tonin (2004) found that fixated stalkers (those who pursued the same target for prolonged periods) were more preoccupied on average than serial stalkers (those who pursued many targets).

Attachment style is not the only factor determining who will become a stalker. If it was, then all stalkers would have preoccupied attachment and no non-stalkers would, which is *not* the case. Note also that individuals with preoccupied attachment are likely to engage in stalking only in particular circumstances. We need to know the processes involved in turning a potential stalker into an actual stalker, an issue to which we now turn.

Findings: processes leading to stalking

The processes leading to stalking are discussed in relational goal pursuit theory (Spitzberg & Cupach, 2007). Three main stages are identified:

1. *Goal linking: motivation*: Our goals in life are organised in a hierarchy, with some being more important than others. We are much more motivated to achieve higher-order goals than lower-order ones, and so devote much more time and effort to them. Goal linking occurs when someone believes a lower-level goal is essential to achieving a higher-order goal. Potential stalkers link their lower-order goal of having a particular relationship with higher-order goals (e.g. having high self-worth; being happy). As a result, huge importance is attached to the relational goal.

KEY TERM

Preoccupied attachment: a style of attachment in which the individual concerned tends to become too involved with another person, idealises that person, and feels almost totally dependent on that person's acceptance in order to feel happy.

2. *Rumination and emotional flooding*: When someone is thwarted in the attainment of a higher-order goal, they engage in rumination—persistent unpleasant thoughts relating to how distressing it would be not to achieve the goal. There is also emotional flooding. This involves intense negative feelings (e.g. anger; frustration; jealousy).

3. *Enhanced motivation*: Rumination and emotional flooding are both very unpleasant and distressing, and successful achievement of the relational goal can be seen as the only way of gaining relief from them. That leads to enhanced motivation and persistence to achieve the relational goal. It also produces a tendency to misinterpret the victim's behaviour as being encouraging. As a result, the potential stalker pursues the relational goal obsessively in the face of rejection from the victim.

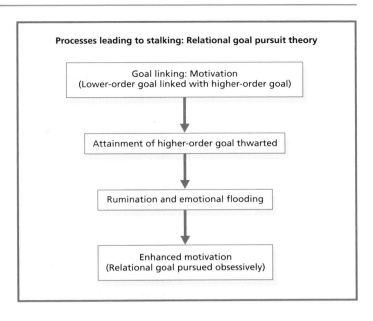

Processes leading to stalking: Relational goal pursuit theory

Goal linking: Motivation
(Lower-order goal linked with higher-order goal)

Attainment of higher-order goal thwarted

Rumination and emotional flooding

Enhanced motivation
(Relational goal pursued obsessively)

Some findings support relational goal pursuit theory. Dutton-Greene (2004) studied individuals who found it difficult to cope with the ending of a romantic relationship. Those who engaged in the most pursuit of the other person were those who experienced the most rumination, anger, and jealousy. Cupach, Spitzberg, Younghans, and Gibbons (2006) also studied romantic relationships that had ended. Persistence of attempts at reconciliation was associated with goal linking, rumination, and emotional flooding as predicted by relational goal pursuit theory.

Findings: violence

Which stalkers are most likely to behave violently towards their victim? The most important factor is the nature of the prior relationship the stalker had with his or her victim—the closer the relationship, the higher the probability of physical violence. Purcell, Pathe, and Mullen (2002) found that 56% of ex-intimates were physically harmed by their stalkers, compared with 36% of estranged friends or relatives, 16% of casual acquaintances, and 8% of strangers. These findings indicate that the strength of the attachment the stalker has to the victim is important, which is consistent with relational goal pursuit theory.

We might expect stalkers with a psychiatric diagnosis or personality disorder to be more likely than other stalkers to resort to physical violence. However, there is little support for this view. McEwan, Mullen, and Purcell (2007) reviewed the evidence; surprisingly, stalkers diagnosed with psychosis are *less* likely than other stalkers to use violence. So far as personality disorder is concerned, stalkers with personality disorders are generally no more likely than other stalkers to resort to violence. In fact, the tendency of stalkers to use physical violence depends far more on the type of relationship they have had with the victim than on whether or not they have a mental illness.

Evaluation

Theory and research on stalking have several strengths. First, there is convincing evidence that the motives of stalkers vary considerably (e.g. intimacy, aggression, and drug-based). Second, there is an increasing understanding of the type of personality possessed by many stalkers (e.g. low agreeableness, high neuroticism). Third, stalking is *not* typically a violent crime carried out by mentally ill individuals. Instead, "Most stalking represents a distorted version of courtship and romantic relationship failure . . . stalking is [generally] a product of relatively normal relationship processes" (Spitzberg & Cupach, 2007, p. 79). This is a powerful insight into many cases of stalking. Fourth, some of the processes involved in the development of stalking have been identified. More specifically, stalkers who feel thwarted engage in rumination and emotional flooding, which often lead to increased motivation to pursue their victim.

What are the limitations of research on stalking? First, nearly all the evidence consists of associations or correlations between stalking and certain motives, personality characteristics, and forms of attachment, and we can't infer causality from associations. For example, there is an association between stalking and preoccupied attachment. This might mean that individuals with preoccupied attachment are more likely to become stalkers. However, it is possible that stalking behaviour leads stalkers to develop a more preoccupied attachment style than previously. Second, although it is very likely that stalkers who pursue celebrity victims have similar psychological characteristics to those who pursue non-celebrities, there is insufficient evidence about celebrity stalkers to be sure. Third, the motives of stalkers are so diverse that it hasn't proved possible to develop a general theory that accounts for most cases of stalking.

SECTION SUMMARY
The Psychology of "Celebrity"

Celebrity worship

❖ It is important to distinguish among three types of celebrity worship: entertainment–social, intense–personal, and borderline–pathological.
❖ Celebrity worship has been accounted for by the Absorption–Addiction Model, which assumes that an initial absorption with a celebrity is often followed by addiction.
❖ Evaluation:

— Some aspects of individual differences (e.g. personality; intelligence) associated with celebrity worship have been identified.
— The evidence is predominantly correlational. As a result, it is very hard to know which factors help to cause celebrity worship.
— The Absorption–Addiction Model seems to provide more of a description than an explanation of celebrity worship.

Stalking

❖ In 80% of stalking cases, the stalker and the victim knew each other before, and this often involved a romantic involvement.
❖ The motives of stalkers include intimacy, aggression, disability-based (e.g. drugs), and issue-based.
❖ Stalkers very often exhibit preoccupied attachment, and respond to being thwarted by rumination and emotional flooding.
❖ Evaluation:

— There is much evidence that most stalkers have severe problems with attachment.

— The diverse motives of stalkers have made it very hard to construct general theories of stalking.

— The evidence is correlational, and so the causes of stalking behaviour haven't been definitely established.

FURTHER READING

Some of the topics in this chapter are covered in greater depth in Clarke, D. (2001). *Pro- and anti-social behaviour* (Routledge Modular Series). London: Routledge. The various theories of persuasion and attitude change are discussed in Hogg, M.A., & Vaughan, G.M. (2005). *Social psychology* (4th Edn). London: Pearson. If you want a good overview of research on celebrity worship, have a look at Giles, D., & Maltby, J. (2006). Praying at the altar of the stars. *The Psychologist*, 19, 82–85. There is an excellent summary of what we know about stalking in the following article: Spitzberg, B.H., & Capach, W.R. (2007). The state of the art of stalking: Taking stock of the emerging literature. *Aggression and Violent Behavior*, 12, 64–86. Finally, there is a brief account of the factors responsible for stalking behaviour in the following article: Scott, A.J. (2008). The psychology of stalking. *Psychology Review*, 13, 2–5.

See *A2-Level Psychology Online* for some interactive quizzes to help you with your revision.

See *A2-Level Psychology Online* for tips on how to answer these revision questions.

REVISION QUESTIONS

In the exam, questions on this topic are out of 25 marks. You should spend about 35 minutes on each of the questions below, which aim to test the material in this chapter. In the exam, make certain you know if you have covered Media Psychology, The Psychology of Addictive Behaviour, or Anomalistic Psychology as your Psychology in Action topic, and then choose the correct question.

1. (a) Violent video and computer games are often blamed by victims, victims' relatives and others for the real life violence in modern society. Discuss, with reference to psychological research, the effects of video and computer games on young people. (15 marks)

    (b) The popularity of reality shows has increased the number of people who become celebrities for being participants. Describe psychological explanations, including social psychological and evolutionary ones, for the attraction of "celebrity". (10 marks)

2. (a) Outline the role of cognitive consistency/dissonance on decision making. (5 marks)

    (b) Discuss models of persuasion and attitude change, including the Hovland–Yale model. (10 marks)

    (c) Outline and evaluate explanations for the effectiveness of television in persuasion. (10 marks)

3. (a) Outline explanations of media influence on pro- and anti-social behaviour. (10 marks)

    (b) Discuss research into intense fandom, for example celebrity worship and stalking. (15 marks)

Psychology in Action: The Psychology of Addictive Behaviour

15

By Mark Griffiths and Philip Banyard

Introduction

> They tried to make me go to rehab but I said "No, no, no".
> (Amy Winehouse)

"Rehab" is the package holiday of choice for celebrities. And all you need to qualify for it is to have an addiction. The term "addiction" appears in nearly every edition of our papers and magazines but what does it mean? The word has a long history and appears in the prologue to Shakespeare's *Henry V* (lines 91–97), written over 400 years ago:

> *Which is a wonder how his grace should glean it,*
> *Since his addiction was to courses vain,*
> *His companies unletter'd, rude and shallow,*
> *His hours fill'd up with riots, banquets, sports,*
> *And never noted in him any study,*
> *Any retirement, any sequestration*
> *From open haunts and popularity.*

Interestingly, Shakespeare is describing a life full of partying and messing about. He is describing addictive behaviours rather than a dependence on a chemical substance. Shakespeare apart, in everyday use the word was not used much until the growth in opium and then heroin use at the beginning of the twentieth century. For the best part of that century, the term "addiction" was commonly taken to refer to a chemical dependency on opiates or alcohol or nicotine. At the end of the twentieth century, ideas changed about addiction and it began to be seen as a set of behaviours rather than just a chemical dependency. The first thing we need to consider in this chapter, then, is what we mean by addiction.

What do we mean by addiction?

How to define addiction has been a matter of great debate for decades. For many people, the concept of addiction involves taking of drugs (Walker, 1989; Rachlin, 1990). Therefore it is perhaps unsurprising that most official definitions concentrate on drug ingestion. Here are some typical definitions:

How do you define addiction?

Addiction is the compulsive uncontrolled use of habit forming drugs. (Webster's New International Dictionary)

An addict is a person addicted to a habit, especially one dependent on a (specified) drug. (Concise Oxford Dictionary)

An addict is one who habitually uses and has an uncontrollable craving for an addictive drug. (Webster's New International Dictionary)

Addiction is a state of periodic or chronic intoxication produced by repeated consumption of a drug, natural or synthetic. (World Health Organization)

Despite such definitions, a growing movement (e.g. Miller, 1980; Orford, 2001; Griffiths, 2006) now views a number of behaviours as potentially addictive, including behaviours that do not involve the ingestion of a drug. These include behaviours diverse as **gambling**, overeating, sex, exercise, playing, love, internet use, and work. In fact, you can become addicted to almost anything. Such diversity has led to new, all-encompassing definitions of what constitutes an addictive behaviour. One such definition is that of Marlatt and colleagues, who define addictive behaviour as:

A repetitive habit pattern that increases the risk of disease and/or associated personal and social problems. Addictive behaviours are often experienced subjectively as "loss of control"—the behaviour contrives to occur despite volitional attempts to abstain or moderate use. These habit patterns are typically characterised by immediate gratification (short term reward), often coupled with delayed deleterious effects (long-term costs). Attempts to change an addictive behaviour (via treatment or self-initiation) are typically marked with high relapse rates. (Marlatt, Baer, Donovan, & Kivlahan, 1988, p. 224)

The key idea here that is common to previous ideas about chemical addictions is "loss of control". Individuals with an addiction are not able to regulate their behaviour as they would like and their behaviour becomes extreme. In truth, we are much less in control of our behaviour then we like to think, and we often find ourselves doing something we said we wouldn't, e.g. in the cafe, the clothes shop, or the bar. We are not necessarily addicted to these behaviours but sometimes we eat that cake, buy that skirt, or drink that gallon of lager when we didn't set out to do that.

In addition, it has been argued that addiction is most usefully described as a process (Krivanek, 1988), with involvement in addictive behaviour being placed on a spectrum of severity of use and abuse (McMurran, 1994). The boundaries of this formulation are flexible enough to include both substance and non-substance behaviours and to account for the inclusion of a wide variety of influencing factors. However, on an ethical level, the emphasis on the "subjective experience" of loss of control means that the above definition does not locate the problem entirely within the individual concerned, but nor does it preclude our **attribution** of some responsibility to that individual. Most people have their own idea or some common sense intuitive component about what "addiction" comprises but actually trying to define it becomes difficult. Defining "addiction" is rather like defining a "mountain" or "window", i.e. no single set of criteria can ever be

KEY TERMS

Gambling: the wagering of money or something of material value on an event with an uncertain outcome with the primary intent of winning additional money and/or material goods. Typically, the outcome of the wager is evident within a short period.

Attribution: the process of giving reasons for why things happen.

necessary or sufficient to define all instances. In essence, the whole is easier to recognise than the parts.

Are chemical addictions the same as behavioural addictions?

Besides the fact that chemical addictions usually involve the excessive use of ingested **psychoactive substances** and behavioural addictions usually involve excessive activity of a particular behaviour, are there really any important distinctions between the two types of addiction? Much of this comes down to how you define addiction in the first place! One way of finding out whether behavioural addictions are addictive in a similar way to chemical addictions is to compare them against **clinical criteria** for other established drug-ingested addictions and see to what extent there is common overlap. This method of making behavioural excesses more clinically identifiable has been proposed for behavioural addictions such as "television addiction" (McIlwraith, Jacobvitz, Kubey, & Alexander, 1991) and "amusement machine addiction" (Griffiths, 1991). Further to this, authors such as Carnes (1991) and Brown (1993) have suggested that addictions consist of a number of common components. Carnes (1991) outlined what he called the "signs of addiction".

> **Ten signs of addiction**
>
> 1. A pattern of out-of-control behaviour
> 2. Severe consequences of behaviour
> 3. Inability to stop behaviour despite adverse consequences
> 4. Persistent pursuit of self-destructive or high-risk behaviour
> 5. Ongoing desire or effort to limit behaviour
> 6. Use of behaviour as a coping strategy
> 7. Increased amounts of behaviour because the current level of activity is no longer sufficient
> 8. Severe mood changes around behaviour
> 9. Inordinate amounts of time spent trying to engage in behaviour and recovering from it
> 10. Important social, occupational, and recreational activities are sacrificed or reduced because of behaviour
>
> Adapted from Carnes (1991).

To a large extent, the ten signs outlined in the box are subsumed within the components outlined by Brown (1993) and later modified by Griffiths (1996a): salience, mood modification, tolerance, withdrawal, conflict, and relapse; these are described below.

Components of addiction
Salience
This refers to how important the behaviour becomes to the individual. The addictive behaviour becomes the most important activity for addicted individuals, so that even when they are not doing it, they are thinking about it. It should also be noted that some addictive behaviours, such as smoking (nicotine) and drinking (alcohol), are activities that can be engaged in concurrently with other activities and therefore do not tend to dominate an addict's thoughts or lead to total preoccupation. For instance, smokers can carry their cigarettes with them and still engage in other day-to-day activities. However, if nicotine-addicted individuals are in a situation in which they are unable to smoke for

Because smoking is an association that can be satisfied fairly regularly, it tends not to dominate the addict's thoughts. However, when the ability to smoke is inhibited for any substantial period of time, e.g. on a long flight, the addict will likely be anxiously preoccupied with the thought of smoking.

KEY TERMS

Psychoactive substance: a chemical substance that exerts psychological effects including changes in mood, cognition, and behaviour.
Clinical criteria: the key features than can be used to diagnose a condition.

a long period (such as a 24-hour plane flight), smoking would be the single most important thing in their life and would totally dominate their thoughts and behaviour. This is what could be termed "reverse salience", with the addictive activity becoming the most important thing in those individuals' lives when they are prevented from engaging in the behaviour.

Mood modification

This is the experience people report when they carrying out their addictive behaviour. People with addictive behaviour patterns commonly report a "rush", a "buzz", or a "high" when they are taking their drugs or when they are gambling, for example. What is interesting is that a person's drug or activity of choice can have the capacity to achieve different mood modifying effects at different times. For instance, nicotine addicts may use cigarettes first thing in the morning to get the arousing "nicotine rush" they need to get going for the day. By the end of the day, they may not be using nicotine for its stimulant qualities but in fact as a way of de-stressing and relaxing. It appears that addicts can use their addiction to bring about mood changes; this is as true for gamblers as it is for drug addicts.

Tolerance

This refers to the increasing amount of activity that is required to achieve the same effect. The classic example of tolerance is a heroin addict's need to increase the size of their "fix" to get the type of feeling (e.g. an intense "rush") they once got from much smaller doses. In gambling, tolerance may involve the gambler gradually having to increase the size of the bet to experience a mood modifying effect that was initially obtained by a much smaller bet. It may also involve spending longer and longer periods gambling. Tolerance is well established in psychoactive substance addictions and there is growing evidence in the field of behavioural addictions.

Withdrawal symptoms

These are the unpleasant feelings and physical effects that occur when the addictive behaviour is suddenly discontinued or reduced. They can include "the shakes", moodiness, and irritability. Withdrawal symptoms are commonly believed to be a response to the removal of a chemical to which the person has developed a tolerance. However, these effects can also be experienced by gamblers (see Orford, 2001), so the effects might be due to withdrawal from the behaviour as well as the substance.

Conflict

People with addictive behaviours develop conflicts with the people around them, often causing great social misery, and also develop conflicts within themselves. Continually choosing short-term pleasure and relief leads to a disregard of adverse consequences and of long-term damage, which in turn increases the apparent need for the addictive activity as a coping strategy.

Relapse

This refers to the tendency for repeated reversions to earlier patterns of the particular activity to recur and for even the most extreme patterns typical of the height of the addiction to be quickly restored after many years of abstinence or control. The classic example of relapse behaviour is in smokers, who often give up for a period only to return to full-time smoking after a few cigarettes. However, such relapses are common in all addictions, including behavioural addictions such as gambling (Griffiths, 2002).

EXAM HINT
Make sure you can explain the components of addiction: salience, mood modification, tolerance, withdrawal, conflict, and relapse.

Griffiths (2002) has argued that all these components need to be present for a behaviour to be operationally defined as addictive. It is clear that some individuals engage in behaviours that have addictive elements without it necessarily being a full-blown addiction. For instance, if someone has no negative withdrawal effects after stopping their excessive cocaine use or gambling, is that person really addicted? If the cocaine use or gambling does not conflict with anything else in that person's life, can it be said to be an addiction? In very simple terms, the difference between an excessive enthusiasm and an addiction is that enthusiasms add to life whereas addictions take away from it.

One thing that is worth adding is that relying on self-report is sometimes problematic. Addicts might simply rationalise their own behaviour by saying "I couldn't help myself!". Because of this, a more temporal and/or dimensional approach is needed. It might be more useful to imagine each of the addiction criteria as being on a continuum.

HOW SCIENCE WORKS: WHAT DO PEOPLE UNDERSTAND BY "ADDICTION"?
People use the term "addiction" in inaccurate ways, such as saying "I am addicted to chocolate/celebrity/football". It would be interesting to ask some non-psychologists what they would say they are addicted to. If they admit a so-called addiction you could then use the Carnes (1991) list from the box earlier in this chapter as a checklist, and ask each participant to tick any of the ten criteria that apply to their named behaviour. This could demonstrate that the scientific, psychological meaning of addiction differs from the street meaning, and should help inform your participants about what addiction as a psychological disorder really means.

SECTION SUMMARY
Introduction

❖ Addiction is much talked about but difficult to define.

❖ Addiction is commonly taken to refer to excessive substance use but it can also refer to other excessive and repetitive behaviours.

❖ Substance and non-substance addictions share the same behavioural features of: salience, mood modification, tolerance, withdrawal symptoms, conflict, and relapse.

MODELS OF ADDICTIVE BEHAVIOUR

The model we use to explain addiction affects how we view the person with the addictive behaviour and also how we decide to "treat" that person's behaviour in order to change it. The word "treat" is in inverted commas because what we are really talking about here is not making someone better from the measles but changing their behaviour to make them more socially acceptable. We can only really call this "treatment" if addiction is a disease.

The numerous models of addictive behaviour can be summarised under the following headings:

- *Biological models*: the idea here is that main causes of addictive behaviours are biological changes in the individual. For example, the disease model suggests that addiction comes from a disorder of the body, such as a neurochemical imbalance. In this model, individuals have limited control over

What reinforces addictive behaviour? Why do smokers suffer the cost, smell, and discomfort of having to stand outside in the cold to smoke if they no longer even enjoy smoking?

their behaviour in the same way that you have limited control over whether you get measles. Another biological approach is the *genetic model*, which suggests that there is a genetic disposition towards addictive behaviour. It is known that the biggest risk factor for becoming a smoker is having parents who smoke. But does this show evidence of a genetic disposition or family influence? There is evidence that shows a higher incidence of certain genes in people with addictive behaviours (see below).

- *Cognitive models*: the idea here is that the best way to understand addictive behaviours is to look at the cognitive processes that drive them. One approach has been to look at the way that we make decisions, and psychologists have developed models of decision making that try to explain why and how we change our behaviour. The cognitive models also look at the faulty thinking that maintains people in their damaging behaviours. These models are very productive in developing therapies to help people change their behaviour.

- *Learning models*: the idea here is that we can best explain addictive behaviours by looking at how they developed. In particular they focus on learning theories (see page 285–297). The most important concept here is reinforcement. What are the reinforcements that encourage someone to, for example, smoke cigarettes and to continue to smoke them even when the individual doesn't really enjoy them and cannot afford them. It must be something pretty powerful to encourage a smoker to pay over £40 a week just to stand outside shivering and sucking in the smoke from burning leaves.

- *Social models*: the idea here is that our social interactions and the sense we make of the world are the most important factor in addictive behaviours. The Experiential Model commonly associated with Peele (1990) suggests that addictive behaviours are much more temporary and more dependent on the situation we are in than either of the previous two models would suggest. In fact, people often move on (or grow out of) their addictive behaviours as their life circumstances change. Alternatively, the Moral Model suggests that the key issue with addiction is a lack of character. In this view, addiction is a result of weakness, or moral failure in the individual. The treatment for this is clearly to get people to repent and then to develop their moral strength.

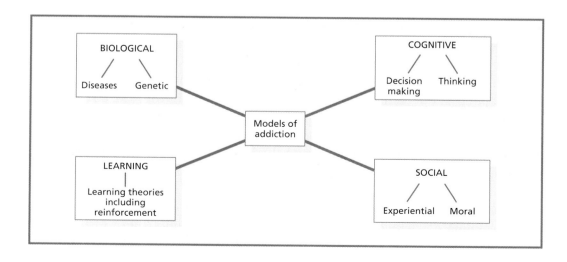

The main models of addiction.

Although there are many more models of addictive behaviours, the above gives a flavour of the different approaches that people take to this issue. These ideas are developed further below.

Explanations of Addictive Behaviours

This section looks at biological, behavioural, and cognitive explanations. Although there are clear differences between the theories, they overlap with each other and all contribute to our understanding of the complex behaviours we call addictions.

Biological explanations of addictive behaviour

The biological explanation is much easier when we are talking about chemical addictions such as nicotine than when we are talking about gambling. Biological explanations of addiction focus on neurotransmitter substances in the brain, and on genetic differences between people with addictions and people without addictions.

Neurotransmitters

Without going into a full biology lesson, a **neurotransmitter** is a chemical that moves across the gaps between nerve cells to transmit messages. If the chemical is blocked or replaced, for example, then the message changes and there is an effect on the physiological systems, and also on cognition, mood, and behaviour. The neurotransmitter that is most commonly implicated in all this is dopamine, but other chemicals have also been found to have an effect (Potenza, 2001). Not only do neurotransmitters play a role in chemical addictions, they have also been implicated in behaviours such as gambling and video-game playing.

Genetics

Until relatively recently, the main way of investigating genetic factors in human behaviour was to study family relationships. More recently, it has been possible to carry out genetic analysis and look for differences in the genetic structure of people with and without addictive behaviours. The two methods tend to point to different answers. The family studies tend to emphasise the role of environmental factors in the development of addictive behaviours. A study of over 300 **monozygotic twins** (identical) and just under 200 same sex **dizygotic twins** (fraternal) estimated the contribution of genetic factors and environmental factors to substance use in adolescence. It concluded that the major influences on the decision to use substances were environmental rather than genetic (Han et al., 1999). Some family studies, however, suggest a link between addictive behaviour and personality traits. For example, a study of monozygotic and dizygotic twins looked at the relationship between alcohol use and personality. The study suggests that there is a connection between genetics and the characteristics of anti-social personality (including attention seeking, not following social norms, and violence), and between these personality characteristics and alcoholism (Jang, Vernon, & Livesley, 2000). Similar findings

---

KEY TERMS

Neurotransmitters: chemical substances that are released at the junction between neurons (a synapse) and that affect the transmission of messages in the nervous system.

Monozygotic twins: identical twins derived from the same fertilised ovum.

Dizygotic twins: fraternal twins derived from two fertilised ova.

have also been found for behavioural addictions such as gambling addiction (Comings et al., 1996).

Reinforcement

The biological explanation overlaps with the behavioural explanation (see below) when we look at **reinforcement**. Reinforcement is defined as being anything that increases the probability that the behaviour will recur in similar circumstances. The term commonly refers to learned associations, acquired through operant or classical conditioning (see pages 285–297), but it may also be applied to other forms of learning.

A possible answer to the question of what makes something reinforcing comes from the discovery of "pleasure centres" in the brain. Olds and Milner (1954) found that rats would press a lever for the reward of mild electrical stimulation in particular areas of the brain. The rats would continue to press the lever in preference to other possible rewards such as food, drink, or sexual activity. The researchers did not record whether the animals had silly smiles on their faces, but these areas of the brain are now commonly referred to as "pleasure centres".

The experience of pleasure is very important for our healthy development. If, for example, we found food or sex boring, then our species would probably starve to death or fail to breed. The feelings of pleasure associated with these activities act as a reinforcement. If we associate these pleasure feelings with other activities, then they too will be reinforced. So, the pleasure that encourages essential behaviours is also the pleasure that can encourage damaging behaviour. Could it be that the threat of addiction is the price we pay for pleasure? This brings us neatly on to consider behavioural theories.

Evaluation of biological explanations for addiction

The difficulty with looking at which neurotransmitter produces which reward is that, to state the blindingly obvious, the brain is remarkably complex and the effects of even one drug can be very diverse. Ashton and Golding (1989) suggest that nicotine can simultaneously affect a number of systems including learning and memory, the control of pain, and the relief of anxiety. In fact, it is generally believed that smoking nicotine can increase arousal and reduce stress—two responses that ought to be incompatible (Parrott, 1998). This means that it is difficult to pin down a single response that follows smoking a cigarette. A deeper problem with the neurochemical explanations is the neglect of the social contexts of the behaviours. The pleasures and escapes associated with taking a drug are highly varied and depend on the person, the dose, the situation they are in, and the wider social context of the society they live in (Orford, 2001).

Studies that analyse the genetic structure of individuals tend to emphasis the role of genetics rather than the environment in addictive behaviours. Some **genes** have attracted particular attention and have been shown to appear more frequently in people with addictive behaviours than in people without. The problem is that these genes do not occur in all people with the addictive behaviour and they do appear in some people without it. For example, a gene referred to as *DRD2* (no, nothing to do with *Star Wars*) has been found in 42% of people with alcoholism. It has also been found in 50% of pathological gamblers, 45% of people with Tourette's syndrome, and 55% of people with autism; it has also been found in 25% of the general population. This means that *DRD2* appears more

KEY TERM

Reinforcement: anything that increases the probability that a behaviour will recur in similar circumstances. The term is usually used of learned associations, acquired through operant or classical conditioning, but it may also be applied to other forms of learning.
Genes: units of inheritance that form part of a chromosome. Some characteristics are determined by one gene, whereas for others many genes are involved.

frequently in people with these behavioural syndromes but that it cannot be the sole explanation for the behaviour (Comings, 1998).

Behavioural (learning) explanations of addictive behaviour

Behavioural (i.e. learning) explanations take as their starting point the theories of classical and operant conditioning (see pages 285–297). These theories say that we change our behaviour in response to changes in the environment such as rewards and punishments. These rewards and punishments can bring about changes in mood (for example, pleasure; see above) or material changes such as money. A striking finding of work with animals is that greater behavioural change can be achieved with less reinforcement rather than more. This effect is amplified if the arrival of these reinforcements is made less predictable. The schedule for producing the strongest behavioural change was the variable ratio that describes a situation where rewards are given not every time you do the behaviour but on average every fifth time you do it, for example (does this remind you of anything?).

In operant explanations for problem gambling (Delfabbro & Winefield, 1999), persistent gambling is seen as a conditioned behaviour maintained by intermittent schedules of reinforcement, most likely a variable-ratio schedule. However, proponents of classical conditioning models argue that people continue to gamble as a result of becoming conditioned to the excitement or arousal associated with gambling, so that they feel bored, unstimulated, and restless when they are not gambling. Both the classical and operant perspectives have been central to the development of measures of "impaired control" over gambling (Dickerson & O'Connor, 2006) and clinical interventions using desensitisation, aversive conditioning, and satiation techniques. In each of these examples, it is assumed that the more a person gambles, the more his or her behaviour is dictated by factors beyond the person's control.

EXAM HINT

Note that the *DRD2* gene evidence provides a useful source of assessment for the contribution of biological factors to addiction because:

1. It is not present in all addicts.
2. It is present to some extent in the general population.
3. It is present across various psychopathologies.

This leads to the conclusion that abnormality may have some universal factors and some specific factors and that social and psychological factors will also contribute to the form the abnormality takes.

Could the addictive element of gambling lie in the excitement and arousal associated with the environment?

Evaluation of behavioural (learning) explanations

Despite evidence supporting both theories, neither is entirely satisfactory on its own. Classical conditioning seems useful to explain people's motivation to commence a gambling session, but appears less useful to explain persistent gambling behaviour. Conversely, while operant conditioning might explain ongoing behaviour, it appears less useful in explaining why people commence gambling or recommence gambling after a prolonged period of abstinence (Griffiths, 1995). Researchers have also raised questions about the extent to which behaviours like excessive gambling adhere to operant theory at all, since gamblers lose more than they win and because reinforcement magnitudes are not independent of player responses, e.g. stake sizes (Delfabbro & Winefield, 1999).

It is important to recognise that these theories cannot stand in isolation. As with other psychological theories, conditioning theories cannot explain why people exposed to similar stimuli respond differently; why some smoke, drink, or gamble whereas others do not or why some people smoke, drink, or gamble more than others. In addition, the effectiveness, or strength, of the conditioning effect may be a function of motivational factors and type of activity. Some, but not all,

? Why do you think some people might recommence gambling after a prolonged period of abstinence?

people engage in these behaviours for excitement or relaxation, and, as discussed above, people satisfy these needs with different activities. Thus, it is unlikely that classical conditioning will affect all types of addictive behaviour in the same way.

Similar difficulties plague attempts to develop general operant theories of very specific activities such as gambling. Some activities appear to suit this form of explanation more than others. Examples include slot machines and scratch cards, where there is a short time interval between stake and outcome, and where outcomes are entirely determined by chance. It is more difficult to apply these principles to skilled gambling games such as blackjack, poker, and sports betting, where player decisions can significantly influence outcomes.

Cognitive explanations of addictive behaviour

Cognitive explanations focus on the way that we process information. If we are making faulty judgements then we might develop addictive behaviours. This explanation is not nearly as clear cut as it sounds because faulty thinking is what keeps us going. Look at it this way, you will exist on this planet for just a few moments in the great expanse of time, and your impact on the whole scheme of things amounts to very little (at best). And yet it does all seem to matter and please don't give up your psychology course now. The faulty thinking around gambling is that you will win or at least be able to control the odds, using your "lucky numbers" on the lottery—so lucky that you've never won anything with them.

Gamblers will keep playing so long as they think there is money to be won.

Despite the fact that the odds of almost all activities are weighted strongly in favour of the gambling operator, gamblers continue to believe they can win money from gambling. This observation leads to the conclusion that gambling may be maintained by irrational or erroneous beliefs. For example, people overestimate the extent to which they can predict or influence gambling outcomes and tend to misjudge how much money they have won or lost. This hypothesis has been confirmed in numerous studies (Langer, 1975; Langer & Roth, 1983) showing that people overestimate the degree of skill or control that can be exerted in chance activities, and also in studies using the so-called "thinking aloud" method (Griffiths, 1994), which reveal high levels of irrationality in verbalised statements made during gambling sessions.

Griffiths (1994) has demonstrated that gamblers have irrational biases concerning their gambling behaviour and that they use a variety of **heuristics** (e.g. flexible attributions, hindsight bias, illusory correlations, etc.). For instance, typical examples for explaining away losses involved hindsight bias with players predicting events after they happen:

> *I had a feeling it wasn't going to pay very much after it had just given me a feature . . . I had a feeling it was going to chew up those tokens fairly rapidly . . . I had a feeling it had paid out earlier because it's not giving me a chance.*

Some players had completely erroneous perceptions:

> *I'm only gonna put one quid in to start with because psychologically I think it's very important . . . it bluffs the machine—it's my own psychology.*

Others personified the machine, usually swearing at it:

> *This machine doesn't like me . . . ooh it does, it's given me a number . . . hates me! It's given me low numbers, I don't think it wants to pay out at all . . . probably thinks I'm a *******—it's not wrong!" (a regular player)*
>
> *It's really ******* me over . . . Am I allowed to change to another machine? . . . I think this machine is not going to pay out happily . . . It stitches me up every time . . . unbelievable.*
>
> *I had a feature held and then it stopped them . . . ******* conned . . . this is where it just takes off your money right at the end 'cos it's out of pocket . . . ******* machine.*

Why the players should demonstrate these biases and where they come from is not so clear. It may be that there is a general tendency to personify machines with which people spend a lot of time. Furthermore, it is difficult to predict when a heuristic will be used. It is also unclear whether use of **heuristics** depends on intrinsic factors (e.g. psychological mood state) and/or extrinsic factors (e.g. gambling history). Based on these findings, it has been suggested that irrational thinking may be related to problematic gambling behaviour (Wagenaar, 1988; Ladouceur & Walker, 1996; Parke, Griffiths, & Parke, 2007), with persistent behaviour thought to be the result of people's overconfidence in their ability to win money (Wagenaar, 1988; Walker, 1992). Evidence suggests that problem gamblers frequently overestimate the amount of control and skill involved in gambling (Griffiths, 1994; Parke et al., 2007). It could be argued that cognitive biases reflect behaviour rather than cause it (particularly if they are used as a justification of the behaviour). However, research on cognitive biases in gambling behaviour may help to provide insights into other types of addictive bias. For instance, smokers and drinkers may rationalise their behaviour following their actions in much the same way that gamblers do.

Gamblers often adopt irrational heuristics in order to justify their behaviour or to "rationalise" any negative outcome of their gambling: claiming they "knew" the machine wasn't going to pay out that time, for example.

Evaluation of cognitive explanations

A problem with the cognitive approach to studying addictions like gambling is that irrationality does not appear to co-vary with other observable facets of gambling, such as the level of risk-taking or reinforcement frequency. Alternatively, where irrationality positively relates to involvement, few differences in behaviour have been observed. As a result, Dickerson and Baron (2000) have concluded that irrational thinking is probably more a reflection of demand characteristics (see page 151) than a rational underlying behaviour. A lot of what people say may only result from the difficulty of trying to come up with rational, meaningful statements in chance-determined situations.

In addition to these conceptual difficulties, it is also possible that contextual factors play a role in cognitive research. For example, Griffiths (1994) found that regular gamblers had greater difficulty than occasional players in verbalising their thoughts while they were gambling. Regular players seemed capable of gambling without attending to what they were doing, suggesting: (1) that cognitive processes did not play a major role in the maintenance of their behaviour; or (2) that the original justifications or rationales for behaviour were less accessible. In either case, Griffiths' observations suggested that temporal factors (namely, how long a person has been gambling) appear to be important. Therefore, all other things being equal, it appears that valid comparisons cannot be drawn between gamblers with differing levels of gambling experience, because what holds for infrequent gamblers might not hold for regular players, and vice versa.

Finally, it is again important to observe that cognitive theories need to take structural variations in activities into account. Many cognitive processes thought to underlie gambling behaviour (e.g. overestimations of control, biased attributions) are more likely to be observed when activities are perceived as having some skill component (Griffiths, 1995). With some activities, there is a genuine possibility for skilful play (e.g. racing, blackjack, table poker). The more people play or know about these activities, the greater their awareness of the skills involved. Thus, beliefs about control and skill are neither completely irrational nor consistent across players. Instead, in these situations, researchers must examine the quality of play; for example, to what extent the person adheres to optimal strategies, rather than look for evidence of irrational thinking (Keren & Wagenaar, 1985).

Even in activities where outcomes are determined by chance, there are likely to be variations in the extent to which gamblers perceive that the outcomes are solely chance-determined (e.g. roulette and craps are probably more likely to be perceived as skilful than slot machines because of the greater complexity of the rules and the possibility for variations in playing strategy). Therefore, it may be ineffective to compare results across studies using different chance activities without controlling for variations in perceived skill.

It should also be noted that psychological explanations are insufficient to explain the full complexity of addiction and that a unified theory of addiction will be complex and **biopsychosocial** (Griffiths, 2006, 2008). Whether ongoing behaviour is explained in terms of biological, behavioural, or cognitive theories, it remains unclear why one person engages more heavily in one behaviour than another. In other words, while it seems likely that increased involvement with a particular behaviour is likely to contribute to loss of control over behaviour, development of irrational beliefs, and greater psychological dependence, it is important to determine what makes some people more susceptible to these factors than others. It is here that research into biological and personality factors becomes important. Central to this research is to ascertain whether addicts possess qualities that would predispose them to excessive behaviour.

Biological and **dispositional** accounts assume that such factors should override other environmental or contextual factors and allow for the development of a general theory of addiction. However, this is clearly not so. If we say that it is all down to the person's character (disposition) then we are ignoring all the factors that have an effect on behaviour. For example, if we look at gambling, some slot machines attract more trade than others because of the way they are designed. Therefore, it appears that addictive gambling is likely to result from both dispositional and psychological factors and the complex interaction between them. Psychological explanations must play a role because of the obvious

---

EXAM HINT

Make sure you can comment on *how* a biopsychosocial approach can better account for addiction that goes beyond the rather simple explanation that it is more complex! You need to be able to discuss how multiple factors may interact to cause addiction. These factors include:

- the person's biological and/or genetic predisposition
- their psychological constitution (personality factors, unconscious motivations, attitudes, expectations, beliefs, etc.)
- their social environment (i.e. situational characteristics)
- the nature of the activity itself (i.e. structural characteristics).

KEY TERMS

Biopsychosocial: an approach that takes account of biological, psychological, and social variables.

Dispositional: where the cause of a particular behaviour is thought to have resulted from the person's own personality or characteristics, rather than from the demands of circumstances.

importance of external factors in the development of gambling habits. However, it is also clear that internal factors influence how certain individuals respond to these situations.

As we have seen from the example of gambling addiction, it is clear that many research perspectives are rather narrow and can only explain a small part of addictive behaviours. Addiction is a multi-faceted behaviour that is strongly influenced by contextual factors that cannot be explained by any single theoretical perspective. These factors include variations in behavioural involvement and motivation across different demographic groups, structural characteristics of activities/substances, and the developmental or temporal nature of addictive behaviour. Research and clinical interventions are best served by a biopsychosocial approach that incorporates the best strands of contemporary psychology, biology, and sociology.

There are a number of things to consider when looking at addictive behaviours and after reading the above you can come to your own decisions about some of them:

- How much control do people have over their behaviour? Your answer to this will affect how strongly you support the various models of addictive behaviour.
- What are similarities and differences between chemical addictions and behavioural addictions?
- Is addiction something that can happen to anyone (like catching measles) or are some people more likely to develop these behaviours than others? If so, then why? Is it due to chemical imbalances or genes or family background or something else inside them?
- How can we obtain evidence for our theories? Are the methods of asking people to describe their experience the best way of capturing what is going on? Are there other ways of collecting reliable evidence?

> ■ **Activity: Why do people become addicts?**
> You could produce simple and clear summaries of the different explanations for addiction in the form of a handout, and ask participants—who should not really be psychology students—to choose which explanation they feel is most likely to be the true one. Then you could explain that each explanation has some credibility, and discuss this with them. You could also finish off by totalling the number of choices for each option to see what the general public believe about addiction.

SECTION SUMMARY
Models of Addictive Behaviour

❖ There are numerous models of addictive behaviour including biological, cognitive, and learning models.

❖ Biological explanations of addictive behaviours focus on neurotransmitters, genetics, and reinforcement centres in the brain.

❖ Problems with these explanations include the varying effect of chemicals on behaviour and experience, and also the low correlation of key genes with addictive behaviours.

Biological explanations

Cognitive explanations

❖ Cognitive explanations of addictive behaviours focus on the ways we process information.

❖ People with addictive behaviours often display irrational biases when reviewing their own behaviour.

❖ Cognitive explanations do not take account of the varying circumstances in which addictive behaviours take place.

Behavioural explanations

❖ Behavioural explanations of addictive behaviours focus on the theories of operant and classical conditioning.

❖ Behavioural explanations can be useful in explaining some behaviours by novice gamblers but they are less useful in explaining the behaviour of skilled gambling games like blackjack.

Biopsychosocial approach

❖ To arrive at a reasonable explanation of addictive behaviours it is helpful to take a biopsychosocial approach that draws on explanations from all of the above.

FACTORS AFFECTING ADDICTIVE BEHAVIOURS

When we are looking for factors that change behaviour we can look inside the individual for personal characteristics that make people vulnerable to addiction and we can look outside the individual for features of the environment that encourage addictive behaviours. The factors within the individual might include their explanations of their behaviour (attributions) and their sense of self-worth. Outside the individual are such issues as availability and media cues.

? What types of attributions may lead to a negative sense of self worth?

Personal Explanations of Addictions

Attributions

What people think about addiction is also important when examining factors that affect use. Attribution theory relates to how people explain the behaviour of others in an attempt to make sense of the world. Attribution theory has been utilised to illustrate how the use of addiction as a label can promote irresponsibility, learned helplessness, and passivity (Preyde & Adams, 2008). Similarly, there is concern regarding the label of the "addict", which might lead to a self-fulfilling prophecy in which the label itself convinces individuals that this is who they are and so makes them feel more hopeless, dependent, and less able to do anything about it (Preyde & Adams, 2008).

CASE STUDY: CYBERLIFE ADDICTION

J is an overweight male college student who admits to spending about 40 hours a week on the internet, with only 3 hours being related to his college work. He doesn't think of himself as an addict, although he does say the internet is the most important thing in his life and says "I tend not to socialise much". He thinks about his online life when not connected and suffers from withdrawal symptoms, such as anxiety, irritability, and shaking—even though he says he is trying to reduce his cyberlife. J enjoys using discussion groups, chat rooms, and message boards and says he meets lots of people in this way. He does not feel he would socialise if he stopped using the internet and thinks he has gained knowledge from this usage. He justifies his habit by saying he plans to make his career in an internet-related field of employment.

Griffiths (1998) thinks J might be a stereotypic example of an addict, being a male teenager, overweight, low in self-esteem and confidence, with little social life, and in denial of his problem.

Possibly, J feels comfortable in the text-based internet environment and would not feel he could be accepted in the same way in the real world because his self-esteem could be reduced due to his obesity.

Davies (1996) argues that the explanations people make for their behaviour are functional. He asserts that people make different attributions for the same event in different contexts. For example, Davies and Baker (1987) showed that heroin users reported different attributions for their drug use to another heroin user and to someone whose drug use was unknown to them. This is because attributions we make about ourselves serve to protect self-esteem and preserve self-concept (Schlenker, Weigold, & Hallam, 1990). Davies argues that attributions help the individual addict to protect themselves from acknowledging their own behaviour.

As addiction develops, Davies suggests five attributional stages through which a person progresses. Each stage is marked by a different attribution style and can vary in terms of:

- *Purposiveness*, i.e. how intentional the behaviour is portrayed.
- **Hedonism**, i.e. how positively the behaviour is described.
- *Contradictoriness*, i.e. whether attributions contradict across the course of a given time period.
- *Addiction self-ascription*, i.e. whether attributions make use of the concept of addiction as an explanation for behaviour.

The five stages outlined by Davies (1996) are as follows:

- *Stage 1*: before the drug-using behaviour become a problem, people's attributions for their drug use are high on purposiveness and hedonism (i.e. people enjoy using the drug and consider it under their control).
- *Stage 2*: as problems begin to arise, peoples' discourse becomes contradictory and varies from context to context (between positive and negative aspects of drug use) and the controlled and uncontrolled aspects of their drug use. These attributions reflect the ambivalence that emerges during the development of addiction.
- *Stage 3*: people refer to themselves as addicted, explain their drug use as out of their control, and view it as negative.
- *Stage 4*: people begin to reject the usefulness of the "addiction" concept in the explanation for their behaviour and their discourse again becomes mixed and contradictory.
- *Stage 5*: people can be either positive or negative. Whatever the version, people's attributions are

In stage 3 of Davies' (1996) five stages of attribution, individuals acknowledge that they have a problem, and view themselves negatively as addicted.

relatively stable at this stage and do not contradict in different contexts. Furthermore, they do not refer to their drug-using behaviour in terms of addiction. In the positive version, people might have given up drugs or alcohol, but return to a view of their past behaviour as controllable and a description of their drug use that highlights both the positive and negative aspects of that behaviour. In the negative version, although the concept of addiction has been dropped, people continue to use drugs and see themselves as "down and out". Here, their behaviour is uncontrollable and their drug use is negative.

KEY TERM

Hedonism: the pursuit of pleasure.

Although these stages tend to relate to the progression of an addiction, people can move back and forth between stages. The one exception to this, according to Davies (1996), is an irreversible transition from the second to third stage that often occurs when people enter treatment and may persist long after. Davies (1996) subsequently tested his attribution model through interviews with 20 drug and alcohol users. Interviews were transcribed and coders rated the attributions given in each interview in terms of the dimensions outlined in the model above. The investigators assigned each respondent to one of the stages based on those ratings. Consensus between four judges rating the same participants was good. The average agreement between the judges was 71% (ranging from 0.49 to 0.75). In all instances, the judges never disagreed by more than one stage.

Evaluation

Although Davies demonstrated the reliability of his model (i.e. the ability of coders to identify the attribution patterns associated with each stage) and stated that these stages related to the stages of an addiction, he did not provide information about how the attributional stages correspond to the actual temporal progression of addiction in his interviewees (e.g. whether the majority of participants classified as stage 3 were in treatment at the time of the interview). Given his claim that movement between at least two of the stages is irreversible, a claim that contradicts established research on addiction stages (see Prochaska, Norcross, & DiClemente, 1994), further research is needed to verify the model. In addition, although Davies developed his model based on years of observations and interviews of drug users, he only tested it on 20 people. Given the theoretical basis of the model (i.e. that attributions vary according to context), it is important to test this model and its stages in different samples of substance users and different settings. Nelson (2004) argues that Davies' model of attribution change needs to be validated, but argues that the model is important for the questions it raises. For instance, how do these different stages of attribution relate to the stages of change described in models that have been highly researched [e.g. Prochaska et al.'s (1994) Stages of Change Model outlined later in this chapter]?

If these attribution patterns reliably correspond to different stages of an addiction, it is important to determine whether these attributions predict change (e.g. provide explanations that refer to being addicted as precursors of treatment-seeking behaviour) or reflect change (e.g. provide explanations that refer to being addicted as an attempt to understand and explain past behaviour within the treatment context).

Both possibilities (i.e. predictive and reflective) stress the importance of a person's subjective understanding and interpretation of behaviour in guiding future behaviour. As Nelson concludes, this attribution-behaviour cycle is a crucial, often neglected piece of the study of addictions. Despite some criticism of Davies' work, Nelson (2004) does say that attributions play a role in all aspects of addiction including:

- People's attributions about their own addictive behaviour differ in predictable ways from attributions they make about others' addictive behaviours.
- Attributions about peers' drinking behaviour affecting a person's own drinking behaviour.
- Being labelled as a heavy smoker altering people's attributions about their smoking.

? When conducting research into the use of alcohol and drug abuse, what safeguards would you bear in mind when selecting participants?

- Attributions people make about their addictions predicting their own chances for recovery or likelihood of relapse.
- Attributions for wins and losses influencing the development of gambling problems.

Self-esteem

In a comprehensive overview of addiction, Orford (2001) noted that **self-esteem** is not well represented in research on taking up alcohol, tobacco, or other drug use. There appears to be more work in areas such as eating disorders/addictions that shows those with lower self-esteem are at significantly greater risk of developing problems with their behaviour (e.g. Button, Loan, Davies, & Sonuga-Barke, 1997). Jessor (1987) reports low self-esteem as predictive of involvement in problematic behaviours such as addiction, although some studies suggest that no such association exists. For instance, Van Hasselt, Hull, Kempton, and Bukstein (1993) compared adolescent substance abusers and a comparative adolescent group who did not abuse drugs. Although the adolescent drug abusers were more likely to be depressed, there were no differences between them in terms of self-esteem. An earlier study by Newcombe, Maddahian, and Bentler (1986) examining risk factors for substance abuse found that in order of importance, self-esteem ranked behind peer drug use, general deviance, perceived drug use by adults, early alcohol use, sensation seeking, poor relationship with parents, low religiosity, poor academic achievement, and psychological distress.

In examining factors that determine addictive behaviour, McMurran (1994) notes that the most important are culture, family, social group, lifestyle, environment, behavioural skills, thoughts, feelings, and physical factors. Somehow, this whole range of different influencing factors has to be accounted for when examining addictive behaviour. A comprehensive study carried out by Sussman, Dent, and Leu (2000) examined prospective predictors of substance abuse using "triadic influence theory". Triadiac influence theory classifies drug use into three substantive domains (interpersonal, attitude/cultural, and intrapersonal). In their study, they sampled 702 youths at high risk for drug abuse from 21 Californian "alternative high schools". They controlled for baseline abuse and dependence, and found that, of 13 predictors, a drug use and intention index, and a concern that one is or will become an addict or alcoholic, were consistently predictive of self-reported substance abuse or dependence 1 year later. Other factors such as poor pro-social coping also predicted later abuse and dependence (Sussman, Skara, & Ames, 2006).

There has been some speculation that some people may be more prone to drug abuse and addiction than others. Research is being carried out into whether there may even be genes that predispose certain people to addiction. Social circumstances are important in drug abuse. Peer pressure, emotional distress, and low self-esteem can all lead individuals to abuse drugs. Ease of access to drugs is another influence. People abuse drugs for a reason. Understanding what the person's motivation is helps to explain why that person is abusing drugs.

The Social Context of Addiction

Some types of addictive behaviour are socially acceptable and others attract a moral panic in our society. For example, the level of acceptance for a particular social drug changes over time, as does the level of moral panic. If you look at response to **opiates**

> **KEY TERM**
>
> **Self-esteem:** the evaluative dimension of the self-concept, which is to do with how worthwhile and/or confident a person feels about him- or herself.
> **Opiates:** a natural or synthetic derivative of opium that has similar pain killing and sedative effects.

(such as opium, morphine, and heroin), although they currently generate a lot of moral concern, this was not always the case. Opium was used for hundreds of years to relieve pain, to induce sleep, and to control common ailments like coughs and colds. The common way it was taken was as laudanum: a mixture of opium and alcohol. Opium was seen as an acceptable medication and it was only during the nineteenth century that concerns began to develop when the use of the drug increased and people started using it for recreational as well as medical purposes. Orford (1985) reports that up to the middle of the nineteenth century it was accepted that many people living in the fens (of Lincolnshire, Cambridgeshire, and Norfolk) were regular users of opium. In fact, the *Morning Chronicle* of 1850 described the fenland town of Ely as the "opium-eating city". The reason for this heavy use was attributed to the damp conditions of fenland and the rheumatism and neuralgia that many people developed.

Once acceptable, but now feared, opiates have changed their position in our society. Contrast this with the position of gin, which is now seen as a smart alcoholic drink and is not associated with excess or disease. In eighteenth-century London, however, gin was a major killer. The gin craze of the early eighteenth century saw Londoners drink on average 35 litres of the stuff each year. The Foundling Hospital was founded in 1756 by Thomas Coram as a response to his horror at the effects of gin. Papers in the archives of the Old Bailey relate the typical story of a mother who "fetched her child from the workhouse, where it has just been 'new-clothed' for the afternoon. She strangled it and left it in a ditch in Bethnal Green in order to sell its clothes. The money was spent on gin" (Humphreys, 2001). The gin problem had an economic cause, in that the country had an enormous surplus of corn and, to keep the prices up and the landowners happy, the manufacture of alcohol was deregulated so that urban areas were flooded with cheap gin. It was only when the government eventually took on the vested interests of the landowners and restricted the sale of gin that the epidemic subsided.

The history of opium and gin could fill a book, but the point to be made here is that in different cultures and in different times, a substance can have a very different social significance and a very different social use. What this means is that the substances that health workers currently choose to look at and create the maximum social concern about are not necessarily the most threatening substances for our health. They are, however, the substances that we are currently most concerned about for all manner of health, financial, moral, and

In modern society, opium generates a moral panic, but it was actually used for hundreds of years to treat common ailments and was used well into the mid-nineteenth century as a hospital drug to control pain.

An engraving from the 1750s by William Hogarth (1697–1764) entitled *Gin Lane* illustrates various problems caused by addiction to gin. Among other things we can see a woman dropping her baby, people fighting, and people pawning their goods.

Change over time

Attitudes to drugs of all types have changed and will continue to change over time. When Freud first tried cocaine he was enthusiastic about its use as a therapeutic drug, and recommended it to many people, including his friends and family. His close friend Fleischl became severely addicted to cocaine, which eventually contributed to his death (Stevens, 1989). Nowadays cocaine would not be seen as therapeutically useful.

In the 1960s and 1970s, amphetamines were prescribed to suppress appetite and help in weight loss. However, once the dramatic side-effect of amphetamine use became known, this practice waned, and is now regarded as very dangerous.

political reasons. Also, as we will see below, the methods that are most commonly used to reduce substance abuse are not necessarily the most effective for reducing health risks. These methods are also affected by the political and moral responses from the rest of the community (e.g. see Higgins, Budney, Bickel, Foerg, Donham, and Badger's (1994) report on treatment for cocaine abusers later in this chapter).

There is currently a lot of concern about the social use of opiates, although the behaviour that is thought to have the most damaging effect on the nation's health is smoking. This behaviour has been singled out for particular attention in government strategies (Department of Health, 1992, 1999), and smokers have now become social outcasts huddled under shelters outside public buildings reading newspaper stories about how they will de denied medical treatment until they give up their habit.

Availability

A number of environmental factors affect the incidence of addictive behaviours in a society. One factor that affects the level of alcoholism is the availability of alcohol and the average consumption of alcohol by the general population. Comparison studies have found near perfect correlations between the number of deaths through liver cirrhosis (generally attributed to alcohol abuse) and the average consumption of alcohol in different countries (for a discussion, see Orford, 1985). The availability factor also affects the consumption of cigarettes as shown in the study below.

If we examine the pattern of cigarette consumption compared with the retail price of cigarettes in this country we can observe a remarkable relationship. The figure shows how the curve for consumption is the mirror image of the curve for retail price (Townsend, 1993).

Since 1970, any increase in price has brought about a decrease in smoking. At the time of the study there was a slight decrease in the price of cigarettes (figures adjusted to take account of inflation) and a corresponding rise in smoking. This rise in smoking was particularly noticeable in young people, and according to Townsend (1993) regular smoking by 15-year-old boys increased from 20 to 25% and by 16- to 19-year-old girls from 28 to 32%. This connection between price and consumption suggests an obvious policy for governments who want to reduce smoking.

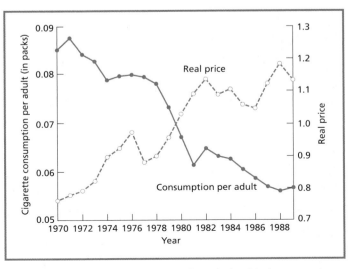

The relationship between the price of cigarettes and consumption 1970–1989.

Social cues: tobacco advertising

In their response to the Health of the Nation strategy (Department of Health, 1992), the British Psychological Society (1993) called for a ban on the advertising of all tobacco products. This call was backed up by the government's own research (Department of Health, 1993), which suggested a relationship between advertising and sales. Also, in four countries that have banned advertising (New Zealand, Canada, Finland, and Norway) there has been a significant drop in consumption.

Public policy, however, is not always driven by research findings, and the powerful commercial lobby for tobacco has considerable influence. In her reply to the British Psychological Society, the Secretary of State for Health (at that time Virginia Bottomley) rejected a ban saying that the evidence was unclear on this issue and efforts should be concentrated elsewhere. This debate highlights how issues of addictive behaviours cannot be discussed just within the context of health. There are also political, economic, social, and moral contexts to consider. The British government and European Union have made commitments to ban tobacco advertising, although they found it difficult to bring these bans in as quickly as they hoped. It is now rare to see smoking advertised anywhere in the UK but there is a new trend in television drama and films to set the action in a time or location where smoking is part of the way of life (for example the US television programme *Mad Men*).

Media influences

The media (television, radio, newspapers, etc.) is an important channel for portraying information and channelling communication. Knowledge about how the mass media works may influence both the promotion of potentially addictive behaviour (as in advertising), and for the promotion of health education (such as promoting abstinence or moderation) (McMurran, 1994). Much of the research done on advertising is done by the companies themselves and thus remains confidential (Wilde, 1993). The media, especially television and film, often portrays addictions (e.g. heroin addiction in the film *Trainspotting*, marijuana use in the TV show *Weeds*, gambling addiction in the TV show *Sunshine*, etc.). Because of this constant portrayal of various addictions, television and film dramas often create controversy because of claims that they glamorise addictive behaviour. The popularity of media dramas depicting various addictions requires an examination of their themes and the potential impact on the public.

The makers of such dramas argue that presenting such material reflects the fact that addictions are everywhere and cut across political, ethnic, and religious lines. Addiction is certainly an issue that impacts all communities. However, it is important to consider possible impacts that such dramas might have on society. Empirical research suggests that the mass media can potentially influence behaviours. For example, research indicates that the more adolescents are exposed to movies with smoking the more likely they are to start smoking (Dalton et al., 2003). Furthermore, research has shown that the likeability of film actors and actresses who smoke (both on-screen and off-screen) relates to their

Many films and TV programmes have depicted issues of addiction. The 1995 Oscar-winning film, *Leaving Las Vegas*, for example, portrays the life of Ben (Nicolas Cage); a former movie executive who loses his wife and family in a sea of alcoholic self-destruction.

adolescent fans' decisions to smoke (Distefan, Gilpin, Sargent, & Pierce, 1999). Perhaps unsurprisingly, films tend to stigmatise drinking and smoking less than other forms of drug taking (Cape, 2003). However, the media transmits numerous positive messages about drug use and other potential addictions (Will, Porter, Geller, & DePasquale, 2005), and it is plausible that such favourable portrayals lead to more use by those that watch them. Anecdotally, some things may be changing. For instance, there appears to be more emphasis on the media's portrayal of alcohol as socially desirable and positive as opposed to smoking, which is increasingly being regarded as anti-social and dangerous.

The issue of glamorisation versus reality is of course complicated. Although the drama producers hope to accurately depict various addictions, they still need to keep ratings up. Clearly, positive portrayals are more likely to increase ratings and programmes might favour acceptance of drug use over depictions of potential harms. More research on how media influences drug use is needed in order to evaluate the impact of such dramas. With media and addiction, it is important to walk with caution, as the line between reality and glamorisation is easy to cross. More research is needed that investigates direct, indirect, and interactive effects of media portrayals on addictive behaviour.

Putting the Explanations Together: The Biopsychosocial Approach

Addictions always result from an interaction and interplay between many factors including the person's biological and/or genetic predisposition, their psychological constitution (personality factors, unconscious motivations, attitudes, expectations, beliefs, etc.), their social environment (i.e. situational characteristics), and the nature of the activity itself (i.e. structural characteristics) (Griffiths, 1999a). This "global" view of addiction highlights the interconnected processes and integration between individual differences (i.e. personal vulnerability factors), situational characteristics, structural characteristics, and the resulting addictive behaviour.

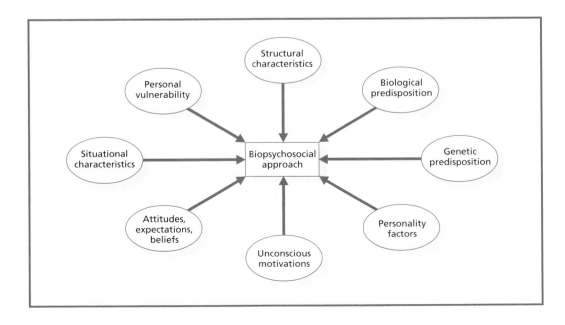

The main factors and characteristics of the biopsychosocial approach to addiction.

KEY TERM

Situational characteristics: a reason for an act or behaviour which implies that it occurred as a result of the situation or circumstances that the person was in at the time.

There are many individual (personal vulnerability) factors that may be involved in the acquisition, development, and maintenance of addiction (e.g. personality traits, biological processes, unconscious motivations, learning and conditioning effects, thoughts, beliefs, and attitudes), although some factors are more personal (e.g. financial motivation and economic pressures in the case of gambling addiction).

On a situational level, there are many factors that are likely to be involved in acquisition elements of addictive behaviour. This is what some researchers have referred to as "object exposure" (i.e. Shaffer, LaPlante, LaBrie, Kidman, Donato, & Stanton, 2004). Other factors central to understanding gambling behaviour are the **situational characteristics** of gambling activities. These are the factors that often facilitate and encourage people to gamble in the first place (Griffiths & Parke, 2003). Situational characteristics are primarily features of the environment (e.g. accessibility factors such as location of the gambling venue, the number of venues in a specified area, and possible membership requirements) but can also include internal features of the venue itself (décor, heating, lighting, colour, background music, floor layout, refreshment facilities) or facilitating factors that may influence gambling in the first place (e.g. advertising, free travel and/or accommodation to the gambling venue, free bets or gambles on particular games) or influence continued gambling (e.g. the placing of a cash dispenser on the casino floor, free food and/or alcoholic drinks while gambling) (Griffiths & Parke, 2003; Abbott, 2007).

Context can be an important factor in the development of addictions. For instance, during the Vietnam War, drug taking amongst the conscript American army was highly prevalent but, on returning to the US, most soldiers' addictive drug use stopped spontaneously when they were in their home environment (Robins, Helzer, & Davis, 1975). Another example is the effects of Ecstasy, which are likely to be different depending on the presence or absence of dance music (Larkin & Griffiths, 2004).

In some activities, such as gambling, structural characteristics can be important in the development of addictive behaviour. For example, slot machines are known to be one of the most addictive types of gambling (Griffiths, 1999a, 2002; Parke & Griffiths, 2006). Almost all of the above factors are unique to slot machines and represent the features that are specifically incorporated into the machine by the designers and operators in the gaming industry to keep people gambling once they have started. They are important in the development and maintenance of gambling addiction. This is what some researchers have referred to as either "object interaction" (i.e. Shaffer et al., 2004) or "psycho-structural interaction" (Griffiths, 1993b). Griffiths (1999a) has noted there is no precise frequency level of a gambling game at which people become addicted since addiction will be an integrated mix of factors in which frequency is just one factor in the overall equation. Other factors and dimensions (external to the person themselves) have been reported in the general gambling literature, and were summarised by Griffiths (1999a; Parke & Griffiths, 2007). Some of the most important ones are outlined below:

? Have you ever been influenced by situational characteristics?

? Here we use gambling as an example of how structural characteristics may influence a person to take up an addictive habit. What are some other examples?

- *Event frequency*: this refers to the number of events that are available for gambling on in any given time period. For example, a lottery draw might occur twice a week but a person may be able to gamble 10–20 times a minute on a slot machine. Games that offer a fast, arousing span of play, frequent wins, and the opportunity for rapid replay are those most associated with problem gambling. Frequency of opportunities to gamble (i.e. event frequency) appears to be a major contributory factor in the development of gambling problems. The general rule is that the higher the event frequency, the more likely it is that the activity will cause gambling problems.

- *Jackpot size*: there is some evidence to suggest that higher jackpots attract more participation in that gambling activity. For instance, more lottery tickets are sold on "rollover" weeks because the potential jackpot is very large (Griffiths & Wood, 2001).

- *The "near miss"*: the definition of a near miss is any non-winning outcome of a gamble that is perceived as being almost successful (and should perhaps more accurately be termed a "near win"). A near miss, (e.g. two matching symbols on a win line with the third matching symbol just off the win line), may still be reinforcing and fun even though it may not cost the operator anything. Essentially, players perceive that they frequently nearly win, as opposed to frequently losing (Griffiths, 1999b).

- *Play features*: the degree of personal participation (i.e. "gambler involvement") and the exercise of skill are interrelated. The use of specialist play features such as "nudge", "hold", and "gamble" buttons creates perceived skill in situations determined by chance. Specialist play features give the illusion of control through personal involvement, perception of skill, and familiarity with a particular machine.

- *Payout interval*: this is the time between the end of the gambling event (i.e. the outcome) and the winning payment. The frequency of playing when linked with two other factors—the result of the gamble (win or loss) and the actual time until winnings are received—exploits the psychological principles of learning (i.e. operant conditioning) by rewarding (i.e. reinforcing) behaviour (i.e. through presentation of a reward such as money).

- *Suspension of judgement*: this refers to a structural characteristic that temporarily disrupts the gambler's financial value system by changing real money into a virtual representation of it (e.g. the use of chips in casinos, tokens on slot machines, e-cash in internet gambling). For most gamblers, the psychological value of virtual representations of money will be less than "real" money. This is exploited by those in commerce and the gaming industry (i.e. people typically spend more on credit and debit cards because it is easier to spend money using plastic).

The "features" of a fruit machine are designed to dupe the player into thinking he or she has an element of control in the winning or losing.

Many other characteristics are used to influence gambling behaviour, including the use of light and colour effects, music and sound effects, and pseudo-skill features.

Evaluation

Each of these differences can have implications for the gambler's motivations and, as a consequence, the social impact of gambling. Although many of these gambling-inducing structural characteristics are dependent on individual psychological factors (e.g. reinforcement) they are a direct result of the structural characteristics and could not have influenced gambling behaviour independently. It is for this reason, above all others, that a structural approach could be potentially useful. For drug addictions, structural characteristics would include things such as the dose amount, the drug's toxicity, and the route of administration.

It is clear that by including the situational and structural characteristics of the addictive process, the aetiology of how and why addiction occurs starts to become very complex. Shaffer et al. (2004) argue that evidence supporting a broader conceptualisation of addiction is emerging. Citing the latest neurobiological research, they claim that addiction disorders may not be independent. Put simply, they suggest that each addiction—whether it be addiction to gambling, drugs, sex, or the internet—might be a distinctive expression of the same underlying syndrome (i.e. addiction is a syndrome with multiple opportunistic expressions). To support their observations, Shaffer et al. report that many commonalities occur across different expressions of addiction, and that these commonalities reflect a shared aetiology.

> **EXAM HINT**
>
> You need to be able to explain how people's attributions, self-esteem, and the social context affect addiction. Note you can comment on how some of these factors are internal and of course the social context is external, and that the factors may be influenced by both nature and nurture. For example, a person's innate disposition may lead them to seek out environments that increase the likelihood of addiction yet this could also be influenced by their learning in different social contexts.

SECTION SUMMARY
Factors Affecting Addictive Behaviours

❖ Factors that affect addictive behaviours can be divided into personal (dispositional) factors, structural (substance or activity) factors, and situational (environmental factors).

❖ One of the key personal factors is the attributional style a person adopts to explain their own behaviour and the behaviour of others.

❖ The stage model of attributions proposed by Davies offers some useful insights into the thinking of people with addictive behaviours.

❖ Self-esteem is commonly thought to be predictive of addictive behaviours but the evidence is mixed.

❖ Availability is a good predictor of addictive behaviours as shown in changes in smoking behaviours.

❖ Social cues such as tobacco advertising influence addictive behaviours.

❖ The acceptability of addictive behaviours changes between cultures and over time.

❖ Media outlets are used in attempts to reduce or eliminate addictive behaviours.

❖ The biopsychosocial approach can bring a number of these factors together.

❖ The structural factors that affect addictive behaviours, like gambling, include like event frequency, jackpot size, and payout interval.

> **KEY TERM**
>
> **Celebrity:** a celebrity is a widely recognised or famous person who commands a high degree of public and media attention. The word stems from the Latin verb *celebrere*, which translates as "empty-headed attention seeker".

REDUCING ADDICTIVE BEHAVIOUR

As we said at the beginning of this chapter, there is something quite fashionable about rehab for the world of **celebrity**. For the rest of us, however, dramatically changing our behaviour and escaping from our addiction to smoking, drinking alcohol, or gambling, is a very difficult and unglamorous activity.

Of course, the best solution to addiction is not to start it in the first place. A lot of effort is put into stopping people starting the behaviours. Unfortunately, there are even more pressures encouraging you start than there are to stop. And the reason for that is that the people selling you the activity, product, or service stand to make a lot of money if you become addicted to it. This is why major tobacco companies give away cigarettes to children in developing countries; they are not being generous they are just investing in their future (e.g. see McGreal, 2008).

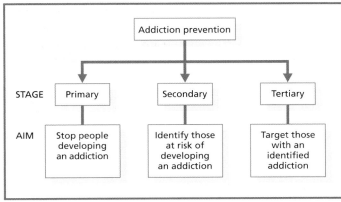

The three types of addiction prevention and their main aims.

Prevention

Prevention efforts targeting mental health and addictive disorders are widely used but there is limited data available on their effectiveness. In the area of substance abuse prevention, there have been large-scale, structured investigations into the effectiveness of individual programmes (e.g. Drug Abuse Resistance Education, or project DARE; Clayton, Cattarello, & Johnstone, 1996), although findings are often inconclusive.

Historically, prevention has been divided into three stages (Force, 1996). The term "primary prevention" has been used to describe measures employed to prevent the onset of a targeted condition. "Secondary prevention" describes measures that identify and treat asymptomatic persons who have already developed risk factors or pre-clinical disease but in whom the condition is not clinically apparent. "Tertiary prevention" describes efforts targeting individuals with identified disease in which the goals involve restoration of function, including minimising or preventing disease-related adverse consequences. These divisions of prevention focus on different targets, with primary efforts tending to target the general population, secondary efforts at-risk or vulnerable groups, and tertiary efforts individuals with an identified disorder.

If we look at how to prevent addictions then, clearly, the best route is to stop people developing the addictive behaviours in the first place. Campaigns intended to achieve this have been spectacular in their failure. Millions of pounds have been spent on campaigns to stop smoking, excessive drinking, and drug taking. Latest evidence suggests a small decline in smoking and rises in the other two. "Just say 'No!'" is not enough. The content and impact of primary prevention is strongly influenced by knowledge of the effect of the behaviour or disorder being prevented. For example, prevention efforts targeting tobacco smoking cessation have changed significantly as more information concerning the health impact of tobacco smoke have become available (Slovic, 2001). General evidence shows that accurate knowledge about healthy and unhealthy behaviours (including, to some degree, attitudes towards these behaviours) does not necessarily affect the behaviour itself (Botvin, 2001; Durlak, 2003). Thus, it is premature to draw a definite conclusion of what type of preventive intervention works in terms of behavioural change related to addiction. It is still unresolved what type of prevention programme works with regard to enduring behavioural changes or if the positive effects reported have any long-lasting effect.

Nevertheless, findings from universal cognitive-based approaches demonstrate that inappropriate perceptions related to addictive activities can be corrected

EXAM HINT

Make sure that you can explain the stages of prevention: primary, secondary, and tertiary and assess the effectiveness of each.

EXAM HINT

To increase AO2 in an essay on reducing addictive behaviour consider which approach works best at reducing the addiction: the social inoculation approach or the fear induction? Can you explain why?

(Hayer, Griffiths, & Meyer, 2005). To increase effectiveness, prevention models must: (1) increase awareness of addiction and its consequences; (2) enhance knowledge about addiction and its consequences; (3) change attitudes towards addiction and adopt a more balanced view; (4) teach effective coping and adaptive skills; and (5) correct inappropriate cognitions related to addiction. In the future, one of the main goals must be to connect research findings, theory, and prevention science with practice. It would seem reasonable that such prevention programmes should be aimed at adolescents given that many addicts report that their first experiences with their drug or behaviour of choice was in their youth (Griffiths, 1995).

Studies dealing with adolescents suggest that simply giving information is not enough to create positive effects (Edmundson, McAlister, Murray, Perry, & Lichtenstein, 1991; Donaldson, Graham, Piccinin, & Hansen, 1997; Van der Pligt, 1998). Furthermore, information in the form of a "teaching session" may not be the optimum method for giving information to adolescents. As research has generally shown that "fear induction" and "information only" techniques are unsuccessful, Evans and colleagues (Evans, 1989, 2001; Evans & Getz, 2001) have explored how psychosocial models and constructs can be applied to the prevention of health-threatening behaviours in adolescents. At the heart of these approaches is the concept of "social inoculation". The **social inoculation** model involves "inoculating" adolescents with the knowledge and social skills (i.e. "resistance skills") necessary to resist various social pressures to engage in risky behaviours to which they may be exposed (including in this case, potentially addictive behaviours).

Models of Behaviour Change and Prevention

Why do we do the things we do? It seems reasonable to suggest that our behaviour is affected by the attitudes we have about particular issues. For example, if people have strong beliefs about the environment then we would expect them to make regular visits to the bottle bank and use recycled paper. This doesn't seem to be the case, however, and over 100 years of research on human behaviour has found the consistent result that attitudes do not predict behaviour. The closeness of the bottle bank is a better predictor on your use of it than your attitudes. Availability, ease, and social norms all seem to have a greater impact on our behaviour than our beliefs and feelings. This means that the simple intuitive model of attitudes and behaviour shown on the left cannot be used to predict how people will behave.

Model one: Intuitive model of attitudes and behaviour

Attitudes ⟶ Behaviour

The Theory of Reasoned Action

The Theory of Reasoned Action first proposed by Fishbein and Ajzen (1975, Azjen & Fishbein, 1980) attempted to improve on the intuitive model and to explain why people make their behavioural choices.

The model suggests that our intention to engage in behaviour is predicted by our attitudes and by subjective norms. Notice that they are talking about intentions to do something (behave) rather than the behaviour itself. There is a

KEY TERM

Social inoculation: giving people the skills to resist social pressure.

slight problem here because, for example, we intend to do a lot of things (like drink less alcohol and be a nicer person) but somehow these things don't seem to happen. In this model, an attitude is a collection of beliefs that you have about a particular behaviour. For example, you might believe that eating healthy foods, like muesli and brown rice, is good for you and will help you live longer and have better bowel movement. You might also believe that it tastes like the scrapings from the bottom of a hamster's cage. This collection of beliefs forms your attitude to eating muesli.

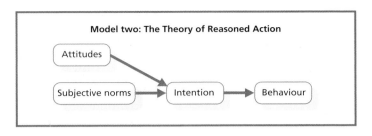

The other predictor of intention to act is subjective norms. These are influences around us including other people. If your housemates all eat muesli and bang on about how good it is for you, then you will be experiencing more cues to eating muesli and so will be more likely to do so. The higher you rate these people, the more likely you are to take their attitudes on board.

This is the essence of the Theory of Reasoned Action. It has been used extensively in a range of areas, such as health and also marketing, to predict and hence try to alter behaviour. Human behaviour, however, is very difficult to predict and this can be seen in the mass social events that take the world by surprise. For example, the credit crunch that began in 2008 represents a mass change of attitude and belief about the value of commodities, which has led to a massive change in the way people, companies, and nations behave; the impact on the world has been massive. This difficulty in predicting behaviour extends to simpler activities like choosing to stop smoking or to take up exercise. To try to take account of a few more of the variables involved in behaviour choice The Theory of Reasoned Action was modified and became The Theory of Planned Behaviour (Ajzen, 1991).

The Theory of Planned Behaviour

The Theory of Planned Behaviour adds another factor to the original model. This additional factor deals with the beliefs we have about the amount of control we have over our behaviour. We might feel we have control over some aspects of our health behaviour, such as choosing not to eat the *superchoccodoublecream* sweet after a big meal, but feel unable to control our smoking behaviour. If you think about most health behaviours, they are easily solved if we are in control of them. If you want to lose weight all you have to do is eat less and move about more. It's not rocket science. Unfortunately, it is also not that easy because we don't seem to be as in control of our behaviour as we would like to think.

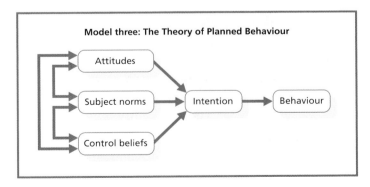

On the plus side, these models help frame a lot of research into behaviour change and they are able to make some predictions about what people will do. The downside is that these predictions are usually quite weak. Another problem with the model is that it is about cognitive processes to the exclusion of emotions. The underlying idea is people behave in thoughtful and rational ways when in fact we often act on impulse and emotion.

The Stages of Change Model

One model that has been used with some success in the changing the behaviour of people with addictions is the Stages of Change Model (Prochaska, DiClemente, & Norcross, 1992). If you have ever attended a smoking cessation clinic then it is likely that this model was behind the structure of the event. This model identifies an individual's "readiness for change" and tries to get a person to a position where they are highly motivated to change their behaviour. The individual stages of this model are outlined below.

Pre-contemplation

In this stage, individuals have no intention to change their behaviour and probably do not even perceive that they have a problem. The problem might be obvious to their family and friends but the individuals themselves might well respond to these concerns by saying "I know I have some faults but there is nothing I really need to change."

Contemplation

In this stage, the individuals are aware that they have a problem and think that they should do something about it. However, they have not yet made a commitment to take action. People can stay in this stage indefinitely, and the authors quote some of their own research that observed some smokers who were stuck in the contemplation stage for the full 2 years of the study.

Preparation

In this stage, individuals intend to take action in the near future and may well have already started to do something. Most commonly, they will have reduced the number of cigarettes they smoke, or delayed the time of the first cigarette each day. If this was a race then people in this stage are at the "get set" point, just before they start to run.

Action

In this stage, people change their behaviour, or their experience, or their environment so that they can overcome their problem. They are said to be in the action stage if they have successfully altered their behaviour for a period of between 1 day and 6 months. In the case of smoking, the change must involve not smoking at all. People often—incorrectly—see the action stage as the main part of change and overlook the importance of the preliminary stages that prepare the person for change, and the efforts that are required to maintain the change.

Maintenance

In this stage, individuals work to prevent a relapse and to consolidate the changes they have made. People are said to be in the maintenance stage if they are able to remain free from the problem behaviour for more than 6 months.

The model shown in the figure presents change as a spiral. This takes account of the observation that most people who take action to change a habit are not successful at the first attempt. Prochaska et al. (1992) suggest that smokers commonly make three or four action attempts before they reach the maintenance stage.

In the action stage, the individual has changed his or her behaviour to overcome the problem; by using nicotine replacement therapy in place of smoking, for example.

People can stay in one stage for a long time and it is also possible for unassisted change, such "maturing out" or "spontaneous remission" (McMurran, 1994). Various techniques that can be used to help people prepare for readiness include motivational techniques, behavioural self-training, skills training, stress management training, anger management training, relaxation training, aerobic exercise, relapse prevention, and lifestyle modification. The goal of treatment can be either abstinence or simply to cut down.

Spiral model of change proposed by Prochaska, DiClemente, and Norcross (1992).

Connections between the theories of behavioural change

Evans and Getz (2004) highlight five distinct (yet overlapping) theoretical paradigms that have been central to understanding health and illness-related behaviour. These are Social Cognitive Theory, Health Belief Model, Theory of Reasoned Action, Theory of Planned Behaviour, Self-regulation/Self-control Theory, and the Subjective Culture and Interpersonal Relations approach. These perspectives converge on a set of eight conditions necessary for the performance of any volitional behaviour. If applied to potentially addictive behaviour (such as smoking cigarettes, drinking alcohol, gambling, or taking drugs) they would be as shown below in the box.

The first three conditions are essential for the action to be performed. The final five conditions either directly influence the strength of intention or the strength of the action, or moderate the relation between intention and action.

As Evans and Getz point out, these eight conditions embody a model of behaviour in general and health behaviour in particular. From a prevention standpoint, the social inoculation approach can be understood as an effort to manipulate each of the variables in this model to facilitate health behaviour and inhibit health-risking behaviour. This may be the way forward in future adolescent addiction prevention schemes.

There have been debates in the addiction field about the extent to which individuals are responsible for their problems and subsequent recovery. One of the most straightforward models relating to the treatment of addictive behaviour was put forward by Brickman and colleagues (1982). Their model provides a good conceptual approach by asking just two simple questions:

1. To what extent is the person considered responsible for the initial devel-opment of the problem?
2. To what extent is the person held responsible for changing the behaviour or solving the problem?

Eight conditions necessary for the performance of any volitional behaviour

1. Strong intention or commitment to engage (or not engage) in the behaviour.
2. Absence of environmental barriers that would make the behaviour impossible.
3. Possession of the skills necessary to engage in the behaviour.
4. Person has a positive attitude towards the behaviour (its benefits are perceived to outweigh its costs).
5. Person perceives the behaviour to be consistent with social norms.
6. Person perceives the behaviour to be consistent with their self-images.
7. Person's emotional reaction to performing the behaviour is positive.
8. Person realistically perceives they have the capability to engage in the behaviour (i.e. self-efficacy).

Evidence: Types of Intervention

The intervention and treatment options for the treatment of addiction include, but are not limited to, counselling/psychotherapies, behavioural therapies, cognitive-behavioural therapies, self-help therapies, pharmacotherapies, residential therapies, minimal interventions, and combinations of these (i.e. multi-modal treatment packages). The following sections includes a selection of interventions that give a flavour of what is on offer.

Biological (medical) interventions

Pharmacological interventions basically consist of addicts being given a drug to help overcome their addiction. These are mainly given to those people with chemical addictions (e.g. nicotine, alcohol, heroin) but are increasingly being used for those with behavioural addictions (e.g. gambling, sex). For instance, some drugs produce an unpleasant reaction when used in combination with the drug of dependence, replacing the positive effects of the drug of dependence with a negative reaction. The only aversive agent available is disulfiram (Antabuse), which, when combined with alcohol, produces nausea and possibly vomiting.

Agonist maintenance (methadone) treatment

Agonist treatment is usually given to opiate addicts in outpatient settings. Here, long-acting synthetic opiates (methadone) are administered orally to prevent withdrawal symptoms, block the effects of illicit opiate use, and decrease craving. Addicts using methadone can engage more readily in counselling and other behavioural interventions essential to recovery and rehabilitation.

Narcotic antagonist (naltrexone) treatment

This treatment is usually given to opiate addicts in outpatient settings although initiation often begins after detoxification in a residential setting. Detoxification provides interventions to ensure that the physical withdrawal process to eliminate the drug of dependence is completed with safety and comfort. Experience in many different countries has shown that relapse following detoxification is extremely common unless followed by an appropriate rehabilitation programme. Naltrexone is a long-acting medication with few side effects that blocks the effects of self-administered opiates (e.g. euphoria). The theory behind this treatment is that the repeated lack of the desired opiate effects breaks the drug habit. Addicts often fail to comply with the treatment programme so effective counselling or psychotherapy are often used alongside the medication. More recently, antagonists have also been used in other addictions such as alcoholism and gambling addiction. Partial agonists (such as buprenorphine) can also be used.

Evaluation

The main criticism of all these treatments is that although the symptoms are being treated, the underlying reasons for the addictions may be being ignored. On a more pragmatic level, what happens when the medication comes to an end? It is very likely that addicts will return to their addiction if this is the only method of treatment used. Methadone maintenance has been shown to be safe and very

? What are some risks associated with the use of methadone?

effective on a variety of measures, including preventing illicit drug use. Buprenorphine is probably equally effective, although it is more expensive in some countries (Luty, 2003). The value of these "substitution therapies" lies in the opportunity it provides for addicts to stabilise their health and social functioning and reduce their exposure to risk behaviours before addressing the physical adaptation dimension of addiction.

Psychological interventions

Behavioural therapies are based on the view that addiction is a learned maladaptive behaviour and can therefore be "unlearned". A wide range of behavioural techniques has been applied on this basis in the treatment of addictions. These have mainly been based on the classical conditioning paradigm and include aversion therapy, in vivo desensitisation, imaginal desensitisation, systematic desensitisation, relaxation therapy, covert sensitisation, and satiation therapy.

Types of behavioural therapy for addictive behaviour

- *Aversion therapy*: involves the pairing of an aversive stimulus (electric shock or an emetic—a drug that makes you feel sick—similar to Pernod) with a specific addiction response or may be randomly interspersed while engaging in the addictive behaviour.

- *In vivo desensitisation*: involves pairing cues for addiction with no addiction behaviour and feelings of boredom. Typically the addict is taken to the environment where the addiction typically takes place such as the casino or the bar and stands by without engaging in the addictive behaviour for extended periods of time. The therapist suggests the whole situation is uninteresting.

- *Imaginal desensitisation*: differs from IVD by having the addict imagine the cues for addiction and then pairing these imagined cues with a competing response such as feelings of boredom.

- *Systematic desensitisation*: refers to a gradient of increasingly powerful cues for the addiction. At each step, any arousal that the addict is experiencing is extinguished by imagined scenes of tranquility or direct muscular relaxation.

- *Relaxation therapy*: consists of training in relaxation techniques that can be used when the urge to engage in the behaviour arises.

- *Satiation therapy*: involves presenting the addict with no other stimuli and no other activities but those associated with the addiction.

Adapted from Walker (1992).

All of these therapies focus on cue exposure and relapse triggers (like the sight and smell of alcohol/drugs, walking through a neighbourhood where casinos are abundant, pay day, arguments, pressure). By repeated exposure to relapse triggers in the absence of the addiction, the addict learns to stay addiction free in high-risk situations.

It would seem that behavioural therapies can curtail addictive behaviour but to achieve a long-term improvement the addict must learn how to satisfy his or her needs in more adaptive ways. It could be argued that if the addiction is caused by some underlying psychological problem (rather than a learned maladaptive behaviour), then behavioural therapy would at best eliminate the behaviour but not the problem. This therefore means that the addictive behaviour may well have been curtailed but the problem is still there so the person will perhaps engage in a different addictive behaviour instead. For instance, there are case studies in the literature of gambling addicts being treated with aversive therapy only for the gambling to stop but for alcohol addiction to take its place (Griffiths, 1995). It is

EXAM HINT

Note that both the biological and behavioural treatments can be criticised as treating symptoms not causes. Make sure you can explain why this is so and how this can lead to symptom substitution in which the original addiction is reduced but a different maladaptive behaviour takes its place.

also hard to evaluate treatment effectiveness in some studies because behavioural therapy has often been used with other treatment techniques (e.g. self-help groups, counselling, pharmacotherapy).

Reinforcement

One way to reduce substance abuse is to give people rewards for not taking the substance. There are two psychological ways of looking at this, one is to see it as reinforcement for the behaviour, the other is to see it as a distracter from the pleasurable reinforcement of the substance. Higgins et al. (1994) tried to change the behaviour of people with a serious cocaine problem. The subjects had their urine tested several times a week for traces of cocaine, and every time it was clear of any cocaine they were given vouchers. The vouchers started with a value of $2.50 but every time they were clear of cocaine the value went up by $1.50, so that if they had ten consecutive clear tests they would receive $17.50 for the next clear test. If they had one test that showed traces of cocaine then the payments went back to $2.50. The best way to cash-in on this programme, then, was to stay clear of cocaine for as long as possible.

The vouchers were backed up with counselling on how best to spend the money, so they were encouraged to spend it on, for example, sports equipment to take up a hobby, or a family meal in a restaurant to help build-up relationships that might have been damaged by the substance use. The voucher-therapy approach was reported to have good results. The norm for drug treatment programmes is a drop out rate of 70% within 6 weeks. On this programme, however, around 85% stayed in the programme for 12 weeks and around two-thirds stayed in for 6 months.

The problem with this approach does not concern its success rate but the reaction of other people to the idea of giving drug users money not to take drugs. It is not difficult to imagine the hostile reaction of politicians and the general public to this sort of programme. It is the same hostile reaction that is met by harm-minimisation programmes that seek to reduce the dangers to health in people carrying out risky behaviours.

Cognitive-behavioural therapy

A more recent development in the treatment of addictive behaviours is the use of **cognitive-behavioural therapies** (CBT) (e.g. Marlatt & Gordon, 1985; Harris, 1989). Many different CBT approaches have been used in the treatment of addictive behaviours, including rational emotive therapy, motivational interviewing, and relapse prevention. The technique assumes that addiction is a means of coping with difficult situations, depressed mood, and peer pressure. Treatment aims to help addicts recognise high-risk situations and either avoid or cope with them without use of the addictive behaviour.

Motivational interviewing

The therapeutic approach of motivational interviewing (MI) has gained many adherents since its inception in the early 1980s. MI borrows strategies from **cognitive therapy**, **client-centred counselling**, systems theory, and the social psychology of persuasion, and contains elements of both directive and non-

KEY TERM

Cognitive-behavioural therapies: a development of cognitive therapy where some elements of behavioural therapy (such as focus on behaviour change) have been added.
Cognitive therapy: a form of treatment involving attempts to change or restructure the client's thoughts and beliefs.
Client-centred counselling: a form of humanistic therapy introduced by Carl Rogers and designed to increase the client's self-esteem.

directive therapeutic approaches. It is based on theories of cognitive dissonance and attempts to promote a favourable attitude change. Briefly, instructing addicts of the problems of dependency and the advantages of abstinence tends to result in the addict making contradictory arguments. Motivational interviewing encourages clients to give their own reasons for attempting to change their drug use.

Miller and Rollnick (2002) are the main proponents of such an approach and advocate that MI is primarily about the motivational aspects of changing people's behaviour in the therapeutic setting, an area that Miller and Rollnick feel is most salient to those people who engage in addictive behaviours (e.g. alcohol and other drug use, gambling, eating disorders). The underlying theme of such a therapeutic approach is the issue of ambivalence (the mixed feelings the addict has to their behaviour), and how the therapist can use MI to resolve it and allow the client to build commitment and reach a decision to change. Miller and Rollnick argue that motivation is not a personality problem and that there is little evidence for an "addictive personality". Such assertions are integral to MI's theoretical basis. The focus for MI highlights Prochaska, DiClemente, and Norcross' (1992) Stages of Change Model (outlined above), which seeks to explain how people change either with or without a therapist. The method employed in MI consists of using a mnemonically structured (A–H) list of eight effective motivational strategies:

- giving Advice
- removing Barriers
- providing Choice
- decreasing Desirability
- practising Empathy
- providing Feedback
- clarifying Goals
- active Helping.

These strategies are intertwined with the five general principles of MI (expressing empathy, developing discrepancy, avoiding argumentation, rolling with resistance, and supporting self-efficacy). The therapist attempts to elicit self-motivational statements (through non-confrontational approaches) to bring them to a point of making a decision to change (e.g. problem recognition, expression of concern, intention to change, optimism about change). MI involves avoiding labelling, asking evocative questions, listing advantages and disadvantages, acknowledging positives, reversing roles, and summarising as methods of getting people to come to a decision themselves about changing their behaviour. Reasonable evidence exists for the effectiveness of motivational interviewing (Luty, 2003).

Relapse prevention

Another common strategy often used as part of cognitive-behaviour therapy in helping people overcome their addictions is relapse prevention (Marlatt & Gordon, 1985). Here, the therapist helps to identify situations that present a risk for relapse (both intrapersonal and interpersonal). On an intrapersonal level, this may include acknowledging unpleasant emotions, physical discomfort, pleasant emotions, testing personal control, and urges/temptations. On an interpersonal level, this is likely to include conflicts and social pressures. Relapse prevention provides the addict with techniques to learn how to cope with temptation (positive self-statements, decision review, and distraction activities), coupled with the use of covert modelling (i.e. practising coping skills in one's imagination). It also provides skills for coping with lapses (by redefining what is happening), and utilises graded practice (a desensitisation technique in which addicts encounter real-life situations slowly) or 12-step approaches in opiate addiction. Overall, CBT approaches are better researched than the other psychological methods in addiction but are probably no more effective (Luty, 2003).

Changing cognitions and changing behaviour

Dijkstra and De Vries (2001) investigated the extent to which self-help interventions change specific cognitions, and the extent to which changes in these cognitions are related to behaviour. They carried out a field experiment with follow-ups after 2 weeks and 12 weeks. Over 1500 smokers were randomly assigned to one of four conditions offering self-help materials to aid giving up smoking. The research used two types of information: (1) information about the outcomes of smoking such as shorter life expectancy and various unpleasant diseases; and (2) self-efficacy information telling people how to be successful at giving up. The four groups were given the information as follows:

- Group 1: just given information about the outcome of continuing to smoke.
- Group 2: just given self-efficacy enhancing information.
- Group 3: given outcome and self-efficacy information.
- Group 4: given no information.

The response rate of the smokers was 81% after 2 weeks and 71% after 12 weeks, which is pretty good for this sort of study. The box on the left shows the proportion of people after 12 weeks who had not smoked for the previous 7 days (7 days quit) and the number of people who had attempted to quit during the previous 12 weeks (quit attempt).

The box shows that about a quarter of the smokers had attempted to quit but that most had started smoking again. This might be a bad thing because it gives them an experience of failure and hence lowers self-efficacy, although it might well be a learning experience that helps them to be successful in the future. The main conclusion from the study is that self-efficacy information seems to be effective and that the outcome information had no significant effect.

Proportion of people reporting smoking behaviour after 12 weeks (data in percentages)

	7 days quit	Quit attempt
Group 1	4.8	25.5
Group 2	8.5	27.3
Group 3	8.1	24.6
Group 4	3.2	15.6

KEY TERM

Psychoanalysis: Freud's set of theories about human behaviour; also the form of treatment for mental disorders he devised.

Psychotherapies

Psychotherapy can include everything from Freudian **psychoanalysis** and transactional analysis, to more recent innovations like drama therapy, family therapy, and minimalist intervention strategies (Griffiths & MacDonald, 1999).

The therapy can take place as an individual, as a couple, as a family, as a group and is basically viewed as a "talking cure" consisting of regular sessions with a psychotherapist over a period of time. Most psychotherapies view maladaptive behaviour as the symptom of other underlying problems. Psychotherapy often is very eclectic by trying to meet the needs of the individual and helping the addict develop coping strategies. If the problem is resolved, the addiction should disappear. In some ways, this is the therapeutic opposite of pharmacotherapy (which treats the symptoms rather than the underlying cause). Discussions can concentrate on such topics as narcissism, manipulative behaviour, guilt, irrational thinking, and low ego strength. There has been little evaluation of its effectiveness, although most addicts go through at least some form of counselling during the treatment process.

> **EXAM HINT**
>
> Note that psychotherapy offers great scope for AO2 because it is difficult to assess its effectiveness. This is due to several factors:
>
> - The treatment is highly individualised and is often combined with other therapies, making it difficult to know which has had the most effect.
> - Attempting to deal with the underlying causes of the addictive behaviour is very challenging and often does not meet with success.
> - There are different interpretations of what constitutes success.

There can be great difficulty evaluating the effectiveness of psychotherapeutic techniques because they are usually used as an adjunct to other therapies although there is some evidence that some forms of psychodynamic psychotherapy do not appear to be particularly effective (Luty, 2003). It is therefore hard to establish whether "success" is due to the psychotherapy, some other treatment intervention (e.g. pharmacotherapy or attendance at a self-help group), or an interaction between therapies. There is also the added problem of defining what a "successful" outcome is. Although abstinence from the behaviour might appear to be a clear objective, many would argue that improvement in the lifestyle of the addict—regardless of whether they have stopped the behaviour or not—is just as valid as an obtainable objective.

Self-help therapies

The most popular self-help therapy worldwide is the Minnesota Model 12-Step Programme (e.g. Alcoholics Anonymous, Gamblers Anonymous, Narcotics Anonymous, Overeaters Anonymous, Sexaholics Anonymous, etc.). This treatment programme uses a group therapy technique and uses only ex-addicts as helpers (Griffiths, 1995). Addicts attending 12-Step groups accept personal responsibility and view their behaviour as an addiction that cannot be cured but merely arrested. To some, it becomes a way of life—both spiritually and socially (Griffiths, 1995)—and, compared with almost all other treatments, it is especially cost-effective (even if other treatments have greater "success" rates) as the organisation makes no financial demands on members or the community. For the therapy to work, the 12-Step Programme asserts that addicts must attend voluntarily and must really want to stop engaging in their addictive behaviour. Further to this, they are only allowed to join once they have reached "rock bottom".

Alcoholics Anonymous, which was founded in 1935, uses ex-addicts as helpers in group therapy.

12-Step groups typically meet once a week and each member of the group talks about their personal experiences. These testimonies are in fact called "therapies". Meetings focus on the 12 steps to recovery (see the box below). The therapeutic aims are to instil hope, openness and self-disclosure, to develop social networks, to focus on abstinence and loss of control, to rely on others for help, and to develop spiritually. However, it should be noted that the spiritual development and references to a "Higher Power" prevent some people from continuing with the group.

The twelve steps

1. We admitted we were powerless over [the addiction] and that our lives had become unmanageable.
2. Came to believe that a Power greater than ourselves could restore us to a normal way of thinking and living.
3. Made a decision to turn our will and our lives over to the care of this Power of our own understanding.
4. Made a searching and fearless moral and financial inventory of ourselves.
5. Admitted to ourselves and another human being the exact nature of our wrongs.
6. Were entirely ready to have these defects of character removed.
7. Humbly asked God (of our understanding) to remove our shortcomings.
8. Made a list of all the persons we had harmed, and became willing to make amends to them all.
9. Made direct amends to such people wherever possible, except when to do so would injure them or others.
10. Continued to take personal inventory and when we were wrong promptly admitted it.
11. Sought through prayer and meditation to improve our conscious contact with God, as we understand him, praying only for knowledge of His will for us and the power to carry that out.
12. Having made an effort to practice these principles in all our affairs, we tried to carry this message to other [addicts].

Adapted from Griffiths (1995).

Outside of the meetings, members are free to call each other whenever they get an urge to engage in the behaviour and they adhere to the motto "One day at a time". 12-Step Programmes claim to help fill the void left by not engaging in the addiction by focusing attention on the demands of the next meeting and social rewards (i.e. praise from other members) for non-participation in the addiction. The programme's other major aim is to direct the addict's energies towards work and leisure activities. For every year members go without engaging in the behaviour, they are awarded a pin, which members consider as important milestones.

To date there has been little systematic study of 12-Step groups. There are a number of problems preventing this, particularly anonymity, sample bias, and criteria for success (Walker, 1992):

- *Anonymity*: no case records are kept, no attempt is made at objective evaluation, and the only evidence is the subjectively based self-report of the member. These self-reports are themselves not available to an outsider on the regular basis necessary for evaluation.
- *Sample bias*: 12-Step groups accept only those who come voluntarily and have reached "rock bottom". Membership is continually changing and some members attend multiple meetings. These factors rule out the possibility of comparison with a control group.

- *Criterion for success*: in 12-Step groups, the criterion for success is complete abstention. Among those who drop out and among those who "fall", there is no measure of the success that the 12-Step Programme has achieved. It is quite possible that many of those who attended for a small number of meetings gained the strength to resist the urge to gamble compulsively without needing to attend further meetings.

The empirical evidence suggests that self-help support groups complement formal treatment options and can support standardised psychosocial interventions (UN Office on Drugs/World Health Organization, 2008).

> **HOW SCIENCE WORKS: EVALUATING THE 12 STEPS TO FREEDOM**
> The 12 Steps self-help therapy model is used by Alcoholics Anonymous and many other similar addiction-therapy groups. Anecdotally it seems a successful model in practice but there are problems that make its efficacy difficult to research empirically. It would be useful to identify as many of these problem issues as you can, and for each one explain clearly just why it is an issue for research. You could start with the ethics of socially sensitive research, and take it on from there. This could even be presented as a series of smaller posters.

Residential therapies

This treatment typically requires prolonged residence (often 9–18 months) depending on the type of addiction and abstinence is usually a prerequisite. Residential addiction treatment centres have traditionally been alcohol- and drug-based but other types of residential treatment for behavioural addictions such as gambling addiction have been reported in the literature (e.g. Griffiths, Bellringer, Farrell-Roberts, & Freestone, 2001). Clients are often closely involved in the management of the programmes, including selecting and discharging residents. Residential rehabilitation programmes provide a safe environment where skills and attitudes that will support an addiction-free lifestyle can be developed. Therapeutic communities represent a subset of residential rehabilitation defined by the emphasis placed on accepting personal responsibility for decisions and actions, and assigning residents tasks of "everyday living" as part of their treatment. Most residential treatment involves multi-modal techniques, including pharmacotherapy, psychotherapy, self-help therapy, and CBT. Several large studies suggest that therapeutic communities are beneficial, although completion rates for prolonged residential programmes are often below 20% from the orders for breach of terms (Luty, 2003).

Why do you think completion rates for prolonged residential programmes are so low?

Minimal interventions

Minimal interventions refer to those treatments that require a smaller amount of professional time and/or resources than are typical of the traditional face-to-face interaction between therapist and individual clients or groups (Heather, 1986; Dickerson, Hinchy, and Legg England, 1990). As Dickerson et al. (1990) point out, such a definition includes a whole range of brief interventions including written self-help materials (with or without therapist contact). Heather (1986) further outlines five factors that have contributed to their growth:

1. The increasing cost of health services.
2. The emergence of the ideology of self-help.

3. An ethos and theoretical base in psychology supportive to such an ideology.
4. The erosion of illness models in areas of personal problems (e.g. alcoholism).
5. Evidence that some traditional treatments are ineffective.

Minimal interventions have been applied successfully to a number of areas of addictive behaviour, including alcohol addiction (e.g. Miller, Gribskov, & Mortell, 1981), benzodiazepine addiction (Cormack & Sinnott, 1983; Cormack, Owens, & Dewey, 1989) and gambling addiction (Dickerson et al., 1990). Dickerson et al. (1990) argued that the minimal intervention approach to some addictions (like problem gambling) may be acceptable to some clients and may be associated with short-term reductions in gambling involvement. They also added that some form of self-help manual may well have a useful part to play in the provision of services for addicts who seek help. As with self-help treatments like the 12-Step Programmes, self-help manuals—even if they are only partially successful—are still very cost effective.

Cyber-therapies
There is also a very recent move towards surfing the internet as a route for guidance, counselling, and treatment (Griffiths & Cooper, 2003; Griffiths, 2005b; Wood & Griffiths, 2007). Treatment and support is provided from a range of different people (with and without formal medical qualifications), including specialist addiction nurses, counsellors, medics, psychologists, and psychiatrists. There are also websites and helplines to access information or discuss addiction problems anonymously, and local support groups where addicts meet other people with similar experiences (e.g. Alcoholics Anonymous, Gamblers Anonymous). Support is also available for friends and family members of addicts (e.g. Al Anon, Gam Anon). Many private and charitable organisations provide support and advice for people with addiction problems. Some focus exclusively on the help, counselling, and treatment of a specific addiction (e.g. Narcotics Anonymous, Overeaters Anonymous), whereas others also work to address addictive behaviours across the spectrum.

The method and style of treatment varies between providers and can range from comprehensive holistic approaches to treating the addiction (e.g. encouraging fitness, nutrition, alternative therapies, and religious counselling), to an abstinence-based approach. Many providers also encourage patients (and sometimes friends and families) to join support groups while others offer confidential one-to-one counselling and advice.

Public health interventions and legislation
Harm minimisation
Health education programmes that encourage people to stop taking drugs are remarkably unsuccessful. The message "Hey kids, just say 'No!'" does not produce much reduction in substance use. An alternative approach is to encourage **harm minimisation**. These controversial campaigns accept that people will engage in risky behaviour and try to reduce the health risks by encouraging users to take the drug safely. One way of reducing the health risks for intravenous drug users is to provide needle exchanges so that they do not share injecting

equipment. Using sterile equipment dramatically reduces the risk of getting blood infections such as hepatitis or HIV and AIDS.

Safer drug use can be encouraged by messages for harm minimisation that involve a hierarchy of behavioural changes such as:

- Do not use drugs.
- If you must use drugs, do not inject.
- If you must inject, do not share equipment.
- If you must share, sterilise the injecting equipment before each injection.

The harm-minimisation programmes also give information on how to sterilise injecting equipment easily and effectively. Instead of treating drug dependency by trying to achieve abstinence, this approach tries to educate drug users about safe practices they can adopt to minimise the risks to themselves and others. Another way of reducing the potential harm to intravenous drug users is to provide medically controlled drugs as a substitute for street drugs. These drugs, such as methadone, are less harmful than street heroin, partly because they are free from impurities. Although harm-minimisation programmes can improve the health of drug users, they attract a lot of criticism because they appear to condone drug use.

The public resistance to the above approaches for dealing with excessive drug use suggests that concerns about personal health are not the only ones that need to be taken into account when designing health programmes. It appears that health workers must balance the moral concerns of society with the health needs of their clients.

Peer-based programmes

We prefer to take advice from people like ourselves or people we have great respect for. It seems reasonable to suggest, then, that health-education programmes led by peers will be more successful than programmes led by adult strangers or by teachers. Bachman, Johnson, O'Malley, & Humphreys (1988) looked at a health-promotion programme that asked students to talk about drugs to each other, to state their disapproval of drugs, and to say that they didn't take drugs. The idea was to create a social norm that was against drug taking and also give people practice in saying no. It is claimed that the programme changed attitudes towards drugs and led to a reduction in cannabis use. A similar programme was reported by Sussman et al. (1995), who compared the effectiveness of teacher-led lessons with lessons that required student participation. The study looked at around 1000 students from schools in the US, and suggested that there were significant changes in attitudes to drugs and intentions to use drugs in the active participation lessons but not in the teacher-led lessons.

> **EXAM HINT**
>
> Harm minimisation programmes are a good source of commentary because you can discuss why they are so controversial. For example, many people have both moral and economic objections to supporting people's addictions. In addition, it is argued that such programmes are more likely to perpetuate rather than reduce the addiction.

The Bleachman Campaign was a major media and community outreach education effort designed to influence San Francisco's 12,000–18,000 intravenous drug users to clean their needles with bleach. The idea was not to promote drug use but was instead a short-term solution aimed to stop the rapid spread of HIV in a high-risk population.

Two of the criticisms of the peer-led health education programmes are that they are not based on sound theory and do not provide much evidence of their effectiveness. However, a number of studies have compared the effectiveness of peer-led health education in schools with adult-led programmes delivering the same material (Mellanby, Rees, & Tripp, 2000). It appears that peer-led programmes were at least as effective as the adult-led programmes, and sometimes more effective. One of the reasons for this might be that information, particularly of a sensitive kind, is more easily shared between people of a similar age.

> ■ Activity: What would you do?
> Imagine that your group has a friend with an addiction and, although this is not immediately life- or health-threatening, you know that it will eventually lead to serious problems. With the knowledge from your studies, you can pool your ideas on how to support your friend and enable him or her to recover—and justify your decisions from the research evidence.

Smoking reduction in the workplace

An attempt to encourage people to quit smoking was carried out at five worksites. All the sites received a 6-week programme in cognitive behaviour therapy that focused on the skills of giving up. The workers who enrolled in the programmes in four of the sites were put into competing teams, with the workers at the fifth site acting as a control. At the end of the programme, 31% of the people in the programme at the control site and 22% at the competition sites had stopped smoking. A follow-up study after 6 months found that 18% of the control group and 14% of the competition groups had stayed off the cigarettes. This appears to suggest that the control group was doing better than the competition group, but this was not the case. At the competition sites, 88% of the smokers joined the programme but only 54% did so at the control site. This suggests that the incentive of competition encouraged more people to attempt to give up and, when the data were compared for the total number of smokers at each site to give up, there was a 16% reduction in the competition sites and only 7% at the control site (Klesges, Vasey, & Glasgow, 1986).

The most dramatic intervention in recent years has been the ban on smoking in all public places introduced in England in 2007 (following the introduction in Scotland a year earlier). It is still too early to measure the full effect of this ban but initial surveys suggest that over 400,000 people have given up smoking as a result of the ban (BBC website, 2008).

Addiction Treatment: Evaluation

When examining all the literature on the treatment of addiction, a number of key conclusions can be drawn (National Institute on Drug Abuse, 1999; Zerger, 2002; United Nations/World Health Organization, 2008):

- Treatment must be readily available.
- No single treatment is appropriate for all individuals.
- It is better for an addict to be treated than not to be treated.

It does not seem to matter which treatment an addict engages in as no single treatment has been shown to be demonstrably better than any other. Psychosocial interventions have demonstrated to be effective in rehabilitation and relapse prevention, both in out-patient and residential settings, in particular cognitive behavioural therapy, motivational interviewing and contingency management, employment and vocational training, counselling, and legal advice.

- A variety of treatments simultaneously appear to be beneficial to the addict.
- Individual needs of the addict have to be met (i.e. the treatment should be fitted to the addict including being gender-specific and culture-specific). Effective treatment attends to the multiple needs of the individual, not just their addiction. An individual's treatment plan must be assessed continually and modified as necessary to ensure that the plan meets the person's changing needs.
- Clients with co-existing addiction disorders should receive services that are integrated.
- Remaining in treatment for an adequate period of time is critical for treatment effectiveness.
- Medications are an important element of treatment for many patients, especially when combined with counselling and other behavioural therapies.
- Recovery from addiction can be a long-term process and frequently requires multiple episodes of treatment.
- There is a direct association between the length of time spent in treatment and positive outcomes. One of the challenges is retaining clients in addiction treatment.
- The duration of treatment interventions is determined by individual needs, and there are no pre-set limits to the duration of treatment.

For all the money and effort put into behaviour change, perhaps people will just give up anyway. Perhaps giving up is a natural process? Some people argue that giving up is a natural consequence of developing a strong or excessive appetite for gambling or alcohol or smoking (Orford, 2001). This argument points out that expert treatments only have a limited success, and that the success occurs regardless of the treatment that is used. Treatments that are very different in intensity or in theory have a similar beneficial effect. Orford concludes that there is a lot of evidence that people give up excessive appetites (or addictions) without the help of experts.

> **EXAM HINT**
>
> Remember to assess:
>
> - the appropriateness of treatments by considering how effective the treatment is across different addictions
> - the patient's level of functioning
> - the effect of the treatment on relapse rates
> - the patient's motivation to use the treatment versus the drop-out rate
> - whether the action of the treatment is fully understood
> - ethical issues.

SECTION SUMMARY
Reducing Addictive Behaviour

- ❖ Changing your behaviour is more difficult than it sounds, and the best way to stop gambling or smoking is not to start.
- ❖ Considerable effort and funds are put into prevention work though many campaigns have had little or no effect.

❖ There are many psychological models of behavioural change and the one that has been most successful with addictive behaviours is the Stages of Change Model by Prochaska, DiClemente, and Norcross.

❖ Biological interventions can be useful in reducing the symptoms and helping addicts stabilise their lives.

❖ There are many psychological therapies that have been applied to addictive behaviours and all have some success but none provides an easy route to behaviour change.

❖ Cognitive behaviour therapy is the current big idea of the UK government and has been shown to have some positive effects of people with addictive behaviours.

❖ Self-help therapies are commonly based on the 12-Step Programme used by Alcoholics Anonymous and others.

❖ Among the many other treatments the most controversial is harm-minimisation, which attempts to help people reduce the risks of their behaviour without necessarily directing them to stop.

FURTHER READING

Griffiths. M.D. (2002). *Gambling and gaming addictions in adolescence*. BPS Blackwells: Oxford

Hayer, T., Meyer, G., & Griffiths, M.D. (2009). *Problem gaming in Europe: Challenges, prevention, and interventions*. New York: Springer.

Orford, J. (2001). *Excessive appetites: A psychological view of the addictions* (2nd Edn). Chichester: Wiley.

Shaffer, H.J., LaPlante, D.A., LaBrie, R.A., Kidman, R.C., Donato, A.N., & Stanton, M.V. (2004). Towards a syndrome model of addiction: Multiple expressions, common etiology. *Harvard Review of Psychiatry, 12*, 1–8.

See *A2-Level Psychology Online* for some interactive quizzes to help you with your revision.

REVISION QUESTIONS

In the exam, questions on this topic are out of 25 marks. You should spend about 35 minutes on each of the questions below, which aim to test the material in this chapter. In the exam, make certain you know if you have covered Media Psychology, The Psychology of Addictive Behaviour, or Anomalistic Psychology as your Psychology in Action topic, and then choose the correct question.

1. A leading psychiatrist from the Tavistock Centre in London published data showing he is treating more young people than ever who are addicted to online gaming. In 2006, in response to this growing problem Europe's first ever clinic for game addiction was opened.
    (a) Discuss the reasons why policy makers base their plans on published data such as that from the Tavistock Centre rather than on anecdotal or media opinion. (5 marks)
    (b) Explain with reference to initiation, maintenance, and relapse, the cognitive model of gaming addiction in young people. (10 marks)
    (c) Online games playing is available to a vast number of people and yet only a small number become addicted. Discuss individual factors affecting addictive behaviour. (10 marks)
2. Reducing addictive behaviour requires a two-pronged approach; not just deciding how to prevent such behaviour from occurring but also what interventions are effective.
    (a) Discuss models of prevention for addictive behaviour, including theory of reasoned action and theory of planned behaviour. (10 marks)
    (b) Describe and evaluate types of intervention for addictive behaviour, such as biological, psychological, public health, and legislation. (15 marks)
3. Two common addictions to legal behaviours in our culture are smoking and gambling addiction. Outline and evaluate two models of addiction, including explanations for initiation, maintenance and relapse, as applied to smoking and/or gambling addiction. (25 marks)
4. (a) Outline explanations of media influence on pro- and anti-social behaviour. (10 marks)
    (b) Discuss research into intense fandom, for example celebrity worship and stalking. (15 marks)

See *A2-Level Psychology Online* for tips on how to answer these revision questions.

Psychology in Action: Anomalistic Psychology

By Craig Roberts

Anomalistic psychology is a relatively new area of study in psychology. It looks at those experiences that a human might have that do not fit in with conventional physical laws and so could be interpreted as being caused by mental processes. Thus it tends to focus on parapsychology and includes phenomena like **clairvoyance**, **telepathy**, **extra-sensory perception**, and **psychokinesis**—experiences that cannot be explained by science and scientific principles. This chapter examines a range of parapsychological phenomena with a focus on theoretical and methodological issues surrounding this fascinating topic.

THEORETICAL AND METHODOLOGICAL ISSUES IN THE STUDY OF ANOMALOUS EXPERIENCE

Issues of Pseudoscience

Pseudoscience refers to when a belief, for example in some parapsychological phenomenon, is based on a body of knowledge or "evidence" that appears to be scientific but that, on closer inspection, does not adhere to scientific principles or methods.

The basic principles of science can be defined as follows:

- *Replicability*: can the study be run again to test whether the results are the same or similar? Therefore, procedures ought to be experimental testing cause and effect.

KEY TERMS

Clairvoyance: comes from the French *clair*, meaning clear, and *voyance*, meaning visibility. The term refers to a supernatural power to see objects, etc. that cannot be perceived by the usual senses.

Telepathy: apparent communication from one mind to another.

Extra-sensory perception: refers to an ability to acquire knowledge and information without the use of our five main senses (sight, touch, taste, hearing, and smell) or from any previous experiences. It is a general term that encompasses things like telepathy, precognition, and clairvoyant abilities.

Psychokinesis: derives from the Greek words *psyche*, meaning mind and *kinesis*, which means movement. Therefore, "psychokinesis" literally means mind movement! This reportedly occurs when the mind can supposedly affect matter, space, time, or energy in a way that cannot be explained by the current laws of physics.

Pseudoscience: refers to when a belief, e.g. in some parapsychological phenomenon, is based on a body of knowledge or "evidence" that appears to be scientific. However, on closer inspection, this may not be the case as it does not adhere to scientific principles or methods.

■ Activity: Objectivity

Which of the following would you describe as objective, and why? Discuss your answers in small groups.

- It will probably rain, now that it is spring.
- The life expectancy of a cat is 15–20 years.
- Deciduous trees all lose their leaves in winter.
- If you eat all that chocolate you will definitely be sick.

- *Falsifiability*: is it possible to test out an idea to confirm or *falsify* it? If we cannot even test out an idea and suggest it *could* be wrong in some way it is not particularly scientific.
- *Observable and measurable evidence*: can the phenomena be measured in an objective way? That is, a pseudoscientist may rely on anecdotal evidence (based on one-off happenings or case studies) rather than experimental evidence (or empirical evidence).

Other researchers have defined pseudoscience differently. Williams (2000) stated the following about pseudoscience:

1. *All pseudoscience is irrational—so, it disregards and rejects rational principles. Therefore, it likes to keep on "open mind" on concepts.*
2. *Pseudoscience does not proceed by trial and error (and some science does)—it proceeds by revelation!*

For point 1 above, Williams (2000) uses a nice example to highlight the problems of irrationality. Keeping an "open mind" over concepts can be quite irrational, especially when evidence points to the opposite being much more rational. For example ". . . on that basis we could demand an open mind on pigs might fly. That is not rational. Pigs have no wings, and their body weight far exceeds the maximum with which an animal can fly, even when an animal does have wings. The only way in which a pig might fly is in a Boeing 747," (Williams, 2000, p. xix).

For point 2, Williams (2000) quotes many examples of when trial and error have been rejected, especially when the errors mount up. The US Military spent a huge amount of resources testing remote viewing (the idea that some people can see hidden or distant locations using psychic powers) to no avail. However, many researchers still believe that the idea of remote viewing has credence–they are simply not deterred. As Williams (2000, p. xix) sums up ". . . failed tests are explained away by the experimenter's tiredness or by the presence of sceptical observers blocking some supernatural mechanism."

One of the major problems (up until relatively recently) is that certain arms of parapsychology and anomalistic psychology have never had any "training arms", so that researchers *can* test out ideas scientifically and conclude cause and effect. Certainly, in my own research with UFO and abduction "researchers" in the UK (Roberts, 2000), I have found that many never apply any scientific principles to data collection, analysis, and reporting, and rarely examine the "psychology of the witness" when researching cases. Any field that allows this to happen must be called a "pseudoscience" and will simply be dismissed by the scientific community.

Taking this further, another distinction between science and pseudoscience is the use of the experimental method with the obvious associated control of the environment. Throughout this chapter (and in your own readings), always ask yourself whether adequate controls have been put into place in any given study. We know that psychology researchers will manipulate an independent variable and measure a dependent variable. With all other variables controlled, the researcher can be quite confident that it is the independent variable *causing* any change seen in the dependent variable. Therefore, science employs strictness in procedure; pseudoscience does not.

However, this is all changing. In The UK, you can now study parapsychology at a range of universities (e.g. Edinburgh, Liverpool John Moores, Coventry, Hertfordshire) and I am sure they are objective in their approach to teaching and researching parapsychology. Therefore, like with any other discipline, it may only be a matter of time before it is all accepted as a true science. Finally, remember how psychology has progressed out of philosophy, then Freud, and then the scientific behaviourists. All of this did not happen overnight!

What evidence is there that parapsychology could be a pseudoscience?

One way in which any scientific community communicates with each other is via the publishing of studies and findings from research. Mousseau (2003) examined studies published in some mainstream scientific journals (e.g. *Experimental Physiology*) and compared them with those in "fringe" journals that examine parapsychology (e.g. *Journal of Parapsychology*). She used content analysis to see how many of the articles conformed to some of the criteria of science. The box below highlights some of the main results—it shows the percentage of articles fulfilling each criterion:

Criterion	Parapsychology journals	Mainstream "scientific" journals
Collected empirical data*	43%	64%
Used the experimental method	24%	57%
Disconfirmed an idea	19%	0%
Percentage who cited their own previous work	12%	0%
* This tests out who used trial-and-error techniques in their study.		

It can be seen that parapsychology uses less empirical data collection and experimental method but does disconfirm more often than the mainstream (taken as a measure of *falsifiability*). One of the main criticisms of pseudoscientific research is that published work is full of self-citations (researchers citing their own work). As can be seen, in this sample, this is not the case.

In addition to these arguments, there are procedures that are experimental and try to establish cause and effect in parapsychology. For example, the **Ganzfeld procedure** for testing out extra-sensory perception is strictly experimental and can easily be replicated given the correct equipment (see page 654 for the procedure).

Hypothesis testing and falsifiability

Any scientific hypothesis must be open to the possibility of being disproved, i.e. it must be falsifiable. An example that is often quoted is the assertion that "All ravens are black." To test this hypothesis fully, one would have to catch and examine every raven in the world, and even then an albino raven might be on the point of hatching out. Although it might be true that, in most people's experience, all ravens are black, it would only take one albino bird for the whole hypothesis to be shown to be false.

KEY TERM

Ganzfeld procedure: in a typical procedure, participants are placed in a room and allowed to relax on a comfortable chair. Halved ping-pong balls are placed over their eyes and a red light is shone into their face. Also, they wear headphones that play them white noise so that they experience mild sensory deprivation.

The argument with anomalistic psychology is that psychologists tend to believe that any evidence is based on pseudoscience. However, the parapsychologists argue that because the phenomenon is anomalistic, it won't fit into conventional science anyway!

Issues of Scientific Fraud

It would appear that the field of parapsychology has had its fair share of controversy in terms of fraud. This element of research was clearly defined by Pinch (1979, pp. 330–331) as:

> . . . *certain experimental results which, it is claimed, establish some variety of telepathy, clairvoyance, psychokinesis or pre-cognition (more generally called "psi phenomena"), can be better interpreted as fraud. The fraud may involve either the subject (the supposed source of the psi phenomenon), the experimenter, or both acting in collusion.*

Interestingly, as Pinch (1979) notes, there have been a fair few cases of fraud in psychology over the years but, when the fraud happens in parapsychology, it is not just the researcher that gets targeted but the entire field!

The case of Walter J. Levy

In one of the first automated ESP experiments, Levy was judging the psi abilities of rats and gerbils, among other species (technically, this is called **anpsi**—the psi ability of animals). The research quickly gathered momentum because human intervention was minimal as the equipment recorded "hits" and "misses". Therefore, the argument about humans affecting the recording of results was nullified. It all appeared that Levy was collating positive result after positive result with his subjects. However, a series of papers, which culminated in Rhine (1975) entitled "a second report on a case of experimenter fraud", exposed Levy as fraudulent.

From the middle of 1974 onwards, Levy's associates—Kennedy, Davis, and Levin—began to notice that Levy was acting strangely near the recording equipment during a series of anpsi experiments. So, for example, in June 1974 Kennedy was helping to run an experiment on the effects of Valium on anpsi. During trials, Levy was seen to be touching the recording equipment, which was not necessary as the computer recorded the results on a "paper-punched" readout. As soon as Levy left the room, Kennedy checked the output to find a string of "hits" being recorded. This reportedly happened on other occasions. The research team had also noted that Levy had stated that if the Valium experiment results proved positive there might be more funding available for subsequent work.

A few days later, Levy was seen "fiddling" with the equipment again. Davis this time checked once Levy had left the room and, as before, a long string of hits had been recorded on the paper-punch readout. Subsequently it was also discovered that the plug for the "misses" was not connected and so could not record them! The nail in the coffin for Levy came about during these trials. The rest of the research team set up an Esterline Angus recording device, which recorded all output from the experimental procedures in the laboratory and could not be tampered with. When the results from this were compared with the paper-punch output, it became clear that the misses had not been recorded by the original recording equipment. Rhine confronted Levy about the claims and Levy admitted to the fraudulent behaviour.

This shook the parapsychological research world and, of course, could be used as ammunition by people who believed that research into this area was fraudulent and that parapsychology as a discipline was not worth pursuing.

Other examples
Project Alpha—James Randi (1983)
Research into fraud tends to be focused on the experimenter, but what if the participants are fraudulent and deceiving the researchers? Randi (1983) set up Project Alpha to test this. He chose two "upcoming" participants who—seemingly—had psychokinetic and ESP powers (Steve Shaw and Michael Edwards). In a long series of "experiments", the two participants produced what looked like parapsychological phenomena. For example, it looked as though they could bend spoons and that they had telepathic skills.

In the spoon-bending trials, Randi had instructed the researchers to put only one object on the table for the participants to bend (to test if the researchers would follow a set protocol). However Shaw and Edwards reported that many objects littered the table and that nothing was permanently marked, each item simply had a tag attached to it via a piece of string. When the experimenter was distracted, one of the participants changed a few tags around so the spoons would have a different measurement after the experiment! The researchers construed these changes as being paranormal events. Also, on some days the participants would ensure they left the room last and that they left a window unlocked. During the night they would come back, enter through the window, bend all of the spoons, and leave. In the morning they would claim that they had done this via psychokinesis during the night.

For the telepathy tasks, the two participants were given an envelope with a target drawing inside it; this was "sealed" using two staples. The participants were left in the room alone so that they could try to "see" what was in the envelope. This was easy—they took out the staples, looked at the picture, and then re-sealed the envelope by placing the staples through the original holes! The participants deliberately got some wrong as 100% accuracy would have been suspicious.

Yes—Randi went to great lengths to show that researchers can be fooled by fraudulent participants, but it is interesting to note the commentary by Thalbourne (1995) about conducting exploratory versus formal research. It would appear that a great deal of the fraud took place when the researchers were simply conducting exploratory research to see what could then be tested more formally in the laboratory.

Smith (1993) investigated how instructions can affect recall of a "psychic" demonstration. People were simply divided into two groups. They watched the same film but one group was told that the film contained trickery; the other that it contained genuine paranormal phenomena. The "trickery" group recalled much more of the film than the "paranormal" group. Wiseman (2001) uses this to explain why fake psychics are eager to encourage people to observe their "abilities"; because people will not be able to recall much about the experience! However, not much is known about *why* this lack of recall occurs (see pages 659–664 for cognitive and personality factors that affect experiences).

Controversies Relating to Ganzfeld Studies of Extra-Sensory Perception

ESP stands for extra-sensory perception, which refers to an ability to acquire knowledge and information without the use of our five main senses (sight, touch, taste, hearing, and smell) or from any previous experiences. It is a general term that encompasses things like telepathy, pre-cognition, and clairvoyant abilities.

One of the classic ways in which ESP has been tested out is with Zener cards using the Ganzfeld procedure (*Ganzfeld* is German for "entire field"). Although there has been a great deal of research into ESP, this section of the book will only focus on what you need to know—Ganzfeld.

In a typical procedure, participants are placed, alone, in a room and allowed to relax on a comfortable chair. Halved ping-pong balls are placed over their eyes and a red light is shone into their face. They also wear headphones, which play white noise so that they experience mild sensory deprivation. In this state, participants are commonly referred to as *receivers*. This procedure tends to last around 30 minutes. At the same time as the receiver is being sensory deprived, a *sender* chooses from the pack of Zener cards and tries mentally to send the shape to the receiver. The receiver then speaks out which shape he or she feels is on the card. The result is then recorded and then when all the cards have been "transmitted" the researchers can calculate whether the amount of correct answers deviates significantly from *chance*. So, for example, if there are 25 cards with five different shapes on (as with the Zener cards) then you should, by chance, get five correct (25 divided by 5).

So, what are the controversies with Ganzfeld–ESP research? The quick answer is: far too many for this book. We will therefore look at a select few that relate to the Ganzfeld–ESP procedure as evidence for something parapsychological or something methodological!

Controversy 1: have early research findings been replicated?

The early research by Rhine (e.g. Rhine & Pratt, 1954) showed that certain individuals had extraordinarily high scores on ESP tasks: as high as 40% accuracy (with chance being at 20%). Many researchers claim that the results of these early trials have "dried-up" because of the tightening of controls and the introduction of Ganzfeld-type procedures. However, as Parker and Brusewitz (2003) point out, this is a myth. In their review of the field, they quote six more case studies of people who scored well above chance in ESP and related tasks. They also state that their list is *not* exhaustive of the field.

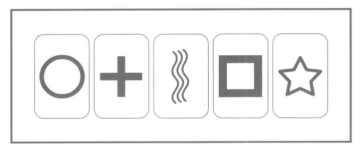

The five Zener cards.

A woman undergoing the Ganzfeld telepathy experiment.

Controversy 2: can the choice of experimental design affect results?

Most research studies into Ganzfeld–ESP use a forced-choice or a free-response design. In a forced-choice design, the participant chooses from a pre-determined set of answers (e.g. Zener cards). However, with a free-response design, participants must simply state what is being transmitted to them without the constraints of pre-determined answers to choose from. It is easy to argue that correct responses will be more likely using a forced-choice design because the targets are known.

Honorton and Ferrari (1989) reviewed forced-choices experiments spanning 52 years via meta-analysis. They found a huge significant effect in favour of ESP, especially if the study had specially selected participants. Milton (1997) conducted a similar analysis of free-response experiments and found a large significant result in the same direction (even when methodologically flawed studies were deleted from the analysis). The results were actually *stronger* for studies that used Ganzfeld procedures. However, with any meta-analysis we must be aware of the **file–drawer effect.**

Controversy 3: can factors bring about positive results without being a case for ESP?

Honorton and the Psychophysical Research Laboratory's Four-factor Model of "success in Ganzfeld" studies

- *Factor 1: prior experience*: Dalton (1997) reports on evidence that participants with prior experience of Ganzfeld–psi tend to produce consistently higher success rates. It is hypothesised that they are better at recognising what appears in the Ganzfeld. The question here is whether participants are screened prior to a Ganzfeld study to see if they have done it before.
- *Factor 2: practice of a mental discipline like meditation*: Dalton (1997) highlights that people who meditate are more likely to have higher success scores in Ganzfeld tasks. This could be due to them being used to attending internal mental processes. Again, how many participants are screened for this pre-study?
- *Factor 3: prior laboratory experience*: Dalton (1997) notes that participants who have had *any* prior experience with laboratory studies (non-Ganzfeld) tend to do better at Ganzfeld tasks. This could be because they experience less stress as the situation is no longer novel and therefore they can focus more on psi activity.
- *Factor 4: feeling/perception preferences on a Myers–Briggs-type indicator*: yet again, Dalton (1997) reports that participants who show a preference for feeling/perception (FP) on this questionnaire tend to generate higher success rates. An FP person is someone who seeks new experiences and is flexible and adaptable in a range of situations. This could help to explain higher success rates because the participant is more motivated as it is a new experience for them.

Therefore, the controversy is based around the experimental design and controlling of potential variables that can "get in the way" of "real" ESP. Research that does not attempt to control these four factors cannot assume cause and effect.

> **KEY TERM**
>
> **File–drawer effect:** the term given to the number of studies that must have been undertaken giving non-significant results that have not been published (and are in a file drawer somewhere) to render a meta-analysis non-significant.

Controversy 4: can the belief of the experimenter affect ESP results?

Parker and Brusewitz (2003, p. 42) stated that this is "perhaps the most reliable and replicable finding in parapsychology." Smith (2003) provides evidence to show that the most successful psi experimenters (e.g. those who report the largest success rates) are more likely to believe in the existence of psi phenomena than experimenters who might be described as sceptical. One idea is that the attitudes towards psi are communicated to the participants, which in turn affects their motivation and subsequent performance on Ganzfeld (or other) tasks.

A startling example of this comes from Wiseman and Schiltz (1997), who set up an experiment during which participants were sometimes watched, via CCTV, by either Wiseman or Schiltz. (The participants didn't know they were being watched.) The participants' galvanic skin response (GSR) was measured throughout. When it was Schiltz (a pro-psi researcher) watching the participants, their GSR was more active than when they were being watched by Wiseman (a psi-sceptic).

In conclusion, Parker and Brusewitz (2003) acknowledged that the experimenter effect cannot explain psi effects if all controls are in place for that study.

Later in this chapter we deal with how cognitive and personality factors may underlie anomalous experiences and these are other controversial ideas that could affect Ganzfeld research.

Controversies solved? Autoganzfeld

Berger and Honorton (1985) attempted to overcome many of the controversies surrounding Ganzfeld research by creating an **autoganzfeld** testing system. Basically, the system automatically randomises the targets and records the responses that eliminate human error and experimenter effects. Also, the entire experimenter procedure is automated, making replication even easier! After Honorton and a range of colleagues ran a series of trials using the system, a review was conducted and the success rate was well above chance, at 33% (Bem & Honorton, 1994).

With the advances of technology, a series of digital autoganzfeld procedures can be used. One in particular was highlighted by Goulding, Westerlund, Parker, and Wackermann (2004) at Göteborg University, Sweden. In this technique, the response from the participant is captured and then automatically stored as a digital audio file. This allows for an examination of the trials in real time. Thus, researchers can examine the lag time between the computer choosing and playing a target event (e.g. a Zener card or film clip) and the participant's response. This was not previously possible, with any degree of certainty. Whether the participant answered after the target was displayed and, if so, how long after, can be checked to see if the timing is consistent throughout the trials.

> **EXAM HINT**
> Make up a mnemonic or draw a mind-map to revise the key issues with the Ganzfeld procedure: replication, forced-choice response bias, prior laboratory experience, feeling/perception personality bias, and the experimenter expectancy effect. Also be able to challenge these criticisms with the autoganzfeld evidence.

> **KEY TERM**
> **Autoganzfeld:** the system automatically randomises the targets and records the responses, thus eliminating human error and experimenter effects. Also, the entire experimenter procedure is automated, making replication even easier!

Psychokinesis (Mind Over Matter)

Psychokinesis (PK) derives from the Greek words *psyche*, meaning "mind", and *kinesis*, which means "movement". Therefore, psychokinesis literally means "mind movement"! This reportedly occurs when the mind is supposed to affect matter, space, time, or energy in a way that cannot be explained by the current laws of physics. One of the most common, well-publicised examples of psychokinesis is spoon-bending.

There are two main types of psychokinesis:

1. *Macro-PK*: the ability to affect objects that can be directly observed (so the effect can be seen), e.g. affecting the throw of a die or spoon-bending.
2. *Micro-PK*: the ability to affect much smaller objects (like a random number generator). Therefore, the effects can be directly observed so the researchers use statistics to see if the results are well above what would be expected by chance.

Spoon bending, as demonstrated here by celebrity psychic Uri Geller, is one of the most well-known examples of psychokinesis.

Significantly less work has been done on PK than on ESP. Nevertheless, there are still controversies surrounding research into PK.

Controversy 1: early research used dice in a potentially biased way

Early researchers were interested in whether participants could influence the throw of dice. For example, participants were asked to influence two dice so that the cumulative score was over 7. If a significant result was obtained (i.e. consistently scoring above 5 hits out of every 12 rolls, which is better than chance), this could easily be used as evidence for PK. Irwin and Watt (2007) reported that when J.B. Rhine obtained results from the above trials that were significantly better than chance, he questioned whether the dice may have been biased. Therefore, he asked participants to try to influence the dice so the cumulative score was less than 7. Furthermore, he ran more trials in which the target was exactly 7. Above-chance performance was seen on all trials, indicating non-biased dice. However, it must be questioned how many other studies have tested for bias in dice.

Also, many critics of PK research noted that early studies allowed subjects to throw the dice from their hand, which could allow them to (somehow) influence the landing of the dice, thus eliminating PK as the source of the influence. This was easily rectified by using a mechanical dice thrower.

Radin and Ferrari (1991) reviewed the field using a meta-analysis of 148 experiments conducted by 52 researchers. In total, this equated to over 2 million dice throws from 2569 participants! The analysis showed a very convincing set of results indicating the potential existence of PK. However, many studies had not used the Rhine protocol outlined above, in which the target score is changed to test for biased dice; only 69 studies did this. Therefore, Radin and Ferrari re-analysed the data for these 69 studies. The results were much weaker than when all studies were used but the overall findings were still statistically significant.

> **EXAM HINT**
>
> Psychokinesis has often been studied through dice throwing. Check you can assess why such studies may lack validity using the problem of biased dice, participants throwing the dice, and the parapsychological experimenter effect!

Controversy 2: potential experimenter effects

As with Ganzfeld research, it could be hypothesised that a researcher's belief or own PK powers can affect the performance of a participant. One way in which this can be tested out is via anpsi—examining if animals have PK powers. Simple procedures can be employed. An electrified grille can be used whereby—randomly—half of it will become active at a given time point. The idea is to test whether the animal can use PK powers to "send" the electric current to the other half of the grille. This might sound highly unusual but Irwin and Watt (2007) report that there has been success using a range of species from cats to guinea pigs to brine shrimps!

One particular study (Schmidt, 1970) using cockroaches yielded strange results that some people use as evidence for an experimenter effect. The results showed a significant effect (as with the other species) but in the *other* direction. That is, the cockroaches sat on the side that became electrified significantly more than chance would suggest! Irwin and Watt (2007) produce an array of possibilities to explain these results, ranging from the cockroaches being masochistic to Schmidt unknowingly affecting the results. In the latter instance, it could be construed that Schmidt might have disliked cockroaches and therefore used his own PK powers to influence which half was electrified (and making it more often than not the half where the poor cockroaches were). This is a long shot, but we have seen that experimenter's beliefs can affect ESP performance. This example, according to Irwin and Watt (2007, p. 100), ". . . illustrates the problematic character of the parapsychological experimenter effect hypothesis."

HOW SCIENCE WORKS: PHENOMENON OR FAKE?

You have the opportunity to research a haunted house—the hauntings having been reported for over 100 years. The reports are of a "grey lady" who comes down the stairs at midnight and then disappears, sometimes leaving a scent of flowers after she has passed by.
    How would you research this phenomenon to find out of it is paranormal or fake?
    You need a hypothesis, a justification for your prediction, and then a procedure. What will you need? How will you do this? What will you record or measure and how? Are there any risks, or ethical issues?
    Why not team up with some classmates and design how this could be done as a piece of scientific, psychological research?

SECTION SUMMARY
Theoretical and Methodological Issues in the Study of Anomalous Experience

Issues of pseudoscience and scientific fraud

❖ Pseudoscience refers to when a belief, for example in some parapsychological phenomenon, is based on a body of knowledge or "evidence" that appears to be scientific.

❖ Science is based on objectivity, falsifiability, and observable behaviour.

❖ Others believe that pseudoscience is based on irrationality and revelation.

❖ Mousseau (2003)—published parapsychological research is less empirical but more falsifiable.

❖ Scientific fraud has plagued the area of parapsychology—Levy tampered with experimental equipment to fake results. Project Alpha exposed researcher flaws when he employed two people who claimed psychokinetic powers.

❖ ESP refers to an ability to acquire knowledge and information without the use of our five main senses (sight, touch, taste, hearing, and smell) or from any previous experiences.

❖ Ganzfeld procedures include a receiver who is sensorily deprived attempting to read the mind of someone else.

❖ Controversies in ESP include non-replication, experimental designs, the Four-factor Model to Success, and experimenter belief.

❖ Non-replication was found not to be true (Parker & Brusewitz, 2003); Milton (1997) reported that Ganzfeld procedures *did* generate significant results more often; Honorton's Four Factors to success are prior experience, meditation, prior laboratory experiences, and feeling/perception personality type; Smith (2003) reported that pro-psi experimenters yield more positive results.

❖ Psychokinesis literally means mind movement! This reportedly occurs when the mind can supposedly affect matter, space, time, or energy in a way that cannot be explained by the current laws of physics.

❖ Controversies in psychokinesis include loaded dice and experimenter effects.

Controversies relating to Ganzfeld studies of ESP

Studies of psychokinesis

FACTORS UNDERLYING ANOMALOUS EXPERIENCE

Cognitive, Personality, and Biological Factors Underlying Anomalous Experience

Cognitive

One of the many cognitive factors that can affect people's experiences of things anomalous is given the title **sheep–goat effect**. People who believe paranormal activity to be real are labelled sheep; disbelievers are labelled goats. This type of cognitive bias has been shown to affect people's judgements on paranormal activity. In a simple design, Jones and Russell (1980) got sheep and goats to observe a demonstration of ESP. One group of each type observed a "successful" demonstration whereas the others witnessed an unsuccessful demonstration. All were then asked to recall the demonstration. The sheep who observed the unsuccessful demonstration tended to distort their memories by recalling that the demonstration had been successful; goats were much better at recalling what actually happened irrespective of whether the demonstration was successful or not.

Wiseman, Smith, and Wiseman (1995) examined the role of eyewitness testimony further by examining people's recollection of a séance. Over a series of three séances, 25 participants completed a short questionnaire prior to séance that highlighted whether they believed paranormal activity to be genuine or not. The

KEY TERM

Sheep–goat effect: refers to belief in the paranormal. A sheep is a believer and a goat is a non-believer.

participants sat in a darkened room with various objects in it on a table at the centre (e.g. a bell, a slate, and a book—all treated with luminous paint). The medium, played by an actor, first got participants to focus on a luminous ball suspended above the centre table. Then he got them to try to move the ball alongside the other objects. In reality, nothing ever moved. However, participants were asked to complete a questionnaire after the séance. In total, about 27% of participants reported something that moved. One key finding from this group was that 14% of disbelievers claimed that an object had moved compared with 40% of believers. Also, 20% of believers thought that something genuine had occurred; this was 0% in the disbeliever group.

? Why do you think so many people reported movement?

Finally, witness reliability is not the only issue. Fiorino and Leone (2001) assessed the reliability of a witness to a classic UFO case in Trans-en-Provence in France. There was some very strong physical evidence that something had occurred (e.g. soil samples showing great changes and a "landing site"). However, witness reliability was questioned by French ufologists. Originally, the key witness (an Italian) had been questioned in French, a language in which he was far from fluent. However, it was later discovered that the contradictions in what the witness told the investigators were the result of lack of care and misinterpretations on the part of the investigators. The witness' supposed comments about "hoaxing" the case were simply witty remarks turned into something more concrete by linguistic misunderstandings on the part of the investigators. Therefore, it is not only the "witness" of anomalistic activity that requires careful investigation; the people doing the investigation could be just as biased!

Cognitive biases can also affect people's belief in horoscopes (Wiseman & Smith, 2002). Participants were simply asked to read and judge four horoscopes. Two of these were labelled "reading from *your* birth sign" whereas the other two were labelled "reading from *another* birth sign". These were counterbalanced for each participant, but all participants were given the same four horoscopes. They simply indicated how accurate and how general they believed each horoscope to be. Prior to this, all 80 participants completed the Belief in Astrology Questionnaire to work out if they were a believer or disbeliever. One main cognitive bias emerged—believers gave much lower generality scores than disbelievers on *all* horoscopes and higher accuracy ratings. Therefore, it would appear that cognitive biases play a role in horoscope readings.

False memories could also affect anomalous experiences (Wilson & French, 2006). In another straightforward design, 100 participants completed questionnaires measuring sheep–goat propensity, dissociativity (a defence mechanism whereby anxiety-provoking thoughts and ideas are separated from the rest of our psyche), anomalous experiences, and a News Coverage Questionnaire. The latter was used to assess false memories. The participants were asked a series of questions about real footage they might have seen (e.g. Twin Towers, Challenger Space Shuttle Disaster) and about one occasion for which CCTV footage was *never* taken (Bali bombings). They were asked where they were at the time, where did you see the footage, etc. Remarkably, 36 participants stated that they saw the non-existent footage and all but one of these could easily state where they had seen it, whether it was black and white or colour footage, and what language it was in! There were several predictors for being part of this group of

EXAM HINT

Use your knowledge of eyewitness testimony from your AS-level studies to assess the problems of evidence from witnesses of parapsychological phenomena.

36: more likely to be a sheep, more likely to believe in anomalous experiences, and higher levels of dissociation. Again, this is evidence that cognitive factors really can affect recall of "events".

Personality

There are arguments that the personality of a believer/experiencer is different from that of a non-believer/non-experiencer. One such personality trait that could affect experiences and beliefs is **fantasy proneness** (FP). This type of personality was proposed by Wilson and Barber (1983), who initially examined 27 excellent hypnotic females and a control group of 26 females who weren't. An excellent hypnotic subject is one who can be easily hypnotised. When examining childhood experiences, the majority of the FP group thought that their toys had feelings and emotions, they assumed the roles of fantasy characters during play, and they were praised by parents for fantasy play as a child. These differences also extended into adulthood. The FP group were more likely to spend more time fantasising during the day, experience fantasies as "real as real", have psychic abilities, and experience apparitions. In a review of studies that examined FP and paranormal experiences linked to UFOs and aliens, Roberts (1997) noted that at the time three main studies had been conducted (Ring & Rosing, 1990; Bartholomew, Basterfield, & Howard, 1991; Spanos, Cross, Dickson, & DuBreuil, 1993), of which only one had noted any significant link to FP. It is therefore unclear as to the role of FP in experiences. Nonetheless, Parnell (1998) concluded that:

> *It is impossible to say if these characteristics were prior and possibly pre-disposing characteristics for reporting such an experience or, at least in some cases, could have been characteristic exhibited subsequent to, or even a consequence of, such an experience. (Parnell, 1998, p.163–164)*

When you are reading the rest of this section, ask yourself "Are the findings cause or effect?"

One contemporary study into FP happened in Australia. Gow, Lurie, Coppin, Popper, Powell, and Basterfield (2001) examined the prevalence of FP in a sample of people who claimed to have seen a UFO or experienced an alien abduction. These were compared with a control group. Participants completed a range of questionnaires to measure childhood memories and imaginings, paranormal beliefs, and UFO experiences. The findings showed that reporting any type of UFO experience was linked to heightened levels of FP and stronger beliefs in paranormal activity. However, as the measures were taken post-event, there is no way of clearly seeing of the FP caused the experience or the experience caused an FP!

Having a creative personality has been linked to anomalous experiences and beliefs. A creative personality is one where the person is imaginative, artistic, and inventive. Thalbourne (2001) reviewed the findings linking this type of

An individual exhibiting fantasy proneness is more likely to believe in paranormal activity, and would be more likely, for example, to report having seen a UFO.

KEY TERM

Fantasy proneness: a personality trait where a person is prone to fantasising and having a vivid imagination.

EXAM HINT

Make sure you can explain fantasy proneness and how this personality variable may account for parapsychological experience.

personality and belief in the paranormal. A total of 15 studies were uncovered and all showed the same positive result—those who have a creative personality are more likely to believe that paranormal activity is real (13/15 were significant results). The idea could be that people who think creatively are more likely to accept experiences that are "strange" and try to work out what happened—they are more open to different explanations. Most of the studies had been conducted on students so there may be limited generalisability.

Other research has investigated the role of personality in ESP–Ganzfeld sessions. Parra and Villaneuva (2003) tested 30 subjects, all of whom completed a simple measure of personality: namely the Eysenck Personality Inventory (EPI) and a Pre-Ganzfeld Questionnaire. The latter questionnaire measures relaxation, mood, motivation, and expectation of success. The EPI measures level of extraversion, a personality trait characterised by being outgoing and seeking new experiences. It was therefore predicted that extraverts would manifest psi better than introverts because they respond much better to new stimuli. Villaneuva was always the "sender" of the message and each participant had to "guess" a target photograph that was being sent. The results clearly demonstrated that extraverts scored significantly better at ESP than the introverts. There was no effect for relaxation, mood, motivation, or expectation. From this, we can see that some results from ESP–Ganzfeld studies could be "contaminated" by the personality of the receiver; in this case, extraverted participants. However, some parapsychologists would see it as evidence that only certain types of people are receptive to ESP. The choice is yours!

In a larger sample of students ($n = 107$), Rattet and Bursik (2001) similarly noted that extraversion played a role in paranormal research. Nevertheless, the findings differed from Parra and Villaneuva's. Rattet and Bursik (2001) concluded that extraversion linked to pre-cognitive experience and not paranormal belief. That is, extraverted participants were more likely to have had some form of pre-cognitive paranormal experience even though their paranormal beliefs were the same as the rest of the sample. This simply indicated that the relationship between personality and paranormal beliefs and experiences is a complex one that warrants more serious research.

Biological

[?] Do you think paranormal experiences could be explained by biological factors?

KEY TERM

Electrohypersensitivity: electromagnetic "pollution" causes anomalous experiences, especially ghosts and alien visitations.
Temporal Lobe Lability Hypothesis: an idea that stimulation of the temporal lobes of the brain cause anomalistic experiences.

Two main ideas link biology to paranormal experiences: temporal lobe lability and **electrohypersensitivity**. As will become apparent, both may be linked. The **Temporal Lobe Lability Hypothesis** was proposed by Persinger (1983). He had noted that there appeared to be a link between electromagnetic energy and paranormal experiences. He investigated the apparent psychological effects of exposure to electromagnetism and believed that it affected brain function, especially the temporal lobes (the bits of your brain near the temples on the side of your head).

The temporal lobe has the lowest electrical output, according to Persinger, and so it would be affected by electromagnetism the most. Direct stimulation of the temporal lobe would "modify consciousness, perceptual processing and memory" (Persinger, 1983, p. 261). Any perceptual episode happening during this time would be vivid in relation to normal functioning. The temporal lobe houses memories and fantasies so, if over-stimulated, people could have strange occurrences. Persinger produced many papers showing differing levels of correlation between temporal lobe stimulation and paranormal beliefs and experiences. Nonetheless, correlations do not state cause and effect.

All of his research culminated in claims that Persinger could "induce" an alien abduction experience in the laboratory by stimulating the temporal lobes. Blackmore (1994) tested this claim for a *Horizon* programme on the BBC. She wore a special helmet that directly stimulated the temporal lobes via magnetic fields. In a procedure similar to Ganzfeld, Blackmore was in a dimly lit room with ping-pong balls over her eyes. After about 10 minutes, it felt like two hands had grabbed her and were pulling her upwards followed by having her leg pulled, distorted, and dragged up to the ceiling!

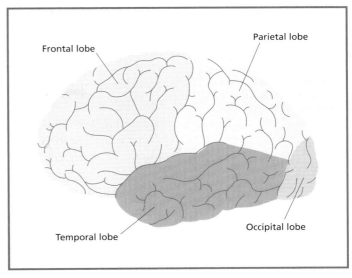

Stimulation of the temporal lobes may bring about anomalistic experiences.

Admittedly, Blackmore knew that her experience had happened due to the temporal lobe stimulation, but what if people did not know the cause? Stimulation of the temporal lobe would probably not be the first thing on their list trying to explain an anomalous experience.

Blackmore and Cox (2000) tested out the Temporal Lobe Lability Hypothesis in 12 people claiming alien abduction. They were compared with 12 matched controls and a group of students. All the participants completed the Personal Philosophy Inventory, which is a questionnaire designed to measure Temporal Lobe Lability. Questions were also asked about sleep paralysis. In general, the abductees scored *lower* on measure of temporal lobe lability. However, for the main features of sleep paralysis (waking paralysed, pressure on chest, and sensed presence) the abductee group scored significantly higher. Despite a small sample, the findings point in the direction of alien abduction being more linked to a sleep paralysis episode than temporal lobe lability. This finding is echoed by Spanos et al. (1993), who discovered no difference between an alien abduction group and control group on a questionnaire measuring temporal lobe lability.

Linked to this is the idea of electrohypersensitivity. Early research (e.g. Budden, 1994) gathered together case studies and anecdotal evidence linking a range of electromagnetic sources to apparitions and alien abduction experiences. Many people who claim visitations appeared to live near electricity sub-stations, mobile-phone transmitters, pylons, or television masts. This was due to electromagnetism affecting the individual in question in a similar way to Persinger's ideas. Therefore, electromagnetic "pollution" as such was causing anomalous experiences, especially ghosts and alien visitation. Taking this further, Budden (1995) explained that certain people who are "targeted" for abduction or who experience a lot of ghostly visitations are electrically hypersensitive. That is, they are more likely to be affected by electromagnetic pollution, as highlighted above. However, Budden never tested out these ideas and

Budden (1994) suggested that electromagnetic pollution may have been a causal factor in the increased number sightings of UFOs and paranormal experiences reported by those living close to electromagnetic sources.

EXAM HINT
Use the methodological criticism that research is retrospective (conducted afterwards) to criticise Budden's (1995) electrohypersensitivity theory.

simply stuck to producing endless case study accounts of the after-effects. The ideas were not tested experimentally or prospectively to "predict" visitations and visions.

Jawer (2006) lends some support to the electrohypersensitivity angle. In a study involving 112 participants, 62 of whom were "sensitives" and 50 constituted a control group, those classified as "sensitive" reported significantly more allergies and electrical sensitivity than the controls; therefore, the groupings appeared to be correct. When asked about apparitional and psi perceptions, the "sensitives" group reported significantly more apparitions and objects moving than the controls. Interestingly, the "sensitives" group had been struck by lightning and affected electrical appliances significantly more often than controls. This, of course, hints at a link between electrohypersensitivity and apparitions that requires further investigation to pinpoint the exact mechanisms that could be causing this.

Overall, it can be clearly seen that cognitive, personality, and biological factors affect people's anomalistic experiences and beliefs, which need to be taken into account when executing any research in this area.

HOW SCIENCE WORKS: DO YOU BELIEVE?

How many of us actually do believe in the paranormal? You could do a survey to find out, perhaps comparing beliefs of your own age group with those of your parents. You could do this quickly and easily by planning a yes/no tick-box set of questions, all starting with "Do you believe . . . ". The list could include the following; any superstitions, extra-sensory perception, out-of-body experiences, psychic healing, psychic mediums, pre-cognition, and so on.

You might trial your questions on someone who has not studied this topic to see if the terms you use are understood. Doing such a pilot study would make your findings more valid. If you scored the answers from each participant you could then produce data showing the range of yes and no answers for each age group as well as totals and mean scores. You could then look at your data, decide how best to present it descriptively, and ask yourself what it tells you.

Functions of Paranormal and Related Beliefs, Including Their Cultural Significance

Functions of paranormal beliefs

This is a relatively new line of research in the field of anomalistic psychology. It attempts to explain the reasons behind why people believe in paranormal activity. On pages 659–664 we discuss the cognitive and personality factors that can affect an experience of an anomalous nature.

One of the main ideas in this area follows one of the general assumptions of psychodynamic psychology—childhood experiences mould adult behaviour and beliefs. Irwin (1992) first developed a coherent idea about this potential link when he reported a link between childhood trauma (e.g. abuse) and a belief in the paranormal. The early idea linked this back to fantasy proneness (Wilson & Barber, 1983) and we will visit this in more depth on page 661. Irwin's idea follows the argument that childhood trauma leads to childhood fantasy (e.g. high imagination, prone to fantasy play, etc.) as a coping mechanism. This manifests itself as either a paranormal experience or a stronger belief in paranormal activities during adolescence and adulthood. As with many things psychodynamic, the idea is that this happens unconsciously as the traumatic events are being dealt with down there. He called this the Psychodynamic Functions Hypothesis.

 Can you think of any ways that paranormal and related beliefs may be adaptive?

Lawrence, Edwards, Barraclough, Church, and Hetherington (1995) tested out this idea using 80 students from the University of Edinburgh. They completed measures on traumatic childhood experiences, belief in the paranormal, and childhood fantasy. The initial correlations clearly showed some relationship between childhood trauma and paranormal *experience*, and also with childhood fantasy. The correlation between childhood trauma and paranormal *belief* just missed out on significance ($P < 0.06$). When sources of childhood trauma were analysed individually, the only factor to be significantly related to paranormal belief was moving home (childhood abuse just missed being significant). As a result of this, Lawrence et al. modified the theory by stating childhood trauma can affect paranormal *experience*, which in turn affects paranormal *beliefs*.

Another separate idea was that paranormal beliefs were affected by locus of control. Rotter (1954) defined two types: internal and external. Internal locus of control refers to when you feel in control of yourself and your life. External locus of control refers to when you feel that other people, a higher authority, or the environment control your decisions for you. Both of these can be used to explain paranormal beliefs. Internal locus of control may explain belief in telepathy and clairvoyance because this is caused by one's own will. External locus of control may explain belief in superstitions and spiritualism because these are fate based and not caused by one's own will.

Dag (1999) tested out this idea on 350 students at a Turkish University. The participants completed questionnaire-based measures of paranormal beliefs and internal–external locus of control. It was reported that internal locus of control was strongly correlated with belief in chance and fate and the overall paranormal belief score. For the former, this went against expectation as fate is an *external* process not *internal*. External locus of control correlated strongly with the overall paranormal belief score, a belief in chance and fate (as predicted) and belief in witchcraft (as predicted too). Therefore, currently, it would appear that external locus of control is a function of paranormal beliefs rather than internal.

> **?** What are the drawbacks of questionnaire-based research?

Both of these approaches have now been merged to give a broader theory as to the functions of paranormal beliefs. It was Irwin (2005) who proposed that paranormal beliefs arise because of a lack of control brought about not just by childhood abuse/trauma but *any* childhood experience characterised by a lack of control (e.g. having older siblings, having authoritarian parents, moving house a lot).

Watts, Watson, and Wilson (2007) tested out this new theory merging childhood experiences and lack of control (e.g. external locus of control). A total of 127 students from the University of Edinburgh completed a range of questionnaires including ones on paranormal beliefs and perceived childhood control. As predicted by Irwin's merged theory, when belief in the paranormal increased, perceived childhood control decreased. The usual correlation between paranormal beliefs and external locus of control was reported but it did not reach significance.

Therefore, the Psychodynamic Functions Hypothesis and subsequent development of it (Irwin, 2002; 2005) has some solid evidence behind it. Traumatic events (and remember, this is not just referring to abuse) lead to a sense

> **EXAM HINT**
>
> Make sure you can explain how a lack of control in childhood has been linked to paranormal belief. Assess this relationship using:
>
> - the lack of significance of research evidence
> - criticisms of correlational research, i.e. lack of cause and effect, and the involvement of other factors.

EXAM HINT

Make sure you can explain the Psychodynamic Functions Hypothesis, i.e. that a possible function of paranormal belief is to avoid facing up to traumatic childhood events. Assess this factor in relation to other factors such as social loneliness, fantasy proneness, attachment style, and coping strategies.

of insecurity and helplessness. This in turn leaves these children with a need to control unpredictable life events using a fantasy-driven unconscious mechanism to cope with everyday uncertainty. This simply manifests itself as a belief in the paranormal in adolescence and adulthood.

Rogers, Qualter, Phelps, and Gardner (2006) investigated whether *how* we cope with traumatic events affects our belief in the paranormal. As highlighted above, the Psychodynamic Functions Hypothesis implies that belief in the paranormal is an *avoidant* coping strategy to deal with unpleasant events. However, ignoring the traumatic event is more of a *passive* coping strategy that is "at odds" with Irwin's (2002) original idea that paranormal beliefs provide us with a "sense of mastery" over unpredictable events. This is obviously an *active* coping strategy. Therefore, Rogers et al. wanted to examine whether active-behavioural coping (when people seek advice or make plans), active-cognitive coping (when people look at past experiences or positively self-talk), or avoidant coping strategies (when people deny and repress events) affect paranormal beliefs.

Rogers et al. (2006) examined these coping strategies by getting 253 participants to complete a set of questionnaires. These included measures on paranormal beliefs, a measure of coping strategies, and one on demographics. After analysis, none of the coping strategies could explain paranormal beliefs. In fact, believers in the paranormal were just as likely to seek advice, positively self-talk, and/or deny events as paranormal sceptics. Therefore coping strategy could not explain belief in the paranormal.

Rogers, Qualter, and Phelps (2007) then took a different avenue of thought. They were interested in whether loneliness and/or attachment style affected paranormal belief. The former was chosen as there is evidence suggesting that people who have experienced childhood trauma are more likely to experience feelings of loneliness in adulthood, especially when seeking partners. The latter was chosen because attachment style can have a bearing on future relationships as adults. By attachment style we mean the quality of relationship with a primary caregiver as a child and its subsequent effect on adult behaviour. These have been split into three distinct groups: secure (more intimate in relationships as adults), avoidant (mistrustful and shun intimacy as adults), and anxious/ambivalent (want intimacy but fear rejection simultaneously). The last two styles can be grouped as insecure attachments. The *avoidant* attachment style may be able to explain paranormal beliefs because it follows the Psychodynamic Functions Hypothesis idea that we ignore and *avoid* dealing with the traumatic events of childhood. This then manifests itself as belief in the paranormal.

Over 250 participants from a range of backgrounds completed questionnaires measuring paranormal beliefs, childhood trauma, loneliness, and attachment style. One of the first clear findings supports the Psychodynamic Functions Hypothesis: childhood trauma was the strongest predictor of paranormal beliefs. Other factors that also significantly predicted belief in the paranormal were proneness to fantasy and social loneliness. Although there was a trend towards insecurely attached individuals believing more in the paranormal, the data suggested that it did not *cause* it.

Overall, it would appear that individuals who experience some form of trauma in childhood are more likely to believe in things paranormal. This appears to be linked to lack of control in childhood that manifests itself as endorsing paranormal beliefs to get back some of the control over unpredictable events.

Social loneliness and proneness to fantasy also appear to be linked to beliefs, whereas, at the moment, coping strategies and attachment style do not. It is clear that much more research needs to be conducted in this area to fully understand all of these links. One drawback from this line of research is that all studies are using questionnaires so we cannot rule out demand characteristics, social desirability, and faulty memories affecting the findings.

Cultural significance

It would appear that the functions of belief in the paranormal are *not* culturally absolute, but culturally relative. Therefore, one culture may perceive a paranormal activity to be that—paranormal—yet another sees it as a human-based skill.

There are many examples of simple cross-cultural differences in things like **superstition**. Some people in the UK are afraid of Friday 13th and believe that bad things may happen. For the Spanish, Friday 13th poses no such problems but Tuesday 13th does!

Jahoda (1969) highlights research with a members of a tribe in New Guinea. Researchers were interested in the transmission of paranormal and supernatural beliefs. They examined beliefs in ghosts, sorcery, and a huge monster called *marsalai*. Whiting, who conducted the initial research, was convinced that it was a simple case of *stimulus generalisation*. That is, the New Guinea peoples were simply generalising fear from *real* dangers onto *paranormal* dangers. For example, children are taught to respect the property of others or be punished by its owner, not to go alone to the swamp otherwise a wild pig or crocodile will attack you, and boys are told not to stare at the genitals of females or they will be punished. Therefore, the fear of real punishment generalises to fear of paranormal activity. This could then be applied to any culture to see if it can explain common beliefs about paranormal activity.

Sleep paralysis is a good example of how the same phenomenon can produce different cultural labelling and explanations. Sleep paralysis occurs when a person is simultaneously awake and asleep during the rapid eye-movement (REM) phase of sleep. The person can look around the room but cannot move his or her body and certainly cannot speak (the author has first-hand experience of this). In addition, it would appear that a sensed presence is felt in the room that usually touches or sits on the person having the paralysis. Many cultures see this as being paranormal in nature as highlighted below.

In Thai and Cambodian culture, the experience is called "pee umm", which describes when ghostly figures hold you down during sleep. In Southern China (Hmong culture) it is referred to as "dab tsog", which means "crushing demon". In Hungary, the experience is definitely more paranormal as they tend to blame witches, fairies, and demon lovers. The Kurdish people keep the theme of ghosts and evil spirits but believe it only happens to people who have done something bad. In New Guinea, the experience is attributed to "Suk Ninmyo", which comes from sacred trees. These trees need human essence to survive and they get this

According to Jahoda (1969), the supernatural beliefs held by the tribes-people of New Guinea demonstrated a generalising of real dangers onto paranormal dangers.

KEY TERM

Superstition: a belief or notion that is not based on reason or knowledge that highlights the "significance" of some behaviour to the individual.

CASE STUDY: THUNDERBIRDS

Rice and Haralambos (2000) report an interesting case of a schoolboy in Minneapolis, USA, who reported seeing thunderbirds—mythical birds.

His teachers were concerned that this was evidence of mental disorder, as hallucinations are a possible sign of, for example, schizophrenia, although assessment by a psychiatrist found no abnormality. However this issue was solved when the boy's parents came into school and told the staff that such sightings were welcome—and an anthropologist confirmed their attitude as correct. The boy's family were Chippewa and in their culture seeing thunderbirds is an honour, something to be proud and not ashamed of.

What one cannot know is whether the boy really believed he had seen the visions, as in confusing fantasy and reality, was using the thunderbirds as a symbol of some personal psychological dilemma, or was just making it all up.

---

during the night; sleep paralysis occurs when the human wakes unnaturally during feeding. The Turks call it "karabasan", which is a creature that attacks people during the night by sitting on their chest and stealing their breath. Finally, in Mexico, the experience is put down to the spirit of a dead person sitting on you. As can be seen, there are lots of different explanations for the same phenomenon.

Irwin (1993) reviewed the field on culture and paranormal beliefs. Studies have been rather mixed in terms of belief. For example, some studies have shown black Americans to have weaker belief in ESP and pre-cognition than white Americans, whereas other studies have found the complete opposite! Irwin commented on a series of studies using the Paranormal Belief Scale, which was standardised on Louisiana university students and therefore is used as a comparison group for other cultures. When this has been done, Finnish students report lower belief scores for witchcraft and superstitions but higher on extraordinary life forms. A similar pattern of low belief in witchcraft and superstitions was found in a sample of Polish students, who instead had stronger beliefs in psi (e.g. ESP and PK). Finally, Australian students had stronger beliefs in spiritualism and pre-cognition. Therefore, Irwin concludes:

> . . . the level of paranormal belief in an individual is in part a function of that person's broader cultural environment. For example, there may be some variation in the extent to which a given paranormal belief is integrated into mainstream culture . . . (Irwin, 1993, p. 11)

This can be highlighted by examining the narratives involved in near-death experiences (see page 680). This could help show how much mainstream culture could be integrated into the experience. Roe (2001) noted that there are some distinct cultural differences when examining the content of reports. For example, North American Indians include snakes, eagles, arrows, and moccasins in their reports whereas Asian Indians report being "sent back to live" as there had been some paranormal bureaucratic error! In terms of religiosity, Roe noted something rather intriguing: when the encounter involves a "God", Hindus do not report seeing Jesus and Christians do not report seeing a Hindu deity.

In a more recent study, Belanti, Perera, and Jagadheesan (2008) examined near-death experiences in the Mapuche, Hawaii, Israel, Thailand, India, and many African regions. There were some marked similarities between the Mapuche people (Southern Chile and Argentina) and Hawaiians in terms of landmarks like volcanoes and the absence of a "life-review" during the event. Both the Thai and Indian narratives had similarities in terms of *no* tunnels, *no* landmarks, and *no* visions of light. There were strong religious undertones to these narratives reflecting the cultural norm (for more about the "standard" near death experience, see page 680 onwards).

In attempting to explain the cultural significance of the narratives, Belanti et al. (2008) examined these cultural "norms". For the Mapuche, as noted above, many narratives featured volcanoes where "dead people" were seen (friends, family, etc.). In their culture, the Mapuche believe that life continues after death in a body that is an exact double, preserving the characteristics of the individual. Also, one narrative featured a German man, which might at first appear odd. However, the area of Chile from which the narrative came was once a German colony and it has therefore affected their culture somewhat. Belanti concluded that ". . . the variability across cultures is most likely due to . . . cultural experiences, religion [and] education . . ." (Belanti, et al., p. 121).

> **EXAM HINT**
>
> Note that cultural relativism means understanding behaviour in the context of a particular culture. This is very important with paranormal belief because it is so culturally relative. In order to illustrate the cultural significance of paranormal beliefs, make sure you have examples of how they differ across cultures.

The Psychology of Deception and Self-deception, Superstition, and Coincidence

Deception and self-deception

Deception

We covered scientific fraud on pages 652–653 Therefore, you are familiar with the cases of Walter Levy (Rhine, 1975) and Project Alpha (Randi, 1983). In these cases, Levy was using **deception** to produce higher success statistics and Randi deliberately asked his two accomplices to deceive the researchers throughout the project.

Hyman (1989, p. 133) defines deception as ". . . an agent acts or speaks so as to induce a false belief in a target or victim". It is clear that, in the previously discussed cases, Levy and Randi used deception.

Delanoy (1987) revealed the deceptive nature of Tim, a 17-year-old who claimed he could bend metal via psychokinesis. As with much research in this area, the first "trials" were very informal and Tim managed to bend several objects, although not when he was being observed. A different parapsychologist tested Tim on an alleged fraud-proof psychokinesis machine and he passed some trials. However, it was later revealed that the researchers had not checked that all the controls on the machine were functional. In a separate incident, Tim claimed to have bent an object in a sealed plastic cube. Later analysis showed it had been tampered with. However, Delanoy persevered with Tim because parapsychologists "need" their participants and in the end admitted that she was probably biased towards him. In some of the final trials, Tim was recorded using a hidden camera, which quickly revealed that he was using blatant trickery. Confronted with the evidence Tim simply confessed to deception—he had practised conjuring since childhood and had actually offered his services to see if he could deceive the researchers.

Other factors can be used to explain why some psychics deceive. One of the strongest incentives is to make money. However, Wiseman (2001) notes that some faith healers assure people that they never accept money for their services to show that there is no motive to deceive. In cases like this, though, people later appear compelled to pay. Morris (1986) noted that other factors could lead to deception. These include personal fame, a desire to look socially helpful, or simply raising self-esteem. In addition, people may deceive to simply have some fun! This has

> **KEY TERM**
>
> **Deception:** Hyman (1989, p. 133) defines deception as ". . . an agent acts or speaks so as to induce a false belief in a target or victim."

This fake photograph of fairies, taken in July 1917, deceived the world for over 60 years, until the 1980s. The fairies were actually drawings, secured in the ground with hat pins. It looks as though the young girls deceived people just to have some fun!

been used to explain why Elsie Wright and Frances Griffiths deceived the world for 66 years with their Cottingley Fairies photographs (which were revealed to be cut-outs fastened to the ground with hat pins).

Wiseman (2001) discusses many examples in which psychics easily deceive their observers. One way is simply to produce the behaviours that an observer tells you are believable. An example would be that an observer believes that objects can move only short distances via psychokinesis. Therefore, the fake psychic simply does that and is somewhat relieved that the observer did not want a levitating table!

A second example, according to Wiseman (2001), is just as straightforward. Some fake psychics or mediums simply say that they have little control over their abilities. This can be used as a clear explanation when nothing happens or no "messages" come through. It is common for the observer to simply accept that as the explanation when in fact they could just have been deceived.

A final example from Wiseman (2001) highlights that the simple use of body language and the positioning of hands, eye contact, etc. can essentially "make" an observer look one way while the clear trickery is happening elsewhere.

To end this section we will look at a case reported by Randi (1982). A certain Dr Lincoln at London Hospital Medical College investigated claims from the Philippines that psychic surgery was being used with great success. He analysed the removed tissue from a patient who had undergone the psychic surgery and found that the blood sample was from a cow and that the supposed tumour was in fact chicken intestine. When confronted with the evidence, the psychic surgeon reported that it is a well-known fact that, during the procedure, supernatural forces change the tumour into something else once it has been removed from the body.

Self-deception

Self-deception is when we mislead ourselves to accept as true what is most likely false. Some psychologists believe it is a way we can justify false beliefs. When it comes to researchers in the field of anomalistic psychology, Gilovich (1993) identifies three ways in which self-deception can occur:

1. Misinterpretation of data: seeing patterns that simply aren't there.
2. Misinterpretation of incomplete or even unrepresentative data: focusing on data that confirm an idea while ignoring or not seeking data that go against an idea (see also page 673 for Lehmann's idea of selective forgetting in superstitious individuals).
3. Having a tendency to be uncritical of research that supports an idea while being highly critical of research that does not support it.

A quick-and-easy solution proposed by Gilovich is that research should be clearly controlled, double-blind in procedure (so participants and the research team conducting the study do not know the true aim of it), randomised where possible, replicable as a result, and published for anyone to read. Although this might appear to be a tall order, the three points listed above would no longer be an issue.

? Can you think of some examples of self-deception?

Another key issue in relation to Gilovich's idea is that it is impossible to run studies that are controlled, randomised, etc. when you are dealing with spontaneous events like ghosts, apparitions, alien abduction accounts, UFO sightings, and poltergeists. Therefore, if we agree with his ideas, all of this research could be tainted by self-deception.

In addition, Irwin (2002) admits that the concept of self-deception is "fuzzy". He states that many psychologists agree it to be the acceptance of a belief in a self-serving way by people who have a motivation to believe in whatever is under investigation. Therefore, there is a tendency for criticisms to focus on the self-deception of researchers! However, Irwin decided to test if there was a relationship between self-deception and belief in paranormal activity in a group of students.

He got 30 Australian university students to complete a range of questionnaires including the Self-Deception Questionnaire and the Revised Paranormal Belief Scale. From the latter a participant was given two scores: a Traditional Paranormal Belief (TPB) score, which looked at belief on witchcraft, the devil, etc., and a New Age Philosophy (NAP) score, which looked at belief in parapsychology, reincarnation, and astrology.

The results showed that TPB scores did not correlate with self-deception but that NAP scores did. That is, beliefs involving NAP are related to self-deception. Intriguingly, the correlation between the two went in the opposite direction than predicted. That is, ". . . people who strongly endorse New Age Philosophy are inclined to avoid self-deception" (Irwin, 2002, p. 84). However, as it was a correlational design, Irwin pointed out that nothing here is causal; the two measures are merely related to each other. Replications of this study using a larger sample would be ideal, as would a similar study using paranormal researchers as participants to see whether a similar trend is reported.

Superstition

Superstition is defined as a belief or notion that is not based on reason or knowledge that highlights the "significance" of some behaviour to the individual. Jahoda (1969) summarises a range of potential explanations for being superstitious. We can all list a whole range of superstitions including never walking under ladders, saluting a magpie, and even wearing lucky underpants! But why do we have such beliefs?

Skinner's view

As you know, Skinner was the proponent of operant conditioning, which is based around the consequences of behaviour. In general terms, we are more likely to repeat a behaviour if it is reinforced and less likely to repeat a behaviour if it is punished. The reward angle can be used to explain why people become superstitious.

One of the main assumptions of the behaviourism is that general laws govern all behaviour (e.g.

Superstitions

Bringers of bad luck:
- Friday 13th
- breaking a mirror
- walking under a ladder
- opening an umbrella indoors
- a black cat crossing one's path

Bringers of good luck:
- finding a horseshoe
- wearing a rabbit's foot
- having a bird poop on you
- finding a four-leafed clover
- a black cat crossing one's path

This humorous photo from the 1950s demonstrates how superstitious beliefs are carried through from generation to generation. The original caption read, "Hoodoos, jinxes, and superstitions apparently mean very little to television actress Joi Lansing. Not content with tempting the fates by breaking a mirror and sitting beneath a ladder, she adds insult to injury by performing the daring deeds on Friday the 13th."

rewards), irrespective of species. Therefore, the behaviour of animals in terms of learning can be applied to that of a human. Bearing this in mind, Skinner (1948) published a paper simply entitled *Superstition in the pigeon*. The experimental procedure for the Skinner (1948) study was simple yet effective. A total of eight hungry pigeons were placed in their own Skinner boxes for just a few minutes per day. The received food pellets every 15 seconds regardless of what they were doing at the time. This procedure lasted for several days. Two observers noted the pigeon's behaviours. Towards the end of the conditioning phase, the length of time between each delivery of pellets increased. Alarmingly, six of the eight pigeons began to show rather repetitive behaviour in between the delivery of food pellets. These included head tossing, pendulum-type swinging of the head, hopping, and turning in an anti-clockwise circle. The observers had noted that these behaviours had not been seen prior to the study. It was also noted that the behaviours were nothing to do with the food appearing (i.e. they were not performed straight after the pigeons received food). When the gap between the delivery of food was increased to 60 seconds, the pigeons exhibited frantic versions of their behaviour until food appeared. Skinner concluded that the pigeons were showing these behaviours as if the delivery of food depended on them doing it (even though in reality it did not!). He believed that this is how human superstitions evolve: we keep a series of behaviours going until we reach a reward (e.g. not walking under a ladder means we get to work safely).

This approach to explaining superstitions has evidence to suggest that "random" rewarding leads to such a notion. However, on the one hand, critics will be quick to point out that elements like not walking under a ladder or not stepping on cracks in the pavement rarely lead to such an observable reward (such as with the pigeons getting food). Hence, it is not a complete explanation. On the other hand, behaviourists would be just as quick to point out that the reward for not walking under a ladder has simply not been identified yet and at some point one will be found.

Superstition as human perceptual errors

Jahoda (1969) highlights evidence that superstitions are formed because of errors or faults in our perceptual and memory systems. Through the mechanisms of "selective forgetting" we remember only superstition-confirming thoughts and behaviours. Alternatively, our perceptual system, in attempting to make sense of some ambiguous stimuli, produces a superstitious-type belief.

Early research by Lehmann (1898) attempted to show errors in observation and memory. Lehmann was initially interested in séances because these are usually held in dimly lit surroundings. However, some mediums allow a bright red light to be used. Lehmann simply placed a blackboard with writing on it at various distances from a white or red light. The figure on the right shows the distances at which it was just possible to read the lettering correctly.

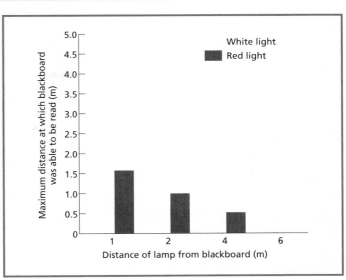

From these results, it was clear that it is very difficult to observe much under red light, so anything that might be seen by a person at a séance could be an error in encoding and then processing information. Lehmann took this a stage further by asking his participants to select a line from a book that was unknown to Lehmann. He had already arranged to have some unintelligible scribble appear on a blackboard. When the participants were shown this, Lehmann was amazed at just how many could make out the line from their book and then confirmed that it was the correct line they had chosen!

Data from Jahoda (1969, p. 37).

So, where does all of this lead to? Well, Lehmann (1898) wanted to use the above as evidence for the fragility of our perceptual system and our ability to selectively forget information. There were two avenues of thought:

1. Error leads *directly* to superstition: some people believe that mythical creatures like the unicorn exist. This could be backed up with evidence that people have seen one when this is, of course, an error of observation. However, these errors are transmitted to other people and the story goes on (very much like the game Chinese whispers).

2. Error leads *indirectly* to superstition: this appears to be a plausible explanation for superstition. In Victorian times, many people had the superstition that something momentous would happen each time a comet was seen. That is, there was an expectation of something evil happening after the appearance of a comet. Such beliefs were perpetuated by selective forgetting, i.e. people would remember only those events that confirmed their beliefs (e.g. only the bad things that *did genuinely happen* after the comet arrived) and selectively forget those that do not fit into the superstition (e.g. getting a new job).

Superstitions and the unconscious

Freud (1901) attempted to explain superstitions through unconscious mechanisms. As we know, thoughts, fears, and wishes are in everyone's unconscious mind. As they tend to be unacceptable, they cannot be accessed into the conscious mind. However, they still motivate our behavioural patterns unknowingly. Freud believed that superstitions are a form of projection whereby the threats from these unconscious thoughts are dealt with by attaching them to things in the outside world. One of Freud's examples starts with a person having a cruel thought. If this is towards someone whom they care a lot about, the guilt aroused by such a thought in the unconscious leads to an expectation of some form of punishment. All of this unconscious "terror" manifests itself in the conscious as a superstition in terms of some form of misfortune happening if a particular set of behavioural patterns are not stuck to. This continually repeats itself as long as the unconscious "terror" still exists.

Marmor (1956) tries to explain superstitions using another familiar unconscious Freudian dilemma: that of the Oedipus/Electra complexes. Marmor was attempting to explain certain superstitious behaviours like knocking on wood three times. He posited that that fear arises from unresolved feelings towards our parents in childhood. During the complexes, the child feels hostility towards the same-sex parent at some point. As the child depends on this parent he or she cannot vent this hostility. Therefore, the hostility is "housed" in the unconscious and manifests itself as anxiety that must be calmed in some way. By knocking three times on wood, anxiety is relieved and therefore we use this superstitious behaviour to stop all of our anxieties.

Obviously, as the ideas are based on unconscious notions, it is extremely difficult to verify or falsify these ideas. How can we know that our anxiety is manifested in Freud's theory or built up hostility according to Marmor that is causing a superstitious behaviour to be maintained?

Contemporary ideas and research

Contemporary research into this area has truly extended Lehmann's (1898) initial work that superstitions could be the result of faulty cognitions. Lindemann and Aarnio (2007) studied whether intuitive processing or analytical processing is common in people who are superstitious. Intuitive thinkers tend to "trust their hunches" so little reasoning happens and analytical thinkers tend to "have explainable reasons for decisions". They give examples of this "hunch" thinking via the work of Rozin, Millman, and Nemeroff (1986), who reported that people would not drink from a cyanide-labelled bottle even though it contained sugared water and that people would not wear Hitler's jumper because somehow his personality was still in it! Intriguingly, the mistakes made by adults are ones seen in children about physical, biological, and psychological phenomena. However, Lindemann and Aarnio were quick to point out that it does not mean that superstitious people have the cognitive ability of a small child. It is all to do with how we process information given to us.

In the Lindemann and Aarnio (2007) study, 239 Finnish volunteers completed a battery of questionnaires aimed to test out things like superstitious beliefs, analytical thinking, and intuitive thinking. Roughly half of the sample were superstitious and the other half sceptics. The findings clearly showed that the superstitious participants relied much more on intuitive thinking than the sceptics and much less on analytical thinking in general decision making.

The argument here could be one of cause and effect. Are the superstitious thoughts being caused by the type of general thinking a person has, or does the general thinking a person has cause them to be superstitious? In a follow-up study using the same participants, Lindemann and Saher (2007) examined the role of intentionality in superstitious beliefs. Intentionality, in the realms of this line of research, is when people attribute intentions to maybe inanimate objects or the role of a part of the body. So, for example, children believe that we eat because our stomach wants to eat or that the moon appears every night because it wants to see the child. The idea was to see if intentionality is more common in superstitious people. As with the previous study, participants completed a battery of questionnaires to assess this. Alongside standard measures of superstition, participants were shown a range of pictures (e.g. a clock, a woman, a tiger's tooth, a mountain, a cloud) and were simply asked if each one had a purpose. They were

Would the results of this study be different in another country?

also asked questions about biological processes like "when we cut our finger, what makes it better?" Both of these could be used as indications of intentionality.

Results from the study clearly showed that the superstitious participants were much more likely to assign purpose to natural objects like mountains and clouds. They were also more likely to endorse statements that showed organ intention (e.g. that a cut finger wants to get better or that when we grow it is because our bones want to do it). However, this is still not to be used as evidence that superstitious individuals are cognitively like children. Lindemann and Saher (2007) noted that the superstitious participants had just the same knowledge of biological processes as the sceptics group. They attempt to explain the superstitious beliefs via dual-coding processes. That is, we all process intuitively and analytically it is just that in superstitious people they process more intuitively when it comes to strange phenomena. They state that using questionnaires may not be the best method to test out these types of processing as it could happen outside of conscious awareness in everyday life. Therefore, future studies should test out implicit knowledge about superstitious beliefs using general population samples (as their sample was superstitious versus sceptic).

Coincidence

Psychologists are obviously interested in **coincidences** because many anomalistic experiences are based on "strange occurrences". But how many are simply coincidences that can be explained by the laws of probability?

Picture this: you walk into your first AS-Level Psychology class. You are the last one to arrive and there are 22 other students sat there. There is one seat left for you. You are asked by your teacher to find out a few things about the person you are sat next to. Within a few minutes you discover that you have the same birthday. You report this back and everyone is astounded by this coincidence. However, the laws of probability can explain this coincidence. It is a classic example, called the birthday problem. In that room there are 253 possible pairings (23 + 22 + 21 . . . + 1 for the amount of pairings that could happen). Using probability equations that are outside the realm of this book, the chance of having the same birthday as someone else in a room of 23 people is 50.7% (if you do not believe this then go to http://www-stat.stanford.edu/~susan/surprise/Birthday.html, where you can randomly choose a certain number of birthdays. Run several trials and see how many bring about a match!). Therefore, this coincidence of having the same birthday is *more* likely to happen than *less* likely to happen with 23 people. Not that remarkable anymore!

Watt (1990–1991) describes a variety of explanations about coincidences:

- *Hidden cause*: this simply states that when a "remarkable coincidence" is reported, there is some hidden cause that has not yet been discovered. An example could be that a person has a "dream" that their favourite actor or pop star has died. The person wakes up and thinks nothing of it until the television is turned on and he or she finds out that it is true. Suddenly, the dreamer believes he or she might have some pre-cognitive power. However, unbeknown to the dreamer, the rest of the family had been watching the newsflash in the next room just as he or she was drifting into sleep. If the family was not questioned thoroughly about this, then it would still be seen as a pre-cognitive experience and not a coincidence.

> ? When was the last time you experienced a coincidence?

> **KEY TERM**
>
> **Coincidence:** an occurrence of two or more events happening at the same time by mere chance.

- *Multiple endpoints*: this simply states that a "close" coincidence is impressive because it has "nearly happened". However, the chances of a "close" coincidence happening is far greater than an "exact" coincidence. Watt (1990–1991) uses an example of a pre-cognitive telephone call. An example would be that you suddenly get a hunch that your Auntie Jayne will call. She hasn't called you in a while. The telephone rings and it is your cousin Elle (Auntie Jayne's daughter). This looks like an impressive coincidence. However, you would be equally "impressed" if it was Auntie Julie, Jayne's husband Martin, or Javier, the guy who walks the dogs of Auntie Jayne. You call your mate Michelle and she is impressed and you chat about how "spooky" that experience was and she tells you of a similar experience she had that was also a "close" coincidence. This shows how multiple endpoints makes the "coincidence" appear more impressive than it actually is! Remember, Auntie Jayne never did phone you yet you feel that you may have some pre-cognitive power now.
- *The Law of Truly Large Numbers*: Diaconis and Mosteller (1989, p. 859) stated that ". . . with a large enough sample, any outrageous thing is likely to happen." That is, coincidences can appear to be impressive but with a very large sample, it was going to happen anyway! Watt (1990–1991) uses population size as an example of this. The UK has a population of around 61 million people. If an event has the probability of occurring to every one in one million people per day, then 61 amazing coincidences should happen (or 22,265 per year!). In the US where the population is over 303 million, then 303 will occur. The argument for this is how many of these are seen as being anomalistic in nature when it is simply what *should* happen by chance!

Coincidence and belief in paranormal activity

One classic study into the link between belief in the paranormal and coincidences and probability was conducted by Blackmore and Troscianko (1985). They ran a series of experiments testing out the beliefs and probability judgements of sheep (believers in psi) and goats (non-believers in psi). There were many parts to the study, but the main focus for this section of the chapter will focus on understanding probability.

In one section of the study, a sample of 50 schoolgirls was presented with 12 examples of random mixtures of boys or girls invited to a party. They had to simply state if the sample was biased or unbiased on a scale of 1–5. Each participant was scored on their ability to spot random samples from ones that showed a distinct pattern. The "goat" participants performed a lot better than the "sheep" participants. Therefore, it was concluded that "sheep" are *less* likely to spot a biased sample or one generated "at random". This means that they are *more* likely to see a coincidence as being something "out of the ordinary" because they cannot spot that it could be down to "pure chance as predicted by mathematical probability." This means that believers in psi and related phenomena are more likely to overlook probability explanations for events in favour of anomalistic explanations. Of course, the sample size was small and only consisted of schoolgirls so the lack of generalisability is apparent here. However, when a second sample of 100 volunteers (aged 12–67) were tested on their understanding of probability (results happening by chance) related to a coin-tossing task the "sheep" performed much worse compared to the "goats". This could lead us to conclude that "sheep" overlook everyday statistical explanations for "coincidence" and tend to focus more on anomalistic ones.

CASE STUDY: MISS A

Miss A, a believer in the paranormal, reports her experience early one evening when she was overwhelmed by what she describes as "a very bad feeling". Her grandfather, to whom she was very close, was very ill at the time and Miss A felt that her feeling related to him. She was very fond of him. However, 4 hours later her boyfriend was knocked down by a car and his skull was fractured in two places. Miss A claims her experience was pre-cognition. Of course, there is no way of testing this but it could be just a coincidence; the interpretation of a feeling based on or caused by perhaps the individual's own thoughts, and then revised as a result of a later occurrence.

SECTION SUMMARY
Factors Underlying Anomalous Experience

❖ Sheep–goat effect: sheep are believers in psi and goats are non-believers.

❖ Jones and Russell (1980) showed that sheep distort memories of psi towards it being successful; goats are more accurate at recalling what has happened.

❖ Cognitive bias can affect experience. Wiseman and Smith (2002) reported that believers in astrology score horoscopes lower for generality than disbelievers.

❖ Having a fantasy-prone personality could explain some experiences. Gow et al. (2001) discovered that people who claim contact with a UFO tend to be more fantasy prone.

❖ A creative personality could also affect experiences. People with this type of personality are more likely to believe psi is real (Thalbourne, 2001).

❖ Temporal lobe lability could explain some strange experiences people have. Electromagnetic stimulation of the temporal lobes may give rise to visions and could help to explain ghost and poltergeist reports.

Cognitive, personality, and biological factors underlying anomalous experience

❖ The Psychodynamic Functions Hypothesis could explain paranormal beliefs. People who have traumatic childhoods are more likely to believe in psi as real (Lawrence et al., 1995).

❖ Irwin (2005) proposed that paranormal beliefs arise because of a lack of control brought about not just by childhood abuse/trauma but *any* childhood experience characterised by a lack of control.

❖ Beliefs in the paranormal are culturally-specific. In New Guinea, children are taught to fear the *marsalai*. Many cultures have different labels for the sensed presence during sleep paralysis.

❖ Near-death experiences appear to be linked to cultural belief (Belanti et al., 2008).

Functions of paranormal and related beliefs, including their cultural significance

❖ Hyman (1989, p. 133) defines deception as ". . . an agent acts or speaks so as to induce a false belief in a target or victim."

❖ Aspects like money, self-esteem, "cannot control own psi-talent", and body language can be effectively used to deceive people.

❖ Self-deception is when we mislead ourselves to accept as true what is most likely false.

The psychology of deception and self-deception, superstition, and coincidence

See *A2-Level Psychology Online* for some interactive quizzes to help you with your revision.

❖ We self-deceive via misinterpreting data patterns, focusing on research that supports our beliefs and being uncritical of favourable research yet highly critical of work that goes against our beliefs.

❖ Superstition is defined as a belief or notion that is not based on reason or knowledge that highlights the "significance" of some behaviour to the individual.

❖ Skinner proposed that we become superstitious due to being rewarded for that behaviour.

❖ Jahoda highlights that there could be some evidence that superstitions are formed because of errors or faults in our perceptual and memory systems (e.g. selective forgetting). Contemporary research tends to favour this explanation.

❖ Freud (1901) attempted to explain superstitions through unconscious mechanisms.

❖ "Coincidences" could be explained via hidden cause, multiple endpoints, and/or the law of truly large numbers.

BELIEF IN EXCEPTIONAL EXPERIENCE

Research into Psychic Healing

There are competing definitions for **psychic healing** as researchers try to differentiate it from spiritual healing, faith healing, and psychic surgery. Therefore, a broad definition is necessary. Benor (1995, p. 234) defines it as ". . . the intentional influence of one or more people upon one or more living system without utilising known physical means of intervention." It is the passing of some form of energy from one person to another living being. This can be the laying of hands on an individual or through prayer.

? What do we mean by reliable?

Throughout the history of healing, there have been many anecdotal accounts about how healers have performed "miracles" and cured people of a variety of ailments. However, this does not constitute *reliable* evidence. Therefore, this section will focus on trials that have been randomised and are double-blind. That is, participants have an equal chance of being in the healing or non-healing group *and* the doctors who examine the participants to see if their condition has improved do not know who had healing or non-healing.

One of the first trials was conducted by Byrd (1998). Over a period of 10 months, 393 patients who were admitted to a coronary care unit were split into two groups—one received prayer healing ($n = 192$) and the remainder acted as a control group ($n = 201$). All participants signed a consent form to take part in the study, knowing that they would be randomly allocated to one of the two groups. Whilst in hospital, the prayer-healing group had directed prayers towards them. In terms of **statistical significance**, there were many outcome measures that

> **KEY TERMS**
>
> **Psychic healing:** Benor (1995, p. 234) defines psychic healing as ". . . the intentional influence of one or more people upon one or more living system without utilising known physical means of intervention."
>
> **Statistical significance:** the idea that the results from a study are not due to chance but by the manipulation of an independent variable (in an experiment) or that two variables are truly correlated. Conventional significance is set at $p = 0.05$, this is, there is a 5% probability that results could be due to chance. A level below this means that the results are statistically significant.

did not change between the groups. However, significant differences occurred in a cluster of outcome measures. These were congestive heart failure, diuretics, cardiopulmonary arrest, pneumonia, use of antibiotics, and intubations (i.e. having a tube inserted into the larynx). All these measures favoured the prayer-healing group. Therefore, initial results appeared to be positive in terms of helping people with chronic heart conditions.

Sicher, Targ, Moore, and Smith (1998) also conducted a double-blind randomised trial on the effects of healing on advanced AIDS patients. A total of 40 patients were randomly allocated to the healing or control group. The control group simply received 10 weeks of standard medical care. The healing group received the same standard medical care but also received distant healing for 1 hour per day, 6 days per week for the 10-week period of study. Patients and healers never met. A series of measures were taken at baseline as a comparison; these included CD4+ count (a measure of immune system efficiency) and a questionnaire measure of mood. During the 10-week period, other measures were taken, like number of days hospitalised, illness severity, and number of outpatient visits. The main differences that were seen after 10 weeks included fewer AIDS-defining illnesses, fewer doctor visits, fewer hospitalisations, and much improved mood. All of these were in favour of the healing group. Thus, there is evidence for the use of distant healing with AIDS patients.

Psychic healing can be described as the passing of some form of energy from one living person to another via touch or prayer.

The final study in this section was conducted by Abbott, Harkness, Stevinson, Marshall, Conn, and Ernst (2001), who investigated the use of spiritual healing in sufferers of chronic pain. Their study had two separate comparisons: face-to-face healing versus simulated face-to-face healing and distant healing versus a control group. As with the previous studies mentioned already in this section, participants were randomly allocated to one of the groups. There were around 25 participants in each of the groups. All participants filled in a standardised pain questionnaire (The McGill Pain Questionnaire). Scores from baseline were compared to those after "treatment". All participants had 30 minutes of "healing" per week for 8 weeks. In general terms, there were no significant differences in pain reduction across all groups. The face-to-face, simulated face-to-face, and control groups reported significant reductions in pain; there was not a significant reduction in pain in the distant healing group. This study does not support the use of healing for the sufferers of chronic pain.

Many psychologists would claim that "positive results" from psychic healing studies are due to the placebo effect. That is, it is the fact that the "patients" are expecting something to happen, or believing it will work, that brings about positive changes, and not the healing procedure itself. So the mere suggestion from a healer that the healing process will work results in the person receiving the healing believing, acting, behaving, and thinking in a different way than usual and it is this that makes the whole procedure look as though it worked. It might look like the healing has been successful but this is not due to the healing at all!

This shows that there are conflicting research findings in terms of using healing to help with medical conditions. Despite this, it should be noted that even in randomised trials there still could be other variables (like participant variables such as belief, current mental health state) that could be affecting the outcome measures in conjunction with or instead of the healing that participants received. Much more research is definitely needed in this area.

EXAM HINT

Make sure that you evaluate research evidence of psychic healing with the placebo effect, personality variables, and variability in health status.

Research Into Out-of-Body Experiences

An **out-of-body experience** (OoBE) is said to occur when individuals believe that they have had a sensation of floating out of their own body and being able to see their own body and the environment surrounding it. Very little research has tested the validity of OoBEs. As Irwin and Watt (2007) point out, with any of the research in this area the accuracy of the description is ". . . assumed rather than proven" (Irwin & Watt, 2007, p. 177). Straightaway, this is a potential weakness in any research into OoBEs. This section examines correlates of experiences and main features, as this is what research into OoBEs tends to focus on.

Alvarado (2000) reviewed the phenomenology of OoBEs to examine if there were any key similarities:

1. Various levels of awareness are linked to OoBEs. Some people simply report a separation from the body; others report seeing themselves come out of their own body and then return to it. Many (62% on average) could see their own body from a short distance.
2. Around 7% of people claim to have seen an "astral cord". This rope-like structure links the OoBE with the physical body to help it return.
3. The description of themselves during the experience can take different forms. Around 50% of people experience being in a body that is not their own. Others claim to be "pure consciousness" (22%), or a ball of light or cloud (28%).

Taking this further, Irwin and Watt (2007) reviewed the circumstances of OoBEs and discovered:

1. In around 60% of cases, the mental state before the event is the same as during the event—calm. For most of the remainder, the experience can be a bit more emotionally arousing, e.g. confronting death during the OoBE.
2. There appears to be no discernible pattern for pre-experience physical state. Many occur during minimal sensory input like simply lying down in a dark room. However, some people report sensory bombardment with lots going on.
3. There can be some profound after-effects of an OoBE. The more complex the experience, the more it is likely to change the attitude of the experient. This is especially true if it happened during a life-threatening scenario so the person then associates death with an afterlife and becomes calmer. The experience will be seen as being "spiritual" if the person is religious or it happened in conjunction with a **near-death experience** (see the next section). However, if the person is atheist it does not convert them to religious practice. Finally, the vast majority of experients are happy to have another one!

CASE STUDY: AN OUT-OF-BODY EXPERIENCE

Wendy describes her earliest out-of-body experience taking place at home when she was 2 or 3 years old. She had cut her foot badly playing outside, and her mother was treating the cut and debris in her foot. Wendy's memory is of being sat on the kitchen counter and then suddenly viewing herself, her mother, and the whole scene from the other side of the room. In addition, this out of body view was a 360° one as she had a panoramic view of the whole room. She recalls making a conscious decision to go back into her body.

What alternative explanations are there for Wendy's memory?

Research into Near-Death Experiences

Generally, a near-death experience (NDE) is the perception reported by someone who was clinically dead but revived or nearly died (this is the crucial difference between this and out-of-body experiences—the latter can occur in non-life threatening situations). The early work of Moody (1975) identified 15 themes that were quite common in NDE reports. These included finding difficulty putting the experience into words, overhearing the news of their own death, a dark tunnel, meeting others, and a review of their own life.

Roe (2001) highlighted five stages of an NDE, which could happen in any order:

1. feelings of deep peace and well-being
2. a sense of separation from the body
3. entering darkness/passing through a tunnel
4. seeing the light
5. entering the light/beautiful garden.

Much research in this area has focused on cardiac-arrest victims and their experiences and this section focuses on three such studies from different countries (the Netherlands, UK, and USA) plus an examination of NDE linked to kidney failure from Taiwan. van Lommel, van Wees, Meyers, and Elfferich (2001) examined NDEs in survivors of cardiac arrest. They examined 244 cardiac patients who were successfully resuscitated. Over 60 patients reported an NDE and these individuals were compared to a group who did not report one. They were examined on demographics, medical and pharmacological data, and psychological assessments. There were no differences between the groups on duration of cardiac arrest, medication taken, or fear of death before the arrest. The main elements reported by those who have experienced NDEs include positive emotions (56%), awareness of being dead (50%), meeting with deceased people (32%), and moving through a tunnel (31%). Some differences between the groups occurred: people younger than 60 had more NDE episodes and females tended to have deeper NDE experiences. Also, those who had a deep NDE experience with a lot of the core elements (see above) were more likely to die within 30 days of their cardiac arrest. A strong positive of this study is that it was *prospective* in nature and not *retrospective*. That is, van Lommel et al. examined the NDE just after it happened and followed it over time (a retrospective study examines the events after they have happened and can be years later so have the problems of memory recall). A sub-group of NDE experients and control group were followed-up 2 years later. There were many differences between these groups. The NDE experients were more loving, empathic, understood others better, got more involved in their family, believed more in life after death, and appreciated the ordinary things in life more so than the control non-NDE group.

Parnia, Waller, Yeates, and Fenwick (2001) interviewed all survivors of cardiac arrest in a South of England hospital over a 1-year period; just over 11% of the sample reported an NDE. The main features reported including coming to a point of no return, feelings of joy and peace, and seeing a bright light (interestingly, all of the NDE were non-practising Christians). When comparing the NDE group

Those who have encountered a near-death experience often describe seeing a bright light at the end of a dark tunnel. However, some studies have discovered that only 30% actually report this.

with the other survivors, there were no physiological differences between the groups except that the NDE had a level of oxygen in their system that was twice as high as the other group. However, instead of being taken as a potential factor in NDEs, Parnia et al. noted that the NDE sample was only four people (the others who had an NDE did not match it on all criteria so were not used in the study). Therefore, generalisability is low to other NDE groups and the high oxygen levels may be skewed data from a small sample (e.g. happened to have four people with high oxygen levels). More research is needed into the role of oxygen in NDEs.

Greyson (2003) also examined NDEs in a cardiac care unit to investigate its incidence rate and potential correlates. He conducted a 30-month survey on 1595 patients admitted to a cardiac care unit. Those who experienced cardiac arrest formed the sample. Those who described an NDE were matched with comparison patients on diagnosis, gender, and age. Around 10% of the entire sample reported having an NDE. Members of the NDE group were more likely to have lost consciousness, have had prior paranormal experiences, and to have an approach-oriented death acceptance. This means that they perceive death as a passage to a pleasant state (it should be noted that there were no differences between the groups on fear of death). Of course, with this we do not know the cause–effect relationship, even though many believe that the experience changes your views, we cannot be sure if we do not measure this before and after an NDE.

Finally in this section, we move away from cardiac arrests and on to dialysis patients (dialysis is used to artificially replace kidney function). Lai et al. (2007) investigated NDEs in 710 dialysis patients across seven health centres in Taipei, Taiwan. Forty-five of these patients reported having an NDE. The most common features included vivid sensations, positive emotions, a sense of deceased spirits, and feelings of peace. The NDE group tended to be younger, female, and to participate in religious ceremonies. After the NDE experience, the group were kinder to others and more motivated than the no-NDE group. Lai et al. are the first to point to the limitations of the study (and of studies into NDEs in general): the incidence of NDEs is based on self-reporting so there is no way of assessing accuracy of reports. Also, at least in this study, many NDEs occurred prior to long-term dialysis therapy. As a result, the "causality" between the NDEs and the after-effects cannot be inferred.

Research into Psychic Mediumship

Psychic mediumship refers to a type of relationship that a living person says they have with spirits. Mediums tend to claim that they can communicate with spirits and pass on messages to loved ones "left behind" in the "earthly" world. It is practised as part of many religions across the globe. There are many hypotheses about mediumship, ranging from the survival hypothesis (i.e. our spirit survives after death and can communicate) to the Sceptical Hypothesis (which predicts that the mediums' messages are so general that they can apply to anyone).

The Sceptical Hypothesis was tested out in a series of studies run by Robertson and Roy (2001; 2004). Ten mediums agreed to participate in their first study, which ran for 2 years (Robertson & Roy, 2001). There were 44 recipients of information from these mediums, with 407 non-recipients. The latter group was used to see if any information from the medium was so general that it could be accepted by them. The mediums were recruited from public meetings and controlled sessions with smaller groups of participants. The researchers were also developing a weighting system for the comments given by the mediums based on mathematical probabilities (called the Robertson–Roy Protocol) to see how many readings "hit target". A hit target, in essence, means that it is not general. The average "hit target" score for a recipient was hugely significantly larger than the non-recipient group. Robertson and Roy rejected the Sceptical Hypothesis; however, they wanted to test it again.

This time, Robertson and Roy (2004) conducted a further set of experiments in England and Scotland. A total of ten mediums generated 73 sets of statements during the sessions run. Again, the Robertson–Roy Protocol was used to score "hit target" responses. As with their 2001 study, they reported that the scores for recipients were much higher than those of the non-recipients. The probability of this happening by chance was one in one million. They ran a series of experiments that tested out other factors like body language and verbal responses of the recipients. When the medium was in a separate room (so body language was not seen) and when the recipient (unknown to the medium) gave no verbal responses to the medium's statements, the scores for recipients were still higher than for non-recipients. Unsurprisingly, this led Robertson and Roy to reject the Sceptical Hypothesis again.

However, this was not the case in a study conducted by O'Keeffe and Wiseman (2005). This research duo was interested in testing out mediumship in a more controlled format that could control for some of the methodological problems of previous studies prior to Robertson and Roy. They wanted to control for:

Harry Houdini is usually remembered as an escapologist rather than an illusionist and magician, but his early career included staging phony seances. He later campaigned against mediums who exploited grieving individuals and, in 1922, he was invited by *Scientific American* to join a committee investigating mediums' claims. A cash prize of $2500 was offered to any medium who could produce a convincing supernatural manifestation. Houdini was able to disprove all the claims that were made—no-one won the prize.

- *Sensory leakage*: mediums pre-searching via the internet or telephone directories for information on their recipients. Also, how quickly the recipient answers "yes" or "no" can be very useful feedback for a medium. All participants were unknown to the medium prior to the study.
- *Generality of mediums' statements*: that is, an assessment of the Sceptical Hypothesis. It should be noted that in the O'Keeffe and Wiseman paper there is no mention of Robertson–Roy Protocol; for this study they used the Pratt–Birge technique. This is when a recipient rates the accuracy of their own reading and then assesses if readings from other recipients apply to them too (called a decoy). Therefore, scores can be easily compared.

A total of five mediums were used in the study alongside five recipients. The design was simple—the five mediums gave a reading to each recipient on separate days counterbalanced for time of day. Each statement given to the recipient was scored on a scale of one (not applicable) to seven (very applicable). The average score for each recipient fell in the range of 3.1 to 3.5 on the 7-point scale. The mediums' average scores across all recipients ranged from 1.78 to 4.46 on the 7-point scale. When all scores were merged for all recipients (using the Pratt–Birge technique), not one recipient had their highest score when they were a recipient. This means that for each recipient a decoy set of statements was rated as more accurate then their own. This naturally led O'Keeffe and Wiseman to accept the Sceptical Hypothesis.

In conclusion, there is conflicting evidence for the genuineness of mediumship but the studies described here used differing techniques to score accuracy. Therefore, it is hard to rule out that it was the technique causing the conclusions not the ability of the mediums. This is another example where a set protocol ought to be agreed by researchers and then studies can be comparable.

SECTION SUMMARY
Belief in Exceptional Experience

Psychic healing

- ❖ Benor (1995, p. 234) defines psychic healing as ". . . the intentional influence of one or more people upon one or more living system without utilising known physical means of intervention."
- ❖ Byrd (1998) reported that healing was successful for people in a coronary care unit.
- ❖ Sicher et al. (1998) reported that psychic healing helped with AIDS patients.
- ❖ Abbott et al. (2001) reported that distance psychic healing did not work with chronic pain sufferers.
- ❖ All of the above studies had control groups to ensure comparability. However, we must question the ethics of research where people, by chance, do not get treatment.

Out-of-body and near-death experiences

- ❖ Out-of-body experiences refer to instances when a person believes that he or she has had a sensation of floating out of their own body and being able to see their own body and the environment surrounding it.
- ❖ Generally, near-death experience is the perception reported by someone who was clinically dead but revived or nearly died.
- ❖ The crucial difference between near-death and out-of-body experiences is that the latter can occur in non-life-threatening situations.
- ❖ van Lommel et al. (2001) reported that people who had a lot of core features in an NDE episode during a heart attack were more likely to die within 30 days of their cardiac arrest.
- ❖ Parnia et al. (2001) discovered that when comparing the NDE group with the other survivors, there were no physiological differences between the groups except that the NDE group had levels of oxygen in their system that were twice as high as the other group.
- ❖ Psychic mediumship refers to a type of relationship that a living person says they have with spirits.

❖ The Robertson–Roy Protocol for examining the generality of content when mediums contact the spirit world showed that statements are not over general and cannot be applied to anyone.

❖ However, O'Keeffe and Wiseman (2005) found that when recipients of messages rated *all* messages reported by a series of mediums, not one recipient had their highest score being when they were a recipient.

Psychic mediumship

FURTHER READING

Irwin, H.J., & Watt, C.A. (2007). *An introduction to parapsychology* (5th Edn). Jefferson, USA: McFarland.

Roberts, R., & Groome, D. (Eds) (2001). *Parapsychology – the science of unusual experience*. London: Hodder.

Henry, J. (Ed.) (2005). *Parapsychology—Research on exceptional experiences*. London: Routledge.

Cardena, E., Lynn, S.J., & Krippner, S. (Eds) (2000). *Varieties of anomalous experience: Examining the scientific evidence*. Washington: APA.

REVISION QUESTIONS

In the exam, questions on this topic are out of 25 marks. You should spend about 35 minutes on each of the questions below, which aim to test the material in this chapter. In the exam, make certain you know if you have covered Media Psychology, The Psychology of Addictive Behaviour, or Anomalistic Psychology as your Psychology in Action topic, and then choose the correct question.

1. (a) Discuss issues of pseudoscience and scientific fraud. (10 marks)
   (b) A PSI Ghostwatch team in Wiltshire reported a variety of paranormal experiences, visual, auditory, olfactory and tactile, but out of 10 hours of video footage and over 100 photos, some showing apparent anomalies, none withstood subsequent analysis (BBC, 2008). Discuss factors, including cognitive and personality, which could underlie anomalous experiences. (15 marks)
2. Many cultures have widespread beliefs in exceptional experiences.
   (a) Discuss the functions of paranormal and related beliefs, including their cultural significance. (10 marks)
   (b) Outline and evaluate research into psychic healing, out-of-body and/or near-death experience, and psychic mediumship. (15 marks)
3. (a) Outline biological factors underlying anomalous experience. (5 marks)
   (b) Discuss the psychology of deception and self-deception, superstition and coincidence. (20 marks)

See *A2-Level Psychology Online* for tips on how to answer these revision questions.

The application of scientific method in psychology p. 687

- What are the major features of science?
- Explain the scientific process, including theory construction, hypothesis testing, use of empirical methods, generation of new laws/principles (e.g. Popper, Kuhn).
- What is the role of peer review in validating new knowledge?

Designing psychological investigations p. 699

- Explain the selection and application of appropriate research methods.
- What are the strengths and weaknesses of different forms of sample methods?
- What are the different types of reliability and how can reliability be assessed and improved?
- What are the different types of validity and how can validity be assessed and improved?
- How should ethical considerations be resolved in psychological research?

Data analysis and reporting on investigations p. 720

- How should you decide which graphs are appropriate for representing the data?
- Use probability to interpret significance and potential type 1/type 2 errors.
- What are the factors that affect the choice of statistical test?
- Explain the use of inferential analysis, including Spearman's rho, Mann–Whitney, Wilcoxon, and chi-squared.
- What are the techniques used for the analysis and interpretation of qualitative data?
- What are the conventions for the reporting of psychological investigations?

Psychological Research and Scientific Method

By Clare Charles and Michael W. Eysenck

THE APPLICATION OF SCIENTIFIC METHOD IN PSYCHOLOGY

The Nature of "Science"

The appropriate starting point for a discussion of whether psychology is a science is to consider the definition of science. This is difficult to do, because views on the nature of science changed during the course of the twentieth century. According to the traditional view, science has the following features (Eysenck & Keane, 1990):

1. It is **objective**.
2. This objectivity is ensured by careful observation and experimentation.
3. The knowledge obtained by scientists is turned into law-like generalisations.

The behaviourists were much influenced by a version of this traditional view known as logical positivism. Logical positivists, such as Ayer and Carnap, argued that the theoretical constructs used in science are meaningful only to the extent that they can be observed. This was very much the position adopted by behaviourists such as Watson and Skinner. As a result, some important concepts within psychology were discarded. For example, Skinner (1980, p. 1209) argued that: "There is no place in a scientific analysis of behaviour for a mind or self."

There are major problems with the traditional view of science held by the behaviourists and others. As is discussed shortly, the notion that behaviour can be observed objectively has been vigorously attacked. Writers such as Kuhn (1970) have argued that the scientific enterprise has important social and subjective aspects to it. This view was taken to extremes by Feyerabend (1975), who argued that science progresses by a sort of "who-shouts-the-loudest" strategy, in which publicity and visibility count for more than the quality of the research. According to this position, objectivity is essentially irrelevant to the conduct of science.

What about the view that science involves forming law-like generalisations? Suppose we test a given hypothesis several times and the findings consistently support the hypothesis. Does this prove that the hypothesis is correct? Popper (1969) argued that it doesn't. Generalisations based on what has been found to be in the past might not hold true in the future. Consider Bertrand Russell's example of a turkey forming the generalisation, "Each day I am fed", because for

> **KEY TERM**
> **Objective:** dealing with facts in a way that is unaffected by feelings or opinions.

Law-like generalisations are not always true.

all of its life that has been true. This generalisation provides no certainty that the turkey will be fed tomorrow, and if tomorrow is Christmas Eve it is likely to be proved false!

A New Definition for Science

In view of the fact that the traditional definition of science is inadequate, it is clear that a new definition is needed. This is easier said than done. As Eysenck and Keane (1990, p. 5) pointed out, the views of Feyerabend and other twentieth-century philosophers of science "have established the point that the division between science and non-science is by no means as clear cut as used to be believed". However, there is probably reasonable agreement that the following are key features of science:

> *What are some examples of controlled observations that you have learned about in this book?*

1. *Controlled observations*: in most sciences (except astronomy and a few others), it is typical for experiments to involve observing the effects of some specific manipulation (e.g. mixing two chemicals together). As applied to psychology, this generally involves observing the effects of some manipulation of the environment on participants' behaviour.
2. *Objectivity*: even if total objectivity is impossible, it is still important for data to be collected in a way as close to objectivity as possible.
3. *Testing theoretical predictions*: scientific experiments are generally carried out to test the predictions of a theory.
4. *Falsifiability*: the notion that scientific theories can potentially be disproved by evidence.
5. *Replicability*: the findings obtained by researchers need to be replicable or repeatable; it would be hard (or impossible) to base a science on inconsistent findings.
6. *Paradigm*: there is a generally accepted theoretical orientation or paradigm within a science.

KEY TERMS

Falsifiability: the notion that scientific theories can potentially be disproved by evidence; it is the hallmark of science according to Popper.
Replicability: the extent to which the findings of research can be repeated.
Paradigm: according to Kuhn, a general theoretical orientation that is accepted by most scientists in a given discipline.

Controlled observations and the experimental method

There are numerous ways of carrying out studies in psychology. However, the approach most in accord with the demands of science is the experimental method. With this method, some aspect of the environment is *controlled* (the independent variable) to assess its impact on participants' behaviour (the dependent variable). Philosophers of science tell us it is impossible to establish causality with certainty. However, the experimental method has the great advantage over other methods in that it allows us to have some confidence that the independent variable has influenced the dependent variable, and so cause and effect can be established.

EXAM HINT

To remember which way round the independent and dependent variables go think of it as id (as in Freud's theory). The IV is first because this CAUSES the EFFECT on the DV.

Objectivity

We have already referred to the importance of data collection or scientific observation as a way of testing hypotheses. According to the traditional view of science, scientific observations are entirely objective. However, Popper (1969, 1972) argued that scientific observations are theory driven rather than objective. He demonstrated this in a famous lecture, which involved him telling the

Goals of science

What are the goals of science? According to Allport (1947), science has the aims of "understanding, prediction and control above the levels achieved by unaided common sense". Thus, three of the main goals of science are as follows:

1. prediction
2. understanding
3. control.

As we will see shortly, psychologists differ among themselves as to the relative importance of these three goals.

Prediction

Scientists put forward theories, which are general explanations or accounts of certain findings or data. These theories can then be used to generate various hypotheses. Hypotheses are predictions or expectations of what will happen in given situations.

One of the best known theories in psychology is Thorndike's (1911) Law of Effect. According to this theory, acts that are rewarded or reinforced are "stamped in", whereas those that are punished are "stamped out". The Law of Effect has generated numerous hypotheses, including predicting the behaviour of rats that are rewarded for lever pressing and the behaviour of pigeons rewarded for pecking at a disc.

The success, or otherwise, of predictions stemming from a theory is very important. Any theory that generates a lot of incorrect predictions is seriously flawed.

Understanding

Even if a theory generates a number of accurate predictions, it does not necessarily follow that the theory gives us a good understanding of what is happening. For example, Craik and Lockhart's (1972) Levels-of-Processing Theory led to the prediction that material that has been processed in terms of its meaning will be remembered better than material that has not been processed in this way. Although this prediction has been confirmed experimentally numerous times (as discussed in your AS level studies), the precise reasons *why* it is beneficial to process meaning still remain unclear.

Control

After prediction and understanding have been achieved, it is sometimes possible to move on to control. For example, behaviourists—such as Thorndike, Skinner, and others—predicted (and found) that people tend to repeat behaviour that is followed by reward (i.e. positive reinforcement). The principles of operant conditioning were put forward in an attempt to understand what is going on when this happens. It is possible to use reinforcement to control human behaviour, as when parents persuade their children to behave well in return for sweets. Skinner (1948), in his utopian novel *Walden Two*, went further, and argued that it would be possible to create an ideal society by arranging matters so that only socially desirable behaviour was rewarded or reinforced.

audience, "Observe!" The obvious and immediate retort was, "Observe what?", which makes the point that no one ever observes without some idea of what they are looking for. Thus, scientific observation is always driven by hypotheses and theories, and what you observe depends in part on what you expect to see.

We can make this argument more concrete by taking a specific example. Over the years, thousands of experiments have been carried out in the Skinner box, a piece of experimental equipment in which the number of lever presses produced by a rat in a given period of time is the key behavioural measure. In most studies, the equipment is designed so that each lever press is recorded automatically. However,

Popper argues that we all see the world from our own particular viewpoints or biases. This influences the topic we choose to look at. How can scientists try to avoid bias in their work?

this procedure is less objective than might be thought. Lever presses with the rat's right paw, with its left paw, and even with its nose or tail are all recorded as a single lever press, even though the rat's actual behaviour differs considerably. Furthermore, the rat sometimes presses the lever too gently to activate the mechanism, and this isn't counted as a lever press at all.

A more sweeping attack on the notion that data in psychology are objective has been made by social constructionists, such as Gergen (1985) and Harré and Secord (1972). Semin (1995, p. 545) described their key assumptions as follows:

> In their view, there are no such things as pure observations. All observations require a prior viewpoint, irrespective of whether these stem from a theoretical perspective, or are due to learning . . . Thus data are socially "manufactured", irrespective of which form these data take.

Wallach and Wallach (1994) agreed that perfect objectivity cannot be achieved, and that it is not possible to be certain that the interpretation of someone's behaviour is correct. However, we can be more confident in our interpretation of behaviour if it is supported by other evidence. According to Wallach and Wallach (1994, p. 234):

> When a [participant] presses a lever that ostensibly [i.e. apparently] delivers shocks to another [participant], it may be far from certain that he or she intends to harm this other [participant]. If the [participant] also asserts that this was his or her intention, or it happens that on the experimenter's declaration that the experiment is over, the [participant] proceeds to punch the other [participant] in the nose, then, all else being equal, it seems likely that harm was intended.

Testing theoretical predictions

It is sensible to design experiments in such a way that they test theoretical predictions. This is because, in principle, there is an infinite number of experiments that could be carried out and scientific theories help in the task of identifying which ones are worthwhile. Science advances when inadequate theories are replaced by ones that are more consistent with the data.

Falsifiability

An extremely influential view of what distinguishes science from non-science was put forward by Popper (1969), who argued that the hallmark of science is falsifiability rather than generalisation from positive instances or findings. Scientists should form theories and hypotheses that can, potentially, be shown to be untrue by experimental tests. According to Popper, the possibility of falsification is what separates science from religions and pseudo-sciences such as psychoanalysis and Marxism. In psychological research, a null hypothesis is stated; this predicts no difference between the conditions. This means the null hypothesis is actually the starting point and it is this that you are setting out to test, not the alternative hypothesis. Research seeks to reject the null hypothesis.

Some theories in psychology are falsifiable; others aren't. For example, H.J. Eysenck (1967) put forward a theory according to which individuals who were high in neuroticism (anxiety and depression) should be more physiologically responsive than those low in neuroticism. Numerous studies have tested this theory, with the great majority failing to support it (Fahrenberg, 1992). Thus, the theory has been falsified.

Another example of a theory that is falsifiable is the frustration–aggression hypothesis, according to which frustration leads to aggression and aggression is caused by frustration; much research has shown that this is a considerable oversimplification of what actually happens.

By contrast, Freud's notion that the mind consists of three parts (ego, superego, and id) is unfalsifiable. It isn't possible to imagine any findings that would disprove such a vague and poorly specified theoretical position. In similar fashion, it is hard to test or to falsify Maslow's (1954) theory of motivation based on a hierarchy of needs. This theory assumes that there are five types of need arranged in a hierarchical way, from the need for survival at the bottom to the need for self-actualisation at the top. The problems associated with falsifying this theory might explain why relatively few studies have tested it.

There are also problems of falsifiability with much of evolutionary psychology. According to evolutionary psychology, most of our behaviour should be adaptive because that maximises the chances of reproduction. However, evolutionary psychologists also claim to be able to "explain" behaviour that is *not* adaptive by using the notion of "genome lag", meaning that evolution of the genome has lagged behind environmental changes. Thus, adaptive and maladaptive behaviour can be "explained", after a fashion. More specifically, evolutionary psychologists have provided explanations of various mental disorders such as schizophrenia and depression (see Chapters 10 and 11). However, these explanations are rather speculative and difficult to falsify.

> [?] What is meant by falsifiable and unfalsifiable?

Replicability

It was indicated earlier that replicability, or repeatability, of findings is an important requirement for a subject to be considered as a science. Replicability of findings in psychology varies enormously as a function of the area of psychology under investigation and the type of study being performed. Replicability tends to be greatest when experiments are conducted in a carefully controlled way, and it tends to be lowest when the experimenter is unable to manipulate the variable or variables of interest.

Clear evidence of replicability is available from studies of operant conditioning. Characteristic patterns of responding are found when animals are put into a Skinner box and rewarded on various schedules of reinforcement. For example, there is the fixed-interval schedule, in which the animal is rewarded with food for the first response after a given interval of time (e.g. 30 seconds). What nearly always happens is that the animal stops responding immediately after receiving food because it has learned that no additional food is available at that time. The animal starts to respond again more and more rapidly as the time at which reward will be available approaches.

> [?] What are the main obstacles to replicability in human psychology?

> [?] If Skinner and Thorndike's theories are correct, then punishment should always be a deterrent, but this is not always true. What could be the reason for this?

? Why do you think replicability tends to be lower when studies are carried out in social psychology?

Replicability tends to be lower when studies are carried out in social psychology, but often remains high when the situation is under good experimental control. An example of this is the Asch situation, in which there is one genuine participant and several participants who are confederates of the experimenter. All the participants are given the task of deciding which of three lines is the same length as another line. The key condition is one in which all the confederates of the experimenter provide the same incorrect decision. Convincing evidence of conformity by the genuine participant has been found in numerous studies in several countries. Milgram's obedience studies (see page 155 and your AS textbook) have also been replicated successfully.

Laboratory experiments

Laboratory experiments permit high control and good replicability. In order for psychology to be regarded as a science, we must have confidence in laboratory (and other) experiments as a way of obtaining valid information about human behaviour. However, not all psychologists respect the experimental approach as a means of investigating human behaviour. For example, at one extreme Boring (1957) argued as follows: "The application of the experimental method to the problem of mind is the great outstanding event in the history of the study of mind, an event to which no other is comparable." By contrast, Nick Heather (1976) was very dismissive of laboratory experiments, arguing that they are very artificial and that all that can be learned from them is how strangers interact in an unusual situation.

Some of the strengths and weaknesses of laboratory research can be made clearer by looking at two kinds of validity:

- *Internal validity*: refers to the validity of research within the context in which it is carried out. For example, if the same experiment is carried out time after time, and the same findings are obtained each time, this would indicate high internal validity. Experiments that can be repeated in this way are high in replicability.
- *External validity*: refers to the validity of the research outside the research situation. Many laboratory experiments are rather low in external validity, meaning that we cannot be confident that what is true in the laboratory is also true of everyday life.

> **EXAM HINT**
> Think of internal validity as TRUTH as this refers to whether the findings are a true effect of the independent variable on the dependent variable. Think of external validity as GENERALISABILITY as this refers to whether the findings generalise beyond the research setting.

> **KEY TERMS**
> **Laboratory experiment:** an experiment conducted in a laboratory setting or other contrived setting away from the participants' normal environments. The experimenter manipulates the independent variable (IV) and accurately measure the dependent variable (DV). Considerable control can be exercised over confounding variables.
> **Internal validity:** refers to the extent to which the experiment measured what it set out to measure, i.e. is the observed effect in the dependent variable (DV) a result of the manipulation of the independent variable (IV)? Thus, internal validity refers to whether the research has *truth* or whether it "worked". Any threats to internal validity reduce the meaningfulness of the findings as they lack truth.
> **External validity:** refers to the validity of the research outside the research situation itself; the extent to which the findings are generalisable to other situations, especially "everyday" situations. The question is whether you would get the same findings in a different setting or whether they are limited to the original research context. If the latter is true then there is a lack of external validity.

Much psychological research on humans is somewhat lacking in external validity. We spend most of our time actively dealing with our environment, deciding which situations to put ourselves into and then responding to those situations as seems appropriate. Much of this dynamic interaction is lacking in laboratory research; the experimenter (rather than the participant) determines the situation in which the participant is placed and what is of interest is the participant's response to that situation. This led Silverman (1977) to argue that the findings obtained from laboratory studies are likely to generalise only to institutions such as prisons, hospitals, or schools.

> ■ **Activity: Validity**
> Construct a brief outline for each of the following:
>
> - An experiment that should show high internal validity.
> - An experiment that will be unlikely to show high internal validity.
> - An experiment that is unlikely to show high ecological validity.

Paradigm: Kuhn's approach

According to Thomas Kuhn (1962, 1970, 1977), the most essential ingredient in a science is what he called a paradigm. This is a general theoretical orientation accepted by the great majority of workers in that field of study. With the advance of knowledge, the dominant paradigm in any science will gradually become less adequate. Eventually, when there is very strong evidence against the current paradigm, it will be replaced by another paradigm.

> ■ **Activity: Causes of schizophrenia**
> The competing theories that exist for the causes of schizophrenia could be indicative of a pre-scientific stage in the psychology of mental disorders.
>
> - Using other sources, research the dominant paradigms that exist in this area and compare them with other, less adequate explanations for schizophrenia.
>
> Can we say that psychologists have established a generally accepted explanation for the causes of certain forms of schizophrenia? If so, are these explanations proof of a scientific approach? What do you think are the chances of a competing explanation resulting in a paradigm shift, for example to environmental and/or social causes?

These considerations led Kuhn (1970) to argue that there are three distinct stages in the development of a science:

1. *Pre-science*: there is no generally accepted paradigm and there is a wide range of opinion about the best theoretical approach to adopt.
2. *Normal science*: there is a generally accepted paradigm that accounts for the phenomena regarded as being central to the field. This paradigm influences the experiments carried out and how the findings are explained. A classic example of normal science is the use of Newtonian mechanics by physicists until the emergence of relativity theory.
3. *Revolutionary science*: when the evidence against the old paradigm reaches a certain point there is what is known as a paradigm shift. This involves replacing the old paradigm with a new one. An example of a paradigm shift is the Copernican revolution, in which the old view that the planets and the sun revolve around the earth was replaced by our present view that the earth and the other planets revolve around the sun.

Before Copernicus showed that the planets, including the earth, revolved around the sun, all astronomical theories had been based on the paradigm that the earth was the centre of the universe. The complete change in science post-Copernicus is an example of a paradigm shift.

The replacement of an old paradigm by a new one does not usually happen in an orderly way. Scientists who support the old paradigm often ignore conflicting evidence or dismiss it as being of little importance. Adherents of the old paradigm resist change for as long as possible, until they can no longer hold out against the onslaught. In other words, social and other pressures lead scientists to stick with paradigms that are clearly inadequate.

Where does psychology fit in?

It is time to return to Kuhn's three stages to consider where psychology fits in. Kuhn (1962) argued that psychology has failed to develop a paradigm and so remains at the pre-science stage. Various arguments support this point of view. First, there are several general theoretical approaches within psychology (e.g. psychodynamic, behaviourist, humanist, cognitive). As a result, it cannot really be argued that most psychologists support the same paradigm.

Second, psychology is an unusually fragmented discipline. It has connections with several other disciplines, including biology, physiology, biochemistry, neurology, and sociology. For example, psychologists studying biochemistry have very little in common with those studying social factors within society. The fragmentation and diversity make it unlikely that agreement can be reached on a common paradigm or general theoretical orientation.

Valentine (1982, 1992) argued for a different position, claiming that behaviourism comes close to being a paradigm. As she pointed out, behaviourism has had a massive influence on psychology through its insistence that psychology is the study of behaviour, and that behaviour should be observed in controlled experiments. It also had a great influence (but one that has declined considerably in recent decades) through its theoretical assumptions that the study of learning is of fundamental importance to psychology, and that learning can be understood in terms of conditioning principles.

It is not clear that behaviourism is a paradigm. Behaviourism's greatest impact on psychology has been at the methodological level, with its emphasis on studying behaviour. However, a paradigm in Kuhn's sense is more concerned with a general theoretical orientation rather than with methodological issues. Thus, behaviourism does not seem to be a paradigm and Kuhn (1962) was probably correct to place psychology at the pre-science stage. This might not make psychology as different from other sciences as is often assumed. Kuhn's view of normal science, in which nearly all scientists within a discipline are working in harmony using the same paradigm, exaggerates the similarity of perspective found among researchers in physics, chemistry, biology, and so on.

Non-scientific Approaches to Psychology

The behaviourists firmly believed that psychology should be a science and they tried hard to achieve this. However, other approaches to psychology attach much less emphasis to the notion of psychology as a science. Humanistic psychologists and social constructionists agreed strongly that psychology should not be a science, and social constructionists went further and argued that it cannot be a science.

Humanistic approaches

The humanistic psychologists (e.g. Maslow, Rogers) were fairly strongly opposed to the traditional scientific approach to psychology. According to Maslow (1968, p. 13), "The uniqueness of the individual does not fit into what we know of science. Then so much the worse for that conception of science. It, too, will have to endure re-creation."

Maslow and Rogers favoured the use of **phenomenology**, in which individuals report their conscious experiences in as pure and undistorted a way as possible. This approach was justified in the following terms by Rogers (1959):

> *This personal, phenomenological type of study—especially when one reads all of the responses—is far more valuable than the traditional "hard-headed" empirical approach. This kind of study, often scorned by psychologists as being "merely self-reports", actually gives the deepest insight into what the experience has meant.*

It will be remembered that three of the major aims of science are understanding, prediction, and control. The humanistic psychologists emphasised the goal of understanding. However, their approach failed to be scientific in part because they attached much less importance to the other two aims of prediction and control.

Social constructionist approaches

Those psychologists who favour **social constructionism** argue that there are no objective data and that our "knowledge" of ourselves and of the world is based on social constructions. Thus, "What we call facts are simply versions of events which, for various reasons, are presently enjoying wide currency" (Burr, 1997, p. 8). Social constructionists have attacked the "so-called objectivity of the 'scientist', disengaged from the cultural and historical circumstances" (Semin, 1995, p. 545). According to them, the observations made by psychologists, and the ways those observations are interpreted, are determined in large measure by the cultural and historical forces influencing them. Thus, for example, teachers nowadays are not allowed to beat disruptive schoolchildren—this is regarded as violent and unacceptable behaviour—but such behaviour was generally tolerated 40 or 50 years ago.

The importance of historical forces was emphasised by Gergen (1973, p. 318): "We must think in terms of a *continuum of historical durability*, with phenomena highly susceptible to historical influence at one extreme and the more stable processes at the other." Behaviourists and other psychologists who favour the scientific approach assume that the historical durability of phenomena is high, whereas social constructionists assume it is often very low.

It follows from what has been said so far that social constructionists believe psychology cannot be a science. How do they think that psychologists should proceed? According to Burr (1997, p. 8), "Since there is no ultimate knowledge of human beings that we can call a final truth, what we must do instead is to try to understand where our current ways of understanding have come from." One of the ways in which this can be done is by means of **discourse analysis**, which involves focusing on analysing people's use of language in order to understand how they perceive the world.

In the past, physical punishment of disobedient children was generally accepted as appropriate. Psychologists today view it differently because the social view of physical punishment has undergone drastic changes.

Wetherell and Potter (1988) carried out discourse analysis on interviews conducted with white New Zealanders. These interviews dealt with the issue of the teaching of Maori culture in schools. What emerged from this discourse analysis was that many white New Zealanders had racist views, even though they claimed not to be racist. They argued in favour of encouraging Maori culture but emphasised the importance of togetherness (all New Zealanders working co-operatively) and of pragmatic realism (being in touch with the modern world). The hidden message was that fostering Maori culture would have adverse effects on togetherness and pragmatic realism, and so should not be done.

However, the study by Wetherell and Potter (1988) fails to meet some of the criteria of science identified earlier. More specifically, the interview data were not obtained under controlled conditions and there was incomplete objectivity because the data were interpreted in a subjective way by the researchers. In addition, we don't know whether the findings are replicable, thus discourse analysis cannot be regarded as falling within a scientific paradigm.

Evaluation

Although there is some validity in the social constructionist position, many psychologists regard it as making exaggerated claims. For example, suppose several people saw a police officer hitting a student hard with a long stick. Regardless of their beliefs, they would probably be able to agree on the basic facts of what had happened. However, there would be much disagreement as to whether the police officer's action was justified or unjustified. In other words, our beliefs can colour our *interpretation* of an action, but they are less likely to influence our *description* of that action.

? What response might a physicist give to the social constructionist approach?

The Scientific Process

The scientific process takes a particular form. It begins with:

Observation of subject matter

This leads to the:

Formulation of theory

The next step is to test the theory:

Hypotheses construction

Hypotheses are tested through research:

Empirical methods

New knowledge cannot be accepted uncritically, it must be checked:

Replication and validation of new knowledge through peer review

The Role of Peer Review in Validating Knowledge

Science is based on repeatable experiment. **Peer review** is a means of assessing the quality of the experiments. The peer review process involves fellow researchers criticising and evaluating the work of their peers before it appears formally in print. Peer review plays an important role—it is intended to provide expert critical review of concepts and ideas to ensure quality and accuracy.

KEY TERM

Peer review: the process by which peers evaluate a researcher's work before it appears formally in print.

The work of specialists is submitted to a qualified adjudicator—an editor—who in turn sends it to fellow specialists—referees—to seek their advice about whether the paper is potentially publishable and, if so, what further work is required to make it acceptable. The paper is not published until and unless the recommended revision can be and is done to the satisfaction of the editor and referees.

Critics of peer review point to the fact that it is plagued by elitism, bias, and abuse. The referees can fail to be sufficiently expert, informed, conscientious, or fair. Editors can be biased in their use of the feedback provided by the referee because they can misinterpret or misapply referees' advice. Thus, it is judged by many as an imperfect system yet it is deemed essential to the scientific process. The internet offers the potential to improve the process by speeding up what can be a quite lengthy process and because the ease of accessibility it offers can result in more referees being used, thereby reducing any selectivity in the feedback.

Summary and Conclusions

It is hard to decide whether psychology should be regarded as a science. In general terms, psychology possesses many of the features of a science. However, it tends to possess them less clearly and less strongly than other sciences such as physics or chemistry.

On the positive side, much research in psychology involves controlled observations and is designed to test theoretical predictions. In addition, some theoretical approaches in psychology have been successful in achieving the goals of prediction, understanding, and control. Many psychological theories fulfil Popper's criterion of falsifiability, as they have been disproved by experimental studies. The findings of numerous experiments in psychology have been replicated successfully, which is another criterion of a science. However, psychology is very variable with respect to falsifiability and replicability. As we have seen, some theories in psychology are not sufficiently precisely expressed to be falsifiable, and many findings are not replicable.

> **?** What are some examples of controlled observations that you have learned about in this book?

On the negative side, there are various legitimate doubts about the scientific nature of psychology. First, at least some of the data obtained are not objective but seem to be influenced by the experimenter's biases, which are determined by his or her social and cultural background. Second, many of the findings obtained from psychological research lack external validity because they have been obtained under the artificial conditions of the laboratory. Third, the experimental method can most easily be used when we want to study the effects of the immediate situation on behaviour. However, as was discussed earlier in the chapter, our behaviour is determined by numerous factors in addition to the immediate situation, and most of these factors cannot be manipulated (e.g. childhood experiences, genetic inheritance, our personality). The fact that we cannot control these factors limits the development of psychology as a science. Fourth, Kuhn (1970) is probably correct in arguing that psychology is a pre-science because it lacks a generally accepted paradigm.

The issue of whether psychology is or is not a science can have important implications for research funding: subjects that are regarded as sciences generally receive more research funding than those not so regarded. The Qualifications and Curriculum Authority's (QCA) move to reclassify A-level psychology as a science

A-level from 2008 is a significant recognition that, at least at an educational level, psychology is classified as a science.

In sum, there are good reasons for arguing that psychology is on the way to becoming a science. At present, however, it should probably be regarded as having only some of the features of a science rather than being a fully fledged science.

SECTION SUMMARY
The Application of Scientific Method in Psychology

What is the definition of "science"?

❖ The traditional view is that science involves the collection of objective data and the drawing of generalisations.
❖ At the opposite extreme some psychologists suggest that objectivity is irrelevant to successful science.
❖ Popper argued that the fundamental scientific belief in testing hypotheses doesn't hold up.
❖ It may be possible to define science as possessing the following features:

— controlled observations
— relatively objective data
— testing theoretical predictions
— falsifiability
— replicability of findings
— use of a paradigm.

Controlled observations

❖ Controlled observations (typically obtained under laboratory conditions using the experimental method) are of key importance.
❖ Science aims to be objective, yet all observations inevitably are influenced by what you expect to see.
❖ According to social constructionists, the observations made by psychologists, and their interpretations of those observations, are determined by cultural forces.

Falsifiability

❖ Popper argued that the hallmark of science is falsifiability (disproving theories and hypotheses by experimental tests).
❖ Not all theories in psychology are falsifiable. Eysenck's theory of physiological responsiveness is falsifiable, while Freud's theory of psychoanalysis is not.
❖ In addition to falsifiability, it is important that findings are replicable—if the findings keep changing, there is no basis for developing theories.

Use of a paradigm

❖ Kuhn described three stages in the development of science: pre-science, normal science, and revolutionary science.
❖ Kuhn claimed psychology has failed to develop a paradigm and remains in the pre-science stage.
❖ This is supported by the variety of theoretical approaches within psychology and the fragmented nature of the subject.
❖ Some approaches within psychology, such as behaviourism, may be paradigms. However, behaviourism is largely methodological (concerned with studying behaviour) rather than a general theoretical orientation.

❖ Humanistic psychologists argue that psychology shouldn't be a science: They suggest phenomenology as an alternative research approach that provides deep insights through self-reporting.

❖ Social constructionists suggest psychology can't be a science: They suggest that the historical durability of phenomena is low and thus research and understanding are best served by qualitative research methods such as discourse analysis.

Non-scientific approaches to psychology

❖ Psychology has some features of a science:

— controlled observations
— testing theoretical predictions
— falsifiability
— replicability.

Is psychology a science?

❖ However, it doesn't fully possess other features:

— paradigm
— objectivity.

❖ There are important implications for the funding of research.

DESIGNING PSYCHOLOGICAL INVESTIGATIONS

The Selection and Application of Appropriate Research Methods

Research methods take either a **quantitative** or **qualitative** approach, which depends on whether the data collected is numerical or non-numerical. Thus, quantitative = numbers and qualitative = words. Quantitative methods are concerned with objective measurement and so try to quantify and describe behaviour. In contrast, qualitative methods are concerned with gaining in-depth data and so try to establish valid (true) explanations for behaviour. All methods can be used in a scientific or non-scientific way, so do not make the mistake of seeing quantitative as the former and qualitative as the latter. To decide which method is the most suitable careful consideration needs to be given to the strengths and weaknesses of the research methods.

Laboratory experiments

The laboratory experiment takes place in a controlled environment and enables the experimenter to test the effect of the IV (independent variable) on the DV (dependent variable). To establish a difference and so detect cause and effect relationships, the IV is systematically varied between two conditions.

Advantages:

1. The highly controlled environment of the laboratory, in particular the direct manipulation of the IV by the experimenter, enables cause and effect to be established. Causal relationships can be identified because, of all the

> **KEY TERMS**
>
> **Quantitative (research methods):** concerned with how data are presented in numerical terms. An example of quantitative data would be a measurement of height or weight.
>
> **Qualitative (research methods):** concerned with how things are expressed, what it feels like, meanings or explanations, i.e. the quality. An example of qualitative data would be that obtained from a media interview.

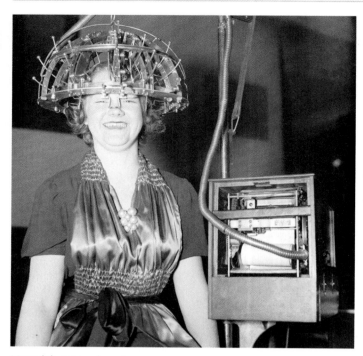

Many laboratory-based psychology experiments show low external validity, that is, their findings do not translate reliably to behaviour outside the laboratory.

experimental methods, this one provides the most confidence that the IV has caused the effect on the DV.

2. Laboratory experiments take the traditional scientific approach and so are objective. They involve precise measurements and so are not as subject to researcher bias as less objective methods.

Weaknesses:

1. The laboratory is an artificial environment and, consequently, the research lacks mundane realism, i.e. it is not like real life. This means that the findings might not generalise to settings other than the laboratory, and so the research lacks external validity. The artificiality of the experiment can also elicit **demand characteristics** (participants guess the research hypothesis from cues in the experimental setting or cues given inadvertently by the experimenter).

2. Laboratory experiments are reductionist because they focus on only two variables. In real life, many interacting variables and multiple causes and effects are involved in behaviour. Therefore, the laboratory experiment is oversimplified.

Field experiments

Field experiments take place in natural settings, e.g. the work environment. The experimenter has control of the IV and so causal relationships can be established. Participants are often not aware they are being researched.

Advantages:

1. As they take place in a natural setting, field experiments usually have greater mundane realism than laboratory experiments, and consequently can have greater generalisability to real life and so high external validity.
2. There is control over the IV and so cause and effect can be established to some extent, although not always, because of the disadvantage of lack of control.

Weaknesses:

1. There is less control in a field experiment, which means confounding variables might be causing the effect on the DV rather than the IV. This means internal validity is lower and it is difficult to infer cause and effect.
2. Most field experiments cannot involve informed consent, right to withdraw, or debriefing, and so the ethical implications are a weakness.

Quasi-experiments

Quasi-experiments take place when the experimenter cannot control the IV—it is said to be naturally occurring. For example, experiments involving gender, age, class, or cultural differences would be classed as quasi because the experimenter cannot manipulate these factors as the IV. However, the experimenter does have control of the research setting.

Advantages:

1. A quasi-experiment enables us to research behaviours that could not otherwise be investigated experimentally because it involves a naturally occurring IV. This means that a quasi-experiment can be used to investigate phenomena that would not be practical or ethical to manipulate in a laboratory or field experiment, where the IV is controlled.
2. The experimental environment is controlled by the experimenter, which enables better control of confounding variables and greater confidence that the IV has been isolated.

Weaknesses:

1. Cause and effect can be inferred only when the experimenter manipulates the IV directly, and so in a quasi-experiment only *association* can be identified, which limits the conclusiveness of the findings, as we cannot conclude that *x* has caused the effect on *y*.
2. Quasi-experiments are reductionist because they focus on only two variables when in real life there are usually many interacting variables and multiple cause and effects involved in behaviour. Thus, quasi-experiments are oversimplified.

Natural experiments

A **natural experiment** is kind of quasi-experiment but the researcher has no control over the IV or the research setting.

Advantages:

1. A natural experiment enables us to research behaviours that could not otherwise be investigated experimentally because it involves a naturally occurring IV. This means that a natural experiment can be used to investigate phenomena that would not be practical or ethical to manipulate in a laboratory or field experiment, where the IV is controlled.
2. Natural experiments take place in a natural setting and so usually have greater mundane realism than the controlled environments of laboratory and quasi-experiments. Consequently, they can have greater generalisability to real life and so high external validity.

Weaknesses:

1. Cause and effect can be inferred only when the experimenter directly manipulates the IV, and so in a natural experiment only *association* can be identified, which limits the conclusiveness of the findings, as we cannot conclude that *x* has caused the effect on *y*.
2. There is less control in a natural experiment, which means confounding variables might be causing the effect on the DV rather than the IV. This means that internal validity is lower and so findings can be difficult to interpret and it might not be possible to infer associations.

? A true experiment involves manipulation of the IV by the experimenter. How is a quasi-experiment different?

? Natural experiments are a good way of doing research, so why are there so few actually done?

KEY TERM

Natural experiment:
a type of experiment in which use is made of some naturally occurring variable(s).

A positive correlation: The taller the player, the higher the score.

A negative correlation: The more time spent playing computer games, the less time spent studying.

No correlation: Where there is no relationship, variables are uncorrelated.

Correlational analysis

Correlational analysis is a technique that measures the strength of the relationship between two variables. The paired scores of the two variables are analysed to establish the strength and direction of the association, e.g. the relationship between stress and illness. This can be illustrated visually through scattergrams and numerically through correlation coefficients. These range from $+1$ to 0 to -1, where the sign shows the direction and the number shows the strength of the association.

Advantages:

1. Correlational analysis shows the direction and strength of relationships and so its greatest use is prediction. One variable can be predicted from the other, e.g. A-level passes from GCSE grades.
2. Correlational analysis is useful when manipulation of the variables is impossible. Thus, a great advantage of this method is that it can be used when an experiment cannot.

Weaknesses:

1. Cause and effect cannot be established because the variables are not manipulated directly and consequently only association can be identified. This means that the findings are descriptive rather than explanatory, as they describe the relationship rather than explaining the effect of one variable on the other.
2. Although only two variables are investigated, other factors (that were not known of or were not accounted for in the research) might be involved. This means that the inferred association would lack validity as the correlation is too reductionist (oversimplified).

Observational techniques

Naturalistic observation

Naturalistic observation involves examining behaviour in a natural setting with minimal intrusion from the researcher because it aims to observe people's natural behaviour. Participants might be aware they are being observed (overt observation), or might not (covert observation).

Advantages:

1. Naturalistic observation involves looking at behaviour as it occurs naturally and so has greater mundane realism than more artificial methods. Consequently, it might have greater generalisability to real life and so high external validity.
2. Naturalistic observation is less biased by participant reactivity, e.g. **demand characteristics**, which means that the behaviour observed is more genuine and so the research might have greater internal validity.

> **KEY TERMS**
> **Correlational analysis:** testing a hypothesis using an association that is found between two variables.
> **Naturalistic observation:** an unobtrusive observational study conducted in a natural setting.
> **Demand characteristics:** features of an experimental situation used by participants to work out what is expected of them and to behave as they think they are expected to.

Weaknesses:

1. Observer bias can lead to imprecise recording or interpretation of findings. Consequently, naturalistic observation might lack **reliability** (lack of consistency) and validity.
2. Naturalistic observations describe behaviour but do not explain it.

Controlled observation

Controlled observation takes place when the researcher has control of the environment in which the observation occurs.

Advantages:

1. If the situation is well controlled there is less risk of unwanted extraneous variables influencing participants' behaviour than is the case with naturalistic observations.
2. Richer and more complete information is often obtained from studies using controlled observations than from conventional experimental studies in which participants are required to produce only limited responses.

Weaknesses:

1. The artificiality of the situation can make it hard to generalise the findings to more natural situations, and so the study might lack external validity and generalisability to real-life settings.
2. Problems such as investigator effects (due to experimenter expectations) and demand characteristics (due to participant expectations) can arise in studies using controlled observations. The Hawthorne effect refers to the fact that participants might change their behaviour because they are being observed. These effects limit internal validity as they will affect the truth of the research.

Self-report techniques

Interviews

As a form of **self-report technique**, interviews take many different forms: they usually take place face to face and can yield rich, in-depth data.

Non-directive interviews. These are led by the participant (the interviewee), who is free to discuss whatever he or she chooses. The interviewer guides the discussion by encouraging the interviewee to elaborate on responses. Such interviews tend to be used in the treatment of mental disorders but have little relevance to psychological research.

Informal interviews. The interviewer has a list of topics that are to be discussed. Informal interviews resemble non-directive interviews in that the interviewee is allowed to discuss the topics in whatever way and order he or she chooses, with the interviewer mainly encouraging more depth and detail.

Semi-structured or guided interviews. All interviewees are asked precisely the same questions in the same order. Thus these interviews possess more structure

> **?** Imagine that you are going to conduct an observation of children in a playgroup with two other researchers. To what extent do you think that you will all record the same behaviours? How might you cope with any disagreements?

> **?** What advantages might be gained by observing children in a naturalistic environment rather than in a laboratory?

> **?** In what way have you altered your own natural behaviour when you were aware of being observed? Was this because of evaluation apprehension or some other reason?

> **KEY TERMS**
>
> **Reliability:** the extent to which a method of measurement or test produces consistent findings.
> **Controlled observation:** the researcher exercises control over some aspects of the environment in which the observations are made.
> **Self-report technique:** a written (questionnaire) or verbal (interview) report method by which the participant answers a series of questions.

? Have you ever been interviewed while out shopping? How would you classify this interview style?

than informal interviews because the interviewer takes control of the issues to be discussed and decides in what order they will be covered.

Clinical interviews. These are often used by clinical psychologists to assess patients with mental disorders. All interviewees are asked the same questions but follow-up questions depend on the answers given. This gives the interviewer flexibility to explore and follow-up on interesting answers.

Structured interviews. A standard set of questions is asked in exactly the same order and the interviewees have a restricted range of answers to select from.

Advantages:

1. Interviews can yield richly detailed data, which has high validity because it is very revealing about how the participants make their experiences meaningful.
2. Interviews can be very flexible as the more unstructured interviews can be led by the participant, as opposed to the researcher.

Weaknesses:

? How would research results be affected by the possibility that people might decide to give the socially acceptable response to statements such as "Smacking children is an appropriate form of punishment"?

1. Interviewer bias is a weakness, because question setting is subjective and data analysis is vulnerable to misinterpretation, either deliberately or unconsciously. The researcher might be drawn to data that corroborate the research hypothesis and disregard data that do not do this, and so validity will be reduced.
2. Participant reactivity is a problem because answers might be biased by evaluation apprehension and social desirability, which means that validity would be low because the answers would lack truth.

Questionnaires

Written questionnaires are a type of interview. They can be conducted face to face, via the telephone, or by post. A questionnaire consists of a standard set of questions, which are either closed (fixed response, e.g. rating scales) or open-ended (requiring detailed responses). Questionnaires are used to survey attitudes, beliefs, and behaviour.

Advantages:

1. The questionnaire is very flexible as open and closed questions can be used and, thus, both quantitative and qualitative data can be gathered. Consequently, a wide range of phenomena can be investigated.
2. On a practical level, questionnaires are quick and economical to conduct and consequently a large sample can be obtained.

Weaknesses:

1. Researcher bias in question setting, implementation, or analysis can reduce validity: the researcher might be drawn to data that corroborate the research hypothesis and might disregard data that does not. Such investigator effects reduce internal validity, i.e. the truth of the research.

2. Participant reactivity is a problem in that answers might be biased by demand characteristics, evaluation apprehension, and social desirability. This would result in low validity, as the answers would lack truth.

Case studies

A **case study** is the in-depth study of an individual or small group. Examples that you will have come across during your studies include: case studies of abnormality (e.g. Little Albert and Anna O), case studies of brain damage (e.g. HM), and case studies of privation (e.g. Genie).

Advantages:

1. Case studies can provide far more information about a specific individual than is usually obtained from studies involving groups of individuals. For example, very detailed information about Genie's intellectual and social development was obtained over a period of several years.
2. Case studies (even limited ones) can provide useful insights that influence future theoretical developments. For example, there is the case study of Little Albert (Watson & Rayner, 1920). This case study influenced the development of behaviour therapy—it showed that fears can be classically conditioned and suggested to behaviour therapists that fears could perhaps be eliminated through conditioning as well.

Weaknesses:

1. A key weakness is the issue of generalisation and drawing general conclusions from case studies. There are two kinds of problem with respect to generalisation. First, the individual might not be representative of individuals of the same age and gender. Second, even if the individual studied is representative, it is still likely that other individuals of the opposite gender and/or a different age would behave differently. For example, strictly speaking, the case study of Little Albert only tells us about fear conditioning in a boy of 11 months—it is perfectly possible that younger or older boys or girls would show different effects.
2. Another weakness with case studies is that of subjective selection, i.e. researcher bias (Coolican, 1994). The therapist often only reports a small fraction of the information obtained from the individual being studied, and what is selected may be influenced by his/her preconceptions

Experimental and Non-Experimental Designs

To account for the application of research methods you need to be able to explain how different methods are implemented.

Experimental research designs

There are three experimental designs that aim to control participant variation (i.e. individual differences between the participants) that could interfere with the effect of the IV (independent variable) on the DV (dependent variable). The three designs share a common characteristic of experiments: there are two conditions,

---

EXAM HINT

Make sure you know two advantages and two disadvantages per method.

? Case studies are often used as a way of understanding unusual behaviours. What are the advantages and weaknesses of using this method of research?

KEY TERM

Case study: detailed study of a single individual, event, or group.

How can an experiment tell us more about "why" the behaviour occurred than an observational study can?

and the IV is varied across these. This usually involves a control condition, which is not exposed to the IV and so acts as a baseline, and an experimental condition, which is influenced by the IV and so shows the effect of the IV in comparison to the control condition. The three experimental designs are discussed below.

Independent groups design

The **independent groups design** involves two groups of different participants. Thus, there are different participants in each of the conditions, and the participants experience *one* condition. A strength of the design is that it avoids **order effects**. As the participants experience only one condition, they are less likely to guess the demand characteristics; they are also less likely to experience other order effects, such as boredom, fatigue, and the practice effect. Another strength of the independent groups design is that random allocation is possible. This means that every participant has an equal chance of being allocated to either condition. This is a strength because it reduces bias in allocation and minimises participant variation.

Weaknesses of this experimental design include **participant variables**. There might be consistent individual differences between the two groups of participants. For example, if one group was more alert than the other then this would systematically distort results on a quick response test. Another weakness is the number of participants: you need more participants than you do with a repeated measures design (see the next page), because there are two groups instead of one.

> **EXAM HINT**
>
> Note the independent measures design generates unrelated data because there are different participants in each condition and the repeated measures design generates related data because the same participants experience both conditions and so the data from the two can be fully related. You will need to know this to understand justification of statistical tests, which comes up further on.

> **KEY TERMS**
>
> **Independent groups design:** a research design in which each participant is in one condition only. Each separate group of participants experiences different levels of the independent variable. Sometimes referred to as an unrelated or between-subjects design.
> **Order effects:** participants' performance on two conditions can be affected by the order in which they are performed, e.g. because of being bored or having more practice.
> **Participant variables:** possible confounding variables if participants are not as similar as possible, e.g. in age, sex, or IQ.
> **Matched participant design:** a research design that matches participants on a one-to-one basis rather than as a whole group.

Matched participant design

The **matched participant design** is as it sounds—the participants in each condition are matched on certain relevant variables. The participants experience only one condition. Thus, there are two groups, which are matched, and each group experiences a different condition. This involves matching the participants on a one-to-one basis, not simply matching the groups as a whole.

A key strength of this design is that it minimises participant variables. Participants are matched on important variables and so there is less participant variation (individual differences) between them. Another strength is that, as in the independent groups design, order effects are avoided. The participants experience only one condition and so are less likely to guess the demand characteristics; they are also less likely to experience other order effects, such as boredom, fatigue, and the practice effect.

Weaknesses of the matched participants design include the fact that the design cannot eliminate participant variables. It is impossible to control for all individual differences and so participant variation is minimised, not eliminated. Another issue is that it is difficult to achieve a good match. It can be difficult to find participants who match on a number of key variables. A large pool of participants is needed, making this approach time consuming and less practical than the other designs.

Repeated measures design

In the **repeated measures design** the same participants experience both conditions; thus, there is one group of participants who take part in *both* conditions. The strengths of this design are that it minimises participant variables. As the same participants are in each condition participant variation is reduced; although it is not eliminated, because there will still be some individual differences between the participants. Another strength is that fewer participants are needed because there is only one group of participants, rather than two different groups as in the independent and matched pairs designs. So to achieve the same-size sample, half the number of participants is needed for repeated measures than for the other two designs.

One of the weaknesses of the repeated measures design is order effects. These are the result of participating in two conditions, e.g. participants can experience practice effect, fatigue, or boredom during the second condition and so differences in their performance might be due to these order effects, rather than the action of the IV. Thus, the internal validity of the research is reduced. Another weakness is that demand characteristics are easier to guess because the participants have experienced two conditions. They are more likely to guess the purpose of the study and so demand characteristics may reduce the internal validity of the research.

Deciding which design to use often comes down to choosing between independent measures and repeated measures, because matched participants is often just too difficult to carry out economically. To decide which design is best, a decision has to be made based on the key weaknesses of the two designs in terms of which will least affect validity, participant variables (independent measures) or order effects, including demand characteristics (repeated measures).

Non-experimental research designs

Observation design

Several factors need to be taken into account when performing non-experimental research. First, researchers need to decide whether to conceal themselves (covert) or not (overt), and this will depend on what is being investigated. A second consideration is whether to conduct a participant or a non-participant observation. Participant observation is when the researcher becomes a member of the group under observation in order to observe more natural behaviour. However, participant observation is not always possible and, for some investigations, non-participant observation will be more practical and ethical, e.g. when investigating alcohol or drug abuse. A further design consideration is how best to sample the behaviour to be observed. To avoid data overload, time, event, and point sampling are used: for time sampling, observations are recorded only during specific time periods; event sampling is when only relevant events or behaviours are recorded; and in point sampling one individual is observed at a time, his or her current behaviour is categorised, and then a second individual is observed, and so on.

Reliability is a key design consideration as observers must be consistent in their judgements if the data are to be reliable and valid. Thus, the recording of the data into **behavioural categories** must be as precise as possible. Precision of the observation criteria and training of observers are of key importance. The issue here is that of reliability or consistency of measurement, i.e. are two observers categorising the same behaviour in the same (i.e. reliable) way? Reliability can be assessed by asking two or more observers to produce observational records at the same time. When these records are correlated, we have a measure of inter-observer reliability (sometimes known as inter-rater or inter-judge reliability). Ethical considerations include the fact that naturalistic observations often cannot involve informed consent, the right to withdraw, or debriefing, and so the ethical implications are a weakness. Deception is also an issue.

Interviews

The first consideration is the format of the interview, which can be structured, semi-structured, or unstructured. A structured interview has a fixed format of questions, which means that the same questions are asked in the same order for each participant. This is researcher led, as the interviewer controls the pace and direction of the interview. Semi-structured interviews also ask the same questions but the order is not fixed, which means they can be selected to suit the flow of the interview and so encourage the participant to be at ease and more forthcoming. Unstructured interviews are participant led in that the participants' answers direct the questions. This is the format taken in the clinical interview.

A key issue is the construction of good questions. This is complex because it is important that the questions are clear and unambiguous—as if they communicate different meanings to different participants then the answers will not be comparable. The questions should also be free from bias and subjectivity, to avoid leading the participant.

Ethical issues involved in the design of interviews include abuse of power, particularly in clinical interviews. Deception, informed consent, and protection of participants are also key issues. For example, participants might feel pressured to answer embarrassing questions if they know their responses are being assessed and compared to others.

Questionnaires

Questionnaire design involves deciding on the format of the questions. Closed questions involve a fixed response, which the participant must choose from, for example, yes/no answers or a Likert scale. This generates quantitative data, which

KEY TERM

Behavioural categories: a way in which the types of behaviour that are expected to be observed are organised and clearly defined using observation criteria to increase the reliability (consistency) of the observation.

are easier to score and analyse. Open questions allow the participants to answer freely and so qualitative analysis is needed, which can be more difficult and time consuming, but can also yield more meaningful data.

A key design issue is that the questions must be free from ambiguity and bias. Ambiguity must be avoided, as data are of little value if answers cannot be compared and they can't be if different participants have interpreted the questions differently. It is also important to avoid biased questions, as these can lead the participants or provoke reactive answers that are not valid if they are not true.

Another design issue is that of construction. A Likert scale is the most usual design; this involves the participants giving self-report ratings on a five-point scale to indicate their level of agreement or non-agreement with whatever was communicated in the question. For positive statements, such as "It is important to get 8 hours' sleep per night", a participant who strongly disagrees with the statement scores 1, whereas someone who strongly agrees scores 5. For negative statements, such as "It is not important to maintain a regular sleep pattern", the scoring is reversed, with strongly disagree scored as 5 and strongly agree as 1. This makes it possible to relate the scores on the questionnaire to each other.

Ethical considerations in the design of questionnaires include deception, informed consent, protection of participants, right to withdraw, debrief, and confidentiality.

Pilot studies

Experimental and non-experimental research designs are often preceded by a **pilot study**, which allows for a trial run of the material so that questions can be checked for clarity and ambiguity, and adjusted if there are problems before the main study. Thus, a pilot study saves time and money, as findings would be valueless if there had been ambiguity in the questions. A pilot study also enables the researcher to check the experimental procedure for design errors and timings. Thus the researcher can ascertain whether the study is replicable, which is essential for testing reliability. For example, the behavioural categories of an observation can be checked to see how appropriately they relate to behaviour and if they are sufficiently well-defined to allow reliable classification of behaviour.

The Strengths and Weaknesses of Different Forms of Sample Methods

Research is conducted on people, and the group of people that the researcher is interested in is called the target population. However, as it is not usually possible to use all of the people in the target population, a **sample** must be selected. Those selected are called "participants" for research purposes. Thus, research is conducted on a sample but the researcher hopes that the findings will be true (valid) for the target population. For this to be the case, the sample must be representative of the target population. If the sample *is* representative then the findings can be generalised back to the target population. If not, the findings lack population validity. Therefore, the key issue is the generalisability of the sample; this is based on two key factors:

- *type* of sampling
- *size* of the sample.

Random sampling

Random methods mean every participant has an equal chance of being selected. They include methods such as selecting names out of a hat, or everybody in the population being assigned a number and a computer or random number table being used to generate the numbers that are selected for the sample.

Evaluation

A positive evaluation is that this sample method is free from the biases that result when the researcher selects the sample (opportunity) or when the participants volunteer themselves (volunteer). It can be difficult to obtain a random sample because of problems in identifying all members of a population. Once identified, it might not be possible to contact all potential participants and they might not be willing to take part. Thus, random sampling is expensive and time-consuming given that it doesn't actually produce a truly representative sample, as this is an impossibility.

Opportunity sampling

Opportunity sampling involves selecting anybody who is available at the time of the study to take part. This is a popular method and as much as 90% of the research discussed in psychology textbooks will have used this method—participants are mainly undergraduates at American universities who were selected based on their availability.

Evaluation

This is a weak form of sampling because opportunity samples are usually drawn from a restricted population and so are not very representative. Also, although anybody who is available can be selected, this doesn't always happen in practice because the researchers might approach people who they think look friendly, or less intimidating, or because they find them attractive. Thus, opportunity sampling is inherently biased by researcher selectivity.

Volunteer sampling

Participants volunteer to take part in a research study, for instance by replying to an advertisement.

Evaluation

It is possible that the people who volunteer for psychological research are different from non-volunteers, for instance in aspects of personality, and so are not a truly representative sample. This is called a volunteer bias, which includes the fact that volunteers are more likely to be sensitive to demand characteristics (the cues used

---

EXAM HINT

Remember random sampling does not mean going up to people at random - this is opportunity sampling as you sample whoever is available, whereas random sampling is when every participant has an equal chance of being selected.

? How do you think students, as research participants, might differ from society in general?

by participants to work out what a study is about) and also that they are more likely to comply with these demand characteristics. This makes generalisations of the findings to the non-volunteering population questionable.

? Why do you think volunteers are more likely than non-volunteers to be sensitive to the demand characteristics of a study?

Reliability: Assessment and Improvement

Reliability is based on consistency. Research that produces the same results every time it is carried out is reliable.

Internal reliability = consistency within the method

Measuring instruments such as a ruler or clock give the same measurements when tested on different occasions. Thus there is consistency within the method of measurement, as the difference between 0cm and 5cm is the same as that between 5cm and 10cm. However, the Likert rating scales lack such consistency, as the difference between 1 and 2 on the scale might not be perceived to be the same as the difference between 4 and 5. This measure is subjective, compared with a ruler, which is objective, and so might lack reliability. Unreliable measures reduce internal validity.

Reliability of observations

Two or more observers are usually used to control for subjectivity, i.e. personal bias in the observations. Problems with reliability arise because it can be difficult to categorise complex behaviour into observation criteria.

External reliability = consistency between uses of the method

To test the consistency of psychological tests over time, the test must be taken once and then again on a later occasion. The time between each test must be long enough to prevent a practice effect but not so long that the measures may have changed in some way.

Internal and external reliability can be checked using correlational techniques.

Techniques to check internal reliability

Split-half technique

The **split-half technique** is used to establish the internal reliability of psychological tests. Half the scores, e.g. the even numbers, are correlated with the other half, e.g. the odd numbers, to see how similar they are. A high degree of similarity would support internal consistency and thus reliability.

Inter-rater reliability (or inter-judge reliability)

Inter-rater reliability is used to test the accuracy of the observations. If the same behaviour is rated the same by two different observers then the observations are reliable. Observers must be well trained and have precise, clear observation criteria. A number of measures are taken and correlated to test for reliability.

Techniques to check external reliability

Test–retest reliability

Test–retest reliability involves testing once and then testing again at a later date, i.e. replicating the original research. Meta-analyses draw on this when they compare the findings from different studies that have tested the same hypothesis,

> **KEY TERMS**
>
> **Split-half technique:** a technique used to establish reliability by assigning items from one test randomly to two sub-tests (split halves). The same person does both sub-tests simultaneously and their scores are compared to see if they are similar, which would suggest that the test items are reliable.
>
> **Inter-rater/inter-judge reliability:** the extent to which ratings from two judges are consistent.
>
> **Test–retest reliability:** a technique used to establish reliability, by giving the same test to participants on two separate occasions to see if their scores remain relatively similar.

EXAM HINT

Questions on reliability may ask you to *explain what it means* and *how you could test for* reliability. Remember:

- Consistency within the research is internal reliability
- Consistency between uses of the measure (e.g. over time) is external reliability.

Check for reliability by the following:

- Replicate to see if the results are consistent over time, test–re-test,
- Check that there is consistency between two observers: this is inter-observer reliability/inter-rater reliability.

e.g. Milgram's study of obedience. Strong consistency between the different findings (i.e. reliability) indicates validity.

Validity: Assessment and Improvement

Campbell and Stanley (1966) distinguished between internal and external validity.

Internal validity/experimental validity

Does the research measure what it set out to? Is the effect genuine? Is the independent variable (IV) really responsible for the effect on the dependent variable (DV)? To be valid, the research must measure what it claims in the hypothesis, i.e. it must be the IV that causes the effect on the DV. If this happens, the research has truth because the effect is genuine and is caused by the IV rather than by a confounding variable.

Coolican (1994) identified threats to internal validity, i.e. other factors that could have caused the effect on the DV:

- *Confounding variables*: situational and participant variables could be responsible for the changes in the DV rather than the IV.
- *Unreliable measures*: measures that are inconsistent, e.g. rating scales lack reliability and validity as there is no "true measure".
- *Standardisation*: a lack of standardisation means participants do not experience the same research process and so findings are not comparable.
- *Randomisation*: bias in allocation due do a lack of randomisation can systematically distort the results and so reduce internal validity, for example, if participants in one condition were picked because they were expected to perform well on a memory test.
- *Demand characteristics*: these can lead to unusual/unnatural participant reactions and behaviour, thus reducing internal validity.
- *Participant reactivity*: evaluation apprehension and social desirability can also lead to behaviour that is not the participants' natural behaviour.
- *Good research design increases internal validity*: accounting for the above in the research design will increase internal validity.

Checking internal validity

If internal validity is high then replication should be possible; if it is low then replication will be difficult. Thus, validity and reliability are interlinked: if the research has truth (validity) it should be consistent (reliable) and so replication is possible. Reliability is also an indicator of validity.

Concurrent validity is another means of testing the internal validity of a new test. The scores from the new test of unknown validity are compared against those of a test where validity has already been established. If the scores are similar then the new test is probably valid, i.e. a true measure.

External validity

Coolican (1994) identified four main aspects to external validity:

1. *Populations*: findings have population validity if they generalise to other populations. Most importantly, it is necessary to determine whether the findings generalise to the target population from which the sample was drawn. Population validity is questionable if a restricted sample was used, e.g. a particular age group, as the findings are less likely to generalise to other age groups.
2. *Locations*: findings have ecological validity if they generalise to other settings. Of particular concern is whether they generalise to real-life situations. A lack of mundane realism is a key weakness of artificial research. This often limits ecological validity because the findings are less likely to generalise to real-life settings.
3. *Measures or constructs*: findings have construct validity if the measures generalise to other measures of the same variable, e.g. does a measure of recall of word lists generalise to everyday memory?
4. *Times*: findings have temporal validity if they generalise to other time periods, e.g. do findings from the past generalise to the current context or do current findings generalise to the past or future? This is difficult to achieve as, to some extent, all research is dependent on era and context.

Checking external validity

A meta-analysis involves the comparison of findings from many studies that have investigated the same hypothesis. Findings that are consistent (reliable) across populations, locations, and periods in time indicate validity (e.g. Van IJzendoorn and Kroonenberg's (1988) meta-analysis of the cross-cultural Strange Situation studies). Thus, if a study has validity then it is likely to replicate, and reliability in the meta-analysis is used as an indicator of validity. So it would seem that you rarely have one without the other, apart from consistently wrong findings!

Predictive validity is another means of checking external validity. It involves using the data from a study to predict behaviour at some point in the future. If the prediction is correct, then this suggests that the original data did generalise to a future context and so has external validity.

Ethical Considerations and Resolutions in Psychological Research

Ethical issues arise when **ethical guidelines** are breached. The need for ethical controls led to the establishment of ethical guidelines, i.e. rules that can

> **EXAM HINT**
>
> Questions on validity may ask you to explain what it means and how you could test research for validity. Remember:
>
> - Internal validity refers to how true the effect of the IV is on the DV, and external validity refers to how far the research will generalise.
> - Check for internal validity with concurrent validity seeing if is gets the same results as a validated measure; and test for external validity through a meta-analysis. If findings are consistent (reliable) across populations, locations, and periods in time then this indicates external validity.

> **KEY TERMS**
>
> **Ethical issues:** can arise in the implementing of research when there is conflict between how the research should be carried out (e.g. no deception of the participants) and the methodological consequences of observing this (e.g. reduced validity of the findings).
>
> **Ethical guidelines:** written code of conduct designed to aid psychologists when designing and running their research. The guidelines set out standards of what is and is not acceptable. The code focuses on the need to treat participants with respect and not to cause them harm or distress. For example, the BPS code of conduct advises of "the need to preserve an overriding high regard for the well-being and dignity of research participants" (BPS, 1993).

? Why do you think that views about the kinds of research that are ethically acceptable have changed over the years?

be used to judge the acceptability of research. For example, the war crimes committed by the Nazis during the Second World War resulted in the establishment of a ten-point "Nuremberg code" after the war. This set out what was acceptable in scientific research and has been adapted by professional bodies all over the world. Most countries now have a psychological organisation that has devised its own code of conduct, such as the BPS (British Psychological Society) guidelines.

The British Psychological Society Guidelines for Research with Human Participants

1. Introduction
Ethical guidelines are necessary to ensure psychological research is acceptable.

2. General
The research must be considered from the viewpoint of all participants. All potential threats to their well-being, etc. should be removed. The best judges of research are members of the target population from which the sample will be taken.

3. Consent
Participants' agreement to take part in research should be based on their full knowledge of the nature and purpose of the research. Thus, they should be given a briefing to ensure they are fully aware of any tasks required of them and their rights as a participant, i.e. the right to withdraw and the right to confidentiality. If the participant is a child (under 16 years) or impaired, adult consent must be gained from the parent or from those in *loco parentis*. If informed consent was not gained at the outset then the safeguards needed for such a deception would be as detailed below in the deception guideline.

4. Deception
Deception of the participants should be avoided wherever possible. Information should not be deliberately withheld and nor should the participants be misled without extremely strong scientific or medical justification. Deception should only be used when alternative procedures, which do not involve deception, have been fully considered and rejected as unfeasible by independent advisors. Also, participants should be fully informed at the earliest possible stage and should be consulted in advance as to how deception would be received.

5. Debriefing
At the end of a study the researcher should provide detailed information about the research and answer any questions the participants might have. The researcher should also monitor the participants for unforeseen negative effects and is responsible for providing active intervention if necessary.

6. Right to withdraw
Participants' right to withdraw from the study must be clearly communicated at the outset of the research. Also, participants have the right to withdraw their consent retrospectively, in which case their data must be destroyed.

? Without ethical guidelines how difficult woud it be to express misgivings about questionable research methods?

7. Confidentiality

In accordance with the Data Protection Act, information disclosed during the research process is confidential and, if the research is published, the anonymity of the participants should be protected. If either of these is likely to be compromised, then the participants' agreement must be sought in advance.

8. Protection of participants from psychological harm

Participants should be protected from psychological harm, such as distress, ridicule, or loss of self-esteem. The risk of harm during the research study should be no greater than that experienced in everyday life. Alternative methodology should be considered and measures must be taken to support participants who have experienced psychological harm. If there is the potential for harm then independent approval must be sought, the participants must be advised, and informed consent gained.

9. Observational research

Studies based on observation must respect the privacy and psychological well-being of the individuals studied. Unless consent has been given, observational research is acceptable in public situations only where one would expect to be observed by strangers.

> **?** What ethical issues would you flag up for observational research? And what issue of validity could there be?

10. Giving advice

Research might reveal physical or psychological problems of which the participant is unaware. It is the researcher's responsibility to inform the participant if it is felt that to not do so would endanger the participant's future well-being.

Ethical Issues and the Steps Taken to Deal With These

Deception

Ethical issues

Participants in Milgram's research into obedience to authority were deceived because they were told the experiment was a test of memory and learning. They were also led to believe that the electric shocks they were encouraged to administer were real when they were not, and that they were painful (particularly in the voice feedback condition, where they thought the cries of the person supposedly receiving the electric shocks were real). They were told that "Mr Wallace" was a real participant like themselves, when he was a confederate of Milgram, and they were deceived into thinking that they had an equal chance of ending up as the "teacher" or the "learner", when in fact the drawing of lots was rigged so that the real participant was always the teacher. Similarly, Asch's participants were deceived because they were told the experiment was a test of visual perception.

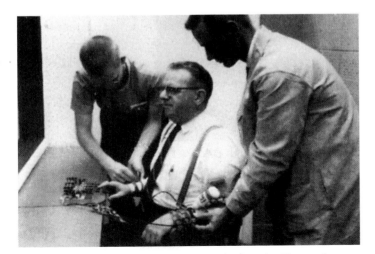

Milgram's research into obedience to authority. The "learner" (seated) was actually a confederate of the experimenter (in the overall). The "teacher" was the true participant and the subject of the experiment.

Deception is an ethical issue because it is often considered necessary to avoid demand characteristics, which would invalidate the findings, and so it might be used despite the potential harm to the participants.

Resolution

Role-play. One way of avoiding the ethical problems associated with deception is the use of role-playing experiments. This approach eliminates many of the ethical problems of deception studies, but there is a danger that the behaviour displayed by role-playing participants is not the same as the behaviour would be if they had been deceived. Zimbardo's (1973) Stanford Prison Experiment is an example of such a role-play experiment: the participants were not deceived (i.e. they knew it wasn't a real prison), but they had to behave as if they weren't aware it was a role-play.

Debrief. Debriefing is an important method for dealing with deception and other ethical issues. At the end of the study, participants should be told the actual nature and purpose of the research and asked not to tell any future participants. In addition, debriefing typically involves providing information about the experimental findings and offering participants the opportunity to have their results excluded from the study if they wish.

Informed consent

Ethical issue

Studies that have involved deception lead to the related issue of informed consent. Participants might have consented to the research but this is not informed consent if they have been deceived. Even in studies such as Zimbardo's, where participants were briefed in advance, it is difficult to be sure that the true nature of the study was grasped, and therefore consent might not have been fully informed. This raises an ethical issue because participants might not have consented had they known the true nature and purpose of the research, and could suffer distress as a consequence of this.

Resolution

Seeking presumptive consent. One way of obtaining consent is to seek presumptive consent by ascertaining the acceptability of a given experiment by asking the opinion of members of the population from which the participants in the research are to be drawn. Milgram did this before his experiments.

Prior general consent. An alternative approach is to gain prior general consent (also known as partially informed consent) by asking participants to take part in research that involves some deception, as the following study illustrates: Gamson, Fireman, and Rytina (1982) conducted a study in which participants were manipulated to produce evidence supporting the unreasonable position of an oil company. All potential participants were asked whether they were willing to take part in any or all of the following kinds of research:

- Research on brand recognition of commercial products.
- Research on product safety.
- Research in which you will be misled about the purpose until afterwards.
- Research involving group standards.

Most people said, "Yes", to all four conditions and were then told that only the last kind of research was in progress. However, they had agreed to the third kind of research and thus consented to be deceived. An obvious limitation is that what the participants had consented to was very vague—"research in which you will be misled about its purpose". They couldn't really give informed consent because they lacked detailed information.

Right to withhold data and retrospective consent. Another means of offering informed consent is to do it afterwards. When the experiment is over, during debriefing, participants should be offered the chance to withhold their data. In essence, this gives them the same power as if they had refused to take part in the first place. If they withhold their data, it is as if they had been informed at the start and not consented to take part. However, participants who exercise their right to withhold data might nevertheless have had experiences during the experiment that they would not have agreed to if they had realised beforehand what was going to happen to them.

Protection of participants
Ethical issues
The key test of whether or not a participant has been harmed is to ask whether the risk of harm was greater than in everyday life.

Physical harm
Excessive anxiety can be thought of as physical harm because the results can be physically evident. For example, if you consider the description of some of Milgram's participants it is clear that they experienced physical as well as psychological harm—some of them had seizures and many perspired and bit their lips. Stress is a psychological state but it has a physical basis.

Psychological harm
Protection of participants from psychological harm is an ethical issue that arises when participants are distressed by the research. Asch's study raises this issue because, at best, his participants experienced embarrassment, although for some this discomfort might have been more severe depending on their level of social anxiety. The studies by Milgram and Zimbardo demonstrate a more obvious lack of protection because of the evident suffering of the participants: sweating, trembling, and seizures in Milgram's study, and crying, screaming, and depression in Zimbardo's study. Of even greater concern is that participants might have suffered long-term harm if they experienced a loss of self-esteem as a result of the study, e.g. Milgram's participants might have felt guilty about delivering the electric shocks. The issue is that participants should have been protected from this psychological harm, particularly as it is debatable whether the ends (findings) justify the means (distress).

> **?** Could the approach adopted by Gamson et al. be adapted to handle the deception issue in most kinds of research?

> **?** If you recall, Watson and Rayner claimed that their experiment with Little Albert was ethical because the psychological harm inflicted was no greater than what he might experience in real life. Is this acceptable?

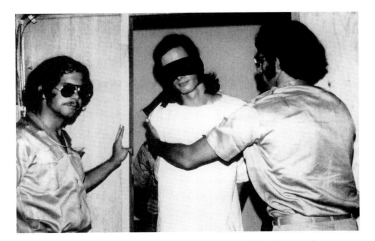

Zimbardo tried to minimise the after-effects of his Stanford prison experiment by asking the participants to sign an informed consent form before the experiment began. However, some of the participants suffered such psychological distress that they had to be released early.

Resolution

Confidentiality.   Confidentiality and the right to privacy protect participants from psychological harm. Confidentiality means that no information (especially sensitive information) about any given participant will be revealed by the experimenter to anyone else. Right to privacy is a matter of concern when conducting observational research. For example, it would not be appropriate to observe a person in situations in which they would not normally be observed by strangers without that person's informed consent.

Right to withdraw.   Participants should be informed of their right to withdraw at the outset of the research so that if they are in any way distressed they can leave the study.

Debriefing.   Debriefing can be used to reduce any distress that might have been caused by the experimenter. According to Aronson (1988), participants should leave the research situation in "a frame of mind that is at least as sound as it was when they entered". However, the debrief might not always achieve this!

Evaluation of the BPS ethical guidelines

The BPS Code of Ethics provides clear guidance and so has helped reduce ethical problems. However, the code is not law and so has limited force. The penalty (disbarment from the BPS) is perhaps not severe enough. It also seems that breaches of the code can be justified and that decisions as to whether research is justifiable can be researcher biased. This has led to the increasingly widespread development of local ethical committees. Most institutions where research takes place (universities, research units, hospitals) have such committees, which makes the decision as to whether the research is justified less biased than if the researcher makes it him- or herself. However, ethical committees are not without bias as most include psychologists, who might be biased in favour of research. It is advisable for the committee also to include non-psychologists and non-expert members of the public.

Cost–benefit analysis

The double-obligation dilemma

The **cost–benefit analysis** is a safeguard that should precede all research. It involves weighing-up whether the ends (i.e. the benefits of the research) justify the means (i.e. the costs). A cost–benefit analysis raises a double obligation dilemma because researchers have an obligation both to their participants and to society. Thus, researchers must weigh-up the potential findings of the research (the benefits for society) against the potential harm (costs to participants). Costs to the participants include harm as a consequence of the research (e.g. distress, ridicule, or loss of self-esteem), and must be balanced against the benefits. The benefits of the research to society include the value of the findings in terms of the understanding they provide and their potential applications.

Evaluation of the cost–benefit analysis

Cost–benefit analysis has a number of weaknesses. It is difficult to predict outcomes (and so the potential costs and benefits) because the outcomes of research are not always clear at the outset. It is also hard accurately to assess the costs and the benefits because they are not objective and so can be difficult to measure and weigh up. Another problem is that the assessment of costs and benefits is open to researcher bias and value judgements. Equally, the subjectivity of the analysis means that judgements might be value laden, and therefore biased. A cost–benefit analysis will be biased if it ignores the rights of the participants and favours the gains to society of the possible usefulness of the research. Judgements will differ across different researchers and across time, meaning the analysis will be era dependent and context bound.

SECTION SUMMARY
Designing Psychological Investigations

❖ The research methods have different strengths and weaknesses and so are more appropriate for some types of research than others. You should know at least two strengths and weaknesses of the following research methods: laboratory experiments, field experiments, quasi-experiments, correlational analysis, controlled and naturalistic observations, interviews, questionnaires, and case studies.

Design and application of appropriate research methods

❖ There are key design issues for each of the methods:

— experimental research: which of the three experimental designs is more appropriate
— observational research: the reliability of the observations
— questionnaire and interview: question formulation as they must be free from bias and ambiguity.

❖ Random sampling means that every participant in the target population has an equal chance of being selected. Opportunity sampling involves selecting whoever is available; volunteer sampling is when participants select themselves.

The strengths and weaknesses of different forms of sampling

❖ Random sampling is most free from bias but is not the most practical method given the difficulties of identifying all members of a target population. Thus, opportunity and volunteer sampling are more economical.

❖ Internal reliability refers to consistency within the method and is best assessed by the split-half technique or, in the case of observations, by inter-rater reliability.

Reliability: assessment and improvement

❖ External reliability refers to consistency between uses of the measure; this can be checked by test–retest.

❖ Internal validity refers to the truth of the findings, i.e. were they due to the manipulation of the IV causing an effect on the DV? Threats to validity include confounding variables and researcher and participant bias, as these can all interfere with the effect of the IV on the DV. Replication is a good test of validity; if the results are valid then they will be the same on both tests. Concurrent validity involves comparing the measure against an already-validated measure of the behaviour being studied.

Validity: assessment and improvement

❖ External validity refers to the generalisability of the results to other settings (ecological validity), other populations (population validity), and other time periods (temporal validity). It is assessed through meta-analysis, which involves comparing the findings of a number of studies, and through predictive validity, which assesses how well the data predict future behaviour.

Ethical considerations and resolutions in psychological research

The BPS guidelines provide guidance on how psychological research should be implemented because they cover ethical concerns such as deception, consent, right to withdraw, debriefing, and confidentiality.

❖ The BPS guidelines provide ways of resolving ethical issues. For example, the debrief resolves deception; retrospective consent, prior general consent, and presumptive consent resolve informed consent; the right to withdraw, confidentiality, and the debrief can resolve protection of participants. However, the guidelines have limitations; they are difficult to enforce and they lack penal power.
❖ A cost–benefit analysis should be conducted at the outset of all research and is another way to resolve ethical issues: the benefits of the research to society should outweigh the costs if the research is justifiable. A weakness of the cost–benefit analysis is that it is subjective and so open to bias.

DATA ANALYSIS AND REPORTING ON INVESTIGATIONS

Descriptive Statistics and Statistical Tests

For the exam, you need to be able to know how to select and interpret statistical tests. There are just four tests you need to cover: Mann–Whitney, Wilcoxon, chi-squared, and Spearman's tests. You will *not* be asked to carry out a statistical analysis during the exam but you must understand which test would be used and when, and the nature of the data each test generates.

Descriptive Statistics

Descriptive statistics give us convenient and easily understood summaries of what we have found. They give an indication of what statistical analysis is likely to reveal. However, to have a clearer idea of what our findings mean, it is generally necessary to carry out one or more **statistical tests**.

Before we consider statistical tests, it is necessary to understand the descriptive statistics these include: graphs, tables, **measures of central tendency**, and **measures of dispersion**. The appropriate descriptive statistics depend on the level of measurement, and so we will consider this first.

KEY TERMS

Statistical tests: various formulae that enable researchers to analyse and compare the data produced in their studies. A statistical test produces a statistic that can be assessed, using tables of significance, to see if the data fit (or do not fit) the hypothesis.
Measures of central tendency: any means of representing the mid-point of a set of data, such as the mean, median, and mode.
Measures of dispersion: any means of expressing the spread of the data, such as range or standard deviation.

Levels of measurement

The four commonly used levels of data measurement relate to the sophistication of the data. The levels of data progress from nominal (the least sophisticated data) to ratio (the most sophisticated data). The following summarises the four levels of measurement:

- *Nominal*: the data consist of the numbers of participants falling into various categories (e.g. fat, thin; men, women).
- *Ordinal*: the data can be placed in rank order, i.e. they can be ordered from lowest to highest (e.g. the finishing positions of athletes in a race or rating scales). Ordinal data are measured on scale of unequal intervals, for example, scores on a test can be put into rank order but it cannot be assumed that the interval between each test score is equal because some questions might have been harder than others.
- *Interval*: at this level the data have fixed intervals and so differ from ordinal data because the units of measurement are fixed throughout the range. For example, there is the same "distance" between a height of 1.82 metres and 1.70 metres as between a height of 1.70 metres and one of 1.58 metres.
- *Ratio*: the data have the same characteristics as interval data, except that they have a meaningful zero point, i.e. an absolute zero. For example, time measurements provide ratio data because the notion of zero time is meaningful, and 10 seconds is twice as long as 5 seconds. The similarities between interval and ratio data are so great that they are sometimes combined and referred to as interval/ratio data.

Nominal

Ordinal

Interval

■ **Activity: Levels of measurement**

To review your understanding of levels of measurement, remember that the data progress in sophistication from nominal to interval/ratio. This means that interval/ratio measures are more precise than nominal and ordinal measures. Data can often can be scaled up or down the levels of measurement, but if they are scaled down to nominal or ordinal then information will be lost at each conversion of the data to a less sophisticated form.

- Using the measurement of time as an example, think about which level of measurement (nominal, ordinal, interval/ratio) the following examples achieve:

1. An observer's estimation of the number of times John sneezes in a 5-minute period.
2. The time between each sneeze as measured on a stop-watch.
3. The number of times John sneezes in a 5-minute period.
4. The time between each sneeze as measured on an analogue clock.
5. An observer's rating of how much John sneezes.

Can you explain why you should have given the same level of measurement for questions 2 and 4 yet the data in question 2 are more precise than the data in question 4?

KEY TERMS

Nominal data: data consisting of the numbers of participants falling into qualitatively different categories.
Ordinal data: data that can be ordered from smallest to largest.
Interval data: data that are measured using units of equal intervals; the intervals reflect a real difference.
Ratio data: as interval data, but with a meaningful zero point.

Ratio

Measures of central tendency and dispersion

You will probably be familiar with the **mean**, **median**, and **mode** (measures of central tendency) and with variation ratio, **range**, interquartile range, and **standard deviation** (measures of dispersion), from your AS studies.

To recap on this: the measures of central tendency—the mode, the median, and the mean—are averages, and so involve the calculation of a single number that is representative of the other numbers with which it is associated. The appropriate measure to use depends on the level of the data.

The mode is the number that occurs most frequently. Advantages of the mode are that it is quick and easy to calculate and can be used whatever the level of data. Thus, it can be used for the least sophisticated nominal data. However, limitations include the fact that it is not widely used in psychological research because it is subject to great variability and provides very limited information; also, it does not tell us about the other values in the score distribution. A further problem is that it is possible to have more than one modal value; two modal values are known as bimodal values, and more than two are called multimodal.

The median is the middle value when the scores are arranged from lowest to highest. So half the values in a score distribution are above the median and half are below it. When there is an even number of scores, the two middle values are added together and then divided by two to give the median. Advantages of the median are that it can be used when you are unsure about the reliability of the extreme values and when you have skewed distributions. The fact that it is based on ordering the data means that it can be used only for data that are ordinal and above. Limitations include the fact that the median is susceptible to minor alterations (variability) in the dataset (score distribution).

The mean is the arithmetic average; it is calculated by adding all the values together and dividing the total by the number of values. The mean is the best measure of central tendency to use because it makes use of all the data in the score distribution. However, limitations include the fact that it should be used only with data that form a normal distribution (remember: the bell-shaped curve) and for data of interval or ratio measurement. The mean should *not* be used when there are extreme outlying values (anomalies) because, as it uses all of the data, it is easily distorted; when there are outliers, the median should be used, not the mean.

The measures of dispersion measure the variability within the data distribution, i.e. are the scores similar to each other or different? Thus, they are a measure of the spread of the scores in the data distribution.

The variation ratio complements the mode because it is the proportion of non-modal scores and so is suitable for nominal data. Advantages include

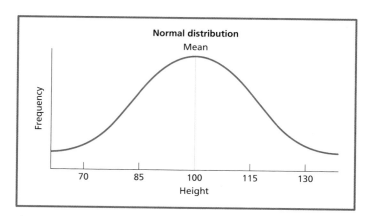

Normal distribution
Mean

Frequency

70   85   100   115   130
Height

This is a normal distribution. It could represent the height of people in your class or the x-axis could be the "life-time" of a light bulb, given in weeks. Most of the scores will be clustered around the mean. The further away from the mean you get, the fewer cases there are.

the fact that it is easy to calculate and can be used on unsophisticated data, i.e. nominal data. The limitation is the same key disadvantage as with the mode: it is not representative of all scores in the distribution and so tends not to be used.

The range is the difference between the highest and lowest scores in a dataset; 1 is added if the scores are all whole numbers, 0.5 is added if values are recorded to the nearest half, 0.1 is added if the values are recorded to one decimal place. The range is used for data that are ordinal and above. The key advantage is that it is easy to calculate. Limitations include the fact that the two most extreme values are used to calculate the range and so if these are outlying the calculated range will not be representative of the distribution. Also, the range does not make use of all the data in the score distribution. The interquartile range solves the problem of outlying values by using only the middle 50% of scores in the calculation. This gives a better idea of the distribution of values around the centre.

The standard deviation is a measure of variability. It measures scores in terms of difference from the mean. Advantages are that, as with the mean, the standard deviation uses all the scores in a set of data and so is the best measure of dispersion to use. We can make inferences based on the relationship between the standard deviation and a normal distribution curve. However, limitations include the fact that data need to be of interval or ratio levels of measurement, and to be approximately normally distributed, which is not always possible because this is the most sophisticated type of data.

Appropriate measures of central tendency and dispersion based on the level of measurement

Level of measurement	Nominal	Ordinal	Interval/ratio
Measure of central tendency	Mode	Median	Mean
Measure of dispersion	Variation ratio	Range and interquartile range	Standard deviation

EXAM HINT

Note the order of the levels of measurement spells NOIR so remember this to remember the order.

Graphs, charts, and tables
Graphs and charts present the data visually. They are a useful way of summarising information as the data is easily accessible in visual format.

Bar charts
Bar charts illustrate data measured at nominal or ordinal level. They are used for non-continuous variables because the bars are separate from each other. This is in comparison to the histogram where bars are adjoined. Bar charts are often used to illustrate the means from different conditions.

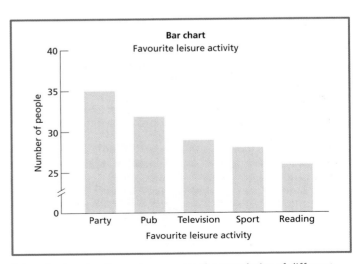

A bar chart makes it easy to compare the popularity of different leisure activities. We can see at a glance that going to a party was the most popular leisure activity, whereas reading a good book was the least popular. The data in this chart are in nominal categories.

Histograms
Histograms are used to present frequencies of continuous data. Thus, the data must be measured at interval or ratio level for the histogram to be

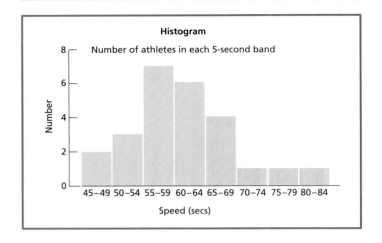

Histogram

Number of athletes in each 5-second band

appropriate. A histogram is similar to a frequency polygon in that the scores are presented on the *x*-axis and the frequencies on the *y*-axis. However, the frequencies are represented by rectangular columns in the histogram, rather than the line graph as in the frequency polygon. Consequently, the frequency polygon provides a clearer picture of the frequency distributions of two conditions.

Frequency polygons

Frequency polygons show the frequencies of continuous data, i.e. data that achieve at interval or ratio level. They are useful when representing results from two conditions at the same time. The *x*-axis shows the scores and the *y*-axis shows the frequency. (See data in the figure below and the resulting frequency polygon on the page opposite.)

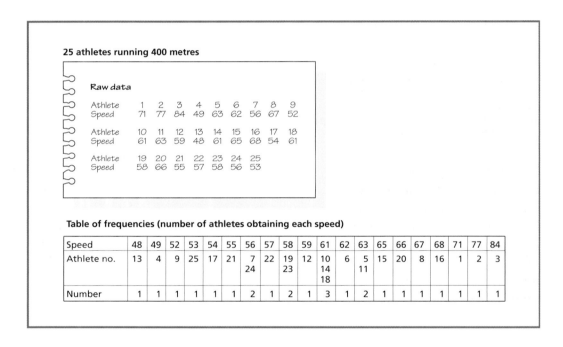

25 athletes running 400 metres

Raw data

Athlete	1	2	3	4	5	6	7	8	9
Speed	71	77	84	49	63	62	56	67	52

Athlete	10	11	12	13	14	15	16	17	18
Speed	61	63	59	48	61	65	68	54	61

Athlete	19	20	21	22	23	24	25
Speed	58	66	55	57	58	56	53

Table of frequencies (number of athletes obtaining each speed)

Speed	48	49	52	53	54	55	56	57	58	59	61	62	63	65	66	67	68	71	77	84
Athlete no.	13	4	9	25	17	21	7 24	22	19 23	12	10 14 18	6	5 11	15	20	8	16	1	2	3
Number	1	1	1	1	1	1	2	1	2	1	3	1	2	1	1	1	1	1	1	1

Scattergraphs

Scattergraphs (or scattergrams) are used to present correlated data (see the figure on the opposite page, far right). It does not matter which variable goes on which axis. Correlations range from perfect positive (+1) to no correlation to perfect negative (−1). The sign indicates the direction, and the correlation coefficient (the number) indicates the strength of the correlation. The closer the correlation coefficient is to 1, the stronger the correlation. If scores are positively correlated they increase and decrease together; if they are negatively correlated, then as the scores on one variable increase the scores on the other variable decrease. Perfect positive and negative correlations are rare in psychological research; imperfect correlations are more common. For example, +0.7 is an imperfect positive correlation and −0.4 is

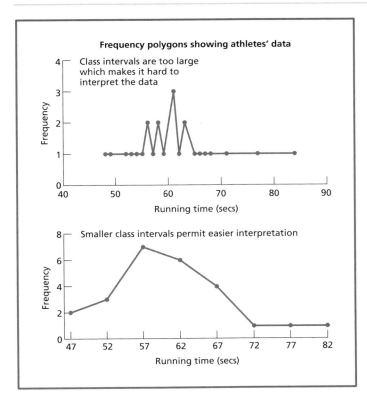

How should we interpret the findings shown in the frequency polygon? It is clear that most of the participants were able to run 400 metres in between about 53 and 67 seconds. Only a few of the athletes were able to better a time of 53 seconds and there was a small number who took longer than 67 seconds.

Examples of scattergrams showing no correlation, positive correlation, and negative correlation.

an imperfect negative correlation. You must be able to interpret the direction and strength of a correlation, so remember: as a rule of thumb, low numbers (0.1 to 0.3) are weak correlations, 0.4 to 0.6 are moderate, and 0.7 to 1 are strong (although it is a little more complex than this because strength depends on the size of the sample). Also remember the weaknesses of correlational data when making interpretations, i.e. be able to explain how lack of cause and effect and the role of other factors limit conclusions.

Tables

A table can be an effective way of summarising a large amount of data, for example, measures of central tendency and dispersion can be provided in the one table. Tables have the advantage of being very precise, e.g. figures are readily apparent, whereas graphs might only allow approximate figures to be worked out. However, tables can be harder to interpret than a graph because it is more difficult to visualise the data.

Statistical Tests

Test of difference, association, or correlation?

The first step in choosing an appropriate statistical test is to decide whether your data were obtained from an experiment in which some aspect of the situation (the independent variable) was manipulated in order to observe its effects on the dependent variable. If so, you need a **test of difference**. However, if you simply have two observations from each of your participants in a non-experimental design, then you need a **test of association** or correlation.

One-tailed or two-tailed test?

When using a statistical test, you need to take account of the alternative hypothesis. If you predicted the direction of any effects (e.g. loud noise will disrupt learning and memory), then you have a **directional hypothesis**, which should be evaluated by a one-tailed test. If you did not predict the direction of any effects (e.g. loud noise will affect learning and memory), then you have a **non-directional hypothesis**, which should be evaluated by a two-tailed test.

Level of precision

Another factor to consider when deciding which statistical test to use is the type of data you have obtained. There are four types of data, of increasing levels of precision (see above).

Statistical Significance

So far, we have discussed some of the issues that influence the choice of statistical test. Shortly, we will consider how to conduct such tests but first we should look at the meaning of **statistical significance**. What happens after we have chosen a statistical test, analysed our data, and we want to interpret our findings? We use the results of the test to choose between the following:

• *Null hypothesis*: which asserts that there is no difference between conditions, e.g. loud noise has no effect on learning.
• *Alternative hypothesis*: e.g. loud noise disrupts learning.

If the statistical test indicates that there is only a small probability of the difference between conditions (e.g. loud noise vs. no noise) having occurred *if the null hypothesis were true*, then we reject the null hypothesis in favour of the alternative hypothesis.

■ **Activity: Devising hypotheses**
Devise suitable null and alternative hypotheses for the following:

- An investigator considers the effect of noise on students' ability to concentrate and complete a word grid. One group only is subjected to the noise in the form of a distractor, i.e. a television programme.
- An investigator explores the view that there might be a link between the amount of television children watch and their behaviour at school.

Why do we focus initially on the null hypothesis rather than the alternative hypothesis? The reason is that the alternative hypothesis is rather imprecise. Although it might state that loud noise will disrupt learning, it does not indicate the *extent* of the disruption. This imprecision makes it hard to evaluate an alternative hypothesis directly. By contrast, a null hypothesis, such as loud noise has no effect on learning, *is* precise, and this precision allows us to use statistical tests to decide the probability that it is correct.

Probability in psychology is used to determine if the probability of our results being due to chance is low enough for the alternative/experimental/correlational hypothesis to be accepted. If so, the results are significant and consequently the null hypothesis can be rejected and the alternative/experimental/correlational hypothesis can be accepted.

The probability of the findings being due to chance is estimated from the level of statistical significance achieved by the data. The conventional minimum level of significance to be accepted is $p < 0.05$ (which is also known as the 5% level); this means that if this level of significance is achieved, the probability of the results being due to chance (i.e. a fluke) is *less than* 5%. Thus, the null hypothesis is rejected (and the alternative hypothesis is accepted) if the probability that the results were due to chance alone is 5% or less. This is often expressed as $p = 0.05$, where $p = $ the probability of the result if the null hypothesis is true. If

From percentage to decimal

10%	= 0.10
5%	= 0.05
1%	= 0.01
2.5%	= 0.025
0.01%	= 0.001

- To go from decimal to percentage: multiply by 100, i.e. move the decimal point two places to the right.
- To go from percentage to decimal: divide by 100, i.e. move the decimal point two places to the left.

the statistical test indicates that the findings do not reach the 5% (i.e. the $p = 0.05$) level of statistical significance, then we retain the null hypothesis and reject the alternative hypothesis. The key decision is whether to reject the null hypothesis, which is why the 0.05 level of statistical significance is so important. The point of doing the statistical test is to reject the null hypothesis by showing that the results are not a fluke. This means that the null hypothesis is actually the starting point and that it is the null hypothesis that you are setting out to test, not the alternative hypothesis.

However, it is also true that, very occasionally, a 10% level is used when the background research supports the null hypothesis (i.e. the prediction is no difference). Setting out to verify the null hypothesis is not the norm because it is contradictory to the purpose of most research, which is—as already stated—to challenge the null hypothesis. Thus, the 10% levels would be used only in the unusual circumstances that the background research predicts no difference.

The data sometimes indicate that the null hypothesis can be rejected with greater confidence, say, at the 1% (i.e. one out of one hundred, shown as 0.01) level. If the null hypothesis can be rejected at the 1% level, it is customary to state that the findings are "highly significant". In general terms, you should state the precise level of statistical significance of your findings, whether it is the 5% level, the 1% level, or whatever.

We can never be totally certain that the results are due to the independent variable, or that the link is real, as there is always a probability of chance even at the most stringent level of significance $p < 0.001$. This is why we never *prove* anything in psychology; there is no such thing as 0% chance and so we can only say the results support or contradict but never prove a hypothesis.

These procedures might seem easy. In fact, two kinds of error might occur when reaching a conclusion on the basis of the results of a statistical test:

- *Type 1 error*: we might reject the null hypothesis in favour of the alternative hypothesis even though the findings are actually due to chance; the probability of this happening is given by the level of statistical significance that is selected.
- *Type 2 error*: we might retain the null hypothesis even though the alternative hypothesis is actually correct.

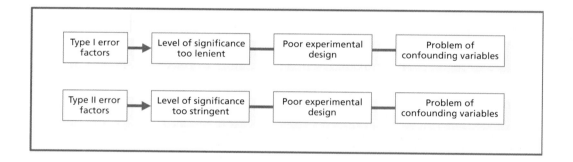

EXAM HINT

Make sure you can explain the levels of significance. Thus, $p < 0.05$ means if achieved that there is a probability of less than 5% that the results are due to chance.

KEY TERMS

Type 1 error: mistakenly rejecting the null hypothesis in favour of the experimental hypothesis when the results are actually due to chance.

Type 2 error: mistakenly retaining the null hypothesis when the experimental hypothesis is actually correct.

It would be possible to reduce the likelihood of a type 1 error by using a more stringent level of significance. For example, if we used the 1% ($p \leq 0.01$) level of significance, this would greatly reduce the probability of a type 1 error. However, use of a more stringent level of significance increases the probability of a type 2 error. We could reduce the probability of a type 2 error by using a less stringent level of significance, such as the 10% ($p \leq 0.10$) level. However, this would increase the probability of a type 1 error. These considerations help to make it clear why most psychologists favour the 5% (or $p \leq 0.05$) level of significance: it allows the probabilities of both type 1 and type 2 errors to remain reasonably low.

Psychologists generally use the 5% level of significance. However, they would use the 1% or even the 0.1% (i.e. one out of one thousand, shown as 0.001) level of significance if it was very important to avoid making a type 1 error. For example, clinical psychologists might require very strong evidence that a new form of therapy was more effective than existing forms of therapy before starting to use it on a regular basis. The 1% or 0.1% level of statistical significance is also used when the alternative hypothesis seems improbable. For example, very few people would accept that telepathy had been proved to exist on the basis of a single study in which the results were only just significant at the 5% level!

Tests of Difference

Here, we will consider those statistical tests that are applicable when we are interested in deciding whether the differences between two conditions or groups are significant. As was discussed in your AS-level studies, there are three kinds of design that can be used when we want to compare two conditions:

1. The independent groups design, in which each participant is allocated to one and only one condition.
2. The repeated measures design, in which the same participants are used in both conditions.
3. The matched participants (matched pairs) design, in which the participants in the two conditions are matched on a one-to-one basis in terms of some variable or variables that might be relevant (e.g. intelligence, age).

When deciding which statistical test to use, it is very important to take account of the particular kind of experimental design that was used:

- If the independent design was used, then the chi-squared test (nominal data) or the Mann–Whitney U test (ordinal and above) is the appropriate test to use.
- If the repeated measures or matched participants design was used, then the Wilcoxon matched pairs signed ranks test (ordinal and above) is the appropriate test to use.

EXAM HINT

If you are asked to explain why a particular statistical test is suitable base this on the experimental design and the level of the data. If the question asks for a third reason, add that it is a test of difference or it is a test of association (depending on whether it refers to an experiment or a correlation).

Selecting a suitable statistical test

If you wish to see if there is a *difference* between one set of data and another, you need a test of difference. Your choice of test depends on the level of measurement; whether the data are measured at the nominal or ordinal/interval level, and whether the groups of data are independent or related.

If you wish to find out whether pairs of variables are associated or *correlated*, then you need a test of correlation. The test you should use is Spearman's rho or chi-squared test depending on the level of measurement.

	Difference test		Correlational test
Level of measurement	Independent data	Related data (obtained from repeated measures and matched pairs designs)	
Nominal	Chi-squared test	Sign test	Chi-squared test
Ordinal and interval	Mann-Whitney U test	Wilcoxon matched pairs signed ranks	Spearman's rho

Note: This chart deals only with the statistical tests described in the text, although other tests do exist.

The chi-squared test

The chi-squared test is a test of association and also a test of difference. It is used when we have nominal data in the form of frequencies, and when each and every observation is independent of all the other observations. For example, suppose that we are interested in the association between eating patterns and cholesterol level. We could divide people into those having a healthy diet with relatively little fat and those having an unhealthy diet. We could also divide them into those having a fairly high level of cholesterol and those having a low level of cholesterol. In essence, the chi-squared test tells us whether membership of a given category on one dimension (e.g. unhealthy diet) is associated with membership of a given category on the other dimension (e.g. high cholesterol level).

In the worked example in the box opposite, we will assume that we have data from 186 individuals with an unhealthy diet and from 128 individuals with a healthy diet. Of those with an unhealthy diet, 116 have a high cholesterol level and 70 have a low cholesterol level. Of those with a healthy diet, 41 have a high cholesterol level and 87 have a low cholesterol level. Our alternative hypothesis is that there is an association between healthiness of diet and low cholesterol level.

The first step is to arrange the frequency data in a 2 × 2 "contingency table", as in the example, with the row and column totals included. The second step is to work out what the four frequencies would be if there were no association at all between diet and cholesterol levels. The expected frequency (by chance alone) in each case is given by the following formula:

$$\frac{\text{row total} \times \text{column total}}{\text{expected frequency}} = \text{overall total}$$

For example, the expected frequency for the number of participants having a healthy diet and high cholesterol is 157 × 128 divided by 314, which comes to 64. The four expected frequencies (those expected by chance alone) are also shown in the worked example in the box. The third step is to apply the following formula to the observed (O) and expected (E) frequencies in each of the four categories:

$$\chi^2 = \sum \frac{(|O-E|-\frac{1}{2})^2}{E} = 26.7$$

In the formula, |O − E| means that the difference between the observed and the expected frequency should be taken, and it should then have a + sign put in front of it regardless of the direction of the difference. The correction factor (i.e. $-\frac{1}{2}$) is used only when there are two rows and two columns.

The fourth step is to add together the four values obtained in the third step in order to provide the chi-squared statistic, shown as χ^2. This is 7.91 + 5.44 + 7.91 + 5.44 = 26.70.

The fifth step is to calculate the number of "degrees of freedom" (*df*). This is given by:

(number of rows − 1) × (number of columns − 1)

For this, we need to refer back to the contingency table. In the example, this is 1 × 1 = 1. Why is there one degree of freedom? Once we know the row and column totals, then only one of the four **observed values** is free to vary. Thus, for example, knowing that the row totals are 157 and 157, the column totals are 128 and 186, and the number of participants having a healthy diet and high

KEY TERM

Observed value: the numerical value calculated using a statistical test. The observed value is also known as the calculated value and is compared with the critical value to determine significance.

Test of association: Chi-squared test: A worked example

Alternative hypothesis: There is an association between healthiness of diet and low cholesterol level.
Null hypothesis: There is no association between healthiness of diet and low cholesterol level.

Contingency table

	Healthy diet	Unhealthy diet	Row total
High cholesterol	41	116	157
Low cholesterol	87	70	157
Column total	128	186	314

Expected frequency if there were no association

Formula: $= \dfrac{\text{row total} \times \text{column total}}{\text{expected frequency}} = \text{overall total}$

	Healthy diet	Unhealthy diet	Row total
High cholesterol	64	93	157
Low cholesterol	64	93	157
Column total	128	186	314

Calculating chi-squared statistic (χ^2)

Formula: $\chi^2 = \sum \dfrac{(|O - E| - \frac{1}{2})^2}{E} = 26.7$

Note: Correction factor $\left(-\frac{1}{2}\right)$ is only used where there are two rows and two columns.

Category	Observed	Expected	|O–E|	$\dfrac{(\|O-E\| - \frac{1}{2})^2}{E}$
Healthy, high cholesterol	41	64	23	7.91
Unhealthy, high cholesterol	116	93	23	5.44
Healthy, low cholesterol	87	64	23	7.91
Unhealthy, low cholesterol	70	93	23	5.44
				26.70

Calculating degrees of freedom

Formula: (no. of rows − 1) × (no. of columns −1) = degrees of freedom $(2 - 1) \times (2 - 1) = 1$

Compare chi-squared statistic with tabled values

Table values

	0.025 level	0.005 level	0.0005 level
df = 1	3.84	6.64	10.83

Question: Is the observed chi-squared value of 26.70 and one degree of freedom the same as or greater than the tabled value?

Conclusion: The chi-squared value is greater than the tabled value, so the null hypothesis can be rejected, and the alternative hypothesis, that there is an association between healthiness of diet and cholesterol level, accepted.

The appropriate table of significance for the chi-squared test can be found on page 752.

cholesterol is 41, we can complete the entire table. In other words, the number of degrees of freedom corresponds to the number of values that are free to vary.

The sixth step is to compare the tabled values in Table 5 in Appendix A (see p. 753) with chi-square = 26.70 and one degree of freedom. The observed value needs to be the same as, or greater than, the tabled value for a one-tailed test in order for the results to be significant.

The tabled value for a one-tailed test with $df = 1$ is 3.84 at the 0.025 level, 6.64 at the 0.005 level, and 10.83 at the 0.0005 level. Thus, we can reject the null hypothesis, and conclude that there is an association between healthiness of diet and cholesterol level ($p = 0.0005$).

It is easy to use the chi-squared test wrongly. According to Robson (1994), "There are probably more inappropriate and incorrect uses of the chi-squared test than of all the other statistical tests put together." To avoid mis-using the chi-squared test, it is important to make use of the following rules:

- Ensure that every observation is independent of every other observation; in other words, each individual should be counted only once and in only *one* category.
- Make sure that each observation is included in the appropriate category; it is not permitted to omit some of the observations (e.g. those from individuals with intermediate levels of cholesterol).
- The total sample should exceed 20; otherwise, the chi-squared test as described here is not applicable. More precisely, the minimum expected frequency should be at least five in every cell of the table.
- The significance level of a chi-squared test is assessed by consulting the one-tailed values in Table 5 in Appendix A (p. 753) if a specific form of association has been predicted and that form was obtained. However, the two-tailed values should always be consulted if there are more than two categories on either dimension.
- Use the correction factor of $-\frac{1}{2}$, applied after the O − E, when there are two rows and two columns.
- Remember that showing there is an association is not the same as showing that there is a causal effect; for example, the association between a healthy diet and low cholesterol does not demonstrate that a healthy diet *causes* low cholesterol.

? Can you think of another example of a situation in which a wrong causal inference could be made, i.e. y followed x, but x did not cause y?

Mann–Whitney U test

The Mann–Whitney U test can be used when an independent design has been used and the data are either ordinal or interval. The worked example in the box opposite shows how this test is calculated.

Suppose we have two conditions. In both conditions, the participants have to fire arrows at a board and their scores are recorded. There are 10 participants in condition A, in which no training is provided before performance is assessed; there are 12 participants in condition B, and they receive extensive training before their performance is assessed. The alternative hypothesis is that extensive

Mann–Whitney U test: A worked example

Alternative hypothesis: extensive training improves performance

Null hypothesis: training has no effect on performance

Participant	Condition A	Rank	Participant	Condition B	Rank
1	4	2	1	21	15
2	10	9	2	26	18
3	12	11	3	20	14
4	28	20	4	22	16
5	7	5	5	32	22
6	13	13	6	5	3
7	12	11	7	12	11
8	2	1	8	6	4
9	9	7.5	9	8	6
10	27	19	10	24	17
			11	29	21
			12	9	7.5

Smaller sample = condition A

Sum of ranks in smaller sample (T) = 98.5

Number of participants in smaller sample (N_A) = 10

Number of participants in larger sample (N_B) = 12

Formula: $U = N_A N_B + \left(\dfrac{N_A(N_A + 1)}{2} \right) - T$

Example: $U = (10 \times 12) + \left(\dfrac{10(10+1)}{2} \right) - 98.5 = 76.5$

Formula for calculating U': $U' = N_A N_B - U$

Example: $U' = (10 \times 12) - 76.5 = 43.5$

Comparing U and U', U' is the smaller value. The calculated value of U' (43.5) is checked against the tabled value for a one-tailed test at 5%.

Table values

	$N_A = 10$
$N_B = 12$	34

Conclusion: As 43.5 is greater than 34, the null hypothesis should be retained, i.e. training has no effect on performance in this task.

The appropriate tables of significance for the Mann-Whitney test can be found on page 748.

training will improve performance; in other words, the scores in condition B should be significantly higher than those in condition A.

The first step is to rank all of the scores from both groups together, with a rank of 1 being given to the smallest score, a rank of 2 to the second smallest score, and so on. If there are tied scores, then the mean of the ranks involved is given to each of the tied participants. For example, two participants were tied for the 7th and 8th ranks, and so they both received a rank of 7.5.

The second step is to work out the sum of the ranks in the smaller sample, which is condition A in our example. This value is known as T; it is 98.5 in the example.

The third step is to calculate U from the formula, in which N_A is the number of participants in the smaller sample and N_B is the number in the larger sample:

$$\left(\frac{N_A(N_A + 1)}{2} \right) - T$$

The fourth step is to calculate U′ (U prime):

$$U' = N_A N_B - U$$

The fifth step is to compare U and U′, selecting whichever is the smaller value provided that the results are in the correct direction. The smaller value (i.e. 43.5) is then looked up in Table 1 in Appendix A (see bottom table on p. 748). Here, we have a one-tailed test, because the alternative hypothesis stated that extensive training would improve performance. With 10 participants in our first condition and 12 in our second condition, the tabled value for significance on a one-tailed test at 0.05 is 34. The observed value must be equal to, or smaller than, the tabled value in order to be significant. As our value of 43.5 is greater than 34, the conclusion is that we retain the null hypothesis. The presence of ties reduces the accuracy of the tables, but the effect is small unless there are several ties.

Wilcoxon matched pairs signed ranks test

The Wilcoxon matched pairs signed ranks test can be used when a repeated measures or matched participants design has been used and the data are at least ordinal. This test can also be used if the data are interval/ratio. The Wilcoxon matched pairs signed ranks test uses more of the information obtained from a study, and so is usually more sensitive and useful than the sign test.

The worked example in the box opposite shows how this test is calculated. The first step is to place all the data in a table in which each participant's two scores are in the same row.

The second step is to subtract the condition B score from the condition A score for each participant.

The third step is to omit all the participants whose two scores are the same, i.e. d = 0.

The fourth step is to rank all the difference scores obtained in the second step from 1 (smallest difference) to 2 (second smallest difference), and so on. For this purpose, ignore the + and − signs, thus taking the absolute size of the difference.

The fifth step is to sum the positive ranks (there are fifty in the example) and—separately—to sum the negative ranks (five in the example). The smaller of these values is T, which in this case is 5.

The sixth step is to work out the number of participants whose two scores are not the same, i.e. d ≠ 0. In the example, N = 10.

The obtained value of T must be the same as, or less than, the tabled value (see Table 3 in Appendix A, on p. 751) in order for the results to be significant. The tabled value for a one-tailed test and N = 10 is 11 at the 5% level of statistical significance, and 5 at the 1% level. Thus, the findings are significant at the 1% level on a one-tailed test. The null hypothesis is rejected in favour of the alternative hypothesis that free recall is better when learning takes place in the absence of noise than in its presence ($p = 0.01$). The presence of ties means that the tables are not completely accurate, but this does not matter providing there are only a few ties.

For the purposes of the exam, you do not need to know the sign test and so a worked example of this has not been included. However, it is useful to know how it compares to the Wilcoxon test. The Wilcoxon test is better able to detect significance than the sign test because the latter is insensitive (or lacking in power)

Wilcoxon matched pairs signed ranks test: A worked example

Alternative hypothesis: Free recall is better when learning takes place in the absence of noise than in its presence.
Null hypothesis: Free recall is not affected by whether or not noise is present during learning.

Participant	Condition A (no noise)	Condition B (loud noise)	Difference (d) (A − B)	Rank
1	12	8	4	7.5
2	10	10	0	—
3	7	8	−1	2.5
4	12	11	1	2.5
5	8	3	5	9
6	10	10	0	—
7	13	7	6	10
8	8	9	−1	2.5
9	14	10	4	7.5
10	11	9	2	5
11	15	12	3	6
12	11	10	1	2.5

Sum of positive ranks (7.5 + 2.5 + 9 + 10 + 7.5 + 5 + 6 + 2.5) = 50
Sum of negative ranks (2.5 + 2.5) = 5
Smaller value (5) = T
Number of participants who scored differently in condition A and B, $N = 10$
Question: For the results to be significant, the value of T must be the same as, or less than, the tabled value.

Table values

	5%	1%
$N = 10$	11	5

Conclusion: In this experiment T is less than the tabled value at the 5% level and the same as the tabled value at the 1% level of significance, so the null hypothesis is rejected in favour of the alternative hypothesis.

The appropriate table of significance for the Wilcoxon test can be found on page 750.

as it takes no account of the *size* of each individual's difference in the dependent variable of the two conditions. It is because this information is made use of in the Wilcoxon test that a significant result can be obtained using that test, whereas it might not be detected using the sign test. This means that the Wilcoxon test is more likely than the sign test to show a significant difference where one exists.

Studies Using Correlational Analysis

In the case of studies using correlational analysis, the data are in the form of two measures of behaviour from each member of a single group of participants. The data are often presented in the form of a scattergraph (also known as a scattergram), so-called because it shows how the individual scores are scattered.

Spearman's rho

Suppose that we have scores on two variables from each of our participants, and we want to see whether there is an association, or correlation, between the two sets of scores. Providing the data are at least ordinal, this can be done using the test known as Spearman's rho. Spearman's rho or r_s indicates the strength of the association. If r_s is −1.0, then there is a perfect positive correlation between

Spearman's rho: A worked example

Alternative hypothesis: There is a positive association between amount of television violence watched and aggressive behaviour.

Null hypothesis: There is no association between amount of television violence watched and aggressive behaviour.

Participant	TV violence seen (*hours*)	Aggressive behaviour (*out of 10*)	Rank A	Rank B	Difference d	d²
1	17	8	7.5	9	−1.50	2.25
2	6	3	2	2	0.00	0.00
3	23	9	10	10.5	−0.50	0.25
4	17	7	7.5	8	−0.50	0.25
5	2	2	1	1	0.00	0.00
6	20	6	9	5.5	+3.50	12.25
7	12	6	4	5.5	−1.50	2.25
8	31	10	12	12	0.00	0.00
9	14	6	5.5	5.5	0.00	0.00
10	26	9	11	10.5	+0.50	0.25
11	9	6	3	5.5	−2.50	6.25
12	14	4	5.5	3	+2.50	6.25

Sum of squared difference scores (Σd^2) = 30

Number of participants (*N*) = 12

Formula: rho $= 1 - \dfrac{(\Sigma d^2 \times 6)}{N(N^2-1)}$

Example: $1 - \dfrac{(30 \times 6)}{12(143)} = 1 - 0.105 = +0.895$

Is the value of rho (+0.895) as great as, or greater than, the tabled value?

Table values

	0.05 level	0.01 level	0.005 level
N = 12	+0.503	+0.671	+0.727

The appropriate table of significance for the Spearman's rho test can be found on page 751.

Conclusion: Null hypothesis rejected in favour of alternative hypothesis, i.e. there is a positive correlation between the amount of television violence watched and aggressive behaviour ($p = 0.005$).

the two variables. If r_s is −1.0, then there is a perfect negative correlation between the two variables. If r_s is 0.0, then there is generally no relationship between the two variables. The working of this test is shown in the box.

An experimenter collects information about the amount of television violence seen in the past month and about the amount of aggressive behaviour exhibited in the past month by 12 participants. She predicts that there will be a positive association between these two variables, i.e. those participants who have seen the most television violence (variable A) will tend to be the most aggressive (variable B). In other words, there is a directional hypothesis.

The first step is to draw up a table in which each participant's scores for the two variables are placed in the same row.

The second step is to rank all the scores for variable A. A rank of 1 is assigned to the smallest score, a rank of 2 to the second smallest score, and so on up to 12. What do we do if there are tied scores? In the example, participants 9 and 12 had the same score for variable A. The ranks that they are competing for are ranks 5 and 6; the average or mean of the ranks at issue is taken: $(5 + 6)/2 = 5.5$.

The third step is to rank all the scores for variable B, with a rank of 1 being assigned to the smallest score. Participants 6, 7, 9, and 11 are all tied, with the ranks at issue being ranks 4, 5, 6, and 7. The mean rank will be $(4 + 5 + 6 + 7)/4 = 5.5$.

The fourth step is to calculate the difference between the two ranks obtained by each individual, with the rank for variable B being subtracted from the rank for variable A. This produces 12 difference (d) scores.

The fifth step is to square all of the d scores obtained in the fourth step. This produces 12 squared difference (d^2) scores.

The sixth step is to add up all of the d^2 scores to obtain the sum of the squared difference scores. This is known as Σd^2, and comes to 30 in the example.

The seventh step is to work out the number of participants. In the example, the number of participants (N) is 12.

The eighth step is to calculate rho from the following formula:

$$rho = 1 - \frac{(\Sigma d^2 \times 6)}{N(N^2 - 1)}$$

In the example, this becomes:

$$1 - \frac{(30 \times 6)}{12(143)} = 1 - 0.105 = + 0.895$$

> Note that the "6" in the equation is always present, and is a feature of the Spearman's rho formula.

The ninth and final step is to work out the significance of the value of rho by referring the result to the table (see Table 4 in Appendix A, p. 752). The obtained value must be as great as, or greater than, the tabled value. The tabled value for a one-tailed test with $N = 12$ is $+0.503$ at the 0.05 level; it is $+0.671$ at the 0.01 level; and it is $+0.727$ at the 0.005 level. Thus, it can be concluded that the null hypothesis should be rejected in favour of the alternative hypothesis that there is a positive correlation between the amount of television violence watched and aggressive behaviour ($p = 0.005$).

An important point about Spearman's rho is that the statistical significance of the obtained value of rho depends very heavily on the number of participants. For example, the tabled value for significance at the 0.05 level on a one-tailed test is $+0.564$ if there are 10 participants. However, it is only $+0.306$ if there are 30 participants. In practical terms, this means that it is very hard to obtain a significant correlation with Spearman's rho if the number of participants is low.

> ? Why is it a good idea to have a reasonable number of participants in a correlational study?

Using Inferential Tests

Choosing a test

The box on the next page summarises the reasons for choosing each test and gives you all the necessary information for justifying your choice of test.

Justifying your choice of test

When justifying your use of a particular statistical test, you need to explain why you chose that test. For example, if you have conducted a study where you are seeking to determine whether there are differences between two independent groups of participants then you might state:

In order to assess the significance of these findings it was necessary to use a statistical test. In this study an appropriate test would be a Mann–Whitney U test because (1) a test of differences was required, (2) the design was independent measures, and (3) the data were at least at an ordinal level.

Calculating the observed value

The next step is to perform the calculations. The outcome of a statistical test is a number, called the observed value. The worked examples in the boxes above show how to calculate each statistical test.

Using a table of significance to compare the observed and critical values

To determine whether the observed value is significant, we consult an appropriate table of significance. These are located in Appendix A, with instructions for their use. Comparing the **critical value** in the table and your own observed value enables you decide whether you can accept or reject the null hypothesis. Thus, to establish significance, your calculated value must be compared with a critical value. The table will tell you if the calculated value has to be *less than or more than* the critical value for significance to be achieved. For the purposes of the exam, you need to know if the observed or calculated value needs to be lower or higher than the critical value. This differs, depending on which statistical test is used.

Comparing the calculated and critical values

Statistical test	Chi-squared test	Mann–Whitney U	Wicoxon signed ranks	Spearman's rho
Calculated compared to critical value	Calculated value must be *greater* than or equal to the critical value	Calculated value must be *less* than or equal to the critical value	Calculated value must be *less* than or equal to the critical value	Calculated value must be *greater* than or equal to the critical value

Reporting the result

The final step is to record the outcome of this whole process. You should include the following information in a statement of significance:

- details of the level of significance
- the critical and observed values
- degrees of freedom or number of participants
- whether the hypothesis was directional or non-directional (one tailed or two-tailed)
- whether it was accepted or rejected.

KEY TERM

Critical value: numerical value found in the statistical tables that are used to determine the significance of the observed value produced by a statistical test.

For example:

For 10 participants, the critical value for rho is 0.564 at the 5% level of significance (p < 0.05, one-tailed). As the observed value of rho is 0.703, this is greater than the critical value and so there is less than a 5% probability that the result is due to chance. The null hypothesis can be rejected and the alternative hypothesis accepted.

Another example:

The calculated value of U = 30, which is greater than the critical value of U = 27, where N1 = 10, N2 = 10, at p < 0.05 (for a one-tailed test). As the observed value needs to be less than the critical value for significance this has not been achieved and so there is greater than a 5% probability that the result is due to chance. This means we must accept the null hypothesis and reject the alternative hypothesis.

Qualitative Analysis

Qualitative data can take many forms:

- written records, e.g. notes or transcripts
- audio or video recordings
- direct quotations from participants.

The process of qualitative analysis

1. Data are gathered using non-experimental methods, which include naturalistic observation, interview, questionnaire, and case study.
2. Data are collected and categorised. Consider the categories suggested by participants; this will avoid researcher bias, which can occur if the researcher constructs the categories. The researcher must note the categories used spontaneously by the participants, arrange items into groups, and then compare these groupings with the categories suggested by the participants themselves. The researcher then forms the final set of categories, although these can change if new information comes to light.
3. Analyse the meanings, attitudes, and interpretations, e.g. discourse analysis. Written transcripts are made and the researcher looks closely at the words people use and the meanings behind them. This is highly subjective and the researcher needs to have excellent interpretative skills. The researcher will look for recurrent themes and patterns in the data, which might or might not fit with the previously constructed categories.
4. Consider the research hypothesis and how this might have changed as a result of the investigation.
5. It might be useful to make the qualitative data quantitative, e.g. content analysis. The researcher might quantify the data by counting the number of items that fall into each category. This can be done to summarise the qualitative data and usually accompanies, rather than replaces, the more in-depth qualitative analysis.

Evaluation of qualitative analysis

Qualitative analysis considers the context and the participants as individuals, providing more depth to the findings. However, it lacks generalisability because the sample is often very small as a result of the time-consuming nature of collecting qualitative data. A key weakness of qualitative analysis is that it is highly subjective, as the analysis and interpretations are very vulnerable to researcher bias. Qualitative analysis is also difficult to replicate and so lacks reliability (consistency) and bias can also reduce validity. However, the data are usually meaningful and so it often has real-life validity. Qualitative analysis provides explanations whereas quantitative analysis is mainly descriptive.

The Conventions for the Reporting of Psychological Research

Psychological research

Psychologists publish their research in magazines called "journals". The intention of these journal reports is to inform other psychologists of new findings and to provide an analysis of what these new findings mean. The journal reports must also provide sufficient detail of the research study so that other psychologists could, if they wanted, replicate the study to confirm the validity of the findings. Journal reports follow a conventional structure as detailed below.

Title

This should be very specific, including the research design and the variables.

Abstract

Invariably, a journal article begins with a summary of the main points of the research study. This enables readers to tell, at a glance, whether the article will be of interest to them. The abstract includes the study aims and a brief description of the methods used in the study and of the findings, including the statistical treatment(s) used and their significance. Finally, conclusions are made, and any limitations or implications identified. An example of an abstract is given here:

Craik and Lockhart's Levels of Processing Theory predicts that the more deeply a word is processed, the more likely it is to be remembered. This study set out to test this prediction by giving participants material that required different levels of processing: shallow (processing words in terms of case), phonetic (processing words in terms of rhyming), and semantic (processing words in terms of meaning). The study was experimental and a repeated measures design. Twenty female participants completed the questionnaire in silence during a school lesson. Comparisons between semantic and shallow processing were analysed using the Wilcoxon test and found to be significant at the $p < 0.05$ level. This suggests that memory is enhanced by deeper processing, as predicted by levels of processing theory. The theory has useful applications to student revision.

[130 words]

Introduction, aims, and hypothesis

The purpose of this part of the report is to identify the background to the study. The background information is often described as the "psychological literature", which refers to research that is already published in books and journals. The introduction should start at a relatively broad level and quickly narrow down to examine two or three particularly relevant pieces of research. Once these studies have been described, it should be obvious what the aims of the study are going to be. For example, if the Levels of Processing Theory has been described in the literature review, it would seem strange to then state that the investigation is of short-term memory. This is not a logical progression. An example of an introduction is given here:

Memory is one of the earliest areas to be studied in psychology, starting with Ebbinghaus' (1985/1913) study of forgetting. Other early research focused on the capacity and duration of different memory stores: sensory memory (which is equivalent to the eyes and ears), short-term memory (STM), and long-term memory (LTM). Information comes to the sensory memory store through the senses and is either forgotten or transferred to the STM. From there, the memory can be forgotten, either because the memory trace disappears or because the material is displaced by newer material. Verbal rehearsal leads a memory to be transferred to LTM. This is called the multi-store model of memory as described by Atkinson and Shiffrin (1968).

Craik and Watkins (1973) found that when participants were asked to remember words from a list they could do this without verbal rehearsal. Instead, if they elaborated the words this also led to enhanced recall. This led to the Levels of Processing Theory. Craik and Lockhart (1972) suggested that it is the kinds of process that are operating at the time of storing data that determine the extent to which something is remembered. They suggested that it is the depth of processing in terms of elaboration that creates a durable memory.

This theory was tested in an experiment by Craik and Tulving (1975). Participants were shown a list of words (five-letter concrete nouns such as "table") and were asked a question for each word; for each question the answer was "yes" or "no". The questions were one of three types: case (shallow processing), such as "Is the word in capital letters?"; rhyme (phonemic processing), such as "Does the word rhyme with 'able'?"; or sentence (semantic or deep processing), such as "Would the word fit in the sentence 'They met a ____ in the street'?" Craik and Tulving found that those words that had been processed semantically were recalled best and those processed phonemically were recalled second best.

Other research has further investigated how depth of processing can be achieved. For example, organisation is a form of elaborative processing. Mandler (1967) showed that organisation alone led to durable memory. Participants were asked to sort 52 word cards into categories. When they had done this repeatedly, they were given an unexpected test of memory and they were quite able to recall the words. The more categories they had used, the better their recall. This shows that deeper processing leads to long-term memory.

Another study showed that distinctiveness can also enhance memory. Eysenck and Eysenck (1980) arranged for participants to say words in a non-semantic, distinctive condition (e.g. pronouncing the "b" in "comb") or a non-semantic, non-distinctive condition (e.g. saying the word "comb" normally). There were also semantic distinctive and non-distinctive conditions where the words were also processed for meaning. Recall was almost as good in the non-semantic, distinctive condition as for the semantic conditions. This shows that distinctiveness can be as powerful as meaning in terms of enhancing memory for words.

The *aim of this study* is to replicate the original work by Craik and Tulving as a means of demonstrating the Levels of Processing Theory. The same design will be followed as in the original study, with all participants being given three conditions: case, phonemic, and semantic in order to see which condition leads to best recall. The original experiment also involved expected and unexpected tests of recall, but these will not be included here. In line with the Levels of Processing Theory, we would expect recall to be highest on the semantic condition and lowest on the case condition. Given the fact that previous research has found that the semantic condition is associated with higher memory, a directional hypothesis would be appropriate.

The hypothesis

- Experimental hypothesis 1: participants recall more words in the semantic condition than in the case condition.
- Null hypothesis: there is no difference in recall between semantic and case conditions.
- Experimental hypothesis 2: participants recall more words in the semantic condition than in the phonemic condition.
- Null hypothesis: there is no difference in recall between semantic and phonemic conditions.

[660 words]

The aims must lead logically from the literature review and act like a buckle to join the introduction to the hypothesis. The hypothesis must be stated clearly and unambiguously, and should be operationalised. This means that it is testable, as the variables have not just been identified but details on how they are to be measured have been included. For example, don't state that "recall is the dependent variable" but operationalise this by being more precise: "the number of words recalled from a list of 20 is the dependent variable".

? What might be an operational definition of fatigue, or hunger?

Method

This section of the report should provide the reader with sufficient detail to replicate the study. It is typically subdivided into the four sections:

1. *Design*: includes design decisions, such as choice of method (e.g. experiment or observation), experimental design, and the key variables. If it is an observation, then details of the observational techniques must be described. If it is a correlational study, the covariables must be operationalised. Any controls or ethical decisions that were taken as part of the design should also be included.
2. *Participants*: includes how many people were involved, plus any relevant demographic details such as age, educational background, and gender; where the participants were tested or observed; and how the particular sample was selected (sampling techniques as discussed above).
3. *Apparatus/materials*: full details of any questionnaires or other materials should be placed in the appendix section of a report, so just a description of the materials is included here. This might include a description of questionnaire construction, observation criteria, standardisation of a test etc.
4. *Standardised procedures*: this should be a clear but detailed summary of exactly how the study was implemented.

? It might be said that the operational definition of "intelligence" is "that which is measured by intelligence tests". What is the main weakness of this definition?

Results

There are three ways to illustrate the results of psychological research:

1. *Raw data*: the numbers prior to any analysis. These should be placed in the appendices but a summary might be included in the results section.
2. *Descriptive statistics*: such as the use of measures of central tendency (mean, median, and mode) and/or spread (range or standard deviation) plus graphical representation.
3. *Statistical tests*: determine whether the findings are significant. This section must state clearly which test was used, justify the choice of statistical test, record details of the test calculations in the appendix, and state the outcome of the statistical test and thus your conclusion regarding the significance of your results in the main body results.

Discussion

The intention of this section is to interpret the findings in terms of previous research, as mentioned in the introduction, or with reference to other research. In addition, this is where the researcher reflects on the strengths and limitations of the study, and on the implications of the research.

Explanation of findings.   The emphasis here is on an *explanation* of what has been found. This includes relating the findings to the original aims and hypotheses. Any unanticipated findings can be discussed.

Relationship to background research.   The findings must be related to the research in the introduction in terms of whether they support or contradict it. New research can also be introduced, in the light of the findings. Theory and/or other research studies should be considered in the light of the research findings.

Limitations and modifications.   The limitations might refer to sampling procedures, design, lack of controls, procedures, and/or statistical treatments. Key limitations are explored by explaining how they were problematic in the study, and improvements to resolve the issues can be discussed.

Implications and suggestions.   Implications include the practical use of the research or theoretical implications not mentioned earlier. The implications should lead logically into suggestions for future research.

References
The reason for full references is so that readers have the details of the original article or book if they wish to research the study/theory further themselves. This is the style used in the reference section of this textbook. An alternative acceptable style is to state the details of a textbook, and list all the studies with page numbers that have been cited from this book. This means that anyone who would like to follow-up one of your references can locate the exact reference and the article.

Appendices
Examples of materials and/or questionnaires, standardised instructions, raw data, and statistical tests are included in the appendices.

See *A2-Level Psychology Online* for some interactive quizzes to help you with your revision.

SECTION SUMMARY
Data Analysis and Reporting on Investigations

- ❖ When we have obtained scores from a group of participants, we can summarise our data using descriptive statistics.
- ❖ Which descriptive statistics are appropriate depend on the level of significance

- ❖ There are four types of data of increasing levels of precision:

  — nominal
  — ordinal
  — interval
  — ratio.

- ❖ Measures of central tendency: mode, median, and mean.
- ❖ Measures of dispersion: the variation ratio, range, interquartile range, and standard deviation.

Descriptive statistics

Levels of significance

Measures of central tendency and dispersion

Graphs, charts, and tables	❖ Bar charts, histograms, frequency polygons, scattergraphs, and tables can all be used to summarise the data. Which graph is most appropriate depends on the nature (continuous, non-continuous, correlational) and the level of the data.
Statistical tests	❖ We determine the significance of the result(s) using a statistical test.
Deciding on the appropriate statistical test	❖ A test of difference is used when data are obtained from a study in which an independent variable was manipulated to observe its effects.
	❖ A test of correlation is used when the data are in the form of scores on two response variables from every participant.
	❖ If the alternative hypothesis predicts the direction of effects (a directional hypothesis), then a one-tailed test should be used.
	❖ Otherwise, a two-tailed test should be used (for a non-directional hypothesis).
Statistical significance	❖ The meaningfulness of research findings is determined through statistical significance.
	❖ If the statistical test indicates that there is only a small probability of the difference between conditions (e.g. loud noise vs. no noise) having occurred if the null hypothesis were true, then we reject the null hypothesis in favour of the alternative hypothesis.
	❖ Psychologists generally use the 5% level of statistical significance. This produces fairly small probabilities of the following errors:
	— type 1 error: incorrectly rejecting the null hypothesis in favour of the alternative hypothesis
	— type 2 error: incorrectly retaining the null hypothesis.
Tests of difference	❖ The chi-squared test:
	— Is used when we have nominal data in the form of frequencies and when each and every observation is independent of all the other observations.
	— All the expected frequencies are 5 or more.
	— Finding an association is not the same as showing the existence of a causal effect.
	❖ The Mann–Whitney U test is the appropriate test of difference if an independent design has been used and the data are at least ordinal.
	❖ The Wilcoxon matched pairs signed ranks test can be used for matched pairs or repeated measures. The data must be at least ordinal.
Studies using correlational analysis	❖ Spearman's rho test: calculates the correlation between two sets of scores, provided the data are at least ordinal.
Comparing the calculated and critical values	❖ Whether the calculated value has to be greater than or less than the critical varies depending on the statistical test.
Reporting the result	❖ Remember to include: details of the level of significance, the critical and observed values, degrees of freedom or number of participants, whether the hypothesis was directional or non-directional (one-tailed or two-tailed), and whether it was accepted or rejected in the statement of significance.

❖ This involves the analysis of words. Two key techniques are discourse analysis, which involves categorising the data by looking for recurring themes and patterns, and content analysis, which involves making the qualitative data quantitative by counting the number of participant responses that fit into particular categories.

❖ The strengths of qualitative analysis include the depth (potential validity) of the data and so its potential to explain, rather than merely describe, behaviour.

❖ Qualitative analysis can lack reliability and generalisability. A further criticism is that it can be biased by subjectivity, which will decrease internal validity. However, this is certainly not true of all qualitative research.

❖ The reporting of psychological research follows a particular scientific format: abstract, introduction, method, results, discussion, references, appendices.

Qualitative analysis

The conventions for the reporting of psychological research

FURTHER READING

These topics are covered in greater depth by A. Searle (1999). *Introducing research and data in psychology* (London: Routledge), which is written specifically for AQA A students. There is detailed but user-friendly coverage of the topics discussed in this section in H. Coolican (2004). *Research methods and statistics in psychology* (4th Edn) (London: Hodder & Stoughton). A shorter version of the Coolican textbook is H. Coolican (2006). *Introduction to research methods and statistics in psychology* (3rd Edn) (London: Hodder & Stoughton).

REVISION QUESTIONS

In the exam the compulsory research methods question carries 35 marks; allow 50 minutes for this. Read the stimulus material very carefully; perhaps even highlight key words and phrases. Make sure you understand what each part of the question is asking you to do. Look at the allocation of marks so you can spend more time on parts with more marks, and less on parts with fewer marks.

There are only 3 AO1 marks, for short, factual answers.

There are just 4 AO2 marks, for accurate descriptions.

There are 28 AO3 marks for appropriate analysis, explanations, extraction of information from the stimulus material, interpretation, and/or applications to unfamiliar contexts.

See page 6 for an example exam question on this topic.

See *A2-Level Psychology Online* for a sample exam question and tips on how to answer it.

APPENDIX

Tables of Significance

Remember that decisions based on statistical tests are open to error, but if you follow the standard procedures outlined in the chapter on Psychological Research and Scientific Method the potential for errors can be minimised. Try to be as unbiased as possible, and try not to assume too much about the results in advance.

How to Use the Tables

In the **Mann–Whitney U test** (on pages 748–749), use the smaller value of U and U′ to look up the critical value of U for a one- or two-tailed test, as appropriate, at 0.05, initially (bottom and top tables, page 749). If the tabled value is equal to or less than your value at that level, the null hypothesis is retained; if it is greater than your value, it is rejected and your experimental hypothesis is proved.

In the **Wilcoxon signed ranks test** (on page 750), look up the critical value of T for a one- or two-tailed test, as appropriate, for N, the number of participants with differing scores, at 0.05, initially. If the tabled value is equal to or less than your value at that level, the null hypothesis is retained; if it is greater than your value, it is rejected and your experimental hypothesis is proved.

In the **Spearman's rho test** (on page 751), look up the critical value of r_s for a one- or two-tailed test, as appropriate, for N, the number of participants, at 0.05, initially. If the tabled value is greater than or equal to your value at that level, the null hypothesis is retained; if it is less than your value, it is rejected and your experimental hypothesis is proved.

In the **chi-squared test** (on page 752), look up the critical value of chi-squared (also shown as χ^2) for a one- or two-tailed test, as appropriate, for df, the degrees of freedom, at 0.05, initially. If the tabled value is greater than or equal to your value at that level, the null hypothesis is retained; if it is less than your value, it is rejected and your experimental hypothesis is proved.

Table 1: Mann–Whitney U test

Critical values of U for a one-tailed test at 0.005; two-tailed test at 0.01*

N_B	| N_A 1	2	3	4	5	6	7	8	9	10	11	12	13	14	15	16	17	18	19	20
1	—	—	—	—	—	—	—	—	—	—	—	—	—	—	—	—	—	—	—	—
2	—	—	—	—	—	—	—	—	—	—	—	—	—	—	—	—	—	—	0	0
3	—	—	—	—	—	—	—	—	0	0	0	1	1	1	2	2	2	2	3	3
4	—	—	—	—	—	0	0	1	1	2	2	3	3	4	5	5	6	6	7	8
5	—	—	—	—	0	1	1	2	3	4	5	6	7	7	8	9	10	11	12	13
6	—	—	—	0	1	2	3	4	5	6	7	9	10	11	12	13	15	16	17	18
7	—	—	—	0	1	3	4	6	7	9	10	12	13	15	16	18	19	21	22	24
8	—	—	—	1	2	4	6	7	9	11	13	15	17	18	20	22	24	26	28	30
9	—	—	0	1	3	5	7	9	11	13	16	18	20	22	24	27	29	31	33	36
10	—	—	0	2	4	6	9	11	13	16	18	21	24	26	29	31	34	37	39	42
11	—	—	0	2	5	7	10	13	16	18	21	24	27	30	33	36	39	42	45	48
12	—	—	1	3	6	9	12	15	18	21	24	27	31	34	37	41	44	47	51	54
13	—	—	1	3	7	10	13	17	20	24	27	31	34	38	42	45	49	53	56	60
14	—	—	1	4	7	11	15	18	22	26	30	34	38	42	46	50	54	58	63	67
15	—	—	2	5	8	12	16	20	24	29	33	37	42	46	51	55	60	64	69	73
16	—	—	2	5	9	13	18	22	27	31	36	41	45	50	55	60	65	70	74	79
17	—	—	2	6	10	15	19	24	29	34	39	44	49	54	60	65	70	75	81	86
18	—	—	2	6	11	16	21	26	31	37	42	47	53	58	64	70	75	81	87	92
19	—	0	3	7	12	17	22	28	33	39	45	51	56	63	69	74	81	87	93	99
20	—	0	3	8	13	18	24	30	36	42	48	54	60	67	73	79	86	92	99	105

*Dashes in the body of the table indicate that no decision is possible at the stated level of significance.
For any N_A and N_B the observed value of U is significant at a given level of significance if it is *equal* to or *less* than the critical values shown.

Source: R. Runyon and A. Haber (1976), *Fundamentals of behavioural statistics (3rd Edn.)*. Reading, MA: McGraw-Hill, Inc. With the kind permission of the publisher.

Critical values of U for a one-tailed test at 0.01; two-tailed test at 0.02*

N_B	| N_A 1	2	3	4	5	6	7	8	9	10	11	12	13	14	15	16	17	18	19	20
1	—	—	—	—	—	—	—	—	—	—	—	—	—	—	—	—	—	—	—	—
2	—	—	—	—	—	—	—	—	—	—	—	0	0	0	0	0	0	0	1	1
3	—	—	—	—	—	—	0	0	1	1	1	2	2	2	3	3	4	4	4	5
4	—	—	—	—	0	1	1	2	3	3	4	5	5	6	7	7	8	9	9	10
5	—	—	—	0	1	2	3	4	5	6	7	8	9	10	11	12	13	14	15	16
6	—	—	—	1	2	3	4	6	7	8	9	11	12	13	15	16	18	19	20	22
7	—	—	0	1	3	4	6	7	9	11	12	14	16	17	19	21	23	24	26	28
8	—	—	0	2	4	6	7	9	11	13	15	17	20	22	24	26	28	30	32	34
9	—	—	1	3	5	7	9	11	14	16	18	21	23	26	28	31	33	36	38	40
10	—	—	1	3	6	8	11	13	16	19	22	24	27	30	33	36	38	41	44	47
11	—	—	1	4	7	9	12	15	18	22	25	28	31	34	37	41	44	47	50	53
12	—	—	2	5	8	11	14	17	21	24	28	31	35	38	42	46	49	53	56	60
13	—	0	2	5	9	12	16	20	23	27	31	35	39	43	47	51	55	59	63	67
14	—	0	2	6	10	13	17	22	26	30	34	38	43	47	51	56	60	65	69	73
15	—	0	3	7	11	15	19	24	28	33	37	42	47	51	56	61	66	70	75	80
16	—	0	3	7	12	16	21	26	31	36	41	46	51	56	61	66	71	76	82	87
17	—	0	4	8	13	18	23	28	33	38	44	49	55	60	66	71	77	82	88	93
18	—	0	4	9	14	19	24	30	36	41	47	53	59	65	70	76	82	88	94	100
19	—	1	4	9	15	20	26	32	38	44	50	56	63	69	75	82	88	94	101	107
20	—	1	5	10	16	22	28	34	40	47	53	60	67	73	80	87	93	100	107	114

*Dashes in the body of the table indicate that no decision is possible at the stated level of significance.
For any N_A and N_B the observed value of U is significant at a given level of significance if it is *equal* to or *less* than the critical values shown.

Source: R. Runyon and A. Haber (1976), *Fundamentals of behavioural statistics (3rd Edn.)*. Reading, MA: McGraw-Hill, Inc. With the kind permission of the publisher.

Critical values of U for a one-tailed test at 0.025; two-tailed test at 0.05*

N_B \ N_A	1	2	3	4	5	6	7	8	9	10	11	12	13	14	15	16	17	18	19	20
1	—	—	—	—	—	—	—	—	—	—	—	—	—	—	—	—	—	—	—	—
2	—	—	—	—	—	—	—	0	0	0	0	1	1	1	1	1	2	2	2	2
3	—	—	—	—	0	1	1	2	2	3	3	4	4	5	5	6	6	7	7	8
4	—	—	—	0	1	2	3	4	4	5	6	7	8	9	10	11	11	12	13	13
5	—	—	0	1	2	3	5	6	7	8	9	11	12	13	14	15	17	18	19	20
6	—	—	1	2	3	5	6	8	10	11	13	14	16	17	19	21	22	24	25	27
7	—	—	1	3	5	6	8	10	12	14	16	18	20	22	24	26	28	30	32	34
8	—	0	2	4	6	8	10	13	15	17	19	22	24	26	29	31	34	36	38	41
9	—	0	2	4	7	10	12	15	17	20	23	26	28	31	34	37	39	42	45	48
10	—	0	3	5	8	11	14	17	20	23	26	29	33	36	39	42	45	48	52	55
11	—	0	3	6	9	13	16	19	23	26	30	33	37	40	44	47	51	55	58	62
12	—	1	4	7	11	14	18	22	26	29	33	37	41	45	49	53	57	61	65	69
13	—	1	4	8	12	16	20	24	28	33	37	41	45	50	54	59	63	67	72	76
14	—	1	5	9	13	17	22	26	31	36	40	45	50	55	59	64	67	74	78	83
15	—	1	5	10	14	19	24	29	34	39	44	49	54	59	64	70	75	80	85	90
16	—	1	6	11	15	21	26	31	37	42	47	53	59	64	70	75	81	86	92	98
17	—	2	6	11	17	22	28	34	39	45	51	57	63	67	75	81	87	93	99	105
18	—	2	7	12	18	24	30	36	42	48	55	61	67	74	80	86	93	99	106	112
19	—	2	7	13	19	25	32	38	45	52	58	65	72	78	85	92	99	106	113	119
20	—	2	8	13	20	27	34	41	48	55	62	69	76	83	90	98	105	112	119	127

*Dashes in the body of the table indicate that no decision is possible at the stated level of significance.
For any N_A and N_B the observed value of U is significant at a given level of significance if it is *equal* to or *less* than the critical values shown.

Source: R. Runyon and A. Haber (1976), *Fundamentals of behavioural statistics (3rd Edn.).* Reading, MA: McGraw-Hill, Inc. With the kind permission of the publisher.

Critical values of U for a one-tailed test at 0.05; two-tailed test at 0.10*

N_B \ N_A	1	2	3	4	5	6	7	8	9	10	11	12	13	14	15	16	17	18	19	20
1	—	—	—	—	—	—	—	—	—	—	—	—	—	—	—	—	—	—	0	0
2	—	—	—	—	0	0	0	1	1	1	1	2	2	2	3	3	3	4	4	4
3	—	—	0	0	1	2	2	3	3	4	5	5	6	7	7	8	9	9	10	11
4	—	—	0	1	2	3	4	5	6	7	8	9	10	11	12	14	15	16	17	18
5	—	0	1	2	4	5	6	8	9	11	12	13	15	16	18	19	20	22	23	25
6	—	0	2	3	5	7	8	10	12	14	16	17	19	21	23	25	26	28	30	32
7	—	0	2	4	6	8	11	13	15	17	19	21	24	26	28	30	33	35	37	39
8	—	1	3	5	8	10	13	15	18	20	23	26	28	31	33	36	39	41	44	47
9	—	1	3	6	9	12	15	18	21	24	27	30	33	36	39	42	45	48	51	54
10	—	1	4	7	11	14	17	20	24	27	31	34	37	41	44	48	51	55	58	62
11	—	1	5	8	12	16	19	23	27	31	34	38	42	46	50	54	57	61	65	69
12	—	2	5	9	13	17	21	26	30	34	38	42	47	51	55	60	64	68	72	77
13	—	2	6	10	15	19	24	28	33	37	42	47	51	56	61	65	70	75	80	84
14	—	2	7	11	16	21	26	31	36	41	46	51	56	61	66	71	77	82	87	92
15	—	3	7	12	18	23	28	33	39	44	50	55	61	66	72	77	83	88	94	100
16	—	3	8	14	19	25	30	36	42	48	54	60	65	71	77	83	89	95	101	107
17	—	3	9	15	20	26	33	39	45	51	57	64	70	77	83	89	96	102	109	115
18	—	4	9	16	22	28	35	41	48	55	61	68	75	82	88	95	102	109	116	123
19	0	4	10	17	23	30	37	44	51	58	65	72	80	87	94	101	109	116	123	130
20	0	4	11	18	25	32	39	47	54	62	69	77	84	92	100	107	115	123	130	138

*Dashes in the body of the table indicate that no decision is possible at the stated level of significance.
For any N_A and N_B the observed value of U is significant at a given level of significance if it is *equal* to or *less* than the critical values shown.

Source: R. Runyon and A. Haber (1976), *Fundamentals of behavioural statistics (3rd Edn.).* Reading, MA: McGraw-Hill, Inc. With the kind permission of the publisher.

Table 2: Wilcoxon signed ranks test

	Levels of significance			
	One-tailed test			
	0.05	0.025	0.01	0.001
	Two-tailed test			
Sample size	0.1	0.05	0.02	0.002
N = 5	T ≤ 0			
6	2	0		
7	3	2	0	
8	5	3	1	
9	8	5	3	
10	11	8	5	0
11	13	10	7	1
12	17	13	9	2
13	21	17	12	4
14	25	21	15	6
15	30	25	19	8
16	35	29	23	11
17	41	34	27	14
18	47	40	32	18
19	53	46	37	21
20	60	52	43	26
21	67	58	49	30
22	75	65	55	35
23	83	73	62	40
24	91	81	69	45
25	100	89	76	51
26	110	98	84	58
27	119	107	92	64
28	130	116	101	71
29	141	125	111	78
30	151	137	120	86
31	163	147	130	94
32	175	159	140	103
33	187	170	151	112

Calculated T must be *equal* to or *less* than the table (critical) value for significance at the level shown.

Source: R. Meddis (1975b), *Statistical handbook for non-statisticians*. London: McGraw-Hill.

Table 3: Spearman's rho test

	Level of significance for two-tailed test			
	0.10	0.05	0.02	0.01
	Level of significance for one-tailed test			
	0.05	0.025	0.01	0.005
N = 4	1.000			
5	0.900	1.000	1.000	
6	0.829	0.886	0.943	1.000
7	0.714	0.786	0.893	0.929
8	0.643	0.738	0.833	0.881
9	0.600	0.700	0.783	0.833
10	0.564	0.648	0.745	0.794
11	0.536	0.618	0.709	0.755
12	0.503	0.587	0.671	0.727
13	0.484	0.560	0.648	0.703
14	0.464	0.538	0.566	0.675
15	0.443	0.521	0.604	0.654
16	0.429	0.503	0.582	0.635
17	0.414	0.485	0.566	0.615
18	0.401	0.472	0.550	0.600
19	0.391	0.460	0.535	0.584
20	0.380	0.447	0.520	0.570
21	0.370	0.435	0.508	0.556
22	0.361	0.425	0.496	0.544
23	0.353	0.415	0.486	0.532
24	0.344	0.406	0.476	0.521
25	0.337	0.398	0.466	0.511
26	0.331	0.390	0.457	0.501
27	0.324	0.382	0.448	0.491
28	0.317	0.375	0.440	0.483
29	0.312	0.368	0.433	0.475
30	0.306	0.362	0.425	0.467

For n > 30, the significance of r_s can be tested by using the formula:

$$t = r_s \sqrt{\frac{n-2}{1-r_s^2}} \qquad df = n - 2$$

and checking the value of t.

Calculated r_s must *equal* or *exceed* the table (critical) value for significance at the level shown.

Source: J.H. Zhar (1972), Significance testing of the Spearman rank correlation coefficient. *Journal of the American Statistical Association, 67*, 578–580. With the kind permission of the publisher. Copyright © 1972 by the American Statistical Association. All rights reserved.

Table 4: Chi-squared test

	Level of significance for one-tailed test					
	0.10	0.05	0.025	0.01	0.005	0.0005
	Level of significance for two-tailed test					
df	0.20	0.10	0.05	0.02	0.01	0.001
1	1.64	2.71	3.84	5.41	6.64	10.83
2	3.22	4.60	5.99	7.82	9.21	13.82
3	4.64	6.25	7.82	9.84	11.34	16.27
4	5.99	7.78	9.49	11.67	13.28	18.46
5	7.29	9.24	11.07	13.39	15.09	20.52
6	8.56	10.64	12.59	15.03	16.81	22.46
7	9.80	12.02	14.07	16.62	18.48	24.32
8	11.03	13.36	15.51	18.17	20.09	26.12
9	12.24	14.68	16.92	19.68	21.67	27.88
10	13.44	15.99	18.31	21.16	23.21	29.59
11	14.63	17.28	19.68	22.62	24.72	31.26
12	15.81	18.55	21.03	24.05	26.22	32.91
13	16.98	19.81	22.36	25.47	27.69	34.53
14	18.15	21.06	23.68	26.87	29.14	36.12
15	19.31	22.31	25.00	28.26	30.58	37.70
16	20.46	23.54	26.30	29.63	32.00	39.29
17	21.62	24.77	27.59	31.00	33.41	40.75
18	22.76	25.99	28.87	32.35	34.80	42.31
19	23.90	27.20	30.14	33.69	36.19	43.82
20	25.04	28.41	31.41	35.02	37.57	45.32
21	26.17	29.62	32.67	36.34	38.93	46.80
22	27.30	30.81	33.92	37.66	40.29	48.27
23	28.43	32.01	35.17	38.97	41.64	49.73
24	29.55	33.20	36.42	40.27	42.98	51.18
25	30.68	34.38	37.65	41.57	44.31	52.62
26	31.80	35.56	38.88	42.86	45.64	54.05
27	32.91	36.74	40.11	44.14	46.96	55.48
28	34.03	37.92	41.34	45.42	48.28	56.89
29	35.14	39.09	42.69	46.69	49.59	58.30
30	36.25	40.26	43.77	43.49	50.89	59.70
32	38.47	42.59	46.19	50.49	53.49	62.49
34	40.68	44.90	48.60	53.00	56.06	65.25
36	42.88	47.21	51.00	55.49	58.62	67.99
38	45.08	49.51	53.38	57.97	61.16	70.70
40	47.27	51.81	55.76	60.44	63.69	73.40
44	51.64	56.37	60.48	65.34	68.71	78.75
48	55.99	60.91	65.17	70.20	73.68	84.04
52	60.33	65.42	69.83	75.02	78.62	89.27
56	64.66	69.92	74.47	79.82	83.51	94.46
60	68.97	74.40	79.08	84.58	88.38	99.61

Calculated value of χ^2 must *equal* or *exceed* the table (critical) value for significance at the level shown.

Abridged from R.A. Fisher and F. Yates (1974), *Statistical tables for biological, agricultural and medical research (6th Edn)*. Harlow, UK: Addison Wesley Longman. Reprinted by permission of Pearson Education Limited.

REFERENCES

Abbott, M.W. (2007). Situational factors that affect gambling behavior. In G. Smith, D. Hodgins, & R. Williams (Eds.), *Research and measurement issues in gambling studies*, pp. 251–278. New York: Elsevier.

Abbott, N.C., Harkness, E.F., Stevinson, C., Marshall, F.P., Conn, D.A., & Ernst, E. (2001). Spiritual healing as a therapy for chronic pain: a randomised, clinical trial. *Pain*, Vol. 91, pp. 79–89.

Abed, R.T., & de Pauw, K.W. (1998). An evolutionary hypothesis for obsessive-compulsive disorder: A psychological immune system? *Behavioural Neurology, 11*, 245–250.

Abhyankar, R.R., Thatte, S.S., Doongaji, D.R. (1981). Idiot savant. *Journal of Postgraduate Medicine, 27*, 44.

Abraham, K. (1927). *Selected papers*. London: Hogarth Press.

Abramowitz, E.S., Baker, A.H., & Fleischer, S.F. (1982). Onset of depressive psychiatric crises and the menstrual cycle. *American Journal of Psychiatry, 139*, 475–478.

Abramowitz, J.S. (1998). Does cognitive-behavioural therapy cure obsessive-compulsive disorder? A meta-analytic evaluation of clinical significance. *Behavior Therapy, 29*, 339–355.

Abramowitz, J.S. (2006). The psychological treatment of obsessive compulsive disorder. *Canadian Journal of Psychiatry, 51*, 407–416.

Abramson, L.Y., Metalsky, G.I., & Alloy, L.B. (1989). Hopelessness depression: A theory-based subtype of depression. *Psychological Review, 96*, 358–372.

Abramson, L.Y., Seligman, M.E., & Teasdale, J. (1978). Learned helplessness in humans: Critique and reformulation. *Journal of Abnormal Psychology, 87*, 49–74.

Ackerman, J.M., Kenrick, D.T., & Schaller, M. (2007). Is friendship akin to kinship? *Evolution and Human Behavior, 28*, 365–374.

Ackermann, R., & DeRubeis, R.J. (1991). Is depressive realism real? *Clinical Psychology Review, 10*, 565–584.

Adolph, K.E. (2000). Specificity of learning: Why infants fall over a veritable cliff. *Psychological Science, 11*, 290–295.

Agnew, Z.K., Bhakoo, K.K., & Puri, B.K. (2007). The human mirror system: A motor resonance theory of mind-reading. *Brain Research Reviews, 54*, 286–293.

Aiello, L.C., & Wheeler, P. (1995). The expensive tissue hypothesis: the brain and the digestive system in human and primate evolution. *Current Anthropology, 36*, 199–221.

Ajzen, I. (1991). Theory of planned behavior. *Organizational Behaviour and Human Decision Processes, 50*, 179–211.

Ajzen, I., & Fishbein, M. (1980). *Understanding attitudes and predicting social behavior*. Englewood Cliffs, NJ: Prentice Hall.

Akerstedt, T. (1977). Inversion of the sleep wakefulness pattern: Effects on circadian variations in psychophysiological activation. *Ergonomics, 20*, 459–474.

Akerstedt, T. (1985). Adjustment of physiological circadian rhythms and the sleep–wake cycle to shiftwork. In Folkard, S. & Monk, T.H. (Eds.), *Hours of work*. Chichester: Wiley.

Akhtar, S., Wig, N.N., Varma, V.K., Pershad, D., & Verma, S.K. (1975). Phenomenological analysis of symptoms in obsessive-compulsive neurosis. *British Journal of Psychiatry, 127*, 342–348.

Alcock, J. (1993). *Animal behaviour* (5th Edn). Sunderland, MA: Sinauer.

Allen, M.G. (1976). Twin studies of affective illness. *Archives of General Psychiatry, 33*, 1476–1478.

Allgood-Merten, B., & Stockland, J. (1991). Sex role identity and self-esteem: A comparison of children and adolescents. *Sex Roles, 25*, 129–139.

Allison, T., & Cicchetti, D.V. (1976). Sleep in mammals: Ecological and constitutional correlates. *Science, 194*, 732–734.

Allport, G.W. (1947). *The use of personal documents in psychological science*. London: Holt, Rinehart, & Winston.

Allport, G.W. (1954). *The nature of prejudice*. Reading, MA: Addison-Wesley.

Allport, G.W., & Pettigrew, T.F. (1957). Cultural influences on the perception of movement: The trapezoidal illusion among Zulus. *Journal of Abnormal and Social Psychology, 55*, 104–113.

Alstadhaug, K.B., Salvesen, R., & Bekkelund, S.I. (2008). 24-hour distribution of migraine attacks. *Headache: The Journal of Head and Face Pain, 48*(1), 95–100.

Alvarado, C.S. (2000). Out-of-body experiences. In E. Cardeña, S.J. Lynnm & S. Krippner (Eds.), *Varieties of anomalous experiences*. Washington, DC: American Psychological Association.

American Psychological Association. (2000). *DSM-IV text revision*. Washington, DC: Author.

Ames, G.J., & Murray, F.B. (1982). When two wrongs make a right: Promoting cognitive change by social conflict. *Developmental Psychology, 18*, 894–897.

Anaki, D., Kaufman, Y., Freedman, M., & Moscovitch, M. (2007). Associative (prosop)agnosia without (apparent) perceptual deficits: A case study. *Neuropsychologia, 45*, 1658–1671.

Ancoli-Israel (2008). Online. Available: http://www.bio-medicine.org/medicine-news-1/Normal-sleep-linked-to-successful-aging-21561-1/

Anderson, C.A., & Bushman, B.J. (2001). Effects of violent video games on aggressive behavior, aggressive cognition, aggressive affect, physiological arousal, and prosocial behavior: A meta-analytic review of the scientific literature. *Psychological Science, 12*(5), 353–359.

Anderson, C.A., & Bushman, B.J. (2002). Human aggression. *Annual Review of Psychology, 53*, 27–51.

Anderson, C.A., Anderson, K.B., & Deuser, W.E. (1996). A general framework for the study of affective aggression: Effects of weapons and extreme temperatures on accessibility of aggressive thoughts, affect, and attitudes. *Personality and Social Psychology Bulletin, 22*, 366–376.

Anderson, C.A., & Dill, K.E. (2000). Video games and aggressive thoughts, feelings, and behavior in the laboratory and in life. *Journal of Personality and Social Psychology*, 78(4), 772–790.

Anderson, J.L., Crawford, C.B., Nadeau, J., & Lindberg, T. (1992). Was the Duchess of Windsor right? A cross-cultural review of the socioecology of ideals of female body shape. *Ethology and Sociobiology*, 13, 197–227.

Andersson, M. (1982). Female choice selects for extreme tail length in a widow-bird. *Nature*, 299, 818–820.

Andreu, J.M., Fujihara, T., Takaya, K., & Ramirez, J. (1998). Justification of interpersonal aggression in Japanese, American, and Spanish students. *Aggressive Behavior*, 25, 185–195.

Andrews, G. (1988). Stressful life events and anxiety. In R. Noyes, M. Roth, & G.D. Burrows (Eds.), *Handbook of anxiety, Vol. 2*. Amsterdam: Elsevier.

Anitei, S. (2006). Male dominance is determined by testosterone levels. Online. Available: http://news.softpedia.com/news/Men-039-Competitiveness-is-Determined-by-Testosterone-Levels-42342.shtml

Annis, R.C., & Frost, B. (1973). Human visual ecology and orientation anisotropies in acuity. *Science*, 182, 729–741.

Apperly, I.A., Samson, D., & Humphreys, G.W. (2005). Domain specificity and theory of mind: Evaluating neuropsychological evidence. *Trends in Cognitive Sciences*, 9, 572–577.

Archer, J. (2006). Testosterone and human aggression: An evaluation of the challenge hypothesis. *Neuroscience and Biobehavior Reviews*, 30, 319–345.

Archer, L., & Yamashita, H. (2003). Theorising inner-city masculinities: 'Race', class, gender, and education. *Gender and Education*, 15, 115–132.

Archer, S. (1982). The lower age boundaries of identity development. *Child Development*, 53, 1551–1556.

Arendt, H. (1963). *Eichmann in Jerusalem: A report on the banality of evil*. New York: Viking Press.

Argyle, M. (1988). Social relationships. In M. Hewstone, W. Stroebe, J.-P. Codol, & G.M. Stephenson (Eds.), *Introduction to social psychology*. Oxford: Blackwell.

Arkin, A.M., Toth, M.F., Baker, J., & Hastey, J.M. (1970). The frequency of sleep-talking in the laboratory among chronic sleeptalkers and good dream recallers. *Journal of Nervous and Mental Disease*, 151, 369–374.

Armstrong K.L., Quinn R.A., & Dadds, M.R. (1994). The sleep patterns of normal children. *Medical Journal of Australia*, 161(3), 202–206.

Aron, A., Aron, E.N., Tudor, M., & Nelson, G. (1991). Close relationships as including other in the self. *Journal of Personality and Social Psychology*, 60, 241–253.

Aron, A., Fisher, H., Mashek, D.J., Strong, G., Li, H., & Brown, L.L. (2005). Reward, motivation, and emotion systems associated with early-stage intense romantic love. *Journal of Neurophysiology*, 94, 327–337.

Aronson, E. (1988). *The social animal* (5th Edn). New York: Freeman.

Aronson, E., & Mills, J. (1959). The effect of severity of initiation on liking for a group. *Journal of Abnormal and Social Psychology*, 59, 177–181.

Arrindell, W.A., Kwee, M.G., Methorst, G.J., van der Ende, J., Pol, E., & Moritz, B.J. (1989). Perceived parental rearing styles of agoraphobic and socially phobic in-patients. *British Journal of Psychiatry*, 155, 526–535.

Arterberry, M., Yonas, A., & Bensen, A.S. (1989). Self-produced locomotion and the development of responsiveness to linear perspective and texture gradients. *Developmental Psychology*, 25, 976–982.

Aschoff, J. (1965). Circadian rhythm of a Russian vocabulary. *Journal of Experimental Psychology: Human learning and memory*, 104, 126–33.

Ashe, D.D., & McCutcheon, L.E. (2001). Shyness, loneliness, and attitude towards celebrities. *Current Research in Social Psychology* (e-journal). Online. Available: http://www.uiowa.edu/~grpproc/crisp.6.9.htm

Ashley, W.R., Harper, R.S., & Runyon, D.L. (1951). The perceived size of coins in normal and hypnotically induced economic states. *American Journal of Psychology*, 64, 564–572.

Ashton, H., & Golding, J. F. (1989). Smoking: motivation and models. In T. Ney & A. Gale (Eds.), *Smoking and human behaviour* (pp. 21–56). Chichester: Wiley.

Astington, J.W., & Jenkins, J.M. (1999). A longitudinal study of the relation between language and theory-of-mind development. *Developmental Psychology*, 35, 1311–1320.

Atkinson, R.C., & Shiffrin, R.M. (1968). Human memory: A proposed system and its control processes. In K.W. Spence & J.T. Spence (Eds.), *The psychology of learning and motivation, Vol. 2*. London: Academic Press.

Avery, D.H., Bolte, M.A., Cohen, S., & Millet, M.S. (1992). Gradual versus rapid dawn simulation treatment of winter depression. *Journal of Clinical Psychiatry*, 53, 359–363.

Avery, D.H., Bolte, M.A., Dager, S.R., Wilson, L.G., Weyer, M., Cox, G.B., & Dunner, D.L. (1993). Dawn simulation treatment and winter depression: A controlled study. *American Journal of Psychiatry*, 150, 113–117.

Awad, A.G., & Voruganti, L.N. (1999). Quality of life and new antipsychotics in schizophrenia: Are patients better off? *International Journal of Social Psychiatry*, 45, 268–275.

Axsom, D., Yates, S., & Chaiken, S. (1987). Audience response as a heuristic cue in persuasion. *Journal of Personality and Social Psychology*, 53, 30–40.

Ayllon, T., & Azrin, N.H. (1968). *The token economy: A motivational system for therapy and rehabilitation*. New York: Appleton-Century-Crofts.

Bachman, J. G., Johnson, L. D., O'Malley, P. M., & Humphreys, H. (1988). Explaining the recent decline in marijuana use: differentiating the effects of perceived risks, disapproval, and general life-style factors. *Journal of Health and Social Behaviour*, 29, 92–112.

Bachner-Melman, R., Lerer, E., Zohar, A.H., Kremer, I., Elizur, Y., Nemanov, L., et al. (2007). Anorexia nervosa, perfectionism, and dopamine D4 receptor (*DRD4*). *American Journal of Medical Genetics, Part B*, 144B, 748–756.

Baillargeon, R., & Graber, M. (1988). Evidence of location memory in 8-month-old infants in a nonsearch AB task. *Developmental Psychology*, 24, 502–511.

Bajpai, N. (2003). *Towards the millennium development goals*. United Nations Development Report.

Baldassari, C.M., Mitchell, R.B., Schubert, C., & Rudnick, E.F. (2008). Pediatric obstructive sleep apnea and quality of life: a meta-analysis. *Otolaryngology and Head and Neck Surgery*, 138(3), 265–273.

Baldessarini, R.J., Tondo, L., & Hennen, J. (1999). Effects of lithium treatment and its discontinuation on suicidal behaviour in bipolar manic-depressive disorders. *Journal of Clinical Psychiatry*, 60, 77–84.

Bandelow, B., Seidler-Brandler, U., Becker, A., Wedekind, D., & Ruther, E. (2007). Meta-analysis of randomised controlled comparisons of psychopharmacological and psychological treatments for anxiety disorders. *World Journal of Biological Psychiatry*, 8, 175–187.

Bandura, A. (1965). Influences of models' reinforcement contingencies on the acquisition of initiative responses. *Journal of Personality and Social Psychology*, 1, 589–593.

Bandura, A. (1977). Self-efficacy: Toward a unifying theory of behavioural change. *Psychological Review*, 84, 191–215.

Bandura, A. (1986). *Social foundations of thought and action: A social cognitive theory.* Englewood Cliffs, NJ: Prentice-Hall.

Bandura, A. (1999). Social cognitive theory of personality. In L. Pervin & O. John (Eds.) *Handbook of personality: theory and research* (2nd Edn), pp. 154–196. New York: Guilford.

Bandura, A., Ross, D., & Ross, S.A. (1961). Transmission of aggression through imitation of aggressive models. *Journal of Abnormal and Social Psychology, 63,* 575–582.

Bandura, A., Ross, D., & Ross, S.A. (1963). Imitation of film-mediated aggressive models. *Journal of Abnormal and Social Psychology, 66,* 3–11.

Banerjee, R., & Lintern, V. (2000). Boys will be boys: The effect of social evaluation concerns on gender-typing. *Social Development, 9,* 397–408.

Banks, M.S., Aslin, R.N., & Letson, R.D. (1975). Sensitive periods for the development of human binocular vision. *Science, 190,* 675–677.

Baran, S.J., Chase, L.J., & Courtright, J.A. (1979). Television drama as a facilitator of prosocial behaviour—Waltons. *Journal of Broadcasting, 23,* 277–284.

Barlett, C.P., Harris, R.J., & Baldassaro, R. (2007). Longer you play, the more hostile you feel: Examination of first person shooter video games and aggression during video game play. *Aggressive Behavior, 33,* 486–497.

Barlow, D.H. (1988). *Anxiety and its disorders: The nature and treatment of anxiety and panic.* New York: Guilford Press.

Barlow, D.H., & Durand, V.M. (1995). *Abnormal psychology: An integrative approach.* New York: Brooks/Cole.

Barnier, G. (1989). L'effet-tuteur dans des situations mettant en jeu des rapports spatiaux chez des enfants de 7–8 ans en interactions dyadiques avec des pairs de 6–7 ans. *European Journal of Psychology of Education, 4,* 385–399.

Baron, R.A., & Richardson, D.R. (1993). *Human aggression* (2nd Edn). New York: Plenum.

Baron-Cohen, S. (1989). The autistic child's theory of mind: A case for specific developmental delay. *Journal of Child Psychology and Psychiatry, 30,* 285–297.

Baron-Cohen, S. (1995). *Mindblindness: An essay on autism and theory of mind.* Boston: MIT Press.

Baron-Cohen, S., Campbell, R., Karmiloff-Smith, A., Grant, J., & Walker, J. (1995). Are children with autism blind to the mentalistic significance of eyes? *British Journal of Developmental Psychology, 13,* 379–398.

Baron-Cohen, S., Cox, A., Baird, G., Swettenham, J., et al. (1996). Psychological markers in the detection of autism in infancy in a large population. *British Journal of Psychiatry, 168,* 158–163.

Baron-Cohen, S., Leslie, A.M., & Frith, U. (1985). Does the autistic child have a "theory of mind"? *Cognition, 21,* 37–46.

Barondes, S.H. (1993). *Molecules and mental illness.* New York: W.H. Freeman & Co.

Barrett, L., & Henzi, P. (2005). The social nature of primate cognition. *Proceedings of the Royal Society B: Biological Sciences, 272,* 1865–1875.

Barry, H., Bacon, M.K., & Child, I.L. (1957). A cross-cultural survey of some sex differences in socialisation. *Journal of Abnormal and Social Psychology, 55,* 327–332.

Bartels, A., & Zeki, S. (2004). The neural correlates of maternal and romantic love. *Neuroimage, 21(3),* 1155–1166.

Bartholomew, K., & Horowitz, L.M. (1991). Attachment styles among young adults: A test of a four-category model. *Journal of Personality and Social Psychology, 61,* 226–244.

Bartholomew, R.E., Basterfield, K., & Howard, G.S. (1991). UFO abductees and contactees: Psychopathology or fantasy proneness? *Professional Psychology: Research and Practice, 22(3),* 215–222.

Bartholow, B.D., Bushman, B.J., & Sestir, M.A. (2006). Chronic violent video game exposure and desensitization to violence: Behavioral and event-related brain potential date. *Journal of Experimental Social Psychology, 42(4),* 532–539.

Bateson, G., Jackson, D.D., Haley, J., & Weakland, J. (1956). Toward a theory of schizophrenia. *Behavioral Science, 1,* 251–264.

Batterham, R.L., Ffytche, D.H., Rosenthal, J.M., Zelaya, F.O., Barker, G.J., Withers, D.J., & Williams, S.C.R. (2007). PYY modulation of cortical and hypothalamic brain areas predicts feeding behaviour in humans. *Nature, 450,* 106–109.

Baumeister, R.F., & Covington, M.V. (1985). Self-esteem, persuasion, and retrospective distortion of initial attitudes. *Electronic Social Psychology, 1,* 1–22.

Baxter, L.R., Schwartz, J.M., Bergman, K.S., Szuba, M.P., et al. (1992). Caudate glucose metabolic-rate changes with both drug and behaviour therapy for obsessive-compulsive disorder. *Archives of General Psychiatry, 49,* 681–689.

BBC (2002). Online. Available: http://news.bbc.co.uk/1/hi/programmes/hooligans/1962084.stm

BBC (2005). Online. Available: http://news.bbc.co.uk/sport1/hi/football/world_football/4483093.stm

BBC (2006). *Murder of baby Ayesha.* Online. Available: http://news.bbc.co.uk/1/hi/england/london/4900530.stm

BBC (2006a) Online. Available: http://www.bbc.co.uk/health/conditions/obesity2.shtml

BBC (2007). *Murder of Jaspal Marsh.* Online. Available: http://news.bbc.co.uk/1/hi/wales/south_west/6520197.stm

BBC (2008). *Smoking ban 'to save many lives'.* Online. Available: http://news.bbc.co.uk/1/hi/health/7480856.stm [accessed December 2008]

BBC (2008a) Online. Available: http://www.bbc.co.uk/food/food_matters/organicfood.shtml

Beck, A.T. (1976). *Cognitive therapy of the emotional disorders.* New York: New American Library.

Beck, A.T., & Clark, D.A. (1988). Anxiety and depression: An information processing perspective. *Anxiety Research, 1,* 23–36.

Beck, A.T., Rush, A.J., Shaw, B.F., & Emery, G. (1979). *Cognitive therapy of depression.* New York: Guilford Press.

Beck, A.T., & Ward, C.H. (1961). Dreams of depressed patients: Characteristic themes in manifest content. *Archives of General Psychiatry, 5,* 462–467.

Beck, A.T., & Weishaar, M.E. (1989). Cognitive therapy. In R.J. Corsini & D. Wedding (Eds.), *Current psychotherapies.* Itacca, IL: Peacock.

Behrend, D.A., Harris, L.L., & Cartwright, K.B. (1992). Morphological cues to verb meaning: Verb inflections and the initial mapping of verb meanings. *Journal of Child Language, 22,* 89–106.

Belanti, J., Perera, M., & Jagadheesan, K. (2008). Phenomenology of near-death experiences: A cross-cultural perspective. *Transcultural Psychiatry, 45(1),* 121–133.

Bellar, A., & Jarosz, P.A. (2008). Implications of the biology of weight regulation and obesity on the treatment of obesity. *Journal of the American Academy of Nurse Practitioners, 20(4),* 230–230.

Bellar, A., Jarosz, P.A., & Bellar, D. (2007). Implications of the biology of weight regulation and obesity on the treatment of obesity. *Journal of the American Academy of Nurse Practitioners, 20(3),* 128–135.

Bellis, M.A., Hughes, K., Hughes, S., & Ashton, J.R. (2005). Measuring paternal discrepancy and its public health consequences. *Journal of Epidemiology and Community Health, 59,* 749–754.

Bem, D.J. (1967). Self-perception: An alternative interpretation of cognitive dissonance phenomena. *Psychological Review, 74*, 183–200.

Bem, D.J. (1972). Self-perception theory. *Advances in Experimental Social Psychology, 1*, 199–218.

Bem, S.L. (1974). The measurement of psychological androgyny. *Journal of Consulting and Clinical Psychology, 42*, 155–162.

Bem, S. (1981). Gender schema theory: A cognitive account of sex-typing. *Psychological Review, 88*, 354–364.

Bem, D., & Honorton, C. (1994). Does psi exist? Replicable evidence of an anomalous process of information transfer. *Psychological Bulletin, 115*, 4–18.

Bem, S.L. (1975). Sex-role adaptability: One consequence of psychological androgyny. *Journal of Personality and Social Psychology, 31*, 634–643.

Bem, S.L. (1978). Beyond Androgyny: Some presumptuous prescriptions for a liberated sexual identity. In J.A. Sherman & F.L. Denmark (Eds.), *The psychology of women: Further directions in research*. New York: Psychological Dimensions.

Benenson, J.C., Apostoleris, N.H., & Parnass, J. (1997). Age and sex differences in dyadic and group interaction. *Developmental Psychology, 33*(3), 538–543.

Benjamin, J., Ben-Zion, I.Z., Karbofsky, E., & Dannon, P. (2000). Double-blind placebo-controlled pilot study of paroxetine for specific phobia. *Psychopharmacology, 149*, 194–196.

Benor, D.J. (1995). Spiritual healing: a unifying influence in complementary medicine. *Complementary Therapies in Medicine, 3*, 234–238.

Bentley, E. (2000). *Awareness: Biorhythms, sleep and dreaming*. London: Routledge.

Benton, D., & Donohoe, R.T. (1999). The effects of nutrients on mood. *Public Health Nutrition, 2*, 403–409.

Berger, R.E., & Honorton, C. (1985). An automated psi Ganzfeld testing system. In *The Parapsychological Association 28th Annual Convention: Proceedings of Presented Papers Volume 1* (pp. 1–36). New York: Parapsychological Association.

Berk, L.E. (1994). Why children talk to themselves. *Scientific American, November*, 60–65.

Berkowitz, L. (1968). Impulse, aggression and the gun. *Psychology Today, September*, 18–22.

Berkowitz, L. (1989). Frustration–aggression hypothesis: Examination and reformulation. *Psychological Bulletin, 106*, 59–73.

Berkowitz, L., & LePage, A. (1967). Weapons as aggression-eliciting stimuli. *Journal of Personality and Social Psychology, 7*, 202–207.

Berns, G.S., Chappelow, J., Zink, C.F., Pagnoni, G., Martin-Skurski, M.E., & Richards, J. (2005). Neurobiological correlates of social conformity and independence during mental rotation. *Biological Psychiatry, 58*, 245–253.

Berrettini, W.H. (2000a). Genetic linkage studies of bipolar disorders. *Neurology, Psychiatry and Brain Research, 8*, 139–146.

Berrettini, W.H. (2000b). Susceptibility loci for bipolar disorder: Overlap with inherited vulnerability to schizophrenia. *Biological Psychiatry, 47*, 245–251.

Berson, D.M., Dunn, F.A., & Takao, M. (2002). Phototransduction by retinal ganglion cells that set the circadian clock. *Science, 8*(295), 1070–1073.

Bhanot, R., & Jovanovic, J. (2005). Do parents' academic gender stereotypes influence whether they intrude on their children's homework? *Sex Roles: A Journal of Research, 52*, 597–607.

Biederman, I., Glass, A.L., & Stacy, E.W. (1973). Searching for objects in real-world scenes. *Journal of Experimental Psychology, 97*, 22–27.

Bienvenu, O.J., Brown, C., Samuels, J.F., Liang, K.Y., et al. (2001). Normal personality traits and comorbidity among phobic, panic and major depressive disorders. *Psychiatry Research, 102*, 73–85.

Bienvenu, O.J., Hettema, J.M., Neale, M.C., Prescott, C.A., & Kendler, K.S. (2007). Low extraversion and high neuroticism as indices of genetic and environmental risk for social phobia, agoraphobia, and animal phobia. *American Journal of Psychiatry, 164*, 1714–1721.

Bifulco, A., Harris, T., & Brown, G.W. (1992). Mourning or early inadequate care? Re-examining the relationship of maternal loss in childhood with adult depression and anxiety. *Development and Psychopathology, 4*, 433–449.

Bilalić, M., McLeod, P., & Gobet, F. (2007). Personality profiles of young chess players. *Personality and Individual Differences, 42*, 901–910.

Biller, H.B. (1974). *Paternal deprivation*. Lexington, MA: D.C. Heath.

Binkley, S. (1979). A timekeeping enzyme in the pineal gland. *Scientific American, 204*(4), 66–71.

Birchwood, M., & Jackson, C. (2001). *Schizophrenia*. Hove, UK: Psychology Press.

Birley, J.L. (1968). Early diagnosis of schizophrenia. *British Medical Journal, 4*, 232–234.

Blackmore, S. (1994). Alien abduction: The inside story. *New Scientist, 1952*(19 November), 29–31.

Blackmore, S., & Cox, M. (2000). Alien abductions, sleep paralysis and the temporal lobe. *European Journal of UFO and Abduction Studies, 1*(2), 113–118.

Blackmore, S.J., & Troscianko, T. (1985). Belief in the paranormal: Probability judgements, illusory control and the chance baseline shift. *British Journal of Psychology, 76*(4), 459–468.

Blake, M.J.F. (1967). Time of day effects on performance on a range of tasks. *Psychonomic Science, 9*, 349–350.

Blakemore, C. (1988). *The mind machine*. London: BBC Publications.

Blazer, D.G., Kessler, R.C., McGonagle, K.A., & Swartz, M.S. (1994). The prevalence and distribution of major depression in a national community sample: The National Comorbidity Survey. *American Journal of Psychiatry, 151*, 979–986.

Bleiberg, E., Jackson, L., & Ross, J.L. (1986). Gender identity disorder and object loss. *Journal of the American Academy of Child and Adolescent Psychiatry, 25*, 58–67.

Bloch, V. (1976). Brain activation and memory consolidation. In M.A. Rosenzweig & E.L. Bennet (Eds.), *Neural mechanisms of learning and memory*. Cambridge, MA: MIT Press.

Block, G. (2005). Keep Time, Stay Healthy. *Science of Aging Knowledge, 19*, 13.

Blomhoff, S., Haug, T.T., Hellstrom, K., Holme, I, et al. (2001). Randomised controlled general practice trial of sertaline, exposure therapy and combined treatment in generalised social phobia. *British Journal of Psychiatry, 179*, 23–30.

Blumenthal, M., Kahn, R.L., Andrews, F.M., & Head, K.B. (1972). *Justifying violence: The attitudes of American men*. Ann Arbor, MI: Institute for Social Research.

Böhner, G. (2001). Attitudes. In M. Hewstone & W. Stroebe (Eds.), *Introduction to social psychology* (3rd Edn). Oxford: Blackwell.

Bolger, K.E., Patterson, C.J., & Kupersmidt, J.B. (1998). Peer relationships and self-esteem among children who have been maltreated. *Child Development, 69*, 1171–1197.

Bollani, L., Dolci, C., Montaruli, A., Rondini, G., & Caran, F. (1997). Temporal structure of body core temperature in twin newborns. *Biological Rhythm Research, 28*(1), 29–35.

Bonnet M.H., & Arand, D.L. (2003). Insomnia, metabolic rate and sleep restoration. *Journal of Internal Medicine, 254*(1), 23–31.

Bonnie, K.E., Horner, V., Whiten, A., & de Waal, F.B.M. (2007). Spread of arbitrary conventions among chimpanzees: A controlled experiment. *Proceedings of the Royal Society B: Biological Sciences, 274*, 367–272.

Bonta, B.D. (1997). Co-operation and competition in peaceful societies. *Psychological Bulletin, 121*, 299–320.

Booker, J.M., & Hellekson, C.J. (1992). Prevalence of SAD in Alaska. *American Journal of Psychiatry, 149*, 1176–1182.

Booth, A., Shelley, G., Mazur, A., Tharp, G., & Kittok, R. (1989). Testosterone, and winning and losing in human competition. *Hormones and Behavior, 23*, 556–571.

Boring, E.G. (1957). *A history of experimental psychology* (2nd Edn). New York: Appleton-Century-Crofts.

Born, J., Rasch, J., & Gais, S. (2006). Sleep to remember. *Neuroscientist, 12*, 410.

Bostwick, J.M., & Pankratz, V.S. (2000). Affective disorders and suicide risk: A re-examination. *American Journal of Psychiatry, 157*, 1925–1932.

Botvin, G.J. (2001). Prevention of substance abuse in adolescents. In N.J. Smelser & P.B. Baltes (Eds.), *International encyclopedia of the social and behavioral sciences* (pp. 15255–15259). Oxford: Pergamon Press.

Bouchard, T.J., Lykken, D.T., McGue, M., Segal, N.L., & Tellegen, A. (1990). Sources of human psychological differences: The Minnesota study of twins reared apart. *Science, 250*, 223–228.

Bouchard, T.J., & McGue, M. (1981). Familial studies of intelligence: A review. *Science, 212*, 1055–1059.

Bower, T.G.R. (1966). The visual world of infants. *Scientific American, 215*, 80–92.

Bower, T.G.R., Broughton, J.M., & Moore, M.K. (1970). The co-ordination of visual and tactual input in infants. *Perception and Psychophysics, 8*, 51–53.

Bowlby, J. (1969). *Attachment and love: Vol. 1. Attachment*. London: Hogarth.

Brace, C.L. (1996). Review of *The Bell Curve*. *Current Anthropology, 37*, 5157–5161.

Bradbard, M.R., Martin, C.L., Endsley, R.C., & Halverson, C.F. (1986). Influence of sex stereotypes on children's exploration and memory: A competence versus performance distinction. *Developmental Psychology, 22*, 481–486.

Braddick, O.J., & Atkinson, J. (1983). Some recent findings on the development of human binocularity: A review. *Behavioural Brain Research, 10*, 141–150.

Bradmetz, J. (1999). Precursors of formal thought: A longitudinal study. *British Journal of Developmental Psychology, 17*, 61–81.

Braga, R.J., & Petrides, G. (2005). The combined use of electroconvulsive therapy and antipsychotics in patients with schizophrenia. *Journal of ECT, 21*, 75–83.

Brainerd, C.J. (1983). Modifiability of cognitive development. In S. Meadows (Ed.), *Developing thinking: Approaches to children's cognitive development*. London: Methuen.

Brainerd, C.J. (2003). Jean Piaget, learning research, and American education. In B.J. Zimmerman & D.H. Schuunk (Eds.), *Educational psychology: A century of contributions*. Mahwah, NJ: Lawrence Erlbaum Associates, Inc.

Brédart, S., Brennen, T., Delchambre, M., McNeill, A., & Burton, A.M. (2005). Naming very familiar people: When retrieving names is faster than retrieving semantic biographical information. *British Journal of Psychology, 96*, 205–214.

Breland, K., & Breland, M. (1961). The misbehaviour of organisms. *American Psychologist, 61*, 681–684.

Brems, C. (1995). Women and depression: A comprehensive analysis. In E.E. Beckham & W. Leber (Eds.), *Handbook of depression* (2nd Edn). New York: Guilford.

Bringuier, J.C. (1980). *Conversations with Jean Piaget*. Chicago: University of Chicago Press.

British Psychological Society (1993). *Response to "The Health of the Nation"*. Leicester, UK: British Psychological Society.

Bromage, T.G., Warshaw, J., Hogg, R., Lacruz, R., Mcfarlin, S.C., Goldmanh. M., Smolyar, I., Enlow, D.H., & Boyde, A. (2008). Bone rhythms correspond to enamel periods and reflect life history. *Proceedings of the 37th Annual Meeting of the American Association for Dental Research*.

Brown, G.W. (1989). Depression. In G.W. Brown & T.O. Harris (Eds.), *Life events and illness*. New York: Guilford Press.

Brown, G.W., & Birley, J.L.T. (1968). Crises and life changes and the onset of schizophrenia. *Journal of Health and Social Behavior, 9*(3), 203–214.

Brown, G.W., & Harris, T. (1978). *Social origins of depression*. London: Tavistock.

Brown, R.C., & Tedeschi, J.T. (1976). Determinants of perceived aggression. *Journal of Social Psychology, 100*, 77–87.

Brown, R.I.F. (1993). Some contributions of the study of gambling to the study of other addictions. In W.R. Eadington & J. Cornelius (Eds.), *Gambling behavior and problem gambling* (pp. 341–372). Reno, NV: University of Nevada Press.

Brown, T.A., DiNardo, P.A., Lehman, C.L., & Campbell, L.A. (2001). Reliability of DSM-IV anxiety and mood disorders: Implications for the classification of emotional disorders. *Journal of Abnormal Psychology, 110*, 49–58.

Bruce, V., Green, P.R., & Georgeson, M.A. (1996). *Visual perception: Physiology, psychology, and ecology* (3rd Edn). Hove, UK: Psychology Press.

Bruce, V., & Young, A.W. (1986). Understanding face recognition. *British Journal of Psychology, 77*, 305–327.

Bruch, H. (1971). Family transactions in eating disorders. *Comprehensive Psychiatry, 12*, 238–248.

Bruch, H. (1975). Obesity and anorexia nervosa: Psychosocial aspects. *Australia and New Zealand Journal of Psychiatry, 9*(3), 159–161.

Bruch, H. (1991). The sleeping beauty: Escape from change. In S.I. Greenspan & G.H. Pollock (Eds.), *The course of life, Vol. 4: Adolescence*. Madison, CT: International Universities Press.

Bruch, M.A., & Heimberg, R.G. (1994). Differences in perceptions of parental and personal between generalized and nongeneralized social phobics. *Journal of Anxiety Disorders, 8*, 155–168.

Brugha, T.S., Bebbington, P.E., Stretch, D.D., MacCarthy, B., & Wykes, T. (1997). Predicting the short-term outcome of first episodes and recurrences of clinical depression: A prospective study of life events, difficulties, and social support networks. *Journal of Clinical Psychiatry, 58*, 298–306.

Bruner, J. (1986). *Actual minds, possible worlds*. New York: Plenum.

Bruner, J. (1990). *Acts of meaning*. Cambridge, MA: Harvard University Press.

Bruner, J.S., & Goodman, C.D. (1947). Value and need as organising factors in perception. *Journal of Abnormal and Social Psychology, 42*, 33–44.

Bruner, J.S., Postman, L., & Rodrigues, J. (1951). Expectations and the perception of colour. *American Journal of Psychology, 64*, 216–227.

Brunner, H.G., Nelen, M., Breakefield, X.O., Ropers, H.H., et al. (1993). Abnormal behavior associated with a point mutation in the structural gene for monoamine oxidase. *Science, 262*(5133), 578–580.

Budden, A. (1994). *Allergies and aliens: The visitation experience: an environmental health issue*. Trowbridge, UK: Discovery Time Press.

Budden, A. (1995). *UFOs: Psychic close encounters*. London: Blandford Press.

Bulik, C.M., & Tozzi, F. (2004). The genetics of bulimia nervosa. *Drugs Today, 40*(9), 741–749.

Bulik, C.M., Thornton, L., Pinheiro, K., Klump, K.L., Brandt, H., Crawford, S., et al. (2008). Suicide attempts in anorexia nervosa. *Journal of Psychosomatic Medicine, 70*(3), 378–383.

Burack, J.A., Flanagan, T., Peled, T., Sutton, H.M., Zygmuntowicz, C., & Manly, J.T. (2006). Social perspective-taking skills in maltreated children and adolescents. *Developmental Psychology, 42*, 207–217.

Burch, J., Yost, M.G., Johnson, W., & Allen, E. (2005). Melatonin, sleep, and shift work adaptation. *Journal of Occupational and Environmental Medicine, 47*(9), 893–901.

Burdakov, D., Alexopoulos, H., Jensen, L.T., & Fugger, L. (2008). Adaptive sugar sensors in hypothalamic feeding circuits. *Proceedings of the National Academy of Science, 105*, 11975–11980.

Burger, J.M., & Caldwell, D.F. (2003). The effects of monetary incentives and labeling on the foot-in-the-door effect: Evidence for a self-perception process. *Basic and Applied Social Psychology, 25*, 235–241.

Burr, V. (1997). Social constructionism and psychology. *The New Psychologist*, April, 7–12.

Burris, C.T., Harmon-Jones, E., & Tarpley, W.R. (1997). "By faith alone": Religious agitation and cognitive dissonance. *Basic and Applied Social Psychology, 19*, 17–31.

Bushman, B.J., & Anderson, C.A. (2002). Violent video games and hostile expectations: A test of the general aggression model. *Personality & Social Psychology Bulletin, 28*(12), 1679–1686.

Bushman, B.J., & Geen, R.G. (1990). Role of cognitive-emotional mediators and individual differences in the effects of media violence on aggression. *Journal of Personality and Social Psychology, 58*, 156–163.

Buss, D.M. (1987). Sex differences in human mate selection criteria: An evolutionary perspective. In C. Crawford, et al. (Eds.), *Sociobiology and psychology: Issues, ideas, and findings*. Hillsdale, NJ: Lawrence Erlbaum Associates.

Buss, D.M. (1989). Sex differences in human mate preferences: Evolutionary hypotheses tested in 37 cultures. *Behavioral and Brain Sciences, 12*, 1–49.

Buss, D.M. (1999). *Evolutionary psychology: The new science of the mind*. Boston: Allyn & Bacon.

Butcher, J.N., Mineka, S., & Hooley, J.M. (2004). *Abnormal psychology* (12th Edn). London: Pearson.

Buttolph, M.L., & Holland, A.D. (1990). Obsessive-compulsive disorders in pregnancy and childbirth. In M. Jenike, L. Baer, & W. Minichiello (Eds.), *Obsessive-compulsive disorders: Theory and management*. Chicago: Year Book Medical.

Button, E.J., Loan, P., Davies, J., & Sonuga-Barke, E.J.S. (1997). Self-esteem, eating problems, and psychological well-being in a cohort of schoolgirls aged 15–16: A questionnaire and interview study. *International Journal of Eating Disorders, 21*, 39–47.

Butzlaff, R.L., & Hooley, J.M. (1998). Expressed emotion and psychiatric relapse: A meta-analysis. *Archives of General Psychiatry, 55*(6), 547–552.

Buunk, B.P. (1996). Affiliation, attraction and close relationships. In M. Hewstone, W. Stroebe, & G.M. Stephenson (Eds.), *Introduction to social psychology* (2nd Edn). Oxford: Blackwell.

Buunk, B.P., Angleitner, A., Oubaid, V., & Buss, D.M. (1996). Sex differences in jealousy in evolutionary and cultural perspective. *Psychological Science, 7*, 359–363.

Buunk, B.P., & VanYperen, N.W. (1991). Referential comparisons, relational comparisons and exchange orientation: Their relation to marital satisfaction. *Personality and Social Psychology Bulletin, 17*, 710–718.

Byrd, R.C. (1998). Positive therapeutic effects of intercessory prayer in a coronary care unit population. *Southern Medical Journal, 81*(7), 826–829.

Byrne, D. (1971). *The attraction paradigm*. New York: Academic Press.

Byrne, R.W. (2004). The manual skills and cognition that lie behind hominid tool use. In A.E. Russon & D.R. Begun (Eds.), *Evolutionary origins of great ape intelligence*. Cambridge: Cambridge University Press.

Byrne, R.W., & Bates, L.A. (2007). Sociality, evolution and cognition. *Current Biology, 17*, R714–R723.

Byrne, R.W., & Corp, N. (2004). Neocortex size predicts deception rate in primates. *Proceedings of the Royal Society of London Series B: Biological Sciences, 271*, 1693–1699.

Byrne, R.W., & Whiten, A. (1988). *Machiavellian intelligence: Social expertise and the evolution of intellect in monkeys, apes and humans*. Oxford: Oxford University Press.

Byrne, R.W., & Whiten, A. (1997). Machiavellian intelligence. In A. Whiten & R.W. Byrne (Eds.), *Machiavellian intelligence II: Extensions and evaluations*. Cambridge: Cambridge University Press.

Cacioppo, J.T., Petty, R.E., Feinstein, J.A., Jarvis, W., & Blaire, G. (1996). Dispositional differences in cognitive motivation: The life and times of individuals varying in need for cognition. *Psychological Bulletin, 119*, 197–253.

Cacioppo, J.T., Petty, R.E., & Morris, K.J. (1983). Effects of need for cognition on message evaluation, recall, and persuasion. *Journal of Personality and Social Psychology, 45*, 805–818.

Cairns, R.B., Gariepy, J., & Hood, K.E. (1990). Development, microevolution and social behaviour. *Psychological Review, 97*, 49–65.

Calder, A.J., Rowland, D., Young, A.W., Nimmo-Smith, I., Keane, J., & Perrett, D.I. (2000). Caricaturing facial expressions. *Cognition, 76*, 105–146.

Caldera, Y.M., & Sciaraffa, M.A. (1998). Parent–toddler play with feminine toys: are all dolls the same? *Sex Roles, 38*, 657–668.

Campbell, A., Shirley, L., & Candy, J. (2004). A longitudinal study of gender-related cognition and behaviour. *Developmental Science, 7*, 1–9.

Campbell, D.T., & Stanley, J.C. (1966). *Experimental and quasiexperimental designs for research*. Chicago: Rand McNally.

Campbell, R., Landis, T., & Regard, M. (1986). Face recognition and lipreading: A neurological dissociation. *Brain, 109*, 509–521.

Cape, G. S. (2003). Addiction, stigma, and movies. *Acta Psychiatrica Scandinavica, 107*, 163–169.

Capron, C., & Duyme, M. (1989). Assessment of effects of socio-economic status on IQ in a full cross-fostering study. *Nature, 340*, 552–554.

Carey, G., & Gottesman, I.I. (1981). Twin and family studies of anxiety, phobic, and obsessive disorders. In D.F. Klein & J.G. Rabkin (Eds.), *Anxiety: New research and changing concepts*. New York: Raven Press.

Carlson, N.R. (1986). *Physiology of behaviour* (3rd Edn). Boston: Alleyn and Bacon.

Carnagey, N.L., & Anderson, C.A. (2005). The effects of reward and punishment in violent video games on aggressive affect, cognition, and behaviour. *Psychological Science, 16*, 882–889.

Carnes, P. (1991). *Don't call it love: Recovery from sexual addiction*. New York: Bantam Books.

Caron, A.J., Caron, R.F., & Carlson, V.R. (1979). Infant perception of the invariant shape of objects varying in slant. *Child Development, 50*, 716–721.

Carrasco, J.L., Diaz-Marsa, M., Hollander, E., Cesar, J., & Saiz-Ruiz, J. (2000). Decreased platelet monoamine oxidase activity in female bulimia nervosa. *European Neuropsychopharmacology*, 10(2), 113–117.

Carroll, B.J. (1991). Psychopathology and neurobiology of manic-depressive disorders. In B.J. Carroll & J.E. Barrett (Eds.), *Psychopathology and the brain*. New York: Raven Press.

Carroll, J.B. (1986). Factor analytic investigations of cognitive abilities. In S.E. Newstead, S.H. Irvine, & P.L. Dann (Eds.), *Human assessment: Cognition and motivation*. Dordrecht, The Netherlands: Nyhoff.

Carroll, J.B. (1993). Human cognitive abilities: A twenty-five retrospective and prospective view. *Educational Researcher*, 18, 26–31.

Carver, K., Joyner, K., & Udry, J.R. (2003). National estimates of adolescent romantic relationships. In P. Florsheim (Ed.), *Adolescent romantic relations and sexual behavior: Theory, research, and practical implications* (pp. 23–56). Mahwah, NJ: Lawrence Erlbaum Associates.

Caspi, A., McClay, J., Moffitt, T.E., Mill, J., Martin, J., Craig, I.W., et al. (2007). Role of genotype in the cycle of violence in maltreated children. *Science*, 297(5582), 851–854.

Ceci, S.J., & Liker, J.K. (1986). A day at the races: A study of IQ, expertise, and cognitive complexity. *Journal of Experimental Psychology: General*, 115, 255–266

Celec, P., Ostatníková, D., Hodosy, J., Skokňová, M., Putz, Z., & Kúdela, M. (2006). Infradian rhythmic variations of salivary estradioland progesterone in healthy men. *Biological Rhythm Research*, 37(1), 37–44.

Central Advisory Council for Education (England) (1967). *Children and their primary schools (The Plowden report)*. London: HMSO.

Chadwick, P., Birchwood, M.J., & Trower, P. (1996). *Cognitive therapy for delusions, voices and paranoia*. Chichester, UK: Wiley.

Chaiken, S., & Eagly, A.H. (1983). Communication modality as a determinant of persuasion: The role of communicator salience. *Journal of Personality and Social Psychology*, 45, 241–256.

Chambry, J., & Gilles, A. (2006). L'anorexie mentale masculine à l'adolescence. *La Psychiatrie de l'enfant*, 49(2), 477–511.

Chanpattana, W. (2007). A questionnaire survey of ECT practice in Australia. *Journal of ECT*, 23, 89–92.

Chapman, L.J., Chapman, J.P., Kwapil, T.R., Eckblad, M., & Zinser, M.C. (1994). Putatively psychosis-prone subjects 10 years later. *Journal of Abnormal Psychology*, 103, 171–183.

Charlton, A. (1998, January 12). TV violence has little impact on children, study finds. *The Times*, p. 5.

Charman, T., Baron-Cohen, S., Swettenham, J., Baird, G., Cox, A., & Drew, A. (2000). Testing joint attention, imitation, and play as infancy precursors to language and theory of mind. *Cognitive Development*, 15, 481–498.

Charness, N., Tuffiash, M., Krampe, R., Reingold, E., & Vasyukova, E. (2005). The role of deliberate practice in chess expertise. *Applied Cognitive Psychology*, 19, 151–165.

Chatard, A., Guimond, S., & Selimbegovic, L. (2007). "How good are you in math?" The effect of gender stereotypes on students' recollection of their school marks. *Journal of Experimental Social Psychology*, 43, 1017–1024.

Cheng, A.T.A., Hawton, K., Chen, T.H.H., Yen, A.M.F., Chen, C.Y., Chen, L.C., & Teng, P.R. (2007). The influence of media coverage of a celebrity suicide on subsequent suicide attempts. *Journal of Clinical Psychiatry*, 68, 862–866.

Cho, K. (2001). Chronic 'jet lag' produces temporal lobe atrophy and spatial cognitive deficits. *Nature Neuroscience*, 4, 567–568.

Choi, I., Choi, K.W., & Cha, J.-H. (1992). *A cross-cultural replication of Festinger and Carlsmith (1959)*. Unpublished manuscript, Seoul National University, Korea.

Choy, Y., Fyer, A.J., & Lipsitz, J.D. (2007). Treatment of specific phobia in adults. *Clinical Psychology Review*, 27, 266–286.

Cirelli, C., & Tononi, G. (2008). Is sleep essential? *Public Library of Science Biology*, 6(8): e216. Also online. Available: http://biology.plosjournals.org/perlserv/?request=get-document&doi=10.1371/journal.pbio.0060216&ct=1&SESSID=bbb1d1d257281e4cdce56434de31d72d

Clamp, A. (2001). *Evolutionary psychology*. London: Hodder and Stoughton.

Clark, D.M., Ehlers, A., Hackmann, A., McManus, F., et al. (2006). Cognitive therapy versus exposure and applied relaxation in social phobia: A randomised controlled trial. *Journal of Consulting and Clinical Psychology*, 74, 568–578.

Clark, D.M., & Wells, A. (1995). A cognitive model of social phobia. In R.R.G. Heimberg, M. Liebowitz, D.A. Hope, & S. Scheier (Eds.), *Social phobia: Diagnosis, assessment and treatment*. New York: Guilford.

Clark, M.S. (1984). Record keeping in two types of relationships. *Journal of Personality and Social Psychology*, 47, 549–557.

Clark, M.S., & Mills, J. (1979). Interpersonal attraction in exchange and communal relationships. *Journal of Personality and Social Psychology*, 37, 12–24.

Clark, R.D., & Hatfield, E. (1989). Gender differences in receptivity to sexual offers. *Journal of Psychology and Human Sexuality*, 2, 39–55.

Clayton, R., Cattarello A.M., & Johnstone, B.M. (1996). The effectiveness of Drug Abuse Resistance Education (project DARE): 5-year follow-up results. *Prevention Medicine*, 25, 307–318.

Clutton-Brock, T.H., & Harvey, P.H. (1980). Primates, brains, and ecology. *Journal of Zoology*, 190, 309–323.

CNN (April 28, 2008). Online. Available: http://www.cnn.com/2008/WORLD/europe/04/28/austria.cellar/index.html

Cogan, J.C., Bhalla, S.K., Sefa-Dedeh, A., & Rathblum, E.D. (1996). A comparison study of United States and African students on perceptions of obesity and thinness. *Journal of Cross-Cultural Psychology*, 27, 98–113.

Cohen, S. (2004). Social relationships and health. *American Psychologist*, 59, 676–684.

Colapinto, J. (2000). *As nature made him*. London: Quartet Books.

Colby, A., & Kohlberg, L. (1987). *The measurement of moral judgement*. Cambridge: Cambridge University Press.

Colby, A., Kohlberg, L., Gibbs, J., & Lieberman, M. (1983). A longitudinal study of moral judgement. *Monographs of the Society for Research in Child Development*, 48(1–2, serial no. 200).

Cole, C.F., Arafat, C., Tidhar, C., Zidan, W.T., Fox, N. A., Killen, M., et al. (2001). The educational impact of Rechov Sumsum/Shara'a Simsim, a Sesame Street television series to promote respect and understanding among children living in Israel, the West Bank, and Gaza. *International Journal of Behavioral Development*, 27, 409–422.

Cole, T., & Leets, L. (1999). Attachment styles and intimate television viewing: Insecurely forming relationships in a parasocial way. *Journal of Social and Personal Relationships*, 16, 495–511.

Collaer, M.L., & Hines, M. (1995). Human behavioural sex differences: A role for gonadal hormones during early development. *Psychological Bulletin*, 118, 55–107.

Collins, W.A. (2003). More than myth: The developmental significance of romantic relationships during adolescence. *Journal of Research on Adolescence, 13*(1), 1–24.

Collins, W.A., & van Dulmen, M.H.M. (2005). The course of true love(s): Origins and pathways in the development of romantic relationships. In A. Crouter & A. Booth (Eds.), *Romance and sex in adolescence and emerging adulthood: Risks and opportunities* (pp. 63–86). Mahwah, NJ: Lawrence Erlbaum Associates.

Colom, F., Vieta, E., Martinez, A., Jorquera, A., & Gasto, C. (1998). What is the role of psychotherapy in the treatment of bipolar disorder? *Psychotherapy and Psychosomatics, 67*, 3–9.

Colquhuon, W.P. (1970). Circadian rhythms, mental efficiency, shift work. *Ergonomics, 13*(5), 558–560.

Comer, R.J. (2001). *Abnormal psychology* (4th Edn). New York: Worth.

Comings, D.E. (1998). Why different rules are required for polygenic inheritance: Lessons from studies of the *DRD2* gene. *Alcohol, 16*, 61–70.

Comings, D.E., Rosenthal, R.J., Lesieur, H.R., Rugle, L.J., Muhleman, D., Chie, C., et al. (1996). A study of dopamine D2 receptor gene in pathological gambling. *Pharmacogenetics, 6*, 223–234.

Comstock, G., & Paik, H. (1991). *Television and the American child*. San Diego, CA: Academic Press.

Condry, J., & Condry, S. (1976). Sex differences: A study in the eye of the beholder. *Child Development, 47*, 812–819.

Conner, D.B., Knight, D.K., & Cross, D.R. (1997). Mothers' and fathers' scaffolding of their 2-year-olds during problem-solving and literary interactions. *British Journal of Developmental Psychology, 15*, 323–338.

Connolly, J., Craig, W., Goldberg, A., & Pepler, D. (1999). Conceptions of cross-sex friendships and romantic relationships in early adolescence. *Journal of Youth and Adolescence, 28*(4), 481–494.

Connolly, J., Craig, W., Goldberg, A., & Pepler, D. (2004). Mixed-gender groups, dating, and romantic relationships. *Journal of Research on Adolescence, 14*(2), 185–207.

Conway, A.R.A., Kane, M.J., & Engle, R.W. (2003). Working memory capacity and its relation to general intelligence. *Trends in Cognitive Sciences, 7*, 547–552.

Cook, M., & Mineka, S. (1989). Observational conditioning of fear to fear-relevant versus fear-irrelevant stimuli in rhesus monkeys. *Journal of Abnormal Psychology, 98*, 448–459.

Coolican, H. (1994). *Research methods and statistics in psychology* (2nd edn). London: Hodder & Stoughton.

Cooper, B. (2005). Immigration and schizophrenia: The social causation hypothesis revisited. *British Journal of Psychiatry, 186*, 361–363.

Cooper, P.J. (1994). Eating disorders. In A.M. Colman (Ed.), *Companion encyclopaedia of psychology, Vol. 2*. London: Routledge.

Cooper, J., & Fazio, R.H. (1984). A new look at dissonance theory. In L. Berkowitz (Ed.), *Advances in experimental social psychology* (Vol. 17). New York: Academic Press.

Cooper, P.J., & Taylor, M.J. (1988). Body image disturbance in bulimia nervosa. *British Journal of Psychiatry, 153*, 32–36.

Coren, S. (1996). *Sleep thieves*. New York: Free Press.

Coren, S., & Girgus, J.S. (1972). Visual spatial illusions: Many explanations. *Science, 179*, 503–504.

Cormack, M., Owens, R.G., & Dewey, M.E. (1989). The effect of minimal interventions by general practitioners on long-term benzodiazepine use. *Journal of the Royal College of General Practitioners, 39*, 408–414.

Cormack, M.A., & Sinnott, A. (1983). Psychological alternatives to long-term benzodiazepine use. *Journal of the Royal College of General Practitioners, 33*, 279–281.

Cottraux, J., Note, I., Yao, S. N., Lafont, S., Note, B., Mollard, E., Bouvard, M., Sauteraud, A., Bourgeois, M., & Dartigues, J.-F. (2001). A randomized controlled trial of cognitive therapy versus intensive behavior therapy in obsessive compulsive disorder. *Psychotherapy and Psychosomatics, 70*, 288–297.

Coyne, S.M., Archer, J., & Eslea, M. (2004). Cruel intentions on television and in real life: Can viewing indirect aggression increase viewers' subsequent indirect aggression? *Journal of Experimental Child Psychology, 88*, 234–253.

Craddock, N., & Jones, I. (1999). Genetics of bipolar disorder. *Journal of Medical Genetics, 36*, 585–594.

Craik, F.I.M., & Lockhart, R.S. (1972). Levels of processing: A framework for memory research. *Journal of Verbal Learning and Verbal Behavior, 11*, 671–684.

Craik, F.I.M., & Tulving, E. (1975). Depth of processing and the retention of words in episodic memory. *Journal of Experimental Psychology, 104*, 268–294.

Craik, F.I., & Watkins, M.J. (1973). The role of rehearsal in short-term memory. *Journal of Verbal Learning and Verbal Behavior, 12*, 599–607.

Cromer, K.R., Schmidt, N.B., & Murphy, D.L. (2007). An investigation of traumatic life events and obsessive-compulsive disorder. *Behaviour Research and Therapy, 45*, 1683–1691.

Crow, T.J. (2000). Schizophrenia as the price that *Homo sapiens* pay for language: A resolution of the central paradox in the origin of the species. *Brain Research Reviews, 31*(2–3), 118–129.

Cumberbatch, G. (1990). Television advertising and sex role stereotyping: A content analysis [Working paper IV for the Broadcasting Standards Council]. Communications Research Group, Aston University, Birmingham, UK.

Cunningham, M.R. (1986). Measuring the physical in physical attractiveness: Quasi experiments on the sociobiology of female facial beauty. *Journal of Personality and Social Psychology, 50*, 925–935.

Cupach, W.R., & Spitzberg, B.H. (2004). *The dark side of relationship pursuit: From attraction to obsession and stalking*. Mahwah, NJ: Lawrence Erlbaum Associates.

Cupach, W.R., Spitzberg, B.H., Younghans, C.M., & Gibbons, B.S. (2006). *Persistence of attempts to reconcile a terminated romantic relationship: An application and partial test of relational goal pursuit theory*. Paper presented at the Western States Communication Association convention, Palm Springs, CA.

Czeisler, C.A., Moore-Ede, M.C., & Coleman, R.M. (1982). Rotating shift work schedules that disrupt sleep are improved by applying circadian principles. *Science, 217*(4558), 460–463.

Dag, I. (1999). The relationship between paranormal beliefs, locus of control and psychopathology in a Turkish sample. *Personality and Individual Differences, 26*, 723–737.

Daley, T.C., Whaley, S.E., Sigman, M.D., Espinosa, M.P., & Neumann, C. (2003). IQ on the rise: The Flynn effect in rural Kenyan children. *Psychological Science, 14*, 215–219.

Dalton, K. (1964). *The premenstrual syndrome*. London: Heinemann.

Dalton, K. (1969). *The menstrual cycle*. London: Penguin.

Dalton, K. (1997). Is there a formula to success in the Ganzfeld? Observations on predictors of psi-Ganzfeld procedures. *European Journal of Parapsychology, 13*, 71–82.

Dalton, M.A., Sargent, J.D., Beach, M.L., Titus-Ernstoff, L., Gibson, J.J., Aherns, M.B., & Heatherton, T.F. (2003). Effect of viewing smoking in movies on adolescent smoking initiation: A cohort study. *The Lancet, 362*, 281–285.

Daneman, M., & Carpenter, P.A. (1980). Individual differences in working memory and reading. *Journal of Verbal Learning and Verbal Behavior, 19*, 450–466.

Daneman, M., & Stainton, M. (1993). The generation effect in reading and proofreading: Is it easier or harder to detect errors in one's own writing? *Reading and Writing*, 5, 297–313.

Dapretto, M., Davies, M.S., Pfeifer, J.H., Scott, A.A., Sigman, M., Bookheimer, S.Y., & Iacoboni, M. (2006). Understanding emotions in others: Mirror neuron dysfunction in children with autism spectrum disorders. *Nature Neuroscience*, 9, 28–30.

Darwin, C. (1859). *The origin of species*. London: Macmillan.

Darwin, C. (1871). *The descent of man and selection in relation to sex*. London: John Murray.

Davey, G.C.L. (1995). Preparedness and phobias: Specific evolved associations or a generalised expectancy bias. *Behavioral and Brain Sciences*, 18, 289–297.

Davies, J.B. (1996). Reasons and causes: Understanding substance users' explanation for their behaviour. *Human Psychopharmacology*, 11(Supplement 1), S39–S48.

Davies, J.B., & Baker, R. (1987). The impact of self-presentation and interviewer bias effects on self-reported heroin use. *British Journal of Addiction*, 82, 907–912.

Davis, S. (1990). Men as success objects and women as sex objects: A study of personal advertisements. *Sex Roles*, 23, 43–50.

Davison, G.C., & Neale, J.M. (2001). *Abnormal psychology* (8th Edn). Chichester: Wiley.

Davison, G.C., Neale, J.M., & Kring, A.M. (2004). *Abnormal psychology* (9th Edn). New York; Wiley.

Davison, G.C., Neale, J.M., & Kring, A.M. (2004). *Abnormal psychology with cases*. Hoboken, NJ: John Wiley & Sons.

Dawson, D., & Campbell, S.S. (1991). Time exposure to bright light improves sleep and alertness during simulated night shifts. *Sleep*, 14, 511–516.

Dawson, G., Toth, K., Abbott, R., Osterling, J., et al. (2004). Early social attention impairments in autism: Social orienting, joint attention, and attention to distress. *Developmental Psychology*, 40, 271–283.

de Araujo, I.E., Gutierrez, R., Pereira Jr., A., Nicolelis, M.A.L., Simon, S.A., & Oliveira-Maia A.J. (2006). Neural Ensemble Coding of Satiety States. *Neuron*, 51, 483–494.

De Castro, J.M., & de Castro, E.S. (1989). Spontaneous meal patterns of humans: Influence of the presence of other people. *American Journal of Clinical Nutrition*, 50, 237–247.

de Saint Hilaire, Z., Straub, J., & Pelissolo, A. (2005). Temperament and character in primary insomnia. *European Psychiatry*, 20(2), 188–192.

De Vreede, I.M., Burger, H., & van Vliet, I.M. (2005). Prediction of response to ECT with routinely collected data in major depression. *Journal of Affective Disorders*, 86, 323–327.

De Waal, F.B.M., Dindo, M., Freeman, C.A., & Hall, M.A. (2005). Monkey in the mirror: Hardly a stranger. *Proceedings of the National Academy of Sciences of the USA*, 102, 11140–11147.

Deary, I.J. (1995). Auditory inspection time and intelligence: What is the direction of causation? *Developmental Psychology*, 31, 237–250.

Deary, I.J., Der, G., & Ford, G. (2001). Reaction times and intelligence differences: A population-based cohort study. *Intelligence*, 29, 389–399.

Deary, I.J., & Stough, C. (1996). Intelligence and inspection time: Achievements, prospects, and problems. *American Psychologist*, 51(6), 599–608.

Delanoy, D.L. (1987). Work with a fraudulent PK metal-bending subject. *Journal of the Society for Psychical Research*, 54, 247–256.

Delfabbro, P.H., & Winefield, A.H. (1999). Poker machine gambling: An analysis of within session characteristics. *British Journal of Psychology*, 90, 425–439.

Delgado, P.L., Charney, D.S., Price, L.H., Aghajanian, G.K., Landis, H., & Heninger, G.R. (1990). Serotonin function and the mechanism of antidepressant action: Reversal of antidepressant induced remission by rapid depletion of plasma tryptophan. *Archives of General Psychiatry*, 47, 411–418.

DeLucia, J.L. (1987). Gender role identity and dating behavior: What is the relationship? *Sex Roles*, 17, 153–161.

DeLucia, P.R., & Hochberg, J. (1991). Geometrical illusions in solid objects under ordinary viewing conditions. *Perception and Psychophysics*, 50, 547–554.

Dement, W.C. (1960). The effects of dream deprivation. *Science*, 131, 1705–1707.

Dement, W. (1972). *Some must watch while some must sleep*. San Francisco: W.H. Freeman.

Dement, W.C., & Kleitman, N. (1957). The relation of eye movements during sleep to dream activity: An objective method for the study of dreaming. *Journal of Experimental Psychology*, 53, 339–346.

Denholtz, M.S., Hall, L.A., & Mann, E. (1978). Automated treatment for flight phobia: 3½ year follow-up. *American Journal of Psychiatry*, 135, 1340–1343.

Denton, K., & Krebs, D. (1990). From the scene to the crime: The effect of alcohol and social context on moral judgement. *Journal of Personality and Social Psychology*, 59, 242–248.

Department of Health (1992). *The health of the nation: A strategy for health in England*. London: HMSO.

Department of Health (1993). *One year on: a report on the progress of "the health of the nation"*. London: HMSO.

Department of Health (1999). *Saving lives: Our healthier nation*: HMSO.

Deregowski, J., Muldrow, E.S., & Muldrow, W.F. (1972). Pictorial recognition in a remote Ethiopian population. *Perception*, 1, 417–425.

DeRubeis, R.J., Hollon, S.D., Amsterdam, J.D., Shelton, R.C., Young, P.R., Salomon, R.M., et al. (2005). Cognitive therapy vs. medications in the treatment of moderate to severe depression. *Archives of General Psychiatry*, 62, 409–416.

Devine, P.G., Tauer, J.M., Barron, K.E., Elliot, A.J., & Vance, K.M. (1999). Moving beyond attitude change in the study of dissonance related processes. In E. Harmon-Jones & J. Mills (Eds.), *Cognitive dissonance: Progress on a pivotal theory in social psychology* (pp. 297–323). Washington, DC: American Psychological Association.

DeVries, R. (2000). Vygotsky, Piaget, and education: A reciprocal assimilation of theories and educational practices. *New Ideas in Psychology*, 18, 187–213.

Di Ceglie, D., (2000). Gender identity disorder in young people. *Advances in Psychiatric Treatment*, 6, 458–466.

Diaconis, P., & Mosteller, F. (1989). Methods for studying coincidences. *Journal of the American Statistical Association*, 84(408), 853–861.

Dickens, W.T., & Flynn, J.R. (2001). Heritability estimates versus large environmental effects: The IQ paradox resolved. *Psychological Review*, 108, 346–369.

Dickerson, F.B., Tenhula, W.N., & Green-Paden, L.D. (2005). The token economy for schizophrenia: Review of the literature and recommendations for future research. *Schizophrenia Research*, 75, 405–416.

Dickerson, M., Hinchy, J., & Legg England, S. (1990). Minimal treatments and problem gamblers: A preliminary investigation. *Journal of Gambling Studies*, 6, 87–102.

Dickerson M.G., & Baron, E. (2000). Contemporary issues and future directions for research into pathological gambling. *Addiction*, 95, 1145–1159.

Dickerson, M.G., & O'Connor, J. (2006). *Gambling as an addictive behaviour: Impaired control and its relationship to other variables*. Cambridge: Cambridge University Press.

Diener, E. (1980). *Psychology of group influence*. Hillsdale, NJ: Lawrence Erlbaum Associates.

Diener, E., Suh, E.M., Lucas, R.E., & Smith, H.E. (1999). Subjective well-being: Three decades of progress. *Psychological Bulletin, 125*, 276–302.

Dijkstra, A., & de Vries, H. (2001). Do self-help interventions in health education lead to cognitive changes, and do cognitive changes lead to behavioural change? *British Journal of Health Psychology, 6*, 121–134.

Dijkstra, M., Buijtels, H.E.J.J.M., & van Raaij, W.F. (2005). Separate and joint effects of medium type on consumer responses: A comparison of television, print, and the internet. *Journal of Business Research, 58*, 377–386.

Dimidjian, S., Hollon, S.D., Dobson, K.S., Schmaling, K.B., Kohlenberg, R. J., Addis, M.E., et al. (2006). Randomised trial of behavioural activation, cognitive therapy, and antidepressant medication in the acute treatment of adults with major depression. *Journal of Consulting and Clinical Psychology, 74*, 658–670.

DiNardo, P.A., Guzy, L.T., Jenkins, J.A., Bak, R.M., Tomasi, S.F., & Copland, M. (1988). Aetiology and maintenance of dog fears. *Behaviour Research and Therapy, 26*, 241–244.

Dinstein, I., Gardner, J.L., Jazayeri, M., & Heeger, D.J. (2008). Executed and observed movements have different distributed representations in human aIPS. *Journal of Neuroscience, 28*, 11231–11239.

Dinstein, I., Hasson, U., Rubin, N., & Heeger, D.J. (2007). Brain areas selective for both observed and executed movements. *Journal of Neurobiology, 98*, 1415–1427.

Distefan, J.M., Gilpin, E.A., Sargent, J.D., & Pierce, J.P. (1999). Do movie stars encourage adolescents to start smoking? Evidence from California. *Preventive Medicine, 28*, 1–11.

Distel, M.A., Vick, J.M., Willemsen, G., Middeldorp, C.M., Merckelbach, H.C.G.J., & Boomsma, D.I. (2008). Heritability of self-reported phobic fear. *Behavior Genetics, 38*, 24–33.

Dohrenwend, B.P., Levav, P.E., Schwartz, S., Naveh, G., Link, B.G., Skodol, A.E., & Stueve, A. (1992). Socioeconomic status and psychiatric disorders: The causation–selection issue. *Science, 255*, 946–952.

Doise, W., & Mugny, G. (1984). *The social development of the intellect*. Oxford: Pergamon.

Dolberg, O.T., Iancu, I., Sasson, Y., & Zohar, J. (1996). The pathogenesis and treatment of obsessive-compulsive disorder. *Clinical Neuropharmacology, 19*, 129–147.

Dolinski, D. (2000). On inferring one's beliefs from one's attempt and consequences for subsequent compliance. *Journal of Personality and Social Psychology, 78*, 260–272.

Dollard, J., Doob, L.W., Miller, N.E., Mowrer, O.H., & Sears, R.R. (1939). *Frustration and aggression*. New Haven, CT: Yale University Press.

Domjan, M. (2005). Pavlovian conditioning: A functional perspective. *Annual Review of Psychology, 56*, 179–206.

Donaldson, S.I., Graham, J.W., Piccinin, A.M., & Hansen, W.B. (1997). Resistant-skills training and onset of alcohol use: Evidence for beneficial and potentially harmful effects in public schools and private Catholic schools. In G.A. Marlatt & G.R. Vanden Bos (Eds.), *Addictive behaviors: readings on etiology, prevention, and treatment* (pp. 215–238). Washington DC: American Psychological Association.

Doob, L.W., & Sears, R.R. (1939). Factors determining substitute behaviour and the overt expression of aggression. *Journal of Abnormal and Social Psychology, 34*, 293–313.

Dougherty, D.D., Baer, L., Cosgrave, G.R., Cassem, E.H., et al. (2002). Prospective long-term follow-up of 44 patients who received cingulotomy for treatment-refractory obsessive-compulsive disorder. *American Journal of Psychiatry, 159*, 269–275.

Downing, P.E., Chan, A.W.Y., Peelen, M.V., Dodds, C.M., & Kanwisher, N. (2006). Domain specificity in visual cortex. *Cerebral Cortex, 16*, 1453–1461.

Drury, V.M., Robinson, E.J., & Birchwood, M. (1998). 'Theory of mind' skills during an acute episode of psychosis and following recovery. *Psychological Medicine, 28*, 1101–1112.

Duchaine, B., & Nakayama, K. (2005). Dissociations of face and object recognition in developmental prosopagnosia. *Journal of Cognitive Neuroscience, 17*, 249–261.

Duchaine, B., & Nakayama, K. (2006). Developmental prosopagnosia: A window to content-specific face processing. *Current Opinion in Neurobiology, 16*, 166–173.

Duchaine, B., Yovel, G., Butterworth, E., & Nakayama, K. (2006). Prosopangosia as an impairment to face-specific mechanisms: Elimination of the alternative hypotheses in a developmental case. *Cognitive Neuropsychology, 23*, 714–747.

Duck, S. (1992). *Human relationships* (2nd Edn). London: Sage.

Dudley, R., (2002). Fermenting fruit and the historical ecology of ethanol ingestion: Is alcoholism in modern humans an evolutionary hangover? *Addiction, 97*(4), 381–388.

Dunbar, R. (1996). *Grooming, gossip and the evolution of language*. London: Faber & Faber.

Dunbar, R., Barrett, L., & Lycett, J. (2005). *Evolutionary psychology: A Beginner's guide*. Oxford: OneWorld.

Dunbar, R.M. (1998). The social brain hypothesis. *Evolutionary Anthropology, 34*, 178–190.

Durkin, K. (1995). *Developmental social psychology: From infancy to old age*. Oxford: Blackwell.

Durkin, K. (2007). Myers, media and modern times. *The Psychologist, 20*(1), 26–29.

Durkin, K., & Nugent, B. (1998). Kindergarten children's gender-role expectations for television actors. *Sex Roles: A Journal of Research, 38*, 387–403.

Durlak, J.A. (2003). Effective prevention and health promotion programming. In T.P. Gullotta & M. Bloom (Eds.), *Encyclopedia of primary prevention and health promotion* (pp. 61–69). New York: Kluwer.

Dutton-Greene, L.B. (2004). *Testing a model of unwanted pursuit and stalking*. Unpublished doctoral dissertation, University of Rhode Island.

Dwyer, D. (2000). *Interpersonal relationships*. London: Routledge.

Eagly, A.H., & Carli, L. (1981). Sex of researchers and sex-typed communications as determinants of sex differences in influenceability: A meta-analysis of social influence studies. *Psychological Bulletin, 90*, 1–20.

Eaton, S., & Konner, M. (1985). Paleolithic nutrition: A consideration of its nature and current implications. *New England Journal of Medicine, 312*(5), 283–289.

Ebbinghaus, H. (1913). *Memory* (H. Ruyer & C.E. Bussenius, Trans.). New York: Teachers College, Columbia University. (Original work published 1885.)

Ebrahim, I.O., & Fenwick, P. (2008). Sleep-related automatism and the law. *Medicine Science and the Law, 48*(2), 124–136.

Economic and Social Research Council (2007). Online. Available: http://www.esrcsocietytoday.ac.uk/ESRCInfoCentre/facts/index55.aspx

Eddy, K.T., Dutra, L., Bradley, R., & Westen, D. (2004). A multidimensional meta-analysis of psychotherapy and pharmacotherapy for obsessive-compulsive disorder. *Clinical Psychology Review, 24*, 1011–1030.

Edmundson, E., McAlister, A., Murray, D., Perry, C., & Lichtenstein, E. (1991). Approaches directed to the individual. In *Strategies to control tobacco use in the United States: A blueprint for public health in the 1990s* (Publication No. 92-3316, pp. 147–199). Washington, DC: National Institutes of Health.

Egeland, B., Gerhard, D.S., Pauls, D.L., Sussex, J.N., Kidd, K.K., Allen, C.R., Hostetter, A.M., & Housman, D.E. (1987). Bipolar affective disorders linked to DNA markers on chromosome 11. *Nature, 325*, 783–787.

Ehrensaft, M.K., Cohen, P., Brown, J., Smailes, E., Chen, H., & Johnson, J.G. (2003). Intergenerational transmission of partner violence: A 20-year prospective study. *Journal of Consulting and Clinical Psychology, 71*(4), 741–753.

Eisenberg, N. (2000). Emotion, regulation, and moral development. *Annual Review of Psychology, 51*, 665–697.

Eisenberg, N. (2002). Emotion-related regulation and its relation to quality of social functioning. *Child psychology in retrospect and prospect: In celebration of the 75th anniversary of the Institute of Child Development, Vol. 32*, 133–171.

Eisenberg, N., & Fabes, R.A. (1998). Prosocial development. In N. Eisenberg (Ed.), *Handbook of child psychology: Vol. 3. Social, emotional, and personality development* (pp. 701–778, W. Damon, Gen. Ed.). New York: Wiley.

Eisenberg, N., Fabes, R.A., Shepard, S.A., Guthrie, I.K., Murphy, B.C., & Reiser, M. (1999). Parental reactions to children's negative emotions: Longitudinal relations to quality of children's social functioning. *Child Development, 70*, 513–534.

Eisenberg, N., Fabes, R.A., Shepard, S.A., Murphy, B.C., Guthrie, I.K., Jones, S., et al. (1997). Contemporaneous and longitudinal prediction of children's social functioning from regulation and emotionality. *Child Development, 68*, 642–664.

Eisenberg, N., Lennon, R., & Roth, K. (1983). Prosocial development: A longitudinal study. *Developmental Psychology, 19*, 846–855.

Eisenberg-Berg, N., & Hand, M. (1979). The relationship of preschoolers' reasoning about prosocial moral conflicts to prosocial behaviour. *Child Development, 50*, 356–363.

Elias, M. F., Nicolson N.A., Bora, C., & Johnston, J. (1986). Sleep/wake patterns of breast-fed infants in the first two years of life. *Pediatrics, 77*, 322–329.

Elkin, I. (1994). The NIMH Treatment of Depression Collaborative Programme: Where we began and where we are. In A.E. Bergin & S.L. Garfield (Eds.), *Handbook of psychotherapy and behaviour change* (4th Edn). New York: Wiley.

Elkin, I., Shea, M.T., Watkins, J.T, Imber, S.D., Sotsky, S.M., Collins, J.F., et al. (1989). National Institute of Mental Health Treatment of Depression Collaborative Research Programme: General effectiveness of treatments. *Archives of General Psychiatry, 46*, 971–982.

Ellis, S., & Gauvain, M. (1992). Social and cultural influences on children's collaborative interactions. In L.T. Winegar & J. Valsiner (Eds.), *Children's development within social context: Vol. 2. Research and methodology*. Hillsdale, NJ: Lawrence Erlbaum Associates.

Else-Quest, N.M., Hyde, J.S., Goldsmith, H.H., & Van Hulle, C.A. (2006). Gender differences in temperament: A meta-analysis. *Psychological Bulletin, 132*, 33–72.

Empson, J.A.C. (1989). *Sleep and dreaming*. London: Faber & Faber.

Empson, J.A.C. (1993). *Sleep and dreaming* (2nd Edn). Hemel Hempstead, UK: Harvester Wheatsheaf.

Endo, Y., Heine, S.J., & Lehman, D.R. (2000). Culture and positive illusions in close relationships: How my relationships are better than yours. *Personality and Social Psychology Bulletin, 26*(12), 1571–1586.

Enticott, P.G., Johnston, P.J., Herring, S.E., Hoy, K.E., & Fitzgerald, P.B. (2008). Mirror neuron activation is associated with facial emotion processing. *Neuropsychologia, 46*(11), 2851–2854.

Ericsson, K.A., & Chase, W.G. (1982). Exceptional memory. *American Scientist, 70*, 607–615.

Ericsson, K.A., & Kintsch, W. (1995). Long-term working memory. *Psychological Review, 102*, 211–245.

Ericsson, K.A., & Lehmann, A.C. (1996). Expert and exceptional performance: evidence of maximal adaptation to task constraints. *Annual Review of Psychology, 47*, 273–305.

Ericsson, K.A., Krampe, R.T., & Tesch-Romer, C. (1993). The role of deliberate practice in the acquisition of expert performance. *Psychological Review, 100*, 363–406.

Erikson, E. (1968). *Identity: Youth and crisis*. New York: Norton.

Erikson, E. (1980). *Identity and the life cycle*. New York: Norton.

Eron, L.D. (1982). Parent–child interaction, television violence, and aggression of children. *American Psychologist, 37*, 197–211.

Esman, A.H. (2001). Obsessive-compulsive disorder: Current views. *Psychoanalytic Inquiry, 21*, 145–156.

Estes, W.K. (1944). An experimental study of punishment. *Psychological Monographs: General and Applied, 54*(No. 263), 1–40.

Evans, D.W., Lewis, M.D., & Iobst, E. (2004). The role of the orbitofrontal cortex in normally developing compulsive-like behaviours and obsessive-compulsive disorder. *Brain and Cognition, 55*, 220–234.

Evans, J., Heron, J., Lewis, G., Araya, R., & Wolke, D. (2005). Negative self-schemas and the onset of depression in women: Longitudinal study. *British Journal of Psychiatry, 186*, 302–307.

Evans, R.I. (1989). The evolution of challenges to health researchers in health psychology. *Health Psychology, 8*, 631–639.

Evans, R.I. (2001). Social influences in etiology and prevention of smoking and other health threatening behaviors in children and adolescents. In A. Baum, T.A. Revenson, & J.E. Singer (Eds.), *Handbook of health psychology* (pp. 459–468). Mahwah, NJ: Lawrence Erlbaum Associates.

Evans, R.I., & Getz, J.G. (2004). Resisting health risk behavior: The social inoculation approach and its extensions. In T.P. Gullotta & M. Bloom (Eds.), *The encyclopedia of primary prevention and health promotion*. New York, NY: Kluwer/Academic.

Eyal, K., & Cohen, J. (2006). When good friends say goodbye: A parasocial breakup study. *Journal of Broadcasting and Electronic Media, 50*, 502–523.

Eysenck, H.J. (1967). *The biological basis of personality*. Springfield, IL: C.C. Thomas.

Eysenck, M.W. (1982). *Attention and arousal: Cognition and performance*. Berlin: Springer.

Eysenck, M.W. (1997). *Anxiety and cognition: A unified theory*. Hove, UK: Psychology Press.

Eysenck, M.W. (2004). *Psychology: An international perspective*. Hove, UK: Psychology Press.

Eysenck, M.W. (2009). *Fundamentals of psychology*. Hove: Psychology Press.

Eysenck, M.W., & Eysenck, M.C. (1980). Effects of processing depth, distinctiveness, and word frequency on retention. *British Journal of Psychology, 71*, 263–274.

Eysenck, M.W., & Keane, M.T. (1990). *Cognitive psychology: A student's handbook* (2nd Edn). Hove, UK: Psychology Press.

Fagot, B.I., & Hagan, R. (1991). Observations of parent reactions to sex-stereotyped behaviours: Age and sex effects. *Child Development, 62*, 617–628.

Fagot, B.I., & Leinbach, M.D. (1989). The young child's gender schema: Environmental input, internal organisation. *Child Development, 60*, 663–672.

Fahrenberg, J. (1992). Psychophysiology of neuroticism and emotionality. In A. Gale & M.W. Eysenck (Eds.), *Handbook of individual differences: Biological perspectives*. Chichester: Wiley.

Fairburn, C., & Harrison, P. (2003). Eating disorders. *The Lancet, 61*(9355), 407–416.

Faller, H., Schilling, S., & Lang, H. (1995). Causal attribution and adaptation among lung-cancer patients. *Journal of Psychosomatic Research, 39*, 619–627.

Falloon, I.R.H., Boyd, J.L., McGill, C.W., Williamson, M., Razani, J., Moss, H.B., et al. (1985). Family management in the prevention of morbidity of schizophrenia. *Archives of General Psychiatry, 42*, 887–896.

Falloon, I.R.H., Montero, I., Sungur, M., Mastoeni, A., Malm, U., et al. (2004). Implementation of evidence-based treatment for schizophrenic disorders: Two-year outcome of an international field trial of optimal treatment. *World Psychiatry, 3*, 104–109.

Farah, M.J. (1999). Relations among the agnosias. In G.W. Humphreys (Ed.), *Case studies in the neuropsychology of vision*. Hove, UK: Psychology Press.

Farah, M.J., Tanaka, J.W., & Drain, H.M. (1995). What causes the face inversion effect? *Journal of Experimental Psychology: Human Perception and Performance, 21*, 628–634.

Farde, L., Wiesel, F.A., Stoneelander, S., Halldin, C., Nordstrom, A.L., Hall, H., & Sedvall, G. (1990). D2 dopamine receptors in neuroleptic naive schizophrenic patients: A positron emission tomography study with [C-11] raclopride. *Archives of General Psychiatry, 47*, 213–219.

Fausto-Sterling, A. (2000). Beyond difference: Feminism and evolutionary psychology. In H. Rose & S. Rose (Eds.), *Alas, poor Darwin: Arguments against evolutionary psychology*. London: Jonathan Cape.

Fazio, R.H., Zanna, M.P., & Cooper, J. (1977). Dissonance versus self-perception: An integrative view of each theory's proper domain of application. *Journal of Experimental Social Psychology, 13*, 464–479.

Feadda, G.L., Tondo, L., Teicher, M.H., Baldessarini, R.J., Gelbard, H.A., & Floris, G.F. (1993). Seasonal mood disorders: Patterns of seasonal recurrence in mania and depression. *Archives of General Psychiatry, 50*, 17–23.

Ferguson, C.J. (2007). Evidence for publication bias in video game violence effects literature: A meta-analytic review. *Aggression and Violent Behavior, 12*, 470–482.

Fery, P., & Morais, J. (2003). A case study of visual agnosia without perceptual processing or structural descriptions' impairment. *Cognitive Neuropsychology, 20*, 595–618.

Festinger, L. (1957). *A theory of cognitive dissonance*. Stanford, CA: Stanford University Press.

Festinger, L., & Carlsmith, J.M. (1959). Cognitive consequences of forced compliance. *Journal of Abnormal and Social Psychology, 47*, 382–389.

Feyerabend, P. (1975). *Against method: Outline of an anarchist theory of knowledge*. London: New Left Books.

Field, A.E., Cheung, L., Wolf, A.M., Herzog, D.B., Gortmaker, S.L., & Colditz, G.A. (1999). Exposure to the mass media and weight concerns among girls. *Pediatrics, 103*, 36.

Fiorino, P., & Leone, M. (2001). Evaluation of witness reliability in the Trans-en-Provence UFO event: The results of an Italian enquiry. *European Journal of UFO and Abduction Studies, 2*(1), 25–38.

Fishbein, M., & Ajzen, I. (1975). *Belief, attitude, intention and behavior: An introduction to theory and research*. Reading, MA: Addison-Wesley.

Fisher, H. (2004). *Why we love: The nature and chemistry of romantic love*. New York: Henry Holt.

Fisher, R.A. (1930). *The genetical theory of natural selection*. Oxford: Clarendon Press.

Fisher-Thompson, D. (1990). Adult sex typing of children's toys. *Sex Roles, 23*, 291–302.

Fiske, S.T. (1993). Social cognition and social perception. *Annual Review of Psychology, 44*, 155–194.

Floody, O.R. (1968). Hormones and aggression in female animals. In B.B. Suare (Ed.), *Hormones and aggressive behaviour*. New York: Plenum Press.

Flynn, E. (2006). A microgenetic investigation of stability and continuity in theory of mind development. *British Journal of Developmental Psychology, 24*, 631–654.

Flynn, J.R. (1987). Massive IQ gains in 14 nations: What IQ tests really measure. *Psychological Bulletin, 101*, 271–291.

Flynn, J.R. (1994). IQ gains over time. In R.J. Sternberg (Ed.), *Encyclopedia of human intelligence*. New York: Macmillan.

Foa, U.G., & Foa, E.B. (1975). *Resource theory of social exchange*. Morristown, NJ: General Learning Press.

Fodor, J.A., & Pylyshyn, Z.W. (1981). How direct is visual perception? Some reflections on Gibson's "ecological approach". *Cognition, 9*, 139–196.

Foley, D. J., Vitiello, M.V., Bliwise, D.L., Ancoli-Israel, S., Monjan, A.A., & Walsh, J.K. (2007). Frequent napping is associated with excessive daytime sleepiness, depression, pain, and nocturia in older adults. Findings from the National Sleep Foundation '2003 Sleep in America' Poll, *American Journal of Geriatric Psychiatry, 15*(4), 344–350.

Folkard, S. (1983). Circadian rhythms and hours of work. In Warr, P. (Ed.), *Psychology at work*. Harmondsworth: Penguin.

Folkard, S. (1996, September 28). Bags of time to play. *Daily Express*.

Fonagy, P., Roth, A., & Higgitt, A. (2005). The outcome of psychodynamic psychotherapy for psychological disorders. *Clinical Neuroscience Research, 4*, 367–377.

Fontenelle, L.F., Mendlowicz, M.V., Marques, C., & Versiani, M. (2004). Trans-cultural aspects of obsessive-compulsive disorder: A description of a Brazilian sample and a systematic review of international clinical studies. *Journal of Psychiatric Research, 38*, 403–411.

Food Standards Agency (2007). Children's attitudes towards food. *Omnibus research report*. Available: http://www.food.gov.uk/multimedia/pdfs/childrensresearchfeb2007.pdf

Food Standards Agency (2008). Online. Available: http://www.food.gov.uk/news/newsarchive/2008/nov/latesttrackingsurvey

Force, U.S.P.T. (1996). *Guide to clinical preventative services* (2nd Edn). Baltimore, MD: Williams & Wilkins.

Fragaszy, D.M., & Perry, S. (Eds.) (2003). *The biology of traditions: Models and evidence*. Cambridge: Cambridge University Press.

Franchini, L., Gasperini, M., Perez, J., Smeraldi, E., & Zanardi, R. (1997). A double-blind study of long-term treatment with sertraline or fluvoxamine for prevention of highly recurrent unipolar depression. *Journal of Clinical Psychiatry, 58*, 104–107.

Francis, B. (2000). *Boys, girls and achievement: Addressing the classroom issues*. London: Routledge.

Franklin, M.E., Abramowitz, J.S., Kozak, M.J., Levitt, J.T., & Foa, E.B. (2000). Effectiveness of exposure and ritual prevention for obsessive-compulsive disorder: Randomised compared with non-randomised samples. *Journal of Consulting and Clinical Psychology, 68,* 594–602.

Franzoi, S.L. (1996). *Social psychology.* Madison, MI: Brown & Benchmark.

Freeston, M.H., Rheaume, J., & Ladouceur, R. (1996). Correcting faulty appraisals of obsessional thoughts. *Behaviour, Research and Therapy, 34,* 433–446.

Freud, S. (1901). *Psychopathology of everyday life.* London: Fisher Unwin (translated by A.A. Brill 1914).

Freud, S. (1910). *On psychotherapy.* London: Hogarth Press.

Freud, S. (1933). *New introductory lectures in psychoanalysis.* New York: Norton.

Freud, S. (1949). *An outline of psychoanalysis.* London: Hogarth Press.

Freud, S. (1950). The effects of cocaine on thought processes. In *Collected Papers, Vol. V.* London: Hogarth. (Original work published 1885.)

Friedrich, L.K., & Stein, A.H. (1973). Aggressive and pro-social television programmes and the natural behaviour of preschool children. *Monographs of the Society for Research in Child Development, 38,* 1–64.

Frith, C.D. (1992). *The cognitive neuropsychology of schizophrenia.* Hove, UK: Psychology Press.

Frith, U., & Happé, F.G.E. (1994). Autism: Beyond 'theory of mind'. *Cognition, 50,* 115–132.

Fromme, K., de Wit, H., Hutchison, K.E., Ray, L., Corbin, W.R., Cook, T.A.R., et al. (2004). Biological and behavioral markers of alcohol sensitivity: neurobiological, behavioral, and environmental relations to drinking. *Alcoholism: Clinical & Experimental Research, 28*(2), 247–256.

Frosdick, S., & Marsh, P. (2005). *Football hooliganism.* Uffculme, UK: Willan Publishing.

Fujii, D.E.M., Ahmed, I., & Takeshita, J. (1999). Neuropsychologic implications in erotomania: Two case studies. *Neuropsychiatry, Neuropsychology, and Behavioral Neurology, 12,* 110–116.

Furlan, R., Barbic, F., Piazza, S., Tinelli, F.M., Seghizzi, P., & Malliani, A. (2000). Modifications of cardiac autonomic profile associated with a shift schedule of work. *Circulation, 102,* 1912–1916.

Fyer, A.J., Mannuzza, S., Chapman, T.F., Liebowitz, M.R., & Klein, D.F. (1993). A direct-interview family study of social phobia. *Archives of General Psychiatry, 50,* 286–293.

Fyer, A.J., Mannuzza, S., Gallops, M.S., Martin, L.Y., et al. (1990). Familial transmission of simple phobias and fears: A preliminary report. *Archives of General Psychiatry, 47*(3), 252–256.

Gaffan, E.A., Hansel, M., & Smith, L. (1983). Does reward depletion influence spatial memory performance? *Learning and Motivation, 14,* 58–74.

Gaffney, J. (2001). Imagined relationships: Political leadership in contemporary democracies. *Parliamentary Affairs, 54,* 120–133.

Gallese, V., Fadiga, L., Fogassi, L., & Rizzolatti, G. (1996). Action recognition in the premotor cortex. *Brain, 119,* 593–609.

Gallese, V., Keysers, C., Rizzolatti, G. (2004). A unifying view of the basis of social cognition *Trends in Cognitive Science*s, *8,* 396–403.

Gallup, G.G. (1970). Chimpanzees: Self-recognition. *Science, 167,* 86–91.

Gallup, G.G., Anderson, J.R., & Shillito, D.J. (2002). The mirror test. In R.L. Mellgren (Ed.), *Animal cognition and behaviour.* Amsterdam: North-Holland.

Gamson, W.B., Fireman, B., & Rytina, S. (1982). *Encounters with unjust authority.* Homewood, IL: Dorsey Press.

Garcia, J., Ervin, F.R., & Koelling, R.A. (1966). Learning with prolonged delay of reinforcement. *Psychonomic Science, 5,* 121–122.

Garcia, J., & Koelling, R.A. (1966). Relation of cue to consequence in avoidance learning. *Psychonomic Science, 4,* 123–124.

Gardner, H. (1983). *Frames of mind: The theory of multiple intelligences.* New York: Basic Books.

Gardner, H. (1998). Are there additional intelligences? The case for naturalist, spiritual, and existential intelligences. In J. Kane (Ed.), *Education, information, and transformation.* Englewood Cliffs, NJ: Prentice-Hall.

Gardner, H., Kornhaber, M.L., & Wake, W.K. (1996). *Intelligence: Multiple perspectives.* Orlando, FL: Harcourt Brace.

Garner, D.M., & Fairburn, C.G. (1988). Relationship between anorexia nervosa and bulimia nervosa: Diagnostic implications. In D.M. Garner & P.E. Garfinkel (Eds.), *Diagnostic issues in anorexia nervosa and bulimia nervosa.* New York: Brunner/Mazel.

Gatward, N. (2007). Anorexia nervosa: An evolutionary puzzle. *European Eating Disorders Review, 15*(1), 1–12.

Gauntlett, D. (2008). *Media, gender and identity* (2nd Edn). Abingdon, UK: Routledge.

Gauthier, I., & Tarr, M.J. (2002). Unravelling mechanisms for expert object recognition: Bridging brain activity and behaviour. *Journal of Experimental Psychology: Human Perception and Performance, 28,* 431–446.

Geary, D.C., Vigil, J., & Byrd-Craven, J. (2004). Evolution of human mate choice. *Journal of Sex Research, 41,* 27–42.

Geddes, J.R., Burgess, S., Hawton, K., Jamison, K., & Goodwin, G.M. (2004). Long-term lithium therapy for bipolar disorder: Systematic review and meta-analysis of randomised controlled trials. *American Journal of Psychiatry, 161,* 217–222.

Geldof, P. (2008). In Peake, A. Peaches: We'll probably get divorced. Retrieved March 18 2009, from http://www.thesun.co.uk/sol/homepage/showbiz/bizarre/artic le1833038.ece

Gentile, D.A., & Anderson, C.A. (2003). Violent video games: The newest media violence hazard. In D.A. Gentile (Ed.), *Media violence and children.* Westport, CT: Praeger Publishing.

Gerbino, L., Oleshansky, M., & Gershon, S. (1978). Clinical use and mode of action of lithium. In M.A. Lipton, A. DiMascio, & F.K. Killam (Eds.), *Psychopharmacology: A generation of progress.* New York: Raven Press.

Gerbner, G. (1994). Reclaiming our cultural mythology. *In Context: A Quarterly of Humane Sustainable Culture, 38,* 40–59.

Gerbner, G., Gross, L., Morgan, M., & Signorielli, N. (1986). Living with television: The dynamics of the cultivation process. In J. Bryant & D. Zillman (Eds.), *Perspectives on media effects* (pp. 17–40). Hillsdale, NJ: Lawrence Erlbaum Associates.

Gergen, K.J. (1973). Social psychology as history. *Journal of Personality and Social Psychology, 26,* 309–320.

Gergen, K.J. (1985). Social constructionist inquiry: Context and implications. In K.J. Gergen & K.E. Davis (Eds.), *The social construction of the person.* New York: Springer-Verlag.

Gergen, K.J. (1997). Social psychology as social construction: The emerging vision. In C. McGarty & A. Haslam (Eds.), *The message of social psychology.* Oxford: Blackwell.

Gergen, K.J., Morse, S.J., & Gergen, M.M. (1980). Behaviour exchange in cross-cultural perspective. In H.C. Triandis & W.W. Lambert (Eds.), *Handbook of cross-cultural psychology: Vol. 5. Social psychology.* Boston: Allyn & Bacon.

Gershon, E.S. (1990). Genetics. In F.K. Goodwin & K.R. Jamison (Eds.), *Manic-depressive illness.* Oxford: Oxford University Press.

Geschwind, D. (2008). When sleep doesn't come, death does. When *ABC News Medical Mystery*. Retrieved March 18 2009, from http://abcnews.go.com/Health/Story?id=3675223&page=3

Gibbons, F.X., Eggleston, T.J., & Benthin, A.C. (1997). Cognitive reactions to smoking relapse: The reciprocal relation between dissonance and self-esteem. *Journal of Personality and Social Psychology, 72*, 184–195.

Gibbs, W.W. (1996, August). Gaining on fat. *Scientific American*, 70–76.

Gibson, E.J., & Walk, R.D. (1960). The visual cliff. *Scientific American, 202*, 64–71.

Gibson, J.J. (1979). *The ecological approach to visual perception*. Boston: Houghton Mifflin.

Giersch, A., Humphreys, G., Boucart, M., & Kovacs, I. (2000). The computation of contours in visual agnosia: Evidence for early computation prior to shape binding and figure–ground coding. *Cognitive Neuropsychology, 17*, 731–759.

Giles, D., & Close, J. (2008). Exposure to lad magazines and drive for muscularity in dating and non-dating young men. *Personality and Individual Differences, 44*(7), 1610–1616.

Giles, D., & Maltby, J. (2006). Praying at the altar of the stars. *Psychologist, 19*, 82–85.

Giles, D.C. (2000). *Illusions of immortality: A psychology of fame and celebrity*. London: Macmillan.

Giles, D.C., & Maltby, J. (2004). The role of media figures in adolescent development: Relations between autonomy, attachment, and interest in celebrities. *Personality and Individual Differences, 36*, 813–822.

Gilligan, C. (1977). In a different voice: Women's conceptions of the self and of morality. *Harvard Educational Review, 47*, 481–517.

Gilligan, C. (1982). *In a different voice: Psychological theory and women's development*. Cambridge, MA: Harvard University Press.

Gilligan, C., & Attanucci, J. (1988). Two moral orientations: Gender differences and similarities. *Merrill-Palmer Quarterly, 34*, 223–237.

Gilovich, T. (1993). *How we know what isn't so: The fallibility of human reason in everyday life*. New York: The Free Press.

Giordano, Peggy C. (2003). Relationships in adolescence. *Annual Review of Sociology, 29*, 257–281.

Girbau, D. (2002). A sequential analysis of private and social speech in children's dyadic communication. *The Spanish Journal of Psychology, 5*, 110–118.

Gjedde, A., & Wong, D.F. (1987). Positron tomographic quantitation of neuroreceptors in human brain in vivo with special reference to the D2 dopamine receptors in caudate nucleus. *Neurosurgical Review, 10*, 9.

Glenn, N.D. (1989) Duration of marriage, family composition and marital happiness. *Journal of Marriage and the Family, 55*, 242–243.

Gold, D.R., Rogacz, S.R., Bock, N., Tosteson, T.D., Baum, T.M., Speizer, F.E., et al. (1992). Rotating shift-work, sleep and accidents related to sleepiness in hospital nurses. *American Journal of Public Health, 82*, 1011–1014.

Goldbart, A.D., Mager, E., Veling, M.C., Goldman, J.L., Kheirandish-Gozal, L., Serpero, L.D., et al. (2007). Neurotrophins and tonsillar hypertrophy in children with obstructive sleep apnea. *Pediatric Research. 62*(4), 489–494.

Goldwyn, E. (1979, May 24). The fight to be male. *Listener*, pp. 709–712.

Goleman, D. (1995). *Emotional intelligence*. New York: Bantam Books.

Gordon, I.E. (1989). *Theories of visual perception*. Chichester: Wiley.

Gordon, N.P. (1986). The prevalence and health impact of shiftwork. *American Journal of Public Health, 76*, 1225–1228.

Gotlib, I.H., & Robinson, L.A. (1982). Responses to depressed individuals: Discrepancies between self-report and observer-rated behaviour. *Journal of Abnormal Psychology, 91*, 231–240.

Gotlib, I.H., Whiffen, V.E., Wallace, P.M., & Mount, J.H. (1991). Prospective investigation of postpartum depression: Factors involved in onset and recovery. *Journal of Abnormal Psychology, 100*, 122–132.

Gottesman, I.I. (1991). *Schizophrenia genesis: The origins of madness*. New York: W.H. Freeman.

Gottesman, I.I., & Bertelsen, A. (1989). Dual mating studies in psychiatry: Offspring of inpatients with examples from reactive (psychogenic) psychoses. *International Review of Psychiatry, 1*, 287–296.

Gottfried, A.W. (1984). Home environment and early cognitive development: Integration, meta-analyses, and conclusions. In A.W. Gottfried (Ed.), *Home environment and early cognitive development: Longitudinal research*. Orlando, FL: Academic Press.

Gould, S.J. (1978). Morton's ranking of races by cranial capacity. *Science, 200*, 503–509.

Gould, S.J. (1981). *The mismeasure of man*. New York: Norton.

Goulding, A., Westerlund, J., Parker, A., & Wackermann, J. (2004). The first digital Autoganzfeld study using a real-time judging procedure. *European Journal of Parapsychology, 19*, 66–97.

Gow, K., Lurie, J., Coppin, S., Popper, A., Powell, A., & Basterfield, K. (2001). Fantasy proneness and other psychological correlates of UFO experience. *European Journal of UFO and Abduction Studies, 2*(2), 45–66.

Grabner, R.H., Stern, E., & Neubauer, A.C. (2007). Individual differences in chess expertise: A psychometric investigation. *Acta Psychologica, 124*, 398–420.

Grammer, K., & Thornhill, R. (1994). Human (*Homo sapiens*) facial attractiveness and sexual selection: The role of symmetry and averageness. *Journal of Comparative Psychology, 108*, 233–242.

Granott, N. (2005). Scaffolding dynamically toward change: Previous and new perspectives. *New Ideas in Psychology, 23*, 140–151.

Gray, P. (2002). *Psychology* (4th Edn). New York: Worth.

Green, S. (1994). *Principles of biopsychology*. Hove, UK: Psychology Press.

Greenfield, P.M. (1984). *Mind and media: The effect of television, video games and computers*. Aylesbury, UK: Fontana.

Gregg, T.R. (2003). Cortical and limbic circuits mediating aggressive behaviour. In M.P. Mattson (Ed.), *The neurobiology of aggression*. New York: Humana Press.

Gregor, A.J., & McPherson, D.A. (1965). A study of susceptibility to geometrical illusion among cultural subgroups of Australian aborigines. *Psychology in Africa, 11*, 1–13.

Gregory, R.L. (1970). *The intelligent eye*. New York: McGraw-Hill.

Gregory, R.L. (1972). Seeing as thinking. *Times Literary Supplement, June 24*, 707–708.

Gregory, R.L. (1973). The confounded eye. In R.L. Gregory & E.H. Gombrich (Eds.), *Illusion in nature and art*. London: Duckworth.

Gregory, R.L., & Wallace, J. (1963). *Recovery from early blindness*. Cambridge, UK: Heffer.

Greyson, B. (2003). Incidence and correlates of near-death experiences in a cardiac care unit. *General Hospital Psychiatry, 25*, 269–276.

Griffit, W.B., & Guay, P. (1969). 'Object' evaluation and conditioned affect. *Journal of Experimental Research in Psychology, 4*, 1–8.

Griffiths, M.D. (1991). Amusement machine playing in childhood and adolescence: A comparative analysis of video games and fruit machines. *Journal of Adolescence, 14,* 53–73.

Griffiths, M.D. (1993). Tolerance in gambling: An objective measure using the psychophysiological analysis of male fruit machine gamblers. *Addictive Behaviors, 18,* 365–372.

Griffiths, M. (1994). The role of cognitive bias and skill in fruit machine gambling. *British Journal of Psychology, 85,* 351–369.

Griffiths, M.D. (1995). *Adolescent gambling.* London: Routledge.

Griffiths, M.D. (1996). Nicotine, tobacco and addiction. *Nature, 384,* 18.

Griffiths, M. (1998). Does internet and computer "addiction" exist?: Some case study evidence. Paper presented at the Internet Research and Information for Social Sciences International Conference, Bristol, UK. Retrieved March 16 2009, from http://www.intute.ac.uk/socialsciences/archive/iriss/papers/paper47.htm

Griffiths, M.D. (1999a). Gambling technologies: Prospects for problem gambling. *Journal of Gambling Studies, 15,* 265–283.

Griffiths, M.D. (1999b). The psychology of the near miss (revisited): A comment on Delfabbro and Winefield. *British Journal of Psychology, 90,* 441–445.

Griffiths, M.D. (2002). *Gambling and gaming addictions in adolescence.* Leicester, UK: British Psychological Society/Blackwells.

Griffiths, M.D. (2005). Online therapy for addictive behaviors. *CyberPsychology and Behavior, 8,* 555–561.

Griffiths, M.D. (2006). An overview of pathological gambling. In T. Plante (Ed.), *Mental disorders of the new millennium. Volume I: Behavioral issues* (pp. 73–98). New York: Greenwood.

Griffiths, M.D. (2008). The biopsychosocial and "complex" systems approach as a unified framework for addiction. *Behavioral and Brain Sciences, 31,* 446–447.

Griffiths, M.D., Bellringer, P., Farrell-Roberts, K., & Freestone, F. (2001). Treating problem gamblers: A residential therapy approach. *Journal of Gambling Studies, 17,* 161–169.

Griffiths, M.D., & Cooper, G. (2003). Online therapy: Implications for problem gamblers and clinicians. *British Journal of Guidance and Counselling, 13,* 113–135.

Griffiths, M.D., Davies, M.N.O., & Chappell, D. (2003). Breaking the stereotype: The case of online gaming. *Cyberpsychology and Behavior, 6,* 81–91.

Griffiths, M.D., & MacDonald, H.F. (1999). Counselling in the treatment of pathological gambling: An overview. *British Journal of Guidance and Counselling, 27,* 179–190.

Griffiths, M.D., & Parke, J. (2003). The environmental psychology of gambling. In G. Reith (Ed.), *Gambling: Who wins? Who loses?* (pp. 277–292). New York: Prometheus Books.

Griffiths, M.D., & Wood, R.T.A. (2001). The psychology of lottery gambling. *International Gambling Studies, 1,* 27–44.

Grigorenko, E.L., Meier, E., Lipka, J., Mohatt, G., Yanez, E., & Sternberg, R.J. (2004). Academic and practical intelligence: A case study of the Yup'ik in Alaska. *Learning and Individual Differences, 14,* 183–207.

Grill-Spector, K., Sayres, R., & Ress, D. (2006). High-resolution imaging reveals highly selective non-face clusters in the fusiform face area. *Nature Neuroscience, 9,* 1177–1185.

Grilo, C.M., & Pogue-Geile, M.F. (1991). The nature of environmental influences on weight and obesity: A behavior genetic analysis. *Psychological Bulletin, 110,* 520–537.

Gross, R. (1996). *Psychology: The science of mind and behaviour* (3rd Edn). London: Hodder & Stoughton.

Grossman, M., Galetta, S., & D'Esposito, M. (1997). Object recognition difficulty in visual apperceptive agnosia. *Brain and Cognition, 33,* 306–342.

Grueter, M., Grueter, T.H., Bell, V., Horst, J., Laskowski, W., Sperling, K., et al. (2007). Hereditary prosopagnosia: The first case series. *Cortex, 43,* 734–749.

Grunhaus, L., Schreiber, S., Dolberg, O.T., Hirshman, S., & Dannon, P.N. (2002). Response to ECT in major depression: Are there differences between unipolar and bipolar depression? *Bipolar Disorders, 4*(Suppl. 1), 91–93.

Grusec, J.E., Davidov, M., & Lundell, L. (2002). Prosocial and helping behaviour. In P.K. Smith & C. Hart (Eds.), *Handbook of childhood social development.* Malden, MA: Blackwell.

Grusser, S.M., Thalemann, R., & Griffiths, M.D. (2007). Excessive computer game playing: Evidence for addiction and aggression? *Cyberpsychology and Behavior, 10,* 290–292.

Guadagno, R. E., Asher, T. Demaine, L. J., & Cialdini, R. B. (2001). When saying yes leads to saying no: Preference for consistency and the reverse foot-in-the-door effect. *Personality and Social Psychology Bulletin, 27,* 859–867.

Guardian (2005). Online. Available: http://www.guardian.co.uk/science/2005/jun/27/sciencenews.research

Guastello, D.D., & Guastello, S.J. (2003). Androgyny, gender role behavior, and emotional intelligence among college students and their parents. *Sex Roles, 49,* 663–673.

Guilleminault, C., Palombini, L., Pelayo, R., & Chervin, R.D. (2003). Sleepwalking and sleep terrors in prepubertal children: What triggers them? *Pediatrics, 111*(1), e17–e25.

Gulevich, G., Dement, W.C., & Johnson, L. (1966). Psychiatric and EEG observations on a case of prolonged (264 hours) wakefulness. *Archives of General Psychiatry, 15,* 29–35.

Gurucharri, C., & Selman, R.L. (1982). The development of interpersonal understanding during childhood, preadolescence, and adolescense: A longitudinal follow-up study. *Child Develoment, 53,* 924–927.

Haart, E.G.O.-de, Carey, D.P., & Milne, A.B. (1999). More thoughts on perceiving and grasping the Müller–Lyer illusion. *Neuropsychologia, 37,* 1437–1444.

Hackmann, A., Clark, D.M., & McManus, F. (2000). Recurrent images and early memories of social phobia. *Behaviour Research and Therapy, 38,* 601–610.

Hadjikhani, N., Joseph, R.M., Snyder, J., & Tager-Flusberg, H. (2006). Anatomical differences in the mirror neuron system and social cognition network in autism. *Cerebral Cortex, 16,* 1276–1282.

Hahn, S., Andersen, G.J., & Saidpour, A. (2003). Static scene analysis for the perception of heading. *Psychological Science, 14,* 543–548.

Haley, A.J. (2001). British soccer superhooligans: Emergence and establishment. *The Sport Journal, 4.*

Halgin, R.P., & Whitbourne, S.K. (1997). *Abnormal psychology: The human experience of psychological disorders.* Madison, WI: Brown & Benchmark.

Haller, J., & Kruk, M. (2003). Neuroendocrine stress responses and aggression. In M.P. Mattson (Ed.), *The neurobiology of aggression.* New York: Humana Press.

Hamilton, M.C., Anderson, D., Broaddus, M., & Young, K. (2006). Gender stereotyping and under-representation of female characters in 200 popular children's picture books: A twenty first century update. *Sex Roles, 55,* 757–765.

Hamilton, M.L. (1977). *Father's influence on children.* Chicago: Nelson-Hall.

Hamilton, W.D., & Zuk, M. (1982). Heritable true fitness and bright birds: A role for parasites? *Science, 218,* 384–387.

Hammen, C. (1997). *Depression.* Hove, UK: Psychology Press.

Han, C., McGue, M.K., & Iacono, W.G. (1999). Lifetime tobacco, alcohol and other substance use in adolescent Minnesota twins: univariate and multivariate behavioral genetic analyses. *Addiction, 94*(7), 981–993.

Happé, F. (1995). The role of age and verbal ability in the theory of mind task performance of subjects with autism. *Child Development, 66,* 843–855.

Hare, B., Call, J., & Tomasello, M. (2001). Do chimpanzees know what conspecifics know? *Animal Behaviour, 61,* 139–151.

Hare, B., Call, J., & Tomasello, M. (2006). Chimpanzees deceive a human competitor by hiding. *Cognition, 101,* 495–514.

Hargreaves, D. (2002). Idealized women in TV ads make girls feel bad. *Journal of Social and Clinical Psychology, 21,* 287–308.

Harré, R., & Secord, P. (1972). *The explanation of social behaviour.* Oxford: Basil Blackwell.

Harris, C.R. (2002). Sexual and romantic jealousy in heterosexual and homosexual adults. *Psychological Science, 13,* 7–12.

Harris, E.L., Noyes, R., Crowe, R.R., & Chaudhry, D.R. (1983). Family study of agoraphobia: Report of a pilot study. *Archives of General Psychiatry, 40,* 1061–1064.

Harris, J.L. (1989). A model for treating compulsive gamblers through cognitive-behavioural approaches. *Psychotherapy Patient, 11,* 211–226.

Harris, M., & Butterworth, G. (2002). *Developmental psychology: A student's handbook.* Hove, UK: Psychology Press.

Harrison, G., Hopper, K., Craig, T., Laska, E., Siegel, C, et al. (2001). *British Journal of Psychiatry, 178,* 506–517.

Harrison, Y. (2004). The relationship between daytime exposure to light and night-time sleep in 6- to 12-week-old infants. *Journal of Sleep Research, 13*(4), 345–352.

Hatfield, E., Utne, M.K., & Traupmann, J. (1979). Equity theory and intimate relationships. In R.L. Burgess & T.L. Huston (Eds.), *Exchange theory in developing relationships.* New York: Academic Press.

Havel, P.J. (2000). Role of adipose tissue in body-weight regulation: Mechanisms regulating leptin production and energy balance. *Proceedings of the Nutrition Society, 59,* 359–371.

Hawkins, L.H., & Armstrong-Esther, C.A. (1978, May 4). Circadian rhythms and night shift working in nurses. *Nursing Times, 74*(18), 49–52.

Hayer, T., Griffiths, M.D., & Meyer, G. (2005). The prevention and treatment of problem gambling in adolescence. In T.P. Gullotta & G. Adams (Eds). *Handbook of adolescent behavioral problems: Evidence-based approaches to prevention and treatment* (pp. 467–486). New York: Springer.

Hayman-White, K., & Happell, B. (2007). Critique of Falloon and the Optimal Treatment Project. *International Journal of Mental Health Nursing, 16,* 44–49.

Hayne, H., Boniface, J., & Barr, R. (2000). The development of declarative memory in human infants: Age-related changes in deferred imitation. *Behavioral Neuroscience, 114,* 77–83.

Hearold, S. (1986). A synthesis of 1043 effects of television on social behaviour. In G. Comstock (Ed.), *Public communication and behaviour, Vol. 1.* Orlando, FL: Academic Press.

Heath, T.P., Melichar, J.K., Nutt, D.J., & Donaldson, L.F. (2006). Human taste thresholds are modulated by serotonin and noradrenaline. *Journal of Neuroscience, 26*(49), 12664–12671.

Heather, N. (1976). *Radical perspectives in psychology.* London: Methuen.

Heather, N. (1986). Minimal intervention treatment interventions for problem drinkers. In G. Edwards & D. Gill (Eds.), *Current issues in clinical psychology.* London: Plenum.

Hedley, L.M., Hoffart, A., & Sexton, H. (2001). The change process in a cognitive-behavioural therapy: Testing a cognitive, a behavioural, and an integrated model of panic disorder with agoraphobia. *Psychotherapy Research, 11,* 401–413.

Heimberg, R.G., Liebowitz, M.R., Hope, D.A., Schneier, F.R., et al. (1998). Cognitive behavioural group therapy vs. phenelzine therapy for social phobia: 12-week outcome. *Archives of General Psychiatry, 55,* 1133–1141.

Hemsley, D.R. (1993). A simple (or simplistic-questionable) cognitive model for schizophrenia. *Behaviour Research and Therapy, 31,* 633–645.

Hemsley, D.R. (2005). The development of a cognitive model of schizophrenia: Placing it in context. *Neuroscience and Biobehavioral Reviews, 29,* 977–988.

Henderson, M. (2008). Online. Available: http://www.timesonline.co.uk/tol/news/uk/science/article3872868.ece

Hendrick, C., & Hendrick, S.S. (2003). Romantic love: Measuring Cupid's arrow. In S. J. Lopez & C.R. Snyder (Eds.), *Positive psychological assessment: A handbook of models and measures* (pp. 235–249). Washington, DC: American Psychological Association.

Hennig, J., Reuter, M., Netter, P., & Burk, C. (2005). Two types of aggression are differentially related to serotonergic activity and the A779C TPH polymorphism. *Behavioral Neuroscience, 119*(1), 16–25.

Hennigan, K.M., Del Rosario, M.L., Cook, T.D., & Calder, B.J. (1982). Impact of the introduction of television on crime in the United States: Empirical findings and theoretical implications. *Journal of Personality and Social Psychology, 42,* 461–477.

Herrmann, E., Melis, A.P., & Tomasello, M. (2006). Apes' use of iconic cues in the object-choice task. *Animal Cognition, 9,* 118–130.

Hersh, S.M. (2004). *American soldiers brutalized Iraqis. How far up does the responsibility go?* Online. Available: http://66.102.1.104/scholar?hl=en&lr=&client=firefox-a&q=cache:v2KGer1bs30J:www.offentlig-dumskap.no/amerikanerane/TORTURE_AT_ABU_GHRAIB.doc+

Hick, W.E. (1952). On the rate of gain of information. *Quarterly Journal of Experimental Psychology, 4,* 11–26.

Higgins, S.T., Budney, A.J., Bickel, W.K., Foerg, F., Donham, R., & Badger, G.J. (1994). Incentives improve outcome in outpatient behavioral treatment of cocaine dependence. *Archives of General Psychiatry, 51,* 568–576.

Highfield, R. (1996). Scientists shed light on the origins of our body clock. *Daily Telegraph,* 5 May.

Hill, E.L., & Frith, U. (2003). Understanding autism: Insights from mind and brain. *Philosophical Transactions of the Royal Society London B, 358,* 281–289.

Hill, J.O., & Peters, J.C. (1998). Environmental contributions to the obesity epidemic. *Science, 280,* 1371–1374.

Hill, N.R., & Beamish, P.M. (2007). Treatment outcomes for obsessive-compulsive disorder: A critical review. *Journal of Counseling and Development, 85,* 504–510.

Hiniker, P.J. (1999). Chinese reactions to forced compliance: Dissonance reduction or national character? *Journal of Social Psychology, 77,* 157–176.

Hiroto, D.S. (1974). Locus of control and learned helplessness. *Journal of Experimental Psychology, 102,* 187–193.

Hirsch, S., Bowen, J., Emami, J., Cramer, P., Jolley, A., Haw, C., & Dickinson, M. (1996). A one-year prospective study of the effect of life events and medication in the aetiology of schizophrenic relapse. *British Journal of Psychiatry, 168,* 49–56.

Hobson, J.A. (1995). Sleeping and dreaming. In D. Kimbly & A.M. Colman (Eds.), *Biological aspects of behaviour*. London: Longman.

Hodgkinson, P.E. (1987). Responding to inpatient suicide. *British Journal of Medical Psychology, 60*, 387–392.

Hofschire, L.J., & Greenberg, B.S. (2002). Media's impact on adolescents' body dissatisfaction. In J. D. Brown, J. R. Steele, & K. Walsh-Childers (Eds.), *Sexual teens, sexual media*. Mahwah, NJ: Lawrence Erlbaum Associates.

Holland, A.J., Sicotte, N., & Treasure, J. (1988). Anorexia nervosa: Evidence for a genetic basis. *Journal of Psychosomatic Research, 32*, 561–572.

Hollis, K.L. (1997). Contemporary research on Pavlovian conditioning: A "new" functional analysis. *American Psychologist, 52*, 956–965.

Hollon, S.D., DeRubeis, R.J., Shelton, R.C., Amsterdam, J.D., Salomon, R.M., O'Reardon, J.P., et al. (2005). Prevention of relapse following cognitive therapy vs. medications in moderate to severe depression. *Archives of General Psychiatry, 62*, 417–422.

Hollon, S.D., Stewart, M.O., & Strunk, D. (2006). Enduring effects for cognitive behaviour therapy in the treatment of depression and anxiety. *Annual Review of Psychology, 57*, 285–315.

Honorton, C., & Ferrari, D. (1989). Future Telling: A meta-analysis of forced-choice precognition experiments. 1935–1987. *Journal of Parapsychology, 53*, 281–302.

Hopko, D.R., Lejuex, C.W., Armento, M.E.A., & Bare, R.L. (2004). Depressive disorders. In M. Hersen (Ed.), *Psychological assessment in clinical practice: A pragmatic guide*. New York: Taylor & Francis.

Horn, J.M. (1983). The Texas adoption project: Adopted children and their intellectual resemblance to biological and adoptive parents. *Child Development, 54*, 268–275.

Horne, J. (1988). *Why do we sleep? The functions of sleep in humans and other mammals*. Oxford: Oxford University Press.

Horne, J. (1992). Stay awake, stay alive. *New Scientist, 4 January*. Online. Available: http://www.newscientist.com/

Horne, J.A., & Minard, A. (1985). Sleep and sleepiness following a behaviourally "active" day. *Ergonomics, 28*, 567–575.

Horvath, T. (2005). The hardship of obesity: A soft-wired hypothalamus. *Nature Neuroscience, 8*, 561–565.

Horwath, E., Johnson, J., Klerman, G.L., & Weissman, M.M. (1992). Depressive symptoms as relative and attributable risk factors for first onset major depression. *Archives of General Psychiatry, 49*, 817–823.

Houran, J., Navik, S., & Zerrusen, K. (2005). Boundary functioning in celebrity worshippers. *Personality and Individual Differences, 38*, 237–248.

Hovland, C.I., Janis, I.L., & Kelley, H.H. (1953). *Communications and persuasion: Psychological studies in opinion change*. New Haven, CT: Yale University Press.

Hovland, C.I., Lumsdaine, A.A., & Sheffield, R.D. (1949). *Experiments in mass communication*. Princeton, NJ: Princeton University Press.

Hovland, C.I., & Sears, R.R. (1940). Minor studies of aggression: VI. Correlation of lynchings with economic indices. *Journal of Psychology, 9*, 301–310.

Hovland, C.I., & Weiss, W. (1951). The influence of source credibility on communication effectiveness. *Public Opinion Quarterly, 151*, 635–650.

Howe, M.J.A. (1998). *Principles of abilities and human learning*. Hove, UK: Psychology Press.

Howe, M.J.A., & Smith, J. (1988). Calendar calculating in idiots savants: How do they do it? *British Journal of Psychology, 79*, 371–386.

Howe, C., Tolmie, A., & Rodgers, C. (1992). The acquisition of conceptual knowledge in science by primary school children: Group interaction and the understanding of motion down an incline. *British Journal of Developmental Psychology, 10*, 113–130.

Howland, R.H., & Thase, M.E. (1991). Biological studies of dysthymia. *Biological Psychiatry, 30*, 283–304.

Hsu, L.K. (1990). *Eating disorders*. New York: Guilford.

Hüber-Weidman, H. (1976). *Sleep, sleep disturbances and sleep deprivation*. Cologne: Kiepenheuser & Witsch.

Hublin, C., Kaprio, J., Partinen, M., Heikkila, K., & Koskenvuo, M. (1997). Prevalence and genetics of sleepwalking: A population-based twin study. *Neurology, 48*, 177–181.

Hudson, W. (1960). Pictorial depth perception in sub-cultural groups in Africa. *Journal of Social Psychology, 52*, 183–208.

Hudziak, J.J., van Beijsterveldt, C.E., Bartels, M., Rietveld, M.J., Rettew, D.C., Derks, E.M., et al. (2003). Individual differences in aggression. *Behavior Genetics, 33*, 575–589.

Huesmann, L.R., & Eron, L.D. (1986). *Television and the aggressive child: A cross-national comparison*. Hillsdale, NJ: Lawrence Erlbaum Associates.

Huesmann, L.R., Lagerspetz, K., & Eron, L.D. (1984). Intervening variables in the TV violence–aggression relation: Evidence from two countries. *Developmental Psychology, 20*, 746–775.

Hughes, C., & Russell, J. (1993). Autistic children's difficulty with mental disengagement from an object: Its implications for executive dysfunction in autism. *Psychological Medicine, 27*, 209–220.

Hughes, M. (1975). *Egocentrism in preschool children*. Unpublished PhD thesis, University of Edinburgh, UK.

Humphrey, L.L., Apple, R.F., & Kirschenbaum, D.S. (1986). Differentiating bulimic-anorexic from normal families using interpersonal and behavioural observational systems. *Journal of Consulting and Clinical Psychology, 54*, 190–195.

Humphreys, G.W., & Riddoch, M.J. (1987). *To see but not to see: A case study of visual agnosia*. Hove, UK: Psychology Press.

Humphreys, K., Avidan, G., & Behrmann, M. (2007). A detailed investigation of facial expression processing in congenital prosopagnosia as compared to acquired prosopagnosia. *Experimental Brain Research, 176*, 356–373.

Humphreys, P. (2001). *Exam success in AQA A psychology*. London: Routledge.

Humphreys, P.W. (1999). Culture-bound syndromes. *Psychology Review, 6*(3), 14–18.

Hunter, J.E. (1983). *Overview of validity generalization for the U.S. Employment Service*. (USES Test Report No. 43). Washington, DC: US Department of Labor, Employment, and Training Administration.

Hunter, J.E. (1986). Cognitive ability, cognitive aptitudes, job knowledge, and job performance. *Journal of Vocational Behavior, 29*, 340–362.

Hunter, J.E., & Schmidt, F.L. (1996). Intelligence and job performance: Economic and social implications. *Psychology, Public Policy and Law, 2*, 447–472.

Huston, A.C. (1985). The development of sex typing: Themes from recent research. *Developmental Review, 5*, 1–17.

Hyman, R. (1989). The psychology of deception. *Annual Review of Psychology, 40*, 133–154.

Iacoboni, M., Molnar–Szakacs, I., Gallese, V., Buccino, G., Mazziotta, J.C., & Rizzolatti, G. (2005). Grasping the intentions of others with one's own mirror neuron system. *PLOS Biology, 3*, 529–535.

Imperato-McGinley, J., Guerro, L., Gautier, T., & Peterson, R.E. (1974). Steroid 5–reductase deficiency in man: An inherited form of male pseudohermaphroditism. *Science, 186*, 1213–1216.

Ingram, N. (2004). Schizophrenia: Destiny in your genes? *Psychology Review, 10*, 26–28.

Inhelder, B., & Piaget, J. (1958). *The growth of logical thinking from childhood to adolescence.* New York: Basic Books.

Irwin H.J. (2005). *The psychology of paranormal belief.* New York: Parapsychology Foundation.

Irwin, H.J. (1992). Origins and functions of paranormal belief: The role of childhood trauma and interpersonal control. *Journal of the American Society for Psychical Research, 86*, 199–208.

Irwin, H.J. (1993). Belief in the paranormal: A review of the empirical literature. *Journal of the American Society for Psychical Research, 87*(1), 1–39.

Irwin, H.J. (2002). Proneness to self-deception and the two-factor model of paranormal belief. *Journal of the Society for Psychical Research, 66*(2), 80–87.

Irwin, H.J., & Watt, C.A. (2007). *An introduction to parapsychology* (5th Edn). Jefferson, NC: McFarland.

Isawa, N. (1992). Postconventional reasoning and moral education in Japan. *Journal of Moral Education, 21*, 3–16.

Ittelson, W.H. (1951). Size as a cue to distance: Static localisation. *American Journal of Psychology, 64*, 54–67.

Ivory, J.D., & Kalyanaraman, S. (2007). The effects of technological advancement and violent content in video games on players' feelings of presence, involvement, physiological arousal, and aggression. *Journal of Communication, 57*, 532–555.

Iyengar, S., & Kinder, D.R. (1987). *News that matters: Television and American opinion.* Chicago, IL: University of Chicago Press.

Jacobs, J. (1887). Experiments on 'prehension'. *Mind, 12*, 75–79.

Jacobson, A., & Kales, A. (1967). Somnambulism: All-night EEG and related studies. In S.S. Kety, E.V. Evarts & H.L. Williams (Eds.), *Sleep and altered states of consciousness.* Baltimore: Williams and Wilkins.

Jacobson, N.S., Dobson, K.S., Truax, P.A., Addis, M.E., Koerner, K., Gollan, J.K., et al. (1996). A component analysis of cognitive-behavioural treatment for depression. *Journal of Consulting and Clinical Psychology, 64*, 295–304.

Jaeger, B., Ruggiero, G.M., Gomez-Peretta, C., Lang, F., Mohammadkhani, P., Sahleen-Veasey, C., et al. (2002). Body dissatisfaction and its interrelations with other risk factors for bulimia nervosa in 12 countries. *Psychotherapy and Psychosomatics, 71*, 54–61.

Jaffee, S., & Hyde, J.S. (2000). Gender differences in moral orientation: A meta-analysis. *Psychological Bulletin, 126*, 703–726.

Jahoda, G. (1969). *The psychology of superstition.* London: Allen Lane/Penguin.

Jakobsen, K.D., Frederiksen, J.N., Hansen, T., et al. (2005). Reliability of clinical ICD-10 schizophrenia diagnoses. *Nordic Journal of Psychiatry, 59*, 209–212.

Jang, K.L., Vernon, P.A., & Livesley, W. J. (2000). Personality disorder traits, family environment and alcohol misuse: a multivariate behavioural genetic analysis. *Addiction, 95*(6), 873–888.

Janicak, P.G., Davis, J.M, Gibbons, R.D., Ericksen, S., Chang, S., & Gallagher, P. (1985). Efficacy of ECT: A meta-analysis. *American Journal of Psychiatry, 142*, 297–302.

Janis, I.L. (1972). *Victims of groupthink.* Boston: Houghton Mifflin.

Jankowiak, W.R., & Fischer, E.F. (1992). A cross-cultural perspective on romantic love. *Ethnology, 31*, 149–155.

Jansz, J., & Martis, R.G. (2007). The Lara phenomenon: Powerful female characters in video games. *Sex Roles, 56*, 141–148.

Jawer, M. (2006). Environmental sensitivity: Inquiry into a possible link with apparitional experience. *Journal of the Society for Psychical Research, 70*(10), 27–46.

Jenkins, H,M., Barrera, C., Ireland, B., & Woodside, B. (1978). Signal-centred action patterns of dogs in appetitive classical conditioning. *Learning and Motivation, 9*, 272–296.

Jerison, H.J. (1973). *Evolution of the brain and intelligence.* New York: Academic Press.

Jessor, R. (1987). Problem behavior theory, psychosocial development, and adolescent problem drinking. *British Journal of Addiction, 82*, 331–342.

Johns, L.C., Rossell, S., Frith, C., Ahmad, F., Hemsley, D., Kuipers, E., & McGuire, P.K. (2001). Verbal self-monitoring and auditory verbal hallucinations in patients with schizophrenia. *Psychological Medicine, 31*, 705–715.

Johnson, F.L., & Young, K. (2002). Gendered voices in children's television advertising. *Critical Studies in Media Communication, 19*, 361–480.

Johnson, M.H., Dziurawiec, S., Ellis, H., & Morton, J. (1991). Newborns' preferential tracking of face-like stimuli and its subsequent decline. *Cognition, 40*, 1–19.

Johnston, J., & Ettema, J. (1986). Using television to best advantage: Research for prosocial television. In J. Bryant & D. Zillman (Eds.), *Perspectives on media effects.* Hillsdale, NJ: Lawrence Erlbaum Associates.

Johnstone et al. (2006). Food or its expectation sparks brain's hunger centers. *ScienceDaily.* Cell Press (2006, October 4). Online. Available: http://www.sciencedaily.com/releases/2006/10/061003191537.htm [accessed 26 January 2009].

Johnstone, L. (1989). *Users and abusers of psychiatry: A critical look at traditional psychiatric practice.* London: Routledge.

Joireman, J., Anderson, J., & Strathman, A. (2003). The aggression paradox: Understanding links among aggression, sensation seeking, and the consideration of future consequences. *Journal of Personality and Social Psychology, 84*, 1287–1302.

Jones, C. (2002). When your boss is a football hooligan. *Northern Echo.* Retrieved March 18 2009 from: http://archive.thenorthernecho.co.uk/2002/3/20/142071.html

Jones, S. (2004). Psychotherapy of bipolar disorder: A review. *Journal of Affective Disorders, 80*, 101–114.

Jones, W.H., & Russell, D. (1980). The selective processing of belief-disconfirming information. *European Journal of Social Psychology, 10*, 309–312.

Joseph, J. (2003). *The gene illusion: Genetic research in psychiatry and psychology under the microscope.* Ross-on-Wye, UK: PCCS Books.

Josephson, W.L. (1987). Television violence and children's aggression: Testing the priming, social script, and disinhibition predictions. *Journal of Personality and Social Psychology, 53*, 882–890.

Jotangia, D., Moody, A., Stamatakis, E., & Wardle, H. (2005). *Obesity among children under 11.* London: Joint Health Surveys Unit.

Jouvet, M. (1967). Mechanisms of the states of sleep: A neuropharmological approach. *Research Publications of the Association for the Research in Nervous and Mental Disorders, 45*, 86–126.

Joyner, K., & Campa, M. (2005). How do adolescent relationships influence the quality of romantic and sexual relationship in young adulthood? In A. Crouter & A. Booth (Eds.), *Romance and sex in adolescence and emerging adulthood: Risks and opportunities* (pp. 93–101). Mahwah, NJ: Lawrence Erlbaum Associates.

Kalat, J.W. (1998). *Biological psychology*. Pacific Grove, CA: Brooks/Cole Publishing Co.

Kalucy, R.S., Crisp, A.H., & Harding, B. (1977). A study of 56 families with anorexia nervosa. *British Journal of Medical Psychology, 50*, 381–395.

Kamieniecki, G.W., Wade, T., & Tsourtos, G. (1997). Interpretive bias for benign sensations in panic disorder with agoraphobia. *Journal of Anxiety Disorders, 11*, 141–156.

Kamin, L.J. (1969). Predictability, surprise, attention and conditioning. In R. Campbell & R. Church (Eds.), *Punishment and aversive behaviour*. New York: Appleton-Century-Crofts.

Kampf, M., Nachson, I., & Babkoff, H. (2002). A serial test of the laterality of familiar face recognition. *Brain and Cognition, 50*, 35–50.

Kamphuis, J.H., Emmelkamp, P.M.G., & de Vries, V. (2004). Informant personality descriptions of postintimate stalkers using the Five Factor Profile. *Journal of Personality Assessment, 82*, 169–178.

Kanner, L. (1943). Autistic disturbances of affective contact. *Nervous Child, 2*, 217–250.

Kariyawasam, S.H., Zaw, F., & Handley, S.L., (2002). Reduced salivary cortisol in children with comorbid attention deficit hyperactivity disorder and oppositional defiant disorder. *Neuroendocrinology Letters, 23*, 45–48.

Karno, M., Golding, J.M., Sorenson, S.B., & Burnham, M.A. (1988). The epidemiology of obsessive-compulsive disorder in 5 United States communities. *Archives of General Psychiatry, 45*, 1094–1099.

Kashima, Y., Siegal, M., Tanaka, K., & Kashima, E.S. (1992). Do people believe behaviours are consistent with attitudes? Towards a cultural psychology of attribution processes. *British Journal of Social Psychology, 31*, 111–124.

Kavanagh, D.J. (1992). Recent developments in expressed emotion and schizophrenia. *British Journal of Psychiatry, 160*, 601–620.

Kayama, Y., & Koyama, Y. (2003). Control of sleep and wakefulness by brainstem monoaminergic and cholinergic neurons. *Acta Neurochirurgica Supplement, 87*, 3–6.

Keating, D.P., & Clark, L.V. (1980). Development of physical and social reasoning in adolescence. *Developmental Psychology, 16*, 23–30.

Keeley, L.H. (1996). *War before civilization: The myth of the peaceful savage*. New York: Oxford University Press.

Keith, S.J., Regier, D.A., & Rae, D.S. (1991). Schizophrenic disorders. In D.A. Regier & L.N. Robins (Eds.), *Psychiatric disorders in America: The Epidemiologic Catchment Area Study*. New York: Free Press.

Kelleher, R.T. (1958). Fixed-ratio schedule of conditioned reinforcement with chimpanzees. *Journal of the Experimental Analysis of Behavior, 1*, 281–289.

Kellman, P.J., & Spelke, E.S. (1983). Perception of partly occluded objects in infancy. *Cognitive Psychology, 15*, 483–524.

Kelly, T.L., Neri, D.F., Grill, D., Ryman, P.D., Hunt, P.D., Dijk, D-J., Shanahan, T.L., & Czeisler, C. (1999). Nonentrained circadian rhythms of melatonin in submariners scheduled to an 18-hour day. *Journal of Biological Rhythms, 14*, 190–196.

Kendall, P.C., & Hammen, C. (1998). *Abnormal psychology* (2nd Edn). Boston: Houghton Mifflin.

Kendler, K.S. (1995). Adversity, stress and psychopathology: A psychiatric genetic perspective. *International Journal of Method in Psychiatric Research, 5*, 163–170.

Kendler, K.S., Gatz, M.D., Gardner, C.O., & Pedersen, N.L. (2006). Swedish national twin study of lifetime major depression. *American Journal of Psychiatry, 163(1)*, 109–114.

Kendler, K.S., Karkowski, L.M., & Prescott, C.A. (1999). Fears and phobias: Reliability and heritability. *Psychological Medicine, 29(3)*, 539–553.

Kendler, K.S., Maclean, C., Neale, M., Kessler, R., Heath, A., & Eaves, L. (1991). The genetic epidemiology of bulimia nervosa. *American Journal of Psychiatry, 148*, 1627–1637.

Kendler, K.S., Neale, M., Kessler, R., Heath, A., & Eaves, L. (1993). A twin study of recent life events and difficulties. *Archives of General Psychiatry, 50*, 789–796.

Kendler, K.S., Pedersen, N.L., Farahmand, B.Y., & Persson, P.G. (1996). The treated incidence of psychotic and affective illness in twins compared with population expectation: A study in the Swedish Twin and Psychiatric Registries. *Psychological Medicine, 26*, 1135–1144.

Kennedy, N., McDonough, M., Kelly, B., & Berrios, G.E. (2002). Erotomania revisited: Clinical course and treatment. *Comprehensive Psychiatry, 43*, 1–6.

Kephart, W.M. (1967). Some correlates of romantic love. *Journal of Marriage and the Family, 29*, 470–474.

Keren, G., & Wagenaar, W.A. (1985). On the psychology of playing blackjack: Normative and descriptive considerations with implications for decision theory. *Journal of Experimental Psychology, 114*, 133–158.

Kessler, R.C. (1997). The effects of stressful life events on depression. *Annual Review of Psychology, 48*, 191–214.

Kessler, R.C., Chiu, W.T., Demier, O., & Walters, E.E. (2005). Prevalence, severity, and comorbidity of 12-month DSM-IV disorders in the National Comorbidity Survey Replication. *Archives of General Psychiatry, 62*, 617–627.

Kety, S.S. (1974). From rationalisation to reason. *American Journal of Psychiatry, 131*, 957–963.

Kety, S.S. (1975). Biochemistry of the major psychoses. In A. Freedman, H. Kaplan, & B. Sadock (Eds.), *Comprehensive textbook of psychiatry*. Baltimore: Williams & Wilkins.

Keuneman, R.J., Pokos, V., Weerasundera, R., & Castle, D.J. (2005). Antipsychotic treatment in obsessive-compulsive disorder: A literature review. *Australian and New Zealand Journal of Psychiatry, 39*, 336–343.

Keuthen, N. (1980). *Subjective probability estimation and somatic structures in phobic individuals*. Unpublished manuscript, State University of New York at Stony Brook.

Khanna, S., Rajendra, P.N., & Channabasavanna, S.M. (1988). Social adjustment in obsessive compulsive disorder. *International Journal of Social Psychiatry, 34*, 118–122.

Kienlen, K.K., Birmingham, D.L., Solberg, K.B., O'Regan, J.T., & Meloy, J.R. (1997). A comparative study of psychotic and nonpsychotic stalking. *Journal of the American Academy of Psychiatry and the Law, 25*, 317–334.

Kim, S.J., Lyoo, I.K., Lee, Y.S., Sung, Y.H., Kim, H.J., Kim, J.H., et al. (2008). Increased GABA levels in medial prefrontal cortex of young adults with narcolepsy. *Sleep, 31(3)*, 342–347.

Kinder, B.N., Pape, N.E., & Walfish, S. (1980. Drug and alcohol education programmes: A review of outcome studies. *International Journal of the Addictions, 15*, 1035–1054.

Kirby, S.D., Ureda, J.R., Rose, R.L., & Hussey, J. (1998). Peripheral cues and involvement level: Influences on acceptance of a mammography message. *Journal of Health Communication, 3*, 119–135.

Klein, K.E., Wegman, H.M., & Hunt, B.I. (1972). Desynchronisation of body temperature and performance circadian rhythm as a result of outgoing and homegoing transmeridian flights. *Aerospace Medicine, 43*, 119–132.

Klein, R., & Armitage, R. (1979). Rhythms in human performance: 1.5 hour oscillations in cognitive style. *Science, 204*, 1326–1327.

Kleiner, L., & Marshall, W.L. (1987). The role of interpersonal problems in the development of agoraphobia with panic attacks. *Journal of Anxiety Disorders, 1*, 313–323.

Kleinmuntz, B. (1974). *Essentials of abnormal psychology.* New York: Harper & Row.

Kleitman, N. (1963). *Sleep and wakefulness.* Chicago: Chicago University Press.

Klesges, R.C., Vasey, B.S., & Glasgow, R.E. (1986). A worksite smoking modification competition: potential for public health impact. *American Journal of Public Health, 76*, 198–200.

Knickmeyer, R., Baron-Cohen, S., Raggatt, P., & Taylor, K. (2005). Foetal testosterone, social relationships, and restricted interests in children. *Journal of Child Psychology and Psychiatry, 46*, 198–210.

Kohlberg, L. (1966). A cognitive-development analysis of children's sex-role concepts and attitudes. In E.E. Maccoby (Ed.), *The development of sex differences.* Stanford, CA: Stanford University Press.

Kohlberg, L. (1969). Stage and sequence: The cognitive-developmental approach to socialisation. In D.A. Goslin (Ed.), *Handbook of socialisation theory and practice.* Skokie, IL: Rand McNally.

Kohlberg, L. (1975). The cognitive-developmental approach to moral education. *Phi Delta Kappan, June*, 670–677.

Kohlberg, L. (1976). Moral stages and moralization. In T. Likona (Ed.), *Moral development and behaviour.* New York: Holt, Rinehart & Winston.

Kohlberg, L. (1981). *Essays on moral development: Vol. 1. The philosophy of moral development.* San Francisco: Harper & Row.

Kraines, S. H. (1948). *The therapy of neuroses and psychoses.* Philadelphia: Lea and Febiger.

Kranzler, J.H., & Jensen, A.R. (1989). Inspection time and intelligence: A meta-analysis. *Intelligence, 13*, 329–347.

Krivanek, J. (1988). *Addictions.* London: Allen and Unwin.

Krosnick, J.A., & Kinder, D.R. (1990). Altering the foundations of support for the President through priming. *American Political Science Review, 84*, 497–512.

Kruijver, F.P.M., Zhou, J-N., Pool, C.W., Hofman, M.A., Gooren, L.J.G., & Swaab, D.F. (2000). Male-to-female transsexuals have female neuron numbers in a limbic nucleus. *Journal of Clinical Endocrinology & Metabolism, 85*(5), 2034–2041.

Kruk, M.R., Halasz, J., Meelis, W., & Haller, J. (2004). Fast positive feedback between the adrenocortical stress response and a brain mechanism involved in aggressive behavior. *Behavioral Neuroscience, 118*, 1062–1070.

Kudielka, B.M., Federenko, I.S., Hellhammer, D.H., & Wüst, S. (2006). Morningness and eveningness: The free cortisol rise after awakening in "early birds" and "night owls". *Biological Psychology, 72*(2), 141–146.

Kuhn, T.S. (1962). *The structure of scientific revolutions.* Chicago: Chicago University Press.

Kuhn, T.S. (1970). *The structure of scientific revolutions* (2nd Edn). Chicago: Chicago University Press.

Kuhn, T.S. (1977). *The essential tension: Selected studies in scientific tradition and change.* Chicago: Chicago University Press.

Kumar, G. (1993). Low mortality and high morbidity in Kerala reconsidered. *Population and Development Review, 19*(1), 103–121.

Kumar, R., Birrer, B.V.X., Macey, P.M., Woo, M.A., Gupta, R.K., Yan-Go, F.L., & Harper, R.M. (2008). Reduced mammillary body volume in patients with obstructive sleep apnea. *Neuroscience Letters, 438*(3), 330–334.

Kutnick, P.J., & Brees, P. (1982). The development of co-operation: Explorations in cognitive and moral competence and social authority. *British Journal of Educational Psychology, 52*, 361–365.

Ladouceur, R., & Walker, M.B. (1996). A cognitive perspective on gambling. In P.M. Salkovkis (Ed.), *Trends in cognitive and behavioural therapies* (pp. 89–120). Chichester: John Wiley & Sons.

LaGuardia, J.G., Ryan, R.M., Couchman, C.E., & Deci, E.L. (2000). Within-person variation in security of attachment: A self-determination theory perspective on attachment, need fulfilment, and well-being. *Journal of Personality and Social Psychology, 79*, 367–384.

Lai, C-F., Kao, T-W., Wu, M-S., Chiang, S-S., Chang, C-H., Lu, C-S., et al. (2007). Impact of near-death experience on dialysis patients: A multicenter collaborative study. *American Journal of Kidney Diseases, 50*(1), 124–132.

Lam, R.W. (1994). Morning light therapy for winter depression: Predictors of response. *Acta Psychiatrica Scandinavia, 89*(2), 97–101.

Lam, R.W., Levitt, A.J., Levitan, R.D., Enns, M.W., Morehouse, R., Michalak, E.E., & Tam, E.M. (2006). The Can-SAD Study: A randomized controlled trial of the effectiveness of light therapy and fluoxetine in patients with winter seasonal affective disorder. *American Journal of Psychiatry, 163*, 805–812.

Lam, R.W., Tam, E.M., Yatham, L.N., Shiah, I.S., & Zis, A.P. (2001). Seasonal depression: the dual vulnerability hypothesis revisited. *Journal of Affective Disorders, 63*, 123–132.

Lamb, M.E. (1997). *The role of the father in child development* (3rd Edn). New York: Wiley.

Lamm, R.W. (1994). Morning light therapy for winter depression: Predictors of response. *Acta Psychiatrica Scandinavia.*

Lamson, R. (2004). Online. Available: http://www.newscientist.com/channel/health/mental-health/mg14219290.700.html

Langer, E.J. (1975). The illusion of control. *Journal of Personality and Social Psychology, 32*, 311–328.

Langer, E.J., & Roth, J. (1983). Heads you win, tails it's chance: The illusion of control as a function of the sequence of outcomes in a purely chance task. *Journal of Personality and Social Psychology, 32*, 951–955.

Langhinrichsen-Rohling, J., Palarea, R.E., Cohen, J., & Roehling, M.L. (2000). Breaking up is hard to do: Unwanted pursuit behaviours following the dissolution of a romantic relationship. *Violence and Victims, 15*, 73–90.

Langlois, J.H., Roggman, L.A., & Musselman, L. (1994). What is average and what is not average about attractive faces. *Psychological Science, 5*, 214–220.

Laposky, A., Bradley, M., Williams, D., Bass, J., & Turek, F. (2008). Sleep–wake regulation is altered in leptin resistant (db/db) genetically obese and diabetic mice. *American Journal of Physiology: Regulatory, Integrative and Comparative Physiology, October 8.* Online. Available: http://ajpregu.physiology.org/cgi/content/abstract/00026.2008v1

Larkin, M., & Griffiths, M.D. (2004). Dangerous sports and recreational drug-use: Rationalising and contextualising risk. *Journal of Community and Applied Social Psychology, 14*, 215–232.

Laruelle, M., Abi-Dargham, A., Gil, R., Kegeles, L., & Innis, R. (1999). Increased dopamine transmission in schizophrenia: Relationship to illness phases. *Biological Psychiatry, 46*, 56–72.

Lavin, J.H., Wittert, G., Sun, W.M., Horowitz, M., Morley, J.E., & Read, N.W. (1996). Appetite regulation by carbohydrate: Role of blood glucose and gastrointestinal hormones. *American Journal of Physiology: Endocrinology and Metabolism, 271*, 209–214.

Lawrence, T., Edwards, C., Barraclough, N., Church, S., & Hetherington, F. (1995). Modelling childhood causes of paranormal belief and experience: Childhood trauma and childhood fantasy. *Personality and Individual Differences*, 19(2), 209–215.

Leader, T., Mullen, B., & Abrams, D. (2007). Without mercy: The immediate impact of group size on lynch mob atrocity. *Personality and Social Psychology Bulletin*, 33(10), 1340–1352.

LeBlanc, M., Beaulieu-Bonneau, S., Mérette, C., Savard, J., Ivers, H., & Morin, C.M. (2007). Psychological and health-related quality of life factors associated with insomnia in a population-based sample. *Journal of Psychosomatic Research*, 63(2), 157–166.

Leenstra, A.S., Ormel, J., & Giel, R. (1995). Positive life changes and recovery from depression and anxiety: A 3-stage longitudinal study of primary care attenders. *British Journal of Psychiatry*, 166, 333–343.

Leff, J., Wig, N.N., Bedi, H., Menon, D.K., et al. (1990). Relatives' expressed emotion and the course of schizophrenia in Chandigarh: A 2-year follow-up of a first-contact sample. *British Journal of Psychiatry*, 156, 351–356.

Lehman, A. (1898). *Aberglaube und Zauberei*. Stuttgart: Enke.

Leibowitz, H., Brislin, R., Permutter, L., & Hennessy, R. (1969). Ponzo perspective illusions as a manifestation of space perception. *Science*, 166, 1174–1176.

Leichsenring, F. (2001). Comparative effects of short-term psychodynamic psychotherapy and cognitive-behavioural therapy in depression: A meta-analytic approach. *Clinical Psychology Review*, 21, 401–419.

Leon, G.R. (1984). *Case histories of deviant behaviour* (3rd Edn). Boston: Allyn & Bacon.

Leonard, W.R. (2002). Food for thought: Dietary change was a driving force in human evolution. *Scientific American*, 287(6), 106–15.

LeUnes, A.D., Nation, J.R., & Turley, N.M. (1980). Male–female performance in learned helplessness. *Journal of Psychology*, 104, 255–258.

Levi, D.M. (2005). Perceptual learning in adults with amblyopia: A re-evaluation of critical periods in human vision. *Developmental Psychobiology*, 46, 222–232.

Levin, R.B., & Gross, A.M. (1985). The role of relaxation in systematic desensitization. *Behavior Research and Therapies*, 23(2), 187–196.

Levine, R., Sato, S., Hashimoto, T., & Verma, J. (1995). Love and marriage in eleven cultures. *Journal of Cross-Cultural Psychology*, 26, 554–571.

Levinson, D.J. (1978). *The seasons of a man's life*. New York: Ballantine.

Levinson, D.J. (1986). A conception of adult development. *American Psychologist*, 41(1), 3–13.

Levinson, D.J., Darrow, C.N., Klein, E.B., Levinson, M.H., & McKee, B. (1978). *The seasons of a man's life*. New York: Knopf.

Levy, M.R. (1979). Watching television news as parasocial interaction. *Journal of Broadcasting*, 23, 69–80.

Lewinsohn, P.M. (1974). A behavioural approach to depression. In R.J. Friedman & M.M. Katz (Eds.), *The psychology of depression: Contemporary theory and research*. Washington, DC: Winston-Wiley.

Lewinsohn, P.M., Hoberman, H.M., & Rosenbaum, M. (1988). A prospective study of risk factors for unipolar depression. *Journal of Abnormal Psychology*, 97, 251–264.

Lewinsohn, P.M., Joiner, T.E., Jr., & Rohde, P. (2001). Evaluation of cognitive diathesis–stress models in predicting major depressive disorder in adolescents. *Journal of Abnormal Psychology*, 110, 203–215.

Lewinsohn, P.M., Munoz, R.F., Youngren, M.A., & Zeiss, A.M. (1992). *Control your depression*. New York: Simon & Schuster.

Lewinsohn, P.M., Rohde, P., & Seeley, J.R. (1995). Adolescent psychopathology 3: The clinical consequences of comorbidity. *Journal of the American Academy of Child and Adolescent Psychiatry*, 34, 510–519.

Lewinsohn, P.M., Youngren, M.A., & Grosscup, S.J. (1979). Reinforcement and depression. In R.A. Dupue (Ed.), The psychobiology of depressive disorders: *Theory, Research, and Practice*, 47, 322–334.

Lewis, S.F., Fremouw, W.J., Del Ben, K., & Farr, C. (2001). An investigation of the psychological characteristics of stalkers: Empathy, problem-solving, attachment and borderline personality features. *Journal of Forensic Sciences*, 46, 80–84.

Leyens, J.-P., Camino, L., Parke, R.D., & Berkowitz, L. (1975). Effects of movie violence on aggression in a field setting as a function of group dominance and cohesion. *Journal of Personality and Social Psychology*, 32, 346–360.

Leykin, Y., Amsterdam, J.D., DeRubeis, R.J., Gallop, R., Shelton, R.C., & Hollon, S.D. (2007). Progressive resistance to a selective serotonin reuptake inhibitor but not to cognitive therapy in the treatment of major depression. *Journal of Consulting and Clinical Psychology*, 75, 267–276.

Liben, L.S., & Signorella, M.L. (1993). Gender-schematic processing in children: The role of initial interpretation of stimuli. *Developmental Psychology*, 29, 141–149.

Lichtman, S., Pisarska, K., Berman, E., Pestone, M., Dowling, H., Offenbacher, E., et al. (1992). Discrepancy between self-reported and actual caloric intake and exercise in obese subjects. *New England Journal of Medicine*, 327, 1947–1948.

Licinio, J., Caglayan, S., Ozata, M., Yildiz, B.O., de Miranda, P.B., O'Kirwan, F, et al. (2004). Phenotypic effects of leptin replacement on morbid obesity, diabetes mellitus, hypogonadism, and behavior in leptin-deficient adults. *Proceedings of the National Academy of Sciences USA*, 101, 4531–4536.

Licinio, J., Milane, M., Thakur, S., Whelan, F., Yildiz, B.O., Delibasi, T., et al. (2007). Effects of leptin on intake of specific micro- and macro-nutrients in a woman with leptin gene deficiency studied off and on leptin at stable body weight. *Appetite*, 49, 594–599.

Licinio, J., Ribeiro, L., Busnello, J.V., Delibasi, T., Thakur, S., Elashoff, R.M., et al. (2007). Effects of leptin replacement on macro- and micronutrient preferences. *International Journal of Obesity*, 31, 1859–1863.

Lieb, R., Wittchen, H.U., Hofler, M., Fuetsch, M., Stein, M.B., & Merikangas, K.R. (2000). Parental psychopathology, parenting styles, and the risk of social phobia in offspring: A prospective longitudinal community study. *Archives of General Psychiatry*, 57, 859–866.

Liebowitz, M.R., Heimberg, R.G., Schneier, F.R., Hope, D.A., et al. (1999). Cognitive-behavioural group therapy versus phenelzine in social phobia: Long-term outcome. *Depression and Anxiety*, 10, 89–98.

Lightweis-Goff, J. (2007). "Blood at the root": Lynching, memory, and Freudian group psychology. *Psychoanalysis, Culture and Society*, 12, 288–295.

Lin, L., Faraco, J., Li, R., Kadotani, H., Rogers, W., Lin, X., et al. (1999). The sleep disorder canine narcolepsy is caused by a mutation in the *hypocretin* (orexin) receptor 2 gene. *Cell*, 98(3), 365–376.

Lindemann, M., & Aarnio, K. (2007). Superstitious, magical and paranormal beliefs: An integrative model. *Journal of Research in Personality*, 4, 731–744.

Lindemann, M., & Saher, M. (2007). Vitalism, purpose and superstition. *British Journal of Psychology, 98,* 33–44.

Linnell, M., & Fluck, M. (2001). The effects of maternal support for counting and cardinal understanding in preschool children. *Social Development, 10,* 202–220.

Lisle, A.M. (2007). Assessing learning styles of adults with intellectual difficulties. *Journal of Intellectual Disabilities, 11,* 23–45.

Lissauer, H. (1890). A case of visual agnosia with a contribution to theory. *Archiv für Psychiatrie, 21,* 222–270. [Translated by T. Shallice & M. Jackson (1988) Lissauer on agnosia. *Cognitive Neuropsychology, 5,* 153–192.]

Lobel, T.E., & Menashri, J. (1993). Relations of conceptions of gender-role transgressions and gender constancy to gender-typed toy preferences. *Developmental Psychology, 29,* 150–155.

Lochner, C., & Stein, D.J. (2003). Heterogeneity of obsessive-compulsive disorder: A literature review. *Harvard Review of Psychiatry, 11,* 113–132.

Loehlin, J.C., Horn, J.M., & Willerman, L. (1989). Modeling IQ change: Evidence from the Texas Adoption Project. *Child Development, 60,* 893–904.

Loehlin, J.C., & Nichols, R.C. (1976). *Heredity, environment and personality.* Austin, TX: University of Texas Press.

Logue, A.W. (2004). *The psychology of eating and drinking.* Routledge: New York.

Lohmann, H., Carpenter, M., & Call, J. (2005). Guessing versus choosing—and seeing versus believing—in false belief tasks. *British Journal of Developmental Psychology, 23,* 451–469.

London, E. (2007). Brain circuits that control hunger identified. *Science Daily,* 30 October. Online. Available: http://www.sciencedaily.com/releases/2007/10/071029172913.htm [accessed 12 October 2008].

Longstreth, W.T. Jr., Koepsell, T.D., Ton, T.G., Hendrickson, A.F., & van Belle, G. (2007). The epidemiology of narcolepsy. *Sleep, 30,* 13–26.

Lopez-Jimenez, F. (2008). *Fat nation: Three out of four UK adults are overweight.* Online. Available: http://www.dailymail.co.uk/health/article-1070029/Fat-nation-Three-UK-adults-overweight.html

Lott, B.E. (1994). *Women's lives: Theories and variations in gender learning.* Pacific Grove, CA: Brooks Cole.

Lourenço, O., & Machado, A. (1996). In defence of Piaget's theory: A reply to 10 common criticisms. *Psychological Review, 103,* 143–164.

Lovelace, V., & Huston, A.C. (1982). Can television teach prosocial behaviour? *Prevention in Human Services, 2,* 93–106.

Luce, G.G. (1971). *Body time: Physiological rhythms and social stress.* New York: Pantheon.

Lugaresi, E., Medori, R., Montagna, P., Baruzzi, A., Cortelli, P., Lugaressi, A., et al. (1986). Fatal familial insomnia and dysautonomia in the selective degeneration of thalamic nuclei. *New England Journal of Medicine, 315,* 997–1003.

Lundy, A., & Rosenberg, J.A. (1987). Androgyny, masculinity, and self-esteem. *Social Behavior and Personality, 15,* 91–95.

Luty, J. (2003). What works in drug addiction? *Advances in Psychiatric Treatment, 9,* 280–288.

Mac an Ghail, M. (1994). *The making of men: Masculinities, sexualities and schooling.* Milton Keynes: Open University Press.

Maccoby, E.E. (1990). The role of gender identity and gender constancy in sex-differentiated development. *New directions for child development, 47,* 5–20.

Maccoby, E. (1998). *The two sexes: Growing up apart, coming together.* Cambridge, MA: Harvard University Press.

Maccoby, E.E., & Jacklin, C.N. (1974). *The psychology of sex differences.* Stanford, CA: Stanford University Press.

Macey, P.M., Henderson, L. A., Macey, K.E., Alger, J.R., Frysinger, R.C., Woo, M.A., et al. (2002). Brain morphology associated with obstructive sleep apnea. *American Journal of Respiratory and Critical Care Medicine, 166,* 1382–1387.

Macht, M., & Dettmer, E.D. (2006). Everyday mood and emotions after eating a chocolate bar or an apple. *Appetite, 46*(33), 332–336.

Mackintosh, N.J. (1998). *IQ and human intelligence.* Oxford: Oxford University Press.

MacLean, P.D. (1970). The triune brain, emotion, and scientific bias. In F.O. Schmitt (Ed.), *The neurosciences: Second study programme.* New York: Rockefeller University Press.

MacLean, P.D. (1982). On the origin and progressive evolution of the triune brain. In E. Armstrong & D. Falk (Eds.), *Primate brain evolution.* New York: Plenum Press.

MacLeod, A. (1998). Abnormal psychology. In M.W. Eysenck (Ed.), *Psychology: An integrated approach.* Harlow, UK: Addison Wesley Longman.

Magee, W.J. (1999). Effects of negative life experiences on phobia onset. *Social Psychiatry and Psychiatric Epidemiology, 34,* 343–351.

Malott, R.W., Malott, M.K., & Pokrzywinski, J. (1967). The effects of outward pointing arrowheads on the Müller–Lyer illusion in pigeons. *Psychonomic Science, 9,* 55–56.

Maltby, J., Day, L., McCutcheon, L.E., Houran, J., & Ashe, D. (2006). Extreme celebrity worship, fantasy proneness and dissociation: Developing the measurement and understanding of celebrity worship within a clinical personality context. *Personality and Individual Differences, 40,* 273–283.

Maltby, J., Houran, J., & McCutcheon, L.E. (2003). A clinical interpretation of attitudes and behaviours associated with celebrity worship. *Journal of Nervous and Mental Disease, 191,* 25–29.

Mandler, G. (1967). Organisation and memory. In K.W. Spence & J.T. Spence (Eds.), *Advances in research and theory: Vol. 1. The psychology of learning and motivation:* London: Academic Press.

Manning, M. (1994). *Undercurrents: A therapist's reckoning with depression.* New York: HarperCollins.

Manuck, S., Flory, J., Ferrell, R., Mann, J., & Muldoon, M. (2000). A regulatory polymorphism of the monoamine oxidase: A gene may be associated with variability in aggression, impulsivity, and central nervous system serotonergic responsivity. *Psychiatry Research, 95*(1), 9–23.

Marder, S.R., Wirshing, W.C., Mintz, J., McKenzie, J. et al. (1996). Two-year outcome of social skills training and group psychotherapy for outpatients with schizophrenia. *American Journal of Psychiatry, 153,* 1585–1592.

Mark, A.L. (2006). Dietary therapy for obesity is a failure and pharmacotherapy is the future: A point of view. *Clinical and Experimental Pharmacology and Physiology, 33*(9), 857–862.

Marks, I.M., Swinson, R.P., Basoglu, M., Kuch, K., et al. (1993). Alprazolam and exposure alone and combined in panic disorder with agoraphobia: A controlled study in London and Toronto. *British Journal of Psychiatry, 162,* 776–787.

Marlatt, G.A., & Gordon, J.R. (1985). *Relapse prevention maintenance strategies in the treatment of addictive behaviors.* New York: Guilford.

Marlatt, G.A., Baer, J.S., Donovan, D.M., & Kivlahan, D.R. (1988). Addictive behaviors: Etiology and treatment. *Annual Review of Psychology, 39,* 223–252.

Marmor, J. (1956). Some observations on superstitions in contemporary life. *American Journal of Orthopsychiatry, 26,* 119–130.

Marsh, P., Rosser, E., & Harré, R. (1978). *The rules of disorder.* London: Routledge & Kegan Paul.

Marteinsdottir, I., Svensson, A., Svedberg, M., Anderberg, U.M., & Von Knorring, L. (2007). The role of life events in social phobia. *Nordic Journal of Psychiatry*, 61, 207–212.

Martin, C.L., & Halverson, C.F. (1983). The effects of sex-typing schemas on young children's memory. *Child Development*, 54, 563–574.

Martin, C.L., & Halverson, C.F. (1987). The roles of cognition in sex role acquisition. In D.B. Carter (Ed.), *Current conceptions of sex roles and sex typing: Theory and research*. New York: Praeger.

Martin, C.L., Wood, C.H., & Little, J.K. (1990). The development of gender stereotype components. *Child Development*, 61, 1891–1904.

Maslow, A.H. (1954). *Motivation and personality*. New York: Harper.

Maslow, A.H. (1968). *Toward a psychology of being* (2nd Edn). New York: Van Nostrand.

Mason, P., Harrison, G., Croudace, T., Glazebrook, C., & Medley, I. (1997). The predictive validity of a diagnosis of schizophrenia: A report from the International Study of Schizophrenia (ISoS) co-ordinated by the World Health Organisation and the Department of Psychiatry, University of Nottingham. *British Journal of Psychiatry*, 170, 321–327.

Masters, J.C., Ford, M.E., Arend, R., Grotevant, H.D., & Clark, L.V. (1979). Modelling and labelling as integrated determinants of children's sex-typed imitative behaviour. *Child Development*, 50, 364–371.

Mataix-Cols, D., Cowley, A.J., Hankin, M., Schneider, A., et al. (2005). Reliability and validity of the Work and Social Adjustment Scale in phobic disorders. *Comprehensive Psychiatry*, 46, 223–228.

Mathalon, D.H., Ford, J.M., Turken, U., Gray, M., Whitfield, S., Kalba, S., et al. (2001). Self-monitoring deficits in schizophrenia: ERP and fMRI evidence. *International Journal of Psychophysiology*, 41, 203.

Matlin, M.W., & Foley, H.J. (1997). *Sensation and perception* (4th. Edn). Boston: Allyn & Bacon.

Matochik, J.A., London, E., Yildiz, B.O., Ozata, M., Caglayan, S., DePaoli, A.M., et al. (2005). Effect of leptin replacement on brain structure in genetically leptin-deficient adults. *The Journal of Clinical Endocrinology & Metabolism*, 90(5), 2851–2854.

Matsumoto, D. (1994). *People: Psychology from a cultural perspective*. California: Brooks/Cole.

Maurer, D., Lewis, T.L., Brent, H.P., & Levin, A.V. (1999). Rapid improvement in the acuity of infants after visual input. *Science*, 286, 108–110.

Maurer, D., Lewis, T.L., & Mondloch, C.J. (2005). Missing sights: Consequences for visual cognitive development. *Trends in Cognitive Sciences*, 9, 144–151.

McCartney, K., Harris, M.J., & Bernieri, F. (1990). Growing up and growing apart: A developmental meta-analysis of twin studies. *Psychological Bulletin*, 107, 226–237.

McClintock, M.K. (1971). Menstrual synchrony and suppression. *Nature*, 229, 244.

McCombs, M.E., & Shaw, D.L. (1972). Agenda-setting function of mass media. *Public Opinion Quarterly*, 36, 176–185.

McConaghy, M.J. (1979). Gender permanence and the genital basis of gender: Stages in the development of constancy of gender identity. *Child Development*, 50, 1223–1226.

McCutcheon, L.E. (2002). Are parasocial relationship styles reflected in love styles? *Current Research in Social Psychology*, 7, 82–94.

McCutcheon, L.E., Ashe, D.D., Houran, J., & Maltby, J. (2003). A cognitive profile of individuals who tend to worship celebrities. *Journal of Psychology*, 137, 309–322.

McCutcheon, L.E., Lange, R., & Houran, J. (2002). Conceptualisation and measurement of celebrity worship. *British Journal of Psychology*, 93, 67–87.

McDaniel, M.A. (2005). Big-brained people are smarter: A meta-analysis of the relationship between in vivo brain volume and intelligence. *Intelligence*, 33, 337–346.

McEwan, T., Mullen, P.E., & Purcell, R. (2007). Identifying risk factors in stalking: A review of current research. *International Journal of Law and Psychiatry*, 30, 1–9.

McFadden, J. (2004). *Warrior blood*. Online. Available: http://www.surrey.ac.uk/qe/articles/The%20TimesJul2004.htm

McFarlane, J., Martin, C.L., & Williams, T.M. (1988). Mood fluctuations: Women versus men and menstrual versus other cycles. *Psychology of Women Quarterly*, 12, 201–223.

McFarlane, W.R., Dixon, L., Lukens, E., & Lucksted, A. (2003). Family psychoeducation and schizophrenia: A review of the literature. *Journal of Marital and Family Therapy*, 29, 223–245.

McGarrigle, J., & Donaldson, M. (1974). Conservation accidents. *Cognition*, 3, 341–350.

McGovern, D., & Cope, R. (1987). First psychiatric admission rates of first and second generation Afro-Caribbeans. *Social Psychiatry*, 22, 139–149.

McGreal, C. (2008). Nigeria takes on big tobacco over campaigns that target the young. *The Guardian*, 15 January.

McGuffin, P., Katz, R., Watkins, S., & Rutherford, J. (1996). A hospital-based twin register of the heritability of DSM-IV unipolar depression. *Archives of General Psychiatry*, 53, 129–136.

McGuigan, F.J. (1966). Covert oral behaviour and auditory hallucinations. *Psychophysiology*, 3, 421–428.

McGuire, P.K., Silbersweig, D.A., Wright, I., Murray, R.M., Frackowiak, R.S.J., & Frith, C.D. (1996). The neural correlates of inner speech and auditory verbal imagery in schizophrenia: Relationship to auditory verbal hallucinations. *British Journal of Psychiatry*, 169, 148–159.

McGurk, H., & MacDonald, J. (1976). Hearing lips and seeing voices. *Nature*, 264, 746–748.

McIlwraith, R., Jacobvitz, R.S., Kubey, R., & Alexander, A. (1991). Television addiction: Theories and data behind the ubiquitous metaphor. *American Behavioral Scientist*, 35, 104–121.

McKenna, S.P. (1996). Measuring quality of life in schizophrenia. *European Psychiatry*, 12, S267–S274.

McKenzie, S.J., Williamson, D.A., & Cubic, B.A. (1993). Stable and reactive body image disturbances in bulimia nervosa. *Behavior Therapy*, 24, 1958–2220.

McKeon, J., Roa, B., & Mann, A. (1984). Life events and personality traits in obsessive-compulsive neurosis. *British Journal of Psychiatry*, 144, 185–189.

McKone, E., Kanwisher, N., & Duchaine, B.C. (2007). Can generic expertise explain special processing for faces? *Trends in Cognitive Sciences*, 11, 8–15.

McMullen, P.A., Shore, D.I., & Henderson, R.B. (2000). Testing a two-component model of face identification: Effects of inversion, contrast reversal, and direction of lighting. *Perception*, 29, 609–619.

McMurran, M. (1994). *The psychology of addiction*. London: Taylor and Francis.

Mead, M. (1935). *Sex and temperament in three primitive societies*. New York: Morrow.

Meddis, R. (1975a). On the function of sleep. *Animal Behaviour*, 23, 676–691.

Meddis, R. (1975b). *Statistical handbook for non-statisticians*. London: McGraw-Hill.

Meddis, R. (1979). The evolution and function of sleep. In D.A. Oakley & H.C. Plotkin (Eds.), *Brain, behaviour and evolution*. London: Methuen.

Mellanby, A. R., Rees, J. B., & Tripp, J. H. (2000). Peer-led and adult-led school health education: a critical review of available comparative research. *Health Education Research, 15*(5), 533–545.

Melville, J. (1978). *Phobias and obsessions*. New York: Penguin.

Meltzer, H.Y. (1999). Outcome in schizophrenia: Beyond symptom reduction. *Journal of Clinical Psychiatry, 60*, 3–8.

Mendoza, C.A. (2006). Structural causes and diffusion processes of collective violence: Understanding lynch mobs in post-conflict Guatemala. Online. Available: http://www.nd.edu/~cmendoz1/collectiveviolencelasa2006.pdf

Menzel, E.W. (1978). Cognitive mapping in chimpanzees. In S.H. Hulse, F. Fowler, & W.K. Honig (Eds.), *Cognitive processes in animal behaviour*. Hillsdale, NJ: Lawrence Erlbaum Associates.

Menzies, R.G., & Clarke, J.C. (1993). The aetiology of childhood water phobia. *Behaviour Research and Therapy, 31*, 499–501.

Merari, A. (2006). Psychological aspects of suicide terrorism in B.M. Bongar, B. Bongar, L.M. Brown, L.E. Beutler, & P.G. Zimbardo (Eds.), *Psychology of Terrorism*. New York: Oxford University Press.

Merckelbach, H., de Jong, P.J., Muris, P., & van den Hout, M.A. (1996). The etiology of specific phobias: A review. *Clinical Psychology Review, 16*, 337–361.

Miele, F. (2002). *Intelligence, race, and genetics: Conversations with Arthur R. Jensen*. Boulder, CO: Westview.

Miles, L.E.M., Raynal, D.M., & Wilson, M.A. (1977). Blind man living in normal society has circadian rhythms of 24.9 hours. *Science, 198*, 421–423.

Milgram, S. (1963). Behavioural study of obedience. *Journal of Abnormal and Social Psychology, 67*, 371–378.

Milgram, S. (1974). *Obedience to authority: An experimental view*. New York: Harper & Row.

Miller, G.R., & Steinberg, M. (1975). *Between people: A new analysis of interpersonal communication*. Palo Alto, CA: Science Research Associates.

Miller, J., & Boggs, M. (2007). *Project everlasting*. Simon & Schuster: New York.

Miller, J.G., Bersoff, D.M., & Harwood, P.L. (1997). Perceptions of social responsibilities in India and the United States: Moral imperatives or personal decisions. In L.A. Peplau & S.E. Taylor (Eds.), *Sociocultural perspectives in social psychology* (pp. 113–144). Upper Saddle River, NJ: Prentice Hall.

Miller, K. (2005). *Communication theories*. New York: McGraw Hill.

Miller, R.R., Barnet, R.C., & Grahame, N.J. (1995). Assessment of the Rescorla–Wagner model. *Psychological Bulletin, 117*, 363–386.

Miller, W.C., Koceja, D.M., & Hamilton, E.J. (1997). A meta-analysis of the past 25 years of weight-loss research using diet, exercise or diet plus exercise intervention. *International Journal of Obesity Related Metabolic Disorders, 21*, 941–947.

Miller, W.R. (1980). *The addictive behaviours*. Oxford: Pergamon Press.

Miller, W.R., & Rollnick, S. (2002). *Motivational interviewing: Preparing people to change addictive behaviour*. New York: Guilford Press.

Miller, W.R., & Seligman, M.E.P. (1975). Depression and learned helplessness in man. *Journal of Abnormal Psychology, 84*, 228–238.

Miller, W.R., Gribskov, C.J., & Mortell, R.L. (1981). Effectiveness of a self-control manual for problem drinkers with and without therapist contact. *International Journal of the Addictions, 16*, 1247–1254.

Milner, A.D., & Goodale, M.A. (1995). *The visual brain in action* (Oxford Psychology series, no. 27, p. xvii). Oxford: Oxford University Press.

Milner, A.D., & Goodale, M.A. (1998). The visual brain in action. *Psyche, 4*, 1–14.

Milton, J. (1997). Meta-analysis of free-response ESP studies without altered states of consciousness. *Journal of Parapsychology, 61*, 279–319.

Mineka, S., Davidson, M., Cook, M., & Kuir, R. (1984). Observational conditioning of snake fear in rhesus monkeys. *Journal of Abnormal Psychology, 93*, 355–372.

Minuchin, S., Roseman, B.L., & Baker, L. (1978). *Psychosomatic families: Anorexia nervosa in context*. Cambridge, MA: Harvard University Press.

Mischler, E.G., & Waxler, N.E. (1968). Interaction in families: An experimental study of family processes and schizophrenia. In A. Smith (Ed.), *Childhood schizophrenia*. New York: Wiley.

Mitchell, R.L.C., & Crow, T.J. (2005). Right hemisphere language functions and schizophrenia: The forgotten hemisphere? *Brain, 128*, 963–978.

Mitte, K. (2005). Meta-analysis of cognitive-behavioural treatments for generalised anxiety disorder: A comparison with pharmacotherapy. *Psychological Bulletin, 131*, 785–795.

Mohanty, A., Gitelman, D.R., Small, D.M., & Mesulam, M.M. (2008). The spatial attention network interacts with limbic and monoaminergic systems to modulate motivation-induced attention shifts. *Cerebral Cortex, 18*(11), 2604–2613. Online. Available: http://cercor.oxfordjournals.org/cgi/content/abstract/bhn021v1

Møller, A.P. (1990). Effects of a haematophagous mite on the barn swallow *Hirundo rustica*: A test of the Hamilton and Zuk hypothesis. *Evolution, 44*, 771–784.

Money, J., & Ehrhardt, A.A. (1972). *Man and woman, boy and girl*. Baltimore: Johns Hopkins University Press.

Monk, T. (2001, December 1). *In space, no one gets to sleep*. Retrieved March 16 2009, from http://www.newscientist.com/article/mg17223192.000-in-space-no-one-gets-to-sleep.html

Monk, T.H., & Folkard, S. (1983). Circadian rhythms and shiftwork. In R. Hockey (Ed.), *Stress and fatigue in human performance*. Chichester: Wiley.

Montagna, P., Gambetti, P., Cortelli, P., & Lugaresi, E. (2003). Familial and sporadic fatal insomnia. *Lancet Neurology, 2*(3), 167–176.

Montague, A. (1968). *The natural superiority of women*. New York: Macmillan.

Monteleone, P., Santonastaso, P., Mauri, M., Bellodi, L., Erzegovesi, S., Fuschino, A., et al. (2007). Investigation of the serotonin transporter regulatory region polymorphism in bulimia nervosa: Relationships to harm avoidance, nutritional parameters, and psychiatric comorbidity. *Psychosomatic Medicine, 68*, 99–103.

Moody, R.A. (1975). *Life after life*. New York: Bantam Books.

Moore, B.R. (1973). The form of the auto-shaped response with food or water reinforcers. *Journal of the Experimental Analysis of Behavior, 20*, 163–181.

Moore-Ede, M., Sulzman, F., & Fuller, C. (1982). *The clocks that time us: Physiology of the circadian timing system*. Cambridge, MA: Harvard University Press.

Morgan, E. (1995). Measuring time with a biological clock. *Biological Sciences Review, 7*, 2–5.

Morris, R.L. (1986). Minimising subject fraud in parapsychology. *European Journal of Parapsychology, 6,* 137–149.

Morton, J., & Johnson, M.H. (1991). CONSPEC and CONLEARN: A two-process theory of infant face recognition. *Psychological Review, 98,* 164–181.

Moscovitch, M., Winocur, G., & Behrmann, M. (1997). What is special about face recognition? Nineteen experiments on a person with visual object agnosia and dyslexia but normal face recognition. *Journal of Cognitive Neuroscience, 9,* 555–604.

Moss, E. (1992). The socioaffective context of joint cognitive activity. In L.T. Winegar & J. Valsiner (Eds.), *Children's development within social context: Vol. 2. Research and methodology.* Hillsdale, NJ: Lawrence Erlbaum Associates, Inc.

Mousseau (2003). Parapsychology – science or pseudoscience? *Journal of Scientific Exploration, 17*(2), 271–282.

Mowrer, O.H. (1947). On the dual nature of learning: A re-interpretation of "conditioning" and "problem-solving". *Harvard Educational Review, 17,* 102–148.

Muhlberger, A., Wiedemann, G., & Pauli, P. (2003). Efficacy of a one-session virtual reality exposure. *Psychotherapy Research, 13*(3), 323–336.

Mukhametov, L.M. (1984). Sleep in marine mammals. In A. Borbely & J.L. Valatx (Eds.), *Sleep mechanisms* [Experimental Brain Research Suppl. 8]. Berlin, Germany: Springer-Verlag.

Mulac, A., Bradac, J.J., & Mann, S.K. (1985). Male/female language differences and attributional consequences in children's television. *Human Communication Research, 11*(4), 481–506.

Müller, U., Zelazo, P.D., & Imrisek, S. (2005). Executive function and children's understanding of false belief: How specific is the relation? *Cognitive Development, 20,* 173–189.

Munroe, R.H., Shimmin, H.S., & Munroe, R.L. (1984). Gender understanding and sex-role preferences in four cultures. *Developmental Psychology, 20,* 673–682.

Muris, P., Merckelbach, H., & Clavan, M. (1997). Abnormal and normal compulsions. *Behaviour Research and Therapy, 35,* 249–252.

Murry, V.M., Kotchick, B.A., Wallace, S., Ketchen, B., Eddings, K., Heller, L., & Collier, I. (2004). Race, culture, and ethnicity: Implications for a community intervention. *Journal of Child & Family Studies, 13*(1), 81–100.

Murstein, B.I., MacDonald, M.G., & Cerreto, M. (1977). A theory and investigation of the effects of exchange-orientation on marriage and friendship. *Journal of Marriage and the Family, 39,* 543–548.

Myhill, A., & Allen, J. (2002). *Rape and sexual assault of women: the extent and nature of the problem.* Home Office Research Study No. 237. London: Home Office.

Myin-Germeys, I., Krabbendam, L., Delespaul, P., et al. (2003). Do life events have their effects on psychosis by influencing the emotional reactivity to daily life stress? *Psychological Medicine, 33,* 327–333.

Nail, P.R., Correll, J.S., Drake, C.E., Glenn, S.B., Scott, G.M., & Stuckey, C. (2001). A validation study of the preference for consistency scale. *Personality and Individual Differences, 31,* 1193–1202.

Naito, T., Lin, W.Y., & Gielen, U.P. (2001). Moral development in East Asian societies: A selective review of the cross-cultural literature. *Psychologia: An International Journal of the Orient, 44,* 148–160.

Nasser, M. (1986). Eating disorders: The cultural dimension. *Social Psychiatry and Psychiatric Epidemiology, 23,* 184–187.

National Institute of Neurological Disorders and Stroke (2007). *Brain basics: Understanding sleep.* Online. Available: http://www.ninds.nih.gov/disorders/brain_basics/understanding_sleep.htm

National Institute on Drug Abuse (NIDA) (1999). *Principles of drug addiction treatment: A research-based guide.* Bethesda, MD: NIDA.

National Television Violence Study (1997). *National Television Violence Study, Volume 2.* Studio City, CA: Mediascope.

Neisser, U. (1976). *Cognition and reality.* San Francisco: W.H. Freeman.

Nelson, S. (2004). Attribution, addiction and gambling: Series conclusion. Brief Addiction Science Information Service (BASIS), 17 March. Online. Available: http://www.basisonline.org/2004/03/the-wager-vol-2.html

Nesse, M., & Williams, C. (1995). *Evolution and healing: The new science of Darwinian medicine.* London: Weidenfeld & Nicolson.

Nesse, R.M. (2000). Is depression an adaptation? *Archives of General Psychiatry, 57,* 14–20.

Nestadt, G., Samuels, J., Riddle, M., Bienvenu, O.J., et al. (2000). A family study of obsessive-compulsive disorder. *Archives of General Psychiatry, 57,* 358–363.

Neubauer, A.C. (1997). The mental speed approach to the assessment of intelligence. In J. Kingma & W. Tomic (Eds.), *Advances in cognition and educational practice: Reflections on the concept of intelligence.* Greenwich, CT: JAI Press.

Nevid, J.S., & Rathus, S. A. (2005). Psychology and the challenges of life: Adjustment in the new millennium. Hoboken, NJ: John Wiley & Sons, Inc.

Newcombe, M.D., Maddahian, E., & Bentler, P.M. (1986). Risk factors for drug abuse among adolescents: Concurrent and longitudinal analyses. *American Journal of Public Health, 76,* 525–531.

Neziroglu, F., Anemone, R., & Yaryuratobias, J.A. (1992). Onset of obsessive-compulsive disorder in pregnancy. *American Journal of Psychiatry, 149,* 947–950.

NINDS (National Institute of Neurological Disorders and Stroke) (2007). Brain basics: Understanding sleep. Retrieved March 18 2009, from http://www.ninds.nih.gov/disorders/brain_basics/understanding_sleep.htm

Nishino, S., Okura, M., & Mignot, E. (2000). Narcolepsy: Genetic prediction and neuropharmacological mechanisms. *Sleep Medicine Reviews, 4*(1), 57–99.

Nishino, S., Ripley, B., Overeem, S., Lammers, G.J., & Mignot, E. (2000). Hypocretin (orexin) deficiency in human narcolepsy. *The Lancet, 355,* 39–41.

Nisoli, E, Brunani, A., Borgomainerio, E., Tonello, C., Dioni, L., Briscini, L., et al. (2007). D2 dopamine receptor (*DRD2*) gene Taq1A polymorphism and the eating-related psychological traits in eating disorders (anorexia nervosa and bulimia) and obesity. *Eating and Weight Disorders, 12*(2), 91–96.

Nolen-Hoeksema, S. (1990). *Sex differences in depression.* Stanford, CA: Stanford University Press.

Nolen-Hoeksema, S. (1991). Responses to depression and their effects on the duration of depressive episodes. *Journal of Abnormal Psychology, 100,* 569–582.

Norlander, T., Erixon, A., & Archer, T. (2000). Psychological androgyny and creativity: Dynamics of gender-role and personality trait. *Social Behavior and Personality, 28,* 423–435.

Norman, G.R., Brooks, L.R., & Allen, S.W. (1989). Recall by expert medical practitioners and novices as a record of processing attention. *Journal of Experimental Psychology: Learning, Memory, and Cognition, 15,* 1166–1174.

Novak, R.D., Smolensky, M.H., Fairchild, E.J., & Reves, R.R. (1990). Shiftwork and industrial injuries at a chemical plant in southeast Texas. *Chronobiology International, 7,* 155–164.

Noyes, R., Crowe, R.R., Harris, E.L., Hamra, B.J., McChesney, C.M., & Chandry, D.R. (1986). Relationship between panic disorder and agoraphobia: A family study. *Archives of General Psychiatry, 43*, 227–232.

O'Callaghan, E., Gibson, T., Colohan, H.A., Buckley, P., Walshe, D.G., Larkin, C., & Waddington, J.L. (1992). Risk of schizophrenia in adults born after obstetric complications and their association with early onset of illness: A controlled study. *British Medical Journal, 305*, 1256–1259.

O'Connor, J. (1980). Intermediate-size transposition and children's operational level. *Developmental Psychology, 16*, 588–596.

O'Donovan, M.C., Williams, N.M., & Owen, M.J. (2003). Recent advances in the genetics of schizophrenia. *Human Molecular Genetics, 12*, R125–R133.

O'Keeffe, C., & Wiseman, R. (2005). Testing alleged mediumship: Methods and results. *British Journal of Psychology, 96*, 165–179.

O'Neill, D. (2008). Online. Available: http://anthro.palomar.edu/homo/homo_3.htm

O'Neill, D.K. (1996). Two-year-old children's sensitivity to parent's knowledge state when making requests. *Child Development, 67*, 659–677.

Oakley, A. (1985). *Sex, gender and society.* Gower Publishing.

Ofcom Communications Market Report (2007). Retrieved March 18 2009 from: http://www.ofcom.org.uk/research/cm/cmr07/

Okagaki, L., & Sternberg, R.J. (1993). Parental beliefs and children's school performance. *Child Development, 64*, 36–56.

Olds, J., & Milner, P. (1954). Positive reinforcement produced by electrical stimulation of septal area and other regions of rat brain. *Journal of Comparative and Physiological Psychology, 47*, 419–427.

Orford, J. (1985). *Excessive appetites: A psychological view of addictions.* Chichester: Wiley.

Orford, J. (2001). *Excessive appetites: A psychological view of the addictions* (2nd Edn). Chichester: Wiley.

Orlofsky, J.L. (1977). Sex role orientation, identity, formation, and self-esteem in college men and women. *Sex Roles, 3*, 561–574.

Orlofosky, J.L., & O'Heron, C.A. (1987). Stereotypic and nonstereotypic sex role trait behaviour organizations: Implications for personal adjustment. *Journal of Personality and Social Psychology, 52*, 1034–1042.

Ost, L.G. (1985). Mode of acquisition of phobias. *Acta Universitatis Uppsaliensis, 529*, 1–45.

Ost, L.G. (1989). *Blood phobia: A specific phobia subtype in DSM-IV.* Paper requested by the Simple Phobia Subcommittee of the DSM-IV Anxiety Disorders Work Group.

Oswald, I. (1970). *Sleep.* Harmondsworth, UK: Penguin Books.

Oswald, I. (1976). The function of sleep. *Postgraduate Medical Journal, 52*(603), 15–18.

Oswald, I. (1980). *Sleep* (4th Edn). Harmondsworth, UK: Penguin Books.

Overbeek, G., ten Have, M., Vollebergh, W., & de Graaf, R. (2007). Parental lack of care and overprotection: Longitudinal associations with DSM-III-R disorders. *Social Psychiatry and Psychiatric Epidemiology, 42*, 87–93.

Owen, F., Crow, T.J., Poulter, M., Cross, A.J., Longden, A., & Riley, A.J. (1978). Increased dopamine-receptor sensitivity in schizophrenia. *The Lancet, 2*, 223–226.

Pagnin, D., de Queiroz, V., Pini, S., & Cassano, G.B. (2004). Efficacy of ECT in depression: A meta-analytic review. *Journal of ECT, 20*, 13–20.

Pahl, J.J., Swayze, V.W., & Andreasen, N.C. (1990). Diagnostic advances in anatomical and functional brain imaging in schizophrenia. In A. Kales, C.N. Stefanis, & J.A. Talbot (Eds.), *Recent advances in schizophrenia.* New York: Springer-Verlag.

Pajer, K., Gardner, W., Rubin, R.T., Perel, J., & Neal, S., (2001). Decreased cortisol levels in adolescent girls with conduct disorder. *Archives of General Psychiatry, 58*, 297–302.

Palinkas, L., Reed, H.L., Reedy, K.R., van Do, N., Case, H.S., & Finney, N.S. (2001). Circannual pattern of hypothalamic-pituitary-thyroid (HPT) function and mood during extended Antarctic residence. *Psychoneuroendocrinology, 26*, 421–431.

Palmer, J.D. (1989). Comparative studies of tidal rhythms: VIII. A translocation experiment involving circalunidian rhythms. *Marine Behaviour and Physiology, 14*, 231–243.

Palmer, S.E. (1975). The effects of contextual scenes on the identification of objects. *Memory and Cognition, 3*, 519–526.

Parke, J., & Griffiths, M.D. (2006). The psychology of the fruit machine: The role of structural characteristics (revisited). *International Journal of Mental Health and Addiction, 4*, 151–179.

Parke, J., & Griffiths, M.D. (2007). The role of structural characteristics in gambling. In G. Smith, D. Hodgins, & R. Williams (Eds.), *Research and measurement issues in gambling studies* (pp. 211–243). New York: Elsevier.

Parke, J., Griffiths, M.D., & Parke, A. (2007). Positive thinking among slot machine gamblers: A case of maladaptive coping? *International Journal of Mental Health and Addiction, 5*, 39–52.

Parker, A., & Brusewitz, G. (2003). A compendium of evidence for Psi. *European Journal of Parapsychology, 18*, 29–48.

Parker, G., Parker, I., & Brotchie, H. (2006). Mood state effects of chocolate. *Journal of Affective Disorders, 92*(2), 149–159.

Parker, S.T., & Gibson, K.R. (1979). A developmental model for the evolution of language and intelligence in early hominids. *Behavioural and Brain Sciences, 2*, 367–408.

Parkin, A.J. (2001). The structure and mechanisms of memory. In B. Rapp (Ed.), *The handbook of cognitive neuropsychology: What deficits reveal about the human mind.* Hove, UK: Psychology Press.

Parnell, J. (1988). Measures personality characteristics of persons claiming UFO experiences. *Psychotherapy in Practice, 6*(3), 159–165.

Parnia, S., Waller, D.G., Yeates, R., & Fenwick, P. (2001). A qualitative and quantitative study of the incidence, features and aetiology of near death experiences in cardiac arrest survivors. *Resuscitation, 48*, 149–156.

Parra, A., & Villaneuva, J. (2003). Personality Factors and ESP during Ganzfeld Sessions. *Journal of the Society for Psychical Research, 67*(1), 26–36.

Parrott, A. C. (1998). Nesbitt's Paradox resolved? Stress and arousal modulation during cigarette smoking. *Addiction, 93*(1), 27–39.

Pascalis, O., de Schonen, S., Morton, J., Deruelle, C., & Fabre-Grenet, M. (1995). Mother's face recognition by neonates: A replication and an extension. *Infant Behavior and Development, 18*, 79–85.

Pastore, N. (1952). The role of arbitrariness in the frustration–aggression hypothesis. *Journal of Abnormal and Social Psychology, 47*, 728–731.

Patterson, G.R., DeBaryshe, B.D., & Ramsey, E. (1989). A developmental perspective on antisocial behaviour. *The American Psychologist, 44*, 329–335.

Patterson, P., Birchwood, M., & Cochrane, R. (2000). Preventing the entrenchment of high expressed emotion in first episode psychosis: Early developmental attachment pathways. *Australian and New Zealand Journal of Psychiatry, 34,* S191–S197.

Paul, G.L., & Lentz, R.J. (1977). *Psychosocial treatment of chronic mental patients: Milieu versus social learning programs.* Cambridge, MA: Harvard University Press.

Pauls, D.L., Alsobrook, J.P., Goodman, W., Rasmussen, S., & Leckman, J.F. (1995). A family study of obsessive-compulsive disorder. *American Journal of Psychiatry, 152,* 76–84.

Pears, R., & Bryant, P. (1990). Transitive inferences by young children about spatial position. *British Journal of Psychology, 81,* 497–510.

Peele, S. (1990). Addiction as a cultural concept. *Annals of the New York Academy of Sciences, 602,* 205–220.

Perez-Barberia, F.J., Shultz, S., & Dunbar, R.I.M. (2007). Evidence for coevolution of sociality and relative brain size in three orders of mammals. *Evolution, 61,* 2811–2821.

Perry, D.G., & Bussey, K. (1979). The social learning theory of sex differences: Imitation is alive and well. *Journal of Personality and Social Psychology, 37,* 1699–1712.

Perry, G.H., Dominy, N.J., Claw, K.G., Lee, A.S., Fiegler, H., Redon, R., et al. (2007). Diet and the evolution of human amylase gene copy number variation. *Nature Genetics, 39*(10), 1256–1260.

Persinger, M.A. (1983). Geophysical variables and behaviour: IX. Expected clinical consequences of close proximity to UFO-related luminosities. *Perceptual and Motor Skills, 56*(1), 259–265.

Persky, S., & Blascovich, J. (2007). Immersive virtual environments versus traditional platforms: Effects of violent and non-violent video game play. *Media Psychology, 10,* 135–156.

Petrides, G., Fink, M., Husain, M.M., Knapp, R.G., et al. (2001). ECT remission rates in psychotic versus nonpsychotic depressed patients: A report from CORE. *Journal of ECT, 17,* 244–253.

Petty, R.E. (1995). Attitude change. In A. Tesser (Ed.), *Advanced social psychology.* New York: McGraw-Hill.

Petty, R.E., & Cacioppo, J.T. (1986). *Communication and persuasion: Central and peripheral routes to attitude change.* New York: Springer-Verlag.

Petty, R.E., Brinol, P., & Tormala, Z.L. (2002). Thought confidence as a determinant of persuasion: The self-validating hypothesis. *Journal of Personality and Social Psychology, 82,* 722–741.

Petty, R.E., Cacioppo, J.T., & Goldman, R. (1981). Personal involvement as a determinant of argument-based persuasion. *Journal of Personality and Social Psychology, 41,* 847–855.

Petty, R.E., Wells, G.L., & Brock, T.C. (1976). Distraction can enhance or reduce yielding to propaganda: Thought disruption versus effort justification. *Journal of Personality and Social Psychology, 34,* 874–884.

Pfammatter, M., Junghan, U.M., & Brenner, H.D. (2006). Efficacy of psychological therapy schizophrenia: Conclusions from meta-analysis. *Schizophrenia Bulletin, 32,* S64–S80.

Phelps, J.A., Davis, J.O., & Schartz, K.M. (1997). Nature, nurture, and twin research strategies. *Current Directions in Psychological Science, 6,* 117–121.

Phillips, D.P. (1986). Natural experiments on the effects of mass media violence on fatal aggression: Strengths and weaknesses of a new approach. In Berkowitz, L. (Ed.) *Advances in experimental social psychology, Volume 19* (pp. 207–250). New York: Academic Press.

Phillips, M.L., Young, A.W., Senior, C., Brammer, M., et al. (1997). A specific neural substrate for facial expressions of disgust. *Nature, 389,* 495–498.

Pierrel, R., & Sherman, J.G. (1963). Train your pet the Barnabus way. *Brown Alumni Monthly,* February, 8–14.

Pike, K.M., & Rodin, J. (1991). Mothers, daughters, and disordered eating. *Journal of Abnormal Psychology, 100,* 198–204.

Pilgrim, D. (2000). Psychiatric diagnosis: More questions than answers. *The Psychologist, 13,* 302–305.

Pilleri, G. (1979). The blind Indus dolphin, *Platanista indi. Endeavour, 3,* 48–56.

Pilon, M., Zadra, A., Joncas, S., & Montplaisir, J. (2008). Hypersynchronous delta waves and somnambulism: Brain topography and effect of sleep deprivation. *Annals of Neurology, 63*(4), 513–519.

Pinch, T. (1979). Normal explanations of the paranormal: The demarcation problem and fraud in parapsychology. *Social Studies of Science, 9,* 329–348.

Pinel, J.P.J. (1993). *Biopsychology* (2nd Edn). Boston: Allyn and Bacon.

Pischon, T., Boeing, H., Hoffmann, K., Bergmann, M., Schulze, M.B., Overvad, K., van der Schouw, Y.T., Spencer, E., Moons, K.G.M., Tjønneland, A., Halkjaer, J., Jensen, M.K., et al. (2008). General and abdominal adiposity and risk of death in Europe. *New England Journal of Medicine, 359*(20), 2105–2120.

Plomin, R. (1988). The nature and nurture of cognitive abilities. In R.J. Sternberg (Ed.), *Advances in the psychology of human intelligence, Volume 4.* Hillsdale, NJ: Lawrence Erlbaum Associates.

Plomin, R. (1990). The role of inheritance in behaviour. *Science, 248,* 183–188.

Plomin, R., DeFries, J.C., & McClearn, G.E. (1997). *Behavioural genetics: A primer* (3rd Edn). New York: Freeman.

Plotnik, J.M., de Waal, F.B.M., & Reiss, D. (2006). Self-recognition in an Asian elephant. *Proceedings of the National Academy of Sciences of the United States of America, 103,* 17053–17057.

Polimeni, J., & Reiss, J. (2002). How shamanism and group selection may reveal the origins of schizophrenia. *Medical Hypotheses, 58,* 244–248.

Pollnac, R.B. (1977). Illusion susceptibility and adaptation to marine environment: Is carpentered world hypothesis seaworthy? *Journal of Cross-cultural Psychology, 8,* 425–434.

Pomerleau, A., Bolduc, D., Malcuit, G., & Cossette, L. (1990). Pink or blue: Environmental gender stereotypes in the first two years of life. *Sex Roles, 22,* 359–367.

Popper, K.R. (1969). *Conjectures and refutations.* London: Routledge & Kegan Paul.

Popper, K.R. (1972). *Objective knowledge.* Oxford: Oxford University Press.

Potenza, M.N. (2001). The neurobiology of pathological gambling. *Seminars in Clinical Neuropsychiatry, 6*(3), 217–226.

Preyde, M., & Adams, G. (2008). Foundations of addictive problems: Developmental, social and neurobiological factors. In C. Essau (Ed.), *Adolescent addiction: Epidemiology, assessment and treatment* (pp. 3–16). San Diego, CA: Elsevier.

Price, J.S., Sloman, L., Gardner, R., & Rohde, P. (1994). The social competition hypothesis of depression. *British Journal of Psychiatry, 164,* 309–315.

Price-Williams, D., Gordon, W., & Ramirez, M. (1969). Skill and conservation: A study of pottery-making children. *Developmental Psychology, 1,* 769.

Priester, J.R., & Petty, R.E. (1995). Source attributions and persuasion: Perceived honesty as a determinant of message scrutiny. *Personality and Social Psychology Bulletin, 21,* 637–654.

Prochaska, J.O., DiClemente, C.C., & Norcross, J.C. (1992). In search of how people change: Applications to addictive behaviours. *American Psychologist, 47*, 1102–1114.

Prochaska, J.O., Norcross, J.C., & DiClemente, C.C. (1994). *Changing for good: A revolutionary six-stage program for overcoming bad habits and moving your life positively forward.* New York: Avon.

Purcell, R., Pathe, M., & Mullen, P.E. (2002). The prevalence and nature of stalking in the Australian community. *Australian and New Zealand Journal of Psychiatry, 36*, 114–120.

Rabbie, J.M., & Horowitz, M. (1960). Arousal of ingroup–outgroup bias by a chance win or loss. *Journal of Personality and Social Psychology, 13*, 269–277.

Rachlin, H. (1990). Why do people gamble and keep gambling despite heavy losses? *Psychological Science, 1*, 294–297.

Rachman, S., & Hodgson, R. (1980). *Obsessions and compulsions.* Englewood Cliffs, NJ: Prentice Hall.

Rachman, S.J. (2004). *Anxiety* (2nd Edn). Hove, UK: Psychology Press.

Rachman, S.J., & de Silva, P. (1978). Abnormal and normal obsessions. *Behaviour Research and Therapy, 16*, 233–238.

Radin, D.I., & Ferrari, D.C. (1991). Effects of consciousness on the fall of dice: A meta-analysis. *Journal of Scientific Exploration, 5*(1), 61–84.

Radke-Yarrow, M., & Zahn-Waxler, C. (1984). Roots, motives, and patterning in children's prosocial behavior. In E. Staub, D. Bar-Tal, J. Karylowski, & J. Raykowski (Eds.), *The development and maintenance of prosocial behavior: International perspectives on positive morality.* New York: Plenum Press.

Raine, A., Buchsbaum, M., & LaCasse, L. (1997). Brain abnormalities in murderers indicated by positron emission tomography. *Biological Psychiatry, 42*, 495–508.

Rajendran, G., & Mitchell, P. (2007). Cognitive theories of autism. *Developmental Review, 27*, 224–260.

Ramm, P. (1979). The locus coeruleus, catecholamines and REM sleep: A critical review. *Behavioural and Neural Biology, 25*, 415–418.

Rampello, L., Nicoletti, F., & Nicoletti, F. (2000). Dopamine and depression: Therapeutic implications. *CNS Drugs, 13*, 35–45.

Randi, J. (1982). *Flim-Flam.* Buffalo, NY: Prometheus Books.

Randi, J. (1983). The Project Alpha Experiment: Part one. The first two years. *Skeptical Inquirer, 7*(4), 24–32.

Rapee, R.M., & Lim, L. (1992). Discrepancy between self- and observer ratings of performance in social phobics. *Journal of Abnormal Psychology, 101*, 728–731.

Rasmussen, S., & Eisen, J. L. (1991). Phenomenology of OCD: Clinical subtypes, heterogeneity and coexistence. In J. Zohar, T. Insel, & S. Rasmussen (Eds.), *The psychobiology of obsessive–compulsive disorder* (pp. 13–43). New York: Springer.

Rattet, S., & Bursik, K. (2001). Investigating the personality correlates of paranormal belief and precognitive experience. *Personality and Individual Differences, 31*, 433–444.

Rauterberg, M. (2004). Positive effects of entertainment technology on human behaviour. *International Federation for Information Processing, 156*, 51–58.

Ravussin, E., Pratley, R.E., Maffei, M., Wang, H., Friedman, J.M., & Bennett, P.H. (1997). Relatively low plasma leptin concentrations precede weight gain in Pima Indians. *Nature Medicine, 3*, 238–240.

Reader, S.M., & Laland, K.N. (2002). Social intelligence, innovation, and enhanced brain size in primates. *Proceedings of the National Academy of Sciences of the United States of America, 99*, 4436–4441.

Rebert, W.M., Stanton, A.L., & Schwarz, R.M. (1991). Influence of personality attributes and daily moods on bulimic eating patterns. *Addictive Behaviors, 16*(6), 497–505.

Rechov Sumsum/Shara'a Simsim Research Symposium (1999). *Israel Education Television.* Al-Quds University Institute of Modern Media and Children's Television Workshop: New York.

Rechtschaffen, A., Bergmann, B.M., Everson, C.A., Kushida, C.A., & Gilliland, M.A. (1989). Sleep deprivation in the rat: 1. Conceptual issues. *Sleep, 12*, 1–4.

Rechtschaffen, A., Gilliland, M., Bergmann, B., & Winter, J. (1983). Physiological correlates of prolonged sleep deprivation in rats. *Science, 221*, 182–184.

Reilly, T., Waterhouse, J., & Edwards, B. (2005). Jet lag and air travel: Implications for performance. *Clinics in Sports Medicine, 24*(2), 367–380.

Reis, H.T., Collins, W.A., & Berscheid, E. (2000). The relationship context of human behavior and development. *Psychological Bulletin, 126*, 844–872.

Reiss, D., & Marino, L. (2001). Mirror self-recognition in the bottlenose dolphin: A case of cognitive divergence. *Proceedings of the National Academy of Sciences of the United States of America, 98*, 5937–5942.

Rekers, G.A. (1986). Inadequate sex role differentiation in childhood: The family and gender identity disorders. *The Journal of Family and Culture, 2*(3), 8–37.

Rekers, G.A., Crandall, B.F., Rosen, A.C., & Bentler, P.M. (1979). Genetic and physical studies of male children with psychological gender disturbances. *Psychological Medicine, 9*, 373–375.

Remington, G., & Kapur, S. (2000). Atypical antipsychotics: Are some more atypical than others? *Psychopharmacology, 148*, 3–15.

Rescorla, R.A., & Wagner, A.R. (1972). A theory of Pavlovian conditioning: Variations in the effectiveness of reinforcement and nonreinforcement. In A.H. Black & W.F. Prokasy (Eds.), *Classical conditioning: II. Current research and theory.* New York: Appleton-Century-Crofts.

Rhee, S.H., & Waldman, I.D. (2002). Genetic and environmental influences on antisocial behavior: A meta-analysis of twin and adoption studies. *Psychology Bulletin, 128*(3), 490–529.

Rhine, J.B. (1975). A Second Report on a Case of Experimenter Fraud. *Journal of Parapsychology, 39*, 306–325.

Rhine, J.B., & Pratt, J.G. (1954). A review of the Pearce-Pratt distance series of ESP tests. *Journal of Parapsychology, 18*, 165–177.

Ribeiro, S.C.M., Tandon, R., Grunhaus, L., & Greden, J.F. (1993). The DST as a predictor of outcome in depression: A meta-analysis. *American Journal of Psychiatry, 150*, 1618–1629.

Rice, D., & Haralambos, M. (Eds.) (2000). *Psychology in focus: AS level.* Ormskirk: Causeway Press

Richards, M.P. (2002). A brief review of the archaeological evidence for Palaeolithic and Neolithic subsistence. *European Journal of Clinical Nutrition, 56*(12), 1270–1278.

Riddoch, M.J., & Humphreys, G.W. (2001). Object recognition. In B. Rapp (Ed.), *The handbook of cognitive neuropsychology: What deficits reveal about the human mind.* Hove, UK: Psychology Press.

Ridley, M. (1999). *Genome.* New York: HarperCollins.

Ring, K., & Rosing, C.J. (1990). The Omega Project: A psychological survey of persons reporting abductions and other UFO encounters. *Journal of UFO Studies, 2*, 59–98.

Ringer, F., & Crittenden, P.M. (2007). Eating disorders and attachment: The effects of hidden family processes on eating disorders. *European Eating Disorders Review, 15*, 119–130.

Ringuette, E.L., & Kennedy, T. (1966). An experimental study of the double bind hypothesis. *Journal of Abnormal Psychology, 71*, 136–141.

Roberts, C.A. (1997). Der Mensch als Teil des UFO-Phanomens, GEP Sonderheft 16 ~ Ludenscheid, German language version of University dissertation. DEGUFO (JUFOF) e.V. Deutschsprachiger Gessellschaft fur UFO Forschung, Germany

Roberts, C.A. (2000). United Kingdom UFO organisations: What do they have knowledge of and what do they investigate? *European Journal of UFO and Abduction Studies, 1*(1), 26–32.

Roberts, M.B.V. (1982). *Biology: A functional approach* (3rd Edn). Walton-on-Thames, UK: Thomas Nelson and Sons.

Robertson, S.I. (2001). *Problem solving*. Hove, UK: Psychology Press.

Robertson, T.J., & Roy, A.E. (2001). A preliminary study of the acceptance by non-recipients of mediums' statements to recipients. *Journal of the Society for Psychical Research, 65*(2), 91–106.

Robertson, T.J., & Roy, A.E. (2004). Results of the application of the Robertson–Roy protocol to a series of experiments with mediums and participants. *Journal of the Society for Psychical Research, 68*(1), 18–34.

Robins, L.N, Helzer, J.E, & Davis, D.H (1975). Narcotic use in Southeast Asia and afterward. *Archives of General Psychiatry, 32*, 955–961.

Robson, C. (1994). *Experimental design and statistics in psychology* (3rd Edn). Harmondsworth: Penguin.

Rode, J.C., Mooney, C.H., Arthaud-Day, M.L., Near, J.P., Baldwin, T.T., Rubin, R., et al. (2007). Emotional intelligence and performance: Evidence of direct and moderated effects. *Journal of Organizational Behavior, 28*, 399–421.

Roe, C.A. (2001). Near-death experiences. In R. Roberts & D. Groome (Eds.). *Parapsychology: The science of unusual experience*. London: Arnold

Rogers, C.R. (1959). A theory of therapy, personality, and interpersonal relationships as developed in the client-centred framework. In S. Koch (Ed.), *Psychology: A study of a science*. New York: McGraw-Hill.

Rogers, P., Qualter, P., & Phelps, G. (2007). The mediating and moderating effects of loneliness and attachment style on belief in the paranormal. *European Journal of Parapsychology, 22*(2), 138–165.

Rogers, P., Qualter, P., Phelps, G., & Gardner, K. (2006). Belief in the paranormal, coping and emotional intelligence. *Personality and Individual Differences, 41*, 1089–1105.

Rogers, P.J., Richardson, N.J., & Elliman, N.A. (1992). Overnight caffeine abstinence and negative reinforcement of preference for caffeine-containing drinks. *Psychopharmacology, 120*(4), 457–462.

Rogers, S.J., Hepburn, S.L., Stackhouse, T., & Wehner, E. (2003). Imitation performance in toddlers with autism and those with other developmental disorders. *Journal of Child Psychology and Psychiatry and Allied Disciplines, 44*, 763–781.

Rose, G.A., & Williams, R.T. (1961). The psychobiology of meals. *British Journal of Nutrition, 15*, 1–9.

Rosen, G.M., Glasgow, R.E., & Barrera, M., Jr. (1976). A controlled study to assess the clinical efficacy of totally self-administered systematic desensitization. *Journal of Consulting and Clinical Psychology, 44*, 208–217.

Rosenblatt, P.C., Walsh, R.P., & Jackson, P.A. (1976). Breaking ties with deceased spouse. In A. Bharati (Ed.), *The realm of the extra-human, Volume 2*. Paris: Mouton.

Rosenhan, D.L. (1973). On being sane in insane places. *Science, 179*, 250–258.

Rosenkoetter, L.I. (1999). The television situation comedy and children's prosocial behaviour. *Journal of Applied Social Psychology, 29*, 979–993.

Rosenthal, D. (1963). *The Genain quadruplets: A case study and theoretical analysis of heredity and environment in schizophrenia*. New York: Basic Books.

Rosenzweig, M.R., Breedlove, S.M., & Leiman, A.L. (2002). *Biological psychology: An introduction to behavioural, cognitive, and clinical neuroscience* (3rd Edn). Sunderland, MA: Sinauer Associates.

Ross, L.R., & Spinner, B. (2001). General and specific attachment representations in adulthood: Is there a relationship? *Journal of Social and Personal Relationships, 18*, 747–766.

Ross, R., Dagnone, D., Jones, P.J.H., Smith, H., Paddags, A., Hudson, R., & Janssen, I., (2000). Reduction in obesity and related comorbid conditions after diet-induced weight loss or exercise-induced weight loss in men: A randomized, controlled trial. *Annals of Internal Medicine, 133*, 92–103.

Rothbaum, F., Rosen, K., Ujiie, T., & Uchida, N. (2002). Family systems theory, attachment theory, and culture. *Family Process, 41*, 328–350.

Rotter, J.B. (1954). *Social learning and clinical psychology*. New York: Prentice Hall.

Rozin, P, Millman, L., & Nemeroff, C. (1986). Operation of the laws of sympathetic magic in disgust and other domains. *Journal of Personality and Social Psychology, 50*, 703–712.

Rubin, J.Z., Provenzano, F.J., & Luria, A. (1974). The eye of the beholder: Parents' views on sex of newborns. *American Journal of Orthopsychiatry, 43*, 720–731.

Rubinstein, S., & Caballero, B. (2000). Is Miss America an undernourished role model? *Journal of the American Medical Association, 283*, 1569.

Ruble, D.N., Balaban, T., & Cooper, J. (1981). Gender constancy and the effects of sex-typed televised toy commercials. *Child Development, 52*, 667–673.

Ruddy, J. (2007, Jan/Feb). Tiny attractors: Boy meets girl. Kids and their elaborate rituals for setting and policing gender boundaries. *Psychology Today*.

Rushton, J.P., & Ankney, C.D. (1995). Brain size matters: A reply. *Canadian Journal of Experimental Psychology, 49*, 562–569.

Rushton, S.K., Harris, J.M., Lloyd, M.R., & Wann, J.P. (1998). Guidance of locomotion on foot uses perceived target direction rather than optic flow. *Current Biology, 8*, 1191–1194.

Russell, M.J., Switz, G.M., & Thompson, K. (1980). Olfactory influences on the human menstrual cycle. *Pharmacology, Biochemistry and Behaviour, 13*, 737–738.

Rust, J., Golomobok, S., Hines, M., Johnson, K., Golding, J., & ALSPAC Study Team (2000). The role of brothers and sisters in gender development of preschool children. *Journal of Experimental Child Psychology, 77*, 292–303.

Ryle, G. (1949). *The concept of mind*. Chicago: University of Chicago Press.

Sageman, M. (2004). Understanding terror networks. Retrieved March 17 2009, from http://www.fpri.org/enotes/20041101.middleeast.sageman.understandingterrornetworks.html

Sagotsky, G., Wood-Schneider, M., & Konop, M. (1981). Learning to co-operate: Effects of modelling and direct instructions. *Child Development, 52*, 1037–1042.

Sajatovic, M., Valenstein, M., Blow, F., Ganoczy, D, & Ignacio, R. (2007). Treatment adherence with lithium and anticonvulsant medications among patients with bipolar disorder. *Psychiatric Services, 58*, 855–863.

Sakai, K. (1985). Anatomical and physiological basis of paradoxical sleep. In McGinty, D., Morrison, A.,

Drucker-Colin, R.R., & Parmeggiani, P.L. (Eds.), *Brain mechanisms of sleep*. New York: Spectrum.

Sakkou, M., Wiedmer, P., Anlag, K., Hamm, A, Seuntjens, E., Ettwiller, L., et al. (2007). A role for brain-specific homeobox factor Bsx in the control of hyperphagia and locomotory behavior. *Cell Metabolism, 5*(6), 450–463.

Salancik, G.R., & Conway, M. (1975). Attitude inferences from salient and relevant cognitive content about behavior. *Journal of Personality and Social Psychology, 32*, 829–840.

Salkovskis, P.M. (1991). The importance of behaviour in the maintenance of anxiety and panic: A cognitive account. *Behavioural Psychotherapy, 19*, 6–19.

Salkovskis, P.M. (1996). The cognitive approach to anxiety: Threat beliefs, safety-seeking behaviour, and the special case of health anxiety and obsessions. In P.M. Salkovskis (Ed.), *Frontiers of cognitive therapy*. New York: Guilford.

Salkovskis, P.M., Hackmann, A., Wells, A., Gelder, M.G., et al. (2007). Belief disconfirmation versus habituation approaches to situational exposure in panic disorder with agoraphobia: A pilot study. *Behaviour Research and Therapy, 45*, 877–885.

Salovey, P., & Mayer, J.D. (1990). Emotional intelligence. *Imagination, Cognition and Personality, 9*, 185–211.

Salzman, L. (1980). *Treatment of the obsessive personality*. New York: J. Aronson.

Salzman, L. (1985). Psychotherapeutic management of obsessive-compulsive patients. *American Journal of Psychotherapy, 39*, 323–330.

Saluja, G., Iachan, R., Schedit, P.C., Overpeck, M.D., Sun, W.Y., & Gledd, J.N. (2004). Prevalence of and risk factors for depressive symptoms among young adolescents. *Archives of Pediatrics & Adolescent Medicine, 158*, 760–765.

Sameroff, A.J., Seifer, R., Baldwin, A., & Baldwin, C. (1993). Stability of intelligence from preschool to adolescence: The influence of social and family risk factors. *Child Development, 64*, 80–97.

Sameroff, A.J., Seifer, R., Barocas, R., Zax, M., & Greenspan, S. (1987). Intelligence quotient scores of 4-year-old children: Social-environmental risk factors. *Pediatrics, 79*, 343–350.

Sampath, G., Shah, A., Krska, J., & Soni, S.D. (1992). Neuroleptic discontinuation in the very stable schizophrenic patient: Relapse rates and serum neuroleptic levels. *Human Psychopharmacology: Clinical and Experimental, 7*, 255–264.

Sands, P. (2008). *Torture team*. London: Penguin.

Sanford, R.N. (1936). The effects of abstinence from food upon imaginal processes. *Journal of Psychology, 2*, 123–136.

Santrock, J.W. (1975). Moral structure: The interrelations of moral behaviour, moral judgement, and moral affect. *Journal of Genetic Psychology, 127*, 201–213.

Saunders, B.E., Villeponteaux, L.A., Lipovsky, J.A., Kilpatrick, D.G., & Veronen, L.J. (1992). Child sexual assault as a risk factor for mental disorders among women: A community survey. *Journal of Interpersonal Violence, 7*, 189–204.

Saxena, S., & Rauch, S.L. (2000). Functional neuroimaging and the neuroanatomy of obsessive-compulsive disorder. *Psychiatric Clinics of North America, 23*(3), 563–586.

Saxena, R., Voight, B.F., Lyssenko, V., Burt, N.P., de Bakker, P.I., Che, H. et al. (2007). Genome-wide association analysis identifies loci for type 2 diabetes and triglyceride levels. *Science, 316*(5829), 1331–1336.

Schafer, R., & Murphy, G. (1943). The role of autism in visual figure–ground relationship. *Journal of Experimental Psychology, 32*, 335–343.

Schaffer, H.R. (1996). *Social development*. Oxford, UK: Blackwell.

Schaller, M. (2006). Cited in E. Harrison, The psychology of celebrity obsession. *Cosmos, 7*, February 2006.

Scher, A. (1991). A longitudinal study of night waking in the first year. *Child: Care, Health and Development, 17*(5), 295–302.

Schillaci, M.A. (2006). Sexual selection and the evolution of brain size in primates. *Public Library of Science, 1*, e62.

Schlenker, B. R., Weigold, M. F., & Hallam, J. R. (1990). Self-serving attributions in social context: Effects of self-esteem and social pressure. *Journal of Personality and Social Psychology, 58*, 855–863.

Schmidt, H. (1970). PK experiments with animals as subjects. *Journal of Parapsychology, 34*, 255–261.

Schneider, F.R., Heckelman, L.R., Garfinkel, R., Campeas, R., et al. (1994). Functional impairment in social phobia. *Journal of Clinical Psychiatry, 55*, 322–329.

Schruers, K., Koning, K., Luermans, J., Haack, M.J., & Griez, E. (2005). Obsessive-compulsive disorder: A critical review of therapeutic perspectives. *Acta Psychiatrica Scandinavica, 111*, 26–271.

Schultz, L.H., Yeates, K.O., & Selman, R.L. (1988). The Interpersonal Negotiation Strategies Manual. Unpublished manual, Harvard University, Cambridge, MA.

Schwartz, J.P., Hage, S.M., Bush, I., & Burns, L.K. (2006). Unhealthy parenting and potential mediators as contributing factors to future intimate violence trauma. *Violence & Abuse, 7*(3), 206–221.

Schwartz, M.F., & Southern, S. (2002). Manifestations of damaged development of the human affectional systems and developmentally based psychotherapies. In P.J. Carnes & K.M. Adams (Eds.). *Clinical management of sex addiction* (pp. 89–100). Hove, UK: Psychology Press.

Schwartz, W., Recht, L., & Lew, R. (1995). Three time zones and you're out. *New Scientist*, 29 October.

Segal, Z.V., Kennedy, S., Gemar, M., Hood, K., Pedersen, R., & Buis, T. (2006). Cognitive reactivity to sad mood provocation and the prediction of depressive relapse. *Archives of General Psychiatry, 63*, 749–755.

Segal, Z.V., Shaw, B.F., Vella, D.D., & Kratz, R. (1992). Cognitive and life stress predictors of relapse in remitted unipolar depressed patients: Test of the congruency hypothesis. *Journal of Abnormal Psychology, 101*, 26–36.

Segall, M.H., Campbell, D.T., & Herskovits, M.J. (1963). Cultural differences in the perception of geometrical illusions. *Science, 139*, 769–771.

Seidman, L.J. (1983). Schizophrenia and brain dysfunction: An integration of recent neurodiagnostic findings. *Psychological Bulletin, 94*, 195–238.

Seidman, L.J. (1990). The neuropsychology of schizophrenia: A neurodevelopmental and case study approach. *Journal of Neuropsychiatry and Clinical Neuroscience, 2*, 301–312.

Seiffge-Krenke, I., & Lang, J. (2002). Forming and maintaining romantic relations from early adolescence to young adulthood: Evidence of a developmental sequence. In S. Shulman & I. Seiffge-Krenke (Co-chairs), *Antecedents of the quality and stability of adolescent romantic relationships*. Symposium conducted at the biennial meeting of the Society for Research on Adolescence. New Orleans: LA.

Selfe, L. (1983). *Normal and anomalous representational drawing ability in children*. London: Academic Press.

Seligman, M.E.P. (1970). On the generality of the laws of learning. *Psychological Review, 77*, 406–418.

Seligman, M.E.P. (1975). *Helplessness: On depression, development and death*. San Francisco: W.H. Freeman.

Seligman, M.E.P. (1995). The effectiveness of psychotherapy: The Consumer Reports study. *American Psychologist, 50*, 965–974.

Seligman, M.E., & Hager, J.L. (1972). *Biological boundaries of learning*. New York: Appleton-Century-Crofts.

Selman, R.L. (1976). Toward a structural-developmental analysis of interpersonal relationship concepts: Research with normal and disturbed pre-adolescent boys. In A. Pick (Ed.), *X Annual Minnesota Symposium on Child Psychology*. Minneapolis: University of Minnesota Press.

Selman, R.L. (1980). *The growth of interpersonal understanding*. New York: Academic Press.

Selman, R.L., Lavin, D.R., & Brion-Meisels, S. (1982). Troubled children's use of self-reflection. In P. Serafica (Ed.), *Social cognitive development in context*. New York: Guilford Press.

Selman, R.L., Schorin, M.Z., Stone, C.R., & Phelps, E. (1983). A naturalistic study of children's social understanding. *Developmental Psychology*, 19, 82–102.

Selye, H. (1936). A syndrome produced by diverse nocuous agents. *Nature*, 138, 32.

Selye, H. (1956). *The stress of life*. New York: McGraw-Hill.

Semin, G.R. (1995). Social constructionism. In A.S.R. Manstead, M. Hewstone, S.T. Fiske, M.A. Hogg, H.T. Reis, & G.R. Semin (Eds.), *The Blackwell encyclopaedia of social psychology*. Oxford: Blackwell.

Sen, A. (1998). In Editor's choice: The morbidity of rich and poor. *British Medical Journal*, 316. Available online: http://www.pubmedcentral.nih.gov/articlerender.fcgi?artid=1112970

Sergent, J., & Signoret, J.L. (1992). Implicit access to knowledge derived from unrecognised faces in prosopagnosia. *Cerebral Cortex*, 2, 389–400.

Serpell, R.S. (1979). How specific are perceptual skills? A cross-cultural study of pattern reproduction. *British Journal of Psychology*, 70, 365–380.

Shackelford, T.K., Schmitt, D.P., & Buss, D.M. (2005). Universal dimensions of human mate preferences. *Personality and Individual Differences*, 39, 447–458.

Shaffer, D.R. (1993). *Developmental psychology: Childhood and adolescence* (3rd Edn). Pacific Grove, CA: Brooks/Cole.

Shaffer, D.R. (1999). *Social and personality development*. Independence, KT: Wadsworth Publishing.

Shaffer, D.R., Pegalis, L.J., & Cornell, (1992). Gender and self disclosure revisited: Personal and contextual variations in self-disclosure to same-sex acquaintances. *Journal of Social Psychology*, 132, 307–315.

Shaffer, H.J., LaPlante, D.A., LaBrie, R.A., Kidman, R.C., Donato, A.N., & Stanton, M.V. (2004). Towards a syndrome model of addiction: Multiple expressions, common etiology. *Harvard Review of Psychiatry*, 12, 1–8.

Sham, P.C., O'Callaghan, E., Takei, N., Murray, G.K., Hare, E.H., & Murray, R.M. (1992). Schizophrenia following prenatal exposure to influenza epidemics between 1939 and 1960. *British Journal of Psychiatry*, 160, 461–466.

Shapiro, C.M., Bortz, R., Mitchell, D., Bartel, P., & Jooste, P. (1981). Slow-wave sleep: A recovery period after exercise. *Science*, 214, 1253–1254.

Shayer, M. (1999). Cognitive acceleration through science education II: Its effects and scope. *International Journal of Science Education*, 21, 883–902.

Shayer, M. (2003). Not just Piaget, not just Vygotsky, and certainly not Vygotsky as *alternative* to Piaget. *Learning and Instruction*, 13, 465–485.

Sheridan, C.L., & King, R.G. (1970). Obedience to authority with an authentic victim. *Proceedings of the 80th Annual Convention of the American Psychological Association*, 7(1), 165–166.

Sherman, S.J. (1980). On the self-erasing nature of errors of prediction. *Journal of Personality and Social Psychology*, 39, 211–221.

Shrum, L.J. (1999). The relation of television viewing with attitude strength and extremity: Implications for the cultivation effect. *Media Psychology*, 1, 3–25.

Shrum, L.J. (2001). Processing strategy moderates the cultivation effect. *Human Communication Research*, 27, 94–120.

Shrum, L.J., Wyer, R.S., & O'Guinn, T.C. (1998). The effects of television consumption on social perceptions: The use of priming procedures to investigate psychological processes. *Journal of Consumer Research*, 24, 447–458.

Shultz, S., & Dunbar, R.I.M. (2007). The evolution of the social brain: Anthropoid primates contrast with other vertebrates. *Proceedings of the Royal Society B: Biological Sciences*, 274, 2429–2436.

Shweder, R.A. (1990). Cultural psychology: What is it? In J.W. Stigler, R.A. Shweder, & G. Gerdt (Eds.), *Cultural psychology* (pp. 1–5). Cambridge. UK: Cambridge University Press.

Sicher, F., Targ, E., Moore II, D., & Smith, H.S. (1998). A randomized double-blind study of the effect of distant healing in a population with advanced AIDS. *Western Journal of Medicine*, 169(6), 356–363.

Siegel, J.M. (2005a). Clues to the functions of mammalian sleep. *Nature*, 437(7063), 1264–1271.

Siegel, J.M. (2005b). Functional implications of sleep development. *Public Library of Science*, 3(5), e178.

Siegel, J.M., Manger, P.R., Nienhuis, R., Fahringer, H.M., & Pettigrew, J.D. (1998). Monotremes and the evolution of rapid eye movement sleep. *Philosophical Transactions of the Royal Society of London: Biological Sciences*, 353(1372), 1147–1157.

Siegler, R.S., & Munakata, Y. (1993). Beyond the immaculate transition: Advances in the understanding of change. *Society for Research in Child Development Newsletter*, 36, 10–13.

Signorielli, N. (1989). Television and conceptions about sex roles: Maintaining conventionality and the status quo. *Sex Roles*, 21, 341–360.

Signorielli, N. (1997). Reflections of girls in the media: A two part study on gender and media. Kaiser Family Foundation. Retrieved March 17 2009, from http://www.kff.org/entmedia/1260-index.cfm

Silber, K. (1999). *The physiological basis of behaviour: Neural and hormonal processes*. London and New York: Routledge.

Silke, A. (2003). Deindividuation, anonymity, and violence: Findings from Northern Ireland. *Journal of Social Psychology*, 143, 493–499.

Silverman, I. (1977). *The human subject in the psychological laboratory*. Oxford: Pergamon.

Sim, K., Chua, T.H., Chan, Y.H., et al. (2006). Psychiatric comorbidity in first episode schizophrenia: A 2-year longitudinal outcome study. *Journal of Psychiatric Research*, 40, 656–663.

Simion, F., Turati, C., Valenza, E., & Leo, I. (2006). The emergence of cognitive specialisation in infancy: The case of face preference. *Attention and peformance*, XX1, 189–208.

Simion, F., Valenza, E., Macchi Cassia, V., Turati, C., & Umiltà, C. (2002). Newborns' preference for up–down asymmetrical configurations. *Developmental Science*, 5, 427–434.

Simons, D.J., & Levin, D.T. (1998). Failure to detect changes to people during a real-world interaction. *Psychonomic Bulletin and Review*, 5, 644–649.

Simpson, H.B., Liebowitz, M.R., Foa, E.B., Kozak, M.J., et al. (2004). Post-treatment effects of exposure therapy and clomipramine in obsessive-compulsive disorder. *Depression and Anxiety*, 19, 225–233.

Simpson, J.P, Collins, W.A., Tran, S., & Haydon, K.C. (2007). Attachment and the experience and expression of emotions in adult romantic relationships: A developmental perspective. *Journal of Personality and Social Psychology*, 92, 355–367.

Simunek, V.Z., & Sizun, J. (2005). Sleep in preterm neonates. Organization, development, deprivation. In J.V. Browne, & J. Sizun (Eds.), *Research on early developmental care for preterm neonates* (pp. 23–32). France: John Libbey Eurotext.

Sing, L. (1994). The Diagnostic Interview Schedule and anorexia nervosa in Hong Kong. *Archives of General Psychiatry, 51,* 251–252.

Singh, D. (1993a). Adaptive significance of female attractiveness: Role of waist-to-hip ratio. *Journal of Personality and Social Psychology, 65,* 293–307.

Singh, D. (1993b). Body shape and women's attractiveness: The critical role of waist-to-hip ratio. *Human Nature: An Interdisciplinary Biosocial Perspective, 4,* 297–321.

Singh, D. (2003). Female mate value at a glance: Relationship of waist-to-hip ratio to health, fecundity and attractiveness. *Human Ethology & Evolutionary Psychology, 23,* 81–91.

Sireteanu, R. (1999). Switching on the infant brain. *Science, 286,* 59–61.

Skinner, B.F. (1938). *The behaviour of organisms.* New York: Appleton-Century-Crofts.

Skinner, B.F. (1948). *Walden two.* New York: Macmillan.

Skinner, B.F. (1953). *Science and human behavior.* New York: Macmillan.

Skre, I., Onstad, S., Torgersen, S., Lygren, S., & Kringlen, E. (1993). A twin study of DSM-III-R anxiety disorders. *Acta Psychiatrica Scandinavica, 88,* 85–92.

Slaby, R.G., & Frey, K.S. (1975). Development of gender constancy and selective attention to same-sex models. *Child Development, 46,* 849–856.

Slater, A.M. (1990). Perceptual development. In M.W. Eysenck (Ed.), *The Blackwell dictionary of cognitive psychology.* Oxford: Blackwell.

Slater, A., & Morison, V. (1985). Shape constancy and slant perception at birth. *Perception, 14,* 337–344.

Slater, A., Mattock, A., & Brown, E. (1990). Newborn infants' responses to retinal and real size. *Journal of Experimental Child Psychology, 49,* 314–322.

Slater, M.D., Rouner, D., & Long, M. (2006). Television dramas and support for controversial public policies: Effects and mechanisms. *Journal of Communication, 56,* 235–252.

Sloboda, J.A., Davidson, J.W., Howe, M.J.A., & Moore, D.G. (1996). The role of practice in the development of performing musicians. *British Journal of Psychology, 87,* 287–309.

Slovic, P. (2001). *Smoking: Risk, perception and policy.* Thousand Oaks, CA: Sage Publications.

Smith, A., Brice, C., Nash, C.J., Rich, N., & Nutt, D.J. (2003). Caffeine and central noradrenaline: Effects on mood, cognitive performance, eye movements and cardiovascular function. *Journal of Psychopharmacology, 17*(3), 283–292.

Smith, L. (1996). The social construction of rational understanding. In A. Tryphon & J. Voneche (Eds.), *Piaget–Vygotsky: The social genesis of thought.* Hove: Psychology Press.

Smith, D.E., & Hochberg, J.E. (1954). The effect of "punishment" (electric shocks) on figure–ground perception. *Journal of Psychology, 38,* 83–87.

Smith, J., & Campfield, L.A. (1993). Meal initiation occurs after experimental induction of transient declines in blood glucose. *American Journal of Physiology: Regulatory, Integrative and Comparative Physiology, 265,* 1423–1429.

Smith, K.A., Clifford, E.M., Hockney, R.A, & Clark, D.M. (1997). Effect of tryptophan depletion on mood in male and female volunteers: A pilot study. *Human Psychopharmacology, Clinical and Experimental, 12,* 111–117.

Smith, L. (1996). The social construction of rational understanding. In A. Tryphon & J. Voneche (Eds.),

Piaget–Vygotsky: *The social genesis of thought.* Hove, UK: Psychology Press.

Smith, M.D. (1993). The effect of belief in the paranormal and prior set upon the observation of a 'psychic' demonstration. *European Journal of Parapsychology, 9,* 24–34.

Smith, M.D. (2003). The role of the experimenter in parapsychological research. *Journal of Consciousness Studies, 10*(6–7), 69–84.

Smith, P.B., & Bond, M.H. (1993). *Social psychology across cultures.* London: Prentice Hall.

Smith, P.K., Cowie, H., & Blades, M. (1998). *Understanding children's development* (3rd Edn). Oxford: Blackwell.

Smith, P.K., Cowie, H., & Blades, M. (2003). *Understanding children's development* (4th Edn). Oxford, UK: Blackwell.

Snarey, J.R. (1985). Cross-cultural universality of social-moral development: A critical review of Kohlbergian research. *Psychological Bulletin, 97,* 202–232.

Soehner, A.M., Kennedy, K.S., & Monk, T.H. (2007). Personality correlates with sleep–wake variable. *Chronobiology International, 24*(5), 889–903.

Solley, C.M., & Haigh, G. (1957). A note to Santa Claus. *Topeka Research Papers: The Menninger Foundation, 18,* 4–5.

Solomon, R.L., & Wynne, L.C. (1953). Traumatic avoidance learning: Acquisition in normal dogs. *Psychological Monographs, 67,* 1–19.

Sørensen, T.I.A. (2003). Weight loss causes increased mortality: PROS. *Obesity Reviews, 4,* 3–7.

Soriano-Mas, C, Pujol, J., Alonso, P., Cardoner, N, et al. (2007). Identifying patients with obsessive-compulsive disorder using whole-brain anatomy. *Neuroimage, 35,* 1028–1037.

Sotirovic, M. (2001). Media use and perceptions of welfare. *Journal of Communication, 51,* 750–774.

Spalding, K.L., Arne, E., Westermark, P.O., Bernard, S., Buchholz, B.A., Bergmann, O., et al. (2008). Dynamics of fat cell turnover in humans. *Nature, 453,* 783–787.

Spanos, N.P., Cross, P.A., Dickson, K., & DuBreuil, S.C. (1993). Close encounters: An examination of UFO experiences. *Journal of Abnormal Psychology, 102*(4), 624–632.

Spearman, C. (1923). *The nature of intelligence and the principles of cognition.* London: Macmillan.

Spence, J.T. (1993). Gender-related traits and gender ideology: Evidence for a multifactorial theory. *Journal of Personality and Social Psychology, 64,* 624–635.

Spitzberg, B.H., & Cupach, W.R. (2007). The state of the art of stalking: Taking stock of the emerging literature. *Aggression and Violent Behavior, 12,* 64–86.

Sprafkin, J.N., Liebert, R.M., & Poulos, R.W. (1975). Effects of a pro-social televised example on children's helping. *Journal of Experimental Child Psychology, 20,* 119–126.

Sprecher, S. (1994). Equity and social exchange in dating couples: Associations with satisfaction, commitment, and stability. *Journal of Marriage and Family, 63*(3), 599–613.

Sprecher, S., & Toro-Morn, M. (2002). A study of men and women from different sides of earth to determine if men are from Mars and women are from Venus in their beliefs about love and romantic relationships. *Sex Roles, 46*(5/6), 131–147.

Steinberger, K., & Schuch, B. (2002). Classification of obsessive-compulsive disorder in childhood and adolescence. *Acta Psychiatrica Scandinavica, 106,* 97–102.

Steinhausen, H.C. (1994). Anorexia and bulimia nervosa. In M. Rutter, E. Taylor, & L. Hersov (Eds.), *Child and adolescent psychiatry.* Oxford: Blackwell.

Steketee, G. (1990). Personality traits and disorders in obsessive-compulsives. *Journal of Anxiety Disorders, 4,* 351–364.

Steketee, G., & Barlow, D.H. (2002). Obsessive compulsive disorder. In D.H. Barlow (Ed.), *Anxiety and its disorder:*

The nature and treatment of anxiety and panic (2nd Edn), New York: Guilford Press.

Stern, W.C., & Morgane, P.J. (1974). Theoretical view of REM sleep function: Maintenance of catecholamine systems in the central nervous system. *Behavioural Biology, 11*, 1–32.

Sternberg, R.J. (1985). *Beyond IQ: A triarchic theory of human intelligence.* Cambridge: Cambridge University Press.

Sternberg, R.J. (1988). Triangulating love. In R.J. Sternberg & M.L. Barnes (Eds.), *The psychology of love* (pp. 119–138). New Haven, CT: Yale University Press.

Sternberg, R.J. (1997). *Successful intelligence.* New York: Plenum.

Sternberg, R.J. (2004). What do we know about the nature of reasoning? In J.P. Leighton & R.J. Sternberg (Eds.), *The nature of reasoning.* New York: Cambridge University Press.

Sternberg, R.J., & Ben-Zeev, T. (2001). *Complex cognition: The psychology of human thought.* Oxford, UK: Oxford University Press.

Sternberg, R.J., & Grajek, S. (1984). The nature of love. *Journal of Personality and Social Psychology, 47*, 312–329.

Sternberg, R.J., & Grigorenko, E.L. (2004). Successful intelligence in the classroom. *Theory into Practice, 43*, 274–280.

Sternberg, R.J., Grigorenko, E.L., Ngorosho, D., Tantufuye, E., Mbise, A., Nokes, C., Jukes, M., & Bundy, D.A. (2002). Assessing intellectual potential in rural Tanzanian school children. *Intelligence, 30*, 141–162.

Sternberg, R.J., & Kaufman, J.C. (1998). Human abilities. *Annual Review of Psychology, 49*, 479–502.

Sternberg, R.J., Nokes, C., Geissler, P.W., Prince, R., Okatcha, F., Bundy, D.A., et al. (2001). The relationship between academic and practical intelligence: A case study in Kenya. *Intelligence, 29*, 401–418.

Stevens, A., & Price, J. (1996). *Evolutionary psychiatry.* London: Routledge.

Stevens, A., & Price, J. (2000). *Evolutionary psychiatry* (2nd Edn). London: Routledge.

Stevens, R. (1989). *Freud and psychoanalysis.* Milton Keynes: Open University Press.

Stewart, R. (1997). *Evolution of the human brain.* Online. Available: http://homepage.mac.com/binck/reports/bevolution/breport:html

Stewart, J., & Amir, S. (1998). Body clocks get tired and emotional. *New Scientist, 21 November 1998.* Online. Available: http://www.newscientist.com/

Stice, E., Cameron, R.P., Killen, J.D. Hayward, C., & Taylor, C.B. (1999). Naturalistic weight-reduction efforts prospectively predict growth in relative weight and onset of obesity among female adolescents. *Journal of Consulting and Clinical Psychology, 67*(6), 967–974.

Stirling, J.D., & Hellewell, J.S.E. (1999). *Psychopathology.* London: Routledge.

Stoller, R.J. (1968). *Sex and gender: On the development of masculinity and femininity, Volume 1.* New York: Science House.

Stopa, L., & Clark, D.M. (1993). Cognitive processes in social phobia. *Behaviour Research and Therapy, 31*, 255–267.

Strassberg, D.S., & Holtz, S. (2003). An experimental study of women's internet personal ads. *Archives of Sexual Behavior, 32*, 253–264.

Stratton, G.M. (1896). Some preliminary experiments on vision without inversion of the retinal image. *Psychological Review, 3*, 611–617.

Straub, J., & Pelissolo, A. (2005). Temperament and character in primary insomnia. *European Psychiatry, 20*(2), 188–192.

Strober, M., & Humphrey, L.L. (1987). Familial contributions to the aetiology and course of anorexia nervosa and bulimia. *Journal of Consulting and Clinical Psychology, 55*, 654–659.

Stunkard, A.J., Sorensen, T.I.A., Hanis, C., Teasdale, T.W., Chakraborty, R., Schull, W.J., & Schulsigner, F. (1986). An adoption study of human obesity. *New England Journal of Medicine, 314*, 193–198.

Sturges, J.W., & Rogers, R.W. (1996). Preventive health psychology from a developmental perspective: An extension of protection motivation theory. *Health Psychology, 15*, 158–166.

Suddath, R.L., Christison, G.W., Torrey, E.F., Casanova, M.F., & Weinberger, D.R. (1990). Anatomical abnormalities in the brains of monozygotic twins discordant for schizophrenia. *New England Journal of Medicine, 322*, 789–794.

Sullivan, P.F., Neale, M.C., & Kendler, K.S. (2000). Genetic epidemiology of major depression: Review and meta-analysis. *American Journal of Psychiatry, 157*, 1552–1562.

Sundet, J.M., Barlaug, D.G., & Torjussen, T.M. (2004). The end of the Flynn effect? A study of secular trends in mean intelligence test scores of Norwegian conscripts during half a century. *Intelligence, 32*, 349–362.

Suppes, T., Baldessarini, R.J., Faedda, G.L., & Tohen, M. (1991). Risk of recurrence following discontinuation of lithium treatment in bipolar disorder. *Archives of General Psychiatry, 48*, 1082–1088.

Susser, E., Neugebauer, R., Hoek, H., Brown, A., Lin, S., Labovitz, D., & Gorman, J. (1996). Schizophrenia after prenatal famine: Further evidence. *Developmental Psychobiology, 29*, 25–31.

Sussman, S., Dent, C.W., & Leu, L. (2000). The one-year prospective prediction of substance abuse and dependence among high-risk adolescents. *Journal of Substance Abuse, 12*, 373–386.

Sussman, S., Dent, C.W., Simon, T.R., Stacy, A.W., Galaif, E.R., Moss, M.A., et al. (1995). Immediate impact of social influence-oriented substance abuse prevention curricula in traditional and continuation high schools. *Drugs and Society, 8*, 65–81.

Sussman, S., Skara, S., & Ames, S.L. (2006). Substance abuse among adolescents. In T. Plante (Ed.), *Mental disorders of the new millennium. Volume II: Public and Social Problems* (pp. 127–169). New York: Greenwood.

Szechtman, H., & Woody, E. (2004). Obsessive-compulsive disorder as a disturbance of security motivation. *Psychological Review, 111*, 111–127.

Szelenberger, W., Niemcewicz, S., Dabrowska, A.J. (2005). Sleepwalking and night terrors: Psychopathological and psychophysiological correlates. *International Review of Psychiatry, 17*(4), 263–270.

Tajfel, H. (1969). Social and cultural factors in perception. In G. Lindzey & E. Aronson (Eds.), *Handbook of social psychology, Volume 3.* Reading, MA: Addison-Wesley.

Tajfel, H., & Jahoda, G. (1966). Development in children of concepts and attitudes about their own and other countries: A cross-national study. *Proceedings of the 18th International Congress of Psychology: Moscow Symposium, 36*, 17–33.

Tajfel, H., & Turner, J.C. (1979). An integrative theory of intergroup conflict. In W. G. Austin & S. Worchel (Eds.), *The social psychology of intergroup relations.* Monterey, CA: Brooks-Cole.

Tallis, F. (1995). *Obsessive-compulsive disorder: A cognitive and neuropsychological perspective.* Chichester, UK: Wiley.

Tarrier, N. (1987). An investigation of residual psychotic symptoms in discharged schizophrenic patients. *British Journal of Clinical Psychology, 26*, 141–143.

Tarrier, N. (2005). Cognitive behaviour therapy for schizophrenia: A review of development, evidence and implementation. *Psychotherapy and Psychosomatics, 74*, 136–144.

Tarrier, N., Beckett, R., Harwood, S., Baker, A., Yusupoff, L., & Ugarteburu, I. (1993). A trial of two cognitive behavioural methods of treating drug-resistant residual psychotic symptoms in schizophrenic patients: 1. Outcome. *British Journal of Psychiatry, 162,* 524–532.

Taylor, S.E. (1975). On inferring one's attitude from one's behavior: Some delimiting conditions. *Journal of Personality and Social Psychology, 31,* 126–131.

Tellegen, A., & Atkinson, G. (1974). Openness to absorbing and self-altering experiences (absorption), a trait related to hypnotic susceptibility. *Journal of Abnormal Psychology, 83,* 268–277.

Teller, D.Y. (1997). First glances: the vision of infants. The Friedenwald lecture. *Investigative Ophthalmology and Visual Science, 38,* 2183–2203.

Terman, M. (1988). On the question of mechanism in phototherapy for seasonal affective disorder: Considerations of clinical efficacy and epidemiology. *Journal of Biological Rhythms, 3,* 155–172.

Teuting, P., Rosen, S., & Hirschfeld, R. (1981). *Special report on depression research* (NIMH-DHHS Publication No. 81–1085). Washington, DC.

Thalbourne, M.A. (1995). Science versus showmanship: A History of the Randi hoax. *The Journal of the American Society for Psychical Research, 89,* 344–366.

Thalbourne, M.A. (2001). Research note: Creative personality and belief in the paranormal. *European Journal of Parapsychology, 20(1),* 79–84.

Thannickal, T.C., Moore, R.Y., Nienhuis, R., Ramanathan, L., Gulyani, S., Aldrich, M., et al. (2000). Reduced number of hypocretin neurons in human narcolepsy. *Neuron, 27,* 469–474.

Tharyan, P. (2005). The Cochrane Schizophrenia Group: Preparing, maintaining and disseminating the evidence for interventions used for people with schizophrenia. *International Review of Psychiatry, 17,* 115–121.

Tharyan, P., & Adams, C.E. (2005). Electroconvulsive therapy for schizophrenia. *Cochrane Database of Systematic Reviews, 2,* CD000076.

Thase, M.E., Rush, A.J., Howland, R.H., Kornstein, S.G., et al. (2002). Double-blind switch study of sertraline treatment of antidepressant-resistant chronic depression. *Archives of General Psychiatry, 59,* 233–239.

Thibaut, J.W., & Kelley, H.H. (1959). *The social psychology of groups.* New York: Wiley.

Thomas, E.M. (1958). *The harmless people.* New York: Random House.

Thomas, M.H., Horton, R.W., Lippincott, E.C., & Drabman, R.S. (1977). Desensitisation to portrayals of real-life aggression as a function of exposure to television violence. *Journal of Personality and Social Psychology, 35,* 450–458.

Thompson, T.L., & Zerbinos, E. (1997). Television cartoons: Do children notice it's a boy's world? *Sex Roles, 37,* 415–432.

Thomson, M. (2006). Human brands: Investigating antecedents to consumers' strong attachments to celebrities. *Journal of Marketing, 70,* 104–119.

Thorndike, E.L. (1911). *Animal intelligence: Experimental studies.* New York: MacMillan.

Thorndike, R.L. (1987). Stability of factor loadings. *Personality and Individual Differences, 8,* 585–586.

Thornhill, R., & Gangestad, S. (1999). Facial attractiveness. *Trends in Cognitive Sciences, 3,* 452–460.

Thorpe, G., & Burns, L. (1983). *The agoraphobic syndrome.* Chichester: Wiley.

Thorpe, S.J., & Salkovskis, P.M. (1995). Phobic beliefs: Do cognitive factors play a role in specific phobias? *Behaviour Research and Therapy, 33,* 805–816.

Thurstone, L.L. (1938). *Primary mental abilities.* Chicago, IL: University of Chicago Press.

Tienari, P. (1991). Interaction between genetic vulnerability and family environment: The Finnish adoptive family study of schizophrenia. *Acta Psychiatrica Scandinavica, 84,* 460–465.

Tiggerman, M., & Pickering, A.S. (1996). Role of television in adolescent women's body dissatisfaction and drive for thinness. *International Journal of Eating Disorders, 20,* 199–203.

Tomarken, A.J., Mineka, S., & Cook, M. (1989). Fear-relevant associations and covariation bias. *Journal of Abnormal Psychology, 98,* 381–394.

Tomlinson-Keasey, C., & Keasey, C.B. (1974). The mediating role of cognitive development in moral judgement. *Child Development, 45,* 291–298.

Tonin, E. (2004). The attachment styles of stalkers. *Journal of Forensic Psychiatry and Psychology, 15,* 584–590.

Torgersen, S. (1983). Genetic factors in anxiety disorders. *Archives of General Psychiatry, 40,* 1085–1089.

Torres, A.R., Prince, M.J., Bebbington, P.E., Bhugra, D., et al. (2006). *American Journal of Psychiatry, 163,* 1978–1985.

Torrey, E.F. (1992). Are we overestimating the genetic contribution to schizophrenia? *Schizophrenia Bulletin, 18,* 159–170.

Townsend, J. (1993). Policies to halve smoking deaths. *Addiction, 88,* 43–52.

Townsend, J.M., & Wasserman, T. (1997). The perception of sexual attractiveness: Sex differences in variability. *Archives of Sexual Behavior, 26,* 243–268.

Townsend, J.M., Kline, J., & Wasserman, T.H. (1995). Low-investment copulation: Sex differences in motivations and emotional reactions. *Ethology and Sociobiology, 16,* 25–51.

Triandis, H.C. (1994). *Culture and social behaviour.* New York: McGraw-Hill.

Trivers, R.L. (1972). Parental investment and sexual selection. In B. Campbell (Ed.), *Sexual selection and the descent of man, 1871–1971.* Chicago: Aldine.

Truby, H., Baic, S., deLooy, A., Fox, K.R., Livingstone, M.B., Logan, C.M., et al. (2006). Randomised controlled trial of four commercial weight loss programmes in the UK: initial findings from the BBC diet trials *British Medical Journal, 332,* 1309–1314.

Tuffiash, M., Roring, R.W., & Ericsson, K.A. (2007). Expert performers in Scrabble®: Implications for the study of the structure and acquisition of complex skills. *Journal of Experimental Psychology: Applied, 13,* 124–134.

Turati, C., Simion, F., Milani, I., & Umiltà, C. (2002). Newborns' preference for faces: What is crucial? *Developmental Psychology, 38,* 875–882.

Turkington, D., Kingdon, D., & Chadwick, P. (2003). Cognitive–behavioural therapy for schizophrenia: Filling the therapeutic vacuum. *British Journal of Psychiatry, 183,* 98–99.

Turner, G. (2006). The mass production of celebrity. *International Journal of Cultural Studies, 9,* 153–165.

Turner, R.J., & Wagonfeld, M.O. (1967). Occupational mobility and schizophrenia. *American Sociological Review, 32,* 104–113.

Turner, T.H., Drummond, S.P.A., Salamat, J.S., & Brown, G.G. (2007). Effects of 42 hr sleep deprivation on component processes of verbal working memory. *Neuropsychology, 21,* 787–795.

Umilta, M.A., Kohler, E., Gallese, V., Fogassi, L., Fadiga, L., Keysers, C., & Rizzolatti, G. (2001). I know what you are doing: A neurophysiological study. *Neuron, 25,* 287–295.

United Nations Office on Drugs and Crime/World Health Organization (UN/WHO) (2008). *Principles of Drug Dependence Treatment: Discussion paper.* UN/WHO.

Unsworth, G., Devilly, G.J., & Ward, T. (2007). The effect of playing violent video games on adolescents: Should parents be quaking in their boots? *Psychology, Crime and Law, 13*, 383–394.

Valentine, C.W. (1946). *The psychology of early childhood* (3rd Edn). London: Hogarth Press.

Valentine, E.R. (1982). *Conceptual issues in psychology.* London: Routledge.

Valentine, E.R. (1992). *Conceptual issues in psychology* (2nd Edn). London: Routledge.

Van Cauter, E., Leproult, E., & Plat, L. (2000). Age-related changes in slow wave sleep and REM sleep and relationship with growth hormone and cortisol levels in healthy men. *Journal of the American Medical Association, 284*, 861–868.

Van den Berg, A.V., & Brenner, E. (1994). Why two eyes are better than one for judgements of heading. *Nature, 371*, 700–702.

Van der Pligt, J. (1998). Perceived risk and vulnerability as predictors of precautionary behaviour. *British Journal of Health Psychology, 3*, 1–14.

Van Goozen, S.H.-M., Fridja, N.H., & van de Poll, N.E. (1995). Anger and aggression during role-playing: Gender differences between hormonally treated male and female transsexuals and controls. *Aggressive Behavior, 21*, 257–273.

van Grootheest, D.S., Cath, D.C., Beekman, A.T., & Boomsma, D.I. (2005). Twin studies on obsessive-compulsive disorder: A review. *Twin Research and Human Genetics, 8*, 450–458.

Van Hassett, V.B.M., Hull, J.A., Kempton, T., & Bukstein, O.G. (1993). Social skills and depression in adolescent substance abusers. *Addictive Behaviors, 18*, 9–18.

Van IJzendoorn, M.H., & Kroonenberg, P.M. (1988). Crosscultural patterns of attachment: A meta-analysis of the Strange Situation. *Child Development, 59*, 147–156.

Van Kammen, D.P., Docherty, J.P., & Bunney, W.E. (1982). Prediction of early relapse after pimozide discontinuation by response to d-amphetamine during pimozide treatment. *Biological Psychiatry, 17*, 223–242.

Van Keer, H. (2004). Fostering reading comprehension in fifth grade by explicit instruction in reading strategies and peer tutoring. *British Journal of Educational Psychology, 74*, 37–70.

van Lommel, P., van Wees, R., Meyers, V., & Elfferich, I. (2001). Near-death experience in survivors of cardiac arrest: A prospective study in the Netherlands. *The Lancet, 358*, 2039–2045.

van Oppen, P., & Arntz, A. (1994). Cognitive therapy for obsessive-compulsive disorder. *Behaviour Research and Therapy, 32*, 79–87.

van Schaik, C. (2006). Why are some animals so smart? *Scientific American, 294*, 64–71.

Vares, M., Ekholm, A., Sedvall, G.C., Hall, H., & Jonsson, E.G. (2006). Characterisation of patients with schizophrenia and related psychoses: Evaluation of different diagnostic procedures. *Psychopathology, 39*, 286–295.

Veitch, R., & Griffitt, W. (1976). Good news, bad news: Affective and interpersonal effects. *Journal of Applied Social Psychology, 6*, 69–75.

Ventura, J., Liberman, R. P., Green, M. F., Shaner, A., & Mintz, J. (1998). Training and quality assurance with the structured Clinical Interview for DSM-IV (SCID-I/P). *Psychiatry Research, 79*, 163–173.

Verburg, K., Griez, E., Meijer, J., & Pols, H. (1995). Respiratory disorders as a possible predisposing factor for panic disorder. *Journal of Affective Disorders, 33*, 129–134.

Vernon, P.E. (1971). *The structure of human abilities*. London: Methuen.

Vgontzas, A.N., Bixler, E.O., Lin, H., Prolo, P., Mastorakos, G., Vela-Bueno, A., et al. (2001). Chronic insomnia is associated with nyctohemeral activation of the hypothalamic-pituitary-adrenal axis: Clinical implications. *The Journal of Clinical Endocrinology & Metabolism, 86*(8), 3787–3794.

Viguera, A.C., Nonacs, R., Cohen, L.S., Tondo, L., Murray, A., & Baldessarini, R.J. (2000). Risk of recurrence of bipolar disorder in pregnant and nonpregnant women after discontinuing lithium maintenance. *American Journal of Psychiatry, 157*, 179–184.

Virkkunen, M. (1985). Urinary free cortisol secretion in habitually violent offenders. *Acta Psychiatria Scandinavia, 72*, 40–44.

Virkkunen, M., Nuutila, A., Goodwin, F.K., & Linnoila, M. (1987). Cerebrospinal fluid monamine metabolite levels in male arsonists. *Archives of General Psychiatry, 44*, 241–247.

Vitousek, K., & Manke, F. (1994). Personality variables and disorders in anorexia nervosa and bulimia nervosa. *Journal of Abnormal Psychology, 103*(1), 137–147.

Vygotsky, L.S. (1976). Play and its role in the mental development of the child. In J.S. Bruner, A. Jolly, & K. Sylva (Eds.), *Play*. Harmondsworth, UK: Penguin.

Vygotsky, L.S. (1978). *Mind in society: The development of higher psychological processes*. Cambridge, MA: MIT Press.

Vygotsky, L.S. (1981). The genesis of higher mental functions. In J.V. Wertsch (Ed.), *The concept of activity in Soviet psychology*. Armonk, NY: Sharpe. (Original work published 1930.)

Vygotsky, L.S. (1986). The genetic roots of thought and speech. In A. Kozulin (Trans. & Ed.), *Thought and language*. Cambridge, MA: MIT Press.

Wade, T.D., Tiggemann, M., Bulik, C.M., Fairburn, C.G., Wray, N.R., & Martin, N.G. (2008). Shared temperament risk factors for anorexia nervosa: A twin study. *Psychosomatic Medicine, 70*, 239–244.

Wagenaar, W.A. (1988). *Paradoxes of gambling behaviour*. London: Lawrence Erlbaum Associates.

Wahlberg, K.E., Lynne, L.C., Oja, H., Keskitalo, P., Pykalainen, L., Lahti, I., et al. (1997). Gene–environment interaction in vulnerability to schizophrenia: Findings from the Finnish adoptive family study of schizophrenia. *American Journal of Psychiatry, 154*, 355–262.

Walker, E.F., Savoie, T., & Davis, D. (1994). Neuromotor precursors of schizophrenia. *Schizophrenia Bulletin, 20*, 441–451.

Walker, L.J. (1980). Cognitive and perspective-taking prerequisites for moral development. *Child Development, 51*, 131–139.

Walker, L.J., de Vries, B., & Trevethan, S.D. (1987). Moral stages and moral orientations in real-life and hypothetical dilemmas. *Child Development, 58*, 842–858.

Walker, L.J., Gustafson, P., & Hennig, K.H. (2001). The consolidation/transition model in moral reasoning development. *Developmental Psychology, 37*, 187–197.

Walker, M.B. (1989). Some problems with the concept of "gambling addiction": Should theories of addiction be generalized to include excessive gambling? *Journal of Gambling Behavior, 5*, 179–200.

Walker, M.B. (1992). *The psychology of gambling*. Oxford: Pergamon Press.

Wallach, L., & Wallach, M.A. (1994). Gergen versus the mainstream: Are hypotheses in social psychology subject to empirical test? *Journal of Personality and Social Psychology, 67*, 233–242.

Walster, E., Walster, G.W., & Berscheid, E. (1978). *Equity: Theory and research*. Boston: Allyn & Bacon.

Walters, R.H., & Thomas, L. (1963). Enhancement of punitiveness by visual and audiovisual displays. *Canadian Journal of Psychology, 16*, 244–255.

Walton, G.E., Bower, N.J.A., & Bower, T.G.R. (1992). Recognition of familiar faces by newborns. *Infant Behaviour and Development, 15*, 265–269.

Wandel, M. (2004). Changes in uncertainty about food safety and trust in nutrition expert advice. *Ecology of Food and Nutrition, 43*(6), 443–462.

Wann, D.L. (1993). Aggression among highly identified spectators as a function of their need to maintain positive social identity. *Journal of Sport & Social Issues, 17*(2), 134–143.

Waring, M., & Ricks, D. (1965). Family patterns of children who became adult schizophrenics. *Journal of Nervous and Mental Disease, 140*, 351–364.

Warren, W.H., & Hannon, D.J. (1988). Direction of self-motion is perceived from optical flow. *Nature, 336*, 162–163.

Warshel, Y. (2007). As though there is peace: Opinions of Jewish–Israeli children about watching Rechov Sumsum/Shara'a Simsim amidst armed political conflict. In D. Lemish & M. Gotz (Eds.) *Children and media at times of conflict and war* (pp. 309–332). Cresskill, NJ: Hampton Press.

Watson, J.B., & Rayner, R. (1920). Conditioned emotional reactions. *Journal of Experimental Psychology, 3*, 1–14.

Watson, P.J., & Andrews, P.W. (2002). Toward a revised evolutionary adaptationist analysis of depression: The social navigation hypothesis. *Journal of Affective Disorders, 72*, 1–14.

Watt, C.A. (1990–1991). Psychology and coincidences. *European Journal of Parapsychology, 8*, 66–84.

Watts, C., Watson, S., & Wilson, L. (2007). Cognitive and psychological mediators of anxiety: Evidence from a study of paranormal belief and perceived childhood control. *Personality and Individual Differences, 42*(2), 335–343.

Waynforth, D., & Dunbar, R.I.M. (1995). Conditional mate choice strategies in humans: Evidence from 'lonely hearts' advertisements. *Behaviour, 132*, 755–779.

Webb, W.B. (1975). *Sleep: The gentle tyrant*. Englewood Cliffs, NJ: Prentice Hall.

Webb, W.B., & Bonnet, M.H. (1978). The sleep of "morning" and "evening" types. *Biological Psychology, 7*(1–2), 29–35.

Webber, D.J., & Walton, F. (2006). Gender specific peer groups and choice at sixteen. *Research in Post-Compulsory Education, 11*(1), 65–84.

Weber, R., Ritterfeld, U., & Mathiak, K. (2006). Does playing violent video games induce aggression? Empirical evidence of a functional magnetic resonance imaging study. *Media Psychology, 8*(1), 39–60.

Weigle, D.S., Cummings, D.E., Newby, P.D., Breen, P.A., Frayo, R.S., Matthys, C.C., et al. (2003). Roles of leptin and ghrelin in the loss of body weight caused by a low fat, high carbohydrate diet. *Journal of Clinical Endocrinology & Metabolism, 88*, 1577–1586.

Weissman, M.M., Klerman, G.L., & Paykel, E.S. (1971). Clinical evaluation of hostility in depression. *American Journal of Psychiatry, 39*, 1397–1403.

Wellman, H.M., Cross, D., & Watson, J. (2001). Meta-analysis of theory-of-mind development: The truth about false belief. *Child Development, 72*, 655–684.

Wender, P.H., Kety, S.S., Rosenthal, D., Schulsinger, F., Ortmann, J., & Lunde, I. (1986). Psychiatric disorders in the biological and adoptive families of adopted individuals with affective disorders. *Archives of General Psychiatry, 43*, 923–929.

Westen, D. (1996). *Psychology: Mind, brain, and culture*. New York: Wiley.

Wetherell, M., & Potter, J. (1988). Discourse analysis and the identification of interpretive repertoires. In C. Antaki (Ed.), *Analysing everyday explanation: A casebook of methods*. London: Sage.

Wheldall, K., & Poborca, B. (1980). Conservation without conversation: An alternative, non-verbal paradigm for assessing conservation of liquid quantity. *British Journal of Psychology, 71*, 117–134.

White, D.P. (2005). Pathogenesis of obstructive and central sleep apnea. *American Journal of Respiratory Critical Care Medicine, 172*, 1363–1370.

Whitehouse, D. (2003). *Study reveals world's most jealous men*. Online. Available: http://news.bbc.co.uk/go/pr/fr/-/1/hi/sci/tech/3045410.stm

Whiten, A. (1998). Imitation of the sequential structure of actions by chimpanzees (*Pan troglodytes*). *Journal of Comparative Psychology, 112*, 270–281.

Whiten, A., & van Schaik, C.P. (2007). The evolution of animal 'cultures' and social intelligence. *Philosophical Transactions of the Royal Society B: Biological Sciences, 362*, 603–620.

WHO (1992). *The ICD-10 classification of mental and behavioural disorders*. Geneva: WHO.

Wicker, A.W. (1969). Attitudes versus actions: The relationship of verbal and overt behavioural responses to attitude objects. *Journal of Social Issues, 25*, 41–78.

Widmeyer, W.N., & McGuire, E.J. (1997). Frequency of competition and aggression in professional ice hockey. *International Journal of Sport Psychology, 28*, 57–66.

Wiegman, O., Kuttschreuter, M., & Baarda, B. (1992). A longitudinal study of the effects of television viewing on aggressive and prosocial behaviours. *British Journal of Social Psychology, 31*, 147–164.

Wilde, G.J.S. (1993). Effects of mass media communications on health and safety habits: An overview of issues and evidence. *Addiction, 88*, 983–996.

Will, K.E., Porter, B.E., Geller, E.S., & DePasquale (2005). Is television a health and safety hazard? A cross-sectional analysis of at-risk behavior on primetime television. *Journal of Applied Social Psychology, 35*, 198–222.

Williams, D. (2004). *Everyday heaven: Journeys beyond the stereotypes of autism*. Philadelphia, PA: Jessica Kingsley Publishers.

Williams, J.E., & Best, D.L. (1982). *Measuring sex stereotypes: A thirty nations study*. London: Sage.

Williams, J.E., & Best, D.L. (1990). *Measuring sex stereotypes: A multination study*. Newbury Park, CA: Sage.

Williams, R.L. (1972). *The BITCH Test (Black Intelligence Test of Cultural Homogeneity)*. St Louis, MI: Washington University.

Williams, T.M. (Ed.). (1986). *The impact of television: A national experiment in three communities*. New York: Academic Press.

Williams, W.F. (2000). Science or pseudoscience? In W.F. Williams (Ed.), *Encyclopedia of pseudoscience: From alien abductions to zone therapy*. New York: Facts on File.

Williamson, A.M., & Feyer, A.-M. (2000). Moderate sleep deprivation produces impairments in cognitive and motor performance equivalent to legally prescribed levels of alcohol intoxication. *Occupational and Environmental Medicine, 57*, 649–655.

Wilner, A., Reich, T., Robins, I., Fishman, R., & van Doren, T. (1976). Obsessive-compulsive neurosis. *Comprehensive Psychiatry, 17*, 527–539.

Wilson, G.T., & Davison, G.C. (1971). Processes of fear reduction in systematic desensitisation: Animal studies. *Psychological Bulletin, 76*, 1–14.

Wilson, K., & French, C.C. (2006). The relationship between susceptibility to false memories, dissociativity, paranormal beliefs and experience. *Personality and Individual Differences, 41*, 1493–1502.

Wilson, S.C., & Barber, T.X. (1983). The fantasy prone personality: Implications for understanding imagery, hypnosis and parapsychological phenomena. In A.A. Sheikh (Ed.). *Imagery: Current theory and application* (pp. 340–387). New York: John Wiley.

Wimmer, H., & Perner, J., (1983). Beliefs about beliefs: Representation and the constraining function of wrong beliefs in young children's understanding of deception. *Cognition, 13*, 103–128.

Windgassen, K. (1992). Treatment with neuroleptics: The patient's perspective. *Acta Psychiatrica Scandinavica, 86*, 405–410.

Winterer, G., & Weinberger, D.R. (2004). Genes, dopamine and cortical signal-to-noise ratio in schizophrenia. *Trends in Neurosciences, 27*, 683–690.

Wiseman, R. (2001). The psychology of psychic fraud. In R. Roberts & D. Groome (Eds.). *Parapsychology: The science of unusual experience* (pp. 51–59). London: Arnold.

Wiseman, R., & Schiltz, M. (1997). Experimenter effects and the remote detection of staring. *Journal of Parapsychology, 61*, 197–207.

Wiseman, R., & Smith, M.D. (2002). Assessing the role of cognitive and motivational biases in belief in the paranormal. *Journal of the Society for Psychical Research, 66*(3), 157–166.

Wiseman, R., Smith, M., & Wiseman, J. (1995). Eyewitness testimony and the paranormal. *Skeptical Inquirer, 19*, 29–32.

Witherington, D.C., Campos, J.J., Anderson, D.I., Lejeune, L., & Seah, E. (2005). Avoidance of heights on the visual cliff in newly walking infants. *Infancy, 7*, 285–298.

Wolpe, J. (1958). *Psychotherapy by reciprocal inhibition*. New York: Pergamon Press.

Wolpe, J. (1969). *The practice of behaviour therapy*. Oxford, UK: Pergamon Press.

Wonderlich, S.A., Crosby, R.D., Joiner, T., Peterson, C.B., Bardone-Cone, A., Klein, M., et al. (2005). Personality subtyping and bulimia nervosa: psychopathological and genetic correlates. *Psychological Medicine, 35*(5), 649–657.

Wonderlich, S.A., Crosby, R.D., Mitchell, J.E., & Engel, S.E. (2007). Testing the validity of eating disorder diagnoses. *International Journal of Eating Disorders, 40*, S3, S40–S45.

Wood, D.J., Bruner, J.S., & Ross, G. (1976). The role of tutoring in problem solving. *Journal of Child Psychology and Psychiatry, 17*, 89–100.

Wood, R.T.A., & Griffiths, M.D. (2007). Online guidance, advice, and support for problem gamblers and concerned relatives and friends: An evaluation of the *Gam-Aid* pilot service. *British Journal of Guidance and Counselling, 35*, 373–389.

Wood, W., & Eagly, A.H. (2002). A cross-cultural analysis of the behaviour of women and men: Implications for the origins of sex differences. *Psychological Bulletin, 128*, 699–727.

Wood, W., Wong, F.Y., & Chachere, J.G. (1991). Effects of media violence on viewers' aggression in unconstrained social interaction. *Psychological Bulletin, 109*, 371–383.

Woodhill, B.M., & Samuels, C.A. (2003). Positive and negative androgyny and their relationship with psychological health and well-being. *Sex Roles, 48*, 555–565.

Woodruff, G., & Premack, D. (1979). Intentional communication in the chimpanzee: Development of deception. *Cognition, 7*, 333–362.

Woods, D., & Twohig, M. (2008). *Trichotillomania: An act-enhanced behaviour therapy approach*. Oxford: Oxford University Press.

Woods, S.C. (1991). The eating paradox: How we tolerate food. *Psychological Review, 98*, 488–505.

Worchel, S., Andreoli, V., & Eason, J. (1975). Is medium message? Study of effects of media, communicator, and message characteristics on attitude change. *Journal of Applied Social Psychology, 5*, 157–172.

Wright, P., Takei, N., Rifkin, L., Murray, R.M., & Shaw, P.C. (1999). Seasonality, prenatal influenza exposure, and schizophrenia. In E.S. Susser, A.S. Brown, & J.M. Gorman (Eds.), *Prenatal exposures in schizophrenia*. Washington, DC: American Psychiatric Press.

Wright, R. (1994). Feminists, meet Mr Darwin. The evolutionary psychology of the female mind. *New Republic, November 28*, 34–46.

Yeates, K.O., Schultz, L.H., & Selman, R.L. (1990). Bridging the gaps in child-clinical assessment: Toward the application of social-cognitive developmental theory. *Clinical Psychology Review, 10*, 567–588.

Yeates, K.O., Schultz, L.H., & Selman, R.L. (1991). The development of interpersonal negotiation strategies in thought and action: A social-cognitive link to behavioural adjustment and social status. *Merrill-Palmer Quarterly Journal of Developmental Psychology, 37*, 369–406.

Yerkes, R.M., & Morgulis, S. (1909). The method of Pavlov in animal psychology. *Psychological Bulletin, 6*, 257–273.

Yonkers, K.A., & O'Brien, P.M. (2008). Premenstrual syndrome. *The Lancet, 371*(9619), 1200–1210.

Young, A.W., Hay, D.C., & Ellis, A.W. (1985). The faces that launched a thousand slips: Everyday difficulties and errors in recognising people. *British Journal of Psychology, 76*, 495–523.

Young, A.W., Hellawell, D., & de Haan, E. (1988). Cross-domain semantic priming in normal subjects and a prosopagnosic patient. *Quarterly Journal of Experimental Psychology, 40*, 561–580.

Young, A.W., McWeeny, K.H., Hay, D.C., & Ellis, A.W. (1986). Naming and categorisation latencies for faces and written names. *Quarterly Journal of Experimental Psychology, 38A*, 297–318.

Young, A.W., Newcombe, F., de Haan, E.H.F., Small, M., & Hay, D.C. (1993). Face perception after brain injury: Selective impairments affecting identity and expression. *Brain, 116*, 941–959.

Young, W.C., Goy, R.W., & Phoenix, C.H. (1964). Hormones and sexual behaviour. *Science, 143*, 212–219.

Zaadstra, B.M., Seidell, J.C., Vannoord, P.A.H., Tevelde, E.R., Habbema, J.D.F., Vrieswijk, B., & Karbaat, J. (1993). Fat and female fecundity: Prospective study of effect of body-fat distribution on conception rates. *British Medical Journal, 306*, 484–487.

Zahavi, A. (1977). The cost of honesty (further remarks on the handicap principle). *Journal of Theoretical Biology, 67*, 603–605.

Zahn-Waxler, C., Robinson, J., & Emde, R.N. (1992). The development of empathy in twins. *Developmental Psychology, 28*, 1038–1047.

Zani, B. (1993). *Dating and interpersonal relationships in adolescence*. Hove, UK: Psychology Press.

Zanna, M.P., & Cooper, J. (1974). Dissonance and the pill: An attribution approach to studying the arousal properties of dissonance. *Journal of Personality and Social Psychology, 29*, 703–709.

Zeki, S. (2007). The neurobiology of love. *FEBS Letters, 12*, 581(14), 2575–2579.

Zerger, S. (2002). *Substance abuse treatment: What works for homeless people? A review of the literature*. Report for the National Health Care for the Homeless Council & HCH Clinicians Network Research Committee.

Zhou, J.N., Hofman, M.A., Gooren, L.J., & Swaab D.F. (1995). A sex difference in the human brain and its relation to transsexuality. *Nature, 378*, 68–70.

Zillmann, D., & Weaver, J.B. (1997). Psychoticism in the effect of prolonged exposure to gratuitous media violence: On the acceptance of violence as a preferred means of conflict resolution. *Personality and Individual Differences, 22*, 613–627.

Zimbardo, P. (1973). On the ethics of intervention in human psychological research: With special reference to the Stanford prison experiment. *Cognition, 2*, 243–256.

Zimbardo, P. (2007). *The Lucifer effect*. London: Random House Group.

Zimbardo, P., McDermott, M., Jansz, J., & Metaal, N. (1995). *Psychology: A European text*. London: HarperCollins.

Zimbardo, P., Weisenberg, M., Firestone, I., & Levy, B. (1965). Communicator effectiveness in producing public conformity and private attitude change. *Journal of Personality, 33*(2), 233–255.

INDEX

Note: References in **bold** are to key terms; those in *italic* are to chapter and section summaries.

ILLUSTRATION CREDITS

CHAPTER 1

Pages 16–19: Marking allocation for AQA specification (draft version) has been reproduced by kind permission of the Assessment and Qualifications Alliance.

CHAPTER 2

Page 22: © Derek Hudson/Sygma/Corbis.
Page 35: © Najlah Feanny/Corbis.
Page 36: © George Hall/Corbis.
Page 37: © Najlah Feanny/Corbis SABA.
Page 40: © Helen King/Corbis.
Page 47 (top and bottom): Jim Wileman/Caters News Agency.
Page 50: © Bettmann/Corbis.

CHAPTER 3

Page 74 (bottom): From J.J. Gibson (1966). *The senses considered as perceptual systems.* © 1966 Wadsworth, a part of Cengage Learning, Inc. Reproduced by permission. www.cengage.com/permissions.
Page 75 (bottom): © Momatiuk – Eastcott/Corbis.
Page 82: Reproduced with permission from R. Schafer and G. Murphy (1943). The role of autism in visual figure-ground relationship. *Journal of Experimental Psychology, 32,* 335–343. Copyright © 1943 American Psychological Association.
Page 86 (bottom left and bottom right): Photographed and supplied by Bip Mistry.
Page 94: From Turati, C., Simion, F., Milani, I., & Umilta, C. (2002). Newborns' preference for faces: What is crucial? *Developmental psychology, 38,* 875–882. Copyright © American Psychological Association. Reproduced with permission.
Page 96: From J.B. Deregowski (1989). Real space and represented space: Cross cultural perspectives. *Behavioural and Brain Sciences,* 12, 51–119. Copyright © 1989 Cambridge University Press. Reproduced with permission.
Page 106: From Duchaine, B.C., & Nakayama, K. (2006). Developmental prosopagnosia: A window to content-specific face processing. *Current Opinion in Neurobiology, 16,* 166–173. Copyright © Elsevier. Reproduced with permission.
Page 110: From Riddoch, M.J. & Humphreys G.W. (2001). Object recognition. In B. Rapp (Ed.), *The handbook of cognitive neuropsychology: What deficits reveal about the human mind.* Hove, UK: Psychology Press.
Page 111: From Fery, P. & Morais, J. (2003). A case study of visual agnosia without perceptual processing or structural descriptions' impairment. *Cognitive Neuropsychology, 20,* 595–618. Copyright © Psychology Press.

CHAPTER 4

Page 129: Photo by Franco Atirador from http://en.wikipedia.org/wiki/Image:Irish_Elk_front.jpg.
Page 131 (top left): © Frank Trapper/Corbis.
Page 131 (top right): © Royalty-Free/Corbis.
Page 131 (bottom left): © Baverel/Lefranc/Corbis KIPA.
Page 131 (bottom right): © Royalty-Free/Corbis.

CHAPTER 5

Page 149: Reproduced by kind permission of Professor Albert Bandura.
Page 154: Reproduced with permission of P.G. Zimbardo Inc.
Page 155: From the film Obedience © 1968 by Stanley Milgram. Copyright © renewed 1991 by Alexandra Milgram and distributed by Penn State Media Sales. Permission granted by Alexandra Milgram.

Page 156 (bottom): © Dave G. Houser/Corbis.
Page 165: © Hulton-Deutsch Collection/Corbis.
Page 173 (top): © Rick Gomez/Corbis.

CHAPTER 6

Page 200: From Logue, A.W. (2004). *The Psychology of Eating and Drinking.* Routledge: New York. Copyright © 2004 by Taylor & Francis Books, Inc.
Page 217: © Steve Marcus/Reuters/Corbis.
Page 221: © Fancy/Veer/Corbis.

CHAPTER 7

Page 231: © Royalty-Free/Corbis.
Page 239: © Jose Luis Pelaez, Inc./Corbis.
Page 241: © Getty Images.
Page 258: © Jim Zuckerman/Corbis.
Page 262: © Wendy Stone/Corbis.

CHAPTER 8

Page 272 (top): From Deary, I.J., Der, G., & Ford, G. (2001). Reaction times and intelligence differences: A population-based cohort study. *Intelligence, 29,* 389–399. Copyright © Elsevier. Reproduced with permission.
Page 272 (bottom): From Deary, I.J., & Stough, C. (1996). Intelligence and inspection time: Achievements, prospects, and problems. *American Psychologist, 51* (6), 599–608. Copyright © American Psychological Association. Reproduced with permission.
Page 281 (left): © Marvin Koner/Corbis.
Page 281 (middle): © Bettmann/Corbis.
Page 281 (right): © Hulton-Deutsch Collection/Corbis.
Page 293: © Bettmann/Corbis.
Page 298: Photos courtesy of the Cognitive Evolution Group, University of Louisiana at Lafayette.

CHAPTER 9

Page 327 (bottom): Doug Goodman / Science Photo Library.
Page 330: © Farrell Grehan/Corbis.
Page 367: © Goodshoot/Corbis.

CHAPTER 10

Page 378: © Royalty-Free/Corbis.
Page 379: AFP/AFP/Getty Images.
Page 393: Images courtesy of Drs. E. Fuller Torrey, M.D., and Daniel Weinberger, The Treatment Advocacy Center. www.treatmentadvocacycenter.org.' Reproduced with permission.
Page 398: © Corbis.
Page 412: Thurston Hopkins/Picture Post/Getty Images.

CHAPTER 11

Page 434 (left): © Peter Foley/epa/Corbis.
Page 434 (right): © Hulton-Deutsch Collection/Corbis.
Page 435: © David Turnley/Corbis.
Page 455: © Joe McNally/Getty Images.
Page 461: © Jose Luis Pelaez, Inc./Corbis.

CHAPTER 12

Page 475 (case study): Blog excerpt from http://www.livingwithagoraphobia. blogspot.com/. Reproduced with kind permission of Lynn Jackson.
Page 486: Reproduced with the kind permission of Benjamin Harris, University of New Hampshire.
Page 492: © Fancy/Veer/Corbis.
Page 502: © Birgid Allig/zefa/Corbis.

CHAPTER 13

Page 527: Wellcome Dept. Of Cognitive Neurology/ Science Photo Library.

Page 533: © Howard C. Smith/isiphotos.com/Corbis.
Page 540: © Rolf Bruderer/Corbis.

CHAPTER 14

Page 552: Reproduced by kind permission of Professor Albert Bandura.
Page 553: © John Springer Collection/Corbis.
Page 556: Courtesy State Archives of Florida.
Page 558: © Royalty-Free/Corbis.
Page 562: © Rockstar Games/Handout/Reuters/Corbis.
Page 563: Reprinted with permission from Anderson, C.A., & Bushman, B.J. (2002). Human aggression. Annual Review of Psychology, 53, 27–51. Copyright © 2002 by Annual Reviews www.annualreviews.org.
Page 569: © Reuters/Corbis.
Page 571: © Business Wire via Getty Images.
Page 578: © Herbert P.Oczeret/EPA/Corbis.
Page 582: © Dave Hogan/Getty Images.
Page 584: © Tim Pannell/Corbis.
Page 587: © Dan Kitwood/Getty Images.
Page 588: © Getty Images.
Page 591 (bottom): © Jeff Vinnick/Getty Images.
Page 593 (left): © Peter Andrews/Corbis.
Page 593 (middle right): © Stephen Hird/Reuters/Corbis.
Page 595: © Jennie Woodcock; Reflections Photolibrary/Corbis.
Page 597: © David Lees/Corbis.
Page 598: © Paul Buck/epa/Corbis.

CHAPTER 15

Page 607: © Stewart Cohen/Blend Images/Corbis.
Page 622 (bottom): From http://upload.wikimedia.org/

wikipedia/commons/d/d0/William_ Hogarth_-_Gin_Lane.jpg.
Page 623: From Townsend, J. (1993). Policies to halve smoking deaths. Addiction, 88, 43–52. Copyright © 1993 by John Wiley & Sons, Inc. All rights reserved. Reproduced with permission.
Page 624: © Corbis Sygma.
Page 630: From Prochaska, J.O., DiClemente, C.C., & Norcross, J.C. (1992). In search of how people change: Applications to addictive behaviours. American Psychologist, 47, 1102–1114. Copyright © American Psychological Association. Reproduced with permission.
Page 632: © moodboard/Corbis.
Page 639: © Bettmann/Corbis.
Page 643: © Roger Ressmeyer/Corbis.

CHAPTER 16

Page 654: © Jeremy Walker / Science Photo Library.
Page 657: © Ina Fassbender/Reuters/Corbis.
Page 661: © John-Francis Bourke/zefa/Corbis.
Page 670: © National Media Museum/SSPL.
Page 672: © Bettmann/Corbis.
Page 683: © Corbis.

CHAPTER 17

Page 693: © Enzo & Paolo Ragazzini/Corbis.
Page 695: © Hulton-Deutsch Collection/Corbis.
Page 700: © Bettmann/Corbis.
Page 715: From the film Obedience © 1968 by Stanley Milgram. Copyright © renewed 1991 by Alexandra Milgram and distributed by Penn State Media Sales. Permission granted by Alexandra Milgram.
Page 717: Reproduced with permission of P.G. Zimbardo Inc.

Fundamentals of Psychology

Michael Eysenck
Royal Holloway, University of London, UK

"This must be surely one of the most comprehensive psychology textbooks in existence. It covers the diverse and multi-leveled discipline that psychology is and it does so in a highly sophisticated yet also readable and interesting way. I appreciated the historical perspective, and the focus on long-standing issues that perplexed and fascinated psychological scientists over the years, and found new framings with the introduction of new methods and techniques of inquiry." – **Arie W. Kruglanski, Distinguished University Professor, University of Maryland**

"Eysenck has written a thorough yet engaging introduction to the science of psychology. The book speaks with a unified voice, pulling in historical examples where they are important, yet still covering cutting-edge research of recent years. He does not shy away from controversial issues in the field, but covers them evenhandedly. The last three chapters on research methods are excellent; I strongly recommend this book." – **Henry Roediger III, Washington University in St. Louis**

"In my opinion Eysenck is the finest textbook author in the world at this level. The sheer breadth of material with which he is comfortable is most impressive, and he has a unique ability to communicate complex and contemporary material so as to make it accessible and interesting." – **Matt Jarvis, Visiting Tutor in Education, Southampton and Keele Universities**

Aimed at those new to the subject, *Fundamentals of Psychology* is a clear and reader-friendly full-color textbook that will help students explore and understand the essentials of psychology. This text offers a balanced and accurate representation of the discipline through a highly accessible synoptic approach, which seamlessly brings together all the various related topics. It also includes substantial coverage of current research.

Combining an authoritative tone, a huge range of psychological material, and an informal, analogy-rich style, the text expertly blends admirably up-to-date empirical research and real-life examples and applications. Both readable and factually dense, the book introduces all the main approaches to psychology, including social, developmental, cognitive, biological, individual differences, and abnormal psychology, as well as psychological research methods. However, it also includes directions for more detailed and advanced study for the interested student.

Fundamentals of Psychology incorporates many helpful textbook features which will aid students and reinforce learning, such as:

- Key-term definitions
- Extremely clear end-of-chapter summaries
- Annotated further reading sections
- Evaluations of significant research findings
- Numerous illustrations presented in attractive full color.

This textbook is also accompanied by a comprehensive program of resources for both students and instructors, which is available free to qualifying adopters. The resources include a web-based Student Learning Program, as well as chapter-by-chapter lecture slides and an interactive chapter-by-chapter multiple-choice question test bank.

Combining exceptional content, abundant pedagogical features, and a lively full-color design, *Fundamentals of Psychology* is an essential resource for anyone new to the subject and more particularly those beginning undergraduate courses. The book will also be ideal for students studying psychology within education, nursing and other healthcare professions.

CONTENTS

Visit **www.psypress.com/fundamentals-of-psychology** to:

- Download a free sample chapter!
- Preview the supplementary resources!
- Instructors: request an examination copy!

January 2009: 8½x11: 712pp
Hb: 978-1-84169-371-2: £49.95 $90.00
Pb: 978-1-84169-372-9: £27.50 $49.95

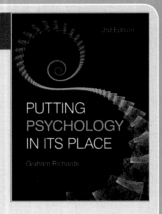

Putting Psychology in its Place

Third Edition
Graham Richards
Former Professor at Staffordshire University, UK

The third edition of *Putting Psychology in its Place* builds on the previous two editions, introducing the history of psychology and placing the discipline within a historical context. It aims to answer questions about the role of psychology in modern society, by critically examining issues such as how psychology developed, why psychoanalysis had such an impact and how the discipline has changed to deal with contemporary social issues such as religion, race and gender.

This new third edition contains two completely new chapters: *Emotion: The Problem or the Whole Point?* and *Psychology, Money and Institutions.* An expanded Epilogue has also been added which incorporates a discussion of the conceptual issues raised in the book and which corresponds with the new BPS requirements for undergraduate courses. Other chapters, including those on psychology and the brain, social psychology and the psychology of madness, as well those on gender, religion and race have also been substantially revised.

Putting Psychology in its Place is imaginatively written and accessible to all. It is an invaluable introductory text for undergraduate students of the history of psychology and will also appeal to postgraduates, academics and anyone interested in psychology or the history of science.

January 2010: 7x10: 264pp
Hb: 978-0-415-45579-4: £45.00
Pb: 978-0-415-45580-0: £19.95
60-day examination copy available

Psychology

The Key Concepts
Graham Richards
Former Professor at Staffordshire University, UK
Routledge Key Guides Series

This book provides a comprehensive overview of 200 concepts central to a solid understanding of Psychology and includes the latest recommendations from the British Psychology Society (BPS). The focus is on practical uses of Psychology in settings such as nursing, education and human resources, with topics ranging from Gender to Psychometrics and Perception.

August 2008: 5½x8½: 266pp
Hb: 978-0-415-43200-9: £60.00
Pb: 978-0-415-43201-6: £14.99
60-day examination copy available